# The Council of State Governments

# STATE DIRECTORY

## Directory I—
## Elective Officials 2017

The Council of State Governments
1776 Avenue of the States
Lexington, KY 40511

Contact the Publication Sales Department at
1-800-800-1910 or sales@csg.org to order:

Directory I—Elective Officials 2017,

Directory II—Legislative Leadership, Committees and Staff 2017,

Directory III—Administrative Officials 2017

or mailing lists of state government officials.

Since 1933, The Council of State Governments has served our nation's state leaders by providing a forum for "sharing capitol ideas." As the only state services organization spanning all three branches of government, CSG offers a unique look into the issues shaping state policy and legislation from the national and regional perspectives. This unique arrangement contributes to a strong national presence for CSG, creating unparalleled opportunities to network, collaborate and form problem-solving partnerships.

## The Council of State Governments Officers

*President* **Gov. Kate Brown**, Ore.

*Chair* **Sen. Kelvin Atkinson**, Nev. ▪ *Chair-Elect* **Sen. Robert Stivers**, Ky. ▪ *Vice Chair* **Rep. Helene Keeley**, Del.

## The Council of State Governments

*David Adkins, Executive Director CEO*

1776 Avenue of the States ▪ Lexington, KY 40511 ▪ (859) 244-8000 ▪ Fax: (859) 244-8001 ▪ www.csg.org

---

**Eastern Office**
*Wendell M. Hannaford, Director*
22 Cortlandt Street, 22nd Floor
New York, NY 10007
(212) 482-2320
Fax: (212) 482-2344
www.csg-erc.org

**Midwestern Office**
*Michael H. McCabe, Director*
701 East 22nd Street, Suite 110
Lombard, IL 60148
(630) 925-1922
Fax: (630) 925-1930
www.csgmidwest.org

**Southern Office**
*Colleen Cousineau, Director*
P.O. Box 98129
Atlanta, GA 30359
(404) 633-1866
Fax: (404) 633-4896
www.slcatlanta.org

**Western Office**
*Edgar E. Ruiz, Director*
1107 9th Street, Suite 730
Sacramento, CA 95814
(916) 553-4423
Fax: (916) 446-5760
www.csgwest.org

**Washington Office**
444 N. Capitol Street, N.W., Suite 401
Washington, DC 20001
(202) 624-5460
Fax: (202) 624-5452
www.csgdc.org

## Editorial Staff

Kelley Arnold ▪ Jessica Clay ▪ Eric Lancaster ▪ Heather Perkins

*Special thanks to the CSG regional offices
and the clerks and secretaries of the legislature for each state.*

# Table of Contents

# Table of Contents by Region

# How to Use This Directory

This volume contains: names of the governor, lieutenant governor, secretary of state, attorney general, auditor, treasurer and other constitutionally elected officials; state court of last resort judges (whether elected or appointed); state legislators who are serving as of January 2017; congressional members and government-related facts about each state.

Elected branch officials are listed with the office title, party affiliation, address, phone number, fax number and email address, if available.

Courts of last resort members, as well as the clerk of the court of last resort, are listed with the name, address, phone number, fax and email address, if available. Since members of these courts are not elected by the public in all states, a two-letter code appears next to the name of the court to indicate the method by which the judges are selected and retained in office.

Legislative rosters for all states and other U.S. jurisdictions are organized by chamber and include the name, party, district, preferred mailing address, phone number, fax number and email address, if available.

Congressional members are listed alphabetically with the party affiliation and district number.

Information current as of press time.

## General Abbreviations

| | |
|---|---|
| N.A. | Not available |
| * | New legislator |

## Party Abbreviations

| | |
|---|---|
| D | Democrat |
| R | Republican |
| REFORM | Reform |
| C | Covenant |
| CONST | Constitution |
| I | Independent |
| L | Libertarian |
| G | Green |
| ICM | Independent Citizen Movement |
| DFL | Democratic-Farmer-Labor |
| NP | Nonpartisan |
| P | Progressive |
| NPP | New Progressive Party |
| PDP | Popular Democratic Party |
| PIP | Puerto Rican Independent Party |
| TRIBAL | Delegate representing a Native American tribe |
| U | Unenrolled |

## Courts of Last Resort Abbreviations

(FA)  Appointed by federal official. In the District of Columbia, U.S. president makes appointments from a list of nominees submitted by the nominating commission. In American Samoa, U.S. secretary of the Interior appoints judges.

(GA)  Gubernatorial appointment. In Delaware, gubernatorial appointment is made with consent of Senate.

(LA)  Legislative appointment.

(MC)  Gubernatorial appointment from a list of nominees submitted by a nominating or selection commission. In Hawaii, appointments require consent of Senate and reappointments are made by the nominating selection commission. In Massachusetts, appointments are for life. In Vermont, judges are retained unless the Legislature votes for removal.

(MR)  Gubernatorial appointment from a list of nominees submitted by a nominating or selection commission; judges run in retention election for subsequent terms. In California, judges are initially appointed by the governor and confirmed by judicial appointments commission.

(NE)  Nonpartisan election.

(PE)  Partisan election. In Illinois and Pennsylvania, judges are selected in partisan elections for initial term and run in nonpartisan retention elections for subsequent terms.

# 2017 Party Control Maps
## (as of Feb. 2017)

## Gubernatorial

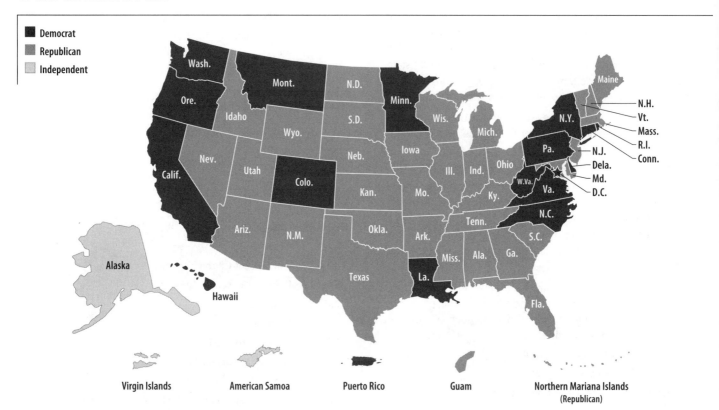

Legend:
- Democrat
- Republican
- Independent

Wash., Ore., Calif., Idaho, Mont., Wyo., Nev., Utah, Ariz., N.M., Colo., N.D., S.D., Neb., Kan., Okla., Texas, Minn., Wis., Iowa, Mo., Ark., La., Mich., Ill., Ind., Ohio, Ky., Tenn., Miss., Ala., Ga., S.C., N.C., Va., W.Va., Fla., Pa., N.Y., Maine, N.H., Vt., Mass., R.I., Conn., N.J., Dela., Md., D.C.

Alaska, Hawaii

Virgin Islands    American Samoa    Puerto Rico    Guam    Northern Mariana Islands (Republican)

## Legislative

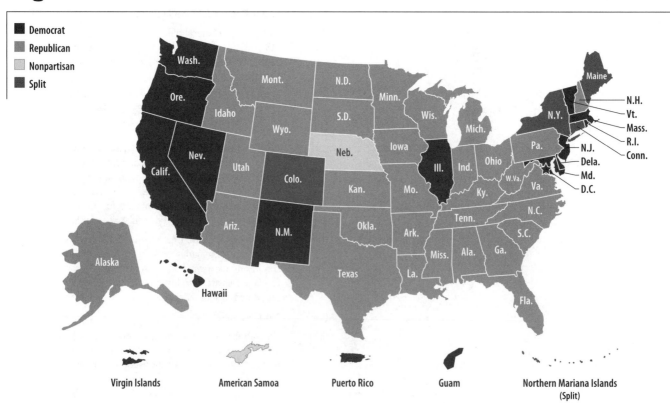

Legend:
- Democrat
- Republican
- Nonpartisan
- Split

Wash., Ore., Calif., Nev., Idaho, Mont., Wyo., Utah, Ariz., N.M., Colo., N.D., S.D., Neb., Kan., Okla., Texas, Minn., Wis., Iowa, Mo., Ark., La., Mich., Ill., Ind., Ohio, Ky., Tenn., Miss., Ala., Ga., S.C., N.C., Va., W.Va., Fla., Pa., N.Y., Maine, N.H., Vt., Mass., R.I., Conn., N.J., Dela., Md., D.C.

Alaska, Hawaii

Virgin Islands    American Samoa    Puerto Rico    Guam    Northern Mariana Islands (Split)

# Alabama

## Executive

### Governor

**The Honorable Robert J. Bentley (R)**
Governor
State Capitol
600 Dexter Avenue
Montgomery, AL 36130
P: (334) 242-7100
F: (334) 353-0004

### Lieutenant Governor

**The Honorable Kay Ivey (R)**
Lieutenant Governor
11 South Union Street, Suite 725
Montgomery, AL 36130
P: (334) 242-7900
F: (334) 242-4661
E: kay.ivey
@ltgov.alabama.gov

### Commissioner of Agriculture & Industries

**The Honorable John McMillan (R)**
Commissioner
Richard Beard Building
1445 Federal Drive
Montgomery, AL 36107
P: (334) 240-7100
F: (334) 240-7190

### Attorney General

**The Honorable Steve Marshall (R)**
Attorney General
501 Washington Avenue
P.O. Box 300152
Montgomery, AL 36130
P: (334) 242-7300

### Public Service Commission

**Mr. Chip Beeker Jr. (R)**
Commissioner
100 North Union Street, Suite 818
P.O. Box 304260
Montgomery, AL 36130
P: (334) 242-5191
E: chip.beeker
@psc.alabama.gov

**Ms. Twinkle Andress Cavanaugh (R)**
President
100 North Union Street, Suite 850
P.O. Box 304260
Montgomery, AL 36130
P: (334) 242-5203
F: (334) 242-0509
E: twinkle.cavanaugh
@psc.alabama.gov

**Mr. Jeremy Oden (R)**
Commissioner
100 North Union Street, Suite 818
P.O. Box 304260
Montgomery, AL 36130
P: (334) 242-5203
E: jeremy.oden
@psc.alabama.gov

### Secretary of State

**The Honorable John Merrill (R)**
Secretary of State
P.O. Box 5616
Montgomery, AL 36103
P: (334) 242-7200
F: (334) 242-4993
E: john.merrill
@sos.alabama.gov

### Treasurer

**The Honorable Young Boozer III (R)**
State Treasurer
600 Dexter Avenue
State Capitol, Room S-106
Montgomery, AL 36104
P: (334) 242-7501
F: (334) 242-7592
E: young.boozer
@treasury.alabama.gov

## Judiciary

### Supreme Court (PE)

**Ms. Julia Jordan Weller**
Clerk
300 Dexter Avenue
Montgomery, AL 36104
P: (334) 229-0700

**The Honorable Lyn Stuart**
Chief Justice
**The Honorable Michael F. Bolin (R)**
**The Honorable Tommy Bryan**
**The Honorable James Allen Main**
**The Honorable Glenn Murdock**
**The Honorable Tom Parker**
**The Honorable Greg Shaw**
**The Honorable Alisa Kelli Wise**

## Legislative Senate

### Senate President

**The Honorable Kay Ivey (R)**
Lieutenant Governor
11 South Union Street, Suite 725
Montgomery, AL 36130
P: (334) 242-7900
F: (334) 242-4661
E: kay.ivey
@ltgov.alabama.gov

### President Pro Tempore of the Senate

**Senator Del Marsh (R)**
Senate President Pro Tempore
State House, Room 722
11 South Union Street
Montgomery, AL 36130
P: (334) 242-7877
F: (334) 242-8819
E: del.marsh@alsenate.gov

### Senate Majority Leader

**Senator Greg Reed (R)**
Senate Majority Leader
State House, Room 726
11 South Union Street
Montgomery, AL 36130
P: (334) 242-7894
F: (334) 242-8819
E: greg.reed@alsenate.gov

### Senate Minority Leader

**Senator Quinton T. Ross Jr. (D)**
Senate Minority Leader
State House, Room 740
11 South Union Street
Montgomery, AL 36130
P: (334) 242-7880
F: (334) 242-8819
E: Quinton.ross
@alsenate.gov

### Secretary of the Senate

**Mr. D. Patrick Harris**
Secretary of the Senate
State House, Senate Chamber
11 South Union Street
Montgomery, AL 36130
P: (334) 242-7803
F: (334) 242-8819

## Members of the Senate

**Albritton, Greg (R, 22)**
State House, Room 735
11 South Union Street
Montgomery, AL 36130
P: (334) 242-7843
F: (334) 242-4759
E: galbritton@att.net

**Allen, Gerald (R, 21)**
State House, Room 729
11 South Union Street
Montgomery, AL 36130
P: (334) 242-7889
F: (334) 353-8277
E: gerald.allen
@alsenate.gov

**Beasley, Billy (D, 28)**
State House, Room 737
11 South Union Street
Montgomery, AL 36130
P: (334) 242-7868
F: (334) 242-8819
E: billy.beasley
@alsenate.gov

**Blackwell, Slade (R, 15)**
State House, Room 729
11 South Union Street
Montgomery, AL 36130
P: (334) 242-7851
F: (334) 242-8819
E: sb@sladeblackwell.com

**Brewbaker, Dick (R, 25)**
State House, Room 734
11 South Union Street
Montgomery, AL 36130
P: (334) 242-7895
F: (334) 242-8819
E: dick.brewbaker
@alsenate.gov

**Bussman, Paul (R, 4)**
State House, Room 733
11 South Union Street
Montgomery, AL 36130
P: (334) 242-7855
F: (334) 242-8819
E: p_bussman@bellsouth.net

**Chambliss Jr., Clyde (R, 30)**
State House, Room 733
11 South Union Street
Montgomery, AL 36130
P: (334) 242-7883
F: (334) 242-8819
E: clyde.chambliss
@alsenate.gov

**Coleman-Madison, Linda (D, 20)**
State House, Room 738
11 South Union Street
Montgomery, AL 36130
P: (334) 242-7864
F: (334) 242-8819
E: linda.coleman
@birminghamal.gov

**Dial, Gerald (R, 13)**
State House, Room 732
11 South Union Street
Montgomery, AL 36130
P: (334) 242-7874
F: (334) 242-8819
E: gerald_dial@yahoo.com

**Dunn, Priscilla (D, 19)**
State House, Room 737
11 South Union Street
Montgomery, AL 36130
P: (334) 242-7793
F: (334) 353-9625

**Figures, Vivian Davis (D, 33)**
State House, Room 736
11 South Union Street
Montgomery, AL 36130
P: (334) 242-7871
F: (334) 242-8819
E: vivian.figures
@alsenate.gov

**Glover, Rusty (R, 34)**
State House, Room 721
11 South Union Street
Montgomery, AL 36130
P: (334) 242-7886
F: (334) 353-3970
E: rusty.glover
@alsenate.gov

**Hightower, Bill (R, 35)**
State House, Room 733
11 South Union Street
Montgomery, AL 36130
P: (334) 242-7882
F: (334) 242-8819
E: bill.hightower
@alsenate.gov

**Holley, Jimmy W. (R, 31)**
State House, Room 732
11 South Union Street
Montgomery, AL 36130
P: (334) 242-7845
F: (334) 242-7191

**Holtzclaw, Bill (R, 2)**
State House, Room 731
11 South Union Street
Montgomery, AL 36130
P: (334) 242-7854
F: (334) 242-8819
E: bill.holtzclaw
@alsenate.gov

**Livingston, Steve (R, 8)**
State House, Room 731
11 South Union Street
Montgomery, AL 36130
P: (334) 242-7858
F: (334) 242-8819
E: steve.livingston
@alsenate.gov

**Marsh, Del (R, 12)**
State House, Room 722
11 South Union Street
Montgomery, AL 36130
P: (334) 242-7877
F: (334) 242-8819
E: del.marsh@alsenate.gov

**McClendon, Jim (R, 11)**
State House, Room 729
11 South Union Street
Montgomery, AL 36130
P: (334) 242-7898
F: (334) 242-4759
E: jimmcc@windstream.net

**Melson, Tim (R, 1)**
State House, Room 735
11 South Union Street
Montgomery, AL 36130
P: (334) 242-7888
F: (334) 242-8819

**Orr, Arthur (R, 3)**
State House, Room 730
11 South Union Street
Montgomery, AL 36130
P: (334) 242-7891
F: (334) 242-8819

**Pittman, Trip (R, 32)**
State House, Room 730
11 South Union Street
Montgomery, AL 36130
P: (334) 242-7897
E: trip.pittman
@alsenate.gov

**Reed, Greg (R, 5)**
State House, Room 726
11 South Union Street
Montgomery, AL 36130
P: (334) 242-7894
F: (334) 242-8819
E: greg.reed@alsenate.gov

**Ross Jr., Quinton T. (D, 26)**
State House, Room 740
11 South Union Street
Montgomery, AL 36130
P: (334) 242-7880
F: (334) 242-8819
E: Quinton.ross
@alsenate.gov

**Sanders, Hank (D, 23)**
State House, Room 736
11 South Union Street
Montgomery, AL 36130
P: (334) 242-7860
F: (334) 242-8819

**Sanford, Paul (R, 7)**
State House, Room 731
11 South Union Street
Montgomery, AL 36130
P: (334) 242-7867
F: (334) 242-8819
E: paul.sanford
@alsenate.gov

**Scofield, Clay (R, 9)**
State House, Room 731
11 South Union Street
Montgomery, AL 36130
P: (334) 242-7876
F: (334) 242-8819
E: clay.scofield
@alsenate.gov

**Shelnutt, Shay (R, 17)**
State House, Room 735
11 South Union Street
Montgomery, AL 36130
P: (334) 242-7794
F: (334) 242-8819
E: shay.sd17@gmail.com

**Singleton, Bobby (D, 24)**
State House, Room 738
11 South Union Street
Montgomery, AL 36130
P: (334) 242-7935
F: (334) 242-7191
E: bsingle362@gmail.com

**Smith, Harri Anne (I, 29)**
State House, Room 737
11 South Union Street
Montgomery, AL 36130
P: (334) 242-7879
F: (334) 242-8819
E: harriannesmith
@graceba.net

**Smitherman, Rodger Mell (D, 18)**
State House, Room 737
11 South Union Street
Montgomery, AL 36130
P: (334) 242-7870
F: (334) 353-8255
E: rodger.smitherman
@alsenate.gov

**Stutts, Larry (R, 6)**
State House, Room 735
11 South Union Street
Montgomery, AL 36130
P: (334) 242-7862
F: (334) 242-8819
E: larry.stutts
@alsenate.gov

**Waggoner, J.T. (R, 16)**
State House, Room 726
11 South Union Street
Montgomery, AL 36130
P: (334) 242-7892
F: (334) 242-2278
E: jabo.waggoner
@alsenate.gov

**Ward, Cam (R, 14)**
State House, Room 719
11 South Union Street
Montgomery, AL 36130
P: (334) 242-7873
F: (334) 242-8819
E: cam@camward.com

**Whatley, Tom (R, 27)**
State House, Room 734
11 South Union Street
Montgomery, AL 36130
P: (334) 242-7865
F: (334) 242-8819
E: tom.whatley@alsenate.gov

**Williams, Phil (R, 10)**
State House, Room 733
11 South Union Street
Montgomery, AL 36130
P: (334) 242-7857
F: (334) 242-8819
E: Phil
@williamsstatesenate.com

# House

## Speaker of the House

**Representative Mac McCutcheon (R)**
Speaker of the House
State House, Room 519-C
11 South Union Street
Montgomery, AL 36130
P: (334) 242-7705
F: (334) 242-4759
E: c.mac.mccutcheon
@gmail.com

## Speaker Pro Tempore of the House

**Representative Victor Gaston (R)**
House Speaker Pro Tempore
State House, Room 519-E
11 South Union Street
Montgomery, AL 36130
P: (334) 242-7664
F: (334) 242-4759
E: hvgaston04@yahoo.com

## House Majority Leader

**Representative Micky Hammon (R)**
House Majority Leader
State House, Room 401
11 South Union Street
Montgomery, AL 36130
P: (334) 242-7709
F: (334) 242-4759
E: mickyhammon@gmail.com

## House Minority Leader

**Representative Craig Ford (D)**
House Minority Leader
State House, Room 434
11 South Union Street
Montgomery, AL 36130
P: (334) 242-7690
F: (334) 242-4759
E: Craig.Ford@alhouse.org

## Clerk of the House

**Mr. Jeff Woodard**
Clerk of the House
State House
11 South Union Street
Montgomery, AL 36130
P: (334) 242-7609
F: (334) 242-2488

## Members of the House

**Ainsworth, Will (R, 27)**
State House, Room 524-B
11 South Union Street
Montgomery, AL 36130
P: (334) 242-7600
F: (334) 242-4759
E: will.ainsworth
@alhouse.gov

**Alexander, Louise (D, 56)**
State House, Room 537-B
11 South Union Street
Montgomery, AL 36130
P: (334) 242-7600
F: (334) 242-4759
E: louise.alexander
@alhouse.gov

**Baker, Alan (R, 66)**
State House, Room 427-B
11 South Union Street
Montgomery, AL 36130
P: (334) 242-7720
F: (334) 242-4759
E: staterep
@co.escambia.al.us

**Ball, Mike (R, 10)**
State House, Room 401-A
11 South Union Street
Montgomery, AL 36130
P: (334) 242-7683
F: (334) 242-4759
E: mikeball@knology.net

**Bandy, George C. (D, 83)**
State House, Room 529
11 South Union Street
Montgomery, AL 36130
P: (334) 242-7721
F: (334) 242-4759
E: George.Bandy@alhouse.org

**Beckman, Paul (R, 88)**
State House, Room 427-D
11 South Union Street
Montgomery, AL 36130
P: (334) 242-7499
F: (334) 242-4759
E: paulbeckmanjr@yahoo.com

**Beech, Elaine (D, 65)**
State House, Room 427-E
11 South Union Street
Montgomery, AL 36130
P: (334) 242-7702
F: (334) 242-4759
E: elainebeech83@gmail.com

**Black, Marcel (D, 3)**
State House, Room 435
11 South Union Street
Montgomery, AL 36130
P: (334) 242-7686
F: (334) 242-4759
E: marcel.black42@gmail.com

**Blackshear, Chris (R, 80)**
State House, Room 427-A
11 South Union Street
Montgomery, AL 36130
P: (334) 232-1683
E: chris.blackshear
@alhouse.gov

**Boothe, Alan C. (R, 89)**
State House, Room 417-H
11 South Union Street
Montgomery, AL 36130
P: (334) 242-7710
F: (334) 242-4759
E: Alan.Boothe@alhouse.org

**Boyd, Barbara B. (D, 32)**
State House, Room 525-C
11 South Union Street
Montgomery, AL 36130
P: (334) 242-7692
F: (334) 242-4759
E: barbara.boyd@alhouse.gov

**Bracy Jr., Napoleon (D, 98)**
State House, Room 540-A
11 South Union Street
Montgomery, AL 36130
P: (334) 242-7756
F: (334) 242-4759
E: Napoleon.Bracy
@alhouse.org

**Brown, K.L. (R, 40)**
State House, Room 423
11 South Union Street
Montgomery, AL 36130
P: (334) 353-1778
F: (334) 242-4759
E: klbrown@cableone.net

**Buskey, James E. (D, 99)**
State House, Room 540-C
11 South Union Street
Montgomery, AL 36130
P: (334) 242-7757
F: (334) 242-4759
E: james.buskey@alhouse.org

**Butler, Mack (R, 30)**
State House, Room 526-A
11 South Union Street
Montgomery, AL 36130
P: (334) 242-7446
F: (334) 242-4759
E: mack.butler@alhouse.gov

**Carns, Jim (R, 48)**
State House, Room 534-C
11 South Union Street
Montgomery, AL 36130
P: (334) 242-7600
F: (334) 242-4759
E: jwcarns@yahoo.com

**Chesteen, Donnie (R, 87)**
State House, Room 427-J
11 South Union Street
Montgomery, AL 36130
P: (334) 242-7742
F: (334) 242-4759
E: dchesteen
@panhandle.rr.com

**Clarke, Adline (D, 97)**
State House, Room 540-B
11 South Union Street
Montgomery, AL 36130
P: (334) 242-7600
F: (334) 242-4759
E: adline.clarke
@alhouse.gov

**Clouse, Steve (R, 93)**
State House, Room 410-D
11 South Union Street
Montgomery, AL 36130
P: (334) 242-7717
F: (334) 242-4759
E: Steve.Clouse@alhouse.org

**Coleman, Merika (D, 57)**
State House, Room 537-A
11 South Union Street
Montgomery, AL 36130
P: (334) 242-7755
F: (334) 242-4759
E: Merika.Coleman
@alhouse.org

**Collins, Terri (R, 8)**
State House, Room 427-A
11 South Union Street
Montgomery, AL 36130
P: (334) 242-7693
F: (334) 242-4759
E: terri@terricollins.org

**Crawford, Danny (R, 5)**
State House, Room 522-A
11 South Union Street
Montgomery, AL 36130
P: (334) 242-1616
E: danny.crawford
@alhouse.gov

**Daniels, Anthony (D, 53)**
State House, Room 522-F
11 South Union Street
Montgomery, AL 36130
P: (334) 242-7600
F: (334) 242-4759
E: anthony.daniels
@alhouse.gov

**Davis, Randy (R, 96)**
State House, Room 417-G
11 South Union Street
Montgomery, AL 36130
P: (334) 242-7724
F: (334) 242-4759
E: rmdavis14@aol.com

**Drake, E. Richard (R, 45)**
State House, Room 528-B
11 South Union Street
Montgomery, AL 36130
P: (334) 242-7727
F: (334) 242-4759
E: ddrake1080@aol.com

**Drummond, Barbara (D, 103)**
State House, Room 536-C
11 South Union Street
Montgomery, AL 36130
P: (334) 242-7600
F: (334) 242-4759
E: drummondbarbara@att.net

**Ellis, Corley (R, 41)***
State House, 5th Floor
11 South Union Street
Montgomery, AL 36130
P: (334) 242-7600
E: corley.ellis@alhouse.gov

**England, Christopher J. (D, 70)**
State House, Room 539-B
11 South Union Street
Montgomery, AL 36130
P: (334) 242-7703
F: (334) 242-4759
E: cengland1@hotmail.com

# Alabama

**Farley, Allen (R, 15)**
State House, Room 427-L
11 South Union Street
Montgomery, AL 36130
P: (334) 242-7767
F: (334) 242-4759
E: allenfarley
@bellsouth.net

**Faulkner, David (R, 46)**
State House, Room 522-B
11 South Union Street
Montgomery, AL 36130
P: (334) 242-7600
F: (334) 242-4759
E: david.faulkner
@alhouse.gov

**Faust, Joe (R, 94)**
State House, Room 426
11 South Union Street
Montgomery, AL 36130
P: (334) 242-7699
F: (334) 242-4759
E: jfaust
@baldwincountyal.gov

**Fincher, Bob (R, 37)**
State House, Room 538-A
11 South Union Street
Montgomery, AL 36130
P: (334) 242-7600
F: (334) 242-4759
E: rsfincher77@gmail.com

**Ford, Craig (D, 28)**
State House, Room 434
11 South Union Street
Montgomery, AL 36130
P: (334) 242-7690
F: (334) 242-4759
E: Craig.Ford@alhouse.org

**Forte, Berry (D, 84)**
State House, Room 540-D
11 South Union Street
Montgomery, AL 36130
P: (334) 242-7553
F: (334) 242-4759
E: berry.forte@alhouse.gov

**Fridy, Matt (R, 73)**
State House, Room 403-E
11 South Union Street
Montgomery, AL 36130
P: (334) 242-7600
E: mdfridy@gmail.com

**Garrett, Danny (R, 44)**
State House, Room 538-B
11 South Union Street
Montgomery, AL 36130
P: (334) 242-7600
E: dannygarrett44@gmail.com

**Gaston, Victor (R, 100)**
State House, Room 519-E
11 South Union Street
Montgomery, AL 36130
P: (334) 242-7664
F: (334) 242-4759
E: hvgaston04@yahoo.com

**Givan, Juandalynn (D, 60)**
State House, Room 528-E
11 South Union Street
Montgomery, AL 36130
P: (334) 242-7684
F: (334) 242-4759
E: Juandalynn.givan
@alhouse.gov

**Greer, Lynn (R, 2)**
State House, Room 403-C
11 South Union Street
Montgomery, AL 36130
P: (334) 242-7576
F: (334) 242-4759
E: Lynn.Greer@alhouse.gov

**Grimsley, Dexter (D, 85)**
State House, Room 537-F
11 South Union Street
Montgomery, AL 36130
P: (334) 242-7740
F: (334) 242-4759
E: wlmdex@hotmail.com

**Hall, Laura (D, 19)**
State House, Room 517-D
11 South Union Street
Montgomery, AL 36130
P: (334) 242-7688
F: (334) 242-4759
E: laura.hall@alhouse.gov

**Hammon, Micky (R, 4)**
State House, Room 401
11 South Union Street
Montgomery, AL 36130
P: (334) 242-7709
F: (334) 242-4759
E: mickyhammon@gmail.com

**Hanes, Tommy (R, 23)**
State House, Room 527-D
11 South Union Street
Montgomery, AL 36130
P: (334) 242-7600
F: (334) 242-4759
E: jhanes55@gmail.com

**Harbison, Corey (R, 12)**
State House, Room 526-F
11 South Union Street
Montgomery, AL 36130
P: (334) 242-7600
F: (334) 242-4759
E: corey.harbison
@alhouse.gov

**Harper, Alan (R, 61)**
State House, Room 403-B
11 South Union Street
Montgomery, AL 36130
P: (334) 242-7732
F: (334) 242-4759
E: salanharper@gmail.com

**Henry, Ed (R, 9)**
State House, Room 401-F
11 South Union Street
Montgomery, AL 36130
P: (334) 242-7736
F: (334) 242-4759
E: Ed.Henry@alhouse.gov

**Hill, Jim (R, 50)**
State House, Room 526-B
11 South Union Street
Montgomery, AL 36130
P: (334) 242-7600
F: (334) 242-4759
E: jim.hill@alhouse.gov

**Holmes, Alvin (D, 78)**
State House, Room 525-A
11 South Union Street
Montgomery, AL 36130
P: (334) 242-7706
F: (334) 242-4759
E: Alvin.Holmes@alhouse.org

**Holmes, Mike (R, 31)**
State House, Room 527-A
11 South Union Street
Montgomery, AL 36130
P: (334) 242-7215
E: mike.holmes@alhouse.gov

**Howard, Ralph (D, 72)**
State House, Room 525-A
11 South Union Street
Montgomery, AL 36130
P: (334) 242-7759
F: (334) 242-4759
E: Ralph.Howard@alhouse.org

**Hurst, Steve (R, 35)**
State House, Room 427-K
11 South Union Street
Montgomery, AL 36130
P: (334) 353-9215
F: (334) 242-4759
E: Steve.Hurst@alhouse.org

**Ingram, Reed (R, 75)**
State House, Room 531
11 South Union Street
Montgomery, AL 36130
P: (334) 242-7600
F: (334) 242-4759
E: reedingram75@gmail.com

**Jackson, Thomas E. (D, 68)**
State House, Room 437-D
11 South Union Street
Montgomery, AL 36130
P: (334) 242-7738
F: (334) 242-4759
E: Thomas.Jackson
@alhouse.org

**Johnson, Ken (R, 7)**
State House, Room 417-E
11 South Union Street
Montgomery, AL 36130
P: (334) 242-7754
F: (334) 242-4759
E: ken.johnson@alhouse.gov

**Johnson, Ronald G. (R, 33)**
State House, Room 413-B
11 South Union Street
Montgomery, AL 36130
P: (334) 242-7777
F: (334) 242-4759
E: Ronald.Johnson
@alhouse.org

**Jones, Mike (R, 92)**
State House, Room 419
11 South Union Street
Montgomery, AL 36130
P: (334) 242-7739
F: (334) 242-4759
E: mljatty@andycable.com

**Knight Jr., John F. (D, 77)**
State House, Room 539-A
11 South Union Street
Montgomery, AL 36130
P: (334) 242-7512
F: (334) 242-4759
E: John.Knight@alhouse.org

**Lawrence, Kelvin (D, 69)**
State House, Room 536-A
11 South Union Street
Montgomery, AL 36130
P: (334) 242-7600
F: (334) 242-4759
E: kelvinj73@gmail.com

**Ledbetter, Nathaniel
(R, 24)**
State House, Room 522-D
11 South Union Street
Montgomery, AL 36130
P: (334) 242-7600
F: (334) 242-4759
E: nathaniel.ledbetter
@alhouse.gov

**Lee, Paul (R, 86)**
State House, Room 410-F
11 South Union Street
Montgomery, AL 36130
P: (334) 242-7675
F: (334) 242-4759
E: pwlee@graceba.net

**Lindsey, Richard J. (D, 39)**
State House, Room 432
11 South Union Street
Montgomery, AL 36130
P: (334) 242-7713
F: (334) 242-4759
E: richard.lindsey
  @alhouse.gov

**Lovvorn, Joe (R, 79)***
State House, 5th Floor
11 South Union
Montgomery, AL 36130
P: (334) 242-7600
E: joe.lovvorn@alhouse.gov

**Martin, James M. (R, 42)**
State House, Room 404
11 South Union Street
Montgomery, AL 36130
P: (334) 242-7600
F: (334) 242-4759
E: jimmy.martin@alhouse.gov

**McCampbell, Artis (D, 71)**
State House, Room 539-F
11 South Union Street
Montgomery, AL 36130
P: (334) 242-7747
F: (334) 242-4759
E: Artis.McCampbell
  @alhouse.org

**McClammy, Thad (D, 76)**
State House, Room 534-A
11 South Union Street
Montgomery, AL 36130
P: (334) 242-7780
F: (334) 242-4759
E: thadmcclammy@aol.com

**McCutcheon, Mac (R, 25)**
State House, Room 519-C
11 South Union Street
Montgomery, AL 36130
P: (334) 242-7705
F: (334) 242-4759
E: c.mac.mccutcheon
  @gmail.com

**McMillan, Stephen A.
  (R, 95)**
State House, Room 532
11 South Union Street
Montgomery, AL 36130
P: (334) 242-7723
F: (334) 242-4759
E: bcld07@gmail.com

**Millican, Michael J.
  (R, 17)**
State House, Room 427-F
11 South Union Street
Montgomery, AL 36130
P: (334) 242-7354
F: (334) 242-4759
E: mike.millican
  @alhouse.gov

**Mooney, Arnold (R, 43)**
State House, Room 538-D
11 South Union Street
Montgomery, AL 36130
P: (334) 242-7600
F: (334) 242-4759
E: arnold.mooney
  @alhouse.gov

**Moore, Barry (R, 91)**
State House, Room 422
11 South Union Street
Montgomery, AL 36130
P: (334) 242-7773
F: (334) 242-4759
E: barry
  @barrymooreindustries.com

**Moore, Mary (D, 59)**
State House, Room 539-D
11 South Union Street
Montgomery, AL 36130
P: (334) 242-7608
F: (334) 242-4759
E: mamoor48@bellsouth.net

**Morrow, Johnny Mack (D, 18)**
State House, Room 517-F
11 South Union Street
Montgomery, AL 36130
P: (334) 242-7698
F: (334) 242-4759
E: Johnny.Morrow
  @alhouse.org

**Nordgren, Becky (R, 29)**
State House, Room 401-D
11 South Union Street
Montgomery, AL 36130
P: (334) 353-9032
F: (334) 242-4759
E: rebeccasnordgren
  @gmail.com

**Patterson, Jim (R, 21)**
State House, Room 427-H
11 South Union Street
Montgomery, AL 36130
P: (334) 242-7531
F: (334) 242-4759
E: jimpattersonhd21
  @gmail.com

**Pettus, Phillip (R, 1)**
State House, Room 524-C
11 South Union Street
Montgomery, AL 36130
P: (334) 242-7600
F: (334) 242-4759
E: phillip.pettus
  @alhouse.gov

**Polizos, Dimitri (R, 74)**
State House, Room 522-C
11 South Union Street
Montgomery, AL 36130
P: (334) 242-7600
F: (334) 242-4759
E: dimitri.polizos
  @alhouse.gov

**Poole, Bill (R, 63)**
State House, Room 514
11 South Union Street
Montgomery, AL 36130
P: (334) 242-7624
F: (334) 242-4759
E: bill.poole@alhouse.gov

**Pringle, Chris (R, 101)**
State House, Room 427-M
11 South Union Street
Montgomery, AL 36130
P: (334) 242-7600
F: (334) 242-4759
E: chrispringle
  @southerntimberlands.com

**Rich, Kerry (R, 26)**
State House, Room 427-C
11 South Union Street
Montgomery, AL 36130
P: (334) 242-7538
F: (334) 242-4759
E: kerryrich@mclo.org

**Rogers Jr., John W. (D, 52)**
State House, Room523-A
11 South Union Street
Montgomery, AL 36130
P: (334) 242-7761
F: (334) 242-4759
E: yke@cec.conteduc.uab.edu

**Rowe, Connie (R, 13)**
State House, Room 537-E
11 South Union Street
Montgomery, AL 36130
P: (334) 242-7600
F: (334) 242-4759
E: connie.rowe@alhouse.gov

**Sanderford, Howard (R, 20)**
State House, Room 413-C
11 South Union Street
Montgomery, AL 36130
P: (334) 242-4368
F: (334) 242-4759
E: hs1989@aol.com

**Scott, Roderick (D, 55)**
State House, Room 425
11 South Union Street
Montgomery, AL 36130
P: (334) 242-7752
F: (334) 242-4759
E: rodhscott@gmail.com

**Sells, Chris (R, 90)**
State House, Room 526-E
11 South Union Street
Montgomery, AL 36130
P: (334) 242-7600
F: (334) 242-4759
E: csea@centurytel.net

**Sessions, David (R, 105)**
State House, Room 417-I
11 South Union Street
Montgomery, AL 36130
P: (334) 242-0947
F: (334) 242-4759
E: d.r.sessions@att.net

**Shedd, Randall (R, 11)**
State House, Room 524-A
11 South Union Street
Montgomery, AL 36130
P: (334) 242-7600
F: (334) 242-4759
E: randall.shedd
  @alhouse.gov

**Shiver, Harry (R, 64)**
State House, Room 526-D
11 South Union Street
Montgomery, AL 36130
P: (334) 242-7745
F: (334) 242-4759
E: harryshiver@aol.com

**South, Kyle (R, 16)**
State House, Room 427-G
11 South Union Street
Montgomery, AL 36130
P: (334) 242-7600
F: (334) 242-4759
E: ksouth@watvc.com

**Standridge, David (R, 34)**
State House, Room 524-D
11 South Union Street
Montgomery, AL 36130
P: (334) 242-7475
E: david.standridge
  @alhouse.gov

**Todd, Patricia (D, 54)**
State House, Room 539-E
11 South Union Street
Montgomery, AL 36130
P: (334) 242-7718
F: (334) 242-4759
E: reptodd@gmail.com

**Treadaway, Allen (R, 51)**
State House, Room 528-A
11 South Union Street
Montgomery, AL 36130
P: (334) 242-7685
F: (334) 242-4759
E: bsketa@aol.com

# Alabama

**Tuggle, Mark (R, 81)**
State House, Room 410-C
11 South Union Street
Montgomery, AL 36130
P: (334) 242-7219
F: (334) 242-4759
E: tughd81@gmail.com

**Wadsworth, Tim (R, 14)**
State House, Room 528-D
11 South Union Street
Montgomery, AL 36130
P: (334) 242-1792
F: (334) 242-4759
E: wadsworth@centurytel.net

**Warren, Pebblin (D, 82)**
State House, Room 517-B
11 South Union Street
Montgomery, AL 36130
P: (334) 242-7734
F: (334) 242-4759
E: tiger9127@bellsouth.net

**Weaver, April (R, 49)**
State House, Room 417-A
11 South Union Street
Montgomery, AL 36130
P: (334) 242-7731
F: (334) 242-4759
E: April.Weaver@alhouse.org

**Whorton, Isaac (R, 38)**
State House, Room 427-C
11 South Union Street
Montgomery, AL 36130
P: (334) 242-7600
F: (334) 242-4759
E: isaacwhorton@charter.net

**Whorton, Ritchie (R, 22)**
State House, Room 526-C
11 South Union Street
Montgomery, AL 36130
P: (334) 242-7600
F: (334) 242-4759
E: ritchiewhorton@gmail.com

**Wilcox, Margie (R, 104)**
State House, Room 524-F
11 South Union Street
Montgomery, AL 36130
P: (334) 242-7600
F: (334) 242-4759
E: margie.wilcox
   @alhouse.gov

**Williams, Jack (R, 47)**
State House, Room 417-A
11 South Union Street
Montgomery, AL 36130
P: (334) 242-7779
F: (334) 242-4759
E: jack@jackwilliams.org

**Williams, Jack W. (R, 102)**
State House, Room 524-F
11 South Union Street
Montgomery, AL 36130
P: (334) 242-7600
F: (334) 242-4759
E: jackwilliams55
   @icloud.com

**Williams, Phil (R, 6)**
State House, Room 401-C
11 South Union Street
Montgomery, AL 36130
P: (334) 242-7704
F: (334) 242-4759
E: philhouse44@gmail.com

**Wingo, Rich (R, 62)**
State House, Room 522-D
11 South Union Street
Montgomery, AL 36130
P: (334) 242-7600
F: (334) 242-4759
E: rich
   @blackwaterresources.com

**Wood, Randy (R, 36)**
State House, Room 424
11 South Union Street
Montgomery, AL 36130
P: (334) 242-7700
F: (334) 242-4759
E: Randy.Wood@alhouse.org

# Alaska

## Executive

### Governor
**The Honorable Bill
 Walker (I)**
Governor
State Capitol
P.O. Box 110001
Juneau, AK 99811
P: (907) 465-3500
F: (907) 465-3532

### Lieutenant Governor
**The Honorable Byron
 Mallot (I)**
Lieutenant Governor
550 West 7th Street, Suite 1700
Anchorage, AK 99501
P: (907) 269-7460
F: (907) 269-0263

### Secretary of State
*Alaska does not have the office
of secretary of state. Some of
the duties of the secretary of
state are performed by the office
of the lieutenant governor.*

### Attorney General
**The Honorable Jahna
 Lindemuth (I)**
 (appointed)
Attorney General
P.O. Box 110300
Juneau, AK 99811
P: (907) 465-2133
F: (907) 465-2075

### Auditor
**The Honorable Kris Curtis**
 (appointed by the Legislature)
Legislative Auditor
P.O. Box 113300
Juneau, AK 99811
P: (907) 465-3830
F: (907) 465-2347

### Treasurer
**The Honorable Pamela Leary**
 (appointed)
State Treasurer
P.O. Box 110400
Juneau, AK 99811
P: (907) 465-3669
F: (907) 465-2389
E: pam.leary@alaska.gov

## Judiciary
### Supreme Court (MR)
**Ms. Marilyn May**
Clerk of the Appellate Courts
303 K Street
Anchorage, AK 99501
P: (907) 264-0612
F: (907) 264-0878
E: mmay
 @appellate.courts.state.ak.us

**The Honorable Craig F.
 Stowers**
Chief Justice
**The Honorable Joel H.
 Bolger**
**The Honorable Susan M.
 Carney**
**The Honorable Peter J.
 Maassen**
**The Honorable Daniel E.
 Winfree**

## Legislative Senate
### Senate President
**Senator Pete Kelly (R)**
Senate President
State Capitol, Room 111
Juneau, AK 98801
P: (907) 465-3709
F: (907) 465-4714
E: Senator.Pete.Kelly
 @akleg.gov

### Senate Majority Leader
**Senator Peter Micciche (R)**
Senate Majority Leader
State Capitol, Room 508
Juneau, AK 99801
P: (907) 465-2828
F: (907) 465-4779
E: Senator.Peter.Micciche
 @akleg.gov

### Senate Minority Leader
**Senator Berta Gardner (D)**
Senate Minority Leader
State Capitol, Room 9
Juneau, AK 99801
P: (907) 465-4930
F: (907) 465-3834
E: Senator.Berta.Gardner
 @akleg.gov

## Secretary of the Senate
**Ms. Liz Clark**
Secretary of the Senate
State Capitol, Room 211
Juneau, AK 99801
P: (907) 465-3701
F: (807) 465-2832
E: liz.clark@akleg.gov

## Members of the Senate
**Begich, Tom (D, J)\***
State Capitol, Room 419
Juneau, AK 99801
P: (907) 465-3704
F: (907) 465-3704
E: Senator.Tom.Begich
 @akleg.gov

**Bishop, Click (R, C)**
State Capitol, Room 121
Juneau, AK 99801
P: (907) 465-2327
F: (907) 465-5241
E: Senator.Click.Bishop
 @akleg.gov

**Coghill Jr., John (R, B)**
State Capitol, Room 119
Juneau, AK 99801
P: (907) 465-3719
F: (907) 465-3258
E: Senator.John.Coghill
 @akleg.gov

**Costello, Mia (R, K)**
State Capitol, Room 504
Juneau, AK 99801
P: (907) 465-4968
F: (907) 465-2040
E: Senator.Mia.Costello
 @akleg.gov

**Dunleavy, Mike (R, E)**
State Capitol, Room 11
Juneau, AK 99801
P: (907) 465-6600
F: (907) 465-3805
E: Senator.Mike.Dunleavy
 @akleg.gov

**Egan, Dennis (D, Q)**
State Capitol, Room 417
Juneau, AK 99801
P: (907) 465-4947
F: (907) 465-2108
E: Senator.Dennis.Egan
 @akleg.gov

**Gardner, Berta (D, I)**
State Capitol, Room 9
Juneau, AK 99801
P: (907) 465-4930
F: (907) 465-3834
E: Senator.Berta.Gardner
 @akleg.gov

**Giessel, Cathy (R, N)**
State Capitol, Room 427
Juneau, AK 99801
P: (907) 465-4843
F: (907) 465-3871
E: Senator.Cathy.Giessel
 @akleg.gov

**Hoffman, Lyman (D, S)**
State Capitol, Room 518
Juneau, AK 99801
P: (907) 465-4453
F: (907) 465-4523
E: Senator.Lyman.Hoffman
 @akleg.gov

**Hughes, Shelley S. (R, F)**
State Capitol, Room 125
Juneau, AK 99801
P: (907) 465-3743
E: Senator.Shelley.Hughes
 @akleg.gov

**Kelly, Pete (R, A)**
State Capitol, Room 111
Juneau, AK 98801
P: (907) 465-3709
F: (907) 465-4714
E: Senator.Pete.Kelly
 @akleg.gov

**MacKinnon, Anna (R, G)**
State Capitol, Room 516
Juneau, AK 99801
P: (907) 465-3777
F: (907) 465-2819
E: Senator.Anna.Fairclough
 @akleg.gov

**Meyer, Kevin (R, M)**
State Capitol, Room 103
Juneau, AK 99801
P: (907) 465-4945
F: (907) 465-3476
E: Senator.Kevin.Meyer
 @akleg.gov

**Micciche, Peter (R, O)**
State Capitol, Room 508
Juneau, AK 99801
P: (907) 465-2828
F: (907) 465-4779
E: Senator.Peter.Micciche
 @akleg.gov

**Olson, Donald (D, T)**
State Capitol, Room 510
Juneau, AK 99801
P: (907) 465-3707
F: (907) 465-4821
E: Senator.Donny.Olson
 @akleg.gov

**Stedman, Bert (R, R)**
State Capitol, Room 30
Juneau, AK 99801
P: (907) 465-3873
F: (907) 465-3922
E: Senator.Bert.Stedman
 @akleg.gov

# Alaska

**Stevens, Gary (R, P)**
State Capitol, Room 429
Juneau, AK 99801
P: (907) 465-4925
F: (907) 465-3517
E: Senator.Gary.Stevens
@akleg.gov

**Von Imhof, Natasha (R, L)***
State Capitol, Room 514
Juneau, AK 99801
P: (907) 465-2995
E: Senator.
Natasha.VonImhof
@akleg.gov

**Wielechowski, Bill (D, H)**
State Capitol, Room 419
Juneau, AK 99801
P: (907) 465-2435
F: (907) 465-6615
E: Senator.
Bill.Wielechowski
@akleg.gov

**Wilson, David S. (R, D)***
State Capitol, Room 115
Juneau, AK 99801
P: (907) 465-3878
F: (907) 465-3265
E: Senator.David.Wilson
@akleg.gov

# House

## Speaker of the House

**Representative Bryce
Edgmon (D)**
Speaker of the House
State Capitol, Room 208
Juneau, AK 99801
P: (907) 465-4451
F: (907) 465-3445
E: Representative.
Bryce.Edgmon@akleg.gov

## House Majority Leader

**Representative Chris
Tuck (D)**
Majority Leader
State Capitol, Room 204
Juneau, AK 99801
P: (907) 465-2095
F: (907) 465-3810
E: Representative.
Chris.Tuck@akleg.gov

## House Minority Leader

**Representative Charisse E.
Millett (R)**
House Minority Leader
State Capitol, Room 404
Juneau, AK 99801
P: (907) 465-3879
F: (907) 465-2069
E: Representative.
Charisse.Millett
@akleg.gov

## Clerk of the House

**Ms. Crys Jones**
Chief Clerk
Thomas B. Stewart Buidling
Room 202
Juneau, AK 99811
P: (907) 465-3725
F: (907) 465-5334
E: crystaline.jones
@akleg.gov

## Members of the House

**Birch, Chris (R, 26)***
State Capitol, Room 112
Juneau, AK 99801
P: (907) 465-4931
E: Representative.
Chris.Birch@akleg.gov

**Chenault, Mike (R, 29)**
State Capitol, Room 434
Juneau, AK 99801
P: (907) 465-3779
F: (907) 465-2833
E: Representative.
Mike.Chenault@akleg.gov

**Claman, Matt (D, 21)**
State Capitol, Room 118
Juneau, AK 99801
P: (907) 465-4919
F: (907) 465-2137
E: Representative.
Matt.Claman@akleg.gov

**Drummond, Harriet (D, 18)**
State Capitol, Room 108
Juneau, AK 99801
P: (907) 465-3875
F: (907) 465-4588
E: Representative.
Harriet.Drummond
@akleg.gov

**Eastman, David (R, 10)***
State Capitol, Room 114
Juneau, AK 99801
P: (907) 465-2186
E: Representative.
David.Eastman@akleg.gov

**Edgmon, Bryce (D, 37)**
State Capitol, Room 208
Juneau, AK 99801
P: (907) 465-4451
F: (907) 465-3445
E: Representative.
Bryce.Edgmon@akleg.gov

**Fansler, Zach (D, 38)***
State Capitol, Room 416
Juneau, AK 99801
P: (907) 465-4942
F: (907) 465-4589
E: Representative.
Zach.Fansler@akleg.gov

**Foster, Neal (D, 39)**
State Capitol, Room 410
Juneau, AK 99801
P: (907) 465-3789
F: (907) 465-3242
E: Representative.
Neal.Foster@akleg.gov

**Gara, Les (D, 20)**
State Capitol, Room 511
Juneau, AK 99801
P: (907) 465-2647
F: (907) 465-3518
E: Representative.Les.Gara
@akleg.gov

**Grenn, Jason S. (I, 22)***
State Capitol, Room 418
Juneau, AK 99801
P: (907) 465-3892
F: (907) 465-6595
E: Representative.
Jason.Grenn@akleg.gov

**Guttenberg, David (D, 4)**
State Capitol, Room 501
Juneau, AK 99801
P: (907) 465-4457
F: (907) 465-3519
E: Representative.
David.Guttenberg
@akleg.gov

**Johnson, DeLena (R, 11)***
State Capitol, Room 405
Juneau, AK 99801
P: (907) 465-4958
F: (907) 465-4928
E: Representative.
DeLena.Johnson@akleg.gov

**Johnston, Jennifer B.
(R, 28)***
State Capitol, Room 430
Juneau, AK 99801
P: (907) 465-4949
E: Representative.
Jennifer.Johnson
@akleg.gov

**Josephson, Andy (D, 17)**
State Capitol, Room 102
Juneau, AK 99801
P: (907) 465-4939
F: (907) 465-2418
E: Representative.
Andy.Josephson@akleg.gov

**Kawasaki, Scott (D, 1)**
State Capitol, Room 502
Juneau, AK 99801
P: (907) 465-3466
F: (907) 465-2937
E: Representative.
Scott.Kawasaki@akleg.gov

**Kito III, Sam (D, 33)**
State Capitol, Room 403
Juneau, AK 99801
P: (907) 465-4766
F: (907) 465-4748
E: Representative.
Sam.Kito.III@akleg.gov

**Knopp, Gary A. (R, 30)***
State Capitol, Room 403
Juneau, AK 99801
P: (907) 465-2693
F: (907) 465-3835
E: Representative.
Gary.Knopp@akleg.gov

**Kopp, Charles (R, 24)***
State Capitol, Room 13
Juneau, AK 99801
P: (907) 465-4993
E: Representative.
Charles.Kopp@akleg.gov

**Kreiss-Tomkins, Jonathan
(D, 35)**
State Capitol, Room 411
Juneau, AK 99801
P: (907) 465-3732
F: (907) 465-2652
E: Representative.
Jonathan.Kreiss-Tomkins
@akleg.gov

**LeDoux, Gabrielle (R, 15)**
State Capitol, Room 216
Juneau, AK 99801
P: (907) 465-4998
F: (907) 465-4419
E: Representative.
Gabrielle.LeDoux
@akleg.gov

**Millett, Charisse E.
(R, 25)**
State Capitol, Room 404
Juneau, AK 99801
P: (907) 465-3879
F: (907) 465-2069
E: Representative.
Charisse.Millett
@akleg.gov

**Neuman, Mark (R, 8)**
State Capitol, Room 104
Juneau, AK 99801
P: (907) 465-2679
F: (907) 465-4822
E: Representative.
 Mark.Neuman@akleg.gov

**Ortiz, Daniel H. (I, 36)**
State Capitol, Room 513
Juneau, AK 99801
P: (907) 465-3824
F: (907) 465-3175
E: Representative.
 Dan.Ortiz@akleg.gov

**Parish, Justin (D, 34)\***
State Capitol, Room 432
Juneau, AK 99801
P: (907) 465-3744
F: (907) 465-2273
E: Representative.
 Justin.Parish@akleg.gov

**Pruitt, Lance (R, 27)**
State Capitol, Room 415
Juneau, AK 99801
P: (907) 465-3438
F: (907) 465-4565
E: Representative.
 Lance.Pruitt@akleg.gov

**Rauscher, George (R, 9)\***
State Capitol, Room 426
Juneau, AK 99801
P: (907) 465-4859
E: Representative.
 George.Rauscher@akleg.gov

**Reinbold, Lora (R, 14)**
State Capitol, Room 409
Juneau, AK 99801
P: (907) 465-3822
F: (907) 465-3756
E: Representative.
 Lora.Reinbold@akleg.gov

**Saddler, Dan (R, 13)**
State Capitol, Room 428
Juneau, AK 99801
P: (907) 465-3783
F: (907) 465-2293
E: Representative.
 Dan.Saddler@akleg.gov

**Seaton, Paul (R, 31)**
State Capitol, Room 505
Juneau, AK 99801
P: (907) 465-2689
F: (907) 465-3472
E: Representative.
 Paul.Seaton@akleg.gov

**Spohnholz, Ivy (D, 16)**
State Capitol, Room 421
Juneau, AK 99801
P: (907) 465-4940
F: (907) 465-3766
E: Representative.
 Ivy.Spohnholz@akleg.gov

**Stutes, Louise B. (R, 32)**
State Capitol, Room 406
Juneau, AK 99801
P: (907) 465-2487
F: (907) 465-4956
E: Representative.
 Louise.Stutes@akleg.gov

**Sullivan-Leonard, Colleen (R, 7)\***
State Capitol, Room 420
Juneau, AK 99801
P: (907) 465-4833
E: Representative.
 colleen.sullivan-leonard
 @akleg.gov

**Talerico, David M. (R, 6)**
State Capitol, Room 110
Juneau, AK 99801
P: (907) 465-4527
F: (907) 465-2197
E: Representative.
 Dave.Talerico@akleg.gov

**Tarr, Geran (D, 19)**
State Capitol, Room 126
Juneau, AK 99801
P: (907) 465-3424
F: (907) 465-3793
E: Representative.
 Geran.Tarr@akleg.gov

**Thompson, Steve (R, 2)**
State Capitol, Room 500
Juneau, AK 99801
P: (907) 465-3004
F: (907) 465-2070
E: Representative.
 Steve.Thompson@akleg.gov

**Tilton, Cathy (R, 12)**
State Capitol, Room 400
Juneau, AK 99801
P: (907) 465-2199
F: (907) 465-4587
E: Representative.
 Cathy.Tilton@akleg.gov

**Tuck, Chris (D, 23)**
State Capitol, Room 204
Juneau, AK 99801
P: (907) 465-2095
F: (907) 465-3810
E: Representative.
 Chris.Tuck@akleg.gov

**Westlake, Dean (D, 40)\***
State Capitol, Room 24
Juneau, AK 99801
P: (907) 465-3473
E: Representative.
 Dean.Westlake@akleg.gov

**Wilson, Tammie (R, 3)**
State Capitol, Room 422
Juneau, AK 99801
P: (907) 465-4797
F: (907) 465-3884
E: Representative.
 Tammie.Wilson@akleg.gov

**Wool, Adam (D, 5)**
State Capitol, Room 412
Juneau, AK 99801
P: (907) 465-4976
F: (907) 465-3883
E: Representative.
 Adam.Wool@akleg.gov

# American Samoa

## Executive

### Governor
**The Honorable Lolo Matalasi Moliga (I)**
Governor
Executive Office Building,
Third Floor
Utulei
Pago Pago, AS 96799
P: (684) 633-4116
F: (684) 633-2269

### Lieutenant Governor
**The Honorable Lemanu Peleti Mauga (I)**
Lieutenant Governor
Territory of American Samoa
Pago Pago, AS 96799
P: (684) 633-4116
F: (684) 633-2269

### Secretary of State
*American Samoa does not have the office of secretary of state. Some of the duties of the secretary of state are performed by the office of the lieutenant governor.*

### Attorney General
**The Honorable Talauega V. Ale**
(appointed)
Attorney General
American Samoa Government
Exeuctive Office Building,
Utulei
Pago Pago, AS 96799
P: (684) 633-4163

### Auditor
**Ms. Liua Fatuesi**
Territorial Auditor
Executive Office Building
AP Lutali - 2nd Floor
Pago Pago, AS 96799
P: (684) 633-5191
F: (684) 633-1039

### Treasurer
**The Honorable Ueli Tonumaipea**
Treasurer
Executive Office Building
Pago Pago, AS 96799
P: (684) 633-4155
F: (684) 633-4100
E: ueli.tonumaipea
@tr.as.gov

## Judiciary

### High Court (FA)
**Mr. Robert Gorniak**
Chief Clerk
American Samoa Government
Pago Pago, AS 96799
P: (684) 633-4131
F: (684) 633-1318

**The Honorable F. Michael Kruse**
Chief Justice
**The Honorable Lyle Richmond**

## Legislative

## Senate

### Senate President
**Senator Gaoteote Palaie Tofau (NP)**
Senate President
Legislature of American Samoa
P.O. Box 485
Pago Pago, AS 96799
P: (684) 633-5853
F: (684) 633-1638

### Secretary of the Senate
**Mr. Leo'o V. Ma'o**
Secretary of the Senate
American Samoa Senate
P.O. Box 127
Pago Pago, AS 96799
P: (684) 633-5866
F: (684) 633-1638

### Members of the Senate
**Aufata, Fonoti Tafa'ifa (NP, 8)**
Legislature of American Samoa
P.O. Box 485
Pago Pago, AS 96799
P: (684) 633-5553
F: (684) 633-1638

**Faauga, Alo (NP, 7)**
Legislature of American Samoa
P.O. Box 485
Pago Pago, AS 96799
P: (684) 633-4553
F: 684) 633-1638

**Faiai, Paepae Iosefa (NP, 12)***
Legislature of American Samoa
P.O. Box 485
Pago Pago, AS 96799
P: (684) 633-4457
F: (684) 633-1638

**Fruen, Tuaolo (NP, 6)**
Legislature of American Samoa
P.O. Box 485
Pago Pago, AS 96799
P: (684) 633-4759
F: 684) 633-1638

**Godinet, Faiivae Iuli (NP, 11)**
Legislature of American Samoa
P.O. Box 485
Pago Pago, AS 96799
P: (684) 633-4568
F: 684) 633-1638

**Hudson, Misaalefua J. (NP, 2)**
Legislature of American Samoa
P.O. Box 485
Pago Pago, AS 96799
P: (684) 633-5663
F: (684) 633-1638

**Logovi'i, Magalei (NP, 8)***
Legislature of American Samoa
P.O. Box 485
Pago Pago, AS 96799
P: (684) 633-4057
F: (684) 633-1638

**Mau Mau Jr., Fa'amausill (NP, 5)**
Legislature of American Samoa
P.O. Box 485
Pago Pago, AS 96799
P: (684) 633-5754
F: (684) 633-1638

**Sao, Nuanuaolefeagaiga (NP, 1)**
Legislature of American Samoa
P.O. Box 485
Pago Pago, AS 96799
P: (684) 633-4656
F: 684) 633-1638

**Satele Jr., Galu (NP, 10)**
Legislature of American Samoa
P.O. Box 485
Pago Pago, AS 96799
P: (684) 633-5757
F: (684) 633-1638

**Shimasaki, Fano Frank (NP, 6)**
Legislature of American Samoa
P.O. Box 485
Pago Pago, AS 96799
P: (684) 633-5359
F: (684) 633-1638

**Solaita Jr., Tulafono Fagamia (NP, 7)**
Legislature of American Samoa
P.O. Box 485
Pago Pago, AS 96799
P: (684) 633-5854
F: (684) 633-1638

**Tauoa, Muagututi'a M.T. (NP, 5)**
Legislature of American Samoa
P.O. Box 485
Pago Pago, AS 96799
P: (684) 633-4869
F: 684) 633-1638

**Tavai, Tuiagamoa (NP, 9)**
Legislature of American Samoa
P.O. Box 485
Pago Pago, AS 96799
P: (684) 633-4654
F: (684) 633-1638

**Tilo, Tilo Vasaga (NP, 6)**
Legislature of American Samoa
P.O. Box 485
Pago Pago, AS 96799
P: (684) 633-4947
F: 684) 633-1638

**Tofau, Gaoteote Palaie (NP, 4)**
Legislature of American Samoa
P.O. Box 485
Pago Pago, AS 96799
P: (684) 633-5853
F: (684) 633-1638

**Tu'ufuli, Galeai (NP, 1)**
Legislature of American Samoa
P.O. Box 485
Pago Pago, AS 96799
P: (685) 633-5453
F: (685) 633-1638

**Vaouli, Tauaa S. (NP, 4)**
Legislature of American Samoa
P.O. Box 485
Pago Pago, AS 96799
P: (684) 633-5668
F: 684) 633-1638

## House

### Speaker of the House
**Representative Savali T. Ale (NP)**
House Speaker
Legislature of American Samoa
P.O. Box 485
Pago Pago, AS 96799
P: (684) 633-5763
F: (684) 633-1681

## Speaker Pro Tempore of the House

**Representative Fetu Fetui Jr. (NP)**
House Vice Speaker
Legislature of American Samoa
P.O. Box 485
Pago Pago, AS 96799
P: (684) 633-4822
F: (684) 633-1681

## Clerk of the House

**Ms. Fialupe Lutu**
Chief Clerk of the House
Legislature of American Samoa
P.O. Box 485
Pago Pago, AS 96799
P: (684) 633-5763
F: (684) 634-1681

## Members of the House

**Afalava, Atualevao Gafatasi (NP, 17)**
Legislature of American Samoa
P.O. Box 485
Pago Pago, AS 96799
P: (684) 633-5763
F: (684) 633-1681

**Ale, Savali T. (NP, 14)**
Legislature of American Samoa
P.O. Box 485
Pago Pago, AS 96799
P: (684) 633-5763
F: (684) 633-1681

**Allen, Faimealelei Anthony F. (NP, 11)**
Legislature of American Samoa
P.O. Box 485
Pago Pago, AS 96799
P: (684) 633-5458
F: (684) 633-1681

**Amituanai, Vailoata Eteuati (NP, 7)**
Legislature of American Samoa
P.O. Box 485
Pago Pago, AS 96799
P: (684) 633-4657
F: (684) 633-1681

**Autele, Toeaina F. (NP, 2)**
Legislature of American Samoa
P.O. Box 485
Pago Pago, AS 96799
P: (684) 633-4754
F: (684) 633-1681

**Fautanu, Vesi Talalelei (NP, 1)**
Legislature of American Samoa
P.O. Box 485
Pago Pago, AS 96799
F: (684) 633-1681

**Fetui Jr., Fetu (NP, 1)**
Legislature of American Samoa
P.O. Box 485
Pago Pago, AS 96799
P: (684) 633-4822
F: (684) 633-1681

**Jennings, Alexander Eli (NP, )**
Legislature of American Samoa
P.O. Box 485
Pago Pago, AS 96799
P: (684) 633-5758
F: (684) 633-1681

**Leasiolagi, Vailiuama Steve (NP, 8)**
Legislature of American Samoa
P.O. Box 485
Pago Pago, AS 96799
P: (684) 633-5457
F: (684) 633-1681

**Mageo, Meauta Lauoi (NP, 9)**
Legislature of American Samoa
P.O. Box 485
Pago Pago, AS 96799
F: (684) 633-1681

**Mauga, Legae'e (NP, 3)**
Legislature of American Samoa
P.O. Box 485
Pago Pago, AS 96799
F: (684) 633-1681

**Mauga, Matagi D.S. (NP, 6)**
Legislature of American Samoa
P.O. Box 485
Pago Pago, AS 96799
P: (684) 633-4059
F: (684) 633-1681

**Meleisea, Samuel Ioka Ale**
Legislature of American Samoa
P.O. Box 485
Pago Pago, AS 96799
P: (684) 633-7876
F: (684) 633-1681

**Moliga, Tuumolimoli Saena (NP, 10)**
Legislature of American Samoa
P.O. Box 485
Pago Pago, AS 96799
P: (684) 633-4058
F: (684) 633-1681

**Salave'a, Fagaoatua Dorian (NP, 13)**
P.O. Box 127
Pago Pago, AS 96799
P: (684) 633-5231
F: (684) 633-1681

**Samuelu, Sataua Mataese (NP, 12)**
Legislature of American Samoa
P.O. Box 485
Pago Pago, AS 96799
P: (684) 633-4822
F: (684) 633-1681

**Saulo, Vui Florence Tuaumu (NP, 15)**
Legislature of American Samoa
P.O. Box 485
Pago Pago, AS 96799
F: (684) 633-1681

**Su'a, Talaimatai Elisara (NP, 4)**
Legislature of American Samoa
P.O. Box 485
Pago Pago, AS 96799
P: (684) 633-5763
F: (684) 633-1681

**Tufele Jr., Puleleiite Li'amatua (NP, 5)**
Legislature of American Samoa
P.O. Box 485
Pago Pago, AS 96799
P: (684) 633-5557
F: (684) 633-1681

**Vaiau, Kitara (NP, 4)**
Legislature of American Samoa
P.O. Box 485
Pago Pago, AS 96799
P: (684) 633-4956
F: (684) 633-1681

**Wilson, Manumaua Wayne (NP, 12)**
Legislature of American Samoa
P.O. Box 485
Pago Pago, AS 96799
F: (684) 633-1681

**Yeun, Timusa Tini Lam (NP, 16)**
Legislature of American Samoa
P.O. Box 485
Pago Pago, AS 96799
P: (684) 633-1681
F: (684) 633-1681

# Arizona

## Executive

### Governor
**The Honorable Doug Ducey (R)**
Governor
State Capitol
1700 West Washington Street
Phoenix, AZ 85007
P: (602) 542-4331
F: (602) 542-7601

### Lieutenant Governor
*This state does not have the office of lieutenant governor. The secretary of state is next in line of succession to the governorship.*

### Attorney General
**The Honorable Mark Brnovich (R)**
Attorney General
1275 West Washington Street
Phoenix, AZ 85007
P: (602) 542-4266
F: (602) 542-4085

### Auditor
**The Honorable Debra K. Davenport**
(appointed by the Legislature)
Auditor General
2910 North 44th Street, Suite 410
Phoenix, AZ 85018
P: (602) 553-0333
F: (602) 553-0051
E: ddavenport@azauditor.gov

### State Mine Inspector
**The Honorable Joe Hart (R)**
State Mine Inspector
1700 West Washington, 4th Floor
Phoenix, AZ 85007
P: (602) 542-5971
F: (602) 542-5335

## Corporation Commission
**The Honorable Robert Burns (R)**
Commissioner
Commissioner's Wing
1200 West Washington, 2nd Floor
Phoenix, AZ 85007
P: (602) 542-3682
F: (602) 542-3708
E: rburns-web@azcc.gov

**The Honorable Boyd Dunn (R)**
Commissioner
Commissioner's Wing
1200 West Washington, 2nd Floor
Phoenix, AZ 85007
P: (602) 542-2237
E: dunn-web@azcc.gov

**The Honorable Tom Forese (R)**
Chair
Commissioner's Wing
1200 West Washington, 2nd Floor
Phoenix, AZ 85007
P: (602) 542-2237
E: forese-web@azcc.gov

**The Honorable Doug Little (R)**
Commissioner
Commissioner's Wing
1200 West Washington, 2nd Floor
Phoenix, AZ 85007
P: (602) 542-2237
F: (602) 542-0752
E: little-web@azcc.gov

**The Honorable Andy M. Tobin (R)**
Commissioner
Commissioner's Wing
1200 West Washington, 2nd Floor
Phoenix, AZ 85007
P: (602) 542-3625
E: tobin-web@azcc.gov

## Secretary of State
**The Honorable Michele Reagan (R)**
Secretary of State
1700 West Washington, Suite 1700
Phoenix, AZ 85007
P: (602) 542-4285
F: (602) 542-1575
E: sosadmin@azsos.gov

## Superintendent of Public Instruction
**The Honorable Diane Douglas (R)**
Superintendent of Public Instruction
1535 West Jefferson Street
Phoenix, AZ 85007
P: (602) 542-5393
E: adeinbox@azed.gov

## Treasurer
**The Honorable Jeff De Wit (R)**
State Treasurer
1701 West Washington Street
Phoenix, AZ 85007
P: (602) 542-7800
F: (602) 542-7176

## Judiciary

### Supreme Court (MR)
**Ms. Janet Johnson**
Clerk of the Court
1501 West Washington, Suite 402
Phoenix, AZ 85007
P: (602) 452-3396
E: scclerk@courts.az.gov

**The Honorable W. Scott Bales**
Chief Justice
**The Honorable Clint Bolick**
**The Honorable Robert Brutinel**
**The Honorable John Pelander**
**The Honorable Ann Scott Timmer**

## Legislative

## Senate

### Senate President
**Senator Steven B. Yarbrough (R)**
Senate President
1700 West Washington
Room 205
Phoenix, AZ 85007
P: (602) 926-5863
F: (602) 417-3121
E: syarbrough@azleg.gov

## President Pro Tempore of the Senate
**Senator Debbie Lesko (R)**
President Pro Tempore
1700 West Washington
Room 200
Phoenix, AZ 85007
P: (602) 926-5413
F: (602) 417-3109
E: dlesko@azleg.gov

## Senate Majority Leader
**Senator Kimberly Yee (R)**
Majority Leader
1700 West Washington
Room 212
Phoenix, AZ 85007
P: (602) 926-3024
F: (602) 417-3110
E: kyee@azleg.gov

## Senate Minority Leader
**Senator Katie Hobbs (D)**
Minority Leader
1700 West Washington
Room 213
Phoenix, AZ 85007
P: (602) 926-5325
F: (602) 417-3149
E: khobbs@azleg.gov

## Members of the Senate
**Allen, Sylvia Tenney (R, 6)**
1700 West Washington
Room 303
Phoenix, AZ 85007
P: (602) 926-5409
F: (602) 417-3105
E: sallen@azleg.gov

**Barto, Nancy K. (R, 15)**
1700 West Washington
Room 307
Phoenix, AZ 85007
P: (602) 926-5766
F: (602) 417-3261
E: nbarto@azleg.gov

**Borrelli, Sonny (R, 5)**
1700 West Washington
Room 304
Phoenix, AZ 85007
P: (602) 926-5051
F: (602) 417-3153
E: sborrelli@azleg.gov

**Bowie, Sean (D, 18)***
1700 West Washington
Room 315
Phoenix, AZ 85007
P: (602) 926-3004
E: sbowie@azleg.gov

**Bradley, David T. (D, 10)**
1700 West Washington
Room 315
Phoenix, AZ 85007
P: (602) 926-5262
F: (602) 926-3429
E: dbradley@azleg.gov

**Brophy McGee, Kate (R, 28)**
1700 West Washington
Room 302
Phoenix, AZ 85007
P: (602) 926-4486
F: (602) 417-3170
E: kbrophymcgee@azleg.gov

**Burges, Judy (R, 22)**
1700 West Washington
Room 302
Phoenix, AZ 85007
P: (602) 926-5861
F: (602) 417-3104
E: jburges@azleg.gov

**Cajero Bedford, Olivia (D, 3)**
1700 West Washington
Room 314
Phoenix, AZ 85007
P: (602) 926-5835
F: (602) 417-3262
E: ocajerobedford@azleg.gov

**Contreras, Lupe Chavira (D, 19)**
1700 West Washington
Room 305
Phoenix, AZ 85007
P: (602) 926-5284
F: (602) 417-3106
E: lcontreras@azleg.gov

**Dalessandro, Andrea (D, 2)**
1700 West Washington
Room 312
Phoenix, AZ 85007
P: (602) 926-5342
F: (602) 417-3169
E: adalessandro@azleg.gov

**Fann, Karen (R, 1)**
1700 West Washington
Room 306
Phoenix, AZ 85007
P: (602) 926-5874
F: (602) 417-3001
E: kfann@azleg.gov

**Farley, Steve (D, 9)**
1700 West Washington
Room 213
Phoenix, AZ 85007
P: (602) 926-3022
F: (602) 417-3128
E: sfarley@azleg.gov

**Farnsworth, David C. (R, 16)**
1700 West Washington
Room 301
Phoenix, AZ 85007
P: (602) 926-3020
F: (602) 417-3119
E: dfarnsworth@azleg.gov

**Griffin, Gail (R, 14)**
1700 West Washington
Room 212
Phoenix, AZ 85007
P: (602) 926-5895
F: (602) 417-3025
E: ggriffin@azleg.gov

**Hobbs, Katie (D, 24)**
1700 West Washington
Room 213
Phoenix, AZ 85007
P: (602) 926-5325
F: (602) 417-3149
E: khobbs@azleg.gov

**Kavanagh, John (R, 23)**
1700 West Washington
Room 300
Phoenix, AZ 85007
P: (602) 926-5170
F: (602) 417-3108
E: jkavanagh@azleg.gov

**Lesko, Debbie (R, 21)**
1700 West Washington
Room 200
Phoenix, AZ 85007
P: (602) 926-5413
F: (602) 417-3109
E: dlesko@azleg.gov

**Mendez, Juan (D, 26)**
1700 West Washington
Room 313
Phoenix, AZ 85007
P: (602) 926-4124
F: (602) 417-3017
E: jmendez@azleg.gov

**Meza, Robert (D, 30)**
1700 West Washington
Room 311
Phoenix, AZ 85007
P: (602) 926-3425
F: (602) 417-3114
E: rmeza@azleg.gov

**Miranda, Catherine (D, 27)**
1700 West Washington
Room 311
Phoenix, AZ 85007
P: (602) 926-4893
F: (602) 417-3116
E: cmiranda@azleg.gov

**Montenegro, Steve (R, 13)**
1700 West Washington
Room 303B
Phoenix, AZ 85007
P: (602) 926-5955
F: (602) 417-3168
E: smontenegro@azleg.gov

**Otondo, Lisa (D, 4)**
1700 West Washington
Room 308
Phoenix, AZ 85007
P: (602) 926-3002
F: (602) 417-3124
E: lotondo@azleg.gov

**Peshlakai, Jamescita (D, 7)**
1700 West Washington
Room 314
Phoenix, AZ 85007
P: (602) 926-5160
E: jpeshlakai@azleg.gov

**Petersen, Warren (R, 12)**
1700 West Washington
Room 309
Phoenix, AZ 85007
P: (602) 926-4136
F: (602) 417-3222
E: wpetersen@azleg.gov

**Pratt, Frank (R, 8)**
1700 West Washington
Room 304
Phoenix, AZ 85007
P: (602) 926-5761
F: (602) 417-3023
E: fpratt@azleg.gov

**Quezada, Martin J. (D, 29)**
1700 West Washington
Room 313
Phoenix, AZ 85007
P: (602) 926-5911
F: (602) 417-3113
E: mquezada@azleg.gov

**Smith, Steve (R, 11)**
1700 West Washington
Room 303
Phoenix, AZ 85007
P: (602) 926-5685
F: (602) 417-3167
E: stsmith@azleg.gov

**Worsley, Bob (R, 25)**
1700 West Washington
Room 310
Phoenix, AZ 85007
P: (602) 926-5760
F: (602) 417-3091
E: bworsley@azleg.gov

**Yarbrough, Steven B. (R, 17)**
1700 West Washington
Room 205
Phoenix, AZ 85007
P: (602) 926-5863
F: (602) 417-3121
E: syarbrough@azleg.gov

**Yee, Kimberly (R, 20)**
1700 West Washington
Room 212
Phoenix, AZ 85007
P: (602) 926-3024
F: (602) 417-3110
E: kyee@azleg.gov

## House
## Speaker of the House

**Representative J. D. Mesnard (R)**
Speaker of the House
1700 West Washington
Room 223
Phoenix, AZ 85007
P: (602) 926-4481
F: (602) 417-3152
E: jmesnard@azleg.gov

## Speaker Pro Tempore of the House

**Representative Thomas R. Shope (R)**
Speaker Pro Tempore
1700 West Washington
Room 204
Phoenix, AZ 85007
P: (602) 926-3012
F: (602) 417-3123
E: tshope@azleg.gov

## House Majority Leader

**Representative John Allen (R)**
Majority Leader
1700 West Washington
Room 208
Phoenix, AZ 85007
P: (602) 926-4916
F: (602) 417-3150
E: jallen@azleg.gov

# Arizona

## House Minority Leader

**Representative Rebecca Rios (D)**
Minority Leader
1700 West Washington
Room 320
Phoenix, AZ 85007
P: (602) 926-3073
F: (602) 417-3288
E: rrios@azleg.gov

## Clerk of the House

**Mr. Jim Drake**
Chief Clerk
Capitol Complex, Room 203
1700 West Washington
Phoenix, AZ 85007
P: (602) 926-3032

## Members of the House

**Allen, John (R, 15)**
1700 West Washington
Room 208
Phoenix, AZ 85007
P: (602) 926-4916
F: (602) 417-3150
E: jallen@azleg.gov

**Alston, Lela (D, 24)**
1700 West Washington
Room 330
Phoenix, AZ 85007
P: (602) 926-5829
F: (602) 417-3115
E: lalston@azleg.gov

**Andrade, Richard C. (D, 29)**
1700 West Washington
Room 337
Phoenix, AZ 85007
P: (602) 926-3130
F: (602) 417-3292
E: randrade@azleg.gov

**Barton, Brenda (R, 6)**
1700 West Washington
Room 114
Phoenix, AZ 85007
P: (602) 926-4129
F: (602) 417-3010
E: bbarton@azleg.gov

**Benally, Wenona (D, 7)***
1700 West Washington
Room 117
Phoenix, AZ 85007
P: (602) 926-5172
E: wbenallyy@azleg.gov

**Blanc, Isela (D, 26)***
1700 West Washington
Room 126
Phoenix, AZ 85007
P: (602) 926-5187
E: iblanc@azleg.gov

**Bolding, Reginald (D, 27)**
1700 West Washington
Room 335
Phoenix, AZ 85007
P: (602) 926-3132
F: (602) 417-3274
E: rbolding@azleg.gov

**Bowers, Russell (R, 25)**
1700 West Washington
Room 310
Phoenix, AZ 85007
P: (602) 926-3128
F: (602) 417-3290
E: rbowers@azleg.gov

**Boyer, Paul (R, 20)**
1700 West Washington
Room 113
Phoenix, AZ 85007
P: (602) 926-4173
F: (602) 417-3153
E: pboyer@azleg.gov

**Butler, Kelli (D, 28)***
1700 West Washington
Room 124
Phoenix, AZ 85007
P: (602) 926-5156
E: kbutler@azleg.gov

**Campbell, Noel (R, 1)**
1700 West Washington
Room 304
Phoenix, AZ 85007
P: (602) 926-3124
F: (602) 417-3287
E: ncampbell@azleg.gov

**Cardenas, Mark (D, 19)**
1700 West Washington
Room 339
Phoenix, AZ 85007
P: (602) 926-3014
F: (602) 417-3048
E: mcardenas@azleg.gov

**Carter, Heather (R, 15)**
1700 West Washington
Room 303
Phoenix, AZ 85007
P: (602) 926-5503
F: (602) 417-3107
E: hcarter@azleg.gov

**Chavez, Cesar (D, 29)***
1700 West Washington
Room 318
Phoenix, AZ 85007
P: (602) 926-4862
E: cchavez@azleg.gov

**Clark, Ken (D, 24)**
1700 West Washington
Room 333
Phoenix, AZ 85007
P: (602) 926-3108
F: (602) 417-3285
E: kenclark@azleg.gov

**Clodfelter, Todd (R, 10)***
1700 West Washington
Room 121
Phoenix, AZ 85007
P: (602) 926-4850
E: tclodfelter@azleg.gov

**Cobb, Regina (R, 5)**
1700 West Washington
Room 302
Phoenix, AZ 85007
P: (602) 926-3126
F: (602) 417-3289
E: rcobb@azleg.gov

**Coleman, Doug (R, 16)**
1700 West Washington
Room 312
Phoenix, AZ 85007
P: (602) 926-3160
F: (602) 417-3151
E: dcoleman@azleg.gov

**Cook, David (R, 8)***
1700 West Washington
Room 341
Phoenix, AZ 85007
P: (602) 926-5162
E: dcook@azleg.gov

**Descheenie, Eric (D, 7)***
1700 West Washington
Room 323
Phoenix, AZ 85007
P: (602) 926-4846
E: edescheenie@azleg.gov

**Engel, Kristen (D, 10)***
1700 West Washington
Room 118
Phoenix, AZ 85007
P: (602) 926-3032
E: kengel@azleg.gov

**Epstein, Denise "Mitzi" (D, 18)***
1700 West Washington
Room 125
Phoenix, AZ 85007
P: (602) 926-4870
E: desptein@azleg.gov

**Espinoza, Diego (D, 19)**
1700 West Washington
Room 338
Phoenix, AZ 85007
P: (602) 926-3134
F: (602) 417-3273
E: despinoza@azleg.gov

**Farnsworth, Eddie (R, 12)**
1700 West Washington
Room 225
Phoenix, AZ 85007
P: (602) 926-5735
F: (602) 417-3122
E: efarnsworth@azleg.gov

**Fernandez, Charlene R. (D, 4)**
1700 West Washington
Room 322
Phoenix, AZ 85007
P: (602) 926-3098
F: (602) 417-3281
E: cfernandez@azleg.gov

**Finchem, Mark (R, 11)**
1700 West Washington
Room 129
Phoenix, AZ 85007
P: (602) 926-3122
F: (602) 417-3286
E: mfinchem@azleg.gov

**Friese, Randall (D, 9)**
1700 West Washington
Room 321
Phoenix, AZ 85007
P: (602) 926-3138
F: (602) 417-3272
E: rfriese@azleg.gov

**Gabaldon, Rosanna (D, 2)**
1700 West Washington
Room 325
Phoenix, AZ 85007
P: (602) 926-3424
F: (602) 417-3129
E: rgabaldon@azleg.gov

**Gonzales, Sally Ann (D, 3)**
1700 West Washington
Room 332
Phoenix, AZ 85007
P: (602) 926-3278
F: (602) 417-3127
E: sgonzales@azleg.gov

**Grantham, Travis (R, 12)***
1700 West Washington
Room 119
Phoenix, AZ 85007
P: (602) 926-4868
E: tgrantham@azleg.gov

**Hernandez, Daniel (D, 2)***
1700 West Washington
Room 115
Phoenix, AZ 85007
P: (602) 926-4840
E: dhernandez@azleg.gov

**John, Drew (R, 14)\***
1700 West Washington
Room 342
Phoenix, AZ 85007
P: (602) 926-5154
E: djohn@azleg.gov

**Kern, Anthony (R, 20)**
1700 West Washington
Room 306
Phoenix, AZ 85007
P: (602) 926-3102
F: (602) 417-3282
E: akern@azleg.gov

**Lawrence, Jay (R, 23)**
1700 West Washington
Room 131
Phoenix, AZ 85007
P: (602) 926-3095
F: (602) 417-3280
E: jlawrence@azleg.gov

**Leach, Vince (R, 11)**
1700 West Washington
Room 226
Phoenix, AZ 85007
P: (602) 926-3106
F: (602) 417-3284
E: vleach@azleg.gov

**Livingston, David (R, 22)**
1700 West Washington
Room 224
Phoenix, AZ 85007
P: (602) 926-4178
F: (602) 417-3154
E: dlivingston@azleg.gov

**Lovas, Phil (R, 22)**
1700 West Washington
Room 205
Phoenix, AZ 85007
P: (602) 926-3297
F: (602) 417-3004
E: plovas@azleg.gov

**Martinez, Ray (D, 30)\***
1700 West Washington
Room 116
Phoenix, AZ 85007
P: (602) 926-5158
E: rmartinez@azleg.gov

**Mesnard, J. D. (R, 17)**
1700 West Washington
Room 223
Phoenix, AZ 85007
P: (602) 926-4481
F: (602) 417-3152
E: jmesnard@azleg.gov

**Mitchell, Darin (R, 13)**
1700 West Washington
Room 313
Phoenix, AZ 85007
P: (602) 926-5894
F: (602) 417-3012
E: dmitchell@azleg.gov

**Mosley, Paul (R, 5)\***
1700 West Washington
Room 309
Phoenix, AZ 85007
P: (602) 926-4844
E: pmosley@azleg.gov

**Navarrete, Tony (D, 30)\***
1700 West Washington
Phoenix, AZ 85007
P: (602) 926-4864
E: onavarrete@azleg.gov

**Norgaard, Jill (R, 18)**
1700 West Washington
Room 112
Phoenix, AZ 85007
P: (602) 926-3140
F: (602) 417-3265
E: jnorgaard@azleg.gov

**Nutt, Becky (R, 14)\***
1700 West Washington
Room 122
Phoenix, AZ 85007
P: (602) 926-4852
E: bnutt@azleg.gov

**Payne, Kevin (R, 21)\***
1700 West Washington
Room 345
Phoenix, AZ 85007
P: (602) 926-4854
E: kpayne@azleg.gov

**Powers Hannley, Pamela (D, 9)\***
1700 West Washington
Room 324
Phoenix, AZ 85007
P: (602) 926-4848
E: ppowershannely@azleg.gov

**Rios, Rebecca (D, 27)**
1700 West Washington
Room 320
Phoenix, AZ 85007
P: (602) 926-3073
F: (602) 417-3288
E: rrios@azleg.gov

**Rivero, Tony (R, 21)**
1700 West Washington
Room 316
Phoenix, AZ 85007
P: (602) 926-3104
F: (602) 417-3283
E: trivero@azleg.gov

**Rubalcava, Jesus (D, 4)\***
1700 West Washington
Room 334
Phoenix, AZ 85007
P: (602) 926-4842
E: jrubalcava@azleg.gov

**Saldate IV, Macario (D, 3)**
1700 West Washington
Room 331
Phoenix, AZ 85007
P: (602) 926-4171
F: (602) 417-3162
E: msaldate@azleg.gov

**Salman, Athena (D, 26)\***
1700 West Washington
Room 123
Phoenix, AZ 85007
P: (602) 926-4858
E: asalman@azleg.gov

**Shooter, Don (R, 13)**
1700 West Washington
Room 222
Phoenix, AZ 85007
P: (602) 926-4139
F: (602) 417-3024
E: dshooter@azleg.gov

**Shope, Thomas R. (R, 8)**
1700 West Washington
Room 204
Phoenix, AZ 85007
P: (602) 926-3012
F: (602) 417-3123
E: tshope@azleg.gov

**Stringer, David (R, 1)\***
1700 West Washington
Room 308
Phoenix, AZ 85007
P: (602) 926-4838
E: dstringer@azleg.gov

**Syms, Maria (R, 28)\***
1700 West Washigton
Room 344
Phoenix, AZ 85007
P: (602) 926-4860
E: msyms@azleg.gov

**Thorpe, Bob (R, 6)**
1700 West Washington
Room 130
Phoenix, AZ 85007
P: (602) 926-5219
F: (602) 417-3118
E: bthorpe@azleg.gov

**Townsend, Kelly (R, 16)**
1700 West Washington
Room 207
Phoenix, AZ 85007
P: (602) 926-4467
F: (602) 417-3018
E: ktownsend@azleg.gov

**Udall, Michelle (R, 25)\***
1700 West Washington
Room 120
Phoenix, AZ 85007
P: (602) 926-4856
E: mudall@azleg.gov

**Ugenti-Rita, Michelle (R, 23)**
1700 West Washington
Room 111
Phoenix, AZ 85007
P: (602) 926-4480
F: (602) 417-3155
E: mugenti@azleg.gov

**Weninger, Jeff (R, 17)**
1700 West Washington
Room 110
Phoenix, AZ 85007
P: (602) 926-3092
F: (602) 417-3279
E: jweninger@azleg.gov

# Arkansas

## Executive

### Governor

**The Honorable Asa Hutchinson (R)**
Governor
State Capitol
Room 250
Little Rock, AR 72201
P: (501) 682-2345
F: (501) 682-1382

### Lieutenant Governor

**The Honorable Tim Griffin (R)**
Lieutenant Governor
270 State Capitol
Little Rock, AR 72201
P: (501) 682-2144
F: (501) 682-2894

### Attorney General

**The Honorable Leslie Rutledge (R)**
Attorney General
323 Center Street, Suite 200
Little Rock, AR 72201
P: (800) 482-8982
F: (501) 682-8084

### Auditor

**The Honorable Andrea Lea (R)**
Auditor of State
State Capitol Building, Room 230
Little Rock, AR 72201
P: (501) 682-6030
F: (501) 682-2521

### Secretary of State

**The Honorable Mark Martin (R)**
Secretary of State
256 State Capitol Building
Little Rock, AR 72201
P: (501) 682-1010
F: (501) 682-3510
E: info@sos.arkansas.gov

### Treasurer

**The Honorable Dennis Milligan**
State Treasurer
220 State Capitol
Little Rock, AR 72201
P: (501) 682-5888
F: (501) 682-3842

## Judiciary

### Supreme Court (PE)

**Ms. Stacey Pectol**
Clerk of the Courts
1320 Justice Building
625 Marshall Street
Little Rock, AR 72201
P: (501) 682-6849
E: stacey.pectol @arcourts.gov

**The Honorable Dan Kemp**
Chief Justice
**The Honorable Karen Baker**
**The Honorable Courtney Goodson**
**The Honorable Josephine L. Hart**
**The Honorable Shawn Womack**
**The Honorable Rhonda Wood**
**The Honorable Robin F. Wynne**

## Legislative
## Senate

### Senate President

**The Honorable Tim Griffin (R)**
Lieutenant Governor
270 State Capitol
Little Rock, AR 72201
P: (501) 682-2144
F: (501) 682-2894

### President Pro Tempore of the Senate

**Senator Jonathan Dismang (R)**
Senate President Pro Tempore
State Capitol
500 Woodlane Street, Suite 320
Little Rock, AR 72201
P: (501) 682-2902
E: dismang28@gmail.com

### Senate Majority Leader

**Senator Jim Hendren (R)**
Senate Majority Leader
State Capitol
500 Woodlane Street, Suite 320
Little Rock, AR 72201
P: (501) 682-2902
E: jim.hendren @senate.ar.gov

## Senate Minority Leader

**Senator Keith M. Ingram (D)**
Senate Minority Leader
State Capitol
500 Woodlane Street, Suite 320
Little Rock, AR 72201
P: (501) 682-2902
E: friendsforkeith @gmail.com

## Secretary of the Senate

**Ms. Ann Cornwell**
Director & Secretary of the Senate
Room 320, State Capitol
Little Rock, AR 72201
P: (501) 682-5951
F: (501) 682-2917
E: ann.cornwell @senate.ar.gov

## Members of the Senate

**Bledsoe, Cecile (R, 3)**
State Capitol
500 Woodlane Street, Suite 320
Little Rock, AR 72201
P: (501) 682-2902
E: cecile.bledsoe @senate.ar.gov

**Bond, Will (D, 32)**
State Capitol
500 Woodlane Street, Suite 320
Little Rock, AR 72201
P: (501) 682-2902
E: will.bond@senate.ar.gov

**Caldwell, Ronald (R, 23)**
State Capitol
500 Woodlane Street, Suite 320
Little Rock, AR 72201
P: (501) 682-2902
E: ronald.caldwell @senate.ar.gov

**Cheatham, Eddie (D, 26)**
State Capitol
500 Woodlane Street, Suite 320
Little Rock, AR 72201
P: (501) 682-2902
E: eddie.cheatham @senate.ar.gov

**Chesterfield, Linda (D, 30)**
State Capitol
500 Woodlane Street, Suite 320
Little Rock, AR 72201
P: (501) 682-2902
E: lchesterfield @comcast.net

**Clark, Alan (R, 13)**
State Capitol
500 Woodlane Street, Suite 320
Little Rock, AR 72201
P: (501) 682-2902
E: alan.clark@senate.ar.gov

**Collins-Smith, Linda (R, 19)**
State Capitol
500 Woodlane Street, Suite 320
Little Rock, AR 72201
P: (501) 682-2902
E: Linda.Collins-Smith @senate.ar.gov

**Cooper, John (R, 21)**
State Capitol
500 Woodlane Street, Suite 320
Little Rock, AR 77201
P: (501) 682-2902
E: john.cooper @senate.ar.gov

**Dismang, Jonathan (R, 28)**
State Capitol
500 Woodlane Street, Suite 320
Little Rock, AR 72201
P: (501) 682-2902
E: dismang28@gmail.com

**Eads, Lance (R, 7)**
State Capitol
500 Woodlane Street, Suite 320
Little Rock, AR 72201
P: (501) 682-2902
E: lance.eads@gmail.com

**Elliott, Joyce (D, 31)**
State Capitol
500 Woodlane Street, Suite 320
Little Rock, AR 72201
P: (501) 682-2902
E: joyce.elliott @senate.ar.gov

**English, Jane (R, 34)**
State Capitol
500 Woodlane Street, Suite 320
Little Rock, AR 72201
P: (501) 682-2902
E: jane.english @senate.ar.gov

**Files, Jake (R, 8)**
State Capitol
500 Woodlane Street, Suite 320
Little Rock, AR 72201
P: (501) 682-2902
E: Jake.Files@senate.ar.gov

**Flippo, Scott (R, 17)**
State Capitol
500 Woodlane Street, Suite 320
Little Rock, AR 72201
P: (501) 682-2902
E: scott.flippo @senate.ar.gov

**Flowers, Stephanie (D, 25)**
State Capitol
500 Woodlane Street, Suite 320
Little Rock, AR 72201
P: (501) 682-2902
E: stephanie.flowers
@senate.ar.gov

**Garner, Trent (R, 27)***
State Capitol
500 Woodlane Street, Suite 320
Little Rock, AR 72201
P: (501) 682-2902
E: trent.garner
@senate.ar.gov

**Hendren, Jim (R, 2)**
State Capitol
500 Woodlane Street, Suite 320
Little Rock, AR 72201
P: (501) 682-2902
E: jim.hendren
@senate.ar.gov

**Hester, Bart (R, 1)**
State Capitol
500 Woodlane Street, Suite 320
Little Rock, AR 72201
P: (501) 682-2902
E: bart.hester
@senate.ar.gov

**Hickey, Jimmy (R, 11)**
State Capitol
500 Woodlane Street, Suite 320
Little Rock, AR 72201
P: (501) 682-2902
E: jimmy.hickey
@senate.ar.gov

**Hutchinson, Jeremy (R, 33)**
State Capitol
500 Woodlane Street, Suite 320
Little Rock, AR 72201
P: (501) 682-2902
E: Jeremy.Hutchinson
@senate.ar.gov

**Ingram, Keith M. (D, 24)**
State Capitol
500 Woodlane Street, Suite 320
Little Rock, AR 72201
P: (501) 682-2902
E: friendsforkeith
@gmail.com

**Irvin, Missy (R, 18)**
State Capitol
500 Woodlane Street, Suite 320
Little Rock, AR 72201
P: (501) 682-2902
E: Missy.Irvin
@senate.ar.gov

**Johnson, Blake (R, 20)**
State Capitol
500 Woodlane Street, Suite 320
Little Rock, AR 72201
P: (501) 682-2902
E: blake.johnson
@senate.ar.gov

**King, Bryan (R, 5)**
State Capitol
500 Woodlane Street, Suite 320
Little Rock, AR 72201
P: (501) 682-2902
E: bryan.king@senate.ar.gov

**Lindsey, Uvalde (D, 4)**
State Capitol
500 Woodlane Street, Suite 320
Little Rock, AR 72201
P: (501) 682-2902
E: uvalde.lindsey
@senate.ar.gov

**Maloch, Bruce (D, 12)**
State Capitol
500 Woodlane Street, Suite 320
Little Rock, AR 72201
P: (501) 682-2902
E: bruce.maloch
@senate.ar.gov

**Rapert, Jason (R, 35)**
State Capitol
500 Woodlane Street, Suite 320
Little Rock, AR 72201
P: (501) 682-2902
E: jason.rapert
@senate.ar.gov

**Rice, Terry (R, 9)**
State Capitol
500 Woodlane Street, Suite 320
Little Rock, AR 72201
P: (501) 682-2902
E: terry.rice@senate.ar.gov

**Sample, Bill (R, 14)**
State Capitol
500 Woodlane Street, Suite 320
Little Rock, AR 72201
P: (501) 682-2902
E: bill.sample
@senate.ar.gov

**Sanders, David (R, 15)**
State Capitol
500 Woodlane Street, Suite 320
Little Rock, AR 72201
P: (501) 682-2902
E: davidjamessanders
@gmail.com

**Standridge, Greg (R, 16)**
State Capitol
500 Woodlane Street, Suite 320
Little Rock, AR 72201
P: (501) 682-2902
E: greg.standridge
@senate.ar.gov

**Stubblefield, Gary (R, 6)**
State Capitol
500 Woodlane Street, Suite 320
Little Rock, AR 72201
P: (501) 682-2902
E: gary.stubblefield
@senate.ar.gov

**Teague, Larry R. (D, 10)**
State Capitol
500 Woodlane Street, Suite 320
Little Rock, AR 72201
P: (501) 682-2902
E: Larry.Teague
@senate.ar.gov

**Wallace, Dave (R, 22)**
State Capitol
500 Woodlane Street, Suite 320
Little Rock, AR 72201
P: (501) 682-2902
E: dave.wallace
@senate.ar.gov

**Williams, Eddie Joe (R, 29)**
State Capitol
500 Woodlane Street, Suite 320
Little Rock, AR 72201
P: (501) 682-2902
E: eddiejoe.williams
@senate.ar.gov

# House

## Speaker of the House

**Representative Jeremy Gillam (R)**
House Speaker
State Capitol
500 Woodlane Street, Suite 350
Little Rock, AR 72201
P: (501) 682-6211
E: jeremy@growing45.com

## Speaker Pro Tempore of the House

**Representative Jon Eubanks (R)**
House Speaker Pro Tempore
State Capitol
500 Woodlane Street, Suite 350
Little Rock, AR 72201
P: (501) 682-6211
E: jon.eubanks
@arkansashouse.org

## House Majority Leader

**Representative Mathew W. Pitsch (R)**
House Majority Leader
State Capitol
500 Woodlane Street, Suite 350
Little Rock, AR 72201
P: (501) 682-6211
E: mathew.pitsch@cox.net

## House Minority Leader

**Representative Michael John Gray (D)**
Minority Leader
State Capitol
500 Woodlane Street, Suite 350
Little Rock, AR 72201
P: (501) 682-6211
E: michael.gray
@arkansashouse.org

## Clerk of the House

**Ms. Sherri Stacks**
Chief Clerk of the House/Fiscal Officer
Room 350, State Capitol
Little Rock, AR 72201
P: (501) 682-7771
E: sherri.stacks
@arkansashouse.org

## Members of the House

**Allen, Fred (D, 30)**
State Capitol
500 Woodlane Street, Suite 350
Little Rock, AR 72201
P: (501) 682-6211
E: FredAllen99@comcast.net

**Armstrong, Eddie L. (D, 37)**
State Capitol
500 Woodlane Street, Suite 350
Little Rock, AR 72201
P: (501) 682-6211
E: earmstrong4rep@gmail.com

# Arkansas

**Ballinger, Bob (R, 97)**
State Capitol
500 Woodlane Street, Suite 350
Little Rock, AR 72201
P: (501) 682-6211
E: bob@bobballinger.com

**Baltz, Scott (D, 61)**
State Capitol
500 Woodlane Street, Suite 350
Little Rock, AR 72201
P: (501) 682-6211
E: scottbaltz@yahoo.com

**Barker, Sonia Eubanks (R, 7)***
State Capitol
500 Woodlane Street, Suite 350
Little Rock, AR 72201
P: (501) 682-6211
E: sonia.barker
@arkansashouse.org

**Beck, Rick (R, 65)**
State Capitol
500 Woodlane Street, Suite 350
Little Rock, AR 72201
P: (501) 682-6211
E: rick.beck
@arkansashouse.org

**Bentley, Mary (R, 73)**
State Capitol
500 Woodlane Street, Suite 350
Little Rock, AR 72201
P: (501) 682-6211
E: mary.bentley
@arkansashouse.org

**Blake, Charles (D, 36)**
State Capitol
500 Woodlane Street, Suite 350
Little Rock, AR 72201
P: (501) 682-6211
E: charles.blake
@arkansashouse.org

**Boyd, Justin (R, 77)**
State Capitol
500 Woodlane Street, Suite 350
Little Rock, AR 72201
P: (501) 682-6211
E: justin.boyd.pharm.d
@gmail.com

**Bragg, Ken (R, 15)**
State Capitol
500 Woodlane Street, Suite 350
Little Rock, AR 72201
P: (501) 682-6211
E: kenwbragg@gmail.com

**Branscum, David (R, 83)**
State Capitol
500 Woodlane Street, Suite 350
Little Rock, AR 72201
P: (501) 682-6211
E: davidbranscum
@hotmail.com

**Brown, Karilyn (R, 41)**
State Capitol
500 Woodlane Street, Suite 350
Little Rock, AR 72201
P: (501) 682-6211
E: karilyn.brown
@arkansashouse.org

**Burch, LeAnne (D, 9)***
Stae Capitol
500 Woodlane Street, Room 350
Little Rock, AR 72201
P: (501) 682-6211
E: leanne.burch
@arkansashouse.org

**Capp, Sarah (R, 82)***
State Capitol
500 Woodlane Street, Suite 350
Little Rock, AR 77201
P: (501) 682-6211
E: sarah.capp
@arknasashouse.org

**Cavenaugh, Frances (R, 60)***
State Capitol
500 Woodlane Street, Suite 350
Little Rock, AR 72201
P: (501) 682-6211
E: frances.cavenaugh
@arkansashouse.org

**Coleman, Bruce (R, 81)***
State Capitol
500 Woodlane Street, Suite 350
Little Rock, AR 72201
P: (501) 682-6211
E: bruce.coleman
@arkansashouse.org

**Collins, Charlie (R, 84)**
State Capitol
500 Woodlane Street, Suite 350
Little Rock, AR 72201
P: (501) 682-6211
E: clcollins6@cox.net

**Cozart, Bruce (R, 24)**
State Capitol
500 Woodlane Street, Suite 350
Little Rock, AR 72201
P: (501) 682-6211
E: bccci@cablelynx.com

**Dalby, Carol (R, 1)***
State Capitol
500 Woodlane Street, Suite 350
Little Rock, AR 72201
P: (501) 682-6211
E: carol.dalby
@arkansashouse.org

**Davis, Andy (R, 31)**
State Capitol
500 Woodlane Street, Suite 350
Little Rock, AR 72201
P: (501) 682-6211
E: andy.davis
@arkansashouse.org

**Deffenbaugh, Gary (R, 79)**
State Capitol
500 Woodlane Street, Suite 350
Little Rock, AR 72201
P: (501) 682-6211
E: gary.deffenbaugh
@arkansashouse.org

**Della Rosa, Jana (R, 90)**
State Capitol
500 Woodlane Street, Suite 350
Little Rock, AR 72201
P: (501) 682-6211
E: jana.dellarosa
@arkansashouse.org

**Dotson, Jim (R, 93)**
State Capitol
500 Woodlane Street, Suite 350
Little Rock, AR 72201
P: (501) 682-6211
E: jim.dotson
@arkansashouse.org

**Douglas, Charlotte Vining (R, 75)**
State Capitol
500 Woodlane Street, Suite 350
Little Rock, AR 72201
P: (501) 682-6211
E: charlotte.douglas
@arkansashouse.org

**Douglas, Dan M. (R, 91)**
State Capitol
500 Woodlane Street, Suite 350
Little Rock, AR 72201
P: (501) 682-6211
E: dan-douglas
@sbcglobal.net

**Drown, Trevor (R, 68)**
State Capitol
500 Woodlane Street, Suite 350
Little Rock, AR 72201
P: (501) 682-6211
E: trevor.drown
@arkansashouse.org

**Eaves, Les (R, 46)**
State Capitol
500 Woodlane Street, Suite 350
Little Rock, AR 72201
P: (501) 682-6211
E: les.eaves
@arkansashouse.org

**Eubanks, Jon (R, 74)**
State Capitol
500 Woodlane Street, Suite 350
Little Rock, AR 72201
P: (501) 682-6211
E: jon.eubanks
@arkansashouse.org

**Farrer, Joe (R, 44)**
State Capitol
500 Woodlane Street, Suite 350
Little Rock, AR 72201
P: (501) 682-6211
E: jfarrer@suddenlink.net

**Ferguson, Deborah (D, 51)**
State Capitol
500 Woodlane Street, Suite 350
Little Rock, AR 72201
P: (501) 682-6211
E: deborah.ferguson
@arkansashouse.org

**Ferguson, Ken (D, 16)**
State Capitol
500 Woodlane Street, Suite 350
Little Rock, AR 72201
P: (501) 682-6211
E: kenneth.ferguson
@arkansashouse.org

**Fielding, David (D, 5)**
State Capitol
500 Woodlane Street, Suite 350
Little Rock, AR 72201
P: (501) 682-6211
E: david.fielding
@arkansashouse.org

**Fite, Charlene (R, 80)**
State Capitol
500 Woodlane Street, Suite 350
Little Rock, AR 72201
P: (501) 682-6211
E: charlenefiteforstaterep
@yahoo.com

**Fite, Lanny (R, 23)**
State Capitol
500 Woodlane Street, Suite 350
Little Rock, AR 72201
P: (501) 682-6211
E: lanny.fite@att.net

**Flowers, Vivian (D, 17)**
State Capitol
500 Woodlane Street, Suite 350
Little Rock, AR 72201
P: (501) 682-6211
E: vivian.flowers
    @arkansashouse.org

**Fortner, Jack (R, 99)***
State Capitol
500 Woodlane Street, Suite 350
Little Rock, AR 72201
P: (501) 682-6211
E: jack.fortner
    @arkansashouse.org

**Gates, Mickey (R, 22)**
State Capitol
500 Woodlane Street, Suite 350
Little Rock, AR 72201
P: (501) 682-6211
E: mickey@mickeygates.com

**Gazaway, Jimmy (R, 57)***
State Capitol
500 Woodlane Street, Suite 350
Little Rock, AR 72201
P: (501) 682-6211
E: jimmy.gazaway
    @arkansashouse.org

**Gillam, Jeremy (R, 45)**
State Capitol
500 Woodlane Street, Suite 350
Little Rock, AR 72201
P: (501) 682-6211
E: jeremy@growing45.com

**Gonzales, Justin (R, 19)**
State Capitol
500 Woodlane Street, Suite 350
Little Rock, AR 72201
P: (501) 682-6211
E: justinrory@yahoo.com

**Gray, Michael John (D, 47)**
State Capitol
500 Woodlane Street, Suite 350
Little Rock, AR 72201
P: (501) 682-6211
E: michael.gray
    @arkansashouse.org

**Gray, Michelle (R, 62)**
State Capitol
500 Woodlane Street, Suite 350
Little Rock, AR 72201
P: (501) 682-6211
E: michelle.gray
    @arkansashouse.org

**Hammer, Kim (R, 28)**
State Capitol
500 Woodlane Street, Suite 350
Little Rock, AR 72201
P: (501) 682-6211
E: kimdhammer@yahoo.com

**Henderson, Kenneth (R, 71)**
State Capitol
500 Woodlane Street, Suite 350
Little Rock, AR 72201
P: (501) 682-6211
E: ken4arkansas@gmail.com

**Hendren, Kim (R, 92)**
State Capitol
500 Woodlane Street, Suite 350
Little Rock, AR 72736
P: (501) 682-6211
E: kim.hendren
    @arkansashouse.org

**Hillman, David (D, 13)**
State Capitol
500 Woodlane Street, Suite 350
Little Rock, AR 72201
P: (501) 682-6211
E: dhillman@futura.net

**Hodges, Grant (R, 96)**
State Capitol
500 Woodlane Street, Suite 350
Little Rock, AR 72201
P: (501) 682-6211
E: grant.hodges
    @arkansashouse.org

**Hodges, Monte (D, 55)**
State Capitol
500 Woodlane Street, Suite 350
Little Rock, AR 72201
P: (501) 682-6211
E: monte.hodges
    @arkansashouse.org

**Holcomb, Mike (R, 10)**
State Capitol
500 Woodlane Street, Suite 350
Little Rock, AR 72201
P: (501) 682-6211
E: mike.holcomb
    @arkansashouse.org

**Hollowell, Steve (R, 49)***
State Capitol
500 Woodlane Street, Suite 350
Little Rock, AR 72736
P: (501) 682-6211
E: steve.hollowell
    @arkansashouse.org

**House, Douglas (R, 40)**
State Capitol
500 Woodlane Street, Suite 350
Little Rock, AR 72201
P: (501) 682-6211
E: housedouglas@gmail.com

**Jean, Lane (R, 2)**
State Capitol
500 Woodlane Street, Suite 350
Little Rock, AR 72201
P: (501) 682-6211
E: l_jean@sbcglobal.net

**Jett, Joe (D, 56)**
State Capitol
500 Woodlane Street, Suite 350
Little Rock, AR 72201
P: (501) 682-6211
E: joe.jett
    @arkansashouse.org

**Johnson, Bob (D, 42)**
State Capitol
500 Woodlane Street, Suite 350
Little Rock, AR 72201
P: (501) 682-6211
E: bobjohnsoncpa@gmail.com

**Ladyman, Jack (R, 59)**
State Capitol
500 Woodlane Street, Suite 350
Little Rock, AR 72201
P: (501) 682-6211
E: jackladyman@gmail.com

**Leding, Greg (D, 86)**
State Capitol
500 Woodlane Street, Suite 350
Little Rock, AR 72201
P: (501) 682-6211
E: greg.leding
    @arkansashouse.org

**Lemons, Tim (R, 43)**
State Capitol
500 Woodlane Street, Suite 350
Little Rock, AR 72201
P: (501) 682-6211
E: arstrep43@gmail.com

**Love, Fredrick J. (D, 29)**
State Capitol
500 Woodlane Street, Suite 350
Little Rock, AR 72201
P: (501) 682-6211
E: fjlove@att.net

**Lowery, Mark (R, 39)**
State Capitol
500 Woodlane Street, Suite 350
Little Rock, AR 72201
P: (501) 682-6211
E: markdlowery@mac.com

**Lundstrum, Robin (R, 87)**
State Capitol
500 Woodlane Street, Suite 350
Little Rock, AR 72201
P: (501) 682-6211
E: robin.lundstrum
    @arkansashouse.org

**Lynch, Roger D. (R, 14)***
State Capitol
500 Woodlane Street, Suite 350
Little Rock, AR 72201
P: (501) 682-6211
E: roger.lynch
    @arkansashouse.org

**Maddox, John (R, 20)***
State Capitol
500 Woodlane Street, Suite 350
Little Rock, AR 72201
P: (501) 682-6211
E: john.maddox
    @arkansashouse.org

**Magie, Stephen (D, 72)**
State Capitol
500 Woodlane Street, Suite 350
Little Rock, AR 72201
P: (501) 682-6211
E: stephen.magie
    @arkansashouse.org

**Mayberry, Andy (R, 27)**
State Capitol
500 Woodlane Street, Suite 350
Little Rock, AR 72201
P: (501) 682-6211
E: andymayberry
    @windstream.net

**McCollum, Austin (R, 95)***
State Capitol
500 Woodlane Street, Suite 350
Little Rock, AR 72201
P: (501) 682-6211
E: austin.mccollum
    @arkansashouse.org

**McElroy, Mark D. (D, 11)**
State Capitol
500 Woodlane Street, Suite 350
Little Rock, AR 72201
P: (501) 682-6211
E: mdmcelroy1@yahoo.com

**McGill, George B. (D, 78)**
State Capitol
500 Woodlane Street, Suite 350
Little Rock, AR 72201
P: (501) 682-6211
E: george.mcgill
    @arkansashouse.org

**McNair, Ron (R, 98)**
State Capitol
500 Woodlane Street, Suite 350
Little Rock, AR 72201
P: (501) 682-6211
E: rmcnair1950@gmail.com

**Meeks, David (R, 70)**
State Capitol
500 Woodlane Street, Suite 350
Little Rock, AR 72201
P: (501) 682-6211
E: David.Meeks
    @arkansashouse.org

# Arkansas

**Meeks, Stephen (R, 67)**
State Capitol
500 Woodlane Street, Suite 350
Little Rock, AR 72201
P: (501) 682-6211
E: stephen.meeks
@arkansashouse.org

**Miller, Josh (R, 66)**
State Capitol
500 Woodlane Street, Suite 350
Little Rock, AR 72201
P: (501) 682-6211
E: josh.miller
@arkansashouse.org

**Murdock, Reginald (D, 48)**
State Capitol
500 Woodlane Street, Suite 350
Little Rock, AR 72201
P: (501) 682-6211
E: rkm_72360@yahoo.com

**Nicks Jr., Milton (D, 50)**
State Capitol
500 Woodlane Street, Suite 350
Little Rock, AR 72201
P: (501) 682-6211
E: milton.nicks
@arkansashouse.org

**Payton, John (R, 64)**
State Capitol
500 Woodlane Street, Suite 350
Little Rock, AR 72201
P: (501) 682-6211
E: john.payton
@arkansashouse.org

**Penzo, Clint (R, 89)***
State Capitol
500 Woodlane Street, Suite 350
Little Rock, AR 72201
P: (501) 682-6211
E: clint.penzo
@arkansashouse.org

**Petty, Rebecca (R, 94)**
State Capitol
500 Woodlane Street, Suite 350
Little Rock, AR 72201
P: (501) 682-6211
E: rebecca.petty
@arkansashouse.org

**Pilkington, Aaron (R, 69)***
State Capitol
500 Woodlane Street, Suite 350
Little Rock, AR 72201
P: (501) 682-6211
E: aaron.pilkington
@arkansashouse.org

**Pitsch, Mathew W. (R, 76)**
State Capitol
500 Woodlane Street, Suite 350
Little Rock, AR 72201
P: (501) 682-6211
E: mathew.pitsch@cox.net

**Richey, Chris (D, 12)**
State Capitol
500 Woodlane Street, Suite 350
Little Rock, AR 72201
P: (501) 682-6211
E: chris.richey
@arkansashouse.org

**Richmond, Marcus E. (R, 21)**
State Capitol
500 Woodlane Street, Suite 350
Little Rock, AR 72201
P: (501) 682-6211
E: marcus.richmond
@arkansashouse.org

**Rushing, Laurie (R, 26)**
State Capitol
500 Woodlane Street, Suite 350
Little Rock, AR 72201
P: (501) 682-6211
E: laurie.rushing
@arkansashouse.org

**Rye, Johnny (R, 54)***
State Capitol
500 Woodlane Street, Suite 350
Little Rock, AR 72201
P: (501) 682-6211
E: johnny.rye
@arkansashouse.org

**Sabin, Warwick (D, 33)**
State Capitol
500 Woodlane Street, Suite 350
Little Rock, AR 72201
P: (501) 682-6211
E: wsabin@wsabin.org

**Shepherd, Matthew (R, 6)**
State Capitol
500 Woodlane Street, Suite 350
Little Rock, AR 72201
P: (501) 682-6211
E: matthew.shepherd
@arkansashouse.org

**Smith, Brandt (R, 58)**
State Capitol
500 Woodlane Street, Suite 350
Little Rock, AR 72201
P: (501) 682-6211
E: brandt.smith
@arkansashouse.org

**Sorvillo, Jim (R, 32)**
State Capitol
500 Woodlane Street, Suite 350
Little Rock, AR 72201
P: (501) 682-6211
E: sorvillo4house@gmail.com

**Speaks, Nelda (R, 100)**
State Capitol
500 Woodlane Street, Suite 350
Little Rock, AR 72201
P: (501) 682-6211
E: nelda@neldaspeaks.com

**Sturch, James (R, 63)**
State Capitol
500 Woodlane Street, Suite 350
Little Rock, AR 72201
P: (501) 682-6211
E: james.sturch
@arkansashouse.org

**Sullivan, Dan (R, 53)**
State Capitol
500 Woodlane Street, Suite 350
Little Rock, AR 72201
P: (501) 682-6211
E: dan.sullivan
@arkansashouse.org

**Tosh, Dwight (R, 52)**
State Capitol
500 Woodlane Street, Suite 350
Little Rock, AR 72201
P: (501) 682-6211
E: dwight.tosh
@arkansashouse.org

**Tucker, Clarke (D, 35)**
State Capitol
500 Woodlane Street, Suite 350
Little Rock, AR 72201
P: (501) 682-6211
E: clarke.tucker
@arkansashouse.org

**Vaught, DeAnn (R, 4)**
State Capitol
500 Woodlane Street, Suite 350
Little Rock, AR 72201
P: (501) 682-6211
E: deann.vaught
@arkansashouse.org

**Walker, John W. (D, 34)**
State Capitol
500 Woodlane Street, Suite 350
Little Rock, AR 72201
P: (501) 682-6211
E: johnwalkeratty@aol.com

**Wardlaw, Jeff (D, 8)**
State Capitol
500 Woodlane Street, Suite 350
Little Rock, AR 72201
P: (501) 682-6211
E: jeff@jeffwardlaw.com

**Warren, Les A. (R, 25)***
State Capitol
500 Woodlane Street, Suite 350
Little Rock, AR 72201
P: (501) 682-6211
E: les@hstitle.com

**Watson, Danny (R, 3)***
State Capitol
500 Woodlane Street, Suite 350
Little Rock, AR 72201
P: (501) 682-6211
E: danny.watson
@arkansashouse.org

**Whitaker, David (D, 85)**
State Capitol
500 Woodlane Street, Suite 350
Little Rock, AR 72201
P: (501) 682-6211
E: david.whitaker
@arkansashouse.org

**Williams, Jeff (R, 89)***
State Capitol
500 Woodlane Street, Suite 350
Little Rock, AR 72201
P: (501) 682-6211
E: jeff.williams
@arkansashouse.org

**Wing, Carlton (R, 38)***
State Capitol
500 Woodlane Street, Suite 350
Little Rock, AR 72201
P: (501) 682-6211
E: carlton.wing
@arkansashouse.org

**Womack, Richard (R, 18)**
State Capitol
500 Woodlane Street, Suite 350
Little Rock, AR 72201
P: (501) 682-6211
E: richard
@richardwomack.com

# California

## Executive

### Governor

The Honorable Edmund G.
Brown Jr. (D)
Governor
State Capitol
Sacramento, CA 95814
P: (916) 445-2841
F: (916) 558-3160

### Lieutenant Governor

The Honorable Gavin
Newsom (D)
Lieutenant Governor
State Capitol, Room 1114
Sacramento, CA 95814
P: (916) 445-8994
F: (916) 323-4998

### Attorney General

The Honorable Xavier
Becerra (D)
Attorney General
1300 I Street, Suite 1740
Sacramento, CA 95814
P: (916) 445-9555

### Auditor

The Honorable Elaine M.
Howle
(appointed)
State Auditor
621 Capitol Mall, Suite 1200
Sacramento, CA 95814
P: (916) 445-0255 Ext. 342
F: (916) 323-0913
E: elaineh@bsa.ca.gov

### Controller

The Honorable Betty T.
Yee (D)
State Controller
300 Capitol Mall, Suite 1850
P.O. Box 942805
Sacramento, CA 94250
P: (916) 445-2636
F: (916) 445-6379

### Secretary of State

Mr. Alex Padilla (D)
Secretary of State
1500 11th Street
Sacramento, CA 95814
P: (916) 653-7244
F: (916) 653-4795
E: secretary.padilla
@sos.ca.gov

## Superintendent of Public Instruction

The Honorable Tom
Torlakson (D)
State Superintendent of Public
Instruction
1430 N Street
Sacramento, CA 95814
P: (916) 319-0800
F: (916) 319-0175
E: superintendent
@cde.ca.gov

## Board of Equalization

The Honorable Diane L.
Harkey (R)
Board Member
400 Capitol Mall, Suite 2580
P.O. Box 942849
Sacramento, CA 94249
P: (916) 319-2073
F: (916) 323-0546

The Honorable Jerome
Horton (D)
Board Member
450 N Street, MIC: 72
Sacramento, CA 95814
P: (916) 445-4154
F: (916) 323-2869

The Honorable Fiona Ma (D)
Board Member
1215 K Street, Suite 1700
Sacramento, CA 94249
P: (916) 445-4081
F: (916) 319-2112

The Honorable George
Runner (R)
Board Member
500 Capitol Mall, Suite 1750
Sacramento, CA 95814
P: (916) 445-2181
F: (916) 327-4003
E: george.runner@boe.ca.gov

## Treasurer

The Honorable John
Chiang (D)
State Treasurer
915 Capitol Mall, Room 110
Sacramento, CA 95814
P: (916) 653-2995
F: (916) 653-3125

## Judiciary

### Supreme Court (MR)

Mr. Frank A. McGuire
Clerk of the Court
350 McAllister Street
San Francisco, CA 94102
P: (415) 865-7000

The Honorable Tani
Cantil-Sakauye
Chief Justice
The Honorable Ming W. Chin
The Honorable Carol A.
Corrigan
The Honorable Mariano
Cuéllar
The Honorable Leondra R.
Kruger
The Honorable Goodwin Liu
The Honorable Kathryn
Werdegar

## Legislative

## Senate

### Senate President

The Honorable Gavin
Newsom (D)
Lieutenant Governor
State Capitol, Room 1114
Sacramento, CA 95814
P: (916) 445-8994
F: (916) 323-4998

### President Pro Tempore of the Senate

Senator Kevin De Leon (D)
Senate President Pro Tem
State Capitol, Room 205
Sacramento, CA 95814
P: (916) 651-4024
F: (916) 651-4924
E: Senator.DeLeon
@senate.ca.gov

### Senate Majority Leader

Senator William W.
Monning (D)
Senate Majority Floor Leader
State Capitol, Room 313
Sacramento, CA 95814
P: (916) 651-4017
F: (916) 651-4917
E: Senator.Monning
@senate.ca.gov

### Senate Minority Leader

Senator Jean Fuller (R)
Senate Minority Leader
State Capitol, Room 305
Sacramento, CA 95814
P: (916) 651-4016
F: (916) 651-4916
E: Senator.Fuller
@senate.ca.gov

## Secretary of the Senate

Mr. Daniel Alvarez
Secretary of the Senate
State Capitol, Room 3044
Sacramento, CA 95814
P: (916) 651-4171
F: (916) 651-4181

## Members of the Senate

Allen, Ben (D, 26)
State Capitol, Room 5072
Sacramento, CA 95814
P: (916) 651-4026
F: (916) 651-4926
E: Senator.Allen
@senate.ca.gov

Anderson, Joel (R, 38)
State Capitol, Room 5052
Sacramento, CA 95814
P: (916) 651-4038
F: (916) 651-4938
E: Senator.Anderson
@senate.ca.gov

Atkins, Toni (D, 39)
State Capitol, Room 4072
Sacramento, CA 95814
P: (916) 651-4039
F: (916) 651-4939
E: Senator.Atkins
@senate.ca.gov

Bates, Patricia C. (R, 36)
State Capitol, Room 4048
Sacramento, CA 95814
P: (916) 651-4036
F: (916) 651-4936
E: Senator.Bates
@senate.ca.gov

Beall Jr., Jim (D, 15)
State Capitol, Room 2082
Sacramento, CA 95814
P: (916) 651-4015
F: (916) 651-4915
E: Senator.Beall
@senate.ca.gov

Berryhill, Tom (R, 8)
State Capitol, Room 3067
Sacramento, CA 95814
P: (916) 651-4008
F: (916) 651-4908
E: Senator.Berryhill
@senate.ca.gov

Bradford, Steven (D, 35)
State Capitol, Room 2054
Sacramento, CA 95814
P: (916) 651-4035
F: (916) 651-4935
E: Senator.Bradford
@senate.ca.gov

# California

**Cannella, Anthony (R, 12)**
State Capitol, Room 5082
Sacramento, CA 95814
P: (916) 651-4012
F: (916) 651-4912
E: Senator.Cannella
@senate.ca.gov

**De Leon, Kevin (D, 24)**
State Capitol, Room 205
Sacramento, CA 95814
P: (916) 651-4024
F: (916) 651-4924
E: Senator.DeLeon
@senate.ca.gov

**Dodd, Bill (D, 3)**
State Capitol, Room 4903
Sacramento, CA 95814
P: (916) 651-4003
E: Senator.Dodd
@senate.ca.gov

**Fuller, Jean (R, 16)**
State Capitol, Room 305
Sacramento, CA 95814
P: (916) 651-4016
F: (916) 651-4916
E: Senator.Fuller
@senate.ca.gov

**Gaines, Ted (R, 1)**
State Capitol, Room 3076
Sacramento, CA 95814
P: (916) 651-4001
F: (916) 651-4901
E: senator.gaines
@senate.ca.gov

**Galgiani, Cathleen (D, 5)**
State Capitol, Room 5097
Sacramento, CA 95814
P: (916) 651-4005
F: (916) 651-4905
E: Senator.Galgiani
@senate.ca.gov

**Glazer, Steve (D, 7)**
State Capitol, Room 5108
Sacramento, CA 95814
P: (916) 651-4007
F: (916) 651-4907
E: Senator.Glazer
@senate.ca.gov

**Hernandez, Edward P.
(D, 22)**
State Capitol, Room 2080
Sacramento, CA 95814
P: (916) 651-4022
F: (916) 651-4922
E: Senator.Hernandez
@senate.ca.gov

**Hertzberg, Robert M.
(D, 18)**
State Capitol, Room 4038
Sacramento, CA 95814
P: (916) 651-4018
F: (916) 651-4918
E: Senator.Hertzberg
@senate.ca.gov

**Hill, Jerry (D, 13)**
State Capitol, Room 5035
Sacramento, CA 95814
P: (916) 651-4013
F: (916) 651-4913
E: Senator.Hill
@senate.ca.gov

**Hueso, Ben (D, 40)**
State Capitol, Room 4035
Sacramento, CA 95814
P: (916) 651-4040
F: (916) 651-4940
E: Senator.Hueso
@senate.ca.gov

**Jackson, Hannah-Beth
(D, 19)**
State Capitol, Room 2032
Sacramento, CA 95814
P: (916) 651-4019
F: (916) 651-4919
E: Senator.Jackson
@senate.ca.gov

**Lara, Ricardo (D, 33)**
State Capitol, Room 5050
Sacramento, CA 95814
P: (916) 651-4033
F: (916) 651-4933
E: Senator.Lara
@senate.ca.gov

**Leyva, Connie M. (D, 20)**
State Capitol, Room 4061
Sacramento, CA 95814
P: (916) 651-4020
F: (916) 651-4920
E: Senator.Leyva
@senate.ca.gov

**McGuire, Mike (D, 2)**
State Capitol, Room 5061
Sacramento, CA 95814
P: (916) 651-4002
F: (916) 651-4902
E: Senator.McGuire
@senate.ca.gov

**Mendoza, Tony (D, 32)**
State Capitol, Room 5100
Sacramento, CA 95814
P: (916) 651-4032
F: (916) 651-4932
E: Senator.Mendoza
@senate.ca.gov

**Mitchell, Holly J. (D, 30)**
State Capitol, Room 5080
Sacramento, CA 95814
P: (916) 651-4030
F: (916) 651-4930
E: Senator.Mitchell
@senate.ca.gov

**Monning, William W. (D, 17)**
State Capitol, Room 313
Sacramento, CA 95814
P: (916) 651-4017
F: (916) 651-4917
E: Senator.Monning
@senate.ca.gov

**Moorlach, John M. W.
(R, 37)**
State Capitol, Room 2048
Sacramento, CA 95814
P: (916) 651-4037
F: (916) 651-4937
E: Senator.Moorlach
@senate.ca.gov

**Morrell, Mike (R, 23)**
State Capitol, Room 3056
Sacramento, CA 95814
P: (916) 651-4023
F: (916) 651-4923
E: Senator.Morrell
@senate.ca.gov

**Newman, Josh (D, 29)***
State Capitol, Room 4082
Sacramento, CA 95814
P: (916) 651-4029
F: (916) 651-4929
E: Senator.Newman
@senate.ca.gov

**Nguyen, Janet (R, 34)**
State Capitol, Room 3048
Sacramento, CA 95814
P: (916) 651-4034
F: (916) 651-4934
E: Senator.Nguyen
@senate.ca.gov

**Nielsen, Jim (R, 4)**
State Capitol, Room 2068
Sacramento, CA 95814
P: (916) 651-4004
F: (916) 651-4904
E: Senator.Nielsen
@senate.ca.gov

**Pan, Richard (D, 6)**
State Capitol, Room 5114
Sacramento, CA 95814
P: (916) 651-4006
F: (916) 651-4906
E: Senator.Pan
@senate.ca.gov

**Portantino, Anthony J.
(D, 25)**
State Capitol, Room 3086
Sacramento, CA 95814
P: (916) 651-4025
E: Assemblymember.
Portantino
@assembly.ca.gov

**Roth, Richard (D, 31)**
State Capitol, Room 4034
Sacramento, CA 95814
P: (916) 651-4031
F: (916) 651-4931
E: Senator.Roth
@senate.ca.gov

**Skinner, Nancy (D, 9)**
State Capitol, Rooom 4909
Sacramento, CA 98514
P: (916) 651-4009
E: Senatorr.Skinner
@senate.ca.gov

**Stern, Henry (D, 27)***
State Capitol, Room 4927
Sacramento, CA 95814
P: (916) 651-4027
E: Senator.Stern
@senate.ca.gov

**Stone, Jeff (R, 28)**
State Capitol, Room 4062
Sacramento, CA 95814
P: (916) 651-4028
F: (916) 651-4928
E: Senator.Stone
@senate.ca.gov

**Vidak, Andy (R, 14)**
State Capitol, Room 3082
Sacramento, CA 95814
P: (916) 651-4014
F: (916) 651-4914
E: Senator.Vidak
@senate.ca.gov

**Wieckowski, Bob (D, 10)**
State Capitol, Room 4085
Sacramento, CA 95814
P: (916) 651-4010
F: (916) 651-4910
E: Senator.Wieckowski
@senate.ca.gov

**Wiener, Scott (D, 11)***
State Capitol, Room 4066
Sacramento, CA 95814
P: (916) 651-4011
F: (916) 651-4911
E: Senator.Wiener
@senate.ca.gov

**Wilk, Scott (R, 21)**
State Capitol, Room 4090
Sacramento, CA 95814
P: (916) 651-4021
F: (916) 651-4921
E: Senator.Wilk
@senate.ca.gov

# Assembly

## Speaker of the Assembly

**Assemblymember Anthony Rendon (D)**
Speaker of the Assembly
State Capitol, Room 219
P.O. Box 942849
Sacramento, CA 94249
P: (916) 319-2063
F: (916) 319-2163
E: Assemblymember.Rendon
@assembly.ca.gov

## Speaker Pro Tempore of the Assembly

**Assemblymember Kevin Mullin (D)**
Assembly Speaker Pro Tempore
State Capitol, Room 3160
P.O. Box 942849
Sacramento, CA 94249
P: (916) 319-2022
F: (916) 319-2122
E: Assemblymember.Mullin
@assembly.ca.gov

## Assembly Majority Leader

**Assemblymember Ian C. Calderon (D)**
Assembly Majority Floor Leader
State Capitol, Room 319
P.O. Box 942849
Sacramento, CA 94249
P: (916) 319-2057
F: (916) 319-2157
E: Assemblymember.Calderon
@assembly.ca.gov

## Assembly Minority Leader

**Assemblymember Chad Mayes (R)**
Assembly Minority Floor Leader
State Capitol, Room 3104
P.O. Box 942849
Sacramento, CA 94249
P: (916) 319-2042
F: (916) 319-2142
E: Assemblymember.Mayes
@assembly.ca.gov

## Clerk of the Assembly

**Mr. E. Dotson Wilson**
Chief Clerk of the Assembly
State Capitol, Room 3196
Sacramento, CA 95814
P: (916) 319-2856
E: Dotson.Wilson@asm.ca.gov

## Members of the Assembly

**Acosta, Dante (R, 38)\***
State Capitol, Room 2002
P.O. Box 942849
Sacramento, CA 94249
P: (916) 319-2038
F: (916) 319-2138
E: Assemblymember.Acosta
@assembly.ca.gov

**Aguiar-Curry, Cecilia M. (D, 4)\***
State Capitol, Room 5144
P.O. Box 942849
Sacramento, CA 94249
P: 916-319-2004
E: assemblymember.
aguiar-curry
@assembly.ca.gov

**Allen, Travis (R, 72)**
State Capitol, Room 4208
P.O. Box 942849
Sacramento, CA 94249
P: (916) 319-2072
F: (916) 319-2172
E: Assemblymember.Allen
@assembly.ca.gov

**Arambula, Joaquin (D, 31)**
State Capitol, Room 5155
P.O. Box 942849
Sacramento, CA 94249
P: (916) 319-2031
F: (916) 319-2131
E: Assemblymember.Arambula
@ca.assembly.gov

**Baker, Catharine (R, 16)**
State Capitol, Room 2130
P.O. Box 942849
Sacramento, CA 94249
P: (916) 319-2016
F: (916) 319-2116
E: Assemblymember.Baker
@asm.ca.gov

**Berman, Marc (D, 24)\***
State Capitol, Room 6011
P.O. Box 942849
Sacramento, CA 94249
P: (916) 319-2024
F: (916) 319-2124
E: Assemblymember.Berman
@assembly.ca.gov

**Bigelow, Franklin E. (R, 5)**
State Capitol, Room 4158
P.O. Box 942849
Sacramento, CA 94249
P: (916) 319-2005
F: (916) 319-2105
E: Assemblymember.Bigelow
@assembly.ca.gov

**Bloom, Richard (D, 50)**
State Capitol, Room 2003
P.O. Box 942849
Sacramento, CA 94249
P: (916) 319-2050
F: (916) 319-2150
E: Assemblymember.Bloom
@assembly.ca.gov

**Bocanegra, Raul (D, 39)**
State Capitol, Room 2175
P.O. Box 942849
Sacramento, CA 94249
P: (916) 619-2039
F: (916) 619-2139
E: Assemblymember.
Bocanegra@assembly.ca.gov

**Bonta, Rob (D, 18)**
State Capitol, Room 2148
P.O. Box 942849
Sacramento, CA 94249
P: (916) 319-2018
F: (916) 319-2118
E: Assemblymember.Bonta
@assembly.ca.gov

**Brough, William (R, 73)**
State Capitol, Room 3141
P.O. Box 942849
Sacramento, CA 94249
P: (916) 319-2073
F: (916) 319-2173
E: Assemblymember.Brough
@asm.ca.gov

**Burke, Autumn (D, 62)**
State Capitol, Room 5150
P.O. Box 942849
Sacramento, CA 94249
P: (916) 319-2062
F: (916) 319-2162
E: Assemblymember.Burke
@asm.ca.gov

**Caballero, Anna M. (D, 30)**
State Capitol, Room 5158
Room 5158
Sacramento, CA 94249
P: (916) 319-2030
F: (916) 319-2130
E: Assemblymember.
Caballero@assembly.ca.gov

**Calderon, Ian C. (D, 57)**
State Capitol, Room 319
P.O. Box 942849
Sacramento, CA 94249
P: (916) 319-2057
F: (916) 319-2157
E: Assemblymember.Calderon
@assembly.ca.gov

**Cervantes, Sabrina (D, 60)\***
State Capitol, Room 5164
P.O. Box 942849
Sacramento, CA 94249
P: (916) 319-2060
F: (916) 319-2161
E: Assemblymember.
Cervantes@assembly.ca.gov

**Chau, Ed (D, 49)**
State Capitol, Room 5016
P.O. Box 942849
Sacramento, CA 94249
P: (916) 319-2049
F: (916) 319-2149
E: Ed.Chau@asm.ca.gov

**Chavez, Rocky I. (R, 76)**
State Capitol, Room 2170
P.O. Box 942849
Sacramento, CA 94249
P: (916) 319-2076
F: (916) 319-2176
E: Assemblymember.Chavez
@assembly.ca.gov

**Chen, Phillip (R, 55)\***
State Capitol, Room 4177
P.O. Box 942849
Sacramento, CA 94249
P: (916) 319-2055
F: (916) 319-2155
E: Assemblymember.Chen
@assembly.ca.gov

# California

**Chiu, David (D, 17)**
State Capitol, Room 4112
P.O. Box 942849
Sacramento, CA 94249
P: (916) 319-2017
F: (916) 319-2117
E: Assemblymember.Chiu
@asm.ca.gov

**Choi, Steven S. (R, 68)***
State Capitol, Room 2016
Room 2016
Sacramento, CA 94249
P: (916) 319-2068
F: (916) 319-2168
E: Assemblymember.Choi
@assembly.ca.gov

**Chu, Kansen (D, 25)**
State Capitol, Room 2160
P.O. Box 942849
Sacramento, CA 94249
P: (916) 319-2025
F: (916) 319-2125
E: Assemblymember.Chu
@assembly.ca.gov

**Cooley, Ken (D, 8)**
State Capitol, Room 3013
P.O. Box 942849
Sacramento, CA 94249
P: (916) 319-2008
F: (916) 319-2108
E: Assemblymember.Cooley
@assembly.ca.gov

**Cooper, Jim (D, 9)**
State Capitol, Room 6025
P.O. Box 942849
Sacramento, CA 94249
P: (916) 319-2009
F: (916) 319-2109
E: Assemblymember.Cooper
@assembly.ca.gov

**Cunningham, Jordan (R, 35)***
State Capitol, Room 4102
P.O. Box 942849
Sacramento, CA 94249
P: (916) 319-2035
F: (916) 319-2135
E: Assemblymember.
Cunningham
@assembly.ca.gov

**Dababneh, Matthew (D, 45)**
State Capitol, Room 6031
P.O. Box 942849
Sacramento, CA 94249
P: (916) 319-2045
F: (916) 319-2145
E: Assemblymember.Dababneh
@assembly.ca.gov

**Dahle, Brian (R, 1)**
State Capitol, Room 4098
P.O. Box 942849
Sacramento, CA 94249
P: (916) 319-2001
F: (916) 319-2101
E: Assemblymember.Dahle
@assembly.ca.gov

**Daly, Tom (D, 69)**
State Capitol, Room 3120
P.O. Box 942849
Sacramento, CA 94249
P: (916) 319-2069
F: (916) 319-2169
E: Assemblymember.Daly
@assembly.ca.gov

**Eggman, Susan Talamantes (D, 13)**
State Capitol, Room 4117
P.O. Box 942849
Sacramento, CA 94249
P: (916) 319-2013
F: (916) 319-2113
E: Assemblymember.Eggman
@assembly.ca.gov

**Flora, Heath (R, 12)***
State Capitol, Room 3149
P.O. Box 942849
Sacramento, CA 94249
P: (916) 319-2012
F: (916) 319-2112
E: Assemblymember.Flora
@assembly.ca.gov

**Fong, Vince (R, 34)***
State Capitol, Room 2134
P.O. Box 942849
Sacramento, CA 94249
P: (916) 319-2034
F: (916) 319-2134
E: Assemblymember.Fong
@assembly.ca.gov

**Frazier, Jim (D, 11)**
State Capitol, Room 3091
P.O. Box 942849
Sacramento, CA 94249
P: (916) 319-2011
F: (916) 319-2111
E: Assemblymember.Frazier
@assembly.ca.gov

**Friedman, Laura (D, 43)***
State Capitol, Room 2137
P.O. Box 942849
Sacramento, CA 94249
P: (916) 319-2043
F: (916) 319-2143
E: Assemblymember.Friedman
@assembly.ca.gov

**Gallagher, James (R, 3)**
State Capitol, Room 2158
P.O. Box 942849
Sacramento, CA 94249
P: (916) 319-2003
F: (916) 319-2103
E: Assemblymember.
Gallagher@assembly.ca.gov

**Garcia, Cristina (D, 58)**
State Capitol, Room 2013
P.O. Box 942849
Sacramento, CA 94249
P: (916) 319-2058
F: (916) 319-2158
E: Assemblymember.Garcia
@assembly.ca.gov

**Garcia, Eduardo (D, 56)**
State Capitol, Room 4140
P.O. Box 942849
Sacramento, CA 94249
P: (916) 319-2056
F: (916) 319-2156
E: assemblymember.
eduardo.garcia
@assembly.ca.gov

**Gipson, Mike (D, 64)**
State Capitol, Room 3173
P.O. Box 942849
Sacramento, CA 94249
P: (916) 319-2064
F: (916) 319-2164
E: Assemblymember.Gipson
@assembly.ca.gov

**Gloria, Todd (D, 78)***
State Capitol, Room 4162
P.O. Box 942849
Sacramento, CA 94249
P: (916) 319-2078
F: (916) 319-2178
E: Assemblymember.Gloria
@assembly.ca.gov

**Gomez, Jimmy (D, 51)**
State Capitol, Room 3126
P.O. Box 942849
Sacramento, CA 94249
P: (916) 319-2051
F: (916) 319-2151
E: Assemblymember.Gomez
@assembly.ca.gov

**Gonzalez, Lorena (D, 80)**
State Capitol, Room 2114
P.O. Box 942849
Sacramento, CA 94249
P: (916) 319-2080
F: (916) 319-2180
E: Assemblymember.Gonzalez
@assembly.ca.gov

**Gray, Adam (D, 21)**
State Capitol, Room 3152
P.O. Box 942849
Sacramento, CA 94249
P: (916) 319-2021
F: (916) 319-2121
E: Assemblymember.Gray
@assembly.ca.gov

**Grayson, Tim (D, 17)***
State Capitol, Room 4164
P.O. Box 942849
Sacramento, CA 94249
P: (916) 319-2014
F: (916) 319-2114
E: Assemblymember.Grayson
@assembly.ca.gov

**Harper, Matthew (R, 74)**
State Capitol, Room 5126
P.O. Box 942849
Sacramento, CA 94249
P: (916) 319-2074
F: (916) 319-2174
E: Assemblymember.Harper
@assembly.ca.gov

**Holden, Chris (D, 41)**
State Capitol, Room 5136
P.O. Box 242849
Sacramento, CA 94249
P: (916) 319-2041
F: (916) 319-2141
E: Assemblymember.Holden
@assembly.ca.gov

**Irwin, Jacqui (D, 44)**
State Capitol, Room 5119
P.O. Box 942849
Sacramento, CA 94249
P: (916) 319-2044
F: (916) 319-2144
E: Assemblymember.Irwin
@assembly.ca.gov

**Jones-Sawyer Sr.,
Reginald B. (D, 59)**
State Capitol, Room 2117
P.O. Box 942849
Sacramento, CA 94249
P: (916) 319-2059
F: (916) 319-2159
E: Assemblymember.
Jones-Sawyer
@assembly.ca.gov

**Kalra, Ash (D, 27)***
State Capitol, Room 5160
P.O. Box 942849
Sacramento, CA 94249
P: (916) 319-2027
F: (916) 317-2127
E: Assemblymember.Kalra
@assembly.ca.gov

**Kiley, Kevin (R, 6)***
State Capitol, Room 4153
P.O. Box 942849
Sacramento, CA 94249
P: (916) 319-2006
F: (916) 319-2116
E: Assemblymember.Kiley
@assembly.ca.gov

**Lackey, Tom (R, 36)**
State Capitol, Room 2174
P.O. Box 942849
Sacramento, CA 94249
P: (916) 319-2036
F: (916) 319-2136
E: Assemblymember.Lackey
@assembly.ca.gov

**Levine, Marc (D, 10)**
State Capitol, Room 5135
P.O. Box 942849
Sacramento, CA 94249
P: (916) 319-2010
F: (916) 319-2110
E: Assemblymember.Levine
@assembly.ca.gov

**Limón, S. Monique (D, 37)***
State Capitol, Room 4167
P.O. Box 942849
Sacramento, CA 94249
P: (916) 319-2037
F: (916) 319-2137
E: Assemblymember.Limon
@assembly.ca.gov

**Low, Evan (D, 28)**
State Capitol, Room 4126
P.O. Box 942849
Sacramento, CA 94249
P: (916) 319-2028
F: (916) 319-2128
E: Assemblymember.Low
@assembly.ca.gov

**Maienschein, Brian (R, 77)**
State Capitol, Room 4139
P.O. Box 942849
Sacramento, CA 94249
P: (916) 317-2077
F: (916) 317-2177
E: Assemblymember.
Maienschein
@assembly.ca.gov

**Mathis, Devon (R, 26)**
State Capitol, Room 2111
P.O. Box 942849
Sacramento, CA 94249
P: (916) 319-2026
F: (916) 319-2126
E: Assemblymember.Mathis
@assembly.ca.gov

**Mayes, Chad (R, 42)**
State Capitol, Room 3104
P.O. Box 942849
Sacramento, CA 94249
P: (916) 319-2042
F: (916) 319-2142
E: Assemblymember.Mayes
@assembly.ca.gov

**McCarty, Kevin (D, 7)**
State Capitol, Room 2136
P.O. Box 942849
Sacramento, CA 94249
P: (916) 319-2007
F: (916) 319-2107
E: Assemblymember.McCarty
@assembly.ca.gov

**Medina, Jose (D, 61)**
State Capitol, Room 2141
P.O. Box 942849
Sacramento, CA 94249
P: (916) 319-2061
F: (916) 319-2161
E: Assemblymember.Medina
@assembly.ca.gov

**Melendez, Melissa A.
(R, 67)**
State Capitol, Room 3098
P.O. Box 942849
Sacramento, CA 94249
P: (916) 319-2067
F: (916) 319-2167
E: Assemblymember.Melendez
@assembly.ca.gov

**Mullin, Kevin (D, 22)**
State Capitol, Room 3160
P.O. Box 942849
Sacramento, CA 94249
P: (916) 319-2022
F: (916) 319-2122
E: Assemblymember.Mullin
@assembly.ca.gov

**Muratsuchi, Al (D, 66)**
State Capitol, Room 2179
P.O. Box 942849
Sacramento, CA 94249
P: (916) 319-2066
F: (916) 319-2166
E: Assemblymember.
Muratsuchi
@assembly.ca.gov

**Nazarian, Adrin (D, 46)**
State Capitol, Room 4146
P.O. Box 942849
Sacramento, CA 94249
P: (916) 319-2046
F: (916) 319-2146
E: Assemblymember.Nazarian
@assembly.ca.gov

**Obernolte, Jay (R, 33)**
State Capitol, Room 4116
P.O. Box 942849
Sacramento, CA 94249
P: (916) 319-2033
F: (916) 319-2133
E: Assemblymember.
Obernolte@assembly.ca.gov

**O'Donnell, Patrick (D, 70)**
State Capitol, Room 2196
P.O. Box 942849
Sacramento, CA 94249
P: (916) 319-2070
F: (916) 319-2170
E: Assemblymember.
O'Donnell@assembly.ca.gov

**Patterson, Jim (R, 23)**
State Capitol, Room 3132
P.O. Box 942849
Sacramento, CA 94249
P: (916) 319-2023
F: (916) 319-2123
E: Assemblymember.
Patterson@assembly.ca.gov

**Quirk, Bill (D, 20)**
State Capitol, Room 2163
P.O. Box 942849
Sacramento, CA 94249
P: (916) 319-2020
F: (916) 319-2120
E: Assemblymember.Quirk
@assembly.ca.gov

**Quirk-Silva, Sharon (D, 47)**
State Capitol, Room 4015
P.O. Box 942849
Sacramento, CA 94249
P: (916) 319-2047
F: (916) 319-2147
E: Assemblymember.
Quirk-Silva
@assembly.ca.gov

**Rendon, Anthony (D, 63)**
State Capitol, Room 219
P.O. Box 942849
Sacramento, CA 94249
P: (916) 319-2063
F: (916) 319-2163
E: Assemblymember.Rendon
@assembly.ca.gov

**Reyes, Eloise Gomez
(D, 47)***
State Capitol, Room 4015
P.O. Box 942849
Sacramento, CA 94249
P: (916) 319-2047
F: (916) 319-2147
E: Assemblymember.Reyes
@assembly.ca.gov

**Ridley-Thomas, Sebastian
(D, 54)**
State Capitol, Room 2176
P.O. Box 942849
Sacramento, CA 94249
P: (916) 319-2054
F: (916) 319-2154
E: Assemblymember.
Ridley-Thomas
@assembly.ca.gov

**Rodriguez, Freddie (D, 52)**
State Capitol, Room 2188
P.O. Box 942849
Sacramento, CA 94249
P: (916) 319-2052
F: (916) 319-2152
E: Assemblymember.
Rodriguez@assembly.ca.gov

**Rubio, Blanca E. (D, 48)***
State Capitol, Room 5175
P.O. Box 942849
Sacramento, CA 94249
P: (916) 319-2048
F: (916) 319-2148
E: Assemblymember.Rubio
@assembly.ca.gov

**Salas Jr., Rudy (D, 32)**
State Capitol, Room 4016
P.O. Box 942849
Sacramento, CA 94249
P: (916) 319-2032
F: (916) 319-2132
E: Assemblymember.Salas
@assembly.ca.gov

**Santiago, Miguel (D, 53)**
State Capitol, Room 6027
P.O. Box 942849
Sacramento, CA 94249
P: (916) 319-2053
F: (916) 319-2153
E: Assemblymember.Santiago
@assembly.ca.gov

**Steinorth, Marc (R, 40)**
State Capitol, Room 5128
P.O. Box 942849
Sacramento, CA 94249
P: (916) 319-2040
F: (916) 319-2140
E: Assemblymember.
Steinorth@assembly.ca.gov

**Stone, Mark (D, 29)**
State Capitol, Room 2146
P.O. Box 942849
Sacramento, CA 94249
P: (916) 319-2029
F: (916) 319-2129
E: Assemblymember.Stone
@assembly.ca.gov

# California

**Thurmond, Tony (D, 15)**
State Capitol, Room 4005
P.O. Box 942849
Sacramento, CA 94249
P: (916) 319-2015
F: (916) 319-2115
E: Assemblymember.Thurmond
   @assembly.ca.gov

**Ting, Philip Y. (D, 19)**
State Capitol, Room 6026
P.O. Box 942849
Sacramento, CA 94249
P: (916) 319-2019
F: (916) 319-2119
E: Assemblymember.Ting
   @assembly.ca.gov

**Voepel, Randy (R, 71)***
P.O. Box 942849
Room 4009
Sacramento, CA 94249
P: (916) 319-2071
E: Assemblymember.Voepel
   @assembly.ca.gov

**Waldron, Marie (R, 75)**
State Capitol, Room 4130
P.O. Box 942849
Sacramento, CA 94249
P: (916) 319-2075
F: (916) 319-2175
E: Assemblymember.Waldron
   @assembly.ca.gov

**Weber, Shirley N. (D, 79)**
State Capitol, Room 3123
P.O. Box 942849
Sacramento, CA 94249
P: (916) 319-2079
F: (916) 319-2179
E: Assemblymember.Weber
   @assembly.ca.gov

**Wood, Jim (D, 2)**
State Capitol, Room 6005
P.O. Box 942849
Sacramento, CA 94249
P: (916) 319-2002
F: (916) 319-2102
E: Assemblymember.Wood
   @assembly.ca.gov

# Colorado

## Executive

### Governor

The Honorable John
Hickenlooper (D)
Governor
136 State Capitol
Denver, CO 80203
P: (303) 866-2471
F: (303) 866-2003

### Lieutenant Governor

The Honorable Donna
Lynne (D)
Lieutenant Governor
130 State Capitol
Denver, CO 80202
P: (303) 866-2087
F: (303) 866-5469

### Attorney General

The Honorable Cynthia
Coffman (R)
Attorney General
Ralph L. Carr Colorado Judicial
Center
1300 Broadway, 10th Floor
Denver, CO 80203
P: (720) 508-6000
F: (720) 508-6030
E: attorney.general
@state.co.us

### Auditor

The Honorable Diane E. Ray
(appointed by the Legislature)
State Auditor
1525 Sherman Street, 7th Floor
Denver, CO 80203
P: (303) 869-2800
F: (303) 869-3060
E: diane.ray@state.co.us

### Secretary of State

The Honorable Wayne
Williams (R)
Secretary of State
1700 Broadway, Suite 200
Denver, CO 80290
P: (303) 894-2200
F: (303) 869-4860
E: wayne.williams
@sos.state.co.us.

## Treasurer

The Honorable Walker
Stapleton (R)
State Treasurer
140 State Capitol Building
Denver, CO 80203
P: (303) 866-2441
F: (303) 866-2123
E: treasurer.stapleton
@state.co.us

## Judiciary

### Supreme Court (MR)

Mr. Christopher T. Ryan
Clerk of the Supreme Court
2 East 14th Avenue
Denver, CO 80203
P: (720) 625-5150
E: Christopher.Ryan
@judicial.state.co.us

The Honorable Nancy E. Rice
Chief Justice
The Honorable Brian D.
Boatright
The Honorable Nathan B.
Coats
The Honorable Allison Eid
The Honorable Richard L.
Gabriel
The Honorable William W.
Hood III
The Honorable Monica M.
Marquez

## Legislative

## Senate

### Senate President

Senator Kevin Grantham (R)
Senate President
200 E. Colfax Avenue
Denver, CO 80203
P: (303) 866-4877
E: kevin.grantham.senate
@state.co.us

### President Pro Tempore of the Senate

Senator Jerry
Sonnenberg (R)
Senate President Pro Tempore
200 E. Colfax Avenue
Denver, CO 80203
P: (303) 866-6360
E: jerry.sonnenberg.senate
@state.co.us

## Senate Majority Leader

Senator Chris Holbert (R)
Senate Majority Leader
200 E. Colfax Avenue
Room 346
Denver, CO 80203
P: (303) 866-4881
E: chris.holbert.senate
@state.co.us

## Senate Minority Leader

Senator Lucia Guzman (D)
Senate Minority Leader
200 E. Colfax Avenue
Room 346
Denver, CO 80203
P: (303) 866-4862
E: lucia.guzman.senate
@state.co.us

## Secretary of the Senate

Ms. Effie Ameen
Secretary of the Senate
State Capitol
200 East Colfax Avenue
Denver, CO 80203
P: (303) 866-4838
F: (303) 866-4543

## Members of the Senate

Aguilar, Irene (D, 32)
200 E. Colfax Avenue
Room 346
Denver, CO 80203
P: (303) 866-4852
E: irene.aguilar.senate
@state.co.us

Baumgardner, Randy L.
(R, 8)
200 E. Colfax Avenue
Denver, CO 80203
P: (303) 866-5292
E: randy.
baumgardner.senate
@state.co.us

Cooke, John (R, 13)
200 E. Colfax Avenue
Room 346
Denver, CO 80203
P: (303) 866-4451
E: john.cooke.senate
@state.co.us

Coram, Don (R, 6)
200 E. Colfax Avenue
Room 346
Denver, CO 80203
P: (303) 866-4884
E: don.coram.senate
@state.co.us

Court, Lois (D, 31)
200 E. Colfax Avenue
Denver, CO 80203
P: (303) 866-4861
E: lois.court.senate
@state.co.us

Crowder, Larry (R, 35)
200 E. Colfax Avenue
Room 346
Denver, CO 80203
P: (303) 866-4875
E: larry.crowder.senate
@state.co.us

Donovan, Kerry (D, 5)
200 E. Colfax Avenue
Denver, CO 80203
P: (303) 866-4871
E: kerry.donovan.senate
@state.co.us

Fenberg, Stephen (D, 18)*
200 E. Colfax Avenue
Denver, CO 80203
P: (303) 866-4872
E: stephen.fenberg.senate
@state.co.us

Fields, Rhonda (D, 29)
200 E. Colfax Avenue
Denver, CO 80203
P: (303) 866-4879
E: rhonda.fields.senate
@state.co.us

Garcia, Leroy M. (D, 3)
200 E. Colfax Avenue
Denver, CO 80203
P: (303) 866-4878
E: leroy.garcia.senate
@state.co.us

Gardner, Bob (R, 12)
200 E. Colfax Avenue
Denver, CO 80203
P: (303) 866-4880
E: bob.gardner.senate
@state.co.us

Grantham, Kevin (R, 2)
200 E. Colfax Avenue
Denver, CO 80203
P: (303) 866-4877
E: kevin.grantham.senate
@state.co.us

# Colorado

**Guzman, Lucia (D, 34)**
200 E. Colfax Avenue
Room 346
Denver, CO 80203
P: (303) 866-4862
E: lucia.guzman.senate
@state.co.us

**Hill, Owen (R, 10)**
200 E. Colfax Avenue
Room 346
Denver, CO 80203
P: (303) 866-2737
E: owen.hill.senate
@state.co.us

**Holbert, Chris (R, 30)**
200 E. Colfax Avenue
Room 346
Denver, CO 80203
P: (303) 866-4881
E: chris.holbert.senate
@state.co.us

**Jahn, Cheri (D, 20)**
200 E. Colfax Avenue
Room 346
Denver, CO 80203
P: (303) 866-4856
E: cheri.jahn.senate
@state.co.us

**Jones, Matt (D, 17)**
200 E. Colfax Avenue
Room 346
Denver, CO 80203
P: (303) 866-5291
E: matt.jones.senate
@state.co.us

**Kagan, Daniel (D, 26)**
200 East Colfax Avenue
Denver, CO 80203
P: (303) 866-4846
E: daniel.kagan.senate
@state.co.us

**Kefalas, John (D, 14)**
200 E. Colfax Avenue
Room 346
Denver, CO 80203
P: (303) 866-4841
E: john.kefalas.senate
@state.co.us

**Kerr, Andy (D, 22)**
200 E. Colfax Avenue
Room 346
Denver, CO 80203
P: (303) 866-4859
E: andy.kerr.senate
@state.co.us

**Lambert, Kent D. (R, 9)**
200 E. Colfax Avenue
Room 346
Denver, CO 80203
P: (303) 866-4835
E: kent.lambert.senate
@state.co.us

**Lundberg, Kevin (R, 15)**
200 E. Colfax Avenue
Room 346
Denver, CO 80203
P: (303) 866-4853
E: kevin.lundberg.senate
@state.co.us

**Marble, Vicki (R, 23)**
200 E. Colfax Avenue
Room 346
Denver, CO 80203
P: (303) 866-4876
E: vicki.marble.senate
@state.co.us

**Martinez Humenik, Beth (R, 24)**
200 E. Colfax Avenue
Room 346
Denver, CO 80203
P: (303) 866-4863
E: beth.
martinezhumenik.senate
@state.co.us

**Merrifield, Michael (D, 11)**
200 E. Colfax Avenue
Room 346
Denver, CO 80203
P: (303) 866-6364
E: michael.
merrifield.senate
@state.co.us

**Moreno, Dominick (D, 21)**
200 E. Colfax Avenue
Denver, CO 80203
P: (303) 866-4857
E: dominick.moreno.senate
@state.co.us

**Neville, Tim (R, 16)**
200 E. Colfax Avenue
Room 346
Denver, CO 80203
P: (303) 866-4873
E: tim.neville.senate
@state.co.us

**Priola, Kevin (R, 25)**
200 E. Colfax Avenue
Denver, CO 80203
P: (303) 866-4855
E: kevin.priola.senate
@state.co.us

**Scott, Ray (R, 7)**
200 E. Colfax Avenue
Denver, CO 80203
P: (303) 866-3077
E: ray.scott.senate
@state.co.us

**Smallwood, Jim (R, 4)\***
200 E Colfax Avenue
Denver, CO 80203
P: (303) 866-4869
E: jim.smallwood.senate
@state.co.us

**Sonnenberg, Jerry (R, 1)**
200 E. Colfax Avenue
Denver, CO 80203
P: (303) 866-6360
E: jerry.sonnenberg.senate
@state.co.us

**Tate, Jack (R, 27)**
200 E. Colfax Avenue
Room 346
Denver, CO 80203
P: (303) 866-4883
E: jack.tate.senate
@state.co.us

**Todd, Nancy (D, 28)**
200 E. Colfax Avenue
Room 346
Denver, CO 80203
P: (303) 866-3432
E: nancy.todd.senate
@state.co.us

**Williams, Angela (D, 33)**
200 E. Colfax Avenue
Denver, CO 80203
P: (303) 866-4864
E: angela.williams.senate
@state.co.us

**Zenzinger, Rachel (D, 19)\***
200 E Colfax Avenue
Room 346
Denver, CO 80203
P: (303) 866-4840
E: rachael.
zenzinger.senate
@state.co.us

# House
## Speaker of the House
**Representative Crisanta Duran (D)**
Speaker of the House
200 E. Colfax Avenue
Room 307
Denver, CO 80203
P: (303) 866-2348
E: crisanta.duran.house
@state.co.us

## Speaker Pro Tempore of the House
**Representative Jessie Danielson (D)**
Speaker Pro Tempore
200 E. Colfax Avenue
Room 307
Denver, CO 80203
P: (303) 866-5522
E: jessie.danielson.house
@state.co.us

## House Majority Leader
**Representative K.C. Becker (D)**
Majority Leader
200 E. Colfax Avenue
Room 307
Denver, CO 80203
P: (303) 866-2578
E: kcbecker.house
@state.co.us

## House Minority Leader
**Representative Patrick Neville (R)**
Minority Leader
200 E. Colfax Avenue
Denver, CO 80203
P: (303) 866-2948
E: patrick.neville.house
@state.co.us

## Clerk of the House
**Ms. Marilyn Eddins**
Chief Clerk of the House
200 East Colfax Avenue, Room 246
Denver, CO 80203
P: (303) 866-2345
E: marilyn.eddins
@state.co.us

## Members of the House
**Arndt, Jeni (D, 53)**
200 E. Colfax Avenue
Denver, CO 80203
P: (303) 866-2917
E: jeni.arndt.house
@state.co.us

**Becker, Jon (R, 65)**
200 E. Colfax Avenue
Denver, CO 80203
P: (303) 866-3706
E: jon.becker.house
@state.co.us

**Becker, K.C. (D, 13)**
200 E. Colfax Avenue
Room 307
Denver, CO 80203
P: (303) 866-2578
E: kcbecker.house
@state.co.us

**Beckman, Susan (R, 38)***
200 E. Colfax Avenue
Room 307
Denver, CO 80203
P: (303) 866-2953
E: Susan.Beckman.house
@state.co.us

**Benavidez, Adrienne (D, 32)***
200 E. Colfax Avenue
Room 307
Denver, CO 80203
P: (303) 866-2964
E: adrienne.
benavidez.house
@state.co.us

**Bridges, Jeff (D, 3)***
200 E. Colfax Avenue
Room 307
Denver, CO 80203
P: (303) 866-2921
E: jeff.bridges.house
@state.co.us

**Buck, Perry (R, 49)**
200 E. Colfax Avenue
Room 307
Denver, CO 80203
P: (303) 866-2907
E: perry.buck.house
@state.co.us

**Buckner, Janet P. (D, 40)**
200 E. Colfax Avenue
Denver, CO 80203
P: (303) 866-2944
E: janet.buckner.house
@state.co.us

**Carver, Terri (R, 20)**
200 E. Colfax Avenue
Room 307
Denver, CO 80203
P: (303) 866-2191
E: terri.carver.house
@state.co.us

**Catlin, Marc (R, 58)***
200 E. Colfax Avenue
Room 307
Denver, CO 80203
P: (303) 866-2955
E: marc.catlin.house
@state.co.us

**Coleman, James (D, 7)***
200 E. Colfax Avenue
Room 307
Denver, CO 80203
P: (303) 866-2909
E: james.coleman.house
@state.co.us

**Covarrubias, Phil (R, 56)***
200 E. Colfax Avenue
Room 307
Denver, CO 80203
P: (303) 866-2912
E: Phil.Covarrubias.house
@state.co.us

**Danielson, Jessie (D, 24)**
200 E. Colfax Avenue
Room 307
Denver, CO 80203
P: (303) 866-5522
E: jessie.danielson.house
@state.co.us

**Duran, Crisanta (D, 5)**
200 E. Colfax Avenue
Room 307
Denver, CO 80203
P: (303) 866-2348
E: crisanta.duran.house
@state.co.us

**Esgar, Daneya (D, 46)**
200 E. Colfax Avenue
Denver, CO 80203
P: (303) 866-2968
E: daneya.esgar.house
@state.co.us

**Everett, Justin (R, 22)**
200 E. Colfax Avenue
Room 307
Denver, CO 80203
P: (303) 866-2927
E: justin.everett.house
@state.co.us

**Exum Sr., Thomas (D, 17)**
200 E. Colfax Avenue
Denver, CO 80203
P: (303) 866-3069
E: tony.exum.house
@state.co.us

**Foote, Mike (D, 12)**
200 E. Colfax Avenue
Room 307
Denver, CO 80203
P: (303) 866-2920
E: mike.foote.house
@state.co.us

**Garnett, Alec (D, 2)**
200 E. Colfax Avenue
Room 307
Denver, CO 80203
P: (303) 866-2911
E: alec.garnett.house
@state.co.us

**Ginal, Joann (D, 52)**
200 E. Colfax Avenue
Room 307
Denver, CO 80203
P: (303) 866-4569
E: joann.ginal.house
@state.co.us

**Gray, Matthew (D, 33)***
200 E. Colfax Avenue
Room 307
Denver, CO 80203
P: (303) 866-4667
E: matthew.gray.house
@state.co.us

**Hamner, Millie (D, 61)**
200 E. Colfax Avenue
Denver, CO 80203
P: (303) 866-2952
E: millie.hamner.house
@state.co.us

**Hansen, Chris (D, 6)***
200 E. Colfax Avenue
Room 307
Denver, CO 80203
P: (303) 866-2967
E: chris.hansen.house
@state.co.us

**Herod, Leslie (D, 8)***
200 E. Colfax Avenue
Room 307
Denver, CO 80203
P: (303) 866-2959
E: leslie.herod.house
@state.co.us

**Hooton, Edie (D, 10)***
200 E. Colfax Avenue
Room 307
Denver, CO 80203
P: (303) 866-2915
E: edie.hooton.house
@state.co.us

**Humphrey, Stephen (R, 48)**
200 East Colfax Avenue
Denver, CO 80203
P: (303) 866-2943
E: stephan.humphrey.house
@state.co.us

**Jackson, Dominique (D, 42)***
200 E. Colfax Avenue
Room 307
Denver, CO 80203
P: (303) 866-3911
E: dominique.jackson.house
@state.co.us

**Jenet, Dafna Michaelson (D, 30)***
200 E. Colfax Avenue
Room 307
Denver, CO 80203
P: (303) 866-2945
E: dafna.
michaelson.jenet.house
@state.co.us

**Kennedy, Chris (D, 23)***
200 E. Colfax Avenue
Room 307
Denver, CO 80203
P: (303) 866-2951
E: chris.kennedy.house
@state.co.us

**Kraft-Tharp, Tracy (D, 29)**
200 E. Colfax Avenue
Room 307
Denver, CO 80203
P: (303) 866-2950
E: tracy.kraft-tharp.house
@state.co.us

**Landgraf, Lois (R, 21)**
200 E. Colfax Avenue
Room 307
Denver, CO 80203
P: (303) 866-2946
E: lois.landgraf.house
@state.co.us

**Lawrence, Polly (R, 39)**
200 E. Colfax Avenue
Denver, CO 80203
P: (303) 866-2935
E: polly.lawrence.house
@state.co.us

**Lebsock, Steve (D, 34)**
200 E. Colfax Avenue
Room 307
Denver, CO 80203
P: (303) 866-2931
E: steve.lebsock.house
@state.co.us

**Lee, Pete (D, 18)**
200 E. Colfax Avenue
Room 307
Denver, CO 80203
P: (303) 866-2932
E: pete.lee.house
@state.co.us

**Leonard, Timothy (R, 25)***
200 E. Colfax Avenue
Room 307
Denver, CO 80203
P: (303) 866-2582
E: tim.leonard.house
@state.co.us

# Colorado

**Lewis, Kimmi (R, 64)***
200 E. Colfax Avenue
Room 307
Denver, CO 80203
P: (303) 866-2398
E: kimmi.lewis.house
@state.co.us

**Liston, Larry G. (R, 16)**
200 E. Colfax Avenue
Room 307
Denver, CO 80203
P: (303) 866-2937
E: larry.liston.house
@state.co.us

**Lontine, Susan (D, 1)**
200 E. Colfax Avenue
Room 307
Denver, CO 80203
P: (303) 866-2966
E: susan.lontine.house
@state.co.us

**Lundeen, Paul (R, 19)**
200 E. Colfax Avenue
Room 307
Denver, CO 80203
P: (303) 866-2924
E: paul.lundeen.house
@state.co.us

**McKean, Hugh (R, 51)***
200 E. Colfax Avenue
Room 307
Denver, CO 80203
P: (303) 866-2947
E: hugh.mckean.house
@state.co.us

**McLachlan, Barbara (D, 59)***
200 E. Colfax Avenue
Room 307
Denver, CO 80203
P: (303) 866-2914
E: barbara.mclachlan.house
@state.co.us

**Melton, Jovan (D, 41)**
200 E. Colfax Avenue
Denver, CO 80203
P: (303) 866-2919
E: jovan.melton.house
@state.co.us

**Mitsch Bush, Diane (D, 26)**
200 E. Colfax Avenue
Room 307
Denver, CO 80203
P: (303) 866-2923
E: diane.mitschbush.house
@state.co.us

**Navarro, Clarice (R, 47)**
200 East Colfax Avenue
Denver, CO 80203
P: (303) 866-2905
E: clarice.navarro.house
@state.co.us

**Neville, Patrick (R, 45)**
200 E. Colfax Avenue
Denver, CO 80203
P: (303) 866-2948
E: patrick.neville.house
@state.co.us

**Nordberg, Dan (R, 14)**
200 E. Colfax Avenue
Room 307
Denver, CO 80203
P: (303) 866-2965
E: dan.nordberg.house
@state.co.us

**Pabon, Dan (D, 4)**
200 E. Colfax Avenue
Room 307
Denver, CO 80203
P: (303) 866-2954
E: dan.pabon.house
@state.co.us

**Pettersen, Brittany (D, 28)**
200 E. Colfax Avenue
Room 307
Denver, CO 80203
P: (303) 866-2939
E: brittany.
    pettersen.house
@state.co.us

**Rankin, Bob (R, 57)**
200 E. Colfax Avenue
Denver, CO 80203
P: (303) 866-2949
E: bob.rankin.house
@state.co.us

**Ransom, Kim (R, 44)**
200 E. Colfax Avenue
Denver, CO 80203
P: (303) 866-2933
E: kim.ransom.house
@state.co.us

**Rosenthal, Paul (D, 9)**
200 E. Colfax Avenue
Room 307
Denver, CO 80203
P: (303) 866-2910
E: paul.rosenthal.house
@state.co.us

**Saine, Lori (R, 63)**
200 E. Colfax Avenue
Denver, CO 80203
P: (303) 866-2906
E: lori.saine.house
@state.co.us

**Salazar, Joseph A. (D, 31)**
200 E. Colfax Avenue
Room 307
Denver, CO 80203
P: (303) 866-2918
E: joseph.salazar.house
@state.co.us

**Sias, Lang (R, 27)**
200 E. Colfax Avenue
Room 307
Denver, CO 80203
P: (303) 866-2962
E: lang.sias.house
@state.co.us

**Singer, Jonathan (D, 11)**
200 E. Colfax Avenue
Room 307
Denver, CO 80203
P: (303) 866-2780
E: jonathan.singer.house
@state.co.us

**Thurlow, Dan (R, 55)**
200 E. Colfax Avenue
Denver, CO 80203
P: (303) 866-3068
E: dan.thurlow.house
@state.co.us

**Valdez, Donald (D, 62)***
200 E Colfax Avenue
Room 307
Denver, CO 80203
P: (303) 866-2916
E: donald.valdez.house
@state.co.us

**Van Winkle, Kevin (R, 43)**
200 E. Colfax Avenue
Denver, CO 80203
P: (303) 866-2936
E: kevin.vanwinkle.house
@state.co.us

**Weissman, Mike (D, 36)***
200 E. Colfax Avenue
Room 307
Denver, CO 80203
P: (303) 866-2942
E: mike.weissman.house
@state.co.us

**Willett, Yeulin (R, 54)**
200 E. Colfax Avenue
Denver, CO 80203
P: (303) 866-2583
E: yeulin.willett.house
@state.co.us

**Williams, Dave (R, 15)***
200 E. Colfax Avenue
Room 307
Denver, CO 80203
P: (303) 866-5525
E: dave.williams.house
@state.co.us

**Wilson, James D. (R, 60)**
200 E. Colfax Avenue
Denver, CO 80203
P: (303) 866-2747
E: james.wilson.house
@state.co.us

**Winter, Faith (D, 35)**
200 E. Colfax Avenue
Room 307
Denver, CO 80203
P: (303) 866-2843
E: faith.winter.house
@state.co.us

**Wist, Cole (R, 37)**
200 E. Colfax Avenue
Room 307
Denver, CO 80203
P: (303) 866-5510
E: cole.wist.house
@state.co.us

**Young, Dave (D, 50)**
200 E. Colfax Avenue
Denver, CO 80203
P: (303) 866-2929
E: dave.young.house
@state.co.us

# Connecticut

## Executive

### Governor
The Honorable Dan Malloy (D)
Governor
210 Capitol Avenue
Hartford, CT 06106
P: (800) 406-1527
F: (860) 524-7395

### Lieutenant Governor
The Honorable Nancy Wyman (D)
Lieutenant Governor
State Capitol, Room 304
210 Capitol Avenue
Hartford, CT 06106
P: (860) 524-7384
F: (860) 524-7304

### Attorney General
The Honorable George C. Jepsen (D)
Attorney General
55 Elm Street
Hartford, CT 06106
P: (860) 808-5318

### Auditor
The Honorable John C. Geragosian
(appointed by the Legislature)
State Auditor
State Capitol
210 Capitol Avenue
Hartford, CT 06106
P: (860) 240-8651
F: (860) 240-8655
E: john.geragosian
@cga.ct.gov

### Secretary of State
The Honorable Denise W. Merrill (D)
Secretary of State
Capitol Office
P.O. Box 150470
Hartford, CT 06115
P: (860) 509-6200
F: (860) 509-6209
E: denise.merrill@ct.gov

### Treasurer
The Honorable Denise L. Nappier (D)
State Treasurer
55 Elm Street, 7th Floor
Hartford, CT 06106
P: (860) 702-3010
F: (860) 702-3043
E: denise.nappier@ct.gov

## Judiciary

### Supreme Court (LA)
Major Paul Hartan
Chief Clerk
231 Capitol Avenue
Hartford, CT 06106
P: (860) 757-2200
F: (860) 757-2217

The Honorable Chase T. Rogers
Chief Justice
The Honorable Carmen E. Espinosa
The Honorable Dennis G. Eveleigh
The Honorable Andrew J. McDonald
The Honorable Richard N. Palmer
The Honorable Richard A. Robinson
The Honorable Christine S. Vertefeuille
The Honorable Peter T. Zarella

## Legislative Senate

### Senate President
The Honorable Nancy Wyman (D)
Lieutenant Governor
State Capitol, Room 304
210 Capitol Avenue
Hartford, CT 06106
P: (860) 524-7384
F: (860) 524-7304

### President Pro Tempore of the Senate
Senator Leonard A. Fasano (R)
Senate Republican President Pro Tempore
Legislative Office Building, Room 3402
300 Capitol Avenue
Hartford, CT 06106
P: (860) 240-8800
F: (860) 240-8306
E: Len.Fasano@cga.ct.gov

Senator Martin M. Looney (D)
Senate President Pro Tempore
Legislative Office Building
Room 3300
Hartford, CT 06106
P: (860) 240-8600
F: (860) 240-0208
E: Looney@senatedems.ct.gov

### Senate Majority Leader
Senator Bob Duff (D)
Senate Majority Leader
Legislative Office Building
Room 3300
Hartford, CT 06106
P: (860) 240-8600
F: (860) 240-0208
E: Bob.Duff@cga.ct.gov

### Secretary of the Senate
Mr. Garey E. Coleman
Clerk of the Senate
State Capitol, Room 305
Hartford, CT 06106
P: (860) 240-0500
E: Garey.Coleman@cga.ct.gov

### Members of the Senate
Boucher, Toni (R, 26)
Legislative Office Building, Room 3701
300 Capitol Avenue
Hartford, CT 06106
P: (860) 240-8800
F: (860) 240-8306
E: Toni.Boucher@cga.ct.gov

Bye, Beth (D, 5)
Legislative Office Building
Room 3900
Hartford, CT 06106
P: (860) 240-8600
F: (860) 240-0208
E: Bye@senatedems.ct.gov

Cassano, Steve (D, 4)
Legislative Office Building
Room 2200
Hartford, CT 06106
P: (860) 240-8600
F: (860) 240-0208

Doyle, Paul R. (D, 9)
Legislative Office Building
Room 2500
Hartford, CT 06106
P: (860) 240-8600
F: (860) 240-0208
E: Doyle@senatedems.ct.gov

Duff, Bob (D, 25)
Legislative Office Building
Room 3300
Hartford, CT 06106
P: (860) 240-8600
F: (860) 240-0208
E: Bob.Duff@cga.ct.gov

Fasano, Leonard A. (R, 34)
Legislative Office Building, Room 3402
300 Capitol Avenue
Hartford, CT 06106
P: (860) 240-8800
F: (860) 240-8306
E: Len.Fasano@cga.ct.gov

Flexer, Mae (D, 29)
Legislative Office Building
Room 1800
Hartford, CT 06106
P: (860) 240-8600
F: (860) 240-0208
E: Mae.Flexer@cga.ct.gov

Fonfara, John W. (D, 1)
Legislative Office Building
Room 3700
Hartford, CT 06106
P: (860) 240-8600
F: (860) 240-0208
E: Fonfara
@senatedems.ct.gov

Formica, Paul (R, 20)
Legislative Office Building, Room 3901
300 Capitol Avenue
Hartford, CT 06106
P: (860) 240-8800
F: (860) 240-8306
E: paul.formica@cga.ct.gov

Frantz, L. Scott (R, 36)
Legislative Office Building, Room 3501
300 Capitol Avenue
Hartford, CT 06106
P: (860) 240-8800
F: (860) 240-8306
E: Scott.Frantz@cga.ct.gov

# Connecticut

**Gerratana, Terry B. (D, 6)**
Legislative Office Building
Room 3000
Hartford, CT 06106
P: (860) 240-8600
F: (860) 240-0208

**Gomes, Edwin A. (D, 23)**
Legislative Office Building
Room 3800
Hartford, CT 06106
P: (860) 240-8600
F: (860) 240-0208
E: gomes@senatedems.ct.gov

**Guglielmo, Anthony (R, 35)**
Legislative Office Building,
Room 3604
300 Capitol Avenue
Hartford, CT 06106
P: (860) 240-8800
F: (860) 240-8306
E: Anthony.Guglielmo
  @cga.ct.gov

**Hartley, Joan V. (D, 15)**
Legislative Office Building
Room 2100
Hartford, CT 06106
P: (860) 240-8600
F: (860) 240-0208
E: Hartley
  @senatedems.ct.gov

**Hwang, Tony (R, 28)**
Legislative Office Building,
Room 3001
300 Capitol Avenue
Hartford, CT 06106
P: (860) 240-8800
F: (860) 240-8306
E: Tony.Hwang@cga.ct.gov

**Kelly, Kevin C. (R, 21)**
Legislative Office Building,
Room 3400
300 Capitol Avenue
Hartford, CT 06106
P: (860) 240-8800
F: (860) 240-8306
E: Kevin.Kelly@cga.ct.gov

**Kennedy Jr., Ted (D, 12)**
Legislative Office Building
Room 3200
Hartford, CT 06106
P: (860) 240-8600
F: (860) 240-0208

**Kissel, John A. (R, 7)**
Legislative Office Building,
Room 2503
300 Capitol Avenue
Hartford, CT 06106
P: (860) 240-8800
F: (860) 240-8306
E: John.A.Kissel@cga.ct.gov

**Larson, Timothy D. (D, 3)**
Legislative Office Building
Room 2800
Hartford, CT 06106
P: (860) 240-8600
F: (860) 240-0208
E: Timothy.Larson
  @cga.ct.gov

**Leone, Carlo (D, 27)**
Legislative Office Building
Room 3500
Hartford, CT 06106
P: (860) 240-8600
F: (860) 240-0208
E: Carlo.Leone@cga.ct.gov

**Linares, Art (R, 33)**
Legislative Office Building,
Room 2705
300 Capitol Avenue
Hartford, CT 06106
P: (860) 240-8800
F: (860) 240-8306
E: Art.Linares@cga.ct.gov

**Logan, George (R, 17)***
Legislative Office Bulding,
Room 3403
300 Capitol Avenue
Hartford, CT 06106
P: (860) 240-8800
E: George.Logan@cga.ct.gov

**Looney, Martin M. (D, 11)**
Legislative Office Building
Room 3300
Hartford, CT 06106
P: (860) 240-8600
F: (860) 240-0208
E: Looney@senatedems.ct.gov

**Markley, Joe (R, 16)**
Legislative Office Building,
Room 2003
300 Capitol Avenue
Hartford, CT 06106
P: (860) 240-8800
F: (860) 240-8306
E: Joe.Markley@cga.ct.gov

**Martin, Henri (R, 31)**
Legislative Office Building,
Room 2403
300 Capitol Avenue
Hartford, CT 06106
P: (860) 240-8800
F: (860) 240-8306
E: Henri.Martin@cga.ct.gov

**McLachlan, Michael A.
  (R, 24)**
Legislative Office Building,
Room 3400
300 Capitol Avenue
Hartford, CT 06106
P: (860) 240-8800
F: (860) 240-8306
E: Michael.McLachlan
  @cga.ct.gov

**Miner, Craig A. (R, 30)**
Legislative Office Building
Room 3403
Hartford, CT 06106
P: (860) 240-8700
F: (860) 240-0207
E: Craig.Miner
  @housegop.ct.gov

**Moore, Marilyn (D, 22)**
Legislative Office Building
Room 2000
Hartford, CT 06106
P: (860) 240-8600
F: (860) 240-0208

**Osten, Cathy (D, 19)**
Legislative Office Building
Room 2700
Hartford, CT 06106
P: (860) 240-8600
F: (860) 240-0208
E: catherine.osten
  @cga.ct.gov

**Slossberg, Gayle S. (D, 14)**
Legislative Office Building
Room 3100
Hartford, CT 06106
P: (860) 240-8600
F: (860) 240-0208
E: Slossberg
  @senatedems.ct.gov

**Somers, Heather (R, 18)***
Legislative Office Building,
Room 3403
300 Capitol Avenue
Hartford, CT 06106
P: (860) 240-8800
E: Heather.Somers
  @cga.ct.gov

**Suzio Jr., Leonard F.
  (R, 13)**
Legislative Office Building
Room 3501
Hartford, CT 06106
P: (860) 240-8800
F: (860) 240-8306
E: Len.Suzio@cga.ct.gov

**Winfield, Gary (D, 10)**
Legislative Office Building
Room 2400
Hartford, CT 06106
P: (860) 240-8600
F: (860) 240-0208
E: Winfield
  @senatedems.ct.gov

**Witkos, Kevin (R, 8)**
Legislative Office Building,
Room 3403
300 Capitol Avenue
Hartford, CT 06106
P: (860) 240-8800
F: (860) 240-8306
E: Kevin.Witkos@cga.ct.gov

# House

## Speaker of the House
**Representative Joe
  Aresimowicz (D)**
Speaker of the House
Legislative Office Building
Room 4105
Hartford, CT 06106
P: (860) 240-8489
E: Joe.Aresimowicz
  @cga.ct.gov

## Speaker Pro Tempore of the House
**Representative Jeffrey J.
  Berger (D)**
House Deputy Speaker
Legislative Office Building
Room 4112
Hartford, CT 06106
P: (860) 240-8500
E: Jeffrey.Berger
  @cga.ct.gov

**Representative Juan R.
  Candelaria (D)**
House Deputy Speaker
Legislative Office Building
Room 4013
Hartford, CT 06106
P: (860) 240-8585
E: Juan.Candelaria
  @cga.ct.gov

**Representative Linda M.
  Gentile (D)**
House Deputy Speaker
Legislative Office Building
Room 4109
Hartford, CT 06106
P: (860) 240-8585
E: Linda.Gentile@cga.ct.gov

**Representative Douglas McCrory (D)**
House Deputy Speaker
Legislative Office Building
Room 4025
Hartford, CT 06106
P: (860) 240-8585
E: Douglas.McCrory
@cga.ct.gov

**Representative Russell A. Morin (D)**
House Deputy Speaker
Legislative Office Building
Room 4110
Hartford, CT 06106
P: (860) 240-8585
E: Russell.Morin@cga.ct.gov

**Representative Bruce V. Morris (D)**
House Deputy Speaker
Legislative Office Building
Room 5004
Hartford, CT 06106
P: (860) 240-8585
E: Bruce.Morris@cga.ct.gov

**Representative Linda A. Orange (D)**
House Deputy Speaker
Legislative Office Building
Room 4012
Hartford, CT 06106
P: (860) 240-8585
E: Linda.Orange@cga.ct.gov

**Representative Kevin Ryan (D)**
House Deputy Speaker
Legislative Office Building
Room 4108
Hartford, CT 06106
P: (860) 240-8585
E: Kevin.Ryan@cga.ct.gov

# House Majority Leader

**Representative Matt Ritter (D)**
House Majority Leader
Legislative Office Building
Room 4106
Hartford, CT 06106
P: (860) 240-8585
E: Matthew.Ritter
@cga.ct.gov

# House Minority Leader

**Representative Themis Klarides (R)**
House Minority Leader
Legislative Office Building
Room 4200
Hartford, CT 06106
P: (860) 240-8700
F: (860) 240-0207
E: Themis.Klarides
@housegop.ct.gov

# Clerk of the House

**Major Martin J. Dunleavy**
Clerk of the House
State Capitol, Room 109
Hartford, CT 06106
P: (860) 240-0400

# Members of the House

**Abercrombie, Catherine F. (D, 83)**
Legislative Office Building
Room 2002
Hartford, CT 06106
P: (860) 240-8500
E: Catherine.Abercrombie
@cga.ct.gov

**Ackert, Timothy (R, 8)**
Legislative Office Building
Room 4200
Hartford, CT 06106
P: (860) 240-8700
F: (860) 240-0207
E: Tim.Ackert
@housegop.ct.gov

**Adams, Terry (D, 146)**
Legislative Office Building
Room 4000
Hartford, CT 06106
P: (860) 240-8500
E: Terry.B.Adams@cga.ct.gov

**Albis, James M. (D, 99)**
Legislative Office Building
Room 3201
Hartford, CT 06106
P: (860) 240-8585
E: James.Albis@cga.ct.gov

**Altobello, Emil (D, 82)**
Legislative Office Building
Room 4015
Hartford, CT 06106
P: (860) 240-8585
E: Emil.Altobello
@cga.ct.gov

**Arce, Angel (D, 4)**
Legislative Office Building
Room 4000
Hartford, CT 06106
P: (860) 240-8585
E: Angel.Arce@cga.ct.gov

**Arconti, David (D, 109)**
Legislative Office Building
Room 4034
Hartford, CT 06106
P: (860) 240-8585
E: David.Arconti@cga.ct.gov

**Aresimowicz, Joe (D, 30)**
Legislative Office Building
Room 4105
Hartford, CT 06106
P: (860) 240-8489
E: Joe.Aresimowicz
@cga.ct.gov

**Baker Jr., Andre (D, 124)**
Legislative Office Building
Room 4037
Hartford, CT 06106
P: (860) 240-8585
E: Andre.Baker@cga.ct.gov

**Baram, David A. (D, 15)**
Legislative Office Building
Room 3504
Hartford, CT 06106
P: (860) 240-8585
E: David.Baram@cga.ct.gov

**Belsito, Sam (R, 53)**
Legislative Office Building
Room 4200
Hartford, CT 06106
P: (860) 240-8700
F: (860) 240-0207
E: sam.belsito
@housegop.ct.gov

**Berger, Jeffrey J. (D, 73)**
Legislative Office Building
Room 4112
Hartford, CT 06106
P: (860) 240-8500
E: Jeffrey.Berger
@cga.ct.gov

**Berthel, Eric (R, 68)**
Legislative Office Building
Room 4200
Hartford, CT 06106
P: (860) 240-8700
F: (860) 240-0207
E: Eric.Berthel
@housegop.ct.gov

**Betts, Whit (R, 78)**
Legislative Office Building
Room 4200
Hartford, CT 06106
P: (860) 240-8700
F: (860) 240-0207
E: Whit.Betts
@housegop.ct.gov

**Bocchino, Mike (R, 150)**
Legislative Office Building
Room 4200
Hartford, CT 06106
P: (860) 240-8700
F: (860) 240-0207
E: Mike.Bocchino
@housegop.ct.gov

**Bolinsky, Mitch (R, 106)**
Legislative Office Building
Room 4200
Hartford, CT 06106
P: (860) 240-8700
F: (860) 240-0207
E: Mitch.Bolinsky
@housegop.ct.gov

**Boyd, Pat (D, 50)***
Legislative Office Building
Room 4005
Hartford, CT 06106
P: (860) 240-8585
E: Pat.Boyd@cga.ct.gov

**Buckbee, William (R, 67)***
Legislative Office Building
Room 4200
Hartford, CT 06106
P: (860) 240-8700
E: Bill.Buckbee
@housegop.ct.gov

**Butler, Larry B. (D, 72)**
Legislative Office Building
Room 5001
Hartford, CT 06106
P: (860) 240-8585
E: Larry.Butler@cga.ct.gov

**Byron, Gary (R, 27)**
Legislative Office Building
Room 4200
Hartford, CT 06106
P: (860) 240-8700
F: (860) 240-0207
E: Gary.Byron
@housegop.ct.gov

**Camillo, Fred (R, 151)**
Legislative Office Building
Room 4200
Hartford, CT 06106
P: (860) 240-8700
F: (860) 240-0207
E: Fred.Camillo
@housegop.ct.gov

# Connecticut

**Candelaria, Juan R. (D, 95)**
Legislative Office Building
Room 4013
Hartford, CT 06106
P: (860) 240-8585
E: Juan.Candelaria
@cga.ct.gov

**Candelora, Vincent J.
(R, 86)**
Legislative Office Building
Room 4200
Hartford, CT 06106
P: (860) 240-8700
F: (860) 240-0207
E: Vincent.Candelora
@housegop.ct.gov

**Carney, Devin (R, 23)**
Legislative Office Building
Room 4200
Hartford, CT 06106
P: (860) 240-8700
F: (860) 240-0207
E: Devin.Carney
@housegop.ct.gov

**Carpino, Christie (R, 32)**
Legislative Office Building
Room 4200
Hartford, CT 06106
P: (860) 240-8700
F: (860) 240-0207
E: Christie.Carpino
@housegop.ct.gov

**Case, Jay (R, 63)**
Legislative Office Building
Room 4200
Hartford, CT 06106
P: (860) 240-8700
F: (860) 240-0207
E: Jay.Case@housegop.ct.gov

**Cheeseman, Holly (R, 37)\***
Legislative Office Building
Room 4200
Hartford, CT 06106
P: (860) 240-8700
E: Holly.Cheeseman
@housegop.ct.gov

**Conley, Christine (D, 40)\***
Legislative Office Building
Room 4009
Hartford, CT 06106
P: (860) 240-8267
E: Christine.Conley
@cga.ct.gov

**Cook, Michelle (D, 65)**
Legislative Office Building
Room 4035
Hartford, CT 06106
P: (860) 240-8585
E: Michelle.Cook@cga.ct.gov

**Cummings, Stephanie
(R, 74)\***
Legislative Office Building
Room 4200
Hartford, CT 06106
P: (860) 240-8700
E: Stephanie.Cummings
@housegop.ct.gov

**Currey, Jeffrey (D, 11)**
Legislative Office Building
Room 4010
Hartford, CT 06106
P: (860) 240-8585
E: Jeff.Currey@cga.ct.gov

**D'Agostino, Mike (D, 91)**
Legislative Office Building
Room 4000
Hartford, CT 06106
P: (860) 240-8585
E: Michael.DAgostino
@cga.ct.gov

**D'Amelio, Anthony J.
(R, 71)**
Legislative Office Building
Room 4200
Hartford, CT 06106
P: (860) 240-8700
F: (860) 240-0207
E: Anthony.DAmelio
@housegop.ct.gov

**Dauphinais, Anne (R, 44)\***
Legislative Office Building
Room 4200
Hartford, CT 06106
P: (860) 240-8700
E: Anne.Dauphinais
@housegop.ct.gov

**Davis, Christopher (R, 57)**
Legislative Office Building
Room 4200
Hartford, CT 06106
P: (860) 240-8700
F: (860) 240-0207
E: Christopher.Davis
@housegop.ct.gov

**De La Cruz, Joe (D, 41)\***
Legislative Office Building
Room 4014
Hartford, CT 06106
P: (860) 240-8267
E: Joe.Delacruz@cga.ct.gov

**Delnicki, Tom (R, 14)\***
Legislative Office Building
Room 4200
Hartford, CT 06106
P: (860) 240-8700
E: Tom.Delnicki
@housegop.ct.gov

**Demicco, Mike (D, 21)**
Legislative Office Building
Room 3201
Hartford, CT 06106
P: (860) 240-8585
E: Mike.Demicco@cga.ct.gov

**Devlin, Laura (R, 134)**
Legislative Office Building
Room 4200
Hartford, CT 06106
P: (860) 240-8700
F: (860) 240-0207
E: Laura.Devlin
@housegop.ct.gov

**Dillon, Patricia A. (D, 92)**
Legislative Office Building
Room 4019
Hartford, CT 06106
P: (860) 240-8585
E: Patricia.Dillon
@cga.ct.gov

**DiMassa, Michael (D, 116)\***
Legislative Office Building
Room 5006
Hartford, CT 06106
P: (860) 240-8267
E: Michael.DiMassa
@cga.ct.gov

**Dubitsky, Doug (R, 47)**
Legislative Office Building
Room 4200
Hartford, CT 06106
P: (860) 240-8700
F: (860) 240-0207
E: Doug.Dubitsky
@housegop.ct.gov

**Duff, William (R, 2)\***
Legislative Office Building
Room 4200
Hartford, CT 06106
P: (860) 240-8700
E: Will.Duff
@housegop.ct.gov

**Dunsby, Adam (R, 135)\***
Legislative Office Building
Room 4200
Hartford, CT 06106
P: (860) 240-8700
E: Adam.Dunsby
@housegop.ct.gov

**Elliott, Joshua (D, 88)\***
Legislative Office Building
Room 4003
Hartford, CT 06106
P: (860) 240-8267
E: Josh.Elliott@cga.ct.gov

**Ferguson, Michael (R, 138)\***
Legislative Office Building
Room 4200
Hartford, CT 06106
P: (860) 240-8700
E: Michael.Ferguson
@housegop.ct.gov

**Ferraro, Charles (R, 117)**
Legislative Office Building
Room 4200
Hartford, CT 06106
P: (860) 240-8700
F: (860) 240-0207
E: Charles.Ferraro
@housegop.ct.gov

**Fishbein, Craig (R, 90)\***
Legislative Office Building
Room 4200
Hartford, CT 06106
P: (860) 240-8700
E: Craig.Fishbein
@housegop.ct.gov

**Fleischmann, Andrew M.
(D, 18)**
Legislative Office Building
Room 3101
Hartford, CT 06106
P: (860) 240-0429
F: (860) 240-0206
E: Andrew.Fleischmann
@cga.ct.gov

**Floren, Livvy R. (R, 149)**
Legislative Office Building
Room 4200
Hartford, CT 06106
P: (860) 240-8700
F: (860) 240-0207
E: Livvy.Floren
@housegop.ct.gov

**Fox, Daniel J. (D, 148)**
Legislative Office Building
Room 2202
Hartford, CT 06106
P: (860) 240-8585
E: Dan.Fox@cga.ct.gov

**France, Mike (R, 42)**
Legislative Office Building
Room 4200
Hartford, CT 06106
P: (860) 240-8700
F: (860) 240-0207
E: Mike.France
@housegop.ct.gov

**Frey, John H. (R, 111)**
Legislative Office Building
Room 4200
Hartford, CT 06106
P: (860) 240-8700
F: (860) 240-0207
E: John.Frey
@housegop.ct.gov

**Fusco, John (R, 81)***
Legislative Office Building
Room 4200
Hartford, CT 06106
P: (860) 240-8700
E: John.Fusco
    @housegop.ct.gov

**Genga, Henry (D, 10)**
Legislative Office Building
Room 4030
Hartford, CT 06106
P: (860) 240-8585
E: Henry.Genga@cga.ct.gov

**Gentile, Linda M. (D, 104)**
Legislative Office Building
Room 4109
Hartford, CT 06106
P: (860) 240-8585
E: Linda.Gentile@cga.ct.gov

**Godfrey, Robert (D, 110)**
Legislative Office Building
Room 4107
Hartford, CT 06106
P: (860) 240-8500
E: Bob.Godfrey@cga.ct.gov

**Gonzalez, Minnie (D, 3)**
Legislative Office Building
Room 4031
Hartford, CT 06106
P: (860) 240-8585
E: Minnie.Gonzalez
    @cga.ct.gov

**Green, Robin (R, 55)***
Legislative Office Building
Room 4200
Hartford, CT 06106
P: (860) 240-8700
E: Robin.Green@cga.ct.gov

**Gresko, Joseph**
Legislative Office Building
Hartford, CT 06106
P: (800) 842-8267
E: joseph.gresko@cga.ct.gov

**Guerrera, Antonio (D, 29)**
Legislative Office Building
Room 2301
Hartford, CT 06106
P: (860) 240-8585
E: Tony.Guerrera@cga.ct.gov

**Haddad, Gregg (D, 54)**
Legislative Office Building
Room 1804
Hartford, CT 06106
P: (860) 240-8585
E: Gregory.Haddad
    @cga.ct.gov

**Hall, Carol (R, 59)***
Legislative Office Building
Room 4200
Hartford, CT 06106
P: (860) 240-8700
E: Carol.Hall
    @housegop.ct.gov

**Hampton, John (D, 16)**
Legislative Office Building
Room 5007
Hartford, CT 06106
P: (860) 240-8568
E: John.Hampton@cga.ct.gov

**Harding, Stephen (R, 107)**
Legislative Office Building
Room 4200
Hartford, CT 06106
P: (860) 240-8700
F: (860) 240-0207
E: Stephen.Harding
    @housegop.ct.gov

**Hennessy, Jack F. (D, 127)**
Legislative Office Building
Room 5002
Hartford, CT 06106
P: (860) 240-8585
E: Jack.Hennessy@cga.ct.gov

**Hoydick, Laura (R, 120)**
Legislative Office Building
Room 4200
Hartford, CT 06106
P: (860) 240-8700
F: (860) 240-0207
E: Laura.Hoydick
    @housegop.ct.gov

**Johnson, Susan (D, 49)**
Legislative Office Building
Room 4029
Hartford, CT 06106
P: (860) 240-8585
E: Susan.Johnson@cga.ct.gov

**Klarides, Themis (R, 114)**
Legislative Office Building
Room 4200
Hartford, CT 06106
P: (860) 240-8700
F: (860) 240-0207
E: Themis.Klarides
    @housegop.ct.gov

**Klarides-Ditria, Nicole
    (R, 105)***
Legislative Office Building
Room 4200
Hartford, CT 06106
P: (860) 240-8700
E: Nicole.Klarides-Ditria
    @housegop.ct.gov

**Kokoruda, Noreen (R, 101)**
Legislative Office Building
Room 4200
Hartford, CT 06106
P: (860) 240-8700
F: (860) 240-0207
E: Noreen.Kokoruda
    @housegop.ct.gov

**Kupchick, Brenda (R, 132)**
Legislative Office Building
Room 4200
Hartford, CT 06106
P: (860) 240-8700
F: (860) 240-0207
E: Brenda.Kupchick
    @cga.ct.gov

**Labriola, David K. (R, 131)**
Legislative Office Building
Room 4200
Hartford, CT 06106
P: (860) 240-8700
F: (860) 240-0207
E: David.Labriola
    @housegop.ct.gov

**Lavielle, Gail (R, 143)**
Legislative Office Building
Room 4200
Hartford, CT 06106
P: (860) 240-8700
F: (860) 240-0207
E: Gail.Lavielle
    @housegop.ct.gov

**LeGeyt, Timothy (R, 17)**
Legislative Office Building
Room 4200
Hartford, CT 06106
P: (860) 240-8700
F: (860) 240-0207
E: Tim.LeGeyt
    @housegop.ct.gov

**Lemar, Roland (D, 96)**
Legislative Office Building
Room 2103
Hartford, CT 06106
P: (860) 240-8585
E: Roland.Lemar@cga.ct.gov

**Lesser, Matthew (D, 100)**
Legislative Office Building
Room 2405
Hartford, CT 06106
P: (860) 240-8585
E: Matthew.Lesser
    @cga.ct.gov

**Linehan, Liz (D, 103)***
Legislative Office Building
Room 4011
Hartford, CT 06106
P: (860) 240-8267
E: Liz.Linehan@cga.ct.gov

**Lopes, Rick (D, 24)**
Legislative Office Building
Room 1802
Hartford, CT 06106
P: (860) 240-8585
E: Rick.Lopes@cga.ct.gov

**Luxenberg, Kelly (D, 12)**
Legislative Office Building
Room 4028
Hartford, CT 06106
P: (860) 240-8585
E: Kelly.Luxenberg
    @cga.ct.gov

**MacLachlan, Jesse (R, 35)**
Legislative Office Building
Room 4200
Hartford, CT 06106
P: (860) 240-8700
F: (860) 240-0207
E: Jesse.MacLachlan
    @housegop.ct.gov

**McCarty, Kathleen (R, 38)**
Legislative Office Building
Room 4200
Hartford, CT 06106
P: (860) 240-8700
F: (860) 240-0207
E: Kathleen.McCarty
    @housegop.ct.gov

**McCrory, Douglas (D, 7)**
Legislative Office Building
Room 4025
Hartford, CT 06106
P: (860) 240-8585
E: Douglas.McCrory
    @cga.ct.gov

**McGee, Brandon L. (D, 5)**
Legislative Office Building
Room 4000
Hartford, CT 06106
P: (860) 240-8585
E: Brandon.McGee@cga.ct.gov

**McGorty, Ben (R, 122)**
Legislative Office Building
Room 4200
Hartford, CT 06106
P: (860) 240-8700
F: (860) 240-0207
E: Ben.McGorty
    @housegop.ct.gov

**Miller, Patricia Billie
    (D, 145)**
Legislative Office Building
Room 4046
Hartford, CT 06106
P: (860) 240-8585
E: Patricia.Miller
    @cga.ct.gov

# Connecticut

**Morin, Russell A. (D, 28)**
Legislative Office Building
Room 4110
Hartford, CT 06106
P: (860) 240-8585
E: Russell.Morin@cga.ct.gov

**Morris, Bruce V. (D, 140)**
Legislative Office Building
Room 5004
Hartford, CT 06106
P: (860) 240-8585
E: Bruce.Morris@cga.ct.gov

**Mushinsky, Mary M. (D, 85)**
Legislative Office Building
Room 4038
Hartford, CT 06106
P: (860) 240-8585
E: Mary.Mushinsky
  @cga.ct.gov

**O'Dea, Thomas (R, 125)**
Legislative Office Building
Room 4200
Hartford, CT 06106
P: (860) 240-8700
F: (860) 240-0207
E: Tom.ODea@housegop.ct.gov

**Ohler, Brian (R, 64)***
Legislative Office Building
Room 4200
Hartford, CT 06106
P: (860) 240-8700
E: Brian.Ohler
  @housegop.ct.gov

**O'Neill, Arthur J. (R, 69)**
Legislative Office Building
Room 4200
Hartford, CT 06106
P: (860) 240-8700
F: (860) 240-0207
E: Arthur.ONeill
  @housegop.ct.gov

**Orange, Linda A. (D, 48)**
Legislative Office Building
Room 4012
Hartford, CT 06106
P: (860) 240-8585
E: Linda.Orange@cga.ct.gov

**Paolillo, Alphonse (D, 97)***
Legislative Office Building
Room 5008
Hartford, CT 06106
P: (860) 240-8585
E: Alphonse.Paolillo
  @cga.ct.gov

**Pavalock-D'Amato,**
  **Cara Christine (R, 77)**
Legislative Office Building
Room 4200
Hartford, CT 06106
P: (860) 240-8700
F: (860) 240-0207
E: Cara.Pavalock-DAmato
  @housegop.ct.gov

**Perillo, Jason (R, 113)**
Legislative Office Building
Room 4200
Hartford, CT 06106
P: (860) 240-8700
F: (860) 240-0207
E: Jason.Perillo
  @housegop.ct.gov

**Perone, Chris (D, 137)**
Legislative Office Building
Room 4111
Hartford, CT 06106
P: (860) 240-8585
E: Chris.Perone@cga.ct.gov

**Petit, William (R, 22)***
Legislative Office Building
Room 4200
Hartford, CT 06106
P: (860) 240-8700
E: William.Petit
  @housegop.ct.gov

**Piscopo, John E. (R, 76)**
Legislative Office Building
Room 4200
Hartford, CT 06106
P: (860) 240-8700
F: (860) 240-0207
E: John.Piscopo
  @housegop.ct.gov

**Porter, Robyn (D, 94)**
Legislative Office Building
Room 3804
Hartford, CT 06106
P: (860) 240-8585
E: Robyn.Porter@cga.ct.gov

**Rebimbas, Rosa C. (R, 70)**
Legislative Office Building
Room 4200
Hartford, CT 06106
P: (860) 240-8700
F: (860) 240-0207
E: Rosa.Rebimbas
  @housegop.ct.gov

**Reed, Lonnie (D, 102)**
Legislative Office Building
Room 3902
Hartford, CT 06106
P: (860) 240-8585
E: Lonnie.Reed@cga.ct.gov

**Riley, Emmett D. (D, 46)**
Legislative Office Building
Room 4114
Hartford, CT 06106
P: (860) 240-8585
E: Emmett.Riley@cga.ct.gov

**Ritter, Matt (D, 1)**
Legislative Office Building
Room 4106
Hartford, CT 06106
P: (860) 240-8585
E: Matthew.Ritter
  @cga.ct.gov

**Rojas, Jason (D, 9)**
Legislative Office Building
Room 3704
Hartford, CT 06106
P: (860) 240-8585
E: Jason.Rojas@cga.ct.gov

**Rosario, Christopher**
  **(D, 128)**
Legislative Office Building
Room 4115
Hartford, CT 06106
P: (860) 240-8585
E: Christopher.Rosario
  @cga.ct.gov

**Rose, Kim (D, 118)**
Legislative Office Building
Room 4002
Hartford, CT 06106
P: (860) 240-8585
E: Kim.Rose@cga.ct.gov

**Rovero, Daniel S. (D, 51)**
Legislative Office Building
Room 4004
Hartford, CT 06106
P: (860) 240-8585
E: Danny.Rovero@cga.ct.gov

**Rutigliano, David (R, 123)**
Legislative Office Building
Room 4200
Hartford, CT 06106
P: (860) 240-8700
F: (860) 240-0207
E: David.Rutigliano
  @housegop.ct.gov

**Ryan, Kevin (D, 139)**
Legislative Office Building
Room 4108
Hartford, CT 06106
P: (860) 240-8585
E: Kevin.Ryan@cga.ct.gov

**Sampson, Rob (R, 80)**
Legislative Office Building
Room 4200
Hartford, CT 06106
P: (860) 240-8700
F: (860) 240-0207
E: Rob.Sampson
  @housegop.ct.gov

**Sanchez, Robert (D, 25)**
Legislative Office Building
Room 4018
Hartford, CT 06106
P: (860) 240-8585
E: Bobby.Sanchez@cga.ct.gov

**Santiago, Ezequiel (D, 130)**
Legislative Office Building
Room 3802
Hartford, CT 06106
P: (860) 240-8585
E: Ezequiel.Santiago
  @cga.ct.gov

**Santiago, Hilda E. (D, 84)**
Legislative Office Building
Room 4027
Hartford, CT 06106
P: (860) 240-8585
E: Hilda.Santiago
  @cga.ct.gov

**Scanlon, Sean (D, 98)**
Legislative Office Building
Room 2802
Hartford, CT 06106
P: (860) 240-8585
E: Sean.Scanlon@cga.ct.gov

**Serra, Joseph C. (D, 33)**
Legislative Office Building
Room 4021
Hartford, CT 06106
P: (860) 240-8585
E: Joseph.Serra@cga.ct.gov

**Siegrist, Robert (R, 36)***
Legislative Office Building
Room 4200
Hartford, CT 06106
P: (860) 240-8700
E: Robert.Siegrist
  @housegop.ct.gov

**Simanski, Bill (R, 62)**
Legislative Office Building
Room 4200
Hartford, CT 06106
P: (860) 240-8700
F: (860) 240-0207
E: Bill.Simanski
  @housegop.ct.gov

**Simmons, Caroline (D, 144)**
Legislative Office Building
Room c110
Hartford, CT 06106
P: (860) 240-8585
E: Caroline.Simmons
@cga.ct.gov

**Skulczyck, Kevin (R, 45)***
Legislative Office Building
Room 4200
Hartford, CT 06106
P: (860) 240-8700
E: Kevin.Skulczyck
@housegop.ct.gov

**Slap, Derek (D, 19)***
Legislative Office Building
Room 4036
Hartford, CT 06106
P: (860) 240-8267
E: Derek.Slap@cga.ct.gov

**Smith, Richard (R, 108)**
Legislative Office Building
Room 4200
Hartford, CT 06106
P: (860) 240-8700
F: (860) 240-0207
E: Richard.Smith
@housegop.ct.gov

**Soto, Chris (D, 39)***
Legislative Office Building
Room 2704
Hartford, CT 06106
P: (860) 240-8267
E: Chris.Soto@cga.ct.gov

**Sredzinski, JP (R, 112)**
Legislative Office Building
Room 4200
Hartford, CT 06106
P: (860) 240-8700
F: (860) 240-0207
E: JP.Sredzinski
@housegop.ct.gov

**Srinivasan, Prasad (R, 31)**
Legislative Office Building
Room 4200
Hartford, CT 06106
P: (860) 240-8700
F: (860) 240-0207
E: Prasad.Srinivasan
@housegop.ct.gov

**Stafstrom, Steven (D, 129)**
Legislative Office Building
Room 2504
Hartford, CT 06106
P: (860) 240-8585
E: Steve.Stafstrom
@cga.ct.gov

**Stallworth, Charlie L.
(D, 126)**
Legislative Office Building
Room 5005
Hartford, CT 06106
P: (860) 240-8585
E: Charlie.Stallworth
@cga.ct.gov

**Staneski, Pam (R, 119)**
Legislative Office Building
Room 4200
Hartford, CT 06106
P: (860) 240-8700
F: (860) 240-0207
E: Pam.Staneski
@housegop.ct.gov

**Steinberg, Jonathan
(D, 136)**
Legislative Office Building
Room 3004
Hartford, CT 06106
P: (860) 240-8585
E: Jonathan.Steinberg
@cga.ct.gov

**Stokes, Greg (R, 58)***
Legislative Office Building
Room 4200
Hartford, CT 06106
P: (860) 240-8700
E: Greg.Stokes
@housegop.ct.gov

**Storms, Scott (R, 60)***
Legislative Office Building
Room 4200
Hartford, CT 06106
P: (860) 240-8700
E: Scott.Storms
@housegop.ct.gov

**Tercyak, Peter A. (D, 26)**
Legislative Office Building
Room 4017
Hartford, CT 06106
P: (860) 240-8585
E: Peter.Tercyak@cga.ct.gov

**Tong, William (D, 147)**
Legislative Office Building
Room 2502
Hartford, CT 06106
P: (860) 240-8585
E: William.Tong@cga.ct.gov

**Tweedie, Mark (R, 13)**
Legislative Office Building
Room 4200
Hartford, CT 06106
P: (860) 240-8700
F: (860) 240-0207
E: Mark.Tweedie
@housegop.ct.gov

**Urban, Diana S. (D, 43)**
Legislative Office Building
Room 4032
Hartford, CT 06106
P: (860) 240-8585
E: Diana.Urban@cga.ct.gov

**Vahey, Cristin McCarthy
(D, 133)**
Legislative Office Building
Room 4001
Hartford, CT 06106
P: (860) 240-8585
E: Cristin.McCarthyVahey
@cga.ct.gov

**Vail, Kurt (R, 52)**
Legislative Office Building
Room 4200
Hartford, CT 06106
P: (860) 240-8700
F: (860) 240-0207
E: Kurt.Vail
@housegop.ct.gov

**Vargas, Edwin (D, 6)**
Legislative Office Building
Room 1003
Hartford, CT 06106
P: (860) 240-8585
E: Edwin.Vargas@cga.ct.gov

**Verrengia, Joe (D, 20)**
Legislative Office Building
Room 3603
Hartford, CT 06106
P: (860) 240-8585
E: Joe.Verrengia@cga.ct.gov

**Walker, Toni E. (D, 93)**
Legislative Office Building
Room 2702
Hartford, CT 06106
P: (860) 240-8585
E: Toni.Walker@cga.ct.gov

**Wilms, Fred (R, 142)**
Legislative Office Building
Room 4200
Hartford, CT 06106
P: (860) 240-8700
F: (860) 240-0207
E: Fred.Wilms
@housegop.ct.gov

**Wilson, David (R, 66)***
Legislative Office Building
Room 4200
Hartford, CT 06106
P: (860) 240-8700
E: David.Wilson
@housegop.ct.gov

**Winkler, Michael (D, 56)***
Legislative Office Building
Room 4026
Hartford, CT 06106
P: (860) 240-8585
E: Michael.Winkler
@cga.ct.gov

**Wood, Terrie E. (R, 141)**
Legislative Office Building
Room 4200
Hartford, CT 06106
P: (860) 240-8700
F: (860) 240-0207
E: Terrie.Wood
@housegop.ct.gov

**Yaccarino, David (R, 87)**
Legislative Office Building
Room 4200
Hartford, CT 06106
P: (860) 240-8700
F: (860) 240-0207
E: dave.yaccarino
@housegop.ct.gov

**Zawistowski, Tami (R, 61)**
Legislative Office Building
Room 4200
Hartford, CT 06106
P: (860) 240-8700
F: (860) 240-0207
E: Tami.Zawistowski
@housegop.ct.gov

**Ziobron, Melissa (R, 34)**
Legislative Office Building
Room 4200
Hartford, CT 06106
P: (860) 240-8700
F: (860) 240-0207
E: Melissa.Ziobron
@housegop.ct.gov

**Ziogas, Christopher
(D, 79)***
Legislative Office Building
Room 4016
Hartford, CT 06106
P: (860) 240-8585
E: Christopher.Ziogas
@cga.ct.gov

**Zupkus, Lezlye (R, 89)**
Legislative Office Building
Room 4200
Hartford, CT 06106
P: (860) 240-8700
F: (860) 240-0207
E: Lezlye.Zupkus
@housegop.ct.gov

# Delaware

## Executive

### Governor

The Honorable John
    Carney Jr. (D)
Governor
Legislative Hall
Dover, DE 19901
P: (302) 744-4101
F: (302) 739-2775

### Lieutenant Governor

The Honorable Bethany A.
    Hall-Long (D)
Lieutenant Governor
Tatnall Building, 3rd Floor
Dover, DE 19901
P: (302) 744-4333
E: bethany.hall-long
    @state.de.us

### Attorney General

The Honorable Matthew
    Denn (D)
Attorney General
Carvel State Office Building
820 North French Street
Wilmington, DE 19801
P: (302) 577-8338
E: matthew.denn@state.de.us

### Auditor

The Honorable R. Thomas
    Wagner Jr. (R)
Auditor of Accounts
401 Federal Street
Townsend Building, Suite 1
Dover, DE 19901
P: (302) 739-5055
F: (302) 739-6707
E: r.thomas.wagner
    @state.de.us

### Commissioner of Insurance

The Honorable Trinidad
    Navarro (D)
Commissioner
841 Silver Lake Boulevard
Dover, DE 19904
P: (302) 674-7300
F: (302) 739-5280

### Treasurer

The Honorable Ken
    Simpler (R)
State Treasurer
820 Silver Lake Boulevard,
Suite 100
Dover, DE 19904
P: (302) 672-6700
F: (302) 739-5635

## Judiciary

### Supreme Court (GA)

Ms. Cathy L. Howard
Clerk of the Court
Carvel State Office Building
820 North French Street, 11th
Floor
Wilmington, DE 19801
P: (302) 739-4187
F: (302) 577-3702

The Honorable Leo E.
    Strine Jr.
Chief Justice
The Honorable Randy J.
    Holland
The Honorable Collins J.
    Seitz Jr.
The Honorable Karen
    Valihura
The Honorable James T.
    Vaughn Jr.

## Legislative Senate

### Senate President

The Honorable Bethany A.
    Hall-Long (D)
Lieutenant Governor
Tatnall Building, 3rd Floor
Dover, DE 19901
P: (302) 744-4333
E: bethany.hall-long
    @state.de.us

### President Pro Tempore of the Senate

Senator David B.
    McBride (D)
Senate President Pro Tempore
411 Legislative Avenue
Dover, DE 19901
P: (302) 744-4167
E: David.McBride
    @state.de.us

### Senate Majority Leader

Senator Margaret Rose
    Henry (D)
Senate Majority Leader
411 Legislative Avenue
Dover, DE 19901
P: (302) 744-4191
E: MargaretRose.Henry
    @state.de.us

### Senate Minority Leader

Senator F. Gary Simpson (R)
Senate Minority Leader
411 Legislative Avenue
Dover, DE 19901
P: (302) 744-4134
F: (302) 739-5049
E: gsimpson@udel.edu

### Secretary of the Senate

Mr. Bernard J. Brady
Secretary of the Senate
Legislative Hall
411 Legislative Avenue
Dover, DE 19901
P: (302) 744-4129
F: (302) 739-7718
E: Bernard.Brady
    @state.de.us

### Members of the Senate

Bonini, Colin R.J. (R, 16)
411 Legislative Avenue
Dover, DE 19901
P: (302) 744-4169
F: (302) 739-5049
E: senator-colin
    @prodigy.net

Bushweller, Brian J.
    (D, 17)
411 Legislative Avenue
Dover, DE 19901
P: (302) 744-4162
F: (302) 739-6890
E: Brian.Bushweller
    @state.de.us

Cloutier, Catherine L.
    (R, 5)
411 Legislative Avenue
Dover, DE 19901
P: (302) 744-4197
F: (302) 739-5049
E: catherine.cloutier
    @state.de.us

Delcollo, Anthony (R, 7)*
411 Legislative Avenue
Dover, DE 19901
P: (302) 744-4114
E: Anthony.Delcollo
    @state.de.us

Ennis, Bruce C. (D, 14)
411 Legislative Avenue
Dover, DE 19901
P: (302) 744-4310
F: (302) 739-6890
E: bruce.ennis@state.de.us

Henry, Margaret Rose (D, 2)
411 Legislative Avenue
Dover, DE 19901
P: (302) 744-4191
E: MargaretRose.Henry
    @state.de.us

Hocker, Gerald W. (R, 20)
411 Legislative Avenue
Dover, DE 19901
P: (302) 744-4144
E: Gerald.Hocker
    @state.de.us

LaVelle, Gregory F. (R, 4)
411 Legislative Avenue
Dover, DE 19901
P: (302) 744-4135
F: (302) 739-5049
E: Greg.Lavelle@state.de.us

Lawson, David G. (R, 15)
411 Legislative Avenue
Dover, DE 19901
P: (302) 744-4237
E: Dave.Lawson@state.de.us

Lopez, Ernesto B. (R, 6)
411 Legislative Avenue
Dover, DE 19901
P: (302) 744-4136
F: (302) 739-5049
E: Ernesto.Lopez
    @state.de.us

Marshall, Robert I. (D, 3)
411 Legislative Avenue
Dover, DE 19901
P: (302) 744-4168
E: robert.marshall
    @state.de.us

McBride, David B. (D, 13)
411 Legislative Avenue
Dover, DE 19901
P: (302) 744-4167
E: David.McBride
    @state.de.us

McDowell III, Harris B.
    (D, 1)
411 Legislative Avenue
Dover, DE 19901
P: (302) 744-4147
E: Harris.McDowell
    @state.de.us

**Pettyjohn, Brian (R, 19)**
411 Legislative Avenue
Dover, DE 19901
P: (302) 744-4117
E: Brian.Pettyjohn
@state.de.us

**Poore, Nicole (D, 12)**
411 Legislative Avenue
Dover, DE 19901
P: (302) 744-4164
F: (302) 739-6890
E: Nicole.Poore@state.de.us

**Richardson, Bryant L. (R, 21)**
411 Legislative Avenue
Dover, DE 19901
P: (302) 744-4298
E: Bryant.Richardson
@state.de.us

**Simpson, F. Gary (R, 18)**
411 Legislative Avenue
Dover, DE 19901
P: (302) 744-4134
F: (302) 739-5049
E: gsimpson@udel.edu

**Sokola, David P. (D, 8)**
411 Legislative Avenue
Dover, DE 19901
P: (302) 744-4139
E: David.Sokola@state.de.us

**Townsend, Bryan (D, 11)**
411 Legislative Avenue
Dover, DE 19901
P: (302) 744-4165
E: Bryan.Townsend
@state.de.us

**Walsh, John (D, 9)\***
411 Legislative Avenue
Dover, DE 19901
P: (302) 744-4163
E: john.walsh@state.de.us

# House

## Speaker of the House

**Representative Peter C. Schwartzkopf (D)**
House Speaker
411 Legislative Avenue
Dover, DE 19901
P: (302) 744-4351
E: Peter.Schwartzkopf
@state.de.us

## Speaker Pro Tempore of the House

**Representative Helene M. Keeley (D)**
House Speaker Pro Tem
411 Legislative Avenue
Dover, DE 19901
P: (302) 744-4351
E: helene.keeley
@state.de.us

## House Majority Leader

**Representative Valerie Longhurst (D)**
House Majority Leader
411 Legislative Avenue
Dover, DE 19901
P: (302) 744-4351
E: Valerie.Longhurst
@state.de.us

## House Minority Leader

**Representative Daniel B. Short (R)**
House Minority Leader
411 Legislative Avenue
Dover, DE 19901
P: (302) 744-4172
F: (302) 739-2773
E: Daniel.Short@state.de.us

## Clerk of the House

**Mr. Richard L. Puffer**
Chief Clerk of the House of
Representatives
411 Legislative Avenue
P.O. Box 1401
Dover, DE 19903
P: (302) 744-4121
F: (302) 739-7854
E: richard.puffer
@state.de.us

## Members of the House

**Baumbach, Paul S. (D, 23)**
411 Legislative Ave
Dover, DE 19901
P: (302) 744-4351
F: (302) 739-2313
E: paul.baumbach
@state.de.us

**Bennett, Andria L. (D, 32)**
411 Legislative Avenue
Dover, DE 19901
P: (302) 744-4351
F: (302) 739-2313
E: andria.bennett
@state.de.us

**Bentz, David (D, 18)**
411 Legislative Avenue
Dover, DE 19901
P: (302) 744-4351
E: David.Bentz@state.de.us

**Bolden, Stephanie T. (D, 2)**
411 Legislative Avenue
Dover, DE 19901
P: (302) 744-4351
F: (302) 739-2313
E: StephanieT.Bolden
@state.de.us

**Brady, Gerald L. (D, 4)**
411 Legislative Avenue
Dover, DE 19901
P: (302) 744-4351
E: gerald.brady@state.de.us

**Carson, William J. (D, 28)**
411 Legislative Avenue
Dover, DE 19901
P: (302) 744-4113
F: (302) 739-2313
E: william.carson
@state.de.us

**Collins, Richard G. (R, 41)**
411 Legislative Avenue
Dover, DE 19901
P: (302) 744-4171
E: R.Collins@state.de.us

**Dukes, Timothy D. (R, 40)**
411 Legislative Avenue
Dover, DE 19901
P: (302) 744-4171
E: timothy.dukes
@state.de.us

**Gray, Ronald E. (R, 38)**
411 Legislative Avenue
Dover, DE 19901
P: (302) 744-4171
E: ronald.gray@state.de.us

**Heffernan, Debra (D, 6)**
411 Legislative Avenue
Dover, DE 19901
P: (302) 744-4351
E: debra.heffernan
@state.de.us

**Hensley, Kevin (R, 9)**
411 Legislative Avenue
Dover, DE 19901
P: (302) 744-4171
F: (302) 739-2773
E: kevin.hensley
@state.de.us

**Hudson, Deborah (R, 12)**
411 Legislative Avenue
Dover, DE 19901
P: (302) 744-4171
E: deborah.hudson
@state.de.us

**Jaques Jr., Earl G. (D, 27)**
411 Legislative Avenue
Dover, DE 19901
P: (302) 744-4142
F: (302) 739-2313
E: earl.jaques@state.de.us

**Johnson, James (D, 16)**
411 Legislative Avenue
Dover, DE 19901
P: (302) 744-4351
F: (302) 739-2313
E: jj.johnson@state.de.us

**Johnson, S. Quinton (D, 8)**
411 Legislative Avenue
Dover, DE 19901
P: (302) 744-4351
F: (302) 739-2313
E: quinton.johnson
@state.de.us

**Keeley, Helene M. (D, 3)**
411 Legislative Avenue
Dover, DE 19901
P: (302) 744-4351
E: helene.keeley
@state.de.us

**Kenton, Harvey R. (R, 36)**
411 Legislative Avenue
Dover, DE 19901
P: (302) 744-4171
F: (302) 739-2773
E: harvey.kenton
@state.de.us

**King, Ruth Briggs (R, 37)**
411 Legislative Avenue
Dover, DE 19901
P: (302) 744-4251
F: (302) 739-2773
E: Ruth.BriggsKing
@state.de.us

**Kowalko Jr., John (D, 25)**
411 Legislative Avenue
Dover, DE 19901
P: (302) 744-4351
F: (302) 739-2313
E: john.kowalko@state.de.us

# Delaware

**Longhurst, Valerie (D, 15)**
411 Legislative Avenue
Dover, DE 19901
P: (302) 744-4351
E: Valerie.Longhurst
@state.de.us

**Lynn, Sean M. (D, 31)**
411 Legislative Avenue
Dover, DE 19901
P: (302) 744-4351
E: sean.lynn@state.de.us

**Matthews, Sean (D, 10)**
411 Legislative Avenue
Dover, DE 19901
P: (302) 744-4351
E: sean.matthews
@state.de.us

**Miro, Joseph E. (R, 22)**
411 Legislative Avenue
Dover, DE 19901
P: (302) 744-4171
E: joseph.miro@state.de.us

**Mitchell Jr., John L. (D, 13)**
411 Legislative Avenue
Dover, DE 19901
P: (302) 744-4351
F: (302) 739-2313
E: john.l.mitchell
@state.de.us

**Mulrooney, Michael P. (D, 17)**
411 Legislative Avenue
Dover, DE 19901
P: (302) 744-4351
E: Michael.Mulrooney
@state.de.us

**Osienski, Edward S. (D, 24)**
411 Legislative Avenue
Dover, DE 19901
P: (302) 744-4351
F: (302) 739-2313
E: Edward.Osienski
@state.de.us

**Outten, William R. (R, 30)**
411 Legislative Avenue
Dover, DE 19901
P: (302) 744-4083
F: (302) 739-2773
E: bobby.outten@state.de.us

**Paradee, W. Charles (D, 29)**
411 Legislative Avenue
Dover, DE 19901
P: (302) 744-4351
F: (302) 739-2313
E: trey.paradee@state.de.us

**Postles Jr., Charles (R, 33)\***
411 Legislative Avenue
Dover, DE 19901
E: Charles.Postles
@state.de.us

**Potter Jr., Charles (D, 1)**
411 Legislative Avenue
Dover, DE 19901
P: (302) 744-4351
F: (302) 739-2313
E: Charles.Potter
@state.de.us

**Ramone, Michael (R, 21)**
411 Legislative Avenue
Dover, DE 19901
P: (302) 744-4108
F: (302) 739-2773
E: Michael.Ramone
@state.de.us

**Schwartzkopf, Peter C. (D, 14)**
411 Legislative Avenue
Dover, DE 19901
P: (302) 744-4351
E: Peter.Schwartzkopf
@state.de.us

**Short, Bryon H. (D, 7)**
411 Legislative Avenue
Dover, DE 19901
P: (302) 744-4297
E: Bryon.Short@state.de.us

**Short, Daniel B. (R, 39)**
411 Legislative Avenue
Dover, DE 19901
P: (302) 744-4172
F: (302) 739-2773
E: Daniel.Short@state.de.us

**Smith, Melanie George (D, 5)**
411 Legislative Avenue
Dover, DE 19901
P: (302) 744-4126
F: (302) 739-2313
E: melanie.g.smith
@state.de.us

**Smyk, Stephen T. (R, 20)**
411 Legislative Avenue
Dover, DE 19901
P: (302) 744-4171
F: (302) 739-2773
E: Steve.Smyk@state.de.us

**Spiegelman, Jeffrey N. (R, 11)**
411 Legislative Avenue
Dover, DE 19901
P: (302) 744-4171
E: jeff.spiegelman
@state.de.us

**Viola, John J. (D, 26)**
411 Legislative Avenue
Dover, DE 19901
P: (302) 744-4351
E: John.Viola@state.de.us

**Williams, Kimberly (D, 19)**
411 Legislative Avenue
Dover, DE 19901
P: (302) 744-4351
E: kimberly.williams
@state.de.us

**Wilson, David L. (R, 35)**
411 Legislative Avenue
Dover, DE 19901
P: (302) 744-4150
F: (302) 739-2773
E: David.L.Wilson
@state.de.us

**Yearick, Lyndon D. (R, 34)**
411 Legislative Ave
Dover, DE 19901
P: (302) 744-4171
E: Lyndon.Yearick
@state.de.us

# District of Columbia

## Executive

### Mayor
**The Honorable Muriel Bowser (D)**
Mayor
1350 Pennsylvania Avenue, Northwest
Suite 316
Washington, DC 20004
P: (202) 727-6300
F: (202) 727-0505
E: eom@dc.gov

### Attorney General
**The Honorable Karl A. Racine**
(appointed)
Attorney General
441 4th Street, Northwest
Suite 1100S
Washington, DC 20001
P: (202) 727-3400
F: (202) 347-8922
E: oag@dc.gov

### Auditor
**The Honorable Kathleen Patterson**
Auditor
717 14th Street, Northwest
Suite 900
Washington, DC 20005
P: (202) 727-3600
F: (202) 724-8814
E: kathleen.patterson
@dc.gov

### Secretary of the District of Columbia
**The Honorable Lauren C. Vaughn**
(appointed)
Secretary of the District
1350 Pennsylvania Avenue, Northwest
Suite 419
Washington, DC 20004
P: (202) 727-6306
F: (202) 727-3582
E: secretary@dc.gov

### Treasurer
**Mr. Jeffrey Barnette**
(appointed)
Deputy CFO & Treasurer
1101 4th Street, Southwest
Suite 850
Washington, DC 20024
P: (202) 442-8200
F: (202) 442-8201

## Judiciary

### Court of Appeals (FA)
**Mr. Julio A. Castillo**
Clerk of the Court of Appeals
Historic Courthouse
430 E Street, Northwest
Washington, DC 20001
P: (202) 879-2700

**The Honorable Eric T. Washington**
Chief Judge
**The Honorable Corinne A. Beckwith**
**The Honorable Anna Blackburne-Rigsby**
**The Honorable Catharine F. Easterly**
**The Honorable John R. Fisher**
**The Honorable Stephen Glickman**
**The Honorable Roy W. McLeese**
**The Honorable Phyllis D. Thompson**

## Council of the District of Columbia

### Council Chair
**Councilman Phil Mendelson (D)**
Council Chair
John A. Wilson Building, Suite 504
1350 Pennsylvania Avenue, Northwest
Washington, DC 20004
P: (202) 724-8032
F: (202) 724-8085
E: pmendelson@dccouncil.us

## Council Chair Pro Tempore
**Councilman Kenyan McDuffie (D)**
Council Chair Pro Tempore
John A. Wilson Building, Suite 506
1350 Pennsylvania Avenue, Northwest
Washington, DC 20004
P: (202) 724-8028
F: (202) 724-8076
E: kmcduffie@dccouncil.us

## Secretary to the Council
**Ms. Nyasha Smith**
Secretary To the Council
John A. Wilson Building, Suite 5
1350 Pennsylvania Avenue Northwest
Washington, DC 20004
P: (202) 724-8080
F: (202) 347-3070
E: nsmith@dccouncil.us

## Members of the Senate

**Allen, Charles (D, 6)**
John A. Wilson Building, Suite 406
1350 Pennsylvania Avenue, Northwest
Washington, DC 20004
P: (202) 724-8072
E: callen@dccouncil.us

**Bonds, Anita (D, At-Large)**
John A. Wilson Building, Suite 110
1350 Pennsylvania Avenue, Northwest
Washington, DC 20004
P: (202) 724-8064
F: (202) 724-8099
E: abonds@dccouncil.us

**Cheh, Mary M. (D, 3)**
John A. Wilson Building, Suite 108
1350 Pennsylvania Avenue, Northwest
Washington, DC 20004
P: (202) 724-8062
F: (202) 724-8118
E: mcheh@dccouncil.us

**Evans, Jack (D, 2)**
John A. Wilson Building, Suite 106
1350 Pennsylvania Avenue, Northwest
Washington, DC 20004
P: (202) 724-8058
F: (202) 727-8023
E: jevans@dccouncil.us

**Gray, Vincent C. (D, 7)**
1350 Pennsylvania Avenue, Northwest
Suite 406
Washington, DC 20004
P: (202) 724-8068
F: (202) 741-0911
E: vgray@dc.gov

**Grosso, David (I, At-Large)**
John A. Wilson Building, Suite 402
1350 Pennsylvania Avenue, Northwest
Washington, DC 20004
P: (202) 724-8105
F: (202) 724-8071
E: dgrosso@dccouncil.us

**McDuffie, Kenyan (D, 5)**
John A. Wilson Building, Suite 506
1350 Pennsylvania Avenue, Northwest
Washington, DC 20004
P: (202) 724-8028
F: (202) 724-8076
E: kmcduffie@dccouncil.us

**Mendelson, Phil (D, At-Large)**
John A. Wilson Building, Suite 504
1350 Pennsylvania Avenue, Northwest
Washington, DC 20004
P: (202) 724-8032
F: (202) 724-8085
E: pmendelson@dccouncil.us

**Nadeau, Brianne (D, 1)**
John A. Wilson Building, Suite 102
1350 Pennsylvania Avenue, Northwest
Washington, DC 20004
P: (202) 724-8181
F: (202) 724-8109
E: bnadeau@dccouncil.us

**Silverman, Elissa (I, At-Large)**
John A. Wilson Building, Suite 408
1350 Pennsylvania Avenue, Northwest
Washington, DC 20004
P: (202) 724-7772
F: (202) 724-8087
E: esilverman@dccouncil.us

# District of Columbia

**Todd, Brandon T. (D, 4)**
John A. Wilson Building, Suite
105
1350 Pennsylvania Avenue,
Northwest
Washington, DC 20004
P: (202) 724-8052
F: (202) 741-0908
E: btodd@dccouncil.us

**White Jr., Robert C.**
    **(D, At-Large)***
John A. Wilson Building, Suite
107
1350 Pennsylvania Avenue,
Northwest
Washington, DC 20004
P: (202) 724-8174
F: (202) 727-8210
E: rwhite@dccouncil.us

**White Sr., Trayon (D, 8)***
John A. Wilson Building, Suite
400
1350 Pennsylvania Avenue
Washington, DC 20004
P: (202) 724-8045
F: (202) 724-8055
E: twhite@dccouncil.us

# Florida

## Executive

### Governor

**The Honorable Rick Scott (R)**
Governor
PL 05, The Capitol
400 South Monroe Street
Tallahassee, FL 32399
P: (850) 488-7146
F: (850) 487-0801

### Lieutenant Governor

**The Honorable Carlos Lopez-Cantera (R)**
Lieutenant Governor
The State Capitol
Tallahassee, FL 32399
P: (850) 488-4711
F: (850) 921-6114

### Commissioner of Agriculture & Consumer Services

**The Honorable Adam H. Putnam (R)**
Commissioner
The Capitol, PL-10
400 South Monroe Street
Tallahassee, FL 32399
P: (850) 488-3022
F: (850) 922-4936

### Attorney General

**The Honorable Pam Bondi (R)**
Attorney General
The Capitol, PL 01
Tallahassee, FL 32399
P: (850) 414-3300
F: (954) 712-4826

### Auditor

**Ms. Sherrill Norman**
(appointed by the Legislature)
Auditor General
Pepper Building, Room G-75
111 West Madison Street
Tallahassee, FL 32399
P: (850) 412-2722
F: (850) 488-6975
E: sherrillnorman
@aud.state.fl.us

### Secretary of State

**The Honorable Kenneth Detzner (R)**
(appointed)
Secretary of State
R.A. Gray Building
500 South Bronough Street, Suite 100
Tallahassee, FL 32399
P: (850) 245-6500
F: (850) 245-6125
E: dossecretaryofstate
@dos.myflorida.com

### Chief Financial Officer

**The Honorable Jeffrey H. Atwater (R)**
Chief Financial Officer
200 East Gaines Street
Tallahassee, FL 32399
P: (850) 413-2850
F: (850) 413-2950
E: allison@jeffatwater.com

## Judiciary

### Supreme Court (MR)

**Mr. John A. Tomasino**
Clerk
500 South Duval Street
Tallahassee, FL 32399
P: (850) 488-0125
E: supremecourt
@flcourts.org

**The Honorable Jorge Labarga**
Chief Justice
**The Honorable Charles T. Canady**
**The Honorable C. Alan Lawson**
**The Honorable R. Fred Lewis**
**The Honorable Barbara J. Pariente**
**The Honorable Ricky Polston**
**The Honorable Peggy A. Quince**

## Legislative

## Senate

### Senate President

**Senator Joe Negron (R)**
Senate President
305 Senate Office Building
404 South Monroe Street
Tallahassee, FL 32399
P: (850) 487-5032
E: negron.joe.web
@flsenate.gov

### President Pro Tempore of the Senate

**Senator Anitere Flores (R)**
President Pro Tempore
404 Senate Office Building
404 South Monroe Street
Tallahassee, FL 32399
P: (850) 487-5037
E: flores.anitere.web
@flsenate.gov

### Senate Majority Leader

**Senator Wilton Simpson (R)**
Senate Majority Leader
330 Senate Office Building
404 South Monroe Street
Tallahassee, FL 32399
P: (850) 487-5018
E: simpson.wilton.web
@flsenate.gov

### Senate Minority Leader

**Senator Oscar Braynon II (D)**
Senate Minority Leader
200 Senate Office Building
404 South Monroe Street
Tallahassee, FL 32399
P: (850) 487-5036
E: braynon.oscar.web
@flsenate.gov

### Secretary of the Senate

**Ms. Debbie Brown**
Secretary of the Senate
Suite 405, The Capitol
404 South Monroe Street
Tallahassee, FL 32399
P: (850) 487-5270
F: (850) 487-5174

### Members of the Senate

**Artiles, Frank (R, 40)**
308 Senate Office Building
404 South Monroe Street
Tallahassee, FL 32399
P: (850) 487-5040
E: artiles.frank.web
@flsenate.gov

**Baxley, Dennis K. (R, 12)**
320 Senate Office Building
404 South Monroe Street
Tallahassee, FL 32399
P: (850) 487-5012
E: baxley.dennis.web
@flsenate.gov

**Bean, Aaron P. (R, 4)**
306 Senate Office Building
404 South Monroe Street
Tallahassee, FL 32399
P: (850) 487-5004
F: (850) 410-4805
E: bean.aaron.web
@flsenate.gov

**Benacquisto, Lizbeth (R, 27)**
400 Senate Office Building
404 South Monroe Street
Tallahassee, FL 32399
P: (850) 487-5030
E: benacquisto.lizbeth.web
@flsenate.gov

**Book, Lauren (D, 32)\***
202 Senate Office Building
404 South Monroe Street
Tallahassee, FL 32399
P: (850) 487-5032
E: book.lauren.web
@flsenate.gov

**Bracy, Randolph (D, 11)**
213 Senate Office Building
404 South Monroe Street
Tallahassee, FL 32399
P: (850) 487-5011
E: bracy.randolph.web
@flsenate.gov

**Bradley, Rob (R, 5)**
414 Senate Office Building
404 South Monroe Street
Tallahassee, FL 32399
P: (850) 487-5007
F: (888) 263-0641
E: bradley.rob.web
@flsenate.gov

**Brandes, Jeffrey P. (R, 24)**
416 Senate Office Building
404 South Monroe Street
Tallahassee, FL 32399
P: (850) 487-5022
E: brandes.jeff.web
@flsenate.gov

**Braynon II, Oscar (D, 35)**
200 Senate Office Building
404 South Monroe Street
Tallahassee, FL 32399
P: (850) 487-5036
E: braynon.oscar.web
@flsenate.gov

**Broxson, Douglas Vaughn (R, 1)**
311 Senate Office Building
404 South Monroe Street
Tallahassee, FL 32399
P: (850) 487-5001
E: broxson.doug.web
@flsenate.gov

# Florida

**Campbell, Daphne D. (D, 38)**
218 Senate Office Building
404 South Monroe Street
Tallahassee, FL 32399
P: (850) 487-5038
E: campbell.daphne.web
@flsenate.gov

**Clemens, Jeff (D, 27)**
210 Senate Office Building
404 South Monroe Street
Tallahassee, FL 32399
P: (850) 487-5027
E: clemens.jeff.web
@flsenate.gov

**Evers, Greg (R, 2)**
308 Senate Office Building
404 South Monroe Street
Tallahassee, FL 32399
P: (850) 487-5002
F: (850) 487-5276
E: evers.greg.web
@flsenate.gov

**Farmer, Gary (D, 34)\***
216 Senate Office Building
404 South Monroe Street
Tallahassee, FL 32399
P: (850) 487-5034
E: farmer.gary.web
@flsenate.gov

**Flores, Anitere (R, 39)**
404 Senate Office Building
404 South Monroe Street
Tallahassee, FL 32399
P: (850) 487-5037
E: flores.anitere.web
@flsenate.gov

**Gainer, George B. (R, 2)\***
302 Senate Office Building
404 South Monroe Street
Tallahassee, FL 32399
P: (850) 487-5002
E: gainer.george.web
@flsenate.gov

**Galvano, Bill (R, 21)**
420 Senate Office Building
404 South Monroe Street
Tallahassee, FL 32399
P: (850) 487-5026
E: galvano.bill.web
@flsenate.gov

**Garcia, Rene (R, 36)**
310 Senate Office Building
404 South Monroe Street
Tallahassee, FL 32399
P: (850) 487-5038
E: garcia.rene.web
@flsenate.gov

**Gibson, Audrey (D, 6)**
405 Senate Office Building
404 South Monroe Street
Tallahassee, FL 32399
P: (850) 487-5009
E: gibson.audrey.web
@flsenate.gov

**Grimsley, Denise (R, 26)**
413 Senate Office Building
404 South Monroe Street
Tallahassee, FL 32399
P: (850) 487-5021
E: grimsley.denise.web
@flsenate.gov

**Hukill, Dorothy L. (R, 14)**
406 Senate Office Building
404 South Monroe Street
Tallahassee, FL 32399
P: (850) 487-5008
E: hukill.dorothy.web
@flsenate.gov

**Hutson, Travis (R, 7)**
314 Senate Office Building
402 South Monroe Street
Tallahassee, FL 32399
P: (850) 487-5006
E: hutson.travis.web
@flsenate.gov

**Latvala, Jack (R, 16)**
412 Senate Office Building
404 South Monroe Street
Tallahassee, FL 32399
P: (850) 487-5020
E: latvala.jack.web
@flsenate.gov

**Lee, Tom (R, 20)**
418 Senate Office Building
404 South Monroe Street
Tallahassee, FL 32399
P: (850) 487-5024
E: lee.tom.web@flsenate.gov

**Mayfield, Debbie (R, 17)**
324 Senate Office Building
404 South Monroe Street
Tallahassee, FL 32399
P: (850) 487-5017
E: mayfield.debbie.web
@flsenate.gov

**Montford, William J. (D, 3)**
410 Senate Office Building
404 South Monroe Street
Tallahassee, FL 32399
P: (850) 487-5003
F: (850) 487-5086
E: montford.bill.web
@flsenate.gov

**Negron, Joe (R, 25)**
305 Senate Office Building
404 South Monroe Street
Tallahassee, FL 32399
P: (850) 487-5032
E: negron.joe.web
@flsenate.gov

**Passidomo, Kathleen (R, 28)**
318 Senate Office Building
404 South Monroe Street
Tallahassee, FL 32399
P: (850) 487-5028
E: passidomo.kathleen.web
@flsenate.gov

**Perry, Keith (R, 8)**
312 Senate Office Building
404 South Monroe Street
Tallahassee, FL 32399
P: (850) 487-5008
E: perry.keith.web
@flsenate.gov

**Powell, Bobby (D, 30)**
214 Senate Office Building
404 South Monroe Street
Tallahassee, FL 32399
P: (850) 487-5030
E: powell.bobby.web
@flsenate.gov

**Rader, Kevin J.G. (D, 29)**
222 Senate Office Building
404 SOuth Monroe Street
Tallahassee, FL 32399
P: (850) 487-5029
E: rader.kevin.web
@flsenate.gov

**Rodriguez, Jose Javier (D, 37)**
212 Senate Office Building
404 South Monroe Street
Tallahassee, FL 32399
P: (850) 487-5037
E: rodriguez.jose.web
@flsenate.gov

**Rouson, Darryl Ervin (D, 19)**
Senate Office Building
404 South Monroe Street
Tallahassee, FL 32399
E: rouson.darryl.web
@flsenate.gov

**Simmons, David (R, 9)**
408 Senate Office Building
404 South Monroe Street
Tallahassee, FL 32399
P: (850) 487-5010
E: simmons.david.web
@flsenate.gov

**Simpson, Wilton (R, 10)**
330 Senate Office Building
404 South Monroe Street
Tallahassee, FL 32399
P: (850) 487-5018
E: simpson.wilton.web
@flsenate.gov

**Stargel, Kelli (R, 22)**
322 Senate Office Building
404 South Monroe Street
Tallahassee, FL 32399
P: (850) 487-5015
E: stargel.kelli.web
@flsenate.gov

**Steube, W. Greg (R, 23)**
326 Senate Office Building
404 South Monroe Street
Tallahassee, FL 32399
P: (850) 487-5023
E: steube.greg.web
@flsenate.gov

**Stewart, Linda (D, 13)**
224 Senate Office Building
404 South Monroe Street
Tallahassee, FL 32399
P: (850) 487-5013
E: stewart.linda.web
@flsenate.gov

**Thurston Jr., Perry E. (D, 33)**
208 Senate Office Building
404 South Monroe Street
Tallahassee, FL 32399
P: (850) 487-5033
E: thurston.perry.web
@flsenate.gov

**Torres Jr., Victor Manuel (D, 15)**
226 Senate Office Building
404 South Monroe Street
Tallahassee, FL 32399
P: (850) 487-5015
E: torres.victor.web
@flsenate.gov

**Young, Dana D. (R, 18)**
316 Senate Office Building
404 South Monroe Street
Tallahassee, FL 32399
P: (850) 487-5018
E: young.dana.web
@flsenate.gov

## House

### Speaker of the House

**Representative Richard Corcoran (R)**
Speaker of the House
420 The Capitol
402 South Monroe Street
Tallahassee, FL 32399
P: (850) 717-5037
E: richard.corcoran
@myfloridahouse.gov

### Speaker Pro Tempore of the House

**Representative Jeanette M. Nunez (R)**
Speaker Pro Tempore
418 The Capitol
402 South Monroe Street
Tallahassee, FL 32399
P: (850) 717-5119
E: jeanette.nunez
@myfloridahouse.gov

### House Majority Leader

**Representative Ray Wesley Rodrigues (R)**
Majority Leader
322 The Capitol
402 South Monroe Street
Tallahassee, FL 32399
P: (850) 717-5076
E: ray.rodrigues
@myfloridahouse.gov

### House Minority Leader

**Representative Janet Cruz (D)**
Democratic Leader
316 The Capitol
402 South Monroe Street
Tallahassee, FL 32399
P: (850) 717-5062
E: janet.cruz
@myfloridahouse.gov

### Clerk of the House

**Mr. Robert L. Ward**
Clerk of the House
513 Capitol
402 South Monroe Street
Tallahassee, FL 32399
P: (850) 717-5400
E: bob.ward
@myfloridahouse.gov

## Members of the House

**Abruzzo, Joseph (D, 81)**
1102 The Capitol
402 South Monroe Street
Tallahassee, FL 32399
P: (850) 717-5081
E: joseph.abruzzo
@myfloridahouse.gov

**Ahern, Lawrence T. (R, 66)**
222 The Capitol
402 South Monroe Street
Tallahassee, FL 32399
P: (850) 717-5066
E: lawrence.ahern
@myfloridahouse.gov

**Albritton, Ben (R, 56)**
222 The Capitol
402 South Monroe Street
Tallahassee, FL 32399
P: (850) 717-5056
E: ben.albritton
@myfloridahouse.gov

**Alexander, Ramon (D, 8)\***
1001 The Capitol
402 South Monroe Street
Tallahassee, FL 32399
P: (850) 717-5008
E: ramon.alexander
@myfloridahouse.gov

**Altman, Thad (R, 52)**
1101 The Capitol
402 South Monroe Street
Tallahassee, FL 32399
P: (850) 717-5052
E: thad.altman
@myfloridahouse.gov

**Antone, Bruce (D, 46)**
300 House Office Building
402 South Monroe Street
Tallahassee, FL 32399
P: (850) 717-5046
E: bruce.antone
@myfloridahouse.gov

**Asencio, Robert (D, 118)\***
1402 The Capitol
402 South Monroe Street
Tallahassee, FL 32399
P: (850) 717-5118
E: robert.asencio
@myfloridahouse.gov

**Ausley, Loranne (D, 9)**
1001 The Capitol
402 South Monroe Street
Tallahassee, FL 32399
P: (850) 717-5009
E: lorrane.ausley
@myfloridahouse.gov

**Avila, Bryan (R, 111)**
303 House Office Building
402 South Monroe Street
Tallahassee, FL 32399
P: (850) 717-5111
E: bryan.avila
@myfloridahouse.gov

**Baez, Daisy J. (D, 114)\***
1003 The Capitol
402 South Monroe Street
Tallahassee, FL 32399
P: (850) 717-5114
E: daisy.baez
@myfloridahouse.gov

**Berman, Lori (D, 90)**
212 The Capitol
402 South Monroe Street
Tallahassee, FL 32399
P: (850) 717-5090
E: lori.berman
@myfloridahouse.gov

**Beshears, Halsey (R, 7)**
303 House Office Building
402 South Monroe Street
Tallahassee, FL 32399
P: (850) 717-5007
E: halsey.beshears
@myfloridahouse.gov

**Bileca, Michael (R, 115)**
313 House Office Building
402 South Monroe Street
Tallahassee, FL 32399
P: (850) 717-5115
E: michael.bileca
@myfloridahouse.gov

**Boyd, Jim (R, 71)**
418 The Capitol
402 South Monroe Street
Tallahassee, FL 32399
P: (850) 717-5071
E: jim.boyd
@myfloridahouse.gov

**Brodeur, Jason T. (R, 28)**
418 The Capitol
402 South Monroe Street
Tallahassee, FL 32399
P: (850) 717-5028
E: jason.brodeur
@myfloridahouse.gov

**Brown, Kamia (D, 45)\***
1402 The Capitol
402 South Monroe Street
Tallahassee, FL 32399
P: (850) 717-5045
E: kamia.brown
@myfloridahouse.gov

**Burgess Jr., Daniel Wright (R, 38)**
303 House Office Building
402 South Monroe Street
Tallahassee, FL 32399
P: (850) 717-5038
E: danny.burgess
@myfloridahouse.gov

**Burton, Colleen (R, 40)**
222 The Capitol
402 South Monroe Street
Tallahassee, FL 32399
P: (850) 717-5040
E: colleen.burton
@myfloridahouse.gov

**Byrd, Cord (R, 11)\***
1101 The Capitol
402 South Monroe Street
Tallahassee, FL 32399
P: (850) 717-5011
E: cord.byrd
@myfloridahouse.gov

**Caldwell, Matthew H. (R, 79)**
209 House Office Building
402 South Monroe Street
Tallahassee, FL 32399
P: (850) 717-5079
E: matthew.caldwell
@myfloridahouse.gov

**Clemons Sr., Charles Wesley (R, 21)\***
1301 The Capitol
402 South Monroe Street
Tallahassee, FL 32399
P: (850) 717-5021
E: chuck.clemons
@myfloridahouse.gov

**Combee, Neil (R, 39)**
209 House Office Building
402 South Monroe Street
Tallahassee, FL 32399
P: (850) 717-5039
E: neil.combee
@myfloridahouse.gov

**Corcoran, Richard (R, 37)**
420 The Capitol
402 South Monroe Street
Tallahassee, FL 32399
P: (850) 717-5037
E: richard.corcoran
@myfloridahouse.gov

**Cortes, Bob (R, 30)**
319 South Monroe Street
Tallahassee, FL 32399
P: (850) 717-5030
E: bob.cortes
@myfloridahouse.gov

# Florida

**Cortes, John (D, 43)**
1003 The Capitol
402 South Monroe Street
Tallahassee, FL 32399
P: (850) 717-5043
E: john.cortes
    @myfloridahouse.gov

**Cruz, Janet (D, 62)**
316 The Capitol
402 South Monroe Street
Tallahassee, FL 32399
P: (850) 717-5062
E: janet.cruz
    @myfloridahouse.gov

**Cummings, W. Travis (R, 18)**
214 House Office Building
402 South Monroe Street
Tallahassee, FL 32399
P: (850) 717-5018
E: travis.cummings
    @myfloridahouse.gov

**Daniels, Kimberly (D, 14)***
1102 The Capitol
402 South Monroe Street
Tallahassee, FL 32399
P: (850) 717-5014
E: kimberly.daniels
    @myfloridahouse.gov

**Davis, Tracie (D, 13)***
1302 The Capitol
402 South Monroe Street
Tallahassee, FL 32399
P: (850) 717-5013
E: tracie.davis
    @myfloridahouse.gov

**Diamond, Ben (D, 68)***
1402 The Capitol
402 South Monroe Street
Tallahassee, FL 32399
P: (850) 717-5068
E: ben.diamond
    @myfloridahouse.gov

**Diaz, Jose Felix (R, 116)**
422 The Capitol
402 South Monroe Street
Tallahassee, FL 32399
P: (850) 717-5116
E: jose.diaz
    @myfloridahouse.gov

**Diaz Jr., Manny (R, 103)**
222 The Capitol
402 South Monroe Street
Tallahassee, FL 32399
P: (850) 717-5103
E: manny.diaz
    @myfloridahouse.gov

**Donalds, Byron (R, 80)***
1101 The Capitol
402 South Monroe Street
Tallahassee, FL 32399
P: (850) 717-5080
E: bryon.donalds
    @myfloridahouse.gov

**Drake, Brad (R, 5)**
209 House Office Building
402 South Monroe Street
Tallahassee, FL 32399
P: (850) 717-5005
E: brad.drake
    @myfloridahouse.gov

**DuBose, Bobby (D, 94)**
212 The Capitol
402 South Monroe Street
Tallahassee, FL 32399
P: (850) 717-5094
E: bobby.dubose
    @myfloridahouse.gov

**Duran, Nicholas X.**
    **(D, 112)***
1102 The Capitol
402 South Monroe Street
Tallahassee, FL 32399
P: (850) 717-5112
E: nicholas.duran
    @myfloridahouse.gov

**Eagle, Dane (R, 77)**
322 The Capitol
402 South Monroe Street
Tallahassee, FL 32399
P: (850) 717-5077
E: dane.eagle
    @myfloridahouse.gov

**Edwards, Katie A. (D, 98)**
300 House Office Building
402 South Monroe Street
Tallahassee, FL 32399
P: (850) 717-5098
E: katie.edwards
    @myfloridahouse.gov

**Eisnaugle, Eric (R, 44)**
317 The Capitol
402 South Monroe Street
Tallahassee, FL 32399
P: (850) 717-5044
E: eric.eisnaugle
    @myfloridahouse.gov

**Fant, Jay (R, 15)**
412 House Office Building
402 South Monroe Street
Tallahassee, FL 32399
P: (850) 717-5015
E: jay.fant
    @myfloridahouse.gov

**Fine, Randy (R, 53)***
1401 The Capitol
402 South Monroe Street
Tallahassee, FL 32399
P: (850) 717-5053
E: randy.fine
    @myfloridahouse.gov

**Fischer, Jason (R, 16)***
1401 The Capitol
402 South Monroe Street
Tallahassee, FL 32399
P: (850) 717-5016
E: jason.fischer
    @myfloridahouse.gov

**Fitzenhagen, Heather Dawes**
    **(R, 78)**
412 House Office Building
402 South Monroe Street
Tallahassee, FL 32399
P: (850) 717-5078
E: heather.fitzenhagen
    @myfloridahouse.gov

**Geller, Joseph S. (D, 100)**
1003 The Capitol
402 South Monroe Street
Tallahassee, FL 32399
P: (850) 717-5100
E: joseph.geller
    @myfloridahouse.gov

**Gonzalez, Julio (R, 74)**
412 House Office Building
402 South Monroe Street
Tallahassee, FL 32399
P: (850) 717-5074
E: julio.gonzalez
    @myfloridahouse.gov

**Goodson, Tom (R, 51)**
317 House Office Building
402 South Monroe Street
Tallahassee, FL 32399
P: (850) 717-5051
E: tom.goodson
    @myfloridahouse.gov

**Grall, Erin (R, 54)***
1101 The Capitol
402 South Monroe Street
Tallahassee, FL 32399
P: (850) 717-5054
E: erin.grall
    @myfloridahouse.gov

**Grant, James W. (R, 64)**
1301 The Capitol
402 South Monroe Street
Tallahassee, FL 32399
P: (850) 717-5064
E: james.grant
    @myfloridahouse.gov

**Grant, Michael J. (R, 75)**
1401 The Capitol
402 South Monroe Street
Tallahassee, FL 32399
P: (850) 717-5075
E: michael.grant
    @myfloridahouse.gov

**Gruters, Joe (R, 73)***
1101 The Capitol
402 South Monroe Street
Tallahassee, FL 32399
P: (850) 717-5073
E: joe.gruters
    @myfloridahouse.gov

**Hager, Bill (R, 89)**
222 The Capitol
402 South Monroe Street
Tallahassee, FL 32399
P: (850) 717-5089
E: bill.hager
    @myfloridahouse.gov

**Hahnfeldt, Don (R, 33)***
1301 The Capitol
402 South Monroe Street
Tallahassee, FL 32399
P: (850) 717-5033
E: don.hahnfeldt
    @myfloridahouse.gov

**Hardemon, Roy (D, 108)***
1302 The Capitol
402 South Monroe Street
Tallahassee, FL 32399
P: (850) 717-5108
E: roy.hardemon
    @myfloridahouse.gov

**Harrell, Gayle B. (R, 83)**
214 House Office Building
402 South Monroe Street
Tallahassee, FL 32399
P: (850) 717-5083
E: gayle.harrell
    @myfloridahouse.gov

**Harrison, Shawn (R, 63)**
406 House Office Building
402 South Monroe Street
Tallahassee, FL 32399
P: (850) 717-5063
E: shawn.harrison
    @myfloridahouse.gov

**Hawkins-Williams,**
    **Patricia (D, 92)***
1102 The Capitol
402 South Monroe Street
Tallahassee, FL 32399
P: (850) 717-5092

**Henry, Patrick (D, 26)***
1402 The Capitol
402 South Monroe Street
Tallahassee, FL 32399
P: (850) 717-5026
E: patrick.henry
   @myfloridahouse.gov

**Ingoglia, Blaise (R, 35)**
1101 The Capitol
402 South Monroe Street
Tallahassee, FL 32399
P: (850) 717-5035
E: blaise.ingoglia
   @myfloridahouse.gov

**Ingram, Clay (R, 1)**
222 The Capitol
402 South Monroe Street
Tallahassee, FL 32399
P: (850) 717-5001
E: clay.ingram
   @myfloridahouse.gov

**Jacobs, Kristin Diane (D, 96)**
200 House Office Building
402 South Monroe Street
Tallahassee, FL 32399
P: (850) 717-5096
E: kristin.jacobs
   @myfloridahouse.gov

**Jacquet, Al (D, 88)***
1302 The Capitol
402 South Monroe Street
Tallahassee, FL 32399
P: (850) 717-5088
E: al.jacquet
   @myfloridahouse.gov

**Jenne, Evan (D, 99)**
316 The Capitol
402 South Monroe Street
Tallahassee, FL 32399
P: (850) 717-5099
E: evan.jenne
   @myfloridahouse.gov

**Jones, Shevrin D. (D, 101)**
405 House Office Building
402 South Monroe Street
Tallahassee, FL 32399
P: (850) 717-5101
E: shevrin.jones
   @myfloridahouse.gov

**Killebrew, Sam (R, 41)***
1101 The Capitol
402 South Monroe Street
Tallahassee, FL 32399
P: (850) 717-5041
E: sam.killebrew
   @myfloridahouse.gov

**La Rosa, Mike (R, 42)**
317 House Office Building
402 South Monroe Street
Tallahassee, FL 32399
P: (850) 717-5042
E: mike.larosa
   @myfloridahouse.gov

**Latvala, Chris (R, 67)**
313 House Office Building
402 South Monroe Street
Tallahassee, FL 32399
P: (850) 717-5067
E: chris.latvala
   @myfloridahouse.gov

**Lee Jr., Larry (D, 84)**
1003 The Capitol
402 South Monroe Street
Tallahassee, FL 32399
P: (850) 717-5084
E: larry.lee
   @myfloridahouse.gov

**Leek, Thomas J. (R, 25)***
1301 The Capitol
402 South Monroe Street
Tallahassee, FL 32399
P: (850) 717-5025
E: tom.leek
   @myfloridahouse.gov

**Magar, MaryLynn (R, 82)**
214 House Office Building
402 South Monroe Street
Tallahassee, FL 32399
P: (850) 717-5082
E: marylynn.magar
   @myfloridahouse.gov

**Mariano, Amber (R, 36)***
1101 The Capitol
402 South Monroe Street
Tallahassee, FL 32399
P: (850) 717-5036
E: amber.mariano
   @myfloridahouse.gov

**Massullo Jr., Ralph (R, 34)***
1301 The Capitol
402 South Monroe Street
Tallahassee, FL 32399
P: (850) 717-5034
E: ralph.massullo
   @myfloridahouse.gov

**McClain, Stan (R, 23)***
1301 The Capitol
402 South Monroe Street
Tallahassee, FL 32399
P: (850) 717-5023
E: stan.mcclain
   @myfloridahouse.gov

**McGhee, Kionne L. (D, 117)**
405 House Office Building
402 South Monroe Street
Tallahassee, FL 32399
P: (850) 717-5117
E: kionne.mcghee
   @myfloridahouse.gov

**Mercado, Amy (D, 48)***
1302 The Capitol
402 South Monroe Street
Tallahassee, FL 32399
P: (850) 717-5048
E: amy.mercado
   @myfloridahouse.gov

**Metz, Larry (R, 32)**
402 House Office Building
402 South Monroe Street
Tallahassee, FL 32399
P: (850) 717-5032
E: larry.metz
   @myfloridahouse.gov

**Miller, Alexandra (R, 72)***
1401 The Capitol
402 South Monroe Street
Tallahassee, FL 32399
P: (850) 717-5072
E: alexandra.miller
   @myfloridahouse.gov

**Miller, Mike (R, 47)**
319 The Capitol
402 South Monroe Street
Tallahassee, FL 32399
P: (850) 717-5047
E: mike.miller
   @myfloridahouse.gov

**Moraitis Jr., George R. (R, 93)**
317 The Capitol
402 South Monroe Street
Tallahassee, FL 32399
P: (850) 717-5093
E: george.moraitis
   @myfloridahouse.gov

**Moskowitz, Jared Evan (D, 97)**
212 The Capitol
402 South Monroe Street
Tallahassee, FL 32399
P: (850) 717-5097
E: jared.moskowitz
   @myfloridahouse.gov

**Newton Sr., Wengay M. (D, 70)***
1302 The Capitol
402 South Monroe Street
Tallahassee, FL 32399
P: (850) 717-5070
E: wengay.newton
   @myfloridahouse.gov

**Nunez, Jeanette M. (R, 119)**
418 The Capitol
402 South Monroe Street
Tallahassee, FL 32399
P: (850) 717-5119
E: jeanette.nunez
   @myfloridahouse.gov

**Oliva, Jose R. (R, 110)**
422 The Capitol
402 South Monroe Street
Tallahassee, FL 32399
P: (850) 717-5110
E: jose.oliva
   @myfloridahouse.gov

**Payne, Bobby (R, 19)***
1301 The Capitol
402 South Monroe Street
Tallahassee, FL 32399
P: (850) 717-5019
E: bobby.payne
   @myfloridahouse.gov

**Peters, Kathleen M. (R, 69)**
303 House Office Building
402 South Monroe Street
Tallahassee, FL 32399
P: (850) 717-5069
E: kathleen.peters
   @myfloridahouse.gov

**Pigman, Cary (R, 55)**
214 House Office Building
402 South Monroe Street
Tallahassee, FL 32399
P: (850) 717-5055
E: cary.pigman
   @myfloridahouse.gov

**Plakon, Scott (R, 29)**
209 House Office Building
402 South Monroe Street
Tallahassee, FL 32399
P: (850) 717-5029
E: scott.plakon
   @myfloridahouse.gov

**Plasencia, Rene (R, 50)**
406 House Office Building
402 South Monroe Street
Tallahassee, FL 32399
P: (850) 717-5050
E: rene.plasencia
   @myfloridahouse.gov

**Ponder, Mel (R, 4)***
1301 The Capitol
402 South Monroe Street
Tallahassee, FL 32399
P: (850) 717-5004
E: mel.ponder
   @myfloridahouse.gov

# Florida

**Porter, Elizabeth W. (R, 10)**
313 House Office Building
402 South Monroe Street
Tallahassee, FL 32399
P: (850) 717-5010
E: elizabeth.porter
@myfloridahouse.gov

**Pritchett, Sharon (D, 102)**
1003 The Capitol
402 South Monroe Street
Tallahassee, FL 32399
P: (850) 717-5102
E: sharon.pritchett
@myfloridahouse.gov

**Raburn, Jake (R, 57)**
313 House Office Building
402 South Monroe Street
Tallahassee, FL 32399
P: (850) 717-5057
E: jake.raburn
@myfloridahouse.gov

**Raschein, Holly Merrill (R, 120)**
209 House Office Building
402 South Monroe Street
Tallahassee, FL 32399
P: (850) 717-5120
E: holly.raschein
@myfloridahouse.gov

**Raulerson, Daniel D. (R, 58)**
209 House Office Building
402 South Monroe Street
Tallahassee, FL 32399
P: (850) 717-5058
E: daniel.raulerson
@myfloridahouse.gov

**Renner, Paul (R, 24)**
1101 The Capitol
402 South Monroe Street
Tallahassee, FL 32399
P: (850) 717-5024
E: paul.renner
@myfloridahouse.gov

**Richardson, David (D, 113)**
200 House Office Building
402 South Monroe Street
Tallahassee, FL 32399
P: (850) 717-5113
E: david.richardson
@myfloridahouse.gov

**Rodrigues, Ray Wesley (R, 76)**
322 The Capitol
402 South Monroe Street
Tallahassee, FL 32399
P: (850) 717-5076
E: ray.rodrigues
@myfloridahouse.gov

**Rommel, Bob (R, 106)***
1401 The Capitol
402 South Monroe Street
Tallahassee, FL 32399
P: (850) 717-5106
E: bob.rommel
@myfloridahouse.gov

**Roth, Rick (R, 85)***
1301 The Capitol
402 South Monroe Street
Tallahassee, FL 32399
P: (850) 717-5085
E: rick.roth
@myfloridahouse.gov

**Russell, Barrington Anthony (D, 95)***
1402 The Capitol
402 South Monroe Street
Tallahassee, FL 32399
P: (850) 717-5095
E: barrington.russell
@myfloridahouse.gov

**Santiago, David (R, 27)**
406 House Office Building
402 South Monroe Street
Tallahassee, FL 32399
P: (850) 717-5027
E: david.santiago
@myfloridahouse.gov

**Shaw, Sean (D, 61)***
1102 The Capitol
402 South Monroe Street
Tallahassee, FL 32399
P: (850) 717-5061
E: sean.shaw
@myfloridahouse.gov

**Silvers, David (D, 87)***
1302 The Capitol
402 South Monroe Street
Tallahassee, FL 32399
P: (850) 717-5087
E: david.silvers
@myfloridahouse.gov

**Slosberg, Emily (D, 91)***
1003 The Capitol
402 South Monroe Street
Tallahassee, FL 32399
P: (850) 717-5091
E: emily.slosberg
@myfloridahouse.gov

**Smith, Carlos Guillermo (D, 49)***
1402 The Capitol
402 South Monroe Street
Tallahassee, FL 32399
P: (850) 717-5049
E: carlos.smith
@myfloridahouse.gov

**Spano, Ross (R, 59)**
412 House Office Building
402 South Monroe Street
Tallahassee, FL 32399
P: (850) 717-5059
E: ross.spano
@myfloridahouse.gov

**Sprowls, Chris (R, 65)**
412 House Office Building
402 South Monroe Street
Tallahassee, FL 32399
P: (850) 717-5065
E: chris.sprowls
@myfloridahouse.gov

**Stafford, Cynthia A. (D, 109)**
316 The Capitol
402 South Monroe Street
Tallahassee, FL 32399
P: (850) 717-5109
E: cynthia.stafford
@myfloridahouse.gov

**Stark, Richard (D, 104)**
405 House Office Building
402 South Monroe Street
Tallahassee, FL 32399
P: (850) 717-5104
E: richard.stark
@myfloridahouse.gov

**Stevenson, Cyndi (R, 17)**
1101 The Capitol
402 South Monroe Street
Tallahassee, FL 32399
P: (850) 717-5017
E: cyndi.stevenson
@myfloridahouse.gov

**Stone, Charlie (R, 22)**
209 House Office Building
402 South Monroe Street
Tallahassee, FL 32399
P: (850) 717-5022
E: charlie.stone
@myfloridahouse.gov

**Sullivan, Jennifer (R, 31)**
402 House Office Building
402 South Monroe Street
Tallahassee, FL 32399
P: (850) 717-5031
E: jennifer.sullivan
@myfloridahouse.gov

**Toledo, Jackie (R, 60)***
1401 The Capitol
402 South Monroe Street
Tallahassee, FL 32399
P: (850) 717-5060
E: jackie.toledo
@myfloridahouse.gov

**Trujillo, Carlos (R, 105)**
418 The Capitol
402 South Monroe Street
Tallahassee, FL 32399
P: (850) 717-5105
E: carlos.trujillo
@myfloridahouse.gov

**Trumbull, Jay (R, 6)**
317 House Office Building
402 South Monroe Street
Tallahassee, FL 32399
P: (850) 717-5006
E: jay.trumbull
@myfloridahouse.gov

**Watson, Barbara (D, 107)**
1003 The Capitol
402 South Monroe Street
Tallahassee, FL 32399
P: (850) 717-5107
E: barbara.watson
@myfloridahouse.gov

**Watson Jr., Clovis (D, 20)**
200 House Office Building
402 South Monroe Street
Tallahassee, FL 32399
P: (850) 717-5020
E: clovis.watson
@myfloridahouse.gov

**White, Frank (R, 2)***
1401 The Capitol
402 South Monroe Street
Tallahassee, FL 32399
P: (850) 717-5002
E: frank.white
@myfloridahouse.gov

**Willhite, Matt (D, 86)***
1102 The Capitol
402 South Monroe Street
Tallahassee, FL 32399
P: (850) 717-5086
E: matt.willhite
@myfloridahouse.gov

**Williamson, Jayer (R, 3)***
1401 The Capitol
402 South Monroe Street
Tallahassee, FL 32399
P: (850) 717-5003
E: jayer.williamson
@myfloridahouse.gov

**Yarborough, Clay (R, 12)***
1401 The Capitol
402 South Monroe Street
Tallahassee, FL 32399
P: (850) 717-5012
E: clay.yarborough
@myfloridahouse.gov

# Georgia

## Executive

### Governor

The Honorable Nathan
    Deal (R)
Governor
203 State Capitol
Atlanta, GA 30334
P: (404) 656-1776
F: (404) 657-7332

### Lieutenant Governor

The Honorable Casey
    Cagle (R)
Lieutenant Governor
240 State Capitol
Atlanta, GA 30334
P: (404) 656-5030
F: (404) 656-6739

### Commissioner of Agriculture

Mr. Gary Black (R)
Commissioner
19 Martin Luther King Jr. Drive,
SW
204 Agricultural Building
Atlanta, GA 30334
P: (404) 656-3600
F: (404) 651-8206

### Attorney General

The Honorable Chris
    Carr (R)
Attorney General
40 Capitol Square, Southwest
Atlanta, GA 30334
P: (404) 656-3300
F: (404) 657-8733

### Auditor

Mr. Greg S. Griffin
    (appointed by the Legislature)
State Auditor
270 Washington Street,
Southwest
Suite 4-113
Atlanta, GA 30334
P: (404) 656-2174
F: (404) 651-9448
E: griffin@audits.ga.gov

## Commissioner of Insurance

The Honorable Ralph T.
    Hudgens (R)
Commissioner
2 Martin Luther King Jr. Drive
West Tower, Suite 704
Atlanta, GA 30334
P: (404) 656-2070
F: (404) 657-8542

## Commissioner of Labor

The Honorable Mark
    Butler (R)
Commissioner
148 International Boulevard
Northeast
Atlanta, GA 30303
P: (404) 232-7300
F: (404) 656-2683
E: commissioner@gdol.ga.gov

## Secretary of State

The Honorable Brian
    Kemp (R)
Secretary of State
214 State Capitol
Atlanta, GA 30334
P: (404) 656-2881
F: (404) 656-0513
E: soscontact@sos.ga.gov

## Superintendent of Schools

The Honorable Richard L.
    Woods (R)
State School Superintendent
2066 Twin Towers East
Atlanta, GA 30334
P: (404) 657-1175
F: (404) 651-8737
E: state.superintendent
    @doe.k12.ga.us

## Treasurer

The Honorable Steve McCoy
    (appointed)
Treasurer & Director
200 Piedmont Avenue
Suite 1204, West Tower
Atlanta, GA 30334
P: (404) 656-2168
F: (404) 656-9048
E: OSTWeb@treasury.ga.gov

## Judiciary

### Supreme Court (NE)

Ms. Therese S. Barnes
Clerk
244 Washington Street
Room 572, State Office Annex
Building
Atlanta, GA 30334
P: (404) 656-3470
F: (404) 656-2253

The Honorable P. Harris
    Hines
Chief Justice
The Honorable Robert Benham
The Honorable Keith R.
    Blackwell
The Honorable Michael P.
    Boggs (D)
The Honorable Britt Grant
The Honorable Carol W.
    Hunstein
The Honorable Harold D.
    Melton
The Honorable David E.
    Nahmias
The Honorable Nels Peterson

## Legislative

## Senate

### Senate President

The Honorable Casey
    Cagle (R)
Lieutenant Governor
240 State Capitol
Atlanta, GA 30334
P: (404) 656-5030
F: (404) 656-6739

### President Pro Tempore of the Senate

Senator David J. Shafer (R)
Senate President Pro Tempore
321 State Capitol
Atlanta, GA 30334
P: (404) 656-0048
F: (404) 463-5220
E: david.shafer
    @senate.ga.gov

## Senate Majority Leader

Senator Bill Cowsert (R)
Senate Majority Leader
236 State Capitol
Atlanta, GA 30334
P: (404) 463-1366
F: (404) 657-9887
E: bill.cowsert
    @senate.ga.gov

## Senate Minority Leader

Senator Steve Henson (D)
Senate Democratic Leader
121-B State Capitol
Atlanta, GA 30334
P: (404) 656-0085
F: (404) 463-2071
E: stevehenson
    @mindspring.com

## Secretary of the Senate

Mr. David A. Cook
Secretary of the Senate
353 State Capitol
Atlanta, GA 30334
P: (404) 656-5040
F: (404) 656-5043
E: David.Cook@senate.ga.gov

## Members of the Senate

Albers, John (R, 56)
110-D State Capitol
Atlanta, GA 30334
P: (404) 463-8055
F: (404) 463-4161
E: info@senatoralbers.com

Anderson, Lee (R, 24)
325-B Legislative Office
Building
Atlanta, GA 30334
P: (404) 656-5114
E: lee.anderson
    @house.ga.gov

Anderson, Tonya (D, 43)
323-B Legislative Office
Building
Atlanta, GA 30334
P: (404) 463-2598
E: tonya.anderson
    @senate.ga.gov

Beach, Brandon (R, 21)
303-B Legislative Office
Building
Atlanta, GA 30334
P: (404) 463-1378
F: (404) 463-1386
E: brandon.beach
    @senate.ga.gov

# Georgia

**Black, C. Ellis (R, 8)**
304-A Legislative Office
Building
Atlanta, GA 30334
P: (404) 656-3932
E: ellis.black
@senate.ga.gov

**Brass, Matt (R, 28)\***
304-B Legislative Office
Building
Atlanta, GA 30334
P: (404) 656-6446
E: matt.brass@senate.ga.gov

**Burke, Dean (R, 11)**
301-A Legislative Office
Building
Atlanta, GA 30334
P: (404) 656-0040
F: (404) 657-7266
E: dean.burke@senate.ga.gov

**Butler, Gloria (D, 55)**
420-C State Capitol
Atlanta, GA 30334
P: (404) 656-0075
F: (404) 657-9728
E: gloria.butler
@senate.ga.gov

**Cowsert, Bill (R, 46)**
236 State Capitol
Atlanta, GA 30334
P: (404) 463-1366
F: (404) 657-9887
E: bill.cowsert
@senate.ga.gov

**Davenport, Gail (D, 44)**
432 State Capitol
Atlanta, GA 30334
P: (404) 463-5260
F: (404) 656-6579
E: gail.davenport
@senate.ga.gov

**Dugan, Mike (R, 30)**
121-J State Capitol
Atlanta, GA 30334
P: (404) 656-2478
F: (404) 651-5795
E: mike.dugan@senate.ga.gov

**Fort, Vincent D. (D, 39)**
121-G State Capitol
Atlanta, GA 30334
P: (404) 656-5091
F: (404) 651-7078
E: vincent.fort
@senate.ga.gov

**Ginn, Frank (R, 47)**
121-I State Capitol
Atlanta, GA 30334
P: (404) 656-4700
F: (404) 657-3248
E: frank.ginn@senate.ga.gov

**Gooch, Steve (R, 51)**
421-F State Capitol
Atlanta, GA 30334
P: (404) 656-9221
F: (404) 651-6768
E: steve.gooch
@senate.ga.gov

**Harbin, M.H. (R, 16)**
302-A Legislative Office
Building
Atlanta, GA 30334
P: (404) 656-0078
F: (404) 656-6484
E: marty.harbin
@senate.ga.gov

**Harbison, Ed (D, 15)**
431 State Capitol
Atlanta, GA 30334
P: (404) 656-0074
F: (404) 463-5547
E: ed.harbison
@senate.ga.gov

**Harper, Tyler (R, 7)**
301-B Legislative Office
Building
Atlanta, GA 30334
P: (404) 463-5263
F: (404) 463-4161
E: tyler.harper
@senate.ga.gov

**Heath, Bill (R, 31)**
110-C State Capitol
Atlanta, GA 30334
P: (404) 656-3943
F: (404) 463-2279
E: billheath@billheath.net

**Henson, Steve (D, 41)**
121-B State Capitol
Atlanta, GA 30334
P: (404) 656-0085
F: (404) 463-2071
E: stevehenson
@mindspring.com

**Hill, Hunter (R, 6)**
421-B State Capitol
Atlanta, GA 30334
P: (404) 463-2518
F: (404) 651-6768
E: hunter.hill
@senate.ga.gov

**Hill, Jack (R, 4)**
234 State Capitol
Atlanta, GA 30334
P: (404) 656-5038
F: (404) 657-7094
E: jack.hill@senate.ga.gov

**Hill, Judson H. (R, 32)**
421-D State Capitol
Atlanta, GA 30334
P: (404) 656-0150
F: (404) 651-6768
E: judson@judsonhill.com

**Hufstetler, Chuck (R, 52)**
121-C State Capitol
Atlanta, GA 30334
P: (404) 656-0034
F: (404) 656-0459
E: chuck.hufstetler
@senate.ga.gov

**Jackson, Lester G. (D, 2)**
110-B State Capitol
Atlanta, GA 30334
P: (404) 463-5261
F: (404) 463-5547
E: lester.jackson
@senate.ga.gov

**James, Donzella J. (D, 35)**
121-D State Capitol
Atlanta, GA 30334
P: (404) 463-1379
F: (404) 656-6579
E: Donzella.James
@senate.ga.gov

**Jeffares, Rick (R, 17)**
327-B Legislative Office
Building
Atlanta, GA 30334
P: (404) 463-1376
F: (404) 651-5795
E: rick.jeffares
@senate.ga.gov

**Jones, Burt (R, 25)**
327-A Legislative Office
Building
Atlanta, GA 30334
P: (404) 656-0082
E: burt.jones@senate.ga.gov

**Jones, Emanuel D. (D, 10)**
420-D State Capitol
Atlanta, GA 30334
P: (404) 656-0502
F: (404) 657-9728
E: emanj@mindspring.com

**Jones II, Harold V. (D, 22)**
323-B Legislative Office
Building
Atlanta, GA 30334
P: (404) 463-3942
E: harold.jones
@senate.ga.gov

**Kennedy, John Flanders
    (R, 18)**
421-C State Capitol
Atlanta, GA 30334
P: (404) 656-7454
F: (404) 651-5795
E: john.kennedy
@senate.ga.gov

**Kirk, Gregory Mark (R, 13)**
320-A Legislative Office
Building
Atlanta, GA 30334
P: (404) 463-5258
E: greg.kirk@senate.ga.gov

**Ligon Jr., William T.
    (R, 3)**
121-E State Capitol
Atlanta, GA 30334
P: (404) 656-0045
F: (404) 651-6768
E: william.ligon
@senate.ga.gov

**Lucas Sr., David E. (D, 26)**
305-B Legislative Office
Building
Atlanta, GA 30334
P: (404) 656-5035
F: (404) 657-7266
E: david.lucas
@senate.ga.gov

**Martin, P. K. (R, 9)**
113 State Capitol
Atlanta, GA 30334
P: (404) 656-7454
F: (404) 656-5795
E: p.k.martin@senate.ga.gov

**McKoon, Joshua (R, 29)**
319-A Legislative Office
Building
Atlanta, GA 30334
P: (404) 463-3931
F: (404) 657-3217
E: jrm2016@yahoo.com

**Millar, Fran (R, 40)**
319-B Legislative Office
Building
Atlanta, GA 30334
P: (404) 463-2260
F: (404) 657-3217
E: fran.millar
@senate.ga.gov

**Miller, Butch (R, 49)**
113 State Capitol
Atlanta, GA 30334
P: (404) 656-7454
F: (404) 651-5795
E: butch.miller
@senate.ga.gov

**Mullis, Jeff E. (R, 53)**
453 State Capitol
Atlanta, GA 30334
P: (404) 656-0057
F: (404) 651-6768
E: jeff.mullis
　@senate.ga.gov

**Orrock, Nan (D, 36)**
420-B State Capitol
Atlanta, GA 30334
P: (404) 463-8054
F: (404) 657-9728
E: nan.orrock@senate.ga.gov

**Parent, Elena C. (D, 42)**
321-B Legislative Office
Building
Atlanta, GA 30334
P: (404) 656-5109
E: elena.parent
　@senate.ga.gov

**Payne, Chuck (R, 54)\***
305-A Legislative Office
Building
Atlanta, GA 30334
P: (404) 463-5402
F: (404) 657-7266
E: chuck.payne
　@senate.ga.gov

**Rhett, Michael A. (D, 33)**
321-A Legislative Office
Building
Atlanta, GA 30334
P: (404) 656-0054
E: michael.rhett
　@senate.ga.gov

**Seay, Valencia (D, 34)**
420-A State Capitol
Atlanta, GA 30334
P: (404) 656-5095
F: (404) 657-9728
E: valencia.seay
　@senate.ga.gov

**Shafer, David J. (R, 48)**
321 State Capitol
Atlanta, GA 30334
P: (404) 656-0048
F: (404) 463-5220
E: david.shafer
　@senate.ga.gov

**Sims, Freddie Powell
　(D, 12)**
110-A State Capitol
Atlanta, GA 30334
P: (404) 463-5259
F: (404) 463-2279
E: freddie.sims
　@senate.ga.gov

**Stone, Jesse (R, 23)**
325-A Legislative Office
Building
Atlanta, GA 30334
P: (404) 463-1314
F: (404) 463-1381
E: jesse.stone
　@senate.ga.gov

**Tate, Horacena (D, 38)**
121-A State Capitol
Atlanta, GA 30334
P: (404) 463-8053
F: (404) 463-7783
E: horacena.tate
　@senate.ga.gov

**Thompson, Bruce (R, 14)**
302-B Legislative Office
Building
Atlanta, GA 30334
P: (404) 656-0065
F: (404) 656-6484
E: Bruce.Thompson
　@senate.ga.gov

**Thompson, Curt (D, 5)**
121-H State Capitol
Atlanta, GA 30334
P: (404) 463-1318
F: (404) 651-7078
E: curt@curtthompson.com

**Tillery, Blake (R, 19)\***
324-B Legislative Office
Building
Altanta, GA 30334
P: (404) 656-0089
E: blake.tillery
　@senate.ga.gov

**Tippins, Lindsey (R, 37)**
303-A Legislative Office
Building
Atlanta, GA 30334
P: (404) 657-0406
F: (404) 657-0459
E: lindsey.tippins
　@senate.ga.gov

**Unterman, Renee S. (R, 45)**
121-F State Capitol
Atlanta, GA 30334
P: (404) 463-1368
F: (404) 651-6767
E: renee.unterman
　@senate.ga.gov

**Walker III, Larry (R, 20)**
113 State Capitol
Atlanta, GA 30334
P: (404) 656-7454
F: (404) 651-5795
E: larry.walker
　@senate.ga.gov

**Watson, Ben (R, 1)**
320-B Legislative Office
Building
Atlanta, GA 30334
P: (404) 656-7880
E: ben.watson@senate.ga.gov

**Wilkinson, John (R, 50)**
421-A State Capitol
Atlanta, GA 30334
P: (404) 463-5257
F: (404) 651-6768
E: john.wilkinson
　@senate.ga.gov

**Williams, Michael E.
　(R, 27)**
324 Legislative Office Building
Atlanta, GA 30334
P: (404) 656-7127
E: michael.williams
　@senate.ga.gov

# House
## Speaker of the House
**Representative David
　Ralston (R)**
House Speaker
332 State Capitol
Atlanta, GA 30334
P: (404) 656-5020
F: (404) 656-5644
E: david.ralston
　@house.ga.gov

## Speaker Pro Tempore of the House
**Representative Jan
　Jones (R)**
House Speaker Pro Tempore
340 State Capitol
Atlanta, GA 30334
P: (404) 656-5072
F: (404) 657-0498
E: jan.jones@house.ga.gov

## House Majority Leader
**Representative Jon G.
　Burns (R)**
House Majority Leader
338 State Capitol
Atlanta, GA 30334
P: (404) 656-5052
F: (404) 656-6897
E: jon.burns@house.ga.gov

## House Minority Leader
**Representative Stacey
　Abrams (D)**
House Minority Leader
609-F Legislative Office
Building
Atlanta, GA 30334
P: (404) 656-5058
E: staceyabrams@gmail.com

## Clerk of the House
**Mr. William L. Reilly**
Clerk of the House
309 State Capitol
Atlanta, GA 30334
P: (404) 656-5015
E: bill.reilly@house.ga.gov

## Members of the House
**Abrams, Stacey (D, 89)**
609-F Legislative Office
Building
Atlanta, GA 30334
P: (404) 656-5058
E: staceyabrams@gmail.com

**Alexander, Kimberly (D, 66)**
512-D Legislative Office
Building
Atlanta, GA 30334
P: (404) 656-7859
E: kimberly.alexander
　@house.ga.gov

**Ballinger, Mandi (R, 23)**
131-B State Capitol
Atlanta, GA 30334
P: (404) 656-5105
E: mandi.ballinger
　@house.ga.gov

**Barr, Timothy (R, 103)**
612-E Legislative Office
Building
Atlanta, GA 30334
P: (404) 656-0325
E: timothy.barr
　@house.ga.gov

**Battles, Paul R. (R, 15)**
401-K State Capitol
Atlanta, GA 30334
P: (404) 657-8441
E: paul.battles
　@house.ga.gov

# Georgia

**Bazemore, Debra (D, 63)***
411-E Legislative Office
Building
Atlanta, GA 30334
P: (404) 656-0126
E: debra.bazemore
   @house.ga.gov

**Beasley-Teague, Sharon
   (D, 65)**
509-A Legislative Office
Building
Atlanta, GA 30334
P: (404) 656-0221
F: (404) 656-7789
E: sharon.beasley-teague
   @house.ga.gov

**Belton, Dave (R, 112)**
401-B Legislative Office
Building
Atlanta, GA 30334
P: (404) 656-0152
E: dave.belton@house.ga.gov

**Bennett, Karen (D, 94)**
507-A Legislative Office
Building
Atlanta, GA 30334
P: (404) 656-0202
E: karen.bennett
   @house.ga.gov

**Bentley, Patty (D, 139)**
607-C Legislative Office
Building
Atlanta, GA 30334
P: (404) 656-0287
E: patty.bentley
   @house.ga.gov

**Benton, Tommy (R, 31)**
217 State Capitol
Atlanta, GA 30334
P: (404) 656-5126
F: (404) 463-2976
E: tommy.benton
   @house.ga.gov

**Beskin, Beth (R, 54)**
601-F Legislative Office
Building
Atlanta, GA 30334
P: (404) 656-0254
E: beth.beskin@house.ga.gov

**Beverly, James (D, 143)**
509-G Legislative Office
Building
Atlanta, GA 30334
P: (404) 656-0220
E: james.beverly
   @house.ga.gov

**Blackmon, Shaw (R, 146)**
501-E Legislative Office
Building
Atlanta, GA 30334
P: (404) 656-0177
E: shaw.blackmon
   @house.ga.gov

**Boddie, William (D, 62)***
404-C Legislative Office
Building
Atlanta, GA 30334
P: (404) 656-0109
E: william.boddie
   @house.ga.gov

**Bonner, Josh (R, 72)***
507-G Legislative Office
Building
Atlanta, GA 30334
P: (404) 656-0202
E: josh.bonner@house.ga.gov

**Broadrick, Bruce (R, 4)**
608-D Legislative Office
Building
Atlanta, GA 30334
P: (404) 656-0298
E: bruce.broadrick
   @house.ga.gov

**Brockway, Buzz (R, 102)**
504-A Legislative Office
Building
Atlanta, GA 30334
P: (404) 656-0188
E: buzz.brockway
   @house.ga.gov

**Bruce, Roger B. (D, 61)**
512-A Legislative Office
Building
Atlanta, GA 30334
P: (404) 656-7859
E: rbruce5347@aol.com

**Buckner, Debbie (D, 137)**
409-A Legislative Office
Building
Atlanta, GA 30334
P: (404) 656-0116
F: (404) 651-8086
E: debbie.buckner
   @house.ga.gov

**Burnough, Rhonda (D, 77)***
409-C Legislative Office
Building
Atlanta, GA 30334
P: (404) 656-0116
E: rhonda.burnough
   @house.ga.gov

**Burns, Jon G. (R, 159)**
338 State Capitol
Atlanta, GA 30334
P: (404) 656-5052
F: (404) 656-6897
E: jon.burns@house.ga.gov

**Caldwell Jr., Johnnie
   (R, 131)**
402 Legislative Office Building
Atlanta, GA 30334
P: (404) 656-5087
E: johnnie.caldwell
   @house.ga.gov

**Caldwell, Michael (R, 20)**
401-F Legislative Office
Building
Atlanta, GA 30334
P: (404) 656-0152
E: michael.caldwell
   @house.ga.gov

**Cannon, Park (D, 58)***
512-F Legislative Office
Building
Atlanta, GA 30334
P: (404) 656-7859
E: park.cannon@house.ga.gov

**Cantrell, Wesley E. (R, 22)**
401 Legislative Office Building
Atlanta, GA 30334
P: (404) 656-0152
E: wesley.cantrell
   @house.ga.gov

**Carson, John (R, 46)**
607-A Legislative Office
Building
Atlanta, GA 30334
P: (404) 656-0287
E: john.carson@house.ga.gov

**Carter, Amy (D, 175)**
245 State Capitol
Atlanta, GA 30334
P: (404) 463-2248
E: amy.carter@house.ga.gov

**Carter, Doreen (D, 92)**
509-D Legislative Office
Building
Atlanta, GA 30334
P: (404) 656-0220
E: doreen.carter
   @house.ga.gov

**Casas, David S. (R, 107)**
601-H Legislative Office
Building
Atlanta, GA 30334
P: (404) 656-0254
E: david.casas@house.ga.gov

**Chandler, Joyce (R, 105)**
601-G Legislative Office
Building
Atlanta, GA 30334
P: (404) 656-0254
E: joyce.chandler
   @house.ga.gov

**Clark, David (R, 98)**
608-C Legislative Office
Building
Atlanta, GA 30334
P: (404) 656-0298
E: david.clark@house.ga.gov

**Clark, Heath Nicholas
   (R, 147)**
408-C Legislative Office
Building
Atlanta, GA 30334
P: (404) 656-1803
E: heath.clark@house.ga.gov

**Coleman, Brooks P. (R, 97)**
416 State Capitol
Atlanta, GA 30334
P: (404) 656-9210
F: (404) 656-5070
E: brooks.coleman
   @house.ga.gov

**Collins, J. (R, 68)***
404-E Legislative Office
Building
Atlanta, GA 30334
P: (404) 656-0109
E: j.collins@house.ga.gov

**Cooke, Kevin (R, 18)**
504-B Legislative Office
Building
Atlanta, GA 30334
P: (404) 656-0188
E: kevin.cooke@house.ga.gov

**Coomer, Christian (R, 14)**
415 State Capitol
Atlanta, GA 30334
P: (404) 656-5024
F: (404) 651-5795
E: christian.coomer
   @house.ga.gov

**Cooper, Sharon (R, 43)**
436 State Capitol
Atlanta, GA 30334
P: (404) 656-5069
E: sharon.cooper
   @house.ga.gov

**Corbett, John I. (R, 174)**
508-C Legislative Office
Building
Atlanta, GA 30334
P: (404) 656-0213
E: john.corbett
   @house.ga.gov

# Georgia

**Cox, Clay (R, 102)**
507-C Legislative Office
Building
Atlanta, GA 30334
P: (404) 656-0202
E: clay.cox@house.ga.gov

**Deffenbaugh, John (R, 1)**
507-D Legislative Office
Building
Atlanta, GA 30334
P: (404) 656-0202
E: john.deffenbaugh
@house.ga.gov

**Dempsey, Katie (R, 13)**
245 State Capitol
Atlanta, GA 30334
P: (404) 463-2247
E: katie.dempsey
@house.ga.gov

**Dickerson, Pamela A. (D, 113)**
611-E Legislative Office
Building
Atlanta, GA 30334
P: (404) 656-0314
E: pam.dickerson
@house.ga.gov

**Dickey, Robert (R, 140)**
245 State Capitol
Atlanta, GA 30334
P: (404) 463-2246
F: (404) 656-0250
E: robert.dickey
@house.ga.gov

**Dollar, Matt (R, 45)**
401-K State Capitol
Atlanta, GA 30334
P: (404) 656-5138
F: (404) 651-8086
E: matt.dollar@house.ga.gov

**Douglas, Demetrius (D, 78)**
512-E Legislative Office
Building
Atlanta, GA 30334
P: (404) 656-7859
E: demetrius.douglas
@house.ga.gov

**Drenner, Karla (D, 85)**
507-H Legislative Office
Building
Atlanta, GA 30334
P: (404) 656-0202
F: (404) 651-8086
E: dren16999@aol.com

**Dreyer, David (D, 59)***
604-D Legislative Office
Building
Atlanta, GA 30334
P: (404) 656-0265
E: david.dreyer
@house.ga.gov

**Dubnik, Matt (R, 29)***
504-F Legislative Office
Building
Atlanta, GA 30334
P: (404) 656-0188
E: matt.dubnik@house.ga.gov

**Dukes, Winfred J. (D, 154)**
411-H Legislative Office
Building
Atlanta, GA 30334
P: (404) 656-0126
E: wdukes_2000@yahoo.com

**Dunahoo, Emory (R, 30)**
401-D Legislative Office
Building
Atlanta, GA 30334
P: (404) 656-0152
E: emory.dunahoo
@house.ga.gov

**Duncan, Geoff (R, 26)**
504-C Legislative Office
Building
Atlanta, GA 30334
P: (404) 656-0188
E: geoff.duncan
@house.ga.gov

**Ealum, Darrel B. (D, 153)**
409-B Legislative Office
Building
Atlanta, GA 30334
P: (404) 656-0116
E: darrel.ealum
@house.ga.gov

**Efstration, Chuck (R, 104)**
113 State Capitol
Atlanta, GA 30334
P: (404) 651-7737
E: chuck.efstration
@house.ga.gov

**Ehrhart, Earl (R, 36)**
245 State Capitol
Atlanta, GA 30334
P: (404) 463-2247
F: (404) 437-2601
E: earl.ehrhart
@house.ga.gov

**England, Terry Lamar (R, 116)**
245 State Capitol
Atlanta, GA 30334
P: (404) 463-2247
E: englandhomeport2
@windstream.net

**Epps, Bubber (R, 144)**
401-E State Capitol
Atlanta, GA 30334
P: (404) 656-7855
E: bubber.epps@house.ga.gov

**Evans, Stacey (D, 42)**
409-G Legislative Office
Building
Atlanta, GA 30334
P: (404) 656-0116
E: stacey@staceyevans.org

**Fleming, Barry A. (R, 121)**
401-H Legislative Office
Building
Atlanta, GA 30334
P: (404) 656-0152
E: barry.fleming
@house.ga.gov

**Frazier, Gloria (D, 126)**
604-C Legislative Office
Building
Atlanta, GA 30334
P: (404) 656-0265
E: frazier26@comcast.net

**Frye, Spencer (D, 118)**
604-B Legislative Office
Building
Atlanta, GA 30334
P: (404) 656-0265
E: spencer.frye
@house.ga.gov

**Gardner, Pat (D, 57)**
604-G Legislative Office
Building
Atlanta, GA 30334
P: (404) 656-0265
F: (404) 463-2634
E: pat@patgardner.org

**Gasaway, Dan (R, 28)**
612-E Legislative Office
Building
Atlanta, GA 30334
P: (404) 656-0325
E: dan.gasaway@house.ga.gov

**Gilliard, Carl (D, 162)***
512-G Legislative Office
Building
Atlanta, GA 30334
P: (404) 656-7859
E: carl.gilliard
@house.ga.gov

**Gilligan, Sheri (R, 24)**
612-F Legislative Office
Building
Atlanta, GA 30334
P: (404) 656-0325
E: sheri.gilligan
@house.ga.gov

**Glanton, Mike (D, 75)**
408-D Legislative Office
Building
Atlanta, GA 30334
P: (404) 657-1803
E: mike.glanton
@house.ga.gov

**Golick, Rich (R, 40)**
218 State Capitol
Atlanta, GA 30334
P: (404) 656-5943
E: rich.golick@house.ga.gov

**Gordon, J. Craig (D, 163)**
607-H Legislative Office
Building
Atlanta, GA 30334
P: (404) 656-0287
E: jcraig.gordon
@house.ga.gov

**Gravley, Micah (R, 67)**
401-C Legislative Office
Building
Atlanta, GA 30334
P: (404) 656-0152
E: micah.gravley
@house.ga.gov

**Greene, Gerald E. (R, 151)**
131-A State Capitol
Atlanta, GA 30334
P: (404) 656-5105
F: (229) 732-2973
E: gerald.greene
@house.ga.gov

**Gurtler, Matt (R, 8)***
504-D Legislative Office
Building
Atlanta, GA 30334
P: (404) 656-0188
E: matt.gurtler
@house.ga.gov

**Hanson, Meagan (R, 80)***
612-D Legislative Office
Building
Atlanta, GA 30334
P: (404) 656-0325
E: meagan.hanson
@house.ga.gov

**Harden, Buddy (R, 148)**
401-B State Capitol
Atlanta, GA 30334
P: (404) 656-7855
E: bharden@planttel.net

**Harrell, Brett A. (R, 106)**
613-D Legislative Office
Building
Atlanta, GA 30334
P: (404) 463-3793
E: brett@voteharrell.com

# Georgia

**Hatchett, Matt (R, 150)**
415 State Capitol
Atlanta, GA 30334
P: (404) 656-5025
F: (404) 657-8278
E: matt.hatchett
@house.ga.gov

**Hawkins, Lee (R, 27)**
508-D Legislative Office
Building
Atlanta, GA 30334
P: (404) 656-0213
E: lee.hawkins@house.ga.gov

**Henson, Michele D. (D, 86)**
512-I Legislative Office
Building
Atlanta, GA 30334
P: (404) 656-7859
F: (404) 651-8086
E: michele.henson
@house.ga.gov

**Hill, Dewayne (R, 3)\***
612-C Legislative Office
Building
Atlanta, GA 30334
P: (404) 656-0325
E: dewayne.hill
@house.ga.gov

**Hilton, Scott (R, 95)\***
507-E Legislative Office
Building
Atlanta, GA 30334
P: (404) 656-0202
E: scott.hilton
@house.ga.gov

**Hitchens, Bill (R, 161)**
401-A Legislative Office
Building
Atlanta, GA 30334
P: (404) 656-0152
E: bill.hitchens
@house.ga.gov

**Hogan, Don (R, 179)\***
404-F Legislative Office
Building
Atlanta, GA 30334
P: (404) 656-0109
E: don.hogan@house.ga.gov

**Holcomb, Scott (D, 81)**
511-E Legislative Office
Building
Atlanta, GA 30334
P: (404) 656-6372
E: scott.holcomb
@house.ga.gov

**Holmes, Susan (R, 129)**
501-F Legislative Office
Building
Atlanta, GA 30334
P: (404) 656-0178
E: sdholmes@bellsouth.net

**Houston, Penny (R, 170)**
245 State Capitol
Atlanta, GA 30334
P: (404) 463-2247
F: (404) 651-8086
E: penny.houston
@house.ga.gov

**Howard, Henry "Wayne" (D, 124)**
511-H Legislative Office
Building
Atlanta, GA 30334
P: (404) 656-6372
E: wayne.howard
@house.ga.gov

**Hugley, Carolyn Fleming (D, 136)**
609-A Legislative Office
Building
Atlanta, GA 30334
P: (404) 656-5058
E: carolyn.hugley
@house.ga.gov

**Jackson, Derrick (D, 64)\***
509-F Legislative Office
Building
Atlanta, GA 30334
P: (404) 656-0220
E: derrick.jackson
@house.ga.gov

**Jackson, Mack (D, 128)**
611-H Legislative Office
Building
Atlanta, GA 30334
P: (404) 656-0314
F: (404) 656-0250
E: mack.jackson
@house.ga.gov

**Jasperse, Rick (R, 11)**
401-H State Capitol
Atlanta, GA 30334
P: (404) 656-7857
E: rick.jasperse
@house.ga.gov

**Jones, Jan (R, 47)**
340 State Capitol
Atlanta, GA 30334
P: (404) 656-5072
F: (404) 657-0498
E: jan.jones@house.ga.gov

**Jones, Jeffrey B. (R, 167)**
501-G Legislative Office
Building
Atlanta, GA 30334
P: (404) 656-0178
E: jeff.jones@house.ga.gov

**Jones, Sheila (D, 53)**
411-D Legislative Office
Building
Atlanta, GA 30334
P: (404) 656-0126
F: (404) 656-8086
E: sheila.jones
@house.ga.gov

**Jones, Todd (R, 25)\***
607-E Legislative Office
Building
Atlanta, GA 30334
P: (404) 656-0287
E: todd.jones@house.ga.gov

**Jones, Vernon (D, 91)\***
607-B Legislative Office
Building
Atlanta, GA 30334
P: (404) 656-0287
E: vernon.jones
@house.ga.gov

**Kelley, Trey (R, 16)**
408-A Legislative Office
Building
Atlanta, GA 30334
P: (404) 657-1803
E: trey.kelley@house.ga.gov

**Kendrick, Dar'shun N. (D, 93)**
409-E Legislative Office
Building
Atlanta, GA 30334
P: (404) 656-0116
F: (404) 651-8086
E: dkendrick
@kendrickforgeorgia.com

**Kirby, Tom (R, 114)**
501-C Legislative Office
Building
Atlanta, GA 30334
P: (404) 656-0177
F: (404) 651-8086
E: tom.kirby@house.ga.gov

**Knight, David (R, 130)**
228-A State Capitol
Atlanta, GA 30334
P: (404) 656-5099
F: (404) 463-1673
E: david.knight
@house.ga.gov

**Lariccia, Dominic Francis (R, 169)**
508-A Legislative Office
Building
Atlanta, GA 30334
P: (404) 656-0213
E: dominic.lariccia
@house.ga.gov

**Lopez, Brenda (D, 99)\***
511-F Legislative Office
Building
Atlanta, GA 30334
P: (404) 656-6372
E: brenda.lopez
@house.ga.gov

**Lott, Jodi (R, 122)**
501-A Legislative Office
Building
Atlanta, GA 30334
P: (404) 656-0177
E: jodi.lott@house.ga.gov

**Lumsden, Eddie (R, 12)**
612-A Legislative Office
Building
Atlanta, GA 30334
P: (404) 656-0325
E: eddie.lumsden
@house.ga.gov

**Marin, Pedro (D, 96)**
611-A Legislative Office
Building
Atlanta, GA 30334
P: (404) 656-0314
F: (404) 651-8086
E: marinstatehouse@aol.com

**Martin Jr., Charles E. (R, 49)**
417-B State Capitol
Atlanta, GA 30334
P: (404) 656-5064
F: (404) 463-2249
E: chuck
@martinforgeorgia.com

**Mathiak, Karen (R, 73)\***
607-F Legislative Office
Building
Atlanta, GA 30334
P: (404) 656-0287
E: karen.mathiak
@house.ga.gov

**Maxwell, Howard R. (R, 17)**
402 State Capitol
Atlanta, GA 30334
P: (404) 656-5143
F: (404) 463-4131
E: howard.maxwell
@house.ga.gov

**McCall, Tom (R, 33)**
228 State Capitol
Atlanta, GA 30334
P: (404) 656-5099
F: (404) 656-6897
E: tommccall@elberton.net

**McClain, Dewey (D, 100)**
509-B Legislative Office
Building
Atlanta, GA 30334
P: (404) 656-0220
E: dewey.mcclain
    @house.ga.gov

**McGowan, Bill (D, 138)***
511-D Legislative Office
Building
Atlanta, GA 30334
P: (404) 656-6372
E: bill.mcgowan
    @house.ga.gov

**Meadows III, John D. (R, 5)**
HM-1 State Capitol
Atlanta, GA 30334
P: (404) 656-5141
E: john.meadows
    @house.ga.gov

**Metze, Marie (D, 55)**
511-G Legislative Office
Building
Atlanta, GA 30334
P: (404) 656-6372
E: marie.metze@house.ga.gov

**Mitchell, Billy (D, 88)**
411-A Legislative Office
Building
Atlanta, GA 30334
P: (404) 656-0126
E: billy.mitchell
    @house.ga.gov

**Morris, Greg (R, 156)**
226 State Capitol
Atlanta, GA 30334
P: (404) 656-5115
F: (404) 463-4122
E: greg.morris@house.ga.gov

**Mosby, Howard (D, 83)**
607-D Legislative Office
Building
Atlanta, GA 30334
P: (404) 656-0287
E: howard.mosby
    @house.ga.gov

**Nelson, Sheila Clark
    (D, 125)***
511-C Legislative Office
Building
Atlanta, GA 30334
P: (404) 656-6372
E: sheila.nelson
    @house.ga.gov

**Newton, Mark (R, 123)***
612-G Legislative Office
Building
Atlanta, GA 30334
P: (404) 656-0325
E: mark.newton@house.ga.gov

**Nimmer, Chad (R, 178)**
401-J State Capitol
Atlanta, GA 30334
P: (404) 656-7857
F: (404) 651-5795
E: chad.nimmer@house.ga.gov

**Nix, Randy (R, 69)**
417-B State Capitol
Atlanta, GA 30334
P: (404) 656-5146
F: (404) 463-2976
E: randy.nix@house.ga.gov

**Oliver, Mary Margaret
    (D, 82)**
604-E Legislative Office
Building
Atlanta, GA 30334
P: (404) 656-0265
F: (404) 463-2634
E: mmo@mmolaw.com

**Paris, Miriam (D, 142)**
404-B Legislative Office
Building
Atlanta, GA 30334
P: (404) 656-0109
E: miriam.paris
    @house.ga.gov

**Park, Samuel (D, 101)***
611-F Legislative Office
Building
Atlanta, GA 30334
P: (404) 656-0314
E: samuel.park@house.ga.gov

**Parrish, Butch (R, 158)**
245 State Capitol
Atlanta, GA 30334
P: (404) 463-2247
E: butch.parrish
    @house.ga.gov

**Parsons, Don (R, 44)**
401 State Capitol
Atlanta, GA 30334
P: (404) 656-9198
E: repdon@donparsons.org

**Peake, Allen (R, 141)**
218-C State Capitol
Atlanta, GA 30334
P: (404) 656-5132
E: allen.peake@house.ga.gov

**Petrea, Jesse I. (R, 166)**
408-B Legislative Office
Building
Atlanta, GA 30334
P: (404) 657-1803
E: jesse.petrea
    @house.ga.gov

**Pezold, John David (R, 133)**
504-E Legislative Office
Building
Atlanta, GA 30334
P: (404) 656-0188
E: john.pezold@house.ga.gov

**Pirkle, Clay (R, 155)**
504-C Legislative Office
Building
Atlanta, GA 30334
P: (404) 656-0188
E: clay.pirkle@house.ga.gov

**Powell, Alan (R, 32)**
613-B Legislative Office
Building
Atlanta, GA 30334
P: (404) 463-3793
F: (404) 651-8086
E: alanpowell23@hotmail.com

**Powell, Jay (R, 171)**
133 State Capitol
Atlanta, GA 30334
P: (404) 656-5103
E: jay.powell@house.ga.gov

**Price, Betty (R, 48)**
507-F Legislative Office
Building
Atlanta, GA 30334
P: (404) 656-0202
E: betty.price@house.ga.gov

**Prince, Brian (D, 127)**
409-D Legislative Office
Building
Atlanta, GA 30334
P: (404) 656-0016
E: brian.prince
    @house.ga.gov

**Pruett, Jimmy (R, 149)**
401-D State Capitol
Atlanta, GA 30334
P: (404) 656-7855
E: jimmy.pruett
    @house.ga.gov

**Quick, Regina (R, 117)**
509-C Legislative Office
Building
Atlanta, GA 30334
P: (404) 656-0220
E: regina.quick
    @house.ga.gov

**Raffensperger, Brad (R, 50)**
601-B Legislative Office
Building
Atlanta, GA 30334
P: (404) 656-0254
E: brad.raffensperger
    @house.ga.gov

**Rakestraw, Paulette (R, 19)**
501-H Legislative Office
Building
Atlanta, GA 30334
P: (404) 656-0177
E: paulette.rakestraw
    @house.ga.gov

**Ralston, David (R, 7)**
332 State Capitol
Atlanta, GA 30334
P: (404) 656-5020
F: (404) 656-5644
E: david.ralston
    @house.ga.gov

**Reeves, Albert Thomas
    (R, 34)**
608-B Legislative Office
Building
Atlanta, GA 30334
P: (404) 656-0298
E: bert.reeves@house.ga.gov

**Rhodes, Trey (R, 120)**
113 State Capitol
Atlanta, GA 30334
P: (404) 651-7737
E: trey.rhodes@house.ga.gov

**Ridley, Jason (R, 6)***
612-B Legislative Office
Building
Atlanta, GA 30334
P: (404) 656-0325
E: jason.ridley
    @house.ga.gov

**Rogers, Terry (R, 10)**
113 State Capitol
Atlanta, GA 30334
P: (404) 651-7737
E: terry.rogers
    @house.ga.gov

**Rutledge, Dale (R, 109)**
601-C Legislative Office
Building
Atlanta, GA 30334
P: (404) 656-0254
E: dale.rutledge
    @house.ga.gov

**Rynders, Ed (R, 152)**
218-D State Capitol
Atlanta, GA 30334
P: (404) 656-6801
F: (404) 463-2249
E: erynders@bellsouth.net

# Georgia

**Scott, Sandra G. (D, 76)**
611-D Legislative Office
Building
Atlanta, GA 30334
P: (404) 656-0314
E: sandra.scott
@house.ga.gov

**Setzler, Ed (R, 35)**
401 State Capitol
Atlanta, GA 30334
P: (404) 656-7857
F: (404) 463-2976
E: ed.setzler@house.ga.gov

**Shannon, Renitta (D, 84)\***
512-B Legislative Office
Building
Atlanta, GA 30334
P: (404) 656-7859
E: renitta.shannon
@house.ga.gov

**Sharper, Dexter (D, 177)**
411-B Legislative Office
Building
Atlanta, GA 30334
P: (404) 656-0126
E: dexter.sharper
@house.ga.gov

**Shaw, Jason (R, 176)**
218-B State Capitol
Atlanta, GA 30334
P: (404) 656-7153
E: jason.shaw@house.ga.gov

**Silcox, Deborah (R, 52)\***
404-D Legislative Office
Building
Atlanta, GA 30334
P: (404) 656-0109
E: deborah.silcox
@house.ga.gov

**Smith, Lynn Ratigan (R, 70)**
228 State Capitol
Atlanta, GA 30334
P: (404) 656-7149
E: lynn.smith@house.ga.gov

**Smith, Michael (D, 41)**
604-F Legislative Office
Building
Atlanta, GA 30334
P: (404) 656-0265
E: michael.smith
@house.ga.gov

**Smith, Richard H. (R, 134)**
220 State Capitol
Atlanta, GA 30334
P: (404) 656-6831
F: (404) 463-1673
E: richard.smith
@house.ga.gov

**Smyre, Calvin (D, 135)**
404-A Legislative Office
Building
Atlanta, GA 30334
P: (404) 656-0109
F: (404) 651-8086
E: calvinsmyre@synovus.com

**Spencer, Jason (R, 180)**
501-D Legislative Office
Building
Atlanta, GA 30334
P: (404) 656-0177
F: (404) 463-2976
E: jason.spencer
@house.ga.gov

**Stephens, Mickey (D, 165)**
604-A Legislative Office
Building
Atlanta, GA 30334
P: (404) 656-0265
E: mickey.stephens
@gmail.com

**Stephens, Ron (R, 164)**
226-A State Capitol
Atlanta, GA 30334
P: (404) 656-5115
F: (404) 463-4122
E: ron.stephens
@house.ga.gov

**Stephenson, Pam (D, 90)**
411-G Legislative Office
Building
Atlanta, GA 30334
P: (404) 656-0126
F: (404) 656-4889
E: pam.stephenson
@house.ga.gov

**Stovall, Valencia (D, 74)**
611-C Legislative Office
Building
Atlanta, GA 30334
P: (404) 656-0314
E: valencia.stovall
@house.ga.gov

**Stover, David (R, 71)**
501-B Legislative Office
Building
Atlanta, GA 30334
P: (404) 656-0177
E: david.stover
@house.ga.gov

**Strickland, Brian (R, 111)**
608-A Legislative Office
Building
Atlanta, GA 30334
P: (404) 656-0298
E: brian.strickland
@house.ga.gov

**Tankersley, Jan (R, 160)**
401-C State Capitol
Atlanta, GA 30334
P: (404) 656-7855
E: jan.tankersley
@house.ga.gov

**Tanner, Kevin (R, 9)**
614-A Legisaltive Office
Building
Atlanta, GA 30334
P: (404) 656-3947
E: kevin.tanner
@house.ga.gov

**Tarvin, Steve (R, 2)**
601-A Legislative Office
Building
Atlanta, GA 30334
P: (404) 656-0254
E: steve.tarvin
@house.ga.gov

**Taylor, Darlene K. (R, 173)**
404-G Legislative Office
Building
Atlanta, GA 30334
P: (404) 656-0109
E: darlene.taylor
@house.ga.gov

**Taylor, Tom (R, 79)**
614-B Legislative Office
Building
Atlanta, GA 30334
P: (404) 656-3947
E: tom.taylor@house.ga.gov

**Teasley, Sam (R, 37)**
415 State Capitol
Atlanta, GA 30334
P: (404) 463-8143
E: sam.teasley@house.ga.gov

**Thomas, Erica Renee (D, 39)**
512-C Legislative Office
Building
Atlanta, GA 30334
P: (404) 656-7859
E: erica.thomas
@house.ga.gov

**Thomas, Mable (D, 56)**
511-B Legislative Office
Building
Atlanta, GA 30334
P: (404) 656-6372
E: mable.thomas
@house.ga.gov

**Trammell, Bob (D, 132)**
611-G Legislative Office
Building
Atlanta, GA 30334
P: (404) 656-0314
E: bob.trammell
@house.ga.gov

**Turner, Scot (R, 21)**
401-G Legislative Office
Building
Atlanta, GA 30334
P: (404) 656-0152
E: scot.turner@house.ga.gov

**Waites, Keisha (D, 60)**
509-E Legislative Office
Building
Atlanta, GA 30334
P: (404) 656-0220
F: (404) 651-8086
E: keisha.waites
@house.ga.gov

**Watson, Sam (R, 172)**
508-A Legislative Office
Building
Atlanta, GA 30334
P: (404) 656-0213
E: sam.watson@house.ga.gov

**Welch, Andrew J. (R, 110)**
220 State Capitol
Atlanta, GA 30334
P: (404) 656-5912
E: awelch@smithwelchlaw.com

**Werkheiser, Bill (R, 157)**
601-D Legislative Office
Building
Atlanta, GA 30334
P: (404) 656-0254
E: bill.werkheiser
@house.ga.gov

**Wilkerson, David (D, 38)**
409-F Legislative Office
Building
Atlanta, GA 30334
P: (404) 656-0116
F: (404) 656-9645
E: david.wilkerson
@house.ga.gov

**Willard, Wendell (R, 51)**
132 State Capitol
Atlanta, GA 30334
P: (404) 656-5125
F: (404) 657-8277
E: wendell.willard
@house.ga.gov

**Williams, Al (D, 168)**
511-A Legislative Office
Building
Atlanta, GA 30334
P: (404) 656-6372
E: al.williams@house.ga.gov

**Williams, Chuck (R, 119)**
601-E Legislative Office
Building
Atlanta, GA 30334
P: (404) 656-0254
E: chuck.williams
@house.ga.gov

**Williams, Earnest (D, 87)**
507-B Legislative Office
Building
Atlanta, GA 30334
P: (404) 656-0202
F: (404) 651-8086
E: earnest.williams
  @house.ga.gov

**Williams, Rick (R, 145)***
607-G Legislative Office
Building
Atlanta, GA 30334
P: (404) 656-0287
E: rick.williams
  @house.ga.gov

**Williamson, Bruce (R, 115)**
415-B State Capitol
Atlanta, GA 30334
P: (404) 656-5025
E: bruce.williamson
  @house.ga.gov

# Guam

## Executive

### Governor

**The Honorable Eddie Baza Calvo (R)**
Governor
Executive Chamber
P.O. Box 2950
Agana, GU 96932
P: (671) 472-8931
F: (671) 477-4826

### Lieutenant Governor

**The Honorable Ray Tenorio (R)**
Lieutenant Governor
R.J. Bordallo Governor's Complex
P.O. Box 2950
Hagatna, GU 96932
P: (671) 475-9380
F: (671) 477-2007
E: webmaster
@guamletgovernor.net

### Secretary of State

*Guam does not have the office of secretary of state. Some of the duties of the secretary of state are performed by the office of the lieutenant governor.*

### Attorney General

**The Honorable Elizabeth Barrett-Anderson**
Attorney General
590 South Marine Corps Drive
ITC Building, Suite 706
Tamuning, GU 96913
P: (671) 475-3324
F: (671) 472-2493
E: law@guamag.org

### Auditor

**The Honorable Doris Flores Brooks**
Public Auditor
DNA Building, Suite 401
238 Archbishop Flores Street
Hagatna, GU 96910
P: (671) 475-0390, Ext. 207
F: (671) 472-7951
E: dfbrooks@guamopa.com

## Treasurer

**The Honorable Rose T. Fejeran**
Treasurer
P.O. Box 884
Hagatna, GU 96928
P: (671) 475-1101
F: (671) 477-6788
E: rtfejeran@doa.guam.gov

## Judiciary

### Supreme Court (MR)

**Ms. Hannah M. Gutierrez-Arroyo**
Clerk of Court
Guam Judicial Center
120 West O'Brien Drive
Hagatna, GU 96910
P: (671) 475-3162
E: hgutierrezarroyo
@guamsupremecourt.com

**The Honorable Katherine A. Maraman**
Chief Justice
**The Honorable F. Phillip Carbullido**
**The Honorable Robert J. Torres Jr.**

## Unicameral Legislature

### Senate President

**Senator Benjamin J.F. Cruz (D)**
Senate Speaker
155 Hesler Street, Suite 107
Hagatna, GU 96910
P: (671) 477-2520
F: (671) 477-2522
E: senator
@senatorbjcruz.com

### Vice Speaker of the Senate

**Senator Therese M. Terlaje (D)**
Senate Vice Speaker
155 Hesler Place, Suite 201
Hagatna, GU 96910
P: (671) 472-3856
F: (671) 472-3589
E: tterlaje@guam.net

## Senate Majority Leader

**Senator Tom C. Ada (D)**
Senate Majority Leader
Suite 207, Ada Plaza Center
173 Aspinall Avenue
Hagatna, GU 96910
P: (671) 473-3301
F: (671) 473-3303
E: office@senatorada.org

## Senate Minority Leader

**Senator James V. Espaldon (R)**
Senate Minority Leader
238 Archebishop Flores Street
Suite 807, DNA Building
Hagatna, GU 96910
P: (671) 475-4546
F: (671) 475-2422
E: senjvespaldon@gmail.com

## Secretary of the Senate

**Ms. Rennae V. Meno**
Clerk of the Legislature
155 Hesler Place
Hagatna, GU 96910
P: (671) 472-3465
F: (671) 472-3524
E: rennae
@guamlegislature.org

## Members of the Senate

**Ada, Tom C. (D)**
Suite 207, Ada Plaza Center
173 Aspinall Avenue
Hagatna, GU 96910
P: (671) 473-3301
F: (671) 473-3303
E: office@senatorada.org

**Aguon Jr., Frank B. (D)**
238 Archebishop Flores Street
Suite 503, DNA Building
Hagatna, GU 96910
P: (671) 475-4861
E: aguon4guam@gmail.com

**Castro, William (R)\***
MVP Center, Unit 108
777 Route 4
Sinjana, GU 96910
P: (671) 969-1225
E: wilcastro671@gmail.com

**Cruz, Benjamin J.F. (D)**
155 Hesler Street, Suite 107
Hagatna, GU 96910
P: (671) 477-2520
F: (671) 477-2522
E: senator
@senatorbjcruz.com

**Espaldon, James V. (R)**
238 Archebishop Flores Street
Suite 807, DNA Building
Hagatna, GU 96910
P: (671) 475-4546
F: (671) 475-2422
E: senjvespaldon@gmail.com

**Esteves, Fernando Barcinas (R, )\***
Bridge Pointe Building, Suite 202
140 Aspinall Avenue
Hagatna, GU 96910
P: (671) 969-3376
E: senatoresteves@gmail.com

**Lee, Regine Biscoe (D)\***
155 Hesler Place, Suite 101
Hagatna, GU 96910
P: (671) 472-3455
E: senatorbiscoelee
@guamlegislature.org

**Morrison, Thomas (R)**
Suite 202/203B, Ada Plaza Center
173 Aspinall Avenue, Building B
Hagatna, GU 96910
P: (671) 478-8669
E: tommy
@senatormorrison.com

**Muna, Louise Borja (R)\***
Bridge Point Building, Suite 201
140 Aspinall Avenue
Hagatna, GU 96910
P: (671) 969-9852
E: senatorlouise@gmail.com

**Nelson, Telena (D)\***
155 Hessler Place, Suite 302
Hagatna, GU 96910
P: (671) 969-7679
E: senatortnelson@gmail.com

**Rodriguez Jr., Dennis G. (D, )**
Ren Care Building, Suite B1
761 South Marine Corps Drive
Tamuning, GU 96931
P: (671) 649-8638
F: (671) 649-0520
E: senatordrodriguez
@gmail.com

**San Agustin, Joe S. (D)\***
Ran Care Building, Suite 3
761 South Marine Corps Drive
Tamuning, GU 96931
P: (671) 989-5445
F: (671) 969-6737
E: senatorjoesssanagustin
@gmail.com

**San Nicolas, Michael F.Q.**
   **(D, )**
238 Archebishop Flores Street
Suite 407, DNA Building
Hagatna, GU 96910
P: (671) 472-6453
E: senatorsannicolas
   @gmail.com

**Terlaje, Therese M. (D)\***
155 Hesler Place, Suite 201
Hagatna, GU 96910
P: (671) 472-3856
F: (671) 472-3589
E: tterlaje@guam.net

**Torres, Mary Camacho (R)**
238 Archebishop Flores Street
Suite 807, DNA Building
Hagatna, GU 96910
P: (671) 475-6279
F: (671) 475-0004
E: marycamachotorres
   @gmail.com

# Hawaii

## Executive

### Governor

**The Honorable David Y. Ige (D)**
Governor
Executive Chambers
State Capitol
Honolulu, HI 96813
P: (808) 586-0034
F: (808) 586-0006

### Lieutenant Governor

**The Honorable Shan S. Tsutsui (D)**
Lieutenant Governor
Executive Chambers
State Capitol
Honolulu, HI 96813
P: (808) 586-0255
F: (808) 586-0231
E: shan.tsusui@hawaii.gov

### Secretary of State

*Hawaii does not have the office of secretary of state. Some of the duties of the secretary of state are performed by the office of the lieutenant governor.*

### Attorney General

**The Honorable Doug Chin (D)**
(appointed)
Attorney General
425 Queen Street
Honolulu, HI 96813
P: (808) 586-1500

### Treasurer

**The Honorable Wesley Machida**
(appointed)
Director of Finance
250 South Hotel Street, Room 305
Honolulu, HI 96813
P: (808) 586-1518
F: (808) 586-1976
E: hi.budgetandfinance
@hawaii.gov

## Judiciary

### Supreme Court (MC)

**Ms. Rochelle Hasuko**
Chief Clerk
Aliiolani Hale
417 South King Street
Honolulu, HI 96813
P: (808) 539-4919
F: (808) 539-4928

**The Honorable Mark E. Recktenwald**
Chief Justice
**The Honorable Sabrina S. McKenna**
**The Honorable Paula A. Nakayama**
**The Honorable Richard W. Pollack**
**The Honorable Michael D. Wilson**

## Legislative

## Senate

### Senate President

**Senator Ronald D. Kouchi (D)**
Senate President
State Capitol, Room 409
415 South Beretania Street
Honolulu, HI 96813
P: (808) 586-6030
F: (808) 586-6031
E: senkouchi
@capitol.hawaii.gov

### Vice President of the Senate

**Senator Michelle N. Kidani (D)**
Senate Vice President
State Capitol, Room 228
415 South Beretania Street
Honolulu, HI 96813
P: (808) 586-7100
F: (808) 586-7109
E: senkidani
@capitol.hawaii.gov

### Senate Majority Leader

**Senator J. Kalani English (D)**
Senate Majority Leader
State Capitol, Room 205
415 South Beretania Street
Honolulu, HI 96813
P: (808) 587-7225
F: (808) 587-7230
E: senenglish
@capitol.hawaii.gov

## Secretary of the Senate

**Ms. Carol Taniguchi**
Chief Clerk of the Senate
State Capitol, Room 010
415 South Beretania Street
Honolulu, HI 96813
P: (808) 586-6720
F: (808) 586-6719
E: sclerk
@Capitol.hawaii.gov

## Members of the Senate

**Baker, Rosalyn H. (D, 6)**
State Capitol, Room 230
415 South Beretania Street
Honolulu, HI 96813
P: (808) 586-6070
F: (808) 586-6071
E: senbaker
@capitol.hawaii.gov

**Chang, Stanley (D, 9)\***
State Capitol, Room 223
415 South Beretania Street
Honolulu, HI 95613
P: (808) 586-8420
F: (808) 586-8426
E: senchang
@capitol.hawaii.gov

**Dela Cruz, Donovan M. (D, 22)**
State Capitol, Room 202
415 South Beretania Street
Honolulu, HI 96813
P: (808) 586-6090
F: (808) 586-6091
E: sendelacruz
@capitol.hawaii.gov

**English, J. Kalani (D, 7)**
State Capitol, Room 205
415 South Beretania Street
Honolulu, HI 96813
P: (808) 587-7225
F: (808) 587-7230
E: senenglish
@capitol.hawaii.gov

**Espero, Will (D, 19)**
State Capitol, Room 226
415 South Beretania Street
Honolulu, HI 96813
P: (808) 586-6360
F: (808) 586-6361
E: senespero
@capitol.hawaii.gov

**Gabbard, Mike (D, 20)**
State Capitol, Room 201
415 South Beretania Street
Honolulu, HI 96813
P: (808) 586-6830
F: (808) 586-6679
E: sengabbard
@capitol.hawaii.gov

**Galuteria, Brickwood (D, 12)**
State Capitol, Room 206
415 South Beretania Street
Honolulu, HI 96813
P: (808) 586-6740
F: (808) 586-6829
E: sengaluteria
@capitol.hawaii.gov

**Green, Josh (D, 3)**
State Capitol, Room 407
415 South Beretania Street
Honolulu, HI 96813
P: (808) 586-9385
F: (808) 586-9391
E: sengreen
@capitol.hawaii.gov

**Harimoto, Breene (D, 16)**
State Capitol, Room 215
415 South Beretania Street
Honolulu, HI 96813
P: (808) 586-6230
F: (808) 586-6231
E: senharimoto
@capitol.hawaii.gov

**Ihara Jr., Les (D, 10)**
State Capitol, Room 220
415 South Beretania Street
Honolulu, HI 96813
P: (808) 586-6250
F: (808) 586-6251
E: senihara
@capitol.hawaii.gov

**Inouye, Lorraine (D, 4)**
State Capitol, Room 210
415 South Beretania Street
Honolulu, HI 96813
P: (808) 586-7335
F: (808) 586-7339
E: seninouye
@capitol.hawaii.gov

**Kahele, Kaiali'i (D, 1)**
State Capitol, Room 213
415 South Berentania Street
Honolulu, HI 96813
P: (808) 586-6760
F: (808) 586-6689
E: senkahele
@capitol.hawaii.gov

**Keith-Agaran, Gilbert (D, 5)**
State Capitol, Room 221
415 South Beretania Street
Honolulu, HI 96813
P: (808) 586-7344
F: (808) 586-7348
E: senkeithagaran
@capitol.hawaii.gov

**Kidani, Michelle N. (D, 18)**
State Capitol, Room 228
415 South Beretania Street
Honolulu, HI 96813
P: (808) 586-7100
F: (808) 586-7109
E: senkidani
@capitol.hawaii.gov

**Kim, Donna Mercado (D, 14)**
State Capitol, Room 218
415 South Beretania Street
Honolulu, HI 96813
P: (808) 587-7200
F: (808) 587-7205
E: senkim
@capitol.hawaii.gov

**Kouchi, Ronald D. (D, 8)**
State Capitol, Room 409
415 South Beretania Street
Honolulu, HI 96813
P: (808) 586-6030
F: (808) 586-6031
E: senkouchi
@capitol.hawaii.gov

**Nishihara, Clarence K. (D, 17)**
State Capitol, Room 214
415 South Beretania Street
Honolulu, HI 96813
P: (808) 586-6970
F: (808) 586-6879
E: sennishihara
@capitol.hawaii.gov

**Rhoads, Karl (D, 13)**
State Capitol, Room 204
415 South Beretania Street
Honolulu, HI 96813
P: (808) 586-6130
F: (808) 586-6131
E: senrhoads
@capitol.hawaii.gov

**Riviere, Gil (D, 23)**
State Capitol, Room 217
415 South Beretania Street
Honolulu, HI 96813
P: (808) 586-7330
F: (808) 586-7334
E: senriviere
@capitol.hawaii.gov

**Ruderman, Russell E. (D, 2)**
State Capitol, Room 203
415 South Beretania Street
Honolulu, HI 96813
P: (808) 586-6890
F: (808) 586-6899
E: senruderman
@capitol.hawaii.gov

**Shimabukuro, Maile S.L. (D, 21)**
State Capitol, Room 222
415 South Beretania Street
Honolulu, HI 96813
P: (808) 586-7793
F: (808) 586-7797
E: senshimabukuro
@capitol.hawaii.gov

**Taniguchi, Brian T. (D, 11)**
State Capitol, Room 219
415 South Beretania Street
Honolulu, HI 96813
P: (808) 586-6460
F: (808) 586-6461
E: sentaniguchi
@capitol.hawaii.gov

**Thielen, Laura H. (D, 25)**
State Capitol, Room 231
415 South Beretania Street
Honolulu, HI 96813
P: (808) 587-8388
F: (808) 587-7240
E: senthielen
@capitol.hawaii.gov

**Tokuda, Jill N. (D, 24)**
State Capitol, Room 207
415 South Beretania Street
Honolulu, HI 96813
P: (808) 587-7215
F: (808) 587-7220
E: sentokuda
@capitol.hawaii.gov

**Wakai, Glenn (D, 15)**
State Capitol, Room 216
415 South Beretania Street
Honolulu, HI 96813
P: (808) 586-8585
F: (808) 586-8588
E: senwakai
@capitol.hawaii.gov

# House

## Speaker of the House

**Representative Joseph M. Souki (D)**
Speaker of the House
State Capitol, Room 431
415 South Beretania Street
Honolulu, HI 96813
P: (808) 586-6100
F: (808) 586-6101
E: repsouki
@capitol.hawaii.gov

## Vice Speaker of the House

**Representative John M. Mizuno (D)**
Vice Speaker
State Capitol, Room 439
415 South Beretania Street
Honolulu, HI 96813
P: (808) 586-6050
F: (808) 586-6051
E: repmizuno
@capitol.hawaii.gov

## House Majority Leader

**Representative Scott K. Saiki (D)**
Majority Leader
State Capitol, Room 434
415 South Beretania Street
Honolulu, HI 96813
P: (808) 586-8485
F: (808) 586-8489
E: repsaiki
@capitol.hawaii.gov

## House Minority Leader

**Representative Andria Tupola (R)**
Minority Leader
State Capitol, Room 317
415 South Beretania Street
Honolulu, HI 96813
P: (808) 586-8465
F: (808) 586-8469
E: reptupola
@Capitol.hawaii.gov

## Clerk of the House

**Mr. Brian Takeshita**
Clerk of the House
State Capitol, Room 027
415 South Beretania Street
Honolulu, HI 96813
P: (808) 586-6400
F: (808) 586-6401
E: hclerk
@capitol.hawaii.gov

## Members of the House

**Aquino, Henry J.C. (D, 38)**
State Capitol, Room 419
415 South Beretania Street
Honolulu, HI 96813
P: (808) 586-6520
F: (808) 586-6521
E: repaquino
@capitol.hawaii.gov

**Belatti, Della Au (D, 24)**
State Capitol, Room 402
415 South Beretania Street
Honolulu, HI 96813
P: (808) 586-9425
F: (808) 586-9431
E: repbelatti
@capitol.hawaii.gov

**Brower, Tom (D, 22)**
State Capitol, Room 315
415 South Beretania Street
Honolulu, HI 96813
P: (808) 586-8520
F: (808) 586-8524
E: repbrower
@capitol.hawaii.gov

**Cachola, Romy M. (D, 30)**
State Capitol, Room 435
415 South Beretania Street
Honolulu, HI 96813
P: (808) 586-6010
F: (808) 586-6011
E: repcachola
@capitol.hawaii.gov

**Choy, Isaac W. (D, 23)**
State Capitol, Room 404
415 South Beretania Street
Honolulu, HI 96813
P: (808) 586-8475
F: (808) 586-8479
E: repchoy
@capitol.hawaii.gov

# Hawaii

**Creagan, Richard (D, 5)**
State Capitol, Room 331
415 South Beretania Street
Honolulu, HI 96813
P: (808) 586-9605
F: (808) 586-9608
E: repcreagan
@Capitol.hawaii.gov

**Cullen, Ty J.K. (D, 39)**
State Capitol, Room 316
415 South Beretania Street
Honolulu, HI 96813
P: (808) 586-8490
F: (808) 586-8494
E: repcullen
@capitol.hawaii.gov

**DeCoite, Lynn (D, 13)**
State Capitol, Room 324
415 South Beretania Street
Honolulu, HI 96813
P: (808) 586-6790
F: (808) 586-6779
E: repdecoite
@capitol.hawaii.gov

**Evans, Cindy (D, 7)**
State Capitol, Room 438
415 South Beretania Street
Honolulu, HI 96813
P: (808) 586-8510
F: (808) 586-8514
E: repevans
@capitol.hawaii.gov

**Fukumoto Chang, Beth (R, 36)**
State Capitol, Room 333
415 South Beretania Street
Honolulu, HI 96813
P: (808) 586-9460
F: (808) 586-9466
E: repfukumoto
@capitol.hawaii.gov

**Gates, Cedric Asuega (D, 44)***
State Capitol, Room 311
415 South Beretania Street
Honolulu, HI 96813
P: 808-586-8460
F: 808-586-8464
E: repgates
@Capitol.hawaii.gov

**Har, Sharon E. (D, 42)**
State Capitol, Room 418
415 South Beretania Street
Honolulu, HI 96813
P: (808) 586-8500
F: (808) 586-8504
E: rephar
@capitol.hawaii.gov

**Hashem, Mark J. (D, 18)**
State Capitol, Room 326
415 South Beretania Street
Honolulu, HI 96813
P: (808) 586-6510
F: (808) 586-6511
E: rephashem
@capitol.hawaii.gov

**Holt, Daniel (D, 29)***
State Capitol, Room 319
415 South Beretania Street
Honolului, HI 96813
P: 808-586-6180
F: 808-586-6189
E: repholt
@Capitol.hawaii.gov

**Ichiyama, Linda (D, 32)**
State Capitol, Room 327
415 South Beretania Street
Honolulu, HI 96813
P: (808) 586-6220
F: (808) 586-6221
E: repichiyama
@capitol.hawaii.gov

**Ing, Kaniela (D, 11)**
State Capitol, Room 427
415 South Beretania Street
Honolulu, HI 96813
P: (808) 586-8525
F: (808) 586-8529
E: reping
@capitol.hawaii.gov

**Ito, Ken (D, 49)**
State Capitol, Room 432
415 South Beretania Street
Honolulu, HI 96813
P: (808) 586-8470
F: (808) 586-8474
E: repito
@capitol.hawaii.gov

**Johanson, Aaron Ling (D, 31)**
State Capitol, Room 426
415 South Beretania Street
Honolulu, HI 96813
P: (808) 586-9470
F: (808) 586-9476
E: repjohanson
@capitol.hawaii.gov

**Keohokalole, Jarrett (D, 48)**
State Capitol, Room 310
415 South Beretania Street
Honolulu, HI 96813
P: (808) 586-8540
F: (808) 586-8544
E: repkeohokalole
@Capitol.hawaii.gov

**Kobayashi, Bertrand (D, 19)**
State Capitol, Room 403
415 South Beretania Street
Honolulu, HI 96813
P: (808) 586-6310
F: (808) 586-6311
E: repkobayashi
@capitol.hawaii.gov

**Kong, Sam (D, 33)**
State Capitol, Room 313
415 South Beretania Street
Honolulu, HI 96813
P: (808) 586-8455
F: (808) 586-8459
E: repkong
@Capitol.hawaii.gov

**Lee, Chris (D, 51)**
State Capitol, Room 436
415 South Beretania Street
Honolulu, HI 96813
P: (808) 586-9450
F: (808) 586-9456
E: repclee
@capitol.hawaii.gov

**Lopresti, Matthew (D, 41)**
State Capitol, Room 328
415 South Beretania Street
Honolulu, HI 96813
P: (808) 586-6080
F: (808) 586-6081
E: replopresti
@Capitol.hawaii.gov

**Lowen, Nicole E. (D, 6)**
State Capitol, Room 425
415 South Beretania Street
Honolulu, HI 96813
P: (808) 586-8400
F: (808) 586-8404
E: replowen
@capitol.hawaii.gov

**Luke, Sylvia (D, 25)**
State Capitol, Room 306
415 South Beretania Street
Honolulu, HI 96813
P: (808) 586-6200
F: (808) 586-6201
E: repluke
@capitol.hawaii.gov

**Matsumoto, Lauren (R, 45)**
State Capitol, Room 303
415 South Beretania Street
Honolulu, HI 96813
P: (808) 586-9490
F: (808) 586-9496
E: repmatsumoto
@capitol.hawaii.gov

**McDermott, Bob (R, 40)**
State Capitol, Room 330
415 South Beretania Street
Honolulu, HI 96813
P: (808) 586-9730
F: (808) 586-9738
E: repmcdermott
@capitol.hawaii.gov

**McKelvey, Angus L.K. (D, 10)**
State Capitol, Room 320
415 South Beretania Street
Honolulu, HI 96813
P: (808) 586-6160
F: (808) 586-6161
E: repmckelvey
@capitol.hawaii.gov

**Mizuno, John M. (D, 28)**
State Capitol, Room 439
415 South Beretania Street
Honolulu, HI 96813
P: (808) 586-6050
F: (808) 586-6051
E: repmizuno
@capitol.hawaii.gov

**Morikawa, Dee (D, 16)**
State Capitol, Room 442
415 South Beretania Street
Honolulu, HI 96813
P: (808) 586-6280
F: (808) 586-6281
E: repmorikawa
@capitol.hawaii.gov

**Nakamura, Nadine (D, 14)***
State Capitol, Room 314
415 South Beretania Street
Honolulu, HI 96813
P: (808) 586-8435
F: (808) 586-8437
E: repnakamura
@Capitol.hawaii.gov

**Nakashima, Mark M. (D, 1)**
State Capitol, Room 406
415 South Beretania Street
Honolulu, HI 96813
P: (808) 586-6680
F: (808) 586-6684
E: repnakashima
@capitol.hawaii.gov

**Nishimoto, Scott Y. (D, 21)**
State Capitol, Room 421
415 South Beretania Street
Honolulu, HI 96813
P: (808) 586-8515
F: (808) 586-8519
E: repnishimoto
@capitol.hawaii.gov

**Ohno, Takashi (D, 27)**
State Capitol, Room 332
415 South Beretania Street
Honolulu, HI 96813
P: (808) 586-9415
F: (808) 586-9421
E: repohno
@capitol.hawaii.gov

**Onishi, Richard H.K. (D, 3)**
State Capitol, Room 441
415 South Beretania Street
Honolulu, HI 96813
P: (808) 586-6120
F: (808) 586-6121
E: reponishi
@capitol.hawaii.gov

**Oshiro, Marcus R. (D, 46)**
State Capitol, Room 424
415 South Beretania Street
Honolulu, HI 96813
P: (808) 586-6700
F: (808) 586-6702
E: repmoshiro
@capitol.hawaii.gov

**Quinlan, Sean (D, 47)***
State Capitol, Room 304
415 South Beretania Street
Honolulu, HI 96813
P: 808-586-6380
F: 808-586-6381
E: repquinlan
@Capitol.hawaii.gov

**Saiki, Scott K. (D, 26)**
State Capitol, Room 434
415 South Beretania Street
Honolulu, HI 96813
P: (808) 586-8485
F: (808) 586-8489
E: repsaiki
@capitol.hawaii.gov

**San Buenaventura, Joy
(D, 4)**
State Capitol, Room 302
415 South Beretania Street
Honolulu, HI 96813
P: (808) 586-6530
F: (808) 586-6531
E: repsanbuenaventura
@Capitol.hawaii.gov

**Say, Calvin K.Y. (D, 20)**
State Capitol, Room 433
415 South Beretania Street
Honolulu, HI 96813
P: (808) 586-6900
F: (808) 586-6910
E: repsay
@capitol.hawaii.gov

**Souki, Joseph M. (D, 8)**
State Capitol, Room 431
415 South Beretania Street
Honolulu, HI 96813
P: (808) 586-6100
F: (808) 586-6101
E: repsouki
@capitol.hawaii.gov

**Takayama, Gregg (D, 34)**
State Capitol, Room 323
415 South Beretania Street
Honolulu, HI 96813
P: (808) 586-6340
F: (808) 586-6341
E: reptakayama
@capitol.hawaii.gov

**Takumi, Roy M. (D, 35)**
State Capitol, Room 444
415 South Beretania Street
Honolulu, HI 96813
P: (808) 586-6170
F: (808) 586-6171
E: reptakumi
@capitol.hawaii.gov

**Thielen, Cynthia (R, 50)**
State Capitol, Room 443
415 South Beretania Street
Honolulu, HI 96813
P: (808) 586-6480
F: (808) 586-6481
E: repthielen
@capitol.hawaii.gov

**Todd, Chris (D, 2)***
State Capitol, Room 305
415 South Beretania Street
Honolulu, HI 96813
P: (808) 586-8480
F: (808) 586-8484
E: reptodd
@capitol.hawaii.gov

**Tokioka, James Kunane
(D, 15)**
State Capitol, Room 322
415 South Beretania Street
Honolulu, HI 96813
P: (808) 586-6270
F: (808) 586-6271
E: reptokioka
@capitol.hawaii.gov

**Tupola, Andria (R, 43)**
State Capitol, Room 317
415 South Beretania Street
Honolulu, HI 96813
P: (808) 586-8465
F: (808) 586-8469
E: reptupola
@Capitol.hawaii.gov

**Ward, Gene (R, 17)**
State Capitol, Room 318
415 South Beretania Street
Honolulu, HI 96813
P: (808) 586-6420
F: (808) 586-6421
E: repward
@capitol.hawaii.gov

**Woodson, Justin (D, 9)**
State Capitol, Room 405
415 South Beretania Street
Honolulu, HI 96813
P: (808) 586-6210
F: (808) 586-6211
E: repwoodson
@capitol.hawaii.gov

**Yamane, Ryan I. (D, 37)**
State Capitol, Room 420
415 South Beretania Street
Honolulu, HI 96813
P: (808) 586-6150
F: (808) 586-6151
E: repyamane
@capitol.hawaii.gov

**Yamashita, Kyle T. (D, 12)**
State Capitol, Room 422
415 South Beretania Street
Honolulu, HI 96813
P: (808) 586-6330
F: (808) 586-6331
E: repyamashita
@capitol.hawaii.gov

# Idaho

## Executive

### Governor
The Honorable C.L. "Butch"
Otter (R)
Governor
700 West Jefferson, Second
Floor
Boise, ID 83702
P: (208) 334-2100
F: (208) 334-2175

### Lieutenant Governor
The Honorable Brad
Little (R)
Lieutenant Governor
State Capitol
Boise, ID 83720
P: (208) 334-2200
F: (208) 334-3259

### Attorney General
The Honorable Lawrence
Wasden (R)
Attorney General
Statehouse
Boise, ID 83720
P: (208) 334-2400
F: (208) 854-8071

### Auditor
*Idaho does not have the office of state auditor by a 1994 amendment to the state constitution.*

### Secretary of State
Mr. Lawerence Denney (R)
Secretary of State
P.O. Box 83720
Boise, ID 83720
P: (208) 334-2300
F: (208) 334-2282
E: ldenney@sos.idaho.gov

### Superintendent of Public Instruction
The Honorable Sherri
Ybarra (R)
Superintendent of Public
Instruction
650 West State Street
Boise, ID 83720
P: (208) 332-6800
F: (208) 334-2228
E: info@sde.idaho.gov

### Treasurer
The Honorable Ron G.
Crane (R)
State Treasurer
700 West Jefferson Street, Suite
E-126
P.O. Box 83720
Boise, ID 83720
P: (208) 334-3200
F: (208) 332-2959
E: ron.crane@sto.idaho.gov

## Judiciary

### Supreme Court (NE)
Mr. Stephen W. Kenyon
Clerk of the Supreme Court
P.O. Box 83720
Boise, ID 83720
P: (208) 334-2210
F: (208) 947-7590

The Honorable Roger S.
Burdick
Chief Justice
The Honorable Robyn Brody
The Honorable Daniel T.
Eismann
The Honorable Joel D.
Horton
The Honorable Warren E.
Jones

## Legislative

### Senate

#### Senate President
The Honorable Brad
Little (R)
Lieutenant Governor
State Capitol
Boise, ID 83720
P: (208) 334-2200
F: (208) 334-3259

#### President Pro Tempore of the Senate
Senator Brent Hill (R)
Senate President Pro Tempore
State Capitol Building
P.O. Box 83720
Boise, ID 83720
P: (208) 332-1300
F: (208) 334-5397
E: bhill@senate.idaho.gov

### Senate Majority Leader
Senator Bart M. Davis (R)
Senate Majority Leader
State Capitol Building
P.O. Box 83720
Boise, ID 83720
P: (208) 332-1305
F: (208) 334-5397
E: bmdavis@senate.idaho.gov

### Senate Minority Leader
Senator Michelle
Stennett (D)
Senate Minority Leader
State Capitol Building
P.O. Box 83720
Boise, ID 83720
P: (208) 332-1410
F: (208) 334-5397
E: mstennett
@senate.idaho.gov

### Secretary of the Senate
Ms. Jennifer Novak
Secretary of the Senate
State Capitol Building, Room
W327
P.O. Box 83720
Boise, ID 83720
P: (208) 332-1309

### Members of the Senate
Agenbroad, Jeff (R, 13)*
State Capitol Building
P.O. Box 83720
Boise, ID 83720
P: (208) 332-1329
F: (208) 334-5397
E: jagenbroad
@senate.idaho.gov

Anthon, Kelly (R, 27)
State Capitol Building
P.O. Box 83720
Boise, ID 83720
P: (208) 334-1327
F: (208) 334-5397
E: kanthon@senate.idaho.gov

Bair, Steve (R, 31)
State Capitol Building
P.O. Box 83720
Boise, ID 83720
P: (208) 332-1346
F: (208) 334-5397
E: sbair@senate.idaho.gov

Bayer, Clifford R. (R, 21)
State Capitol Building
P.O. Box 83720
Boise, ID 83720
P: (208) 332-1331
F: (208) 334-5397
E: cbayer@senate.idaho.gov

Brackett, Bert (R, 23)
State Capitol Building
P.O. Box 83720
Boise, ID 83720
P: (208) 332-1336
F: (208) 334-5397
E: bbrackett
@senate.idaho.gov

Buckner-Webb, Cherie
(D, 19)
State Capitol Building
P.O. Box 83720
Boise, ID 83720
P: (208) 332-1411
F: (208) 334-5397
E: cbucknerwebb
@senate.idaho.gov

Burgoyne, Grant (D, 16)
State Capitol Building
P.O. Box 83720
Boise, ID 83720
P: (208) 332-1409
F: (208) 334-5397
E: gburgoyne
@house.idaho.gov

Crabtree, Carl (R, 7)*
State Capitol Bulding
P.O. Box 83720
Boise, ID 83720
P: (208) 334-1355
F: (208) 334-5397
E: ccrabtree
@senate.idaho.gov

Davis, Bart M. (R, 33)
State Capitol Building
P.O. Box 83720
Boise, ID 83720
P: (208) 332-1305
F: (208) 334-5397
E: bmdavis@senate.idaho.gov

Den Hartog, Lori (R, 22)
State Capitol Building
P.O. Box 83720
Boise, ID 83720
P: (208) 332-1340
F: (208) 334-5397
E: ldenhartog
@senate.idaho.gov

Foreman, Dan (R, 5)*
State Capitol Building
P.O. Box 83720
Boise, ID 83720
P: (208) 332-1405
F: (208) 334-5397
E: dforeman
@senate.idaho.gov

**Guthrie, Jim (R, 28)**
State Capitol Building
P.O. Box 83720
Boise, ID 83720
P: (208) 332-1348
F: (208) 334-5397
E: jguthrie
   @senate.idaho.gov

**Hagedorn, Marv (R, 14)**
State Capitol Building
P.O. Box 83720
Boise, ID 83720
P: (208) 332-1334
F: (208) 334-5397
E: mhagedorn
   @senate.idaho.gov

**Harris, Mark (R, 32)**
State Capitol Building
P.O. Box 83720
Boise, ID 83720
P: (208) 332-1429
F: (208) 334-5397
E: mharris@senate.idaho.gov

**Heider, Lee (R, 24)**
State Capitol Building
P.O. Box 83720
Boise, ID 83720
P: (208) 332-1347
F: (208) 334-5397
E: lheider@senate.idaho.gov

**Hill, Brent (R, 34)**
State Capitol Building
P.O. Box 83720
Boise, ID 83720
P: (208) 332-1300
F: (208) 334-5397
E: bhill@senate.idaho.gov

**Johnson, Dan G. (R, 6)**
State Capitol Building
P.O. Box 83720
Boise, ID 83720
P: (208) 332-1421
F: (208) 334-5397
E: djohnson
   @senate.idaho.gov

**Jordan, Maryanne (D, 17)**
State Capitol Building
P.O. Box 83720
Boise, ID 83720
P: (208) 332-1412
F: (208) 334-5397
E: mjordan@senate.idaho.gov

**Keough, Shawn (R, 1)**
State Capitol Building
P.O. Box 83720
Boise, ID 83720
P: (208) 332-1349
F: (208) 334-5397
E: skeough@senate.idaho.gov

**Lakey, Todd (R, 12)**
State Capitol Building
P.O. Box 83720
Boise, ID 83720
P: (208) 332-1304
F: (208) 334-5397
E: tlakey@senate.idaho.gov

**Lee, Abby (R, 9)**
State Capitol Building
P.O. Box 83720
Boise, ID 83720
P: (208) 332-1325
F: (208) 334-5397
E: alee@senate.idaho.gov

**Lodge, Patti Anne (R, 11)**
State Capitol Building
P.O. Box 83720
Boise, ID 83720
P: (208) 332-1320
F: (208) 334-5397
E: palodge@senate.idaho.gov

**Martin, Fred (R, 15)**
State Capitol Building
P.O. Box 83720
Boise, ID 83720
P: (208) 332-1407
F: (208) 334-5397
E: fmartin@senate.idaho.gov

**Mortimer, Dean M. (R, 30)**
State Capitol Building
P.O. Box 83720
Boise, ID 83720
P: (208) 332-1358
F: (208) 334-5397
E: dmortimer
   @senate.idaho.gov

**Nonini, Bob (R, 3)**
State Capitol Building
P.O. Box 83720
Boise, ID 83720
P: (208) 332-1338
F: (208) 334-5397
E: bnonini@senate.idaho.gov

**Nye, Mark (D, 29)**
State Capitol Building
P.O. Box 83720
Boise, ID 83720
P: (208) 332-1406
F: (208) 334-5397
E: mnye@house.idaho.gov

**Patrick, Jim (R, 25)**
State Capitol Building
P.O. Box 83720
Boise, ID 83720
P: (208) 332-1318
F: (208) 334-5397
E: jpatrick
   @senate.idaho.gov

**Rice, Jim (R, 10)**
State Capitol Building
P.O. Box 83720
Boise, ID 83720
P: (208) 332-1423
F: (208) 334-5397
E: jrice@senate.idaho.gov

**Siddoway, Jeff C. (R, 35)**
State Capitol Building
P.O. Box 83720
Boise, ID 83720
P: (208) 332-1342
F: (208) 334-5397
E: jsiddoway
   @senate.idaho.gov

**Souza, Mary (R, 4)**
State Capitol Building
P.O. Box 83720
Boise, ID 83720
P: (208) 332-1322
F: (208) 334-5397
E: msouza@senate.idaho.gov

**Stennett, Michelle (D, 26)**
State Capitol Building
P.O. Box 83720
Boise, ID 83720
P: (208) 332-1410
F: (208) 334-5397
E: mstennett
   @senate.idaho.gov

**Thayn, Steven P. (R, 8)**
State Capitol Building
P.O. Box 83720
Boise, ID 83720
P: (208) 332-1344
F: (208) 334-5397
E: sthayn@senate.idaho.gov

**Vick, Steve (R, 2)**
State Capitol Building
P.O. Box 83720
Boise, ID 83720
P: (208) 332-1345
F: (208) 334-5397
E: sjvick@senate.idaho.gov

**Ward-Engelking, Janie
   (D, 18)**
State Capitol Building
P.O. Box 83720
Boise, ID 83720
P: (208) 332-1425
F: (208) 334-5397
E: jwardengelking
   @senate.idaho.gov

**Winder, Chuck (R, 20)**
State Capitol Building
P.O. Box 83720
Boise, ID 83720
P: (208) 332-1308
F: (208) 334-5397
E: cwinder@senate.idaho.gov

# House

## Speaker of the House

**Representative Scott
   Bedke (R)**
Speaker of the House
State Capitol Building
P.O. Box 83720
Boise, ID 83720
P: (208) 332-1123
F: (208) 334-5397
E: sbedke@house.idaho.gov

## House Majority Leader

**Representative Mike
   Moyle (R)**
House Majority Leader
State Capitol Building
P.O. Box 83720
Boise, ID 83720
P: (208) 332-1122
F: (208) 334-5397
E: mmoyle@house.idaho.gov

## House Minority Leader

**Representative Mat
   Erpelding (D)**
House Minority Leader
State Capitol Building
P.O. Box 83720
Boise, ID 83720
P: (208) 332-1078
F: (208) 334-5397
E: merpelding
   @house.idaho.gov

## Clerk of the House

**Ms. Carrie Maulin**
Chief Clerk
State Capitol Building, Room
E311
P.O. Box 83720
Boise, ID 83720
P: (208) 332-1141
F: (208) 334-5397
E: cmaulin@house.idaho.gov

## Members of the House

**Amador, Paul (R, 4B)***
State Capitol Building
P.O. Box 83720
Boise, ID 83720
P: (208) 332-1048
F: (208) 334-5397
E: pamador@house.idaho.gov

# Idaho

**Anderson, Neil (R, 31A)**
State Capitol Building
P.O. Box 83720
Boise, ID 83720
P: (208) 332-1086
F: (208) 334-5397
E: nanderson
   @house.idaho.gov

**Anderst, Robert (R, 12A)**
State Capitol Building
P.O. Box 83720
Boise, ID 83720
P: (208) 332-1178
F: (208) 334-5397
E: randerst@house.idaho.gov

**Armstrong, Randy (R, 28A)***
State Capitol Building
P.O. Box 83720
Boise, ID 83720
P: (208) 332-1046
F: (208) 334-5397
E: rarmstrong
   @house.idaho.gov

**Barbieri, Vito (R, 2A)**
State Capitol Building
P.O. Box 83720
Boise, ID 83720
P: (208) 332-1177
F: (208) 334-5397
E: vbar@house.idaho.gov

**Bedke, Scott (R, 27A)**
State Capitol Building
P.O. Box 83720
Boise, ID 83720
P: (208) 332-1123
F: (208) 334-5397
E: sbedke@house.idaho.gov

**Bell, Maxine T. (R, 25A)**
State Capitol Building
P.O. Box 83720
Boise, ID 83720
P: (208) 334-4734
F: (208) 334-5397
E: mbell@house.idaho.gov

**Blanksma, Megan (R, 23B)***
State Capitol Building
P.O. Box 83720
Boise, ID 83720
P: (208) 332-1054
F: (208) 334-5397
E: mblanksma
   @house.idaho.gov

**Boyle, Judy (R, 9B)**
State Capitol Building
P.O. Box 83720
Boise, ID 83720
P: (208) 332-1064
F: (208) 334-5397
E: jboyle@house.idaho.gov

**Burtenshaw, Van (R, 35A)**
State Capitol Building
P.O. Box 83720
Boise, ID 83720
P: (208) 332-1179
F: (208) 334-5397
E: vburtenshaw
   @house.idaho.gov

**Chaney, Greg (R, 10B)**
State Capitol Building
P.O. Box 83720
Boise, ID 83720
P: (208) 332-1055
F: (208) 334-5397
E: gchaney@house.idaho.gov

**Cheatham, Don (R, 3B)**
State Capitol Building
P.O. Box 83720
Boise, ID 83720
P: (208) 332-1060
F: (208) 334-5397
E: dcheatham
   @house.idaho.gov

**Chew, Sue B. (D, 17B)**
State Capitol Building
P.O. Box 83720
Boise, ID 83720
P: (208) 332-1049
F: (208) 334-5397
E: schew@house.idaho.gov

**Clow, Lance (R, 24A)**
State Capitol Building
P.O. Box 83720
Boise, ID 83720
P: (208) 332-1188
F: (208) 334-5397
E: lclow@house.idaho.gov

**Collins, Gary E. (R, 13B)**
State Capitol Building
P.O. Box 83720
Boise, ID 83720
P: (208) 332-1063
F: (208) 334-5397
E: gcollins@house.idaho.gov

**Crane, Brent (R, 13A)**
State Capitol Building
P.O. Box 83720
Boise, ID 83720
P: (208) 332-1058
F: (208) 334-5397
E: bcrane@house.idaho.gov

**Dayley, Thomas (R, 21B)**
State Capitol Building
P.O. Box 83720
Boise, ID 83720
P: (208) 332-1072
F: (208) 334-5397
E: tdayley@house.idaho.gov

**DeMordaunt, Gayann
(R, 14B)***
State Capitol Building
PO Box 83720
Boise, ID 83720
P: (208) 332-1057
F: (208) 334-5397
E: gdemordaunt
   @house.idaho.gov

**Dixon, Sage (R, 1B)**
State Capitol Building
P.O. Box 83720
Boise, ID 83720
P: (208) 332-1185
F: (302) 334-5397
E: sdixon@house.idaho.gov

**Erpelding, Mat (D, 19A)**
State Capitol Building
P.O. Box 83720
Boise, ID 83720
P: (208) 332-1078
F: (208) 334-5397
E: merpelding
   @house.idaho.gov

**Gannon, John (D, 17A)**
State Capitol Building
P.O. Box 83720
Boise, ID 83720
P: (208) 332-1082
F: (208) 334-5397
E: jgannon@house.idaho.gov

**Gestrin, Terry (R, 8A)**
State Capitol Building
P.O. Box 83720
Boise, ID 83720
P: (208) 332-1124
F: (208) 334-5397
E: tgestrin@house.idaho.gov

**Gibbs, Marc (R, 32A)**
State Capitol Building
P.O. Box 83720
Boise, ID 83720
P: (208) 332-1042
F: (208) 334-5397
E: mgibbs@house.idaho.gov

**Giddings, Priscilla
(R, 7A)***
State Capitol Building
P.O. Box 83720
Boise, ID 83720
P: (208) 332-1033
F: (208) 334-5397
E: pgiddings
   @house.idaho.gov

**Hanks, Karey (R, 35B)***
State Capitol Building
P.O. Box 83720
Boise, ID 83720
P: (208) 332-1056
F: (208) 334-5397
E: khanks@house.idaho.gov

**Harris, Steven (R, 21A)**
State Capitol Building
P.O. Box 83720
Boise, ID 83720
P: (208) 332-1043
F: (208) 334-5397
E: sharris@house.idaho.gov

**Hartgen, Stephen (R, 24B)**
State Capitol Building
P.O. Box 83720
Boise, ID 83720
P: (208) 332-1061
F: (208) 334-5397
E: shartgen@house.idaho.gov

**Hixon, Brandon (R, 10A)**
State Capitol Building
P.O. Box 83720
Boise, ID 83720
P: (208) 332-1052
F: (208) 334-5397
E: bhixon@house.idaho.gov

**Holtzclaw, James (R, 20B)**
State Capitol Building
P.O. Box 83720
Boise, ID 83720
P: (208) 332-1041
F: (208) 334-5397
E: jholtzclaw
   @house.idaho.gov

**Horman, Wendy (R, 30B)**
State Capitol Building
P.O. Box 83720
Boise, ID 83720
P: (208) 332-1071
F: (208) 334-5397
E: WendyHorman
   @house.idaho.gov

**Jordan, Paulette E. (D, 5A)**
State Capitol Building
P.O. Box 83720
Boise, ID 83720
P: (208) 332-1175
F: (208) 334-5397
E: pjordan@house.idaho.gov

**Kauffman, Clark (R, 25B)**
State Capitol Building
P.O. Box 83720
Boise, ID 83720
P: (208) 332-1182
F: (208) 332-5397
E: ckauffman
   @house.idaho.gov

**Kerby, Ryan (R, 9A)**
State Capitol Building
P.O. Box 83720
Boise, ID 83720
P: (208) 332-1166
F: (208) 334-5397
E: rkerby@house.idaho.gov

**King, Phylis K. (D, 18B)**
State Capitol Building
P.O. Box 83720
Boise, ID 83720
P: (208) 332-1080
F: (208) 334-5397
E: pking@house.idaho.gov

**Kingsley, Mike (R, 6B)***
State Capitol Building
P.O. Box 83720
Boise, ID 83720
P: (208) 332-1133
F: (208) 334-5397
E: mkingsley
    @house.idaho.gov

**Kloc, Hy (D, 16B)**
State Capitol Building
P.O. Box 83720
Boise, ID 83720
P: (208) 332-1075
F: (208) 334-5397
E: hkloc@house.idaho.gov

**Loertscher, Thomas F.
    (R, 32B)**
State Capitol Building
P.O. Box 83720
Boise, ID 83720
P: (208) 332-1183
F: (208) 334-5397
E: tloertscher
    @house.idaho.gov

**Luker, Lynn M. (R, 15A)**
State Capitol Building
P.O. Box 83720
Boise, ID 83720
P: (208) 332-1039
F: (208) 334-5397
E: lluker@house.idaho.gov

**Malek, Luke (R, 4A)**
State Capitol Building
P.O. Box 83720
Boise, ID 83720
P: (208) 332-1065
F: (208) 334-5397
E: lmalek@house.idaho.gov

**Manwaring, Dustin (R, 29A)***
State Capitol Building
P.O. Box 83720
Boise, ID 83720
P: (208) 332-1079
F: (208) 334-5397
E: dmanwaring
    @house.idaho.gov

**McCrostie, John (D, 16A)**
State Capitol Building
P.O. Box 83720
Boise, ID 83720
P: (208) 332-1083
F: (208) 334-5397
E: jmccrostie
    @house.idaho.gov

**McDonald, Patrick (R, 15A)**
State Capitol Building
P.O. Box 83720
Boise, ID 83720
P: (208) 332-1176
F: (208) 334-5397
E: pmcdonald
    @house.idaho.gov

**Mendive, Ron (R, 3A)**
State Capitol Building
P.O. Box 83720
Boise, ID 83720
P: (208) 332-1040
F: (208) 334-5397
E: rmendive@house.idaho.gov

**Miller, Steven (R, 26A)**
State Capitol Building
P.O. Box 83720
Boise, ID 83720
P: (208) 332-1174
F: (208) 334-5397
E: smiller@house.idaho.gov

**Monks, Jason (R, 22B)**
State Capitol Building
P.O. Box 83720
Boise, ID 83720
P: (208) 332-1036
F: (208) 334-5397
E: jmonks@house.idaho.gov

**Moon, Dorothy (R, 8B)***
State Capitol Building
P.O. Box 83720
Boise, ID 83720
P: (208) 332-1180
F: (208) 334-5397
E: dmoon@house.idaho.gov

**Moyle, Mike (R, 14A)**
State Capitol Building
P.O. Box 83720
Boise, ID 83720
P: (208) 332-1122
F: (208) 334-5397
E: mmoyle@house.idaho.gov

**Nate, Ronald M. (R, 34A)**
State Capitol Building
P.O. Box 83720
Boise, ID 83720
P: (208) 332-1053
F: (208) 334-5397
E: nater@house.idaho.gov

**Packer, Kelley (R, 28B)**
State Capitol Building
P.O. Box 83720
Boise, ID 83720
P: (208) 322-1045
F: (208) 334-5397
E: kpacker@house.idaho.gov

**Palmer, Joe A. (R, 20A)**
State Capitol Building
P.O. Box 83720
Boise, ID 83720
P: (208) 332-1062
F: (208) 334-5397
E: jpalmer@house.idaho.gov

**Perry, Christy (R, 11B)**
State Capitol Building
P.O. Box 83720
Boise, ID 83720
P: (208) 332-1044
F: (208) 334-5397
E: cperry@house.idaho.gov

**Raybould, Dell (R, 34B)**
State Capitol Building
P.O. Box 83720
Boise, ID 83720
P: (208) 332-1173
F: (208) 334-5397
E: draybould
    @house.idaho.gov

**Redman, Eric (R, 2B)**
State Capitol Building
P.O. Box 83720
Boise, ID 83720
P: (208) 332-1070
F: (208) 334-5397
E: eredman@house.idaho.gov

**Rubel, Ilana (D, 18A)**
State Capitol Building
P.O. Box 83720
Boise, ID 83720
P: (208) 332-1034
F: (208) 334-5397
E: irubel@house.idaho.gov

**Scott, Heather (R, 1A)**
State Capitol Building
P.O. Box 83720
Boise, ID 83720
P: (208) 332-1190
F: (208) 334-5397
E: hscott@house.idaho.gov

**Shepherd, Paul E. (R, 7B)**
State Capitol Building
P.O. Box 83720
Boise, ID 83720
P: (208) 332-1067
F: (208) 334-5397
E: pshepherd
    @house.idaho.gov

**Smith, Elaine (D, 29B)**
State Capitol Building
P.O. Box 83720
Boise, ID 83720
P: (208) 332-1031
F: (208) 334-5397
E: esmith@house.idaho.gov

**Stevenson, Thyra (R, 6A)**
State Capitol Building
P.O. Box 83720
Boise, ID 83720
P: (208) 332-1184
F: (208) 334-5397
E: tstevenson
    @house.idaho.gov

**Syme, Scott (R, 11A)***
State Capitol Building
P.O. Box 83720
Boise, ID 83720
P: (208) 332-1047
F: (208) 334-5397
E: ssyme@house.idaho.gov

**Thompson, Jeff (R, 30A)**
State Capitol Building
P.O. Box 83720
Boise, ID 83720
P: (208) 332-1081
F: (208) 334-5397
E: jthompson
    @house.idaho.gov

**Toone, Sally (D, 26B)***
State Capitol Building
P.O. Box 83720
Boise, ID 83720
P: (208) 332-1032
F: (208) 334-5397
E: stoone@house.idaho.gov

**Troy, Caroline (R, 5B)**
State Capitol Building
P.O. Box 83720
Boise, ID 83720
P: (208) 332-1035
F: (208) 334-5397
E: cntroy@house.idaho.gov

**Trujillo, Janet (R, 33A)**
State Capitol Building
P.O. Box 83720
Boise, ID 83720
P: (208) 332-1189
F: (208) 334-5397
E: jtrujillo
    @house.idaho.gov

**Vander Woude, John (R, 22A)**
State Capitol Building
P.O. Box 83720
Boise, ID 83720
P: (208) 332-1037
F: (208) 334-5397
E: jvanderwoude
    @house.idaho.gov

**VanOrden, Julie (R, 31B)**
State Capitol Building
P.O. Box 83720
Boise, ID 83720
P: (208) 332-1038
F: (208) 334-5397
E: jvanorden
    @house.idaho.gov

# Idaho

**Wintrow, Melissa (D, 19B)**
State Capitol Building
P.O. Box 83720
Boise, ID 83720
P: (208) 332-1076
F: (208) 334-5397
E: mwintrow@house.idaho.gov

**Wood, Fred (R, 27B)**
State Capitol Building
P.O. Box 83720
Boise, ID 83720
P: (208) 332-1074
F: (208) 334-5397
E: fwood@house.idaho.gov

**Youngblood, Rick (R, 12B)**
State Capitol Building
P.O. Box 83720
Boise, ID 83720
P: (208) 332-1059
F: (208) 334-5397
E: ryoungblood
    @house.idaho.gov

**Zito, Christy (R, 23A)\***
State Capitol Building
P.O. Box 83720
Boise, ID 83720
P: (208) 332-1181
F: (208) 334-5397
E: czito@house.idaho.gov

**Zollinger, Bryan (R, 33B)\***
State Capitol Building
P.O. Box 83720
Boise, ID 83720
P: (208) 332-1073
F: (208) 334-5397
E: bzollinger
    @house.idaho.gov

# Illinois

## Executive

### Governor
The Honorable Bruce Rauner (R)
Governor
State Capitol
207 Statehouse
Springfield, IL 62706
P: (217) 782-0244
F: (217) 524-4049

### Lieutenant Governor
The Honorable Evelyn Sanguinetti (R)
Lieutenant Governor
214 State House
Springfield, IL 62706
P: (217) 558-3085
F: (217) 558-3086

### Attorney General
The Honorable Lisa Madigan (D)
Attorney General
James R. Thompson Center
100 West Randolph Street
Chicago, IL 60601
P: (312) 814-3000

### Auditor
Mr. Frank J. Mautino (D)
  (appointed by the Legislature)
Auditor General
Iles Park Plaza
740 East Ash Street
Springfield, IL 62703
P: (217) 782-3536
F: (217) 785-8222
E: auditor@mail.state.il.us

### Secretary of State
The Honorable Jesse White (D)
Secretary of State
213 State Capitol
Springfield, IL 62756
P: (217) 782-2201
F: (217) 785-0358
E: jessewhite@ilsos.net

### Treasurer
The Honorable Michael W. Frerichs (D)
State Treasurer
Statehouse
Executive Office 203
Springfield, IL 62706
P: (217) 782-2211
F: (217) 785-2777

## Judiciary

### Supreme Court (PE)
Ms. Carolyn Taft Grosboll
Clerk of the Supreme Court
Supreme Court Building
200 East Capitol
Springfield, IL 62701
P: (217) 782-2035

The Honorable Lloyd A. Karmeier (R)
Chief Justice
The Honorable Anne M. Burke
The Honorable Charles E. Freeman
The Honorable Rita B. Garman
The Honorable Thomas L. Kilbride
The Honorable Mary Jane Theis
The Honorable Robert R. Thomas

## Legislative

## Senate

### Senate President
Senator John J. Cullerton (D)
President of the Senate
327 Capitol Building
Springfield, IL 62706
P: (217) 782-2728
F: (217) 782-3242
E: john @senatorcullerton.com

### President Pro Tempore of the Senate
Senator Don Harmon (D)
Senate President Pro Tempore
329B Capitol Building
Springfield, IL 62706
P: (217) 782-8176
F: (217) 558-6013
E: info@donharmon.org

### Senate Majority Leader
Senator James F. Clayborne Jr. (D)
Senate Majority Leader
329A Capitol Building
Springfield, IL 62706
P: (217) 782-5399
F: (217) 558-6013
E: jclaybourne @senatedem.ilga.gov

### Senate Minority Leader
Senator Christine Radogno (R)
Senate Minority Leader
309G Capitol Building
Springfield, IL 62706
P: (217) 782-7730
F: (217) 782-7818
E: cradogno@sbcglobal.net

### Secretary of the Senate
Mr. Tim Anderson
Secretary of the Senate
Room 401, Capitol Building
Springfield, IL 62706
P: (217) 782-5715

### Members of the Senate
Althoff, Pamela J. (R, 32)
309L Capitol Building
Springfield, IL 62706
P: (217) 782-8000
F: (217) 782-9586
E: pamela@pamelaalthoff.net

Anderson, Neil (R, 36)
105-C State House
Springfield, IL 62706
P: (217) 782-5957
F: (217) 782-0116
E: senatorneilanderson @gmail.com

Aquino, Omar (D, 2)
M120 Capitol Building
Springfield, IL 62706
P: (217) 782-5652
E: Aquino.senate2il @gmail.com

Barickman, Jason (R, 53)
M103-C Capitol Building
Springfield, IL 62706
P: (217) 782-6597
E: jason@jasonbarickman.org

Bennett, Scott M. (D, 52)
218B Capitol Building
Springfield, IL 62706
P: (217) 782-2507

Bertino-Tarrant, Jennifer (D, 49)
119B Capitol Building
Springfield, IL 62706
P: (217) 782-0052

Biss, Daniel (D, 9)
M121 Capitol Building
Springfield, IL 62706
P: (217) 782-2119
E: daniel@danielbiss.com

Bivins, Tim (R, 45)
M103A Capitol Building
Springfield, IL 62706
P: (217) 782-0180
F: (217) 782-9586
E: senatorbivins@grics.net

Brady, Bill (R, 44)
103A Capitol Building
Springfield, IL 62706
P: (217) 782-6216
F: (217) 782-0116
E: billbrady @senatorbillbrady.com

Bush, Melinda (D, 31)
M120 Capitol Building
Springfield, IL 62706
P: (217) 782-7353
F: (218) 782-2115
E: Melinda @senatormelindabush.com

Castro, Cristina (D, 22)*
M121 Capitol Building
Springfield, IL 62706
P: (217) 782-7746

Clayborne Jr., James F. (D, 57)
329A Capitol Building
Springfield, IL 62706
P: (217) 782-5399
F: (217) 558-6013
E: jclaybourne @senatedem.ilga.gov

Collins, Jacqueline Y. (D, 16)
M114 Capitol Building
Springfield, IL 62706
P: (217) 782-1607
F: (217) 782-2115
E: jcollins @senatedem.ilga.gov

Connelly, Michael G. (R, 21)
309 I Capitol Building
Springfield, IL 62706
P: (217) 782-8192
F: (217) 782-9586
E: senatorconnelly21 @gmail.com

# Illinois

**Cullerton, John J. (D, 6)**
327 Capitol Building
Springfield, IL 62706
P: (217) 782-2728
F: (217) 782-3242
E: john
@senatorcullerton.com

**Cullerton, Thomas (D, 23)**
122 Capitol Building
Springfield, IL 62706
P: (217) 782-9463
E: tom
@senatormcullerton.com

**Cunningham, William (D, 18)**
M115 Capitol Building
Springfield, IL 62706
P: (217) 782-5145
F: (217) 782-2115
E: staterepbillcunningham
@gmail.com

**Fowler, Dale (R, 59)***
Capitol Building
Springfield, IL 62706
P: (217) 782-5509

**Haine, William R. (D, 56)**
311C Capitol Building
Springfield, IL 62706
P: (217) 782-5247
F: (217) 782-8287
E: whaine
@senatedem.ilga.gov

**Harmon, Don (D, 39)**
329B Capitol Building
Springfield, IL 62706
P: (217) 782-8176
F: (217) 558-6013
E: info@donharmon.org

**Harris III, Napoleon
(D, 15)**
M122 Capitol Building
Springfield, IL 62706
P: (217) 782-8066

**Hastings, Michael (D, 19)**
118 Capitol Building
Springfield, IL 62706
P: (217) 782-9595

**Holmes, Linda (D, 42)**
129 Capitol Building
Springfield, IL 62706
P: (217) 782-0422
F: (217) 782-2115
E: info
@lindaholmesforsenate.com

**Hunter, Mattie (D, 3)**
619 Capitol Building
Springfield, IL 62706
P: (217) 782-5966
F: (217) 782-1631
E: mhunter
@senatedem.ilga.gov

**Hutchinson, Toi W. (D, 40)**
121C Capitol Building
Springfield, IL 62706
P: (217) 782-7419
F: (217) 557-3930
E: hutchinson
@senatedem.ilga.gov

**Jones III, Emil (D, 14)**
121D Capitol Building
Springfield, IL 62706
P: (217) 782-9573
F: (217) 557-3930
E: jones@senatedem.ilga.gov

**Koehler, David (D, 46)**
M113 Capitol Building
Springfield, IL 62706
P: (217) 782-8250
F: (217) 782-2115
E: dkoehler
@senatedem.ilga.gov

**Landek, Steven M. (D, 12)**
113 Capitol Building
Springfield, IL 62706
P: (217) 782-0054
F: (217) 782-2331
E: SenatorLandek@gmail.com

**Lightford, Kimberly A.
(D, 4)**
323B Capitol Building
Springfield, IL 62706
P: (217) 782-8505
F: (217) 558-2068
E: klightford
@senatedem.ilga.gov

**Link, Terry (D, 30)**
321 Capitol Building
Springfield, IL 62706
P: (217) 782-8181
F: (217) 782-4450
E: senator@link30.org

**Manar, Andy (D, 48)**
119A Capitol Building
Springfield, IL 62706
P: (217) 782-0228
E: amanar
@senatedem.ilga.gov

**Martinez, Iris Y. (D, 20)**
413 Capitol Building
Springfield, IL 62706
P: (217) 782-8191
F: (217) 782-3088
E: ilsenate20@sbcglobal.net

**McCann, Wm. Sam (R, 50)**
108E Capitol Building
Springfield, IL 62706
P: (217) 782-8206
F: (217) 782-0116
E: senatorsam@frontier.com

**McCarter, Kyle (R, 54)**
103C Capitol Building
Springfield, IL 62706
P: (217) 782-5755
F: (217) 782-0116

**McConchie, Daniel (R, 26)**
108B Capitol Building
Springfield, IL 62706
P: (217) 782-8010
E: dan@danmcconchie.com

**McConnaughay, Karen (R, 33)**
103-D Capitol Building
Springfield, IL 62706
P: (217) 782-1977
E: senator
@karenmcconnaughay.com

**McGuire, Pat (D, 43)**
417C Capitol Building
Springfield, IL 62706
P: (217) 782-8800
F: (217) 558-6006
E: pmcguire
@senatedem.ilga.gov

**Morrison, Julie A. (D, 29)**
M108 Capitol Building
Springfield, IL 62706
P: (217) 782-3650
E: ilsenate29@gmail.com

**Mulroe, John G. (D, 10)**
127 Capitol Building
Springfield, IL 62706
P: (217) 782-1035
F: (217) 782-2331
E: senatorjohnmulroe
@att.net

**Munoz, Antonio (D, 1)**
323A Capitol Building
Springfield, IL 62706
P: (217) 782-9415
F: (217) 558-1042
E: munoz@senatedem.ilga.gov

**Murphy, Laura M. (D, 28)**
124 Capitol Building
Springfield, IL 62706
P: (217) 782-3875
F: (217) 558-6006
E: info
@lauramurphy4senate.com

**Nybo, Chris (R, 24)**
105-B Capitol Building
Springfield, IL 62706
P: (217) 782-8148
F: (217) 782-0116
E: chris@chrisnybo.org

**Oberweis, Jim (R, 25)**
105A Capitol Building
Springfield, IL 62706
P: (217) 782-0471
F: (217) 782-0116
E: senatoroberweis
@gmail.com

**Radogno, Christine (R, 41)**
309G Capitol Building
Springfield, IL 62706
P: (217) 782-7730
F: (217) 782-7818
E: cradogno@sbcglobal.net

**Raoul, Kwame (D, 13)**
123 Capitol Building
Springfield, IL 62706
P: (217) 782-5338
F: (217) 558-6006
E: kraoul
@senatedem.ilga.gov

**Rezin, Sue (R, 38)**
309J Capitol Building
Springfield, IL 62706
P: (217) 782-3840
F: (217) 782-0116
E: senatorrezin@gmail.com

**Righter, Dale A. (R, 55)**
309M Capitol Building
Springfield, IL 62706
P: (217) 782-6674
F: (217) 782-7818
E: drighter
@consolidated.net

**Rooney, Tom (R, 27)**
309H Capitol Building
Springfield, IL 62706
P: (217) 782-4471
F: (217) 782-7818

**Rose, Chapin (R, 51)**
M103F Capitol Building
Springfield, IL 62706
P: (217) 558-1006
E: senatorchapinrose
@gmail.com

**Sandoval, Martin A. (D, 11)**
111 Capitol Building
Springfield, IL 62706
P: (217) 782-5304
F: (217) 558-6006
E: msandoval
@senatedem.ilga.gov

**Schimpf, Paul (R, 58)***
105 D Capitol Building
Springfield, IL 62706
P: (217) 782-8137

**Silverstein, Ira I. (D, 8)**
121B Capitol Building
Springfield, IL 62706
P: (217) 782-5500
F: (217) 782-5340
E: isilverstein
@senatedem.ilga.gov

**Stadelman, Steve (D, 34)**
121A Capitol Building
Springfield, IL 62706
P: (217) 782-8022
E: steve
@senatorstadelman.com

**Steans, Heather (D, 7)**
122 Capitol Building
Springfield, IL 62706
P: (217) 782-8492
F: (217) 782-2115
E: hsteans
@senatedem.ilga.gov

**Syverson, Dave (R, 35)**
108A Capitol Building
Springfield, IL 62706
P: (217) 782-5413
F: (217) 782-9586
E: info
@senatordavesyverson.com

**Tracy, Jil (R, 47)**
M103-A Capitol Building
Springfield, IL 62706
P: (217) 782-3613
F: (217) 558-3055
E: jiltracy@jiltracy.com

**Trotter, Donne E. (D, 17)**
627 Capitol Building
Springfield, IL 62706
P: (217) 782-3201
F: (217) 782-8201
E: dtrotter
@senatedem.ilga.gov

**Van Pelt, Patricia (D, 5)**
218A Capitol Building
Springfield, IL 62706
P: (217) 782-6252

**Weaver, Chuck (R, 37)**
M103D Capitol Building
Springfield, IL 62706
P: (217) 782-1942
F: (217) 782-9586
E: chuck@senweaver.com

# House
## Speaker of the House
**Speaker Michael J. Madigan (D)**
Speaker of the House
300 Capitol Building
Springfield, IL 62706
P: (217) 782-5350
F: (217) 524-1794
E: mmadigan@hds.ilga.gov

## House Majority Leader
**Representative Barbara F. Currie (D)**
House Majority Leader
300 Capitol Building
Springfield, IL 62706
P: (217) 782-8121
F: (217) 524-1794

## House Minority Leader
**Representative Jim B. Durkin (R)**
House Minority Leader
316 Capitol Building
Springfield, IL 62706
P: (217) 782-0494
F: (217) 782-7012
E: repdurkin@hotmail.com

## Clerk of the House
**Mr. Tim Mapes**
Clerk of the House/Chief of
Staff To the Speaker
300 State House
Springfield, IL 62706
P: (217) 782-6360

## Members of the House
**Ammons, Carol (D, 103)**
240A-W Stratton Office
Building
Springfield, IL 62706
P: (217) 558-1009
E: assistance
@staterepcarolammons.com

**Andersson, Steven (R, 65)**
211-N Stratton Office Building
Springfield, IL 62706
P: (217) 782-5457
E: steve@staterep65.com

**Andrade Jr., Jaime M. (D, 40)**
260-W Stratton Office Building
Springfield, IL 62706
P: (217) 782-8117
F: (217) 558-4551
E: staterep40@gmail.com

**Arroyo, Luis (D, 3)**
109 Capitol Building
Springfield, IL 62706
P: (217) 782-0480
F: (217) 557-9609
E: RepDistrict3@gmail.com

**Batinick, Mark (R, 97)**
200-8N Stratton Office Building
Springfield, IL 62706
P: (217) 782-1331
E: repbatinick@gmail.com

**Beiser, Daniel V. (D, 111)**
263-S Stratton Office Building
Springfield, IL 62706
P: (217) 782-5996
F: (217) 558-0493
E: dvbeiser@sbcglobal.net

**Bellock, Patricia R. (R, 47)**
217-N Stratton Office Building
Springfield, IL 62706
P: (217) 782-1448
F: (217) 782-2289
E: rep@pbellock.com

**Bennett, Thomas (R, 106)**
220-N Stratton Office Building
Springfield, IL 62706
P: (217) 558-1039
E: tom@tom4illinois.com

**Bourne, Avery (R, 95)**
227-N Stratton Office Building
Springfield, IL 62706
P: (217) 782-8071
F: (217) 782-1336
E: bourne@ilhousegop.org

**Brady, Dan (R, 105)**
314 Capitol Building
Springfield, IL 62706
P: (217) 782-1118
F: (217) 558-6271
E: dan@rep-danbrady.com

**Breen, Peter (R, 48)**
210-N Stratton Office Building
Springfield, IL 62706
P: (217) 782-8037
E: info@votebreen.com

**Bryant, Terri (R, 115)**
207-N Stratton Office Building
Springfield, IL 62706
P: (217) 782-0387
E: stateprterribryant
@gmail.com

**Burke, Daniel J. (D, 1)**
109 Capitol Building
Springfield, IL 62706
P: (217) 782-1117
F: (217) 782-0927
E: burkedj2@ilga.gov

**Burke, Kelly (D, 36)**
246-W Stratton Office Building
Springfield, IL 62706
P: (217) 782-0515
F: (217) 558-4553
E: kburke
@kellyburkerep36.org

**Butler, Tim (R, 87)**
1128-E Stratton Office Building
Springfield, IL 62706
P: (217) 782-0053
F: (217) 782-0897
E: butler@ilhousegop.org

**Cabello, John (R, 68)**
632 Capitol Building
Springfield, IL 62706
P: (217) 782-0455
F: (217) 782-1141
E: cabello@ilhouse.gop

**Cassidy, Kelly M. (D, 14)**
271-S Stratton Office Building
Springfield, IL 62706
P: (217) 782-8088
F: (217) 782-6592
E: repcassidy@gmail.com

**Cavaletto, John (R, 107)**
205-N Stratton Office Building
Springfield, IL 62706
P: (217) 782-0066
F: (217) 782-1336
E: john@johncavaletto.com

**Chapa LaVia, Linda (D, 83)**
233-E Stratton Office Building
Springfield, IL 62706
P: (217) 558-1002
F: (217) 782-0927
E: chapa-laviali@ilga.gov

**Conroy, Deborah (D, 46)**
275-W Stratton Office Building
Springfield, IL 62706
P: (217) 782-8158
E: repdebconroy@gmail.com

**Conyears-Ervin, Melissa (D, 10)***
252-W Stratton Office Building
Springfield, IL 62706
P: (217) 782-8077
E: rep@conyearservin.com

# Illinois

**Costello, Jerry F. (D, 116)**
200-7S Stratton Office Building
Springfield, IL 62706
P: (217) 782-1018
F: (217) 558-4502
E: staterepcostello
@gmail.com

**Crespo, Fred (D, 44)**
245-E Stratton Office Building
Springfield, IL 62706
P: (217) 782-0347
F: (217) 557-4622
E: repfredcrespo@um.att.com

**Currie, Barbara F. (D, 25)**
300 Capitol Building
Springfield, IL 62706
P: (217) 782-8121
F: (217) 524-1794

**D'Amico, John (D, 15)**
279-S Stratton Office Building
Springfield, IL 62706
P: (217) 782-8198
F: (217) 782-2906
E: johnd@ilga.gov

**Davidsmeyer, C.D. (R, 100)**
201-N Stratton Office Building
Springfield, IL 62706
P: (217) 782-1840
F: (217) 558-3743
E: repcddavidsmeyer
@gmail.com

**Davis, William (D, 30)**
254-W Stratton Building
Springfield, IL 62706
P: (217) 782-8197
F: (217) 782-3220

**DeLuca, Anthony (D, 80)**
271-S Stratton Office Building
Springfield, IL 62706
P: (217) 782-1719
F: (217) 558-4944
E: repdeluca@sbcglobal.net

**Demmer, Tom (R, 90)**
314 Capitol Building
Springfield, IL 62706
P: (217) 782-0535
E: demmer@ilhousegop.org

**Drury, Scott (D, 58)**
292-S Stratton Office Building
Springfield, IL 62706
P: (217) 782-0902
E: repdrury@gmail.com

**Durkin, Jim B. (R, 82)**
316 Capitol Building
Springfield, IL 62706
P: (217) 782-0494
F: (217) 782-7012
E: repdurkin@hotmail.com

**Evans Jr., Marcus C.
(D, 33)**
268-S Stratton Office Building
Springfield, IL 62706
P: (217) 782-8272
F: (217) 782-2404
E: repevans33@gmail.com

**Feigenholtz, Sara (D, 12)**
300 Capitol Building
Springfield, IL 62706
P: (217) 782-8062
F: (217) 557-7203
E: sara@staterepsara.com

**Fine, Laura (D, 17)**
247-E Stratton Office Building
Springfield, IL 62706
P: (217) 782-4194
F: (217) 524-0449
E: repfine@gmail.com

**Flowers, Mary E. (D, 31)**
251-E Stratton Office Building
Springfield, IL 62706
P: (217) 782-4207
F: (217) 782-1130
E: maryeflowers@ilga.gov

**Ford, La Shawn K. (D, 8)**
239-E Stratton Office Building
Springfield, IL 62706
P: (217) 782-5962
F: (217) 557-4502
E: repford@lashawnford.com

**Fortner, Mike (R, 49)**
200-4N Stratton Office Building
Springfield, IL 62706
P: (217) 782-1653
F: (217) 282-1275
E: mike.fortner
@sbcglobal.net

**Frese, Randy (R, 94)**
225-N Stratton Office Building
Springfield, IL 62706
P: (217) 782-8096
E: repfrese@adams.net

**Gabel, Robyn (D, 18)**
248-W Stratton Office Building
Springfield, IL 62706
P: (217) 782-8052
F: (217) 558-4553
E: staterepgabel
@robyngabel.com

**Gordon-Booth, Jehan (D, 92)**
200-8S Stratton Office Building
Springfield, IL 62706
P: (217) 782-3186
F: (217) 558-4552
E: repjgordon@gmail.com

**Greenwood, LaToya (D, 114)\***
265-S Stratton Office Building
Springfield, IL 62706
P: (217) 782-5951
E: staterepgreenwood
@gmail.com

**Guzzardi, Will (D, 39)**
284-S Stratton Office Building
Springfield, IL 62706
P: (217) 558-1032
E: will@repguzzardi.com

**Halbrook, Brad E. (R, 110)**
204-N Stratton Office Building
Springfield, IL 62706
P: (217) 558-1040
F: (217) 558-3481
E: staterephalbrook
@gmail.com

**Halpin, Michael (D, 72)\***
242A-W Stratton Office
Building
Springfield, IL 62706
P: (217) 782-5970
E: RepHalpin@gmail.com

**Hammond, Norine (R, 93)**
203-N Stratton Office Building
Springfield, IL 62706
P: (217) 782-0416
F: (217) 557-4530
E: rephammond@macomb.com

**Harper, Sonya Marie (D, 6)**
276-S Stratton Office Building
Springfield, IL 62706
P: (217) 782-5971
F: (217) 558-6370
E: repsonyaharper@gmail.com

**Harris, David (R, 53)**
221-N Stratton Office Building
Springfield, IL 62706
P: (217) 782-3739
E: repharris@yahoo.com

**Harris, Greg (D, 13)**
253-S Stratton Office Building
Springfield, IL 62706
P: (217) 782-3835
F: (217) 557-6470
E: greg@gregharris.org

**Hays, Chad (R, 104)**
202-N Stratton Office Building
Springfield, IL 62706
P: (217) 782-4811

**Hernandez, Elizabeth
(D, 24)**
229-E Stratton Office Building
Springfield, IL 62706
P: (217) 782-8173
F: (217) 558-1844
E: repehernandez@yahoo.com

**Hoffman, Jay C. (D, 113)**
261-S Stratton Office Building
Springfield, IL 62706
P: (217) 782-0104
E: repjayhoffman@gmail.com

**Hurley, Frances Ann (D, 35)**
281-S Stratton Office Building
Springfield, IL 62706
P: (217) 782-8200
E: repfranhurley@gmail.com

**Ives, Jeanne (R, 42)**
218-N Stratton Office Building
Springfield, IL 62706
P: (217) 558-1037
F: (217) 782-1275
E: ives@jeanneives.org

**Jesiel, Sheri (R, 61)**
223-N State Office Buiding
Springfield, IL 62706
P: (217) 782-8151
F: (217) 557-7207
E: jesiel@ilhousegop.org

**Jimenez, Sara Wojcicki
(R, 99)**
E-1 Stratton Office Building
Springfield, IL 62706
P: (217) 782-0044
F: (217) 782-0897
E: sjimenez@ilhousegop.org

**Jones, Thaddeus (D, 29)**
274-S Stratton Office Building
Springfield, IL 62706
P: (217) 782-8087
F: (217) 558-6433
E: repjones.jones@gmail.com

**Kifowit, Stephanie (D, 84)**
200-1S Stratton Office Building
Springfield, IL 62706
P: (217) 782-8028
E: stephanie.kifowit
@att.net

**Lang, Lou (D, 16)**
300 Capitol Building
Springfield, IL 62706
P: (217) 782-1252
F: (217) 782-9903
E: langli@ilga.gov

**Lilly, Camille Y. (D, 78)**
270-S Stratton Office Building
Springfield, IL 62706
P: (217) 782-6400
F: (217) 558-1054
E: stateplilly@yahoo.com

**Long, Jerry (R, 76)\***
210A-W Stratton Office
Building
Springfield, IL 62706
P: (217) 782-0140

**Madigan, Michael J. (D, 22)**
300 Capitol Building
Springfield, IL 62706
P: (217) 782-5350
F: (217) 524-1794
E: mmadigan@hds.ilga.gov

**Mah, Theresa (D, 2)\***
244-W Stratton Office Building
Springfield, IL 62706
P: (217) 782-2855
E: theresa@theresamah.com

**Manley, Natalie (D, 98)**
231-E Stratton Office Building
Springfield, IL 62706
P: (217) 782-3316
E: repmanley@gmail.com

**Martwick, Robert (D, 19)**
290-S Stratton Office Building
Springfield, IL 62706
P: (217) 782-8400
E: repmartwick@gmail.com

**Mayfield, Rita (D, 60)**
278-S Stratton Office Building
Springfield, IL 62706
P: (217) 558-1012
F: (217) 558-1092
E: 60thdistrict@gmail.com

**McAsey, Emily (D, 85)**
259-S Stratton Office Building
Springfield, IL 62706
P: (217) 782-4179
F: (217) 557-7204
E: repemily@gmail.com

**McAuliffe, Michael P.
  (R, 20)**
219-N Stratton Office Building
Springfield, IL 62706
P: (217) 782-8182
F: (217) 558-1073
E: mmcauliffe20@yahoo.com

**McCombie, Tony (R, 71)\***
205A-N Stratton Office
Building
Springfield, IL 62706
P: (217) 782-3992
E: McCombie@ilhousegop.gov

**McDermed, Margo (R, 37)**
209-N Stratton Office Building
Springfield, IL 62706
P: (217) 782-0424
E: mcdermed@ilhousegop.org

**McSweeney, David (R, 52)**
226-N Stratton Office Building
Springfield, IL 62706
P: (217) 782-1517
E: mcsweeney@ilhousegop.org

**Meier, Charles E. (R, 108)**
200-7N Stratton Office Building
Springfield, IL 62706
P: (217) 782-6401
E: repcmeier@gmail.com

**Mitchell, Bill (R, 101)**
632 Capitol Building
Springfield, IL 62706
P: (217) 782-8163
F: (217) 557-0571
E: repmitchell
  @earthlink.net

**Mitchell, Christian (D, 26)**
256-W Stratton Office Building
Springfield, IL 62706
P: (217) 782-2023
F: (217) 558-1092
E: MitchellDistrict26
  @att.net

**Moeller, Anna (D, 43)**
235-E Stratton Office Building
Springfield, IL 62706
P: (217) 782-8020
F: (217) 557-4459
E: staterepmoeller
  @gmail.com

**Morrison, Thomas (R, 54)**
234-N Stratton Office Building
Springfield, IL 62706
P: (217) 782-8026
F: (217) 558-7016
E: Repmorrison54@gmail.com

**Moylan, Martin (D, 55)**
200-3S Stratton Office Building
Springfield, IL 62706
P: (217) 782-8007
E: staterepmoylan@gmail.com

**Mussman, Michelle (D, 56)**
257-S Stratton Office Building
Springfield, IL 62706
P: (217) 782-3725
F: (217) 557-6271
E: staterepmussman
  @gmail.com

**Nekritz, Elaine (D, 57)**
241-E Stratton Office Building
Springfield, IL 62706
P: (217) 558-1004
F: (217) 558-4554
E: enekritz@repnekritz.org

**Olsen, David (R, 81)**
632 Capitol Building
Springfield, IL 62706
P: (217) 782-6578
E: olsen@ilhousegop.org

**Parkhurst, Lindsay (R, 79)\***
232-N Stratton Office Building
Springfield, IL 62706
P: (217) 782-5981

**Phelps, Brandon W. (D, 118)**
200-9S Stratton Office Building
Springfield, IL 62706
P: (217) 782-5131
F: (217) 557-0521
E: bphelps118@gmail.com

**Phillips, Reginald (R, 110)**
200-1N Stratton Office Building
Springfield, IL 62706
P: (217) 558-1040

**Pritchard, Robert W.
  (R, 70)**
200-3N Stratton Office Building
Springfield, IL 62706
P: (217) 782-0425
F: (217) 782-1275
E: bob
  @pritchardstaterep.com

**Reick, Steven (R, 63)\***
230-N Stratton Office Building
Springfield, IL 62706
P: (217) 782-1717

**Reis, David (R, 109)**
632 Capitol Building
Springfield, IL 62706
P: (217) 782-2087
F: (217) 557-0571
E: david@davidreis.org

**Riley, Al (D, 38)**
262-W Stratton Office Building
Springfield, IL 62706
P: (217) 558-1007
F: (217) 557-1664
E: rep.riley38
  @sbcglobal.net

**Rita, Robert (D, 28)**
267-S Stratton Office Building
Springfield, IL 62706
P: (217) 558-1000
F: (217) 558-1091

**Sauer, Nick (R, 51)\***
242-W Stratton Office Building
Springfield, IL 62706
P: (217) 782-3696
E: sauer@ilhousegop.org

**Scherer, Sue (D, 96)**
E-2 Stratton Office Building
Springfield, IL 62706
P: (217) 524-0353
F: (217) 524-0354
E: staterepsue@gmail.com

**Sente, Carol (D, 59)**
272-S Stratton Office Building
Springfield, IL 62706
P: (217) 782-0499
F: (217) 524-0443
E: repsente@gmail.com

**Severin, Dave (R, 117)\***
208-N Stratton Office Building
Springfield, IL 62706
P: (217) 782-1051

**Sims Jr., Elgie R. (D, 34)**
275-S Stratton Office Building
Springfield, IL 62706
P: (217) 782-6476
F: (217) 782-0952
E: Info@RepElgieSims34.com

**Skillicorn, Allen (R, 66)\***
222-N Stratton Office Building
Springfield, IL 62706
P: (217) 782-0432
E: skillicorn
  @ilhousegop.org

**Slaughter, Justin (D, 27)\***
266-S Stratton Office Building
Springfield, IL 62706
P: (217) 782-0010
E: slaughterj@ilga.gov

**Sommer, Keith P. (R, 88)**
216-N Stratton Office Building
Springfield, IL 62706
P: (217) 782-0221
F: (217) 557-1098
E: sommer@mtco.com

**Sosnowski, Joe (R, 69)**
200-2N Stratton Office Building
Springfield, IL 62706
P: (217) 782-0548
F: (217) 782-1141
E: repsosnowski@gmail.com

**Soto, Cynthia (D, 4)**
288-S Stratton Office Building
Springfield, IL 62706
P: (217) 782-0150
F: (217) 557-7210
E: 4repsoto@gmail.com

**Spain, Ryan (R, 73)\***
228-N Stratton Office Building
Springfield, IL 62706
P: (217) 782-8108

**Stewart, Brian W. (R, 89)**
228-N Stratton Office Building
Springfield, IL 62706
P: (217) 782-8186
F: (217) 558-7016
E: repstewart@gmail.com

**Stratton, Juliana (D, 5)\***
258-W Stratton Office Building
Springfield, IL 62706
P: (217) 782-4535
E: repstratton5@gmail.com

# Illinois

**Stuart, Katie (D, 112)***
250-W Stratton Office Building
Springfield, IL 62706
P: (217) 782-8018
E: katie.
    stuart.district112
    @gmail.com

**Swanson, Daniel (R, 74)***
240-W Stratton Office Building
Springfield, IL 62706
P: (217) 782-8032
E: danswanson74@gmail.com

**Tabares, Silvana (D, 21)**
247-E Stratton Office Building
Springfield, IL 62706
P: (217) 782-7752
F: (217) 524-0450
E: rep.tabares@gmail.com

**Thapedi, Andre (D, 32)**
249-E Stratton Office Building
Springfield, IL 62706
P: (217) 782-1702
F: (217) 557-0543
E: illinois32district
    @gmail.com

**Turner, Arthur L. (D, 9)**
109 Capitol Building
Springfield, IL 62706
P: (217) 782-8116
F: (217) 782-0888
E: arthurt@ilga.gov

**Unes, Michael (R, 91)**
224-N Stratton Office Building
Springfield, IL 62706
P: (217) 782-8152
F: (217) 782-1275
E: repunes@gmail.com

**Wallace, Litesa (D, 67)**
280-S Stratton Office Building
Springfield, IL 62706
P: (217) 782-3167
F: (217) 557-7654
E: litesa
    @staterepwallace.com

**Walsh Jr., Lawrence M.
(D, 86)**
269-S Stratton Office Building
Springfield, IL 62706
P: (217) 782-8090
E: statereplarrywalshjr
    @gmail.com

**Wehrli, Grant (R, 41)**
228-N Stratton Office Building
Springfield, IL 62706
P: (217) 782-6507
E: 41districtdirector
    @gmail.com

**Welch, Emanuel Chris (D, 7)**
200-5S Stratton Office Building
Springfield, IL 62706
P: (217) 782-8120
E: repwelch
    @emanuelchriswelch.com

**Welter, David (R, 75)**
214-N Stratton Office Building
Springfield, IL 62706
P: (217) 782-5997
E: welter@ilhousegop.org

**Wheeler, Barbara (R, 64)**
314 Capitol Building
Springfield, IL 62706
P: (217) 782-1664
F: (217) 782-1275
E: wheeler@ilhousegop.org

**Wheeler, Keith (R, 50)**
200-5N Stratton Office Building
Springfield, IL 62706
P: (217) 782-1486
E: office
    @repkeithwheeler.org

**Williams, Ann (D, 11)**
273-S Stratton Office Building
Springfield, IL 62706
P: (217) 782-2458
F: (217) 557-7214
E: ann@repannwilliams.com

**Willis, Kathleen (D, 77)**
264-S Stratton Office Building
Springfield, IL 62706
P: (217) 782-3374
E: repwillis77@gmail.com

**Winger,
Christine Jennifer (R, 45)**
206-N Stratton Office Building
Springfield, IL 62706
P: (217) 782-4014
E: winger@ilhousegop.org

**Yingling, Sam (D, 62)**
237-E Stratton Office Building
Springfield, IL 62706
P: (217) 782-7320
E: repsamyingling@gmail.com

**Zalewski, Michael J.
(D, 23)**
243-E Stratton Office Building
Springfield, IL 62706
P: (217) 782-5280
F: (217) 524-0449
E: repzalewski@gmail.com

# Indiana

## Executive

### Governor

**The Honorable Eric Holcomb (R)**
Governor
State Capitol, Room 206
Indianapolis, IN 46204
P: (317) 232-4567
F: (317) 232-43443

### Lieutenant Governor

**The Honorable Suzanne Crouch (R)**
Lieutenant Governor
State House, Room 240
200 West Washington Street
Indianapolis, IN 46204
P: (317) 232-3300
F: (317) 234-1916

### Attorney General

**The Honorable Curtis Hill (R)**
Attorney General
302 West Washington Street
Indianapolis, IN 46204
P: (317) 232-6201
E: chill@in.gov

### Auditor

**Mr. Paul D. Joyce**
State Examiner
200 West Washington Street
Room E-418
Indianapolis, IN 46204
P: (317) 232-2524
F: (317) 232-4711

**Ms. Tera Klutz**
State Auditor
200 West Washington Street
Suite 240
Indianapolis, IN 46204
P: (317) 232-3300
E: comments@auditor.in.gov

### Secretary of State

**The Honorable Connie Lawson (R)**
Secretary of State
201 State House
Indianapolis, IN 46204
P: (317) 232-6536
F: (317) 233-3283
E: sos@sos.in.gov

## Superintendent of Public Instruction

**The Honorable Jennifer McCormick (R)**
Superintendent of Public
Instruction
151 West Ohio Street
Indianapolis, IN 46204
P: (317) 232-6613
F: (317) 232-8004
E: superintendent
@doe.in.gov

## Treasurer

**The Honorable Kelly Mitchell (R)**
State Treasurer
242 State House
Indianapolis, IN 46204
P: (317) 232-6386
F: (317) 233-1780

## Judiciary

### Supreme Court (MR)

**Mr. Kevin Smith**
Clerk/Administrator
200 West Washington Street
315 State House
Indianapolis, IN 46204
P: (317) 232-2540
F: (317) 232-8372
E: Kevin.Smith
@courts.in.gov

**The Honorable Loretta H. Rush**
Chief Justice
**The Honorable Steven H. David**
**The Honorable Mark Massa**
**The Honorable Robert D. Rucker**
**The Honorable Geoffrey Slaughter**

## President Pro Tempore of the Senate

**Senator David C. Long (R)**
President Pro Tempore
Indiana State Capitol
200 West Washington Street
Indianapolis, IN 46204
P: (317) 232-9416
E: senator.long@iga.in.gov

## Senate Minority Leader

**Senator Tim Lanane (D)**
Senate Minority Floor Leader
Indiana State Capitol
200 West Washington Street
Indianapolis, IN 46204
P: (317) 232-9427
F: (317) 233-4275
E: senator.lanane
@iga.in.gov

## Secretary of the Senate

**Ms. Jennifer Mertz**
Principal Secretary of the Senate
200 West Washington Street
Room 3A-N
Indianapolis, IN 46204
P: (317) 232-9421
E: jmertz@iga.in.gov

## Members of the Senate

**Alting, Ron J. (R, 22)**
Indiana State Capitol
200 West Washington Street
Indianapolis, IN 46204
P: (317) 232-9517
E: senator.alting
@iga.in.gov

**Bassler, Eric (R, 39)**
Indiana State Capitol
200 West Washington Street
Indianapolis, IN 46204
P: (317) 232-9443
E: senator.bassler
@iga.in.gov

**Becker, Vaneta G. (R, 50)**
Indiana State Capitol
200 West Washington Street
Indianapolis, IN 46204
P: (317) 232-9494
E: senator.becker
@iga.in.gov

**Bohacek, Mike (R, 8)***
Indiana State Capitol
200 West Washington Street
Indianapolis, IN 46204
P: (317) 232-9541
E: senator.bohacek
@iga.in.gov

**Boots, Phil (R, 23)**
Indiana State Capitol
200 West Washington Street
Indianapolis, IN 46204
P: (317) 234-9054
E: senator.boots@iga.in.gov

**Bray, Rodric (R, 37)**
Indiana State Capitol
200 West Washington Street
Indianapolis, IN 46204
P: (317) 234-9426
E: senator.bray@iga.in.gov

**Breaux, Jean D. (D, 34)**
Indiana State Capitol
200 West Washington Street
Indianapolis, IN 46204
P: (317) 232-9534
F: (317) 233-4275
E: Senator.Breaux
@iga.in.gov

**Brown, Liz (R, 15)**
Indiana State Capitol
200 West Washington Street
Indianapolis, IN 46204
P: (317) 296-9807
E: senator.brown@iga.in.gov

**Buck, Jim (R, 21)**
Indiana State Capitol
200 West Washington Street
Indianapolis, IN 46204
P: (317) 232-9466
E: senator.buck@iga.in.gov

**Charbonneau, Ed (R, 5)**
Indiana State Senate
200 West Washington Street
Indianapolis, IN 46204
P: (317) 232-9494
E: senator.charbonneau
@iga.in.gov

**Crane, John (R, 24)***
Indiana State Capitol
200 West Washington Street
Indianapolis, IN 46204
P: (317) 232-9984
E: senator.crane@iga.in.gov

**Crider, Michael (R, 28)**
Indiana State Capitol
200 West Washington Street
Indianapolis, IN 46204
P: (317) 234-9054
E: Senator.Crider
@iga.in.gov

**Delph, Mike (R, 29)**
Indiana State Capitol
200 West Washington Street
Indianapolis, IN 46204
P: (317) 232-9541
E: senator.delph@iga.in.gov

**Doriot, Blake (R, 12)***
Indiana State Capitol
200 West Washington Street
Indianapolis, IN 46204
P: (317) 232-9808
E: senator.doriot
@iga.in.gov

# Indiana

**Eckerty, Doug (R, 26)**
Indiana State Capitol
200 West Washington Street
Indianapolis, IN 46204
P: (317) 232-9466
E: senator.eckerty
 @iga.in.gov

**Ford, Jon (R, 38)**
Indiana State Capitol
200 West Washington Street
Indianapolis, IN 46204
P: (317) 234-9443
E: senator.ford@iga.in.gov

**Freeman, Aaron (R, 32)\***
Indiana State Capitol
200 West Washington Street
Indianapolis, IN 46204
P: (317) 232-9490
E: senator.freeman
 @iga.in.gov

**Glick, Susan (R, 13)**
Indiana State Capitol
200 West Washington Street
Indianapolis, IN 46204
P: (317) 232-9493
E: senator.glick@iga.in.gov

**Grooms, Ron (R, 46)**
Indiana State Capitol
200 West Washington Street
Indianapolis, IN 46204
P: (317) 2349425
E: senator.grooms
 @iga.in.gov

**Head, Randall (R, 18)**
Indiana State Capitol
200 West Washington Street
Indianapolis, IN 46204
P: (317) 232-9488
F: (317) 232-9224
E: senator.head@iga.in.gov

**Hershman, Brandt (R, 7)**
Indiana State Capitol
200 West Washington Street
Indianapolis, IN 46204
P: (317) 232-9840
F: (317) 232-9664
E: senator.hershman
 @iga.in.gov

**Holdman, Travis (R, 19)**
Indiana State Capitol
200 West Washington Street
Indianapolis, IN 46204
P: (317) 232-9807
E: senator.holdman
 @iga.in.gov

**Houchin, Erin (R, 47)**
Indiana State Capitol
200 West Washington Street
Indianapolis, IN 46204
P: (317) 296-9814
E: senator.houchin
 @iga.in.gov

**Kenley, Luke (R, 20)**
Indiana State Capitol
200 West Washington Street
Indianapolis, IN 46204
P: (317) 232-9453
E: senator.kenley
 @iga.in.gov

**Koch, Eric (R, 44)**
Indiana State Capitol
200 West Washington Street
Indianapolis, IN 46204
P: (317) 232-9674
E: Senator.Koch@iga.in.gov

**Kruse, Dennis K. (R, 14)**
Indiana State Capitol
200 West Washington Street
Indianapolis, IN 46204
P: (317) 233-0930
E: senator.kruse@iga.in.gov

**Lanane, Tim (D, 25)**
Indiana State Capitol
200 West Washington Street
Indianapolis, IN 46204
P: (317) 232-9427
F: (317) 233-4275
E: senator.lanane
 @iga.in.gov

**Leising, Jean (R, 42)**
Indiana State Capitol
200 West Washington Street
Indianapolis, IN 46204
P: (317) 234-9054
E: senator.leising
 @iga.in.gov

**Long, David C. (R, 16)**
Indiana State Capitol
200 West Washington Street
Indianapolis, IN 46204
P: (317) 232-9416
E: senator.long@iga.in.gov

**Melton, Eddie (D, 3)\***
Indiana State Capitol
200 West Washington Street
Indianapolis, IN 46204
E: senator.melton
 @iga.in.gov

**Merritt Jr., James W.
 (R, 31)**
Indiana State Capitol
200 West Washington Street
Indianapolis, IN 46204
P: (317) 232-9533
E: senator.merritt
 @iga.in.gov

**Messmer, Mark (R, 48)**
Indiana State Capitol
200 West Washington Street
Indianapolis, IN 46204
P: (317) 232-9441
E: senator.messmer
 @iga.in.gov

**Mishler, Ryan D. (R, 9)**
Indiana State Capitol
200 West Washington Street
Indianapolis, IN 46204
P: (317) 233-0930
E: senator.mishler
 @iga.in.gov

**Mrvan Jr., Frank (D, 1)**
Indiana State Capitol
200 West Washington Street
Indianapolis, IN 46204
P: (317) 232-9532
F: (317) 233-4275
E: senator.mrvan@iga.in.gov

**Niemeyer, Rick (R, 6)**
Indiana State Capitol
200 West Washington Street
Indianapolis, IN 46204
P: (317) 232-9490
E: senator.niemeyer
 @iga.in.gov

**Niezgodski, David L.
 (D, 10)**
Indiana State Capitol
200 West Washington Street
Indianapolis, IN 46204
P: (317) 232-9827
E: Senator.Niezgodski
 @iga.in.gov

**Perfect, Chip (R, 43)**
Indiana State Capitol
200 West Washington Street
Indianapolis, IN 46204
P: (317) 232-9489
E: senator.perfect
 @iga.in.gov

**Raatz, Jeff (R, 27)**
Indiana State Capitol
200 West Washington Street
Indianapolis, IN 46204
P: (317) 233-0930
E: senator.raatz@iga.in.gov

**Randolph, Lonnie Marcus
 (D, 2)**
Indiana State Senate
200 West Washington Street
Indianapolis, IN 46204
P: (317) 232-9532
F: (317) 233-4275
E: senator.randolph
 @iga.in.gov

**Ruckelshaus, John (R, 30)\***
Indiana State Capitol
200 West Washington Street
Indianapolis, IN 46204
P: (317) 232-9808
E: senator.ruckelshaus
 @iga.in.gov

**Sandlin, Jack (R, 36)\***
Indiana State Capitol
200 West Washington Street
Indianapolis, IN 46204
P: (317) 232-9414
E: senator.sandlin
 @iga.in.gov

**Smith, Jim (R, 45)**
Indiana State Capitol
200 West Washington Street
Indianapolis, IN 46204
P: (317) 232-9426
E: senator.smith@iga.in.gov

**Stoops, Mark (D, 40)**
Indiana State Capitol
200 West Washington Street
Indianapolis, IN 46204
P: (317) 232-9847
E: Senator.Stoops
 @iga.in.gov

**Tallian, Karen R. (D, 4)**
Indiana State Senate
200 West Washington Street
Indianapolis, IN 46204
P: (317) 232-9847
F: (317) 233-4275
E: karen.tallian@iga.in.gov

**Taylor, Greg (D, 33)**
Indiana State Capitol
200 West Washington Street
Indianapolis, IN 46204
P: (317) 232-9432
F: (317) 233-4275
E: Senator.Taylor
 @iga.in.gov

**Tomes, Jim (R, 49)**
Indiana State Capitol
200 West Washington Street
Indianapolis, IN 46204
P: (317) 232-9414
E: senator.tomes@iga.in.gov

**Walker, Greg (R, 41)**
Indiana State Capitol
200 West Washington Street
Indianapolis, IN 46204
P: (317) 232-9984
E: senator.walker
@iga.in.gov

**Young, R. Michael (R, 35)**
Indiana State Capitol
200 West Washington Street
Indianapolis, IN 46204
P: (317) 232-9517
E: senator.young@iga.in.gov

**Zakas, Joe (R, 11)**
Indiana State Capitol
200 West Washington Street
Indianapolis, IN 46204
P: (317) 232-9490
E: senator.zakas@iga.in.gov

**Zay, Andy (R, 17)***
Indiana State Capitol
200 West Washington Street
Indianapolis, IN 46204
P: (317) 232-9441
E: senator.zay@iga.in.gov

# House
## Speaker of the House
**Speaker Brian C. Bosma (R)**
Speaker of the House
Indiana State Capitol
200 West Washington Street
Indianapolis, IN 46204
P: (317) 232-9677
E: brian.bosma@iga.in.gov

## Speaker Pro Tempore of the House
**Representative William C. Friend (R)**
Speaker Pro Tem
Indiana State Capitol
200 West Washington Street
Indianapolis, IN 46204
P: (317) 232-9981
E: william.friend
@iga.in.gov

## House Minority Leader
**Representative Scott Pelath (D)**
House Minority Leader
Indiana State Capitol
200 West Washington Street
Indianapolis, IN 46204
P: (317) 232-9628
E: h9@in.gov

## Clerk of the House
**Ms. M. Carolyn Spotts**
Principal House Clerk
200 West Washington Street,
Room 3A-8
Indianapolis, IN 46204
P: (317) 232-9608
E: cspotts@iga.in.gov

## Members of the House
**Arnold, Lloyd (R, 74)**
Indiana State Capitol
200 West Washington Street
Indianapolis, IN 46204
P: (317) 232-9793
E: lloyd.arnold@iga.in.gov

**Austin, Terri J. (D, 36)**
Indiana State Capitol
200 West Washington Street
Indianapolis, IN 46204
P: (317) 232-9794
E: terri.austin@iga.in.gov

**Aylesworth, Michael (R, 11)**
Indiana State Capitol
200 West Washington Street
Indianapolis, IN 46204
P: (317) 234-9447
E: michael.aylesworth
@iga.in.gov

**Bacon, Ron (R, 75)**
Indiana State Capitol
200 West Washington Street
Indianapolis, IN 46204
P: (317) 232-9833
E: ron.bacon@iga.in.gov

**Baird, James (R, 44)**
Indiana State Capitol
200 West Washington Street
Indianapolis, IN 46204
P: (317) 232-9509
E: james.baird@iga.in.gov

**Bartlett, John (D, 95)**
Indiana State Capitol
200 West Washington Street
Indianapolis, IN 46204
P: (317) 232-9987
E: h95@in.gov

**Bauer, B. Patrick (D, 6)**
Indiana State Capitol
200 West Washington Street
Indianapolis, IN 46204
P: (317) 232-9987
E: h6@in.gov

**Behning, Robert W. (R, 91)**
Indiana State Capitol
200 West Washington Street
Indianapolis, IN 46204
P: (317) 232-9643
E: robert.behning
@iga.in.gov

**Beumer, Greg (R, 33)**
Indiana State Capitol
200 West Washington Street
Indianapolis, IN 46204
P: (317) 232-9643
E: greg.beumer@iga.in.gov

**Borders, Bruce (R, 45)**
Indiana State Capitol
200 West Washington Street
Indianapolis, IN 46204
P: (317) 232-9753
E: bruce.borders@iga.in.gov

**Bosma, Brian C. (R, 88)**
Indiana State Capitol
200 West Washington Street
Indianapolis, IN 46204
P: (317) 232-9677
E: brian.bosma@iga.in.gov

**Braun, Mike (R, 63)**
Indiana State Capitol
200 West Washington Street
Indianapolis, IN 46204
P: (317) 234-9447
E: mike.braun@iga.in.gov

**Brown, Charlie (D, 3)**
Indiana State Capitol
200 West Washington Street
Indianapolis, IN 46204
P: (317) 232-9798
E: charlie.brown@iga.in.gov

**Brown, Timothy (R, 41)**
Indiana State Capitol
200 West Washington Street
Indianapolis, IN 46204
P: (317) 232-9651
E: timothy.brown@iga.in.gov

**Burton, Woody (R, 58)**
Indiana State Capitol
200 West Washington Street
Indianapolis, IN 46204
P: (317) 232-9648
E: woody.burton@iga.in.gov

**Carbaugh, Martin (R, 81)**
Indiana State Capitol
200 West Washington Street
Indianapolis, IN 46204
P: (317) 232-9643
E: h81@in.gov

**Cherry, Bob (R, 53)**
Indiana State Capitol
200 West Washington Street
Indianapolis, IN 46204
P: (317) 232-9651
E: h53@in.gov

**Clere, Ed (R, 72)**
Indiana State Capitol
200 West Washington Street
Indianapolis, IN 46204
P: (317) 232-9753
E: ed.clere@iga.in.gov

**Cook, Tony (R, 32)**
Indiana State Capitol
200 West Washington Street
Indianapolis, IN 46204
P: (317) 232-9815
E: tony.cook@iga.in.gov

**Culver, Wesley (R, 49)**
Indiana State Capitol
200 West Washington Street
Indianapolis, IN 46204
P: (317) 232-9678
E: wesley.culver@iga.in.gov

**Davisson, Steve (R, 73)**
Indiana State Capitol
200 West Washington Street
Indianapolis, IN 46204
P: (317) 232-9753
E: steve.davisson
@iga.in.gov

**DeLaney, Edward O. (D, 86)**
Indiana State Capitol
200 West Washington Street
Indianapolis, IN 46204
P: (317) 232-9798
E: edward.delaney
@iga.in.gov

**DeVon, Dale (R, 5)**
Indiana State Capitol
200 West Washington Street
Indianapolis, IN 46204
P: (317) 232-9678
E: dale.devon@iga.in.gov

**Dvorak, Ryan (D, 8)**
Indiana State Capitol
200 West Washington Street
Indianapolis, IN 46204
P: (317) 234-9048
E: ryan.dvorak@iga.in.gov

# Indiana

**Eberhart, Sean (R, 57)**
Indiana State Capitol
200 West Washington Street
Indianapolis, IN 46204
P: (317) 232-9793
E: sean.eberhart@iga.in.gov

**Ellington, Jeff (R, 62)**
Indiana State Capitol
200 West Washington Street
Indianapolis, IN 46204
P: (317) 232-9863
E: jeff.ellington
    @iga.in.gov

**Engleman, Karen (R, 70)***
Indiana State Capitol
200 West Washington Street
Indianapolis, IN 46204
E: karen.engleman
    @iga.in.gov

**Errington, Sue (D, 34)**
Indiana State Capitol
200 West Washington Street
Indianapolis, IN 46204
P: (317) 232-9976
E: sue.errington@iga.in.gov

**Forestal, Dan (D, 100)**
Indiana State Capitol
200 West Washington Street
Indianapolis, IN 46204
P: (317) 232-9827
E: dan.forestal@iga.in.gov

**Friend, William C. (R, 23)**
Indiana State Capitol
200 West Washington Street
Indianapolis, IN 46204
P: (317) 232-9981
E: william.friend
    @iga.in.gov

**Frizzell, David N. (R, 93)**
Indiana State Capitol
200 West Washington Street
Indianapolis, IN 46204
P: (317) 232-9981
E: david.frizzell
    @iga.in.gov

**Frye, Randy (R, 67)**
Indiana State Capitol
200 West Washington Street
Indianapolis, IN 46204
P: (317) 234-3827
E: randy.frye@iga.in.gov

**GiaQuinta, Phil (D, 80)**
Indiana State Capitol
200 West Washington Street
Indianapolis, IN 46204
P: (317) 233-5248
E: phil.giaquinta
    @iga.in.gov

**Goodin, Terry (D, 66)**
Indiana State Capitol
200 West Washington Street
Indianapolis, IN 46204
P: (317) 232-9798
E: terry.goodin@iga.in.gov

**Gutwein, Douglas (R, 16)**
Indiana State Capitol
200 West Washington Street
Indianapolis, IN 46204
P: (317) 232-9509
E: douglas.gutwein
    @iga.in.gov

**Hamilton, Carey (D, 87)***
Indiana State Capitol
200 West Washington Street
Indianapolis, IN 46204
E: carey.hamilton
    @iga.in.gov

**Hamm, Richard (R, 56)**
Indiana State Capitol
200 West Washington Street
Indianapolis, IN 46204
P: (317) 232-9769
E: richard.hamm@iga.in.gov

**Harris Jr., Earl (D, 2)***
Indiana State Capitol
200 West Washington Street
Indianapolis, IN 46204
E: earl.harris@iga.in.gov

**Hatfield, Ryan (D, 77)***
Indiana State Capitol
200 West Washington Street
Indianapolis, IN 46204
E: ryan.hatfield@iga.in.gov

**Heaton, Bob (R, 46)**
Indiana State Capitol
200 West Washington Street
Indianapolis, IN 46204
P: (317) 232-9620
E: bob.heaton@iga.in.gov

**Heine, Dave (R, 85)***
Indiana State Capitol
200 West Washington Street
Indianapolis, IN 46204
E: dave.heine@iga.in.gov

**Huston, Todd (R, 37)**
Indiana State Capitol
200 West Washington Street
Indianapolis, IN 46204
P: (317) 234-3827
E: todd.huston@iga.in.gov

**Jordan, Jack (R, 17)***
Indiana State Capitol
200 West Washington Street
Indianapolis, IN 46204
E: jack.jordan@iga.in.gov

**Judy, Christopher (R, 83)**
Indiana State Capitol
200 West Washington Street
Indianapolis, IN 46204
P: (317) 294-2993
E: christopher.judy
    @iga.in.gov

**Karickhoff, Mike (R, 30)**
Indiana State Capitol
200 West Washington Street
Indianapolis, IN 46204
P: (317) 234-3827
E: mike.karickhoff
    @iga.in.gov

**Kersey, Clyde (D, 43)**
Indiana State Capitol
200 West Washington Street
Indianapolis, IN 46204
P: (317) 232-9991
E: clyde.kersey@iga.in.gov

**Kirchhofer, Cindy (R, 89)**
Indiana State Capitol
200 West Washington Street
Indianapolis, IN 46204
P: (317) 232-9793
E: cindy.kirchhofer
    @iga.in.gov

**Klinker, Sheila J. (D, 27)**
Indiana State Capitol
200 West Washington Street
Indianapolis, IN 46204
P: (317) 232-9875
E: sheila.klinker@in.gov

**Lawson, Linda (D, 1)**
Indiana State Capitol
200 West Washington Street
Indianapolis, IN 46204
P: (317) 232-0243
E: h1@in.gov

**Lehe, Don (R, 25)**
Indiana State Capitol
200 West Washington Street
Indianapolis, IN 46204
P: (317) 232-9509
E: don.lehe@iga.in.gov

**Lehman, Matthew S. (R, 79)**
Indiana State Capitol
200 West Washington Street
Indianapolis, IN 46204
P: (317) 232-9499
E: matthew.lehman
    @iga.in.gov

**Leonard, Dan (R, 50)**
Indiana State Capitol
200 West Washington Street
Indianapolis, IN 46204
P: (317) 232-9793
E: dan.leonard@iga.in.gov

**Lucas, Jim (R, 69)**
Indiana State Capitol
200 West Washington Street
Indianapolis, IN 46204
P: (317) 232-9499
E: jim.lucas@iga.in.gov

**Lyness, Randy (R, 68)**
Indiana State Capitol
200 West Washington Street
Indianapolis, IN 46204
P: (317) 232-9600
E: randy.lyness@iga.in.gov

**Macer, Karlee (D, 92)**
Indiana State Capitol
200 West Washington Street
Indianapolis, IN 46204
P: (317) 232-9834
E: karlee.macer@iga.in.gov

**Mahan, Kevin (R, 31)**
Indiana State Capitol
200 West Washington Street
Indianapolis, IN 46204
P: (317) 232-9509
E: kevin.mahan@iga.in.gov

**May, Christopher (R, 65)***
Indiana State Capitol
200 West Washington Street
Indianapolis, IN 46204
E: christopher.may
    @iga.in.gov

**Mayfield, Peggy (R, 60)**
Indiana State Capitol
200 West Washington Street
Indianapolis, IN 46204
P: (317) 232-9816
E: peggy.mayfield
    @iga.in.gov

**McNamara, Wendy (R, 76)**
Indiana State Capitol
200 West Washington Street
Indianapolis, IN 46204
P: (317) 232-9816
E: wendy.mcnamara
    @iga.in.gov

**Miller, Doug (R, 48)**
Indiana State Capitol
200 West Washington Street
Indianapolis, IN 46204
P: (317) 296-920
E: doug.miller@iga.in.gov

**Moed, Justin (D, 97)**
Indiana State Capitol
200 West Washington Street
Indianapolis, IN 46204
P: (317) 232-9834
E: justin.moed@iga.in.gov

**Morris, Bob (R, 84)**
Indiana State Capitol
200 West Washington Street
Indianapolis, IN 46204
P: (317) 232-9769
E: bob.morris@iga.in.gov

**Morrison, Alan (R, 42)**
Indiana State Capitol
200 West Washington Street
Indianapolis, IN 46204
P: (317) 234-2993
E: h42@in.gov

**Moseley, Charles (D, 10)**
Indiana State Capitol
200 West Washington Street
Indianapolis, IN 46204
P: (317) 233-5248
E: charles.moseley
   @iga.in.gov

**Negele, Sharon (R, 13)**
Indiana State Capitol
200 West Washington Street
Indianapolis, IN 46204
P: (317) 232-9816
E: sharon.negele@iga.in.gov

**Nisly, Curt (R, 22)**
Indiana State Capitol
200 West Washington Street
Indianapolis, IN 46204
P: (317) 296-9678
E: curt.nisly@iga.in.gov

**Ober, David (R, 82)**
Indiana State Capitol
200 West Washington Street
Indianapolis, IN 46204
P: (317) 232-9643
E: david.ober@iga.in.gov

**Olthoff, Julie (R, 19)**
Indiana State Capitol
200 West Washington Street
Indianapolis, IN 46204
P: (317) 296-9850
E: julie.olthoff@iga.in.gov

**Pelath, Scott (D, 9)**
Indiana State Capitol
200 West Washington Street
Indianapolis, IN 46204
P: (317) 232-9628
E: h9@in.gov

**Pierce, Matt (D, 61)**
Indiana House of
Representatives
200 West Washington Street
Indianapolis, IN 46204
P: (317) 232-9794
E: h61@in.gov

**Porter, Gregory W. (D, 96)**
Indiana State Capitol
200 West Washington Street
Indianapolis, IN 46204
P: (317) 232-9875
F: (317) 233-8184
E: gregory.porter
   @iga.in.gov

**Pressel, Jim (R, 20)***
Indiana State Capitol
200 West Washington Street
Indianapolis, IN 46204
E: jim.pressel@iga.in.gov

**Pryor, Cherrish S. (D, 94)**
Indiana State Capitol
200 West Washington Street
Indianapolis, IN 46204
P: (317) 232-9794
E: cherrish.pryor
   @iga.in.gov

**Reardon, Mara Candelaria
   (D, 12)**
Indiana State Capitol
200 West Washington Street
Indianapolis, IN 46204
P: (317) 232-9600
E: h12@in.gov

**Richardson, Kathy Kreag
   (R, 29)**
Indiana State Capitol
200 West Washington Street
Indianapolis, IN 46204
P: (317) 234-9380
E: kathy.richardson
   @iga.in.gov

**Saunders, Thomas E. (R, 54)**
Indiana State Capitol
200 West Washington Street
Indianapolis, IN 46204
P: (317) 232-9753
E: thomas.saunders
   @iga.in.gov

**Schaibley, Donna (R, 24)**
Indiana State Capitol
200 West Washington Street
Indianapolis, IN 46204
P: (317) 232-9863
E: donna.schaibley
   @iga.in.gov

**Shackleford, Robin (D, 98)**
Indiana State Capitol
200 West Washington Street
Indianapolis, IN 46204
P: (317) 234-9048
E: rshackle@iga.in.gov

**Siegrist, Sally (R, 26)***
Indiana State Capitol
200 West Washington Street
Indianapolis, IN 46204
E: sally.siegrist
   @iga.in.gov

**Slager, Hal (R, 15)**
Indiana State Capitol
200 West Washington Street
Indianapolis, IN 46204
P: (317) 232-9671
E: hal.slager@iga.in.gov

**Smaltz, Ben (R, 52)**
Indiana State Capitol
200 West Washington Street
Indianapolis, IN 46204
P: (317) 232-9648
E: ben.smaltz@iga.in.gov

**Smith, Milo (R, 59)**
Indiana State Capitol
200 West Washington Street
Indianapolis, IN 46204
P: (317) 232-9620
E: milo.smith@iga.in.gov

**Smith, Vernon G. (D, 14)**
Indiana State Capitol
200 West Washington Street
Indianapolis, IN 46204
P: (317) 232-9976
E: vernon.smith@iga.in.gov

**Soliday, Edmond (R, 4)**
Indiana State Capitol
200 West Washington Street
Indianapolis, IN 46204
P: (317) 232-9619
E: ed.soliday@iga.in.gov

**Speedy, Mike (R, 90)**
Indiana State Capitol
200 West Washington Street
Indianapolis, IN 46204
P: (317) 232-9619
E: mike.speedy@iga.in.gov

**Stemler, Steven R. (D, 71)**
Indiana State Capitol
200 West Washington Street
Indianapolis, IN 46204
P: (317) 232-9834
E: steven.stemler
   @iga.in.gov

**Steuerwald, Greg (R, 40)**
Indiana State Capitol
200 West Washington Street
Indianapolis, IN 46204
P: (317) 232-9833
E: greg.steuerwald
   @iga.in.gov

**Sullivan, Holli (R, 78)**
Indiana State Capitol
200 West Washington Street
Indianapolis, IN 46204
P: (317) 232-9671
E: h78@in.gov

**Summers, Vanessa (D, 99)**
Indiana State Capitol
200 West Washington Street
Indianapolis, IN 46204
P: (317) 234-9048
E: vanessa.summers
   @iga.in.gov

**Taylor, Joe (D, 7)***
Indiana State Capitol
200 West Washington Street
Indianapolis, IN 46204
E: joe.taylor@iga.in.gov

**Thompson, Jeff (R, 28)**
Indiana State Capitol
200 West Washington Street
Indianapolis, IN 46204
P: (317) 232-9651
E: jeff.thompson@iga.in.gov

**Torr, Jerry R. (R, 39)**
Indiana State Capitol
200 West Washington Street
Indianapolis, IN 46204
P: (317) 232-9677
E: jerry.torr@iga.in.gov

**VanNatter, Heath (R, 38)**
Indiana State Capitol
200 West Washington Street
Indianapolis, IN 46204
P: (317) 232-9619
E: heath.vannatter
   @iga.in.gov

**Washburne, Tom (R, 64)**
Indiana State Capitol
200 West Washington Street
Indianapolis, IN 46204
P: (317) 234-2993
E: tom.washburne@iga.in.gov

**Wesco, Tim (R, 21)**
Indiana State Capitol
200 West Washington Street
Indianapolis, IN 46204
P: (317) 232-9648
E: tim.wesco@iga.in.gov

**Wolkins, David A. (R, 18)**
Indiana State Capitol
200 West Washington Street
Indianapolis, IN 46204
P: (317) 232-9671
E: david.wolkins@iga.in.gov

# Indiana

**Wright, Melanie (D, 35)**
Indiana State Capitol
200 West Washington Street
Indianapolis, IN 46204
P: (317) 296-9628
E: melanie.wright
    @iga.in.gov

**Young, John (R, 47)\***
Indiana State Capitol
200 West Washington Street
Indianapolis, IN 46204
E: john.young@iga.in.gov

**Zent, Denny (R, 51)**
Indiana State Capitol
200 West Washington Street
Indianapolis, IN 46204
P: (317) 232-9674
E: denny.zent@iga.in.gov

**Ziemke, Cindy (R, 55)**
Indiana State Capitol
200 West Washington Street
Indianapolis, IN 46204
P: (317) 232-9815
E: cindy.ziemke@iga.in.gov

# Iowa

## Executive

### Governor

**The Honorable Terry Branstad (R)**
Governor
State Capitol
Des Moines, IA 50319
P: (515) 281-5211
F: (515) 281-6611

### Lieutenant Governor

**The Honorable Kim Reynolds (R)**
Lieutenant Governor
State Capitol, Room 9
Des Moines, IA 50319
P: (515) 281-5211
F: (515) 725-3527

### Secretary of Agriculture

**Mr. Bill Northey (R)**
Secretary of Agriculture
Wallace Building
502 East 9th Street
Des Moines, IA 50319
P: (515) 281-5321
F: (515) 281-6236

### Attorney General

**The Honorable Tom Miller (D)**
Attorney General
Hoover State Office Building
1305 East Walnut
Des Moines, IA 50319
P: (515) 281-5164
F: (515) 281-4209

### Auditor

**Ms. Mary Mosiman**
Auditor of State
Room 111, State Capitol Building
Des Moines, IA 50319
P: (515) 281-5835
F: (515) 242-6134

### Secretary of State

**The Honorable Paul Pate (R)**
Secretary of State
State Capitol, Room 105
Des Moines, IA 50319
P: (515) 281-6230
F: (515) 242-5952
E: paul.pate@sos.iowa.gov

### Treasurer

**The Honorable Michael L. Fitzgerald (D)**
State Treasurer
State Capitol Building
Des Moines, IA 50319
P: (515) 281-5368
F: (515) 281-7562
E: mike.fitzgerald@iowa.gov

## Judiciary

### Supreme Court (MR)

**Ms. Donna Humpal**
Clerk
Iowa Judicial Branch Building
1111 East Court Avenue
Des Moines, IA 50319
P: (515) 281-5911
E: Donna.Humpal
@iowacourts.gov

**The Honorable Mark S. Cady**
Chief Justice
**The Honorable Brent R. Appel**
**The Honorable Daryl L. Hecht**
**The Honorable Edward Mansfield**
**The Honorable Thomas D. Waterman**
**The Honorable David S. Wiggins**
**The Honorable Bruce Zager**

## Legislative

## Senate

### Senate President

**Senator Jack Whitver (R)**
Senate President
State Capitol
1007 East Grand Avenue
Des Moines, IA 50319
P: (515) 281-3371
E: jack.whitver
@legis.iowa.gov

### President Pro Tempore of the Senate

**Senator Jerry Behn (R)**
Senate President Pro Tem
State Capitol
1007 East Grand Avenue
Des Moines, IA 50319
P: (515) 281-3371
E: jerry.behn
@legis.iowa.gov

### Senate Majority Leader

**Senator Bill Dix (R)**
Senate Majority Leader
State Capitol
1007 East Grand Avenue
Des Moines, IA 50319
P: (515) 281-5841
E: bill.dix@legis.iowa.gov

### Senate Minority Leader

**Senator Robert M. Hogg (D)**
Senate Minority Leader
State Capitol
1007 East Grand Avenue
Des Moines, IA 50319
P: (515) 281-3371
E: rob.hogg@legis.iowa.gov

### Secretary of the Senate

**Mr. Michael E. Marshall**
Secretary of the Senate
State Capitol
1007 East Grand Avenue
Des Moines, IA 50319
P: (515) 281-5307
E: Mike.Marshall
@legis.iowa.gov

### Members of the Senate

**Allen, Chaz (D, 15)**
State Capitol
1007 East Grand Avenue
Des Moines, IA 50319
P: (515) 281-3371
E: chaz.allen
@legis.iowa.gov

**Anderson, Bill (R, 3)**
State Capitol
1007 East Grand Avenue
Des Moines, IA 50319
P: (515) 281-3371
E: bill.anderson
@legis.iowa.gov

**Behn, Jerry (R, 24)**
State Capitol
1007 East Grand Avenue
Des Moines, IA 50319
P: (515) 281-3371
E: jerry.behn
@legis.iowa.gov

**Bertrand, Rick (R, 7)**
State Capitol
1007 East Grand Avenue
Des Moines, IA 50319
P: (515) 281-3371
E: rick.bertrand
@legis.iowa.gov

**Bisignano, Tony (D, 17)**
State Capitol
1007 East Grand Avenue
Des Moines, IA 50319
P: (515) 281-3371
E: tony.bisignano
@legis.iowa.gov

**Bolkcom, Joe (D, 43)**
State Capitol
1007 East Grand Avenue
Des Moines, IA 50319
P: (515) 281-3371
E: joe.bolkcom
@legis.iowa.gov

**Boulton, Nate (D, 16)***
State Capitol
1007 East Grand Avenue
Des Moines, IA 50319
E: nate.boulton
@legis.iowa.gov

**Bowman, Tod (D, 29)**
State Capitol
1007 East Grand Avenue
Des Moines, IA 50319
P: (515) 281-3371
E: tod.bowman
@legis.iowa.gov

**Breitbach, Michael (R, 28)**
State Capitol
1007 East Grand Avenue
Des Moines, IA 50319
P: (515) 281-3371
E: michael.breitbach
@legis.iowa.gov

**Brown, Waylon (R, 26)***
State Capitol
1007 East Grand Avenue
Des Moines, IA 50319
E: waylon.brown
@legis.iowa.gov

**Chapman, Jake (R, 10)**
State Capitol
1007 East Grand Avenue
Des Moines, IA 50319
P: (515) 281-3371
E: jake.chapman
@legis.iowa.gov

**Chelgren, Mark (R, 41)**
State Capitol
1007 East Grand Avenue
Des Moines, IA 50319
P: (515) 281-3371
E: mark.chelgren
@legis.iowa.gov

**Costello, Mark (R, 12)**
State Capitol
1007 East Grand Avenue
Des Moines, IA 50319
P: (515) 281-3221
E: mark.costello
@legis.iowa.gov

# Iowa

**Danielson, Jeff (D, 30)**
State Capitol
1007 East Grand Avenue
Des Moines, IA 50319
P: (515) 281-3371
E: jeffdanielson@gmail.com

**Dawson, Dan (R, 8)***
State Capitol
1007 East Grand Avenue
Des Moines, IA 50319
E: dan.dawson
　@legis.iowa.gov

**Dix, Bill (R, 25)**
State Capitol
1007 East Grand Avenue
Des Moines, IA 50319
P: (515) 281-5841
E: bill.dix@legis.iowa.gov

**Dotzler Jr., William A.
　(D, 31)**
State Capitol
1007 East Grand Avenue
Des Moines, IA 50319
P: (515) 281-3371
E: bill.dotzler
　@legis.iowa.gov

**Dvorsky, Robert E. (D, 37)**
State Capitol
1007 East Grand Avenue
Des Moines, IA 50319
P: (515) 281-3371
E: robert.dvorsky
　@legis.iowa.gov

**Edler, Jeff (R, 36)***
State Capitol
1007 East Grand Avenue
Des Moines, IA 50319
E: jeff.edler
　@legis.iowa.gov

**Feenstra, Randy (R, 2)**
State Capitol
1007 East Grand Avenue
Des Moines, IA 50319
P: (515) 281-3371
E: randy.feenstra
　@legis.iowa.gov

**Garrett, Julian (R, 13)**
State Capitol
1007 East Grand Avenue
Des Moines, IA 50319
P: (515) 281-3371
E: julian.garrett
　@legis.iowa.gov

**Greene, Thomas (R, 44)***
State Capitol
1007 East Grand Avenue
Des Moines, IA 50319
E: tom.greene
　@legis.iowa.gov

**Guth, Dennis (R, 4)**
State Capitol
1007 East Grand Avenue
Des Moines, IA 50319
P: (515) 281-3371
E: dennis.guth
　@legis.iowa.gov

**Hart, Rita (D, 49)**
State Capitol
1007 East Grand Avenue
Des Moines, IA 50319
P: (515) 281-3371
E: rita.hart@legis.iowa.gov

**Hogg, Robert M. (D, 33)**
State Capitol
1007 East Grand Avenue
Des Moines, IA 50319
P: (515) 281-3371
E: rob.hogg@legis.iowa.gov

**Horn, Wally E. (D, 35)**
State Capitol
1007 East Grand Avenue
Des Moines, IA 50319
P: (515) 281-3371
E: wally.horn
　@legis.iowa.gov

**Jochum, Pam (D, 50)**
State Capitol
1007 East Grand Avenue
Des Moines, IA 50319
P: (515) 281-5804
E: pam.jochum
　@legis.iowa.gov

**Johnson, Craig (R, 32)***
State Capitol
1007 East Grand Avenue
Des Moines, IA 50319
E: craig.johnson
　@legis.iowa.gov

**Johnson, David (I, 1)**
State Capitol
1007 East Grand Avenue
Des Moines, IA 50319
P: (515) 281-3371
E: david.johnson
　@legis.iowa.gov

**Kapucian, Tim L. (R, 38)**
State Capitol
1007 East Grand Avenue
Des Moines, IA 50319
P: (515) 281-3371
E: tim.kapucian
　@legis.iowa.gov

**Kinney, Kevin (D, 39)**
State Capitol
1007 East Grand Avenue
Des Moines, IA 50319
P: (515) 281-3371
E: kevin.kinney
　@legis.iowa.gov

**Kraayenbrink, Tim (R, 5)**
State Capitol
1007 East Grand Avenue
Des Moines, IA 50319
P: (515) 281-3371
E: tim.kraayenbrink
　@legis.iowa.gov

**Lofgren, Mark (R, 46)**
State Capitol
1007 East Grand Avenue
Des Moines, IA 50319
P: (515) 281-3221
E: mark.lofgren
　@legis.iowa.gov

**Lykam, Jim (D, 45)**
State Capitol
1007 East Grand Avenue
Des Moines, IA 50319
P: (515) 281-3221
E: jim.lykam@legis.iowa.gov

**Mathis, Liz (D, 34)**
State Capitol
1007 East Grand Avenue
Des Moines, IA 50319
P: (515) 281-3371
E: liz.mathis
　@legis.iowa.gov

**McCoy, Matt (D, 21)**
State Capitol
1007 East Grand Avenue
Des Moines, IA 50319
P: (515) 281-3371
E: matt.mccoy
　@legis.iowa.gov

**Petersen, Janet (D, 18)**
State Capitol
1007 East Grand Avenue
Des Moines, IA 50319
P: (515) 281-3371
E: janet.petersen
　@legis.iowa.gov

**Quirmbach, Herman C.
　(D, 23)**
State Capitol
1007 East Grand Avenue
Des Moines, IA 50319
P: (515) 281-3371
E: herman.quirmbach
　@legis.iowa.gov

**Ragan, Amanda (D, 27)**
State Capitol
1007 East Grand Avenue
Des Moines, IA 50319
P: (515) 281-3371
E: amanda.ragan
　@legis.iowa.gov

**Rozenboom, Ken (R, 40)**
State Capitol
1007 East Grand Avenue
Des Moines, IA 50319
P: (515) 281-3371
E: ken.rozenboom
　@legis.iowa.gov

**Schneider, Charles (R, 22)**
State Capitol
1007 East Grand Avenue
Des Moines, IA 50319
P: (515) 281-3371
E: charles.schneider
　@legis.iowa.gov

**Schultz, Jason (R, 9)**
State Capitol
1007 East Grand Avenue
Des Moines, IA 50319
P: (515) 281-3221
E: jason.schultz
　@legis.iowa.gov

**Segebart, Mark (R, 6)**
State Capitol
1007 East Grand Avenue
Des Moines, IA 50319
P: (515) 281-3371
E: mark.segebart
　@legis.iowa.gov

**Shipley, Tom (R, 11)**
State Capitol
1007 East Grand Avenue
Des Moines, IA 50319
P: (515) 281-3371
E: tom.shipley
　@legis.iowa.gov

**Sinclair, Amy (R, 14)**
State Capitol
1007 East Grand Avenue
Des Moines, IA 50319
P: (515) 281-3371
E: amy.sinclair
　@legis.iowa.gov

**Smith, Roby (R, 47)**
State Capitol
1007 East Grand Avenue
Des Moines, IA 50319
P: (515) 281-3371
E: roby.smith
　@legis.iowa.gov

**Taylor, Rich (D, 42)**
State Capitol
1007 East Grand Avenue
Des Moines, IA 50319
P: (515) 281-3371
E: rich.taylor
　@legis.iowa.gov

**Whitver, Jack (R, 19)**
State Capitol
1007 East Grand Avenue
Des Moines, IA 50319
P: (515) 281-3371
E: jack.whitver
@legis.iowa.gov

**Zaun, Brad (R, 20)**
State Capitol
1007 East Grand Avenue
Des Moines, IA 50319
P: (515) 281-3371
E: brad.zaun@legis.iowa.gov

**Zumbach, Dan (R, 48)**
State Capitol
1007 East Grand Avenue
Des Moines, IA 50319
P: (515) 281-3371
E: dan.zumbach
@legis.iowa.gov

# House

## Speaker of the House

**Speaker Linda Upmeyer (R)**
Speaker of the House
State Capitol
1007 East Grand Avenue
Des Moines, IA 50319
P: (515) 281-5137
E: linda.upmeyer
@legis.iowa.gov

## Speaker Pro Tempore of the House

**Representative Matt W. Windschitl (R)**
House Speaker Pro Tempore
State Capitol
1007 East Grand Avenue
Des Moines, IA 50319
P: (515) 281-3221
E: matt.windschitl
@legis.iowa.gov

## House Majority Leader

**Representative Chris Hagenow (R)**
House Majority Leader
State Capitol
1007 East Grand Avenue
Des Moines, IA 50319
P: (515) 281-3221
E: chris.hagenow
@legis.iowa.gov

## House Minority Leader

**Representative Mark D. Smith (D)**
House Minority Leader
State Capitol
1007 East Grand Avenue
Des Moines, IA 50319
P: (515) 281-5230
E: mark.smith
@legis.iowa.gov

## Clerk of the House

**Ms. Carmine Boal**
Chief Clerk of the House
State Capitol
1007 East Grand Avenue
Des Moines, IA 50319
P: (515) 281-4280
F: (515) 281-4758
E: carmine.boal
@legis.iowa.gov

## Members of the House

**Abdul-Samad, Ako (D, 35)**
State Capitol
1007 East Grand Avenue
Des Moines, IA 50319
P: (515) 281-6356
E: ako.abdul-samad
@legis.iowa.gov

**Anderson, Marti (D, 36)**
State Capitol
1007 East Grand Avenue
Des Moines, IA 50319
P: (515) 281-3221
E: marti.anderson
@legis.iowa.gov

**Bacon, Rob (R, 48)**
State Capitol
1007 East Grand Avenue
Des Moines, IA 50319
P: (515) 281-3221
E: rob.bacon@legis.iowa.gov

**Baltimore, Chip (R, 47)**
State Capitol
1007 East Grand Avenue
Des Moines, IA 50319
P: (515) 281-3221
E: chip.baltimore
@legis.iowa.gov

**Baudler, Clel (R, 20)**
State Capitol
1007 East Grand Avenue
Des Moines, IA 50319
P: (515) 281-3221
E: clel.baudler
@legis.iowa.gov

**Baxter, Terry (R, 8)**
State Capitol
1007 East Grand Avenue
Des Moines, IA 50319
P: (515) 281-3221
E: terry.baxter
@legis.iowa.gov

**Bearinger, Bruce (D, 64)**
State Capitol
1007 East Grand Avenue
Des Moines, IA 50319
P: (515) 281-3221
E: bruce.bearinger
@legis.iowa.gov

**Bennett, Liz (D, 65)**
State Capitol
1007 East Grand Avenue
Des Moines, IA 50319
P: (515) 281-3221
E: liz.bennett
@legis.iowa.gov

**Bergan, Michael (R, 55)***
State Capitol
1007 East Grand Avenue
Des Moines, IA 50319
E: michael.bergan
@legis.iowa.gov

**Best, Brian (R, 12)**
State Capitol
1007 East Grand Avenueitol
Des Moines, IA 50319
P: (515) 281-3221
E: brian.best
@legis.iowa.gov

**Bloomingdale, Jane (R, 51)***
State Capitol
1007 East Grand Avenue
Des Moines, IA 50319
E: jane.bloomingdale
@legis.iowa.gov

**Breckenridge, Wesley (D, 29)***
State Capitol
1007 East Grand Avenue
Des Moines, IA 50319
E: wes.breckenridge
@legis.iowa.gov

**Brown-Powers, Timi (D, 61)**
State Capitol
1007 East Grand Avenue
Des Moines, IA 50319
P: (515) 281-7330
E: timi.brown-powers
@legis.iowa.gov

**Carlin, Jim (R, 6)***
State Capitol
1007 East Grand Avenue
Des Moines, IA 50319
E: jim.carlin
@legis.iowa.gov

**Carlson, Gary (R, 91)**
State Capitol
1007 East Grand Avenue
Des Moines, IA 50319
P: (515) 281-3221
E: gary.carlson
@legis.iowa.gov

**Cohoon, Dennis (D, 87)**
State Capitol
1007 East Grand Avenue
Des Moines, IA 50319
P: (515) 281-3221
E: dennis.cohoon
@legis.iowa.gov

**Cownie, Peter (R, 42)**
State Capitol
1007 East Grand Avenue
Des Moines, IA 50319
P: (515) 281-7481
E: peter.cownie
@legis.iowa.gov

**Deyoe, Dave (R, 49)**
State Capitol
1007 East Grand Avenue
Des Moines, IA 50319
P: (515) 281-3221
E: dave.deyoe
@legis.iowa.gov

**Dolecheck, Cecil (R, 24)**
State Capitol
1007 East Grand Avenue
Des Moines, IA 50319
P: (515) 281-3221
E: cecil.dolecheck
@legis.iowa.gov

**Finkenauer, Abby (D, 99)**
State Capitol
1007 East Grand Avenue
Des Moines, IA 50319
P: (515) 281-3221
E: abby.finkenauer
@legis.iowa.gov

**Fisher, Dean (R, 72)**
State Capitol
1007 East Grand Avenue
Des Moines, IA 50319
P: (515) 281-3221
E: dean.fisher
@legis.iowa.gov

**Forbes, John (D, 40)**
State Capitol
1007 East Grand Avenue
Des Moines, IA 50319
P: (515) 281-3221
E: john.forbes
@legis.iowa.gov

# Iowa

**Forristall, Greg (R, 22)**
State Capitol
1007 East Grand Avenue
Des Moines, IA 50319
P: (515) 281-3221
E: greg.forristall
   @legis.iowa.gov

**Fry, Joel (R, 27)**
State Capitol
1007 East Grand Avenue
Des Moines, IA 50319
P: (515) 281-7486
E: joel.fry@legis.iowa.gov

**Gaines, Ruth Ann (D, 32)**
State Capitol
1007 East Grand Avenue
Des Moines, IA 50319
P: (515) 281-3221
E: ruthann.gaines
   @legis.iowa.gov

**Gaskill, Mary (D, 81)**
State Capitol
1007 East Grand Avenue
Des Moines, IA 50319
P: (515) 281-3221
E: mary.gaskill
   @legis.iowa.gov

**Gassman, Tedd (R, 7)**
State Capitol
1007 East Grand Avenue
Des Moines, IA 50319
P: (515) 281-3221
E: tedd.gassman
   @legis.iowa.gov

**Grassley, Pat (R, 50)**
State Capitol
1007 East Grand Avenue
Des Moines, IA 50319
P: (515) 281-3221
E: pat.grassley
   @legis.iowa.gov

**Gustafson, Stan (R, 25)**
State Capitol
1007 East Grand AVenue
Des Moines, IA 50319
P: (515) 281-3221
E: stan.gustafson
   @legis.iowa.gov

**Hagenow, Chris (R, 43)**
State Capitol
1007 East Grand Avenue
Des Moines, IA 50319
P: (515) 281-3221
E: chris.hagenow
   @legis.iowa.gov

**Hager, Kristi (R, 56)***
State Capitol
1007 East Grand Avenue
Des Moines, IA 50319
E: kristi.hager
   @legis.iowa.gov

**Hall, Chris (D, 13)**
State Capitol
1007 East Grand Avenue
Des Moines, IA 50319
P: (515) 281-3221
E: chris.hall
   @legis.iowa.gov

**Hanson, Curt (D, 82)**
State Capitol
1007 East Grand Avenue
Des Moines, IA 50319
P: (515) 281-3221
E: curt.hanson
   @legis.iowa.gov

**Hanusa, Mary Ann (R, 16)**
State Capitol
1007 East Grand Avenue
Des Moines, IA 50319
P: (515) 281-3221
E: maryann.hanusa
   @legis.iowa.gov

**Heartsill, Greg (R, 28)**
State Capitol
1007 East Grand Avenue
Des Moines, IA 50319
P: (515) 281-3221
E: greg.heartsill
   @legis.iowa.gov

**Heaton, Dave E. (R, 84)**
State Capitol
1007 East Grand Avenue
Des Moines, IA 50319
P: (515) 281-3221
E: dave.heaton
   @legis.iowa.gov

**Heddens, Lisa (D, 46)**
State Capitol
1007 East Grand Avenue
Des Moines, IA 50319
P: (515) 281-3221
E: lisa.heddens
   @legis.iowa.gov

**Hein, Lee (R, 96)**
State Capitol
1007 East Grand Avenue
Des Moines, IA 50319
P: (515) 281-3221
E: lee.hein@legis.iowa.gov

**Highfill, Jake (R, 39)**
State Capitol
1007 East Grand Avenue
Des Moines, IA 50319
P: (515) 281-3221
E: jake.highfill
   @legis.iowa.gov

**Hinson, Ashley (R, 67)***
State Capitol
1007 East Grand Avenue
Des Moines, IA 50319
E: ashley.hinson
   @legis.iowa.gov

**Holt, Steven (R, 18)**
State Capitol
1007 East Grand Avenue
Des Moines, IA 50319
P: (515) 281-3221
E: steven.holt
   @legis.iowa.gov

**Holz, Chuck (R, 5)**
State Capitol
1007 East Grand Avenue
Des Moines, IA 50319
E: chuck.holz
   @legis.iowa.gov

**Hunter, Bruce (D, 34)**
State Capitol
1007 East Grand Avenue
Des Moines, IA 50319
P: (515) 281-3221
E: bruce.hunter
   @legis.iowa.gov

**Huseman, Daniel A. (R, 3)**
State Capitol
1007 East Grand Avenue
Des Moines, IA 50319
P: (515) 281-3221
E: dan.huseman
   @legis.iowa.gov

**Isenhart, Charles (D, 100)**
State Capitol
1007 East Grand Avenue
Des Moines, IA 50319
P: (515) 281-3221
E: charles.isenhart
   @legis.iowa.gov

**Jacoby, David (D, 74)**
State Capitol
1007 East Grand Avenue
Des Moines, IA 50319
P: (515) 281-3221
E: david.jacoby
   @legis.iowa.gov

**Jones, Megan (R, 2)**
State Capitol
1007 East Grand Avenue
Des Moines, IA 50319
P: (515) 281-3221
E: megan.jones
   @legis.iowa.gov

**Kacena, Timothy (D, 14)***
State Capitol
1007 East Grand Avenue
Des Moines, IA 50319
E: timothy.kacena
   @legis.iowa.gov

**Kaufmann, Bobby (R, 73)**
State Capitol
1007 East Grand Avenue
Des Moines, IA 50319
P: (515) 281-3221
E: bobby.kaufmann
   @legis.iowa.gov

**Kearns, Jerry (D, 83)**
State Capitol
1007 East Grand Avenue
Des Moines, IA 50319
P: (515) 281-3221
E: jerry.kearns
   @legis.iowa.gov

**Kerr, David (R, 88)***
State Capitol
1007 East Grand Avenue
Des Moines, IA 50319
E: david.kerr
   @legis.iowa.gov

**Klein, Jarad (R, 78)**
State Capitol
1007 East Grand Avenue
Des Moines, IA 50319
P: (515) 281-3221
E: jarad.klein
   @legis.iowa.gov

**Koester, Kevin (R, 38)**
State Capitol
1007 East Grand Avenue
Des Moines, IA 50319
P: (515) 281-3221
E: kevin.koester
   @legis.iowa.gov

**Kressig, Bob (D, 59)**
State Capitol
1007 East Grand Avenue
Des Moines, IA 50319
P: (515) 281-3221
E: bob.kressig
   @legis.iowa.gov

**Kurth, Monica (D, 89)***
State Capitol
1007 E Grand Ave
Des Moines, IA 50319
E: monica.kurth
   @legis.iowa.gov

**Landon, John (R, 37)**
State Capitol
1007 East Grand Avenue
Des Moines, IA 50319
P: (515) 282-
E: john.landon
@legis.iowa.gov

**Lensing, Vicki (D, 85)**
State Capitol
1007 East Grand Avenue
Des Moines, IA 50319
P: (515) 281-7333
E: vicki.lensing
@legis.iowa.gov

**Lundgren, Shannon (R, 57)***
State Capitol
1007 East Grand Avenue
Des Moines, IA 50319
E: shannon.lundgren
@legis.iowa.gov

**Mascher, Mary (D, 86)**
State Capitol
1007 East Grand Avenue
Des Moines, IA 50319
P: (515) 282.6445
E: mary.mascher
@legis.iowa.gov

**Maxwell, Dave (R, 76)**
State Capitol
1007 East Grand Avenue
Des Moines, IA 50319
P: (515) 281-3221
E: dave.maxwell
@legis.iowa.gov

**McConkey, Charlie (D, 15)**
State Capitol
1007 East Grand Avenue
Des Moines, IA 50319
P: (515) 281-3221
E: charlie.mcconkey
@legis.iowa.gov

**McKean, Andy (R, 58)**
State Capitol
1007 East Grand Avenue
Des Moines, IA 50319
E: andy.mckean
@legis.iowa.gov

**Meyer, Brian (D, 33)**
State Capitol
1007 East Grand Avenue
Des Moines, IA 50319
P: (515) 281-3221
E: brian.meyer
@legis.iowa.gov

**Miller, Helen (D, 9)**
State Capitol
1007 East Grand Avenue
Des Moines, IA 50319
P: (515) 281-3221
E: helen.miller
@legis.iowa.gov

**Mohr, Gary (R, 94)***
State Capitol
1007 East Grand Avenue
Des Moines, IA 50319
E: gary.mohr@legis.iowa.gov

**Mommsen, Norlin (R, 97)**
State Capitol
1007 East Grand Avenue
Des Moines, IA 50319
P: (515) 281-3221
E: norlin.mommsen
@legis.iowa.gov

**Moore, Tom (R, 21)**
State Capitol
1007 East Grand Avenue
Des Moines, IA 50319
P: (515) 281-3221
E: tom.moore@legis.iowa.gov

**Nielsen, Amy (D, 77)***
State Capitol
1007 East Grand Avenue
Des Moines, IA 50319
E: amy.nielsen
@legis.iowa.gov

**Nunn, Zach (R, 30)**
State Capitol
1007 East Grand Avenue
Des Moines, IA 50319
E: zach.nunn@legis.iowa.gov

**Oldson, Jo (D, 41)**
State Capitol
1007 East Grand Avenue
Des Moines, IA 50319
P: (515) 281-3221
E: jo.oldson@legis.iowa.gov

**Olson, Rick (D, 31)**
State Capitol
1007 East Grand Avenue
Des Moines, IA 50319
P: (515) 281-3221
E: rick.olson
@legis.iowa.gov

**Ourth, Scott (D, 26)**
State Capitol
1007 East Grand Avenue
Des Moines, IA 50319
P: (515) 281-3221
E: scott.ourth
@legis.iowa.gov

**Paustian, Ross (R, 92)**
State Capitol
1007 East Grand Avenue
Des Moines, IA 50319
P: (515) 281-3221
E: Ross.Paustian
@legis.iowa.gov

**Pettengill, Dawn (R, 75)**
State Capitol
1007 East Grand Avenue
Des Moines, IA 50319
P: (515) 281-7487
E: dawn.pettengill
@legis.iowa.gov

**Prichard, Todd (D, 52)**
State Capitol
1007 East Grand Avenue
Des Moines, IA 50319
P: (515) 281-3221
E: todd.prichard
@legis.iowa.gov

**Rizer, Ken (R, 68)**
State Capitol
1007 East Grand Avenue
Des Moines, IA 50319
P: (515) 281-3221
E: ken.rizer@legis.iowa.gov

**Rogers, Walt (R, 60)**
State Capitol
1007 East Grand Avenue
Des Moines, IA 50319
P: (515) 281-3221
E: walt.rogers
@legis.iowa.gov

**Running-Marquardt,
Kirsten (D, 69)**
State Capitol
1007 East Grand Avenue
Des Moines, IA 50319
P: (515) 281-3221
E: kirsten.
running-marquardt
@legis.iowa.gov

**Salmon, Sandy (R, 63)**
State Capitol
1007 East Grand Avenue
Des Moines, IA 50319
P: (515) 281-3221
E: sandy.salmon
@legis.iowa.gov

**Sexton, Mike (R, 10)**
State Capitol
1007 East Grand Avenue
Des Moines, IA 50319
P: (515) 281-6055
E: mike.sexton
@legis.iowa.gov

**Sheets, Larry (R, 80)**
State Capitol
1007 East Grand Avenue
Des Moines, IA 50319
P: (515) 281-3221
E: larry.sheets
@legis.iowa.gov

**Sieck, David (R, 23)**
State Capitol
1007 East Grand Avenue
Des Moines, IA 50319
P: (515) 281-3221
E: david.sieck
@legis.iowa.gov

**Smith, Mark D. (D, 71)**
State Capitol
1007 East Grand Avenue
Des Moines, IA 50319
P: (515) 281-5230
E: mark.smith
@legis.iowa.gov

**Smith, Ras (D, 62)***
State Capitol
1007 East Grand Avenue
Des Moines, IA 50319
E: ras.smith@legis.iowa.gov

**Staed, Art (D, 66)**
State Capitol
1007 East Grand Avenue
Des Moines, IA 50319
P: (515) 281-3221
E: art.staed@legis.iowa.gov

**Steckman, Sharon (D, 53)**
State Capitol
1007 East Grand Avenue
Des Moines, IA 50319
P: (515) 281-3221
E: sharon.steckman
@legis.iowa.gov

**Taylor, Rob (R, 44)**
State Capitol
1007 East Grand Avenue
Des Moines, IA 50319
P: (515) 281-3221
E: rob.taylor
@legis.iowa.gov

**Taylor, Todd E. (D, 70)**
State Capitol
1007 East Grand Avenue
Des Moines, IA 50319
P: (515) 281-3221
E: todd.taylor
@legis.iowa.gov

**Thede, Phyllis (D, 93)**
State Capitol
1007 East Grand Avenue
Des Moines, IA 50319
P: (515) 281-3221
E: phyllis.thede
@legis.iowa.gov

# Iowa

**Upmeyer, Linda (R, 54)**
State Capitol
1007 East Grand Avenue
Des Moines, IA 50319
P: (515) 281-5137
E: linda.upmeyer
    @legis.iowa.gov

**Vander Linden, Guy (R, 79)**
State Capitol
1007 East Grand Avenue
Des Moines, IA 50319
P: (515) 281-3221
E: guy.vander.linden
    @legis.iowa.gov

**Watts, Ralph C. (R, 19)**
State Capitol
1007 East Grand Avenue
Des Moines, IA 50319
P: (515) 281-3221
E: ralph.watts
    @legis.iowa.gov

**Wessel-Kroeschell, Beth
    (D, 45)**
State Capitol
1007 East Grand Avenue
Des Moines, IA 50319
P: (515) 281-3221
E: beth.wessel-kroeschell
    @legis.iowa.gov

**Wheeler, Skyler (R, 4)***
State Capitol
1007 East Grand Avenue
Des Moines, IA 50319
P: (515) 281-7330
E: skyler.wheeler
    @legis.iowa.gov

**Wills, John (R, 1)**
State Capitol
1007 East Grand Avenue
Des Moines, IA 50319
P: (515) 281-3221
E: john.wills
    @legis.iowa.gov

**Winckler, Cindy (D, 90)**
State Capitol
1007 East Grand Avenue
Des Moines, IA 50319
P: (515) 281-3221
E: cindy.winckler
    @legis.iowa.gov

**Windschitl, Matt W. (R, 17)**
State Capitol
1007 East Grand Avenue
Des Moines, IA 50319
P: (515) 281-3221
E: matt.windschitl
    @legis.iowa.gov

**Wolfe, Mary (D, 98)**
State Capitol
1007 East Grand Avenue
Des Moines, IA 50319
P: (515) 281-3221
E: mary.wolfe
    @legis.iowa.gov

**Worthan, Gary (R, 11)**
State Capitol
1007 East Grand Avenue
Des Moines, IA 50319
P: (515) 281-3221
E: gary.worthan
    @legis.iowa.gov

**Zumbach, Louis (R, 95)***
State Capitol
1007 East Grand Avenue
Des Moines, IA 50319
E: louie.zumbach
    @legis.iowa.gov

# Kansas

## Executive

### Governor

**The Honorable Sam Brownback (R)**
Governor
300 Southwest 10th Avenue,
Suite 212S
Topeka, KS 66612
P: (785) 296-3232
F: (785) 296-7973

### Lieutenant Governor

**The Honorable Jeff Colyer (R)**
Lieutenant Governor
State Capitol, 2nd Floor
300 Southwest 10th Avenue
Topeka, KS 66612
P: (785) 296-2214
F: (785) 296-5669

### Attorney General

**The Honorable Derek Schmidt (R)**
Attorney General
120 Southwest 10th Avenue,
2nd Floor
Topeka, KS 66612
P: (785) 296-2215
F: (785) 296-6296

### Auditor

**Mr. Scott E. Frank**
(appointed by the Legislature)
Legislative Post Auditor
800 Southwest Jackson Street
Suite 1200
Topeka, KS 66612
P: (785) 296-5180
F: (785) 296-4482
E: scott.frank@lpa.ks.gov

### Commissioner of Insurance

**The Honorable Ken Selzer (R)**
Commissioner
420 Southwest 9th Street
Topeka, KS 66612
P: (785) 296-3071
F: (785) 296-7805
E: commissioner
@ksinsurance.org

### Secretary of State

**The Honorable Kris Kobach (R)**
Secretary of State
120 Southwest 10th Avenue
Topeka, KS 66612
P: (785) 296-4564
F: (785) 368-8033
E: sos@sos.ks.gov

### Treasurer

**The Honorable Ron Estes (R)**
State Treasurer
900 Southwest Jackson Street,
Suite 201
Topeka, KS 66612
P: (785) 296-3171
F: (785) 296-7950
E: ron@treasurer.ks.gov

## Judiciary

### Supreme Court (MR)

**Ms. Heather L. Smith**
Clerk of the Appellate Courts
Judicial Center
301 Southwest 10th Avenue,
Room 374
Topeka, KS 66612
P: (785) 296-3229
F: (785) 296-1028
E: appellateclerk
@kscourts.org

**The Honorable Lawton R. Nuss**
Chief Justice
**The Honorable Carol A. Beier**
**The Honorable Dan Biles**
**The Honorable Lee A. Johnson**
**The Honorable Marla J. Luckert**
**The Honorable Eric S. Rosen**
**The Honorable Caleb Stegall**

## Legislative

## Senate

### Senate President

**Senator Susan Wagle (R)**
Senate President
300 Southwest 10th Avenue
Room 333-E
Topeka, KS 66612
P: (785) 296-2419
E: susan.wagle
@senate.ks.gov

### Senate Majority Leader

**Senator Jim Denning (R)**
Senate Majority Leader
300 Southwest 10th Avenue
Room 330-E
Topeka, KS 66612
P: (785) 296-7394
E: jim.denning
@senate.ks.gov

### Senate Minority Leader

**Senator Anthony Hensley (D)**
Senate Minority Leader
300 Southwest 10th Avenue
Room 318-E
Topeka, KS 66612
P: (785) 296-3245
E: anthony.hensley
@senate.ks.gov

### Secretary of the Senate

**Mr. Corey Carnahan**
Secretary of the Senate
300 Southwest 10th Avenue
Room 325-E
Topeka, KS 66612
P: (785) 296-2456
F: (785) 276-6718
E: corey.carnahan
@senate.ks.gov

### Members of the Senate

**Alley, Larry W. (R, 32)***
300 Southwest 10th Avenue
Room 541-E
Topeka, KS 66612
P: (785) 296-7381
E: larry.alley
@senate.ks.gov

**Baumgardner, Molly (R, 37)**
300 Southwest 10th Avenue
Room 224-E
Topeka, KS 66612
P: (785) 296-7368
E: molly.baumgardner
@senate.ks.gov

**Berger, Edward E. (R, 34)***
300 Southwest 10th Avenue
Room 235-E
Topeka, KS 66612
P: (785) 296-6981
E: edward.berger
@senate.ks.gov

**Billinger, Rick (R, 40)**
300 Southwest 10th Avenue
Room 236-E
Topeka, KS 66612
P: (785) 296-7659
E: rick.billinger
@senate.ks.gov

**Bollier, Barbara (R, 7)**
300 Southwest 10th Avenue
Room 237-E
Topeka, KS 66612
P: (785) 296-7686
E: barbara.bollier
@senate.ks.gov

**Bowers, Elaine S. (R, 36)**
300 Southwest 10th Avenue
Room 223-E
Topeka, KS 66612
P: (785) 296-7389
E: elaine.bowers
@senate.ks.gov

**Denning, Jim (R, 8)**
300 Southwest 10th Avenue
Room 330-E
Topeka, KS 66612
P: (785) 296-7394
E: jim.denning
@senate.ks.gov

**Doll, John (R, 39)**
300 Southwest 10th Avenue
Room 235-E
Topeka, KS 66612
P: (785) 296-7380
E: john.doll@senate.ks.gov

**Estes, Bud (R, 38)**
300 Southwest 10th Avenue
Room 445-E
Topeka, KS 66612
P: (785) 296-6287
E: bud.estes@senate.ks.gov

**Faust-Goudeau, Oletha (D, 29)**
300 Southwest 10th Avenue
Room 135-E
Topeka, KS 66612
P: (785) 296-7387
E: oletha.faust-goudeau
@senate.ks.gov

**Fitzgerald, Steve (R, 5)**
300 Southwest 10th Avenue
Room 124-E
Topeka, KS 66612
P: (785) 296-7357
E: steve.fitzgerald
@senate.ks.gov

**Francisco, Marci (D, 2)**
300 Southwest 10th Avenue
Room 134-E
Topeka, KS 66612
P: (785) 296-7364
E: marci.francisco
@senate.ks.gov

# Kansas

**Givens, Bruce (R, 14)***
300 Southwest 10th Avenue
Room 225-E
Topeka, KS 66612
P: (785) 296-7678
E: bruce.givens
@senate.ks.gov

**Goddard, Dan (R, 15)***
300 Southwest 10th Avenue
Room 541-E
Topeka, KS 66612
P: (785) 296-7742
E: dan.goddard
@senate.ks.gov

**Haley, David (D, 4)**
300 Southwest 10th Avenue
Room 134-E
Topeka, KS 66612
P: (785) 296-7376
E: david.haley
@senate.ks.gov

**Hardy, Randall R. (R, 24)***
300 Southwest 10th Avenue
Room 223-E
Topeka, KS 66612
P: (785) 296-7369
E: randall.hardy
@senate.ks.gov

**Hawk, Tom (D, 22)**
300 Southwest 10th Avenue
Room 135-E
Topeka, KS 66612
P: (785) 296-7360
E: tom.hawk@senate.ks.gov

**Hensley, Anthony (D, 19)**
300 Southwest 10th Avenue
Room 318-E
Topeka, KS 66612
P: (785) 296-3245
E: anthony.hensley
@senate.ks.gov

**Holland, Tom (D, 3)**
300 Southwest 10th Avenue
Room 134-E
Topeka, KS 66612
P: (785) 296-7372
E: tom.holland
@senate.ks.gov

**Kelly, Laura (D, 18)**
300 Southwest 10th Avenue
Room 125-E
Topeka, KS 66612
P: (785) 296-7365
E: laura.kelly
@senate.ks.gov

**Kerschen, Dan (R, 26)**
300 Southwest 10th Avenue
Room 225-E
Topeka, KS 66612
P: (785) 296-7353
E: dan.kerschen
@senate.ks.gov

**LaTurner, Jacob (R, 13)**
300 Southwest 10th Avenue
Room 136-E
Topeka, KS 66612
P: (785) 296-7370
E: jacob.laturner
@senate.ks.gov

**Longbine, Jeff (R, 17)**
300 Southwest 10th Avenue
Room 341-E
Topeka, KS 66612
P: (785) 296-7384
E: jeff.longbine
@senate.ks.gov

**Lynn, Julia (R, 9)**
300 Southwest 10th Avenue
Room 445-S
Topeka, KS 66612
P: (785) 296-7382
E: julia.lynn@senate.ks.gov

**Masterson, Ty (R, 16)**
300 Southwest 10th Avenue
Room 237-E
Topeka, KS 66612
P: (785) 296-7388
E: ty.masterson
@senate.ks.gov

**McGinn, Carolyn (R, 31)**
300 Southwest 10th Avenue
Room 545-S
Topeka, KS 66612
P: (785) 296-7377
E: carolyn.mcginn
@senate.ks.gov

**Olson, Robert (R, 23)**
300 Southwest 10th Avenue
Room 236-E
Topeka, KS 66612
P: (785) 296-7358
E: robert.olson
@senate.ks.gov

**Petersen, Mike (R, 28)**
300 Southwest 10th Avenue
Room 345-S
Topeka, KS 66612
P: (785) 296-7355
E: mike.petersen
@senate.ks.gov

**Pettey, Pat Huggins (D, 6)**
300 Southwest 10th Avenue
Room 125-E
Topeka, KS 66612
P: (785) 296-7375
E: pat.pettey@senate.ks.gov

**Pilcher-Cook, Mary (R, 10)**
300 Southwest 10th Avenue
Room 234-E
Topeka, KS 66612
P: (785) 296-7362
E: mary.pilchercook
@senate.ks.gov

**Pyle, Dennis (R, 1)**
300 Southwest 10th Avenue
Room 234-E
Topeka, KS 66612
P: (785) 296-7379
E: dennis.pyle
@senate.ks.gov

**Rogers, Lynn W. (D, 25)***
300 Southwest 10th Avenue
Room 135-E
Topeka, KS 66612
P: (785) 296-7391
E: lynn.rogers
@senate.ks.gov

**Schmidt, Vicki (R, 20)**
300 Southwest 10th Avenue
Room 441-E
Topeka, KS 66612
P: (785) 296-7374
E: vicki.schmidt
@senate.ks.gov

**Skubal, John (R, 11)***
300 Southwest 10th Avenue
Room 124-E
Topeka, KS 66612
P: (785) 296-7301
E: john.skubal
@senate.ks.gov

**Suellentrop, Gene (R, 27)**
300 Southwest 10th Avenue
Room 224-E
Topeka, KS 66612
P: (785) 296-7681
E: gene.suellentrop
@Senate.ks.gov

**Sykes, Dinah H. (R, 21)***
300 Southwest 10th Avenue
Room 237-E
Topeka, KS 66612
P: (785) 296-7367
E: dinah.sykes
@senate.ks.gov

**Taylor, Mary Jo (R, 33)***
300 Southwest 10th Avenue
Room 441-E
Topeka, KS 66612
P: (785) 296-7667
E: maryjo.taylor
@senate.ks.gov

**Tyson, Caryn (R, 12)**
300 Southwest 10th Avenue
Room 123-E
Topeka, KS 66612
P: (785) 296-6838
E: caryn.tyson
@senate.ks.gov

**Wagle, Susan (R, 30)**
300 Southwest 10th Avenue
Room 333-E
Topeka, KS 66612
P: (785) 296-2419
E: susan.wagle
@senate.ks.gov

**Wilborn, Richard (R, 35)**
300 Southwest 10th Avenue
Room 541-E
Topeka, KS 66612
P: (785) 296-7354
E: richard.wilborn
@senate.ks.gov

# House

## Speaker of the House

**Speaker Ron Ryckman Jr. (R)**
Speaker of the House
300 Southwest 10th Avenue
Room 370-W
Topeka, KS 66612
P: (785) 296-5481
E: ron.ryckman@house.ks.gov

## Speaker Pro Tempore of the House

**Representative Scott
   Schwab (R)**
House Speaker Pro Tempore
300 Southwest 10th Avenue
Room 381-W
Topeka, KS 66612
P: (785) 296-7501
E: scott.schwab
@house.ks.gov

## House Majority Leader

**Representative Don
  Hineman (R)**
House Majority Leader
300 Southwest 10th Avenue
Room 372-W
Topeka, KS 66612
P: (785) 296-7636
E: don.hineman@house.ks.gov

## House Minority Leader

**Representative Jim Ward (D)**
House Minority Leader
300 Southwest 10th Avenue
Room 359-W
Topeka, KS 66612
P: (785) 296-7698
E: jim.ward@house.ks.gov

## Clerk of the House

**Ms. Susan W. Kannarr**
Chief Clerk of the House
300 Southwest 10th Avenue,
Room 272-W
Topeka, KS 66612
P: (785) 296-7633
F: (785) 291-3531
E: susan.kannarr
  @house.ks.gov

## Members of the House

**Alcala, John (D, 57)**
300 Southwest 10th Avenue
Room 173-S
Topeka, KS 66612
P: (785) 296-7371
E: john.alcala@house.ks.gov

**Alford, Steve (R, 124)**
300 Southwest 10th Avenue
Room 187-N
Topeka, KS 66612
P: (785) 296-7656
E: j.stephen.alford
  @house.ks.gov

**Arnberger, Tory M.
  (R, 112)***
300 Southwest 10th Avenue
Room 352-S
Topeka, KS 66612
P: (785) 296-7363
E: tory.arnberger
  @house.ks.gov

**Aurand, Clay (R, 106)***
300 Southwest 10th Avenue
Room 286-N
Topeka, KS 66612
P: (785) 296-7672
E: clay.aurand@house.ks.gov

**Awerkamp, Francis (R, 61)***
300 Southwest 10th Avenue
Room 166-W
Topeka, KS 66612
P: (785) 296-6989
E: francis.awerkamp
  @house.ks.gov

**Baker, Dave (R, 68)***
300 Southwest 10th Avenue
Room 167-W
Topeka, KS 66612
P: (785) 296-6997
E: dave.baker@house.ks.gov

**Ballard, Barbara W. (D, 44)**
300 Southwest 10th Avenue
Room 451-S
Topeka, KS 66612
P: (785) 296-7697
E: barbara.ballard
  @house.ks.gov

**Barker, John (R, 70)**
300 Southwest 10th Avenue
Room 285-N
Topeka, KS 66612
P: (785) 296-7674
E: john.barker@house.ks.gov

**Becker, Steven (R, 104)**
300 Southwest 10th Avenue
Room 512-N
Topeka, KS 66612
P: (785) 296-7196
E: steven.becker
  @house.ks.gov

**Bishop, Elizabeth (D, 88)***
300 Southwest 10th Avenue
Room 559-W
Topeka, KS 66612
P: (785) 296-5016
E: elizabeth.bishop
  @house.ks.gov

**Blex, Doug (R, 12)***
300 Southwest 10th Avenue
Room 168-W
Topeka, KS 66612
P: (785) 296-5863
E: doug.blex@house.ks.gov

**Brim, Shelee (R, 39)***
300 Southwest 10th Avenue
Room 519-N
Topeka, KS 66612
P: (785) 296-7675
E: shelee.brim@house.ks.gov

**Burroughs, Tom (D, 33)**
300 Southwest 10th Avenue
Room 50-S
Topeka, KS 66612
P: (785) 296-7630
E: tom.burroughs
  @house.ks.gov

**Campbell, Larry (R, 26)**
300 Southwest 10th Avenue
Room 286-N
Topeka, KS 66612
P: (785) 296-7632
E: larry.campbell
  @house.ks.gov

**Carlin, Sydney (D, 66)**
300 Southwest 10th Avenue
Room 451-S
Topeka, KS 66612
P: (785) 296-7649
E: sydney.carlin
  @house.ks.gov

**Carmichael, John (D, 92)**
300 Southwest 10th Avenue
Room 451-S
Topeka, KS 66612
P: (785) 296-7650
E: john.carmichael
  @house.ks.gov

**Carpenter, Blake (R, 81)**
300 Southwest 10th Avenue
Room 512-N
Topeka, KS 66612
P: (785) 296-7567
E: blake.carpenter
  @house.ks.gov

**Claeys, J.R. (R, 69)**
300 Southwest 10th Avenue
Room 274-W
Topeka, KS 66612
P: (785) 296-7670
E: jrclaeys@house.ks.gov

**Clark, Lonnie (R, 65)**
300 Southwest 10th Avenue
Room 352-S
Topeka, KS 66612
P: (785) 296-7483
E: lonnie.clark
  @house.ks.gov

**Clayton, Stephanie (R, 19)**
300 Southwest 10th Avenue
Room 512-N
Topeka, KS 66612
P: (785) 296-7655
E: stephanie.clayton
  @house.ks.gov

**Concannon, Susan (R, 107)**
300 Southwest 10th Avenue
Room 149-S
Topeka, KS 66612
P: (785) 296-7677
E: susan.concannon
  @house.ks.gov

**Corbet, Ken (R, 54)**
300 Southwest 10th Avenue
Room 179-N
Topeka, KS 66612
P: (785) 296-7679
E: ken.corbet@house.ks.gov

**Cox, Tom (R, 17)***
300 Southwest 10th Avenue
Room 165-W
Topeka, KS 66612
P: (785) 296-7331
E: tom.cox@house.ks.gov

**Crum, Steven G. (D, 98)***
300 Southwest 10th Avenue
Room 173-W
Topeka, KS 66612
P: (785) 296-7468
E: steven.crum@house.ks.gov

**Curtis, Pam (D, 32)**
300 Southwest 10th Avenue
Room 452-S
Topeka, KS 66612
P: (785)-296-7371
E: pam.curtis@house.ks.gov

**Davis, Erin (R, 15)**
300 Southwest 10th Avenue
Room 151-S
Topeka, KS 66612
P: (785) 296-3971
E: erin.davis@house.ks.gov

**Deere, Debbie (D, 40)***
300 Southwest 10th Avenue
Room 174-W
Topeka, KS 66612
P: (785) 296-7653
E: debbie.deere
  @house.ks.gov

**DeGraaf, Peter (R, 82)**
300 Southwest 10th Avenue
Room 458-W
Topeka, KS 66612
P: (785) 296-7693
E: pete.degraaf
  @house.ks.gov

**Delperdang, Leo (R, 94)***
300 Southwest 10th Avenue
Room 352-S
Topeka, KS 66612
P: (785) 296-7663
E: leo.delperdang
  @house.ks.gov

# Kansas

**Dierks, Diana (D, 71)**
300 Southwest 10th Avenue
Room 519-N
Topeka, KS 66612
P: (785) 296-7642
E: diana.dierks
@house.ks.gov

**Dietrich, Brenda S.
(R, 52)***
300 Southwest 10th Avenue
Room 166-W
Topeka, KS 66612
P: (785) 296-7648
E: brenda.dietrich
@house.ks.gov

**Dove, Willie (R, 38)**
300 Southwest 10th Avenue
Room 149-S
Topeka, KS 66612
P: (785) 296-7670
E: willie.dove@house.ks.gov

**Elliott, Roger A. (R, 87)***
300 Southwest 10th Avenue
Room 168-W
Topeka, KS 66612
P: (785) 296-7476
E: roger.elliott
@house.ks.gov

**Ellis, Ronald B. (R, 47)***
300 Southwest 10th Avenue
Room 166-W
Topeka, KS 66612
P: (785) 296-5623
E: ronald.ellis
@house.ks.gov

**Eplee, John R. (R, 63)***
300 Southwest 10th Avenue
Room 512-N
Topeka, KS 66612
P: (785) 296-8621
E: john.eplee@house.ks.gov

**Esau, Keith (R, 14)**
300 Southwest 10th Avenue
Room 151-S
Topeka, KS 66612
P: (785) 296-7631
E: keith.esau@house.ks.gov

**Finch, Blaine (R, 59)**
300 Southwest 10th Avenue
Room 519-N
Topeka, KS 66612
P: (785) 296-7655
E: blaine.finch
@house.ks.gov

**Finney, Gail (D, 84)**
300 Southwest 10th Avenue
Room 451-S
Topeka, KS 66612
P: (785) 296-7648
E: gail.finney@house.ks.gov

**Francis, Shannon (R, 125)**
300 Southwest 10th Avenue
Room 561-W
Topeka, KS 66612
P: (785) 296-7655
E: shannon.francis
@house.ks.gov

**Frownfelter, Stan S.
(D, 37)**
300 Southwest 10th Avenue
Room 359-W
Topeka, KS 66612
P: (785) 296-7648
E: stan.frownfelter
@house.ks.gov

**Gallagher, Linda (R, 23)**
300 Southwest 10th Avenue
Room 187-N
Topeka, KS 66612
P: (785) 296-7548
E: linda.gallagher
@house.ks.gov

**Garber, Randy (R, 62)**
300 Southwest 10th Avenue
Room 459-W
Topeka, KS 66612
P: (785) 296-7665
E: randy.garber
@house.ks.gov

**Gartner, Jim (D, 53)**
300 Southwest 10th Avenue
Room 43-S
Topeka, KS 66612
P: (785) 296-7668
E: jim.gartner@house.ks.gov

**Good, Mary Martha (R, 75)***
300 Southwest 10th Avenue
Room 168-W
Topeka, KS 66612
E: marymartha.good
@house.ks.gov

**Hawkins, Daniel (R, 100)**
300 Southwest 10th Avenue
Room 186-N
Topeka, KS 66612
P: (785) 296-7631
E: dan.hawkins@house.ks.gov

**Helgerson Jr., Henry
(D, 83)**
300 Southwest 10th Avenue
Room 174-W
Topeka, KS 66612
P: (785) 296-7355
E: henry.helgerson
@house.ks.gov

**Henderson, Broderick T.
(D, 35)**
300 Southwest 10th Avenue
Room 451-S
Kansas City, KS 66612
P: (785) 296-7697
E: broderick.henderson
@house.ks.gov

**Hibbard, Larry (R, 13)**
300 Southwest 10th Avenue
Room 512-N
Topeka, KS 66612
P: (785) 296-7380
E: larry.hibbard
@house.ks.gov

**Highberger, Dennis (D, 46)**
300 Southwest 10th Avenue
Room 174-W
Topeka, KS 66612
P: (785) 296-7122
E: dennis.boog.highberger
@house.ks.gov

**Highland, Ron (R, 51)**
300 Southwest 10th Avenue
Room 561-W
Topeka, KS 66612
P: (785) 296-7310
E: ron.highland
@house.ks.gov

**Hineman, Don (R, 118)**
300 Southwest 10th Avenue
Room 372-W
Topeka, KS 66612
P: (785) 296-7636
E: don.hineman@house.ks.gov

**Hodge, Tim (D, 72)***
300 Southwest 10th Avenue
Room 176-W
Topeka, KS 66612
P: (785) 296-2361
E: tim.hodge@house.ks.gov

**Hoffman, Kyle (R, 116)**
300 Southwest 10th Avenue
Room 481-W
Topeka, KS 66612
P: (785) 296-7643
E: kyle.hoffman
@house.ks.gov

**Holscher, Cindy (D, 16)***
300 Southwest 10th Avenue
Room 173-W
Topeka, KS 66612
P: (785) 296-7659
E: cindy.holscher
@house.ks.gov

**Houser, Michael (R, 1)**
300 Southwest 10th Avenue
Room 179-N
Topeka, KS 66612
P: (785) 296-7679
E: michael.houser
@house.ks.gov

**Huebert, Steve (R, 90)**
300 Southwest 10th Avenue
Room 512-N
Topeka, KS 66612
P: (785) 296-1754
E: steve.huebert
@house.ks.gov

**Humphries, Susan (R, 99)***
300 Southwest 10th Avenue
Room 512-N
Topeka, KS 66612
P: (785) 296-7699
E: susan.humphries
@house.ks.gov

**Jacobs, Trevor (R, 4)***
300 Southwest 10th Avenue
Room 167-W
Topeka, KS 66612
P: (785) 296-7616
E: trevor.jacobs
@house.ks.gov

**Jennings, Russell (R, 122)**
300 Southwest 10th Avenue
Room 151-S
Topeka, KS 66612
P: (785) 296-7196
E: russ.jennings
@house.ks.gov

**Johnson, Steven (R, 108)**
300 Southwest 10th Avenue
Room 185-N
Topeka, KS 66612
P: (785) 296-7696
E: steven.johnson
@house.ks.gov

**Jones, Kevin (R, 5)**
300 Southwest 10th Avenue
Room 151-S
Topeka, KS 66612
P: (785) 296-6287
E: kevin.jones@house.ks.gov

**Judd-Jenkins, Anita
(R, 80)***
300 Southwest 10th Avenue
Room 166-W
Topeka, KS 66612
P: (785) 296-7671
E: anita.judd-jenkins
@house.ks.gov

**Karleskint, Jim (D, 42)***
300 Southwest 10th Avenue
Room 512-N
Topeka, KS 66612
P: (785) 296-7683
E: jim.karleskint
@house.ks.gov

**Kelly, Jim (R, 11)**
300 Southwest 10th Avenue
Room 581-W
Topeka, KS 66612
P: (785) 296-6014
E: jim.kelly@house.ks.gov

**Kessinger, Jan H. (R, 20)***
300 Southwest 10th Avenue
Room 268-W
Topeka, KS 66612
P: (785) 296-7436
E: jan.kessinger
@house.ks.gov

**Kiegerl, S. Mike (R, 121)**
300 Southwest 10th Avenue
Room 512-N
Topeka, KS 66612
P: (785) 296-7636
E: mike.kiegerl
@house.ks.gov

**Koesten, Joy (R, 28)***
300 Southwest 10th Avenue
Room 268-W
Topeka, KS 66612
P: (785) 296-7646
E: joy.koesten@house.ks.gov

**Kuether, Annie (D, 55)**
300 Southwest 10th Avenue
Room 43-S
Topeka, KS 66612
P: (785) 296-7669
E: annie.kuether
@house.ks.gov

**Lakin, Greg (R, 91)***
300 Southwest 10th Avenue
Room 352-S
Topeka, KS 66612
P: (785) 296-7681
E: greg.lakin@house.ks.gov

**Landwehr, Brenda (R, 105)***
300 Southwest 10th Avenue
Room 352-S
Topeka, KS 66612
P: (785) 296-7683
E: brenda.landwehr
@house.ks.gov

**Lewis, Greg (R, 113)**
300 Southwest 10th Avenue
Room 268-W
Topeka, KS 66612
P: (785) 296-7682
E: greg.lewis@house.ks.gov

**Lusk, Nancy (D, 22)**
300 Southwest 10th Avenue
Room 54-S
Topeka, KS 66612
P: (785) 296-7651
E: nancy.lusk@house.ks.gov

**Lusker, Adam (D, 2)**
300 Southwest 10th Avenue
Room 50-S
Topeka, KS 66612
P: (785) 296-7698
E: adam.lusker@house.ks.gov

**Markley, Patty (R, 8)***
300 Southwest 10th Avenue
Room 165-W
Topeka, KS 66612
P: (785) 296-7695
E: patty.markley
@house.ks.gov

**Mason, Les (R, 73)**
300 Southwest 10th Avenue
Room 521-E
Topeka, KS 66612
P: (785) 296-7640
E: les.mason@house.ks.gov

**Mastroni, Leonard A.
(R, 117)***
300 Southwest 10th Avenue
Room 167-W
Topeka, KS 66612
P: (785) 296-7396
E: leonard.mastroni
@house.ks.gov

**Miller, Vic (D, 58)***
300 Southwest 10th Avenue
Room 176-W
Topeka, KS 66612
P: (785) 296-7656
E: vic.miller@house.ks.gov

**Murnan, Monica (D, 3)***
300 Southwest 10th Avenue
Room 54-S
Topeka, KS 66612
P: (785) 296-7462
E: monica.murnan
@house.ks.gov

**Neighbor, Cindy (D, 18)**
300 Southwest 10th Avenue
Room 43-S
Topeka, KS 66612
P: (785) 296-7690
E: cindy.neighbor
@house.ks.gov

**Ohaebosim, KC (D, 89)***
300 Southwest 10th Avenue
Room 173-W
Topeka, KS 66612
E: kc.ohaebosim
@house.ks.gov

**Orr, Boyd (R, 115)***
300 Southwest 10th Avenue
Room 168-W
Topeka, KS 66612
P: (785) 296-7392
E: boyd.orr@house.ks.gov

**Osterman, Leslie (R, 97)**
300 Southwest 10th Avenue
Room 149-S
Topeka, KS 66612
P: (785) 296-7689
E: leslie.osterman
@house.ks.gov

**Ousley, Jarrod (D, 24)**
300 Southwest 10th Avenue
Room 452-S
Topeka, KS 66612
P: (785) 296-7366
E: jarrod.ousley
@house.ks.gov

**Parker, Brett (D, 29)***
300 Southwest 10th Avenue
Room 451-S
Topeka, KS 66612
P: (785) 296-5413
E: brett.parker
@house.ks.gov

**Patton, Fred (R, 50)**
300 Southwest 10th Avenue
Room 274-W
Topeka, KS 66612
P: (785) 296-7460
E: fred.patton@house.ks.gov

**Phelps, Eber (D, 111)***
300 Southwest 10th Avenue
Room 43-S
Topeka, KS 66612
P: (785) 296-7691
E: eber.phelps@house.ks.gov

**Phillips, Tom (R, 67)**
300 Southwest 10th Avenue
Room 512-N
Topeka, KS 66612
P: (785) 296-6014
E: tom.phillips
@house.ks.gov

**Pittman, Jeff (D, 41)***
300 Southwest 10th Avenue
Room 559-S
Topeka, KS 66612
P: (785) 296-7522
E: jeff.pittman
@house.ks.gov

**Powell, Randy (R, 30)**
300 Southwest 10th Avenue
Room 459-W
Topeka, KS 66612
P: (785) 296-5593
E: randy.powell
@house.ks.gov

**Proehl, Richard J. (R, 7)**
300 Southwest 10th Avenue
Room 581-W
Topeka, KS 66612
P: (785) 296-7639
E: richard.proehl
@house.ks.gov

**Rafie, Abraham (R, 48)***
State Capitol
300 Southwest 10th Avenue
Topeka, KS 66612
P: (785) 296-7680
E: abraham.rafie
@house.ks.gov

**Rahjes, Ken (R, 110)**
300 Southwest 10th Avenue
Room 352-S
Topeka, KS 66612
P: 785 296-7676
E: ken.rahjes@house.ks.gov

**Ralph, Bradley (R, 119)***
300 Southwest 10th Avenue
Room 512-N
Topeka, KS 66612
P: (785) 296-7501
E: bradley.ralph
@house.ks.gov

**Rooker, Melissa (R, 25)**
300 Southwest 10th Avenue
Room 168-W
Topeka, KS 66612
P: (785) 296-7686
E: melissa.rooker
@house.ks.gov

**Ruiz, Louis E. (D, 31)**
300 Southwest 10th Avenue
Room 47-S
Topeka, KS 66612
P: (785) 296-7122
E: louis.ruiz@house.ks.gov

**Ryckman Jr., Ron (R, 78)**
300 Southwest 10th Avenue
Room 370-W
Topeka, KS 66612
P: (785) 296-5481
E: ron.ryckman@house.ks.gov

**Sawyer, Tom (D, 95)**
300 Southwest 10th Avenue
Room 174-W
Topeka, KS 66612
P: (785) 296-7691
E: tom.sawyer@house.ks.gov

**Schreiber, Mark (R, 60)***
300 Southwest 10th Avenue
Room 167-W
Topeka, KS 66612
E: mark.schreiber
@house.ks.gov

# Kansas

**Schroeder, Don (R, 74)**
300 Southwest 10th Avenue
Room 149-S
Topeka, KS 66612
P: (785) 296-7500
E: don.schroeder
  @house.ks.gov

**Schwab, Scott (R, 49)**
300 Southwest 10th Avenue
Room 381-W
Topeka, KS 66612
P: (785) 296-7501
E: scott.schwab
  @house.ks.gov

**Seiwert, Joe (R, 101)**
300 Southwest 10th Avenue
Room 481-W
Topeka, KS 66612
P: (785) 296-7647
E: joe.seiwert@house.ks.gov

**Sloan, Tom (R, 45)**
300 Southwest 10th Avenue
Room 521-E
Topeka, KS 66612
P: (785) 296-7654
E: tom.sloan@house.ks.gov

**Smith, Adam (R, 120)***
300 Southwest 10th Avenue
Room 512-N
Topeka, KS 66612
E: adam.smith@house.ks.gov

**Smith, Eric L. (R, 76)***
300 Southwest 10th Avenue
Room 167-W
Topeka, KS 66612
P: (785) 296-7557
E: eric.smith@house.ks.gov

**Stogsdill, Jerry (D, 21)***
300 Southwest 10th Avenue
Room 452-S
Topeka, KS 66612
P: (785) 296-7692
E: jerry.stogsdill
  @house.ks.gov

**Sutton, William (R, 43)**
300 Southwest 10th Avenue
Room 274-W
Topeka, KS 66612
P: (785) 296-7676
E: bill.sutton@house.ks.gov

**Swanson, Susie (R, 64)**
300 Southwest 10th Avenue
Room 519-N
Topeka, KS 66612
P: (785) 296-7642
E: susie.swanson
  @house.ks.gov

**Tarwater Sr., Sean E.**
  **(R, 27)***
300 Southwest 10th Avenue
Room 268-W
Topeka, KS 66612
P: (785) 296-7685
E: sean.tarwater
  @house.ks.gov

**Terrell, Patsy (D, 102)***
300 Southwest 10th Avenue
Room 174-W
Topeka, KS 66612
P: (785) 296-7645
E: patsy.terrell
  @house.ks.gov

**Thimesch, Jack (R, 114)**
300 Southwest 10th Avenue
Room 561-W
Topeka, KS 66612
P: (785) 296-7105
E: jack.thimesch
  @house.ks.gov

**Thompson, Kent (R, 9)**
300 Southwest 10th Avenue
Room 187-N
Topeka, KS 66612
P: (785) 296-7673
E: kent.thompson
  @house.ks.gov

**Trimmer, Ed (D, 79)**
300 Southwest 10th Avenue
Room 174-W
Topeka, KS 66612
P: (785) 296-7122
E: ed.trimmer@house.ks.gov

**Vickrey, Jene (R, 6)**
300 Southwest 10th Avenue
Room 276-W
Topeka, KS 66612
P: (785) 296-7662
E: jene.vickrey
  @house.ks.gov

**Victors, Ponka-We (D, 103)**
300 Southwest 10th Avenue
Room 54-S
Topeka, KS 66612
P: (785) 296-7651
E: ponka-we.victors
  @house.ks.gov

**Ward, Jim (D, 86)**
300 Southwest 10th Avenue
Room 359-W
Topeka, KS 66612
P: (785) 296-7698
E: jim.ward@house.ks.gov

**Waymaster, Troy (R, 109)**
300 Southwest 10th Avenue
Room 111-N
Topeka, KS 66612
P: (785) 296-7672
E: troy.waymaster
  @house.ks.gov

**Weber, Chuck (R, 85)**
300 Southwest 10th Avenue
Room 512-N
Topeka, KS 66612
P: 785-296-7688
E: chuck.weber@house.ks.gov

**Wheeler Jr., John P.**
  **(R, 123)***
300 Southwest 10th Avenue
Room 167-W
Topeka, KS 66612
P: (785) 296-7461
E: john.wheeler
  @house.ks.gov

**Whipple, Brandon (D, 96)**
300 Southwest 10th Avenue
Room 452-S
Topeka, KS 66612
P: (785) 296-7366
E: brandon.whipple
  @house.ks.gov

**Whitmer, John (R, 93)**
300 Southwest 10th Avenue
Room 512-N
Topeka, KS 66612
P: (785) 296-7567
E: john.whitmer
  @house.ks.gov

**Williams, Kristey (R, 77)**
300 Southwest 10th Avenue
Room 165-W
Topeka, KS 66612
P: (785) 296-3971
E: kristey.williams
  @house.ks.gov

**Wilson, John (D, 10)**
300 Southwest 10th Avenue
Room 54-S
Topeka, KS 66612
P: (785) 296-7652
E: john.wilson@house.ks.gov

**Winn, Valdenia C. (D, 34)**
300 Southwest 10th Avenue
Room 451-S
Topeka, KS 66612
P: (785) 296-7657
E: valdenia.winn
  @house.ks.gov

**Wolfe Moore, Kathy (D, 36)**
300 Southwest 10th Avenue
Room 47-S
Topeka, KS 66612
P: (785) 296-7688
E: kathy.wolfemoore
  @house.ks.gov

# Kentucky

## Executive

### Governor

**The Honorable Matt Bevin (R)**
Governor
700 Capital Avenue, Suite 100
Frankfort, KY 40601
P: (502) 564-2611
F: (502) 564-0437

### Lieutenant Governor

**The Honorable Jenean Hampton (R)**
Lieutenant Governor
700 Capital Avenue, Suite 142
Frankfort, KY 40601
P: (502) 564-2611
F: (502) 564-2849

### Commissioner of Agriculture

**The Honorable Ryan Quarles (R)**
Commissioner of Agriculture
105 Corporate Drive
Frankfort, KY 40601
P: (502) 573-0282
F: (502) 573-0046
E: ag.web@ky.gov

### Attorney General

**The Honorable Andy Beshear (D)**
Attorney General
700 Capitol Avenue
Capitol Building, Suite 118
Frankfort, KY 40601
P: (502) 696-5300
F: (502) 564-2894

### Auditor

**The Honorable Mike Harmon (R)**
Auditor of Public Accounts
209 St. Clair Street
Frankfort, KY 40601
P: (502) 564-5841
F: (502) 564-2912

## Secretary of State

**The Honorable Alison L. Grimes (D)**
Secretary of State
700 Capital Avenue, Suite 152
Frankfort, KY 40601
P: (502) 564-3490
F: (502) 564-5687
E: sos.secretary@ky.gov

## Treasurer

**The Honorable Allison Ball (R)**
State Treasurer
1050 U.S. Highway 127 South
Suite 100
Frankfort, KY 40601
P: (502) 564-4722
F: (502) 567-6545
E: allison.ball@ky.gov

# Judiciary

## Supreme Court (NE)

**Ms. Susan Stokley Clary**
Clerk of the Supreme Court
State Capitol
700 Capitol Avenue, Room 235
Frankfort, KY 40601
P: (502) 564-5444
F: (502) 564-2665

**The Honorable John D. Minton Jr.**
Chief Justice
**The Honorable William Cunningham**
**The Honorable Lisabeth T. Hughes**
**The Honorable Michelle M. Keller**
**The Honorable Laurance VanMeter**
**The Honorable Daniel J. Venters**
**The Honorable Samuel T. Wright III**

# Legislative

## Senate

### Senate President

**Senator Robert Stivers (R)**
Senate President
Capitol Annex, Room 236
702 Capitol Avenue
Frankfort, KY 40601
P: (502) 564-3120
E: robert.stivers @lrc.ky.gov

## President Pro Tempore of the Senate

**Senator David Givens (R)**
Senate President Pro Tempore
Capitol Annex, Room 236
702 Capitol Avenue
Frankfort, KY 40601
P: (502) 564-3120
E: david.givens@lrc.ky.gov

## Senate Majority Leader

**Senator Damon Thayer (R)**
Senate Majority Floor Leader
Capitol Annex, Room 242
702 Capitol Avenue
Frankfort, KY 40601
P: (502) 564-2450
E: Damon.Thayer@lrc.ky.gov

## Senate Minority Leader

**Senator Ray S. Jones II (D)**
Senate Minority Floor Leader
Capitol Annex, Room 254
702 Capitol Avenue
Frankfort, KY 40601
P: (502) 564-2470
E: Ray.Jones@lrc.ky.gov

## Secretary of the Senate

**Ms. Donna Holiday**
Senate Clerk
702 Capital Avenue
Frankfort, KY 40601
P: (502) 564-5320
E: donna.holiday@lrc.ky.gov

## Members of the Senate

**Adams, Julie Raque (R, 36)**
Capitol Annex, Room 209
702 Capitol Avenue
Frankfort, KY 40601
P: (502) 564-8100 Ext. 682
E: Julie.Adams@lrc.ky.gov

**Alvarado, Ralph (R, 28)**
Capitol Annex, Room 229
702 Capitol Avenue
Frankfort, KY 40601
P: (502) 564-8100 Ext. 681
E: Ralph.Alvarado @lrc.ky.gov

**Angel, Denise Harper (D, 35)**
Capitol Annex, Room 255
702 Capitol Avenue
Frankfort, KY 40601
P: (502) 564-8100 Ext. 633
E: denise.harperangel @lrc.ky.gov

**Bowen, Joe R. (R, 8)**
Capitol Annex, Room 228
702 Capitol Avenue
Frankfort, KY 40601
P: (502) 564-8100 Ext. 662
E: Joe.Bowen@lrc.ky.gov

**Buford, Tom (R, 22)**
Capitol Annex, Room 252
702 Capitol Avenue
Frankfort, KY 40601
P: (502) 564-8100 Ext. 610
F: (502) 564-2466
E: Tom.Buford@lrc.ky.gov

**Carpenter, Jared (R, 34)**
Capitol Annex, Room 203
702 Capitol Avenue
Frankfort, KY 40601
P: (502) 564-8100 Ext. 730
E: Jared.Carpenter @lrc.ky.gov

**Carroll, Danny (R, 2)**
Capitol Annex, Room 229
702 Capitol Avenue
Frankfort, KY 40601
P: (502) 564-8100 Ext. 712
E: danny.carroll@lrc.ky.gov

**Carroll, Julian (D, 7)**
Capitol Annex, Room 254
702 Capitol Avenue
Frankfort, KY 40601
P: (502) 564-2470
E: julian.carroll @lrc.ky.gov

**Clark, Perry B. (D, 37)**
Capitol Annex, Room 255
702 Capitol Avenue
Frankfort, KY 40601
P: (502) 564-8100 Ext. 715
E: Perry.Clark@lrc.ky.gov

**Embry Jr., C.B. (R, 6)**
Capitol Annex, Room 252
702 Capitol Avenue
Frankfort, KY 40601
P: (502) 564-8100 Ext. 710
E: CB.Embry@lrc.ky.gov

**Girdler, Rick (R, 15)\***
Capitol Annex, Room 209
702 Capitol Avenue
Frankfort, KY 40601
P: (501) 564-8100 Ext. 656
E: rick.girdler@lrc.ky.gov

# Kentucky

**Givens, David (R, 9)**
Capitol Annex, Room 236
702 Capitol Avenue
Frankfort, KY 40601
P: (502) 564-3120
E: david.givens@lrc.ky.gov

**Harris, Ernie (R, 26)**
Capitol Annex, Room 204
702 Capitol Avenue
Frankfort, KY 40601
P: (502) 564-8100 Ext. 605
E: Ernie.Harris@lrc.ky.gov

**Higdon, Jimmy (R, 14)**
Capitol Annex, Room 242
702 Capitol Avenue
Frankfort, KY 40601
P: (502) 564-2450
E: Jimmy.Higdon@lrc.ky.gov

**Hornback, Paul (R, 20)**
Capitol Annex, Room 203
702 Capitol Avenue
Frankfort, KY 40601
P: (502) 564-8100 Ext. 648
E: Paul.Hornback@lrc.ky.gov

**Humphries, Stan (R, 1)**
Capitol Annex, Room 209
702 Capitol Avenue
Frankfort, KY 40601
P: (502) 564-8100 Ext. 870
E: stan.humphries
    @lrc.ky.gov

**Jones II, Ray S. (D, 31)**
Capitol Annex, Room 254
702 Capitol Avenue
Frankfort, KY 40601
P: (502) 564-2470
E: Ray.Jones@lrc.ky.gov

**Kerr, Alice Forgy (R, 12)**
Capitol Annex, Room 203
702 Capitol Avenue
Frankfort, KY 40601
P: (502) 564-8100 Ext. 625
E: alice.kerr@lrc.ky.gov

**McDaniel, Chris (R, 23)**
Capitol Annex, Room 204
702 Capitol Avenue
Frankfort, KY 40601
P: (502) 564-8100 Ext. 615
E: christ.mcdaniel
    @lrc.ky.gov

**McGarvey, Morgan (D, 19)**
Capitol Annex, Room 255
702 Capitol Avenue
Frankfort, KY 40601
P: (502) 564-8100 Ext. 621
E: morgan.mcgarvey
    @lrc.ky.gov

**Meredith, Stephen L.
    (R, 5)\***
Capitol Annex, Room 229
702 Capitol Avenue
Frankfort, KY 40601
P: (502) 564-8100 Ext. 644
E: stephen.meredith
    @lrc.ky.gov

**Neal, Gerald A. (D, 33)**
Capitol Annex, Room 255
702 Capitol Avenue
Frankfort, KY 40601
P: (502) 564-8100 Ext. 655
E: Gerald.Neal@lrc.ky.gov

**Parrett, Dennis (D, 10)**
Capitol Annex, Room 255
702 Capitol Avenue
Frankfort, KY 40601
P: (502) 564-8100 Ext. 645
E: Dennis.Parrett
    @lrc.ky.gov

**Ridley, Dorsey (D, 4)**
Capitol Annex, Room 254
702 Capitol Avenue
Frankfort, KY 40601
P: (502) 564-2470
E: Dorsey.Ridley@lrc.ky.gov

**Robinson, Albert (R, 21)**
Capitol Annex, Room 228
702 Capitol Avenue
Frankfort, KY 40601
P: (502) 564-8100 Ext. 604
E: Albert.Robinson
    @lrc.ky.gov

**Schickel, John (R, 11)**
Capitol Annex, Room 209
702 Capitol Avenue
Frankfort, KY 40601
P: (502) 564-8100 Ext. 617
E: John.Schickel@lrc.ky.gov

**Schroder, Wil (R, 24)**
Capitol Annex, Room 209
702 Capitol Avenue
Frankfort, KY 40601
P: (502) 564-8100 Ext. 624
E: Wil.Schroder@lrc.ky.gov

**Seum, Dan (R, 38)**
Capitol Annex, Room 242
702 Capitol Avenue
Frankfort, KY 40601
P: (502) 564-2450
E: dan.seum@lrc.ky.gov

**Smith, Brandon (R, 30)**
Capitol Annex, Room 252
702 Capitol Avenue
Frankfort, KY 40601
P: (502) 564-8100 Ext. 646
E: Brandon.Smith@lrc.ky.gov

**Stivers, Robert (R, 25)**
Capitol Annex, Room 236
702 Capitol Avenue
Frankfort, KY 40601
P: (502) 564-3120
E: robert.stivers
    @lrc.ky.gov

**Thayer, Damon (R, 17)**
Capitol Annex, Room 242
702 Capitol Avenue
Frankfort, KY 40601
P: (502) 564-2450
E: Damon.Thayer@lrc.ky.gov

**Thomas, Reginald (D, 13)**
Capitol Annex, Room 255
702 Capitol Avenue
Frankfort, KY 40601
P: (502) 564-8100 Ext. 608
F: (502) 564-0777
E: reginald.thomas
    @lrc.ky.gov

**Turner, Johnny Ray (D, 29)**
Capitol Annex, Room 254
702 Capitol Avenue
Frankfort, KY 40601
P: (502) 564-8100 Ext. 6136
E: JohnnyRay.Turner
    @lrc.ky.gov

**Webb, Robin L. (D, 18)**
Capitol Annex, Room 255
702 Capitol Avenue
Frankfort, KY 40601
P: (502) 564-8100 Ext. 676
E: Robin.Webb@lrc.ky.gov

**West, Steve (R, 27)**
Capitol Annex, Room 229
702 Capitol Avenue
Frankfort, KY 40601
P: (502) 564-8100 Ext. 806
E: steve.west@lrc.ky.gov

**Westerfield, Whitney (R, 3)**
Capitol Annex, Room 228
702 Capitol Avenue
Frankfort, KY 40601
P: (502) 564-8100 Ext. 622
E: whitney.westerfield
    @lrc.ky.gov

**Wilson, Mike (R, 32)**
Capitol Annex, Room 204
702 Capitol Avenue
Frankfort, KY 40601
P: (502) 564-8100 Ext. 717
E: Mike.Wilson@lrc.ky.gov

**Wise, Max (R, 16)**
Capitol Annex, Room 229
702 Capitol Avenue
Frankfort, KY 40601
P: (502) 564-8100 Ext. 673
E: Max.Wise@lrc.ky.gov

# House

## Speaker of the House

**Representative Jeffrey
    Hoover (R)**
Speaker of the House
Capitol Annex, Room 332
702 Capitol Avenue
Frankfort, KY 40601
P: (502) 564-4334
E: Jeff.Hoover@lrc.ky.gov

## Speaker Pro Tempore of the House

**Representative David
    Osborne (R)**
Speaker Pro Tempore
Capitol Annex, Room 332C
702 Capitol Avenue
Frankfort, KY 40601
P: (502) 564-4334
E: David.Osborne@lrc.ky.gov

## House Majority Leader

**Representative Jonathan
    Shell (R)**
Majority Floor Leader
Capitol Annex, Room 370D
702 Capitol Avenue
Frankfort, KY 40601
P: (502) 564-2217
E: jonathan.shell
    @lrc.ky.gov

## House Minority Leader

**Representative Rocky
    Adkins (D)**
House Majority Floor Leader
Capitol Annex, Room 472
702 Capitol Avenue
Frankfort, KY 40601
P: (502) 564-5565
E: Rocky.Adkins@lrc.ky.gov

## Clerk of the House

**Mr. Brad Metcalf**
Chief Clerk of the House
State Capitol, Room 309
700 Capital Avenue
Frankfort, KY 40601
P: (502) 564-3366
F: (502) 564-7178

# Members of the House

**Adkins, Rocky (D, 99)**
Capitol Annex, Room 472
702 Capitol Avenue
Frankfort, KY 40601
P: (502) 564-5565
E: Rocky.Adkins@lrc.ky.gov

**Bechler, Lynn (R, 4)**
Capitol Annex, Room 316C
702 Capitol Avenue
Frankfort, KY 40601
P: (502) 564-8100 Ext. 665
E: lynn.bechler@lrc.ky.gov

**Bentley, Danny R. (R, 98)***
Capitol Annex, Room 329J
702 Capitol Avenue
Frankfort, KY 40601
P: (502) 564-8100 Ext. 678
E: danny.bentley@lrc.ky.gov

**Benvenuti III, Robert (R, 88)**
Capitol Annex, Room 376
702 Capitol Avenue
Frankfort, KY 40601
P: (502) 564-8100 Ext. 628
E: robert.benvenuti@lrc.ky.gov

**Blanton, John C. (R, 92)***
Capitol Annex, Room 329H
702 Capitol Avenue
Frankfort, KY 40601
P: (502) 564-8100 Ext. 668
E: john.blanton@lrc.ky.gov

**Bratcher, Kevin D. (R, 29)**
Capitol Annex, Room 370
702 Capitol Avenue
Frankfort, KY 40601
P: (502) 564-2217
E: Kevin.Bratcher@lrc.ky.gov

**Brown Jr., George A. (D, 77)**
Capitol Annex, Room 429B
702 Capitol Avenue
Frankfort, KY 40601
P: (502) 564-8100 Ext. 620
E: George.Brown@lrc.ky.gov

**Brown, Larry D. (R, 95)***
Capitol Annex, Room 329I
702 Capitol Avenue
Frankfort, KY 40601
P: (502) 564-8100 Ext. 649
E: larry.brown@lrc.ky.gov

**Bunch, Regina (R, 82)**
Capitol Annex, Room 367A
702 Capitol Avenue
Frankfort, KY 40601
P: (502) 564-8100 Ext. 683
E: Regina.Bunch@lrc.ky.gov

**Burch, Tom (D, 30)**
Capitol Annex, Room 472
702 Capitol Avenue
Frankfort, KY 40601
P: (502) 564-8100 Ext. 601
E: Tom.Burch@lrc.ky.gov

**Cantrell, McKenzie (D, 38)***
Capitol Annex, Room 424A
702 Capitol Avenue
Frankfort, KY 40601
P: (502) 564-8100 Ext. 670
E: mckenzie.cantrell@lrc.ky.gov

**Carney, John (R, 51)**
Capitol Annex, Room 309
702 Capitol Avenue
Frankfort, KY 40601
P: (502) 564-8100 Ext. 660
E: John.Carney@lrc.ky.gov

**Castlen, Matt (R, 14)***
Capitol Annex, Room 329D
702 Capitol Avenue
Frankfort, KY 40601
P: (502) 564-8100 Ext. 688
E: matt.castlen@lrc.ky.gov

**Couch, Tim (R, 90)**
Capitol Annex, Room 329C
702 Capitol Avenue
Frankfort, KY 40601
P: (502) 564-8100 Ext. 632
E: Tim.Couch@lrc.ky.gov

**Coursey, Will (D, 6)**
Capitol Annex, Room 424D
702 Capitol Avenue
Frankfort, KY 40601
P: (502) 564-8100 Ext. 659
E: Will.Coursey@lrc.ky.gov

**DeCesare, Jim (R, 17)**
Capitol Annex, Room 373A
702 Capitol Avenue
Frankfort, KY 40601
P: (502) 564-8100 Ext. 640
E: dj951@twc.com

**Donohue, Jeffrey (D, 37)**
Capitol Annex, Room 451C
702 Capitol Avenue
Frankfort, KY 40601
P: (502) 564-8100 Ext. 629
E: jeffrey.donohue@lrc.ky.gov

**Dossett, Myron (R, 9)**
Capitol Annex, Room 401
702 Capitol Avenue
Frankfort, KY 40601
P: (502) 564-8100 Ext. 657
E: Myron.Dossett@lrc.ky.gov

**DuPlessis, Jim (R, 25)**
Capitol Annex, Room 373C
702 Capitol Avenue
Frankfort, KY 40601
P: (502) 564-8100 Ext. 650
E: Jim.DuPlessis@lrc.ky.gov

**Elliott, Daniel (R, 54)**
Capitol Annex, Room 329F
702 Capitol Avenue
Frankfort, KY 40601
P: (502) 564-8100 Ext. 677
E: daniel.elliott@lrc.ky.gov

**Fischer, Joseph M. (R, 68)**
Capitol Annex, Room 313
702 Capitol Avenue
Frankfort, KY 40601
P: (502) 564-8100 Ext. 742
E: Joe.Fischer@lrc.ky.gov

**Fleming, Ken (R, 48)***
Capitol Annex, Room 351D
702 Capitol Avenue
Frankfort, KY 40601
P: (502) 564-8100 Ext. 698
E: ken.fleming@lrc.ky.gov

**Flood, Kelly (D, 75)**
Capitol Annex, Room 432G
702 Capitol Avenue
Frankfort, KY 40601
P: (502) 564-8100 Ext. 675
E: Kelly.Flood@lrc.ky.gov

**Fugate, Chris (R, 84)***
Capitol Annex, Room 329G
702 Capitol Avenue
Frankfort, KY 40601
P: (502) 564-8100 Ext. 697
E: chris.fugate@lrc.ky.gov

**Gentry, Alan (D, 46)***
Capitol Annex, Room 432D
702 Capitol Avenue
Frankfort, KY 40601
P: (502) 564-8100 Ext. 699
E: al.gentry@lrc.ky.gov

**Gooch, Jim (R, 12)**
Capitol Annex, Room 376
702 Capitol Avenue
Frankfort, KY 40601
P: (502) 564-8100 Ext. 687
E: Jim.Gooch@lrc.ky.gov

**Graham, Derrick W. (D, 57)**
Capitol Annex, Room 429J
702 Capitol Avenue
Frankfort, KY 40601
P: (502) 564-8100 Ext. 639
E: Derrick.Graham@lrc.ky.gov

**Greer, Jeff (D, 27)**
Capitol Annex, Room 424F
702 Capitol Avenue
Frankfort, KY 40601
P: (502) 564-8100 Ext. 603
E: Jeff.Greer@lrc.ky.gov

**Hale, David (R, 74)**
Capitol Annex, Room 405B
702 Capitol Avenue
Frankfort, KY 40601
P: (502) 564-8100 Ext. 642
E: David.Hale@lrc.ky.gov

**Harris, Chris (D, 93)**
Capitol Annex, Room 457C
702 Capitol Avenue
Frankfort, KY 40601
P: (502) 564-8100 Ext. 635
E: Chris.Harris@lrc.ky.gov

**Hart, Mark (R, 78)***
Capitol Annex, Room 316E
702 Capitol Avenue
Frankfort, KY 40601
P: (502) 564-8100 Ext. 667
E: mark.hart@lrc.ky.gov

**Hatton, Angie (D, 94)***
Capitol Annex, Room 429I
702 Capitol Avenue
Frankfort, KY 40601
P: (502) 564-8100 Ext. 669
E: angie.hatton@lrc.ky.gov

**Heath, Richard (R, 2)**
Capitol Annex, Room 405E
702 Capitol Avenue
Frankfort, KY 40601
P: (502) 564-8100 Ext. 638
E: richard.heath@lrc.ky.gov

**Herald, Toby (R, 91)**
Capitol Annex, Room 329B
702 Capitol Avenue
Frankfort, KY 40601
P: (502) 564-8100 Ext. 641
E: toby.herald@lrc.ky.gov

**Hoover, Jeffrey (R, 83)**
Capitol Annex, Room 332
702 Capitol Avenue
Frankfort, KY 40601
P: (502) 564-4334
E: Jeff.Hoover@lrc.ky.gov

# Kentucky

**Horlander, Dennis (D, 40)**
Capitol Annex, Room 457E
702 Capitol Avenue
Frankfort, KY 40601
P: (502) 564-8100 Ext. 636
E: Dennis.Horlander
@lrc.ky.gov

**Imes, Kenny (R, 5)**
Capitol Annex, Room 324A
702 Capitol Avenue
Frankfort, KY 40601
P: (502) 564-8100 Ext. 611
E: Kenny.Imes@lrc.ky.gov

**Jenkins, Joni L. (D, 44)**
Capitol Annex, Room 432A
702 Capitol Avenue
Frankfort, KY 40601
P: (502) 564-8100 Ext. 692
E: Joni.Jenkins@lrc.ky.gov

**Johnson, D.J. (R, 13)***
Capitol Annex, Room 352B
702 Capitol Avenue
Frankfort, KY 40601
P: (502) 564-8100 Ext. 705
E: DJ.Johnson@lrc.ky.gov

**Johnson, Dan (R, 49)***
Capitol Annex, Room 413E
702 Capitol Avenue
Frankfort, KY 40601
P: (502) 564-8100 Ext. 651
E: Dan.Johnson@lrc.ky.gov

**Kay II, James (D, 56)**
Capitol Annex, Room 451A
702 Capitol Avenue
Frankfort, KY 40601
P: (502) 564-8100 Ext. 736
E: james.kay@lrc.ky.gov

**Keene, Dennis (D, 67)**
Capitol Annex, Room 472
702 Capitol Avenue
Frankfort, KY 40601
P: (502) 564-5565
E: Dennis.Keene@lrc.ky.gov

**King, Kim (R, 55)**
Capitol Annex, Room 405C
702 Capitol Avenue
Frankfort, KY 40601
P: (502) 564-8100 Ext. 763
E: Kim.King@lrc.ky.gov

**Koenig, Adam (R, 69)**
Capitol Annex, Room 329E
702 Capitol Avenue
Frankfort, KY 40601
P: (502) 564-8100 Ext. 689
E: Adam.Koenig@lrc.ky.gov

**Lee, Stan (R, 45)**
Capitol Annex, Room 357D
702 Capitol Avenue
Frankfort, KY 40601
P: (502) 564-8100 Ext. 693
E: Stan.Lee@lrc.ky.gov

**Linder, Brian (R, 61)**
Capitol Annex, Room 316D
702 Capitol Avenue
Frankfort, KY 40601
P: (502) 564-8100 Ext. 627
E: brian.linder@lrc.ky.gov

**Marzian, Mary Lou (D, 34)**
Capitol Annex, Room 451E
702 Capitol Avenue
Frankfort, KY 40601
P: (502) 564-8100 Ext. 643
E: MaryLou.Marzian
@lrc.ky.gov

**Mayfield, Donna (R, 73)**
Capitol Annex, Room 358B
702 Capitol Avenue
Frankfort, KY 40601
P: (502) 564-8100 Ext. 630
E: Donna.Mayfield
@lrc.ky.gov

**McCoy, D. Chad (R, 50)***
Capitol Annex, Room 416B
702 Capitol Avenue
Frankfort, KY 40601
P: (502) 564-8100 Ext. 664
E: chad.mccoy@lrc.ky.gov

**Meade, David (R, 80)**
Capitol Annex, Room 370
702 Capitol Avenue
Frankfort, KY 40601
P: (502) 564-2217
E: david.meade@lrc.ky.gov

**Meeks, Reginald K. (D, 42)**
Capitol Annex, Room 432B
702 Capitol Avenue
Frankfort, KY 40601
P: (502) 564-8100 Ext. 653
E: Reginald.Meeks
@lrc.ky.gov

**Meredith, Michael (R, 19)**
Capitol Annex, Room 416A
702 Capitol Avenue
Frankfort, KY 40601
P: (502) 564-8100 Ext. 719
E: Michael.Meredith
@lrc.ky.gov

**Meyer, Russ (D, 39)**
Capitol Annex, Room 457B
702 Capitol Avenue
Frankfort, KY 40601
P: (502) 564-8100 Ext. 623
E: Russ.Meyer@lrc.ky.gov

**Miles, Suzanne (R, 7)**
Capitol Annex, Room 367B
702 Capitol Avenue
Frankfort, KY 40601
P: (502) 564-8100 Ext. 709
E: suzanne.miles@lrc.ky.gov

**Miller, Charles (D, 28)**
Capitol Annex, Room 457D
702 Capitol Avenue
Frankfort, KY 40601
P: (502) 564-8100 Ext. 631
E: Charlie.Miller
@lrc.ky.gov

**Miller, Jerry T. (R, 36)**
Capitol Annex, Room 357C
702 Capitol Avenue
Frankfort, KY 40601
P: (502) 564-8100 Ext. 718
E: Jerry.Miller@lrc.ky.gov

**Mills, Robert M. (R, 11)***
Capitol Annex, Room 413C
702 Capitol Avenue
Frankfort, KY 40601
P: (502) 564-8100 Ext. 700
E: Robby.Mills@lrc.ky.gov

**Moffett, Phil (R, 32)**
Capitol Annex, Room 357E
702 Capitol Avenue
Frankfort, KY 40601
P: (502) 564-8100 Ext. 708
E: Phil.Moffett@lrc.ky.gov

**Moore, Tim (R, 18)**
Capitol Annex, Room 358C
702 Capitol Avenue
Frankfort, KY 40601
P: (502) 564-8100 Ext. 702
E: Tim.Moore@lrc.ky.gov

**Morgan, C. Wesley (R, 81)***
Capitol Annex, Room 405D
702 Capitol Avenue
Frankfort, KY 40601
P: (502) 564-8100 Ext. 607
E: wesley.morgan@lrc.ky.gov

**Moser, Kimberly Poore
(R, 64)***
Capitol Annex, Room 351C
702 Capitol Avenue
Frankfort, KY 40601
P: (502) 564-8100 Ext. 694
E: kimberly.moser
@lrc.ky.gov

**Nelson, Rick (D, 87)**
Capitol Annex, Room 424G
702 Capitol Avenue
Frankfort, KY 40601
P: (502) 564-8100 Ext. 612
E: Rick.Nelson@lrc.ky.gov

**Nemes, Jason Michael
(R, 33)***
Capitol Annex, Room 416C
702 Capitol Avenue
Frankfort, KY 40601
P: (502) 564-8100 Ext. 706
E: jason.nemes@lrc.ky.gov

**Osborne, David (R, 59)**
Capitol Annex, Room 332C
702 Capitol Avenue
Frankfort, KY 40601
P: (502) 564-4334
E: David.Osborne@lrc.ky.gov

**Overly, Sannie (D, 72)**
Capitol Annex, Room 457A
702 Capitol Avenue
Frankfort, KY 40601
P: (502) 564-8100 Ext. 661
E: sannie.overly@lrc.ky.gov

**Owens, Darryl T. (D, 43)**
Capitol Annex, Room 429A
702 Capitol Avenue
Frankfort, KY 40601
P: (502) 564-8100 Ext. 685
E: Darryl.Owens@lrc.ky.gov

**Palumbo, Ruth Ann (D, 76)**
Capitol Annex, Room 432E
702 Capitol Avenue
Frankfort, KY 40601
P: (502) 564-8100 Ext. 600
E: RuthAnn.Palumbo
@lrc.ky.gov

**Petrie, Jason (R, 16)***
Capitol Annex, Room 351B
702 Capitol Avenue
Frankfort, KY 40601
P: (502) 564-8100 Ext. 618
E: jason.petrie@lrc.ky.gov

**Pratt, Phillip (R, 62)***
Capitol Annex, Room 316A
702 Capitol Avenue
Frankfort, KY 40601
P: (502) 564-8100 Ext. 671
E: phillip.pratt@lrc.ky.gov

**Prunty, Melinda Gibbons
(R, 15)***
Capitol Annex, Room 413G
702 Capitol Avenue
Frankfort, KY 40601
P: (502) 564-8100 Ext. 686
E: melinda.prunty
@lrc.ky.gov

**Rader, Marie L. (R, 89)**
Capitol Annex, Room 405C
702 Capitol Avenue
Frankfort, KY 40601
P: (502) 564-8100 Ext. 720
E: Marie.Rader@lrc.ky.gov

# Kentucky

**Rand, Rick (D, 47)**
Capitol Annex, Room 303
702 Capitol Avenue
Frankfort, KY 40601
P: (502) 564-8100 Ext. 720
F: (502) 564-1010
E: Rick.Rand@lrc.ky.gov

**Reed, William Brandon
(R, 24)***
Capitol Annex, Room 402
702 Capitol Avenue
Frankfort, KY 40601
P: (502) 564-8100 Ext. 684
E: brandon.reed@lrc.ky.gov

**Richards, Jody (D, 20)**
Capitol Annex, Room 429H
702 Capitol Avenue
Frankfort, KY 40601
P: (502) 564-8100 Ext. 672
E: Jody.Richards@lrc.ky.gov

**Riggs, Steve (D, 31)**
Capitol Annex, Room 429F
702 Capitol Avenue
Frankfort, KY 40601
P: (502) 564-8100 Ext. 674
F: (502) 564-6543
E: steve.riggs@lrc.ky.gov

**Riley, Steve (R, 23)***
Capitol Annex, Room 352C
702 Capitol Avenue
Frankfort, KY 40601
P: (502) 564-8100 Ext. 680
E: steve.riley@lrc.ky.gov

**Rothenburger, Rob (R, 58)***
Capitol Annex, Room 351E
702 Capitol Avenue
Frankfort, KY 40601
P: (502) 564-8100 Ext. 609
E: rob.rothenburger
@lrc.ky.gov

**Rowland, Bart (R, 21)**
Capitol Annex, Room 416D
702 Capitol Avenue
Frankfort, KY 40601
P: (502) 564-8100 Ext. 613
E: bart.rowland@lrc.ky.gov

**Rudy, Steven J. (R, 1)**
Capitol Annex, Room 304
702 Capitol Avenue
Frankfort, KY 40601
P: (502) 564-8100 Ext. 637
E: Steven.Rudy@lrc.ky.gov

**Santoro, Sal (R, 60)**
Capitol Annex, Room 351A
702 Capitol Avenue
Frankfort, KY 40601
P: (502) 564-8100 Ext. 691
E: Sal.Santoro@lrc.ky.gov

**Schamore, Dean (D, 10)**
Capitol Annex, Room 429G
702 Capitol Avenue
Frankfort, KY 40601
P: (502) 564-8100 Ext. 704
E: Dean.Schamore@lrc.ky.gov

**Scott, Attica Woodson
(D, 41)***
Capitol Annex, Room 432C
702 Capitol Avenue
Frankfort, KY 40601
P: (502) 564-8100 Ext. 606
E: attica.scott@lrc.ky.gov

**Shell, Jonathan (R, 71)**
Capitol Annex, Room 370D
702 Capitol Avenue
Frankfort, KY 40601
P: (502) 564-2217
E: jonathan.shell
@lrc.ky.gov

**Simpson, Arnold (D, 65)**
Capitol Annex, Room 429D
702 Capitol Avenue
Frankfort, KY 40601
P: (502) 564-8100 Ext. 695
E: Arnold.Simpson
@lrc.ky.gov

**Sims Jr., John (D, 70)***
Capitol Annex, Room 429C
702 Capitol Avenue
Frankfort, KY 40601
P: (502) 564-8100 Ext. 696
E: john.sims@lrc.ky.gov

**Sinnette, Kevin P. (D, 100)**
Capitol Annex, Room 424C
702 Capitol Avenue
Frankfort, KY 40601
P: (502) 564-8100 Ext. 703
E: Kevin.Sinnette
@lrc.ky.gov

**St. Onge, Diane (R, 63)**
Capitol Annex, Room 357B
702 Capitol Avenue
Frankfort, KY 40601
P: (502) 564-8100 Ext. 701
E: Diane.StOnge@lrc.ky.gov

**Stewart, Jim (R, 86)**
Capitol Annex, Room 358A
702 Capitol Avenue
Frankfort, KY 40601
P: (502) 564-8100 Ext. 690
E: Jim.Stewart@lrc.ky.gov

**Stone, Wilson (D, 22)**
Capitol Annex, Room 472
702 Capitol Avenue
Frankfort, KY 40601
P: (502) 564-8100 Ext. 672
E: Wilson.Stone@lrc.ky.gov

**Thomas, Walker Wood (R, 8)***
Capitol Annex, Room 413F
702 Capitol Avenue
Frankfort, KY 40601
P: (502) 564-8100 Ext. 658
E: Walker.Thomas@lrc.ky.gov

**Tipton, James A. (R, 53)**
Capitol Annex, Room 316B
702 Capitol Avenue
Frankfort, KY 40601
P: (502) 564-8100 Ext. 793
E: James.Tipton@lrc.ky.gov

**Turner, Tommy (R, 85)**
Capitol Annex, Room 324B
702 Capitol Avenue
Frankfort, KY 40601
P: (502) 564-8100 Ext. 716
E: Tommy.Turner@lrc.ky.gov

**Upchurch, Ken (R, 52)**
Capitol Annex, Room 373B
702 Capitol Avenue
Frankfort, KY 39201
P: (502) 564-8100 Ext. 784
E: Ken.Upchurch@lrc.ky.gov

**Watkins, Gerald (D, 3)**
Capitol Annex, Room 429G
702 Capitol Avenue
Frankfort, KY 40601
P: (502) 564-8100 Ext. 634
E: Gerald.Watkins
@lrc.ky.gov

**Wayne, Jim (D, 35)**
Capitol Annex, Room 451B
702 Capitol Avenue
Frankfort, KY 40601
P: (502) 564-8100 Ext. 616
E: Jim.Wayne@lrc.ky.gov

**Webber, Russell (R, 26)**
Capitol Annex, Room 352A
702 Capitol Avenue
Frankfort, KY 40601
P: (502) 564-8100 Ext. 663
E: russell.webber
@lrc.ky.gov

**Wells, William Scott
(R, 97)***
Capitol Annex, Room 413D
702 Capitol Avenue
Frankfort, KY 40601
P: (502) 564-8100 Ex. 654
E: scott.wells@lrc.ky.gov

**Westrom, Susan (D, 79)**
Capitol Annex, Room 424E
702 Capitol Avenue
Frankfort, KY 40601
P: (502) 564-8100 Ext. 740
E: Susan.Westrom@lrc.ky.gov

**Wuchner, Addia (R, 66)**
Capitol Annex, Room 315
702 Capitol Avenue
Frankfort, KY 40601
P: (502) 564-8100 Ext. 707
E: AddiaKathryn.Wuchner
@lrc.ky.gov

**York, Jill (R, 96)**
Capitol Annex, Room 367C
702 Capitol Avenue
Frankfort, KY 40601
P: (502) 564-8100 Ext. 602
E: jill.york@lrc.ky.gov

*State Elective Officials 2017*    97

# Louisiana

## Executive

### Governor
**The Honorable John Bel Edwards (D)**
Governor
P.O. Box 94004
Baton Rouge, LA 70804
P: (225) 342-7015
F: (225) 342-7099

### Lieutenant Governor
**The Honorable Billy Nungesser (R)**
Lieutenant Governor
1051 North 3rd Street, Capitol Annex
P.O. Box 44243
Baton Rouge, LA 70804
P: (225) 342-7009
F: (225) 342-1949
E: ltgov@crt.la.gov

### Commissioner of Agriculture & Forestry
**Dr. Michael G. Strain (R)**
Commissioner
5825 Florida Boulevard, Suite 2000
Baton Rouge, LA 70806
P: (225) 922-1234
F: (225) 923-4880
E: commissioner @ldaf.state.la.us

### Attorney General
**The Honorable Jeffrey Landry (R)**
Attorney General
P.O. Box 94095
Baton Rouge, LA 70804
P: (225) 326-6000
F: (225) 326-6797

### Auditor
*Louisiana does not have the office of auditor.*

### Commissioner of Insurance
**The Honorable James J. Donelon (R)**
Commissioner
1702 North 3rd Street
P.O. Box 94214
Baton Rouge, LA 70804
P: (225) 342-5900
F: (225) 342-8622

### Secretary of State
**The Honorable Tom Schedler (R)**
Secretary of State
P.O. Box 94125
Baton Rouge, LA 70804
P: (225) 922-2880
F: (225) 922-2003
E: admin@sos.la.gov

## Judiciary

### Supreme Court (NE)
**Mr. John Tarlton Olivier**
Clerk of Court
400 Royal Street, Suite 4200
New Orleans, LA 70130
P: (504) 310-2300

**The Honorable Bernette J. Johnson**
Chief Justice
**The Honorable Marcus R. Clark**
**The Honorable Scott J. Crichton**
**The Honorable James Genovese**
**The Honorable Greg Guidry**
**The Honorable Jefferson D. Hughes III**
**The Honorable John L. Weimer**

## Legislative

## Senate

### Senate President
**Senator John A. Alario Jr. (R)**
Senate President
State Capitol
P.O. Box 94183
Baton Rouge, LA 70804
P: (225) 342-2040
F: (225) 342-0617
E: alarioj@legis.la.gov

### President Pro Tempore of the Senate
**Senator Gerald Long (R)**
Senate President Pro Tempore
State Capitol
P.O. Box 94183
Baton Rouge, LA 70804
P: (225) 342-2040
F: (225) 342-0617
E: longg@legis.la.gov

### Secretary of the Senate
**Mr. Glenn Koepp**
Secretary of the Senate
Basement, State Capitol
900 North 3rd Street
Baton Rouge, LA 70804
P: (225) 342-5997
F: (225) 342-1140
E: koeppg@legis.la.gov

### Members of the Senate
**Alario Jr., John A. (R, 8)**
State Capitol
P.O. Box 94183
Baton Rouge, LA 70804
P: (225) 342-2040
F: (225) 342-0617
E: alarioj@legis.la.gov

**Allain II, R.L. Bret (R, 21)**
State Capitol
P.O. Box 94183
Baton Rouge, LA 70804
P: (225) 342-2040
F: (225) 342-0617
E: allainb@legis.la.gov

**Appel, Conrad (R, 9)**
State Capitol
P.O. Box 94183
Baton Rouge, LA 70804
P: (225) 342-2040
F: (225) 342-0617
E: appelc@legis.la.gov

**Barrow, Regina Ashford (D, 15)**
State Capitol
P.O. Box 94183
Baton Rouge, LA 70804
P: (225) 342-2040
F: (225) 342-0617
E: barrowr@legis.la.gov

**Bishop, Wesley T. (D, 4)**
State Capitol
P.O. Box 94183
Baton Rouge, LA 70804
P: (225) 342-2040
F: (225) 342-0617
E: bishopw@legis.la.gov

**Boudreaux, Gerald (D, 24)**
State Capitol
P.O. Box 94183
Baton Rouge, LA 70804
P: (225) 342-2040
F: (225) 342-0617
E: boudreauxg@legis.la.gov

**Brown, Troy E. (D, 2)**
State Capitol
P.O. Box 94183
Baton Rouge, LA 70804
P: (225) 342-2040
F: (225) 342-0617
E: brownte@legis.la.gov

**Carter, Troy (D, 7)**
State Capitol
P.O. Box 94183
Baton Rouge, LA 70804
P: (225) 342-2040
F: (225) 342-0617
E: cartert@legis.la.gov

**Chabert, Norby (R, 20)**
State Capitol
P.O. Box 94183
Baton Rouge, LA 70804
P: (225) 342-2040
F: (225) 342-0617
E: chabertn@legis.la.gov

**Claitor, Dan (R, 16)**
State Capitol
P.O. Box 94183
Baton Rouge, LA 70804
P: (225) 342-2040
F: (225) 342-0617
E: claitord@legis.la.gov

**Colomb, Yvonne (D, 14)**
State Capitol
P.O. Box 94183
Baton Rouge, LA 70804
P: (225) 342-2040
F: (225) 342-0617
E: dorseyy@legis.la.gov

**Cortez, Patrick Page (R, 23)**
State Capitol
P.O. Box 94183
Baton Rouge, LA 70804
P: (225) 342-2040
F: (225) 342-0617
E: cortezp@legis.la.gov

**Donahue, Jack (R, 11)**
State Capitol
P.O. Box 94183
Baton Rouge, LA 70804
P: (225) 342-2040
F: (225) 342-0617
E: donahuej@legis.la.gov

**Erdey, Dale (R, 13)**
State Capitol
P.O. Box 94183
Baton Rouge, LA 70804
P: (225) 342-2040
F: (225) 342-0617
E: erdeyd@legis.la.gov

**Fannin, James R. (R, 35)**
State Capitol
P.O. Box 94183
Baton Rouge, LA 70804
P: (225) 342-2040
F: (225) 342-0617
E: fanninj@legis.la.gov

**Gatti, Ryan (R, 36)**
State Capitol
P.O. Box 94183
Baton Rouge, LA 70804
P: (225) 342-2040
F: (225) 342-0617
E: gattir@legis.la.gov

**Hewitt, Sharon (R, 1)**
State Capitol
P.O. Box 94183
Baton Rouge, LA 70804
P: (225) 342-2040
F: (225) 342-0617
E: hewitts@legis.la.gov

**Johns, Ronnie (R, 27)**
State Capitol
P.O. Box 94183
Baton Rouge, LA 70804
P: (225) 342-2040
F: (225) 342-0617
E: johnsr@legis.la.gov

**LaFleur, Eric (D, 28)**
State Capitol
P.O. Box 94183
Baton Rouge, LA 70804
P: (225) 342-2040
F: (225) 342-0617
E: lafleure@legis.la.gov

**Lambert, Eddie J. (R, 18)**
State Capitol
P.O. Box 94183
Baton Rouge, LA 70804
P: (225) 342-2040
F: (225) 342-0617
E: lamberte@legis.la.gov

**Long, Gerald (R, 31)**
State Capitol
P.O. Box 94183
Baton Rouge, LA 70804
P: (225) 342-2040
F: (225) 342-0617
E: longg@legis.la.gov

**Luneau, Jay (D, 29)**
State Capitol
P.O. Box 94183
Baton Rouge, LA 70804
P: (225) 342-2040
F: (225) 342-0617
E: luneauj@legis.la.gov

**Martiny, Daniel R. (R, 10)**
State Capitol
P.O. Box 94183
Baton Rouge, LA 70804
P: (225) 342-2040
F: (225) 342-0617
E: martinyd@legis.la.gov

**Milkovich, John (D, 38)**
State Capitol
P.O. Box 94183
Baton Rouge, LA 70804
P: (225) 342-2040
F: (225) 342-0617
E: milkovichj@legis.la.gov

**Mills Jr., Fred H. (R, 22)**
State Capitol
P.O. Box 94183
Baton Rouge, LA 70804
P: (225) 342-2040
F: (225) 342-0617
E: millsf@legis.la.gov

**Mizell, Beth (R, 12)**
State Capitol
P.O. Box 94183
Baton Rouge, LA 70804
P: (225) 342-2040
F: (225) 342-0617
E: mizellb@legis.la.gov

**Morrell, Jean-Paul J. (D, 3)**
State Capitol
P.O. Box 94183
Baton Rouge, LA 70804
P: (225) 342-2040
F: (225) 342-0617
E: morrelljp@legis.la.gov

**Morrish, Dan W. (R, 25)**
State Capitol
P.O. Box 94183
Baton Rouge, LA 70804
P: (225) 342-2040
F: (225) 342-0617
E: morrishd@legis.la.gov

**Peacock, Barrow (R, 37)**
State Capitol
P.O. Box 94183
Baton Rouge, LA 70804
P: (225) 342-2040
F: (225) 342-0617
E: peacockb@legis.la.gov

**Perry, Jonathan (R, 26)**
State Capitol
P.O. Box 94183
Baton Rouge, LA 70804
P: (225) 342-2040
F: (225) 342-0617
E: perryj@legis.la.gov

**Peterson, Karen Carter (D, 5)**
State Capitol
P.O. Box 94183
Baton Rouge, LA 70804
P: (225) 342-2040
F: (225) 342-0617
E: petersonk@legis.la.gov

**Riser, Neil (R, 32)**
State Capitol
P.O. Box 94183
Baton Rouge, LA 70804
P: (225) 342-2040
F: (225) 342-0617
E: risern@legis.la.gov

**Smith Jr., Gary L. (D, 19)**
State Capitol
P.O. Box 94183
Baton Rouge, LA 70804
P: (225) 342-2040
F: (225) 342-0617
E: smithgl@legis.la.gov

**Smith, John R. (R, 30)**
State Capitol
P.O. Box 94183
Baton Rouge, LA 70804
P: (225) 342-2040
F: (225) 342-0617
E: smithj@legis.la.gov

**Tarver Sr., Gregory W. (D, 39)**
State Capitol
P.O. Box 94183
Baton Rouge, LA 70804
P: (225) 342-2040
F: (225) 342-0617
E: tarverg@legis.la.gov

**Thompson, Francis C. (D, 34)**
State Capitol
P.O. Box 94183
Baton Rouge, LA 70804
P: (225) 342-2040
F: (225) 342-0617
E: thompsof@legis.la.gov

**Walsworth, Michael A. (R, 33)**
State Capitol
P.O. Box 94183
Baton Rouge, LA 70804
P: (225) 342-2040
F: (225) 342-0617
E: walsworthm@legis.la.gov

**Ward III, Rick (R, 17)**
State Capitol
P.O. Box 94183
Baton Rouge, LA 70804
P: (225) 342-2040
F: (225) 342-0617
E: wardr@legis.la.gov

**White Jr., Mack A. (R, 6)**
State Capitol
P.O. Box 94183
Baton Rouge, LA 70804
P: (225) 342-2040
F: (225) 342-0617
E: whitem@legis.la.gov

# House

## Speaker of the House

**Representative Taylor F. Barras (R)**
Speaker of the House
State Capitol
P.O. Box 94062
Baton Rouge, LA 70804
P: (225) 342-6945
F: (225) 342-8336
E: barrast@legis.la.gov

## Speaker Pro Tempore of the House

**Representative Walt Leger III (D)**
House Speaker Pro Tempore
State Capitol
P.O. Box 94062
Baton Rouge, LA 70804
P: (225) 342-6945
F: (225) 342-8336
E: legerw@legis.la.gov

## House Majority Leader

**Representative Lance Harris (R)**
House Majority Leader
State Capitol
P.O. Box 94062
Baton Rouge, LA 70804
P: (225) 342-6945
F: (225) 342-8336
E: harrisl@legis.la.gov

# Louisiana

## Clerk of the House

**Mr. Alfred W. Speer**
Clerk of the House
P.O. Box 44281
Room G-106
Baton Rouge, LA 70804
P: (225) 342-7259
F: (225) 342-5045
E: speera@legis.state.la.us

## Members of the House

**Abraham, Mark (R, 36)**
State Capitol
P.O. Box 94062
Baton Rouge, LA 70804
P: (225) 342-6945
F: (225) 342-8336
E: abrahamm@legis.la.gov

**Abramson, Neil (D, 98)**
State Capitol
P.O. Box 94062
Baton Rouge, LA 70804
P: (225) 342-6945
F: (225) 342-8336
E: abramson@legis.la.gov

**Amedee, Beryl A. (R, 51)**
State Capitol
P.O. Box 94062
Baton Rouge, LA 70804
P: (225) 342-6945
F: (225) 342-8336
E: amedee@legis.la.gov

**Anders, John F. (D, 21)**
State Capitol
P.O. Box 94062
Baton Rouge, LA 70804
P: (225) 342-6945
F: (225) 342-8336
E: larep021@legis.la.gov

**Armes III, James K. (D, 30)**
State Capitol
P.O. Box 94062
Baton Rouge, LA 70804
P: (225) 342-6945
F: (225) 342-8336
E: armesj@legis.la.gov

**Bacala, Tony (R, 59)**
State Capitol
P.O. Box 94062
Baton Rouge, LA 70804
P: (225) 342-6945
F: (225) 342-8336
E: bacalat@legis.la.gov

**Bagley, Lawrence A. (R, 7)**
State Capitol
P.O. Box 94062
Baton Rouge, LA 70804
P: (225) 342-6945
F: (225) 342-8336
E: bagleyl@legis.la.gov

**Bagneris, John (D, 100)**
State Capitol
P.O. Box 94062
Baton Rouge, LA 70804
P: (225) 342-6945
F: (225) 342-8336
E: bagnerisj@legis.la.gov

**Barras, Taylor F. (R, 48)**
State Capitol
P.O. Box 94062
Baton Rouge, LA 70804
P: (225) 342-6945
F: (225) 342-8336
E: barrast@legis.la.gov

**Berthelot, John A. (R, 88)**
State Capitol
P.O. Box 94062
Baton Rouge, LA 70804
P: (225) 342-6945
F: (225) 342-8336
E: berthelotj@legis.la.gov

**Billiot, Robert E. (D, 83)**
State Capitol
P.O. Box 94062
Baton Rouge, LA 70804
P: (225) 342-6945
F: (225) 342-8336
E: billiotr@legis.la.gov

**Bishop, Stuart J. (R, 43)**
State Capitol
P.O. Box 94062
Baton Rouge, LA 70804
P: (225) 342-6945
F: (225) 342-8336
E: bishops@legis.la.gov

**Bouie Jr., Joseph (D, 97)**
State Capitol
P.O. Box 94062
Baton Rouge, LA 70804
P: (225) 342-6945
F: (225) 342-8336
E: bouiej@legis.la.gov

**Broadwater, Christopher (R, 86)**
State Capitol
P.O. Box 94062
Baton Rouge, LA 70804
P: (225) 342-6945
F: (225) 342-8336
E: broadwaterc@legis.la.gov

**Brown, Chad (D, 60)**
State Capitol
P.O. Box 94062
Baton Rouge, LA 70804
P: (225) 342-6945
F: (225) 342-8336
E: larep060@legis.la.gov

**Brown, Terry R. (I, 22)**
State Capitol
P.O. Box 94062
Baton Rouge, LA 70804
P: (225) 342-6945
F: (225) 342-8336
E: browntr@legis.la.gov

**Carmody Jr., Thomas G. (R, 6)**
State Capitol
P.O. Box 94062
Baton Rouge, LA 70804
P: (225) 342-6945
F: (225) 342-8336
E: carmodyt@legis.la.gov

**Carpenter, Barbara W. (D, 63)**
State Capitol
P.O. Box 94062
Baton Rouge, LA 70804
P: (225) 342-6945
F: (225) 342-8336
E: carpenterb@legis.la.gov

**Carter Jr., Gary (D, 102)**
State Capitol
P.O. Box 94062
Baton Rouge, LA 70804
P: (225) 342-6945
F: (225) 342-8336
E: carterg@legis.la.gov

**Carter, Robert J. (D, 72)**
State Capitol
P.O. Box 94062
Baton Rouge, LA 70804
P: (225) 342-6945
F: (225) 342-8336
E: larep072@legis.la.gov

**Carter, Steve F. (R, 68)**
State Capitol
P.O. Box 94062
Baton Rouge, LA 70804
P: (225) 342-6945
F: (225) 342-8336
E: carters@legis.la.gov

**Chaney, Charles R. (R, 19)**
State Capitol
P.O. Box 94062
Baton Rouge, LA 70804
P: (225) 342-6945
F: (225) 342-8336
E: chaneyb@legis.la.gov

**Connick, Patrick (R, 84)**
State Capitol
P.O. Box 94062
Baton Rouge, LA 70804
P: (225) 342-6945
F: (225) 342-8336
E: connickp@legis.la.gov

**Coussan, Jean-Paul (R, 45)**
State Capitol
P.O. Box 94062
Baton Rouge, LA 70804
P: (225) 342-6945
F: (225) 342-8336
E: coussanjp@legis.la.gov

**Cox, Kenny R. (D, 23)**
State Capitol
P.O. Box 94062
Baton Rouge, LA 70804
P: (225) 342-6945
F: (225) 342-8336
E: coxk@legis.la.gov

**Cromer, George Gregory (R, 90)**
State Capitol
P.O. Box 94062
Baton Rouge, LA 70804
P: (225) 342-6945
F: (225) 342-8336
E: cromerg@legis.la.gov

**Danahay, Michael E. (D, 33)**
State Capitol
P.O. Box 94062
Baton Rouge, LA 70804
P: (225) 342-6945
F: (225) 342-8336
E: danahaym@legis.la.gov

**Davis, Paula (R, 69)**
State Capitol
P.O. Box 94062
Baton Rouge, LA 70804
P: (225) 342-6945
F: (225) 342-8336
E: davisp@legis.la.gov

**DeVillier, Phillip (R, 41)**
State Capitol
P.O. Box 94062
Baton Rouge, LA 70804
P: (225) 342-6945
F: (225) 342-8336
E: devillierp@legis.la.gov

**Dwight, Stephen (R, 35)**
State Capitol
P.O. Box 94062
Baton Rouge, LA 70804
P: (225) 342-6945
F: (225) 342-8336
E: dwights@legis.la.gov

**Edmonds, Rick (R, 66)**
State Capitol
P.O. Box 94062
Baton Rouge, LA 70804
P: (225) 342-6945
F: (225) 342-8336
E: edmondsr@legis.la.gov

**Emerson, Julie (R, 39)**
State Capitol
P.O. Box 94062
Baton Rouge, LA 70804
P: (225) 342-6945
F: (225) 342-8336
E: emersonj@legis.la.gov

**Falconer, Reid (R, 89)**
State Capitol
P.O. Box 94062
Baton Rouge, LA 70804
P: (225) 342-6945
F: (225) 342-8336
E: falconerr@legis.la.gov

**Foil, Franklin J. (R, 70)**
State Capitol
P.O. Box 94062
Baton Rouge, LA 70804
P: (225) 342-6945
F: (225) 342-8336
E: foilf@legis.la.gov

**Franklin, A.B. (D, 34)**
State Capitol
P.O. Box 94062
Baton Rouge, LA 70804
P: (225) 342-6945
F: (225) 342-8336
E: franklina@legis.la.gov

**Gaines, Randal L. (D, 57)**
State Capitol
P.O. Box 94062
Baton Rouge, LA 70804
P: (225) 342-6945
F: (225) 342-8336
E: gainesr@legis.la.gov

**Garofalo Jr., Raymond E. (R, 103)**
State Capitol
P.O. Box 94062
Baton Rouge, LA 70804
P: (225) 342-6945
F: (225) 342-8336
E: garofalor@legis.la.gov

**Gisclair, Jerry (D, 54)**
State Capitol
P.O. Box 94062
Baton Rouge, LA 70804
P: (225) 342-6945
F: (225) 342-8336
E: gisclairj@legis.la.gov

**Glover, Cedric B. (D, 4)**
State Capitol
P.O. Box 94062
Baton Rouge, LA 70804
P: (225) 342-6945
F: (225) 342-8336
E: larep004@legis.la.gov

**Guinn, John E. (R, 37)**
State Capitol
P.O. Box 94062
Baton Rouge, LA 70804
P: (225) 342-6945
F: (225) 342-8336
E: guinnj@legis.la.gov

**Hall, Jeff (D, 26)**
State Capitol
P.O. Box 94062
Baton Rouge, LA 70804
P: (225) 342-6945
F: (225) 342-8336
E: hallj@legis.la.gov

**Harris, Jimmy (D, 99)**
State Capitol
P.O. Box 94062
Baton Rouge, LA 70804
P: (225) 342-6945
F: (225) 342-8336
E: harrisj@legis.la.gov

**Harris, Lance (R, 25)**
State Capitol
P.O. Box 94062
Baton Rouge, LA 70804
P: (225) 342-6945
F: (225) 342-8336
E: harrisl@legis.la.gov

**Havard, Kenneth E. (R, 62)**
State Capitol
P.O. Box 94062
Baton Rouge, LA 70804
P: (225) 342-6945
F: (225) 342-8336
E: havardk@legis.la.gov

**Hazel, Lowell C. (R, 27)**
State Capitol
P.O. Box 94062
Baton Rouge, LA 70804
P: (225) 342-6945
F: (225) 342-8336
E: hazelc@legis.la.gov

**Henry, Cameron (R, 82)**
State Capitol
P.O. Box 94062
Baton Rouge, LA 70804
P: (225) 342-6945
F: (225) 342-8336
E: henryc@legis.la.gov

**Hensgens, Bob (R, 47)**
State Capitol
P.O. Box 94062
Baton Rouge, LA 70804
P: (225) 342-6945
F: (225) 342-8336
E: hensgensb@legis.la.gov

**Hilferty, Stephanie (R, 94)**
State Capitol
P.O. Box 94062
Baton Rouge, LA 70804
P: (225) 342-6945
F: (225) 342-8336
E: hilfertys@legis.la.gov

**Hill, Dorothy Sue (D, 32)**
State Capitol
P.O. Box 94062
Baton Rouge, LA 70804
P: (225) 342-6945
F: (225) 342-8336
E: hilld@legis.la.gov

**Hodges, Valarie (R, 64)**
State Capitol
P.O. Box 94062
Baton Rouge, LA 70804
P: (225) 342-6945
F: (225) 342-8336
E: hodgesv@legis.la.gov

**Hoffmann, Frank A. (R, 15)**
State Capitol
P.O. Box 94062
Baton Rouge, LA 70804
P: (225) 342-6945
F: (225) 342-8336
E: hoffmannf@legis.la.gov

**Hollis, Paul B. (R, 104)**
State Capitol
P.O. Box 94062
Baton Rouge, LA 70804
P: (225) 342-6945
F: (225) 342-8336
E: hollisp@legis.la.gov

**Horton, Dodie (R, 9)**
State Capitol
P.O. Box 94062
Baton Rouge, LA 70804
P: (225) 342-6945
F: (225) 342-8336
E: hortond@legis.la.gov

**Howard, Frank A. (R, 24)**
State Capitol
P.O. Box 94062
Baton Rouge, LA 70804
P: (225) 342-6945
F: (225) 342-8336
E: howardf@legis.la.gov

**Hunter, Marcus L. (D, 17)**
State Capitol
P.O. Box 94062
Baton Rouge, LA 70804
P: (225) 342-6945
F: (225) 342-8336
E: hunterm@legis.la.gov

**Huval, Mike (R, 46)**
State Capitol
P.O. Box 94062
Baton Rouge, LA 70804
P: (225) 342-6945
F: (225) 342-8336
E: huvalm@legis.la.gov

**Ivey, Barry (R, 65)**
State Capitol
P.O. Box 94062
Baton Rouge, LA 70804
P: (225) 342-6945
F: (225) 342-8336
E: iveyb@legis.la.gov

**Jackson, Katrina R. (D, 16)**
State Capitol
P.O. Box 94062
Baton Rouge, LA 70804
P: (225) 342-6945
F: (225) 342-8336
E: jacksonk@legis.la.gov

**James II, Edward C. (D, 101)**
State Capitol
P.O. Box 94062
Baton Rouge, LA 70804
P: (225) 342-6945
F: (225) 342-8336
E: james.ted@legis.la.gov

**Jefferson, Patrick O. (D, 11)**
State Capitol
P.O. Box 94062
Baton Rouge, LA 70804
P: (225) 342-6945
F: (225) 342-8336
E: jeffersonpo@legis.la.gov

**Jenkins Jr., Samuel L. (D, 2)**
State Capitol
P.O. Box 94062
Baton Rouge, LA 70804
P: (225) 342-6945
F: (225) 342-8336
E: jenkinss@legis.la.gov

**Johnson, Robert A. (D, 28)**
State Capitol
P.O. Box 94062
Baton Rouge, LA 70804
P: (225) 342-6945
F: (225) 342-8336
E: johnsoro@legis.la.gov

# Louisiana

**Jones, Sam (D, 50)**
State Capitol
P.O. Box 94062
Baton Rouge, LA 70804
P: (225) 342-6945
F: (225) 342-8336
E: joness@legis.la.gov

**Jordan, Edmond (D, 29)**
State Capitol
P.O. Box 94062
Baton Rouge, LA 70804
P: (225) 342-6945
F: (225) 342-8336
E: jordane@legis.la.gov

**Landry, Nancy (R, 31)**
State Capitol
P.O. Box 94062
Baton Rouge, LA 70804
P: (225) 342-6945
F: (225) 342-8336
E: landryn@legis.la.gov

**Landry, Terry (D, 96)**
State Capitol
P.O. Box 94062
Baton Rouge, LA 70804
P: (225) 342-6945
F: (225) 342-8336
E: landryt@legis.la.gov

**LeBas, H. Bernard (D, 38)**
State Capitol
P.O. Box 94062
Baton Rouge, LA 70804
P: (225) 342-6945
F: (225) 342-8336
E: lebasb@legis.la.gov

**Leger III, Walt (D, 91)**
State Capitol
P.O. Box 94062
Baton Rouge, LA 70804
P: (225) 342-6945
F: (225) 342-8336
E: legerw@legis.la.gov

**Leopold, Christopher J. (R, 105)**
State Capitol
P.O. Box 94062
Baton Rouge, LA 70804
P: (225) 342-6945
F: (225) 342-8336
E: leopoldc@legis.la.gov

**Lyons Sr., Rodney (D, 87)**
State Capitol
P.O. Box 94062
Baton Rouge, LA 70804
P: (225) 342-6945
F: (225) 342-8336
E: lyonsr@legis.la.gov

**Mack, Sherman Q. (R, 95)**
State Capitol
P.O. Box 94062
Baton Rouge, LA 70804
P: (225) 342-6945
F: (225) 342-8336
E: macks@legis.la.gov

**Magee, Tanner (R, 53)**
State Capitol
P.O. Box 94062
Baton Rouge, LA 70804
P: (225) 342-6945
F: (225) 342-8336
E: mageet@legis.la.gov

**Marcelle, C. Denise (D, 61)**
State Capitol
P.O. Box 94062
Baton Rouge, LA 70804
P: (225) 342-6945
F: (225) 342-8336
E: marcelled@legis.la.gov

**Marino, Joseph (I, 85)**
State Capitol
P.O. Box 94062
Baton Rouge, LA 70804
P: (225) 342-6945
F: (225) 342-8336
E: marinoj@legis.la.gov

**McFarland, Jack (R, 13)**
State Capitol
P.O. Box 94062
Baton Rouge, LA 70804
P: (225) 342-6945
F: (225) 342-8336
E: mcfarlandj@legis.la.gov

**Miguez, Blake (R, 49)**
State Capitol
P.O. Box 94062
Baton Rouge, LA 70804
P: (225) 342-6945
F: (225) 342-8336
E: miguezb@legis.la.gov

**Miller, Dustin (D, 40)**
State Capitol
P.O. Box 94062
Baton Rouge, LA 70804
P: (225) 342-6945
F: (225) 342-8336
E: millerd@legis.la.gov

**Miller, Gregory A. (R, 56)**
State Capitol
P.O. Box 94062
Baton Rouge, LA 70804
P: (225) 342-6945
F: (225) 342-8336
E: millerg@legis.la.gov

**Moreno, Helena N. (D, 93)**
State Capitol
P.O. Box 94062
Baton Rouge, LA 70804
P: (225) 342-6945
F: (225) 342-8336
E: morenoh@legis.la.gov

**Morris, James H. (R, 1)**
State Capitol
P.O. Box 94062
Baton Rouge, LA 70804
P: (225) 342-6945
F: (225) 342-8336
E: larep001@legis.la.gov

**Morris III, John C. (R, 14)**
State Capitol
P.O. Box 94062
Baton Rouge, LA 70804
P: (225) 342-6945
F: (225) 342-8336
E: morrisjc@legis.la.gov

**Norton, Barbara (D, 3)**
State Capitol
P.O. Box 94062
Baton Rouge, LA 70804
P: (225) 342-6945
F: (225) 342-8336
E: nortonb@legis.la.gov

**Pearson, J. Kevin (R, 76)**
State Capitol
P.O. Box 94062
Baton Rouge, LA 70804
P: (225) 342-6945
F: (225) 342-8336
E: pearsonk@legis.la.gov

**Pierre, Vincent J. (D, 44)**
State Capitol
P.O. Box 94062
Baton Rouge, LA 70804
P: (225) 342-6945
F: (225) 342-8336
E: pierrev@legis.la.gov

**Pope, J. Rogers (R, 71)**
State Capitol
P.O. Box 94062
Baton Rouge, LA 70804
P: (225) 342-6945
F: (225) 342-8336
E: poper@legis.la.gov

**Price, Edward J. (D, 58)**
State Capitol
P.O. Box 94062
Baton Rouge, LA 70804
P: (225) 342-6945
F: (225) 342-8336
E: pricee@legis.la.gov

**Pugh, Stephen E. (R, 73)**
State Capitol
P.O. Box 94062
Baton Rouge, LA 94062
P: (225) 342-6945
F: (225) 342-8336
E: pughs@legis.la.gov

**Pylant, Steven E. (R, 20)**
State Capitol
P.O. Box 94062
Baton Rouge, LA 70804
P: (225) 342-6945
F: (225) 342-8336
E: pylants@legis.la.gov

**Reynolds, H. Eugene (D, 10)**
State Capitol
P.O. Box 94062
Baton Rouge, LA 70804
P: (225) 342-6945
F: (225) 342-8336
E: reynoldsg@legis.la.gov

**Richard, Jerome (I, 55)**
State Capitol
P.O. Box 94062
Baton Rouge, LA 70804
P: (225) 342-6945
F: (225) 342-8336
E: richardj@legis.la.gov

**Schexnayder, Clay (R, 81)**
State Capitol
P.O. Box 94062
Baton Rouge, LA 70804
P: (225) 342-6945
F: (225) 342-8336
E: schexnayderc
   @legis.la.gov

**Schroder Sr., John M. (R, 77)**
State Capitol
P.O. Box 94062
Baton Rouge, LA 70804
P: (225) 342-6945
F: (225) 342-8336
E: schrodej@legis.la.gov

**Seabaugh, Alan (R, 5)**
State Capitol
P.O. Box 94062
Baton Rouge, LA 70804
P: (225) 342-6945
F: (225) 342-8336
E: seabaugha@legis.la.gov

**Shadoin, Robert E. (R, 12)**
State Capitol
P.O. Box 94062
Baton Rouge, LA 70804
P: (225) 342-6945
F: (225) 342-8336
E: shadoinr@legis.la.gov

**Simon, Scott (R, 74)**
State Capitol
P.O. Box 94062
Baton Rouge, LA 70804
P: (225) 342-6945
F: (225) 342-8336
E: simons@legis.la.gov

**Smith, Patricia Haynes
   (D, 67)**
State Capitol
P.O. Box 94062
Baton Rouge, LA 70804
P: (225) 342-6945
F: (225) 342-8336
E: smithp@legis.la.gov

**Stokes, Julie (R, 79)**
State Capitol
P.O. Box 94062
Baton Rouge, LA 70804
P: (225) 342-6945
F: (225) 342-8336
E: stokesj@legis.la.gov

**Talbot, Kirk (R, 78)**
State Capitol
P.O. Box 94062
Baton Rouge, LA 70804
P: (225) 342-6945
F: (225) 342-8336
E: talbotk@legis.la.gov

**Thibaut Jr., Major (D, 18)**
State Capitol
P.O. Box 94062
Baton Rouge, LA 70804
P: (225) 342-6945
F: (225) 342-8336
E: thibautm@legis.la.gov

**Thomas, Polly (R, 80)**
P.O. Box 94062
Baton Rouge, LA 70804
P: (225) 342-6945
F: (225) 342-8336
E: thomaspj@legis.la.gov

**White, Malinda B. (D, 75)**
State Capitol
P.O. Box 94062
Baton Rouge, LA 70804
P: (225) 342-6945
F: (225) 342-8336
E: whitem@legis.la.gov

**Zeringue, Jerome (R, 52)**
State Capitol
P.O. Box 94062
Baton Rouge, LA 70804
P: (225) 342-6945
F: (225) 342-8336
E: zeringuej@legis.la.gov

# Maine

## Executive

### Governor
**The Honorable Paul LePage (R)**
Governor
#1 State House Station
Augusta, ME 04333
P: (207) 287-3531
F: (207) 287-1034

### Lieutenant Governor
*This state does not have the office of lieutenant governor. The president (or speaker) of the Senate is next in line of succession to the governorship.*

### Attorney General
**The Honorable Janet T. Mills (D)**
Attorney General
State House Station 6
Augusta, ME 04333
P: (207) 626-8800

### Auditor
**The Honorable Pola Buckley**
(elected by the Legislature)
State Auditor
66 State House Station
Augusta, ME 04333
P: (207) 624-6250
F: (207) 624-6273

### Secretary of State
**The Honorable Matthew Dunlap (D)**
Secretary of State
148 State House Station
Augusta, ME 04333
P: (207) 626-8400
F: (207) 287-8598
E: sos.office@maine.gov

### Treasurer
**The Honorable Terry Hayes (I)**
State Treasurer
39 State House Station
Augusta, ME 04333
P: (207) 624-7477
F: (207) 287-2367
E: terry.hayes@maine.gov

## Judiciary

### Supreme Judicial Court (GA)
**Mr. Matthew Pollack**
Clerk of the Law Court
205 Newbury Street, Room 139
Portland, ME 04101
P: (207) 822-4146

**The Honorable Leigh I. Saufley**
Chief Justice
**The Honorable Donald G. Alexander**
**The Honorable Ellen A. Gorman**
**The Honorable Jeffrey L. Hjelm**
**The Honorable Thomas E. Humphrey**
**The Honorable Joseph M. Jabar**
**The Honorable Andrew M. Mead**

## Legislative

## Senate

### Senate President
**Senator Michael D. Thibodeau (R)**
Senate President
3 State House Station
Augusta, ME 04333
P: (207) 287-1500
F: (207) 287-1527
E: senatorthibodeau@aol.com

### Senate Majority Leader
**Senator Garrett P. Mason (R)**
Senate Majority Leader
3 State House Station
Augusta, ME 04333
P: (207) 287-1505
F: (207) 287-1527
E: Garrett.Mason
@legislature.maine.gov

### Senate Minority Leader
**Senator Troy D. Jackson (D)**
Senate Minority Leader
3 State House Station
Augusta, ME 04333
P: (207) 287-1515
F: (207) 287-1527
E: Troy.Jackson
@legislature.maine.gov

## Secretary of the Senate
**Ms. Heather J.R. Priest**
Secretary of the Senate
3 State House Station
Augusta, ME 04333
P: (207) 287-1540
F: (207) 287-1900
E: heather.priest
@legislature.maine.gov

## Members of the Senate
**Bellows, Shenna (D, 14)***
3 State House Station
Augusta, ME 04333
P: (207) 287-1515
F: (207) 287-1527
E: Shenna.Bellows
@legislature.maine.gov

**Brakey, Eric (R, 20)**
3 State House Station
Augusta, ME 04333
P: (207) 287-1505
F: (207) 287-1527
E: sen.eric.brakey
@gmail.com

**Breen, Catherine (D, 25)**
3 State House Station
Augusta, ME 04333
P: (207) 287-1515
F: (207) 287-1527
E: cathy.breen
@legislature.maine.gov

**Carpenter, Michael (D, 2)***
3 State House Station
Augusta, ME 04333
P: (207) 287-1515
F: (207) 287-1527
E: Mike.Carpenter
@legislature.maine.gov

**Carson, Everett (D, 24)***
3 State House Station
Augusta, ME 04333
P: (207) 287-1515
F: (207) 287-1527
E: Everett.Carson
@legislature.maine.gov

**Chenette, Justin Mark (D, 31)**
3 State House Station
Augusta, ME 04333
P: (207) 287-1515
F: (207) 287-1527
E: Justin.Chenette
@legislature.maine.gov

**Chipman, Benjamin M. (D, 27)**
3 State House Station
Augusta, ME 04333
P: (207) 287-1515
F: (207) 287-1527
E: Ben.Chipman
@legislature.maine.gov

**Collins, Ronald F. (R, 34)**
3 State House Station
Augusta, ME 04333
P: (207) 287-1505
F: (207) 287-1527
E: RCollins7@maine.rr.com

**Cushing III, Andre E. (R, 10)**
3 State House Station
Augusta, ME 04333
P: (207) 287-1505
F: (207) 287-1527
E: andre@andrecushing.com

**Cyrway, Scott (R, 16)**
3 State House Station
Augusta, ME 04333
P: (207) 287-1505
F: (207) 287-1527
E: scyrway@roadrunner.com

**Davis Sr., Paul T. (R, 4)**
3 State House Station
Augusta, ME 04333
P: (207) 287-1505
F: (207) 287-1527
E: sendavis@myottmail.com

**Deschambault, Susan (D, 32)**
3 State House Station
Augusta, ME 04333
P: (207) 287-1515
F: (207) 287-1527
E: Susan.Deschambault
@legislature.maine.gov

**Diamond, Bill (D, 26)**
3 State House Station
Augusta, ME 04333
P: (207) 287-1515
F: (207) 287-1527
E: diamondhollyd@aol.com

**Dill, James F. (D, 5)**
3 State House Station
Augusta, ME 04333
P: (207) 287-1515
F: (207) 287-1527
E: jdill@umext.maine.edu

**Dion, Mark N. (D, 28)**
3 State House Station
Augusta, ME 04333
P: (207) 287-1515
F: (207) 287-1527
E: Mark.Dion
@legislature.maine.gov

**Dow, Dana L. (R, 13)**
3 State House Station
Augusta, ME 04333
P: (207) 287-1505
F: (207) 287-1527
E: Dana.Dow
   @legislative.maine.gov

**Gratwick, Geoffrey M. (D, 9)**
3 State House Station
Augusta, ME 04333
P: (207) 287-1515
F: (207) 287-1527
E: geoffrey.gratwick
   @legislature.maine.gov

**Hamper, James Michael (R, 19)**
3 State House Station
Augusta, ME 04333
P: (207) 287-1505
F: (207) 287-1527
E: senatorhamp@gmail.com

**Hill, Dawn (D, 35)**
3 State House Station
Augusta, ME 04333
P: (207) 287-1515
F: (207) 287-1527
E: Dawn.Hill
   @legislature.maine.gov

**Jackson, Troy D. (D, 1)**
3 State House Station
Augusta, ME 04333
P: (207) 287-1515
F: (207) 287-1527
E: Troy.Jackson
   @legislature.maine.gov

**Katz, Roger J. (R, 15)**
3 State House Station
Augusta, ME 04333
P: (207) 287-1505
F: (207) 287-1527
E: Roger.Katz
   @legislature.maine.gov

**Keim, Lisa (R, 18)\***
3 State House Station
Augusta, ME 04333
P: (207) 287-1505
F: (207) 271-1527
E: Lisa.Keim
   @legislature.maine.gov

**Langley, Brian D. (R, 7)**
3 State House Station
Augusta, ME 04333
P: (207) 287-1505
F: (207) 287-1527
E: Brian.Langley
   @legislature.maine.gov

**Libby, Nathan L. (D, 21)**
3 State House Station
Augusta, ME 04333
P: (207) 287-1515
F: (207) 287-1527
E: nathan.libby@gmail.com

**Maker, Joyce A. (R, 6)**
3 State House Station
Augusta, ME 04333
P: (207) 287-1505
F: (207) 287-1456
E: Joyce.Maker
   @legislature.maine.gov

**Mason, Garrett P. (R, 22)**
3 State House Station
Augusta, ME 04333
P: (207) 287-1505
F: (207) 287-1527
E: Garrett.Mason
   @legislature.maine.gov

**Millett, Rebecca J. (D, 29)**
3 State House Station
Augusta, ME 04333
P: (207) 287-1515
F: (207) 287-1527
E: senrebeccamillett
   @gmail.com

**Miramant, David (D, 12)**
3 State House Station
Augusta, ME 04333
P: (207) 287-1515
F: (207) 287-1527
E: davemiramant@gmail.com

**Rosen, Kimberley C. (R, 8)**
3 State House Station
Augusta, ME 04333
P: (207) 287-1505
F: (207) 287-1527
E: kimberley.rosen
   @legislature.maine.gov

**Saviello, Thomas B. (R, 17)**
3 State House Station
Augusta, ME 04333
P: (207) 287-1505
F: (207) 287-1527
E: drtom16@hotmail.com

**Thibodeau, Michael D. (R, 11)**
3 State House Station
Augusta, ME 04333
P: (207) 287-1500
F: (207) 287-1527
E: senatorthibodeau@aol.com

**Vitelli, Eloise (D, 23)**
3 State House Station
Augusta, ME 04333
P: (207) 287-1515
F: (207) 287-1527
E: Eloise.Vitelli
   @legislature.maine.gov

**Volk, Amy (R, 30)**
3 State House Station
Augusta, ME 04333
P: (207) 287-1505
F: (207) 287-1527
E: amy.volk
   @legislature.maine.gov

**Whittemore, Rodney L. (R, 3)**
3 State House Station
Augusta, ME 04333
P: (207) 287-1505
F: (207) 287-1527
E: Rodwhittemore@gmail.com

**Woodsome, David (R, 33)**
3 State House Station
Augusta, ME 04333
P: (207) 287-1505
F: (207) 287-1527
E: david.woodsome
   @legislature.maine.gov

# House

## Speaker of the House

**Representative Sara Gideon (D)**
Speaker of the House
Room 333, State House
2 State House Station
Augusta, ME 04333
P: (207) 287-1430
F: (207) 287-1456
E: Sara.Gideon
   @legislature.maine.gov

## House Majority Leader

**Representative Erin D. Herbig (D)**
Majority Leader
Room 333, State House
2 State House Station
Augusta, ME 04333
P: (207) 287-1430
F: (207) 287-1456
E: Erin.Herbig
   @legislature.maine.gov

## House Minority Leader

**Representative Kenneth Wade Fredette (R)**
House Minority Floor Leader
Room 332, State House
2 State House Station
Augusta, ME 04333
P: (207) 287-1440
F: (207) 287-1456
E: Kenneth.Fredette
   @legislature.maine.gov

## Clerk of the House

**Mr. Robert B. Hunt**
Clerk of the House
Room 300, State House
2 State House Station
Augusta, ME 04333
P: (207) 287-1400
F: (207) 287-1456
E: RepRob.Hunt
   @legislature.maine.gov

## Members of the House

**Ackley, Kent (I, 82)\***
2 State House Station
Augusta, ME 04333
P: (207) 287-1400
E: Kent.Ackley
   @legislature.maine.gov

**Alley Sr., Robert (D, 138)**
Room 333, State House
2 State House Station
Augusta, ME 04333
P: (207) 287-1430
F: (207) 287-1456
E: Robert.Alley
   @legislature.maine.gov

**Austin, Betty A. (D, 107)\***
Room 333, State House
2 State House Station
Augusta, ME 04333
P: (207) 287-1430
F: (207) 287-1456
E: Betty.Austin
   @legislature.maine.gov

**Austin, Susan (R, 67)**
Room 332, State House
2 State House Station
Augusta, ME 04333
P: (207) 287-1440
F: (207) 287-1456
E: Sue.Austin
   @legislature.maine.gov

# Maine

**Babbidge, Christopher W. (D, 8)**
Room 333, State House
2 State House Station
Augusta, ME 04333
P: (207) 287-1430
F: (207) 287-1456
E: Chris.Babbidge
@legislature.maine.gov

**Bailey, Donna (D, 14)***
Room 333, State House
2 State House Station
Augusta, ME 04333
P: (207) 287-1430
F: (207) 287-1456
E: Donna.Bailey
@legislature.maine.gov

**Bates, Dillon (D, 35)**
Room 333, State House
2 State House Station
Augusta, ME 04333
P: (207) 287-1430
F: (207) 287-1456
E: Dillon.Bates
@legislature.maine.gov

**Battle, Kevin (R, 33)**
Room 332, State House
2 State House Station
Augusta, ME 04333
P: (207) 287-1440
F: (207) 287-1456
E: Kevin.Battle
@legislature.maine.gov

**Bear, Henry John (TRIBAL)**
2 State House Station
Augusta, ME 04333
P: (207) 287-1400
F: (207) 287-1456
E: Henry.Bear
@legislature.maine.gov

**Beebe-Center, Pinny (D, 93)**
Room 333, State House
2 State House Station
Augusta, ME 04333
P: (207) 287-1430
F: (207) 287-1456
E: Pinny.Beebe-Center
@legislature.maine.gov

**Berry, Seth A. (D, 55)**
Room 333, State House
2 State House Station
Augusta, ME 04333
P: (207) 287-1430
F: (207) 287-1456
E: Seth.Berry
@legislature.maine.gov

**Bickford, Bruce A. (R, 63)**
Room 332, State House
2 State House Station
Augusta, ME 04333
P: (207) 287-1440
F: (207) 287-1456
E: Bruce.Bickford
@legislature.maine.gov

**Black, Russell J. (R, 114)**
Room 332, State House
2 State House Station
Augusta, ME 04333
P: (207) 287-1440
F: (207) 287-1456
E: Russell.Black
@legislature.maine.gov

**Blume, Lydia (D, 3)**
Room 333, State House
2 State House Station
Augusta, ME 04333
P: (207) 287-1430
F: (207) 287-1456
E: Lydia.Blume
@legislature.maine.gov

**Bradstreet, Richard T. (R, 80)***
Room 332, State House
2 State House Station
Augusta, ME 04333
P: (207) 287-1440
F: (207) 287-1456
E: Richard.Bradstreet
@legislature.maine.gov

**Brooks, Heidi (D, 61)**
Room 333, State House
2 State House Station
Augusta, ME 04333
P: (207) 287-1430
F: (207) 287-1456
E: Heidi.Brooks
@legislature.maine.gov

**Bryant, Mark E. (D, 24)**
Room 333, State House
2 State House Station
Augusta, ME 04333
P: (207) 287-1430
F: (207) 287-1456
E: Mark.Bryant
@legislature.maine.gov

**Campbell, Richard H. (R, 130)**
Room 332, State House
2 State House Station
Augusta, ME 04333
P: (207) 287-1440
F: (207) 287-1456
E: Richard.Campbell
@legislature.maine.gov

**Cardone, Barbara A. (D, 127)***
Room 333, State House
2 State House Station
Augusta, ME 04333
P: (207) 287-1430
F: (207) 287-1456
E: Barbara.Cardone
@legislature.maine.gov

**Casas, Owen D. (I, 94)***
2 State House Station
Augusta, ME 04333
P: (207) 287-1400
E: Owen.Casas
@legislature.maine.gov

**Cebra, Richard M. (R, 68)**
Room 332, State House
2 State House Station
Augusta, ME 04333
P: (207) 287-1440
F: (207) 287-1456
E: Rich.Cebra
@legislature.maine.gov

**Chace, Paul (R, 46)**
Room 332, State House
2 State House Station
Augusta, ME 04333
P: (207) 287-1440
F: (207) 287-1456
E: Paul.Chace
@legislature.maine.gov

**Chapman, Ralph (D, 133)**
Room 333, State House
2 State House Station
Augusta, ME 04333
P: (207) 287-1430
F: (207) 287-1456
E: Ralph.Chapman
@legislature.maine.gov

**Collings, Benjamin T. (D, 42)***
Room 333, State Capitol
2 State House Station
Augusta, ME 04333
P: (207) 287-1430
F: (207) 287-1456
E: Benjamin.Collings
@legislature.maine.gov

**Cooper, Janice E. (D, 47)**
Room 333, State House
2 State House Station
Augusta, ME 04333
P: (207) 287-1430
F: (207) 287-1456
E: Janice.Cooper
@legislature.maine.gov

**Corey, Patrick (R, 25)**
Room 332, State House
2 State House Station
Augusta, ME 04333
P: (207) 287-1440
F: (207) 287-1456
E: Patrick.Corey
@legislature.maine.gov

**Craig, Garrel Robert (R, 128)***
Room 332, State House
2 State House Station
Augusta, ME 04333
P: (207) 287-1440
F: (207) 287-1456
E: Garrel.Craig
@legislature.maine.gov

**Dana II, Matthew (TRIBAL, Passamaquoddy Tribe)**
2 State House Station
Augusta, ME 04333
P: (207) 287-1440
F: (207) 287-1456
E: Matthew.Dana
@legislature.maine.gov

**Daughtry, Matthea E. L. (D, 49)**
Room 333, State House
2 State House Station
Augusta, ME 04333
P: (207) 287-1430
F: (207) 287-1456
E: mattie.daughtry
@legislature.maine.gov

**DeChant, Jennifer (D, 52)**
Room 333, State House
2 State House Station
Augusta, ME 04333
P: (207) 287-1430
F: (207) 287-1456
E: Jennifer.DeChant
@legislature.maine.gov

**Denno, Dale J. (D, 45)***
Room 333, State House
2 State House Station
Augusta, ME 04333
P: (207) 287-1430
F: (207) 287-1456
E: Dale.Denno
@legislature.maine.gov

**Devin, Michael (D, 90)**
Room 333, State House
2 State House Station
Augusta, ME 04333
P: (207) 287-1430
F: (207) 287-1456
E: Michael.Devin
@legislature.maine.gov

**Dillingham,
Kathleen Jackson (R, 72)**
Room 332, State House
2 State House Station
Augusta, ME 04333
P: (207) 287-1440
F: (207) 287-1456
E: Kathleen.Dillingham
@legislature.maine.gov

**Doore, Donna (D, 85)**
Room 333, State House
2 State House Station
Augusta, ME 04333
P: (207) 287-1430
F: (207) 287-1456
E: Donna.Doore
@legislature.maine.gov

**Duchesne, Robert S.
(D, 121)**
Room 333, State House
2 State House Station
Augusta, ME 04333
P: (207) 287-1430
F: (207) 287-1456
E: Bob.Duchesne
@legislature.maine.gov

**Dunphy, Michelle Ann
(D, 122)**
Room 333, State House
2 State House Station
Augusta, ME 04333
P: (207) 287-1430
F: (207) 287-1456
E: Michelle.Dunphy
@legislature.maine.gov

**Espling, Eleanor M. (R, 65)**
Room 332, State House
2 State House Station
Augusta, ME 04333
P: (207) 287-1440
F: (207) 287-1456
E: Ellie.Espling
@legislature.maine.gov

**Farnsworth, Richard R.
(D, 37)**
Room 333, State House
2 State House Station
Augusta, ME 04333
P: (207) 287-1430
F: (207) 287-1456
E: Richard.Farnsworth
@legislature.maine.gov

**Farrin, Bradlee (R, 111)**
Room 332, State House
2 State House Station
Augusta, ME 04333
P: (207) 287-1440
F: (207) 287-1456
E: Bradlee.Farrin
@legislature.maine.gov

**Fay, Jessica L. (D, 66)\***
Room 333, State House
2 State House Station
Augusta, ME 04333
P: (207) 287-1430
F: (207) 287-1456
E: Jessica.Fay
@legislature.maine.gov

**Fecteau, Ryan (D, 11)**
Room 333, State House
2 State House Station
Augusta, ME 04333
P: (207) 287-1430
F: (207) 287-1456
E: Ryan.Fecteau
@legislature.maine.gov

**Foley, Robert (R, 7)**
Room 332, State House
2 State House Station
Augusta, ME 04333
P: (207) 287-1440
F: (207) 287-1456
E: Robert.Foley
@legislature.maine.gov

**Fredette, Kenneth Wade
(R, 100)**
Room 332, State House
2 State House Station
Augusta, ME 04333
P: (207) 287-1440
F: (207) 287-1456
E: Kenneth.Fredette
@legislature.maine.gov

**Frey, Aaron M. (D, 124)**
Room 333, State House
2 State House Station
Augusta, ME 04333
P: (207) 287-1430
F: (207) 287-1456
E: Aaron.Frey
@legislature.maine.gov

**Fuller, Roger Jason
(D, 59)\***
Room 333, State House
2 State House Station
Augusta, ME 04333
P: (207) 287-1430
F: (207) 287-1456
E: Roger.Fuller
@legislature.maine.gov

**Gattine, Drew W. (D, 34)**
Room 333, State House
2 State House Station
Augusta, ME 04333
P: (207) 287-1430
F: (207) 287-1456
E: Drew.Gattine
@legislature.maine.gov

**Gerrish, Karen (R, 20)**
Room 332, State House
2 State House Station
Augusta, ME 04333
P: (207) 287-1440
F: (207) 287-1456
E: Karen.Gerrish
@legislature.maine.gov

**Gideon, Sara (D, 48)**
Room 333, State House
2 State House Station
Augusta, ME 04333
P: (207) 287-1430
F: (207) 287-1456
E: Sara.Gideon
@legislature.maine.gov

**Gillway, James S. (R, 98)**
Room 332, State House
2 State House Station
Augusta, ME 04333
P: (207) 287-1440
F: (207) 287-1456
E: James.Gillway
@legislature.maine.gov

**Ginzler, Phyllis (R, 69)**
Room 332, State House
2 State House Station
Augusta, ME 04333
P: (207) 287-1440
F: (207) 287-1456
E: Phyllis.Ginzler
@legislature.maine.gov

**Golden, Jared (D, 60)**
Room 333, State House
2 State House Station
Augusta, ME 04333
P: (207) 287-1430
F: (207) 287-1456
E: Jared.Golden
@legislature.maine.gov

**Grant, Gay M. (D, 83)**
Room 333, State House
2 State House Station
Augusta, ME 04333
P: (207) 287-1430
F: (207) 287-1456
E: Gay.Grant
@legislature.maine.gov

**Grignon, Chad Wayne
(R, 118)\***
Room 332, State House
2 State House Station
Augusta, ME 04333
P: (207) 287-1440
F: (207) 287-1456
E: Chad.Grignon
@legislature.maine.gov

**Grohman, Martin (D, 12)**
Room 333, State House
2 State House Station
Augusta, ME 04333
P: (207) 287-1430
F: (207) 287-1456
E: Martin.Grohman
@legislature.maine.gov

**Guerin, Stacey K. (R, 102)**
Room 332, State House
2 State House Station
Augusta, ME 04333
P: (207) 287-1440
F: (207) 287-1456
E: Stacey.Guerin
@legislature.maine.gov

**Haggan, David G (R, 101)\***
Room 332, State House
2 State House Station
Augusta, ME 04333
P: (207) 287-1440
F: (207) 287-1456
E: David.Haggan
@legislature.maine.gov

**Hamann, Scott M. (D, 32)**
Room 333, State House
2 State House Station
Augusta, ME 04333
P: (207) 287-1430
F: (207) 287-1456
E: Scott.Hamann
@legislature.maine.gov

**Handy, James R. (D, 58)\***
Room 333, State House
2 State House Station
Augusta, ME 04333
P: (207) 287-1430
F: (207) 287-1456
E: James.Handy
@legislature.maine.gov

**Hanington, Sheldon Mark
(R, 142)**
Room 332, State House
2 State House Station
Augusta, ME 04333
P: (207) 287-1440
F: (207) 287-1456
E: Sheldon.Hanington
@legislature.maine.gov

**Hanley, Jeffery (R, 87)**
Room 332, State House
2 State House Station
Augusta, ME 04333
P: (207) 287-1440
F: (207) 287-1456
E: Jeff.Hanley
@legislature.maine.gov

# Maine

**Harlow, Denise Patricia (D, 36)**
Room 333, State House
2 State House Station
Augusta, ME 04333
P: (207) 287-1430
F: (207) 287-1456
E: Denise.Harlow
@legislature.maine.gov

**Harrington, Matthew A. (R, 19)**
Room 332, State House
2 State House Station
Augusta, ME 04333
P: (207) 287-1440
F: (207) 287-1456
E: Matthew.Harrington
@legislature.maine.gov

**Harvell, Lance Evans (R, 113)**
Room 332, State House
2 State House Station
Augusta, ME 04333
P: (207) 287-1440
F: (207) 287-1456
E: Lance.Harvell
@legislature.maine.gov

**Hawke, Stephanie (R, 89)**
Room 332, State House
2 State House Station
Augusta, ME 04333
P: (207) 287-1440
F: (207) 287-1456
E: Stephanie.Hawke
@legislature.maine.gov

**Head, Frances (R, 117)**
Room 332, State House
2 State House Station
Augusta, ME 04333
P: (207) 287-1440
F: (207) 287-1456
E: Frances.Head
@legislature.maine.gov

**Herbig, Erin D. (D, 97)**
Room 333, State House
2 State House Station
Augusta, ME 04333
P: (207) 287-1430
F: (207) 287-1456
E: Erin.Herbig
@legislature.maine.gov

**Herrick, Lloyd (R, 73)**
Room 332, State House
2 State House Station
Augusta, ME 04333
P: (207) 287-1440
F: (207) 287-1456
E: Skip.Herrick
@legislature.maine.gov

**Hickman, Craig V. (D, 81)**
Room 333, State House
2 State House Station
Augusta, ME 04333
P: (207) 287-1430
F: (207) 287-1456
E: Craig.Hickman
@legislature.maine.gov

**Higgins, Norman (R, 120)**
Room 332, State House
2 State House Station
Augusta, ME 04333
P: (207) 287-1440
F: (207) 287-1456
E: Norman.Higgins
@legislature.maine.gov

**Hilliard, Gary (R, 76)**
Room 332, State House
2 State House Station
Augusta, ME 04333
P: (207) 287-1440
F: (207) 287-1456
E: Gary.Hilliard
@legislature.maine.gov

**Hogan, George W. (D, 13)**
Room 333, State House
2 State House Station
Augusta, ME 04333
P: (207) 287-1430
F: (207) 287-1456
E: George.Hogan
@legislature.maine.gov

**Hubbell, Brian L. (D, 135)**
Room 333, State House
2 State House Station
Augusta, ME 04333
P: (207) 287-1430
F: (207) 287-1456
E: Brian.Hubbell
@legislature.maine.gov

**Hymanson, Patricia (D, 4)**
Room 333, State House
2 State House Station
Augusta, ME 04333
P: (207) 287-1430
F: (207) 287-1456
E: Patricia.Hymanson
@legislature.maine.gov

**Johanson, Chris A. (R, 145)\***
Room 332, State House
2 State House Station
Augusta, ME 04333
P: (207) 287-1440
F: (207) 287-1456
E: Chris.Johanson
@legislature.maine.gov

**Jorgensen, Erik C. (D, 41)**
Room 333, State House
2 State House Station
Augusta, ME 04333
P: (207) 287-1430
F: (207) 287-1456
E: Erik.Jorgensen
@legislature.maine.gov

**Kinney, Jonathan L. (R, 22)**
Room 332, State House
2 State House Station
Augusta, ME 04333
P: (207) 287-1440
F: (207) 287-1456
E: Jonathan.Kinney
@legislature.maine.gov

**Kinney, Mary Anne (R, 99)**
Room 332, State House
2 State House Station
Augusta, ME 04333
P: (207) 287-1440
F: (207) 287-1456
E: MaryAnne.Kinney
@legislature.maine.gov

**Kornfield, Victoria P. (D, 125)**
Room 333, State House
2 State House Station
Augusta, ME 04333
P: (207) 287-1430
F: (207) 287-1456
E: Tori.Kornfield
@legislature.maine.gov

**Kumiega III, Walter A. (D, 134)**
Room 333, State House
2 State House Station
Augusta, ME 04333
P: (207) 287-1430
F: (207) 287-1456
E: Walter.Kumiega
@legislature.maine.gov

**Lawrence, Mark W. (D, 2)**
Room 333, State House
2 State House Station
Augusta, ME 04333
P: (207) 287-1430
F: (207) 287-1456

**Lockman, Lawrence E. (R, 137)**
Room 332, State House
2 State House Station
Augusta, ME 04333
P: (207) 287-1440
F: (207) 287-1456
E: Lawrence.Lockman
@legislature.maine.gov

**Longstaff, Thomas R.W. (D, 109)**
Room 333, State House
2 State House Station
Augusta, ME 04333
P: (207) 287-1430
F: (207) 287-1456
E: Thomas.Longstaff
@legislature.maine.gov

**Luchini, Louis J. (D, 132)**
Room 333, State House
2 State House Station
Augusta, ME 04333
P: (207) 287-1430
F: (207) 287-1456
E: Louis.Luchini
@legislature.maine.gov

**Lyford, Peter (R, 129)**
Room 332, State House
2 State House Station
Augusta, ME 04333
P: (207) 287-1440
F: (207) 287-1456
E: Peter.Lyford
@legislature.maine.gov

**Madigan, Colleen M. (D, 110)\***
Room 333, State House
2 State House Station
Augusta, ME 04333
P: (207) 287-1430
F: (207) 287-1456
E: Colleen.Madigan
@legislature.maine.gov

**Madigan Jr., John E. (D, 115)\***
Room 333, State House
2 State House Station
Augusta, ME 04333
P: (207) 287-1430
F: (207) 287-1456
E: John.Madigan
@legislature.maine.gov

**Malaby, Richard S. (R, 136)**
Room 332, State House
2 State House Station
Augusta, ME 04333
P: (207) 287-1440
F: (207) 287-1456
E: Richard.Malaby
@legislature.maine.gov

**Marean, Donald G. (R, 16)**
Room 332, State House
2 State House Station
Augusta, ME 04333
P: (207) 287-1440
F: (207) 287-1456
E: Donald.Marean
@legislature.maine.gov

**Martin, John L. (D, 151)**
Room 333, State House
2 State House Station
Augusta, ME 04333
P: (207) 287-1430
F: (207) 287-1456
E: John.Martin
@legislature.maine.gov

**Martin, Roland Daniel (D, 150)**
Room 333, State House
2 State House Station
Augusta, ME 04333
P: (207) 287-1430
F: (207) 287-1456
E: Danny.Martin
@legislature.maine.gov

**Mason, Gina M. (R, 56)***
Room 332, State House
2 State House Station
Augusta, ME 04333
P: (207) 287-1440
F: (207) 287-1456
E: Gina.Mason
@legislature.maine.gov

**Mastraccio, Anne-Marie (D, 18)**
Room 333, State House
2 State House Station
Augusta, ME 04333
P: (207) 287-1430
F: (207) 287-1456
E: Anne-Marie.Mastraccio
@legislature.maine.gov

**McCrea, David Harold (D, 148)***
Room 333, State House
2 State House Station
Augusta, ME 04333
P: (207) 287-1430
F: (207) 287-1456
E: David.McCrea
@legislature.maine.gov

**McCreight, Joyce (D, 51)**
Room 333, State House
2 State House Station
Augusta, ME 04333
P: (207) 287-1430
F: (207) 287-1456
E: Jay.McCreight
@legislature.maine.gov

**McElwee, Carol A. (R, 149)**
Room 332, State House
2 State House Station
Augusta, ME 04333
P: (207) 287-1440
F: (207) 287-1456
E: Carol.McElwee
@legislature.maine.gov

**McLean, Andrew J. (D, 27)**
Room 333, State House
2 State House Station
Augusta, ME 04333
P: (207) 287-1430
F: (207) 287-1456
E: Andrew.McLean
@legislature.maine.gov

**Melaragno, Gina (D, 62)**
Room 333, State House
2 State House Station
Augusta, ME 04333
P: (207) 287-1430
F: (207) 287-1456
E: Gina.Melaragno
@legislature.maine.gov

**Monaghan, Kimberly J. (D, 30)**
Room 333, State House
2 State House Station
Augusta, ME 04333
P: (207) 287-1430
F: (207) 287-1456
E: Kimberly.Monaghan
@legislature.maine.gov

**Moonen, Matthew W. (D, 38)**
Room 333, State House
2 State House Station
Augusta, ME 04333
P: (207) 287-1430
F: (207) 287-1456
E: Matthew.Moonen
@legislature.maine.gov

**Nadeau, Catherine M. (D, 78)**
Room 333, State House
2 State House Station
Augusta, ME 04333
P: (207) 287-1430
F: (207) 287-1456
E: Catherine.Nadeau
@legislature.maine.gov

**O'Connor, Beth A. (R, 5)**
Room 332, State House
2 State House Station
Augusta, ME 04333
P: (207) 287-1440
F: (207) 287-1456
E: Beth.O'Connor
@legislature.maine.gov

**O'Neil, Margaret (D, 15)***
Room 333, State House
2 State House Station
Augusta, ME 04333
P: (207) 287-1430
F: (207) 287-1456
E: Margaret.O'Neil
@legislature.maine.gov

**Ordway, Lester S. (R, 23)**
Room 332, State House
2 State House Station
Augusta, ME 04333
P: (207) 287-1440
F: (207) 287-1456
E: Lester.Ordway
@legislature.maine.gov

**Parker, Jennifer (D, 6)***
Room 333, State House
2 State House Station
Augusta, ME 04333
P: (207) 287-1430
F: (207) 287-1456
E: Jennifer.Parker
@legislature.maine.gov

**Parry, Wayne R. (R, 10)**
Room 332, State House
2 State House Station
Augusta, ME 04333
P: (207) 287-1440
F: (207) 287-1456
E: Wayne.Parry
@legislature.maine.gov

**Perkins, Michael D. (R, 77)***
Room 332, State House
2 State House Station
Augusta, ME 04333
P: (207) 287-1440
F: (207) 287-1456
E: Michael.Perkins
@legislature.maine.gov

**Perry, Anne C. (D, 140)**
Room 333, State House
2 State House Station
Augusta, ME 04333
P: (207) 287-1430
F: (207) 287-1456
E: Anne.Perry
@legislature.maine.gov

**Picchiotti, John J. (R, 108)**
Room 332, State House
2 State House Station
Augusta, ME 04333
P: (207) 287-1440
F: (207) 287-1456
E: John.Picchiotti
@legislature.maine.gov

**Pickett, Richard (R, 116)**
Room 332, State House
2 State House Station
Augusta, ME 04333
P: (207) 287-1440
F: (207) 287-1456
E: Richard.Pickett
@legislature.maine.gov

**Pierce, Jeffrey (R, 53)**
Room 332, State House
2 State House Station
Augusta, ME 04333
P: (207) 287-1440
F: (207) 287-1456
E: Jeff.Pierce
@legislature.maine.gov

**Pierce, Teresa (D, 44)**
Room 333, State House
2 State House Station
Augusta, ME 04333
P: (207) 287-1430
F: (207) 287-1456
E: Teresa.Pierce
@legislature.maine.gov

**Pouliot, Matthew G. (R, 86)**
Room 332, State House
2 State House Station
Augusta, ME 04333
P: (207) 287-1440
F: (207) 287-1456
E: Matthew.Pouliot
@legislature.maine.gov

**Prescott, Dwayne (R, 17)**
Room 332, State House
2 State House Station
Augusta, ME 04333
P: (207) 287-1440
F: (207) 287-1456
E: Dwayne.Prescott
@legislature.maine.gov

**Reckitt, Lois Galgay (D, 31)***
Room 333, State House
2 State House Station
Augusta, ME 04333
P: (207) 287-1430
F: (207) 287-1456
E: Lois.Reckitt
@legislature.maine.gov

**Reed, Roger E. (R, 103)**
Room 332, State House
2 State House Station
Augusta, ME 04333
P: (207) 287-1440
F: (207) 287-1456
E: Roger.Reed
@legislature.maine.gov

**Riley, Christina (D, 74)***
Room 333, State House
2 State House Station
Augusta, ME 04333
P: (207) 287-1430
F: (207) 287-1456
E: Christina.Riely
@legislature.maine.gov

# Maine

**Ross, Rachel Talbot (D, 40)***
Room 333, State House
2 State House Station
Augusta, ME 04333
P: (207) 287-1430
F: (207) 287-1456
E: Rachel.TablotRoss
@legislature.maine.gov

**Rykerson, Deane (D, 1)**
Room 333, State House
2 State House Station
Augusta, ME 04333
P: (207) 287-1430
F: (207) 287-1456
E: Deane.Rykerson
@legislature.maine.gov

**Sampson, Heidi H. (R, 21)***
Room 332, State House
2 State House Station
Augusta, ME 04333
P: (207) 287-1440
F: (207) 287-1456
E: Heidi.Sampson
@legislature.maine.gov

**Sanborn, Heather B. (D, 43)***
Room 333, State House
2 State House Station
Augusta, ME 04333
P: (207) 287-1430
F: (207) 287-1456
E: Heather.Sanborn
@legislature.maine.gov

**Sanderson, Deborah J. (R, 88)**
Room 332, State House
2 State House Station
Augusta, ME 04333
P: (207) 287-1440
F: (207) 287-1456
E: Deborah.Sanderson
@legislature.maine.gov

**Schneck, John C. (D, 126)**
Room 333, State House
2 State House Station
Augusta, ME 04333
P: (207) 287-1430
F: (207) 287-1456
E: John.Schneck
@legislature.maine.gov

**Seavey, H. Stedman (R, 9)**
Room 332, State House
2 State House Station
Augusta, ME 04333
P: (207) 287-1440
F: (207) 287-1456
E: Stedman.Seavey
@legislature.maine.gov

**Sheats, Bettyann W. (D, 64)***
Room 333, State House
2 State House Station
Augusta, ME 04333
P: (207) 287-1430
F: (207) 287-1456
E: Bettyann.Sheats
@legislature.maine.gov

**Sherman, Roger L. (R, 144)**
Room 332, State House
2 State House Station
Augusta, ME 04333
P: (207) 287-1440
F: (207) 287-1456
E: Rsherm
@legislature.maine.gov

**Simmons, Abden S. (R, 91)***
Room 332, State House
2 State House Station
Augusta, ME 04333
P: (207) 287-1440
F: (207) 287-1456
E: Abden.Simmons
@legislature.maine.gov

**Sirocki, Heather W. (R, 28)**
Room 332, State House
2 State House Station
Augusta, ME 04333
P: (207) 287-1440
F: (207) 287-1456
E: Heather.Sirocki
@legislature.maine.gov

**Skolfield, Thomas (R, 112)**
Room 332, State House
2 State House Station
Augusta, ME 04333
P: (207) 287-1440
F: (207) 287-1456
E: Thomas.Skolfield
@legislature.maine.gov

**Spear, John Alden (D, 92)***
Room 333, State House
2 State House Station
Augusta, ME 04333
P: (207) 287-1430
F: (207) 287-1456
E: John.Spear
@legislature.maine.gov

**Stanley, Stephen S. (D, 143)**
Room 333, State House
2 State House Station
Augusta, ME 04333
P: (207) 287-1430
F: (207) 287-1456
E: Stephen.Stanley
@legislature.maine.gov

**Stearns, Paul (R, 119)**
Room 332, State House
2 State House Station
Augusta, ME 04333
P: (207) 287-1440
F: (207) 287-1456
E: Paul.Stearns
@legislature.maine.gov

**Stetkis, Joel (R, 105)**
Room 332, State House
2 State House Station
Augusta, ME 04333
P: (207) 287-1440
F: (207) 287-1456
E: Joel.Stetkis
@legislature.maine.gov

**Stewart III, Harold L. (R, 147)***
Room 332, State House
2 State House Station
Augusta, ME 04333
P: (207) 287-1440
F: (207) 287-1456
E: Trey.Stewart
@legislature.maine.gov

**Strom, Scott Walter (R, 106)***
Room 332, State House
2 State House Station
Augusta, ME 04333
P: (207) 287-1440
F: (207) 287-1456
E: Scott.Strom
@legislature.maine.gov

**Sutton, Paula G. (R, 95)***
Room 332, State House
2 State House Station
Augusta, ME 04333
P: (207) 287-1440
F: (207) 287-1456
E: Paula.Sutton
@legislature.maine.gov

**Sylvester, Michael (D, 39)***
Room 333, State House
2 State House Station
Augusta, ME 04333
P: (207) 287-1430
F: (207) 287-1456
E: Mike.Sylvester
@legislature.maine.gov

**Tepler, Denise (D, 54)**
Room 333, State House
2 State House Station
Augusta, ME 04333
P: (207) 287-1430
F: (207) 287-1456
E: Denise.Tepler
@legislature.maine.gov

**Terry, Maureen Fitzgerald (D, 26)***
Room 333, State House
2 State House Station
Augusta, ME 04333
P: (207) 287-1430
F: (207) 287-1456
E: Maureen.Terry
@legislature.maine.gov

**Theriault, Timothy (R, 79)**
Room 332, State House
2 State House Station
Augusta, ME 04333
P: (207) 287-1440
F: (207) 287-1456
E: tim.theriault
@legislature.maine.gov

**Timberlake, Jeffrey L. (R, 75)**
Room 332, State House
2 State House Station
Augusta, ME 04333
P: (207) 287-1440
F: (207) 287-1456
E: Jeffrey.Timberlake
@legislature.maine.gov

**Tipping, Ryan D. (D, 123)**
Room 333, State House
2 State House Station
Augusta, ME 04333
P: (207) 287-1430
F: (207) 287-1456
E: Tipping-Spitz
@legislature.maine.gov

**Tucker, Ralph (D, 50)**
Room 333, State House
2 State House Station
Augusta, ME 04333
P: (207) 287-1430
F: (207) 287-1456
E: Ralph.Tucker
@legislature.maine.gov

**Tuell, William (R, 139)**
Room 332, State House
2 State House Station
Augusta, ME 04333
P: (207) 287-1440
F: (207) 287-1456
E: Will.Tuell
@legislature.maine.gov

**Turner, Beth P. (R, 141)**
Room 332, State House
2 State House Station
Augusta, ME 04333
P: (207) 287-1440
F: (207) 287-1456
E: Beth.Turner
@legislature.maine.gov

**Vachon, Karen (R, 29)**
Room 332, State House
2 State House Station
Augusta, ME 04333
P: (207) 287-1440
F: (207) 287-1456
E: Karen.Vachon
    @legislature.maine.gov

**Wadsworth, Nathan (R, 70)**
Room 332, State House
2 State House Station
Augusta, ME 04333
P: (207) 287-1440
F: (207) 287-1456
E: Nathan.Wadsworth
    @legislature.maine.gov

**Wallace, Raymond A.
    (R, 104)**
Room 332, State House
2 State House Station
Augusta, ME 04333
P: (207) 287-1440
F: (207) 287-1456
E: Raymond.Wallace
    @legislature.maine.gov

**Ward, Karleton (R, 131)**
Room 332, State House
2 State House Station
Augusta, ME 04333
P: (207) 287-1440
F: (207) 287-1456
E: Karl.Ward
    @legislature.maine.gov

**Warren, Charlotte (D, 84)**
Room 333, State House
2 State House Station
Augusta, ME 04333
P: (207) 287-1430
F: (207) 287-1456
E: Charlotte.Warren
    @legislature.maine.gov

**White, Dustin Michael
    (R, 146)**
Room 332, State House
2 State House Station
Augusta, ME 04333
P: (207) 287-1440
F: (207) 287-1456
E: Dustin.White
    @legislature.maine.gov

**Winsor, Tom J. (R, 71)**
Room 332, State House
2 State House Station
Augusta, ME 04333
P: (207) 287-1440
F: (207) 287-1456
E: Tom.Winsor
    @legislature.maine.gov

**Wood, Stephen J. (R, 57)**
Room 332, State House
2 State House Station
Augusta, ME 04333
P: (207) 287-1440
F: (207) 287-1456
E: Stephen.Wood
    @legislature.maine.gov

**Zeigler Jr., Stanley Paige
    (D, 96)***
Room 333, State House
2 State House Station
Augusta, ME 04333
P: (207) 287-1430
F: (207) 287-1456
E: Stanley.Zeigler
    @legislature.maine.gov

# Maryland

## Executive

### Governor

**The Honorable Larry Hogan (R)**
Governor
State House
100 State Circle
Annapolis, MD 21401
P: (410) 974-3901
F: (410) 974-3275

### Lieutenant Governor

**The Honorable Boyd Rutherford (R)**
Lieutenant Governor
100 State Circle
Annapolis, MD 21401
P: (410) 974-2804
E: ltgov@gov.state.md.us

### Attorney General

**The Honorable Brian E. Frosh (D)**
Attorney General
200 Saint Paul Place
Baltimore, MD 21202
P: (410) 576-6300
F: (410) 576-6404
E: oag@oag.state.md.us

### Auditor

**Mr. Thomas J. Barnickel III**
(appointed by the Legislature)
Legislative Auditor
301 West Preston Street, Room 1202
Baltimore, MD 21201
P: (410) 946-5900
F: (410) 946-5998
E: tbarnickel
@ola.state.md.us

### Comptroller

**The Honorable Peter Franchot (D)**
Comptroller
L.L. Goldstein Treasury Building
P.O. Box 466
Annapolis, MD 21404
P: (410) 260-7801
F: (410) 974-3808
E: mdcomptroller
@comp.state.md.us

### Secretary of State

**The Honorable John C. Wobensmith**
(appointed)
Secretary of State
16 Francis Street
Annapolis, MD 21401
P: (410) 974-5521
F: (410) 841-5527
E: dlmdsos_sos@maryland.gov

### Treasurer

**The Honorable Nancy K. Kopp**
(elected by the Legislature)
State Treasurer
80 Calvert Street
Annapolis, MD 21401
P: (410) 260-7160
F: (410) 260-6056
E: nkopp
@treasurer.state.md.us

## Judiciary

### Court of Appeals (MR)

**Ms. Bessie M. Decker**
Clerk of Court of Appeals
Robert Murphy Courts of Appeal Building
361 Rowe Boulevard
Annapolis, MD 21401
P: (410) 260-1500

**The Honorable Mary Ellen Barbera**
Chief Judge
**The Honorable Sally D. Adkins**
**The Honorable Joseph M. Getty (R)**
**The Honorable Clayton Greene Jr.**
**The Honorable Michele D. Hotten**
**The Honorable Robert N. McDonald**
**The Honorable Shirley M. Watts**

## Legislative

## Senate

### Senate President

**Senator Thomas V. Mike Miller Jr. (D)**
Senate President
State House, H-107
100 State Circle
Annapolis, MD 21401
P: (410) 841-3700
F: (410) 841-3910
E: thomas.v.mike.miller
@senate.state.md.us

### President Pro Tempore of the Senate

**Senator Nathaniel J. McFadden (D)**
Senate President Pro Tem
Miller Senate Office Building, Room 422
11 Bladen Street
Annapolis, MD 21401
P: (410) 841-3165
F: (410) 841-3138
E: nathaniel.mcfadden
@senate.state.md.us

### Senate Majority Leader

**Senator Douglas J.J. Peters (D)**
Senate Majority Leader
James Senate Office Building, Room 120
11 Bladen Street
Annapolis, MD 21401
P: (410) 841-3631
F: (301) 858-3174
E: douglas.peters
@senate.state.md.us

### Senate Minority Leader

**Senator J.B. Jennings (R)**
Senate Minority Leader
James Senate Office Building, Room 423
11 Bladen Street
Annapolis, MD 21401
P: (410) 841-3706
F: (410) 841-3750
E: jb.jennings
@senate.state.md.us

### Secretary of the Senate

**Mr. William B.C. Addison Jr.**
Secretary of the Senate
Room H-105, State House
100 State Circle
Annapolis, MD 21401
P: (410) 841-3908
F: (410) 841-3910

## Members of the Senate

**Astle, John C. (D, 30)**
James Senate Office Building, Room 123
11 Bladen Street
Annapolis, MD 21401
P: (410) 841-3578
F: (410) 841-3156
E: john.astle
@senate.state.md.us

**Bates, Gail H. (R, 9)**
James Senate Office Building, Room 401
11 Bladen Street
Annapolis, MD 21401
P: (410) 841-3671
F: (401) 841-3395
E: gail.bates
@senate.state.md.us

**Benson, Joanne Claybon (D, 24)**
James Senate Office Building, Room 214
11 Bladen Street
Annapolis, MD 21401
P: (410) 841-3148
F: (301) 858-3149
E: joanne.benson
@senate.state.md.us

**Brochin, James (D, 42)**
James Senate Office Building, Room 221
11 Bladen Street
Annapolis, MD 21401
P: (410) 841-3648
F: (410) 841-3643
E: jim.brochin
@senate.state.md.us

**Cassilly, Bob (R, 34)**
James Senate Office Building, Room 321
11 Bladen Street
Annapolis, MD 21401
P: (410) 841-3158
E: Bob.Cassilly
@senate.state.md.us

**Conway, Joan Carter (D, 43)**
Miller Senate Building, 2 West Wing
11 Bladen Street
Annapolis, MD 21401
P: (410) 841-3145
F: (410) 841-3145
E: joan.carter.conway
@senate.state.md.us

**Currie, Ulysses (D, 25)**
James Senate Office Building,
Room 201
11 Bladen Street
Annapolis, MD 21401
P: (410) 841-3127
F: (301) 858-3733
E: ulysses.currie
@senate.state.md.us

**DeGrange Sr., James E.
(D, 32)**
James Senate Office Building,
Room 101
11 Bladen Street
Annapolis, MD 21401
P: (410) 841-3593
F: (410) 841-3589
E: james.degrange
@senate.state.md.us

**Eckardt, Adelaide C.
(R, 37)**
James Senate Office Building,
Room 322
11 Bladen Street
Annapolis, MD 21401
P: (410) 841-3590
F: (410) 841-3299
E: adelaide.eckardt
@house.state.md.us

**Edwards, George C. (R, 1)**
James Senate Office Building,
Room 323
11 Bladen Street
Annapolis, MD 21401
P: (410) 841-3565
F: (301) 858-3552
E: george.edwards
@senate.state.md.us

**Feldman, Brian J. (D, 15)**
James Senate Office Building,
Room 104
11 Bladen Street
Annapolis, MD 21401
P: (410) 841-3169
F: (410) 841-3607
E: brian.feldman
@senate.state.md.us

**Ferguson IV, William C.
(D, 46)**
Miller Senate Building, Room
401
11 Bladen Street
Annapolis, MD 21401
P: (410) 841-3600
F: (410) 841-3161
E: bill.ferguson
@senate.state.md.us

**Guzzone, Guy (D, 13)**
James Senate Office Building,
Room 121
11 Bladen Street
Annapolis, MD 21401
P: (410) 841-3572
F: (410) 841-3438
E: guy.guzzone
@senate.state.md.us

**Hershey Jr., Stephen S.
(R, 36)**
James Senate Office Building,
Room 420
11 Bladen Street
Annapolis, MD 21401
P: (410) 841-3639
F: (410) 841-3762
E: steve.hershey
@senate.state.md.us

**Hough, Michael (R, 4)**
James Senate Office Building,
Room 403
11 Bladen Street
Annapolis, MD 21401
P: (410) 841-3704
E: michael.hough
@senate.state.md.us

**Jennings, J.B. (R, 7)**
James Senate Office Building,
Room 423
11 Bladen Street
Annapolis, MD 21401
P: (410) 841-3706
F: (410) 841-3750
E: jb.jennings
@senate.state.md.us

**Kagan, Cheryl C. (D, 17)**
James Senate Office Building,
Room 203
11 Bladen Street
Annapolis, MD 21401
P: (410) 841-3134

**Kasemeyer, Edward J.
(D, 12)**
Miller Senate Building, 3 West
Wing
11 Bladen Street
Annapolis, MD 21401
P: (410) 841-3653
F: (410) 841-3091
E: edward.kasemeyer
@senate.state.md.us

**Kelley, Delores Goodwin
(D, 10)**
James Senate Office Building,
Room 302
11 Bladen Street
Annapolis, MD 21401
P: (410) 841-3606
F: (410) 841-3399
E: delores.kelley
@senate.state.md.us

**King, Nancy J. (D, 39)**
James Senate Office Building,
Room 223
11 Bladen Street
Annapolis, MD 21401
P: (301) 858-3686
F: (301) 858-6370
E: nancy.king
@senate.state.md.us

**Klausmeier, Katherine A.
(D, 8)**
James Senate Office Building,
Room 103
11 Bladen Street
Annapolis, MD 21401
P: (410) 841-3620
F: (410) 841-3085
E: katherine.klausmeier
@senate.state.md.us

**Lee, Susan C. (D, 16)**
James Senate Office Building,
Room 222
11 Bladen Street
Annapolis, MD 21401
P: (410) 841-3124
F: (301) 858-3424
E: susan.lee
@senate.state.md.us

**Madaleno Jr.,
Richard Stuart (D, 18)**
Miller Senate Building, 3 West
Wing
11 Bladen Street
Annapolis, MD 21401
P: (410) 841-3137
F: (301) 858-3676
E: richard.madaleno
@senate.state.md.us

**Manno, Roger (D, 19)**
James Senate Office Building,
Room 102
11 Bladen Street
Annapolis, MD 21401
P: (410) 841-3151
F: (301) 858-3740
E: roger.manno
@senate.state.md.us

**Mathias Jr., James N.
(D, 38)**
James Senate Office Building,
Room 216
11 Bladen Street
Annapolis, MD 21401
P: (410) 841-3645
F: (410) 841-3006
E: james.mathias
@senate.state.md.us

**McFadden, Nathaniel J.
(D, 45)**
Miller Senate Office Building,
Room 422
11 Bladen Street
Annapolis, MD 21401
P: (410) 841-3165
F: (410) 841-3138
E: nathaniel.mcfadden
@senate.state.md.us

**Middleton, Thomas McLain
(D, 28)**
Miller Senate Building, 3 East
Wing
11 Bladen Street
Annapolis, MD 21401
P: (410) 841-3616
F: (301) 858-3682
E: thomas.mclain.middleton
@senate.state.md.us

**Miller Jr., Thomas V. Mike
(D, 27)**
State House, H-107
100 State Circle
Annapolis, MD 21401
P: (410) 841-3700
F: (410) 841-3910
E: thomas.v.mike.miller
@senate.state.md.us

**Muse, C. Anthony (D, 26)**
Miller Senate Building, Room
420
11 Bladen Street
Annapolis, MD 21401
P: (410) 841-3092
F: (301) 858-3410
E: anthony.muse
@senate.state.md.us

**Nathan-Pulliam, Shirley
(D, 44)**
James Senate Office Building,
Room 304
11 Bladen Street
Annapolis, MD 21401
P: (410) 841-3612
F: (410) 841-3612
E: shirley.nathan.pulliam
@senate.state.md.us

# Maryland

**Norman, Wayne (R, 35)**
James Senate Office Building,
Room 315
11 Bladen Street
Annapolis, MD 21401
P: (410) 841-3603
F: (410) 841-3115
E: wayne.norman
    @senate.state.md.us

**Peters, Douglas J.J.**
  **(D, 23)**
James Senate Office Building,
Room 120
11 Bladen Street
Annapolis, MD 21401
P: (410) 841-3631
F: (301) 858-3174
E: douglas.peters
    @senate.state.md.us

**Pinsky, Paul G. (D, 22)**
James Senate Office Building,
Room 220
11 Bladen Street
Annapolis, MD 21401
P: (410) 841-3155
F: (301) 858-3144
E: paul.pinsky
    @senate.state.md.us

**Ramirez, Victor R. (D, 47)**
James Senate Office Building,
Room 303
11 Bladen Street
Annapolis, MD 21401
P: (410) 841-3745
F: (301) 858-3387
E: victor.ramirez
    @senate.state.md.us

**Ready, Justin D. (R, 5)**
James Senate Office Building,
Room 414
11 Bladen Street
Annapolis, MD 21401
P: (410) 841-3683
E: justin.ready
    @senate.state.md.us

**Reilly, Edward R. (R, 33)**
James Senate Office Building,
Room 316
11 Bladen Street
Annapolis, MD 21401
P: (410) 841-3568
F: (410) 841-3067
E: edward.reilly
    @senate.state.md.us

**Robinson, Barbara A.**
  **(D, 40)**
Miller Senate Building, Room
401
11 Bladen Street
Annapolis, MD 21401
P: (410) 841-3656
E: barbara.robinson
    @senate.state.md.us

**Rosapepe, James C. (D, 21)**
James Senate Office Building,
Room 314
11 Bladen Street
Annapolis, MD 21401
P: (410) 841-3141
F: (410) 841-3195
E: jim.rosapepe
    @senate.state.md.us

**Salling, Johnny Ray (R, 6)**
James Senate Office Building,
Room 416
11 Bladen Street
Annapolis, MD 21401
P: (410) 841-3587
E: JohnnyRay.Salling
    @senate.state.md.us

**Serafini, Andrew A. (R, 2)**
James Senate Office Building,
Room 402
11 Bladen Street
Annapolis, MD 21401
P: (410) 841-3903
E: andrew.serafini
    @senate.state.md.us

**Simonaire, Bryan W. (R, 31)**
James Senate Office Building,
Room 320
11 Bladen Street
Annapolis, MD 21401
P: (410) 841-3658
F: (410) 841-3586
E: bryan.simonaire
    @senate.state.md.us

**Smith, Will (D, 20)**
Miller Senate Building, 2 East
Wing
11 Bladen Street
Annapolis, MD 21401
P: (410) 841-3634
E: wiil.smith
    @senate.state.md.us

**Waugh, Steve (R, 29)**
Miller Senate Building, 2 West
Wing
11 Bladen Street
Annapolis, MD 21401
P: (410) 841-3673
E: Steve.Waugh
    @senate.state.md.us

**Young, Ronald N. (D, 3)**
James Senate Office Building,
Room 301
11 Bladen Street
Annapolis, MD 21401
P: (410) 841-3575
F: (301) 858-3193
E: ronald.young
    @senate.state.md.us

**Zirkin, Robert A. (D, 11)**
Miller Senate Building, 2 East
Wing
11 Bladen Street
Annapolis, MD 21401
P: (410) 841-3131
F: (410) 841-3737
E: bobby.zirkin
    @senate.state.md.us

# House

## Speaker of the House

**Delegate Michael Erin**
  **Busch (D)**
House Speaker
State House, H-101
State Circle
Annapolis, MD 21401
P: (410) 841-3800
F: (410) 841-3880
E: michael.busch
    @house.state.md.us

## Speaker Pro Tempore of the House

**Delegate Adrienne A.**
  **Jones (D)**
House Speaker Pro Tem
House Office Building, Room
312
6 Bladen Street
Annapolis, MD 21401
P: (410) 841-3391
F: (410) 841-3157
E: adrienne.jones
    @house.state.md.us

## House Majority Leader

**Delegate Bill Frick (D)**
House Majority Leader
House Office Building, Room
350
6 Bladen Street
Annapolis, MD 21401
P: (410) 841-3454
F: (301) 858-3457
E: bill.frick
    @house.state.md.us

## House Minority Leader

**Delegate Nicholaus R.**
  **Kipke (R)**
House Minority Leader
House Office Building, Room
212
6 Bladen Street
Annapolis, MD 21401
P: (410) 841-3421
F: (410) 841-3553
E: nicholaus.kipke
    @house.state.md.us

## Clerk of the House

**Ms. Sylvia Siegert**
Chief Clerk
Room H-104, State House
100 State Circle
Annapolis, MD 21401
P: (410) 841-3999
E: hseclerk
    @mlis.state.md.us

## Members of the House

**Adams, Christopher (R, 37B)**
House Office Building, Room
326
6 Bladen Street
Annapolis, MD 21401
P: (410) 841-3343
E: Christopher.Adams
    @house.state.md.us

**Afzali, Kathryn L. (R, 4)**
House Office Building, Room
326
6 Bladen Street
Annapolis, MD 21401
P: (410) 841-3288
F: (301) 858-3184
E: kathy.afzali
    @house.state.md.us

**Ali, Bilal (D, 41)\***
House Office Building, Room
217
6 Bladen Street
Annapolis, MD 21401
P: (410) 841-3268
E: bilal.ali
    @house.state.md.us

**Anderson, Curtis Stovall**
  **(D, 43)**
House Office Building, Room
314
6 Bladen Street
Annapolis, MD 21401
P: (410) 841-3291
F: (410) 841-3024
E: curt.anderson
    @house.state.md.us

**Anderton Jr., Carl (R, 38B)**
House Office Building, Room 317
6 Bladen Street
Annapolis, MD 21401
P: (410) 841-3431
E: Carl.Anderton
@house.state.md.us

**Angel, Angela (D, 25)**
House Office Building, Room 216
6 Bladen Street
Annapolis, MD 21401
P: (410) 841-3707
E: Angela.Angel
@house.state.md.us

**Arentz, Steven J. (R, 36)**
House Office Building, Room 308
6 Bladen Street
Annapolis, MD 21401
P: (410) 841-3543
F: (410) 841-3098
E: steven.arentz
@house.state.md.us

**Atterbeary, Vanessa (D, 13)**
House Office Building, Room 424
6 Bladen Street
Annapolis, MD 21401
P: (410) 841-3471
E: Vanessa.Atterbeary
@house.state.md.us

**Aumann, Susan L.M. (R, 42B)**
House Office Building, Room 303
6 Bladen Street
Annapolis, MD 21401
P: (410) 841-3258
F: (410) 841-3163
E: susan.aumann
@house.state.md.us

**Barkley, Charles E. (D, 39)**
House Office Building, Room 223
6 Bladen Street
Annapolis, MD 21401
P: (401) 841-3001
F: (301) 858-3009
E: charles.barkley
@house.state.md.us

**Barnes, Benjamin S. (D, 21)**
House Office Building, Room 151
6 Bladen Street
Annapolis, MD 21401
P: (410) 841-3046
F: (410) 841-3346
E: ben.barnes
@house.state.md.us

**Barnes, Darryl (D, 25)**
House Office Building, Room 206
6 Bladen Street
Annapolis, MD 21401
P: (410) 841-3557
E: Darryl.Barnes
@house.state.md.us

**Barron, Erek (D, 24)**
House Office Building, Room 216
6 Bladen Street
Annapolis, MD 21401
P: (410) 841-3692
E: Erek.Barron
@house.state.md.us

**Barve, Kumar P. (D, 17)**
House Office Building, Room 251
6 Bladen Street
Annapolis, MD 21401
P: (410) 841-3990
F: (301) 858-3850
E: kumar.barve
@house.state.md.us

**Beidle, Pamela G. (D, 32)**
House Office Building, Room 165
6 Bladen Street
Annapolis, MD 21401
P: (410) 841-3370
F: (410) 841-3347
E: pamela.beidle
@house.state.md.us

**Beitzel, Wendell R. (R, 1A)**
House Office Building, Room 309
6 Bladen Street
Annapolis, MD 21401
P: (410) 841-3435
F: (301) 858-3040
E: wendell.beitzel
@house.state.md.us

**Branch, Talmadge (D, 45)**
House Office Building, Room 151
6 Bladen Street
Annapolis, MD 21401
P: (410) 841-3398
F: (410) 841-3550
E: talmadge.branch
@house.state.md.us

**Bromwell, Eric M. (D, 8)**
House Office Building, Room 415
6 Bladen Street
Annapolis, MD 21401
P: (410) 841-3766
F: (410) 841-3850
E: eric.bromwell
@house.state.md.us

**Brooks, Benjamin (D, 10)**
House Office Building, Room 304
6 Bladen Street
Annapolis, MD 21401
P: (410) 841-3352
E: Benjamin.Brooks
@house.state.md.us

**Buckel, Jason (R, 1B)**
House Office Building, Room 309
6 Bladen Street
Annapolis, MD 21401
P: (410) 841-3404
E: Jason.Buckel
@house.state.md.us

**Busch, Michael Erin (D, 30A)**
State House, H-101
State Circle
Annapolis, MD 21401
P: (410) 841-3800
F: (410) 841-3880
E: michael.busch
@house.state.md.us

**Carey, Ned (D, 31A)**
House Office Building, Room 161
6 Bladen Street
Annapolis, MD 21401
P: (410) 841-3047
E: Ned.Carey
@house.state.md.us

**Carozza, Mary Beth (R, 38C)**
House Office Building, Room 203
6 Bladen Street
Annapolis, MD 21401
P: (410) 841-3356
E: MaryBeth.Carozza
@house.state.md.us

**Carr Jr., Alfred C. (D, 18)**
House Office Building, Room 222
6 Bladen Street
Annapolis, MD 21401
P: (410) 841-3638
F: (301) 858-3053
E: alfred.carr
@house.state.md.us

**Cassilly, Andrew (R, 35B)**
House Office Building, Room 316
6 Bladen Street
Annapolis, MD 21401
P: (410) 841-3444
E: Andrew.Cassilly
@house.state.md.us

**Chang, Mark (D, 32)**
House Office Building, Room 160
6 Bladen Street
Annapolis, MD 21401
P: (410) 841-3511
E: Mark.Chang
@house.state.md.us

**Ciliberti, Barrie S. (R, 4)**
House Office Building, Room 324
6 Bladen Street
Annapolis, MD 21401
P: (410) 841-3080
F: (410) 841-3028
E: Barrie.Ciliberti
@house.state.md.us

**Clark, Jerry (R, 29)***
House Office Building, Room 303
6 Bladen Street
Annapolis, MD 21401
P: (410) 841-3314
E: jerry.clark
@house.state.md.us

**Clippinger, Luke H. (D, 46)**
House Office Building, Room 350
6 Bladen Street
Annapolis, MD 21401
P: (410) 841-3303
F: (410) 841-3537
E: luke.clippinger
@house.state.md.us

**Cluster, Joe (R, 8)**
House Office Building, Room 308
6 Bladen Street
Annapolis, MD 24101
P: (410) 841-3526
E: joseph.cluster
@house.state.md.us

**Conaway Jr., Frank M. (D, 40)**
House Office Building, Room 314
6 Bladen Street
Annapolis, MD 21401
P: (410) 841-3189
F: (410) 841-3079
E: frank.conaway
@house.state.md.us

**Cullison, Bonnie L. (D, 19)**
House Office Building, Room 350
6 Bladen Street
Annapolis, MD 21401
P: (410) 841-3883
F: (301) 858-3882
E: bonnie.cullison
@house.state.md.us

# Maryland

**Davis, Dereck E. (D, 25)**
House Office Building, Room 231
6 Bladen Street
Annapolis, MD 21401
P: (410) 841-3519
F: (301) 858-3558
E: dereck.davis
@house.state.md.us

**Dumais, Kathleen M. (D, 15)**
House Office Building, Room 101
6 Bladen Street
Annapolis, MD 21401
P: (410) 841-3052
F: (301) 858-3219
E: kathleen.dumais
@house.state.md.us

**Ebersole, Eric (D, 12)**
House Office Building, Room 305
6 Bladen Street
Annapolis, MD 21401
P: (410) 841-3328
E: Eric.Ebersole
@house.state.md.us

**Fennell, Diana (D, 47A)**
House Office Building, Room 209
6 Bladen Street
Annapolis, MD 21401
P: (410) 841-3478
E: Diana.Fennell
@house.state.md.us

**Fisher, Mark (R, 27C)**
House Office Building, Room 202
6 Bladen Street
Annapolis, MD 21401
P: (410) 841-3231
F: (301) 858-3335
E: mark.fisher
@house.state.md.us

**Flanagan, Bob (R, 9B)**
House Office Building, Room 430
6 Bladen Street
Annapolis, MD 21401
P: (410) 841-3077
F: (410) 841-3241
E: Bob.Flanagan
@house.state.md.us

**Folden, William (R, 3B)**
House Office Building, Room 405
6 Bladen Street
Annapolis, MD 21401
P: (410) 841-3240
F: (410) 841-3481
E: William.Folden
@house.state.md.us

**Fraser-Hidalgo, David (D, 15)**
House Office Building, Room 226
6 Bladen Street
Annapolis, MD 21401
P: (410) 841-3186
F: (301) 858-3112
E: david.fraser.hidalgo
@house.state.md.us

**Frick, Bill (D, 16)**
House Office Building, Room 350
6 Bladen Street
Annapolis, MD 21401
P: (410) 841-3454
F: (301) 858-3457
E: bill.frick
@house.state.md.us

**Frush, Barbara A. (D, 21)**
House Office Building, Room 364
6 Bladen Street
Annapolis, MD 21401
P: (410) 841-3114
F: (410) 841-3116
E: barbara.frush
@house.state.md.us

**Gaines, Tawanna P. (D, 22)**
House Office Building, Room 121
6 Bladen Street
Annapolis, MD 21401
P: (410) 841-3058
F: (301) 858-3119
E: tawanna.gaines
@house.state.md.us

**Ghrist, Jeff (R, 36)**
House Office Building, Room 410
6 Bladen Street
Annapolis, MD 21401
P: (410) 841-3555
F: (410) 841-3434
E: Jeff.Ghrist
@house.state.md.us

**Gilchrist, James W. (D, 17)**
House Office Building, Room 219
6 Bladen Street
Annapolis, MD 21401
P: (410) 841-3744
F: (301) 858-3057
E: jim.gilchrist
@house.state.md.us

**Glass, Glen (R, 34A)**
House Office Building, Room 325
6 Bladen Street
Annapolis, MD 21401
P: (410) 841-3280
F: (410) 841-3754
E: glen.glass
@house.state.md.us

**Glenn, Cheryl D. (D, 45)**
House Office Building, Room 413
6 Bladen Street
Annapolis, MD 21401
P: (410) 841-3257
F: (410) 841-3019
E: cheryl.glenn
@house.state.md.us

**Grammer Jr., Robin (R, 6)**
House Office Building, Room 307
6 Bladen Street
Annapolis, MD 21401
P: (410) 841-3298
E: Robin.Grammer
@house.state.md.us

**Gutierrez, Ana Sol (D, 18)**
House Office Building, Room 404
6 Bladen Street
Annapolis, MD 21401
P: (410) 841-3181
F: (301) 858-3232
E: ana.gutierrez
@house.state.md.us

**Hayes, Antonio (D, 40)**
House Office Building, Room 315
6 Bladen Street
Annapolis, MD 21401
P: (410) 841-3545
E: Antonio.Hayes
@house.state.md.us

**Haynes, Keith E. (D, 44A)**
House Office Building, Room 363
6 Bladen Street
Annapolis, MD 21401
P: (401) 841-3801
F: (410) 841-3530
E: keith.haynes
@house.state.md.us

**Healey, Anne (D, 22)**
House Office Building, Room 361
6 Bladen Street
Annapolis, MD 21401
P: (410) 841-3961
F: (301) 858-3223
E: anne.healey
@house.state.md.us

**Hettleman, Shelly (D, 11)**
House Office Building, Room 311
6 Bladen Street
Annapolis, MD 21401
P: (410) 841-3833
E: Shelly.Hettleman
@house.state.md.us

**Hill, Terri (D, 12)**
House Office Building, Room 215
6 Bladen Street
Annapolis, MD 21401
P: (410) 841-3378
E: Terri.Hill
@house.state.md.us

**Hixson, Sheila Ellis (D, 20)**
House Office Building, Room 131
6 Bladen Street
Annapolis, MD 21401
P: (410) 841-3469
F: (410) 841-3777
E: sheila.hixson
@house.state.md.us

**Holmes Jr., Marvin E. (D, 23B)**
House Office Building, Room 313
6 Bladen Street
Annapolis, MD 21401
P: (410) 841-3310
F: (410) 841-3017
E: marvin.holmes
@house.state.md.us

**Hornberger, Kevin Bailey (R, 35A)**
House Office Building, Room 410
6 Bladen Street
Annapolis, MD 21401
P: (410) 841-3284
E: Kevin.Hornberger
@house.state.md.us

**Howard, Carolyn J.B. (D, 24)**
House Office Building, Room 301
6 Bladen Street
Annapolis, MD 21401
P: (410) 841-3919
F: (410) 841-3925
E: carolyn.howard
@house.state.md.us

**Howard, Seth (R, 30B)**
House Office Building, Room 159
6 Bladen Street
Annapolis, MD 21401
P: (410) 841-3439
E: Seth.Howard
@house.state.md.us

**Impallaria, Rick (R, 7)**
House Office Building, Room 310
6 Bladen Street
Annapolis, MD 21401
P: (410) 841-3289
F: (410) 841-3598
E: rick.impallaria
@house.state.md.us

**Jackson, Michael (D, 27B)**
House Office Building, Room 204
6 Bladen Street
Annapolis, MD 21401
P: (410) 841-3103
E: Michael.Jackson
@house.state.md.us

**Jacobs, Jay A. (R, 36)**
House Office Building, Room 321
6 Bladen Street
Annapolis, MD 21401
P: (410) 841-3449
F: (410) 841-3093
E: jay.jacobs
@house.state.md.us

**Jalisi, Jay (D, 10)**
House Office Building, Room 304
6 Bladen Street
Annapolis, MD 21401
P: (410) 841-3358
F: (410) 841-3100
E: Jay.Jalisi
@house.state.md.us

**Jameson, Sally Young (D, 28)**
House Office Building, Room 231
6 Bladen Street
Annapolis, MD 21401
P: (410) 841-3337
F: (301) 858-3277
E: sally.jameson
@house.state.md.us

**Jones, Adrienne A. (D, 10)**
House Office Building, Room 312
6 Bladen Street
Annapolis, MD 21401
P: (410) 841-3391
F: (410) 841-3157
E: adrienne.jones
@house.state.md.us

**Kaiser, Anne R. (D, 14)**
House Office Building, Room 350
6 Bladen Street
Annapolis, MD 21401
P: (410) 841-3036
F: (301) 858-3060
E: anne.kaiser
@house.state.md.us

**Kelly, Ariana B. (D, 16)**
House Office Building, Room 210
6 Bladen Street
Annapolis, MD 21401
P: (410) 841-3642
F: (301) 858-3026
E: ariana.kelly
@house.state.md.us

**Kipke, Nicholaus R. (R, 31B)**
House Office Building, Room 212
6 Bladen Street
Annapolis, MD 21401
P: (410) 841-3421
F: (410) 841-3553
E: nicholaus.kipke
@house.state.md.us

**Kittleman, Trent (R, 9A)**
House Office Building, Room 202
6 Bladen Street
Annapolis, MD 21401
P: (410) 841-3556
E: Trent.Kittleman
@house.state.md.us

**Knotts, Tony (D, 26)**
House Office Building, Room 204
6 Bladen Street
Annapolis, MD 21401
P: (410) 841-3212
E: Tony.Knotts
@house.state.md.us

**Korman, Marc (D, 16)**
House Office Building, Room 210
6 Bladen Street
Annapolis, MD 21401
P: (410) 841-3649
E: Marc.Korman
@house.state.md.us

**Kramer, Benjamin F. (D, 19)**
House Office Building, Room 226
6 Bladen Street
Annapolis, MD 21401
P: (410) 841-3485
F: (301) 858-3875
E: benjamin.kramer
@house.state.md.us

**Krebs, Susan W. (R, 5)**
House Office Building, Room 324
6 Bladen Street
Annapolis, MD 21401
P: (410) 841-3200
F: (410) 841-3200
E: susan.krebs
@house.state.md.us

**Krimm, Carol (D, 3A)**
House Office Building, Room 215
6 Bladen Street
Annapolis, MD 21401
P: (410) 841-3472
E: Carol.Krimm
@house.state.md.us

**Lafferty, Stephen W. (D, 42A)**
House Office Building, Room 305
6 Bladen Street
Annapolis, MD 21401
P: (410) 841-3487
F: (410) 841-3501
E: stephen.lafferty
@house.state.md.us

**Lam, Clarence (D, 12)**
House Office Building, Room 214
6 Bladen Street
Annapolis, MD 21401
P: (410) 841-3205
E: Clarence.Lam
@house.state.md.us

**Lewis, Robbyn (D, 46)***
House Office Building, Room 304
6 Bladen Street
Annapolis, MD 21401
P: (410) 841-3772
E: robbyn.lewis
@house.state.md.us

**Lierman, Brooke Elizabeth (D, 46)**
House Office Building, Room 311
6 Bladen Street
Annapolis, MD 21401
P: (410) 841-3319
E: Brooke.Lierman
@house.state.md.us

**Lisanti, Mary Ann (D, 34A)**
House Office Building, Room 217
6 Bladen Street
Annapolis, MD 21401
P: (410) 841-3331
E: MaryAnn.Lisanti
@house.state.md.us

**Long, Bob (R, 6)**
House Office Building, Room 325
6 Bladen Street
Annapolis, MD 21401
P: (410) 841-3458
E: Bob.Long
@house.state.md.us

**Luedtke, Eric G. (D, 14)**
House Office Building, Room 222
6 Bladen Street
Annapolis, MD 21401
P: (410) 841-3110
F: (301) 858-3053
E: eric.luedtke
@house.state.md.us

**Malone, Michael E. (R, 33)**
House Office Building, Room 154
6 Bladen Street
Annapolis, MD 21401
P: (410) 841-3510
E: Michael.Malone
@house.state.md.us

**Mautz, Johnny (R, 37B)**
House Office Building, Room 323
6 Bladen Street
Annapolis, MD 21401
P: (410) 841-3429
E: Johnny.Mautz
@house.state.md.us

**McComas, Susan K. (R, 34B)**
House Office Building, Room 319
6 Bladen Street
Annapolis, MD 21401
P: (410) 841-3272
F: (410) 841-3202
E: susan.mccomas
@house.state.md.us

**McConkey, Tony (R, 33)**
House Office Building, Room 163
6 Bladen Street
Annapolis, MD 21401
P: (410) 841-3406
F: (410) 841-3209
E: tony.mcconkey
@house.state.md.us

# Maryland

**McCray, Cory (D, 45)**
House Office Building, Room 315
6 Bladen Street
Annapolis, MD 21401
P: (410) 841-3486
E: Cory.McCray
@house.state.md.us

**McDonough, Patrick L. (R, 7)**
House Office Building, Room 310
6 Bladen Street
Annapolis, MD 21401
P: (410) 841-3334
F: (410) 841-3598
E: pat.mcdonough
@house.state.md.us

**McIntosh, Maggie (D, 43)**
House Office Building, Room 121
6 Bladen Street
Annapolis, MD 21401
P: (410) 841-3407
F: (410) 841-3509
E: maggie.mcintosh
@house.state.md.us

**McKay, Mike (R, 1C)**
House Office Building, Room 322
6 Bladen Street
Annapolis, MD 21401
P: (410) 841-3321
E: Mike.McKay
@house.state.md.us

**McMillan, Herbert H. (R, 30A)**
House Office Building, Room 164
6 Bladen Street
Annapolis, MD 21401
P: (410) 841-3211
F: (410) 841-3386
E: herb.mcmillan
@house.state.md.us

**Metzgar, Ric (R, 6)**
House Office Building, Room 307
6 Bladen Street
Annapolis, MD 21401
P: (410) 841-3332
E: Ric.Metzgar
@house.state.md.us

**Miele, Christian (R, 8)**
House Office Building, Room 316
6 Bladen Street
Annapolis, MD 21401
P: (410) 841-3365
E: Christian.Miele
@house.state.md.us

**Miller, Aruna (D, 15)**
House Office Building, Room 426
6 Bladen Street
Annapolis, MD 21401
P: (410) 841-3090
F: (401) 841-3120
E: aruna.miller
@house.state.md.us

**Miller, Warren E. (R, 9A)**
House Office Building, Room 403
6 Bladen Street
Annapolis, MD 21401
P: (410) 841-3582
F: (410) 841-3571
E: warren.miller
@house.state.md.us

**Moon, David (D, 20)**
House Office Building, Room 220
6 Bladen Street
Annapolis, MD 21401
P: (410) 841-3474
E: David.Moon
@house.state.md.us

**Morales, Maricé (D, 19)**
House Office Building, Room 225
6 Bladen Street
Annapolis, MD 21401
P: (410) 841-3528
E: Marice.Morales
@house.state.md.us

**Morgan, Matt (R, 29A)**
House Office Building, Room 317
6 Bladen Street
Annapolis, MD 21401
P: (410) 841-3170
E: Matt.Morgan
@house.state.md.us

**Morhaim, Dan K. (D, 11)**
House Office Building, Room 362
6 Bladen Street
Annapolis, MD 21401
P: (410) 841-3054
F: (410) 841-3385
E: dan.morhaim
@house.state.md.us

**Mosby, Nick (D, 40)\***
House Office Building, Room 217
6 Bladen Street
Annapolis, MD 21401
P: (410) 841-3520
F: (410) 841-3199
E: nick.mosby
@house.state.md.us

**Oaks, Nathaniel T. (D, 41)**
House Office Building, Room 411
6 Bladen Street
Annapolis, MD 21401
P: (410) 841-3283
F: (410) 841-3267
E: nathaniel.oaks
@house.state.md.us

**Otto, Charles J. (R, 38A)**
House Office Building, Room 321
6 Bladen Street
Annapolis, MD 21401
P: (410) 841-3433
F: (410) 841-3463
E: charles.otto
@house.state.md.us

**Parrott, Neil C. (R, 2A)**
House Office Building, Room 213
6 Bladen Street
Annapolis, MD 21401
P: (410) 841-3636
F: (301) 858-3308
E: neil.parrott
@house.state.md.us

**Patterson, Edith (D, 28)**
House Office Building, Room 221
6 Bladen Street
Annapolis, MD 21401
P: (410) 841-3247
E: Edith.Patterson
@house.state.md.us

**Pena-Melnyk, Joseline A. (D, 21)**
House Office Building, Room 425
6 Bladen Street
Annapolis, MD 21401
P: (410) 841-3502
F: (410) 841-3342
E: joseline.pena.melnyk
@house.state.md.us

**Pendergrass, Shane E. (D, 13)**
House Office Building, Room 241
6 Bladen Street
Annapolis, MD 21401
P: (410) 841-3139
F: (410) 841-3409
E: shane.pendergrass
@house.state.md.us

**Platt, Andrew (D, 17)**
House Office Building, Room 220
6 Bladen Street
Annapolis, MD 21401
P: (410) 841-3037
E: Andrew.Platt
@house.state.md.us

**Proctor, Elizabeth (D, 27A)**
House Office Building, Room 207
6 Bladen Street
Annapolis, MD 21401
P: (410) 841-3083
F: (410) 841-3459
E: elizabeth.proctor
@house.state.md.us

**Queen, Pam (D, 14)**
House Office Building, Room 224
6 Bladen Street
Annapolis, MD 21401
P: (410) 841-3380
E: pam.queen
@house.state.md.us

**Reilly, Teresa (R, 35B)**
House Office Building, Room 203
6 Bladen Street
Annapolis, MD 21401
P: (410) 841-3278
F: (410) 841-3190
E: Teresa.Reilly
@house.state.md.us

**Rey, Deb (R, 29B)**
House Office Building, Room 319
6 Bladen Street
Annapolis, MD 21401
P: (410) 841-3227
E: Deborah.Rey
@house.state.md.us

**Reznik, Kirill (D, 39)**
House Office Building, Room 225
6 Bladen Street
Annapolis, MD 21401
P: (410) 841-3039
F: (301) 858-3126
E: kirill.reznik
@house.state.md.us

**Robinson, A. Shane (D, 39)**
House Office Building, Room 223
6 Bladen Street
Annapolis, MD 21401
P: (410) 841-3021
F: (301) 858-3375
E: shane.robinson
@house.state.md.us

**Rose, April (R, 5)**
House Office Building, Room 320
6 Bladen Street
Annapolis, MD 21401
P: (410) 841-3070
E: April.Rose
@house.state.md.us

**Rosenberg, Samuel I. (D, 41)**
House Office Building, Room 365
6 Bladen Street
Annapolis, MD 21401
P: (410) 841-3297
F: (410) 841-3179
E: samuel.rosenberg
@house.state.md.us

**Saab, Sid (R, 33)**
House Office Building, Room 157
6 Bladen Street
Annapolis, MD 21401
P: (410) 841-3551
E: Sid.Saab
@house.state.md.us

**Sample-Hughes, Sheree (D, 37A)**
House Office Building, Room 221
6 Bladen Street
Annapolis, MD 21401
P: (410) 841-3427
E: Sheree.Sample.Hughes
@house.state.md.us

**Sanchez, Carlo (D, 47B)**
House Office Building, Room 206
6 Bladen Street
Annapolis, MD 21401
P: (410) 841-3340
F: (410) 841-3239
E: carlo.sanchez
@house.state.md.us

**Shoemaker, Haven (R, 5)**
House Office Building, Room 320
6 Bladen Street
Annapolis, MD 21401
P: (410) 841-3359
E: Haven.Shoemaker
@house.state.md.us

**Simonaire, Meagan (R, 31B)**
House Office Building, Room 156
6 Bladen Street
Annapolis, MD 21401
P: (410) 841-3206
E: Meagan.Simonaire
@house.state.md.us

**Sophocleus, Theodore J. (D, 32)**
House Office Building, Room 162
6 Bladen Street
Annapolis, MD 21401
P: (410) 841-3372
F: (410) 841-3437
E: ted.sophocleus
@house.state.md.us

**Stein, Dana M. (D, 11)**
House Office Building, Room 251
6 Bladen Street
Annapolis, MD 21401
P: (410) 841-3527
F: (410) 841-3373
E: dana.stein
@house.state.md.us

**Sydnor III, Charles (D, 44B)**
House Office Building, Room 306
6 Bladen Street
Annapolis, MD 21401
P: (410) 841-3802
E: Charles.Sydnor
@house.state.md.us

**Szeliga, Kathy (R, 7)**
House Office Building, Room 212
6 Bladen Street
Annapolis, MD 21401
P: (410) 841-3698
F: (410) 841-3023
E: kathy.szeliga
@house.state.md.us

**Tarlau, Jimmy (D, 47A)**
House Office Building, Room 209
6 Bladen Street
Annapolis, MD 21401
P: (410) 841-3326
E: Jimmy.Tarlau
@house.state.md.us

**Turner, Frank S. (D, 13)**
House Office Building, Room 131
6 Bladen Street
Annapolis, MD 21401
P: (410) 841-3246
F: (410) 841-3986
E: frank.turner
@house.state.md.us

**Valderrama, Kriselda (D, 26)**
House Office Building, Room 205
6 Bladen Street
Annapolis, MD 21401
P: (410) 841-3210
F: (301) 858-3525
E: kris.valderrama
@house.state.md.us

**Valentino-Smith, Geraldine (D, 23A)**
House Office Building, Room 427
6 Bladen Street
Annapolis, MD 21401
P: (410) 841-3101
F: (301) 858-3294
E: geraldine.
valentino.smith
@house.state.md.us

**Vallario Jr., Joseph F. (D, 23B)**
House Office Building, Room 101
6 Bladen Street
Annapolis, MD 21401
P: (410) 841-3488
F: (301) 858-3495
E: joseph.vallario
@house.state.md.us

**Vogt III, David E. (R, 4)**
House Office Building, Room 326
6 Bladen Street
Annapolis, MD 21401
P: (410) 841-3118
E: David.Vogt
@house.state.md.us

**Waldstreicher, Jeffrey D. (D, 18)**
House Office Building, Room 414
6 Bladen Street
Annapolis, MD 21401
P: (410) 841-3130
F: (301) 858-3233
E: jeff.waldstreicher
@house.state.md.us

**Walker, Jay (D, 26)**
House Office Building, Room 207
6 Bladen Street
Annapolis, MD 21401
P: (301) 858-3581
F: (301) 858-3078
E: jay.walker
@house.state.md.us

**Washington, Alonzo T. (D, 22)**
House Office Building, Room 205
6 Bladen Street
Annapolis, MD 21401
P: (410) 841-3652
F: (301) 858-3699
E: alonzo.washington
@house.state.md.us

**Washington, Mary L. (D, 43)**
House Office Building, Room 429
6 Bladen Street
Annapolis, MD 21401
P: (410) 841-3476
F: (410) 841-3295
E: mary.washington
@house.state.md.us

**West, Chris (R, 42B)**
House Office Building, Room 303
6 Bladen Street
Annapolis, MD 21401
P: (410) 841-3793
E: Chris.West
@house.state.md.us

**Wilkins, Jheanelle K. (D, 20)\***
House Office Building, Room 224
6 Bladen Street
Annapolis, MD 21401
P: (410) 841-3493
E: jheanelle.wilkins
@house.state.md.us

**Wilson, Brett (R, 2B)**
House Office Building, Room 213
6 Bladen Street
Annapolis, MD 21401
P: (410) 841-3125
E: brett.wilson
@house.state.md.us

**Wilson, C. T. (D, 28)**
House Office Building, Room 422
6 Bladen Street
Annapolis, MD 21401
P: (410) 841-3325
F: (410) 841-3367
E: ct.wilson
@house.state.md.us

**Wivell, William J. (R, 2A)**
House Office Building, Room 322
6 Bladen Street
Annapolis, MD 21401
P: (410) 841-3447
E: william.wivell
@house.state.md.us

# Maryland

**Young, Karen Lewis (D, 3A)**
House Office Building, Room
217
6 Bladen Street
Annapolis, MD 21401
P: (410) 841-3436
E: Karen.Young
   @house.state.md.us

**Young, Pat (D, 44B)**
House Office Building, Room
306
6 Bladen Street
Annapolis, MD 21401
P: (410) 841-3544
E: pat.young
   @house.state.md.us

# Massachusetts

## Executive

### Governor
The Honorable Charles Baker (R)
Governor
Room 360
Boston, MA 02133
P: (617) 725-4005
F: (617) 727-9725

### Lieutenant Governor
The Honorable Karyn E. Polito (R)
Lieutenant Governor
State House, Suite 109B
24 Beacon Street
Boston, MA 02133
P: (617) 727-7030
F: (617) 742-4528

### Attorney General
The Honorable Maura Healey (D)
Attorney General
1 Ashburton Place
Boston, MA 02108
P: (617) 727-2200

### Auditor
The Honorable Suzanne M. Bump (D)
Auditor of the Commonwealth
State House, Room 230
Boston, MA 02133
P: (617) 727-2075
F: (617) 727-2383
E: suzanne.bump
@sao.state.ma.us

### Secretary of the Commonwealth
The Honorable William F. Galvin (D)
Secretary of the Commonwealth
State House, Room 337
24 Beacon Street
Boston, MA 02133
P: (617) 727-9180
F: (617) 742-4722
E: cis@sec.state.ma.us

### Treasurer
The Honorable Deb Goldberg (D)
State Treasurer
State House, Room 227
Boston, MA 02133
P: (617) 367-3900
F: (617) 248-0372

## Judiciary

### Supreme Judicial Court (MC)
Mr. Francis V. Kenneally
Clerk
John Adams Courthouse, Suite 1-400
One Pemberton Square
Boston, MA 02108
P: (617) 557-1020
F: (617) 557-1145
E: SJCCommClerk
@sjc.state.ma.us

The Honorable Ralph D. Gants
Chief Justice
The Honorable Margot Botsford
The Honorable Kimberly S. Budd
The Honorable Frank M. Gaziano
The Honorable Geraldine S. Hines
The Honorable Barbara A. Lenk
The Honorable David A. Lowy

## Legislative

## Senate

### Senate President
Senator Stanley C. Rosenberg (D)
Senate President
Room 332, State House
Boston, MA 02133
P: (617) 722-1500
F: (617) 722-1072
E: Stan.Rosenberg
@masenate.gov

### President Pro Tempore of the Senate
Senator Marc R. Pacheco (D)
Senate President Pro Tempore
Room 312B, State House
Boston, MA 02133
P: (617) 722-1551
F: (617) 722-1074
E: Marc.Pacheco
@masenate.gov

### Senate Majority Leader
Senator Harriette L. Chandler (D)
Senate Majority Leader
Room 333, State House
Boston, MA 02133
P: (617) 722-1544
F: (617) 722-1357
E: Harriette.Chandler
@masenate.gov

### Senate Minority Leader
Senator Bruce E. Tarr (R)
Senate Minority Leader
Room 308, State House
Boston, MA 02133
P: (617) 722-1600
F: (617) 722-1310
E: Bruce.Tarr@masenate.gov

### Secretary of the Senate
Mr. William F. Welch
Clerk of the Senate
Room 335, State House
24 Beacon Street
Boston, MA 02133
P: (617) 722-1276
E: william.welch
@state.ma.us

## Members of the Senate
Barrett, Michael (D, SP62)
Room 416, State House
Boston, MA 02133
P: (617) 722-1572
F: (617) 626-0898
E: Mike.Barrett
@masenate.gov

Boncore, Joseph (D, SP185)
Room 109D, State House
Boston, MA 02133
P: (617) 722-1634
E: Joseph.Boncore
@masenate.gov

Brady, Michael D. (D, SP183)
Room 109E, State House
Boston, MA 02133
P: (617) 722-1200
E: Michael.Brady
@masenate.gov

Brownsberger, William (D, SP186)
Room 504, State House
Boston, MA 02133
P: (617) 722-1280
F: (617) 722-2339
E: William.Brownsberger
@masenate.gov

Chandler, Harriette L. (D, SP143)
Room 333, State House
Boston, MA 02133
P: (617) 722-1544
F: (617) 722-1357
E: Harriette.Chandler
@masenate.gov

Chang-Diaz, Sonia Rosa (D, SP125)
Room 111, State House
Boston, MA 02133
P: (617) 722-1673
F: (617) 722-1079
E: Sonia.Chang-Diaz
@masenate.gov

Creem, Cynthia Stone (D, SP174)
Room 312A, State House
Boston, MA 02133
P: (617) 722-1639
F: (617) 722-1266
E: Cynthia.Creem
@masenate.gov

Cyr, Julian Andre (D, SP165)*
Room 405, State House
Boston, MA 02133
P: (617) 722-1570
E: Julian.Cyr@masenate.gov

DeMacedo, Viriato Manuel (R, SP181)
Room 313A, State House
Boston, MA 02133
P: (617) 722-1330
F: (617) 722-2390
E: Vinny.deMacedo
@mahouse.gov

DiDomenico, Sal N. (D, SP176)
Room 208, State House
Boston, MA 02133
P: (617) 722-1650
F: (617) 722-1323
E: Sal.DiDomenico
@masenate.gov

Donnelly, Kenneth J. (D, SP63)
Room 413D, State House
Boston, MA 02133
P: (617) 722-1432
F: (617) 722-1004
E: Kenneth.Donnelly
@masenate.gov

# Massachusetts

**Donoghue, Eileen M.
(D, SP60)**
Room 112, State House
Boston, MA 02133
P: (617) 722-1630
F: (617) 722-1001
E: Eileen.Donoghue
@masenate.gov

**Eldridge, James B.
(D, SP177)**
Room 218, State House
Boston, MA 02133
P: (617) 722-1120
F: (617) 722-1089
E: James.Eldridge
@masenate.gov

**Fattman, Ryan C. (R, SP190)**
Room 520, State House
Boston, MA 02133
P: (617) 722-1420
F: (617) 722-1944
E: Ryan.Fattman@mahouse.gov

**Flanagan, Jennifer L.
(D, SP189)**
Room 312D, State House
Boston, MA 02133
P: (617) 722-1230
F: (617) 722-1130
E: Jennifer.Flanagan
@masenate.gov

**Forry, Linda Dorcena
(D, SP124)**
Room 410, State House
Boston, MA 02133
P: (617) 722-1150
E: Linda.DorcenaForry
@mahouse.gov

**Gobi, Anne M. (D, SP188)**
Room 513, State House
Boston, MA 02133
P: (617) 722-1540
F: (617) 722-1078
E: Anne.Gobi@mahouse.gov

**Hinds, Adam G. (D, SP161)***
Room 413-F, State House
Boston, MA 02133
P: (617) 722-1625
E: Adam.Hinds@masenate.gov

**Humason Jr., Donald F.
(R, SP171)**
Room 213A, State House
Boston, MA 02133
P: (617) 722-1415
F: 617-722-1506
E: Donald.Humason
@masenate.gov

**Jehlen, Patricia D.
(D, SP61)**
Room 424, State House
Boston, MA 02133
P: (617) 722-1578
F: (617) 722-1117
E: Patricia.Jehlen
@masenate.gov

**Keenan, John F. (D, SP180)**
Room 413B, State House
Boston, MA 02133
P: (617) 722-1494
F: (617) 722-1055
E: John.Keenan@masenate.gov

**Lesser, Eric Philip
(D, SP170)**
Room 519, State House
Boston, MA 02133
P: (617) 722-1291
F: (617) 722-1014
E: eric.lesser@masenate.gov

**Lewis, Jason M. (D, SP64)**
Room 511B, State House
Boston, MA 02133
P: (617) 722-1206
E: Jason.Lewis@masenate.gov

**L'Italien, Barbara A.
(D, SP167)**
State House Rm 413-C
Boston, MA 02133
P: (617) 722-1612
F: (617) 722-1058
E: Barbara.L'Italien
@mahouse.gov

**Lovely, Joan (D, SP26)**
Room 413A, State House
Boston, MA 02133
P: (617) 722-1410
F: (617) 722-1347
E: Joan.Lovely@masenate.gov

**McGee, Thomas M. (D, SP27)**
Room 109C, State House
Boston, MA 02133
P: (617) 722-1350
E: Thomas.McGee
@masenate.gov

**Montigny, Mark C.
(D, SP164)**
Room 312C, State House
Boston, MA 02133
P: (617) 722-1440
F: (617) 722-1068
E: Mark.Montigny
@masenate.gov

**Moore, Michael O.
(D, SP144)**
Room 109-B, State House
Boston, MA 02133
P: (617) 722-1485
F: (617) 722-1066
E: Michael.Moore
@masenate.gov

**O'Connor, Patrick
(R, SP184)**
Room 520, State House
Boston, MA 02133
P: (617) 722-1646
E: Patrick.OConnor
@masenate.gov

**O'Connor Ives, Kathleen
(D, SP25)**
Room 215, State House
Boston, MA 02133
P: (617) 722-1604
F: (617) 722-1999
E: Kathleen.OConnorIves
@masenate.gov

**Pacheco, Marc R. (D, SP182)**
Room 312B, State House
Boston, MA 02133
P: (617) 722-1551
F: (617) 722-1074
E: Marc.Pacheco
@masenate.gov

**Rodrigues, Michael J.
(D, SP163)**
Room 213B, State House
Boston, MA 02133
P: (617) 722-1114
F: (617) 722-1498
E: Michael.Rodrigues
@masenate.gov

**Rosenberg, Stanley C.
(D, SP172)**
Room 332, State House
Boston, MA 02133
P: (617) 722-1500
F: (617) 722-1072
E: Stan.Rosenberg
@masenate.gov

**Ross, Richard J. (R, SP179)**
Room 419, State House
Boston, MA 02133
P: (617) 722-1555
F: (617) 722-1054
E: Richard.Ross
@masenate.gov

**Rush, Michael F. (D, SP187)**
Room 511C, State House
Boston, MA 02133
P: (617) 722-1348
F: (617) 722-1071
E: Mike.Rush@masenate.gov

**Spilka, Karen E. (D, SP175)**
Room 212, State House
Boston, MA 02133
P: (617) 722-1640
F: (617) 722-1077
E: Karen.Spilka
@masenate.gov

**Tarr, Bruce E. (R, SP166)**
Room 308, State House
Boston, MA 02133
P: (617) 722-1600
F: (617) 722-1310
E: Bruce.Tarr@masenate.gov

**Timilty, James E.
(D, SP162)**
Room 507, State House
Boston, MA 02133
P: (617) 722-1222
F: (617) 722-1056
E: James.Timilty
@masenate.gov

**Timilty, Walter F.
(D, SP178)**
Room 320, State House
Boston, MA 02133
P: (617) 722-1643
E: Walter.Timilty
@masenate.gov

**Welch, James T. (D, SP169)**
Room 309, State House
Boston, MA 02133
P: (617) 722-1660
F: (413) 737-7747
E: James.Welch@masenate.gov

# House

## Speaker of the House
**Representative Robert A.
DeLeo (D)**
House Speaker
Room 356, State House
Boston, MA 02133
P: (617) 722-2500
F: (617) 722-2008
E: Robert.DeLeo@mahouse.gov

## Speaker Pro Tempore of the House
**Representative Patricia A.
Haddad (D)**
House Speaker Pro Tempore
Room 370, State House
Boston, MA 02133
P: (617) 722-2600
F: (617) 722-2313
E: Patricia.Haddad
@mahouse.gov

## House Majority Leader

**Representative Ronald Mariano (D)**
House Majority Leader
Room 343, State House
Boston, MA 02133
P: (617) 722-2300
F: (617) 722-2750
E: Ronald.Mariano
@mahouse.gov

## House Minority Leader

**Representative Bradley H. Jones Jr. (R)**
House Minority Leader
Room 124, State House
Boston, MA 02133
P: (617) 722-2100
F: (617) 722-2390
E: Bradley.Jones
@mahouse.gov

## Clerk of the House

**Mr. Steven T. James**
Clerk of the House
Room 145, State House
24 Beacon Street
Boston, MA 02133
P: (617) 722-2356
F: (617) 722-2798
E: steven.james
@hou.state.ma.us

## Members of the House

**Arciero, James (D, SP61)**
Room 172, State House
Boston, MA 02133
P: (617) 722-2019
F: (617) 722-2798
E: James.Arciero
@mahouse.gov

**Ashe, Brian Michael (D, SP46)**
Room 466, State House
Boston, MA 02133
P: (617) 722-2017
F: (617) 722-2813
E: Brian.Ashe@mahouse.gov

**Atkins, Cory (D, SP73)**
Room 195, State House
Boston, MA 02133
P: (617) 722-2015
F: (617) 722-2822
E: Cory.Atkins@mahouse.gov

**Ayers, Bruce J. (D, SP97)**
Room 167, State House
Boston, MA 02133
P: (617) 722-2230
E: Bruce.Ayers@mahouse.gov

**Balser, Ruth B. (D, SP71)**
Room 136, State House
Boston, MA 02133
P: (617) 722-2396
F: (617) 626-0119
E: Ruth.Balser@mahouse.gov

**Barber, Christine P. (D, SP93)**
Room 236, State House
Boston, MA 02133
P: (617) 722-2430
E: Christine.Barber
@mahouse.gov

**Barrows, F. Jay (R, SP11)**
Room 542, State House
Boston, MA 02133
P: (617) 722-2488
F: (617) 722-2390
E: F.JayBarrows@mahouse.gov

**Benson, Jennifer (D, SP96)**
Room 42, State House
Boston, MA 02133
P: (617) 722-2014
F: (617) 722-2813
E: Jennifer.Benson
@mahouse.gov

**Berthiaume Jr., Donald R. (R, SP147)**
Room 540, State House
Boston, MA 02133
P: (617) 722-2090
E: Donald.Berthiaume
@mahouse.gov

**Boldyga, Nicholas (R, SP47)**
Room 167, State House
Boston, MA 02133
P: (617) 722-2810
F: (617) 626-0137
E: Nicholas.Boldyga
@mahouse.gov

**Brodeur, Paul A. (D, SP91)**
Room 160, State House
Boston, MA 02133
P: (617) 722-2304
F: (617) 626-2215
E: Paul.Brodeur@mahouse.gov

**Cabral, Antonio F.D. (D, SP23)**
Room 466, State House
Boston, MA 02133
P: (617) 722-2017
F: (617) 722-2813
E: Antonio.Cabral
@mahouse.gov

**Cahill, Daniel (D, SP34)**
Room 527A, State House
Boston, MA 02133
P: (617) 722-2020
E: David.Cahill@mahouse.gov

**Calter III, Thomas J. (D, SP123)**
Room 446, State House
Boston, MA 02133
P: (617) 722-2460
F: (617) 722-2598
E: Thomas.Calter
@mahouse.gov

**Campanale, Kate D. (R, SP159)**
Room 542, State House
Boston, MA 02133
P: (617) 722-2488
E: Kate.Campanale
@mahouse.gov

**Campbell, Linda Dean (D, SP39)**
Room 236, State House
Boston, MA 02133
P: (617) 722-2430
F: (617) 722-9278
E: Linda.Campbell
@mahouse.gov

**Cantwell, James M. (D, SP115)**
Room 22, State House
Boston, MA 02133
P: (617) 722-2140
F: (617) 626-0835
E: James.Cantwell
@mahouse.gov

**Cariddi, Gailanne M. (D, SP7)**
Room 36, State House
Boston, MA 02133
P: (617) 722-2370
F: (617) 626-0143
E: Gailanne.Cariddi
@mahouse.gov

**Carvalho, Evandro (D, SP128)**
Room 446, State House
Boston, MA 02133
P: (617) 722-2460
F: (617) 626-0802
E: Evandro.Carvalho
@mahouse.gov

**Cassidy, Gerard (D, SP120)**
Room 134, State House
Boston, MA 02133
P: (617) 722-2400
E: Gerard.Cassidy
@mahouse.gov

**Chan, Tackey (D, SP98)**
Room 26, State House
Boston, MA 02133
P: (617) 722-2080
F: (617) 626-0146
E: Tackey.Chan@mahouse.gov

**Collins, Nick (D, SP127)**
Room 39, State House
Boston, MA 01233
P: (617) 722-2014
F: (617) 626-0154
E: Nick.Collins@mahouse.gov

**Connolly, Mike (D, SP85)***
Room 437, State House
Boston, MA 02133
P: 617-722-2425
E: Mike.Connolly
@mahouse.gov

**Coppinger, Edward F. (D, SP133)**
Room 160, State House
Boston, MA 02133
P: (617) 722-2304
F: (617) 626-0158
E: Edward.Coppinger
@mahouse.gov

**Crighton, Brendan P. (D, SP35)**
Room 130, State House
Boston, MA 02133
P: (617) 722-2130
E: brendan.crighton
@mahouse.gov

**Crocker, William L. (R, SP2)***
Room 437, State House
Boston, MA 02133
P: (617) 722-2425
E: William.Crocker
@mahouse.gov

**Cronin, Claire (D, SP122)**
Room 136, State House
Boston, MA 02133
P: (617) 722-2396
F: (617) 626-0285
E: Claire.Cronin
@mahouse.gov

**Cullinane, Daniel R. (D, SP135)**
Room 121, State House
Boston, MA 02133
P: (617) 722-2006
F: (617) 626-0456
E: Daniel.Cullinane
@mahouse.gov

# Massachusetts

**Cusack, Mark J. (D, SP101)**
Room 544, State House
Boston, MA 02133
P: (617) 722-2637
F: (617) 626-0159
E: Mark.Cusack@mahouse.gov

**Cutler, Josh (D, SP117)**
Room 473F, State House
Boston, MA 02133
P: (617) 722-2010
F: (617) 626-0325
E: Josh.Cutler@mahouse.gov

**Day, Michael Seamus
(D, SP90)**
Room 448, State House
Boston, MA 02133
P: (617) 722-2582
E: Michael.Day@mahouse.gov

**Decker, Marjorie (D, SP84)**
Room 155, State House
Boston, MA 02133
P: (617) 722-2450
F: (617) 626-0337
E: Marjorie.Decker
@mahouse.gov

**Decoste, David F.
(R, SP116)**
Room 236, State House
Boston, MA 02133
P: (617) 722-2430
E: David.DeCoste
@mahouse.gov

**DeLeo, Robert A. (D, SP142)**
Room 356, State House
Boston, MA 02133
P: (617) 722-2500
F: (617) 722-2008
E: Robert.DeLeo@mahouse.gov

**D'Emilia, Angelo L.
(R, SP119)**
Room 548, State House
Boston, MA 02133
P: (617) 722-2488
F: (617) 626-0170
E: Angelo.D'Emilia
@mahouse.gov

**Dempsey, Brian S. (D, SP27)**
Room 243, State House
Boston, MA 02133
P: (617) 722-2990
F: (617) 722-2215
E: Brian.Dempsey
@mahouse.gov

**Diehl, Geoffrey G.
(R, SP118)**
Room 167, State House
Boston, MA 02133
P: (617) 722-2810
E: Geoff.Diehl@mahouse.gov

**DiZoglio, Diana (D, SP38)**
Room 33, State House
Boston, MA 02133
P: (617) 722-2060
F: (617) 626-0191
E: Diana.DiZoglio
@mahouse.gov

**Donahue, Daniel M.
(D, SP158)**
Room 122, State House
Boston, MA 02133
P: (617) 722-2006
F: (617) 626-0457
E: Daniel.Donahue
@mahouse.gov

**Donato, Paul J. (D, SP94)**
Room 481, State House
Boston, MA 02133
P: (617) 722-2180
F: (617) 722-2347
E: Paul.Donato@mahouse.gov

**Dooley, Shawn (R, SP105)**
Room 167, State House
Boston, MA 02133
P: (617) 722-2810
E: Shawn.Dooley@mahouse.gov

**Driscoll Jr., William J.
(D, SP103)\***
Room 437, State House
Boston, MA 02133
P: (617) 722-2425
E: William.Driscoll
@mahouse.gov

**Dubois, Michelle M.
(D, SP121)**
Room 146, State House
Boston, MA 02133
P: (617) 722-2011
E: michelle.dubois
@mahouse.gov

**Durant, Peter (R, SP148)**
Room 33, State House
Boston, MA 02133
P: (617) 722-2060
E: Peter.Durant@mahouse.gov

**Dwyer, James J. (D, SP89)**
Room 254, State House
Boston, MA 02133
P: (617) 722-2220
F: (617) 626-0831
E: James.Dwyer@mahouse.gov

**Dykema, Carolyn C.
(D, SP67)**
Room 127, State House
Boston, MA 02133
P: (617) 722-2680
F: (617) 722-2239
E: Carolyn.Dykema
@mahouse.gov

**Ehrlich, Lori A. (D, SP32)**
Room 236, State House
Boston, MA 02133
P: (617) 722-2430
E: Lori.Ehrlich@mahouse.gov

**Farley-Bouvier, Tricia
(D, SP9)**
Room 156, State House
Boston, MA 02133
P: (617) 722-2240
E: Tricia.Farley-Bouvier
@mahouse.gov

**Ferguson, Kimberly N.
(R, SP143)**
Room 473B, State House
Boston, MA 02133
P: (617) 722-2263
F: (617) 626-0182
E: Kimberly.Ferguson
@mahouse.gov

**Fernandes, Dyan A.
(D, SP6)\***
Room 437, State House
Boston, MA 02133
P: (617) 722-2425
E: Dyan.Fernandes
@mahouse.gov

**Ferrante, Ann-Margaret
(D, SP29)**
Room 26, State House
Boston, MA 02133
P: (617) 722-2080
F: (617) 722-2339
E: Ann-Margaret.Ferrante
@mahouse.gov

**Finn, Michael J. (D, SP50)**
Room 134, State House
Boston, MA 02133
P: (617) 722-2400
F: (617) 626-0189
E: Michael.Finn@mahouse.gov

**Fiola, Carole (D, SP16)**
Room 443, State House
Boston, MA 02133
P: (617) 722-2460
F: (617) 626-0460
E: Carole.Fiola@mahouse.gov

**Frost, Paul K. (R, SP149)**
Room 542, State House
Boston, MA 02133
P: (617) 722-2489
E: Paul.Frost@mahouse.gov

**Galvin, William C.
(D, SP102)**
Room 166, State House
Boston, MA 02133
P: (617) 722-2692
E: William.Galvin
@mahouse.gov

**Garballey, Sean (D, SP82)**
Room 540, State House
Boston, MA 02133
P: (617) 722-2090
F: (617) 722-2848
E: Sean.Garballey
@mahouse.gov

**Garlick, Denise C.
(D, SP109)**
Room 167, State House
Boston, MA 02133
P: (617) 722-2810
F: (617) 626-0197
E: Denise.Garlick
@mahouse.gov

**Garry, Colleen M. (D, SP95)**
Room 238, State House
Boston, MA 02133
P: (617) 722-2380
F: (617) 722-2847
E: Colleen.Garry
@mahouse.gov

**Gentile, Carmine Lawrence
(D, SP72)**
Room 39, State House
Boston, MA 02133
P: (617) 722-2014
E: carmine.gentile
@mahouse.gov

**Gifford, Susan Williams
(R, SP113)**
Room 124, State House
Boston, MA 02133
P: (617) 722-2100
F: (617) 722-2848
E: Susan.Gifford
@mahouse.gov

**Golden Jr., Thomas A.
(D, SP75)**
Room 473B, State House
Boston, MA 02133
P: (617) 722-2263
F: (617) 570-6578
E: Thomas.Golden
@mahouse.gov

**Goldstein-Rose,
Solomon Israel (D, SP59)\***
Room 437, State House
Boston, MA 02133
P: (617) 722-2425
E: Solomon.Goldstein-Rose
@mahouse.gov

**Gonzalez, Carlos (D, SP54)**
Room 26, State House
Boston, MA 02133
P: (617) 722-2080
E: Carlos.Gonzalez
@mahouse.gov

**Gordon, Kenneth (D, SP80)**
Room 472, State House
Boston, MA 02133
P: (617) 722-2013
F: (617) 626-0320
E: Ken.Gordon@mahouse.gov

**Gregoire, Danielle W.**
**(D, SP63)**
Room 473G, State House
Boston, MA 02133
P: (617) 722-2070
F: (617) 626-0323
E: Danielle.Gregoire
@mahouse.gov

**Haddad, Patricia A.**
**(D, SP15)**
Room 370, State House
Boston, MA 02133
P: (617) 722-2600
F: (617) 722-2313
E: Patricia.Haddad
@mahouse.gov

**Harrington, Sheila C.**
**(R, SP60)**
Room 237, State House
Boston, MA 02133
P: (617) 722-2305
F: (617) 626-0199
E: Sheila.Harrington
@mahouse.gov

**Hay, Stephan (D, SP145)**
Room 33, State House
Boston, MA 02133
P: (617) 722-2060
E: Stephan.Hay@mahouse.gov

**Hecht, Jonathan (D, SP88)**
Room 22, State House
Boston, MA 02133
P: (617) 722-2140
F: (617) 626-0199
E: Jonathan.Hecht
@mahouse.gov

**Heroux, Paul (D, SP12)**
Room 540, State House
Boston, MA 02133
P: (617) 722-2090
F: (617) 626-0335
E: Paul.Heroux@mahouse.gov

**Higgins, Natalie**
**(D, SP146)\***
Room 437, State House
Boston, MA 02133
P: (617) 722-2425
E: Natalie.Higgins
@mahouse.gov

**Hill, Bradford (R, SP28)**
Room 128, State House
Boston, MA 02133
P: (617) 722-2100
E: Brad.Hill@mahouse.gov

**Hogan, Kate (D, SP62)**
Room 130, State House
Boston, MA 02133
P: (617) 722-2130
E: Kate.Hogan@mahouse.gov

**Holmes, Russell (D, SP129)**
Room 254, State House
Boston, MA 02133
P: (617) 722-2220
F: (617) 626-0205
E: Russell.Holmes
@mahouse.gov

**Honan, Kevin G. (D, SP140)**
Room 38, State House
Boston, MA 02133
P: (617) 722-2470
F: (617) 722-2162
E: Kevin.Honan@mahouse.gov

**Howitt, Steven S. (R, SP14)**
Room 237, State House
Boston, MA 02133
P: (617) 722-2305
F: (617) 626-0211
E: Steven.Howitt
@mahouse.gov

**Hunt, Daniel (D, SP136)**
Room 473B, State House
Boston, MA 02133
P: (617) 722-2263
E: Daniel.Hunt@mahouse.gov

**Hunt, Randy (R, SP5)**
Room 136, State House
Boston, MA 02133
P: (617) 722-2396
F: (617) 626-0218
E: Randy.Hunt@mahouse.gov

**Jones Jr., Bradley H.**
**(R, SP79)**
Room 124, State House
Boston, MA 02133
P: (617) 722-2100
F: (617) 722-2390
E: Bradley.Jones
@mahouse.gov

**Kafka, Louis L. (D, SP104)**
Room 185, State House
Boston, MA 02133
P: (617) 722-2960
F: (617) 722-2713
E: Louis.Kafka@mahouse.gov

**Kane, Hannah (R, SP153)**
Room 236, State House
Boston, MA 02133
P: (617) 722-2430
E: Hannah.Kane@mahouse.gov

**Kaufman, Jay R. (D, SP74)**
Room 34, State House
Boston, MA 02133
P: (617) 722-2320
F: (617) 722-2415
E: Jay.Kaufman@mahouse.gov

**Keefe, Mary (D, SP157)**
Room 473F, State House
Boston, MA 02133
P: (617) 722-2210
F: (617) 626-0286
E: Mary.Keefe@mahouse.gov

**Kelcourse, James M.**
**(R, SP25)**
Room 130, State House
Boston, MA 02133
P: (617) 722-2130
E: james.kelcourse
@mahouse.gov

**Khan, Kay (D, SP70)**
Room 146, State House
Boston, MA 02133
P: (617) 722-2011
F: (617) 722-2238
E: Kay.Khan@mahouse.gov

**Kocot, Peter V. (D, SP57)**
Room 22, State House
Boston, MA 02133
P: (617) 722-2140
F: (617) 722-2347
E: Peter.Kocot@mahouse.gov

**Koczera, Robert M.**
**(D, SP21)**
Room 448, State House
Boston, MA 02133
P: (617) 722-2582
E: Robert.Koczera
@mahouse.gov

**Kulik, Stephen (D, SP43)**
Room 238, State House
Boston, MA 02133
P: (617) 722-2380
F: (617) 722-2847
E: Stephen.Kulik
@mahouse.gov

**Kuros, Kevin J. (R, SP150)**
Room 443, State House
Boston, MA 02133
P: (617) 722-2460
F: (617) 722-2353
E: Kevin.Kuros@mahouse.gov

**Lawn, John J. (D, SP69)**
Room 254, State House
Boston, MA 02133
P: (617) 722-2220
F: (617) 626-0150
E: John.Lawn@mahouse.gov

**Lewis, Jack Patrick**
**(D, SP66)\***
Room 437, State House
Boston, MA 02133
P: (617) 722-2425
E: Jack.Lewis@mahouse.gov

**Linsky, David P. (D, SP64)**
Room 146, State House
Boston, MA 02133
P: (617) 722-2575
F: (617) 722-2238
E: David.Linsky@mahouse.gov

**Livingstone, Jay (D, SP131)**
Room 136, State House
Boston, MA 02133
P: (617) 722-2396
E: Jay.Livingstone
@mahouse.gov

**Lombardo, Marc T. (R, SP81)**
Room 443, State House
Boston, MA 02133
P: (617) 722-2460
F: (617) 626-0240
E: Marc.Lombardo
@mahouse.gov

**Lyons Jr., James J.**
**(R, SP42)**
Room 443, State House
Boston, MA 02133
P: (617) 722-2460
F: (617) 626-0246
E: James.Lyons@mahouse.gov

**Madaro, Adrian (D, SP124)**
Room 544, State House
Boston, MA 02133
P: (617) 722-2637
E: Adrian.Madaro
@mahouse.gov

**Mahoney, John J. (D, SP155)**
Room 443, State House
Boston, MA 02133
P: (617) 722-2460
F: (617) 626-0247
E: John.Mahoney@mahouse.gov

**Malia, Elizabeth A.**
**(D, SP134)**
Room 33, State House
Boston, MA 02133
P: (617) 722-2060
E: Liz.Malia@mahouse.gov

**Mariano, Ronald (D, SP99)**
Room 343, State House
Boston, MA 02133
P: (617) 722-2300
F: (617) 722-2750
E: Ronald.Mariano
@mahouse.gov

# Massachusetts

**Mark, Paul W. (D, SP8)**
Room 166, State House
Boston, MA 02133
P: (617) 722-2692
F: (617) 626-0249
E: Paul.Mark@mahouse.gov

**Markey, Christopher (D, SP19)**
Room 527A, State House
Boston, MA 02133
P: (617) 722-2020
F: (617) 626-0250
E: Christopher.Markey
@mahouse.gov

**Matias, Juana B. (D, SP40)***
Room 437, State House
Boston, MA 02133
P: (617) 722-2425
E: Juana.Matais@mahouse.gov

**McGonagle, Joseph W. (D, SP87)**
Room 134, State House
Boston, MA 02133
P: (617) 722-2400
E: Joseph.McGonagle
@mahouse.gov

**McKenna, Joseph D. (R, SP160)**
Room 33, State House
Boston, MA 02133
P: (617) 722-2060
E: joseph.mckenna
@mahouse.gov

**McMurtry, Paul (D, SP107)**
Room 448, State House
Boston, MA 02133
P: (617) 722-2582
F: (617) 626-0413
E: Paul.McMurtry
@mahouse.gov

**Meschino, Joan (D, SP114)***
Room 437, State House
Boston, MA 02133
P: (617) 722-2425
E: Joan.Meschino
@mahouse.gov

**Miceli, James R. (D, SP78)**
Room 237, State House
Boston, MA 02133
P: (617) 722-2305
E: James.Miceli@mahouse.gov

**Michlewitz, Aaron M. (D, SP126)**
Room 254, State House
Boston, MA 02133
P: (617) 722-2220
F: (617) 570-6575
E: Aaron.M.Michlewitz
@mahouse.gov

**Mirra, Leonard (R, SP26)**
Room 548, State House
Boston, MA 02133
P: (617) 722-2488
F: (617) 626-0339
E: Lenny.Mirra@mahouse.gov

**Mom, Rady (D, SP77)**
Room 443, State House
Boston, MA 02133
P: (617) 722-2460
E: Rady.Mom@mahouse.gov

**Moran, Frank (D, SP41)**
Room 279, State House
Boston, MA 02133
P: (617) 722-2017
F: (617) 626-0288
E: Frank.Moran@mahouse.gov

**Moran, Michael (D, SP141)**
Room 42, State House
Boston, MA 02133
P: (617) 722-2014
E: Michael.Moran
@mahouse.gov

**Muradian Jr., David K. (R, SP151)**
Room 156, State House
Boston, MA 02133
P: (617) 722-2240
E: David.Muradian
@mahouse.gov

**Muratore, Mathew J. (R, SP112)**
Room 39, State House
Boston, MA 02133
P: (617) 722-2014
E: Mathew.Muratore
@mahouse.gov

**Murphy, James M. (D, SP100)**
Room 156, State House
Boston, MA 02133
P: (617) 722-2240
E: James.Murphy@mahouse.gov

**Murray, Brian W. (D, SP152)***
Room 437, State House
Boston, MA 02133
P: (617) 722-2425
E: Brian.Murray@mahouse.gov

**Nangle, David M. (D, SP76)**
Room 146, State House
Boston, MA 02133
P: (617) 722-2575
F: (617) 722-2215
E: David.Nangle@mahouse.gov

**Naughton Jr., Harold P. (D, SP154)**
Room 167, State House
Boston, MA 02133
P: (617) 722-2230
F: (617) 722-9278
E: Harold.Naughton
@mahouse.gov

**O'Connell, Shaunna (R, SP13)**
Room 237, State House
Boston, MA 02133
P: (617) 722-2305
E: Shaunna.O'Connell
@mahouse.gov

**O'Day, James J. (D, SP156)**
Room 540, State House
Boston, MA 02133
P: (617) 722-2090
F: (617) 626-0884
E: James.O'Day@mahouse.gov

**Orrall, Keiko M. (R, SP22)**
Room 540, State House
Boston, MA 02133
P: (617) 722-2090
F: (617) 626-0477
E: Keiko.Orrall@mahouse.gov

**Parisella, Jerald A. (D, SP30)**
Room 174, State House
Boston, MA 02133
P: (617) 722-2877
F: (617) 626-0261
E: Jerald.Parisella
@mahouse.gov

**Peake, Sarah K. (D, SP4)**
Room 163, State House
Boston, MA 02133
P: (617) 722-2040
F: (617) 722-2239
E: Sarah.Peake@mahouse.gov

**Peisch, Alice Hanlon (D, SP110)**
Room 473G, State House
Boston, MA 02133
P: (617) 722-2070
E: Alice.Peisch@mahouse.gov

**Petrolati, Thomas M. (D, SP51)**
Room 171, State House
Boston, MA 02133
P: (617) 722-2255
F: (617) 722-2846
E: Thomas.Petrolati
@mahouse.gov

**Pignatelli, William Smitty (D, SP10)**
Room 466, State House
Boston, MA 02133
P: (617) 722-2017
F: (617) 722-2879
E: rep.smitty@mahouse.gov

**Poirier, Elizabeth A. (R, SP24)**
Room 124, State House
Boston, MA 02133
P: (617) 722-2100
F: (617) 626-0108
E: Elizabeth.Poirier
@mahouse.gov

**Provost, Denise (D, SP24)**
Room 473B, State House
Boston, MA 02133
P: (617) 722-2263
F: (617) 626-0548
E: Denise.Provost
@mahouse.gov

**Puppolo, Angelo (D, SP56)**
Room 236, State House
Boston, MA 02133
P: (617) 722-2430
F: (617) 722-2848
E: Angelo.Puppolo
@mahouse.gov

**Rogers, David (D, SP83)**
Room 472, State House
Boston, MA 02133
P: (617) 722-2013
F: (617) 626-0275
E: Dave.Rogers@mahouse.gov

**Rogers, John H. (D, SP108)**
Room 162, State House
Boston, MA 02133
P: (617) 722-2092
F: (617) 722-2347
E: John.Rogers@mahouse.gov

**Roy, Jeffrey (D, SP106)**
Room 527A, State House
Boston, MA 02133
P: (617) 722-2020
F: (617) 626-0279
E: Jeffrey.Roy@mahouse.gov

**Rushing, Byron (D, SP132)**
Room 234, State House
Boston, MA 02133
P: (617) 722-2783
F: (617) 722-2238
E: Byron.Rushing
@mahouse.gov

**Ryan, Daniel J. (D, SP125)**
Room 146, State House
Boston, MA 02133
P: (617) 722-2575
E: Dan.Ryan@mahouse.gov

**Sanchez, Jeffrey (D, SP138)**
Room 236, State House
Boston, MA 02133
P: (617) 722-2430
E: Jeffrey.Sanchez
@mahouse.gov

**Scaccia, Angelo M.
(D, SP137)**
Room 33, State House
Boston, MA 02133
P: (617) 722-2060
F: (617) 722-2849
E: Angelo.Scaccia
@mahouse.gov

**Schmid, Paul A. (D, SP18)**
Room 473F, State House
Boston, MA 02133
P: (617) 722-2210
F: (617) 626-0267
E: Paul.Schmid@mahouse.gov

**Scibak, John W. (D, SP58)**
Room 43, State House
Boston, MA 02133
P: (617) 722-2030
F: (617) 722-2215
E: John.Scibak@mahouse.gov

**Silvia, Alan (D, SP17)**
Room 174, State House
Boston, MA 02133
P: (617) 722-2877
F: (617) 626-0168
E: Alan.Silvia@mahouse.gov

**Smizik, Frank Israel
(D, SP111)**
Room 274, State House
Boston, MA 02133
P: (617) 722-2676
F: (617) 722-2239
E: Frank.Smizik@mahouse.gov

**Smola, Todd M. (R, SP45)**
Room 124, State House
Boston, MA 02133
P: (617) 722-2100
E: Todd.Smola@mahouse.gov

**Speliotis, Theodore C.
(D, SP37)**
Room 20, State House
Boston, MA 02133
P: (617) 722-2410
E: Theodore.Speliotis
@mahouse.gov

**Stanley, Thomas M.
(D, SP68)**
Room 167, State House
Boston, MA 02133
P: (617) 722-2230
E: Thomas.Stanley
@mahouse.gov

**Straus, William M.
(D, SP20)**
Room 134, State House
Boston, MA 02133
P: (617) 722-2400
F: (617) 722-2387
E: William.Straus
@mahouse.gov

**Tosado, Jose F. (D, SP53)**
Room 34, State House
Boston, MA 02133
P: (617) 722-2320
E: Jose.Tosado@mahouse.gov

**Tucker, Paul F. (D, SP31)**
Room 134, State House
Boston, MA 02133
P: (617) 722-2400
E: Paul.Tucker@mahouse.gov

**Tyler, Chynah (D, SP130)\***
Room 437, State House
Boston, MA 02133
P: (617) 722-2425
E: Chynah.Tyler@mahouse.gov

**Ultrino, Steven (D, SP92)**
Room 443, State House
Boston, MA 02133
P: (617) 722-2460
E: Steven.Ultrino
@mahouse.gov

**Vega, Aaron (D, SP49)**
Room 146, State House
Boston, MA 02133
P: (617) 722-2011
F: (617) 626-2224
E: Aaron.Vega@mahouse.gov

**Velis, John (D, SP48)**
Room 448, State House
Boston, MA 02133
P: (617) 722-2582
E: john.velis@mahouse.gov

**Vieira, David T. (R, SP3)**
Room 167, State House
Boston, MA 02133
P: (617) 722-2230
E: David.Vieira@mahouse.gov

**Vincent, RoseLee (D, SP139)**
Room 473F, State House
Boston, MA 02133
P: (617) 722-2210
E: RoseLee.Vincent
@mahouse.gov

**Wagner, Joseph F. (D, SP52)**
Room 42, State House
Boston, MA 02133
P: (617) 722-2370
E: Joseph.Wagner
@MAhouse.gov

**Walsh, Chris (D, SP65)**
Room 472, State House
Boston, MA 02133
P: (617) 722-2013
F: (617) 626-0291
E: Chris.Walsh@mahouse.gov

**Walsh, Thomas (D, SP36)**
Room 276, State House
Boston, MA 02133
P: (617) 722-2676
E: Thomas.Walsh@mahouse.gov

**Whelan, Timothy R. (R, SP1)**
Room 39, State House
Boston, MA 02133
P: (617) 722-2014
E: Timothy.Whelan
@mahouse.gov

**Whipps Lee, Susannah M.
(R, SP44)**
Room 540, State House
Boston, MA 02133
P: (617) 722-2090
E: Susannah.WhippsLee
@mahouse.gov

**Williams, Bud L. (D, SP55)\***
Room 437, State House
Boston, MA 02133
P: (617) 722-7300
E: Bud.Williams@mahouse.gov

**Wong, Donald H. (R, SP33)**
Room 541, State House
Boston, MA 02133
P: (617) 722-2488
F: (617) 626-0299
E: Donald.Wong@mahouse.gov

**Zlotnik, Jonathan
(D, SP144)**
Room 26, State House
Boston, MA 02133
P: (617) 722-2080
F: (617) 626-0333
E: Jon.Zlotnik@mahouse.gov

# Michigan

## Executive

### Governor

**The Honorable Rick Snyder (R)**
Governor
P.O. Box 30013
Lansing, MI 48909
P: (517) 373-3400
F: (517) 335-6863

### Lieutenant Governor

**The Honorable Brian Calley (R)**
Lieutenant Governor
P.O. Box 30013
Lansing, MI 48909
P: (517) 373-6800
F: (517) 241-5026

### Attorney General

**The Honorable Bill Schuette (R)**
Attorney General
525 West Ottawa Street
P.O. Box 30212
Lansing, MI 48909
P: (517) 373-1110

### Auditor

**The Honorable Doug Ringler**
(appointed by the Legislature)
Auditor General
201 North Washington Square
Victor Center, Suite 600
Lansing, MI 48913
P: (517) 334-8050
F: (517) 334-8079
E: dringler
@audgen.michigan.gov

### Secretary of State

**The Honorable Ruth Johnson (R)**
Secretary of State
430 West Allegan Street, 4th Floor
Lansing, MI 48918
P: (517) 373-2510
F: (517) 373-0727
E: secretary@michigan.gov

## Treasurer

**The Honorable Nick Khouri**
(appointed)
State Treasurer
430 West Allegan Street
Lansing, MI 48922
P: (517) 373-3223
F: (517) 335-1785

## Judiciary

### Supreme Court (NE)

**Mr. Larry Royster**
Clerk
P.O. Box 30052
Lansing, MI 48909
P: (517) 373-0120
E: MSC_Clerk@courts.mi.gov

**The Honorable Stephen J. Markman**
Chief Justice
**The Honorable Richard Bernstein**
**The Honorable Joan L. Larsen**
**The Honorable Bridget Mary McCormack**
**The Honorable David F. Viviano**
**The Honorable Brian Zahra**

## Legislative
## Senate

### Senate President

**The Honorable Brian Calley (R)**
Lieutenant Governor
P.O. Box 30013
Lansing, MI 48909
P: (517) 373-6800
F: (517) 241-5026

### President Pro Tempore of the Senate

**Senator Tonya Schuitmaker (R)**
Senate President Pro Tempore
7400 Binsfeld Building
P.O. Box 30036
Lansing, MI 48909
P: (517) 373-0793
F: (517) 373-5607
E: SenTSchuitmaker
@senate.michigan.gov

## Senate Majority Leader

**Senator Arlan Meekhof (R)**
Senate Majority Leader
S-106 Capitol Building
P.O. Box 30036
Lansing, MI 48909
P: (517) 373-6920
F: (517) 373-2751
E: SenAMeekhof
@senate.michigan.gov

## Senate Minority Leader

**Senator Jim Ananich (D)**
Senate Minority Leader
S-105 Capitol Building
P.O. Box 30036
Lansing, MI 48909
P: (517) 373-0142
F: (517) 373-3938
E: SenJAnanich
@senate.michigan.gov

## Members of the Senate

**Ananich, Jim (D, 27)**
S-105 Capitol Building
P.O. Box 30036
Lansing, MI 48909
P: (517) 373-0142
F: (517) 373-3938
E: SenJAnanich
@senate.michigan.gov

**Bieda, Steve (D, 9)**
6300 Binsfeld Building
P.O. Box 30036
Lansing, MI 48909
P: (517) 373-8360
F: (517) 373-9230
E: SenSBieda
@senate.michigan.gov

**Booher, Darwin (R, 35)**
3200 Binsfeld Building
P.O. Box 30036
Lansing, MI 48909
P: (517) 373-1725
F: (517) 373-0741
E: SenDBooher
@senate.michigan.gov

**Brandenburg, Jack (R, 8)**
7500 Binsfeld Building
P.O. Box 30036
Lansing, MI 48909
P: (517) 373-7670
F: (517) 373-5958
E: SenJBrandenburg
@senate.michigan.gov

**Casperson, Tom (R, 38)**
4100 Binsfeld Building
P.O. Box 30036
Lansing, MI 48909
P: (517) 373-7840
F: (517) 373-3932
E: SenTCasperson
@senate.michigan.gov

**Colbeck, Patrick (R, 7)**
3400 Binsfeld Building
P.O. Box 30036
Lansing, MI 48909
P: (517) 373-7350
F: (517) 373-9228
E: SenPColbeck
@senate.michigan.gov

**Emmons, Judy (R, 33)**
4400 Binsfeld Building
P.O. Box 30036
Lansing, MI 48909
P: (517) 373-3760
F: (517) 373-8661
E: SenJEmmons
@senate.michigan.gov

**Green, Mike (R, 31)**
6100 Binsfeld Building
P.O. Box 30036
Lansing, MI 48909
P: (517) 373-1777
F: (517) 373-5871
E: SenMGreen
@senate.michigan.gov

**Gregory, Vincent (D, 11)**
6400 Binsfeld Building
P.O. Box 30036
Lansing, MI 48909
P: (517) 373-7888
F: (517) 373-2983
E: SenVGregory
@senate.michigan.gov

**Hansen, Goeff (R, 34)**
7100 Binsfeld Building
P.O. Box 30036
Lansing, MI 48909
P: (517) 373-1635
F: (517) 373-3300
E: SenGHansen
@senate.michigan.gov

**Hertel Jr., Curtis (D, 23)**
7600 Binsfeld Building
P.O. Box 30036
Lansing, MI 48909
P: (517) 373-1734
F: (517) 373-5397
E: senchertel
@senate.michigan.gov

**Hildenbrand, Dave (R, 29)**
S-324 Capitol Building
P.O. Box 30036
Lansing, MI 48909
P: (517) 373-1801
F: (517) 373-5801
E: SenDHildenbrand
@senate.michigan.gov

**Hood III, Morris (D, 3)**
S-9 Capitol Building
P.O. Box 30036
Lansing, MI 48909
P: (517) 373-0990
F: (517) 373-5338
E: SenMHood
@senate.michigan.gov

**Hopgood, Hoon-Yung (D, 6)**
4500 Binsfeld Building
P.O. Box 30036
Lansing, MI 48909
P: (517) 373-7800
F: (517) 373-9310
E: senhhopgood
@senate.michigan.gov

**Horn, Ken (R, 32)**
7200 Binsfeld Building
P.O. Box 30036
Lansing, MI 48909
P: (517) 373-1760
F: (517) 373-3487
E: SenKHorn
@senate.michigan.gov

**Hune, Joe (R, 22)**
6600 Binsfeld Building
P.O. Box 30036
Lansing, MI 48909
P: (517) 373-2420
F: (517) 373-2764
E: SenJHune
@senate.michigan.gov

**Johnson, Bert (D, 2)**
3300 Binsfeld Building
P.O. Box 30036
Lansing, MI 48909
P: (517) 373-7748
F: (517) 373-1387
E: SenBJohnson
@senate.michigan.gov

**Jones, Rick (R, 24)**
4200 Binsfeld Building
P.O. Box 30036
Lansing, MI 48909
P: (517) 373-3447
F: (517) 373-5849
E: SenRJones
@senate.michigan.gov

**Knezek, David (D, 5)**
5500 Binsfeld Building
P.O. Box 30036
Lansing, MI 48909
P: (517) 373-0994
F: (517) 373-5981
E: DavidKnezek
@senate.michigan.gov

**Knollenberg, Marty (R, 13)**
3100 Binsfeld Building
P.O. Box 30036
Lansing, MI 48909
P: (517) 373-2523
F: (517) 373-5669
E: senmknollenberg
@senate.michigan.gov

**Kowall, Michael (R, 15)**
S-309 Capitol Building
P.O. Box 30036
Lansing, MI 48909
P: (517) 373-1758
F: (517) 373-0938
E: SenMKowall
@senate.michigan.gov

**MacGregor, Peter (R, 28)**
5600 Binsfeld Building
P.O. Box 30036
Lansing, MI 48909
P: (517) 373-0797
F: (517) 373-5236
E: senpmacgregor
@senate.michigan.gov

**Marleau, James (R, 12)**
S-2 Capitol Building
P.O. Box 30036
Lansing, MI 48909
P: (517) 373-2417
F: (517) 373-2694
E: senjmarleau
@senate.michigan.gov

**Meekhof, Arlan (R, 30)**
S-106 Capitol Building
P.O. Box 30036
Lansing, MI 48909
P: (517) 373-6920
F: (517) 373-2751
E: SenAMeekhof
@senate.michigan.gov

**Nofs, Mike (R, 19)**
S-132 Capitol Building
P.O. Box 30036
Lansing, MI 48909
P: (517) 373-2426
F: (517) 373-2964
E: SenMNofs
@senate.michigan.gov

**O'Brien, Margaret E. (R, 20)**
5400 Binsfeld Building
P.O. Box 30036
Lansing, MI 48909
P: (517) 373-5100
F: (517) 373-5115
E: senmobrien
@senate.michigan.gov

**Pavlov, Phillip (R, 25)**
6200 Binsfeld Building
P.O. Box 30036
Lansing, MI 48909
P: (517) 373-7708
F: (517) 373-1450
E: SenPPavlov
@senate.michigan.gov

**Proos, John (R, 21)**
S-8 Capitol Building
P.O. Box 30036
Lansing, MI 48909
P: (517) 373-6960
F: (517) 373-0897
E: SenJProos
@senate.michigan.gov

**Robertson, David B. (R, 14)**
6500 Binsfeld Building
P.O. Box 30036
Lansing, MI 48909
P: (517) 373-1636
F: (517) 373-1453
E: SenDRobertson
@senate.michigan.gov

**Rocca, Tory (R, 10)**
3600 Binsfeld Building
P.O. Box 30036
Lansing, MI 48909
P: (517) 373-7315
F: (517) 373-3126
E: SenTRocca
@senate.michigan.gov

**Schmidt, Wayne A. (R, 37)**
4600 Binsfeld Building
P.O. Box 30036
Lansing, MI 48909
P: (517) 373-2413
F: (517) 373-5144
E: senwschmidt
@senate.michigan.gov

**Schuitmaker, Tonya (R, 26)**
7400 Binsfeld Building
P.O. Box 30036
Lansing, MI 48909
P: (517) 373-0793
F: (517) 373-5607
E: SenTSchuitmaker
@senate.michigan.gov

**Shirkey, Michael (R, 16)**
5300 Binsfeld Building
P.O. Box 30036
Lansing, MI 48909
P: (517) 373-5932
F: (517) 373-5944
E: senmshirkey
@senate.michigan.gov

**Stamas, Jim (R, 36)**
5200 Binsfeld Building
P.O. Box 30036
Lansing, MI 48909
P: (517) 373-7946
F: (517) 373-2678
E: senjstamas
@senate.michigan.gov

**Warren, Rebekah (D, 18)**
7300 Binsfeld Building
P.O. Box 30036
Lansing, MI 48909
P: (517) 373-2406
F: (517) 373-5679
E: SenRWarren
@senate.michigan.gov

**Young II, Coleman (D, 1)**
4300 Binsfeld Building
P.O. Box 30036
Lansing, MI 48909
P: (517) 373-7346
F: (517) 373-9320
E: SenCYoung
@senate.michigan.gov

**Zorn, Dale (R, 17)**
5100 Binsfeld Building
P.O. Box 30036
Lansing, MI 48909
P: (517) 373-3543
F: (517) 373-0927
E: sendzorn
@senate.michigan.gov

# House

## Speaker of the House

**Speaker Tom Leonard (R)**
Speaker of the House
164 Capitol Building
P.O. Box 30014
Lansing, MI 48909
P: (517) 373-1778
E: TomLeonard@house.mi.gov

# Michigan

## Speaker Pro Tempore of the House

**Representative Lee Chatfield (R)**
House Speaker Pro Tempore
251 Capitol Building
P.O. Box 30014
Lansing, MI 48909
P: (517) 373-2629
E: leechatfield
    @house.mi.gov

## House Minority Leader

**Representative Sam Singh (D)**
House Minority Leader
167 Capitol Building
P.O. Box 30014
Lansing, MI 48909
P: (517) 373-1786
E: SamSingh@house.mi.gov

## Clerk of the House

**Mr. Gary Randall**
Clerk of the House
Capitol Building, Room 70
P.O. Box 30014
Lansing, MI 48909
P: (517) 373-0135
E: clerk@house.mi.gov

## Members of the House

**Afendoulis, Chris (R, 73)**
House Office Building, N-1092
P.O. Box 30014
Lansing, MI 48909
P: (517) 373-0218
E: chrisafendoulis
    @house.mi.gov

**Albert, Thomas (R, 86)\***
House Office Building 1190-N
PO Box 30014
Lansing, MI 48909
P: (517) 373-0846
E: thomasalbert
    @house.mi.gov

**Alexander, Julie (R, 64)\***
House Office Building 998-N
PO Box 30014
Lansing, MI 48909
P: (517) 373-1795
E: juliealexander
    @house.mi.gov

**Allor, Sue (R, 106)\***
House Office Building 1485-S
PO Box 30014
Lansing, MI 48909
P: (517) 373-0833
E: sueallor@house.mi.gov

**Barrett, Tom (R, 71)**
House Office Building, N-1090
P.O. Box 30014
Lansing, MI 48909
P: (517) 373-0853
E: tombarrett@house.mi.gov

**Bellino, Joseph (R, 17)\***
House Office Building 696-N
PO Box 30014
Lansing, MI 48909
P: (517) 373-1530
E: josephbellino
    @house.mi.gov

**Bizon, John (R, 62)**
House Office Building, N0996
P.O. Box 30014
Lansing, MI 48909
P: (517) 373-0555
E: drjohnbizon@house.mi.gov

**Brann, Tommy (R, 77)\***
House Office Building 1096-N
PO Box 30014
Lansing, MI 48909
P: (517) 373-2277
E: tommybrann@house.mi.gov

**Brinks, Winnie (D, 76)**
House Office Building, N-1095
P.O. Box 30014
Lansing, MI 48909
P: (517) 373-0822
E: winniebrinks
    @house.mi.gov

**Byrd, Wendell L. (D, 3)**
House Office Building, S-587
P.O. Box 30014
Lansing, MI 48909
P: (517) 373-0144
E: wendellbyrd@house.mi.gov

**Calley, Julie (R, 87)\***
House Office Building 1191-N
PO Box 30014
Lansing, MI 48909
P: (517) 373-0842
E: juliecalley@house.mi.gov

**Camilleri, Darrin (D, 23)\***
House Office Building 787-S
PO Box 30014
Lansing, MI 48909
P: (517) 373-0855
E: darrincamilleri
    @house.mi.gov

**Canfield, Edward (R, 84)**
House Office Building, S-1188
P.O. Box 30014
Lansing, MI 48909
P: (517) 373-0476
E: edwardcanfield
    @house.mi.gov

**Chang, Stephanie (D, 6)**
House Office Building, S-685
P.O. Box 30014
Lansing, MI 48909
P: (517) 373-0823
E: stephaniechang
    @house.mi.gov

**Chatfield, Lee (R, 107)**
251 Capitol Building
P.O. Box 30014
Lansing, MI 48909
P: (517) 373-2629
E: leechatfield
    @house.mi.gov

**Chirkun, John (D, 22)**
House Office Building, S-786
P.O. Box 30014
Lansing, MI 48909
P: (517) 373-0854
E: johnchirkun@house.mi.gov

**Clemente, Cara (D, 14)\***
House Office Building 693-N
PO Box 30014
Lansing, MI 48909
P: (517) 373-0140
E: caraclemente
    @house.mi.gov

**Cochran, Tom (D, 67)**
House Office Building, S-1086
P.O. Box 30014
Lansing, MI 48909
P: (517) 373-0587
E: TomCochran@house.mi.gov

**Cole, Triston (R, 105)**
House Office Building, S-1389
P.O. Box 30014
Lansing, MI 48909
P: (517) 373-0829
E: tristoncole@house.mi.gov

**Cox, Laura (R, 19)**
351 Capitol Building
P.O. Box 30014
Lansing, MI 48909
P: (517) 373-3920
E: lauracox@house.mi.gov

**Crawford, Kathy (R, 38)**
House Office Building, S-887
P.O. Box 30014
Lansing, MI 48909
P: (517) 373-0827
E: kathycrawford
    @house.mi.gov

**Dianda, Scott (D, 110)**
House Office Building, S-1489
P.O. Box 30014
Lansing, MI 48909
P: (517) 373-0850
E: ScottDianda@house.mi.gov

**Durhal III, Fred (D, 5)**
House Office Building, S-589
P.O. Box 30014
Lansing, MI 48909
P: (517) 373-0844
E: freddurhal@house.mi.gov

**Elder, Brian (D, 96)\***
House Office Building 1285-S
PO Box 30014
Lansing, MI 48909
P: (517) 373-0158
E: brianelder@house.mi.gov

**Ellison, Jim (D, 26)\***
House Office Building 790-N
PO Box 30014
Lansing, MI 48909
P: (517) 373-3818
E: jimellison@house.mi.gov

**Faris, Pam (D, 48)**
House Office Building, N-897
P.O. Box 30014
Lansing, MI 48909
P: (517) 373-7557
E: PamFaris@house.mi.gov

**Farrington, Diana (R, 30)\***
House Office Building 794-N
PO Box 30014
Lansing, MI 48909
P: (517) 373-7768
E: dianafarrington
    @house.mi.gov

**Frederick, Ben (R, 85)\***
House Office Building 1189-S
PO Box 30014
Lansing, MI 48909
P: (517) 373-0841
E: benfrederick
    @house.mi.gov

**Garcia, Daniela Rosa (R, 90)**
House Office Building, N-1194
P.O. Box 30014
Lansing, MI 48909
P: (517) 373-0830
E: danielagarcia
    @house.mi.gov

**Garrett, LaTanya (D, 7)**
House Office Building, S-686
P.O. Box 30014
Lansing, MI 48909
P: (517) 373-2276
E: latanyagarrett
    @house.mi.gov

**Gay-Dagnogo, Sherry (D, 8)**
House Office Building,687-S
P.O. Box 30014
Lansing, MI 48909
P: (517) 373-3815
E: sherrygay-dagnogo
    @house.mi.gov

**Geiss, Erika (D, 12)**
N691 House Office Building
P.O. Box 30014
Lansing, MI 48909
P: (517) 373-0852
E: erikageiss@house.mi.gov

**Glenn, Gary (R, 98)**
House Office Building, S-1287
P.O. Box 30014
Lansing, MI 48909
P: (517) 373-1791
E: garyglenn@house.mi.gov

**Graves, Joseph (R, 51)**
House Office Building, S-985
P.O. Box 30014
Lansing, MI 48909
P: (517) 373-1780
E: JosephGraves
    @house.mi.gov

**Green, Patrick (D, 28)***
House Office Building 792-N
PO Box 30014
Lansing, MI 48909
P: (517) 373-1772
E: patrickgreen
    @house.mi.gov

**Greig, Christine (D, 37)**
141 Capitol Building
P.O. Box 30014
Lansing, MI 48909
P: (517) 373-1793
E: cgreig@house.mi.gov

**Greimel, Tim (D, 29)**
House Office Building, 793-N
P.O. Box 30014
Lansing, MI 48909
P: (517) 373-0475
E: TimGreimel@house.mi.gov

**Griffin, Beth (R, 66)***
House Office Building 1085-S
PO Box 30014
Lansing, MI 48909
P: (517) 373-0839
E: bethgriffin@house.mi.gov

**Guerra, Vanessa (D, 95)**
House Office Building, N-1199
P.O. Box 30014
Lansing, MI 48909
P: (517) 373-0152
E: vanessaguerra
    @house.mi.gov

**Hammoud, Abdullah (D, 15)***
House Office Building 694-N
PO Box 30014
Lansing, MI 48909
P: (517) 373-0847
E: abdullahhammoud
    @house.mi.gov

**Hauck, Roger (R, 99)***
House Office Building 1288-S
PO Box 30014
Lansing, MI 48909
P: (517) 373-1789
E: rogerhauck@house.mi.gov

**Hernandez, Shane (R, 83)***
House Office Building 1187-S
PO Box 30014
Lansing, MI 48909
P: (517) 373-0835
E: shanehernandez
    @house.mi.gov

**Hertel, Kevin (D, 18)***
House Office Building 697-N
PO Box 30014
Lansing, MI 48909
P: (517) 373-1180
E: kevinhertel@house.mi.gov

**Hoadley, Jon (D, 60)**
House Office Building, N-994
P.O. Box 30014
Lansing, MI 48909
P: (517) 373-1785
E: jonhoadley@house.mi.gov

**Hoitenga, Michele (R, 102)***
House Office Building 1386-S
PO Box 30014
Lansing, MI 48909
P: (517) 373-1747
E: michelehoitenga
    @house.mi.gov

**Hornberger, Pamela (R, 32)***
House Office Building 796-N
PO Box 30014
Lansing, MI 48909
P: (517) 373-8931
E: pamelahornberger
    @house.mi.gov

**Howell, Gary (R, 82)**
House Office Building, S-1186
PO Box 30014
Lansing, MI 48909
P: (517) 373-1800
E: garyhowell@house.mi.gov

**Howrylak, Martin (R, 41)**
House Office Building, N-890
P.O. Box 30014
Lansing, MI 48909
P: (517) 373-1783
E: MartinHowrylak
    @house.mi.gov

**Hughes, Holly (R, 91)**
House Office Building, N-1195
P.O. Box 30014
Lansing, MI 48909
P: (517) 373-3436
F: (517) 373-9698
E: HollyHughes@house.mi.gov

**Iden, Brandt (R, 61)**
House Office Building, N-995
P.O. Box 30014
Lansing, MI 48909
P: (517) 373-1774
E: brandtiden@house.mi.gov

**Inman, Larry (R, 104)**
House Office Building, S-1388
P.O. Box 30014
Lansing, MI 48909
P: (517) 373-1766
E: larryinman@house.mi.gov

**Johnson, Steven (R, 72)***
House Office Building 1091-N
PO Box 30014
Lansing, MI 48909
P: (517) 373-0840
E: stevenjohnson
    @house.mi.gov

**Jones, Jewell (D, 11)***
House Office Building 690-N
PO Box 30014
Lansing, MI 48909
P: (517) 373-0849
E: jewelljones@house.mi.gov

**Kahle, Bronna (R, 57)***
House Office Building 991-N
PO Box 30014
Lansing, MI 48909
P: (517) 373-1706
E: bronnakahle@house.mi.gov

**Kelly, Tim (R, 94)**
House Office Building, N-1198
P.O. Box 30014
Lansing, MI 48909
P: (517) 373-0837
E: TimKelly@house.mi.gov

**Kesto, Klint (R, 39)**
House Office Building, S-888
P.O. Box 30014
Lansing, MI 48909
P: (517) 373-1799
E: KlintKesto@house.mi.gov

**Kivela, John (D, 109)**
House Office Building, S-1488
P.O. Box 30014
Lansing, MI 48909
P: (517) 373-0498
E: JohnKivela@house.mi.gov

**Kosowski, Robert L. (D, 16)**
House Office Building, N-695
P.O. Box 30014
Lansing, MI 48909
P: (517) 373-2576
E: RobertKosowski
    @house.mi.gov

**LaFave, Beau (R, 108)***
House Office Building 1487-S
PO Box 30014
Lansing, MI 48909
P: (517) 373-0156
E: beaulafave@house.mi.gov

**LaGrand, David (D, 75)**
House Office Building, 1094-N
P.O. Box 30014
Lansing, MI 48909
P: (517) 373-2668
E: davidlagrand
    @house.mi.gov

**LaSata, Kim (R, 79)***
House Office Building 1098-N
PO Box 30014
Lansing, MI 48909
P: (517) 373-1403
E: kimlasata@house.mi.gov

**Lasinski, Donna (D, 52)***
House Office Building 986-S
PO Box 30014
Lansing, MI 48909
P: (517) 373-0828
E: donnalasinski
    @house.mi.gov

**Lauwers, Dan (R, 81)**
151 Capitol Building
P.O. Box 30014
Lansing, MI 48909
P: (517) 373-1790
E: DanLauwers@house.mi.gov

**Leonard, Tom (R, 93)**
164 Capitol Building
P.O. Box 30014
Lansing, MI 48909
P: (517) 373-1778
E: TomLeonard@house.mi.gov

**Leutheuser, Eric (R, 58)**
House Office Building, N-992
P.O. Box 30014
Lansing, MI 48909
P: (517) 373-1794
E: ericleutheuser
    @house.mi.gov

**Liberati, Frank (D, 13)**
House Office Building, N-692
P.O. Box 30014
Lansing, MI 48909
P: (517) 373-0845
E: frankliberati
    @house.mi.gov

# Michigan

**Lilly, Jim (R, 89)***
House Office Building 1193-N
PO Box 30014
Lansing, MI 48909
P: (517) 373-0838
E: jimlilly@house.mi.gov

**Love, Leslie (D, 10)**
House Office Building, S-689
P.O. Box 30014
Lansing, MI 48909
P: (517) 373-0857
E: leslielove@house.mi.gov

**Lower, James (R, 70)***
House Office Building 1089-S
PO Box 30014
Lansing, MI 48909
P: (517) 373-1786
E: jameslower@house.mi.gov

**Lucido, Peter (R, 36)**
House Office Building, S-885
P.O. Box 30014
Lansing, MI 48909
P: (517) 373-0843
E: peterlucido@house.mi.gov

**Marino, Steve (R, 24)***
House Office Building 788-S
PO Box 30014
Lansing, MI 48909
P: (517) 373-0113
E: smarino@house.mi.gov

**Maturen, David (R, 63)**
House Office Building, N-997
P.O. Box 30014
Lansing, MI 48909
P: (517) 373-1787
E: davidmaturen
   @house.mi.gov

**McCready, Mike (R, 40)**
House Office Building, S-889
P.O. Box 30014
Lansing, MI 48909
P: (517) 373-8670
E: MikeMcCready
   @house.mi.gov

**Miller, Aaron (R, 59)**
House Office Building, N-993
P.O. Box 30014
Lansing, MI 48909
P: (517) 373-0832
E: aaronmiller@house.mi.gov

**Moss, Jeremy (D, 35)**
House Office Building, 799-N
P.O. Box 30014
Lansing, MI 48909
P: (517) 373-1788
E: jeremymoss@house.mi.gov

**Neeley, Sheldon (D, 34)**
House Office Building, N-798
P.O. Box 30014
Lansing, MI 48909
P: (517) 373-8808
E: sheldonneeley
   @house.mi.gov

**Noble, Jeff (R, 20)***
House Office Building 699-N
PO Box 30014
Lansing, MI 48909
P: (517) 373-3816
E: jeffnoble@house.mi.gov

**Pagan, Kristy (D, 21)**
House Office Building, S-785
P.O. Box 30014
Lansing, MI 48909
P: (517) 373-2575
E: kristypagan@house.mi.gov

**Pagel, David (R, 78)**
House Office Building, N-1097
P.O. Box 30014
Lansing, MI 48909
P: (517) 373-1796
E: DavePagel@house.mi.gov

**Peterson, Ronnie (D, 54)***
House Office Building 988-S
PO Box 30014
Lansing, MI 48909
P: (517) 373-1771
E: ronniepeterson
   @house.mi.gov

**Phelps, Phil (D, 49)**
House Office Building, N-898
P.O. Box 30014
Lansing, MI 48909
P: (517) 373-7515
F: (517) 373-5817
E: RepPhelps@house.mi.gov

**Rabhi, Yousef (D, 53)***
House Office Building 987-S
PO Box 30014
Lansing, MI 48909
P: (517) 373-2577
E: yousefrabhi@house.mi.gov

**Reilly, John (R, 46)***
House Office Building 895-N
PO Box 30014
Lansing, MI 48909
P: (517) 373-1798
E: johnreilly@house.mi.gov

**Rendon, Daire (R, 103)***
House Office Building 1387-S
PO Box 30014
Lansing, MI 48909
P: (517) 373-3817
E: dairerendon@house.mi.gov

**Roberts, Brett (R, 65)**
House Office Building, N-999
P.O. Box 30014
Lansing, MI 48909
P: (517) 373-1775
E: brettroberts
   @house.mi.gov

**Robinson, Rose Mary (D, 4)**
House Office Building, S-588
P.O. Box 30014
Lansing, MI 48909
P: (517) 373-1008
E: RoseMaryRobinson
   @house.mi.gov

**Runestad, Jim (R, 44)**
House Office Building, N-893
P.O. Box 30014
Lansing, MI 48909
P: (517) 373-2616
E: jimrunestad@house.mi.gov

**Sabo, Terry (D, 92)***
House Office Building 1196-N
PO Box 30014
Lansing, MI 48909
P: (517) 373-2646
E: terrysabo@house.mi.gov

**Santana, Sylvia (D, 9)***
House Office Building 688-S
PO Box 30014
Lansing, MI 48909
P: (517) 373-6990
E: sylviasantana
   @house.mi.gov

**Schor, Andy (D, 68)**
House Office Building, S-1087
P.O. Box 30014
Lansing, MI 48909
P: (517) 373-0826
E: AndySchor@house.mi.gov

**Scott, Bettie Cook (D, 2)**
House Office Building, 586-S
P.O. Box 30014
Lansing, MI 48909
P: (517) 373-1776
F: (517) 373-8502
E: bettiecookscott
   @house.mi.gov

**Sheppard, Jason (R, 56)**
House Office Building, N-990
P.O. Box 30014
Lansing, MI 48909
P: (517) 373-2617
E: jasonsheppard
   @house.mi.gov

**Singh, Sam (D, 69)**
167 Capitol Building
P.O. Box 30014
Lansing, MI 48909
P: (517) 373-1786
E: SamSingh@house.mi.gov

**Sneller, Tim (D, 50)***
House Office Building 899-N
PO Box 30014
Lansing, MI 48909
P: (517) 373-3906
E: timsneller@house.mi.gov

**Sowerby, William (D, 31)***
House Office Building 795-N
PO Box 30014
Lansing, MI 48909
P: (517) 373-0159
E: williamsowerby
   @house.mi.gov

**Tedder, Jim (R, 43)**
House Office Building, N-892
P.O. Box 30014
Lansing, MI 48909
P: (517) 373-0615
E: jimtedder@house.mi.gov

**Theis, Lana (R, 42)**
House Office Building, N-891
P.O. Box 30014
Lansing, MI 48909
P: (517) 373-1784
E: lanatheis@house.mi.gov

**VanderWall, Curt (R, 101)***
House Office Building 1385-S
PO Box 30014
Lansing, MI 48909
P: (517) 373-0825
E: curtvanderwall
   @house.mi.gov

**VanSingel, Scott (R, 100)***
House Office Building 1289-S
PO Box 30014
Lansing, MI 48909
P: (517) 373-7317
E: scottvansingel
   @house.mi.gov

**Vaupel, Henry (R, 47)**
House Office Building, N-896
P.O. Box 30014
Lansing, MI 48909
P: (517) 373-8835
E: hankvaupel@house.mi.gov

**VerHeulen, Rob (R, 74)**
House Office Building, N-1093
P.O. Box 30014
Lansing, MI 48909
P: (517) 373-8900
E: RobVerHeulen
   @house.mi.gov

**Victory, Roger (R, 88)**
House Office Building, N-1192
P.O. Box 30014
Lansing, MI 48909
P: (517) 373-1830
E: RogerVictory
   @house.mi.gov

**Webber, Michael (R, 45)**
House Office Building, N-894
P.O. Box 30014
Lansing, MI 48909
P: (517) 373-1773
E: michaelwebber
@house.mi.gov

**Wentworth, Jason (R, 97)***
House Office Building 1286-S
PO Box 30014
Lansing, MI 48909
P: (517) 373-8962
E: jasonwentworth
@house.mi.gov

**Whiteford, Mary (R, 80)**
House Office Building, 1099N
P.O. Box 30014
Lansing, MI 48909
P: (517) 373-0836
E: marywhiteford
@house.mi.gov

**Wittenberg, Robert (D, 27)**
House Office Building, N-791
P.O. Box 30014
Lansing, MI 48909
P: (517) 373-0478
E: robertwittenberg
@house.mi.gov

**Yanez, Henry (D, 25)**
House Office Building, S-789
P.O. Box 30014
Lansing, MI 48909
P: (517) 373-2275
E: henryyanez@house.mi.gov

**Yaroch, Jeff (R, 33)***
House Office Building 797-N
PO Box 30014
Lansing, MI 48909
P: (517) 373-0820
E: jeffyaroch@house.mi.gov

**Zemke, Adam F. (D, 55)**
House Office Building, S-989
P.O. Box 30014
Lansing, MI 48909
P: (517) 373-1792
E: AdamZemke@house.mi.gov

# Minnesota

## Executive

### Governor

**The Honorable Mark Dayton (D)**
Governor
130 State Capitol
75 Rev. Martin Luther King Jr. Boulevard
St. Paul, MN 55155
P: (651) 201-3400
F: (651) 797-1850

### Lieutenant Governor

**The Honorable Tina Smith (D)**
Lieutenant Governor
130 State Capitol
75 Rev. Martin Luther King Jr. Boulevard
St. Paul, MN 55155
P: (651) 201-3400
F: (651) 797-1850

### Attorney General

**The Honorable Lori Swanson (DFL)**
Attorney General
1400 Bremer Tower
445 Minnesota Street
St. Paul, MN 55101
P: (651) 296-3353
F: (651) 297-4193
E: Attorney.General
@ag.state.mn.us

### Auditor

**The Honorable Rebecca Otto (DFL)**
State Auditor
525 Park Street, Suite 500
St. Paul, MN 55103
P: (615) 296-2551
F: (615) 296-4755
E: rebecca.otto@state.mn.us

### Secretary of State

**The Honorable Steve Simon (DFL)**
Secretary of State
180 State Office Building
100 Martin Luther King Jr. Boulevard
St. Paul, MN 55155
P: (651) 201-1324
F: (651) 269-9073
E: secretary.state
@state.mn.us

## Commissioner of Management & Budget

**Mr. Myron Frans**
(appointed)
Commissioner
658 Cedar Street
400 Centennial Building
St. Paul, MN 55155
P: (651) 201-8000
F: (651) 797-1300
E: myron.frans@state.mn.us

## Judiciary

### Supreme Court (NE)

**Ms. AnnMarie O'Neill**
Clerk of Appellate Courts
305 Minnesota Judicial Center
25 Martin Luther King Jr. Boulevard
St. Paul, MN 55155
P: (651) 296-2581

**The Honorable Lorie S. Gildea**
Chief Justice
**The Honorable Grant Barry Anderson**
**The Honorable Margaret H. Chutich**
**The Honorable Natalie E. Hudson**
**The Honorable David L. Lillehaug**
**The Honorable Anne McKeig**
**The Honorable David R. Stras**

## Legislative Senate

### Senate President

**Senator Michelle L. Fischbach (R)**
Senate President
95 University Avenue W
Minnesota Senate Building, Room 2113
St. Paul, MN 55155
P: (651) 296-2084
E: sen.michelle.fischbach
@senate.mn

## President Pro Tempore of the Senate

**Senator Warren Limmer (R)**
Senate President Pro Tempore
95 University Avenue West
Minnesota Senate Building, Room 3221
St. Paul, MN 55155
P: (651) 296-2159
E: sen.warren.limmer
@senate.mn

## Senate Majority Leader

**Senator Paul E. Gazelka (R)**
Senate Majority Leader
95 University Avenue W
Minnesota Senate Building, Room 3113
St. Paul, MN 55155
P: (651) 296-4875
E: sen.paul.gazelka
@senate.mn

## Senate Minority Leader

**Senator Thomas M. Bakk (DFL)**
Senate Minority Leader
95 University Avenue W.
Minnesota Senate Building, Room 2221
St. Paul, MN 55155
P: (651) 296-8881
E: sen.tom.bakk@senate.mn

## Secretary of the Senate

**Ms. JoAnne Zoff**
Secretary of the Senate
231 State Capitol Building
75 Martin Luther King Jr. Boulevard
St. Paul, MN 55155
P: (651) 296-2344
E: joanne.zoff@senate.mn

## Members of the Senate

**Abeler, Jim (R, 35)**
95 University Avenue W
Minnesota Senate Building, Room 3215
St. Paul, MN 55155
P: (651) 296-3733
E: sen.jim.abeler@senate.mn

**Anderson, Bruce (R, 29)**
95 University Avenue West
Minnesota Senate Building, Room 3209
St. Paul, MN 55155
P: (651) 296-5981
E: sen.bruce.anderson
@senate.mn

**Anderson, Paul (R, 44)***
95 University Avenue W
Minnesota Senate Building, Room 2103
St. Paul, MN 55155
P: (651) 296-9261
E: sen.paul.anderson
@senate.mn

**Bakk, Thomas M. (DFL, 3)**
95 University Avenue W.
Minnesota Senate Building, Room 2221
St. Paul, MN 55155
P: (651) 296-8881
E: sen.tom.bakk@senate.mn

**Benson, Michelle R. (R, 31)**
95 University Avenue West
Minnesota Senate Building, Room 3109
St. Paul, MN 55155
P: (651) 296-3219
E: sen.michelle.benson
@senate.mn

**Carlson, Jim (DFL, 51)**
95 University Avenue W
Minnesota Senate Building, Room 2207
St. Paul, MN 55155
P: (651) 297-8073
E: sen.jim.carlson
@senate.mn

**Chamberlain, Roger C. (R, 38)**
95 University Avenue West
Minnesota Senate Building, Room 3225
St. Paul, MN 55155
P: (651) 296-1253
E: sen.roger.chamberlain
@senate.mn

**Champion, Bobby Joe (DFL, 59)**
95 University Avenue W
Minnesota Senate Building, Room 2303
St. Paul, MN 55155
P: (651) 296-9246
E: sen.bobby.champion
@senate.mn

# Minnesota

**Clausen, Greg D. (DFL, 57)**
95 University Avenue W
Minnesota Senate Building,
Room 2233
St. Paul, MN 55155
P: (651) 296-4120
E: sen.greg.clausen
@senate.mn

**Cohen, Richard J. (DFL, 64)**
95 University Avenue W
Minnesota Senate Building,
Room 2301
St. Paul, MN 55155
P: (651) 296-5931
E: sen.richard.cohen
@senate.mn

**Cwodzinski, Steve (D, 48)***
95 University Avenue W
Minnesota Senate Building,
Room 2319
St. Paul, MN 55155
P: (651) 296-1314
E: sen.steve.cwodzinski
@senate.mn

**Dahms, Gary H. (R, 16)**
95 University Avenue West
Minnesota Senate Building,
Room 2111
St. Paul, MN 55155
P: (651) 296-8138
E: sen.gary.dahms@senate.mn

**Dibble, D. Scott (DFL, 61)**
95 University Avenue W
Minnesota Senate Building,
Room 2213
St. Paul, MN 55155
P: (651) 296-4191
E: sen.scott.dibble
@senate.mn

**Draheim, Rich (R, 20)***
95 University Avenue W
Minnesota Senate Building,
Room 3227
St. Paul, MN 55155
P: (651) 296-5558
E: sen.rich.draheim
@senate.mn

**Dziedzic, Kari (DFL, 60)**
95 University Avenue W
Minnesota Senate Building,
Room 2203
St. Paul, MN 55155
P: (651) 296-7809
E: sen.kari.dziedzic
@senate.mn

**Eaton, Chris A. (DFL, 40)**
95 University Avenue W
Minnesota Senate Building,
Room 2403
St. Paul, MN 55155
P: (651) 296-8869
E: sen.chris.eaton
@senate.mn

**Eichorn, Justin (R, 5)***
95 University Ave W
Minnesota Senate Building,
Room 3213
St. Paul, MN 55155
P: (651) 296-7079
E: sen.justin.eichorn
@senate.mn

**Eken, Kent (DFL, 4)**
95 University Avenue W
Minnesota Senate Building,
Room 2227
St. Paul, MN 55155
P: (651) 296-3205
E: sen.kent.eken@senate.mn

**Fischbach, Michelle L. (R, 13)**
95 University Avenue W
Minnesota Senate Building,
Room 2113
St. Paul, MN 55155
P: (651) 296-2084
E: sen.michelle.fischbach
@senate.mn

**Franzen, Melisa (DFL, 49)**
95 University Avenue W
Minnesota Senate Building,
Room 2229
St. Paul, MN 55155
P: (651) 296-6238
E: sen.melisa.franzen
@senate.mn

**Frentz, Nick (D, 19)***
95 University Avenue W
Minnesota Senate Building,
Room 2415
St. Paul, MN 55155
P: (651) 296-6153
E: sen.nick.frentz
@senate.mn

**Gazelka, Paul E. (R, 9)**
95 University Avenue W
Minnesota Senate Building,
Room 3113
St. Paul, MN 55155
P: (651) 296-4875
E: sen.paul.gazelka
@senate.mn

**Goggin, Mike (R, 21)***
95 University Avenue W
Minnesota Senate Building,
Room 3203
St. Paul, MN 55155
P: (651) 296-5612
E: sen.mike.goggin
@senate.mn

**Hall, Dan D. (R, 56)**
95 University Avenue W
Minnesota Senate Building,
Room 3111
St. Paul, MN 55155
P: (651) 296-5975
E: sen.dan.hall@senate.mn

**Hawj, Foung (DFL, 67)**
95 University Avenue W
Minnesota Senate Building,
Room 3413
St. Paul, MN 55155
P: (651) 296-5285
E: sen.foung.hawj@senate.mn

**Hayden, Jeff (DFL, 62)**
95 University Avenue W
Minnesota Senate Building,
Room 2209
St. Paul, MN 55155
P: (651) 296-4261
E: sen.jeff.hayden
@senate.mn

**Hoffman, John A. (DFL, 36)**
95 University Avenue W
Minnesota Senate Building,
Room 2231
St. Paul, MN 55155
P: (651) 296-4154
E: sen.john.hoffman
@senate.mn

**Housley, Karin (R, 39)**
95 University Avenue W
Minnesota Senate Building,
Room 3217
St. Paul, MN 55155
P: (651) 296-4351
E: sen.karin.housley
@senate.mn

**Ingebrigtsen, Bill G. (R, 8)**
95 University Avenue W
Minnesota Senate Building,
Room 3207
St. Paul, MN 55155
P: (651) 297-8063
E: sen.bill.ingebrigtsen
@senate.mn

**Isaacson, Jason (DFL, 42)**
95 University Ave W
Minnesota Senate Building,
Room 2321
St. Paul, MN 55155
P: (651) 296-5537
E: sen.jason.isaacson
@senate.mn

**Jasinski, John (R, 24)***
95 University Avenue West
Minnesota Senate Building,
Room 2101
St. Paul, MN 55155
P: (651) 296-0284
E: sen.john.jasinski
@senate.mn

**Jensen, Scott (R, 47)***
95 University Avenue West
Minnesota Senate Building,
Room 3229
St. Paul, MN 55155
P: (651) 296-4837
E: sen.scott.jensen
@senate.mn

**Johnson, Mark (R, 1)***
95 University Avenue West
Minnesota Senate Building,
Room 2105
St. Paul, MN 55155
P: (651) 296-5782
E: sen.mark.johnson
@senate.mn

**Kent, Susan (DFL, 53)**
95 University Avenue West
Minnesota Senate Building,
2325
St. Paul, MN 55155
P: (651) 296-4166
E: sen.susan.kent@senate.mn

**Kiffmeyer, Mary (R, 30)**
95 University Avenue West
Minnesota Senate Building,
Room 3103
St. Paul, MN 55155
P: (651) 296-5655
E: sen.mary.kiffmeyer
@senate.mn

**Klein, Matt (D, 52)***
95 University Avenue West
Minnesota Senate Building,
Room 2409
St. Paul, MN 55155
P: (651) 296-4370
E: sen.matt.klein@senate.mn

**Koran, Mark (R, 32)***
95 University Avenue West
Minnesota Senate Building,
Room 3101
St. Paul, MN 55155
P: (651) 296-5419
E: sen.mark.koran@senate.mn

# Minnesota

**Laine, Carolyn (DFL, 41)**
95 University Avenue West
Minnesota Senate Building,
Room 2327
St. Paul, MN 55155
P: (651) 296-4334
E: sen.carolyn.laine
@senate.mn

**Lang, Andrew (R, 17)***
95 University Avenue West
Minnesota Senate Building,
Room 3205
St. Paul, MN 55155
P: (651) 296-4918
E: sen.andrew.lang
@senate.mn

**Latz, Ron (DFL, 46)**
95 University Avenue West
Minnesota Senate Building,
Room 2215
St. Paul, MN 55155
P: (651) 297-8065
E: sen.ron.latz@senate.mn

**Limmer, Warren (R, 34)**
95 University Avenue West
Minnesota Senate Building,
Room 3221
St. Paul, MN 55155
P: (651) 296-2159
E: sen.warren.limmer
@senate.mn

**Little, Matt (D, 58)***
95 University Avenue West
Minnesota Senate Building,
Room 3411
St. Paul, MN 55155
P: (651) 296-5252
E: sen.matt.little
@senate.mn

**Lourey, Tony (DFL, 11)**
95 University Avenue West
Minnesota Senate Building,
Room 2211
St. Paul, MN 55155
P: (651) 296-0293
E: sen.tony.lourey
@senate.mn

**Marty, John (DFL, 66)**
95 University Avenue West
Minnesota Senate Building,
Room 2401
St. Paul, MN 55155
P: (651) 296-5645
E: sen.john.marty@senate.mn

**Mathews, Andrew (R, 15)***
95 University Avenue West
Minnesota Senate Building,
Room 3409
St. Paul, MN 55155
P: (651) 296-8075
E: sen.andrew.mathews
@senate.mn

**Miller, Jeremy R. (R, 28)**
95 University Avenue West
Minnesota Senate Building,
Room 3107
St. Paul, MN 55155
P: (651) 296-5649
E: sen.jeremy.miller
@senate.mn

**Nelson, Carla J. (R, 26)**
95 University Avenue West
Minnesota Senate Building,
Room 3231
St. Paul, MN 55155
P: (651) 296-4848
E: sen.carla.nelson
@senate.mn

**Newman, Scott J. (R, 18)**
95 University Avenue West
Minnesota Senate Building,
Room 3105
St. Paul, MN 55155
P: (651) 296-4131
E: sen.scott.newman
@senate.mn

**Newton, Jerry (DFL, 37)**
95 University Avenue West
Minnesota Senate Building,
Room 2411
St. Paul, MN 55155
P: (651) 296-2556
E: sen.jerry.newton
@senate.mn

**Osmek, David J. (R, 33)**
95 University Avenue West
Minnesota Senate Building,
Room 2107
St. Paul, MN 55155
P: (651) 296-1282
E: sen.david.osmek
@senate.mn

**Pappas, Sandra L. (DFL, 65)**
95 University Avenue West
Minnesota Senate Building,
Room 2205
St. Paul, MN 55155
P: (651) 296-1802
E: sen.sandra.pappas
@senate.mn

**Pratt, Eric R. (R, 55)**
95 University Avenue West
Minnesota Senate Building,
Room 3219
St. Paul, MN 55155
P: (651) 296-4123
E: sen.eric.pratt@senate.mn

**Relph, Jerry (R, 14)***
95 University Avenue West
Minnesota Senate Building,
Room 3211
St. Paul, MN 55155
P: (651) 296-6455
E: sen.jerry.relph
@senate.mn

**Rest, Ann H. (D, 45)**
95 University Avenue W
Minnesota Senate Building,
Room 2217
St. Paul, MN 55155
P: (651) 296-2889
E: sen.ann.rest@senate.mn

**Rosen, Julie A. (R, 23)**
95 University Avenue West
Minnesota Senate Building,
Room 3235
St. Paul, MN 55155
P: (651) 296-5713
E: sen.julie.rosen
@senate.mn

**Ruud, Carrie L. (R, 10)**
95 University Avenue West
Minnesota Senate Building,
Room 3233
St. Paul, MN 55155
P: (651) 296-4913
E: sen.carrie.ruud
@senate.mn

**Schoen, Dan (DFL, 54)**
95 University Avenue West
Minnesota Senate Building,
Room 2413
St. Paul, MN 55155
P: (651) 296-8060
E: sen.dan.schoen@senate.mn

**Senjem, David H. (R, 25)**
95 University Avenue West
Minnesota Senate Building,
Room 3401
St. Paul, MN 55155
P: (651) 296-3903
E: sen.david.senjem
@senate.mn

**Simonson, Erik (DFL, 7)**
95 University Avenue West
Minnesota Senate Building,
Room 2417
St. Paul, MN 55155
P: (651) 296-4188
E: sen.erik.simonson
@senate.mn

**Sparks, Dan (DFL, 27)**
95 University Avenue West
Minnesota Senate Building,
Room 2201
St. Paul, MN 55155
P: (651) 296-9248
E: sen.dan.sparks@senate.mn

**Tomassoni, David J.
(DFL, 6)**
95 University Avenue West
Minnesota Senate Building,
Room 2235
St. Paul, MN 55155
P: (651) 296-8017
E: sen.david.tomassoni
@senate.mn

**Torres Ray, Patricia
(DFL, 63)**
95 University Avenue West
Minnesota Senate Building,
Room 2225
St. Paul, MN 55155
P: (651) 296-4274
E: sen.patricia.torres.ray
@senate.mn

**Utke, Paul (R, 2)***
95 University Avenue West
Minnesota Senate Building,
Room 3403
St. Paul, MN 55155
P: (651) 296-9651
E: sen.paul.utke@senate.mn

**Weber, Bill (R, 22)**
95 University Avenue West
Minnesota Senate Building,
Room 2109
St. Paul, MN 55155
P: (651) 296-5650
E: sen.bill.weber@senate.mn

**Westrom, Torrey N. (R, 12)**
95 University Avenue West
Minnesota Senate Building,
Room 3201
St. Paul, MN 55155
P: (651) 296-3826
E: sen.torrey.westrom
@senate.mn

**Wiger, Charles W. (DFL, 43)**
95 University Avenue West
Minnesota Senate Building,
Room 2219
St. Paul, MN 55155
P: (651) 296-6820
E: sen.chuck.wiger
@senate.mn

**Wiklund, Melissa H. (DFL, 50)**
95 University Avenue West
Minnesota Senate Building, Room 2323
St. Paul, MN 55155
P: (651) 297-8061
E: sen.melissa.wiklund
@senate.mn

# House

## Speaker of the House

**Speaker Kurt Daudt (R)**
Speaker of the House
463 State Office Building
100 Martin Luther King Jr. Boulevard
St. Paul, MN 55155
P: (651) 296-5364
E: rep.kurt.daudt@house.mn

## Speaker Pro Tempore of the House

**Representative Tony Albright (R)**
House Speaker Pro Tempore
407 State Office Building
100 Martin Luther King Jr. Boulevard
St. Paul, MN 55155
P: (651) 296-5185
E: rep.tony.albright
@house.mn

## House Majority Leader

**Representative Joyce Peppin (R)**
House Majority Leader
459 State Office Building
100 Martin Luther King Jr. Boulevard
St. Paul, MN 55155
P: (651) 296-7806
E: rep.joyce.peppin
@house.mn

## House Minority Leader

**Representative Melissa Hortman (DFL)**
House Minority Leader
267 State Office Building
100 Martin Luther King Jr. Boulevard
St. Paul, MN 55155
P: (651) 296-4280
E: rep.melissa.hortman
@house.mn

## Clerk of the House

**Mr. Al Mathiowetz**
Chief Clerk of the House
211 State Capitol
100 Martin Luther King Jr. Boulevard
St. Paul, MN 55155
P: (651) 296-2314
E: Al.Mathiowetz@house.mn

## Members of the House

**Albright, Tony (R, 55B)**
407 State Office Building
100 Martin Luther King Jr. Boulevard
St. Paul, MN 55155
P: (651) 296-5185
E: rep.tony.albright
@house.mn

**Allen, Susan (DFL, 62B)**
229 State Office Building
100 Martin Luther King Jr. Boulevard
St. Paul, MN 55155
P: (651) 296-7152
E: rep.susan.allen@house.mn

**Anderson, Paul H. (R, 12B)**
369 State Office Building
100 Rev Dr Martin Luther King Jr Blvd
St. Paul, MN 55155
P: (651) 296-4317
E: rep.paul.anderson
@senate.mn

**Anderson, Paul H. (R, 12B)**
369 State Office Building
100 Rev Dr Martin Luther King Jr Blvd
St. Paul, MN 55155
P: (651) 296-4317
E: rep.paul.anderson
@senate.mn

**Anderson, Sarah (R, 44A)**
583 State Office Building
100 Martin Luther King Jr. Boulevard
St. Paul, MN 55155
P: (651) 296-5511
E: rep.sarah.anderson
@house.mn

**Anselmo, Dario (R, 49A)\***
579 State Office Building
100 Dr Rev Martin Luther King Jr. Blvd
St. Paul, MN 55155
P: (651) 296-4363
E: rep.dario.anselmo
@house.mn

**Applebaum, Jon (DFL, 44B)**
281 State Office Building
100 Rev. Dr. Martin Luther King Jr. Blvd
St. Paul, MN 55155
P: (651) 296-9934
E: rep.jon.applebaum
@house.mn

**Backer, Jeff (R, 12A)**
593 State Office Building
100 Rev. Dr. Martin Luther King Jr. Blvd
St. Paul, MN 55155
P: (651) 296-4929
E: rep.jeff.backer@house.mn

**Bahr, Calvin (R, 31B)\***
387 State Office Building
100 Rev Dr Martin Luther King Jr Blvd
St. Paul, MN 55155
P: (651) 296-2439
E: rep.cal.bahr@house.mn

**Baker, Dave (R, 17B)**
539 State Office Building
100 Rev. Dr. Martin Luther King Jr. Blvd
St. Paul, MN 55155
P: (651) 296-6206
E: rep.dave.baker@house.mn

**Barr, Regina (R, 52B)\***
553 State Office Building
100 Dr. Rev Martin Luther King
St. Paul, MN 55155
P: (651) 296-4192
E: rep.regina.barr@house.mn

**Becker-Finn, Jamie (D, 42B)\***
307 State Office Building
100 Rev Dr Martin Luther King
St. Paul, MN 55155
P: (651) 296-7153
E: rep.jamie.becker-finn
@house.mn

**Bennett, Peggy (R, 27A)**
507 State Office Building
100 Rev. Dr. Martin Luther King Jr. Blvd
St. Paul, MN 55155
P: (651) 296-8216
E: rep.peggy.bennett
@house.mn

**Bernardy, Connie (DFL, 41A)**
253 State Office Building
100 Martin Luther King Jr. Boulevard
St. Paul, MN 55155
P: (651) 296-5510
E: rep.connie.bernardy
@house.mn

**Bliss, Matt (R, 5A)\***
529 State Office Building
100 Rev Dr Martin Luther King Jr Blvd
St. Paul, MN 55155
P: (651) 296-5516
E: rep.matt.bliss@house.mn

**Bly, David (DFL, 20B)**
301 State Office Building
100 Martin Luther King Jr. Boulevard
St. Paul, MN 55155
P: (651) 296-0171
E: rep.david.bly@house.mn

**Carlson, Andrew (D, 50B)\***
211 State Office Building
100 Dr Rev Martin Luther King
St. Paul, MN 55155
P: (651) 296-4218
E: rep.andrew.carlson
@house.mn

**Carlson, Lyndon (DFL, 45A)**
283 State Office Building
100 Martin Luther King Jr. Boulevard
St. Paul, MN 55155
P: (651) 296-4255
E: rep.lyndon.carlson
@house.mn

**Christensen, Drew (R, 56A)**
575 State Office Building
100 Rev. Dr. Martin Luther King Jr. Blvd
St. Paul, MN 55155
P: (651) 296-4212
E: rep.drew.christensen
@house.mn

**Clark, Karen (DFL, 62A)**
273 State Office Building
100 Martin Luther King Jr. Boulevard
St. Paul, MN 55155
P: (651) 296-0294
E: rep.karen.clark@house.mn

# Minnesota

**Considine, Jack (DFL, 19B)**
323 State Office Building
100 Rev. Dr. Martin Luther
King Jr. Blvd
St. Paul, MN 55155
P: (651) 296-3248
E: rep.jack.considine
@house.mn

**Cornish, Tony (R, 23B)**
365 State Office Building
100 Martin Luther King Jr.
Boulevard
St. Paul, MN 55155
P: (651) 296-4240
E: rep.tony.cornish
@house.mn

**Daniels, Brian (R, 24B)**
551 State Office Building
100 Rev. Dr. Martin Luther
King Jr. Blvd
St. Paul, MN 55155
P: (651) 296-8237
E: rep.brian.daniels
@house.mn

**Daudt, Kurt (R, 31A)**
463 State Office Building
100 Martin Luther King Jr.
Boulevard
St. Paul, MN 55155
P: (651) 296-5364
E: rep.kurt.daudt@house.mn

**Davids, Greg (R, 28B)**
585 State Office Building
100 Martin Luther King Jr.
Boulevard
St. Paul, MN 55155
P: (651) 296-9278
E: rep.greg.davids@house.mn

**Davnie, Jim (DFL, 63A)**
393 State Office Building
100 Martin Luther King Jr.
Boulevard
St. Paul, MN 55155
P: (651) 296-0173
E: rep.jim.davnie@house.mn

**Dean, Matt (R, 38B)**
401 State Office Building
100 Martin Luther King Jr.
Boulevard
St. Paul, MN 55155
P: (651) 296-3018
E: rep.matt.dean@house.mn

**Dehn, Raymond (DFL, 59B)**
279 State Office Building
100 Martin Luther King Jr.
Boulevard
St. Paul, MN 55155
P: (651) 296-8659
E: rep.raymond.dehn
@house.mn

**Dettmer, Bob (R, 39A)**
565 State Office Building
100 Martin Luther King Jr.
Boulevard
St. Paul, MN 55155
P: (651) 296-4124
E: rep.bob.dettmer@house.mn

**Drazkowski, Steve (R, 21B)**
591 State Office Building
100 Martin Luther King Jr.
Boulevard
St. Paul, MN 55155
P: (651) 296-2273
E: rep.steve.drazkowski
@house.mn

**Ecklund, Rob (DFL, 3A)**
311 State Office Building
100 Rev. Dr. Martin Luther
King Jr. Blvd
St. Paul, MN 55155
P: (651) 296-2190
E: rep.rob.ecklund@house.mn

**Erickson, Sondra (R, 15A)**
479 State Office Building
100 Martin Luther King Jr.
Boulevard
St. Paul, MN 55155
P: (651) 296-6746
E: rep.sondra.erickson
@house.mn

**Fabian, Dan (R, 1A)**
359 State Office Building
100 Martin Luther King Jr.
Boulevard
St. Paul, MN 55155
P: (651) 296-9635
E: rep.dan.fabian@house.mn

**Fenton, Kelly (R, 53B)**
525 State Office Building
100 Rev. Dr. Martin Luther
King Jr. Blvd
St. Paul, MN 55155
P: (651) 296-1147
E: rep.kelly.fenton
@house.mn

**Fischer, Peter (DFL, 43A)**
201 State Office Building
100 Martin Luther King Jr.
Boulevard
St. Paul, MN 55155
P: (651) 296-5363
E: rep.peter.fischer
@house.mn

**Flanagan, Peggy (DFL, 46A)**
309 State Office Building
100 Rev. Dr. Martin Luther
King Jr. Blvd
St. Paul, MN 55155
P: (651) 296-7026
E: rep.peggy.flanagan
@house.mn

**Franke, Keith (R, 54A)***
567 State Office Building
100 Rev Dr Martin Luther King
Jr Blvd
St. Paul, MN 55155
P: (651) 296-4342
E: rep.keith.franke
@house.mn

**Franson, Mary (R, 8B)**
545 State Office Building
100 Martin Luther King Jr.
Boulevard
St. Paul, MN 55155
P: (651) 296-3201
E: rep.mary.franson
@house.mn

**Freiberg, Mike (DFL, 45B)**
239 State Office Building
100 Martin Luther King Jr.
Boulevard
St. Paul, MN 55155
P: (651) 296-4176
E: rep.mike.freiberg
@house.mn

**Garofalo, Patrick (R, 58B)**
485 State Office Building
100 Martin Luther King Jr.
Boulevard
St. Paul, MN 55155
P: (651) 296-1069
E: rep.pat.garofalo
@house.mn

**Green, Steve (R, 2B)**
413 State Office Building
100 Martin Luther King Jr.
Boulevard
St. Paul, MN 55155
P: (651) 296-9918
E: rep.steve.green@house.mn

**Grossell, Matthew (R, 2B)***
429 State Office Building
100 Martin Luther King Jr Blvd
St. Paul, MN 55155
P: (651) 296-4265
E: rep.matt.grossell
@house.mn

**Gruenhagen, Glenn (R, 18B)**
487 State Office Building
100 Martin Luther King Jr.
Boulevard
St. Paul, MN 55155
P: (651) 296-4229
E: rep.glenn.gruenhagen
@house.mn

**Gunther, Bob (R, 23A)**
563 State Office Building
100 Martin Luther King Jr.
Boulevard
St. Paul, MN 55155
P: (651) 296-3240
E: rep.bob.gunther@house.mn

**Haley, Barb (R, 21A)***
451 State Office Building
100 Rev Dr Martin Luther King
Jr Blvd
St. Paul, MN 55155
P: (651) 296-8635
E: rep.barb.haley@house.mn

**Halverson, Laurie
(DFL, 51B)**
233 State Office Building
100 Martin Luther King Jr.
Boulevard
St. Paul, MN 55155
P: (651) 296-4128
E: rep.laurie.halverson
@house.mn

**Hamilton, Rod (R, 22B)**
443 State Office Building
100 Martin Luther King Jr.
Boulevard
St. Paul, MN 55155
P: (651) 296-5373
E: rep.rod.hamilton
@house.mn

**Hansen, Rick (D, 52A)**
247 State Office Building
100 Martin Luther King Jr.
Boulevard
St. Paul, MN 55155
P: (651) 296-6828
E: rep.rick.hansen@house.mn

**Hausman, Alice (DFL, 66A)**
255 State Office Building
100 Martin Luther King Jr.
Boulevard
St. Paul, MN 55155
P: (651) 296-3824
E: rep.alice.hausman
@house.mn

**Heintzeman, Joshua (R, 10A)**
357 State Office Building
100 Rev. Dr. Martin Luther
King Jr. Blvd
St. Paul, MN 55155
P: (651) 296-4333
E: rep.josh.heintzeman
@house.mn

**Hertaus, Jerry (R, 33A)**
403 State Office Building
100 Martin Luther King Jr.
Boulevard
St. Paul, MN 55155
P: (651) 296-9188
E: rep.jerry.hertaus
@house.mn

**Hilstrom, Debra (DFL, 40B)**
245 State Office Building
100 Martin Luther King Jr.
Boulevard
St. Paul, MN 55155
P: (651) 296-3709
E: rep.debra.hilstrom
@house.mn

**Hoppe, Joe (R, 47B)**
543 State Office Building
100 Martin Luther King Jr.
Boulevard
St. Paul, MN 55155
P: (651) 296-5066
E: rep.joe.hoppe@house.mn

**Hornstein, Frank (DFL, 61A)**
243 State Office Building
100 Martin Luther King Jr.
Boulevard
St. Paul, MN 55155
P: (651) 296-9281
E: rep.frank.hornstein
@house.mn

**Hortman, Melissa (DFL, 36B)**
267 State Office Building
100 Martin Luther King Jr.
Boulevard
St. Paul, MN 55155
P: (651) 296-4280
E: rep.melissa.hortman
@house.mn

**Howe, Jeff (R, 13A)**
527 State Office Building
100 Martin Luther King Jr.
Boulevard
St. Paul, MN 55155
P: (651) 296-4373
E: rep.jeff.howe@house.mn

**Jessup, Randy (R, 42A)***
477 State Office Building
100 Rev Dr Martin Luther King
St. Paul, MN 55155
P: (651) 296-0141
E: rep.randy.jessup
@house.mn

**Johnson, Brian (R, 32A)**
421 State Office Building
100 Martin Luther King Jr.
Boulevard
St. Paul, MN 55155
P: (651) 296-4346
E: rep.brian.johnson
@house.mn

**Johnson, Clark (DFL, 19A)**
289 State Office Building
100 Martin Luther King Jr.
Boulevard
St. Paul, MN 55155
P: (651) 296-8634
E: rep.clark.johnson
@house.mn

**Johnson, Sheldon (DFL, 67B)**
259 State Office Building
100 Martin Luther King Jr.
Boulevard
St. Paul, MN 55155
P: (651) 296-4201
E: rep.sheldon.johnson
@house.mn

**Jurgens, Tony (R, 54B)***
523 State Office Building
100 Rev Dr Martin Luther King
Jr Blvd
St. Paul, MN 55155
P: (651) 296-3135
E: rep.tony.jurgens
@house.mn

**Kiel, Deb (R, 1B)**
537 State Office Building
100 Martin Luther King Jr.
Boulevard
St. Paul, MN 55155
P: (651) 293-5091
E: rep.deb.kiel@house.mn

**Knoblach, Jim (R, 14B)**
453 State Office Building
100 Rev.Dr. Martin Luther King
Jr. Blvd
St. Paul, MN 55155
P: (651) 296-6612
E: rep.jim.knoblach
@house.mn

**Koegel, Erin (D, 37A)***
213 State Office Building
100 Rev Dr Martin Luther King
Jr Blvd
St. Paul, MN 55155
P: (651) 296-5369
E: rep.erin.koegel@house.mn

**Koznick, Jon (R, 58A)**
367 State Office Building
100 Rev. Dr. Martin Luther
King Jr. Blvd
St. Paul, MN 55155
P: (651) 296-6926
E: rep.jon.koznick@house.mn

**Kresha, Ron (R, 9B)**
531 State Office Building
100 Martin Luther King Jr.
Boulevard
St. Paul, MN 55155
P: (651) 296-4247
E: rep.ron.kresha@house.mn

**Kunesh-Podein, Mary
(D, 41B)***
303 State Office Building
100 Rev Dr Martin Luther King
Jr Blvd
St. Paul, MN 55155
P: (651) 296-4331
E: rep.mary.kuneshpodein
@house.mn

**Layman, Sandy (R, 5B)***
533 State Office Building
100 Rev Dr Martin Luther King
Jr Blvd
St. Paul, MN 55155
P: (651) 296-4936
E: rep.sandy.layman
@house.mn

**Lee, Fue (D, 59A)***
223 State Office Building
100 Rev Dr Martin Luther King
Jr Blvd
St. Paul, MN 55155
P: (651) 296-4262
E: rep.fue.lee@house.mn

**Lesch, John (DFL, 66B)**
217 State Office Building
100 Martin Luther King Jr.
Boulevard
St. Paul, MN 55155
P: (651) 296-4224
E: rep.john.lesch@house.mn

**Liebling, Tina (DFL, 26A)**
237 State Office Building
100 Martin Luther King Jr.
Boulevard
St. Paul, MN 55155
P: (651) 296-0573
E: rep.tina.liebling
@house.mn

**Lien, Ben (DFL, 4A)**
241 State Office Building
100 Martin Luther King Jr.
Boulevard
St. Paul, MN 55155
P: (651) 296-5515
E: rep.ben.lien@house.mn

**Lillie, Leon (DFL, 43B)**
277 State Office Building
100 Martin Luther King Jr.
Boulevard
St. Paul, MN 55155
P: (651) 296-1188
E: rep.leon.lillie@house.mn

**Loeffler, Diane (DFL, 60A)**
349 State Office Building
100 Martin Luther King Jr.
Boulevard
St. Paul, MN 55155
P: (651) 296-4219
E: rep.diane.loeffler
@house.mn

**Lohmer, Kathy (R, 39B)**
501 State Office Building
100 Martin Luther King Jr.
Boulevard
St. Paul, MN 55155
P: (651) 296-4244
E: rep.kathy.lohmer
@house.mn

**Loon, Jenifer (R, 48B)**
449 State Office Building
100 Martin Luther King Jr.
Boulevard
St. Paul, MN 55155
P: (651) 296-7449
E: rep.jenifer.loon
@house.mn

**Loonan, Bob (R, 55A)**
597 State Office Building
100 Rev. Dr. Martin Luther
King Jr. Blvd
St. Paul, MN 55155
P: (651) 296-8872
E: rep.bob.loonan@house.mn

**Lucero, Eric (R, 30B)**
515 State Office Building
100 Rev. Dr. Martin Luther
King Jr. Blvd
St. Paul, MN 55155
P: (651) 296-1534
E: rep.eric.lucero@house.mn

**Lueck, Dale K. (R, 10B)**
423 State Office Building
100 Rev. Dr. Martin Luther
King Jr. Blvd
St. Paul, MN 55155
P: (651) 296-2365
E: rep.dale.lueck@house.mn

**Mahoney, Tim (DFL, 67A)**
345 State Office Building
100 Martin Luther King Jr.
Boulevard
St. Paul, MN 55155
P: (651) 296-4277
E: rep.tim.mahoney@house.mn

**Mariani, Carlos (DFL, 65B)**
203 State Office Building
100 Martin Luther King Jr.
Boulevard
St. Paul, MN 55155
P: (651) 296-9714
E: rep.carlos.mariani
@house.mn

**Marquart, Paul (DFL, 4B)**
261 State Office Building
100 Martin Luther King Jr.
Boulevard
St. Paul, MN 55155
P: (651) 296-6829
E: rep.paul.marquart
@house.mn

**Masin, Sandra (DFL, 51A)**
335 State Office Building
100 Martin Luther King Jr.
Boulevard
St. Paul, MN 55155
P: (651) 296-3533
E: rep.sandra.masin
@house.mn

# Minnesota

**Maye Quade, Erin (D, 57A)***
389 State Office Building
100 Rev Dr Martin Luther King
Jr. Blvd
St. Paul, MN 55155
P: (651) 296-5506
E: rep.erin.mayequade
@house.mn

**McDonald, Joe (R, 29A)**
503 State Office Building
100 Martin Luther King Jr.
Boulevard
St. Paul, MN 55155
P: (651) 296-4336
E: rep.joe.mcdonald
@house.mn

**Metsa, Jason (DFL, 6B)**
313 State Office Building
100 Martin Luther King Jr.
Boulevard
St. Paul, MN 55155
P: (651) 296-0170
E: rep.jason.metsa@house.mn

**Miller, Tim (R, 17A)**
415 State Office Building
100 Rev. Dr. Martin Luther
King Jr. Blvd
St. Paul, MN 55155
P: (651) 296-4228
E: rep.tim.miller@house.mn

**Moran, Rena (DFL, 65A)**
329 State Office Building
100 Martin Luther King Jr.
Boulevard
St. Paul, MN 55155
P: (651) 296-5158
E: rep.rena.moran@house.mn

**Murphy, Erin (DFL, 64A)**
331 State Office Building
100 Martin Luther King Jr,
Boulevard
St. Paul, MN 55155
P: (651) 296-8799
E: rep.erin.murphy@house.mn

**Murphy, Mary (DFL, 3B)**
343 State Office Building
100 Martin Luther King Jr.
Boulevard
St. Paul, MN 55155
P: (651) 296-2676
E: rep.mary.murphy@house.mn

**Nash, Jim (R, 47A)**
557 State Office Building
100 Rev. Dr. Martin Luther
King Jr. Blvd
St. Paul, MN 55155
P: (651) 296-4282
E: rep.jim.nash@house.mn

**Nelson, Michael V.
(DFL, 40A)**
351 State Office Building
100 Martin Luther King Jr.
Boulevard
St. Paul, MN 55155
P: (651) 296-3751
E: rep.michael.nelson
@house.mn

**Neu, Anne (R, 32B)***
327 State Office Building
100 Rev Dr Martin Luther King
Blvd
St. Paul, MN 55155
P: (651) 296-5377
E: rep.anne.neu@house.mn

**Newberger, Jim (R, 15B)**
371 State Office Building
100 Martin Luther King Jr.
Boulevard
St. Paul, MN 55155
P: (651) 296-2451
E: rep.jim.newberger
@house.mn

**Nornes, Bud (R, 8A)**
471 State Office Building
100 Martin Luther King Jr.
Boulevard
St. Paul, MN 55155
P: (651) 296-4946
E: rep.bud.nornes@house.mn

**O'Driscoll, Tim (R, 13B)**
559 State Office Building
100 Martin Luther King Jr.
Boulevard
St. Paul, MN 55155
P: (651) 296-7808
E: rep.tim.odriscoll
@house.mn

**Olson, Liz (D, 7B)***
221 State Office Building
100 Rev Dr Martin Luther King
Jr Blvd
St. Paul, MN 55155
P: (651) 296-4246
E: rep.liz.olson@house.mn

**Omar, Ilhan (D, 60B)***
327 State Office Building
100 Rev Dr Martin Luther KIng
St. Paul, MN 55155
P: (651) 296-4257
E: rep.ilhan.omar@house.mn

**O'Neill, Marion (R, 29B)**
549 State Office Building
100 Martin Luther King Jr.
Boulevard
St. Paul, MN 55155
P: (651) 296-5063
E: rep.marion.oneill
@house.mn

**Pelowski Jr., Gene
(DFL, 28A)**
295 State Office Building
100 Martin Luther King Jr.
Boulevard
St. Paul, MN 55155
P: (651) 296-8637
E: rep.gene.pelowski
@house.mn

**Peppin, Joyce (R, 34A)**
459 State Office Building
100 Martin Luther King Jr.
Boulevard
St. Paul, MN 55155
P: (651) 296-7806
E: rep.joyce.peppin
@house.mn

**Petersburg, John (R, 24A)**
577 State Office Building
100 Martin Luther King Jr.
Boulevard
St. Paul, MN 55155
P: (651) 296-5368
E: rep.john.petersburg
@house.mn

**Peterson, Roz (R, 56B)**
521 State Office Building
100 Rev. Dr. Martin Luther
King Jr. Blvd
St. Paul, MN 55155
P: (651) 296-5387
E: rep.roz.peterson
@house.mn

**Pierson, Nels T. (R, 26B)**
379 State Office Building
100 Rev. Dr. Martin Luther
King Jr. Blvd
St. Paul, MN 55155
P: (651) 296-4378
E: rep.nels.pierson
@house.mn

**Pinto, Dave (DFL, 64B)**
321 State Office Building
100 Rev. Dr. Martin Luther
King Jr. Blvd
St. Paul, MN 55155
P: (651) 296-4199
E: rep.dave.pinto@house.mn

**Poppe, Jeanne (DFL, 27B)**
291 State Office Building
100 Martin Luther King Jr.
Boulevard
St. Paul, MN 55155
P: (651) 296-4193
E: rep.jeanne.poppe
@house.mn

**Poston, John (R, 9A)***
517 State Office Building
100 Rev Dr Martin Luther King
Jr Blvd
St. Paul, MN 55155
P: (651) 296-4293
E: rep.john.poston@house.mn

**Pryor, Laurie (D, 48A)***
227 State Office Building
100 Rev Dr Martin Luther King
St. Paul, MN 55155
P: (651) 296-3964
E: rep.laurie.pryor
@house.mn

**Pugh, Cindy (R, 33B)**
411 State Office Building
100 Martin Luther King Jr.
Boulevard
St. Paul, MN 55155
P: (651) 296-4315
E: rep.cindy.pugh@house.mn

**Quam, Duane (R, 25A)**
571 State Office Building
100 Martin Luther King Jr.
Boulevard
St. Paul, MN 55155
P: (651) 296-9236
E: rep.duane.quam@house.mn

**Rarick, Jason (R, 11B)**
431 State Office Building
100 Rev. Dr. Martin Luther
King Jr. Blvd
St. Paul, MN 55155
P: (651) 296-0518
E: rep.jason.rarick
@house.mn

**Rosenthal, Paul (DFL, 49B)**
209 State Office Building
100 Martin Luther King Jr.
Boulevard
St. Paul, MN 55155
P: (651) 296-7803
E: rep.paul.rosenthal
@house.mn

**Runbeck, Linda (R, 38A)**
417 State Office Building
100 Martin Luther King Jr.
Boulevard
St. Paul, MN 55155
P: (651) 296-2907
E: rep.linda.runbeck
@house.mn

**Sandstede, Julie (D, 6A)***
337 State Office Building
100 Dr Rev Martin Luther King
Jr Blvd
St. Paul, MN 55155
P: (651) 296-0172
E: rep.julie.sandstede
@house.mn

**Sauke, Duane (D, 25B)***
287 State Office Building
100 Rev Dr Martin Luther King
Jr Blvd
St. Paul, MN 55155
P: (651) 296-9249
E: rep.duane.sauke@house.mn

**Schomacker, Joe (R, 22A)**
509 State Office Building
100 Martin Luther King Jr.
Boulevard
St. Paul, MN 55155
P: (651) 296-5505
E: rep.joe.schomacker
@house.mn

**Schultz, Jennifer (DFL, 7A)**
215 State Office Building
100 Rev. Dr. Martin Luther
King Jr. Blvd
St. Paul, MN 55155
P: (651) 296-2228
E: rep.jennifer.schultz
@house.mn

**Scott, Peggy (R, 35B)**
437 State Office Building
100 Martin Luther King Jr.
Boulevard
St. Paul, MN 55155
P: (651) 296-4231
E: rep.peggy.scott@house.mn

**Slocum, Linda (DFL, 50A)**
207 State Office Building
100 Martin Luther King Jr.
Boulevard
St. Paul, MN 55155
P: (651) 296-7158
E: rep.linda.slocum
@house.mn

**Smith, Dennis (R, 34B)**
375 State Office Building
100 Rev. Dr. Martin Luther
King Jr. Blvd
St. Paul, MN 55155
P: (651) 296-5502
E: rep.dennis.smith
@house.mn

**Sundin, Mike (DFL, 11A)**
315 State Office Building
100 Martin Luther King Jr.
Boulevard
St. Paul, MN 55155
P: (651) 296-4308
E: rep.mike.sundin@house.mn

**Swedzinski, Chris (R, 16A)**
409 State Office Building
100 Martin Luther King Jr.
Boulevard
St. Paul, MN 55155
P: (651) 296-5374
E: rep.chris.swedzinski
@house.mn

**Theis, Tama (R, 14A)**
445 State Office Building
100 Martin Luther King Jr.
Boulevard
St. Paul, MN 55155
P: (651) 296-6316
E: rep.tama.theis@house.mn

**Thissen, Paul (DFL, 61B)**
317 State Office Bldg
100 Martin Luther King Jr. Blvd
Saint Paul, MN 55155
P: (651) 296-5375
F: (651) 296-3869
E: rep.paul.thissen
@house.mn

**Torkelson, Paul (R, 16B)**
381 State Office Building
100 Martin Luther King Jr.
Boulevard
St. Paul, MN 55155
P: (651) 296-9303
E: rep.paul.torkelson
@house.mn

**Uglem, Mark (R, 36A)**
569 State Office Building
100 Martin Luther King Jr.
Boulevard
St. Paul, MN 55155
P: (651) 296-5513
E: rep.mark.uglem@house.mn

**Urdahl, Dean (R, 18A)**
473 State Office Building
100 Martin Luther King Jr.
Boulevard
St. Paul, MN 55155
P: (651) 296-4344
E: rep.dean.urdahl@house.mn

**Vogel, Bob (R, 20A)**
581 State Office Building
100 Rev. Dr. Martin Luther
King Jr. Blvd
St. Paul, MN 55155
P: (651) 296-7065
E: rep.bob.vogel@house.mn

**Wagenius, Jean (DFL, 63B)**
251 State Office Building
100 Martin Luther King Jr.
Boulevard
St. Paul, MN 55155
P: (651) 296-4200
E: rep.jean.wagenius
@house.mn

**Ward, JoAnn (DFL, 53A)**
231 State Office Building
100 Martin Luther King Jr.
Boulevard
St. Paul, MN 55155
P: (651) 296-7807
E: rep.joann.ward@house.mn

**West, Nolan (R, 37B)***
377 State Office Building
100 Rev Dr Martin Luther King
St. Paul, MN 55155
P: (651) 296-4226
E: rep.nolan.west@house.mn

**Whelan, Abigail (R, 35A)**
439 State Office Building
100 Rev. Dr. Martin Luther
King Jr. Blvd
St. Paul, MN 55155
P: (651) 296-1729
E: rep.abigail.whelan
@house.mn

**Wills, Anna (R, 57B)**
491 State Office Building
100 Martin Luther King Jr.
Boulevard
St. Paul, MN 55155
P: (651) 296-4306
E: rep.anna.wills@house.mn

**Youakim, Cheryl (DFL, 46B)**
225 State Office Building
100 Rev. Dr. Martin Luther
King Jr. Blvd
St. Paul, MN 55155
P: (651) 296-9889
E: rep.cheryl.youakim
@house.mn

**Zerwas, Nick (R, 30A)**
433 State Office Building
100 Martin Luther King Jr.
Boulevard
St. Paul, MN 55155
P: (651) 296-4237
E: rep.nick.zerwas@house.mn

# Mississippi

## Executive

### Governor

**The Honorable Phil Bryant (R)**
Governor
P.O. Box 139
Jackson, MS 39205
P: (601) 359-3150
F: (601) 359-3741
E: governor
@governor.state.ms.us

### Lieutenant Governor

**The Honorable Tate Reeves (R)**
Lieutenant Governor
New Capitol, Room 315
P.O. Box 1018
Jackson, MS 39215
P: (601) 359-3200
F: (601) 359-2001
E: ltgov@senate.ms.gov

### Commissioner of Agriculture & Commerce

**The Honorable Cindy Hyde-Smith (R)**
Commissioner
121 North Jefferson Street
Jackson, MS 39201
P: (601) 359-1100
F: (601) 354-7710

### Attorney General

**The Honorable Jim Hood (D)**
Attorney General
Department of Justice
P.O. Box 220
Jackson, MS 39205
P: (601) 359-3680
E: msag05@ago.state.ms.us

### Auditor

**The Honorable Stacey E. Pickering (R)**
State Auditor
Woolfolk Building, Suite 801
501 North West Street, P.O. Box 956
Jackson, MS 39205
P: (601) 576-2641
F: (601) 576-2650
E: stacey.pickering
@osa.ms.gov

### Commissioner of Insurance

**The Honorable Mike Chaney (R)**
Commissioner
1001 Woolfolk State Office Building
501 North West Street, P.O. Box 79
Jackson, MS 39205
P: (601) 359-3569
F: (601) 359-2474
E: mike.chaney
@mid.state.ms.us

### Secretary of State

**The Honorable C. Delbert Hosemann Jr. (R)**
Secretary of State
125 South Congress Street
Jackson, MS 39201
P: (601) 359-1350
F: (601) 359-6700
E: delbert.hosemann
@sos.ms.gov

### Treasurer

**The Honorable Lynn Fitch (R)**
State Treasurer
P.O. Box 138
Jackson, MS 39205
P: (601) 359-3600
F: (601) 576-4495

## Judiciary

### Supreme Court (PE)

**Ms. Muriel B. Ellis**
Clerk
450 High Street
P.O. Box 117
Jackson, MS 39201
P: (601) 359-3694
F: (601) 359-2407
E: sctclerk
@mssc.state.ms.us

**The Honorable William L. Waller Jr.**
Chief Justice
**The Honorable Dawn H. Beam**
**The Honorable Robert P. Chamberlin (R)**
**The Honorable Josiah D. Coleman**
**The Honorable Jess H. Dickinson**
**The Honorable Leslie D. King**
**The Honorable James W. Kitchens**
**The Honorable James D. Maxwell II**

**The Honorable Michael K. Randolph**

## Legislative Senate

### Senate President

**The Honorable Tate Reeves (R)**
Lieutenant Governor
New Capitol, Room 315
P.O. Box 1018
Jackson, MS 39215
P: (601) 359-3200
F: (601) 359-2001
E: ltgov@senate.ms.gov

### President Pro Tempore of the Senate

**Senator Terry C. Burton (R)**
President Pro Tempore
New Capitol, Room 215 B
P.O. Box 1018
Jackson, MS 39215
P: (601) 359-3234
F: (601) 359-5345
E: tburton@senate.ms.gov

### Secretary of the Senate

**Ms. Liz Welch**
Secretary of the Senate
New Capitol, Room 308
P.O. Box 1018
Jackson, MS 39215
P: (601) 359-3202
F: (601) 359-3935

### Members of the Senate

**Barnett, Juan (D, 34)**
New Capitol, Room 407
P.O. Box 1018
Jackson, MS 39215
E: jbarnett@senate.ms.gov

**Blackmon, Barbara (D, 21)**
New Capitol, Room 213-F
P.O. Box 1018
Jackson, MS 39215
P: (601) 359-3237
E: bblackmon@senate.ms.gov

**Blackwell, Kevin (R, 19)**
New Capitol, Room 212-B
P.O. Box 1018
Jackson, MS 39215
P: (601) 359-3234
E: kblackwell@senate.ms.gov

**Blount, David (D, 29)**
New Capitol, Room 405-D
P.O. Box 1018
Jackson, MS 39215
P: (601) 359-3232
F: (601) 359-5957
E: dblount@senate.ms.gov

**Branning, Jenifer B. (R, 18)**
New Capitol, Room 215
P.O. Box 1018
Jackson, MS 39215
P: (601) 359-3246
E: jbranning@senate.ms.gov

**Browning, Nickey (R, 3)**
New Capitol, Room 213 C
P.O. Box 1018
Jackson, MS 39215
P: (601) 359-3252
F: (601) 359-3063
E: nbrowning@senate.ms.gov

**Bryan, Hob (D, 7)**
New Capitol, Room 409 A
P.O. Box 1018
Jackson, MS 39215
P: (601) 359-3237
F: (601) 359-2879
E: hbryan@senate.ms.gov

**Burton, Terry C. (R, 31)**
New Capitol, Room 215 B
P.O. Box 1018
Jackson, MS 39215
P: (601) 359-3234
F: (601) 359-5345
E: tburton@senate.ms.gov

**Butler, Albert (D, 36)**
New Capitol, Room 213
P. O. Box 1018
Jackson, MS 39215
P: (601) 359-3232
F: (601) 359-5957
E: abutler@senate.ms.gov

**Carmichael, Videt (R, 33)**
New Capitol, Room 213 A
P.O. Box 1018
Jackson, MS 39215
P: (601) 359-3244
F: (601) 359-9210
E: vcarmichael
@senate.ms.gov

**Caughman, Chris (R, 35)**
New Capitol, Room 405
P.O. Box 1018
Jackson, MS 39215
P: (601) 359-3244
E: ccaughman@senate.ms.gov

**Chassaniol, Lydia (R, 14)**
New Capitol, Room 212 A
P.O. Box 1018
Jackson, MS 39215
P: (601) 359-3246
F: (601) 359-3063
E: lchassaniol
@senate.ms.gov

**Clarke, Eugene (R, 22)**
New Capitol, Room 214 D
P.O. Box 1018
Jackson, MS 39215
P: (601) 359-3250
F: (601) 359-5110
E: bclarke@senate.ms.gov

**Dawkins, Deborah Jeanne (D, 48)**
New Capitol, Room 405B
P.O. Box 1018
Jackson, MS 39215
P: (601) 359-3237
F: (601) 359-2879
E: ddawkins@senate.ms.gov

**Dearing, Bob M. (D, 37)**
New Capitol, Room 405C
P.O. Box 1018
Jackson, MS 39215
P: (601) 359-3244
F: (601) 359-9210
E: bdearing@senate.ms.gov

**DeBar, Dennis (R, 43)**
New Capitol, Room 407
P.O. Box 1018
Jackson, MS 39215
P: (601) 359-3221
E: ddebar@senate.ms.gov

**Doty, Sally (R, 39)**
New Capitol, Room 404
P.O. Box 1018
Jackson, MS 39215
P: (601) 359-2395
F: (601) 359-2879
E: sdoty@senate.ms.gov

**Fillingane, Joey (R, 41)**
New Capitol, Room 215 C
P.O. Box 1018
Jackson, MS 39215
P: (601) 359-3246
F: (601) 359-3063
E: jfillingane
@senate.ms.gov

**Frazier, Hillman (D, 27)**
New Capitol, Room 117 A
P.O. Box 1018
Jackson, MS 39215
P: (601) 359-3246
F: (601) 359-3063
E: hfrazier@senate.ms.gov

**Gollott, Tommy A. (R, 50)**
New Capitol, Room 408
P.O. Box 1018
Jackson, MS 39215
P: (601) 359-2886
F: (601) 359-2889
E: tgollott@senate.ms.gov

**Harkins, Josh (R, 20)**
New Capitol, Room 215
P.O. Box 1018
Jackson, MS 39215
P: (601) 359-2886
F: (601) 359-2889
E: jharkins@senate.ms.gov

**Hill, Angela Burks (R, 40)**
New Capitol, Room 408
P.O. Box 1018
Jackson, MS 39215
P: (601) 359-2886
F: (601) 359-2889
E: ahill@senate.ms.gov

**Hopson III, W. Briggs (R, 23)**
New Capitol, Room 409 B
P.O. Box 1018
Jackson, MS 39215
P: (601) 359-3237
F: (601) 359-2879
E: bhopson@senate.ms.gov

**Horhn, John (D, 26)**
New Capitol, Room 212 B
P.O. Box 1018
Jackson, MS 39215
P: (601) 359-3237
F: (601) 359-2879
E: jhorhn@senate.ms.gov

**Hudson, Billy (R, 45)**
New Capitol, Room 404
P.O. Box 1018
Jackson, MS 39215
P: (601) 359-2395
F: (601) 359-3938
E: bhudson@senate.ms.gov

**Jackson, Gary (R, 15)**
New Capitol, Room 212 C
P.O. Box 1018
Jackson, MS 39215
P: (601) 359-3234
F: (601) 359-5345
E: gjackson@senate.ms.gov

**Jackson, Robert L. (D, 11)**
New Capitol, Room 404 D
P.O. Box 1018
Jackson, MS 39215
P: (601) 359-3221
F: (601) 359-2166
E: rjackson@senate.ms.gov

**Jackson II, Sampson (D, 32)**
New Capitol, Room 407
P.O. Box 1018
Jackson, MS 39215
P: (601) 359-2886
F: (601) 359-2889
E: sjackson@senate.ms.gov

**Jolly, Russell (D, 8)**
New Capitol, Room 408
P.O. Box 1018
Jackson, MS 39215
P: (601) 359-2886
F: (601) 359-2889
E: rjolly@senate.ms.gov

**Jordan, David (D, 24)**
New Capitol, Room 405 A
P.O. Box 1018
Jackson, MS 39215
P: (601) 359-3244
F: (601) 359-9210
E: djordan@senate.ms.gov

**Kirby, Dean (R, 30)**
New Capitol, Room 212 D
P.O. Box 1018
Jackson, MS 39215
P: (601) 359-3234
F: (601) 359-5345
E: dkirby@senate.ms.gov

**Massey, Chris (R, 1)**
New Capitol, Room 214B
P.O. Box 1018
Jackson, MS 39215
P: (601) 359-2886
F: (601) 359-2889
E: cmassey@senate.ms.gov

**McDaniel, Chris (R, 42)**
New Capitol, Room 404
P.O. Box 1018
Jackson, MS 39215
P: (601) 359-2395
F: (601) 359-3935
E: cmcdaniel@senate.ms.gov

**McMahan, Chad (R, 6)**
New Capitol, Room 405
P.O. Box 1018
Jackson, MS 39215
P: (601) 359-3244
F: (601) 359-9210
E: cmcmahan@senate.ms.gov

**Michel, J. Walter (R, 25)**
New Capitol, Room 407
P.O. Box 1018
Jackson, MS 39215
P: (601) 359-3221
F: (601) 359-2166
E: wmichel@senate.ms.gov

**Moran, Philip (R, 46)**
New Capitol, Room 214B
P.O. Box 1018
Jackson, MS 39215
P: (601) 359-3221
F: (601) 359-2166
E: pmoran@senate.ms.gov

**Norwood, Sollie B. (D, 28)**
New Capitol, Room 407
P. O. Box 1018
Jackson, MS 39215
P: (601) 359-3221
F: (601) 359-2166
E: snorwood@senate.ms.gov

**Parker, David (R, 2)**
New Capitol, Room 408
P.O. Box 1018
Jackson, MS 39215
P: (601) 359-2886
F: (601) 359-2889
E: dparker@senate.ms.gov

**Parks, Rita Potts (R, 4)**
New Capitol, Room 213
P.O. Box 1018
Jackson, MS 39215
P: (601) 359-3252
F: (601) 359-5957
E: rparks@senate.ms.gov

**Polk, John A. (R, 44)**
New Capitol, Room 404C
P.O. Box 1018
Jackson, MS 39215
P: (601) 359-3246
F: (601) 359-3063
E: jpolk@senate.ms.gov

**Seymour, Joseph M. (R, 47)**
New Capitol, Room 408
P.O. Box 1018
Jackson, MS 39215
P: (601) 359-2886
F: (601) 359-2889
E: jseymour@senate.ms.gov

**Simmons, Derrick T. (D, 12)**
New Capitol, Room 407
P.O. Box 1018
Jackson, MS 39215
P: (601) 359-3221
F: (601) 359-2166
E: dsimmons@senate.ms.gov

**Simmons, Willie (D, 13)**
New Capitol, Room 410
P.O. Box 1018
Jackson, MS 39215
P: (601) 359-3237
F: (601) 359-2879
E: wsimmons@senate.ms.gov

# Mississippi

**Stone, Bill (D, 10)**
New Capitol, Room 209
P.O. Box 1018
Jackson, MS 39215
P: (601) 359-3221
F: (601) 359-2166
E: bstone@senate.ms.gov

**Tindell, Sean J. (R, 49)**
New Capitol, Room 409B
P.O. Box 1018
Jackson, MS 39215
P: (601) 359-2395
F: (601) 359-3935
E: stindell@senate.ms.gov

**Tollison, Gray (R, 9)**
New Capitol, Room 404 A
P.O. Box 1018
Jackson, MS 39215
P: (601) 359-2395
F: (601) 359-3935
E: gtollison@senate.ms.gov

**Turner, Angela (D, 16)**
New Capitol, Room 409
P.O. Box 1018
Jackson, MS 39215
P: (601) 359-3237
F: (601) 359-2879
E: aturner@senate.ms.gov

**Watson, Michael (R, 51)**
New Capitol, Room 404
P.O. Box 1018
Jackson, MS 39215
P: (601) 359-2395
F: (601) 359-3935
E: mwatson@senate.ms.gov

**Wiggins, Brice (R, 52)**
New Capitol, Room 404B
P.O. Box 1018
Jackson, MS 39215
P: (601) 359-3232
F: (601) 359-5957
E: bwiggins@senate.ms.gov

**Wilemon Jr., J.P. (D, 5)**
New Capitol, Room 213B
P.O. Box 1018
Jackson, MS 39215
P: (601) 359-3232
F: (601) 359-5957
E: jwilemon@senate.ms.gov

**Witherspoon, Tammie (D, 38)**
New Capitol, Room 407
P.O. Box 1018
Jackson, MS 39215
P: (601) 359-3221
F: (601) 359-2166
E: twitherspoon
   @senate.ms.gov

**Younger, Charles (R, 17)**
New Capitol, Room 215
P.O. Box 1018
Jackson, MS 39215
P: (601) 359-2395
F: (601) 359-3938
E: Cyounger@senate.ms.gov

# House

## Speaker of the House

**Representative Philip Gunn (R)**
House Speaker
New Capitol, Room 306
P.O. Box 1018
Jackson, MS 39215
P: (601) 359-3300

## Speaker Pro Tempore of the House

**Representative Greg Snowden (R)**
House Speaker Pro Tempore
New Capitol, Room 302
P.O. Box 1018
Jackson, MS 39215
P: (601) 359-3304
E: gsnowden@house.ms.gov

## Clerk of the House

**Mr. Andrew Ketchings**
Clerk of the House
305 New Capitol Building
P.O. Box 1018
Jackson, MS 39215
P: (601) 359-3360
E: aketchings@house.ms.gov

## Members of the House

**Aguirre, Shane (R, 17)**
New Capitol, 100-C
P.O. Box 1018
Jackson, MS 39215
P: (601) 359-3374
E: saguirre@house.ms.gov

**Anderson, Jeramey D. (D, 110)**
New Capitol, Room 400-F
P.O. Box 1018
Jackson, MS 39215
P: (601) 359-2438
E: janderson@house.ms.gov

**Arnold, William Tracy (R, 3)**
New Capitol, Room 400-E
P.O. Box 1018
Jackson, MS 39215
P: (601) 359-2438
E: warnold@house.ms.gov

**Bailey, Willie L. (D, 49)**
New Capitol, Room 100-C
P.O. Box 1018
Jackson, MS 39215
P: (601) 359-9311
E: wbailey@house.ms.gov

**Bain, Nick (D, 2)**
New Capitol, Room 400-F
P.O. Box 1018
Jackson, MS 39215
P: (601) 359-3338
E: nbain@house.ms.gov

**Baker, Mark (R, 74)**
New Capitol, Room 112-A
P.O. Box 1018
Jackson, MS 39215
P: (601) 359-3388
E: mbaker@house.ms.gov

**Banks, Earle S. (D, 67)**
New Capitol, Room 100-C
P.O. Box 1018
Jackson, MS 39215
P: (601) 359-9392
E: ebanksjax@aol.com

**Baria, David (D, 122)**
New Capitol, Room 201
P.O. Box 1018
Jackson, MS 39215
P: (601) 359-3133
E: dbaria@house.ms.gov

**Barker, Toby (R, 102)**
New Capitol, Room 100
P.O. Box 1018
Jackson, MS 39215
P: (601) 359-3362
E: tbarker@house.ms.gov

**Barnett, Shane (R, 86)**
New Capitol, Room 400-F
P.O. Box 1018
Jackson, MS 39215
P: (601) 359-2426
E: sbarnett@house.ms.gov

**Barton, Manly (R, 109)**
New Capitol, Room BSMNT
P.O. Box 1018
Jackson, MS 39215
P: (601) 359-3354
E: mbarton@house.ms.gov

**Beckett, Charles Jim (R, 23)**
New Capitol, Room 205-C
P.O. Box 1018
Jackson, MS 39215
P: (601) 359-3335
E: jbeckett@house.ms.gov

**Bell, Christopher (D, 65)**
New Capitol, Room 400-F
P.O. Box 1018
Jackson, MS 39215
P: (601) 359-2461
E: cbell@house.ms.gov

**Bell, Donnie (R, 21)**
New Capitol, Room 400-B
P.O. Box 1018
Jackson, MS 39215
P: (601) 359-3396
E: dbell@house.ms.gov

**Bennett, Richard (R, 120)**
New Capitol, Room 201M-3
P.O. Box 1018
Jackson, MS 39215
P: (601) 359-2860
E: rbennett@house.ms.gov

**Blackmon Jr., Edward (D, 57)**
New Capitol, Room 400-H
P.O. Box 1018
Jackson, MS 39215
P: (601) 359-3371
E: eblackmon@house.ms.gov

**Bomgar, Joel (R, 58)**
New Capitol, Room 400-F
P.O. Box 1018
Jackson, MS 39215
P: (601) 359-9485
E: jbomgar@house.ms.gov

**Bounds, C. Scott (R, 44)**
New Capitol, Room 115-B
P.O. Box 1018
Jackson, MS 39215
P: (601) 359-3334
E: sbounds@house.ms.gov

**Boyd, Randy P. (R, 19)**
New Capitol, Room 400-F
P.O. Box 1018
Jackson, MS 39215
P: (601) 359-3305
E: rboyd@house.ms.gov

**Brown, Chris (R, 20)**
New Capitol, Room 400-F
P.O. Box 1018
Jackson, MS 39215
P: (601) 359-2434
E: crbrown@house.ms.gov

**Burnett, Cedric (D, 9)**
New Capitol, Room 400-E
P.O. Box 1018
Jackson, MS 39215
P: (601) 359-2422
E: cburnett@house.ms.gov

**Busby, Charles (R, 111)**
New Capitol, Room 400-F
P.O. Box 1018
Jackson, MS 39215
P: (601) 359-3373
E: cbusby@house.ms.gov

**Byrd, Larry (R, 104)**
New Capitol, Room 201M-7
P.O. Box 1018
Jackson, MS 39215
P: (601) 359-3352
E: lbyrd@house.ms.gov

**Calhoun, Credell (D, 68)**
New Capitol, Room 102-C
P.O. Box 1018
Jackson, MS 39215
P: (601) 359-2429
E: ccalhoun@house.ms.gov

**Carpenter, Lester (R, 1)**
New Capitol, Room 102-C
P.O. Box 1018
Jackson, MS 39215
P: (601) 359-2425
E: lcarpenter@house.ms.gov

**Chism, Gary A. (R, 37)**
New Capitol, Room 400-G
P.O. Box 1018
Jackson, MS 39215
P: (601) 359-3364
E: gchism@house.ms.gov

**Clark, Bryant W. (D, 47)**
New Capitol, Room BSMNT-B
P.O. Box 1018
Jackson, MS 39215
P: (601) 359-2845
E: bclark@house.ms.gov

**Clarke, Alyce Griffin
(D, 69)**
New Capitol, Room 204-D
P.O. Box 1018
Jackson, MS 39215
P: (601) 359-9465
E: aclarke@house.ms.gov

**Cockerham, Angela (D, 96)**
New Capitol, Room 201
P.O. Box 1018
Jackson, MS 39215
P: (601) 359-3333
E: acockerham@house.ms.gov

**Crawford, Carolyn (R, 121)**
New Capitol, Room 400-F
P.O. Box 1018
Jackson, MS 39215
P: (601) 359-2430
E: ccrawford@house.ms.gov

**Criswell, Dana (R, 6)**
New Capitol, Room 400-F
P.O. Box 1018
Jackson, MS 39215
P: (601) 359-2861
E: dcriswell@house.ms.gov

**Currie, Becky (R, 92)**
New Capitol, Room 401-C
P.O. Box 1018
Jackson, MS 39215
P: (601) 359-5334
E: bcurrie@house.ms.gov

**DeLano, Scott (R, 117)**
New Capitol, Room 401-B
P.O. Box 1018
Jackson, MS 39215
P: (601) 359-3349
E: sdelano@house.ms.gov

**Denny Jr., Bill C. (R, 64)**
New Capitol, Room 400-D
P.O. Box 1018
Jackson, MS 39215
P: (601) 359-3369
E: bdenny@house.ms.gov

**Denton, Oscar (D, 55)**
New Capitol, Room 400-F
P.O. Box 1018
Jackson, MS 39215
P: (601) 359-2438
E: odenton@house.ms.gov

**Dixon, Deborah Butler
(D, 63)**
New Capitol, Room 400-F
P.O. Box 1018
Jackson, MS 39215
P: (601) 359-3339
E: ddixon@house.ms.gov

**Dortch, Jarvis (D, 66)**
New Capitol, Room 400-F
P.O. Box 1018
Jackson, MS 39215
P: (601) 359-3339
E: jdortch@house.ms.gov

**Ellis, Tyrone (D, 38)**
New Capitol, Room BSMNT
P.O. Box 1018
Jackson, MS 39215
P: (601) 359-4084
E: tellis@house.ms.gov

**Eubanks, Dan (R, 25)**
New Capitol, BSMNT
P.O. Box 1018
Jackson, MS 39215
P: (601) 359-4082
E: deubanks@house.ms.gov

**Eure, Casey (R, 116)**
New Capitol, Room 119-B
P.O. Box 1018
Jackson, MS 39215
P: (601) 359-9466
E: ceure@house.ms.gov

**Evans, Bob (D, 91)**
New Capitol, Room BSMNT
P.O. Box 1018
Jackson, MS 39215
P: (601) 359-3354
E: bevans@house.ms.gov

**Evans, Michael T. (D, 45)**
New Capitol, Room 400-F
P.O. Box 1018
Jackson, MS 39215
P: (601) 359-3311
E: mevans@house.ms.gov

**Faulkner, John G. (D, 5)**
New Capitol, Room 400-F
P.O. Box 1018
Jackson, MS 39215
P: (601) 359-2432
E: jfaulkner@house.ms.gov

**Formby, Mark (R, 108)**
New Capitol, Room 402-B
P.O. Box 1018
Jackson, MS 39215
P: (601) 359-3359
E: mformby@house.ms.gov

**Foster, Robert (R, 28)**
New Capitol, BSMNT
P.O. Box 1018
Jackson, MS 39215
P: (601) 359-3287
E: rfoster@house.ms.gov

**Gibbs, Debra (D, 72)\***
New Capitol
P.O. Box 1018
Jackson, MS 39215

**Gibbs, Karl (D, 36)**
New Capitol, Room 400-F
P. O. Box 1018
Jackson, MS 39215
P: (601) 359-3253
E: kgibbs@house.ms.gov

**Gipson, Andy (R, 77)**
New Capitol, Room 112-B
P.O. Box 1018
Jackson, MS 39215
P: (601) 359-1541
E: agipson@house.ms.gov

**Guice, Jeffrey S. (R, 114)**
New Capitol, Room 119
P.O. Box 1018
Jackson, MS 39215
P: (601) 359-2508
E: jguice@house.ms.gov

**Gunn, Philip (R, 56)**
New Capitol, Room 306
P.O. Box 1018
Jackson, MS 39215
P: (601) 359-3300

**Hale, Jeff (R, 24)**
New Capitol, Room 400-F
P.O. Box 1018
Jackson, MS 39215
P: (601) 359-9395
E: jhale@house.ms.gov

**Haney, Greg (R, 118)**
New Capitol, Room 400-F
P.O. Box 1018
Jackson, MS 39215
P: (601) 359-3338
E: ghaney@house.ms.gov

**Henley, Ashley (R, 40)**
New Capitol, Room 400-F
P.O. Box 1018
Jackson, MS 39215
P: (601) 359-2429
E: ahenley@house.ms.gov

**Hines Sr., John W. (D, 50)**
New Capitol, Room 112-D
P.O. Box 1018
Jackson, MS 39215
P: (601) 359-3755
E: jhines@house.ms.gov

**Holland, D. Stephen (D, 16)**
New Capitol, Room 201
P.O. Box 1018
Jackson, MS 39215
P: (601) 359-3348
E: sholland@house.ms.gov

**Holloway Sr., Gregory
(D, 76)**
New Capitol, Room 400-F
P.O. Box 1018
Jackson, MS 39215
P: (601) 359-2435
E: gholloway@house.ms.gov

**Hood, Joey (R, 35)**
New Capitol, Room 400-F
P.O. Box 1018
Jackson, MS 39215
P: (601) 359-3339
E: jhood@house.ms.gov

**Hopkins, Steve (R, 7)**
New Capitol, Room 400-F
P.O. Box 1018
Jackson, MS 39215
P: (601) 359-9393
E: shopkins@house.ms.gov

# Mississippi

**Horan, Kevin (D, 34)**
New Capitol, Room 400-F
P.O. Box 1018
Jackson, MS 39215
P: (601) 359-2438
E: khoran@house.ms.gov

**Horne, Steve A. (R, 81)**
New Capitol, Room 400-E
P.O. Box 1018
Jackson, MS 39215
P: (601) 359-2424
E: shorne@house.ms.gov

**Huddleston, Mac (R, 15)**
New Capitol, Room 201
P.O. Box 1018
Jackson, MS 39215
P: (601) 359-3340
E: mhuddleston@house.ms.gov

**Huddleston, Robert E.
(D, 30)**
New Capitol, Room 400-E
P.O. Box 1018
Jackson, MS 39215
P: (601) 359-2418
E: rhuddleston@house.ms.gov

**Hudson, Abe (D, 29)**
New Capitol
P.O. Box 1018
Jackson, MS 39215
E: ahudson@house.ms.gov

**Hughes, Jay (D, 12)**
New Capitol, Room 400-F
P.O. Box 1018
Jackson, MS 39215
P: (601) 359-3339
E: jhughes@house.ms.gov

**Jackson, Lataisha (D, 11)**
New Capitol, Room 201M-7
P.O. Box 1018
Jackson, MS 39215
P: (601) 359-3348
E: ljackson@house.ms.gov

**Johnson, Chris (R, 87)**
New Capitol, BSMNT
P.O. Box 1018
Jackson, MS 39215
P: (601) 359-3362
E: cjohnson@house.ms.gov

**Johnson III, Robert L.
(D, 94)**
New Capitol, Room 100-D
P.O. Box 1018
Jackson, MS 39215
P: (601) 359-3355
E: rjohnson@house.ms.gov

**Karriem, Kabir (D, 41)**
New Capitol, Room 400-F
P.O. Box 1018
Jackson, MS 39215
P: (601) 359-3339
E: kkarriem@house.ms.gov

**Kinkade, Bill (R, 52)**
New Capitol, Room 112-C
P.O. Box 1018
Jackson, MS 39215
P: (601) 359-3367
E: bkinkade@house.ms.gov

**Ladner, Timmy (R, 93)**
New Capitol, Room 400-F
P.O. Box 1018
Jackson, MS 39215
P: (601) 359-2438
E: tladner@house.ms.gov

**Lamar, John Thomas (R, 8)**
New Capitol, Room 400-F
P.O. Box 1018
Jackson, MS 39215
P: (601) 359-2431
E: jlamar@house.ms.gov

**Mangold, Vince (R, 53)**
New Capitol, BSMNT
P.O. Box 1018
Jackson, MS 39215
P: (601) 359-5140
E: vmangold@house.ms.gov

**Massengill, Steve (R, 13)**
New Capitol, Room 400-F
P.O. Box 1018
Jackson, MS 39215
P: (601) 359-3338
E: smassengill@house.ms.gov

**McLeod, Doug (R, 107)**
New Capitol, Room 400-F
P.O. Box 1018
Jackson, MS 39215
P: (601) 359-3311
E: dmcleod@house.ms.gov

**McNeal, Roun (R, 105)**
New Capitol, Room 400-F
P.O. Box 1018
Jackson, MS 39215
P: (601) 359-3352
E: rmcneal@house.ms.gov

**Mettetal, Nolan (R, 10)**
New Capitol, Room 205-A
P.O. Box 1018
Jackson, MS 39215
P: (601) 359-3331
E: nmettetal@house.ms.gov

**Mickens, Carl (D, 42)**
New Capitol, Room 400-F
P.O. Box 1018
Jackson, MS 39215
P: (601) 359-2439
E: cmickens@house.ms.gov

**Middleton, America Chuck
(D, 85)**
New Capitol, Room 400-F
P.O. Box 1018
Jackson, MS 39215
P: (601) 359-2436
E: amiddleton@house.ms.gov

**Miles, Tom (D, 75)**
New Capitol, Room 400-F
P.O. Box 1018
Jackson, MS 39215
P: (601) 359-3311
E: tmiles@house.ms.gov

**Mims, Sam C. (R, 97)**
New Capitol, Room 104-B
P.O. Box 1018
Jackson, MS 39215
P: (601) 359-3320
E: smims@house.ms.gov

**Monsour, Alex (R, 54)**
New Capitol, Room 102-B
P.O. Box 1018
Jackson, MS 39215
P: (601) 359-9382
E: amonsour@house.ms.gov

**Moore, John L. (R, 60)**
New Capitol, Room 205-B
P.O. Box 1018
Jackson, MS 39215
P: (601) 359-3330
E: jmoore@house.ms.gov

**Morgan, Ken (R, 100)**
New Capitol, Room 102-C
P.O. Box 1018
Jackson, MS 39215
P: (601) 359-2426
E: kmorgan@house.ms.gov

**Myers, David W. (D, 98)**
New Capitol, Room 201M-6
P.O. Box 1018
Jackson, MS 39215
P: (601) 359-9393
E: dmyers@house.ms.gov

**Oliver, Karl (R, 46)**
New Capitol, Room 400-F
P.O. Box 1018
Jackson, MS 39215
P: (601) 359-2430
E: koliver@house.ms.gov

**Paden, Orlando (D, 26)**
New Capitol, Room 400-F
P.O. Box 1018
Jackson, MS 39215
P: (601) 359-2439
E: opaden@house.ms.gov

**Patterson, Randall H.
(R, 115)**
New Capitol, BSMNT
P.O. Box 1018
Jackson, MS 39215
P: (601) 359-4074
E: rhpatterson@house.ms.gov

**Perkins Sr., Willie J.
(D, 32)**
New Capitol, Room BSMNT
P.O. Box 1018
Jackson, MS 39215
P: (601) 359-4082
E: wperkins@house.ms.gov

**Pigott, Bill (R, 99)**
New Capitol, Room 201M-7
P.O. Box 1018
Jackson, MS 39215
P: (601) 359-5140
E: bpigott@house.ms.gov

**Powell, Brent (R, 59)**
New Capitol, Room 119
P.O. Box 1018
Jackson, MS 39215
P: (601) 359-3349
E: bpowell@house.ms.gov

**Read, John O. (R, 112)**
New Capitol, Room 201M-2
P.O. Box 1018
Jackson, MS 39215
P: (601) 359-3366
E: jread@house.ms.gov

**Reynolds, Thomas U. (D, 33)**
New Capitol, Room 201M-6
P.O. Box 1018
Jackson, MS 39215
P: (601) 359-9394
E: treynolds@house.ms.gov

**Roberson, Rob (R, 43)**
New Capitol, Room 201M-7
P.O. Box 1018
Jackson, MS 39215
P: (601) 359-9465
E: rroberson@house.ms.gov

**Rogers, Margaret Ellis
(R, 14)**
New Capitol, Room 100-C
P.O. Box 1018
Jackson, MS 39215
P: (601) 359-9390
E: mrogers@house.ms.gov

**Rogers, Ray (R, 61)**
New Capitol, Room 201
P.O. Box 1018
Jackson, MS 39215
P: (601) 359-3343
E: rrogers@house.ms.gov

**Rushing, Randal (R, 78)**
New Capitol, Room 400-F
P.O. Box 1018
Jackson, MS 39215
P: (601) 359-2435
E: rrushing@house.ms.gov

**Sanford, Noah (R, 90)**
New Capitol, Room 400-F
P.O. Box 1018
Jackson, MS 39215
P: (601) 359-9489
E: nsanford@house.ms.gov

**Scott, Omeria (D, 80)**
New Capitol, BSMNT
P.O. Box 1018
Jackson, MS 39215
P: (601) 359-4084
E: oscott@house.ms.gov

**Shirley, William (R, 84)**
New Capitol, Room 400-F
P.O. Box 1018
Jackson, MS 39215
P: (601) 359-2434
E: wshirley@house.ms.gov

**Smith, Jeffrey C. (R, 39)**
New Capitol, Room 201-F
P.O. Box 1018
Jackson, MS 39215
P: (601) 359-3343
E: jsmith@house.ms.gov

**Snowden, Greg (R, 83)**
New Capitol, Room 302
P.O. Box 1018
Jackson, MS 39215
P: (601) 359-3304
E: gsnowden@house.ms.gov

**Staples, Gary V. (R, 88)**
New Capitol, Room 201M-4
P.O. Box 1018
Jackson, MS 39215
P: (601) 359-3017
E: gstaples@house.ms.gov

**Steverson, Jody (R, 4)**
New Capitol, Room 400-F
P.O. Box 1018
Jackson, MS 39215
P: (601) 359-3305
E: jsteverson@house.ms.gov

**Straughter, Rufus E.
(D, 51)**
New Capitol, Room 400-E
P.O. Box 1018
Jackson, MS 39215
P: (601) 359-2421
E: rstraughter@house.ms.gov

**Sullivan, Preston E.
(D, 22)**
New Capitol, Room 202
P.O. Box 1018
Jackson, MS 39215
P: (601) 359-3332
E: psullivan@house.ms.gov

**Sykes, Kathy (D, 70)**
New Capitol, Room 400-F
P.O. Box 1018
Jackson, MS 39215
P: (601) 359-2436
E: ksykes@house.ms.gov

**Thomas, Sara Richardson
(D, 31)**
New Capitol, Room BSMNT
P.O. Box 1018
Jackson, MS 39215
P: (601) 359-2845
E: sthomas@house.ms.gov

**Touchstone, Brad (R, 101)**
New Capitol, BSMNT
P.O. Box 1018
Jackson, MS 39215
P: (601) 359-2419
E: btouchstone@house.ms.gov

**Tullos, Mark (R, 79)**
New Capitol
P.O. Box 1018
Jackson, MS 39215
E: mtullos@house.ms.gov

**Turner, Jerry R. (R, 18)**
New Capitol, Room 201M-4
P.O. Box 1018
Jackson, MS 39215
P: (601) 359-9473
E: jturner@house.ms.gov

**Walker, Kenneth (D, 27)**
New Capitol, Room 400-F
P.O. Box 1018
Jackson, MS 39215
P: (601) 359-2439
E: kwalker@house.ms.gov

**Watson, Percy W. (D, 103)**
New Capitol, Room 201M-7
P.O. Box 1018
Jackson, MS 39215
P: (601) 359-3351
E: pwatson@house.ms.gov

**Weathersby, Tom (R, 62)**
New Capitol, Room 115-A
P.O. Box 1018
Jackson, MS 39215
P: (601) 359-3336
E: tweathersby@house.ms.gov

**White, Jason (R, 48)**
New Capitol, Room BSMNT-B
P.O. Box 1018
Jackson, MS 39215
P: (601) 359-2861
E: jwhite@house.ms.gov

**Williams-Barnes, Sonya
(D, 119)**
New Capitol, Room 400-F
P.O. Box 1018
Jackson, MS 39215
P: (601) 359-2432
E: swilliams-barnes
@house.ms.gov

**Willis, Patricia H. (R, 95)**
New Capitol, Room 112-D
P. O. Box 1018
Jackson, MS 39215
P: (601) 359-3744
E: pwillis@house.ms.gov

**Wilson, Cory (R, 73)**
New Capitol, Room 112-E
P.O. Box 1018
Jackson, MS 39215
P: (601) 359-3742
E: cwilson@house.ms.gov

**Wooten, Adrienne (D, 71)**
New Capitol, Room 400-F
P.O. Box 1018
Jackson, MS 39215
P: (601) 359-2433
E: adrienneahooper
@yahoo.com

**Young Jr., Charles (D, 82)**
New Capitol, Room 400-F
P.O. Box 1018
Jackson, MS 39215
P: (601) 359-2432
E: cyoung@house.ms.gov

**Zuber III, Henry (R, 113)**
New Capitol, Room 402-C
P.O. Box 1018
Jackson, MS 39215
P: (601) 359-3328
E: hzuber@house.ms.gov

# Missouri

## Executive

### Governor

**The Honorable Eric Greitens (R)**
Governor
P.O. Box 270
Jefferson City, MO 65102
P: (573) 751-4917
F: (573) 751-1906

### Lieutenant Governor

**The Honorable Michael Parson (R)**
Lieutenant Governor
State Capitol, Room 224
Jefferson City, MO 65101
P: (573) 751-4727
F: (573) 526-8793

### Auditor

**Ms. Nicole Galloway**
State Auditor
State Capitol, Room 224
Jefferson City, MO 65102
P: (573) 751-4824
F: (573) 751-6539

### Secretary of State

**The Honorable Jay Ashcroft (R)**
Secretary of State
600 West Main
P.O. Box 1767
Jefferson City, MO 65101
P: (573) 751-4936
F: (573) 526-4903

### Treasurer

**The Honorable Eric Schmitt (R)**
State Treasurer
State Capitol, Room 229
P.O. Box 210
Jefferson City, MO 65102
P: (573) 751-2411
F: (573) 751-9443
E: eric.schmitt
@treasurer.mo.gov

## Judiciary

### Supreme Court (MR)

**Ms. Betsy AuBuchon**
Supreme Court Clerk
P.O. Box 150
Jefferson City, MO 65102
P: (573) 751-4144

**The Honorable Patricia Breckenridge**
Chief Justice
**The Honorable George W. Draper III**
**The Honorable Zel M. Fischer**
**The Honorable Mary Russell**
**The Honorable Laura Denvir Stith**
**The Honorable Richard B. Teitelman**
**The Honorable Paul C. Wilson**

## Legislative Senate

### Senate President

**The Honorable Michael Parson (R)**
Lieutenant Governor
State Capitol, Room 224
Jefferson City, MO 65101
P: (573) 751-4727
F: (573) 526-8793

### President Pro Tempore of the Senate

**Senator Ron Richard (R)**
Senate President Pro Tem
State Capitol, Room 326
201 West Capitol Avenue
Jefferson City, MO 65101
P: (573) 751-2173
F: (573) 526-5813
E: Ron.Richard
@senate.mo.gov

### Senate Majority Leader

**Senator Mike Kehoe (R)**
Senate Majority Floor Leader
State Capitol, Room 321
201 West Capitol Avenue
Jefferson City, MO 65101
P: (573) 751-2076
F: (573) 751-2582
E: Mike.Kehoe@senate.mo.gov

### Senate Minority Leader

**Senator Gina Walsh (D)**
Senate Minority Floor Leader
State Capitol, Room 333
201 West Capitol Avenue
Jefferson City, MO 65101
P: (573) 751-2420
F: (573) 751-1598
E: Gina.Walsh@senate.mo.gov

### Secretary of the Senate

**Ms. Julie Bochat**
Secretary of the Senate
State Capitol, Room 325
201 West Capitol Avenue
Jefferson City, MO 65101
P: (573) 751-3766
E: jbochat@senate.mo.gov

### Members of the Senate

**Brown, Dan W. (R, 16)**
State Capitol, Room 422
201 West Capitol Avenue
Jefferson City, MO 65101
P: (573) 751-5713
F: (573) 751-0733
E: Dan.Brown@senate.mo.gov

**Chappelle-Nadal, Maria (D, 14)**
State Capitol, Room 428
201 West Capitol Avenue
Jefferson City, MO 65101
P: (573) 751-4106
F: (573) 751-0467
E: Maria.ChappelleNadal
@senate.mo.gov

**Cunningham, Mike (R, 33)**
State Capitol, Room 331
201 West Capitol Avenue
Jefferson City, MO 65101
P: (573) 751-1882
E: Mike.Cunningham
@senate.mo.gov

**Curls, Shalonn Kiki (D, 9)**
State Capitol, Room 434
201 West Capitol Avenue
Jefferson City, MO 65101
P: (573) 751-3158
E: Shalonn.Curls
@senate.mo.gov

**Dixon, Bob (R, 30)**
State Capitol, Room 221
201 West Capitol Avenue
Jefferson City, MO 65101
P: (573) 751-2583
F: (573) 526-1305
E: Bob.Dixon@senate.mo.gov

**Eigel, Bill (R, 23)***
State Capitol, Room 226
201 W Capitol Ave
Jefferson City, MO 65101
P: (573) 751-1141
E: bill.eigel@senate.mo.gov

**Emery, Ed (R, 31)**
State Capitol, Room 420
201 West Capitol Avenue
Jefferson City, MO 65101
P: (573) 751-2108
E: Ed.Emery@senate.mo.gov

**Hegeman, Daniel J. (R, 12)**
State Capitol, Room 332
201 West Capitol Avenue
Jefferson City, MO 65101
P: (573) 751-1415
E: Dan.Hegeman
@senate.mo.gov

**Holsman, Jason R. (D, 7)**
State Capitol, Room 421
201 West Capitol Avenue
Jefferson City, MO 65101
P: (573) 751-6607
F: (573) 522-9495
E: Jason.Holsman
@senate.mo.gov

**Hoskins, Denny L. (R, 21)**
State Capitol, Room 431
201 West Capitol Avenue
Jefferson City, MO 65101
P: (573) 751-4302
E: Denny.Hoskins
@senate.mo.gov

**Hummel, Jacob (D, 4)**
State Capitol, Room 328
201 West Capitol Avenue
Jefferson City, MO 65101
P: (573) 751-3599
E: Jake.Hummel
@senate.mo.gov

**Kehoe, Mike (R, 6)**
State Capitol, Room 321
201 West Capitol Avenue
Jefferson City, MO 65101
P: (573) 751-2076
F: (573) 751-2582
E: Mike.Kehoe@senate.mo.gov

**Koenig, Andrew (R, 15)**
State Capitol, Room 220
201 West Capitol Avenue
Jefferson City, MO 65101
P: (573) 751-5568
E: Andrew.Koenig
@senate.mo.gov

**Kraus, Will (R, 8)**
State Capitol, Room 320
201 West Capitol Avenue
Jefferson City, MO 65101
P: (573) 751-1464
E: Will.Kraus@senate.mo.gov

**Libla, Doug (R, 25)**
State Capitol, Room 219
201 West Capitol Avenue
Jefferson City, MO 65101
P: (573) 751-4843
E: Doug.Libla@senate.mo.gov

**Munzlinger, Brian (R, 18)**
State Capitol, Room 319
201 West Capitol Avenue
Jefferson City, MO 65101
P: (573) 751-7985
F: (573) 522-3722
E: Brian.Munzlinger
@senate.mo.gov

**Nasheed, Jamilah (D, 5)**
State Capitol, Room 330
201 West Capitol Avenue
Jefferson City, MO 65101
P: (573) 751-4415
F: (573) 522-9180
E: Jamilah.Nasheed
@senate.mo.gov

**Onder Jr., Robert F. (R, 2)**
State Capitol, Room 227
201 West Capitol Avenue
Jefferson City, MO 65101
P: (573) 751-1282
F: (573) 526-4766
E: Bob.Onder@senate.mo.gov

**Richard, Ron (R, 32)**
State Capitol, Room 326
201 West Capitol Avenue
Jefferson City, MO 65101
P: (573) 751-2173
F: (573) 526-5813
E: Ron.Richard
@senate.mo.gov

**Riddle, Jeanie (R, 10)**
State Capitol, Room 417
201 West Capitol Avenue
Jefferson City, MO 65101
P: (573) 751-2757
E: Jeanie.Riddle
@senate.mo.gov

**Rizzo, John (D, 11)**
State Capitol, Room 425
201 West Capitol Avenue
Jefferson City, MO 65101
P: (573) 751-3074
E: John.Rizzo@senate.mo.gov

**Romine, Gary (R, 3)**
State Capitol, Room 429
201 West Capitol Avenue
Jefferson City, MO 65101
P: (573) 751-4008
E: Gary.Romine
@senate.mo.gov

**Rowden, Caleb (R, 19)**
State Capitol, Room 433
201 West Capitol Avenue
Jefferson City, MO 65101
P: (573) 751-3931
E: Caleb.Rowden
@senate.mo.gov

**Sater, David (R, 29)**
State Capitol, Room 416
201 West Capitol Avenue
Jefferson City, MO 65101
P: (573) 751-1480
F: (573) 522-1466
E: David.Sater
@senate.mo.gov

**Schaaf, Robert (R, 34)**
State Capitol, Room 423
201 West Capitol Avenue
Jefferson City, MO 65101
P: (573) 751-2183
F: (573) 526-9851
E: Robert.Schaaf
@senate.mo.gov

**Schatz, Dave (R, 26)**
State Capitol, Room 419
201 West Capitol Avenue
Jefferson City, MO 65101
P: (573) 751-3678
E: Dave.Schatz
@senate.mo.gov

**Schupp, Jill (D, 24)**
State Capitol, Room 329
201 West Capitol Avenue
Jefferson City, MO 65101
P: (573) 751-9762
E: Jill.Schupp
@senate.mo.gov

**Sifton, Scott (D, 1)**
State Capitol, Room 427
201 West Capitol Avenue
Jefferson City, MO 65101
P: (573) 751-0220
F: (573) 751-4564
E: Scott.Sifton
@senate.mo.gov

**Silvey, Ryan (R, 17)**
State Capitol, Room 331A
201 West Capitol Avenue
Jefferson City, MO 65101
P: (573) 751-5282
E: Ryan.Silvey
@senate.mo.gov

**Wallingford, Wayne (R, 27)**
State Capitol, Room 225
201 West Capitol Avenue
Jefferson City, MO 65101
P: (573) 751-2459
E: Wayne.Wallingford
@senate.mo.gov

**Walsh, Gina (D, 13)**
State Capitol, Room 333
201 West Capitol Avenue
Jefferson City, MO 65101
P: (573) 751-2420
F: (573) 751-1598
E: Gina.Walsh@senate.mo.gov

**Wasson, Jay (R, 20)**
State Capitol, Room 323
201 West Capitol Avenue
Jefferson City, MO 65101
P: (573) 751-1503
F: (573) 522-6233
E: Jay.Wasson@senate.mo.gov

**Wieland, Paul (R, 22)**
State Capitol, Room 334
201 West Capitol Avenue
Jefferson City, MO 65101
P: (573) 751-1492
E: Paul.Wieland
@senate.mo.gov

# House

## Speaker of the House

**Representative Todd Richardson (R)**
Speaker of the House
State Capitol, Room 308
201 West Capitol Avenue
Jefferson City, MO 65101
P: (573) 751-4039
F: (573) 751-5271
E: Todd.Richardson
@house.mo.gov

## Speaker Pro Tempore of the House

**Representative Elijah Haahr (R)**
Speaker Pro Tem
State Capitol, Room 301
201 West Capitol Avenue
Jefferson City, MO 65101
P: (573) 751-2210
E: Elijah.Haahr
@house.mo.gov

## House Majority Leader

**Representative Mike Cierpiot (R)**
House Majority Floor Leader
State Capitol, Room 302-A
201 West Capitol Avenue
Jefferson City, MO 65101
P: (573) 751-0907
E: Mike.Cierpiot
@house.mo.gov

## House Minority Leader

**Representative Gail McCann Beatty (D)**
House Minority Floor Leader
State Capitol, Room 204
201 West Capitol Avenue
Jefferson City, MO 65101
P: (573) 751-2124
F: (573) 522-9796
E: Gail.Beatty@house.mo.gov

## Clerk of the House

**Mr. D. Adam Crumbliss**
Chief Clerk
State Capitol, Room 306C
201 West Capitol Avenue
Jefferson City, MO 65101
P: (573) 751-4017
E: adam.crumbliss
@house.mo.gov

## Members of the House

**Adams, Joe (D, 86)**
State Capitol, Room 106-A
201 West Capitol Avenue
Jefferson City, MO 65101
P: (573) 751-4265
E: Joe.Adams@house.mo.gov

**Alferman, Justin (R, 61)**
State Capitol, Room 102-BB
201 West Capitol Avenue
Jefferson City, MO 65101
P: (573) 751-6668
E: Justin.Alferman
@house.mo.gov

**Anders, Ira (D, 21)**
State Capitol, Room 101E
201 West Capitol Avenue
Jefferson City, MO 65101
P: (573) 751-5701
F: (573) 526-7337
E: Ira.Anders@house.mo.gov

**Anderson, Sonya (R, 131)**
State Capitol, Room 234
201 West Capitol Avenue
Jefferson City, MO 65101
P: (573) 751-2948
E: Sonya.Anderson
@house.mo.gov

**Andrews, Allen (R, 1)**
State Capitol, Room 406-B
201 West Capitol Avenue
Jefferson City, MO 65101
P: (573) 751-9465
E: Allen.Andrews
@house.mo.gov

# Missouri

**Arthur, Lauren (D, 18)**
State Capitol, Room 101-D
201 West Capitol Avenue
Jefferson City, MO 65101
P: (573) 751-2199
E: Lauren.Arthur
@house.mo.gov

**Austin, Kevin (R, 136)**
State Capitol, Room 302B
201 West Capitol Avenue
Jefferson City, MO 65101
P: (573) 751-0232
E: Kevin.Austin
@house.mo.gov

**Bahr, Kurt (R, 102)**
State Capitol, Room 200-A
201 West Capitol Avenue
Jefferson City, MO 65101
P: (573) 751-9768
F: (573) 526-1423
E: Kurt.Bahr@house.mo.gov

**Bangert, Gretchen (D, 69)***
State Capitol, Room 109E
201 West Capitol Avenue
Jefferson City, MO 65101
P: (573) 751-5365
E: gretchen.bangert
@house.mo.gov

**Baringer, Donna (D, 82)***
State Capitol, Room 109I
201 West Capitol Avenue
Jefferson City, MO 65101
P: (573) 751-4220
E: donna.baringer
@house.mo.gov

**Barnes, Jay (R, 60)**
State Capitol, Room 306A
201 West Capitol Avenue
Jefferson City, MO 65101
P: (573) 751-2412
F: (573) 526-9774
E: Jay.Barnes@house.mo.gov

**Barnes, Jerome (D, 28)***
State Capitol, Room 103BB
201 West Capitol Avenue
Jefferson City, MO 65101
P: (573) 751-9851
E: jerome
@barnes@house.mo.gov

**Basye, Chuck (R, 47)**
State Capitol, Room 236-B
201 West Capitol Avenue
Jefferson City, MO 65101
P: (573) 751-1501
E: Chuck.Basye@house.mo.gov

**Beard, Nathan (R, 52)**
State Capitol, Room 409A
201 West Capitol Avenue
Jefferson City, MO 65101
P: (573) 751-9774
E: Nathan.Beard
@house.mo.gov

**Beatty, Gail McCann (D, 26)**
State Capitol, Room 204
201 West Capitol Avenue
Jefferson City, MO 65101
P: (573) 751-2124
F: (573) 522-9796
E: Gail.Beatty@house.mo.gov

**Beck, Doug (D, 92)***
State Capitol, Room 109D
201 West Capitol Avenue
Jefferson City, MO 65101
P: (573) 751-9472
E: doug.beck@house.mo.gov

**Bernskoetter, Mike (R, 59)**
State Capitol, Room 414
201 West Capitol Avenue
Jefferson City, MO 65101
P: (573) 751-0665
F: (573) 526-3278
E: Mike.Bernskoetter
@house.mo.gov

**Berry, T.J. (R, 38)**
State Capitol, Room 205
201 West Capitol Avenue
Jefferson City, MO 65101
P: (573) 751-2238
F: (573) 522-9320
E: TJ.Berry@house.mo.gov

**Black, Rusty (R, 7)***
State Capitol, Room 115C
201 West Capitol Avenue
Jefferson City, MO 65101
P: (573) 751-2917
E: rusty.black@house.mo.gov

**Bondon, Jack (R, 56)**
State Capitol, Room 201F
201 West Capitol Avenue
Jefferson City, MO 65101
P: (573) 751-2175
E: Jack.Bondon@house.mo.gov

**Brattin, Rick (R, 55)**
State Capitol, Room 114C
201 West Capitol Avenue
Jefferson City, MO 65101
P: (573) 751-3783
F: (573) 522-6078
E: Rick.Brattin
@house.mo.gov

**Brown, Cloria (R, 94)**
State Capitol, Room 206-C
201 West Capitol Avenue
Jefferson City, MO 65101
P: (573) 751-3719
F: (573) 522-2628
E: Cloria.Brown
@house.mo.gov

**Brown, Richard (D, 27)***
State Capitol, Room 109G
201 West Capitol Avenue
Jefferson City, MO 65101
P: (573) 751-7639
E: richard.brown
@house.mo.gov

**Brown, Wanda (R, 57)**
State Capitol, Room 315
201 West Capitol Avenue
Jefferson City, MO 65101
P: (573) 751-3971
F: (573) 526-1889
E: Wanda.Brown@house.mo.gov

**Burnett, Ingrid (D, 19)***
State Capitol, Room 105G
201  West Capitol Avenue
Jefferson City, MO 65101
P: (573) 751-3310
E: ingrid.burnett
@house.mo.gov

**Burns, Bob (D, 93)**
State Capitol, Room 105D
201 West Capitol Avenue
Jefferson City, MO 65101
P: (573) 751-0211
E: Bob.Burns@house.mo.gov

**Butler, Michael (D, 79)**
State Capitol, Room 101B
201 West Capitol Avenue
Jefferson City, MO 65101
P: (573) 751-6800
E: Michael.Butler
@house.mo.gov

**Carpenter, Jon (D, 15)**
State Capitol, Room 103-BC
201 West Capitol Avenue
Jefferson City, MO 65101
P: (573) 751-4787
E: Jon.Carpenter
@house.mo.gov

**Chipman, Jason (R, 120)**
State Capitol, Room 415-B
201 West Capitol Avenue
Jefferson City, MO 65101
P: (573) 751-1688
E: Jason.Chipman
@house.mo.gov

**Christofanelli, Phil
(R, 105)***
State Capitol, Room 116-1
201 West Capitol Avenue
Jefferson City, MO 65101
P: (573) 751-2949
E: phil.christofanelli
@house.mo.gov

**Cierpiot, Mike (R, 30)**
State Capitol, Room 302-A
201 West Capitol Avenue
Jefferson City, MO 65101
P: (573) 751-0907
E: Mike.Cierpiot
@house.mo.gov

**Conway, Kathie (R, 104)**
State Capitol, Room 114B
201 West Capitol Avenue
Jefferson City, MO 65101
P: (573) 751-2250
F: (573) 522-2070
E: Kathie.Conway
@house.mo.gov

**Conway, Pat (D, 10)**
State Capitol, Room 109C
201 West Capitol Avenue
Jefferson City, MO 65101
P: (573) 751-9755
F: (573) 526-1965
E: Pat.Conway@house.mo.gov

**Cookson, Steve (R, 153)**
State Capitol, Room 411-A
201 West Capitol Avenue
Jefferson City, MO 65101
P: (573) 751-1066
F: (573) 526-9842
E: Steve.Cookson
@house.mo.gov

**Corlew, Kevin (R, 14)**
State Capitol, Room 201BA
201 West Capitol Avenue
Jefferson City, MO 65101
P: (573) 751-3618
E: Kevin.Corlew
@house.mo.gov

**Cornejo, Robert (R, 64)**
State Capitol, Room 410-B
201 West Capitol Avenue
Jefferson City, MO 65101
P: (573) 751-1484
E: Robert.Cornejo
@house.mo.gov

**Crawford, Sandy (R, 129)**
State Capitol, Room 312
201 West Capitol Avenue
Jefferson City, MO 65101
P: (573) 751-1167
F: (573) 526-0821
E: Sandy.Crawford
@house.mo.gov

**Cross, Gary (R, 35)**
State Capitol, Room 112
201 West Capitol Avenue
Jefferson City, MO 65101
P: (573) 751-1459
F: (573) 526-0932
E: Gary.Cross@house.mo.gov

**Curtis, Courtney Allen (D, 73)**
State Capitol, Room 135BB
201 West Capitol Avenue
Jefferson City, MO 65101
P: (573) 751-0855
E: Courtney.Curtis
@house.mo.gov

**Curtman, Paul (R, 109)**
State Capitol, Room 306B
201 West Capitol Avenue
Jefferson City, MO 65101
P: (573) 751-3776
E: Paul.Curtman
@house.mo.gov

**Davis, Charlie (R, 162)**
State Capitol, Room 207-B
201 West Capitol Avenue
Jefferson City, MO 65101
P: (573) 751-7082
F: (573) 526-9847
E: Charlie.Davis
@house.mo.gov

**DeGroot, Bruce (R, 101)***
State Capitol, Room 116-2
201 West Capitol Avenue
Jefferson City, MO 65101
P: (573) 751-1247
E: bruce.degroot
@house.mo.gov

**Dogan, Shamed (R, 98)**
State Capitol, Room 412-B
201 West Capitol Avenue
Jefferson City, MO 65101
P: (573) 751-4392
E: Shamed.Dogan
@house.mo.gov

**Dohrman, Dean (R, 51)**
State Capitol, Room 415-A
201 West Capitol Avenue
Jefferson City, MO 65101
P: (573) 751-2204
E: Dean.Dohrman
@house.mo.gov

**Dunn, Randy (D, 23)**
State Capitol, Room 130-DA
201 West Capitol Avenue
Jefferson City, MO 65101
P: (573) 751-0538
E: Randy.Dunn@house.mo.gov

**Eggleston, J. (R, 2)**
State Capitol, Room 405-B
201 West Capitol Avenue
Jefferson City, MO 65101
P: (573) 751-4285
E: J.Eggleston@house.mo.gov

**Ellebracht, Mark (D, 17)***
State Capitol, Room 135BA
200 West Capitol Avenue
Jefferson City, MO 65101
P: (573) 751-1218
E: mark.ellebracht
@house.mo.gov

**Ellington, Brandon (D, 22)**
State Capitol, Room 101C
201 West Capitol Avenue
Jefferson City, MO 65101
P: (573) 751-3129
E: Brandon.Ellington
@house.mo.gov

**Engler, Kevin (R, 116)**
State Capitol, Room 313-3
201 West Capitol Avenue
Jefferson City, MO 65101
P: (573) 751-3455
E: Kevin.Engler
@house.mo.gov

**Evans, Jean (R, 99)***
State Capitol, Room 405A
201 West Capitol Avenue
Jefferson City, MO 65101
P: (573) 751-3859
E: jean.evans@house.mo.gov

**Fitzpatrick, Scott (R, 158)**
State Capitol, Room 309
201 West Capitol Avenue
Jefferson City, MO 65101
P: (608) 266-5660
E: Scott.Fitzpatrick
@house.mo.gov

**Fitzwater, Paul (R, 144)**
State Capitol, Room 110B
201 West Capitol Avenue
Jefferson City, MO 65101
P: (573) 751-2112
F: (573) 526-6856
E: Paul.Fitzwater
@house.mo.gov

**Fitzwater, Travis (R, 49)**
State Capitol, Room 410-A
201 West Capitol Avenue
Jefferson City, MO 65101
P: (573) 751-5226
E: Travis.Fitzwater
@house.mo.gov

**Fraker, Lyndall (R, 137)**
State Capitol, Room 304A
201 West Capitol Avenue
Jefferson City, MO 65101
P: (573) 751-3819
F: (573) 526-1888
E: Lyndall.Fraker
@house.mo.gov

**Francis, Rick (R, 145)***
State Capitol, Room 115I
201 West Capitol Avenue
Jefferson City, MO 65101
P: (573) 751-5912
E: rick.francis
@house.mo.gov

**Franklin, Diane (R, 123)**
State Capitol, Room 206B
201 West Capitol Avenue
Jefferson City, MO 65101
P: (573) 751-1119
F: (573) 526-9803
E: Diane.Franklin
@house.mo.gov

**Franks Jr., Bruce (D, 78)***
State Capitol, Room 101I
201 West Capitol Avenue
Jefferson City, MO 65101
P: (573) 751-2383
E: bruce.franks
@house.mo.gov

**Frederick, Keith (R, 121)**
State Capitol, Room 411-B
201 West Capitol Avenue
Jefferson City, MO 65101
P: (573) 751-3834
F: (573) 751-0733
E: Keith.Frederick
@house.mo.gov

**Gannon, Elaine (R, 115)**
State Capitol, Room 304B
201 West Capitol Avenue
Jefferson City, MO 65101
P: (573) 751-7735
E: Elaine.Gannon
@house.mo.gov

**Gray, Alan (D, 75)***
State Capitol, Room 105F
201 West Capitol Avenue
Jefferson City, MO 65101
P: (573) 751-5538
E: alan.gray@house.mo.gov

**Green, Alan (D, 67)**
State Capitol, Room 135-AB
201 West Capitol Avenue
Jefferson City, MO 65101
P: (573) 751-2135
E: Alan.Green@house.mo.gov

**Gregory, David (R, 96)***
State Capitol, Room 116-5
201 West Capitol Avenue
Jefferson City, MO 65101
P: (573) 751-2150
E: david.gregory
@house.mo.gov

**Grier, Derek (R, 100)***
State Capitol, Room 115G
201 West Capitol Avenue
Jefferson City, MO 65101
P: (573) 751-9765
E: derek.grier@house.mo.gov

**Haahr, Elijah (R, 134)**
State Capitol, Room 301
201 West Capitol Avenue
Jefferson City, MO 65101
P: (573) 751-2210
E: Elijah.Haahr
@house.mo.gov

**Haefner, Marsha (R, 95)**
State Capitol, Room 311
201 West Capitol Avenue
Jefferson City, MO 65101
P: (573) 751-3762
F: (573) 526-4767
E: Marsha.Haefner
@house.mo.gov

**Hannegan, Tom (R, 65)***
State Capitol, Room 201G
201 West Capitol Avenue
Jefferson City, MO 65101
P: (573) 751-3717
E: tom.hannegan
@house.mo.gov

**Hansen, Jim (R, 40)**
State Capitol, Room 111
201 West Capitol Avenue
Jefferson City, MO 65101
P: (573) 751-4028
E: Jim.Hansen@house.mo.gov

**Harris, Ben (D, 118)**
State Capitol, Room 109-A
201 West Capitol Avenue
Jefferson City, MO 65101
P: (573) 751-2398
F: (573) 526-1963
E: Ben.Harris@house.mo.gov

**Helms, Steve (R, 135)***
State Capitol, Room 203A
201 West Capitol Avenue
Jefferson City, MO 65101
P: (573) 751-9809
E: steve.helms@house.mo.gov

# Missouri

**Henderson, Mike (R, 117)***
State Capitol, Room 115H
201 West Capitol Avenue
Jefferson City, MO 65101
P: (573) 751-2317
E: mike.henderson
@house.mo.gov

**Higdon, Galen (R, 11)**
State Capitol, Room 411-2
201 West Capitol Avenue
Jefferson City, MO 65101
P: (573) 751-3643
F: (573) 522-5025
E: Galen.Higdon
@house.mo.gov

**Hill, Justin (R, 108)**
State Capitol, Room 203-C
201 West Capitol Avenue
Jefferson City, MO 65101
P: (573) 751-3572
E: Justin.Hill@house.mo.gov

**Houghton, Jay (R, 43)**
State Capitol, Room 413-A
201 West Capitol Avenue
Jefferson City, MO 65101
P: (573) 751-3649
F: (573) 526-0905
E: Jay.Houghton
@house.mo.gov

**Houx, Dan (R, 54)***
State Capitol, Room 116A-1
201 West Capitol Avenue
Jefferson City, MO 65101
P: (573) 751-3850
E: dan.houx@house.mo.gov

**Hubrecht, Tila (R, 151)**
State Capitol, Room 201-B
201 West Capitol Avenue
Jefferson City, MO 65101
P: (573) 751-1494
E: Tila.Hubrecht
@house.mo.gov

**Hurst, Tom (R, 62)**
State Capitol, Room 412-A
201 West Capitol Avenue
Jefferson City, MO 65101
P: (573) 751-1344
E: Tom.Hurst@house.mo.gov

**Johnson, Delus (R, 9)**
State Capitol, Room 302-1
201 West Capitol Avenue
Jefferson City, MO 65101
P: (573) 751-3666
E: Delus.Johnson
@house.mo.gov

**Justus, Jeffery (R, 156)**
State Capitol, Room 407-B
201 West Capitol Avenue
Jefferson City, MO 65101
P: (573) 751-1309
E: Jeffery.Justus
@house.mo.gov

**Kelley, Mike (R, 127)**
State Capitol, Room 207-A
201 West Capitol Avenue
Jefferson City, MO 65101
P: (573) 751-2165
F: (573) 526-2577
E: Mike.Kelley@house.mo.gov

**Kelly, Hannah (R, 141)***
State Capitol, Room 116A-2
201 West Capitol Avenue
Jefferson City, MO 65101
P: (573) 751-2205
E: hannah.kelly
@house.mo.gov

**Kendrick, Kip (D, 45)**
State Capitol, Room 106B
201 West Capitol Avenue
Jefferson City, MO 65101
P: (573) 751-4189
E: Kip.Kendrick
@house.mo.gov

**Kidd, Bill (R, 20)**
State Capitol, Room 236-A
201 West Capitol Avenue
Jefferson City, MO 65101
P: (573) 751-3674
E: Bill.Kidd@house.mo.gov

**Kolkmeyer, Glen (R, 53)**
State Capitol, Room 402
201 West Capitol Avenue
Jefferson City, MO 65101
P: (573) 751-1462
E: Glen.Kolkmeyer
@house.mo.gov

**Korman, Bart (R, 42)**
State Capitol, Room 113
201 West Capitol Avenue
Jefferson City, MO 65101
P: (573) 751-2689
F: (573) 526-0559
E: Bart.Korman@house.mo.gov

**Lant, Bill (R, 159)**
State Capitol, Room 300
201 West Capitol Avenue
Jefferson City, MO 65101
P: (573) 751-9801
F: (573) 522-5505
E: Bill.Lant@house.mo.gov

**Lauer, Jeanie (R, 32)**
State Capitol, Room 413B
201 West Capitol Avenue
Jefferson City, MO 65101
P: (573) 751-1487
F: (573) 526-2619
E: Jeanie.Lauer
@house.mo.gov

**Lavender, Deb (D, 90)**
State Capitol, Room 105J
201 West Capitol Avenue
Jefferson City, MO 65101
P: (573) 751-4069
E: Deb.Lavender
@house.mo.gov

**Lichtenegger, Donna
(R, 146)**
State Capitol, Room 314
201 West Capitol Avenue
Jefferson City, MO 65101
P: (573) 751-6662
F: (573) 522-6191
E: Donna.Lichtenegger
@house.mo.gov

**Love, Warren (R, 125)**
State Capitol, Room 235BA
201 West Capitol Avenue
Jefferson City, MO 65101
P: (573) 751-4065
E: Warren.Love@house.mo.gov

**Lynch, Steve (R, 122)**
State Capitol, Room 313-I
201 West Capitol Avenue
Jefferson City, MO 65101
P: (573) 751-1446
E: Steve.Lynch@house.mo.gov

**Marshall, Nick (R, 13)**
State Capitol, Room 134
201 West Capitol Avenue
Jefferson City, MO 65101
P: (573) 751-6593
F: (573) 522-9278
E: Nick.Marshall
@house.mo.gov

**Mathews, Kirk (R, 110)**
State Capitol, Room 406-A
201 West Capitol Avenue
Jefferson City, MO 65101
P: (573) 751-0562
E: Kirk.Mathews
@house.mo.gov

**Matthiesen, Mark (R, 70)***
State Capitol, Room 305A
201 West Capitol Avenue
Jefferson City, MO 65101
P: (573) 751-4163
E: mark.matthiesen
@house.mo.gov

**May, Karla (D, 84)**
State Capitol, Room 101J
201 West Capitol Avenue
Jefferson City, MO 65101
P: (573) 751-2198
F: (573) 526-9004
E: Karla.May@house.mo.gov

**McCaherty, John (R, 97)**
State Capitol, Room 401B
201 West Capitol Avenue
Jefferson City, MO 65101
P: (573) 751-3751
F: (573) 522-1582
E: John.McCaherty
@house.mo.gov

**McCreery, Tracy (D, 88)**
State Capitol, Room 130-DB
201 West Capitol Avenue
Jefferson City, MO 65101
P: (573) 751-7535
E: Tracy.McCreery
@house.mo.gov

**McDaniel, Andrew (R, 150)**
State Capitol, Room 115-E
201 West Capitol Avenue
Jefferson City, MO 65101
P: (573) 751-3629
E: Andrew.McDaniel
@house.mo.gov

**McGaugh, Joe Don (R, 39)**
State Capitol, Room 305-B
201 West Capitol Avenue
Jefferson City, MO 65101
P: (573) 751-1468
E: JoeDon.McGaugh
@house.mo.gov

**McGee, DaRon (D, 36)**
State Capitol, Room 135-AA
201 West Capitol Avenue
Jefferson City, MO 65101
P: (573) 751-9469
E: DaRon.McGee@house.mo.gov

**Meredith, Sue (D, 71)**
State Capitol, Room 105-B
201 West Capitol Avenue
Jefferson City, MO 65101
P: (573) 751-4183
E: Susan.Meredith
@house.mo.gov

**Merideth, Peter (D, 80)***
State Capitol, Room 105H
201 West Capitol Avenue
Jefferson City, MO 65101
P: (573) 751-6736
E: peter.merideth
@house.mo.gov

**Messenger, Jeffrey (R, 130)**
State Capitol, Room 313-2
201 West Capitol Avenue
Jefferson City, MO 65101
P: (573) 751-2381
E: Jeff.Messenger
@house.mo.gov

**Miller, Rocky (R, 124)**
State Capitol, Room 233B
201 West Capitol Avenue
Jefferson City, MO 65101
P: (573) 751-3604
E: Rocky.Miller
@house.mo.gov

**Mitten, Gina (D, 83)**
State Capitol, Room 107
201 West Capitol Avenue
Jefferson City, MO 65101
P: (573) 751-2883
E: Gina.Mitten@house.mo.gov

**Moon, Mike (R, 157)**
State Capitol, Room 203B
201 West Capitol Avenue
Jefferson City, MO 65101
P: (573) 751-4077
E: Mike.Moon@house.mo.gov

**Morgan, Judy (D, 24)**
State Capitol, Room 105-A
201 West Capitol Avenue
Jefferson City, MO 65101
P: (573) 751-4485
E: Judy.Morgan@house.mo.gov

**Morris, Lynn A. (R, 140)**
State Capitol, Room 200BC
201 West Capitol Avenue
Jefferson City, MO 65101
P: (573) 751-2565
E: Lynn.Morris@house.mo.gov

**Mosley, Jay (D, 68)***
State Capitol, Room 101G
201 West Capitol Avenue
Jefferson City, MO 65101
P: (573) 751-9628
E: jay.mosley@house.mo.gov

**Muntzel, Dave (R, 48)**
State Capitol, Room 235BB
201 West Capitol Avenue
Jefferson City, MO 65101
P: (573) 751-0169
E: Dave.Muntzel
@house.mo.gov

**Neely, Jim (R, 8)**
State Capitol, Room 110A
201 West Capitol Avenue
Jefferson City, MO 65101
P: (573) 751-0246
E: Jim.Neely@house.mo.gov

**Newman, Stacey (D, 87)**
State Capitol, Room 101K
201 West Capitol Avenue
Jefferson City, MO 65101
P: (573) 751-0100
F: (573) 526-9866
E: Stacey.Newman
@house.mo.gov

**Nichols, Mary (D, 72)**
State Capitol, Room 101A
201 West Capitol Avenue
Jefferson City, MO 65101
P: (573) 751-1832
F: (573) 526-2649
E: Mary.Nichols
@house.mo.gov

**Peters, Joshua (D, 76)**
State Capitol, Room 130-DC
201 West Capitol Avenue
Jefferson City, MO 65101
P: (573) 751-7605
E: Joshua.Peters
@house.mo.gov

**Pfautsch, Donna (R, 33)**
State Capitol, Room 404-B
201 West Capitol Avenue
Jefferson City, MO 65101
P: (573) 751-9766
E: Donna.Pfautsch
@house.mo.gov

**Phillips, Don (R, 138)**
State Capitol, Room 135
201 West Capitol Avenue
Jefferson City, MO 65101
P: (573) 751-3851
F: (573) 526-9794
E: Don.Phillips
@house.mo.gov

**Pierson Jr., Tommie (D, 66)***
State Capitol, Room 101H
201 West Capitol Avenue
Jefferson City, MO 65101
P: (573) 751-6845
E: tommie.pierson
@house.mo.gov

**Pietzman, Randy (R, 41)**
State Capitol, Room 408-B
201 West Capitol Avenue
Jefferson City, MO 65101
P: (573) 751-9459
E: Randy.Pietzman
@house.mo.gov

**Pike, Patricia (R, 126)**
State Capitol, Room 400CB
201 West Capitol Avenue
Jefferson City, MO 65101
P: (573) 751-5388
E: Patricia.Pike
@house.mo.gov

**Plocher, Dean (R, 89)**
State Capitol, Room 115-D
201 West Capitol Avenue
Jefferson City, MO 65101
P: (573) 751-1544
E: Dean.Plocher
@house.mo.gov

**Pogue, Jeff (R, 143)**
State Capitol, Room 400CC
201 West Capitol Avenue
Jefferson City, MO 65101
P: (573) 751-2264
E: Jeff.Pogue@house.mo.gov

**Quade, Crystal (D, 132)***
State Capitol, Room 105-I
201 West Capitol Avenue
Jefferson City, MO 65101
P: (573) 751-3795
E: crystal.quade
@house.mo.gov

**Razer, Greg (D, 25)***
State Capitol, Room 103BA
201 West Capitol Avenue
Jefferson City, MO 65101
P: (573) 751-2437
E: greg.razer@house.mo.gov

**Redmon, Craig (R, 4)**
State Capitol, Room 317-B
201 West Capitol Avenue
Jefferson City, MO 65101
P: (573) 751-3644
E: Craig.Redmon
@house.mo.gov

**Rehder, Holly (R, 148)**
State Capitol, Room 403-A
201 West Capitol Avenue
Jefferson City, MO 65101
P: (573) 751-5471
E: Holly.Rehder
@house.mo.gov

**Reiboldt, Bill (R, 160)**
State Capitol, Room 303B
201 West Capitol Avenue
Jefferson City, MO 65101
P: (573) 751-9781
F: (573) 522-9287
E: Bill.Reiboldt
@house.mo.gov

**Reisch, Cheri Toalson (R, 44)***
State Capitol, Room 115J
201 West Capitol Avenue
Jefferson City, MO 65101
P: (573) 751-1169
E: cheri.reisch
@house.mo.gov

**Remole, Tim (R, 6)**
State Capitol, Room 408-A
201 West Capitol Avenue
Jefferson City, MO 65101
P: (573) 751-6566
E: Tim.Remole@house.mo.gov

**Rhoads, Shawn (R, 154)**
State Capitol, Room 403B
201 West Capitol Avenue
Jefferson City, MO 65101
P: (573) 751-1455
E: Shawn.Rhoads
@house.mo.gov

**Richardson, Todd (R, 152)**
State Capitol, Room 308
201 West Capitol Avenue
Jefferson City, MO 65101
P: (573) 751-4039
F: (573) 751-5271
E: Todd.Richardson
@house.mo.gov

**Roberts, Steven (D, 77)***
State Capitol, Room 109H
201 West Capitol Avenue
Jefferson City, MO 65101
P: (573) 751-1400
E: steven.roberts
@house.mo.gov

**Roden, Shane (R, 111)**
State Capitol, Room 201-E
201 West Capitol Avenue
Jefferson City, MO 65101
P: (573) 751-4567
E: Shane.Roden@house.mo.gov

**Roeber, Rebecca (R, 34)**
State Capitol, Room 102-BA
201 West Capitol Avenue
Jefferson City, MO 65101
P: (573) 751-1456
E: Rebecca.Roeber
@house.mo.gov

**Rone, Don (R, 149)**
State Capitol, Room 201-C
201 West Capitol Avenue
Jefferson City, MO 65101
P: (573) 751-4085
E: Don.Rone@house.mo.gov

**Ross, Robert (R, 142)**
State Capitol, Room 114A
201 West Capitol Avenue
Jefferson City, MO 65101
P: (573) 751-1490
E: Robert.Ross@house.mo.gov

# Missouri

**Rowland, Lyle (R, 155)**
State Capitol, Room 310
201 West Capitol Avenue
Jefferson City, MO 65101
P: (573) 751-2042
F: (573) 526-0575
E: Lyle.Rowland
　@house.mo.gov

**Rowland, Rory (D, 29)**
State Capitol, Room 109-F
201 West Capitol Avenue
Jefferson City, MO 65101
P: (573) 751-3623
E: Rory.Rowland
　@house.mo.gov

**Runions, Joe (D, 37)**
State Capitol, Room 109-B
201 West Capitol Avenue
Jefferson City, MO 65101
P: (573) 751-0238
E: Joe.Runions@house.mo.gov

**Ruth, Becky (R, 114)**
State Capitol, Room 115-A
201 West Capitol Avenue
Jefferson City, MO 65101
P: (573) 751-4451
E: Becky.Ruth@house.mo.gov

**Schroer, Nick (R, 107)***
State Capitol, Room 400CA
201 West Capitol Avenue
Jefferson City, MO 65101
P: (573) 751-1470
E: nick.schroer
　@house.mo.gov

**Shaul, Dan (R, 113)**
State Capitol, Room 201-A
201 West Capitol Avenue
Jefferson City, MO 65101
P: (573) 751-2504
E: Dan.Shaul@house.mo.gov

**Shull, Noel (R, 16)**
State Capitol, Room 412-C
201 West Capitol Avenue
Jefferson City, MO 65101
P: (573) 751-9458
E: Noel.Shull@house.mo.gov

**Shumake, Lindell F. (R, 5)**
State Capitol, Room 404A
201 West Capitol Avenue
Jefferson City, MO 65101
P: (573) 751-3613
F: (573) 751-7928
E: Lindell.Shumake
　@house.mo.gov

**Smith, Clem (D, 85)**
State Capitol, Room 105C
201 West Capitol Avenue
Jefferson City, MO 65101
P: (573) 751-4468
F: (573) 526-1239
E: Clem.Smith@house.mo.gov

**Smith, Cody (R, 163)***
State Capitol, Room 115B
201 West Capitol Avenue
Jefferson City, MO 65101
P: (573) 751-5458
E: cody.smith@house.mo.gov

**Sommer, Chrissy (R, 106)**
State Capitol, Room 401A
201 West Capitol Avenue
Jefferson City, MO 65101
P: (573) 751-1452
E: Chrissy.Sommer
　@house.mo.gov

**Spencer, Bryan (R, 63)**
State Capitol, Room 200B
201 West Capitol Avenue
Jefferson City, MO 65101
P: (573) 751-1460
E: Bryan.Spencer
　@house.mo.gov

**Stacy, Dan (R, 31)***
State Capitol, Room 116-3
201 West Capitol Avenue
Jefferson City, MO 65101
P: (573) 751-8636
E: dan.stacy@house.mo.gov

**Stephens, Mike (R, 128)***
State Capitol, Room 201D
201 West Capitol Avenue
Jefferson City, MO 65101
P: (573) 751-1347
E: mike.stephens
　@house.mo.gov

**Stevens, Martha (D, 46)***
State Capitol, Room 105E
201 West Capitol Avenue
Jefferson City, MO 65101
P: (573) 751-9753
E: martha.stevens
　@house.mo.gov

**Swan, Kathryn (R, 147)**
State Capitol, Room 233-A
201 West Capitol Avenue
Jefferson City, MO 65101
P: (573) 751-1443
E: Kathryn.Swan
　@house.mo.gov

**Tate, Nate (R, 119)***
State Capitol, Room 115F
201 West Capitol Avenue
Jefferson City, MO 65101
P: (573) 751-0549
E: nate.tate@house.mo.gov

**Taylor, Jered (R, 139)**
State Capitol, Room 201-CA
201 West Capitol Avenue
Jefferson City, MO 65101
P: (573) 751-3833
E: Jered.Taylor
　@house.mo.gov

**Trent, Curtis (R, 133)***
State Capitol, Room 116-4
201 West Capitol Avenue
Jefferson City, MO 65101
P: (573) 751-0136
E: curtis.trent
　@house.mo.gov

**Unsicker, Sarah (D, 91)***
State Capitol, Room 135BC
201 West Capitol Avenue
Jefferson City, MO 65101
P: (573) 751-1285
E: sarah.unsicker
　@house.mo.gov

**Vescovo, Rob (R, 112)**
State Capitol, Room 409B
201 West Capitol Avenue
Jefferson City, MO 65101
P: (573) 751-3607
E: Rob.Vescovo@house.mo.gov

**Walker, Cora (D, 74)***
State Capitol, Room 101F
201 West Capitol Avenue
Jefferson City, MO 65101
P: (573) 751-4726
E: cora.walker@house.mo.gov

**Walker, Nate (R, 3)**
State Capitol, Room 316
201 West Capitol Avenue
Jefferson City, MO 65101
P: (573) 751-3647
E: Nate.Walker@house.mo.gov

**Wessels, Fred (D, 81)***
State Capitol, Room 135AC
201 West Capitol Avenue
Jefferson City, MO 65101
P: (573) 751-0438
E: fred.wessels
　@house.mo.gov

**White, Bill (R, 161)**
State Capitol, Room 400
201 West Capitol Avenue
Jefferson City, MO 65101
P: (573) 751-3791
E: Bill.White@house.mo.gov

**Wiemann, John (R, 103)**
State Capitol, Room 407-A
201 West Capitol Avenue
Jefferson City, MO 65101
P: (573) 751-2176
E: John.Wiemann
　@house.mo.gov

**Wilson, Kenneth (R, 12)**
State Capitol, Room 206A
201 West Capitol Avenue
Jefferson City, MO 65101
P: (573) 751-9760
E: Ken.Wilson@house.mo.gov

**Wood, David (R, 58)**
State Capitol, Room 235
201 West Capitol Avenue
Jefferson City, MO 65101
P: (573) 751-2077
E: David.Wood@house.mo.gov

# Montana

## Executive

### Governor

**The Honorable Steve Bullock (D)**
Governor
State Capitol
Helena, MT 59620
P: (406) 444-3111
F: (404) 444-5529

### Lieutenant Governor

**The Honorable Mike Cooney (D)**
Lieutenant Governor
Capitol Station, Room 207
P.O. Box 200801
Helena, MT 59620
P: (406) 444-5665
F: (406) 444-4648

### Attorney General

**The Honorable Tim Fox (R)**
Attorney General
Justice Building
215 North Sanders
Helena, MT 59620
P: (406) 444-2026
F: (406) 444-3549
E: contactdoj@mt.gov

### Auditor

**The Honorable Matt Rosendale (R)**
Commissioner of Securities & Insurance, State Auditor
840 Helena Avenue
Helena, MT 59601
P: (406) 444-2040
F: (406) 444-3497
E: stateauditor@mt.gov

### Public Service Commission

**Mr. Brad Johnson (R)**
Chair
1701 Prospect Avenue
P.O. Box 202601
Helena, MT 59620
P: (406) 444-6169
F: (406) 444-7618
E: bjohnson@mt.gov

**Mr. Travis Kavulla (R)**
Commissioner
1701 Prospect Avenue
P.O. Box 202601
Helena, MT 59620
P: (406) 444-6166
F: (406) 444-7618
E: tkavulla@mt.gov

**Mr. Roger Koopman (R)**
Commissioner
1701 Prospect Avenue
P.O. Box 202601
Helena, MT 59620
P: (406) 444-6168
E: rkoopman@mt.gov

**Mr. Bob Lake (R)**
Commissioner
1701 Prospect Avenue
P.O. Box 202601
Helena, MT 59620
P: (406) 444-6167
E: blake@mt.gov

**Mr. Tony O'Donnell (R)**
Commissioner
1701 Prospect Avenue
P.O. Box 202601
Helena, MT 59620
P: (406) 444-6165

### Secretary of State

**The Honorable Corey Stapleton (R)**
Secretary of State
P.O. Box 200801
Helena, MT 59620
P: (406) 444-2034
F: (406) 444-4249
E: sos@mt.gov

### Superintendent of Public Instruction

**The Honorable Elsie Arntzen (R)**
Superintendent of Public Instruction
P.O. Box 202501
Helena, MT 59620
P: (406) 444-5658
F: (406) 444-9299
E: opisupt@mt.gov

### Treasurer

**The Honorable Sheila Hogan** (appointed)
Director
125 North Roberts Street, Room 155
P.O. Box 200101
Helena, MT 59620
P: (406) 444-3033
F: (406) 444-6194
E: shogan@mt.gov

## Judiciary

### Supreme Court (NE)

**Mr. Ed Smith**
Clerk
215 North Sanders, Room 323
P.O. Box 203003
Helena, MT 59620
P: (406) 444-3858
F: (406) 444-5705

**The Honorable Mike McGrath**
Chief Justice
**The Honorable Beth Baker**
**The Honorable Laurie McKinnon**
**The Honorable James A. Rice**
**The Honorable Dirk M. Sandefur**
**The Honorable James J. Shea**
**The Honorable Michael Wheat**

## Legislative
## Senate

### Senate President

**Senator Scott Sales (R)**
Senate President
P.O. Box 200500
Helena, MT 59620
P: (406) 444-4800
F: (406) 444-4875
E: sales4mtsenate @hotmail.com

### President Pro Tempore of the Senate

**Senator Bob Keenan (R)**
President Pro Tempore
P.O. Box 200500
Helena, MT 59620
P: (406) 444-4800
F: (406) 444-4875
E: bob@bobkeenan.us

### Senate Majority Leader

**Senator Fred Thomas (R)**
Senate Majority Leader
P.O. Box 200500
Helena, MT 59620
P: (406) 444-4800
F: (406) 444-4875
E: sfredthomas@yahoo.com

### Senate Minority Leader

**Senator Jon Sesso (D)**
Senate Minority Leader
P.O. Box 200500
Helena, MT 59620
P: (406) 444-4800
F: (406) 444-4875
E: jonsesso@yahoo.com

### Secretary of the Senate

**Ms. Marilyn Miller**
Secretary of the Senate
Room 302B, State Capitol
P.O. Box 200500
Helena, MT 59620
P: (406) 444-4801
F: (406) 444-4875
E: mmiller2@mt.gov

### Members of the Senate

**Ankney, Duane (R, 20)**
P.O. Box 200500
Helena, MT 59620
P: (406) 444-4800
F: (406) 444-4875
E: goodwind1.duane @gmail.com

**Barrett, Dick (D, 45)**
P.O. Box 200500
Helena, MT 59620
P: (406) 444-4800
F: (406) 444-4875
E: rnewbar@gmail.com

**Blasdel, Mark (R, 4)**
P.O. Box 200500
Helena, MT 59620
P: (406) 444-4800
F: (406) 444-4875
E: Sen.Mark.Blasdel@mt.gov

**Boland, Cydnie (D, 12)**
P.O. Box 200500
Helena, MT 59620
P: (406) 444-4800
F: (406) 444-4825
E: sen.carlie.boland@mt.gov

**Brown, Dee L. (R, 2)**
P.O. Box 200500
Helena, MT 59620
P: (406) 444-4800
F: (406) 444-4875
E: Sen.Dee.Brown@mt.gov

**Buttrey, Edward (R, 11)**
P.O. Box 200500
Helena, MT 59620
P: (406) 444-4800
F: (406) 444-4875
E: ebuttrey@senate13.com

# Montana

**Caferro, Mary (D, 41)**
P.O. Box 200500
Helena, MT 59620
P: (406) 444-4800
F: (406) 444-4875
E: marycaferro@gmail.com

**Cohenour, Jill (D, 42)**
P.O. Box 200500
Helena, MT 59620
P: (406) 444-4800
F: (406) 444-4875
E: Sen.Jill.Cohenour@mt.gov

**Connell, Pat (R, 43)**
P.O. Box 200500
Helena, MT 59620
P: (406) 444-4800
F: (406) 444-4875
E: connell4sd43@yahoo.com

**Facey, Tom (D, 50)**
P.O. Box 200500
Helena, MT 59620
P: (406) 444-4800
F: (406) 444-4875
E: TFacey@mt.gov

**Fielder, Jennifer (R, 7)**
P.O. Box 200500
Helena, MT 59620
P: (406) 444-4800
F: (406) 444-4875
E: Sen.Jennifer.Fielder
    @mt.gov

**Fitzpatrick, Steve (R, 10)**
P.O. Box 200500
Helena, MT 59620
P: (406) 444-4800
F: (406) 444-4875
E: Sen.Steve.Fitzpatrick
    @mt.gov

**Gauthier, Terry (R, 40)***
P.O. Box 200500
Helena, MT 59620
P: (406) 444-4800
F: (406) 444-4875
E: Mrmac570@me.com

**Gross, Jen (D, 25)***
P.O. Box 200500
Helena, MT 59620
P: (406) 444-4800
F: (406) 444-4875
E: Sen.Jen.Gross@mt.gov

**Hinebauch, Steve (R, 18)***
P.O. Box 200500
Helena, MT 59620
P: (406) 444-4800
F: (406) 444-4875
E: Sen.Steve.Hinebauch
    @mt.gov

**Hinkle, Jedediah (R, 32)**
P.O. Box 200500
Helena, MT 59620
P: (406) 444-4800
F: (406) 444-4875
E: Sen.Jedediah.Hinkle
    @mt.gov

**Hoven, Brian E. (R, 13)**
P.O. Box 200500
Helena, MT 59620
P: (406) 444-4800
F: (406) 444-4875
E: brian@hovenequipment.com

**Howard, David (R, 29)**
P.O. Box 200500
Helena, MT 59620
P: (406) 444-4800
F: (406) 444-4875
E: sendavidhoward@gmail.com

**Jones, Llew (R, 9)**
P.O. Box 200500
Helena, MT 59620
P: (406) 444-4800
F: (406) 444-4875
E: Sen.Llew.Jones@mt.gov

**Kary, Douglas (R, 22)**
P.O. Box 200500
Helena, MT 59620
P: (406) 444-4800
F: (406) 444-4875
E: Sen.Doug.Kary@mt.gov

**Keenan, Bob (R, 5)**
P.O. Box 200500
Helena, MT 59620
P: (406) 444-4800
F: (406) 444-4875
E: bob@bobkeenan.us

**Lang, Mike (R, 17)**
P.O. Box 200500
Helena, MT 59620
P: (406) 444-4800
F: (406) 444-4875
E: Sen.Mike.Lang@mt.gov

**MacDonald, Margie (D, 26)**
P.O. Box 200500
Helena, MT 59620
P: (406) 444-4800
F: (406) 444-4875
E: Sen.Margie.MacDonald
    @mt.gov

**Malek, Sue (D, 46)**
P.O. Box 200500
Helena, MT 59620
P: (406) 444-4800
F: (406) 444-4875
E: suemalek@gmail.com

**McClafferty, Edie L.
    (D, 38)**
P.O. Box 200500
Helena, MT 59620
P: (406) 444-4800
F: (406) 444-4875
E: ediemcclafferty
    @gmail.com

**McNally, Mary (D, 24)**
P.O. Box 200500
Helena, MT 59620
P: (406) 444-4800
F: (406) 444-4875
E: Sen.Mary.McNally@mt.gov

**Moore, Eric (R, 19)**
P.O. Box 200500
Helena, MT 59620
P: (406) 444-4800
F: (406) 444-4875
E: mail
    @senatoricmoore.com

**Olszewski, Albert D. (R, 6)**
P.O. Box 200500
Helena, MT 59620
P: (406) 444-4800
F: (406) 444-4875
E: Sen.Albert.Olszewski
    @mt.gov

**Osmundson, Ryan (R, 15)**
P.O. Box 200500
Helena, MT 59620
P: (406) 444-4800
F: (406) 444-4875
E: ryanosmundson@gmail.com

**Phillips, Mike (D, 31)**
P.O. Box 200500
Helena, MT 59620
P: (406) 444-4800
F: (406) 444-4875
E: mikephillips@montana.net

**Pomnichowski, J.P. (D, 33)**
P.O. Box 200500
Helena, MT 59620
P: (406) 444-4800
F: (406) 444-4875
E: Sen.JP@mt.gov

**Regier, Keith (R, 3)**
P.O. Box 200500
Helena, MT 59620
P: (406) 444-4800
F: (406) 444-4875
E: Sen.Keith.Regier@mt.gov

**Richmond, Tom (R, 28)**
P.O. Box 200500
Helena, MT 59620
P: (406) 444-4800
F: (406) 444-4875
E: tomrichmondmt@gmail.com

**Sales, Scott (R, 35)**
P.O. Box 200500
Helena, MT 59620
P: (406) 444-4800
F: (406) 444-4875
E: sales4mtsenate
    @hotmail.com

**Salomon, Daniel (R, 47)**
P.O. Box 200500
Helena, MT 59620
P: (406) 444-4800
F: (406) 444-4875
E: dansalomon12@gmail.com

**Sands, Diane (D, 49)**
P.O. Box 200500
Helena, MT 59620
P: (406) 444-4800
F: (406) 444-4875
E: senatorsands@gmail.com

**Sesso, Jon (D, 37)**
P.O. Box 200500
Helena, MT 59620
P: (406) 444-4800
F: (406) 444-4875
E: jonsesso@yahoo.com

**Small, Jason (R, 21)***
P.O. Box 200500
Helena, MT 59620
P: (406) 444-4800
F: (406) 444-4875
E: Sen.Jason.Small@mt.gov

**Smith, Cary L. (R, 27)**
P.O. Box 200500
Helena, MT 59620
P: (406) 444-4800
F: (406) 444-4875
E: Sen.Cary.Smith@mt.gov

**Smith, Frank J. (D, 16)***
P.O. Box 200500
Helena, MT 59620
P: (406) 444-4800
F: (406) 444-4875
E: clairena@hughes.net

**Swandal, Nels (R, 30)**
P.O. Box 200500
Helena, MT 59620
P: (406) 444-4800
F: (406) 444-4875
E: Sen.Nels.Swandal@mt.gov

**Tempel, Russell (R, 14)***
P.O. Box 200500
Helena, MT 59620
P: (406) 444-4800
F: (406) 444-4875
E: Sen.Russ.Tempel@mt.gov

**Thomas, Fred (R, 44)**
P.O. Box 200500
Helena, MT 59620
P: (406) 444-4800
F: (406) 444-4875
E: sfredthomas@yahoo.com

**Vance, Gordon (R, 34)**
P.O. Box 200500
Helena, MT 59620
P: (406) 444-4800
F: (406) 444-4875
E: vancesd34@gmail.com

**Vincent, Chas V. (R, 1)**
P.O. Box 200500
Helena, MT 59620
P: (406) 444-4800
F: (406) 444-4875
E: cvvincent@hotmail.com

**Vuckovich, Gene (D, 39)**
P.O. Box 200500
Helena, MT 59620
P: (406) 444-4800
F: (406) 444-4875
E: Sen.Gene.Vuckovich
  @mt.gov

**Webb, Roger (R, 23)**
P.O. Box 200500
Helena, MT 59620
P: (406) 444-4800
F: (406) 444-4875
E: webb4mt@hotmail.com

**Welborn, Jeffrey W. (R, 36)**
P.O. Box 200500
Helena, MT 59620
P: (406) 444-4800
F: (406) 444-4875
E: jeffwelborn@hotmail.com

**Whitford, Lea (D, 8)**
P.O. Box 200500
Helena, MT 59620
P: (406) 444-4800
F: (406) 444-4875
E: lea.whitford@gmail.com

**Wolken, Cynthia (D, 48)**
P.O. Box 200500
Helena, MT 59620
P: (406) 444-4800
F: (406) 444-4875
E: Sen.Cynthia.Wolken
  @mt.gov

# House
## Speaker of the House
**Representative Austin Knudsen (R)**
Speaker of the House
P.O. Box 200400
Helena, MT 59620
P: (406) 444-4800
F: (406) 444-4825
E: austinforhouse@yahoo.com

## Speaker Pro Tempore of the House
**Representative Greg Hertz (R)**
P.O. Box 200400
Helena, MT 59620
P: (406) 444-4800
F: (406) 444-4825
E: greghertz11@gmail.com

## House Majority Leader
**Representative Ron Ehli (R)**
Majority Leader
P.O. Box 200400
Helena, MT 59620
P: (406) 444-4800
F: (406) 444-4825
E: Rep.Ron.Ehli@mt.gov

## House Minority Leader
**Representative Jenny Eck (D)**
Minority Leader
P.O. Box 200400
Helena, MT 59620
P: (406) 444-4800
F: (406) 444-4825
E: jennyeck4mt@gmail.com

## Clerk of the House
**Ms. Lindsey Grovom**
Chief Clerk of the House
Room 370, State Capitol
P.O. Box 200400
Helena, MT 59620
P: (406) 444-4819
F: (406) 444-4825
E: lvroegindewey@mt.gov

# Members of the House
**Abbott, Kim (D, 83)***
P.O. Box 200400
Helena, MT 59620
P: (406) 444-4800
F: (406) 444-4825
E: Rep.Kim.Abbott@mt.gov

**Anderson, Fred (R, 20)***
P.O. Box 200400
Helena, MT 59620
P: (406) 444-4800
F: (406) 444-4825

**Bachmeier, Jacob (D, 28)***
P.O. Box 200400
Helena, MT 59620
P: (406) 444-4800
F: (406) 444-4825

**Ballance, Nancy (R, 87)**
P.O. Box 200400
Helena, MT 59620
P: (406) 444-4800
F: (406) 444-4825
E: nancyballance@aol.com

**Bartel, Dan (R, 29)***
P.O. Box 200400
Helena, MT 59620
P: (406) 444-4800
F: (406) 444-4825
E: Danbartel2@gmail.com

**Beard, Becky (R, 80)***
P.O. Box 200400
Helena, MT 59620
P: (406) 444-4800
F: (406) 444-4825
E: becky4hd80@blackfoot.net

**Bennett, Bryce (D, 91)**
P.O. Box 200400
Helena, MT 59620
P: (406) 444-4800
F: (406) 444-4825
E: bennettforhouse
  @gmail.com

**Berglee, Seth (R, 58)**
P.O. Box 200400
Helena, MT 59620
P: (406) 444-4800
F: (406) 444-4825
E: Rep.Seth.Berglee@mt.gov

**Bishop, Laurie (D, 60)***
P.O. Box 200400
Helena, MT 59620
P: (406) 444-4800
F: (406) 444-4825
E: Rep.Laurie.Bishop@mt.gov

**Brodehl, Randy (R, 9)**
P.O. Box 200400
Helena, MT 59620
P: (406) 444-4800
F: (406) 444-4825
E: randybrodehl57@gmail.com

**Brown, Bob (R, 13)**
P.O. Box 200400
Helena, MT 59620
P: (406) 444-4800
F: (406) 444-4825
E: Rep.Bob.Brown@mt.gov

**Brown, Zach D. (D, 63)**
P.O. Box 200400
Helena, MT 59620
P: (406) 444-4800
F: (406) 444-4825
E: brownformontana
  @gmail.com

**Burnett, Tom (R, 67)**
P.O. Box 200400
Helena, MT 59620
P: (406) 444-4800
F: (406) 444-4825
E: burnetthd67@gmail.com

**Cook, Rob (R, 18)**
P.O. Box 200400
Helena, MT 59620
P: (406) 444-4800
F: (406) 444-4825
E: Rep.Rob.Cook@mt.gov

**Court, Virginia (D, 50)**
P.O. Box 200400
Helena, MT 59620
P: (406) 444-4800
F: (406) 444-4825
E: vcourtforlegislature
  @yahoo.com

**Cuffe, Mike (R, 2)**
P.O. Box 200400
Helena, MT 59620
P: (406) 444-4800
F: (406) 444-4825
E: Rep.Mike.Cuffe@mt.gov

**Curdy, Willis (D, 98)**
P.O. Box 200400
Helena, MT 59620
P: (406) 444-4800
F: (406) 444-4825
E: Rep.Willis.Curdy@mt.gov

**Curtis, Amanda (D, 74)***
P.O. Box 200400
Helena, MT 59620
P: (406) 444-4800
F: (406) 444-4825
E: amanda
  @curtisforbutte.com

# Montana

**Custer, Geraldine (R, 39)**
P.O. Box 200400
Helena, MT 59620
P: (406) 444-4800
F: (406) 444-4825
E: Rep.Geraldine.Custer
@mt.gov

**Doane, Alan (R, 36)**
P.O. Box 200400
Helena, MT 59620
P: (406) 444-4800
F: (406) 444-4825
E: alandoane@midrivers.com

**Dudik, Kimberly (D, 94)**
P.O. Box 200400
Helena, MT 59620
P: (406) 444-4800
F: (406) 444-4825
E: kimberly.dudik@gmail.com

**Dunwell, Mary Ann (D, 84)**
P.O. Box 200400
Helena, MT 59620
P: (406) 444-4800
F: (406) 444-4825
E: Rep.MaryAnn.Dunwell
@mt.gov

**Eck, Jenny (D, 79)**
P.O. Box 200400
Helena, MT 59620
P: (406) 444-4800
F: (406) 444-4825
E: jennyeck4mt@gmail.com

**Ehli, Ron (R, 86)**
P.O. Box 200400
Helena, MT 59620
P: (406) 444-4800
F: (406) 444-4825
E: Rep.Ron.Ehli@mt.gov

**Ellis, Janet (D, 81)**
P.O. Box 200400
Helena, MT 59620
P: (406) 444-4800
F: (406) 444-4825
E: Rep.Janet.Ellis@mt.gov

**Essmann, Jeff (R, 54)**
P.O. Box 200400
Helena, MT 59620
P: (406) 444-4800
F: (406) 444-4825
E: jessmann@mt.gov

**Fern, Dave (D, 5)***
P.O. Box 200400
Helena, MT 59630
P: (406) 444-4800
F: (406) 444-4825
E: Rep.Dave.Fern@mt.gov

**Fitzgerald, Ross (R, 17)***
P.O. Box 200400
Helena, MT 59620
P: (406) 444-4800
F: (406) 444-4825
E: Rep.Ross.Fitzgerald
@mt.gov

**Fleming, John (D, 93)***
P.O. Box 200400
Helena, MT 59620
P: (406) 444-4800
F: (406) 444-4825
E: fleming@stignatius.net

**Flynn, Kelly (R, 70)**
P.O. Box 200400
Helena, MT 59620
P: (406) 444-4800
F: (406) 444-4825
E: Rep.Kelly.Flynn@mt.gov

**Funk, Moffie (D, 82)**
P.O. Box 200400
Helena, MT 59620
P: (406) 444-4800
F: (406) 444-4825
E: Rep.Moffie.Funk@mt.gov

**Galt, E. Wylie (R, 30)***
P.O. Box 200400
Helena, MT 59620
P: (406) 444-4800
F: (406) 444-4825
E: wyliegaltformt@gmail.com

**Garner, Frank (R, 7)**
P.O. Box 200400
Helena, MT 59620
P: (406) 444-4800
F: (406) 444-4825
E: Rep.Frank.Gardner@mt.gov

**Glimm, Carl (R, 6)**
P.O. Box 200400
Helena, MT 59620
P: (406) 444-4800
F: (406) 444-4825
E: Rep.Carl.Glimm@mt.gov

**Greef, Edward (R, 88)**
P.O. Box 200400
Helena, MT 59620
P: (406) 444-4800
F: (406) 444-4825
E: edgreef@hotmail.com

**Grubbs, Bruce (R, 68)***
P.O. Box 200400
Helena, MT 59620
P: (406) 444-4800
F: (406) 444-4825
E: rep.bruce.grubbs@mt.gov

**Gunderson, Steve (R, 1)***
P.O. Box 200400
Helena, MT 59620
P: (406) 444-4800
F: (406) 444-4825
E: Rep.Steve.Gunderson
@mt.gov

**Hamilton, Jim (D, 61)***
P.O. Box 200400
Helena, MT 59620
P: (406) 444-4800
F: (406) 444-4825
E: Rep.Jim.Hamilton@mt.gov

**Hamlett, Bradley Maxon
(D, 23)**
P.O. Box 200400
Helena, MT 59620
P: (406) 444-4800
F: (406) 444-4825
E: Rep.Bradley.Hamlett
@mt.gov

**Harris, Bill (R, 37)**
P.O. Box 200400
Helena, MT 59620
P: (406) 444-4800
F: (406) 444-4825
E: harris@midrivers.com

**Hayman, Denise (D, 66)**
P.O. Box 200400
Helena, MT 59620
P: (406) 444-4800
F: (406) 444-4825
E: Rep.Denise.Hayman@mt.gov

**Hertz, Adam (R, 96)***
P.O. Box 200400
Helena, MT 59620
P: (406) 444-4800
F: (406) 444-4825
E: Rep.Adam.Hertz@mt.gov

**Hertz, Greg (R, 12)**
P.O. Box 200400
Helena, MT 59620
P: (406) 444-4800
F: (406) 444-4825
E: greghertz11@gmail.com

**Holmlund, Kenneth (R, 38)**
P.O. Box 200400
Helena, MT 59620
P: (406) 444-4800
F: (406) 444-4825
E: Rep.Ken.Holmlund@mt.gov

**Hopkins, Mike (R, 92)***
P.O. Box 200400
Helena, MT 59620
P: (406) 444-4800
F: (406) 444-4825
E: Mikeformontana@gmail.com

**Jacobson, Tom (D, 21)**
P.O. Box 200400
Helena, MT 59620
P: (406) 444-4800
F: (406) 444-4825
E: tomjacobsonmt@gmail.com

**Jones, Donald W. (R, 46)**
P.O. Box 200400
Helena, MT 59620
P: (406) 444-4800
F: (406) 444-4825
E: donjonesmt@gmail.com

**Karjala, Jessica (D, 48)**
P.O. Box 200400
Helena, MT 59620
P: (406) 444-4800
F: (406) 444-4825
E: Rep.Jessica.Karjala
@mt.gov

**Keane, Jim (D, 73)**
P.O. Box 200400
Helena, MT 59620
P: (406) 444-4800
F: (406) 444-4825

**Kelker, Katharin A. (D, 47)**
P.O. Box 200400
Helena, MT 59620
P: (406) 444-4800
F: (406) 444-4825
E: Rep.Kathy.Kelker@mt.gov

**Kipp III, George G. (D, 15)**
P.O. Box 200400
Helena, MT 59620
P: (406) 444-4800
F: (406) 444-4825
E: Rep.George.Kipp@mt.gov

**Knokey, Jon (R, 65)***
P.O. Box 200400
Helena, MT 59620
P: (406) 444-4800
F: (406) 444-4825
E: Rep.Jon.Knokey@mt.gov

**Knudsen, Austin (R, 34)**
P.O. Box 200400
Helena, MT 59620
P: (406) 444-4800
F: (406) 444-4825
E: austinforhouse@yahoo.com

**Knudsen, Casey (R, 33)***
P.O. Box 200400
Helena, MT 59620
P: (406) 444-4800
F: (406) 444-4825
E: Rep.Casey.Knudsen@mt.gov

**Lavin, Steve (R, 8)**
P.O. Box 200400
Helena, MT 59620
P: (406) 444-4800
F: (406) 444-4825
E: Rep.Steve.Lavin@mt.gov

**Lenz, Dennis (R, 53)***
P.O. Box 200400
Helena, MT 59620
P: (406) 444-4800
F: (406) 444-4825
E: Rep.Dennis.Lenz@mt.gov

**Loge, Denley (R, 14)***
P.O. Box 200400
Helena, MT 59620
P: (406) 444-4800
F: (406) 444-4825
E: Denleylogehd14@gmail.com

**Lynch, Ryan (D, 76)**
P.O. Box 200400
Helena, MT 59620
P: (406) 444-4800
F: (406) 444-4825
E: Rep.Ryan.Lynch@mt.gov

**Mandeville, Forrest J.
   (R, 57)**
P.O. Box 200400
Helena, MT 59620
P: (406) 444-4800
F: (406) 444-4825
E: Rep.Forrest.Mandeville
   @mt.gov

**Manzella, Theresa (R, 85)**
P.O. Box 200400
Helena, MT 59620
P: (406) 444-4800
F: (406) 444-4825
E: Rep.Theresa.Manzella
   @mt.gov

**McCarthy, Kelly (D, 49)**
P.O. Box 200400
Helena, MT 59620
P: (406) 444-4800
F: (406) 444-4825
E: kelly
   @kellyformontana.org

**McConnell, Nate (D, 89)**
P.O. Box 200400
Helena, MT 59620
P: (406) 444-4800
F: (406) 444-4825
E: nateforhd89@gmail.com

**McKamey, Wendy (R, 19)**
P.O. Box 200400
Helena, MT 59620
P: (406) 444-4800
F: (406) 444-4825
E: Rep.Wendy.McKamey@mt.go

**Morigeau, Shane A. (D, 95)***
P.O. Box 200400
Helena, MT 59620
P: (406) 444-4800
F: (406) 444-4825
E: Rep.Shane.Morigeau
   @mt.gov

**Mortensen, Dale (R, 44)**
P.O. Box 200400
Helena, MT 59620
P: (406) 444-4800
F: (406) 444-4825
E: Rep.Dale.Mortensen
   @mt.gov

**Noland, Mark R. (R, 10)**
P.O. Box 200400
Helena, MT 59620
P: (406) 444-4800
F: (406) 444-4825
E: marknolandhd10@gmail.com

**O'Hara, James (R, 27)***
P.O. Box 200400
Helena, MT 59620
P: (406) 444-4800
F: (406) 444-4825
E: rep.james.ohara@mt.gov

**Olsen, Andrea (D, 100)**
P.O. Box 200400
Helena, MT 59620
P: (406) 444-4800
F: (406) 444-4825
E: Rep.Andrea.Olsen@mt.gov

**Patelis, Jimmy (R, 52)***
P.O. Box 200400
Helena, MT 59620
P: (406) 444-4800
F: (406) 444-4825
E: Rep.Jimmy.Patelis@mt.gov

**Peppers, Patricia Rae
   (D, 41)**
P.O. Box 200400
Helena, MT 59620
P: (406) 444-4800
F: (406) 444-4825
E: Rep.Rae.Peppers@mt.gov

**Perry, Zac (D, 3)**
P.O. Box 200400
Helena, MT 59620
P: (406) 444-4800
F: (406) 444-4825
E: Rep.Zac.Perry@mt.gov

**Pierson, Gordon (D, 78)**
P.O. Box 200400
Helena, MT 59620
P: (406) 444-4800
F: (406) 444-4825
E: Rep.Gordon.Pierson
   @mt.gov

**Price, Jean (D, 24)**
P.O. Box 200400
Helena, MT 59620
P: (406) 444-4800
F: (406) 444-4825
E: jeanbigskybigwin
   @gmail.com

**Redfield, Alan (R, 59)**
P.O. Box 200400
Helena, MT 59620
P: (406) 444-4800
F: (406) 444-4825
E: Rep.Alan.Redfield@mt.gov

**Reiger, Matt (R, 4)***
P.O. Box 200400
Helena, MT 59620
P: (406) 444-4800
F: (406) 444-4825
E: Rep.Matt.Regier@mt.gov

**Ricci, Vince (R, 55)**
P.O. Box 200400
Helena, MT 59620
P: (406) 444-4800
F: (406) 444-4825
E: Rep.Vince.Ricci@mt.gov

**Rosendale, Adam (R, 51)***
P.O. Box 200400
Helena, MT 59620
P: (406) 444-4800
F: (406) 444-4825
E: Atomicrosie@gmail.com

**Ryan, Marilyn (D, 99)***
P.O. Box 200400
Helena, MT 59620
P: (406) 444-4800
F: (406) 444-4825
E: Rep.Marilyn.Ryan@mt.gov

**Sales, Walt (R, 69)***
P.O. Box 200400
Helena, MT 59620
P: (406) 444-4800
F: (406) 444-4825
E: Rep.Walt.Sales@mt.gov

**Schreiner, Casey (D, 26)**
P.O. Box 200400
Helena, MT 59620
P: (406) 444-4800
F: (406) 444-4825
E: Rep.Casey.Schreiner
   @mt.gov

**Shaw, Ray (R, 71)**
P.O. Box 200400
Helena, MT 59620
P: (406) 444-4800
F: (406) 444-4825
E: Rep.Ray.Shaw@mt.gov

**Sheldon-Galloway, Lola
   (R, 22)***
P.O. Box 200400
Helena, MT 59620
P: (406) 444-4800
F: (406) 444-4825
E: Rep.
   Lola.Sheldon-Galloway
   @mt.gov

**Skees, Derek (R, 11)***
P.O. Box 200400
Helena, MT 59620
P: (406) 444-4800
F: (406) 444-4825
E: derekskees@gmail.com

**Smith, Bridget (D, 31)**
P.O. Box 200400
Helena, MT 59620
P: (406) 444-4800
F: (406) 444-4825
E: repbsmith@gmail.com

**Smith, Ellie Hill (D, 90)**
PO Box 200400
Helena, MT 59620
P: (406) 444-4800
F: (406) 444-4825
E: elliehillhd94@gmail.com

**Staffanson, Scott (R, 35)**
P.O. Box 200400
Helena, MT 59620
P: (406) 444-4800
F: (406) 444-4825
E: scottstaffanson
   @gmail.com

**Stewart-Peregoy, Sharon
   (D, 42)**
P.O. Box 200400
Helena, MT 59620
P: (406) 444-4800
F: (406) 444-4825
E: Rep.
   Sharon.Stewart-Peregoy
   @mt.gov

**Swanson, Kathy (D, 77)**
P.O. Box 200400
Helena, MT 59620
P: (406) 444-4800
F: (406) 444-4825
E: Rep.Kathy.Swanson@mt.gov

**Trebas, Jeremy (R, 25)***
P.O. Box 200400
Helena, MT 59620
P: (406) 444-4800
F: (406) 444-4825
E: Rep.Jeremy.Trebas@mt.gov

**Tschida, Brad (R, 97)**
P.O. Box 200400
Helena, MT 59620
P: (406) 444-4800
F: (406) 444-4825
E: Rep.Brad.Tschida@mt.gov

**Usher, Barry (R, 40)***
P.O. Box 200400
Helena, MT 59620
P: (406) 444-4800
F: (406) 444-4825
E: Rep.Barry.Usher@mt.gov

# Montana

**Vinton, Sue (R, 56)***
P.O. Box 200400
Helena, MT 59620
P: (406) 444-4800
F: (406) 444-4825
E: Rep.Sue.Vinton@mt.gov

**Wagoner, Kirk (R, 75)**
P.O. Box 200400
Helena, MT 59620
P: (406) 444-4800
F: (406) 444-4825
E: kirk@kirkbwagoner.org

**Webb, Peggy (R, 43)***
P.O. Box 200400
Helena, MT 59620
P: (406) 444-4800
F: (406) 444-4825
E: Webb4house@gmail.com

**Webber, Susan A. (D, 16)**
P.O. Box 200400
Helena, MT 59620
P: (406) 444-4800
F: (406) 444-4825
E: Rep.Susan.Webber
   @gmail.com

**Welch, Tom (R, 72)***
P.O. Box 200400
Helena, MT 59620
P: (406) 444-4800
F: (406) 444-4825
E: Twelch1213@gmail.com

**White, Kerry (R, 64)**
P.O. Box 200400
Helena, MT 59620
P: (406) 444-4800
F: (406) 444-4825
E: winwithwhite@gmail.com

**Windy Boy, Jonathan (D, 32)**
P.O. Box 200400
Helena, MT 59620
P: (406) 444-4800
F: (406) 444-4825
E: SenatorJWB@gmail.com

**Woods, Tom (D, 62)**
P.O. Box 200400
Helena, MT 59620
P: (406) 444-4800
F: (406) 444-4825
E: tomwoods4mt@gmail.com

**Zolnikov, Daniel (R, 45)**
P.O. Box 200400
Helena, MT 59620
P: (406) 444-4800
F: (406) 444-4825
E: Rep.Daniel.Zolnikov
   @mt.gov

# Nebraska

## Executive

### Governor
The Honorable Pete
  Ricketts (R)
Governor
P.O. Box 94848
Lincoln, NE 68509
P: (402) 471-2244
F: (402) 741-6031

### Lieutenant Governor
The Honorable Mike
  Foley (R)
Lieutenant Governor
State Capitol, Room 2315
P.O. Box 94863
Lincoln, NE 68509
P: (402) 471-2256
F: (402) 471-6031
E: mike.foley@nebraska.gov

### Attorney General
The Honorable Doug
  Peterson (R)
Attorney General
State Capitol
P.O. Box 98920
Lincoln, NE 68509
P: (402) 471-2682
F: (402) 471-3297

### Auditor
The Honorable Charlie
  Janssen (R)
State Auditor
Room 2303, State Capitol
P.O. Box 98917
Lincoln, NE 68509
P: (402) 471-2111
F: (402) 471-3301
E: charlie.janssen
  @nebraska.gov

### Secretary of State
The Honorable John A.
  Gale (R)
Secretary of State
P.O. Box 94608-4608
Lincoln, NE 68509
P: (402) 471-2554
F: (402) 471-3237
E: sos.info@nebraska.gov

### Treasurer
The Honorable Don B.
  Stenberg (R)
State Treasurer
State Capitol, Room 2005
Lincoln, NE 68509
P: (402) 471-2455
F: (402) 471-4390
E: Don.Stenberg
  @nebraska.gov

## Judiciary

### Supreme Court (MR)
Ms. Teresa Brown
Clerk
2413 State Capitol
P.O. Box 98910
Lincoln, NE 68509
P: (402) 471-3731
F: (402) 471-3480
E: terri.a.brown
  @nebraska.gov

The Honorable Michael G.
  Heavican
Chief Justice
The Honorable William B.
  Cassel
The Honorable Jeffrey J.
  Funke
The Honorable Max J. Kelch
The Honorable Lindsey
  Miller-Lerman
The Honorable Stephanie F.
  Stacy
The Honorable John F.
  Wright

## Clerk of the Legislature
Mr. Patrick J. O'Donnell
Clerk of the Legislature
State Capitol, Room 2018
P.O. Box 94604
Lincoln, NE 68509
P: (402) 471-2271
F: (402) 471-2126
E: podonnell@leg.ne.gov

## Members of the Senate
Albrecht, Joni (NP, 17)*
State Capitol, Room 2010
PO Box 94604
Lincoln, NE 68509
P: (402) 471-2716
E: jalbrecht@leg.ne.gov

Baker, Roy (NP, 30)
State Capitol, Room 1208
P.O. Box 94604
Lincoln, NE 68509
P: (402) 471-2620
E: rbaker@leg.ne.gov

Blood, Carol (NP, 3)*
State Capitol, Room 1021
PO Box 94604
Lincoln, NE 68509
P: (402) 471-2627
E: cblood@leg.ne.gov

Bolz, Kate (NP, 29)
State Capitol, Room 1015
P.O. Box 94604
Lincoln, NE 68509
P: (402) 471-2734
F: (402) 471-2126
E: kbolz@leg.ne.gov

Bostelman, Bruce (NP, 23)*
State Capitol
PO Box 94604
Lincoln, NE 68509

Brasch, Lydia (NP, 16)
State Capitol, Room 1022
P.O. Box 94604
Lincoln, NE 68509
P: (402) 471-2728
F: (402) 471-2126
E: lbrasch@leg.ne.gov

Brewer, Tom (NP, 43)*
State Capitol, Room 1202
PO Box 94604
Lincoln, NE 68509
P: (402) 471-2628
E: tbrewer@leg.ne.gov

Chambers, Ernie (NP, 11)
State Capitol, Room 1302
P.O. Box 94604
Lincoln, NE 68509
P: (402) 471-2612
F: (402) 471-2126
E: echambers@leg.ne.gov

Clements, Richard (NP, 2)*
State Capitol, Room 1523
PO Box 94604
Lincoln, NE 68509
P: (402) 471-2613
E: rclements@leg.ne.gov

Craighead, Joni (NP, 6)
State Capitol, Room 2107
P.O. Box 94604
Lincoln, NE 68509
P: (402) 471-2714
E: jcraighead@leg.ne.gov

Crawford, Sue (NP, 45)
State Capitol, Room 1016
P.O. Box 94604
Lincoln, NE 68509
P: (402) 471-2628
F: (402) 471-2126
E: scrawford@leg.ne.gov

Ebke, Laura (NP, 32)
State Capitol, Room 1103
P.O. Box 94604
Lincoln, NE 68509
P: (402) 471-2711
E: lebke@leg.ne.gov

Erdman, Steve (NP, 47)*
State Capitol, Room 1529
PO Box 94604
Lincoln, NE 68509
P: (402) 471-2616
E: serdman@leg.ne.gov

Friesen, Curt (NP, 34)
State Capitol, Room 1110
P.O. Box 94604
Lincoln, NE 68509
P: (402) 471-2630
E: cfriesen@leg.ne.gov

Geist, Suzanne (NP, 25)*
State Capitol, Room 2115
PO Box 94604
Lincoln, NE 68509
P: (402) 471-2731
E: sgeist@leg.ne.gov

Groene, Michael (NP, 42)
State Capitol, Room 1107
P.O. Box 94604
Lincoln, NE 68509
P: (402) 471-2729
E: mgroene@leg.ne.gov

Halloran, Steve (NP, 33)*
State Capitol, Room 1306
PO Box 94604
Lincoln, NE 68509
P: (402) 471-2712
E: shalloran@leg.ne.gov

Hansen, Matt (NP, 26)
State Capitol, Room 1017
P.O. Box 94604
Lincoln, NE 68509
P: (402) 471-2610
E: mhansen@leg.ne.gov

Harr, Burke (NP, 8)
State Capitol, Room 2011
P.O. Box 94604
Lincoln, NE 68509
P: (402) 471-2722
F: (402) 471-2126
E: bharr@leg.ne.gov

Hilgers, Mike (NP, 21)*
State Capitol, Room 1404
PO Box 94604
Lincoln, NE 68509
P: (402) 471-2673
E: mhilgers@leg.ne.gov

Hilkemann, Robert (NP, 4)
State Capitol, Room 2028
P.O. Box 94604
Lincoln, NE 68509
P: (402) 471-2621
E: rhilkemann@leg.ne.gov

# Nebraska

**Howard, Sara (NP, 9)**
State Capitol, Room 1012
P.O. Box 94604
Lincoln, NE 68509
P: (402) 471-2723
F: (402) 471-2126
E: showard@leg.ne.gov

**Hughes, Dan (NP, 44)**
State Capitol, Room 1210
P.O. Box 94604
Lincoln, NE 68509
P: (402) 471-2805
E: dhughes@leg.ne.gov

**Kintner, Bill (NP, 2)**
State Capitol, Room 1000
P.O. Box 94604
Lincoln, NE 68509
P: (402) 471-2613
F: (402) 471-2126
E: bkintner@leg.ne.gov

**Kolowski, Rick (NP, 31)**
State Capitol, Room 1018
P.O. Box 94604
Lincoln, NE 68509
P: (402) 471-2327
F: (402) 471-2126
E: rkolowski@leg.ne.gov

**Kolterman, Mark (NP, 24)**
State Capitol, Room 2004
P.O. Box 94604
Lincoln, NE 68509
P: (402) 471-2756
E: mkolterman@leg.ne.gov

**Krist, Bob (NP, 10)**
State Capitol, Room 1114
P.O. Box 94604
Lincoln, NE 68509
P: (402) 471-2718
F: (402) 471-2126
E: bkrist@leg.ne.gov

**Kuehn, John (NP, 38)**
State Capitol, Room 2000
P.O. Box 94604
Lincoln, NE 68509
P: (402) 471-2732
E: jkuehn@leg.ne.gov

**Larson, Tyson (NP, 40)**
State Capitol, Room 1019
P.O. Box 94604
Lincoln, NE 68509
P: (402) 471-2801
F: (402) 471-2126
E: tlarson@leg.ne.gov

**Lindstrom, Brett (NP, 18)**
State Capitol, Room 1401
P.O. Box 94604
Lincoln, NE 68509
P: (402) 471-2618
E: blindstrom@leg.ne.gov

**Linehan, Lou Ann (NP, 39)\***
State Capitol, Room 1117
PO Box 94604
Lincoln, NE 68509
P: (402) 471-2885
E: llinehan@leg.ne.gov

**Lowe Sr., John S. (NP, 37)\***
State Capitol, Room 1528
PO Box 94604
Lincoln, NE 68509
P: (402) 471-2726
E: jlowe@leg.ne.gov

**McCollister, John (NP, 20)**
State Capitol, Room 1101
P.O. Box 94604
Lincoln, NE 68509
P: (402) 471-2622
E: jmccollister@leg.ne.gov

**McDonnell, Mike (NP, 5)\***
State Capitol, Room 1522
PO Box 94604
Lincoln, NE 68509
P: (402) 471-2710
E: mmcdonnell@leg.ne.gov

**Morfeld, Adam (NP, 46)**
State Capitol, Room 1008
P.O. Box 94604
Lincoln, NE 68509
P: (402) 471-2720
E: amorfeld@leg.ne.gov

**Murante, John (NP, 49)**
State Capitol, Room 1423
P.O. Box 94604
Lincoln, NE 68509
P: (402) 471-2725
F: (402) 471-2126
E: jmurante@leg.ne.gov

**Pansing Brooks, Patty
   (NP, 28)**
State Capitol, Room 1206
P.O. Box 94604
Lincoln, NE 68509
P: (402) 471-2633
E: ppansingbrooks
   @leg.ne.gov

**Quick, Dan (NP, 35)\***
State Capitol, Room 1406
PO Box 94604
Lincoln, NE 68509
P: (402) 471-2617
E: dquick@leg.ne.gov

**Riepe, Merv (NP, 12)**
State Capitol, Room 1402
P.O. Box 94604
Lincoln, NE 68509
P: (402) 471-2623
E: mriepe@leg.ne.gov

**Scheer, Jim (NP, 19)**
State Capitol, Room 2103
P.O. Box 94604
Lincoln, NE 68509
P: (402) 471-2929
F: (402) 471-2126
E: jscheer@leg.ne.gov

**Schumacher, Paul (NP, 22)**
State Capitol, Room 1124
P.O. Box 94604
Lincoln, NE 68509
P: (402) 471-2715
F: (402) 471-2126
E: pschumacher@leg.ne.gov

**Smith, Jim (NP, 14)**
State Capitol, Room 1116
P.O. Box 94604
Lincoln, NE 68509
P: (402) 471-2730
F: (402) 471-2126
E: jsmith@leg.ne.gov

**Stinner Sr., John (NP, 48)**
State Capitol, Room 1004
P.O. Box 94604
Lincoln, NE 68509
P: (402) 471-2802
E: jstinner@leg.ne.gov

**Vargas, Tony (NP, 7)\***
State Capitol, Room 1523
PO Box 94604
Lincoln, NE 68509
P: (402) 471-2721
E: tvargas@leg.ne.gov

**Walz, Lynne M. (NP, 15)\***
StateCapitol
PO Box 94604
Lincoln, NE 68509
P: (402) 471-2625
E: lwalz@leg.ne.gov

**Watermeier, Dan (NP, 1)**
State Capitol, Room 2108
P.O. Box 94604
Lincoln, NE 68509
P: (402) 471-2733
F: (402) 471-2126
E: dwatermeier@leg.ne.gov

**Wayne, Justin (NP, 13)\***
State Capitol, Room 1212
PO Box 94604
Lincoln, NE 68509
P: (402) 471-2727
E: jwayne@leg.ne.gov

**Williams, Matt (NP, 36)**
State Capitol, Room 2015
P.O. Box 94604
Lincoln, NE 68509
P: (402) 471-2642
E: mwilliams@leg.ne.gov

**Wishart, Anna (NP, 27)\***
State Capitol, Room 1308
PO Box 94604
Lincoln, NE 68509
P: (402) 471-2632
E: awishart@leg.ne.gov

# House

## Speaker of the House

**Speaker Jim Scheer (NP)**
Speaker of the Legislature
State Capitol, Room 2103
P.O. Box 94604
Lincoln, NE 68509
P: (402) 471-2929
F: (402) 471-2126
E: jscheer@leg.ne.gov

# Nevada

## Executive

### Governor

The Honorable Brian
  Sandoval (R)
Governor
Capitol Building
Carson City, NV 89701
P: (775) 684-5670
F: (775) 684-5683

### Lieutenant Governor

The Honorable Mark
  Hutchison (R)
Lieutenant Governor
101 North Carson Street, Suite 2
Carson City, NV 89701
P: (775) 684-7111
F: (775) 684-7110

### Attorney General

The Honorable Adam Paul
  Laxalt (R)
Attorney General
Old State Capitol Building
100 North Carson Street
Carson City, NV 89701
P: (775) 684-1100
F: (775) 684-1108
E: aginfo@ag.state.nv.us

### Auditor

Mr. Rocky J. Cooper
Legislative Auditor
401 South Carson Street
Carson City, NV 89701
P: (775) 684-6815
F: (775) 684-6435

### Controller

The Honorable Ron
  Knecht (R)
State Controller
State Capitol Building
101 North Carson Street, Suite 5
Carson City, NV 89701
P: (775) 684-5632
F: (775) 684-5696

### Secretary of State

The Honorable Barbara
  Cegavske (R)
Secretary of State
101 North Carson Street, Suite 3
Carson City, NV 89701
P: (775) 684-5708
F: (775) 684-5724
E: sosexec@sos.nv.gov

### Treasurer

The Honorable Dan
  Schwartz (R)
State Treasurer
101 North Carson Street, Suite 4
Carson City, NV 89701
P: (775) 684-7109
F: (775) 684-5623
E: statetreasurer
  @nevadatreasurer.gov

## Judiciary

### Supreme Court (NE)

Ms. Elizabeth Brown
Chief Clerk
201 South Carson Street
Carson City, NV 89701
P: (775) 684-1600
F: (775) 684-1601
E: nvscclerk
  @nvcourts.nv.gov

The Honorable Michael A.
  Cherry
Chief Justice
The Honorable Michael L.
  Douglas
The Honorable Mark Gibbons
The Honorable James W.
  Hardesty
The Honorable Ron
  Parraguirre
The Honorable Kristina
  Pickering

## Legislative

## Senate

### Senate President

The Honorable Mark
  Hutchison (R)
Lieutenant Governor
101 North Carson Street, Suite 2
Carson City, NV 89701
P: (775) 684-7111
F: (775) 684-7110

### President Pro Tempore of the Senate

Senator Mo Denis (D)
Senate President Pro Tempore
Room 2128
401 South Carson Street
Carson City, NV 89701
P: (775) 684-1431
F: (775) 684-6522
E: Moises.Denis
  @sen.state.nv.us

### Senate Majority Leader

Senator Aaron D. Ford (D)
Senate Majority Leader
Room 1222
401 South Carson Street
Carson City, NV 89701
P: (775) 684-6502
F: (775) 684-6522
E: Aaron.Ford
  @sen.state.nv.us

### Senate Minority Leader

Senator Michael
  Roberson (R)
Senate Minority Leader
Room 2160
401 South Carson Street
Carson City, NV 89701
P: (775) 684-1481
F: (775) 684-6522
E: Michael.Roberson
  @sen.state.nv.us

### Secretary of the Senate

Ms. Claire J. Clift
Secretary of the Senate
401 South Carson Street
Carson City, NV 89701
P: (775) 684-1400
E: cclift@lcb.state.nv.us

### Members of the Senate

Atkinson, Kelvin D. (D, 4)
Room 1224
401 South Carson Street
Carson City, NV 89701
P: (775) 684-1429
F: (775) 684-6522
E: Kelvin.Atkinson
  @sen.state.nv.us

Cancela, Yvanna (D, 10)*
Room 2127
401 South Carson Street
Carson City, NV 89701
P: (775) 684-1427
E: yvanna.cancela
  @sen.state.nv.us

Cannizzaro, Nicole (D, 6)*
Room 2143
401 South Carson Street
Carson City, NV 89701
P: (775) 684-1475
E: Nicole.Cannizzaro
  @sen.state.nv.us

Denis, Mo (D, 2)
Room 2128
401 South Carson Street
Carson City, NV 89701
P: (775) 684-1431
F: (775) 684-6522
E: Moises.Denis
  @sen.state.nv.us

Farley, Patricia (R, 8)
Room 2145
401 South Carson Street
Carson City, NV 89701
P: (775) 684-1445
F: (775) 684-6522
E: Patricia.Farley
  @sen.state.nv.us

Ford, Aaron D. (D, 11)
Room 1222
401 South Carson Street
Carson City, NV 89701
P: (775) 684-6502
F: (775) 684-6522
E: Aaron.Ford
  @sen.state.nv.us

Gansert, Heidi S. (R, 15)
Room 2103
401 South Carson Street
Carson City, NV 89701
P: (775) 684-1419
E: Heidi.Gansert
  @sen.state.nv.us

Goicoechea, Pete (R, 19)
Room 2100
401 South Carson Street
Carson City, NV 89701
P: (775) 684-1447
F: (775) 684-6522
E: Pete.Goicoechea
  @sen.state.nv.us

Gustavson, Donald G.
  (R, 14)
Room 2104
401 South Carson Street
Carson City, NV 89701
P: (775) 684-1480
F: (775) 684-6522
E: Don.Gustavson
  @sen.state.nv.us

Hammond, Scott (R, 18)
Room 2102
401 South Carson Street
Carson City, NV 89701
P: (775) 684-1442
F: (775) 684-6522
E: Scott.Hammond
  @sen.state.nv.us

# Nevada

**Hardy, Joseph P. (R, 12)**
Room 2158
401 South Carson Street
Carson City, NV 89701
P: (775) 684-1462
F: (775) 684-6522
E: Joe.Hardy
   @sen.state.nv.us

**Harris, Becky (R, 9)**
Room 2101
401 South Carson Street
Carson City, NV 89701
P: (775) 684-1421
F: (775) 684-6522
E: Becky.Harris
   @sen.state.nv.us

**Kieckhefer, Ben (R, 16)**
Room 2156
401 South Carson Street
Carson City, NV 89701
P: (775) 684-1450
F: (775) 684-6522
E: Ben.Kieckhefer
   @sen.state.nv.us

**Manendo, Mark A. (D, 21)**
Room 2129
401 South Carson Street
Carson City, NV 89701
P: (775) 684-6503
F: (775) 684-6522
E: Mark.Manendo
   @sen.state.nv.us

**Parks, David R. (D, 7)**
Room 2125
401 South Carson Street
Carson City, NV 89701
P: (775) 684-6504
F: (775) 684-6522
E: David.Parks
   @sen.state.nv.us

**Ratti, Julia (D, 13)***
Room 2121
401 South Carson Street
Carson City, NV 89701
P: (775) 684-1429
E: Julia.Ratti
   @sen.state.nv.us

**Roberson, Michael (R, 20)**
Room 2160
401 South Carson Street
Carson City, NV 89701
P: (775) 684-1481
F: (775) 684-6522
E: Michael.Roberson
   @sen.state.nv.us

**Segerblom, Tick (D, 3)**
Room 2132
401 South Carson Street
Carson City, NV 89701
P: (775) 684-1422
F: (775) 684-6522
E: Tick.Segerblom
   @sen.state.nv.us

**Settelmeyer, James (R, 17)**
Room 2107
401 South Carson Street
Carson City, NV 89701
P: (775) 684-1470
F: (775) 684-6522
E: James.Settelmeyer
   @sen.state.nv.us

**Spearman, Pat (D, 1)**
Room 2124
401 South Carson Street
Carson City, NV 89701
P: (775) 684-1424
F: (775) 684-6522
E: Pat.Spearman
   @sen.state.nv.us

**Woodhouse, Joyce (D, 5)**
Room 2126
401 South Carson Street
Carson City, NV 89701
P: (775) 684-1457
F: (775) 684-6522
E: Joyce.Woodhouse
   @sen.state.nv.us

# Assembly

## Speaker of the Assembly

**Assemblyman Jason Frierson (D)**
Speaker of the Assembly
Room 1104
401 South Carson Street
Carson City, NV 89701
P: (775) 684-8537
F: (775) 684-8533
E: Jason.Frierson
   @asm.state.nv.us

## Speaker Pro Tempore of the Assembly

**Assemblywoman Irene Bustamante Adams (D)**
Assembly Speaker Pro Tempore
Room 4108
401 South Carson Street
Carson City, NV 89701
P: (775) 684-8803
F: (775) 684-8533
E: Irene.BustamanteAdams
   @asm.state.nv.us

## Assembly Majority Leader

**Assemblywoman Teresa Benitez-Thompson (D)**
Assembly Majority Floor Leader
Room 3105E
401 South Carson Street
Carson City, NV 89701
P: (775) 684-8845
F: (775) 684-8533
E: Teresa.BenitezThompson
   @asm.state.nv.us

## Assembly Minority Leader

**Assemblyman Paul Anderson (R)**
Assembly Minority Floor Leader
Room 3105
401 South Carson Street
Carson City, NV 89701
P: (775) 684-8853
F: (775) 684-8533
E: Paul.Anderson
   @asm.state.nv.us

## Clerk of the Assembly

**Ms. Susan Furlong**
Chief Clerk of the Assembly
401 South Carson Street
Carson City, NV 89701
P: (775) 684-8555
E: Susan.Furlong
   @asm.state.nv.us

## Members of the Assembly

**Anderson, Elliot T. (D, 15)**
Room 3125
401 South Carson Street
Carson City, NV 89701
P: (775) 684-8835
F: (775) 684-8533
E: Elliot.Anderson
   @asm.state.nv.us

**Anderson, Paul (R, 13)**
Room 3105
401 South Carson Street
Carson City, NV 89701
P: (775) 684-8853
F: (775) 684-8533
E: Paul.Anderson
   @asm.state.nv.us

**Araujo, Nelson (D, 3)**
Room 3140
401 South Carson Street
Carson City, NV 89701
P: (775) 684-8599
F: (775) 684-8533
E: Nelson.Araujo
   @asm.state.nv.us

**Benitez-Thompson, Teresa (D, 27)**
Room 3105E
401 South Carson Street
Carson City, NV 89701
P: (775) 684-8845
F: (775) 684-8533
E: Teresa.BenitezThompson
   @asm.state.nv.us

**Bilbray-Axelrod, Shannon (D, 34)***
Room 3129
401 South Carson Street
Carson City, NV 89701
P: (775) 684-8847
E: Shannon.BilbrayAxelRod
   @asm.state.nv.us

**Brooks, Chris (D, 10)***
Room 4107
401 South Carson Street
Carson City, NV 89701
P: (775) 684-8541
E: Chris.Brooks
   @asm.state.nv.us

**Bustamante Adams, Irene (D, 42)**
Room 4108
401 South Carson Street
Carson City, NV 89701
P: (775) 684-8803
F: (775) 684-8533
E: Irene.BustamanteAdams
   @asm.state.nv.us

**Carlton, Maggie (D, 14)**
Room 3133
401 South Carson Street
Carson City, NV 89701
P: (775) 684-8597
F: (775) 684-8533
E: Maggie.Carlton
   @asm.state.nv.us

**Carrillo, Richard (D, 18)**
Room 3119
401 South Carson Street
Carson City, NV 89701
P: (775) 684-8801
F: (775) 684-8533
E: Richard.Carrillo
   @asm.state.nv.us

**Cohen, Lesley E. (D, 29)**
Room 3156
401 South Carson Street
Carson City, NV 89701
P: (775) 684-8855
E: Lesley.Cohen
@asm.state.nv.us

**Daly, Skip (D, 31)**
Room 4122
401 South Carson Street
Carson City, NV 89701
P: (775) 684-8563
F: (775) 684-8533
E: Skip.Daly
@asm.state.nv.us

**Diaz, Olivia (D, 11)**
Room 3128
401 South Carson Street
Carson City, NV 89701
P: (775) 684-8553
F: (775) 684-8533
E: Olivia.Diaz
@asm.state.nv.us

**Edwards, Chris (R, 19)**
Room 3134
401 South Carson Street
Carson City, NV 89701
P: (775) 684-8857
F: (775) 684-8533
E: Chris.Edwards
@asm.state.nv.us

**Ellison, John (R, 33)**
Room 3116
401 South Carson Street
Carson City, NV 89701
P: (775) 684-8831
F: (775) 684-8533
E: John.Ellison
@asm.state.nv.us

**Flores, Edgar R. (D, 28)**
Room 4115
401 South Carson Street
Carson City, NV 89701
P: (775) 684-8583
F: (775) 684-8533
E: Edgar.Flores
@asm.state.nv.us

**Frierson, Jason (D, 8)**
Room 1104
401 South Carson Street
Carson City, NV 89701
P: (775) 684-8537
F: (775) 684-8533
E: Jason.Frierson
@asm.state.nv.us

**Fumo, Ozzie (D, 21)***
Room 4118
401 South Carson Street
Carson City, NV 89701
P: (775) 684-8839
E: Ozzie.Fumo
@asm.state.nv.us

**Hambrick, John (R, 2)**
Room 3160
401 South Carson Street
Carson City, NV 89701
P: (775) 684-8827
F: (775) 684-8533
E: John.Hambrick
@asm.state.nv.us

**Hansen, Ira (R, 32)**
Room 4123
401 South Carson Street
Carson City, NV 89701
P: (775) 684-8851
F: (775) 684-8533
E: Ira.Hansen
@asm.state.nv.us

**Jauregui, Sandra (D, 41)***
Room 4104
401 South Carson Street
Carson City, NV 89701
P: (775) 684-8821
E: Sandra.Jauregui
@asm.state.nv.us

**Joiner, Amber J. (D, 24)**
Room 4113
401 South Carson Street
Carson City, NV 89701
P: (775) 684-8559
F: (775) 684-8533
E: Amber.Joiner
@asm.state.nv.us

**Kramer, Al (R, 40)***
Room 3130
401 South Carson Street
Carson City, NV 89701
P: (775) 684-8825
E: Al.Kramer
@asm.state.nv.us

**Krasner, Lisa (R, 26)***
Room 3124
401 South Carson Street
Carson City, NV 89701
P: (775) 684-8848
E: Lisa.Krasner
@asm.state.nv.us

**Marchant, Jim (R, 37)***
Room 4102
401 South Carson Street
Carson City, NV 89701
P: (775) 684-8505
E: Jim.Marchant
@asm.state.nv.us

**McArthur, Richard (R, 4)**
Room 4121
401 South Carson Street
Carson City, NV 89701
P: (775) 684-8829
E: rmcarthur
@asm.state.nv.us

**McCurdy II, William (D, 6)***
Room 4112
401 South Carson Street
Carson City, NV 89701
P: (775) 684-8545
E: William.McCurdy
@asm.state.nv.us

**Miller, Brittney (D, 5)***
Room 3131
401 South Carson Street
Carson City, NV 89701
P: (775) 684-8833
E: Brittney.Miller
@asm.state.nv.us

**Monroe-Moreno, Daniele (D, 1)***
Room 4117
401 South Carson Street
Carson City, NV 89701
P: (775) 684-8509
E: Daniele.MonroeMoreno
@asm.state.nv.us

**Neal, Dina (D, 7)**
Room 4109
401 South Carson Street
Carson City, NV 89701
P: (775) 684-8587
F: (775) 684-8533
E: Dina.Neal
@asm.state.nv.us

**Ohrenschall, James (D, 12)**
Room 3123
401 South Carson Street
Carson City, NV 89701
P: (775) 684-8819
F: (775) 684-8533
E: James.Ohrenschall
@asm.state.nv.us

**Oscarson, James (R, 36)**
Room 3105
401 South Carson Street
Carson City, NV 89701
P: (775) 684-8805
F: (775) 684-8533
E: James.Oscarson
@asm.state.nv.us

**Pickard, Keith (R, 22)***
Room 4105
401 South Carson Street
Carson City, NV 89701
P: (775) 684-8823
E: Keith.Pickard
@asm.state.nv.us

**Spiegel, Ellen B. (D, 20)**
Room 3154
401 South Carson Street
Carson City, NV 89701
P: (775) 684-8577
F: (775) 684-8533
E: Ellen.Spiegel
@asm.state.nv.us

**Sprinkle, Michael (D, 30)**
Room 3132
401 South Carson Street
Carson City, NV 89701
P: (775) 684-8841
F: (775) 684-8533
E: Mike.Sprinkle
@asm.state.nv.us

**Swank, Heidi (D, 16)**
Room 3158
401 South Carson Street
Carson City, NV 89701
P: (775) 684-8595
F: (775) 684-8533
E: Heidi.Swank
@asm.state.nv.us

**Thompson, Tyrone (D, 17)**
Room 4114
401 South Carson Street
Carson City, NV 89701
P: (775) 684-8569
F: (775) 684-8533
E: Tyrone.Thompson
@asm.state.nv.us

**Titus, Robin I. (R, 38)**
Room 411
401 South Carson Street
Carson City, NV 89701
P: (775) 684-8507
F: (775) 684-8533
E: Robin.Titus
@asm.state.nv.us

**Tolles, Jill (R, 25)***
Room 4103
401 South Carson Street
Carson City, NV 89701
P: (775) 684-8837
E: Jill.Tolles
@asm.state.nv.us

**Watkins, Justin (D, 35)***
Room 4110
401 South Carson Street
Carson City, NV 89701
P: (775) 684-8573
E: Justin.Watkins
@asm.state.nv.us

# Nevada

**Wheeler, Jim (R, 39)**
Room 3105
401 South Carson Street
Carson City, NV 89701
P: (775) 684-8843
F: (775) 684-8533
E: Jim.Wheeler
   @asm.state.nv.us

**Woodbury, Melissa (R, 23)**
Room 3159
401 South Carson Street
Carson City, NV 89701
P: (775) 684-8503
F: (775) 684-8533
E: Melissa.Woodbury
   @asm.state.nv.us

**Yeager, Steve (D, 9)\***
Room 3127
401 South Carson Street
Carson City, NV 89701
P: (775) 684-8549
E: Steve.Yeager
   @asm.state.nv.us

# New Hampshire

## Executive

### Governor

**The Honorable Chris Sununu (R)**
Governor
107 North Main Street, Room 208
Concord, NH 03301
P: (603) 271-2121
F: (603) 271-7640

### Lieutenant Governor

*This state does not have the office of lieutenant governor. The president (or speaker) of the Senate is next in line of succession to the governorship.*

### Attorney General

**The Honorable Joseph Foster**
(appointed)
Attorney General
33 Capitol Street
Concord, NH 03301
P: (603) 271-3658
F: (603) 271-2110
E: attorneygeneral
@doj.nh.gov

### Auditor

**Mr. Michael Kane**
(appointed by the Legislature)
Legislative Budget Assistant
State House, Room 102
107 North Main Street
Concord, NH 03301
P: (603) 271-2389
F: (603) 271-1097

### Secretary of State

**The Honorable William M. Gardner (D)**
(elected by the Legislature)
Secretary of State
State House, Room 204
Concord, NH 03301
P: (603) 271-3242
F: (603) 271-6316
E: kladd@sos.state.nh.us

## Treasurer

**The Honorable William Dwyer**
(elected by the Legislature)
State Treasurer
25 Capitol Street
Concord, NH 03301
P: (603) 271-2621
F: (603) 271-3922

## Judiciary

### Supreme Court (GA)

**Ms. Eileen Fox**
Clerk of Court
Supreme Court Building
One Charles Doe Drive
Concord, NH 03301
P: (603) 271-2646
F: (603) 271-6630

**The Honorable Linda S. Dalianis**
Chief Justice
**The Honorable James P. Bassett**
**The Honorable Carol Ann Conboy**
**The Honorable Gary E. Hicks**
**The Honorable Robert J. Lynn**

## Legislative Senate

### Senate President

**Senator Chuck Morse (R)**
Senate President
State House, Room 302
107 North Main Street
Concord, NH 03301
P: (603) 271-8472
E: chuck.morse
@leg.state.nh.us

### President Pro Tempore of the Senate

**Senator Sharon M. Carson (R)**
Senate President Pro Tempore
State House, Room 106
107 North Main Street
Concord, NH 03301
P: (603) 271-1403
E: sharon.carson
@leg.state.nh.us

## Senate Majority Leader

**Senator Jeb E. Bradley (R)**
Senate Majority Leader
State House, Room 302
107 North Main Street
Concord, NH 03301
P: (603) 271-2106
E: jeb.bradley
@leg.state.nh.us

## Senate Minority Leader

**Senator Jeff Woodburn (D)**
Senate Minority Leader
State House, Room 120
107 North Main Street
Concord, NH 03301
P: (603) 271-3207
E: Jeff.Woodburn
@leg.state.nh.us

## Secretary of the Senate

**Ms. Tammy L. Wright**
Clerk of the Senate
Senate Chamber
107 North Main Street
Concord, NH 03301
P: (603) 271-3420
F: (603) 271-2545
E: tammy.wright
@leg.state.nh.us

## Members of the Senate

**Avard, Kevin A (R, 12)**
State House, Room 105-A
107 North Main Street
Concord, NH 03301
P: (603) 271-4151
F: (603) 521-7657
E: kevin.avard
@leg.state.nh.us

**Birdsell, Regina M. (R, 19)**
State House, Room 105-A
107 North Main Street
Concord, NH 03301
P: (603) 271-4151
E: regina.birdsell
@leg.state.nh.us

**Bradley, Jeb E. (R, 3)**
State House, Room 302
107 North Main Street
Concord, NH 03301
P: (603) 271-2106
E: jeb.bradley
@leg.state.nh.us

**Carson, Sharon M. (R, 14)**
State House, Room 106
107 North Main Street
Concord, NH 03301
P: (603) 271-1403
E: sharon.carson
@leg.state.nh.us

**Clark, Martha Fuller (D, 21)**
State House, Room 115
107 North Main Street
Concord, NH 03301
P: (603) 271-3076
E: martha.fullerclark
@leg.state.nh.us

**D'Allesandro, Lou (D, 20)**
State House, Room 117
107 North Main Street
Concord, NH 03301
P: (603) 271-2117
E: dalas@leg.state.nh.us

**Daniels, Gary L. (R, 11)**
State House, Room 302
107 North Main Street
Concord, NH 03301
P: (603) 271-2609
E: Gary.Daniels
@leg.state.nh.us

**Feltes, Dan (D, 15)**
Legislative Office Building, Room 5
33 North State Street
Concord, NH 03301
P: (603) 271-3067
E: Dan.Feltes
@leg.state.nh.us

**French, Harold F. (R, 7)**
State House, Room 107
107 North Main Street
Franklin, NH 03301
P: (603) 271-4063
E: harold.french
@leg.state.nh.us

**Gannon, William M. (R, 23)**
State House, Room 124
107 North Main Street
Concord, NH 03301
P: (603) 271-3091
E: William.Gannon
@leg.state.nh.us

**Gray, James P. (R, 6)**
State House, Room 302
107 North Main Street
Concord, NH 03301
P: (603) 271-3042
E: james.gray
@leg.state.nh.us

# New Hampshire

**Guida, Bob (R, 2)***
State House, Room 302
107 North Main Street
Concord, NH 03301
P: (603) 271-2111
E: Bob.Guida
    @leg.state.nh.us

**Hennessey, Martha (D, 5)**
Legislative Office Building,
Room 5
33 North State Street
Concord, NH 03301
P: (603) 271-3067
E: martha.hennessey
    @leg.state.nh.us

**Innis, Daniel (R, 24)***
State House, Room 115
107 North Main Street
Concord, NH 03301
P: (603) 271-3077
E: Daniel.Innis
    @leg.state.nh.us

**Kahn, Jay (D, 10)***
Legislative Office Building,
Room 101-A
33 North State Street
Concord, NH 03301
P: (603) 271-8631
E: Jay.Kahn@leg.state.nh.us

**Lasky, Bette R. (D, 13)**
State House, Room 124
107 North Main Street
Concord, NH 03301
P: (603) 271-3091
E: Bette.Lasky
    @leg.state.nh.us

**McGilvray, Scott (D, 16)***
Legislative Office Building,
Room 5
33 North State Street
Concord, NH 03301
P: (603) 271-3067
E: Scott.McGilvray
    @leg.state.nh.us

**Morse, Chuck (R, 22)**
State House, Room 302
107 North Main Street
Concord, NH 03301
P: (603) 271-8472
E: chuck.morse
    @leg.state.nh.us

**Reagan, John (R, 17)**
State House, Room 107
107 North Main Street
Concord, NH 03301
P: (603) 271-4063
E: john.reagan111@gmail.com

**Sanborn, Andy (R, 9)**
State House, Room 302
107 North Main Street
Concord, NH 03301
P: (603) 271-2609
E: andy.sanborn
    @leg.state.nh.us

**Soucy, Donna M. (D, 18)**
State House, Room 120
107 North Main Street
Concord, NH 03301
P: (603) 271-3207
E: donna.soucy
    @leg.state.nh.us

**Ward, Ruth (R, 8)***
State House, Room 105-A
107 North Main Street
Concord, NH 03301
P: (603) 271-4151
E: Ruth.Ward
    @leg.state.nh.us

**Watters, David H. (D, 4)**
Legislative Office Building,
Room 101-A
33 North State Street
Concord, NH 03301
P: (603) 271-8631
E: david.watters
    @leg.state.nh.us

**Woodburn, Jeff (D, 1)**
State House, Room 120
107 North Main Street
Concord, NH 03301
P: (603) 271-3207
E: Jeff.Woodburn
    @leg.state.nh.us

# House
## Speaker of the House
**Representative Shawn N. Jasper (R)**
Speaker of the House
107 North Main Street
Concord, NH 03301
P: (603) 271-3661
F: (603) 882-2056
E: shawn.jasper
    @leg.state.nh.us

## Deputy Speaker of the House
**Representative Sherman A. Packard (R)**
House Speaker Pro Tem
107 North Main Street
Concord, NH 03301
P: (603) 271-3661
F: (603) 421-0902
E: sherman.packard
    @leg.state.nh.us

## House Majority Leader
**Representative Richard W. Hinch (R)**
House Majority Leader
107 North Main Street
Concord, NH 03301
P: (603) 271-3661
E: dick.hinch
    @leg.state.nh.us

## House Minority Leader
**Representative Stephen J. Shurtleff (D)**
House Minority Leader
107 North Main Street
Concord, NH 03303
P: (603) 271-3661
E: steve.shurtleff
    @leg.state.nh.us

## Clerk of the House
**Ms. Karen O. Wadsworth**
Clerk of the House
State House, Room 317
107 North Main Street
Concord, NH 03301
P: (603) 271-2548
F: (603) 271-3309
E: karen.wadsworth
    @leg.state.nh.us

## Members of the House
**Abbott, Michael D. (D, SP18)**
107 North Main Street
Concord, NH 03301
P: (603) 271-3661
E: Michael.Abbott
    @leg.state.nh.us

**Abear, Marc (R, SP2)**
107 North Main Street
Concord, NH 03301
P: (603) 271-3661
E: sea1mra@gmail.com

**Abel, Richard (D, SP53)**
107 North Main Street
Concord, NH 03301
P: (603) 271-3661
E: Richard.Abel

**Abrami, Patrick F. (R, SP150)**
107 North Main Street
Concord, NH 03301
P: (603) 271-3661
F: (781) 272-5666
E: patrick.abrami
    @leg.state.nh.us

**Aldrich, Glen (R, SP2)**
107 North Main Street
Concord, NH 03301
P: (603) 271-3661
E: glenaldrich@gmail.com

**Alicea, Caroletta C. (D, SP110)**
107 North Main Street
Concord, NH 03301
P: (603) 271-3661
E: caroletta.alicea
    @leg.state.nh.us

**Allen, Mary M. (R, SP146)**
107 North Main Street
Concord, NH 03301
P: (603) 271-3661

**Almy, Susan W. (D, SP53)**
107 North Main Street
Concord, NH 03301
P: (603) 271-3661
E: susan.almy@comcast.net

**Altschillier, Debra (D, SP150)***
107 North Main Street
Concord, NH 03301
P: (603) 271-3661
E: debra.altschillier
    @leg.state.nh.us

**Ames, Richard (D, SP26)**
107 North Main Street
Concord, NH 03301
P: (603) 271-3661
E: Richard.Ames
    @leg.state.nh.us

**Ammon, Keith (R, SP97)**
107 North Main Street
Concord, NH 03301
P: (603) 271-3661
E: Keith.Ammon
    @leg.state.nh.us

**Avellani, Lino (R, SP14)**
107 North Main Street
Concord, NH 03301
P: (603) 271-3661
E: lino.avellani
    @leg.state.nh.us

**Ayala, Jessica (D, SP88)**
107 North Main Street
Concord, NH 03301
P: (603) 271-3661
E: jpfaith@comcast.net

**Azarian, Gary S. (R, SP139)**
107 North Main Street
Concord, NH 03301
P: (603) 271-3661
E: gazarian@comcast.net

**Backus, Robert A. (D, SP76)**
107 North Main Street
Concord, NH 03301
P: (603) 271-3661
E: Bob.Backus
    @leg.state.nh.us

**Bailey, Brad (R, SP54)**
107 North Main Street
Concord, NH 03301
P: (603) 271-3661
E: brad.bailey
    @leg.state.nh.us

**Baldasaro, Alfred P.
    (R, SP136)**
107 North Main Street
Concord, NH 03301
P: (603) 271-3661
E: al.baldasaro
    @leg.state.nh.us

**Barnes III, Arthur E.
    (R, SP139)**
107 North Main Street
Concord, NH 03301
P: (603) 271-3661
E: arthur.barnes
    @leg.state.nh.us

**Baroody, Benjamin C.
    (D, SP100)**
107 North Main Street
Concord, NH 03301
P: (603) 271-3661
F: (603) 218-6780
E: ben.baroody
    @leg.state.nh.us

**Barry, Richard W. (R, SP78)**
107 North Main Street
Concord, NH 03301
P: (603) 271-3661
F: (603) 880-0582
E: richard.barry
    @leg.state.nh.us

**Bartlett, Christy D.
    (D, SP121)**
107 North Main Street
Concord, NH 03301
P: (603) 271-3661
E: christydbartlett
    @gmail.com

**Bates, David (R, SP138)**
107 North Main Street
Concord, NH 03301
P: (603) 271-3661
E: rep.bates@live.com

**Bean, Philip (R, SP152)***
107 North Main Street
Concord, NH 03301
P: (603) 271-3661
E: philip.bean
    @leg.state.nh.us

**Beaudoin, Steven P.
    (R, SP177)**
107 North Main Street
Concord, NH 03301
P: (603) 271-3661
E: steven.beaudoin
    @leg.state.nh.us

**Beaulieu, Jane E.
    (D, SP102)**
107 North Main Street
Concord, NH 03301
P: (603) 271-3661
E: jane.beaulieu
    @leg.state.nh.us

**Belanger, James P.
    (R, SP84)**
107 North Main Street
Concord, NH 03301
P: (603) 271-3661
E: jim.belanger
    @leg.state.nh.us

**Belanger, Ronald J.
    (R, SP139)**
107 North Main Street
Apartment 201
Concord, NH 03301
P: (603) 271-3661
E: ronald.belanger
    @leg.state.nh.us

**Bennett, Travis (D, SP48)**
107 North Main Street
Concord, NH 03301
P: (603) 271-3661
E: travisrbennett1
    @gmail.com

**Berch, Paul S. (D, SP18)**
107 North Main Street
Concord, NH 03301
P: (603) 271-3661
E: pberch@myfairpoint.net

**Berrien, Skip (D, SP149)**
107 North Main Street
Concord, NH 03301
P: (603) 271-3661
E: skip.berrien
    @leg.state.nh.us

**Berube, Roger R. (D, SP186)**
107 North Main Street
Concord, NH 03301
P: (603) 271-3661
E: rogerrberube@hotmail.com

**Biggie, Barbara (R, SP80)**
107 North Main Street
Concord, NH 03301
P: (603) 271-3661
E: barbara.biggie
    @leg.state.nh.us

**Binford, David W.
    (R, SP55)***
107 North Main Street
Concord, NH 03301
P: (603) 271-3661
E: david.binford
    @leg.state.nh.us

**Bixby, Peter W. (D, SP185)**
107 North Main Street
Concord, NH 03301
P: (603) 271-3661
E: peter.bixby
    @leg.state.nh.us

**Bordenet, John (D, SP22)**
107 North Main Street
Concord, NH 03301
P: (603) 271-3661
E: John.Bordenet
    @leg.state.nh.us

**Bouldin, Amanda (D, SP69)**
107 North Main Street
Manchester, NH 03103
P: (972) 834-7302
E: Amanda.Bouldin
    @leg.state.nh.us

**Boutin, Skylar (R, SP42)***
107 North Main Street
Concord, NH 03301
P: (603) 271-3661
E: skylar.boutin
    @leg.state.nh.us

**Bove, Martin N. (R, SP136)**
107 North Main Street
Concord, NH 03301
P: (603) 271-3661
E: martin.bove
    @leg.state.nh.us

**Brewster, Michael
    (R, SP123)**
107 North Main Street
Concord, NH 03301
P: (603) 271-3661

**Brown, Duane R. (R, SP56)**
107 North Main Street
Concord, NH 03301
P: (603) 271-3661
E: duane.brown
    @leg.state.nh.us

**Buco, Thomas L. (D, SP11)**
107 North Main Street
Concord, NH 03301
P: (603) 271-3661
E: tom.buco@leg.state.nh.us

**Burns, Charlie (R, SP80)***
107 North Main Street
Concord, NH 03301
P: (603) 271-3661
E: Charles.Burns
    @leg.state.nh.us

**Burridge, Delmar D.
    (D, SP33)**
107 North Main Street
Concord, NH 03301
P: (603) 271-3661
F: (603) 543-1844
E: dburridge@ne.rr.com

**Burt, John A. (R, SP96)**
107 North Main Street
Concord, NH 03301
P: (603) 271-3661
F: (603) 641-1135
E: john.burt
    @leg.state.nh.us

**Burton, Wayne M. (D, SP174)**
107 North Main Street
Concord, NH 03301
P: (603) 271-3661
E: Wayne.Burton
    @leg.state.nh.us

**Butler, Edward A. (D, SP16)**
107 North Main Street
Concord, NH 03301
P: (603) 271-3661
F: (603) 374-6168
E: edofthenotch@gmail.com

**Byron, Frank A. (R, SP77)**
107 North Main Street
Concord, NH 03301
P: (603) 271-3661
E: frank.byron
    @leg.state.nh.us

**Cahill, Michael D.
    (D, SP148)**
107 North Main Street
Concord, NH 03301
P: (603) 271-3661
E: michael.cahill
    @leg.state.nh.us

**Cali-Pitts, Jacqueline A.
    (D, SP161)**
107 North Main Street
Concord, NH 03301
P: (603) 271-3661
E: cali0917@aol.com

# New Hampshire

**Campion, Polly Kent (D, SP52)***
107 North Main Street
Concord, NH 03301
P: (603) 271-3661

**Carr, John J. (R, SP83)**
107 North Main Street
Concord, NH 03301
P: (603) 271-3661
E: john.carr
@leg.state.nh.us

**Carson, Clyde J. (D, SP109)**
107 North Main Street
Concord, NH 03301
P: (603) 271-3661
E: clyde.carson
@leg.state.nh.us

**Chandler, Gene G. (R, SP10)**
107 North Main Street
Concord, NH 03301
P: (603) 271-3661
E: gene.chandler
@leg.state.nh.us

**Chandley, Shannon E. (D, SP79)**
107 North Main Street
Concord, NH 03301
P: (603) 271-3661
E: Shannon.Chandley.NH
@aol.com

**Chase, Francis (R, SP151)**
107 North Main Street
Concord, NH 03301
P: (603) 271-3661
E: CHD5100@outlook.com

**Chirichiello, Brian (R, SP137)**
107 North Main Street
Concord, NH 03301
P: (603) 271-3661
E: brian.chirichiello
@verani.com

**Christensen, Chris (R, SP78)**
107 North Main Street
Concord, NH 03301
P: (603) 271-3661
E: c.christensen
@leg.state.nh.us

**Christie, Rick (R, SP63)**
107 North Main Street
Concord, NH 03301
P: (603) 271-3661
E: Rick.Christie
@leg.state.nh.us

**Cilley, Jacalyn L. (D, SP172)**
107 North Main Street
Concord, NH 03301
P: (603) 271-3661
E: jcilley@aol.com

**Cleaver, Skip (D, SP92)***
107 North Main Street
Concord, NH 03301
P: (603) 271-3661
E: skipcleaver@comcast.net

**Cloutier, John R. (D, SP203)**
107 North Main Street
Concord, NH 03301
P: (603) 271-3661
E: jocloutier@comcast.net

**Comeau, Ed (R, SP14)**
107 North Main Street
Concord, NH 03301
P: (603) 271-3661
E: ed@edcomeau.org

**Comtois, Barbara (R, SP7)***
107 North Main Street
Concord, NH 03301
P: (603) 271-3661
E: barbara.comtois
@leg.state.nh.us

**Cook, Allen W. (R, SP142)**
107 North Main Street
Concord, NH 03301
P: (603) 271-3661
E: Allen.cook
@leg.state.nh.us

**Copp, Anne (R, SP103)***
107 North Main Street
Concord, NH 03301
P: (603) 271-3661
E: anne.copp
@leg.state.nh.us

**Cordelli, Glenn (R, SP13)**
107 North Main Street
Concord, NH 03301
P: (603) 271-3661
E: glenn.cordelli
@leg.state.nh.us

**Cornell, Patricia (D, SP75)**
107 North Main Street
Manchester, NH 03102
P: (603) 644-5480
E: patricia.cornell
@leg.state.nh.us

**Costable Jr., Michael (R, SP134)***
107 North Main Street
Concord, NH 03301
P: (603) 271-3661

**Cote, David E. (D, SP88)**
107 North Main Street
Concord, NH 03301
P: (603) 271-3661
E: david.cote
@leg.state.nh.us

**Crawford, Karel A. (R, SP13)**
107 North Main Street
Concord, NH 03301
P: (603) 271-3661
E: karel.crawford
@leg.state.nh.us

**Cushing, Robert R. (D, SP152)**
107 North Main Street
Hampton, NH 03842
P: (617) 926-2737
E: renny.cushing
@leg.state.nh.us

**Danielson, David J. (R, SP64)**
107 North Main Street
Concord, NH 03301
P: (603) 271-3661
E: bedrep7@gmail.com

**Darrow, Stephen (R, SP57)**
107 North Main Street
Concord, NH 03301
P: (603) 271-3661
E: stephen.darrow
@leg.state.nh.us

**Dean-Bailey, Yvonne (R, SP163)**
107 North Main Street
Concord, NH 03301
P: (603) 271-3661
E: ydb@leg.state.nh.us

**DeTreville, Andrew N. (D, SP120)***
107 North Main Street
Concord, NH 03301
P: (603) 271-3661

**Dickey, Glen (R, SP62)***
107 North Main Street
Concord, NH 03301
P: (603) 271-3661
E: glen.dickey
@leg.state.nh.us

**DiLorenzo, Charlotte I. (D, SP148)***
107 North Main Street
Concord, NH 03301
P: (603) 271-3661
E: charlotte.dilorenzo
@leg.state.nh.us

**DiSilvestro, Linda A. (D, SP66)**
107 North Main Street
Concord, NH 03301
P: (603) 271-3661
E: linda.disilvestro
@leg.state.nh.us

**Doherty, David (D, SP122)**
107 North Main Street
Pembroke, NH 03275
P: (603) 485-2788
E: David.Doherty
@leg.state.nh.us

**Donovan, Daniel A. (R, SP59)**
107 North Main Street
Concord, NH 03301
P: (603) 271-3661
F: (603) 487-3591
E: daniel.donovan
@leg.state.nh.us

**Dontonville, Roger W. (D, SP50)***
107 North Main Street
Concord, NH 03301
P: (603) 271-3661
E: rdontonville@gmail.com

**Doucette, Fred (R, SP139)**
107 North Main Street
Concord, NH 03301
P: (603) 271-3661
E: fred.doucette
@leg.state.nh.us

**Dowling, Patricia A. (R, SP137)**
107 North Main Street
Concord, NH 03301
P: (603) 271-3661
E: pat.dowling@verani.com

**Dyer, Caleb Q. (R, SP94)***
107 North Main Street
Concord, NH 03301
P: (603) 271-3661

**Eaton, Daniel A. (D, SP20)**
107 North Main Street
Concord, NH 03301
P: (603) 271-3661
F: (603) 446-3535
E: Daniel.Eaton
@leg.state.nh.us

**Ebel, Karen E. (D, SP107)**
107 North Main Street
Concord, NH 03301
P: (603) 271-3661
E: karen.ebel
@leg.state.nh.us

**Edgar, Michael (D, SP152)***
107 North Main Street
Concord, NH 03301
P: (603) 271-3661
E: michael.edgar
@leg.state.nh.us

**Edwards, Elizabeth
(D, SP68)**
107 North Main Street
Concord, NH 03301
P: (603) 271-3661
E: ecomstockedwards
@gmail.com

**Edwards, Jess (R, SP135)***
107 North Main Street
Concord, NH 03301
P: (603) 271-3661
E: jess.edwards
@leg.state.nh.us

**Elber, Joel (D, SP76)***
107 North Main Street
Concord, NH 03301
P: (603) 271-3661

**Elliott, Robert J.
(R, SP139)**
107 North Main Street
Concord, NH 03301
P: (603) 271-3661
E: bob.elliott
@leg.state.nh.us

**Ellis, Donna (D, SP176)***
107 North Main Street
Concord, NH 03301
P: (603) 271-3661

**Emerick, J. Tracy
(R, SP152)**
107 North Main Street
Concord, NH 03301
P: (603) 271-3661
E: tracy.emerick
@leg.state.nh.us

**Epstein, Isaac (D, SP181)***
107 North Main Street
Concord, NH 03301
P: (603) 271-3661
E: isaac.epstein
@state.nh.us

**Farnham, Betsey (D, SP149)***
107 North Main Street
Concord, NH 03301
P: (603) 271-3661
E: efarnham@exeter.edu

**Faulkner, Barry (D, SP29)***
107 North Main Street
Concord, NH 03301
P: (603) 271-3661
E: fbfaulkner@outlook.com

**Fedolfi, James L.
(R, SP58)***
107 North Main Street
Concord, NH 03301
P: (603) 271-3661

**Fenton, Donovan (D, SP25)***
107 North Main Street
Concord, NH 03301
P: (603) 271-3661
E: donovan.fenton
@leg.state.nh.us

**Ferreira, Elizabeth
(R, SP85)**
107 North Main Street
Concord, NH 03301
P: (603) 271-3661
E: Elizabeth.Ferreira.NH
@gmail.com

**Fesh, Bob M. (R, SP137)**
107 North Main Street
Concord, NH 03301
P: (603) 271-3661
E: rmfesh@comcast.net

**Fields, Dennis H. (R, SP4)**
107 North Main Street
Concord, NH 03301
P: (603) 271-3661
E: dennis.fields
@leg.state.nh.us

**Fisher, Robert (R, SP9)**
107 North Main Street
Concord, NH 03301
P: (603) 271-3661
E: robert.fisher
@leg.state.nh.us

**Flanders, Donald H.
(R, SP3)**
1107 North Main Street
Concord, NH 03301
P: (603) 271-3661
F: (603) 524-0748
E: dflanders@metrocast.net

**Fontneau, Timothy
(D, SP175)***
107 North Main Street
Concord, NH 03301
P: (603) 271-3661
E: timfornh@yahoo.com

**Forest, Armand D. (D, SP75)**
107 North Main Street
Concord, NH 03301
P: (603) 271-3661
E: armand.forest
@leg.state.nh.us

**Fothergill, John (R, SP34)**
107 North Main Street
Concord, NH 03301
P: (603) 271-3661
E: john.Fothergill
@leg.state.nh.us

**Francese, Paula (D, SP149)**
107 North Main Street
Concord, NH 03301
P: (603) 271-3661
E: Paula.Francese
@leg.state.nh.us

**Fraser, Valerie (R, SP1)**
107 North Main Street
Concord, NH 03301
P: (603) 271-3661
E: valerie.fraser
@leg.state.nh.us

**Freeman, Lisa M. (R, SP69)***
107 North Main Street
Concord, NH 03301
P: (603) 271-3661
E: boscward5@mansd.org

**Freitas, Mary C. (D, SP71)**
107 North Main Street
Concord, NH 03301
P: (603) 271-3661
E: Mary.Freitas
@leg.state.nh.us

**Friel, William G.
(R, SP145)**
107 North Main Street
Concord, NH 03301
P: (603) 271-3661
E: william.friel
@leg.state.nh.us

**Fromuth, Bart (R, SP64)**
107 North Main Street
Concord, NH 03301
P: (603) 271-3661
E: bart@voteforbart.com

**Frost, Sherry (D, SP184)***
107 North Main Street
Concord, NH 03301
P: (603) 271-3661
E: sherry.frost
@leg.state.nh.us

**Gagne, Larry (R, SP70)**
107 North Main Street
Concord, NH 03301
P: (603) 271-3661
E: lgagne25@comcast.net

**Gagnon, Raymond G.
(D, SP198)**
107 North Main Street
Concord, NH 03301
P: (603) 271-3661
E: raymond.gagnon
@leg.state.nh.us

**Gargasz, Carolyn M.
(R, SP84)**
107 North Main Street
Concord, NH 03301
P: (603) 271-3661
F: (603) 465-7463
E: carolyn.gargasz
@leg.state.nh.us

**Gauthier, Francis
(R, SP196)***
107 North Main Street
Concord, NH 03301
P: (603) 271-3661
E: fgauthier1776@gmail.com

**Gay, Betty I. (R, SP139)***
107 North Main Street
Concord, NH 03301
P: (603) 271-3661
E: betty.gay
@leg.state.nh.us

**Gidge, Kenneth N. (D, SP90)**
107 North Main Street
Concord, NH 03301
P: (603) 271-3661
E: kgidge@aol.com

**Gile, Mary Stuart
(D, SP129)**
107 North Main Street
Concord, NH 03301
P: (603) 271-3661
E: mary.gile
@leg.state.nh.us

**Gilman, Julie (D, SP149)***
107 North Main Street
Concord, NH 03301
P: (603) 271-3661

**Goley, Jeff P. (D, SP65)**
107 North Main Street
Concord, NH 03301
P: (603) 271-3661
E: jgoley03104@yahoo.com

**Gordon, Pamela S.
(D, SP160)**
107 North Main Street
Concord, NH 03301
P: (603) 271-3661
E: Pamela.Gordon
@leg.state.nh.us

**Gordon, Richard E.
(R, SP166)**
107 North Main Street
Concord, NH 03301
P: (603) 271-3661
E: dick.gordon
@leg.state.nh.us

# New Hampshire

**Gottling, Suzanne H.
(D, SP195)**
107 North Main Street
Concord, NH 03301
P: (603) 271-3661
E: sgottling@comcast.net

**Gould, Linda (R, SP64)**
107 North Main Street
Concord, NH 03301
P: (603) 271-3661
E: linda.gould
@leg.state.nh.us

**Gourgue, Amanda (D, SP193)***
107 North Main Street
Concord, NH 03301
P: (603) 271-3661
E: amanda.gourgue
@leg.state.nh.us

**Graham, John A. (R, SP64)**
107 North Main Street
Concord, NH 03301
P: (603) 271-3661
E: graham4rep@hotmail.com

**Graham, Robert V.
(R, SP169)**
107 North Main Street
Concord, NH 03301
P: (603) 271-3661
E: Robert.Graham
@leg.state.nh.us

**Grassie, Chuck (D, SP179)***
107 North Main Street
Concord, NH 03301
P: (603) 271-3661
E: cwgrassie@msn.com

**Green, Dennis (R, SP144)**
107 North Main Street
Concord, NH 03301
P: (603) 271-3661
E: Dennis.Green
@leg.state.nh.us

**Grenier, James L.
(R, SP200)**
107 North Main Street
Concord, NH 03301
P: (603) 271-3661
E: jimgreniersullivan7
@gmail.com

**Griffin, Barbara (R, SP63)**
84 Merrill Road
Goffstown, NH 03045
P: (603) 497-8286
E: barbara.griffin
@leg.state.nh.us

**Griffin, Gerald (R, SP62)***
107 North Main Street
Concord, NH 03301
P: (603) 271-3661
E: NHLPM@myfairpoint.net

**Griffin, Mary E. (R, SP138)**
107 North Main Street
Concord, NH 03301
P: (603) 271-3661
E: mary.griffin
@leg.state.nh.us

**Guthrie, Joseph A.
(R, SP144)**
107 North Main Street
Concord, NH 03301
P: (603) 271-3661
E: joseph.guthrie
@leg.state.nh.us

**Hagan, Joseph M. (R, SP135)**
107 North Main Street
Concord, NH 03301
P: (603) 271-3661
E: josephhaganmd@gmail.com

**Halstead, Carolyn (R, SP80)**
107 North Main Street
Concord, NH 03301
P: (603) 271-3661
E: carolyn.halstead
@leg.state.nh.us

**Ham, Bonnie D. (R, SP45)**
107 North Main Street
Concord, NH 03301
P: (603) 271-3661
E: bdham@roadrunner.com

**Hansen, Peter (R, SP79)**
107 North Main Street
Amherst, NH 03031
P: (603) 673-5987
E: peter.hansen
@leg.state.nh.us

**Harrington, Michael D.
(R, SP171)**
107 North Main Street
Concord, NH 03301
P: (603) 271-3661
E: harringt@metrocast.net

**Harvey, Suzanne (D, SP86)**
107 North Main Street
Concord, NH 03301
P: (603) 271-3661
E: suzanne.harvey
@leg.state.nh.us

**Hatch, William A. (D, SP39)**
107 North Main Street
Concord, NH 03301
P: (603) 271-3661
E: William.Hatch
@leg.state.nh.us

**Heath, Mary (D, SP71)**
107 North Main Street
Concord, NH 03301
P: (603) 271-3661
E: mary.heath
@leg.state.nh.us

**Hellwig, Steve D. (R, SP94)**
107 North Main Street
Concord, NH 03301
P: (603) 271-3661
E: steve.hellwig
@leg.state.nh.us

**Henle, Paul J. (D, SP114)**
107 North Main Street
Concord, NH 03301
P: (603) 271-3661
E: paul.henle
@leg.state.nh.us

**Hennessey, Erin Tapper
(R, SP41)**
107 North Main Street
Concord, NH 03301
P: (603) 271-3661
E: erin.hennessey
@leg.state.nh.us

**Herbert, Christopher J.
(D, SP100)**
85 Watts Street
Manchester, NH 03104
P: (603) 669-2838
E: Chris.Herbert
@leg.state.nh.us

**Higgins, Patricia C.
(D, SP52)**
107 North Main Street
Concord, NH 03301
P: (603) 271-3661
E: patricia.higgins
@leg.state.nh.us

**Hill, Gregory (R, SP105)**
107 North Main Street
Concord, NH 03301
P: (603) 271-3661
E: greg.hill
@leg.state.nh.us

**Hinch, Richard W. (R, SP78)**
107 North Main Street
Concord, NH 03301
P: (603) 271-3661
E: dick.hinch
@leg.state.nh.us

**Hoell, J.R. (R, SP125)**
107 North Main Street
Concord, NH 03301
P: (603) 271-3661
E: jr.hoell@leg.state.nh.us

**Hoelzel, Kathleen M.
(R, SP134)**
107 North Main Street
Concord, NH 03301
P: (603) 271-3661
E: kathleen.hoelzel
@leg.state.nh.us

**Hopper, Gary S. (R, SP59)**
107 North Main Street
Concord, NH 03281
P: (603) 271-3661
E: gary.hopper
@leg.state.nh.us

**Horgan, James (R, SP170)***
107 North Main Street
Concord, NH 03301
P: (603) 271-3661
E: james.horgan
@leg.state.nh.us

**Horn, Werner D. (R, SP104)**
107 North Main Street
Concord, NH 03301
P: (603) 271-3661
E: werner.horn
@leg.state.nh.us

**Horrigan, Timothy
(D, SP174)**
107 North Main Street
Concord, NH 03301
P: (603) 271-3661
F: (866) 542-0665
E: Timothy.Horrigan
@leg.state.nh.us

**Howard, Raymond (R, SP8)**
107 North Main Street
Concord, NH 03301
P: (603) 271-3661
E: brhowardjr@yahoo.com

**Hull, Robert (R, SP49)**
107 North Main Street
Concord, NH 03301
P: (603) 271-3661
E: robert.hull
@leg.state.nh.us

**Hunt, John B. (R, SP28)**
107 North Main Street
Concord, NH 03301
P: (603) 271-3661
F: (603) 899-6160
E: jbhunt@prodigy.net

**Huot, David O. (D, SP3)**
107 North Main Street
Concord, NH 03301
P: (603) 271-3661
E: david.huot
@leg.state.nh.us

**Hynes, Dan (R, SP78)***
107 North Main Street
Concord, NH 03301
P: (603) 271-3661

**Irwin, Virginia (D, SP202)**
107 North Main Street
Concord, NH 03301
P: (603) 271-3661
E: virginia.irwin
@leg.state.nh.us

**Itse, Daniel C. (R, SP141)**
107 North Main Street
Concord, NH 03301
P: (603) 271-3661
E: itsenh@comcast.net

**Jack, Martin L. (D, SP93)**
107 North Main Street
Concord, NH 03301
P: (603) 271-3661
E: martin.jack
    @leg.state.nh.us

**Janigian, John (R, SP139)***
107 North Main Street
Concord, NH 03301
P: (603) 271-3661
E: john.janigian
    @leg.state.nh.us

**Janvrin, Kevin (R, SP151)**
107 North Main Street
Concord, NH 03301
P: (603) 271-3661

**Jasper, Shawn N. (R, SP94)**
107 North Main Street
Concord, NH 03301
P: (603) 271-3661
F: (603) 882-2056
E: shawn.jasper
    @leg.state.nh.us

**Jeudy, Jean L. (D, SP67)**
107 North Main Street
Concord, NH 03301
P: (603) 271-3661
E: Jean.jeudy@gmail.com

**Johnsen, Gladys (D, SP24)**
107 North Main Street
Concord, NH 03301
P: (603) 271-3661
F: (603) 398-5164
E: johnsengladys@gmail.com

**Johnson, Tiffany (R, SP47)***
107 North Main Street
Concord, NH 03301
P: (603) 271-3661
E: tiffany.johnson
    @leg.state.nh.us

**Josephson, Timothy
    (D, SP51)***
107 North Main Street
Concord, NH 03301
P: (603) 271-3661
E: timothy.josephson
    @leg.state.nh.us

**Judd, Bing (R, SP34)***
107 North Main Street
Concord, NH 03301
P: (603) 271-3661

**Kaczynski Jr., Thomas L.
    (R, SP190)**
107 North Main Street
Concord, NH 03301
P: (603) 271-3661
E: hampoul@metrocast.net

**Katsakiores, Phyllis M.
    (R, SP137)**
107 North Main Street
Concord, NH 03301
P: (603) 271-3661
E: pkatsakiores@comcast.net

**Katsiantonis, Thomas
    (D, SP72)**
107 North Main Street
Concord, NH 03301
P: (603) 271-3661
E: thomaskatsiantonis
    @gmail.com

**Keane, Amelia (D, SP88)***
107 North Main Street
Concord, NH 03301
P: (603) 271-3661

**Keans, Sandra Balomenos
    (D, SP191)**
107 North Main Street
Concord, NH 03301
P: (603) 271-3661
E: sandra.keans@yahoo.com

**Kenison, Linda B.
    (D, SP117)**
107 North Main Street
Concord, NH 03301
P: (603) 271-3661
E: Linda.Kenison
    @leg.state.nh.us

**Kent Campion, Polly
    (D, SP52)***
107 North Main Street
Concord, NH 03301
P: (603) 271-3661

**Khan, Aboul B. (R, SP151)**
107 North Main Street
Concord, NH 03301
P: (603) 271-3661

**King, Mark (D, SP90)***
107 North Main Street
Concord, NH 03301
P: (603) 271-3661
E: mark.king
    @leg.state.nh.us

**Klee, Patricia S.
    (D, SP87)***
107 North Main Street
Concord, NH 03301
P: (603) 271-3661
E: patricia.klee
    @leg.state.nh.us

**Klose, John F. (R, SP123)**
107 North Main Street
Concord, NH 03301
P: (603) 271-3661
E: john.klose
    @leg.state.nh.us

**Knirk, Jerry (D, SP12)***
107 North Main Street
Concord, NH 03301
P: (603) 271-3661

**Kolodziej, Walter
    (R, SP138)**
107 North Main Street
Concord, NH 03301
P: (603) 271-3661

**Kotowski, Frank R.
    (R, SP126)**
107 North Main Street
Concord, NH 03301
P: (603) 271-3661
E: frkotowski@comcast.net

**Krans, Hamilton (D, SP182)***
107 North Main Street
Concord, NH 03301
P: (603) 271-3661

**Kuch, Bill (R, SP125)**
107 North Main Street
Concord, NH 03304
P: (603) 271-3661
E: Bill.Kuch
    @leg.state.nh.us

**Kurk, Neal M. (R, SP59)**
107 North Main Street
Concord, NH 03281
P: (603) 271-3661
E: rep03281@aol.com

**Ladd, Rick (R, SP44)**
107 North Main Street
Concord, NH 03765
P: (603) 271-3661
E: ladd.nhhouse@charter.net

**Laflamme, Larry L.
    (D, SP36)***
107 North Main Street
Concord, NH 03301
P: (603) 271-3661
E: laflamme@ne.rr.com

**Lang, Timothy (R, SP4)***
107 North Main Street
Concord, NH 03301
P: (603) 271-3661

**Lascelles, Richard W.
    (R, SP77)***
107 North Main Street
Concord, NH 03301
P: (603) 271-3661
E: richard.lascelles
    @leg.state.nh.us

**Laware, Thomas (R, SP201)**
107 North Main Street
Concord, NH 03603
P: (603) 271-3661
F: (603) 826-3137
E: thomas.laware
    @leg.state.nh.us

**Le, Tamara (D, SP161)***
107 North Main Street
Concord, NH 03301
P: (603) 271-3661
E: tamara.le
    @leg.state.nh.us

**Leavitt, John A.
    (R, SP126)***
107 North Main Street
Concord, NH 03301
P: (603) 271-3661
E: leavittbrothersauto
    @hotmail.com

**LeBrun, Donald (R, SP89)**
107 North Main Street
Concord, NH 03062
P: (603) 271-3661
E: donald.lebrun
    @leg.state.nh.us

**Leishman, Peter R.
    (D, SP81)**
107 North Main Street
Concord, NH 03458
P: (603) 271-3661
E: PRLeishman@aol.com

**Lewicke, John (R, SP83)***
107 North Main Street
Concord, NH 03301
P: (603) 271-3661

**Ley, Douglas A. (D, SP26)**
107 North Main Street
Concord, NH 03452
P: (603) 271-3661
E: douglas.ley
    @leg.state.nh.us

**L'Heureux, Robert J.
    (R, SP78)**
107 North Main Street
Concord, NH 03301
P: (603) 271-3661
E: bob.lheureux
    @leg.state.nh.us

**Lisle, David (D, SP92)***
107 North Main Street
Concord, NH 03301
P: (603) 271-3661
E: david.lisle
    @leg.state.nh.us

# New Hampshire

**Long, Douglas B. (R, SP106)**
107 North Main Street
Concord, NH 03287
P: (603) 271-3661
E: longbroscon
@mcttelecom.com

**Long, Patrick T. (D, SP67)**
107 North Main Street
Concord, NH 03101
P: (603) 271-3661
E: long55@comcast.net

**Lovejoy, Patricia
(D, SP167)**
107 North Main Street
Concord, NH 03885
P: (603) 271-3661
E: patty.lovejoy
@leg.state.nh.us

**Lundgren, David C.
(R, SP136)**
107 North Main Street
Concord, NH 03053
P: (603) 271-3661
F: (603) 432-4142
E: qtipnh@aol.com

**Luneau, David (I, SP112)**
107 North Main Street
Concord, NH 03229
P: (603) 271-3661
E: dluneauNH@gmail.com

**MacKay, James R. (D, SP116)**
107 North Main Street
Concord, NH 03301
P: (603) 271-3661
E: james.mackay@mygait.com

**MacKay, Mariellen J.
(D, SP87)**
107 North Main Street
Concord, NH 03064
P: (603) 271-3661
E: mariellen.mackay
@leg.state.nh.us

**Mackenzie, Mark S.
(D, SP74)***
107 North Main Street
Concord, NH 03301
P: (603) 271-3661
E: mackenziedist17
@gmail.com

**Maes, Kevin G. (D, SP46)**
107 North Main Street
Concord, NH 03266
P: (603) 271-3661
E: Kevin.Maes
@leg.state.nh.us

**Major, Norman L. (R, SP145)**
107 North Main Street
Concord, NH 03865
P: (603) 271-3661
F: (603) 382-8117
E: norman.major
@leg.state.nh.us

**Malloy, Dennis J.
(D, SP154)**
107 North Main Street
Concord, NH 03301
P: (603) 271-3661
E: dennis.malloy
@leg.state.nh.us

**Maloney, Michael F.
(R, SP5)**
107 North Main Street
Concord, NH 03301
P: (603) 271-3661

**Mangipudi, Latha (D, SP92)**
107 North Main Street
Concord, NH 03062
P: (603) 271-3661
E: Latha.Mangipudi
@leg.state.nh.us

**Manley, Jonathan F.
(D, SP60)**
107 North Main Street
Concord, NH 03442
P: (603) 271-3661
E: jonathan.manley
@leg.state.nh.us

**Mann, John E. (D, SP19)**
107 North Main Street
Concord, NH 03602
P: (603) 271-3661
E: john.mann
@leg.state.nh.us

**Manning Jr., John J.
(R, SP139)**
107 North Main Street
Concord, NH 03079
P: (603) 271-3661
E: john.manning
@leg.state.nh.us

**Marple, Richard (R, SP126)**
107 North Main Street
Concord, NH 03106
P: (603) 271-3661
F: (603) 627-1837
E: dick.marple
@leg.state.nh.us

**Marsh, Henry (R, SP153)***
107 North Main Street
Concord, NH 03301
P: (603) 271-3661

**Marsh, William M.
(R, SP17)***
107 North Main Street
Concord, NH 03301
P: (603) 271-3661
E: william.marsh
@leg.state.nh.us

**Martin, Joelle (R, SP80)***
107 North Main Street
Concord, NH 03301
P: (603) 271-3661

**Martineau, Jesse J.
(D, SP99)**
107 North Main Street
Concord, NH 03301
P: (603) 271-3661
E: jess.martineau
@leg.state.nh.us

**Massimilla, Linda (D, SP41)**
107 North Main Street
Concord, NH 03561
P: (603) 271-3661
E: linda.massimilla
@leg.state.nh.us

**Matthews, Carolyn L.
(R, SP134)**
107 North Main Street
Concord, NH 03077
P: (603) 271-3661
E: Carolyn.Matthews
@leg.state.nh.us

**McBeath, Rebecca (D, SP157)**
107 North Main Street
Concord, NH 03801
P: (603) 271-3661
E: NHStateHouse@gmail.com

**McCarthy, Frank (R, SP11)**
107 North Main Street
Concord, NH 03818
P: (603) 271-3661
E: serendipity922@gmail.com

**McCarthy, Michael (R, SP86)**
107 North Main Street
Concord, NH 03301
P: (603) 271-3661
E: mike.mccarthy
@leg.state.nh.us

**McConkey, Mark E. (R, SP12)**
107 North Main Street
Concord, NH 03836
P: (603) 271-3661
E: mcconkey2@hotmail.com

**McConnell, Jim (R, SP29)**
107 North Main Street
Concord, NH 03431
P: (603) 271-3661
E: Jim.McConnell
@leg.state.nh.us

**McGuire, Carol (R, SP131)**
107 North Main Street
Concord, NH 03234
P: (603) 271-3661
E: carol@mcguire4house.com

**McKinney, Betsy (R, SP136)**
107 North Main Street
Londonderry, NH 03053
P: (603) 271-3661
E: betsy.mckinney
@leg.state.nh.us

**McMahon, Charles E.
(R, SP138)**
107 North Main Street
Windham, NH 03087
P: (603) 271-3661
F: (603) 432-6854
E: cmcmahon55@gmail.com

**McNally, Jody (R, SP178)***
107 North Main Street
Concord, NH 03301
P: (603) 271-3661
E: mcnally-jody-usmc
@yahoo.com

**McNamara, Richard D.
(D, SP95)**
107 North Main Street
Concord, NH 03301
P: (603) 271-3661

**Meader, David R. (D, SP23)**
107 North Main Street
Concord, NH 03301
P: (603) 271-3661
E: david.meader
@leg.state.nh.us

**Merner, Troy (R, SP40)***
107 North Main Street
Concord, NH 03301
P: (603) 271-3661

**Messmer, Mindi (D, SP155)***
107 North Main Street
Concord, NH 03301
P: (603) 271-3661
E: mindi.messmer
@leg.state.nh.us

**Milz, David E. (R, SP137)**
107 North Main Street
Concord, NH 03038
P: (603) 271-3661
E: david.milz
@leg.state.nh.us

**Moffett, Howard M.
(D, SP111)**
107 North Main Street
Concord, NH 03224
P: (603) 271-3661
E: howard.moffett
@leg.state.nh.us

**Moffett, Michael (R, SP111)**
107 North Main Street
Concord, NH 03301
P: (603) 271-3661
E: mofmichael@aim.com

**Moore, Craig C. (R, SP82)***
107 North Main Street
Concord, NH 03301
P: (603) 271-3661
E: moore4nh@gmail.com

**Moore, Josh (R, SP78)**
107 North Main Street
Concord, NH 03054
P: (603) 271-3661
E: josh.moore
@leg.state.nh.us

**Morrison, Sean D.
(R, SP140)***
107 North Main Street
Concord, NH 03301
P: (603) 271-3661

**Moynihan, Wayne T.
(D, SP35)**
107 North Main Street
Concord, NH 03588
P: (603) 271-3661
E: wayne.moynihan
@leg.state.nh.us

**Mullen, John A. (R, SP169)**
107 North Main Street
Concord, NH 03887
P: (603) 271-3661
E: john.mullen
@leg.state.nh.us

**Mulligan, Mary Jane
(D, SP52)***
107 North Main Street
Concord, NH 03301
P: (603) 271-3661
E: maryjane.mulligan
@leg.state.nh.us

**Murotake, David K.
(R, SP89)**
17 Portchester Drive
Nashua, NH 03062
P: (603) 889-4568
E: david.murotake
@leg.state.nh.us

**Murphy, Keith (R, SP64)**
107 North Main Street
Concord, NH 03301
P: (603) 271-3661
F: (603) 644-3537
E: rep.keithmurphy
@gmail.com

**Murray, Kate (D, SP155)***
107 North Main Street
Concord, NH 03301
P: (603) 271-3661

**Myler, Mel (D, SP112)**
107 North Main Street
Concord, NH 03301
P: (603) 271-3661
E: mel.myler
@leg.state.nh.us

**Nasser, Jim (R, SP133)***
107 North Main Street
Concord, NH 03301
P: (603) 271-3661

**Negron, Steve (R, SP89)***
107 North Main Street
Concord, NH 03301
P: (603) 271-3661
E: steve.negron
@leg.state.nh.us

**Nelson, Bill G. (R, SP14)**
107 North Main Street
Concord, NH 03301
P: (603) 271-3661
E: bill.nelson
@leg.state.nh.us

**Newman, Sue (D, SP86)***
107 North Main Street
Concord, NH 03301
P: (603) 271-3661
E: snewmannh@aol.com

**Nigrello, Robert L.
(R, SP147)**
107 North Main Street
Concord, NH 03301
P: (603) 271-3661
E: bob.nigrello
@leg.state.nh.us

**Nordgren, Sharon L.
(D, SP52)**
107 North Main Street
Concord, NH 03301
P: (603) 271-3661
F: (603) 643-8567
E: sharon.nordgren
@leg.state.nh.us

**Notter, Jeanine (R, SP78)**
107 North Main Street
Concord, NH 03301
P: (603) 271-3661
E: jeanine.notter
@leg.state.nh.us

**Nutting, Allison (D, SP91)***
107 North Main Street
Concord, NH 03301
P: (603) 271-3661
E: allison.nutting
@leg.stae.nh.us

**Ober, Lynne M. (R, SP94)**
107 North Main Street
Concord, NH 03301
P: (603) 271-3661
E: lynne.ober@comcast.net

**Ober III, Russell T.
(R, SP94)**
107 North Main Street
Concord, NH 03301
P: (603) 271-3661

**O'Brien Sr., Michael B.
(D, SP93)**
107 North Main Street
Concord, NH 03301
P: (603) 271-3661
E: michael.o'brien
@leg.state.nh.us

**O'Connor, John J.
(R, SP197)***
107 North Main Street
Concord, NH 03301
P: (603) 271-3661

**O'Connor, John T.
(R, SP137)**
107 North Main Street
Concord, NH 03301
P: (603) 271-3661
E: john.o'connor
@leg.state.nh.us

**O'Day, John E. (R, SP28)***
107 North Main Street
Concord, NH 03301
P: (603) 271-3661
E: joday603@gmail.com

**Ohm, Bill (R, SP93)**
107 North Main Street
Concord, NH 03301
P: (603) 271-3661
F: (413) 691-6187
E: billohm2010@aol.com

**O'Leary, Richard (D, SP70)***
107 North Main Street
Concord, NH 03301
P: (603) 271-3661

**O'Neil, William (D, SP66)**
107 North Main Street
Concord, NH 03301
P: (603) 271-3661
E: william.oneil
@leg.state.nh.us

**Opderbecke, Linn
(D, SP183)***
107 North Main Street
Concord, NH 03301
P: (603) 271-3661

**Osborne, Jason (R, SP135)**
107 North Main Street
Concord, NH 03301
P: (603) 271-3661
E: Jason@Osborne4NH.com

**Oxenham, Lee Walker
(D, SP194)**
107 North Main Street
Concord, NH 03301
P: (603) 271-3661
E: Lee.Oxenham
@leg.state.nh.us

**Packard, Sherman A.
(R, SP136)**
107 North Main Street
Concord, NH 03301
P: (603) 271-3661
F: (603) 421-0902
E: sherman.packard
@leg.state.nh.us

**Panasiti, Reed (R, SP79)***
107 North Main Street
Concord, NH 03301
P: (603) 271-3661
E: reed.panasiti
@leg.state.nh.us

**Pantelakos, Laura C.
(D, SP156)**
107 North Main Street
Concord, NH 03301
P: (603) 271-3661
E: lcpantelakos@comcast.net

**Parkhurst, Henry A.L.
(D, SP30)**
107 North Main Street
Concord, NH 03301
P: (603) 271-3661
E: hank.parkhurst
@leg.state.nh.us

**Patten, Dick (D, SP119)**
107 North Main Street
Concord, NH 03301
P: (603) 271-3661
F: (603) 715-1648
E: Dick.Patten
@leg.state.nh.us

**Pearl, Howard (R, SP128)***
107 North Main Street
Concord, NH 03301
P: (603) 271-3661
E: howard.pearl
@leg.state.nh.us

**Pearson, Mark A. (R, SP165)**
107 North Main Street
Concord, NH 03301
P: (603) 271-3661
E: mark.pearson
@leg.state.nh.us

**Pearson, William (D, SP21)**
107 North Main Street
Concord, NH 03301
P: (603) 271-3661
E: William.Pearson
@leg.state.nh.us

# New Hampshire

**Pellegrino, Tony J.
(R, SP78)**
107 North Main Street
Concord, NH 03301
P: (603) 271-3661
E: anthony.pellegrino
@leg.state.nh.us

**Phinney, Brandon
(R, SP192)\***
107 North Main Street
Concord, NH 03301
P: (603) 271-3661
E: brandon.phinney
@leg.state.nh.us

**Pierce, David W. (R, SP63)**
107 North Main Street
Concord, NH 03301
P: (603) 271-3661
E: david.w.pierce
@leg.state.nh.us

**Pitre, Joseph (R, SP170)**
107 North Main Street
Concord, NH 03301
P: (603) 271-3661
F: (603) 755-2447
E: joe@joepitre.com

**Plumer, John (R, SP6)**
107 North Main Street
Concord, NH 03301
P: (603) 271-3661
E: john.plumer
@leg.state.nh.us

**Polewarczyk, William
(R, SP135)\***
107 North Main Street
Concord, NH 03301
P: (603) 271-3661
E: william.polewarczyk
@leg.state.nh.us

**Porter, Marjorie A.
(D, SP58)**
107 North Main Street
Concord, NH 03301
P: (603) 271-3661
E: marjorie.porter
@leg.state.nh.us

**Proulx, Mark (R, SP101)**
107 North Main Street
Concord, NH 03301
P: (603) 271-3661
F: (603) 669-7179
E: mark.proulx
@leg.state.nh.us

**Prout, Andrew (R, SP94)\***
107 North Main Street
Concord, NH 03301
P: (603) 271-3661
E: andrew.prout
@leg.state.nh.us

**Rand, Steven (D, SP48)\***
107 North Main Street
Concord, NH 03301
P: (603) 271-3661
E: RStevenRand@yahoo.com

**Read, Ellen (D, SP148)\***
107 North Main Street
Concord, NH 03301
P: (603) 271-3661
E: ellen.read
@leg.state.nh.us

**Renzullo, Andrew (R, SP94)**
107 North Main Street
Concord, NH 03301
P: (603) 271-3661
E: andrew.renzullo
@leg.state.nh.us

**Rice, Chip L. (D, SP129)**
107 North Main Street
Concord, NH 03301
P: (603) 271-3661
E: chip.rice
@leg.state.nh.us

**Rice, Kimberly (R, SP94)**
107 North Main Street
Concord, NH 03301
P: (603) 271-3661
E: kimberly.rice
@leg.state.nh.us

**Richards, Beth (D, SP115)\***
107 North Main Street
Concord, NH 03301
P: (603) 271-3661

**Richardson, Herbert D.
(R, SP37)**
107 North Main Street
Concord, NH 03301
P: (603) 271-3661
E: honhdr@yahoo.com

**Rimol, Bob (R, SP136)\***
107 North Main Street
Concord, NH 03301
P: (603) 271-3661
E: rrimol@rimol.com

**Roberts, Carol R. (D, SP61)**
107 North Main Street
Concord, NH 03301
P: (603) 271-3661
E: Carol.Roberts
@leg.state.nh.us

**Rodd, Beth (D, SP108)**
107 North Main Street
Concord, NH 03301
P: (603) 271-3661
E: beth.rodd
@leg.state.nh.us

**Rogers, Katherine D.
(D, SP130)**
107 North Main Street
Concord, NH 03301
P: (603) 271-3661
E: katherine.rogers
@leg.state.nh.us

**Rollins, Skip (R, SP199)**
107 North Main Street
Concord, NH 03301
P: (603) 271-3661
E: skip@lavalleys.com

**Rosenwald, Cindy (D, SP87)**
107 North Main Street
Concord, NH 03301
P: (603) 271-3661
E: cindy.rosenwald
@leg.state.nh.us

**Rouillard, Claire (R, SP63)**
107 North Main Street
Concord, NH 03301
P: (603) 271-3661
E: Claire.Rouillard
@leg.state.nh.us

**Salloway, Jeffrey
(D, SP173)\***
107 North Main Street
Concord, NH 03301
P: (603) 271-3661

**Sanborn, Laurie J.
(R, SP98)**
107 North Main Street
Concord, NH 03301
P: (603) 271-3661
E: repsanborn@gmail.com

**Sandler, Catt (D, SP189)\***
107 North Main Street
Concord, NH 03301
P: (603) 271-3661

**Sapareto, Frank V.
(R, SP137)**
107 North Main Street
Concord, NH 03301
P: (603) 271-3661
E: sapareto@comcast.net

**Schleien, Eric (R, SP94)**
107 North Main Street
Concord, NH 03301
P: (603) 271-3661
E: eric.schleien
@leg.state.nh.us

**Schmidt, Andrew (D, SP194)**
107 North Main Street
Concord, NH 03301
P: (603) 271-3661
E: andrew.schmidt
@leg.state.nh.us

**Schmidt, Janice E.
(D, SP85)**
107 North Main Street
Concord, NH 03301
P: (603) 271-3661

**Schmidt, Peter B.
(D, SP187)**
107 North Main Street
Concord, NH 03301
P: (603) 271-3661
E: reppbs@ttlc.net

**Schmidt, Stephen (R, SP15)**
107 North Main Street
Concord, NH 03301
P: (603) 271-3661
E: stephen.schmidt
@leg.state.nh.us

**Schuett, Dianne E.
(D, SP122)**
107 North Main Street
Concord, NH 03301
P: (603) 271-3661
E: dianne.schuett
@leg.state.nh.us

**Schwaegler, Vicki
(R, SP43)\***
107 North Main Street
Concord, NH 03301
P: (603) 271-3661

**Scruton, Mathew (R, SP180)\***
107 North Main Street
Concord, NH 03301
P: (603) 271-3661
E: matthew.scruton
@leg.state.nh.us

**Scully, Kevin (R, SP90)\***
107 North Main Street
Concord, NH 03301
P: (603) 271-3661

**Seaworth, G. Brian
(R, SP122)**
107 North Main Street
Concord, NH 03275
P: (603) 271-3661
E: brian.seaworth
@leg.state.nh.us

**Seidel, Carl W. (R, SP85)**
107 North Main Street
Concord, NH 03063
P: (603) 271-3661
F: (603) 598-3412
E: seidel4staterep
@mindspring.com

**Shackett, Jeffrey (R, SP49)**
107 North Main Street
Concord, NH 03222
P: (603) 271-3661
E: jeffrey.shackett
@leg.state.nh.us

**Shaw, Barbara E. (D, SP73)**
107 North Main Street
Concord, NH 03103
P: (603) 271-3661
E: beshaw3@comcast.net

**Shepardson, Marjorie J.
   (D, SP27)**
107 North Main Street
Concord, NH 03455
P: (603) 271-3661
E: marge.shepardson
   @gmail.com

**Shurtleff, Stephen J.
   (D, SP113)**
107 North Main Street
Concord, NH 03303
P: (603) 271-3661
E: steve.shurtleff
   @leg.state.nh.us

**Silber, Norman (R, SP2)***
107 North Main Street
Concord, NH 03301
P: (603) 271-3661
E: njs@silbersnh.com

**Smith, Gregory (R, SP94)**
107 North Main Street
Concord, NH 03076
P: (603) 271-3661
E: gregory.smith
   @leg.state.nh.us

**Smith, Marjorie K.
   (D, SP174)**
107 North Main Street
Concord, NH 03824
P: (603) 271-3661
E: msmithpen@aol.com

**Smith, Ryan (R, SP105)***
107 North Main Street
Concord, NH 03301
P: (603) 271-3661

**Smith, Steven (R, SP204)**
107 North Main Street
Concord, NH 03603
P: (603) 271-3661
E: nhfirst@gmail.com

**Smith, Suzanne (D, SP48)**
107 North Main Street
Concord, NH 03241
P: (603) 271-3661
E: suzanne.smith
   @leg.state.nh.us

**Smith, Timothy J. (D, SP74)**
107 North Main Street
Concord, NH 03102
P: (603) 271-3661
E: tim.smith
   @leg.state.nh.us

**Snow, Kendall A. (D, SP99)**
107 North Main Street
Concord, NH 03104
P: (603) 271-3661
E: Ken.Snow@leg.state.nh.us

**Sofikitis, Catherine
   (D, SP91)***
107 North Main Street
Concord, NH 03301
P: (603) 271-3661
E: csofikitis@gmail.com

**Somero, Paul (R, SP82)***
107 N Main St
Concord, NH 03301
P: (603) 271-3661
E: paulsomero@msn.com

**Somssich, Peter (D, SP158)***
107 North Main Street
Concord, NH 03301
P: (603) 271-3661
E: peter.somssich
   @leg.state.nh.us

**Soucy, Timothy (D, SP91)**
107 North Main Street
Concord, NH 03301
P: (603) 271-3661
E: timothy.soucy
   @leg.state.nh.us

**Southworth, Tom (D, SP188)**
107 North Main Street
Concord, NH 03820
P: (603) 271-3661
E: Thomas.Southworth
   @leg.state.nh.us

**Souza, Kathleen F.
   (R, SP100)**
107 North Main Street
Concord, NH 03104
P: (603) 271-3661
E: irishsouza@netscape.com

**Spang, Judith T. (D, SP174)**
107 North Main Street
Concord, NH 03824
P: (603) 271-3661
E: judith@kestrelnet.net

**Spanos, Peter (R, SP3)**
107 North Main Street
Concord, NH 03289
P: (603) 271-3661
E: peterjspanos@gmail.com

**Spencer, Matthew
   (R, SP186)***
107 North Main Street
Concord, NH 03301
P: (603) 271-3661
E: matthew.spencer
   @leg.state.nh.us

**Spillane, James (R, SP133)**
107 North Main Street
Concord, NH 03037
P: (603) 271-3661
E: james@jamesspillane.org

**Sprague, Dale R. (D, SP186)**
107 North Main Street
Concord, NH 03878
P: (603) 271-3661
E: dale.sprague
   @leg.state.nh.us

**Stallcop, Joseph (D, SP21)***
107 North Main Street
Concord, NH 03301
P: (603) 271-3661
E: joseph.stallcop
   @leg.state.nh.us

**Sterling Jr., Franklin W.
   (R, SP31)**
107 North Main Street
Concord, NH 03452
P: (603) 271-3661
E: fwsterling@comcast.net

**Sullivan, Daniel J.
   (D, SP99)**
107 North Main Street
Concord, NH 03104
P: (603) 271-3661
E: dan.sullivan
   @leg.state.nh.us

**Sullivan, Victoria L.
   (R, SP73)**
107 North Main Street
Concord, NH 03103
P: (603) 271-3661
E: patchessul@comcast.net

**Sykes, George E. (D, SP53)**
3 Avon Avenue
Concord, NH 03766
P: (603) 271-3661
E: george.sykes
   @leg.state.nh.us

**Sylvia, Michael J. (R, SP6)**
107 North Main Street
Concord, NH 03220
P: (603) 271-3661
E: mike.sylvia
   @leg.state.nh.us

**Sytek, John J. (R, SP139)**
107 North Main Street
Concord, NH 03079
P: (603) 271-3661
F: (603) 893-0000
E: john.sytek
   @leg.state.nh.us

**Tanner, Linda L. (D, SP202)**
107 North Main Street
Concord, NH 03301
P: (603) 271-3661
E: linda.tanner
   @leg.state.nh.us

**Tatro, Bruce (D, SP32)**
107 North Main Street
Concord, NH 03446
P: (603) 271-3661
E: bruce.tatro
   @leg.state.nh.us

**Testerman, Dave (R, SP104)***
107 North Main Street
Concord, NH 03301
P: (603) 271-3661
E: Dave@sanbornhall.net

**Theberge, Robert L.
   (D, SP36)**
107 North Main Street
Concord, NH 03570
P: (603) 271-3661
E: robert.theberge
   @leg.state.nh.us

**Thomas, Doug (R, SP136)**
107 North Main Street
Concord, NH 03053
P: (603) 271-3661
E: doug.thomasnh@gmail.com

**Thomas, Yvonne D. (D, SP36)**
107 North Main Street
Concord, NH 03570
P: (603) 271-3661
E: yvonne.thomas
   @leg.state.nh.us

**Tilton, Franklin T.
   (R, SP3)**
107 North Main Street
Concord, NH 03246
P: (603) 271-3661
E: franklin.tilton
   @leg.state.nh.us

**Tilton, Rio (R, SP151)**
107 North Main Street
Concord, NH 03874
P: (603) 271-3661

**Torosian, Peter E.
   (R, SP145)***
107 North Main Street
Concord, NH 03301
P: (603) 271-3661
E: peter.torosian
   @leg.state.nh.us

**Treleaven, Susan (D, SP185)**
107 North Main Street
Concord, NH 03820
P: (603) 271-3661
E: streleaven@comcast.net

# New Hampshire

**Tripp, Richard P.
(R, SP137)\***
107 North Main Street
Concord, NH 03301
P: (603) 271-3661

**True, Chris (R, SP135)**
107 North Main Street
Concord, NH 03873
P: (603) 271-3661
E: chris.true
@leg.state.nh.us

**Tucker, Edith (D, SP38)\***
107 North Main Street
Concord, NH 03301
P: (603) 271-3661

**Turcotte, Alan J.
(D, SP124)**
107 North Main Street
Concord, NH 03301
P: (603) 271-3661
E: alanturcotte4rep
@gmail.com

**Turcotte, Len (R, SP172)**
107 North Main Street
Concord, NH 03301
P: (603) 271-3661
E: len.turcotte
@leg.state.nh.us

**Twombly, Timothy L.
(R, SP91)**
107 North Main Street
Concord, NH 03301
P: (603) 271-3661
F: (603) 888-4466
E: timothy.twombly
@leg.state.nh.us

**Ulery, Jordan G. (R, SP94)**
107 North Main Street
Concord, NH 03301
P: (603) 271-3661
F: (603) 882-6863
E: repulery@comcast.net

**Umberger, Karen C.
(R, SP11)**
P.O. Box 186
Kearsarge, NH 03847
P: (603) 356-6881
E: karen.umberger
@leg.state.nh.us

**Vadney, Herbert R. (R, SP2)**
107 North Main Street
Concord, NH 03301
P: (603) 271-3661
E: herb.vadney
@leg.state.nh.us

**Vaillancourt, Steve
(R, SP72)**
107 North Main Street
Concord, NH 03301
P: (603) 271-3661

**Valera, John (R, SP95)\***
107 North Main Street
Concord, NH 03301
P: (603) 271-3661

**Van Houten, Connie
(D, SP102)\***
107 North Main Street
Concord, NH 03301
P: (603) 271-3661
E: constance.vanhouten
@leg.state.nh.us

**Vann, Ivy (D, SP81)**
107 North Main Street
Concord, NH 03301
P: (603) 271-3661
E: Ivy.Vann@leg.state.nh.us

**Varney, Peter (R, SP5)**
107 North Main Street
Concord, NH 03301
P: (603) 271-3661
E: pvarney@atsnh.com

**Verville, Kevin (R, SP133)\***
107 North Main Street
Concord, NH 03301
P: (603) 271-3661
E: kevin.verville
@leg.state.nh.us

**Vincent, Kenneth
(D, SP185)\***
107 North Main Street
Concord, NH 03301
P: (603) 271-3661
E: kvincentNHrep
@comcast.net

**Vose, Michael (R, SP140)**
75 Olde Bridge Lane
Concord, NH 03301
P: (603) 271-3661
E: michael.vose
@leg.state.nh.us

**Wall, Janet G. (D, SP174)**
107 North Main Street
Concord, NH 03301
P: (603) 271-3661
F: (603) 749-3051
E: janet.wall
@leg.state.nh.us

**Wallace, Scott (R, SP164)\***
107 North Main Street
Concord, NH 03301
P: (603) 271-3661
E: scott.wallace
@leg.state.nh.us

**Wallner, Mary Jane
(D, SP112)**
107 North Main Street
Concord, NH 03301
P: (603) 271-3661
E: Maryjane.Wallner
@leg.state.nh.us

**Walsh, Robert M. (D, SP68)**
107 North Main Street
Concord, NH 03301
P: (603) 271-3661
E: bobwalsh2@comcast.net

**Walsh, Thomas C. (R, SP126)**
107 North Main Street
Concord, NH 03301
P: (603) 271-3661
E: tcwiv1966@aol.com

**Ward, Gerald W.R.
(D, SP159)**
107 North Main Street
Concord, NH 03301
P: (603) 271-3661
E: ward4staterep@gmail.com

**Webb, James (R, SP137)**
107 North Main Street
Concord, NH 03301
P: (603) 271-3661
E: james.webb
@leg.state.nh.us

**Weber, Lucy McV. (D, SP18)**
107 North Main Street
Concord, NH 03301
P: (603) 271-3661
E: lwmcv@comcast.net

**Welch, David A. (R, SP144)**
107 North Main Street
Concord, NH 03301
P: (603) 271-3661
E: v-chcj@outlook.com

**Wells, Natalie J.
(R, SP127)\***
107 North Main Street
Concord, NH 03301
P: (603) 271-3661
E: natalie.wells
@leg.state.nh.us

**Weyler, Kenneth L.
(R, SP144)**
107 North Main Street
Concord, NH 03301
P: (603) 271-3661
E: kweyler@aol.com

**White, Andrew (D, SP53)**
107 North Main Street
Concord, NH 03301
P: (603) 271-3661
E: andrew.white
@leg.state.nh.us

**Williams, Kermit R.
(D, SP61)**
107 North Main Street
Concord, NH 03301
P: (603) 271-3661
E: kermit.williams
@leg.state.nh.us

**Willis, Brenda (R, SP137)\***
107 North Main Street
Concord, NH 03301
P: (603) 271-3661

**Woitkun, Steven J.
(R, SP164)**
107 North Main Street
Concord, NH 03301
P: (603) 271-3661
E: steven.woitkun
@leg.state.nh.us

**Wolf, Dan (R, SP107)\***
107 North Main Street
Concord, NH 03301
P: (603) 271-3661

**Wolf, Terry (R, SP64)**
107 North Main Street
Concord, NH 03301
P: (603) 271-3661
E: terry.wolf
@leg.state.nh.us

**Woolpert, David (D, SP108)\***
107 North Main Street
Concord, NH 03301
P: (603) 271-3661
E: dave.woolpert@lpl.com

**Wuelper, Kurt (R, SP171)**
107 North Main Street
Concord, NH 03301
P: (603) 271-3661
E: kurt.wuelper
@leg.state.nh.us

**Zaricki, Nick (R, SP63)**
107 North Main Street
Concord, NH 03301
P: (603) 271-3661
E: nick.zaricki
@leg.state.nh.us

# New Jersey

## Executive

### Governor
**The Honorable Chris Christie (R)**
Governor
The State House
P.O. Box 001
Trenton, NJ 08625
P: (609) 292-6000
F: (609) 292-3454

### Lieutenant Governor
**The Honorable Kim Guadagno (R)**
Lieutenant Governor
P.O. Box 300
Trenton, NJ 08625
P: (609) 292-6000
F: (609) 292-3454
E: lt.governor
   @gov.state.nj.us

### Attorney General
**The Honorable Robert Lougy**
   (appointed)
Acting Attorney General
25 Market Street, Box 080
Trenton, NJ 08625
P: (609) 292-4925
F: (609) 292-3508

### Auditor
**The Honorable Stephen M. Eells**
   (appointed by the Legislature)
State Auditor
P.O. Box 067
Trenton, NJ 08625
P: (609) 847-3470
F: (609) 633-0834
E: seells@njleg.org

### Treasurer
**The Honorable Ford M. Scudder**
   (appointed)
State Treasurer
State House
P.O. Box 002
Trenton, NJ 08625
P: (609) 292-6748
F: (609) 984-3888

## Judiciary
### Supreme Court (GA)
**Ms. Michelle Smith**
Clerk
Rihcard J. Hughes Justice Complex
P.O. Box 970
Trenton, NJ 08625
P: (609) 292-4837

**The Honorable Stuart Rabner**
Chief Justice
**The Honorable Barry T. Albin**
**The Honorable Faustino J. Fernandez-Vina**
**The Honorable Jaynee LaVecchia**
**The Honorable Anne M. Patterson**
**The Honorable Lee A. Solomon**
**The Honorable Walter F. Timpone**

## Legislative
## Senate
### Senate President
**Senator Stephen M. Sweeney (D)**
Senate President
State House
P.O. Box 099
Trenton, NJ 08625
P: (609) 847-3700
F: (609) 984-1235
E: SenSweeney@njleg.org

### President Pro Tempore of the Senate
**Senator Nia H. Gill (D)**
Senate President Pro Tempore
State House
P.O. Box 099
Trenton, NJ 08625
P: (609) 847-3700
F: (609) 984-1235
E: SenGill@njleg.org

## Senate Majority Leader
**Senator Loretta Weinberg (D)**
Senate Majority Leader
State House
P.O. Box 099
Trenton, NJ 08625
P: (609) 847-3700
F: (609) 984-1235
E: SenWeinberg@njleg.org

## Senate Minority Leader
**Senator Thomas H. Kean Jr. (R)**
Senate Republican Leader
State House
P.O. Box 099
Trenton, NJ 08625
P: (609) 847-3600
F: (609) 984-8148
E: SenKean@njleg.org

## Secretary of the Senate
**Ms. Jennifer A. McQuaid**
Secretary of the Senate
State House, Room 115
P.O. Box 099
Trenton, NJ 08625
P: (609) 847-3915

## Members of the Senate
**Addiego, Dawn Marie (R, 8)**
State House
P.O. Box 099
Trenton, NJ 08625
P: (609) 847-3600
F: (609) 984-8148
E: SenAddiego@njleg.org

**Allen, Diane B. (R, 7)**
State House
P.O. Box 099
Trenton, NJ 08625
P: (609) 847-3600
F: (609) 984-8148
E: SenAllen@njleg.org

**Bateman, Christopher (R, 16)**
State House
P.O. Box 099
Trenton, NJ 08625
P: (609) 847-3600
F: (609) 984-8148
E: SenBateman@njleg.org

**Beach, James (D, 6)**
State House
P.O. Box 099
Trenton, NJ 08625
P: (609) 847-3700
F: (609) 984-1235
E: SenBeach@njleg.org

**Beck, Jennifer (R, 11)**
State House
P.O. Box 099
Trenton, NJ 08625
P: (609) 847-3600
F: (609) 984-8148
E: SenBeck@njleg.org

**Bucco, Anthony R. (R, 25)**
State House
P.O. Box 099
Trenton, NJ 08625
P: (609) 847-3600
F: (609) 984-8148
E: SenBucco@njleg.org

**Cardinale, Gerald (R, 39)**
State House
P.O. Box 099
Trenton, NJ 08625
P: (609) 847-3600
F: (609) 984-8148
E: SenCardinale@njleg.org

**Codey, Richard J. (D, 27)**
State House
P.O. Box 099
Trenton, NJ 08625
P: (609) 847-3700
F: (609) 984-1235
E: SenCodey@njleg.org

**Connors, Christopher J. (R, 9)**
State House
P.O. Box 099
Trenton, NJ 08625
P: (609) 847-3600
F: (609) 984-8148
E: SenConnors@njleg.org

**Cruz-Perez, Nilsa (D, 5)**
State House
P.O. Box 099
Trenton, NJ 08625
P: (609) 847-3700
F: (609) 984-1235
E: sencruzperez@njleg.org

**Cunningham, Sandra Bolden (D, 31)**
State House
P.O. Box 099
Trenton, NJ 08625
P: (609) 847-3700
F: (609) 984-1235
E: SenCunningham@njleg.org

# New Jersey

**Diegnan Jr., Patrick J. (D, 18)**
State House
P.O. Box 098
Trenton, NJ 08625
P: (609) 847-3500
F: (609) 292-2386
E: SenDiegnan@njleg.org

**Doherty, Michael J. (R, 23)**
State House
P.O. Box 099
Trenton, NJ 08625
P: (609) 847-3600
F: (609) 984-8148
E: SenDoherty@njleg.org

**Gill, Nia H. (D, 34)**
State House
P.O. Box 099
Trenton, NJ 08625
P: (609) 847-3700
F: (609) 984-1235
E: SenGill@njleg.org

**Gordon, Robert M. (D, 38)**
State House
P.O. Box 099
Trenton, NJ 08625
P: (609) 847-3700
F: (609) 984-1235
E: SenGordon@njleg.org

**Greenstein, Linda R. (D, 14)**
State House
P.O. Box 099
Trenton, NJ 08625
P: (609) 847-3700
F: (609) 984-1235
E: SenGreenstein@njleg.org

**Holzapfel, James W. (R, 10)**
State House
P.O. Box 099
Trenton, NJ 08625
P: (609) 847-3600
F: (609) 984-8148
E: SenHolzapfel@njleg.org

**Kean Jr., Thomas H. (R, 21)**
State House
P.O. Box 099
Trenton, NJ 08625
P: (609) 847-3600
F: (609) 984-8148
E: SenKean@njleg.org

**Kyrillos Jr., Joseph M. (R, 13)**
State House
P.O. Box 099
Trenton, NJ 08625
P: (609) 847-3600
F: (609) 984-8148
E: SenKyrillos@njleg.org

**Lesniak, Raymond J. (D, 20)**
State House
P.O. Box 099
Trenton, NJ 08625
P: (609) 847-3700
F: (609) 984-1235
E: SenLesniak@njleg.org

**Madden Jr., Fred H. (D, 4)**
State House
P.O. Box 099
Trenton, NJ 08625
P: (609) 847-3700
F: (609) 984-1235
E: SenMadden@njleg.org

**Oroho, Steven V. (R, 24)**
State House
P.O. Box 099
Trenton, NJ 08625
P: (609) 847-3600
F: (609) 984-8148
E: SenOroho@njleg.org

**O'Toole, Kevin J. (R, 40)**
State House
P.O. Box 099
Trenton, NJ 08625
P: (609) 847-3600
F: (609) 984-8148
E: SenOToole@njleg.org

**Pennacchio, Joseph (R, 26)**
State House
P.O. Box 099
Trenton, NJ 08625
P: (609) 847-3600
F: (609) 984-8148
E: SenPennacchio@njleg.org

**Pou, Nellie (D, 35)**
State House
P.O. Box 099
Trenton, NJ 08625
P: (609) 847-3700
F: (609) 984-1235
E: SenPou@njleg.org

**Rice, Ronald L. (D, 28)**
State House
P.O. Box 099
Trenton, NJ 08625
P: (609) 847-3700
F: (609) 984-1235
E: SenRice@njleg.org

**Ruiz, M. Teresa (D, 29)**
State House
P.O. Box 099
Trenton, NJ 08625
P: (609) 847-3700
F: (609) 984-1235
E: SenRuiz@njleg.org

**Sacco, Nicholas J. (D, 32)**
State House
P.O. Box 099
Trenton, NJ 08625
P: (609) 847-3700
F: (609) 984-1235
E: SenSacco@njleg.org

**Sarlo, Paul A. (D, 36)**
State House
P.O. Box 099
Trenton, NJ 08625
P: (609) 847-3700
F: (609) 984-1235
E: SenSarlo@njleg.org

**Scutari, Nicholas P. (D, 22)**
State House
P.O. Box 099
Trenton, NJ 08625
P: (609) 847-3700
F: (609) 984-1235
E: SenScutari@njleg.org

**Singer, Robert W. (R, 30)**
State House
P.O. Box 099
Trenton, NJ 08625
P: (609) 847-3600
F: (609) 984-8148
E: SenSinger@njleg.org

**Smith, Bob (D, 17)**
State House
P.O. Box 099
Trenton, NJ 08625
P: (609) 847-3700
F: (609) 984-1235
E: senbsmith@njleg.org

**Stack, Brian P. (D, 33)**
State House
P.O. Box 099
Trenton, NJ 08625
P: (609) 847-3700
F: (609) 984-1235
E: SenStack@njleg.org

**Sweeney, Stephen M. (D, 3)**
State House
P.O. Box 099
Trenton, NJ 08625
P: (609) 847-3700
F: (609) 984-1235
E: SenSweeney@njleg.org

**Thompson, Samuel D. (R, 12)**
State House
P.O. Box 099
Trenton, NJ 08625
P: (609) 847-3600
F: (609) 984-8148
E: SenThompson@njleg.org

**Turner, Shirley K. (D, 15)**
State House
P.O. Box 099
Trenton, NJ 08625
P: (609) 847-3700
F: (609) 984-1235
E: SenTurner@njleg.org

**Van Drew, Jeff (D, 1)**
State House
P.O. Box 099
Trenton, NJ 08625
P: (609) 847-3700
F: (609) 984-1235
E: SenVanDrew@njleg.org

**Vitale, Joseph F. (D, 19)**
State House
P.O. Box 099
Trenton, NJ 08625
P: (609) 847-3700
F: (609) 984-1235
E: SenVitale@njleg.org

**Weinberg, Loretta (D, 37)**
State House
P.O. Box 099
Trenton, NJ 08625
P: (609) 847-3700
F: (609) 984-1235
E: SenWeinberg@njleg.org

**Whelan, Jim (D, 2)**
State House
P.O. Box 099
Trenton, NJ 08625
P: (609) 847-3700
F: (609) 984-1235
E: SenWhelan@njleg.org

# General Assembly

## Speaker of the General Assembly

**Assemblyman Vincent Prieto (D)**
Assembly Speaker
State House
P.O. Box 098
Trenton, NJ 08625
P: (609) 847-3500
F: (609) 292-2386
E: AsmPrieto@njleg.org

## Speaker Pro Tempore of the General Assembly

**Assemblyman Jerry Green (D)**
Assembly Speaker Pro Tempore
State House
P.O. Box 098
Trenton, NJ 08625
P: (609) 847-3500
F: (609) 292-2386
E: AsmGreen@njleg.org

## General Assembly Majority Leader

**Assemblyman Louis D. Greenwald (D)**
Assembly Majority Leader
State House
P.O. Box 098
Trenton, NJ 08625
P: (609) 847-3500
F: (609) 292-2386
E: AsmGreenwald@njleg.org

## General Assembly Minority Leader

**Assemblyman Jon M. Bramnick (R)**
Assembly Republican Leader
State House
P.O. Box 098
Trenton, NJ 08625
P: (609) 847-3400
F: (609) 633-9806
E: AsmBramnick@njleg.org

## Clerk of the General Assembly

**Ms. Dana M. Burley**
Clerk of the General Assembly
State House, Room 214
P.O. Box 098
Trenton, NJ 08625
P: (609) 847-3115

## Members of the General Assembly

**Andrzejczak, Bob (D, 1)**
State House
P.O. Box 098
Trenton, NJ 08625
P: (609) 847-3500
F: (609) 292-2386
E: AsmAndrzejczak@njleg.org

**Auth, Robert (R, 39)**
State House
P.O. Box 098
Trenton, NJ 08625
P: (609) 847-3400
F: (609) 633-9806
E: AsmAuth@njleg.org

**Barclay, Arthur (D, 5)**
State House
P.O. Box 098
Trenton, NJ 08625
P: (609) 847-3500
E: AsmBarclay@njleg.org

**Benson, Daniel R. (D, 14)**
State House
P.O. Box 098
Trenton, NJ 08625
P: (609) 847-3500
F: (609) 292-2386
E: AsmBenson@njleg.org

**Bramnick, Jon M. (R, 21)**
State House
P.O. Box 098
Trenton, NJ 08625
P: (609) 847-3400
F: (609) 633-9806
E: AsmBramnick@njleg.org

**Brown, Chris A. (R, 2)**
State House
P.O. Box 098
Trenton, NJ 08625
P: (609) 847-3400
F: (609) 633-9806
E: asmchrisabrown@njleg.org

**Bucco, Anthony M. (R, 25)**
State House
P.O. Box 098
Trenton, NJ 08625
P: (609) 847-3400
F: (609) 633-9806
E: AsmBucco@njleg.org

**Burzichelli, John J. (D, 3)**
State House
P.O. Box 098
Trenton, NJ 08625
P: (609) 847-3500
F: (609) 292-2386
E: AsmBurzichelli@njleg.org

**Caputo, Ralph R. (D, 28)**
State House
P.O. Box 098
Trenton, NJ 08625
P: (609) 847-3500
F: (609) 292-2386
E: AsmCaputo@njleg.org

**Caride, Marlene (D, 36)**
State House
P.O. Box 098
Trenton, NJ 08625
P: (609) 292-7065
F: (609) 292-2386
E: AswCaride@njleg.org

**Carroll, Michael Patrick (R, 25)**
State House
P.O. Box 098
Trenton, NJ 08625
P: (609) 847-3400
F: (609) 633-9806
E: AsmCarroll@njleg.org

**Chaparro, Annette (D, 33)**
State House
P.O. Box 098
Trenton, NJ 08625
P: (609) 847-3500
E: AswChaparro@njleg.org

**Chiaravalloti, Nicholas (D, 31)**
State House
P.O. Box 098
Trenton, NJ 08625
P: (609) 847-3500
E: AsmChiaravalloti
@njleg.org

**Ciattarelli, Jack M. (R, 16)**
State House
P.O. Box 098
Trenton, NJ 08625
P: (609) 847-3400
F: (609) 633-9806
E: AsmCiattarelli@njleg.org

**Clifton, Robert (R, 12)**
State House
P.O. Box 098
Trenton, NJ 08625
P: (609) 847-3400
F: (609) 633-9806
E: AsmClifton@njleg.org

**Conaway Jr., Herb (D, 7)**
State House
P.O. Box 098
Trenton, NJ 08625
P: (609) 847-3500
F: (609) 292-2386
E: AsmConaway@njleg.org

**Coughlin, Craig J. (D, 19)**
State House
P.O. Box 098
Trenton, NJ 08625
P: (609) 847-3500
F: (609) 292-2386
E: AsmCoughlin@njleg.org

**Dancer, Ronald S. (R, 12)**
State House
P.O. Box 098
Trenton, NJ 08625
P: (609) 847-3400
F: (609) 633-9806
E: AsmDancer@njleg.org

**Danielsen, Joseph (D, 17)**
State House
P.O. Box 098
Trenton, NJ 08625
P: (609) 847-3500
F: (609) 292-2386
E: AsmDanielsen@njleg.org

**DeAngelo, Wayne P. (D, 14)**
State House
P.O. Box 098
Trenton, NJ 08625
P: (609) 847-3500
F: (609) 292-2386
E: AsmDeAngelo@njleg.org

**DeCroce, BettyLou (R, 26)**
State House
P.O. Box 098
Trenton, NJ 08625
P: (609) 847-3400
F: (609) 633-9806
E: AswDeCroce@njleg.org

**DiMaio, John (R, 23)**
State House
P.O. Box 098
Trenton, NJ 08625
P: (609) 847-3400
F: (609) 633-9806
E: AsmDiMaio@njleg.org

**Downey, Joann (D, 11)**
State House
P.O. Box 098
Trenton, NJ 08625
P: (609) 847-3500
E: AswDowney@njleg.org

**Egan, Joseph V. (D, 17)**
State House
P.O. Box 098
Trenton, NJ 08625
P: (609) 847-3500
F: (609) 292-2386
E: AsmEgan@njleg.org

**Egan Jones, Patricia (D, 5)**
State House
P.O. Box 098
Trenton, NJ 08625
P: (609) 847-3500

**Eustace, Timothy J. (D, 38)**
State House
P.O. Box 098
Trenton, NJ 08625
P: (609) 847-3500
F: (609) 292-2386
E: AsmEustace@njleg.org

# New Jersey

**Giblin, Thomas P. (D, 34)**
State House
P.O. Box 098
Trenton, NJ 08625
P: (609) 847-3500
F: (609) 292-2386
E: AsmGiblin@njleg.org

**Gove, Dianne C. (R, 9)**
State House
P.O. Box 098
Trenton, NJ 08625
P: (609) 847-3400
F: (609) 633-9806
E: AswGove@njleg.org

**Green, Jerry (D, 22)**
State House
P.O. Box 098
Trenton, NJ 08625
P: (609) 847-3500
F: (609) 292-2386
E: AsmGreen@njleg.org

**Greenwald, Louis D. (D, 6)**
State House
P.O. Box 098
Trenton, NJ 08625
P: (609) 847-3500
F: (609) 292-2386
E: AsmGreenwald@njleg.org

**Gusciora, Reed (D, 15)**
State House
P.O. Box 098
Trenton, NJ 08625
P: (609) 847-3500
F: (609) 292-2386
E: AsmGusciora@njleg.org

**Handlin, Amy H. (R, 13)**
State House
P.O. Box 098
Trenton, NJ 08625
P: (609) 847-3400
F: (609) 633-9806
E: AswHandlin@njleg.org

**Holley, Jamel (D, 20)**
State House
P.O. Box 098
Trenton, NJ 08625
P: (609) 847-3500

**Houghtaling, Eric (D, 11)**
State House
P.O. Box 098
Trenton, NJ 08625
P: (609) 847-3500
E: AsmHoughtaling@njleg.org

**Howarth, Joe (R, 8)**
State House
P.O. Box 098
Trenton, NJ 08625
P: (609) 847-3400

**Huttle, Valerie Vainieri (D, 37)**
State House
P.O. Box 098
Trenton, NJ 08625
P: (609) 847-3500
F: (609) 292-2386
E: AswVainieriHuttle@njleg.org

**Jasey, Mila M. (D, 27)**
State House
P.O. Box 098
Trenton, NJ 08625
P: (609) 847-3500
F: (609) 292-2386
E: AswJasey@njleg.org

**Jimenez, Angelica M. (D, 32)**
State House
P.O. Box 098
Trenton, NJ 08625
P: (609) 847-3500
F: (609) 292-2386
E: AswJimenez@njleg.org

**Johnson, Gordon M. (D, 37)**
State House
P.O. Box 098
Trenton, NJ 08625
P: (609) 847-3500
F: (609) 292-2386
E: AsmJohnson@njleg.org

**Karabinchak, Robert (D, 18)**
State House
P.O. Box 099
Trenton, NJ 08625
P: (609) 847-3700
F: (609) 984-1235
E: AsmKarabinchak@njleg.org

**Kean, Sean T. (R, 30)**
State House
P.O. Box 098
Trenton, NJ 08625
P: (609) 847-3400
F: (609) 633-9806
E: AsmKean@njleg.org

**Kennedy, James J. (D, 22)**
State House
P.O. Box 098
Trenton, NJ 08625
P: (609) 847-3500
E: AsmKennedy@njleg.org

**Lagana, Joseph A. (D, 38)**
State House
P.O. Box 098
Trenton, NJ 08625
P: (609) 847-3500
F: (609) 292-2386
E: AsmLagana@njleg.org

**Lampitt, Pamela Rosen (D, 6)**
State House
P.O. Box 098
Trenton, NJ 08625
P: (609) 847-3500
F: (609) 292-2386
E: AswLampitt@njleg.org

**Land, R. Bruce (D, 1)**
State House
P.O. Box 098
Trenton, NJ 08625
P: (609) 847-3500
E: AsmLand@njleg.org

**Mazzeo, Vincent (D, 2)**
State House
P.O. Box 098
Trenton, NJ 08625
P: (609) 847-3500
F: (609) 292-2386
E: AsmMazzeo@njleg.org

**McGuckin, Gregory P. (R, 10)**
State House
P.O. Box 098
Trenton, NJ 08625
P: (609) 847-3400
F: (609) 633-9806
E: AsmMcGuckin@njleg.org

**McKeon, John F. (D, 27)**
State House
P.O. Box 098
Trenton, NJ 08625
P: (609) 847-3500
F: (609) 292-2386
E: AsmMcKeon@njleg.org

**McKnight, Angela (D, 31)**
State House
P.O. Box 098
Trenton, NJ 08625
P: (609) 847-3500
E: AswMcKnight@njleg.org

**Moriarty, Paul D. (D, 4)**
State House
P.O. Box 098
Trenton, NJ 08625
P: (609) 847-3500
F: (609) 292-2386
E: AsmMoriarty@njleg.org

**Mosquera, Gabriela (D, 4)**
State House
P.O. Box 098
Trenton, NJ 08625
P: (609) 847-3500
F: (609) 292-2386
E: AswMosquera@njleg.org

**Mukherji, Raj (D, 33)**
State House
P.O. Box 098
Trenton, NJ 08625
P: (609) 847-3500
F: (609) 292-2386
E: AsmMukherji@njleg.org

**Munoz, Nancy (R, 21)**
State House
P.O. Box 098
Trenton, NJ 08625
P: (609) 847-3400
F: (609) 633-9806
E: AswMunoz@njleg.org

**Muoio, Elizabeth Mahar (D, 15)**
State House
P.O. Box 98
Trenton, NJ 08625
P: (609) 847-3500
F: (609) 292-2386
E: AswMuoio@njleg.org

**Oliver, Sheila Y. (D, 34)**
State House
P.O. Box 098
Trenton, NJ 08625
P: (609) 847-3500
F: (609) 292-2386
E: AswOliver@njleg.org

**O'Scanlon Jr., Declan (R, 13)**
State House
P.O. Box 098
Trenton, NJ 08625
P: (609) 847-3400
F: (609) 633-9806
E: AsmOScanlon@njleg.org

**Peterson, Erik (R, 23)**
State House
P.O. Box 098
Trenton, NJ 08625
P: (609) 847-3400
F: (609) 633-9806
E: AsmPeterson@njleg.org

**Phoebus, Gail (R, 24)**
State House
P.O. Box 098
Trenton, NJ 08625
P: (609) 847-3400
E: AswPhoebus@njleg.org

**Pinkin, Nancy J. (D, 18)**
State House
P.O. Box 098
Trenton, NJ 08625
P: (609) 847-3500
F: (609) 292-2386
E: AswPinkin@njleg.org

**Pintor Marin, Eliana
(D, 29)**
State House
P.O. Box 098
Trenton, NJ 08625
P: (609) 847-3500
F: (609) 292-2386
E: AswPintorMarin@njleg.org

**Prieto, Vincent (D, 32)**
State House
P.O. Box 098
Trenton, NJ 08625
P: (609) 847-3500
F: (609) 292-2386
E: AsmPrieto@njleg.org

**Quijano, Annette (D, 20)**
State House
P.O. Box 098
Trenton, NJ 08625
P: (609) 847-3500
F: (609) 292-2386
E: AswQuijano@njleg.org

**Rible, David P. (R, 30)**
State House
P.O. Box 098
Trenton, NJ 08625
P: (609) 847-3400
F: (609) 633-9806
E: AsmRible@njleg.org

**Rodriguez-Gregg, Maria
(R, 8)**
State House
P.O. Box 098
Trenton, NJ 08625
P: (609) 847-3400
F: (609) 633-9806
E: AswRodriguez-Gregg
  @njleg.org

**Rooney, Kevin J. (R, 40)\***
State House
P.O. Box 098
Trenton, NJ 08625
P: (609) 847-3500
F: (609) 292-2386
E: AsmRooney@njleg.org

**Rumpf, Brian E. (R, 9)**
State House
P.O. Box 098
Trenton, NJ 08625
P: (609) 847-3400
F: (609) 633-9806
E: AsmRumpf@njleg.org

**Russo, David C. (R, 40)**
State House
P.O. Box 098
Trenton, NJ 08625
P: (609) 847-3400
F: (609) 633-9806
E: AsmRusso@njleg.org

**Schaer, Gary S. (D, 36)**
State House
P.O. Box 098
Trenton, NJ 08625
P: (609) 847-3500
F: (609) 292-2386
E: AsmSchaer@njleg.org

**Schepisi, Holly (R, 39)**
State House
P.O. Box 098
Trenton, NJ 08625
P: (609) 847-3400
F: (609) 633-9806
E: AswSchepisi@njleg.org

**Singleton, Troy (D, 7)**
State House
P.O. Box 098
Trenton, NJ 08625
P: (609) 847-3500
F: (609) 292-2386
E: AsmSingleton@njleg.org

**Space, Parker (R, 24)**
State House
P.O. Box 098
Trenton, NJ 08625
P: (609) 847-3400
F: (609) 633-9806
E: asmspace@njleg.org

**Sumter, Shavonda E. (D, 35)**
State House
P.O. Box 098
Trenton, NJ 08625
P: (609) 847-3500
F: (609) 292-2386
E: AswSumter@njleg.org

**Taliaferro, Adam (D, 3)**
State House
P.O. Box 98
Trenton, NJ 08625
P: (609) 847-3500
F: (609) 292-2386
E: AsmTaliaferro@njleg.org

**Tucker, Cleopatra G.
(D, 28)**
State House
P.O. Box 098
Trenton, NJ 08625
P: (609) 847-3500
F: (609) 292-2386
E: AswTucker@njleg.org

**Watson, Blonnie R. (D, 29)**
State House
P.O. Box 098
Trenton, NJ 08625
P: (609) 847-3500
F: (609) 292-2386
E: AswWatson@njleg.org

**Webber, Jay (R, 26)**
State House
P.O. Box 098
Trenton, NJ 08625
P: (609) 847-3400
F: (609) 633-9806
E: AsmWebber@njleg.org

**Wimberly, Benjie E. (D, 35)**
State House
P.O. Box 098
Trenton, NJ 08625
P: (609) 847-3500
F: (609) 292-2386
E: AsmWimberly@njleg.org

**Wisniewski, John S. (D, 19)**
State House
P.O. Box 098
Trenton, NJ 08625
P: (609) 847-3500
F: (609) 292-2386
E: AsmWisniewski@njleg.org

**Wolfe, David W. (R, 10)**
State House
P.O. Box 098
Trenton, NJ 08625
P: (609) 847-3400
F: (609) 633-9806
E: AsmWolfe@njleg.org

**Zwicker, Andrew (D, 16)**
State House
P.O. Box 098
Trenton, NJ 08625
P: (609) 847-3500
E: AsmZwicker@njleg.org

# New Mexico

## Executive

### Governor

**The Honorable Susana Martinez (R)**
Governor
State Capitol, Fourth Floor
Santa Fe, NM 87501
P: (505) 476-2200
F: (505) 476-2226

### Lieutenant Governor

**The Honorable John A. Sanchez (R)**
Lieutenant Governor
State Capitol, Suite 417
Santa Fe, NM 87501
P: (505) 476-2250
F: (505) 476-2257

### Attorney General

**The Honorable Hector H. Balderas (D)**
Attorney General
P.O. Drawer 1508
Santa Fe, NM 87504
P: (505) 827-6000
F: (505) 827-5826

### Auditor

**The Honorable Timothy Keller (D)**
State Auditor
2540 Camino Edward Ortiz, Suite A
Santa Fe, NM 87507
P: (505) 476-3800
F: (505) 827-3512
E: timothy.keller
@osa.state.nm.us

### Commissioner of Public Lands

**The Honorable Aubrey Dunn (R)**
Commissioner
310 Old Santa Fe Trail
P.O. Box 1148
Santa Fe, NM 87504
P: (505) 827-5760
F: (505) 827-5766
E: adunn@slo.state.nm.us

## Secretary of State

**The Honorable Maggie Oliver (D)**
Secretary of State
325 Don Gaspar, Suite 300
Santa Fe, NM 87501
P: (505) 827-3600

## Treasurer

**The Honorable Tim Eichenberg (D)**
State Treasurer
2055 South Pacheco Street, Suite 100
Santa Fe, NM 85008
P: (505) 955-1172
F: (505) 955-1195

## Judiciary

### Supreme Court (PE)

**Mr. Joey D. Moya**
Chief Clerk
237 Don Gaspar Avenue, Room 104
P.O. Box 848
Santa Fe, NM 87504
P: (505) 827-4860
F: (505) 827-4837

**The Honorable Charles W. Daniels**
Chief Justice
**The Honorable Edward L. Chavez**
**The Honorable Petra Jimenez Maes**
**The Honorable Judith K. Nakamura**
**The Honorable Barbara J. Vigil**

## Legislative Senate

### Senate President

**The Honorable John A. Sanchez (R)**
Lieutenant Governor
State Capitol, Suite 417
Santa Fe, NM 87501
P: (505) 476-2250
F: (505) 476-2257

## President Pro Tempore of the Senate

**Senator Mary Kay Papen (D)**
Senate President Pro Tempore
State Capitol Building, Room 105
Santa Fe, NM 87501
P: (505) 986-4733
E: marykay.papen
@nmlegis.gov

## Senate Majority Leader

**Senator Peter Wirth (D)**
Senate Majority Floor Leader
State Capitol Building, Room 119
Santa Fe, NM 87501
P: (505) 986-4861
E: peter.wirth@nmlegis.gov

## Senate Minority Leader

**Senator Stuart Ingle (R)**
Senate Minority Floor Leader
State Capitol Building, Room 109A
Santa Fe, NM 87501
P: (505) 986-4702
E: stuart.ingle@nmlegis.gov

## Secretary of the Senate

**Ms. Lenore Naranjo**
Chief Clerk of the Senate
State Capitol Building, Room 115
Santa Fe, NM 87501
P: (505) 986-4714
F: (505) 986-4280
E: lenore.naranjo
@nmlegis.gov

## Members of the Senate

**Baca, Gregory (R, 29)***
State Capitol Building, Room 415I
Santa Fe, NM 87501
P: (505) 986-4877
E: greg.baca@nmlegis.gov

**Brandt, Craig (R, 40)**
State Capitol Building, Room 414C
Santa Fe, NM 87501
P: (505) 986-4267
E: craig.brandt@nmlegis.gov

**Burt, William F. (R, 33)**
State Capitol Building, Room 415A
Santa Fe, NM 87501
P: (505) 986-4366
E: bill.burt@nmlegis.gov

**Campos, Pete (D, 8)**
State Capitol Building, Room 302B
Santa Fe, NM 87501
P: (505) 986-4311
E: pete.campos@nmlegis.gov

**Candelaria, Jacob (D, 26)**
State Capitol Building, Room 218B
Santa Fe, NM 87501
P: (505) 986-4391
E: jacob.candelaria
@nmlegis.gov

**Cervantes, Joseph (D, 31)**
State Capitol Building, Room 328B
Santa Fe, NM 87501
P: (505) 986-4385
E: joseph.cervantes
@nmlegis.gov

**Cisneros, Carlos R. (D, 6)**
State Capitol Building, Room 325B
Santa Fe, NM 87501
P: (505) 986-4362
E: carlos.cisneros
@nmlegis.gov

**Gould, Candace (R, 10)***
State Capitol Building, Room 415F
Santa Fe, NM 87114
P: (505) 986-4266
E: candace.gould
@nmlegis.gov

**Griggs, Ron (R, 34)**
State Capitol Building, Room 414A
Santa Fe, NM 87501
P: (505) 986-4276
E: ron.griggs@nmlegis.gov

**Ingle, Stuart (R, 27)**
State Capitol Building, Room 109A
Santa Fe, NM 87501
P: (505) 986-4702
E: stuart.ingle@nmlegis.gov

**Ivey-Soto, Daniel A. (D, 15)**
State Capitol Building, Room 300B
Santa Fe, NM 87501
P: (505) 986-4270
E: daniel.ivey-soto
@nmlegis.gov

**Kernan, Gay G. (R, 42)**
State Capitol Building, Room 415E
Santa Fe, NM 87501
P: (505) 986-4274
E: gay.kernan@nmlegis.gov

**Leavell, Carroll H. (R, 41)**
State Capitol Building, Room 415C
Santa Fe, NM 87501
P: (505) 986-4278
E: carroll.leavell
    @nmlegis.gov

**Lopez, Linda M. (D, 11)**
State Capitol Building, Room 320
Santa Fe, NM 87501
P: (505) 986-4737
E: linda.lopez@nmlegis.gov

**Martinez, Richard C. (D, 5)**
State Capitol Building, Room 319
Santa Fe, NM 87501
P: (505) 986-4487
E: richard.martinez
    @nmlegis.gov

**McSorley, Cisco (D, 16)**
State Capitol Building, Room 217
Santa Fe, NM 87501
P: (505) 986-4389
E: cisco.mcsorley
    @nmlegis.gov

**Moores, Mark (R, 21)**
State Capitol Building, Room 414D
Santa Fe, NM 87501
P: (505) 986-4859
E: mark.moores@nmlegis.gov

**Morales, Howie C. (D, 28)**
State Capitol Building, Room 300D
Santa Fe, NM 87501
P: (505) 986-4863
E: howie.morales
    @nmlegis.gov

**Munoz, George K. (D, 4)**
State Capitol Building, Room 218A
Santa Fe, NM 87501
P: (505) 986-4371
E: george.munoz@mnlegis.gov

**Neville, Steven P. (R, 2)**
State Capitol Building, Room 109C
Santa Fe, NM 87501
P: (505) 986-4701
E: steven.neville
    @nmlegis.gov

**O'Neill, Bill B. (D, 13)**
State Capitol Building, Room 300C
Santa Fe, NM 87501
P: (505) 986-4260
E: oneillsd13
    @billoneillfornm.com

**Ortiz Y Pino, Gerald P. (D, 12)**
State Capitol Building, Room 300A
Santa Fe, NM 87501
P: (505) 986-4482
E: gerald.ortizypino
    @nmlegis.gov

**Padilla, Michael (D, 14)**
State Capitol Building, Room 120
Santa Fe, NM 87501
P: (505) 986-4726
E: michael.padilla
    @nmlegis.gov

**Papen, Mary Kay (D, 38)**
State Capitol Building, Room 105
Santa Fe, NM 87501
P: (505) 986-4733
E: marykay.papen
    @nmlegis.gov

**Payne, William H. (R, 20)**
State Capitol Building, Room 109B
Santa Fe, NM 87501
P: (505) 986-4703
E: william.payne
    @nmlegis.gov

**Pinto, John (D, 3)**
State Capitol Building, Room 301B
Santa Fe, NM 87501
P: (505) 986-4835
E: john.pinto@nmlegis.gov

**Pirtle, Cliff R. (R, 32)**
State Capitol Building, Room 414B
Santa Fe, NM 87501
P: (505) 986-4862
E: cliff.pirtle@nmlegis.gov

**Rodriguez, Nancy (D, 24)**
State Capitol Building, Room 301A
Santa Fe, NM 87501
P: (505) 986-4264
E: nancy.rodriguez
    @nmlegis.gov

**Rue, Sander (R, 23)**
State Capitol Building, Room 415B
Santa Fe, NM 87501
P: (505) 986-4375
E: sander.rue@nmlegis.gov

**Sanchez, Clemente (D, 30)**
State Capitol Building, Room 323
Santa Fe, NM 87501
P: (505) 986-4369
E: clemente.sanchez
    @nmlegis.gov

**Sapien, John M. (D, 9)**
State Capitol Building, Room 416G
Santa Fe, NM 87501
P: (505) 986-4834
E: john.sapien@nmlegis.gov

**Sharer, William E. (R, 1)**
State Capitol Building, Room 415H
Santa Fe, NM 87501
P: (505) 986-4381
E: william.sharer
    @nmlegis.gov

**Shendo Jr., Benny (D, 22)**
State Capitol Building, Room 302A
Santa Fe, NM 87501
P: (505) 986-4310
E: benny.shendo@nmlegis.gov

**Smith, John Arthur (D, 35)**
State Capitol Building, Room 325A
Santa Fe, NM 87501
P: (505) 986-4365
E: john.smith@nmlegis.gov

**Soules, Bill (D, 37)**
State Capitol Building, Room 328C
Santa Fe, NM 87501
P: (505) 986-4380
E: bill.soules@nmlegis.gov

**Stefanics, Elizabeth (D, 39)\***
State Capitol Building, Room 416C
Santa Fe, NM 87501
P: (505) 986-4377
E: liz.stefanics
    @nmlegis.gov

**Steinborn, Jeff (D, 36)**
State Capitol Building, Room 416E
Santa Fe, NM 87501
P: (505) 986-4436
E: jeff.steinborn
    @nmlegis.gov

**Stewart, Mimi (D, 17)**
State Capitol Building, Room 416F
Santa Fe, NM 87501
P: (505) 986-4856
E: mimi.stewart@nmlegis.gov

**Tallman, Bill (D, 18)\***
State Capitol Building, Room 416D
Santa Fe, NM 87501
P: (505) 9864373
E: bill.tallman@nmlegis.gov

**White, James P. (R, 19)**
State Capitol Building, Room 415G
Santa Fe, NM 87501
P: (505) 986-4395
E: james.white@nmlegis.gov

**Wirth, Peter (D, 25)**
State Capitol Building, Room 119
Santa Fe, NM 87501
P: (505) 986-4861
E: peter.wirth@nmlegis.gov

**Woods, Pat (R, 7)**
State Capitol Building, Room 415D
Santa Fe, NM 87501
P: (505) 986-4393
E: pat.woods@nmlegis.gov

# House

## Speaker of the House
**Representative Brian F. Egolf Jr. (D)**
Speaker of the House
State Capitol Building, Room 104
Santa Fe, NM 87501
P: (505) 986-4782
E: brian.egolf@nmlegis.gov

## House Majority Leader
**Representative Sheryl W. Stapleton (D)**
Majority Floor Leader
State Capitol Building, Room 134
Santa Fe, NM 87501
P: (505) 986-4780
E: sheryl.stapleton
    @nmlegis.gov

# New Mexico

## House Minority Leader

**Representative Nate Gentry (R)**
Minority Floor Leader
State Capitol Building, Room 125
Santa Fe, NM 87501
P: (505) 986-4757
E: natefornm@gmail.com

## Clerk of the House

**Ms. Denise Greenlaw Ramonas**
Chief Clerk of the House
State Capitol, Room 100
Santa Fe, NM 87501
P: (505) 986-4751
F: (505) 986-4755
E: Denise.Ramonas
@nmlegis.gov

## Members of the House

**Adkins, David Edward (R, 29)**
State Capitol Building, Room 203F CN
Santa Fe, NM 87501
P: (505) 986-4467
E: david.adkins@nmlegis.gov

**Alcon, Eliseo Lee (D, 6)**
State Capitol Building, Room 314B
Santa Fe, NM 87501
P: (505) 986-4425
E: eliseo.alcon@nmlegis.gov

**Armstrong, Deborah (D, 17)**
State Capitol Building, Room 312B
Santa Fe, NM 87501
P: (505) 986-4840
E: deborah.armstrong
@nmlegis.gov

**Armstrong, Gail (R, 49)***
State Capitol Building, Room 203F CN
Santa Fe, NM 87501
P: (505) 986-4467
E: gail
@gailfornewmexico.com

**Baldonado, Alonzo (R, 8)**
State Capitol Building, Room 203B
Santa Fe, NM 87501
P: (505) 986-4226
E: alonzo.baldonado
@nmlegis.gov

**Bandy, Paul C. (R, 3)**
State Capitol Building, Room 201B
Santa Fe, NM 87501
P: (505) 986-4214
E: paul@paulbandy.org

**Brown, Cathrynn N. (R, 55)**
State Capitol Building, Room 204B
Santa Fe, NM 87501
P: (505) 986-4210
E: cathy@cathrynnbrown.com

**Chasey, Gail (D, 18)**
State Capitol Building, Room 308
Santa Fe, NM 87501
P: (505) 986-4411
E: gail@gailchasey.com

**Clahchischilliage, Sharon (R, 4)**
State Capitol Building, Room 203H CN
Santa Fe, NM 87501
P: (505) 986-4453
E: sharon.clahchischill
@nmlegis.gov

**Cook, Zachary (R, 56)**
State Capitol Building, Room 205A
Santa Fe, NM 87501
P: (505) 986-4233
E: zachary.cook@nmlegis.gov

**Crowder, Randal S. (R, 64)**
State Capitol Building, Room 205A
Santa Fe, NM 87501
P: (505) 986-4243
E: randal.crowder
@nmlegis.gov

**Dines, James Mitchell (R, 20)**
State Capitol Building, Room 205B
Santa Fe, NM 87501
P: (505) 986-4242
E: jim.dines@nmlegis.gov

**Dodge Jr., George (D, 63)**
State Capitol Building, Room 304C
Santa Fe, NM 87501
P: (505) 986-4318
E: george.dodgejr
@nmlegis.gov

**Dow, Rebecca (R, 38)***
State Capitol Building, Room 203H CN
Santa Fe, NM 87901
P: (505) 986-4453
E: rebecca.dow@nmlegis.gov

**Egolf Jr., Brian F. (D, 47)**
State Capitol Building, Room 104
Santa Fe, NM 87501
P: (505) 986-4782
E: brian.egolf@nmlegis.gov

**Ely, Daymon (D, 23)***
State Capitol Building, Room 203D CN
Santa Fe, NM 87501
P: (505) 986-4336
E: daymon.ely@nmlegis.gov

**Ezzell, Candy Spence (R, 58)**
State Capitol Building, Room 203E CN
Santa Fe, NM 87501
P: (505) 986-4211
E: csecows@aol.com

**Fajardo, Kelly K. (R, 7)**
State Capitol Building, Room 202A
Santa Fe, NM 87501
P: (505) 986-4221
E: kelly.fajardo
@nmlegis.gov

**Ferrary, Joanne J. (D, 37)***
State Capitol Building, Room 203D CN
Santa Fe, NM 87501
P: (505) 986-4336
E: joanne.ferrary
@nmlegis.gov

**Gallegos, David (R, 61)**
State Capitol Building, Room 203I CN
Santa Fe, NM 87501
P: (505) 986-4454
E: david.rsi@hotmail.com

**Gallegos, Doreen Y. (D, 52)**
State Capitol Building, Room 134
Santa Fe, NM 87501
P: (505) 986-4780
E: doreen.gallegos
@nmlegis.gov

**Garcia, Harry (D, 69)**
State Capitol Building, Room 413E
Santa Fe, NM 87501
P: (505) 986-4433
E: harry.garcia@nmlegis.gov

**Garcia, Miguel P. (D, 14)**
State Capitol Building, Room 413C
Santa Fe, NM 87501
P: (505) 986-4844
E: miguel.garcia
@nmlegis.gov

**Garcia Richard, Stephanie (D, 43)**
State Capitol Building, Room 313B CN
Santa Fe, NM 87501
P: (505) 986-4846
E: stephanie.garciarichard
@nmlegis.gov

**Gentry, Nate (R, 30)**
State Capitol Building, Room 125
Santa Fe, NM 87501
P: (505) 986-4757
E: natefornm@gmail.com

**Gomez, Bill (D, 34)**
State Capitol Building, Room 313A
Santa Fe, NM 87501
P: (505) 986-4341
E: bealquin.gomez
@nmlegis.gov

**Gonzales, Roberto J. (D, 42)**
State Capitol Building, Room 327
Santa Fe, NM 87501
P: (505) 986-4333
E: roberto.gonzales
@nmlegis.gov

**Hall, Jimmie C. (R, 28)**
State Capitol Building, Room 201A
Santa Fe, NM 87501
P: (505) 986-4215
E: jimmie.hall@nmlegis.gov

**Harper, Jason (R, 57)**
State Capitol Building, Room 203A
Santa Fe, NM 87501
P: (505) 986-4227
E: JasonHarperNM@gmail.com

**Herrell, Yvette (R, 51)**
State Capitol Building, Room 204B
Santa Fe, NM 87501
P: (505) 986-4210
E: yherrell@yahoo.com

**Johnson, D. Wonda (D, 5)**
State Capitol Building, Room 413D
Santa Fe, NM 87501
P: (505) 986-4236
E: dwonda.johnson
@nmlegis.gov

**Larranaga, Larry A. (R, 27)**
State Capitol Building, Room 201A
Santa Fe, NM 87501
P: (505) 986-4215
E: larry@larranaga.com

**Lente, Derrick J. (D, 65)***
State Capitol Building, Room 413E
Santa Fe, NM 87501
P: (505) 986-4433
E: derrick.lente
   @nmlegis.gov

**Lewis, Tim D. (R, 60)**
State Capitol Building, Room 202B
Santa Fe, NM 87501
P: (505) 986-4220
E: lewisfornm@gmail.com

**Little, Rick (R, 53)**
State Capitol Building, Room 202B
Santa Fe, NM 87501
P: (505) 986-4220
E: rick.little@nmlegis.gov

**Louis, Georgene (D, 26)**
State Capitol Building, Room 312A
Santa Fe, NM 87501
P: (505) 986-4327
E: georgene.louis
   @nmlegis.gov

**Lundstrom, Patricia A.
   (D, 9)**
State Capitol Building, Room 304B
Santa Fe, NM 87501
P: (505) 986-4316
E: patricia.lundstrom
   @nmlegis.gov

**Maestas, Antonio (D, 16)**
State Capitol Building, Room 413B
Santa Fe, NM 87501
P: (505) 986-4438
E: antonio.maestas
   @nmlegis.gov

**Maestas Barnes, Sarah
   (R, 15)**
State Capitol Building, Room 202A
Santa Fe, NM 87501
P: (505) 986-4221
E: sarah.maestasbarnes
   @nmlegis.gov

**Martinez, Javier I. (D, 11)**
State Capitol Building, Room 413C
Santa Fe, NM 87501
P: (505) 986-4436
E: javier.martinez
   @nmlegis.gov

**Martinez, Rodolfo S.
   (D, 39)**
State Capitol Building, Room 206B
Santa Fe, NM 87501
P: (505) 986-4248
E: rodolpho.martinez
   @nmlegis.gov

**McCamley, Bill (D, 33)**
State Capitol Building, Room 314A
Santa Fe, NM 87501
P: (505) 986-4415
E: bill.mccamley
   @nmlegis.gov

**McQueen, Matthew (D, 50)**
State Capitol Building, Room 316A
Santa Fe, NM 87501
P: (505) 986-4421
E: matthew.mcqueen
   @nmlegis.gov

**Montoya, Rodney D. (R, 1)**
State Capitol Building, Room 125
Santa Fe, NM 87501
P: (505) 986-4757
E: roddmontoya@gmail.com

**Nibert, Greg (R, 59)***
State Capitol Building, Room 203E CN
Santa Fe, NM 87501
P: (505) 986-4211
E: greg.nibert@nmlegis.gov

**Powdrell-Culbert, Jane E.
   (R, 44)**
State Capitol Building, Room 205A
Santa Fe, NM 87501
P: (505) 986-4243
E: jpandp@comcast.net

**Rehm, Bill R. (R, 31)**
State Capitol Building, Room 201B
Santa Fe, NM 87501
P: (505) 986-4214
E: bill.rehm@nmlegis.gov

**Roch, Dennis J. (R, 67)**
State Capitol Building, Room 203A
Santa Fe, NM 87501
P: (505) 986-4227
E: denroch@hotmail.com

**Rodella, Debbie A. (D, 41)**
State Capitol Building, Room 306
Santa Fe, NM 87501
P: (505) 986-4329
E: debbie.rodella
   @nmlegis.gov

**Romero, G. Andres (D, 10)**
State Capitol Building, Room 413F
Santa Fe, NM 87501
P: (505) 986-4433
E: andres.romero
   @nmlegis.gov

**Roybal Caballero,
   Patricia (D, 13)**
State Capitol Building, Room 206B
Santa Fe, NM 87501
P: (505) 986-4248
E: pat.roybalcaballero
   @nmlegis.gov

**Rubio, Angelica (D, 35)***
State Capitol Building, Room 203B CN
Santa Fe, NM 87501
P: (505) 986-4464
E: angelica.rubio
   @nmlegis.gov

**Ruiloba, Patricio R.
   (D, 12)**
State Capitol Building, Room 413F
Santa Fe, NM 87501
P: (505) 986-4433
E: patricio.ruiloba
   @nmlegis.gov

**Salazar, Nick L. (D, 40)**
State Capitol Building, Room 413E
Santa Fe, NM 87501
P: (505) 986-4432

**Salazar, Tomás (D, 70)**
State Capitol Building, Room 413C
Santa Fe, NM 87501
P: (505) 986-4436
E: tomas.salazar
   @nmlegis.gov

**Sarinana, Debra M. (D, 21)***
State Capitol Buildling, Room 203B CN
Santa Fe, NM 87501
P: (505) 986-4464
E: debbie.sarinana
   @nmlegis.gov

**Scott, Larry R. (R, 62)**
State Capitol Building, Room 203G CN
Santa Fe, NM 87501
P: (505) 986-4450
E: larry.scott@nmlegis.gov

**Small, Nathan P. (D, 36)***
State Capitol Building, Room 203C CN
Santa Fe, NM 87501
P: (505) 986-4254
E: nathan.small@nmlegis.gov

**Smith, James E. (R, 22)**
State Capitol Building, Room 204A
Santa Fe, NM 87501
P: (505) 986-4233
E: jim@jimsmithnm.com

**Stapleton, Sheryl W.
   (D, 19)**
State Capitol Building, Room 134
Santa Fe, NM 87501
P: (505) 986-4780
E: sheryl.stapleton
   @nmlegis.gov

**Strickler, James R.J.
   (R, 2)**
State Capitol Building, Room 203B
Santa Fe, NM 87501
P: (505) 986-4226
E: jamesstrickler@msn.com

**Sweetser, Candie G.
   (D, 32)***
State Capitol Building, Room 203A CN
Santa Fe, NM 87501
P: (505) 986-4255
E: candie.sweetser
   @nmlegis.gov

**Thomson, Elizabeth (D, 24)**
State Capitol Building, Room 206A
Santa Fe, NM 87501
P: (505) 986-4249
E: liz.thomson@nmlegis.gov

**Townsend, James G. (R, 54)**
State Capitol Building, Room 203G CN
Santa Fe, NM 87501
P: (505) 986-4450
E: townsend@pvtn.net

**Trujillo, Carl (D, 46)**
State Capitol Building, Room 413D
Santa Fe, NM 87501
P: (505) 986-4236
E: carl.trujillo
   @nmlegis.gov

# New Mexico

**Trujillo, Christine (D, 25)**
State Capitol Building, Room
206A
Santa Fe, NM 87501
P: (505) 986-4249
E: christine.trujillo
   @nmlegis.gov

**Trujillo, Jim R. (D, 45)**
State Capitol Building, Room
316B
Santa Fe, NM 87501
P: (505) 986-4420
E: jimtrujillo@msn.com

**Trujillo, Linda M. (D, 48)\***
State Capitol Building, Room
203A CN
Santa Fe, NM 87501
P: (505) 986-4255
E: linda.trujillo
   @nmlegis.gov

**Wooley, Bob (R, 66)**
State Capitol Building, Room
203I CN
Santa Fe, NM 87501
P: (505) 986-4454
E: bobwooley66@gmail.com

**Youngblood, Monica (R, 68)**
State Capitol Building, Room
205B
Santa Fe, NM 87501
P: (505) 986-4242
E: monica@MyNMStateRep.com

# New York

## Executive

### Governor
The Honorable Andrew M.
 Cuomo (D)
Governor
State Capitol
Albany, NY 12224
P: (518) 474-7516

### Lieutenant Governor
The Honorable Kathy
 Hochul (D)
Lieutenant Governor
State Capitol
Albany, NY 12224
P: (518) 474-8390
F: (518) 474-1513

### Attorney General
The Honorable Eric T.
 Schneiderman (D)
Attorney General
Department of Law
The Capitol, 2nd Floor
Albany, NY 12224
P: (518) 474-7330

### Auditor
Mr. Andrew SanFilippo
110 State Street
Albany, NY 12236
P: (518) 474-4040
F: (518) 473-8940

### Comptroller
The Honorable Thomas P.
 DiNapoli (D)
Comptroller
110 State Street
Albany, NY 12236
P: (518) 474-4040
F: (518) 474-3004
E: tdinapoli
 @osc.state.ny.us

### Secretary of State
The Honorable Rossana
 Rosado
 (appointed)
Secretary of State
One Commerce Plaza
99 Washington Avenue, Suite
1100
Albany, NY 12231
P: (518) 486-9846
E: info@dos.ny.gov

## Treasurer
The Honorable Christopher
 Curtis
 (appointed)
Deputy Commissioner &
Treasurer
Division of the Treasury
P.O. Box 22119
Albany, NY 12201
P: (518) 474-4250
F: (518) 402-4118

## Judiciary

### Court of Appeals (GA)
Mr. John P. Asiello
Clerk of the Court
20 Eagle Street
Albany, NY 12207
P: (518) 455-7700
F: (518) 463-6869

The Honorable Janet DiFiore
Chief Judge
The Honorable Sheila
 Abdus-Salaam
The Honorable Eugene M.
 Fahey
The Honorable Michael J.
 Garcia
The Honorable Jenny Rivera
The Honorable Leslie E.
 Stein

## Legislative
## Senate

### Senate President
Senator John J.
 Flanagan (R)
Temporary President & Majority
Leader
330 State Capitol Building
Albany, NY 12247
P: (518) 455-2071
F: (518) 426-6904
E: flanagan@nysenate.gov

The Honorable Kathy
 Hochul (D)
Lieutenant Governor
State Capitol
Albany, NY 12224
P: (518) 474-8390
F: (518) 474-1513

## Senate Coalition Co-Leader & Independent Democratic Conference Leader
Senator Jeffrey D.
 Klein (D)
Senate Independent Democratic
Conference Leader
913 Legislative Office Building
Albany, NY 12247
P: (518) 455-3595
E: jdklein@nysenate.gov

## Senate Democratic Conference Leader
Senator Andrea
 Stewart-Cousins (D)
Senate Democratic Conference
Leader
907 Legislative Office Building
Albany, NY 12247
P: (518) 455-2585
F: (518) 426-6811
E: scousins@nysenate.gov

## Secretary of the Senate
Mr. Frank Patience
Secretary of the Senate
State Capitol, Room 321
Albany, NY 12247
P: (518) 455-2051
F: (518) 455-3332

## Members of the Senate
Addabbo, Joseph P. (D, 15)
613 Legislative Office Building
Albany, NY 12247
P: (518) 455-2322
F: (518) 426-6875
E: addabbo@nysenate.gov

Akshar II, Frederick J.
 (R, 52)
805 Legislative Office Building
Albany, NY 12247
P: (518) 455-2673
F: (518) 426-6720
E: akshar@nysenate.gov

Alcantara, Marisol (D, 31)*
311 Legislative Office Building
Albany, NY 12247
P: (518) 455-2041
E: alcantara@nysenate.gov

Amedore Jr., George (R, 46)
802 Legislative Office Building
Albany, NY 12247
P: (518) 455-2350
F: (518) 426-6751
E: Amedore@nysenate.gov

Avella, Tony (D, 11)
902 Legislative Office Building
Albany, NY 12247
P: (518) 455-2210
F: (518) 426-6736
E: avella@nysenate.gov

Bailey, Jamaal (D, 36)*
707 Legislative Office Building
Albany, NY 12247
P: (518) 455-2061
E: bailey@nysenate.gov

Bonacic, John J. (R, 42)
503 Legislative Office Building
Albany, NY 12247
P: (518) 455-3181
F: (518) 426-6948
E: bonacic@nysenate.gov

Boyle, Philip M. (R, 4)
814 Legislative Office Building
Albany, NY 12247
P: (518) 455-3411
E: pboyle@nysenate.gov

Breslin, Neil D. (D, 44)
414 State Capitol Building
Albany, NY 12247
P: (518) 455-2225
F: (518) 426-6807
E: breslin@nysenate.gov

Brooks, John E. (D, 8)*
513 Legislative Office Building
Albany, NY 12247
P: (518) 455-2760
E: brooks@nysenate.gov

Carlucci, David (D, 38)
509 Legislative Office Building
Albany, NY 12247
P: (518) 455-2991
F: (518) 426-6737
E: carlucci@nysenate.gov

Comrie, Leroy (D, 14)
617 Legislative Office Building
Albany, NY 12247
P: (518) 455-2701
E: Comrie@nysenate.gov

Croci, Tom (R, 3)
306 Legislative Office Building
Albany, NY 12247
P: (518) 455-3570
E: Croci@nysenate.gov

DeFrancisco, John A.
 (R, 50)
416 State Capitol Building
Albany, NY 12247
P: (518) 455-3511
E: jdefranc@nysenate.gov

# New York

**Diaz Sr., Ruben (D, 32)**
606 Legislative Office Building
Albany, NY 12247
P: (518) 455-2511
F: (518) 426-6945
E: diaz@nysenate.gov

**Dilan, Martin Malave
(D, 18)**
711B Legislative Office
Building
Albany, NY 12247
P: (518) 455-2177
F: (518) 426-6947
E: dilan@nysenate.gov

**Felder, Simcha (D, 17)**
944 Legislative Office Building
Albany, NY 12247
P: (518) 455-2754
F: (518) 426-6931
E: felder@nysenate.gov

**Flanagan, John J. (R, 2)**
330 State Capitol Building
Albany, NY 12247
P: (518) 455-2071
F: (518) 426-6904
E: flanagan@nysenate.gov

**Funke, Rich (R, 55)**
905 Legislative Office Building
Albany, NY 12247
P: (518) 455-2215
F: (518) 426-6745
E: Funke@nysenate.gov

**Gallivan, Patrick M.
(R, 59)**
512 Legislative Office Building
Albany, NY 12247
P: (518) 455-3471
F: (518) 426-6949
E: gallivan@nysenate.gov

**Gianaris, Michael N.
(D, 12)**
413 Legislative Office Building
Albany, NY 12247
P: (518) 455-3486
F: (518) 426-6929
E: gianaris@nysenate.gov

**Golden, Martin J. (R, 22)**
409 Legislative Office Building
Albany, NY 12247
P: (518) 455-2730
F: (518) 426-6910
E: golden@nysenate.gov

**Griffo, Joseph A. (R, 47)**
612 Legislative Office Building
Albany, NY 12247
P: (518) 455-3334
F: (518) 426-6921
E: griffo@nysenate.gov

**Hamilton, Jesse (D, 20)**
915 Legislative Office Building
Albany, NY 12247
P: (518) 455-2431
F: (518) 426-6856
E: Hamilton@nysenate.gov

**Hannon, Kemp (R, 6)**
420 State Capitol Building
Albany, NY 12247
P: (518) 455-2200
E: hannon@nysenate.gov

**Helming, Pamela (R, 54)***
946 Legislative Office Building
Albany, NY 12247
P: (518) 455-2366
E: helming@nysenate.gov

**Hoylman, Brad (D, 27)**
413 Legislative Office Building
Albany, NY 12247
P: (518) 455-2451
F: (518) 426-6846
E: hoylman@nysenate.gov

**Jacobs, Christopher
(R, 60)***
947 Legislative Office Building
Albany, NY 12247
P: (518) 455-3240
E: jacobs@nysenate.gov

**Kaminsky, Todd (D, 20)**
302 Legislative Office Building
Albany, NY 12248
P: (518) 455-3028
E: kaminskyt
@assembly.state.ny.us

**Kennedy, Timothy M. (D, 63)**
506 Legislative Office Building
Albany, NY 12247
P: (518) 455-2426
F: (518) 426-6851
E: kennedy@nysenate.gov

**Klein, Jeffrey D. (D, 34)**
913 Legislative Office Building
Albany, NY 12247
P: (518) 455-3595
E: jdklein@nysenate.gov

**Krueger, Liz (D, 28)**
808 Legislative Office Building
Albany, NY 12247
P: (518) 455-2297
F: (518) 426-6874
E: lkrueger@nysenate.gov

**Lanza, Andrew J. (R, 24)**
708 Legislative Office Building
Albany, NY 12247
P: (518) 455-3215
F: (518) 426-6852
E: lanza@nysenate.gov

**Larkin, William (R, 39)**
502 Legislative Office Building
Albany, NY 12247
P: (518) 455-2770
F: (518) 426-6923
E: larkin@nysenate.gov

**Latimer, George S. (D, 37)**
615 Legislative Office Building
Albany, NY 12247
P: (518) 455-2031
F: (518) 426-6860
E: latimer@nysenate.gov

**LaValle, Kenneth P. (R, 1)**
806 Legislative Office Building
Albany, NY 12247
P: (518) 455-3121
E: lavalle@nysenate.gov

**Little, Elizabeth (R, 45)**
310 Legislative Office Building
Albany, NY 12247
P: (518) 455-2811
E: little@nysenate.gov

**Marcellino, Carl L. (R, 5)**
811 Legislative Office Building
Albany, NY 12247
P: (518) 455-2390
F: (518) 426-6975
E: marcelli@nysenate.gov

**Marchione, Kathleen A.
(R, 43)**
917 Legislative Office Building
Albany, NY 12247
P: (518) 455-2381
F: (518) 426-6985
E: marchione@nysenate.gov

**Montgomery, Velmanette
(D, 25)**
903 Legislative Office Building
Albany, NY 12247
P: (518) 455-3451
F: (518) 426-6854
E: montgome@nysenate.gov

**Murphy, Terrence P. (R, 40)**
817 Legislative Office Building
Albany, NY 12247
P: (518) 455-3111
F: (518) 426-6977
E: murphy@nysenate.gov

**O'Mara, Thomas F. (R, 58)**
307 Legislative Office Building
Albany, NY 12247
P: (518) 455-2091
F: (518) 426-6976
E: omara@nysenate.gov

**Ortt, Robert (R, 62)**
815 Legislative Office Building
Albany, NY 12247
P: (518) 455-2024
F: (518) 426-6987
E: Ortt@nysenate.gov

**Parker, Kevin S. (D, 21)**
604 Legislative Office Building
Albany, NY 12247
P: (518) 455-2580
F: (518) 426-6843
E: parker@nysenate.gov

**Peralta, Jose R. (D, 13)**
415 Legislative Office Building
Albany, NY 12247
P: (518) 455-2529
F: (518) 426-6909
E: jperalta@nysenate.gov

**Perkins, Bill (D, 30)**
517 Legislative Office Building
Albany, NY 12247
P: (518) 455-2441
F: (518) 426-6809
E: perkins@nysenate.gov

**Persaud, Roxanne (D, 19)**
504 Legislative Office Building
Albany, NY 12247
P: (518) 455-2788
E: persaud@nysenate.gov

**Phillips, Elaine (R, 7)***
848 Legislative Office Building
Albany, NY 12247
P: (518) 455-3265
E: ephillips@nysenate.gov

**Ranzenhofer, Michael H.
(R, 61)**
609 Legislative Office Building
Albany, NY 12247
P: (518) 455-3161
F: (518) 426-6963
E: ranz@nysenate.gov

**Ritchie, Patricia A.
(R, 48)**
412 Legislative Office Building
Albany, NY 12247
P: (518) 455-3438
F: (518) 426-6740
E: ritchie@nysenate.gov

**Rivera, J. Gustavo (D, 33)**
408 Legislative Office Building
Albany, NY 12247
P: (518) 455-3395
F: (518) 426-6858
E: grivera@nysenate.gov

**Robach, Joseph E. (R, 56)**
711 Legislative Office Building
Albany, NY 12247
P: (518) 455-2909
E: robach@nysenate.gov

**Sanders, James (D, 10)**
508 Legislative Office Building
Albany, NY 12247
P: (518) 455-3531
F: (718) 523-3670
E: sanders@nysenate.gov

Savino, Diane J. (D, 23)
315 Legislative Office Building
Albany, NY 12247
P: (518) 455-2437
F: (518) 426-6943
E: savino@nysenate.gov

Serino, Sue (R, 41)
812 Legislative Office Building
Albany, NY 12247
P: (518) 455-2945
F: (518) 426-6770
E: Serino@nysenate.gov

Serrano, Jose M. (D, 29)
406 Legislative Office Building
Albany, NY 12247
P: (518) 455-2795
F: (518) 426-6886
E: serrano@nysenate.gov

Seward, James L. (R, 51)
430 Legislative Office Building
Albany, NY 12247
P: (518) 455-3131
E: seward@nysenate.gov

Squadron, Daniel L. (D, 26)
515 Legislative Office Building
Albany, NY 12247
P: (518) 455-2625
F: (518) 426-6956
E: squadron@nysenate.gov

Stavisky, Toby Ann (D, 16)
706 Legislative Office Building
Albany, NY 12247
P: (518) 455-3461
F: (518) 426-6857
E: stavisky@nysenate.gov

Stewart-Cousins, Andrea
  (D, 35)
907 Legislative Office Building
Albany, NY 12247
P: (518) 455-2585
F: (518) 426-6811
E: scousins@nysenate.gov

Tedisco, James (R, 49)
803 Legislative Office Building
Albany, NY 12248
P: (518) 455-5772
E: tedisco@nysenate.gov

Valesky, David J. (D, 53)
514 Legislative Office Building
Albany, NY 12247
P: (518) 455-2838
F: (518) 426-6885
E: valesky@nysenate.gov

Young, Catharine M. (R, 57)
428 Legislative Office Building
Albany, NY 12247
P: (518) 455-3563
F: (518) 426-6905
E: cyoung@nysenate.gov

# Assembly

## Speaker of the Assembly

**Assemblyman Carl E. Heastie (D)**
Speaker of the Assembly
932 Legislative Office Building
Albany, NY 12248
P: (518) 455-3791
F: (518) 455-4812
E: Speaker
  @assembly.state.ny.us

## Speaker Pro Tempore of the Assembly

**Assemblyman Jeffrion L. Aubry (D)**
Assembly Speaker Pro Tempore
646 Legislative Office Building
Albany, NY 12248
P: (518) 455-4561
F: (518) 455-4565
E: AubryJ
  @assembly.state.ny.us

## Assembly Majority Leader

**Assemblyman Joseph D. Morelle (D)**
Assembly Majority Leader
926 Legislative Office Building
Albany, NY 12248
P: (518) 455-5373
F: (518) 455-5647
E: morellej
  @assembly.state.ny.us

## Assembly Minority Leader

**Assemblyman Brian M. Kolb (R)**
Assembly Minority Leader
933 Legislative Office Building
Albany, NY 12248
P: (518) 455-3751
E: KolbB
  @assembly.state.ny.us

## Clerk of the Assembly

**Ms. Laurene R. Kretzler**
Clerk of the Assembly
State Capitol, Room 437
Albany, NY 12248
P: (518) 455-4242

# Members of the Assembly

**Abbate Jr., Peter J. (D, 49)**
839 Legislative Office Building
Albany, NY 12248
P: (518) 455-3053
E: abbatep
  @assembly.state.ny.us

**Abinanti, Thomas J. (D, 92)**
744 Legislative Office Building
Albany, NY 12248
P: (518) 455-5753
E: abinantit
  @assembly.state.ny.us

**Amato, Stacey Pheffer
  (D, 23)***
542 Legislative Office Building
Albany, NY 12248
P: (518) 455-4292
E: amatos@nyassembly.gov

**Arroyo, Carmen E. (D, 84)**
734 Legislative Office Building
Albany, NY 12248
P: (518) 455-5402
E: ArroyoC
  @assembly.state.ny.us

**Aubry, Jeffrion L. (D, 35)**
646 Legislative Office Building
Albany, NY 12248
P: (518) 455-4561
F: (518) 455-4565
E: AubryJ
  @assembly.state.ny.us

**Barclay, William A.
  (R, 120)**
521 Legislative Office Building
Albany, NY 12248
P: (518) 455-5841
E: BarclaW@nyassembly.gov

**Barnwell, Brian (D, 30)***
921 Legislative Office Building
Albany, NY 12248
P: (518) 455-3791
E: barnwellb@nyassembly.gov

**Barrett, Didi (D, 106)**
553 Legislative Office Building
Albany, NY 12248
P: (518) 455-5177
F: (518) 455-5418
E: BarrettD
  @assembly.state.ny.us

**Barron, Charles (D, 60)**
532 Legislative Office Building
Albany, NY 12248
P: (518) 455-5912
E: barronc
  @assembly.state.ny.us

**Benedetto, Michael (D, 82)**
842 Legislative Office Building
Albany, NY 12248
P: (518) 455-5296
E: benedettom
  @assembly.state.ny.us

**Bichotte, Rodneyse (D, 42)**
833 Legislative Office Building
Albany, NY 12248
P: (518) 455-5385
E: bichotter
  @assembly.state.ny.us

**Blake, Michael (D, 79)**
919 Legislative Office Building
Albany, NY 12248
P: (518) 455-5272
E: blakem
  @assembly.state.ny.us

**Blankenbush, Ken (R, 117)**
322 Legislative Office Building
Albany, NY 12248
P: (518) 455-5797
F: (518) 455-5289
E: blankenbushk
  @assembly.state.ny.us

**Brabenec, Karl (R, 98)**
723 Legislative Office Building
Albany, NY 12248
P: (518) 455-5991
F: (518) 455-5929
E: brabeneck
  @assembly.state.ny.us

**Braunstein, Edward (D, 26)**
557 Legislative Office Building
Albany, NY 12248
P: (518) 455-5425
F: (518) 455-4648
E: braunsteine
  @assembly.state.ny.us

**Brindisi, Anthony J.
  (D, 119)**
538 Legislative Office Building
Albany, NY 12248
P: (518) 455-5454
F: (518) 455-5928
E: brindisia
  @assembly.state.ny.us

**Bronson, Harry (D, 138)**
502 Legislative Office Building
Albany, NY 12248
P: (518) 455-4527
E: bronsonh
  @assembly.state.ny.us

**Buchwald, David (D, 93)**
331 Legislative Office Building
Albany, NY 12248
P: (518) 455-5397
E: BuchwaldD
  @assembly.state.ny.us

# New York

**Butler, Marc W. (R, 118)**
525 Legislative Office Building
Albany, NY 12248
P: (518) 455-5393
E: ButlerM
  @assembly.state.ny.us

**Byrne, Kevin M. (R, 94)***
629 Legislative Office Building
Albany, NY 12248
P: (518) 455-5783
E: byrnek@nyassembly.gov

**Cahill, Kevin A. (D, 103)**
716 Legislative Office Building
Albany, NY 12248
P: (518) 455-4436
E: CahillK
  @assembly.state.ny.us

**Carroll, Robert C. (D, 44)***
429 Legislative Office Building
Albany, NY 12248
P: (518) 455-5377
E: carrollr@nyassembly.gov

**Castornia Jr., Ron (R, 62)**
428 Legislative Office Building
Albany, NY 12248
P: (518) 455-4495
F: (518) 455-4501
E: castorniar
  @nyassembly.gov

**Colton, William (D, 47)**
733 Legislative Office Building
Albany, NY 12248
P: (518) 455-5828
E: ColtonW
  @assembly.state.ny.us

**Cook, Vivian E. (D, 32)**
939 Legislative Office Building
Albany, NY 12248
P: (518) 455-4203
E: CookV
  @assembly.state.ny.us

**Crespo, Marcos A. (D, 85)**
454 Legislative Office Building
Albany, NY 12248
P: (518) 455-5514
E: CrespoM
  @assembly.state.ny.us

**Crouch, Clifford W.
  (R, 122)**
450 Legislative Office Building
Albany, NY 12248
P: (518) 455-5741
E: CrouchC
  @assembly.state.ny.us

**Curran, Brian (R, 21)**
318 Legislative Office Building
Albany, NY 12248
P: (518) 455-4656
E: curranb
  @assembly.state.ny.us

**Cusick, Michael (D, 63)**
724 Legislative Office Building
Albany, NY 12248
P: (518) 455-5526
E: CusickM
  @assembly.state.ny.us

**Cymbrowitz, Steven (D, 45)**
943 Legislative Office Building
Albany, NY 12248
P: (518) 455-5214
E: CymbroS
  @assembly.state.ny.us

**Davila, Maritza (D, 53)**
631 Legislative Office Building
Albany, NY 12248
P: (518) 455-5537
F: (518) 455-5789
E: DavilaM
  @assembly.state.ny.us

**De La Rosa, Carmen N.
  (D, 72)***
528 Legislative Office Building
Albany, NY 12248
P: (518) 455-5807
E: delarosac@nyassembly.gov

**DenDekker, Michael G.
  (D, 34)**
841 Legislative Office Building
Albany, NY 12248
P: (518) 455-4545
E: DenDekkerM
  @assembly.state.ny.us

**Dickens, Inez E. (D, 70)***
650 Legislative Office Building
Albany, NY 12248
P: (518) 455-4793
E: dickensi@nyassembly.gov

**Dilan, Erik (D, 54)**
921 Legislative Office Building
Albany, NY 12248
P: (518) 455-5821
E: dilane
  @assembly.state.ny.us

**Dinowitz, Jeffrey (D, 81)**
422 Legislative Office Building
Albany, NY 12248
P: (518) 455-5965
F: (518) 455-4437
E: DinowiJ
  @assembly.state.ny.us

**DiPietro, David (R, 147)**
543 Legislative Office Building
Albany, NY 12248
P: (518) 455-5314
E: DiPietroD
  @assembly.state.ny.us

**D'Urso, Anthony (D, 16)***
920 Legislative Office Building
Albany, NY 12248
P: (518) 455-5192
E: dursoa@nyassembly.gov

**Englebright, Steve (D, 4)**
621 Legislative Office Building
Albany, NY 12248
P: (518) 455-4804
E: EngleS
  @assembly.state.ny.us

**Errigo, Joseph A. (R, 133)**
527 Legislative Office Building
Albany, NY 12248
P: (518) 455-5662
E: errigoj@nyassembly.gov

**Fahy, Patricia (D, 109)**
452 Legislative Office Building
Albany, NY 12248
P: (518) 455-4178
E: FahyP
  @assembly.state.ny.us

**Farrell Jr., Herman D.
  (D, 71)**
923 Legislative Office Building
Albany, NY 12248
P: (518) 455-5491
E: FarrelH
  @assembly.state.ny.us

**Finch, Gary D. (R, 126)**
448 Legislative Office Building
Albany, NY 12248
P: (518) 455-5878
E: FinchG
  @assembly.state.ny.us

**Fitzpatrick, Michael J.
  (R, 8)**
458 Legislative Office Building
Albany, NY 12248
P: (518) 455-5021
F: (518) 455-4394
E: FitzpatrickM
  @assembly.state.ny.us

**Friend, Christopher
  (R, 124)**
938 Legislative Office Building
Albany, NY 12248
P: (518) 455-4538
E: friendc
  @assembly.state.ny.us

**Galef, Sandy (D, 95)**
641 Legislative Office Building
Albany, NY 12248
P: (518) 455-5348
E: GalefS
  @assembly.state.ny.us

**Gantt, David F. (D, 137)**
830 Legislative Office Building
Albany, NY 12248
P: (518) 455-5606
E: GanttD
  @assembly.state.ny.us

**Garbarino, Andrew R. (R, 7)**
529 Legislative Office Building
Albany, NY 12248
P: (518) 455-4611
E: GarbarinoA
  @assembly.state.ny.us

**Giglio, Joe (R, 148)**
439 Legislative Office Building
Albany, NY 12248
P: (518) 455-5241
E: GiglioJ
  @assembly.state.ny.us

**Gjonaj, Mark (D, 80)**
633 Legislative Office Building
Albany, NY 12248
P: (518) 455-5844
E: GjonajM
  @assembly.state.ny.us

**Glick, Deborah J. (D, 66)**
717 Legislative Office Building
Albany, NY 12248
P: (518) 455-4841
E: GlickD
  @assembly.state.ny.us

**Goodell, Andy (R, 150)**
545 Legislative Office Building
Albany, NY 12248
P: (518) 455-4511
E: goodella
  @assembly.state.ny.us

**Gottfried, Richard N.
  (D, 75)**
822 Legislative Office Building
Albany, NY 12248
P: (518) 455-4941
F: (518) 455-5939
E: GottfriedR
  @assembly.state.ny.us

**Graf, Al (R, 5)**
433 Legislative Office Building
Albany, NY 12248
P: (517) 455-5937
E: grafa
  @assembly.state.ny.us

**Gunther, Aileen M. (D, 100)**
826 Legislative Office Building
Albany, NY 12248
P: (518) 455-5355
E: GuntheA
  @assembly.state.ny.us

**Harris, Pamela (D, 46)**
324 Legislative Office Building
Albany, NY 12248
P: (518) 455-4811
E: HarrisP
@assembly.state.ny.us

**Hawley, Stephen (R, 139)**
329 Legislative Office Building
Albany, NY 12248
P: (518) 455-5811
E: HawleyS
@assembly.state.ny.us

**Heastie, Carl E. (D, 83)**
932 Legislative Office Building
Albany, NY 12248
P: (518) 455-3791
F: (518) 455-4812
E: Speaker
@assembly.state.ny.us

**Hevesi, Andrew (D, 28)**
844 Legislative Office Building
Albany, NY 12248
P: (518) 455-4926
E: HevesiA
@assembly.state.ny.us

**Hikind, Dov (D, 48)**
551 Legislative Office Building
Albany, NY 12248
P: (518) 455-5721
F: (518) 455-5948
E: HikindD
@assembly.state.ny.us

**Hooper, Earlene (D, 18)**
739 Legislative Office Building
Albany, NY 12248
P: (518) 455-5861
E: hoopere
@assembly.state.ny.us

**Hunter, Pamela J. (D, 128)**
432 Legislative Office Building
Albany, NY 12248
P: (518) 455-5383
E: HunterP
@assembly.state.ny.us

**Hyndman, Alicia (D, 29)**
820 Legislative Office Building
Albany, NY 12248
P: (518) 455-4451
E: HyndmanA
@assembly.state.ny.us

**Jaffee, Ellen (D, 97)**
650 Legislative Office Building
Albany, NY 12248
P: (518) 455-5118
E: JaffeeE
@assembly.state.ny.us

**Jean-Pierre, Kimberly (D, 11)**
530 Legislative Office Building
Albany, NY 12248
P: (518) 455-5787
F: (518) 455-3976
E: jeanpierrek
@assembly.state.ny.us

**Jenne, Addie (D, 116)**
456 Legislative Office Building
Albany, NY 12248
P: (518) 455-5545
E: JenneA
@assembly.state.ny.us

**Johns, Mark (R, 135)**
549 Legislative Office Building
Albany, NY 12248
P: (518) 455-5784
E: johnsm
@assembly.state.ny.us

**Jones, D. Billy (D, 115)***
639 Legislative Office Building
Albany, NY 12248
P: (518) 455-5943
E: jonesb
@assembly.state.ny.us

**Joyner, Latoya (D, 77)**
427 Legislative Office Building
Albany, NY 12248
P: (518) 455-5671
F: (518) 455-5461
E: joynerl
@assembly.state.ny.us

**Kavanagh, Brian P. (D, 74)**
419 Legislative Office Building
Albany, NY 12248
P: (518) 455-5506
E: KavanaghB
@assembly.state.ny.us

**Kearns, Michael P. (D, 142)**
431 Legislative Office Building
Albany, NY 12248
P: (518) 455-4691
E: kearnsm
@assembly.state.ny.us

**Kim, Ron (D, 40)**
419 Legislative Office Building
Albany, NY 12248
P: (518) 455-5411
E: KimR
@assembly.state.ny.us

**Kolb, Brian M. (R, 131)**
933 Legislative Office Building
Albany, NY 12248
P: (518) 455-3751
E: KolbB
@assembly.state.ny.us

**Lalor, Kieran Michael (R, 105)**
531 Legislative Office Building
Albany, NY 12248
P: (518) 455-5725
E: LalorK
@assembly.state.ny.us

**Lavine, Charles D. (D, 13)**
441 Legislative Office Building
Albany, NY 12248
P: (518) 455-5456
F: (518) 455-5467
E: LavineC
@assembly.state.ny.us

**Lawrence, Peter (R, 134)**
722 Legislative Office Building
Albany, NY 12248
P: (518) 455-4664
F: (518) 455-3093
E: lawrencep
@assembly.state.ny.us

**Lentol, Joseph R. (D, 50)**
632 Legislative Office Building
Albany, NY 12248
P: (518) 455-4477
E: LentolJ
@assembly.state.ny.us

**Lifton, Barbara (D, 125)**
555 Legislative Office Building
Albany, NY 12248
P: (518) 455-5444
E: LiftonB
@assembly.state.ny.us

**Lopez, Peter D. (R, 102)**
402 Legislative Office Building
Albany, NY 12248
P: (518) 455-5363
E: LopezP
@assembly.state.ny.us

**Lupardo, Donna (D, 123)**
626 Legislative Office Building
Albany, NY 12248
P: (518) 455-5431
E: LupardoD
@assembly.state.ny.us

**Lupinacci, Chad A. (R, 10)**
937 Legislative Office Building
Albany, NY 12248
P: (518) 455-5732
E: lupinaccic
@assembly.state.ny.us

**Magee, William (D, 121)**
828 Legislative Office Building
Albany, NY 12248
P: (518) 455-4807
E: MageeW
@assembly.state.ny.us

**Magnarelli, William B. (D, 129)**
837 Legislative Office Building
Albany, NY 12248
P: (518) 455-4826
E: MagnarW
@assembly.state.ny.us

**Malliotakis, Nicole (R, 64)**
404 Legislative Office Building
Albany, NY 12248
P: (518) 455-5716
E: malliotakisn
@assembly.state.ny.us

**Mayer, Shelley (D, 90)**
327 Legislative Office Building
Albany, NY 12248
P: (518) 455-3662
F: (518) 455-5499
E: MayerS
@assembly.state.ny.us

**McDonald III, John T. (D, 108)**
417 Legislative Office Building
Albany, NY 12248
P: (518) 455-4474
E: McDonaldJ
@assembly.state.ny.us

**McDonough, David G. (R, 14)**
443 Legislative Office Building
Albany, NY 12248
P: (518) 455-4633
E: mcdonoughd
@assembly.state.ny.us

**McKevitt, Tom (R, 17)**
446 Legislative Office Building
Albany, NY 12248
P: (518) 455-5341
E: MckeviT
@assembly.state.ny.us

**McLaughlin, Steven F. (R, 107)**
533 Legislative Office Building
Albany, NY 12248
P: (518) 455-5777
E: mclaughlins
@assembly.state.ny.us

**Miller, Brian D. (R, 101)***
544 Legislative Office Building
Albany, NY 12248
P: (518) 455-5334
E: millerb@nyassembly.gov

**Miller, Melissa L. (R, 20)***
426 Legislative Office Building
Albany, NY 12248
P: (518) 455-3028
E: millerml@nyassembly.gov

# New York

**Miller, Michael (D, 38)**
519 Legislative Office Building
Albany, NY 12248
P: (518) 455-4621
E: MillerMG
@assembly.state.ny.us

**Montesano, Michael A.**
**(R, 15)**
437 Legislative Office Building
Albany, NY 12248
P: (518) 455-4684
E: MontesanoM
@assembly.state.ny.us

**Morelle, Joseph D. (D, 136)**
926 Legislative Office Building
Albany, NY 12248
P: (518) 455-5373
F: (518) 455-5647
E: morellej
@assembly.state.ny.us

**Morinello, Angelo J.**
**(R, 145)\***
721 Legislative Office Building
Albany, NY 12248
P: (518) 455-5284
E: morinelloa
@nyassembly.gov

**Mosley, Walter T. (D, 57)**
528 Legislative Office Building
Albany, NY 12248
P: (518) 455-5325
E: MosleyW
@assembly.state.ny.us

**Moya, Francisco P. (D, 39)**
727 Legislative Office Building
Albany, NY 12248
P: (518) 455-4567
E: moyaf
@assembly.state.ny.us

**Murray, Dean (R, 3)**
430 Legislative Office Building
Albany, NY 12248
P: (518) 455-4901
F: (518) 455-5908
E: MurrayD
@assembly.state.ny.us

**Niou, Yuh-Line (D, 65)\***
818 Legislative Office Building
Albany, NY 12248
P: (518) 455-3640
E: niouy@nyassembly.gov

**Nolan, Catherine (D, 37)**
836 Legislative Office Building
Albany, NY 12248
P: (518) 455-4851
E: NolanC
@assembly.state.ny.us

**Norris, Michael J.**
**(R, 144)\***
718 Legislative Office Building
Albany, NY 12248
P: (518) 455-4601
E: norrism@nyassembly.gov

**Oaks, Bob (R, 130)**
Capitol 444
Albany, NY 12248
P: (518) 455-5655
E: OaksR
@assembly.state.ny.us

**O'Donnell, Daniel J.**
**(D, 69)**
526 Legislative Office Building
Albany, NY 12248
P: (518) 455-5603
E: OdonnellD
@assembly.state.ny.us

**Ortiz, Felix (D, 51)**
731 Legislative Office Building
Albany, NY 12248
P: (518) 455-3821
E: OrtizF
@assembly.state.ny.us

**Otis, Steven (D, 91)**
325 Legislative Office Building
Albany, NY 12248
P: (518) 455-4897
E: OtisS
@assembly.state.ny.us

**Palmesano, Philip A.**
**(R, 132)**
320 Legislative Office Building
Albany, NY 12248
P: (518) 455-5791
F: (518) 455-4644
E: palmesanop
@assembly.state.ny.us

**Palumbo, Anthony H. (R, 2)**
719 Legislative Office Building
Albany, NY 12248
P: (518) 455-5294
E: palumboa
@assembly.state.ny.us

**Paulin, Amy (D, 88)**
713 Legislative Office Building
Albany, NY 12248
P: (518) 455-5585
E: PaulinA
@assembly.state.ny.us

**Peoples-Stokes, Crystal D.**
**(D, 141)**
625 Legislative Office Building
Albany, NY 12248
P: (518) 455-5005
E: PeopleC
@assembly.state.ny.us

**Perry, N. Nick (D, 58)**
736 Legislative Office Building
Albany, NY 12248
P: (518) 455-4166
E: PerryN
@assembly.state.ny.us

**Pichardo, Victor M. (D, 86)**
920 Legislative Office Building
Albany, NY 12248
P: (518) 455-5511
E: PichardoV
@assembly.state.ny.us

**Pretlow, J. Gary (D, 89)**
845 Legislative Office Building
Albany, NY 12248
P: (518) 455-5291
E: PretloJ
@assembly.state.ny.us

**Quart, Dan (D, 73)**
741 Legislative Office Building
Albany, NY 12248
P: (518) 455-4794
E: quartd
@assembly.state.ny.us

**Ra, Edward P. (R, 19)**
546 Legislative Office Building
Albany, NY 12248
P: (518) 455-4627
E: rae@assembly.state.ny.us

**Raia, Andrew P. (R, 12)**
635 Legislative Office Building
Albany, NY 12248
P: (518) 455-5952
E: RaiaA
@assembly.state.ny.us

**Ramos, Phil (D, 6)**
648 Legislative Office Building
Albany, NY 12248
P: (518) 455-5185
E: RamosP
@assembly.state.ny.us

**Richardson, Diana C.**
**(D, 43)**
834 Legislative Office Building
Albany, NY 12248
P: (518) 455-5262
E: district43
@assembly.state.ny.us

**Rivera, Jose (D, 78)**
536 Legislative Office Building
Albany, NY 12248
P: (518) 455-5414
E: RiveraJ
@assembly.state.ny.us

**Rodriguez, Robert (D, 68)**
729 Legislative Office Building
Albany, NY 12248
P: (518) 455-4781
E: rodriguezrj
@assembly.state.ny.us

**Rosenthal, Linda B. (D, 67)**
627 Legislative Office Building
Albany, NY 12248
P: (518) 455-5802
E: RosentL
@assembly.state.ny.us

**Rozic, Nily (D, 25)**
547 Legislative Office Building
Albany, NY 12248
P: (518) 455-5172
F: (518) 455-5479
E: RozicN
@assembly.state.ny.us

**Ryan, Sean (D, 149)**
540 Legislative Office Building
Albany, NY 12248
P: (518) 455-4886
F: (518) 455-4890
E: ryans
@assembly.state.ny.us

**Santabarbara, Angelo**
**(D, 111)**
654 Legislative Office Building
Albany, NY 12248
P: (518) 455-5197
E: SantabarbaraA
@assembly.state.ny.us

**Schimminger, Robin (D, 140)**
847 Legislative Office Building
Albany, NY 12248
P: (518) 455-4767
E: SchimmR
@assembly.state.ny.us

**Seawright, Rebecca (D, 76)**
650 Legislative Office Building
Albany, NY 12248
P: (518) 455-5676
E: seawrightr
@assembly.state.ny.us

**Sepulveda, Luis R. (D, 87)**
746 Legislative Office Building
Albany, NY 12248
P: (518) 455-5102
E: SepulvedaL
@assembly.state.ny.us

**Simanowitz, Michael (D, 27)**
742 Legislative Office Building
Albany, NY 12248
P: (518) 455-4404
E: simanowitzm
@assembly.state.ny.us

**Simon, Jo Anne (D, 52)**
326 Legislative Office Building
Albany, NY 12248
P: (518) 455-5426
E: simonj
@assembly.state.ny.us

# New York

**Simotas, Aravella (D, 36)**
652 Legislative Office Building
Albany, NY 12248
P: (518) 455-5014
E: simotasa
@assembly.state.ny.us

**Skartados, Frank K.
(D, 104)**
435 Legislative Office Building
Albany, NY 12248
P: (518) 455-5762
F: (518) 455-5593
E: SkartadosF
@assembly.state.ny.us

**Skoufis, James (D, 99)**
704 Legislative Office Building
Albany, NY 12248
P: (518) 455-5441
E: SkoufisJ
@assembly.state.ny.us

**Solages, Michaelle C.
(D, 22)**
619 Legislative Office Building
Albany, NY 12248
P: (518) 455-4465
F: (518) 455-5560
E: SolagesM
@assembly.state.ny.us

**Stec, Dan (R, 114)**
940 Legislative Office Building
Albany, NY 12248
P: (518) 455-5565
E: StecD
@assembly.state.ny.us

**Steck, Phil (D, 110)**
819 Legislative Office Building
Albany, NY 12248
P: (518) 455-5931
F: (518) 455-5840
E: SteckP
@assembly.state.ny.us

**Stirpe Jr., Albert A.
(D, 127)**
656 Legislative Office Building
Albany, NY 12248
P: (518) 455-4505
E: StirpeA
@assembly.state.ny.us

**Thiele Jr., Fred W. (D, 1)**
622 Legislative Office Building
Albany, NY 12248
P: (518) 455-5997
E: ThieleF
@assembly.state.ny.us

**Titone, Matthew (D, 61)**
643 Legislative Office Building
Albany, NY 12248
P: (518) 455-4677
E: TitoneM
@assembly.state.ny.us

**Titus, Michele R. (D, 31)**
522 Legislative Office Building
Albany, NY 12248
P: (518) 455-5668
E: TitusM
@assembly.state.ny.us

**Vanel, Clyde (D, 33)***
547 Legislative Office Building
Albany, NY 12248
P: (518) 455-4711
F: (518) 455-3740
E: vanelc@nyassembly.gov

**Walker, Latrice (D, 55)**
628 Legislative Office Building
Albany, NY 12248
P: (518) 455-4466
E: walkerl
@assembly.state.ny.us

**Wallace, Monica P.
(D, 143)***
721 Legislative Office Building
Albany, NY 12248
P: (518) 455-5921
F: (518) 455-3962
E: wallacem@nyassembly.gov

**Walsh, Mary Beth (R, 112)***
725 Legislative Office Building
Albany, NY 12248
P: (518) 455-5772
E: walshm@nyassembly.gov

**Walter, Raymond (R, 146)**
550 Legislative Office Building
Albany, NY 12248
P: (518) 455-4618
F: (518) 455-5023
E: walterr
@assembly.state.ny.us

**Weinstein, Helene E.
(D, 41)**
831 Legislative Office Building
Albany, NY 12248
P: (518) 455-5462
E: weinsth
@assembly.state.ny.us

**Weprin, David I. (D, 24)**
602 Legislative Office Building
Albany, NY 12248
P: (518) 455-5806
E: weprind
@assembly.state.ny.us

**Williams, Jaime (D, 59)**
523 Legislative Office Building
Albany, NY 12248
P: (518) 455-5211
E: WilliamsJ@nyassembly.gov

**Woerner, Carrie (D, 113)**
323 Legislative Office Building
Albany, NY 12248
P: (518) 455-5404
F: (518) 455-3727
E: woernerc
@assembly.state.ny.us

**Wright, Tremaine S.
(D, 56)***
424 Legislative Office Building
Albany, NY 12248
P: (518) 455-5474
E: wrightt@nyassembly.gov

**Zebrowski, Kenneth P.
(D, 96)**
424 Legislative Office Building
Albany, NY 12248
P: (518) 455-5735
E: ZebrowskiK
@assembly.state.ny.us

# North Carolina

## Executive

### Governor

**The Honorable Roy A. Cooper III (D)**
Governor
20301 Mail Service Center
Raleigh, NC 27699
P: (919) 733-4240
F: (919) 733-2120

### Lieutenant Governor

**The Honorable Dan Forest (R)**
Lieutenant Governor
310 North Blount Street
Raleigh, NC 27601
P: (919) 733-7350
F: (919) 733-6595
E: lt.gov@nc.gov

### Commissioner of Agriculture & Consumer Services

**Mr. Steve Troxler (R)**
Commissioner
1001 Mail Service Center
Raleigh, NC 27699
P: (919) 707-3000
F: (919) 733-1141

### Attorney General

**The Honorable Josh Stein (D)**
Attorney General
Department of Justice
P.O. Box 629
Raleigh, NC 27602
P: (919) 716-6400
F: (919) 716-6750
E: jstein@ncdoj.gov

### Auditor

**The Honorable Beth Wood (D)**
State Auditor
2 South Salisbury Street
20601 Mail Service Center
Raleigh, NC 27699
P: (919) 807-7500
F: (919) 807-7600
E: Beth_Wood@ncauditor.net

### Commissioner of Insurance

**The Honorable Mike Causey (R)**
Commissioner
430 North Salisburg Street
Dobbs Building, 1201 Mail Service Center
Raleigh, NC 27699
P: (919) 807-6000
F: (919) 733-6495

### Commissioner of Labor

**The Honorable Cherie K. Berry (R)**
Commissioner
1101 Mail Service Center
Raleigh, NC 27699
P: (919) 807-2796
F: (919) 733-7640
E: cherie.berry @labor.nc.gov

### Secretary of State

**The Honorable Elaine F. Marshall (D)**
Secretary of State
P.O. Box 29622
Raleigh, NC 27626
P: (919) 807-2005
F: (919) 807-2010
E: emarshal@sosnc.com

### Superintendent of Public Instruction

**The Honorable Mark Johnson (R)**
Superintendent of Public Instruction
Education Building
301 North Wilmington Street
Raleigh, NC 27699
P: (919) 807-3300
F: (919) 807-3445

### Treasurer

**The Honorable Dale R. Folwell (R)**
State Treasurer
325 North Salisbury Street
P.O. Box 25903
Raleigh, NC 27603
P: (919) 508-5176
F: (919) 508-5167
E: assistantsecretary @nccommerce.com

## Judiciary

### Supreme Court (PE)

**Mr. J. Bryan Boyd**
2 East Morgan Street
P.O. Box 2170
Raleigh, NC 27602
P: (919) 831-5700

**The Honorable Mark D. Martin**
Chief Justice
**The Honorable Cheri Beasley**
**The Honorable Sam J. Ervin**
**The Honorable Robin E. Hudson**
**The Honorable Barbara Jackson**
**The Honorable Michael Morgan**
**The Honorable Paul Martin Newby**

## Legislative

## Senate

### Senate President

**The Honorable Dan Forest (R)**
Lieutenant Governor
310 North Blount Street
Raleigh, NC 27601
P: (919) 733-7350
F: (919) 733-6595
E: lt.gov@nc.gov

### President Pro Tempore of the Senate

**Senator Phil Berger (R)**
Senate President Pro Tempore
2007 Legislative Building
16 West Jones Street
Raleigh, NC 27601
P: (919) 733-5708
F: (919) 733-2599
E: Phil.Berger@ncleg.net

### Senate Majority Leader

**Senator Harry Brown (R)**
Senate Majority Leader
300-B Legislative Office Building
300 North Salisbury Street
Raleigh, NC 27603
P: (919) 715-3034
F: (919) 733-3113
E: Harry.Brown@ncleg.net

### Senate Minority Leader

**Senator Dan Blue Jr. (D)**
Senate Democratic Leader
1129 Legislative Building
16 West Jones Street
Raleigh, NC 27601
P: (919) 733-5752
F: (919) 733-2599
E: Dan.Blue@ncleg.net

### Secretary of the Senate

**Ms. Sarah Lang**
Principal Clerk of the Senate
2020 Legislative Building
16 West Jones Street
Raleigh, NC 27601
P: (919) 733-7761
E: sarahc@ncleg.net

### Members of the Senate

**Alexander Jr., John McKnitt (R, 15)**
625 Legislative Office Building
300 North Salisbury Street
Raleigh, NC 27603
P: (919) 733-5850
F: (919) 733-2599
E: John.Alexander@ncleg.net

**Ballard, Deanna (R, 45)**
521 Legislative Office Building
300 North Salisbury Street
Raleigh, NC 27603
P: (919) 733-5742
E: deanna.ballard@ncleg.net

**Barefoot, Chad (R, 18)**
406 Legislative Office Building
300 North Salisbury Street
Raleigh, NC 27603
P: (919) 715-3036
F: (919) 733-3113
E: Chad.Barefoot@ncleg.net

**Barringer, Tamara (R, 17)**
629 Legislative Office Building
300 North Salisbury Street
Raleigh, NC 27603
P: (919) 733-5653
F: (919) 733-3113
E: Tamara.Barringer @ncleg.net

**Berger, Phil (R, 26)**
2007 Legislative Building
16 West Jones Street
Raleigh, NC 27601
P: (919) 733-5708
F: (919) 733-2599
E: Phil.Berger@ncleg.net

**Bishop, Dan (R, 39)**
2108 Legislative Building
16 West Jones Street
Raleigh, NC 27601
P: (919) 715-3009
F: (919) 733-3113
E: Dan.Bishop@ncleg.net

**Blue Jr., Dan (D, 14)**
1129 Legislative Building
16 West Jones Street
Raleigh, NC 27601
P: (919) 733-5752
F: (919) 733-2599
E: Dan.Blue@ncleg.net

**Britt, Danny Earl (R, 13)\***
2117 Legislative Building
16 West Jones Street
Raleigh, NC 27601
P: (919) 733-5651
E: danny.britt@ncleg.net

**Brock, Andrew C. (R, 34)**
310 Legislative Office Building
300 North Salisbury Street
Raleigh, NC 27603
P: (919) 715-0690
F: (919) 733-3113
E: Andrew.Brock@ncleg.net

**Brown, Harry (R, 6)**
300-B Legislative Office
Building
300 North Salisbury Street
Raleigh, NC 27603
P: (919) 715-3034
F: (919) 733-3113
E: Harry.Brown@ncleg.net

**Bryant, Angela R. (D, 4)**
516 Legislative Office Building
300 North Salisbury Street
Raleigh, NC 27603
P: (919) 733-5878
F: (919) 733-3113
E: Angela.Bryant@ncleg.net

**Chaudhuri, Jay (D, 16)**
1121 Legislative Building
16 West Jones Street
Raleigh, NC 27601
P: 919) 715-6400
E: Jay.Chaudhuri@ncleg.net

**Clark, Ben (D, 21)**
1117 Legislative Building
16 West Jones Street
Raleigh, NC 27601
P: (919) 733-9349
F: (919) 733-2599
E: Ben.Clark@ncleg.net

**Cook, Bill (R, 1)**
1026 Legislative Building
16 West Jones Street
Raleigh, NC 27601
P: (919) 715-8293
F: (919) 733-3113
E: Bill.Cook@ncleg.net

**Curtis, David L. (R, 44)**
410 Legislative Office Building
300 North Salisbury Street
Raleigh, NC 27603
P: (919) 715-3038
F: (919) 733-3113
E: David.Curtis@ncleg.net

**Daniel, Warren (R, 46)**
627  Legislative Office Building
300 North Salisbury Street
Raleigh, NC 27603
P: (919) 715-7823
F: (919) 733-3113
E: Warren.Daniel@ncleg.net

**Davis, Donald (D, 5)**
519 Legislative Office Building
300 North Salisbury Street
Raleigh, NC 27603
P: (919) 715-8363
F: (919) 733-3113
E: Don.Davis@ncleg.net

**Davis, Jim (R, 50)**
621 Legislative Office Building
300 North Salisbury Street
Raleigh, NC 27603
P: (919) 733-5875
F: (919) 733-3113
E: Jim.Davis@ncleg.net

**Dunn, Cathy (R, 33)\***
2113 Legislative Building
16 West Jones Street
Raleigh, NC 27601
P: (919) 733-5665
E: cathy.dunn@ncleg.net

**Edwards, Chuck (R, 48)\***
2115 Legislative Building
16 West Jones Street
Raleigh, NC 27601
P: (919) 733-5745
E: chuck.edwards@ncleg.net

**Ford, Joel D.M. (D, 38)**
520 Legislative Office Building
300 North Salisbury Street
Raleigh, NC 27603
P: (919) 733-5955
F: (919) 733-2599
E: Joel.Ford@ncleg.net

**Foushee, Valerie P. (D, 23)**
517 Legislative Office Building
300 North Salisbury Street
Raleigh, NC 27603
P: (919) 733-5804
F: (919) 733-3113
E: Valerie.Foushee
@ncleg.net

**Gunn, Rick (R, 24)**
523 Legislative Office Building
300 North Salisbury Street
Raleigh, NC 27603
P: (919) 301-1446
F: (919) 733-3113
E: Rick.Gunn@ncleg.net

**Harrington, Kathy (R, 43)**
300-C Legislative Office
Building
300 North Salisbury Street
Raleigh, NC 27603
P: (919) 733-5734
F: (919) 733-3113
E: Kathy.Harrington
@ncleg.net

**Hise, Ralph (R, 47)**
312 Legislative Office Building
300 North Salisbury Street
Raleigh, NC 27603
P: (919) 733-3460
F: (919) 733-2599
E: Ralph.Hise@ncleg.net

**Horner, Rick (R, 11)\***
2106 Legislative Building
16 West Jones Street
Raleigh, NC 27603
P: (919) 715-3030
E: rick.horner@ncleg.net

**Jackson, Brent (R, 10)**
2022 Legislative Building
16 West Jones Street
Raleigh, NC 27601
P: (919) 733-5705
F: (919) 733-2599
E: Brent.Jackson@ncleg.net

**Jackson, Jeff (D, 37)**
1104 Legislative Building
16 West Jones Street
Raleigh, NC 27601
P: (919) 715-8331
F: (919) 733-2599
E: Jeff.Jackson@ncleg.net

**Krawiec, Joyce (R, 31)**
308 Legislative Office Building
300 North Salisbury Street
Raleigh, NC 27603
P: (919) 733-7850
F: (919) 733-2599
E: Joyce.Krawiec@ncleg.net

**Lee, Michael V. (R, 9)**
408 Legislative Office Building
300 North Salisbury Street
Raleigh, NC 27603
P: (919) 715-2525
F: (919) 733-2599
E: Michael.Lee@ncleg.net

**Lowe Jr., Paul A. (D, 32)**
1119 Legislative Building
16 West Jones Street
Raleigh, NC 27601
P: (919) 733-5620
F: (919) 733-2599
E: Paul.Lowe@ncleg.net

**McInnis, Thomas Moses
(R, 25)**
620 Legislative Office Building
300 North Salisbury Street
Raleigh, NC 27603
P: (919) 733-5953
F: (919) 733-2599
E: Tom.McInnis@ncleg.net

**McKissick Jr., Floyd B.
(D, 20)**
515 Legislative Office Building
300 North Salisbury Street
Raleigh, NC 27603
P: (919) 733-4599
F: (919) 733-3113
E: Floyd.McKissick
@ncleg.net

**Meredith, Wesley (R, 19)**
314 Legislative Office Building
300 North Salisbury Street
Raleigh, NC 27603
P: (919) 733-5776
F: (919) 733-3113
E: Wesley.Meredith
@ncleg.net

**Newton, Paul (R, 36)\***
2111 Legislative Building
16 West Jones Street
Raleigh, NC 27601
P: (919) 733-7223
E: paul.newton@ncleg.net

**Pate Jr., Louis M. (R, 7)**
311 Legislative Office Building
300 North Salisbury Street
Raleigh, NC 27603
P: (919) 733-5621
F: (919) 733-2599
E: Louis.Pate@ncleg.net

**Rabin, Ronald J. (R, 12)**
411 Legislative Office Building
300 North Salisbury Street
Raleigh, NC 27603
P: (919) 733-5748
F: (919) 733-3113
E: Ron.Rabin@ncleg.net

# North Carolina

**Rabon, Bill (R, 8)**
2010 Legislative Building
16 West Jones Street
Raleigh, NC 27301
P: (919) 733-5963
F: (919) 733-3113
E: Bill.Rabon@ncleg.net

**Randleman, Shirley B.
(R, 30)**
628 Legislative Office Building
300 North Salisbury Street
Raleigh, NC 27603
P: (919) 733-5743
F: (919) 733-3113
E: Shirley.Randleman
@ncleg.net

**Robinson, Gladys A. (D, 28)**
1120 Legislative Building
16 West Jones Street
Raleigh, NC 27601
P: (919) 715-3042
F: (919) 733-2599
E: Gladys.Robinson
@ncleg.net

**Sanderson, Norman W. (R, 2)**
1127 Legislative Building
16 West Jones Street
Raleigh, NC 27601
P: (919) 733-5706
F: (919) 733-3113
E: Norman.Sanderson
@ncleg.net

**Smith-Ingram,
Erica Danette (D, 3)**
1118 Legislative Building
16 West Jones Street
Raleigh, NC 27601
P: (919) 715-3040
F: (919) 733-2599
E: Erica.Smith-Ingram
@ncleg.net

**Tarte, Jeff (R, 41)**
623 Legislative Office Building
300 North Salisbury Street
Raleigh, NC 27603
P: (919) 715-3050
F: (919) 733-2599
E: Jeff.Tarte@ncleg.net

**Tillman, Jerry W. (R, 29)**
309 Legislative Office Building
300 North Salisbury Street
Raleigh, NC 27603
P: (919) 733-5870
F: (919) 733-3113
E: Jerry.Tillman@ncleg.net

**Tucker, Tommy (R, 35)**
300-A Legislative Office
Building
300 North Salisbury Street
Raleigh, NC 27603
P: (919) 733-7659
F: (919) 733-2599
E: Tommy.Tucker@ncleg.net

**Van Duyn, Terry (D, 49)**
1025 Legislative Building
16 West Jones Street
Raleigh, NC 27601
P: (919) 715-3001
F: (919) 733-2599
E: Terry.VanDuyn@ncleg.net

**Waddell, Joyce D. (D, 40)**
1113 Legislative Building
16 West Jones Street
Raleigh, NC 27601
P: (919) 733-5650
F: (919) 733-3113
E: Joyce.Waddell@ncleg.net

**Wade, Trudy (R, 27)**
525 Legislative Office Building
300 North Salisbury Street
Raleigh, NC 27603
P: (919) 733-5856
F: (919) 733-3113
E: Trudy.Wade@ncleg.net

**Wells Jr., Andy (R, 42)**
1028 Legislative Building
16 West Jones Street
Raleigh, NC 27601
P: (919) 733-5876
F: (919) 733-2599
E: Andy.Wells@ncleg.net

**Woodard, Mike (D, 22)**
518 Legislative Office Building
300 North Salisbury Street
Raleigh, NC 27603
P: (919) 733-4809
F: (919) 733-3113
E: Mike.Woodard@ncleg.net

# House

## Speaker of the House

**Representative Tim
Moore (R)**
Speaker of the House
2304 Legislative Building
16 West Jones Street
Raleigh, NC 27601
P: (919) 733-3451
F: (919) 733-2599
E: Tim.Moore@ncleg.net

## Speaker Pro Tempore of the House

**Representative Sarah
Stevens (R)**
Speaker Pro Tempore
419 Legislative Office Building
300 North Salisbury Street
Raleigh, NC 27603
P: (919) 715-1883
F: (919) 733-3113
E: Sarah.Stevens@ncleg.net

## House Majority Leader

**Representative John R.
Bell IV (R)**
Majority Leader
301F Legislative Office
Building
300 North Salisbury Street
Raleigh, NC 27603
P: (919) 715-3017
F: (919) 733-3113
E: John.Bell@ncleg.net

## House Minority Leader

**Representative Darren G.
Jackson (D)**
Democratic Leader
506 Legislative Office Building
300 North Salisbury Street
Raleigh, NC 27603
P: (919) 733-5974
F: (919) 733-2599
E: Darren.Jackson@ncleg.net

## Clerk of the House

**Mr. James White**
Principal Clerk of the House
2319 Legislative Building
16 West Jones Street
Raleigh, NC 27601
P: (919) 733-7760
F: (919) 733-2599
E: jamesw@ncleg.net

## Members of the House

**Adams Jr., James Cecil
(R, 96)**
2223 Legislative Building
16 West Jones Street
Raleigh, NC 27601
P: (919) 733-5988
F: (919) 733-2599
E: Jay.Adams@ncleg.net

**Adcock, Gale B. (D, 41)**
1211 Legislative Building
16 West Jones Street
Raleigh, NC 27601
P: (919) 733-5602
F: (919) 733-2599
E: Gale.Adcock@ncleg.net

**Ager Jr., John Curtis
(D, 115)**
1315 Legislative Building
16 West Jones Street
Raleigh, NC 27601
P: (919) 733-5746
F: (919) 733-2599
E: John.Ager@ncleg.net

**Alexander Jr., Kelly M.
(D, 107)**
404 Legislative Office Building
300 North Salisbury Street
Raleigh, NC 27603
P: (919) 733-5778
F: (919) 733-3113
E: Kelly.Alexander
@ncleg.net

**Arp, Dean (R, 69)**
529 Legislative Office Building
300 North Salisbury Street
Raleigh, NC 27603
P: (919) 715-3007
F: (919) 733-3113
E: Dean.Arp@ncleg.net

**Autry, John (D, 100)\***
1019 Legislative Building
16 West Jones Street
Raleigh, NC 27601
P: (919) 715-0706
E: john.autry@ncleg.net

**Ball, Cynthia (D, 47)\***
1319 Legislative Building
16 West Jones Street
Raleigh, NC 27601
P: (919) 733-5860
E: cynthia.ball@ncleg.net

**Beasley, Chaz (D, 92)\***
403 Legislative Office Building
300 North Salisbury Street
Raleigh, NC 27603
P: (919) 733-5654
E: chaz.beasley@ncleg.net

**Belk, Mary (D, 88)\***
1313 Legislative Building
16 West Jones Street
Raleigh, NC 27601
P: (919) 733-5607
E: mary.belk@ncleg.net

**Bell IV, John R. (R, 10)**
301F Legislative Office
Building
300 North Salisbury Street
Raleigh, NC 27603
P: (919) 715-3017
F: (919) 733-3113
E: John.Bell@ncleg.net

**Bell, Larry M. (D, 21)**
510 Legislative Office Building
300 North Salisbury Street
Raleigh, NC 27603
P: (919) 733-5863
F: (919) 733-3113
E: Larry.Bell@ncleg.net

**Blackwell, Hugh (R, 86)**
541 Legislative Office Building
300 North Salisbury Street
Raleigh, NC 27603
P: (919) 733-5805
F: (919) 733-3113
E: Hugh.Blackwell@ncleg.net

**Blust, John M. (R, 62)**
2208 Legislative Building
16 West Jones Street
Raleigh, NC 27601
P: (919) 733-5781
F: (919) 733-2599
E: John.Blust@ncleg.net

**Boles Jr., James L. (R, 52)**
528 Legislative Office Building
300 North Salisbury Street
Raleigh, NC 27603
P: (919) 733-5903
F: (919) 733-3113
E: Jamie.Boles@ncleg.net

**Boswell, Beverly (R, 6)***
531 Legislative Office Building
300 North Salisbury Street
Raleigh, NC 27603
P: (919) 733-5906
E: beverly.boswell
    @ncleg.net

**Bradford III, John Ray
    (R, 98)**
2123 Legislative Building
16 West Jones Street
Raleigh, NC 27601
P: (919) 733-5825
F: (919) 733-2599
E: John.Bradford@ncleg.net

**Brawley, William (R, 103)**
534 Legislative Office Building
300 North Salisbury Street
Raleigh, NC 27603
P: (919) 733-5800
F: (919) 733-3113
E: Bill.Brawley@ncleg.net

**Brisson, William (D, 22)**
405 Legislative Office Building
300 North Salisbury Street
Raleigh, NC 27603
P: (919) 733-5772
F: (919) 733-3113
E: William.Brisson
    @ncleg.net

**Brockman, Cecil Antonio
    (D, 60)**
1311 Legislative Building
16 West Jones Street
Raleigh, NC 27601
P: (919) 733-5825
F: (919) 733-2599
E: Cecil.Brockman@ncleg.net

**Brody, Mark (R, 55)**
2219 Legislative Building
16 West Jones Street
Raleigh, NC 27601
P: (919) 715-3029
F: (919) 733-2599
E: Mark.Brody@ncleg.net

**Bumgardner, Dana (R, 109)**
2119 Legislative Building
16 West Jones Street
Raleigh, NC 27601
P: (919) 733-5809
F: (919) 733-2599
E: Dana.Bumgardner
    @ncleg.net

**Burr, Justin P. (R, 67)**
307A Legislative Office
Building
300 North Salisbury Street
Raleigh, NC 27603
P: (919) 733-5908
F: (919) 733-3113
E: Justin.Burr@ncleg.net

**Carney, Becky (D, 102)**
1221 Legislative Building
16 West Jones Street
Raleigh, NC 27601
P: (919) 733-5827
F: (919) 733-2599
E: Becky.Carney@ncleg.net

**Clampitt, Mike (R, 119)***
1420 Legislative Building
16 West Jones Street
Raleigh, NC 27601
P: (919) 715-3005
E: mike.clampitt@ncleg.net

**Cleveland, George G.
    (R, 14)**
417A Legislative Office
Building
300 North Salisbury Street
Raleigh, NC 27603
P: (919) 715-6707
F: (919) 733-3113
E: George.Cleveland
    @ncleg.net

**Collins, Jeff (R, 25)**
1106 Legislative Building
16 West Jones Street
Raleigh, NC 27601
P: (919) 733-5802
F: (919) 733-2599
E: Jeff.Collins@ncleg.net

**Conrad, Debra (R, 74)**
416B Legislative Office
Building
300 North Salisbury Street
Raleigh, NC 27603
P: (919) 733-5787
F: (919) 733-3113
E: Debra.Conrad@ncleg.net

**Corbin, Kevin (R, 120)***
2215 Legislative Building
16 West Jones Street
Raleigh, NC 27601
P: (919) 733-5859
E: kevin.corbin@ncleg.net

**Cunningham, Carla D.
    (D, 106)**
1109 Legislative Building
16 West Jones Street
Raleigh, NC 27601
P: (919) 733-5807
F: (919) 733-2599
E: Carla.Cunningham
    @ncleg.net

**Davis Jr., Ted (R, 19)**
417B Legislative Office
Building
300 North Salisbury Street
Raleigh, NC 27603
P: (919) 733-5786
F: (919) 733-3113
E: Ted.Davis@ncleg.net

**Dixon, Jimmy (R, 4)**
2226 Legislative Building
16 West Jones Street
Raleigh, NC 27601
P: (919) 715-3021
F: (919) 733-3113
E: Jimmy.Dixon@ncleg.net

**Dobson, Josh (R, 85)**
301N Legislative Office
Building
300 North Salisbury Street
Raleigh, NC 27603
P: (919) 733-5862
F: (919) 733-3113
E: Josh.Dobson@ncleg.net

**Dollar, Nelson (R, 36)**
307B Legislative Office
Building
300 North Salisbury Street
Raleigh, NC 27603
P: (919) 715-0795
F: (919) 733-3113
E: Nelson.Dollar@ncleg.net

**Dulin, Andy (R, 104)***
609 Legislative Office Building
300 North Salisbury Street
Raleigh, NC 27603
P: (919) 715-3009
E: andy.dulin@ncleg.net

**Earle, Beverly M. (D, 101)**
514 Legislative Office Building
300 North Salisbury Street
Raleigh, NC 27603
P: (919) 715-2530
F: (919) 733-3113
E: Beverly.Earle@ncleg.net

**Elmore, Jeffrey (R, 94)**
306A3 Legislative Office
Building
300 North Salisbury Street
Raleigh, NC 27603
P: (919) 733-5935
F: (919) 733-3113
E: Jeffrey.Elmore@ncleg.net

**Faircloth, John (R, 61)**
613 Legislative Office Building
300 North Salisbury Street
Raleigh, NC 27603
P: (919) 733-5877
F: (919) 733-3113
E: John.Faircloth@ncleg.net

**Farmer-Butterfield, Jean
    (D, 24)**
1220 Legislative Building
16 West Jones Street
Raleigh, NC 27601
P: (919) 733-5898
F: (919) 733-2599
E: Jean.Farmer-Butterfield
    @ncleg.net

**Fisher, Susan C. (D, 114)**
504 Legislative Office Building
300 North Salisbury Street
Raleigh, NC 27603
P: (919) 715-2013
F: (919) 733-3113
E: Susan.Fisher@ncleg.net

# North Carolina

**Floyd, Elmer (D, 43)**
1325 Legislative Building
16 West Jones Street
Raleigh, NC 27601
P: (919) 733-5959
F: (919) 733-2599
E: Elmer.Floyd@ncleg.net

**Ford, Carl (R, 76)**
608 Legislative Office Building
300 North Salisbury Street
Raleigh, NC 27603
P: (919) 733-5881
F: (919) 733-3113
E: Carl.Ford@ncleg.net

**Fraley, John A. (R, 95)**
637 Legislative Office Building
300 North Salisbury Street
Raleigh, NC 27603
P: (919) 733-5741
F: (919) 733-3113
E: John.Fraley@ncleg.net

**Garrison, Terry (D, 32)***
1017 Legislative Building
16 West Jones Street
Raleigh, NC 27601
P: (919) 733-5824
E: terry.garrison@ncleg.net

**Gill, Rosa U. (D, 33)**
1303 Legislative Building
16 West Jones Street
Raleigh, NC 27601
P: (919) 733-5880
F: (919) 733-2599
E: Rosa.Gill@ncleg.net

**Goodman, Ken (D, 66)**
542 Legislative Office Building
300 North Salisbury Street
Raleigh, NC 27603
P: (919) 733-5823
F: (919) 733-3113
E: Ken.Goodman@ncleg.net

**Graham, Charles (D, 47)**
1309 Legislative Building
16 West Jones Street
Raleigh, NC 27601
P: (919) 715-0875
F: (919) 733-2599
E: Charles.Graham@ncleg.net

**Graham, George (D, 12)**
1321 Legislative Building
16 West Jones Street
Raleigh, NC 27601
P: (919) 733-5995
F: (919) 733-2599
E: George.Graham@ncleg.net

**Grange, Holly (R, 20)**
604 Legislative Office Building
300 North Salisbury Street
Raleigh, NC 27603
P: (919) 733-5830
E: Holly.Grange@ncleg.net

**Hall, Destin (R, 87)***
306C Legislative Office
Building
300 North Salisbury Street
Raleigh, NC 27603
P: (919) 733-5931
E: destin.hall@ncleg.net

**Hall, Duane (D, 11)**
1004 Legislative Building
16 West Jones Street
Raleigh, NC 27601
P: (919) 733-5755
F: (919) 733-2599
E: Duane.Hall@ncleg.net

**Hall, Kyle (R, 91)**
536 Legislative Office Building
300 North Salisbury Street
Raleigh, NC 27603
P: (919) 733-5609
E: Kyle.Hall@ncleg.net

**Hanes Jr., Edward (D, 72)**
1006 Legislative Building
16 West Jones Street
Raleigh, NC 27601
P: (919) 733-5829
F: (919) 733-2599
E: Edward.Hanes@ncleg.net

**Hardister, Jon (R, 59)**
638 Legislative Office Building
300 North Salisbury Street
Raleigh, NC 27603
P: (919) 733-5191
F: (919) 733-3113
E: Jon.Hardister@ncleg.net

**Harrison, Pricey (D, 57)**
1218 Legislative Building
16 West Jones Street
Raleigh, NC 27601
P: (919) 733-5771
F: (919) 733-2599
E: Pricey.Harrison
@ncleg.net

**Hastings, Kelly E. (R, 110)**
1206 Legislative Building
16 West Jones Street
Raleigh, NC 27601
P: (919) 715-2002
F: (919) 733-2599
E: Kelly.Hastings@ncleg.net

**Henson, Cody (R, 113)***
537 Legislative Office Building
300 North Salisbury Street
Raleigh, NC 27603
P: (919) 715-4466
E: cody.henson@ncleg.net

**Holley, Yvonne Lewis
(D, 38)**
1219 Legislative Building
16 West Jones Street
Raleigh, NC 27601
P: (919) 733-5758
F: (919) 733-2599
E: Yvonne.Holley@ncleg.net

**Horn, D. Craig (R, 68)**
305 Legislative Office Building
300 North Salisbury Street
Raleigh, NC 27603
P: (919) 733-2406
F: (919) 733-3113
E: Craig.Horn@ncleg.net

**Howard, Julia C. (R, 79)**
302 Legislative Office Building
300 North Salisbury Street
Raleigh, NC 27603
P: (919) 733-5904
F: (919) 733-3113
E: Julia.Howard@ncleg.net

**Hunter III, Howard Jacque
(D, 5)**
1307 Legislative Building
16 West Jones Street
Raleigh, NC 27601
P: (919) 733-5780
F: (919) 733-2599
E: Howard.Hunter@ncleg.net

**Hurley, Pat B. (R, 70)**
532 Legislative Office Building
300 North Salisbury Street
Raleigh, NC 27603
P: (919) 733-5865
F: (919) 733-3113
E: Pat.Hurley@ncleg.net

**Iler, Frank (R, 17)**
639 Legislative Office Building
300 North Salisbury Street
Raleigh, NC 27603
P: (919) 301-1450
F: (919) 733-3113
E: Frank.Iler@ncleg.net

**Insko, Verla (D, 56)**
502 Legislative Office Building
300 North Salisbury Street
Raleigh, NC 27603
P: (919) 733-7208
F: (919) 733-3113
E: Verla.Insko@ncleg.net

**Jackson, Darren G. (D, 39)**
506 Legislative Office Building
300 North Salisbury Street
Raleigh, NC 27603
P: (919) 733-5974
F: (919) 733-2599
E: Darren.Jackson@ncleg.net

**John, Joe (D, 40)***
1013 Legislative Building
16 West Jones Street
Raleigh, NC 27601
P: (919) 733-5530
E: joe.john@ncleg.net

**Johnson, Linda P. (R, 83)**
301-D Legislative Office
Building
300 North Salisbury Street
Raleigh, NC 27603
P: (919) 733-5861
F: (919) 733-3113
E: Linda.Johnson2@ncleg.net

**Jones, Bert (R, 65)**
416-A Legislative Office
Building
300 North Salisbury Street
Raleigh, NC 27603
P: (919) 733-5779
F: (919) 733-3113
E: Bert.Jones@ncleg.net

**Jones, Brenden (R, 46)***
2217 Legislative Building
16 West Jones Street
Raleigh, NC 27601
P: (919) 733-5821
E: brenden.jones@ncleg.net

**Jordan, Jonathan C. (R, 93)**
420 Legislative Office Building
300 North Salisbury Street
Raleigh, NC 27603
P: (919) 733-7727
F: (919) 733-3113
E: Jonathan.Jordan
@ncleg.net

**Lambeth, Donny (R, 75)**
303 Legislative Office Building
300 North Salisbury Street
Raleigh, NC 27603
P: (919) 733-5747
F: (919) 733-3113
E: Donny.Lambeth@ncleg.net

**Lehman, Philip (D, 30)***
1111 Legislative Building
16 West Jones Street
Raleigh, NC 27601
P: 919733-7663
E: Philip.Lehman@ncleg.net

**Lewis, David R. (R, 53)**
2301 Legislative Building
16 West Jones Street
Raleigh, NC 27601
P: (919) 715-3015
F: (919) 733-2599
E: David.Lewis@ncleg.net

**Lucas, Marvin W. (D, 42)**
509 Legislative Office Building
300 North Salisbury Street
Raleigh, NC 27603
P: (919) 733-5775
F: (919) 733-3113
E: Marvin.Lucas@ncleg.net

**Malone, Chris (R, 35)**
1229 Legislative Building
16 West Jones Street
Raleigh, NC 27601
P: (919) 715-3010
F: (919) 733-3113
E: Chris.Malone@ncleg.net

**Martin, Grier (D, 34)**
1023 Legislative Building
16 West Jones Street
Raleigh, NC 27601
P: (919) 733-5773
F: (919) 733-2599
E: Grier.Martin@ncleg.net

**Martin, Susan (R, 8)**
526 Legislative Office Building
300 North Salisbury Street
Raleigh, NC 27603
P: (919) 715-3023
F: (919) 733-3113
E: Susan.Martin@ncleg.net

**McElraft, Pat (R, 13)**
634 Legislative Office Building
300 North Salisbury Street
Raleigh, NC 27603
P: (919) 733-6275
F: (919) 733-3113
E: Pat.McElraft@ncleg.net

**McGrady, Chuck (R, 117)**
304 Legislative Office Building
300 North Salisbury Street
Raleigh, NC 27603
P: (919) 733-5956
F: (919) 733-3113
E: Chuck.McGrady@ncleg.net

**McNeill, Allen (R, 78)**
418D Legislative Office
Building
300 North Salisbury Street
Raleigh, NC 27603
P: (919) 715-4946
F: (919) 733-3113
E: Allen.McNeill@ncleg.net

**Meyer, Graig R. (D, 50)**
1426 Legislative Building
16 West Jones Street
Raleigh, NC 27601
P: (919) 715-3019
F: (919) 733-2599
E: Graig.Meyer@ncleg.net

**Michaux Jr., Henry M. (D, 31)**
1227 Legislative Building
16 West Jones Street
Raleigh, NC 27601
P: (919) 715-2528
F: (919) 733-2599
E: Mickey.Michaux@ncleg.net

**Millis, Chris (R, 16)**
633 Legislative Office Building
300 North Salisbury Street
Raleigh, NC 27603
P: (919) 715-9664
F: (919) 733-3113
E: Chris.Millis@ncleg.net

**Moore, Rodney W. (D, 99)**
402 Legislative Office Building
300 North Salisbury Street
Raleigh, NC 27603
P: (919) 733-5606
F: (919) 733-2599
E: Rodney.Moore@ncleg.net

**Moore, Tim (R, 111)**
2304 Legislative Building
16 West Jones Street
Raleigh, NC 27601
P: (919) 733-3451
F: (919) 733-2599
E: Tim.Moore@ncleg.net

**Murphy, Gregory F. (R, 9)**
632 Legislative Office Building
300 North Salisbury Street
Raleigh, NC 27603
P: (919) 733-5757
E: Gregory.Murphy@ncleg.net

**Pierce, Garland E. (D, 48)**
1204 Legislative Building
16 West Jones Street
Raleigh, NC 27601
P: (919) 733-5803
F: (919) 733-2599
E: Garland.Pierce@ncleg.net

**Pittman, Larry G. (R, 82)**
1010 Legislative Building
16 West Jones Street
Raleigh, NC 27601
P: (919) 715-2009
F: (919) 733-2599
E: Larry.Pittman@ncleg.net

**Potts, Larry (R, 81)***
607 Legislative Office Building
300 North Salisbury Street
Raleigh, NC 27603
P: (919) 715-0873
E: larry.potts@ncleg.net

**Presnell, Michele D. (R, 118)**
418A Legislative Office
Building
300 North Salisbury Street
Raleigh, NC 27603
P: (919) 733-5732
F: (919) 733-3113
E: Michele.Presnell
@ncleg.net

**Quick, Amos (D, 58)***
1317 Legislative Building
16 West Jones Street
Raleigh, NC 27601
P: (919) 733-5902
E: amos.quick@ncleg.net

**Reives II, Robert T. (D, 54)**
1323 Legislative Building
16 West Jones Street
Raleigh, NC 27601
P: (919) 733-0057
F: (919) 733-2599
E: Robert.Reives@ncleg.net

**Richardson, Bobbie (D, 7)**
1217 Legislative Building
16 West Jones Street
Raleigh, NC 27601
P: (919) 715-3032
F: (919) 733-2599
E: Bobbie.Richardson
@ncleg.net

**Richardson, William O. (D, 44)**
1021 Legislative Building
16 West Jones Street
Raleigh, NC 27601
P: (919) 733-5601
E: William.Richardson
@ncleg.net

**Riddell, Dennis (R, 64)**
533 Legislative Office Building
300 North Salisbury Street
Raleigh, NC 27603
P: (919) 733-5905
F: (919) 733-3113
E: Dennis.Riddell@ncleg.net

**Rogers, David (R, 112)**
418C Legislative Office
Building
300 North Salisbury Street
Raleigh, NC 27603
P: (919) 733-5749
E: David.Rogers@ncleg.net

**Ross, Stephen M. (R, 63)**
635 Legislative Office Building
300 North Salisbury Street
Raleigh, NC 27603
P: (919) 733-5820
F: (919) 733-2599
E: Stephen.Ross@ncleg.net

**Saine, Jason (R, 97)**
1326 Legislative Building
16 West Jones Street
Raleigh, NC 27601
P: (919) 733-5782
F: (919) 733-2599
E: Jason.Saine@ncleg.net

**Sauls, John (R, 51)**
610 Legislative Office Building
16 West Jones Street
Raleigh, NC 27603
P: (919) 715-3026
E: john.sauls@ncleg.net

**Setzer, Mitchell S. (R, 89)**
2204 Legislative Building
16 West Jones Street
Raleigh, NC 27601
P: (919) 733-4948
F: (919) 733-2599
E: Mitchell.Setzer
@ncleg.net

**Shepard, Phil R. (R, 15)**
530 Legislative Office Building
300 North Salisbury Street
Raleigh, NC 27603
P: (919) 715-9644
F: (919) 733-3113
E: Phil.Shepard@ncleg.net

**Speciale, Michael (R, 3)**
1008 Legislative Building
16 West Jones Street
Raleigh, NC 27601
P: (919) 733-5853
F: (919) 733-2599
E: Michael.Speciale
@ncleg.net

**Steinburg, Bob (R, 1)**
301B Legislative Office
Building
300 North Salisbury Street
Raleigh, NC 27603
P: (919) 733-0010
F: (919) 733-3113
E: Bob.Steinburg@ncleg.net

**Stevens, Sarah (R, 90)**
419 Legislative Office Building
300 North Salisbury Street
Raleigh, NC 27603
P: (919) 715-1883
F: (919) 733-3113
E: Sarah.Stevens@ncleg.net

# North Carolina

**Stone, Scott (R, 105)**
2213 Legislative Building
16 West Jones Street
Raleigh, NC 27601
P: (919) 733-5886
E: scott.stone@ncleg.net

**Strickland, Larry (R)***
602 Legislative Office Building
300 North Salisbury Street
Raleigh, NC 27603
P: (919) 733-5849
E: larry.strickland
    @ncleg.net

**Szoka, John (R, 45)**
2207 Legislative Building
16 West Jones Street
Raleigh, NC 27601
P: (919) 733-9892
F: (919) 733-2599
E: John.Szoka@ncleg.net

**Terry, Evelyn (D, 71)**
1015 Legislative Building
16 West Jones Street
Raleigh, NC 27601
P: (919) 733-5777
F: (919) 733-2599
E: Evelyn.Terry@ncleg.net

**Torbett, John A. (R, 108)**
538 Legislative Office Building
300 North Salisbury Street
Raleigh, NC 27603
P: (919) 733-5868
F: (919) 733-3113
E: John.Torbett@ncleg.net

**Turner, Brian Mills
    (D, 116)**
1209 Legislative Building
16 West Jones Street
Raleigh, NC 27601
P: (919) 715-3012
F: (919) 733-2599
E: Brian.Turner@ncleg.net

**Turner, Rena W. (R, 84)**
606 Legislative Office Building
300 North Salisbury Street
Raleigh, NC 27603
P: (919) 733-5661
F: (919) 733-3113
E: Rena.Turner@ncleg.net

**Warren, Harry (R, 77)**
611 Legislative Office Building
300 North Salisbury Street
Raleigh, NC 27603
P: (919) 733-5784
F: (919) 733-3113
E: Harry.Warren@ncleg.net

**Watford, Samuel Lee (R, 80)**
2121 Legislative Building
16 West Jones Street
Raleigh, NC 27601
P: (919) 715-2526
F: (919) 733-2599
E: Sam.Watford@ncleg.net

**White, Donna McDowell (R)***
306A2 Legislative Office
Building
300 North Salisbury Street
Raleigh, NC 27603
P: (919) 733-5605
E: donna.white@ncleg.net

**Williams, Linda Hunt
    (R, 37)***
603 Legislative Office Building
300 North Salisbury Street
Raleigh, NC 27601
P: (919) 733-2962
E: linda.williams@ncleg.net

**Willingham, Shelly (D, 23)**
513 Legislative Office Building
300 North Salisbury Street
Raleigh, NC 27603
P: (919) 715-3024
F: (919) 733-3113
E: Shelly.Willingham
    @ncleg.net

**Wray, Michael H. (D, 27)**
503 Legislative Office Building
300 North Salisbury Street
Raleigh, NC 27603
P: (919) 733-5662
F: (919) 733-3113
E: Michael.Wray@ncleg.net

**Yarborough, Lawrence (R, 2)**
1301 Legislative Building
16 West Jones Street
Raleigh, NC 27601
P: (919) 715-0850
F: (919) 733-2599
E: Larry.Yarborough
    @ncleg.net

**Zachary Jr., Walter Lee
    (R, 73)**
1002 Legislative Building
16 West Jones Street
Raleigh, NC 27601
P: (919) 715-8361
F: (919) 733-2599
E: Lee.Zachary@ncleg.net

# North Dakota

## Executive

### Governor

**The Honorable Doug Burgum (R)**
Governor
600 East Boulevard Avenue
Bismarck, ND 58505
P: (701) 328-2200
F: (701) 328-2205

### Lieutenant Governor

**The Honorable Brent Sanford (R)**
Lieutenant Governor
State Capitol
Bismarck, ND 58505
P: (701) 328-2200
F: (701) 328-2205

### Commissioner of Agriculture

**Mr. Doug Goehring (R)**
Commissioner
600 East Boulevard Avenue
Department 602
Bismarck, ND 58505
P: (701) 328-2231
F: (701) 328-4567
E: ndda@nd.gov

### Attorney General

**The Honorable Wayne Stenehjem (R)**
Attorney General
State Capitol
600 East Boulevard Avenue
Bismarck, ND 58505
P: (701) 328-2210
F: (701) 328-2226
E: wstenehjem@nd.gov

### Auditor

**The Honorable Josh Gallion (R)**
State Auditor
600 East Boulevard, 3rd Floor
Bismarck, ND 58505
P: (701) 328-2241
E: jgallion@nd.gov

### Commissioner of Insurance

**The Honorable John Godfread (R)**
Commissioner
State Capitol, 5th Floor
600 East Boulevard Avenue
Bismarck, ND 58505
P: (701) 328-2440
F: (701) 328-4880

### Public Service Commission

**The Honorable Randy Christmann (R)**
Commissioner
600 East Boulevard Avenue
Department 408
Bismarck, ND 58505
P: (701) 328-2400
F: (701) 328-2410
E: rchristmann@nd.gov

**Ms. Julie Fedorchak (R)**
Commissioner
600 East Boulevard Avenue
Department 408
Bismarck, ND 58505
P: (701) 328-2400
F: (701) 328-2410
E: jfedorchak@nd.gov

**The Honorable Brian Kalk (R)**
Chair
600 East Boulevard Avenue
Department 408
Bismarck, ND 58505
P: (701) 328-4195
F: (701) 328-2410
E: bkalk@nd.gov

### Secretary of State

**The Honorable Alvin A. Jaeger (R)**
Secretary of State
600 East Boulevard
Department 108
Bismarck, ND 58505
P: (701) 328-2900
F: (701) 328-1690
E: ajaeger@nd.gov

### Superintendent of Public Instruction

**The Honorable Kirsten Baesler**
Superintendent of Public Instruction
600 East Boulevard Avenue
Department 201
Bismarck, ND 58505
P: (701) 328-4570
F: (701) 328-2461
E: kbaesler@nd.gov

### Tax Commissioner

**The Honorable Ryan Rauschenberger (R)**
Commissioner
600 East Boulevard Avenue
Department 127
Bismarck, ND 58505
P: (701) 328-7088
F: (701) 328-3700
E: rrauschenberger@nd.gov

### Treasurer

**The Honorable Kelly L. Schmidt (R)**
State Treasurer
600 East Boulevard, Department 120
State Capital, 3rd Floor
Bismarck, ND 58505
P: (701) 328-2643
F: (701) 328-3002
E: treasurer@nd.gov

## Judiciary

### Supreme Court (NE)

**Ms. Penny Miller**
Clerk of Supreme Court
Judicial Wing, 1st Floor
600 East Boulevard Avenue
Bismarck, ND 58505
P: (701) 328-2221
F: (701) 328-4480
E: PMiller@ndcourts.gov

**The Honorable Gerald W. VandeWalle**
Chief Justice
**The Honorable Daniel J. Crothers**
**The Honorable Carol Ronning Kapsner**
**The Honorable Lisa Fair McEvers**
**The Honorable Jerod Tufte**

## Legislative

## Senate

### Senate President

**The Honorable Brent Sanford (R)**
Lieutenant Governor
State Capitol
Bismarck, ND 58505
P: (701) 328-2200
F: (701) 328-2205

### President Pro Tempore of the Senate

**Senator Gary A. Lee (R)**
Senate President Pro Tempore
State Capitol
600 East Boulevard Avenue
Bismarck, ND 58505
P: (701) 328-3373
E: galee@nd.gov

### Senate Majority Leader

**Senator Rich Wardner (R)**
Senate Majority Leader
State Capitol
600 East Boulevard Avenue
Bismarck, ND 58505
P: (701) 328-3373
E: rwardner@nd.gov

### Senate Minority Leader

**Senator Joan Heckaman (D)**
Senate Minority Leader
State Capitol
600 East Boulevard Avenue
Bismarck, ND 58505
P: (701) 328-3373
E: jheckaman@nd.gov

### Secretary of the Senate

**Mr. William R. Horton**
Secretary of the Senate
State Capitol
600 East Boulevard Avenue
Bismarck, ND 58505
P: (701) 328-2916
F: (701) 328-3615

### Members of the Senate

**Anderson Jr., Howard C. (R, 8)**
State Capitol
600 East Boulevard Avenue
Bismarck, ND 58505
P: (701) 328-3373
E: hcanderson@nd.gov

**Armstrong, Kelly M. (R, 36)**
State Capitol
600 East Boulevard Avenue
Bismarck, ND 58505
P: (701) 328-3373
E: karmstrong@nd.gov

# North Dakota

**Bekkedahl, Brad (R, 1)**
State Capitol
600 East Boulevard Avenue
Bismarck, ND 58505
P: (701) 328-3373
E: bbekkedahl@nd.gov

**Bowman, Bill L. (R, 39)**
State Capitol
600 East Boulevard Avenue
Bismarck, ND 58505
P: (701) 328-3373
E: bbowman@nd.gov

**Burckhard, Randall (R, 5)**
State Capitol
600 East Boulevard Avenue
Bismarck, ND 58505
P: (701) 328-3373
E: raburckhard@nd.gov

**Campbell, Tom (R, 19)**
State Capitol
600 East Boulevard Avenue
Bismarck, ND 58505
P: (701) 328-3373
E: tomcampbell@nd.gov

**Casper, Jonathan (R, 27)**
State Capitol
600 East Boulevard Avenue
Bismarck, ND 58505
P: (701) 328-3373
E: jcasper@nd.gov

**Clemens, David (R, 16)\***
State Capitol
600 East Boulevard Avenue
Bismarck, ND 58505
P: (701) 328-3373
E: dclemens@nd.gov

**Cook, Dwight (R, 34)**
State Capitol
600 East Boulevard Avenue
Bismarck, ND 58505
P: (701) 328-3373
E: dcook@nd.gov

**Davison, Kyle (R, 41)**
State Capitol
600 East Boulevard Avenue
Bismarck, ND 58505
P: (701) 328-3373
E: kdavison@nd.gov

**Dever, Dick (R, 32)**
State Capitol
600 East Boulevard Avenue
Bismarck, ND 58505
P: (701) 328-3373
E: ddever@nd.gov

**Dotzenrod, Jim (D, 26)**
State Capitol
600 East Boulevard Avenue
Bismarck, ND 58505
P: (701) 328-3373
E: jdotzenrod@nd.gov

**Erbele, Robert S. (R, 28)**
State Capitol
600 East Boulevard Avenue
Bismarck, ND 58505
P: (701) 328-3373
E: rerbele@nd.gov

**Grabinger, John (D, 12)**
State Capitol
600 East Boulevard Avenue
Bismarck, ND 58505
P: (701) 328-3373
E: jgrabinger@nd.gov

**Heckaman, Joan (D, 23)**
State Capitol
600 East Boulevard Avenue
Bismarck, ND 58505
P: (701) 328-3373
E: jheckaman@nd.gov

**Hogue, David (R, 38)**
State Capitol
600 East Boulevard Avenue
Bismarck, ND 58505
P: (701) 328-3373
E: dhogue@nd.gov

**Holmberg, Ray (R, 17)**
State Capitol
600 East Boulevard Avenue
Bismarck, ND 58505
P: (701) 328-3373
E: rholmberg@nd.gov

**Kannianen, Jordan (R, 4)\***
State Capitol
600 East Boulevard Avenue
Bismarck, ND 58505
P: (701) 328-3373
E: jkannianen@nd.gov

**Kilzer, Ralph L. (R, 47)**
State Capitol
600 East Boulevard Avenue
Bismarck, ND 58505
P: (701) 328-3373
E: rkilzer@nd.gov

**Klein, Jerry (R, 14)**
State Capitol
600 East Boulevard Avenue
Bismarck, ND 58505
P: (701) 328-3373
E: jklein@nd.gov

**Krebsbach, Karen K. (R, 40)**
State Capitol
600 East Boulevard Avenue
Bismarck, ND 58505
P: (701) 328-3373
E: kkrebsbach@nd.gov

**Kreun, Curt (R, 42)\***
State Capitol
600 East Boulevard Avenue
Bismarck, ND 58505
P: (701) 328-3373
E: ckreun@nd.gov

**Laffen, Lonnie (R, 43)**
State Capitol
600 East Boulevard Avenue
Bismarck, ND 58505
P: (701) 328-3373
E: llaffen@nd.gov

**Larsen, Oley (R, 3)**
State Capitol
600 East Boulevard Avenue
Bismarck, ND 58505
P: (701) 328-3373
E: olarsen@nd.gov

**Larson, Diane (R, 30)**
State Capitol
600 East Boulevard Avenue
Bismarck, ND 58505
P: (701) 328-3373
E: dklarson@nd.gov

**Lee, Gary A. (R, 22)**
State Capitol
600 East Boulevard Avenue
Bismarck, ND 58505
P: (701) 328-3373
E: galee@nd.gov

**Lee, Judy (R, 13)**
State Capitol
600 East Boulevard Avenue
Bismarck, ND 58505
P: (701) 328-3373
E: jlee@nd.gov

**Luick, Larry (R, 25)**
State Capitol
600 East Boulevard Avenue
Bismarck, ND 58505
P: (701) 328-3373
E: lluick@nd.gov

**Marcellais, Richard (D, 9)**
State Capitol
600 East Boulevard Avenue
Bismarck, ND 58505
P: (701) 328-3373
E: rmarcellais@nd.gov

**Mathern, Tim (D, 11)**
State Capitol
600 East Boulevard Avenue
Bismarck, ND 58505
P: (701) 328-3373
E: tmathern@nd.gov

**Meyer, Scott (R, 18)\***
State Capitol
600 East Boulevard Avenue
Bismarck, ND 58505
P: (701) 328-3373
E: scottmeyer@nd.gov

**Myrdal, Janne (R, 10)\***
State Capitol
600 East Boulevard Avenue
Bismarck, ND 58505
P: (701) 328-3373
E: jmyrdal@nd.gov

**Nelson, Carolyn C. (D, 21)**
State Capitol
600 East Boulevard Avenue
Bismarck, ND 58505
P: (701) 328-3373
E: cnelson@nd.gov

**Oban, Erin (D, 35)**
State Capitol
600 East Boulevard Avenue
Bismarck, ND 58505
P: (701) 328-3373
E: eoban@nd.gov

**Oehlke, Dave (R, 15)**
State Capitol
600 East Boulevard Avenue
Bismarck, ND 58505
P: (701) 328-3373
E: doehlke@nd.gov

**Osland, Arne (R, 20)\***
State Capitol
600 East Boulevard Avenue
Bismarck, ND 58505
P: (701) 328-3373
E: aosland@nd.gov

**Piepkorn, Merrill (D, 44)\***
State Capitol
600 East Boulevard Avenue
Bismarck, ND 58505
P: (701) 328-3373
E: mpiepkorn@nd.gov

**Poolman, Nicole (R, 7)**
State Capitol
600 East Boulevard Avenue
Bismarck, ND 58505
P: (701) 328-3373
E: npoolman@nd.gov

**Robinson, Larry J. (D, 24)**
State Capitol
600 East Boulevard Avenue
Bismarck, ND 58505
P: (701) 328-3373
E: lrobinson@nd.gov

**Roers, Jim (R, 46)\***
State Capitol
600 East Boulevard Ave
Bismarck, ND 58505
E: jroers@nd.gov

**Rust, David S. (R, 2)**
State Capitol
600 East Boulevard Avenue
Bismarck, ND 58505
P: (701) 328-3373
E: drust@nd.gov

**Schaible, Donald (R, 31)**
State Capitol
600 East Boulevard Avenue
Bismarck, ND 58505
P: (701) 328-3373
E: dgschaible@nd.gov

**Sorvaag, Ronald (R, 45)**
State Capitol
600 East Boulevard Avenue
Bismarck, ND 58505
P: (701) 328-3373
E: rsorvaag@nd.gov

**Unruh, Jessica K. (R, 33)**
State Capitol
600 East Boulevard Avenue
Bismarck, ND 58505
P: (701) 328-3373
E: jkunruh@nd.gov

**Vedaa, Shawn (R, 6)***
State Capitol
600 East Boulevard Avenue
Bismarck, ND 58505
F: svedaa@nd.gov

**Wanzek, Terry M. (R, 29)**
State Capitol
600 East Boulevard Avenue
Bismarck, ND 58505
P: (701) 328-3373
E: tmwanzek@nd.gov

**Wardner, Rich (R, 37)**
State Capitol
600 East Boulevard Avenue
Bismarck, ND 58505
P: (701) 328-3373
E: rwardner@nd.gov

# House

## Speaker of the House

**Speaker Larry Bellew (R)**
Speaker of the House
State Capitol
600 East Boulevard Avenue
Bismarck, ND 58505
P: (701) 328-3373
E: lbellew@nd.gov

## House Majority Leader

**Representative Al Carlson (R)**
House Majority Leader
State Capitol
600 East Boulevard Avenue
Bismarck, ND 58505
P: (701) 328-3373
E: acarlson@nd.gov

## House Minority Leader

**Representative Corey Mock (D)**
House Minority Leader
State Capitol
600 East Boulevard Avenue
Bismarck, ND 58505
P: (701) 328-3373
E: crmock@nd.gov

## Clerk of the House

**Mr. Buell Reich**
Chief Clerk of the House
State Capitol
600 East Boulevard Avenue
Bismarck, ND 58505
P: (701) 328-2916
F: (701) 328-3615

## Members of the House

**Anderson, Bert (R, 2)**
State Capitol
600 East Boulevard Avenue
Bismarck, ND 58505
P: (701) 328-3373
E: bertanderson@nd.gov

**Anderson, Dick (R, 6)**
State Capitol
600 East Boulevard Avenue
Bismarck, ND 58505
P: (701) 328-3373
E: dickanderson@nd.gov

**Anderson, Pamela (D, 41)**
State Capitol
600 East Boulevard Avenue
Bismarck, ND 58505
P: (701) 328-3373
E: pkanderson@nd.gov

**Beadle, Thomas (R, 27)**
State Capitol
600 East Boulevard Avenue
Bismarck, ND 58505
P: (701) 328-3373
E: tbeadle@nd.gov

**Becker, Rich (R, 43)**
State Capitol
600 East Boulevard Avenue
Bismarck, ND 58505
P: (701) 328-3373
E: rsbecker@nd.gov

**Becker, Rick C. (R, 7)**
State Capitol
600 East Boulevard Avenue
Bismarck, ND 58505
P: (701) 328-3373
E: rcbecker@nd.gov

**Bellew, Larry (R, 38)**
State Capitol
600 East Boulevard Avenue
Bismarck, ND 58505
P: (701) 328-3373
E: lbellew@nd.gov

**Blum, Jake (R, 42)***
State Capitol
600 East Boulevard Avenue
Bismarck, ND 58505
E: jblum@nd.gov

**Boe, Tracy (D, 9)**
State Capitol
600 East Boulevard Avenue
Bismarck, ND 58505
E: tboe@nd.gov

**Boehning, Randy (R, 27)**
State Capitol
600 East Boulevard Avenue
Bismarck, ND 58505
P: (701) 328-3373
E: rboehning@nd.gov

**Bosch, Glenn (R, 30)***
State Capitol
600 East Boulevard Avenue
Bismarck, ND 58505
P: (701) 328-3373
E: mhowe@nd.gov

**Boschee, Joshua A. (D, 44)**
State Capitol
600 East Boulevard Avenue
Bismarck, ND 58505
P: (701) 328-3373
E: jboschee@nd.gov

**Brabandt, Roger (R, 5)**
State Capitol
600 East Boulevard Avenue
Bismarck, ND 58505
P: (701) 328-3373
E: rbrabandt@nd.gov

**Brandenburg, Mike D. (R, 28)**
State Capitol
600 East Boulevard Avenue
Bismarck, ND 58505
P: (701) 328-3373
E: mbrandenburg@nd.gov

**Carlson, Al (R, 41)**
State Capitol
600 East Boulevard Avenue
Bismarck, ND 58505
P: (701) 328-3373
E: acarlson@nd.gov

**Damschen, Chuck (R, 10)**
State Capitol
600 East Boulevard Avenue
Bismarck, ND 58505
P: (701) 868-3281
E: cdamschen@nd.gov

**Delmore, Lois (D, 43)**
State Capitol
600 East Boulevard Avenue
Bismarck, ND 58505
P: (701) 328-3373
E: ldelmore@nd.gov

**Delzer, Jeff (R, 8)**
State Capitol
600 East Boulevard Avenue
Bismarck, ND 58505
P: (701) 328-3373
E: jdelzer@nd.gov

**Devlin, Bill (R, 23)**
State Capitol
600 East Boulevard Avenue
Bismarck, ND 58505
P: (701) 328-3373
E: bdevlin@nd.gov

**Dobervich, Gretchen (D, 11)**
State Capitol
600 East Boulevard Avenue
Bismarck, ND 58505
P: (701) 328-3373
E: gdobervich@nd.gov

**Dockter, Jason (R, 7)**
State Capitol
600 East Boulevard Avenue
Bismarck, ND 58505
P: (701) 328-3373
E: jddockter@nd.gov

**Ertelt, Sebastian (R, 26)***
State Capitol
600 East Boulevard Avenue
Bismarck, ND 58505
P: (701) 328-3373
F: (701) 328-3373
E: sertelt@nd.gov

**Grueneich, Jim (R, 12)***
State Capitol
600 East Boulevard Avenue
Bismarck, ND 58505
P: (701) 328-3373
E: jgrueneich@nd.gov

**Guggisberg, Ron (D, 11)**
State Capitol
600 East Boulevard Avenue
Bismarck, ND 58505
P: (701) 328-3373
E: rguggisberg@nd.gov

**Hanson, Karla Rose (D, 44)***
State Capitol
600 East Boulevard Avenue
Bismarck, ND 58505
P: (701) 328-3373
E: krhanson@nd.gov

# North Dakota

**Hatlestad, Patrick R.**
**(R, 1)**
State Capitol
600 East Boulevard Avenue
Bismarck, ND 58505
P: (701) 328-3373
E: phatlestad@nd.gov

**Headland, Craig (R, 29)**
State Capitol
600 East Boulevard Avenue
Bismarck, ND 58505
P: (701) 328-3373
E: cheadland@nd.gov

**Heinert, Patrick (R, 32)***
State Capitol
600 East Boulevard Avenue
Bismarck, ND 58505
P: (701) 328-3373
E: pdheinert@nd.gov

**Hogan, Kathy (D, 21)**
State Capitol
600 East Boulevard Avenue
Bismarck, ND 58505
P: (701) 328-3373
E: khogan@nd.gov

**Holman, Richard G. (D, 20)**
State Capitol
600 East Boulevard Avenue
Bismarck, ND 58505
P: (701) 328-3373
E: rholman@nd.gov

**Howe, Michael (R, 22)***
State Capitol
600 East Boulevard Avenue
Bismarck, ND 58505
P: (701) 328-3373
E: mchowe@nd.gov

**Johnson, Craig (R, 6)***
State Capitol
600 East Boulevard Ave
Bismarck, ND 58505
E: craigjohnson@nd.gov

**Johnson, Dennis (R, 15)**
State Capitol
600 East Boulevard Avenue
Bismarck, ND 58505
P: (701) 328-3373
E: djohnson@nd.gov

**Johnson, Mary C. (R, 45)**
State Capitol
600 East Boulevard Avenue
Bismarck, ND 58505
P: (701) 328-3373
E: marycjohnson@nd.gov

**Johnston, Daniel (R, 24)***
State Capitol
600 East Boulevard Avenue
Bismarck, ND 58505
P: (701) 328-3373
E: dljohnston@nd.gov

**Jones, Terry (R, 4)***
State Capitol
600 East Boulevard Avenue
Bismarck, ND 58505
P: (701) 328-3373
E: tbjones@nd.gov

**Kading, Tom (R, 45)**
State Capitol
600 East Boulevard Avenue
Bismarck, ND 58505
P: (701) 328-3373
E: tkading@nd.gov

**Karls, Karen (R, 35)**
State Capitol
600 East Boulevard Avenue
Bismarck, ND 58505
P: (701) 328-3373
E: kkarls@nd.gov

**Kasper, Jim (R, 46)**
State Capitol
600 East Boulevard Avenue
Bismarck, ND 58505
P: (701) 328-3373
E: jkasper@nd.gov

**Keiser, George J. (R, 47)**
State Capitol
600 East Boulevard Avenue
Bismarck, ND 58505
P: (701) 328-3373
E: gkeiser@nd.gov

**Kempenich, Keith (R, 39)**
State Capitol
600 East Boulevard Avenue
Bismarck, ND 58505
P: (701) 328-3373
E: kkempenich@nd.gov

**Kiefert, Dwight (R, 24)**
State Capitol
600 East Boulevard Avenue
Bismarck, ND 58505
P: (701) 328-3373
E: dhkiefert@nd.gov

**Klemin, Lawrence R. (R, 47)**
State Capitol
600 East Boulevard Avenue
Bismarck, ND 58505
P: (701) 328-3373
E: lklemin@nd.gov

**Koppelman, Ben (R, 16)**
State Capitol
600 East Boulevard Avenue
Bismarck, ND 58505
P: (701) 328-3373
E: bkoppelman@nd.gov

**Koppelman, Kim (R, 13)**
State Capitol
600 East Boulevard Avenue
Bismarck, ND 58505
P: (701) 328-3373
E: kkoppelman@nd.gov

**Kreidt, Gary (R, 33)**
State Capitol
600 East Boulevard Avenue
Bismarck, ND 58505
P: (701) 328-3373
E: gkreidt@nd.gov

**Laning, Vernon R. (R, 8)**
State Capitol
600 East Boulevard Avenue
Bismarck, ND 58505
P: (701) 328-3373
E: vrlaning@nd.gov

**Lefor, Mike (R, 37)**
State Capitol
600 East Boulevard Avenue
Bismarck, ND 58505
P: (701) 328-3373
E: mlefor@nd.gov

**Longmuir, Donald (R, 2)***
State Capitol
600 East Boulevard Ave
Bismarck, ND 58505
E: dlongmuir@nd.gov

**Louser, Scott (R, 5)**
State Capitol
600 East Boulevard Avenue
Bismarck, ND 58505
P: (701) 328-3373
E: sclouser@nd.gov

**Magrum, Jeffery (R, 28)***
State Capitol
600 East Boulevard Avenue
Bismarch, ND 58505
P: (701) 328-3373
E: jmagrum@nd.gov

**Maragos, Andrew G. (R, 3)**
State Capitol
600 East Boulevard Avenue
Bismarck, ND 58505
P: (701) 328-3373
E: amaragos@nd.gov

**Marschall, Andrew (R, 16)***
State Capitol
600 East Boulevard Avenue
Bismarck, ND 58505
P: (701) 328-3373
E: amarschall@nd.gov

**Martinson, Bob (R, 35)**
State Capitol
600 East Boulevard Avenue
Bismarck, ND 58505
P: (701) 328-3373
E: bmartinson@nd.gov

**McWilliams, Aaron (R, 20)***
State Capitol
600 East Boulevard Avenue
Bismarck, ND 58505
P: (701) 328-3373
E: amcwilliams@nd.gov

**Meier, Lisa (R, 32)**
State Capitol
600 East Boulevard Avenue
Bismarck, ND 58505
P: (701) 328-3373
E: lmeier@nd.gov

**Mitskog, Alisa (D, 25)**
State Capitol
600 East Boulevard Avenue
Bismarck, ND 58505
P: (701) 328-3373
E: amitskog@nd.gov

**Mock, Corey (D, 18)**
State Capitol
600 East Boulevard Avenue
Bismarck, ND 58505
P: (701) 328-3373
E: crmock@nd.gov

**Monson, David (R, 10)**
State Capitol
600 East Boulevard Avenue
Bismarck, ND 58505
P: (701) 328-3373
E: dmonson@nd.gov

**Nathe, Mike (R, 30)**
State Capitol
600 East Boulevard Avenue
Bismarck, ND 58505
P: (701) 328-3373
E: mrnathe@nd.gov

**Nelson, Jon O. (R, 14)**
State Capitol
600 East Boulevard Avenue
Bismarck, ND 58505
P: (701) 328-3373
E: jonelson@nd.gov

**Nelson, Marvin (D, 9)**
State Capitol
600 East Boulevard Avenue
Bismarck, ND 58505
P: (701) 328-3373
E: menelson@nd.gov

**O'Brien, Emily (R, 42)***
State Capitol
600 East Boulevard Avenue
Bismarck, ND 58505
P: (701) 328-3373
E: eobrien@nd.gov

**Oliver, Bill (R, 4)***
State Capitol
600 East Boulevard Avenue
Bismarck, ND 58505
P: (701) 328-3373
E: boliver@nd.gov

**Olson, Christopher (R, 13)**
State Capitol
600 East Boulevard Avenue
Bismarck, ND 58505
P: (701) 328-3373
E: cdolson@nd.gov

**Owens, Mark S. (R, 17)**
State Capitol
600 East Boulevard Avenue
Bismarck, ND 58505
P: (701) 328-3373
E: mowens@nd.gov

**Paur, Gary (R, 19)**
State Capitol
600 East Boulevard Avenue
Bismarck, ND 58505
P: (701) 328-3373
E: gpaur@nd.gov

**Pollert, Chet (R, 29)**
State Capitol
600 East Boulevard Avenue
Bismarck, ND 58505
P: (701) 328-3373
E: cpollert@nd.gov

**Porter, Todd (R, 34)**
State Capitol
600 East Boulevard Avenue
Bismarck, ND 58505
P: (701) 328-3373
E: tkporter@nd.gov

**Pyle, Brandy (R, 22)***
State Capitol
600 East Boulevard Avenue
Bismarck, ND 58505
P: (701) 328-3373
E: bpyle@nd.gov

**Roers Jones, Shannon (R, 46)***
State Capitol
600 East Boulevard Avenue
Bismarck, ND 58505
P: (701) 328-3373
E: sroersjones@nd.gov

**Rohr, Karen (R, 31)**
State Capitol
600 East Boulevard Avenue
Bismarck, ND 58505
P: (701) 328-3373
E: kmrohr@nd.gov

**Ruby, Dan J. (R, 38)**
State Capitol
600 East Boulevard Avenue
Bismarck, ND 58505
P: (701) 328-3373
E: druby@nd.gov

**Ruby, Matthew (R, 40)***
State Capitol
600 East Boulevard Avenue
Bismarck, ND 58505
P: (701) 328-3373
E: mruby@nd.gov

**Sanford, Mark (R, 17)**
State Capitol
600 East Boulevard Avenue
Bismarck, ND 58505
P: (701) 328-3373
E: masanford@nd.gov

**Satrom, Bernie (R, 12)***
State Capitol
600 East Boulevard Avenue
Bismarck, ND 58505
P: (701) 328-3373
E: blsatrom@nd.gov

**Schatz, Mike (R, 36)**
State Capitol
600 East Boulevard Avenue
Bismarck, ND 58505
P: (701) 328-3373
E: mischatz@nd.gov

**Schmidt, James E. (R, 31)**
State Capitol
600 East Boulevard Avenue
Bismarck, ND 58505
P: (701) 328-3373
E: jeschmidt@nd.gov

**Schneider, Mary (D, 21)**
State Capitol
600 East Boulevard Avenue
Bismarck, ND 58505
P: (701) 328-3373
E: mschneider@nd.gov

**Schobinger, Randy A. (R, 40)***
State Capitol
600 East Boulevard Avenue
Bismarck, ND 58505
P: (701) 328-3373
E: rschobinger@nd.gov

**Schreiber Beck, Cynthia (R, 25)**
State Capitol
600 East Boulevard Avenue
Bismarck, ND 58505
P: (701) 328-3373
E: cschreiberbeck@nd.gov

**Seibel, Jay (R, 33)**
State Capitol
600 East Boulevard Avenue
Bismarck, ND 58505
P: (701) 328-3373
E: jayseibel@nd.gov

**Simons, Luke (R, 36)***
State Capitol
600 East Boulevard Avenue
Bismarck, ND 58505
P: (701) 328-3373
E: lsimons@nd.gov

**Skroch, Kathy (R, 26)***
State Capitol
600 East Boulevard Avenue
Bismarck, ND 58505
P: (701) 328-3373
E: kskroch@nd.gov

**Steiner, Vicky (R, 37)**
State Capitol
600 East Boulevard Avenue
Bismarck, ND 58505
P: (701) 328-3373
E: vsteiner@nd.gov

**Streyle, Roscoe K. (R, 3)**
State Capitol
600 East Boulevard Avenue
Bismarck, ND 58505
P: (701) 328-3373
E: rstreyle@nd.gov

**Sukut, Gary (R, 1)**
State Capitol
600 East Boulevard Avenue
Bismarck, ND 58505
P: (701) 328-3373
E: gsukut@nd.gov

**Toman, Nathan (R, 34)**
State Capitol
600 East Boulevard Avenue
Bismarck, ND 58505
P: (701) 328-3373
E: nptoman@nd.gov

**Trottier, Wayne (R, 19)**
State Capitol
600 East Boulevard Avenue
Bismarck, ND 58505
P: (701) 328-3373
E: wtrottier@nd.gov

**Vetter, Steve (R, 18)***
State Capitol
600 E Boulevard Ave
Bismarck, ND 58505
E: smvetter@nd.gov

**Vigesaa, Don (R, 23)**
State Capitol
600 East Boulevard Avenue
Bismarck, ND 58505
P: (701) 328-3373
E: dwvigesaa@nd.gov

**Weisz, Robin (R, 14)**
State Capitol
600 East Boulevard Avenue
Bismarck, ND 58505
P: (701) 328-3373
E: rweisz@nd.gov

**Westlind, Greg (R, 15)***
State Capitol
600 East Boulevard Avenue
Bismarck, ND 58505
E: gwestlind@nd.gov

**Zubke, Denton (R, 39)**
State Capitol
600 East Boulevard Avenue
Bismarck, ND 58505
P: (701) 328-3373
E: dzubke@nd.gov

# Northern Mariana Islands

## Executive

### Governor
**The Honorable Ralph D.G. Torres (R)**
Governor
Caller Box 10007
Saipan, MP 96950
P: (670) 664-2280
F: (670) 664-2211

### Lieutenant Governor
**The Honorable Victor B. Hocog (R)**
Lieutenant Governor
Caller Box 10007
Capitol Hill
Saipan, MP 96950
P: (670) 664-2300
F: (670) 664-2311

### Secretary of State
*Northern Mariana Islands does not have the office of secretary of state.*

### Attorney General
**The Honorable Edward Manibusan**
Attorney General
Administration Building
P.O. Box 10007
Saipan, MP 96950
P: (670) 664-2341

### Auditor
**Mr. Michael S. Pai**
Public Auditor
P.O. Box 501399
Saipan, MP 96950
P: (670) 322-6481
F: (670) 322-7812
E: mpai@opacnmi.com

### Treasurer
**Mr. Mark O. Rabauliman**
Secretary of Commerce
Office of the Insurance Commissioner
Caller Box 10007 CK
Saipan, MP 96950
P: (670) 664-3077
F: (670) 664-3067

## Judiciary

### Commonwealth Supreme Court
**Ms. Deanna Ogo**
Clerk
P.O. Box 502165
Saipan, MP 96950
P: (670) 236-9800
F: (670) 236-9702
E: supreme.court@saipan.com

**The Honorable Alexandro C. Castro**
Chief Justice
**The Honorable Perry Borja Inos**
**The Honorable John A. Manglona**

## Commonwealth Legislature

### Senate President
**Senator Arnold I. Palacios (R)**
Senate President
P.O. Box 500129
Saipan, MP 96950
P: (670) 664-8807
F: (670) 664-8809
E: sen.palaciosa
@cnmileg.gov.mp

### Vice President of the Senate
**Senator Steven King Mesngon (R)**
Senate Vice President
P.O. Box 500129
Saipan, MP 96950
P: (670) 664-8803
F: (670) 664-8824
E: sen.mesngons
@cnmileg.gov.mp

### Senate Majority Leader
**Senator Francisco M. Borja (I)**
Senate Majority Floor Leader
P.O. Box 500129
Saipan, MP 96950
P: (670) 664-8807
F: (670) 664-8810
E: sen.borjaf
@cnmileg.gov.mp

## Secretary of the Senate
**Ms. Dolores S. Bermudes**
Senate Clerk
P.O. Box 500129
Saipan, MP 96950
P: (670) 664-8850
F: (670) 664-8849
E: bermudesd@cnmileg.gov.mp

## Members of the Senate
**Borja, Francisco M. (I, 2)**
P.O. Box 500129
Saipan, MP 96950
P: (670) 664-8807
F: (670) 664-8810
E: sen.borjaf
@cnmileg.gov.mp

**Cruz, Francisco Q. (R, 2)**
P.O. Box 500129
Saipan, MP 96950
P: (670) 664-8922
F: (670) 664-8938
E: sen.cruzf@cnmileg.gov.mp

**Hofschneider, Jude U. (R, 2)**
P.O. Box 500129
Saipan, MP 96950
P: (670) 664-8868
F: (670) 664-8908
E: sen.hofschneiderj
@cnmileg.gov.mp

**Igisomar, Sixto K. (R, 3)**
P.O. Box 500129
Saipan, MP 96950
P: (670) 664-8812
F: (670) 664-8813
E: sen.igisomars
@cnmileg.gov.mp

**Manglona, Paul A. (I, 1)**
P.O. Box 500129
Saipan, MP 96950
P: (670) 664-8967
F: (670) 664-8919
E: sen.manglonap
@cnmileg.gov.mp

**Mesngon, Steven King (R, 1)**
P.O. Box 500129
Saipan, MP 96950
P: (670) 664-8803
F: (670) 664-8824
E: sen.mesngons
@cnmileg.gov.mp

**Palacios, Arnold I. (R, 3)**
P.O. Box 500129
Saipan, MP 96950
P: (670) 664-8807
F: (670) 664-8809
E: sen.palaciosa
@cnmileg.gov.mp

**Quitugua, Justo S. (I, 3)**
P.O. Box 500129
Saipan, MP 96950
P: (670) 664-8874
F: (670) 664-8976
E: sen.quituguaj
@cnmileg.gov.mp

**Santos, Teresita A. (R, 1)**
P.O. Box 500129
Saipan, MP 96950
P: (670) 664-8814
F: (670) 664-8815
E: sen.santost
@cnmileg.gov.mp

## House

### Speaker of the House
**Representative Rafael S. Demapan (R)**
House Speaker
P.O. Box 500586
Saipan, MP 96950
P: (670) 664-8971
F: (670) 664-8900
E: rep.demapanr
@cnmileg.gov.mp

### Vice President of the House
**Representative Rafael S. Demapan (R)**
House Speaker
P.O. Box 500586
Saipan, MP 96950
P: (670) 664-8971
F: (670) 664-8900
E: rep.demapanr
@cnmileg.gov.mp

**Representative Janet Ulloa Maratita (R)**
House Vice Speaker
P.O. Box 500586
Saipan, MP 96950
P: (670) 664-8974
F: (670) 664-8864
E: rep.maratitaj
@cnmileg.gov.mp

### House Majority Leader
**Representative Glenn L. Maratita (R)**
House Majority Floor Leader
P.O. Box 500586
Saipan, MP 96950
P: (670) 664-8836
F: (670) 664-8985
E: rep.maratitag
@cnmileg.gov.mp

## Clerk of the House

**Ms. Linda B. Muna**
Clerk of the House
P.O. Box 500586
Saipan, MP 96950
P: (670) 664-8848
F: (670) 664-8849
E: munal@cnmileg.gov.mp

## Members of the House

**Aguon, Francisco (R, 5)***
P.O. Box 500586
Saipan, MP 96950
P: (670) 664-8881
F: (670) 664-8895
E: rep.aguonf
    @cnmileg.gov.mp

**Aldan, Edwin P. (I, 6)**
P.O. Box 500586
Saipan, MP 96950
P: (670) 664-8890
F: (670) 664-8892
E: rep.aldane
    @cnmileg.gov.mp

**Attao, Blass Jonathan (I, 3)**
P.O. Box 500586
Saipan, MP 96950
P: (670) 664-8925
F: (670) 664-8871
E: rep.attaob
    @cnmileg.gov.mp

**Barcinas, Donald C. (R, 3)***
P.O. Box 500586
Saipan, MP 96950
P: (670) 664-8931
F: (670) 664-8880
E: rep.barcinasd
    @cnmileg.gov.mp

**Blanco, Ivan (R, 3)***
P.O. Box 500586
Saipan, MP 96950
P: (670) 664-8841
F: (670) 664-8827
E: rep.blancoi
    @cnmileg.gov.mp

**Dela Cruz, Francisco S. (R, 3)**
P.O. Box 500586
Saipan, MP 96950
P: (670) 664-8903
F: (670) 664-8842
E: rep.delacruzf
    @cnmileg.gov.mp

**Deleon Guerrero, Joseph P. (I, 1)**
P.O. Box 500586
Saipan, MP 96950
P: (670) 664-8923
F: (670) 664-8926
E: rep.dlguerreroj
    @cnmileg.gov.mp

**Deleon Guerrero, Lorenzo I. (I, 5)**
P.O. Box 500586
Saipan, MP 96950
P: (670) 664-8888
F: (670) 664-8889
E: rep.dlguerrerol
    @cnmileg.gov.mp

**Demapan, Angel A. (R, 1)**
P.O. Box 500586
Saipan, MP 96950
P: (670) 664-8983
F: (670) 664-8985
E: rep.demapana
    @cnmileg.gov.mp

**Demapan, Rafael S. (R, 2)**
P.O. Box 500586
Saipan, MP 96950
P: (670) 664-8971
F: (670) 664-8900
E: rep.demapanr
    @cnmileg.gov.mp

**Guerrero, Joseph L. (R, 1)**
P.O. Box 500586
Saipan, MP 96950
P: (670) 664-8899
F: (670) 664-8948
E: rep.guerreroj
    @cnmileg.gov.mp

**Igitol, Alice S. (R, 4)***
P.O. Box 500586
Saipan, MP 96950
P: (670) 664-8806
F: (670) 664-8952
E: rep.igitola
    @cnmileg.gov.mp

**Itibus, Jose I. (R, 3)***
P.O. Box 500586
Saipan, MP 96950
P: (670) 664-8826
F: (670) 664-8822
E: rep.itibusj
    @cnmileg.gov.mp

**Maratita, Glenn L. (R, 7)**
P.O. Box 500586
Saipan, MP 96950
P: (670) 664-8836
F: (670) 664-8985
E: rep.maratitag
    @cnmileg.gov.mp

**Maratita, Janet Ulloa (R, 1)**
P.O. Box 500586
Saipan, MP 96950
P: (670) 664-8974
F: (670) 664-8864
E: rep.maratitaj
    @cnmileg.gov.mp

**Propst, Edward K. (I, 1)**
P.O. Box 500586
Saipan, MP 96950
P: (670) 664-8829
F: (670) 664-8816
E: propste@cnmileg.gov.mp

**Sablan Jr., Gregorio (R, 1)***
P.O. Box 500586
Saipan, MP 96950
P: (670) 664-8830
F: (670) 664-8831
E: rep.sablang
    @cnmileg.gov.mp

**Sablan, John Paul (R, 2)**
P.O. Box 500586
Saipan, MP 96950
P: (670) 664-8965
F: (670) 664-8966
E: rep.sablanj
    @cnmileg.gov.mp

**Sablan, Vison E. (I, 4)**
P.O. Box 500586
Saipan, MP 96950
P: (670) 664-8928
F: (670) 664-8930
E: rep.sablanv
    @cnmileg.gov.mp

**Villagomez, Edmund S. (I, 3)**
P.O. Box 500586
Saipan, MP 96950
P: (670) 664-8897
F: (670) 664-8902
E: rep.villagomeze
    @cnmileg.gov.mp

# Ohio

## Executive

### Governor

**The Honorable John Kasich (R)**
Governor
77 South High Street, 30th Floor
Columbus, OH 43215
P: (614) 466-3555
F: (614) 466-9354

### Lieutenant Governor

**The Honorable Mary Taylor (R)**
Lieutenant Governor
77 High Street, 30th Floor
Columbus, OH 43215
P: (614) 644-0935
F: (614) 466-9354

### Attorney General

**The Honorable Mike DeWine (R)**
Attorney General
State Office Tower
30 East Broad Street
Columbus, OH 43266
P: (614) 466-4320

### Auditor

**The Honorable David A. Yost (R)**
Auditor of State
88 East Broad Street, 5th Floor
P.O. Box 1140
Columbus, OH 43216
P: (614) 466-4514
F: (614) 466-4490
E: contactus
@auditor.state.oh.us

### Secretary of State

**The Honorable Jon Husted (R)**
Secretary of State
180 East Broad Street, 16th Floor
Columbus, OH 43215
P: (614) 466-2655
F: (614) 644-0649
E: jhusted
@ohiosecretaryofstate.gov

### Treasurer

**The Honorable Josh Mandel (R)**
Treasurer of State
30 East Broad Street
9th Floor
Columbus, OH 43215
P: (614) 466-2160
F: (614) 644-7313

## Judiciary

### Supreme Court (NE)

**Ms. Sandra Huth Grosko**
Clerk of Court
65 South Front Street, 8th Floor
Columbus, OH 43215
P: (614) 387-9530

**The Honorable Maureen O'Connor (R)**
Chief Justice
**The Honorable R. Patrick DeWine**
**The Honorable Pat Fischer**
**The Honorable Judith L. French**
**The Honorable Sharon L. Kennedy**
**The Honorable Terrence O'Donnell**
**The Honorable William M. O'Neill**

## President Pro Tempore of the Senate

**Senator Larry Obhof (R)**
Senate President Pro Tempore
Statehouse
2nd Floor
Columbus, OH 43215
P: (614) 466-7505
E: Obhof@ohiosenate.gov

**Senator Bob Peterson (R)**
Senate President Pro Tempore
Senate Building
1 Capitol Square, 1st Floor
Columbus, OH 43215
P: (614) 644-8156
E: Peterson@ohiosenate.gov

## Senate Minority Leader

**Senator Joe Schiavoni (D)**
Senate Minority Leader
Statehouse
3rd Floor
Columbus, OH 43215
P: (614) 466-8285
E: Schiavoni@ohiosenate.gov

## Secretary of the Senate

**Mr. Vincent Keeran**
Clerk of the Senate
Statehouse, Second Floor
Columbus, OH 43215
P: (614) 466-4900
F: (614) 466-8261

## Members of the Senate

**Bacon, Kevin (R, 3)**
Senate Building
1 Capitol Square, Ground Floor
Columbus, OH 43215
P: (614) 466-8064
E: Bacon@ohiosenate.gov

**Balderson, Troy (R, 20)**
Senate Building
1 Capitol Square, 1st Floor
Columbus, OH 43215
P: (614) 466-8076
E: Balderson@ohiosenate.gov

**Beagle, Bill (R, 5)**
Senate Building
1 Capitol Square, 2nd Floor
Columbus, OH 43215
P: (614) 466-6247
E: Beagle@ohiosenate.gov

**Brown, Edna (D, 11)**
Senate Building
1 Capitol Square, 2nd Floor
Columbus, OH 43215
P: (614) 466-5204
E: Brown@ohiosenate.gov

**Burke, David (R, 26)**
Senate Building
1 Capitol Square, Ground Floor
Columbus, OH 43215
P: (614) 466-8049
E: Burke@ohiosenate.gov

**Coley II, William P. (R, 4)**
Senate Building
1 Capitol Square, 1st Floor
Columbus, OH 43215
P: (614) 466-8072
E: Coley@ohiosenate.gov

**Dolan, Matthew J. (R, 24)**
Senate Building
1 Capitol Square, Ground Floor
Columbus, OH 43215
P: (614) 466-8056
E: dolan@ohiosenate.gov

**Eklund, John (R, 18)**
Senate Building
1 Capitol Square, 1st Floor
Columbus, OH 43215
P: (614) 644-7718
E: Eklund@ohiosenate.gov

**Gardner, Randy (R, 2)**
Senate Building
1 Capitol Square, 2nd Floor
Columbus, OH 43215
P: (614) 466-8060
E: Gardner@ohiosenate.gov

**Hackett, Robert D. (R, 10)**
Senate Building
1 Capitol Square, Ground Floor
Columbus, OH 43215
P: (614) 466-3780
E: hackett@ohiosenate.gov

**Hite, Cliff (R, 1)**
Senate Building
1 Capitol Square, 1st Floor
Columbus, OH 43215
P: (614) 466-8150
E: Hite@ohiosenate.gov

**Hoagland, Frank (R, 30)\***
Senate Building
1 Capitol Square, 1st Floor
Columbus, OH 43215
P: (614) 466-6508
E: hoagland@ohiosenate.gov

**Hottinger, Jay (R, 31)**
Senate Building
1 Capitol Square, Ground Floor
Columbus, OH 43215
P: (614) 466-5838
F: (614) 719-3971
E: hottinger@ohiosenate.gov

**Huffman, Matt (R, 12)**
Senate Building
1 Capitol Square, 1st Floor
Columbus, OH 43215
P: (614) 466-7584
E: huffman@ohiosenate.gov

**Jordan, Kris (R, 19)**
Senate Building
1 Capitol Square, Ground Floor
Columbus, OH 43215
P: (614) 466-8086
E: Jordan@ohiosenate.gov

**Kunze, Stephanie (R, 16)**
Capitol
1 Capitol Square, 1st Floor
Columbus, OH 43215
P: (614) 466-5981
E: kunze@ohiosenate.gov

**LaRose, Frank (R, 27)**
Senate Building
1 Capitol Square, 2nd Floor
Columbus, OH 43215
P: (614) 466-4823
E: LaRose@ohiosenate.gov

**Lehner, Peggy (R, 6)**
Senate Building
1 Capitol Square, 1st Floor
Columbus, OH 43215
P: (614) 466-4538
E: Lehner@ohiosenate.gov

**Manning, Gayle (R, 13)**
Senate Building
1 Capitol Square, 1st Floor
Columbus, OH 43215
P: (614) 644-7613
E: Manning@ohiosenate.gov

**Obhof, Larry (R, 22)**
Statehouse
2nd Floor
Columbus, OH 43215
P: (614) 466-7505
E: Obhof@ohiosenate.gov

**O'Brien, Sean (D, 32)**
Senate Building
1 Capitol Square, Ground Floor
Columbus, OH 43215
E: obrien@ohiosenate.gov

**Oelslager, Scott (R, 29)**
Senate Building
1 Capitol Square, 1st Floor
Columbus, OH 43215
P: (614) 466-0626
E: Oelslager@ohiosenate.gov

**Peterson, Bob (R, 17)**
Senate Building
1 Capitol Square, 1st Floor
Columbus, OH 43215
P: (614) 644-8156
E: Peterson@ohiosenate.gov

**Schiavoni, Joe (D, 33)**
Statehouse
3rd Floor
Columbus, OH 43215
P: (614) 466-8285
E: Schiavoni@ohiosenate.gov

**Skindell, Michael J.
(D, 23)**
Senate Building
1 Capitol Square, Ground Floor
Columbus, OH 43215
P: (614) 466-5123
E: Skindell@ohiosenate.gov

**Tavares, Charleta B.
(D, 15)**
Senate Building
1 Capitol Square, 2nd Floor
Columbus, OH 43215
P: (614) 466-5131
E: Tavares@ohiosenate.gov

**Terhar, Louis (R, 8)**
Capitol Building
1 Capitol Square, Ground Floor
Columbus, OH 43215
P: (614) 466-8068
E: terhar@ohiosenate.gov

**Thomas, Cecil (D, 9)**
Senate Building
1 Capitol Square, 3rd Floor
Columbus, OH 43215
P: (614) 466-5980
E: thomas@ohiosenate.gov

**Uecker, Joseph (R, 14)**
Senate Building
1 Capitol Square, Ground Floor
Columbus, OH 43215
P: (614) 466-8082
E: Uecker@ohiosenate.gov

**Williams, Sandra (D, 21)**
Senate Building
1 Capitol Square, Ground Floor
Columbus, OH 43215
P: (614) 466-4857
E: williams@ohiosenate.gov

**Wilson, Steven (R, 7)\***
Senate Building
1 Capitol Square,
Columbus, OH 43215
P: (614) 466-9737
E: wilson@ohiosenate.gov

**Yuko, Kenny (D, 25)**
Senate Building
1 Capitol Square, Ground Floor
Columbus, OH 43215
P: (614) 466-4583
E: yuko@ohiosenate.gov

# House

## Speaker of the House

**Speaker Cliff
Rosenberger (R)**
Speaker of the House
77 South High Street
14th Floor
Columbus, OH 43215
P: (614) 466-3506
E: Rep91@ohiohouse.gov

## Speaker Pro Tempore of the House

**Representative Kirk
Schuring (R)**
House Speaker Pro Tempore
77 South High Street
14th Floor
Columbus, OH 43215
P: (614) 752-2438
E: Rep48@ohiohouse.gov

## House Majority Leader

**Representative Dorothy
Pelanda (R)**
House Majority Leader
77 South High Street
14th Floor
Columbus, OH 43215
P: (614) 466-8147
E: Rep86@ohiohouse.gov

## House Minority Leader

**Representative Fred
Strahorn (D)**
House Minority Leader
77 South High Street
14th Floor
Columbus, OH 43215
P: (614) 466-1607
E: Rep39@ohiohouse.gov

## Clerk of the House

**Mr. Bradley J. Young**
Legislative Clerk of the House
Statehouse
Columbus, OH 43215
P: (614) 466-3357

## Members of the House

**Anielski, Marlene (R, 6)**
77 South High Street
12th Floor
Columbus, OH 43215
P: (614) 644-6041
E: Rep06@ohiohouse.gov

**Antani, Niraj J. (R, 42)**
77 South High Street
11th Floor
Columbus, OH 43215
P: (614) 466-6504
E: rep42@ohiohouse.gov

**Antonio, Nickie (D, 13)**
77 South High Street
14th Floor
Columbus, OH 43215
P: (614) 466-5921
F: (614) 719-3913
E: Rep13@ohiohouse.gov

**Arndt, Steven (R, 89)**
77 South High Street
11th Floor
Columbus, OH 43215
P: (614) 644-6011
E: rep89@ohiohouse.gov

**Ashford, Mike (D, 44)**
77 South High Street
10th Floor
Columbus, OH 43215
P: (614) 466-1401
E: Rep44@ohiohouse.gov

**Barnes Jr., John E. (D, 12)**
77 South High Street
11th Floor
Columbus, OH 43215
P: (614) 466-1408
F: (614) 719-3912
E: Rep12@ohiohouse.gov

**Becker, John (R, 65)**
77 South High Street
12th Floor
Columbus, OH 43215
P: (614) 466-8134
E: Rep65@ohiohouse.gov

**Bishoff, Heather (D, 20)**
77 South High Street
10th Floor
Columbus, OH 43215
P: (614) 644-6002
E: Rep20@ohiohouse.gov

**Blessing III, Louis W.
(R, 29)**
77 South High Street
13th Floor
Columbus, OH 43215
P: (614) 466-9091
E: Rep29@ohiohouse.gov

**Boccieri, John (D, 59)**
77 South High Street
10th Floor
Columbus, OH 43215
P: (614) 466-6107
E: rep59@ohiohouse.gov

**Boggs, Kristin (D, 18)**
77 South High Street
10th Floor
Columbus, OH 43215
P: (614) 466-1896
F: (614) 719-6974
E: Rep18@ohiohouse.gov

**Boyd, Janine (D, 9)**
77 South High Street
10th Floor
Columbus, OH 43215
P: (614) 644-5079
E: rep09@ohiohouse.gov

**Brenner, Andrew (R, 67)**
77 South High Street
13th Floor
Columbus, OH 43215
P: (614) 644-6711
F: (614) 719-0002
E: Rep67@ohiohouse.gov

# Ohio

**Brinkman Jr., Tom (R, 27)**
77 South High Street
11th Floor
Columbus, OH 43215
P: (614) 644-6886
E: rep27@ohiohouse.gov

**Butler, James (R, 41)**
77 South High Street
13th Floor
Columbus, OH 43215
P: (614) 644-6008
E: Rep41@ohiohouse.gov

**Carfagna, Rick (R, 68)\***
77 South High Street
13th Floor
Columbus, OH 43215
P: (614) 466-1431
E: rep68@ohiohouse.gov

**Celebrezze, Nicholas J.
(D, 15)**
77 South High Street
14th Floor
Columbus, OH 43215
P: (614) 466-3485
F: (614) 719-3911
E: Rep15@ohiohouse.gov

**Cera, Jack (D, 96)**
77 South High Street
10th Floor
Columbus, OH 43215
P: (614) 466-3735
E: Rep96@ohiohouse.gov

**Clyde, Kathleen (D, 75)**
77 South High Street
10th Floor
Columbus, OH 43215
P: (614) 466-2004
E: Rep75@ohiohouse.gov

**Conditt, Margaret (R, 52)**
77 South High Street
11th Floor
Columbus, OH 43215
P: (614) 466-8550
E: Rep52@ohiohouse.gov

**Craig, Hearcel F. (D, 26)**
77 South High Street
10th Floor
Columbus, OH 43215
P: (614) 466-8010
E: hearcel.craig
    @ohiohouse.gov

**Cupp, Robert R. (R, 4)**
77 South High Street
13th Floor
Columbus, OH 43215
P: (614) 466-4895
E: rep04@ohiohouse.gov

**Dean, Bill (R, 74)**
77 South High Street
12th Floor
Columbus, OH 43215
P: (614) 466-1470
F: (614) 719-0010
E: bill.dean@ohiohouse.gov

**Dever, Jonathan (R, 28)**
77 South High Street
13th Floor
Columbus, OH 43215
P: (614) 466-8120
E: jonathan.dever
    @ohiohouse.gov

**DeVitis, Anthony (R, 36)**
77 South High Street
11th Floor
Columbus, OH 43215
P: (614) 466-1790
E: Rep36@ohiohouse.gov

**Duffey, Mike (R, 21)**
77 South High Street
13th Floor
Columbus, OH 43215
P: (614) 644-6030
F: (614) 719-6960
E: mike.duffey
    @ohiohouse.gov

**Edwards, Jay (R, 94)\***
77 South High Street
11th Floor
Columbus, OH 43215
P: (814) 466-2158
E: rep94@ohiohouse.gov

**Faber, Keith (R, 84)**
77 South High Street
13th Floor
Columbus, OH 43215
P: (614) 466-6344
E: rep84@ohiohouse.gov

**Fedor, Teresa (D, 45)**
77 South High Street
10th Floor
Columbus, OH 43215
P: (614) 644-6017
E: Rep45@ohiohouse.gov

**Gavarone, Theresa (R, 3)**
77 South High Street
11th Floor
Columbus, OH 43215
P: (614) 466-8104
F: (614) 719-0006
E: rep03@ohiohouse.gov

**Ginter, Tim (R, 5)**
77 South High Street
13th Floor
Columbus, OH 43215
P: (614) 466-8022
E: rep05@ohiohouse.gov

**Gonzales, Anne (R, 19)**
77 South High Street
13th Floor
Columbus, OH 43215
P: (614) 466-4847
F: (614) 719-6958
E: Rep19@ohiohouse.gov

**Goodman, Wes (R, 87)**
77 South High Street
11th Floor
Columbus, OH 43215
P: (614) 644-6265
E: rep87@ohiohouse.gov

**Green, Doug (R, 66)**
77 South High Street
13th Floor
Columbus, OH 43215
P: (614) 644-6034
E: Rep66@ohiohouse.gov

**Greenspan, Dave (R, 16)\***
77 South High Street
11th Floor
Columbus, OH 43215
P: (614) 466-0961
E: rep16@ohiohouse.gov

**Hagan, Christina (R, 50)**
77 South High Street
13th Floor
Columbus, OH 43215
P: (614) 466-9078
F: (614) 719-6950
E: Rep50@ohiohouse.gov

**Hambley, Stephen D. (R, 69)**
77 South High Street
11th Floor
Columbus, OH 43215
P: (614) 466-8140
E: rep69@ohiohouse.gov

**Henne, Michael (R, 40)**
77 South High Street
13th Floor
Columbus, OH 43215
P: (614) 644-8051
F: (614) 719-3590
E: Rep40@ohiohouse.gov

**Hill, Brian (R, 97)**
77 South High Street
13th Floor
Columbus, OH 43215
P: (614) 644-6014
E: Rep97@ohiohouse.gov

**Holmes, Glenn (D, 63)\***
77 South High Street
10th Floor
Columbus, OH 43215
P: (614) 466-3488
E: rep63@ohiohouse.gov

**Hood, Ron (R, 78)**
77 South High Street
12th Floor
Columbus, OH 43215
P: (614) 466-1464
E: Rep78@ohiohouse.gov

**Householder, Larry (R, 72)\***
77 South High Street
11th Floor
Columbus, OH 43215
P: (614) 466-2500
E: rep72@ohiohouse.gov

**Howse, Stephanie (D, 11)**
77 South High Street
10th Floor
Columbus, OH 43215
P: (614) 466-1414
E: rep11@ohiohouse.gov

**Huffman, Stephen A. (R, 80)**
77 South High Street
12th Floor
Columbus, OH 43215
P: (614) 466-8114
E: rep80@ohiohouse.gov

**Hughes, Jim (R, 24)**
77 South High Street
13th Floor
Columbus, OH 43215
P: (614) 466-8012
E: rep24@ohiohouse.gov

**Ingram, Catherine (D, 32)\***
77 South High Street
10th Floor
Columbus, OH 43215
P: 614466645
E: rep32@ohiohouse.gov

**Johnson, Greta (D, 35)**
77 South High Street
10th Floor
Columbus, OH 43215
P: (614) 644-6037
E: rep35@ohiohouse.gov

**Johnson, Terry (R, 90)**
77 South High Street
11th Floor
Columbus, OH 43215
P: (614) 466-2124
E: Rep90@ohiohouse.gov

**Keller, Candice (R, 53)**
77 South High Street
11th Floor
Columbus, OH 43215
P: (614) 644-5094
E: rep53@ohiohouse.gov

**Kelly, Brigid (D, 31)\***
77 South High Street
10th Floor
Columbus, OH 43215
P: (614) 466-5786
E: rep31@ohiohouse.gov

**Kennedy Kent, Bernadine (D, 25)***
77 South High Street
10th Floor
Columbus, OH 43215
P: (614) 466-5343
E: rep25@ohiohouse.gov

**Kick, Darrell (R, 70)***
77 South High Street
11th Floor
Columbus, OH 43215
P: (614) 466-2994
E: rep70@ohiohouse.gov

**Koehler, Kyle (R, 79)**
77 South High Street
11th Floor
Columbus, OH 43215
P: (614) 466-2038
E: rep79@ohiohouse.gov

**Landis, Al (R, 98)**
77 South High Street
11th Floor
Columbus, OH 43215
P: (614) 466-8035
E: Rep98@ohiohouse.gov

**Lanese, Laura (R, 23)***
77 South High Street
11th Floor
Columbus, OH 43215
P: (614) 466-9690
E: rep23@ohiohouse.gov

**LaTourette, Sarah (R, 76)**
77 South High Street
14th Floor
Columbus, OH 43215
P: (614) 644-5088
E: rep76@ohiohouse.gov

**Leland, David (D, 22)**
77 South High Street
10th Floor
Columbus, OH 43215
P: (614) 466-2473
E: rep22@ohiohouse.gov

**Lepore-Hagan, Michele (D, 58)**
77 South High Street
10th Floor
Columbus, OH 43215
P: (614) 466-9435
E: rep58@ohiohouse.gov

**Lipps, Scott (R, 62)***
77 South High Street
13th Floor
Columbus, OH 43215
P: 616446023
E: rep62@ohiohouse.gov

**Manning, Nathan H. (R, 55)**
77 South High Street
10th Floor
Columbus, OH 43215
P: (614) 644-5076
E: rep55@ohiohouse.gov

**McColley, Robert (R, 81)**
77 South High Street
14th Floor
Columbus, OH 43215
P: (614) 466-3760
E: rep81@ohiohouse.gov

**Merrin, Derek (R, 47)**
77 South High Street
11th Floor
Columbus, OH 43215
P: (614) 466-1731
E: rep47@ohiohouse.gov

**Miller, Adam (D, 17)***
77 South High Street
10th Floor
Columbus, OH 43215
P: (614) 644-6005
E: rep17@ohiohouse.gov

**O'Brien, Michael J. (D, 64)**
77 South High Street
10th Floor
Columbus, OH 43215
P: (614) 466-5358
E: rep64@ohiohouse.gov

**Patmon, Bill (D, 10)**
77 South High Street
11th Floor
Columbus, OH 43215
P: (614) 466-7954
F: (614) 719-0010
E: Rep10@ohiohouse.gov

**Patterson, John (D, 99)**
77 South High Street
10th Floor
Columbus, OH 43215
P: (614) 466-1405
E: Rep99@ohiohouse.gov

**Patton, Thomas F. (R, 7)**
77 South High Street
14th Floor
Columbus, OH 43215
P: (614) 466-4895
E: rep07@ohiohouse.gov

**Pelanda, Dorothy (R, 86)**
77 South High Street
14th Floor
Columbus, OH 43215
P: (614) 466-8147
E: Rep86@ohiohouse.gov

**Perales, Rick (R, 73)**
77 South High Street
13th Floor
Columbus, OH 43215
P: (614) 644-6020
E: Rep73@ohiohouse.gov

**Ramos, Dan (D, 56)**
77 South High Street
10th Floor
Columbus, OH 43215
P: (614) 466-5141
F: (614) 719-3956
E: Rep56@ohiohouse.gov

**Reece, Alicia (D, 33)**
77 South High Street
10th Floor
Columbus, OH 43215
P: (614) 466-1308
F: (614) 719-3587
E: Rep33@ohiohouse.gov

**Reineke Jr., Bill (R, 88)**
77 South High Street
13th Floor
Columbus, OH 43215
P: (614) 466-1374
E: rep88@ohiohouse.gov

**Retherford, Wes (R, 51)**
77 South High Street
13th Floor
Columbus, OH 43215
P: (614) 644-6721
E: Rep51@ohiohouse.gov

**Rezabek, Jeff (R, 43)**
77 South High Street
12th Floor
Columbus, OH 43215
P: (614) 466-2960
E: rep43@ohiohouse.gov

**Riedel, Craig (R, 82)***
77 South High Street
11th Floor
Columbus, OH 43215
P: (614) 644-5091
E: rep82@ohiohouse.gov

**Roegner, Kristina (R, 37)**
77 South High Street
11th Floor
Columbus, OH 43215
P: (614) 466-1177
E: Rep37@ohiohouse.gov

**Rogers, John M. (D, 60)**
77 South High Street
10th Floor
Columbus, OH 43215
P: (614) 466-7251
E: Rep60@ohiohouse.gov

**Romanchuk, Mark J. (R, 2)**
77 South High Street
11th Floor
Columbus, OH 43215
P: (614) 466-5802
E: Rep02@ohiohouse.gov

**Rosenberger, Cliff (R, 91)**
77 South High Street
14th Floor
Columbus, OH 43215
P: (614) 466-3506
E: Rep91@ohiohouse.gov

**Ryan, Scott K. (R, 71)**
77 South High Street
13th Floor
Columbus, OH 43215
P: (614) 466-1482
E: rep71@ohiohouse.gov

**Schaffer, Timothy (R, 77)**
77 South High Street
11th Floor
Columbus, OH 43215
P: (614) 466-8100
E: rep77@ohiohouse.gov

**Scherer, Gary (R, 92)**
77 South High Street
12th Floor
Columbus, OH 43215
P: (614) 644-7928
E: Rep92@ohiohouse.gov

**Schuring, Kirk (R, 48)**
77 South High Street
14th Floor
Columbus, OH 43215
P: (614) 752-2438
E: Rep48@ohiohouse.gov

**Seitz, Bill (R, 30)**
77 South High Street
13th Floor
Columbus, OH 43215
P: (614) 466-8258
E: rep30@ohiohouse.gov

**Sheehy, Michael (D, 46)**
77 South High Street
10th Floor
Columbus, OH 43215
P: (614) 466-1418
E: Rep46@ohiohouse.gov

**Slaby, Marilyn (R, 38)**
77 South High Street
11th Floor
Columbus, OH 43215
P: (614) 644-5085
F: (614) 719-6941
E: Rep38@ohiohouse.gov

# Ohio

**Smith, Kent (D, 8)**
77 South High Street
10th Floor
Columbus, OH 43215
P: (614) 466-5441
E: rep08@ohiohouse.gov

**Smith, Ryan (R, 93)**
77 South High Street
13th Floor
Columbus, OH 43215
P: (614) 466-1366
E: Rep93@ohiohouse.gov

**Sprague, Robert (R, 83)**
77 South High Street
13th Floor
Columbus, OH 43215
P: (614) 466-3819
E: Rep83@ohiohouse.gov

**Stein, Dick (R, 57)***
77 South High Street
11th Floor
Columbus, OH 43215
P: (614) 466-9628
E: rep57@ohiohouse.gov

**Strahorn, Fred (D, 39)**
77 South High Street
14th Floor
Columbus, OH 43215
P: (614) 466-1607
E: Rep39@ohiohouse.gov

**Sweeney, Martin J. (D, 14)**
77 South High Street
11th Floor
Columbus, OH 43215
P: (614) 466-3350
E: rep14@ohiohouse.gov

**Sykes, Emilia Strong
   (D, 34)**
77 South High Street
10th Floor
Columbus, OH 43215
P: (614) 466-3100
E: rep34@ohiohouse.gov

**Thompson, Andy (R, 95)**
77 South High Street
11th Floor
Columbus, OH 43215
P: (614) 644-8728
E: Rep95@ohiohouse.gov

**Vitale, Nino (R, 85)**
77 South High Street
11th Floor
Columbus, OH 43215
P: (614) 466-1507
E: rep85@ohiohouse.gov

**West, Thomas (D, 49)***
77 South High Street
10th Floor
Columbus, OH 43215
P: (614) 466-8030
E: rep49@ohiohouse.gov

**Wiggam, Scott (R, 1)***
77 South High Street
11th Floor
Columbus, OH 43215
P: (614) 466-1474
E: rep01@ohiohouse.gov

**Young, Ron (R, 61)**
77 South High Street
13th Floor
Columbus, OH 43215
P: (614) 644-6074
E: Rep61@ohiohouse.gov

**Zeltwanger, Paul (R, 54)**
77 South High Street
12th Floor
Columbus, OH 43215
P: (614) 644-6027
E: rep54@ohiohouse.gov

# Oklahoma

## Executive

### Governor

**The Honorable Mary Fallin (R)**
Governor
Capitol Building
2300 Lincoln Boulevard, Room 212
Oklahoma City, OK 73105
P: (405) 521-2342
F: (405) 521-3353

### Lieutenant Governor

**The Honorable Todd Lamb (R)**
Lieutenant Governor
State Capitol, Room 211
Oklahoma City, OK 73105
P: (405) 521-2161
F: (405) 522-8694

### Auditor

**The Honorable Gary Jones (R)**
State Auditor & Inspector
2300 North Lincoln Boulevard
State Capitol Building, Room 100
Oklahoma City, OK 73105
P: (405) 521-3495
F: (405) 521-3426
E: gjones@sai.ok.gov

### Commissioner of Insurance

**The Honorable John D. Doak**
Commissioner
Five Corporate Plaza
3625 Northwest 56th Street, Suite 100
Oklahoma City, OK 73112
P: (405) 521-2828
F: (405) 521-6635

### Corporation Commission

**The Honorable Bob Anthony (R)**
Commissioner
2101 North Lincoln Boulevard
P.O. Box 52000
Oklahoma City, OK 73152
P: (405) 521-2261
F: (405) 521-4532
E: b.anthony@occemail.com

**The Honorable Todd Hiett (R)**
Vice Chair
2101 North Lincoln Boulevard
P.O. Box 52000
Oklahoma City, OK 73152
P: (405) 521-2264
F: (405) 522-1623
E: t.hiett@occemail.com

**The Honorable Dana Murphy (R)**
Chair
2101 North Lincoln Boulevard
P.O. Box 52000
Oklahoma City, OK 73152
P: (405) 521-2267
F: (405) 522-1623
E: d.murphy@occemail.com

### Secretary of State

**The Honorable Mike Hunter**
(appointed)
Secretary of State
State Capitol Building, Room 101
2300 Lincoln Boulevard
Oklahoma City, OK 73105
P: (405) 521-3912

### Superintendent of Public Instruction

**The Honorable Joy Hofmeister (R)**
Superintendent of Public Instruction
2500 North Lincoln Boulevard
Oklahoma City, OK 73105
P: (405) 521-3301
F: (405) 521-6205
E: Joy.Hofmeister@sde.ok.gov

### Treasurer

**The Honorable Ken Miller (R)**
State Treasurer
Room 217, State Capitol Building
2300 North Lincoln Boulevard
Oklahoma City, OK 73105
P: (405) 521-3191
F: (405) 521-4994

## Judiciary

### Supreme Court (MR)

**Mr. Michael S. Richie**
Supreme Court Clerk
P.O. Box 53126
Oklahoma City, OK 73152
P: (405) 521-2163

**The Honorable Doug Combs**
Chief Justice
**The Honorable Tom Colbert**

**The Honorable James E. Edmondson**
**The Honorable Noma Gurich**
**The Honorable Yvonne Kauger**
**The Honorable John F. Reif**
**The Honorable Joseph M. Watt**
**The Honorable James R. Winchester**
**The Honorable Patrick Wyrick**

## Legislative Senate

### Senate President

**The Honorable Todd Lamb (R)**
Lieutenant Governor
State Capitol, Room 211
Oklahoma City, OK 73105
P: (405) 521-2161
F: (405) 522-8694

### President Pro Tempore of the Senate

**Senator Mike Schulz (R)**
President Pro Tempore
Room 422
2300 North Lincoln Boulevard
Oklahoma City, OK 73105
P: (405) 521-5612
E: schulz@oksenate.gov

### Senate Majority Leader

**Senator Greg Treat (R)**
Senate Majority Floor Leader
Room 418
2300 North Lincoln Boulevard
Oklahoma City, OK 73105
P: (405) 521-5632
E: treat@oksenate.gov

### Senate Minority Leader

**Senator John Sparks (D)**
Senate Democratic Floor Leader
Room 519
2300 North Lincoln Boulevard
Oklahoma City, OK 73105
P: (405) 521-5553
E: sparks@oksenate.gov

### Secretary of the Senate

**Mr. Paul Ziriax**
Secretary
Room 6, State Capitol
Oklahoma City, OK 73105
P: (405) 522-6615
F: (405) 521-6457
E: pziriax@elections.ok.gov

### Members of the Senate

**Allen, Mark (R, 4)**
Room 234
2300 North Lincoln Boulevard
Oklahoma City, OK 73105
P: (405) 521-5576
E: allen@oksenate.gov

**Bass, Randy (D, 32)**
Room 521B
2300 North Lincoln Boulevard
Oklahoma City, OK 73105
P: (405) 521-5567
E: bass@oksenate.gov

**Bergstrom, Michael (R, 1)***
Room 527A
2300 North Lincoln Boulevard
Oklahoma City, OK 73105
P: (405) 521-5561
E: bergstrom@oksenate.gov

**Bice, Stephanie (R, 22)**
Room 424A
2300 North Lincoln Boulevard
Oklahoma City, OK 73105
P: (405) 521-5592
E: bice@oksenate.gov

**Boggs, Larry (R, 7)**
Room 425
2300 North Lincoln Boulevard
Oklahoma City, OK 73105
P: (405) 521-5604
E: boggs@oksenate.gov

**Brecheen, Josh (R, 6)**
Room 417C
2300 North Lincoln Boulevard
Oklahoma City, OK 73105
P: (405) 521-5586
E: brecheen@oksenate.gov

**Brown, Bill (R, 36)**
Room 232
2300 North Lincoln Boulevard
Oklahoma City, OK 73105
P: (405) 521-5602
E: brownb@oksenate.gov

**Dahm, Nathan (R, 33)**
Room 237
2300 North Lincoln Boulevard
Oklahoma City, OK 73105
P: (405) 521-5551
E: dahm@oksenate.gov

# Oklahoma

**Daniels, Julie (R, 29)***
Room 531
2300 North Lincoln Boulevard
Oklahoma City, OK 73105
P: (405) 521-5634
E: daniels@oksenate.gov

**David, Kim (R, 18)**
Room 537
2300 North Lincoln Boulevard
Oklahoma City, OK 73105
P: (405) 521-5590
E: david@oksenate.gov

**Dossett, Joseph (D, 34)**
Room 522B
2300 North Lincoln Boulevard
Oklahoma City, OK 73105
P: (405) 521-5566
E: dossett@oksenate.gov

**Dugger, Tom (R, 21)***
Room 524
2300 North Lincoln Boulevard
Oklahoma City, OK 73105
P: (405) 521-5572
E: dugger@oksenate.gov

**Fields, Eddie (R, 10)**
Room 530
2300 North Lincoln Boulevard
Oklahoma City, OK 73105
P: (405) 521-5581
E: efields@oksenate.gov

**Floyd, Kay (D, 46)**
Room 610
2300 North Lincoln Boulevard
Oklahoma City, OK 73105
P: (405) 521-5610
E: floyd@oksenate.gov

**Fry, Jack (R, 42)**
Room 413A
2300 North Lincoln Boulevard
Oklahoma City, OK 73105
P: (405) 521-5584
E: fry@oksenate.gov

**Griffin, AJ (R, 20)**
Room 534
2300 North Lincoln Boulevard
Oklahoma City, OK 73105
P: (405) 521-5628
E: griffin@oksenate.gov

**Holt, David (R, 30)**
Room 424
2300 North Lincoln Boulevard
Oklahoma City, OK 73105
P: (405) 521-5636
E: holt@oksenate.gov

**Jech, Darcy A. (R, 26)**
Room 415
2300 North Lincoln Boulevard
Oklahoma City, OK 73105
P: (405) 521-5545
E: jech@oksenate.gov

**Kidd, Chris (R, 31)***
Room 411A
2300 North Lincoln Boulevard
Oklahoma City, OK 73105
P: (405) 521-5563
E: kidd@oksenate.gov

**Leewright, James (R, 12)**
Room 427A
2300 North Lincoln Boulevard
Oklahoma City, OK 73105
P: (405) 521-5528
E: leewright@oksenate.gov

**Loveless, Kyle (R, 45)**
Room 238
2300 North Lincoln Boulevard
Oklahoma City, OK 73105
P: (405) 521-5618
E: loveless@oksenate.gov

**Marlatt, Bryce (R, 27)**
Room 526
2300 North Lincoln Boulevard
Oklahoma City, OK 73105
P: (405) 521-5626
E: marlatt@oksenate.gov

**Matthews, Kevin (D, 11)**
Room 522A
2300 North Lincoln Boulevard
Oklahoma City, OK 73105
P: (405) 521-5598
E: matthews@oksenate.gov

**McCortney, Greg (R, 13)***
Room 233
2300 North Lincoln Boulevard
Oklahoma City, OK 73105
P: (405) 521-5600
E: mccortney@oksenate.gov

**Newberry, Dan (R, 37)**
Room 233
2300 North Lincoln Boulevard
Oklahoma City, OK 73105
P: (405) 521-5600
E: newberry@oksenate.gov

**Newhouse, Joe (R, 25)***
Room 527B
2300 North Lincoln Boulevard
Oklahoma City, OK 73105
P: (405) 521-5675
E: newhouse@oksenate.gov

**Paxton, Lonnie (R, 23)***
Room 428B
2300 North Lincoln Boulevard
Oklahoma City, OK 73105
P: (405) 521-5537
E: paxton@oksenate.gov

**Pederson, Roland (R, 19)***
Room 630
2300 North Lincoln Boulevard
Oklahoma City, OK 73105
P: (405) 521-5630
E: pederson@oksenate.gov

**Pemberton, Dewayne (R, 9)***
Room 427
2300 North Lincoln Boulevard
Oklahoma City, OK 73105
P: (405) 521-5533
E: pemberton@oksenate.gov

**Pittman, Anastasia (D, 48)**
Room 521A
2300 North Lincoln Boulevard
Oklahoma City, OK 73105
P: (405) 521-5531
E: pittman@oksenate.gov

**Pugh, Adam (R, 41)***
Room 528A
2300 North Lincoln Boulevard
Oklahoma City, OK 73105
P: (405) 521-5622
E: pugh@oksenate.gov

**Quinn, Marty (R, 2)**
Room 417B
2300 North Lincoln Boulevard
Oklahoma City, OK 73105
P: (405) 521-5555
E: quinn@oksenate.gov

**Rader, Dave (R, 39)***
Room 426
2300 North Lincoln Boulevard
Oklahoma City, OK 73105
P: (405) 521-5620
E: rader@oksenate.gov

**Schulz, Mike (R, 38)**
Room 422
2300 North Lincoln Boulevard
Oklahoma City, OK 73105
P: (405) 521-5612
E: schulz@oksenate.gov

**Scott, Paul (R, 43)***
Room 529A
2300 North Lincoln Boulevard
Oklahoma City, OK 73105
P: (405) 521-5522
E: scott@oksenate.gov

**Sharp, Ron (R, 17)**
Room 429
2300 North Lincoln Boulevard
Oklahoma City, OK 73105
P: (405) 521-5539
E: sharp@oksenate.gov

**Shaw, Wayne (R, 3)**
Room 235
2300 North Lincoln Boulevard
Oklahoma City, OK 73105
P: (405) 521-5574
E: shaw@oksenate.gov

**Shortey, Ralph (R, 44)**
Room 412
2300 North Lincoln Boulevard
Oklahoma City, OK 73105
P: (405) 521-5557
E: shortey@oksenate.gov

**Silk, Joseph W. (R, 5)**
Room 536
2300 North Lincoln Boulevard
Oklahoma City, OK 73105
P: (405) 521-5614
E: silk@oksenate.gov

**Simpson, Frank (R, 14)**
Room 414
2300 North Lincoln Boulevard
Oklahoma City, OK 73105
P: (405) 521-5607
E: simpson@oksenate.gov

**Smalley, Jason (R, 28)**
Room 416
2300 North Lincoln Boulevard
Oklahoma City, OK 73105
P: (405) 521-5547
E: smalley@oksenate.gov

**Sparks, John (D, 16)**
Room 519
2300 North Lincoln Boulevard
Oklahoma City, OK 73105
P: (405) 521-5553
E: sparks@oksenate.gov

**Standridge, Rob (R, 15)**
Room 417A
2300 North Lincoln Boulevard
Oklahoma City, OK 73105
P: (405) 521-5535
E: standridge@oksenate.gov

**Stanislawski, Gary (R, 35)**
Room 428
2300 North Lincoln Boulevard
Oklahoma City, OK 73105
P: (405) 521-5624
E: stanislawski
    @oksenate.gov

**Sykes, Anthony (R, 24)**
Room 423
2300 North Lincoln Boulevard
Oklahoma City, OK 73105
P: (405) 521-5569
E: lewis@oksenate.gov

**Thompson, Roger (R, 8)**
Room 523
2300 North Lincoln Boulevard
Oklahoma City, OK 73105
P: (405) 521-5588
E: thompson@oksenate.gov

**Treat, Greg (R, 47)**
Room 418
2300 North Lincoln Boulevard
Oklahoma City, OK 73105
P: (405) 521-5632
E: treat@oksenate.gov

**Yen, Ervin (R, 40)**
Room 413
2300 North Lincoln Boulevard
Oklahoma City, OK 73105
P: (405) 521-5543
E: yen@oksenate.gov

# House

## Speaker of the House

**Representative Charles A. McCall (R)**
Speaker of the House
Room 401
2300 North Lincoln Boulevard
Oklahoma City, OK 73105
P: (405) 557-7412
E: charles.mccall
   @okhouse.gov

## Speaker Pro Tempore of the House

**Representative Harold Wright (R)**
Speaker Pro Tempore
Room 411
2300 North Lincoln Boulevard
Oklahoma City, OK 73105
P: (405) 557-7325
E: harold.wright
   @okhouse.gov

## House Majority Leader

**Representative Jon Echols (R)**
Majority Floor Leader
Room 442
2300 North Lincoln Boulevard
Oklahoma City, OK 73105
P: (405) 557-7354
E: jon.echols@okhouse.gov

## House Minority Leader

**Representative Scott Inman (D)**
House Democrat Minority Leader
Room 548
2300 North Lincoln Boulevard
Oklahoma City, OK 73105
P: (405) 557-7370
E: scott.inman@okhouse.gov

## Clerk of the House

**Ms. Jan Harrison**
Chief Clerk Of The House
2300 North Lincoln Boulevard
Oklahoma City, OK 73105
P: (405) 521-2711
E: harrisonja@okhouse.gov

## Members of the House

**Babinec, Greg (R, 33)***
Room 301
2300 North Lincoln Boulevard
Oklahoma City, OK 73105
P: (401) 557-7304
E: greg.babinec@okhouse.gov

**Baker, Rhonda (R, 60)***
Room 202A
2300 North Lincoln Boulevard
Oklahoma City, OK 73105
P: (405) 557-7311
E: rhonda.baker@okhouse.gov

**Bennett, Forrest (D, 92)***
Room 543
2300 North Lincoln Boulevard
Oklahoma City, OK 73105
P: (405) 557-7404
E: forrest.bennett
   @okhouse.gov

**Bennett, John (R, 2)**
Room 301A
2300 North Lincoln Boulevard
Oklahoma City, OK 73105
P: (405) 557-7315
E: john.bennett@okhouse.gov

**Biggs, Scott R. (R, 51)**
Room 244
2300 North Lincoln Boulevard
Oklahoma City, OK 73105
P: (405) 557-7405
E: scott.biggs@okhouse.gov

**Blancett, Meloyde (D, 78)***
Room 510
2300 North Lincoln Boulevard
Oklahoma City, OK 73105
P: (405) 557-7334
E: meloyde.blancett
   @okhouse.gov

**Brumbaugh, David (R, 76)**
Room 400B
2300 North Lincoln Boulevard
Oklahoma City, OK 73105
P: (405) 557-7347
E: david.brumbaugh
   @okhouse.gov

**Bush, Carol (R, 70)***
Room 204A
2300 North Lincoln Boulevard
Oklahoma City, OK 73105
P: (405) 557-7359
E: carol.bush@okhouse.gov

**Caldwell, Chad (R, 40)**
Room 332
2300 North Lincoln Boulevard
Oklahoma City, OK 73105
P: (405) 557-7317
E: chad.caldwell
   @okhouse.gov

**Calvey, Kevin (R, 82)**
Room 435
2300 North Lincoln Boulevard
Oklahoma City, OK 73105
P: (405) 557-7357
E: kevincalvey@okhouse.gov

**Cannaday, Ed (D, 15)**
Room 546
2300 North Lincoln Boulevard
Oklahoma City, OK 73105
P: (405) 557-7375
E: ed.cannaday@okhouse.gov

**Casey, Dennis (R, 35)**
Room 331
2300 North Lincoln Boulevard
Oklahoma City, OK 73105
P: (405) 557-7344
E: dennis.casey@okhouse.gov

**Cleveland, Bobby (R, 20)**
Room 434
2300 North Lincoln Boulevard
Oklahoma City, OK 73105
P: (405) 557-7308
E: bob.cleveland
   @okhouse.gov

**Cockroft, Josh (R, 27)**
Room 408
2300 North Lincoln Boulevard
Oklahoma City, OK 73105
P: (405) 557-7349
E: josh.cockroft
   @okhouse.gov

**Condit, Donnie (D, 18)**
Room 502
2300 North Lincoln Boulevard
Oklahoma City, OK 73105
P: (405) 557-7376
E: donnie.condit
   @okhouse.gov

**Coody, Jeff (R, 63)**
Room 337
2300 North Lincoln Boulevard
Oklahoma City, OK 73105
P: (405) 557-7307
E: jeff.coody@okhouse.gov

**Derby, Dale (R, 74)***
Room 500
2300 North Lincoln Boulevard
Oklahoma City, OK 73105
P: (405) 557-7377
E: dale.derby@okhouse.gov

**Dollens, Mickey (D, 93)***
Room 510B
2300 North Lincoln Boulevard
Oklahoma City, OK 73105
P: (405) 557-7371
E: mickey.dollens
   @okhouse.gov

**Downing, Tim (R, 42)***
Room 300A
2300 North Lincoln Boulevard
Oklahoma City, OK 73105
P: (405) 557-7365
E: tim.downing@okhouse.gov

**Dunlap, Travis (R, 10)**
Room 250
2300 North Lincoln Boulevard
Oklahoma City, OK 73105
P: (405) 557-7402
E: travis.dunlap
   @okhouse.gov

**Dunnington, Jason (D, 88)**
Room 539
2300 North Lincoln Boulevard
Oklahoma City, OK 73105
P: (405) 557-7396
E: jason.dunnington
   @okhouse.gov

**Echols, Jon (R, 90)**
Room 442
2300 North Lincoln Boulevard
Oklahoma City, OK 73105
P: (405) 557-7354
E: jon.echols@okhouse.gov

**Enns, John (R, 41)**
Room 440
2300 North Lincoln Boulevard
Oklahoma City, OK 73105
P: (405) 557-7321
E: john.enns@okhouse.gov

**Faught, George (R, 14)**
Room 301B
2300 North Lincoln Boulevard
Oklahoma City, OK 73105
P: (405) 557-7310
E: george.faught
   @okhouse.gov

**Fetgatter, Scott (R, 16)***
Room 248A
2300 North Lincoln Boulevard
Oklahoma City, OK 73105
P: (405) 557-7373
E: scott.fetgatter
   @okhouse.gov

# Oklahoma

**Ford, Roger (R, 95)***
Room 301
2300 North Lincoln Boulevard
Oklahoma City, OK 73105
P: (405) 557-7314
E: roger.ford@okhouse.gov

**Fourkiller, William (D, 86)**
Room 542
2300 North Lincoln Boulevard
Oklahoma City, OK 73105
P: (405) 557-7394
E: will.fourkiller
   @okhouse.gov

**Frix, Avery (R, 13)***
Room 328B
2300 North Lincoln Boulevard
Oklahoma City, OK 73105
P: (405) 557-7302
E: avery.frix@okhouse.gov

**Gann, Tom (R, 8)***
Room 500
2300 North Lincoln Boulevard
Oklahoma City, OK 73105
P: (405) 557-7364
E: tom.gann@okhouse.gov

**Goodwin, Regina (D, 73)**
Room 510
2300 North Lincoln Boulevard
Oklahoma City, OK 73105
P: (405) 557-7406
E: Regina.Goodwin
   @okhouse.gov

**Griffith, Claudia (D, 45)**
Room 539
2300 North Lincoln Boulevard
Oklahoma City, OK 73105
P: (405) 557-7386
E: claudia.griffith
   @okhouse.gov

**Hall, Elise (R, 100)**
Room 200A
2300 North Lincoln Boulevard
Oklahoma City, OK 73105
P: (405) 557-7403
E: elise.hall@okhouse.gov

**Hardin, Tommy (R, 49)**
Room 336
2300 North Lincoln Boulevard
Oklahoma City, OK 73105
P: (405) 557-7383
E: tommy.hardin@okhouse.gov

**Henke, Katie (R, 71)**
Room 244B
2300 North Lincoln Boulevard
Oklahoma City, OK 73105
P: (405) 557-7361
E: katie.henke@okhouse.gov

**Hilbert, Kyle (R, 29)***
Room 330
2300 North Lincoln Boulevard
Oklahoma City, OK 73105
P: (405) 557-7353
E: kyle.hilbert@okhouse.gov

**Hoskin, Chuck (D, 6)**
Room 509
2300 North Lincoln Boulevard
Oklahoma City, OK 73105
P: (405) 557-7319
E: chuck.hoskin@okhouse.gov

**Humphrey, Justin (R, 19)***
Room 329B
2300 North Lincoln Boulevard
Oklahoma City, OK 73105
P: (405) 557-7382
E: justin.humphrey
   @okhouse.gov

**Inman, Scott (D, 94)**
Room 548
2300 North Lincoln Boulevard
Oklahoma City, OK 73105
P: (405) 557-7370
E: scott.inman@okhouse.gov

**Jordan, John Paul (R, 43)**
Room 410
2300 North Lincoln Boulevard
Oklahoma City, OK 73105
P: (405) 557-7352
E: jp.jordan@okhouse.gov

**Kannady, Chris (R, 91)**
Room 246A
2300 North Lincoln Boulevard
Oklahoma City, OK 73105
P: (405) 557-7337
E: chris.kannady
   @okhouse.gov

**Kerbs, Dell (R, 26)***
Room 335
2300 North Lincoln Boulevard
Oklahoma City, OK 73105
P: (405) 557-7345
E: dell.kerbs@okhouse.gov

**Kirby, Dan (R, 75)**
Room 328
2300 North Lincoln Boulevard
Oklahoma City, OK 73105
P: (405) 557-7356
E: dan.kirby@okhouse.gov

**Kouplen, Steve (D, 24)**
Room 541
2300 North Lincoln Boulevard
Oklahoma City, OK 73105
P: (405) 557-7306
E: steve.kouplen
   @okhouse.gov

**Lawson, Mark (R, 30)***
Room 300B
2300 North Lincoln Boulevard
Oklahoma City, OK 73105
P: (405) 557-7414
E: mark.lawson@okhouse.gov

**Lepak, Mark Paul (R, 9)**
Room 328A
2300 North Lincoln Boulevard
Oklahoma City, OK 73105
P: (405) 557-7380
E: mark.lepak@okhouse.gov

**Loring, Ben (D, 7)**
Room 539B
2300 North Lincoln Boulevard
Oklahoma City, OK 73105
P: (405) 557-7399
E: ben.loring@okhouse.gov

**Lowe, Jason (D, 97)***
Room 539
2300 North Lincoln Boulevard
Oklahoma City, OK 73105
P: (405) 557-7367
E: jason.lowe@okhouse.gov

**Martin, Scott (R, 46)**
Room 441
2300 North Lincoln Boulevard
Oklahoma City, OK 73105
P: (405) 557-7329
E: scott.martin@okhouse.gov

**Martinez, Ryan (R, 39)***
Room 338
2300 North Lincoln Boulevard
Oklahoma City, OK 73105
P: (405) 557-7342
E: ryan.martinez
   @okhouse.gov

**McBride, Mark (R, 53)**
Room 433B
2300 North Lincoln Boulevard
Oklahoma City, OK 73105
P: (405) 557-7346
E: mark.mcbride@okhouse.gov

**McCall, Charles A. (R, 22)**
Room 401
2300 North Lincoln Boulevard
Oklahoma City, OK 73105
P: (405) 557-7412
E: charles.mccall
   @okhouse.gov

**McDaniel, Randy (R, 83)**
Room 438
2300 North Lincoln Boulevard
Oklahoma City, OK 73105
P: (405) 557-7409
E: randy.mcdaniel
   @okhouse.gov

**McDugle, Kevin (R, 12)***
Room 242B
2300 North Lincoln Boulevard
Oklahoma City, OK 73105
P: (405) 557-7388
E: kevin.mcdugle
   @okhouse.gov

**McEachin, Scott (R, 67)***
Room 409
2300 North Lincoln Boulevard
Oklahoma City, OK 73105
P: (405) 557-7341
E: scott.mceachin
   @okhouse.gov

**McEntire, Marcus (R, 50)***
Room 204B
2300 North Lincoln Boulevard
Oklahoma City, OK 73105
P: (405) 557-7327
E: marcus.mcentire
   @okhouse.gov

**Meredith, Matt (D, 4)***
Room 545
2300 North Lincoln Boulevard
Oklahoma City, OK 73105
P: (405) 557-7408
E: matt.meredith
   @okhouse.gov

**Montgomery, John Michael
(R, 62)**
Room 304
2300 North Lincoln Boulevard
Oklahoma City, OK 73105
P: (405) 557-7374
E: john.montgomery
   @okhouse.gov

**Moore, Lewis H. (R, 96)**
Room 329
2300 North Lincoln Boulevard
Oklahoma City, OK 73105
P: (405) 557-7400
E: lewis.moore@okhouse.gov

**Mulready, Glen (R, 68)**
Room 200
2300 North Lincoln Boulevard
Oklahoma City, OK 73105
P: (405) 557-7340
E: glen.mulready
   @okhouse.gov

**Munson, Cyndi (D, 85)**
Room 539
2300 North Lincoln Boulevard
Oklahoma City, OK 73105
P: (405) 557-7392
E: cyndi.munson@okhouse.gov

# Oklahoma

**Murdock, Casey (R, 61)**
Room 303A
2300 North Lincoln Boulevard
Oklahoma City, OK 73105
P: (405) 557-7384
E: casey.murdock
   @okhouse.gov

**Murphey, Jason (R, 31)**
Room 432D
2300 North Lincoln Boulevard
Oklahoma City, OK 73105
P: (405) 557-7350
E: jason.murphey
   @okhouse.gov

**Newton, Carl (R, 58)\***
Room 300
2300 North Lincoln Boulevard
Oklahoma City, OK 73105
P: (405) 557-7339
E: carl.newton@okhouse.gov

**Nichols, Monroe (D, 72)\***
Room 510
2300 North Lincoln Boulevard
Oklahoma City, OK 73105
P: (405) 557-7391
E: monroe.nichols
   @okhouse.gov

**Nollan, Jadine (R, 66)**
Room 407
2300 North Lincoln Boulevard
Oklahoma City, OK 73105
P: (405) 557-7390
E: jadine.nollan
   @okhouse.gov

**O'Donnell, Terry (R, 23)**
Room 433
2300 North Lincoln Boulevard
Oklahoma City, OK 73105
P: (405) 557-7379
E: terry.odonnell
   @okhouse.gov

**Ortega, Charles L. (R, 52)**
Room 305A
2300 North Lincoln Boulevard
Oklahoma City, OK 73105
P: (405) 557-7369
E: charles.ortega
   @okhouse.gov

**Osborn, Leslie (R, 47)**
Room 240
2300 North Lincoln Boulevard
Oklahoma City, OK 73105
P: (405) 557-7333
E: leslie.osborn
   @okhouse.gov

**Osburn, Mike (R, 81)\***
Room 338
2300 North Lincoln Boulevard
Oklahoma City, OK 73105
P: (405) 557-7360
E: mike.osburn@okhouse.gov

**Ownbey, Pat (R, 48)**
Room 334
2300 North Lincoln Boulevard
Oklahoma City, OK 73105
P: (405) 557-7326
E: pat.ownbey@okhouse.gov

**Park, Scooter (R, 65)**
Room 303B
2300 North Lincoln Boulevard
Oklahoma City, OK 73105
P: (405) 557-7305
E: scooter.park@okhouse.gov

**Perryman, David L. (D, 56)**
Room 540
2300 North Lincoln Boulevard
Oklahoma City, OK 73105
P: (405) 557-7401
E: david.perryman
   @okhouse.gov

**Pfeiffer, John (R, 38)**
Room 302B
2300 North Lincoln Boulevard
Oklahoma City, OK 73105
P: (405) 557-7332
E: john.pfeiffer
   @okhouse.gov

**Proctor, Eric (D, 77)**
Room 540A
2300 North Lincoln Boulevard
Oklahoma City, OK 73105
P: (405) 557-7410
E: eric.proctor@okhouse.gov

**Renegar, Brian (D, 17)**
Room 504
2300 North Lincoln Boulevard
Oklahoma City, OK 73105
P: (405) 557-7381
E: brian.renegar
   @okhouse.gov

**Ritze, Mike (R, 80)**
Room 436
2300 North Lincoln Boulevard
Oklahoma City, OK 73105
P: (405) 557-7338
E: mike.ritze@okhouse.gov

**Roberts, Dustin (R, 21)**
Room 303
2300 North Lincoln Boulevard
Oklahoma City, OK 73105
P: (405) 557-7366
E: dustin.roberts
   @okhouse.gov

**Roberts, Sean (R, 36)**
Room 250
2300 North Lincoln Boulevard
Oklahoma City, OK 73105
P: (405) 557-7322
E: sean.roberts@okhouse.gov

**Rogers, Michael (R, 98)**
Room 302
2300 North Lincoln Boulevard
Oklahoma City, OK 73105
P: (405) 557-7362
E: michael.rogers
   @okhouse.gov

**Russ, Todd (R, 55)**
Room 406
2300 North Lincoln Boulevard
Oklahoma City, OK 73105
P: (405) 557-7312
E: todd.russ@okhouse.gov

**Sanders, Mike (R, 59)**
Room 205
2300 North Lincoln Boulevard
Oklahoma City, OK 73105
P: (405) 557-7407
E: mike.sanders@okhouse.gov

**Sears, Earl (R, 11)**
Room 439
2300 North Lincoln Boulevard
Oklahoma City, OK 73105
P: (405) 557-7358
E: earl.sears@okhouse.gov

**Stone, Shane (D, 89)**
Room 510A
2300 North Lincoln Boulevard
Oklahoma City, OK 73105
P: (405) 557-7397
E: shane.stone@okhouse.gov

**Strohm, Chuck (R, 69)**
Room 302A
2300 North Lincoln Boulevard
Oklahoma City, OK 73105
P: (405) 557-7331
E: chuck.strohm@okhouse.gov

**Tadlock, Johnny (D, 1)**
Room 539B
2300 North Lincoln Boulevard
Oklahoma City, OK 73105
P: (405) 557-7363
E: johnny.tadlock
   @okhouse.gov

**Teague, Tess (R, 101)\***
Room 329A
2300 North Lincoln Boulevard
Oklahoma City, OK 73105
P: (405) 557-7395
E: tess.teague@okhouse.gov

**Thomsen, Todd (R, 25)**
Room 437
2300 North Lincoln Boulevard
Oklahoma City, OK 73105
P: (405) 557-7336
E: todd.thomsen@okhouse.gov

**Vaughan, Steve (R, 37)**
Room 435A
2300 North Lincoln Boulevard
Oklahoma City, OK 73105
P: (405) 557-7355
E: steve.vaughan
   @okhouse.gov

**Virgin, Emily (D, 44)**
Room 500
2300 North Lincoln Boulevard
Oklahoma City, OK 73105
P: (405) 557-7323
E: emily.virgin@okhouse.gov

**Walke, Collin (D, 87)\***
Room 510
2300 North Lincoln Boulevard
Oklahoma City, OK 73105
P: (405) 557-7335
E: collin.walke@okhouse.gov

**Wallace, Kevin (R, 32)**
Room 246B
2300 North Lincoln Boulevard
Oklahoma City, OK 73105
P: (405) 557-7368
E: kevin.wallace
   @okhouse.gov

**Watson, Weldon (R, 79)**
Room 405
2300 North Lincoln Boulevard
Oklahoma City, OK 73105
P: (405) 557-7330
E: weldon.watson
   @okhouse.gov

**West, Josh (R, 5)\***
Room 242A
2300 North Lincoln Boulevard
Oklahoma City, OK 73105
P: (405) 557-7415
E: josh.west@okhouse.gov

**West, Kevin (R, 54)\***
Room 248B
2300 North Lincoln Boulevard
Oklahoma City, OK 73105
P: (405) 557-7343
E: kevin.west@okhouse.gov

**West, Rick (R, 3)\***
Room 333
2300 North Lincoln Boulevard
Oklahoma City, OK 73105
P: (405) 557-7413
E: rick.west@okhouse.gov

# Oklahoma

**West, Tammy (R, 84)***
Room 202B
2300 North Lincoln Boulevard
Oklahoma City, OK 73105
P: (405) 557-7348
E: tammy.west@okhouse.gov

**Williams, Cory T. (D, 34)**
Room 544
2300 North Lincoln Boulevard
Oklahoma City, OK 73105
P: (405) 557-7411
E: cory.williams
   @okhouse.gov

**Worthen, Rande (R, 64)***
Room 300C
2300 North Lincoln Boulevard
Oklahoma City, OK 73105
P: (405) 557-7398
E: rande.worthen
   @okhouse.gov

**Wright, Harold (R, 57)**
Room 411
2300 North Lincoln Boulevard
Oklahoma City, OK 73105
P: (405) 557-7325
E: harold.wright
   @okhouse.gov

**Young Sr., George E.
   (D, 99)**
Room 510B
2300 North Lincoln Boulevard
Oklahoma City, OK 73105
P: (405) 557-7393
E: george.young@okhouse.gov

# Oregon

## Executive

### Governor

**The Honorable Kate Brown (D)**
Governor
State Capitol, Room 160
900 Court Street North
Salem, OR 97301
P: (503) 378-3111
F: (503) 378-8970

### Lieutenant Governor

*This state does not have the office of lieutenant governor. The secretary of state is next in line of succession to the governorship.*

### Attorney General

**The Honorable Ellen Rosenblum (D)**
Attorney General
Justice Building
1162 Court Street, Northeast
Salem, OR 97301
P: (503) 378-6002
F: (503) 378-4017

### Auditor

**Ms. Mary Wenger**
(appointed)
Interim Director
255 Capitol Street, Northeast
Suite 500
Salem, OR 97310
P: (503) 986-2355
F: (503) 378-4829

### Secretary of State

**The Honorable Dennis Richardson (R)**
Secretary of State
136 State Capitol
Salem, OR 37310
P: (503) 986-1523
F: (503) 986-1616
E: oregon.sos@state.or.us

### Treasurer

**The Honorable Tobias Read (D)**
State Treasurer
900 Court Street, Room 159
Salem, OR 97301
P: (503) 378-4329
F: (503) 373-7051

## Judiciary

### Supreme Court (NE)

**Ms. Kingsley W. Click**
State Court Administrator
Supreme Court Building
1163 State Street
Salem, OR 97301
P: (503) 986-5500
F: (503) 986-5503
E: kingsley.w.click
@state.or.us

**The Honorable Thomas A. Balmer**
Chief Justice
**The Honorable Richard C. Baldwin**
**The Honorable David V. Brewer**
**The Honorable Rives Kistler**
**The Honorable Jack L. Landau**
**The Honorable Lynn Nakamoto**
**The Honorable Martha Lee Walters**

## Legislative Senate

### Senate President

**Senator Peter Courtney (D)**
Senate President
900 Court Street, Northeast
S-201
Salem, OR 97301
P: (503) 986-1600
F: (503) 986-1004
E: Sen.PeterCourtney
@oregonlegislature.gov

### President Pro Tempore of the Senate

**Senator Laurie Monnes Anderson (D)**
Senate President Pro Tempore
900 Court Street, Northeast
S-211
Salem, OR 97301
P: (503) 986-1725
E: Sen.
LaurieMonnesAnderson
@oregonlegislature.gov

### Senate Majority Leader

**Senator Ginny Burdick (D)**
Senate Democratic Leader
900 Court Street, Northeast
S-223
Salem, OR 97301
P: (503) 986-1700
E: Sen.GinnyBurdick
@oregonlegislature.gov

### Senate Minority Leader

**Senator Ted Ferrioli (R)**
Senate Republican Leader
900 Court Street, Northeast
S-323
Salem, OR 97301
P: (503) 986-1950
E: Sen.TedFerrioli
@oregonlegislature.gov

### Secretary of the Senate

**Ms. Lori Brocker**
Secretary of the Senate
900 Court Street, Northeast
Room 233
Salem, OR 97301
P: (503) 986-1851
E: lori.l.brocker
@oregonlegislature.gov

### Members of the Senate

**Baertschiger, Herman (R, 2)**
900 Court Street, Northeast
S-403
Salem, OR 97301
P: (503) 986-1702
E: Sen.HermanBaertschiger
@oregonlegislature.gov

**Beyer, Lee (D, 6)**
900 Court Street, Northeast
S-411
Salem, OR 97301
P: (503) 986-1706
E: Sen.LeeBeyer
@oregonlegislature.gov

**Boquist, Brian (R, 12)**
900 Court Street, Northeast
S-311
Salem, OR 97301
P: (503) 986-1712
E: Sen.BrianBoquist
@oregonlegislature.gov

**Burdick, Ginny (D, 18)**
900 Court Street, Northeast
S-223
Salem, OR 97301
P: (503) 986-1700
E: Sen.GinnyBurdick
@oregonlegislature.gov

**Courtney, Peter (D, 11)**
900 Court Street, Northeast
S-201
Salem, OR 97301
P: (503) 986-1600
F: (503) 986-1004
E: Sen.PeterCourtney
@oregonlegislature.gov

**DeBoer, Alan (R, 3)***
900 Court Street Northeast
S-421
Salem, OR 97301
P: (503) 986-1703
E: sen.AlanDeBoer
@oregonlegislature.gov

**Dembrow, Michael E. (D, 23)**
900 Court Street, Northeast
S-407
Salem, OR 97301
P: (503) 986-1723
E: Sen.MichaelDembrow
@oregonlegislature.gov

**Devlin, Richard (D, 19)**
900 Court Street, Northeast
S-213
Salem, OR 97301
P: (503) 986-1719
E: Sen.RichardDevlin
@oregonlegislature.gov

**Ferrioli, Ted (R, 30)**
900 Court Street, Northeast
S-323
Salem, OR 97301
P: (503) 986-1950
E: Sen.TedFerrioli
@oregonlegislature.gov

**Frederick, Lew (D, 22)**
900 Court Street, Northeast
S-419
Salem, OR 97301
P: (503) 986-1722
E: Sen.LewFrederick
@oregonlegislature.gov

**Gelser, Sara (D, 8)**
900 Court Street, Northeast
S-405
Salem, OR 97301
P: (503) 986-1708
E: Sen.SaraGelser
@oregonlegislature.gov

# Oregon

**Girod, Fred (R, 9)**
900 Court Street, Northeast
S-401
Salem, OR 97301
P: (503) 986-1709
E: Sen.FredGirod
@oregonlegislature.gov

**Hansell, Bill (R, 29)**
900 Court Street, Northeast
S-415
Salem, OR 97301
P: (503) 986-1729
E: Sen.BillHansell
@oregonlegislature.gov

**Hass, Mark (D, 14)**
900 Court Street, Northeast
S-207
Salem, OR 97301
P: (503) 986-1714
E: Sen.MarkHass
@oregonlegislature.gov

**Johnson, Betsy (D, 16)**
900 Court Street, Northeast
S-209
Salem, OR 97301
P: (503) 986-1716
E: Sen.BetsyJohnson
@oregonlegislature.gov

**Knopp, Tim (R, 27)**
900 Court Street, Northeast
S-309
Salem, OR 97301
P: (503) 986-1727
E: sen.timknopp
@oregonlegislature.gov

**Kruse, Jeff (R, 1)**
900 Court Street, Northeast
S-315
Salem, OR 97301
P: (503) 986-1701
E: sen.jeffkruse
@state.or.us

**Linthicum, Dennis (R, 28)***
900 Court Street Northeast
S-305
Salem, OR 97301
P: (503) 986-1728
E: Sen.DennisLinthicum
@oregonlegislature.gov

**Manning Jr., James I.
(D, 7)***
900 Court Street Northeast
S-205
Salem, OR 97301
P: (503) 986-1707
E: Sen.JamesManning
@oregonlegislature.gov

**Monnes Anderson, Laurie
(D, 25)**
900 Court Street, Northeast
S-211
Salem, OR 97301
P: (503) 986-1725
E: Sen.
LaurieMonnesAnderson
@oregonlegislature.gov

**Monroe, Rod (D, 24)**
900 Court Street, Northeast
S-409
Salem, OR 97301
P: (503) 986-1724
E: Sen.RodMonroe
@oregonlegislature.gov

**Olsen, Alan (R, 20)**
900 Court Street, Northeast
S-425
Salem, OR 97301
P: (503) 986-1720
E: Sen.AlanOlsen
@oregonlegislature.gov

**Prozanski, Floyd (D, 4)**
900 Court Street, Northeast
S-413
Salem, OR 97301
P: (503) 986-1704
E: Sen.FloydProzanski
@oregonlegislature.gov

**Riley, Chuck (D, 15)**
900 Court Street, Northeast
S-303
Salem, OR 97301
P: (503) 986-1715
E: Sen.ChuckRiley
@oregonlegislature.gov

**Roblan, Arnie (D, 5)**
900 Court Street, Northeast
S-417
Salem, OR 97301
P: (503) 986-1705
E: Sen.ArnieRoblan
@staoregonlegislature.gov

**Steiner Hayward,
Elizabeth (D, 17)**
900 Court Street, Northeast
S-215
Salem, OR 97301
P: (503) 986-1717
E: Sen.
ElizabethSteinerHayward
@oregonlegislature.gov

**Taylor, Kathleen (D, 21)**
900 Court Street, Northeast
S-423
Salem, OR 97301
P: (503) 986-1441
E: Sen.KathleenTaylor
@oregonlegislature.gov

**Thatcher, Kim (R, 13)**
900 Court Street, Northeast
S-307
Salem, OR 97301
P: (503) 986-1713
E: Sen.KimThatcher
@oregonlegislature.gov

**Thomsen, Chuck (R, 26)**
900 Court Street, Northeast
S-316
Salem, OR 97301
P: (503) 986-1726
E: Sen.ChuckThomsen
@oregonlegislature.gov

**Winters, Jackie (R, 10)**
900 Court Street, Northeast
S-301
Salem, OR 97301
P: (503) 986-1710
E: Sen.JackieWinters
@oregonlegislature.gov

# House
## Speaker of the House
**Representative Tina
Kotek (D)**
House Speaker
900 Court Street, Northeast
H-269
Salem, OR 97301
P: (503) 986-1200
E: Rep.TinaKotek
@state.or.us

## Speaker Pro Tempore of the House
**Representative Paul
Holvey (D)**
House Speaker Pro Tempore
900 Court Street, Northeast
H-277
Salem, OR 97301
P: (503) 986-1408
E: Rep.PaulHolvey
@oregonlegislature.gov

## House Majority Leader
**Representative Jennifer
Williamson (D)**
House Majority Leader
900 Court Street, Northeast
H-295
Salem, OR 97301
P: (503) 986-1436
E: Rep.JenniferWilliamson
@oregonlegislature.gov

## House Minority Leader
**Representative Michael
McLane (R)**
House Republican Leader
900 Court Street, Northeast
H-395
Salem, OR 97301
P: (503) 986-1455
E: Rep.MikeMcLane
@oregonlegislature.gov

## Clerk of the House
**Mr. Tim Sekerak**
Chief Clerk of the House
900 Court Street, Northeast
H-271
Salem, OR 97301
P: (503) 986-1870
F: (503) 986-1876
E: tim.sekerak
@oregonlegislature.gov

## Members of the House
**Alonso Leon, Teresa
(D, 22)***
900 Court Street Northeast
H-283
Salem, OR 97301
P: (503) 986-1422
E: Rep.TeresaAlonsoLeon
@oregonlegislature.gov

**Barker, Jeff (D, 28)**
900 Court Street, Northeast
H-480
Salem, OR 97301
P: (503) 986-1428
E: Rep.JeffBarker
@oregonlegislature.gov

**Barnhart, Phil (D, 11)**
900 Court Street, Northeast
H-279
Salem, OR 97301
P: (503) 986-1411
E: Rep.PhilBarnhart
@oregonlegislature.gov

**Barreto, Greg (R, 58)**
900 Court Street, Northeast
H-384
Salem, OR 97301
P: (503) 986-1458
E: Rep.GregBarreto
@oregonlegislature.gov

**Bentz, Cliff (R, 60)**
900 Court Street, Northeast
H-475
Salem, OR 97301
P: (503) 986-1460
E: Rep.CliffBentz
   @oregonlegislature.gov

**Boone, Deborah (D, 32)**
900 Court Street, Northeast
H-481
Salem, OR 97301
P: (503) 986-1432
E: Rep.DeborahBoone
   @oregonlegislature.gov

**Brock Smith, David (R, 1)\***
H-379
Salem, OR 97301
P: (503) 986-1401
E: Rep.DavidBrockSmith
   @oregonlegislature.gov

**Buehler, Knute C. (R, 54)**
900 Court Street, Northeast
H-389
Salem, OR 97301
P: (503) 986-1454
E: Rep.KnuteBuehler
   @oregonlegislature.gov

**Bynum, Janelle (D, 51)\***
900 Court Street Northeast
H-284
Salem, OR 97301
P: (503) 986-1451
E: Rep.JanelleBynum
   @oregonlegislature.gov

**Clem, Brian (D, 21)**
900 Court Street, Northeast
H-478
Salem, OR 97301
P: (503) 986-1421
E: Rep.BrianClem
   @oregonlegislature.gov

**Doherty, Margaret (D, 35)**
900 Court Street, Northeast
H-282
Salem, OR 97301
P: (503) 986-1435
E: Rep.MargaretDoherty
   @oregonlegislature.gov

**Esquivel, Sal (R, 6)**
900 Court Street, Northeast
H-382
Salem, OR 97301
P: (503) 986-1406
E: Rep.SalEsquivel
   @oregonlegislature.gov

**Evans, Paul (D, 20)**
900 Court Street, Northeast
H-281
Salem, OR 97301
P: (503) 986-1420
E: Rep.PaulEvans
   @oregonlegislature.gov

**Fahey, Julie (D, 14)\***
900 Court Street, Northeast
H-474
Salem, OR 97301
P: (503) 986-1414
E: Rep.JulieFahey
   @oregonlegislature.gov

**Gomberg, David (D, 10)**
900 Court Street, Northeast
H-471
Salem, OR 97301
P: (503) 986-1410
E: Rep.DavidGomberg
   @oregonlegislature.gov

**Gorsek, Chris (D, 49)**
900 Court Street, Northeast
H-486
Salem, OR 97301
P: (503) 986-1449
E: Rep.ChrisGorsek
   @oregonlegislature.gov

**Greenlick, Mitch (D, 33)**
900 Court Street, Northeast
H-493
Salem, OR 97301
P: (503) 986-1433
E: Rep.MitchGreenlick
   @oregonlegislature.gov

**Hack, Jodi L. (R, 19)**
900 Court Street, Northeast
H-385
Salem, OR 97301
P: (503) 986-1419
E: Rep.JodiHack
   @oregonlegislature.gov

**Hayden, Cedric (R, 7)**
900 Court Street, Northeast
H-492
Salem, OR 97301
P: (503) 986-1407
E: Rep.CedricHayden
   @oregonlegislature.gov

**Heard, Dallas (R, 2)**
900 Court Street, Northeast
H-386
Salem, OR 97301
P: (503) 986-1402
E: Rep.DallasHeard
   @oregonlegislature.gov

**Helm, Ken (D, 34)**
900 Court Street, Northeast
H-490
Salem, OR 97301
P: (503) 986-1434
E: Rep.KenHelm
   @oregonlegislature.gov

**Hernanadez, Diego (D, 47)\***
900 Court Street, Northeast
H-373
Salem, OR 97301
P: (503) 986-1447
E: Rep.DiegoHernandez
   @oregonlegislature.gov

**Holvey, Paul (D, 8)**
900 Court Street, Northeast
H-277
Salem, OR 97301
P: (503) 986-1408
E: Rep.PaulHolvey
   @oregonlegislature.gov

**Huffman, John E. (R, 59)**
900 Court Street, Northeast
H-483
Salem, OR 97301
P: (503) 986-1459
E: Rep.JohnHuffman
   @oregonlegislature.gov

**Johnson, Mark (R, 52)**
900 Court Street, Northeast
H-489
Salem, OR 97301
P: (503) 986-1452
E: Rep.MarkJohnson
   @oregonlegislature.gov

**Kennemer, Bill (R, 39)**
900 Court Street, Northeast
H-380
Salem, OR 97301
P: (503) 986-1439
E: Rep.BillKennemer
   @oregonlegislature.gov

**Keny-Guyer, Alissa (D, 46)**
900 Court Street, Northeast
H-272
Salem, OR 97301
P: (503) 986-1446
E: Rep.AlissaKenyGuyer
   @oregonlegislature.gov

**Kotek, Tina (D, 44)**
900 Court Street, Northeast
H-269
Salem, OR 97301
P: (503) 986-1200
E: Rep.TinaKotek
   @state.or.us

**Lininger, Ann (D, 38)**
900 Court Street Northeast,
H-485
Salem, OR 97301
P: (503) 986-1438
E: Rep.AnnLininger
   @oregonlegislature.gov

**Lively, John (D, 12)**
900 Court Street, Northeast
H-488
Salem, OR 97301
P: (503) 986-1412
E: Rep.JohnLively
   @oregonlegislature.gov

**Malstrom, Sheri (D, 27)\***
900 Court Street, Northeast
H-280
Salem, OR 97301
P: (503) 986-1427
E: Rep.SheriMalstrom
   @oregonlegislature.gov

**Marsh, Pam (D, 5)\***
900 Court Street, Northeast
H-375
Salem, OR 97301
P: (503) 986-1405
E: Rep.PamMarsh
   @oregonlegislature.gov

**McKeown, Caddy (D, 9)**
900 Court Street, Northeast
H-476
Salem, OR 97301
P: (503) 986-1409
E: Rep.CaddyMcKeown
   @oregonlegislature.gov

**McLain, Susan (D, 29)**
900 Court Street, Northeast
H-477
Salem, OR 97301
P: (503) 986-1429
E: Rep.SusanMclain
   @oregonlegislature.gov

**McLane, Michael (R, 55)**
900 Court Street, Northeast
H-395
Salem, OR 97301
P: (503) 986-1455
E: Rep.MikeMcLane
   @oregonlegislature.gov

**Meek, Mark (D, 40)\***
900 Court Street Northeast
H-285
Salem, OR 97301
P: (503) 986-1440
E: Rep.MarkMeek
   @oregonlegislature.gov

# Oregon

**Nathanson, Nancy (D, 13)**
900 Court Street, Northeast
H-276
Salem, OR 97301
P: (503) 986-1413
E: Rep.NancyNathanson
    @oregonlegislature.gov

**Nearman, Mike (R, 23)**
900 Court Street, Northeast
H-378
Salem, OR 97301
P: (503) 986-1423
E: Rep.MikeNearman
    @oregonlegislature.gov

**Noble, Ron (R, 24)***
900 Court Street, Northeast
H-376
Salem, OR 97301
P: (503) 986-1424
E: Rep.RonNoble
    @oregonlegislature.gov

**Nosse, Rob (D, 42)**
900 Court Street, Northeast
H-472
Salem, OR 97301
P: (503) 986-1442
E: Rep.RobNosse
    @oregonlegislature.gov

**Olson, Andy (R, 15)**
900 Court Street, Northeast
H-478
Salem, OR 97301
P: (503) 986-1415
E: Rep.AndyOlson
    @oregonlegislature.gov

**Parrish, Julie (R, 37)**
900 Court Street, Northeast
H-371
Salem, OR 97301
P: (503) 986-1437
E: Rep.JulieParrish
    @oregonlegislature.gov

**Piluso, Carla C. (D, 50)**
900 Court Street, Northeast
H-491
Salem, OR 97301
P: (503) 986-1450
E: Rep.CarlaPiluso
    @oregonlegislature.gov

**Post, Bill (R, 25)**
900 Court Street, Northeast
H-373
Salem, OR 97301
P: (503) 986-1425
E: Rep.BillPost
    @oregonlegislature.gov

**Power, Karin (D, 41)***
900 Court Street, Northeast
H-274
Salem, OR 97301
P: (503) 986-1441
E: Rep.KarinPower
    @oregonlegislature.gov

**Rayfield, Dan (D, 16)**
900 Court Street, Northeast
H-375
Salem, OR 97301
P: (503) 986-1416
E: Rep.DanRayfield
    @oregonlegislature.gov

**Reardon, Jeff (D, 48)**
900 Court Street, Northeast
H-473
Salem, OR 97301
P: (503) 986-1448
E: Rep.JeffReardon
    @oregonlegislature.gov

**Reschke, E. Werner (R, 56)***
900 Court Street Northeast
H-377
Salem, OR 97301
P: (503) 986-1456
E: Rep.EWernerReschke
    @oregonlegislature.gov

**Sanchez, Tawna (D, 43)***
900 Court Street Northeast
H-273
Salem, OR 97301
P: (503) 986-1443
E: Rep.TawnaSanchez
    @oregonlegislature.gov

**Smith, Greg (R, 57)**
900 Court Street, Northeast
H-482
Salem, OR 97301
P: (503) 986-1457
E: Rep.GregSmith
    @oregonlegislature.gov

**Smith Warner, Barbara (D, 45)**
900 Court Street, Northeast
H-275
Salem, OR 97301
P: (503) 986-1445
E: Rep.BarbaraSmithWarner
    @oregonlegislature.gov

**Sollman, Janeen (D, 30)***
900 Court Street Northeast
H-487
Salem, OR 97301
P: (503) 986-1430
E: Rep.JaneenSollman
    @oregonlegislature.gov

**Sprenger, Sherrie (R, 17)**
900 Court Street, Northeast
H-388
Salem, OR 97301
P: (503) 986-1417
E: Rep.SherrieSprenger
    @oregonlegislature.gov

**Stark, Duane A. (R, 4)**
900 Court Street, Northeast
H-372
Salem, OR 97301
P: (503) 986-1404
E: Rep.DuaneStark
    @oregonlegislature.gov

**Vial, A. Richard (R, 26)***
900 Court Street, Northeast
H-484
Salem, OR 97301
P: (503) 986-1426
E: Rep.RichVial
    @oregonlegislature.gov

**Whisnant, Gene (R, 53)**
900 Court Street, Northeast
H-383
Salem, OR 97301
P: (503) 986-1453
E: Rep.GeneWhisnant
    @oregonlegislature.gov

**Williamson, Jennifer (D, 36)**
900 Court Street, Northeast
H-295
Salem, OR 97301
P: (503) 986-1436
E: Rep.JenniferWilliamson
    @oregonlegislature.gov

**Wilson, Carl (R, 3)**
900 Court Street, Northeast
H-390
Salem, OR 97301
P: (503) 986-1403
E: Rep.CarlWilson
    @oregonlegislature.gov

**Witt, Brad (D, 31)**
900 Court Street, Northeast
H-374
Salem, OR 97301
P: (503) 986-1431
E: Rep.BradWitt
    @oregonlegislature.gov

# Pennsylvania

## Executive

### Governor

**The Honorable Thomas W. Wolf (D)**
Governor
Room 225, Main Capitol Building
Harrisburg, PA 17120
P: (717) 787-2500
F: (717) 772-8284

### Lieutenant Governor

**The Honorable Michael J. Stack (D)**
Lieutenant Governor
200 Main Capitol Building
Harrisburg, PA 17120
P: (717) 787-3300
F: (717) 783-0150

### Attorney General

**The Honorable Josh Shapiro (D)**
Attorney General
1600 Strawberry Square
Harrisburg, PA 17120
P: (717) 787-3391
F: (717) 787-8242

### Auditor

**The Honorable Eugene DePasquale (D)**
Auditor General
Finance Building, Room 229
Harrisburg, PA 17120
P: (717) 787-2543
F: (717) 783-4407
E: auditorgen
    @auditorgen.state.pa.us

### Secretary of State

**The Honorable Pedro A. Cortes (D)**
    (appointed)
Secretary of the Commonwealth
302 North Office Building
Harrisburg, PA 17120
P: (717) 787-6458
F: (717) 787-1734
E: ST-PRESS@pa.gov

### Treasurer

**The Honorable Joseph Torsella (D)**
State Treasurer
129 Finance Building
Harrisburg, PA 17120
P: (717) 787-2465
F: (717) 783-9760

## Judiciary

### Supreme Court (PE)

**Ms. Patricia Johnson**
Chief Clerk
468 City Hall
Philadelphia, PA 19107
P: (215) 560-6370

**Ms. Patricia A. Nicola**
Chief Clerk
801 City-County Building
Pittsburgh, PA 15219
P: (412) 565-2816

**Ms. Elizabeth Zisk**
Chief Clerk
601 Commonwealth Avenue, Suite 4500
P.O. Box 62575
Harrisburg, PA 17106
P: (717) 787-6181

**The Honorable Thomas G. Saylor**
Chief Justice
**The Honorable Max Baer**
**The Honorable Christine Donohue**
**The Honorable Kevin M. Dougherty**
**The Honorable Sallie Updyke Mundy**
**The Honorable Debra M. Todd**
**The Honorable David N. Wecht**

## Legislative

## Senate

### Senate President

**The Honorable Michael J. Stack (D)**
Lieutenant Governor
200 Main Capitol Building
Harrisburg, PA 17120
P: (717) 787-3300
F: (717) 783-0150

### President Pro Tempore of the Senate

**Senator Joseph B. Scarnati III (R)**
Senate President Pro Tempore
292 Main Capitol
Senate Box 203025
Harrisburg, PA 17120
P: (717) 787-7084
F: (717) 772-2755
E: jscarnati@pasen.gov

### Senate Majority Leader

**Senator Jake Corman (R)**
Senate Majority Leader
350 Main Capitol
Senate Box 203034
Harrisburg, PA 17120
P: (717) 787-1377
F: (717) 772-3146
E: jcorman@pasen.gov

### Senate Minority Leader

**Senator Jay Costa (D)**
Senate Minority Floor Leader
535 Main Capitol
Senate Box 203043
Harrisburg, PA 17120
P: (717) 787-7683
F: (717) 783-5976
E: costa@pasenate.com

### Secretary of the Senate

**Ms. Megan Martin**
Secretary-Parliamentarian of the Senate
462 Capitol Building
Senate Box 203053
Harrisburg, PA 17120
P: (717) 787-5920
E: mconsedine@os.pasen.gov

### Members of the Senate

**Alloway, Richard (R, 33)**
172 Main Capitol
Senate Box 203033
Harrisburg, PA 17120
P: (717) 787-4651
F: (717) 772-2753
E: alloway@pasen.gov

**Argall, David G. (R, 29)**
171 Main Capitol
Senate Box 203029
Harrisburg, PA 17120
P: (717) 787-2637
F: (717) 783-8657
E: dargall@pasen.gov

**Aument, Ryan P. (R, 36)**
15 East Wing
Senate Box 203036
Harrisburg, PA 17120
P: (717) 787-4420
F: (717) 783-3156
E: raument@pasen.gov

**Baker, Lisa (R, 20)**
362 Main Capitol
Senate Box 203020
Harrisburg, PA 17120
P: (717) 787-7428
F: (717) 787-9242
E: lbaker@pasen.gov

**Bartolotta, Camera (R, 46)**
459 Main Capitol
Senate Box 203046
Harrisburg, PA 17120
P: (717) 787-1463
F: (717) 772-2108
E: cbartolotta@pasen.gov

**Blake, John P. (D, 22)**
17 East Wing
Senate Box 203022
Harrisburg, PA 17120
P: (717) 787-6481
F: (717) 783-5198
E: senatorblake
    @pasenate.com

**Boscola, Lisa M. (D, 18)**
458 Capitol Building
Senate Box 203018
Harrisburg, PA 17120
P: (717) 787-4236
F: (717) 783-1257
E: boscola@pasenate.com

**Brewster, James R. (D, 45)**
458 Main Capitol
Senate Box 203045
Harrisburg, PA 17120
P: (717) 787-5580
F: (717) 772-3588
E: brewster@pasenate.com

**Brooks, Michele (R, 50)**
351 Main Capitol
Senate Box 203050
Harrisburg, PA 17120
P: (717) 787-1322
F: (717) 772-0577
E: mbrooks@pasen.gov

**Browne, Patrick M. (R, 16)**
281 Main Capitol
Senate Box 203016
Harrisburg, PA 17120
P: (717) 787-1349
F: (717) 772-3458
E: pbrowne@pasen.gov

# Pennsylvania

**Corman, Jake (R, 34)**
350 Main Capitol
Senate Box 203034
Harrisburg, PA 17120
P: (717) 787-1377
F: (717) 772-3146
E: jcorman@pasen.gov

**Costa, Jay (D, 43)**
535 Main Capitol
Senate Box 203043
Harrisburg, PA 17120
P: (717) 787-7683
F: (717) 783-5976
E: costa@pasenate.com

**Dinniman, Andrew E. (D, 19)**
182 Main Capitol
Senate Box 203019
Harrisburg, PA 17120
P: (717) 787-5709
F: (717) 787-4384
E: andy@pasenate.com

**DiSanto, John (R, 15)***
352 Main Capitol
Senate Box 203015
Harrisburg, PA 17120
P: (717) 787-6801
F: (717) 783-3722

**Eichelberger, John H.
   (R, 30)**
173 Main Capitol
Senate Box 203030
Harrisburg, PA 17120
P: (717) 787-5490
F: (717) 783-5192
E: jeichelberger@pasen.gov

**Farnese Jr., Lawrence M.
   (D, 1)**
543 Main Capitol
Senate Box 203001
Harrisburg, PA 17120
P: (717) 787-5662
F: (717) 787-4531
E: farnese@pasenate.com

**Folmer, Mike (R, 48)**
337 Main Capitol
Senate Box 203048
Harrisburg, PA 17120
P: (717) 787-5708
F: (717) 787-3455
E: mfolmer@pasen.gov

**Fontana, Wayne D. (D, 42)**
543 Main Capitol
Senate Box 203042
Harrisburg, PA 17120
P: (717) 787-5300
F: (717) 772-5484
E: fontana@pasenate.com

**Gordner, John R. (R, 27)**
177 Main Capitol
Senate Box 203027
Harrisburg, PA 17120
P: (717) 787-8928
F: (717) 787-9715
E: jgordner@pasen.gov

**Greenleaf, Stewart J.
   (R, 12)**
19 East Wing
Senate Box 203012
Harrisburg, PA 17120
P: (717) 787-6599
F: (717) 783-7328
E: sgreenleaf@pasen.gov

**Haywood, Art (D, 4)**
10 East Wing
Senate Box 203004
Harrisburg, PA 17120
P: (717) 787-1427
F: (717) 772-0572
E: senatorhaywood
   @pasenate.com

**Hughes, Vincent J. (D, 7)**
545 Capitol Building
Senate Box 203007
Harrisburg, PA 17120
P: (717) 787-7112
F: (717) 772-0579
E: hughes@pasenate.com

**Hutchinson, Scott E.
   (R, 21)**
170 Main Capitol
Senate Box 203021
Harrisburg, PA 17120
P: (717) 787-9684
F: (717) 787-6088
E: shutchinson@pasen.gov

**Killion, Thomas H. (R, 9)**
463 Main Capitol
Senate Box 203009
Harrisburg, PA 17120
P: (717) 787-4712
F: (717) 783-7490
E: tkillion@pasenate.gov

**Langerholc, Wayne (R, 35)***
185 Main Capitol
Senate Box 203035
Harrisburg, PA 17120
P: (717) 787-5400
F: (717) 772-0573
E: wlangerholc@pasen.gov

**Laughlin, Daniel (R, 49)***
184 Main Capitol
Senate Box 203049
Harrisburg, PA 17120
P: (717) 787-8927
E: dlaughlin@pasen.gov

**Leach, Daylin (D, 17)**
543 Main Capitol
Senate Box 203017
Harrisburg, PA 17120
P: (717) 787-5544
F: (717) 705-7741
E: senatorleach
   @pasenate.com

**Martin, Scott (R, 13)***
183 Main Capitol
Senate Box 203013
Harrisburg, PA 17120
P: (717) 878-6535

**McGarrigle, Thomas (R, 26)**
187 Main Capitol
Senate Box 203026
Harrisburg, PA 17120
P: (717) 787-1350
F: (717) 787-0196

**McIlhinney Jr., Chuck T.
   (R, 10)**
187 Main Capitol
Senate Box 203010
Harrisburg, PA 17120
P: (717) 787-7305
F: (717) 783-5962
E: cmcilhinney@pasen.gov

**Mensch, Bob (R, 24)**
16 East Wing
Senate Box 203024
Harrisburg, PA 17120
P: (717) 787-3110
F: (717) 787-8004
E: bmensch@pasen.gov

**Rafferty Jr., John C.
   (R, 44)**
20 East Wing
Senate Box 203044
Harrisburg, PA 17120
P: (717) 787-1398
F: (717) 783-4587
E: jrafferty@pasen.gov

**Regan, Mike (R, 31)**
460 Main Capitol
Senate Box 203031
Harrisburg, PA 17120
P: (717) 787-8524
E: mregan@pasen.gov

**Reschenthaler, Guy (R, 37)**
366 Main Capitol Building
Senate Box 203037
Harrisburg, PA 17120
P: (717) 787-5839
F: (717) 772-4437

**Sabatina Jr., John P.
   (D, 5)**
457 Main Capitol
Senate Box 203005
Harrisburg, PA 17120
P: (717) 787-9608
F: (717) 772-2162

**Scarnati III, Joseph B.
   (R, 25)**
292 Main Capitol
Senate Box 203025
Harrisburg, PA 17120
P: (717) 787-7084
F: (717) 772-2755
E: jscarnati@pasen.gov

**Scavello, Mario M. (R, 40)**
168 Main Capitol
Senate Box 203040
Harrisburg, PA 17120
P: (717) 787-6123
F: (717) 772-3695
E: mscavello@pasen.gov

**Schwank, Judith L. (D, 11)**
457 Main Capitol
Senate Box 203011
Harrisburg, PA 17120
P: (717) 787-8925
F: (717) 772-0578
E: SenatorSchwank
   @pasenate.com

**Stefano, Pat (R, 32)**
169 Main Capitol
Senate Box 203032
Harrisburg, PA 17120
P: (717) 787-7175

**Street, Sharif (D, 3)***
535 Main Capitol
Senate Box 203003
Harrisburg, PA 17120
P: (717) 787-6735
E: info
   @senatorsharifstreet.com

**Tartaglione, Christine M.
   (D, 2)**
458 Main Capitol
Senate Box 203002
Harrisburg, PA 17120
P: (717) 787-1141
F: (717) 787-7439
E: tartaglione@pasenate.com

**Tomlinson, Robert M. (R, 6)**
281 Capitol Building
Senate Box 203006
Harrisburg, PA 17120
P: (717) 787-5072
F: (717) 772-2991
E: rtomlinson@pasen.gov

**Vogel Jr., Elder A. (R, 47)**
362 Main Capitol
Senate Box 203047
Harrisburg, PA 17120
P: (717) 787-3076
F: (717) 772-2756
E: evogel@pasen.gov

**Vulakovich, Randy (R, 38)**
168 Main Capitol
Senate Box 203038
Harrisburg, PA 17120
P: (717) 787-6538
F: (717) 787-8625
E: rvulakovich@pasen.gov

**Wagner, Scott (R, 28)**
9 East Wing
Senate Box 203028
Harrisburg, PA 17120
P: (717) 787-3817
F: (717) 783-1900
E: swagner@pasen.gov

**Ward, Kim L. (R, 39)**
168 Main Capitol
Senate Box 203039
Harrisburg, PA 17120
P: (717) 787-6063
F: (717) 772-0580
E: kward@pasen.gov

**White, Donald C. (R, 41)**
286 Capitol Building
Senate Box 203041
Harrisburg, PA 17120
P: (717) 787-8724
F: (717) 772-1589
E: dwhite@pasen.gov

**Williams, Anthony H. (D, 8)**
11 East Wing
Senate Box 203008
Harrisburg, PA 17120
P: (717) 787-5970
F: (717) 772-0574
E: williams@pasenate.com

**Yaw, Gene (R, 23)**
362 Main Capitol
Senate Box 203023
Harrisburg, PA 17120
P: (717) 787-3280
F: (717) 772-0575
E: gyaw@pasen.gov

**Yudichak, John T. (D, 14)**
458 Main Capitol
Senate Box 203014
Harrisburg, PA 17120
P: (717) 787-7105
F: (717) 783-4141
E: yudichak@pasenate.com

# House

## Speaker of the House
**Representative Mike Turzai (R)**
Speaker of the House
139 Main Capitol
P.O. Box 202028
Harrisburg, PA 17120
P: (717) 772-9943
F: (717) 772-2470
E: mturzai@pahousegop.com

## House Majority Leader
**Representative Dave Reed (R)**
House Majority Leader
110 Main Capitol Building
P.O. Box 202062
Harrisburg, PA 17120
P: (717) 705-7173
F: (717) 705-1947
E: dreed@pahousegop.com

## House Minority Leader
**Representative Frank Dermody (D)**
House Democratic Leader
423 Main Capitol Building
P.O. Box 202033
Harrisburg, PA 17120
P: (717) 787-3566
F: (717) 787-8060
E: fdermody@pahouse.net

## Clerk of the House
**Mr. Dave Reddecliff**
Chief Clerk of the House
129 Main Capitol Building
Harrisburg, PA 17120
P: (717) 787-2372

## Members of the House
**Baker, Matthew E. (R, 68)**
213 Ryan Office Building
P.O. Box 202068
Harrisburg, PA 17120
P: (717) 772-5371
F: (717) 705-1835
E: mbaker@pahousegop.com

**Barbin, Bryan (D, 71)**
321 Irvin Office Building
P.O. Box 202071
Harrisburg, PA 17120
P: (717) 783-1491
F: (717) 705-7001

**Barrar, Stephen E. (R, 160)**
18 East Wing
P.O. Box 202160
Harrisburg, PA 17120
P: (717) 783-3038
F: (717) 787-7604
E: parep160@aol.com

**Benninghoff, Kerry A. (R, 171)**
147 Main Capitol Building
P.O. Box 202171
Harrisburg, PA 17120
P: (717) 783-1918
F: (717) 260-6528
E: kbenning@pahousegop.com

**Bernstine, Aaron (R, 10)***
5 East Wing
P.O. Box 202010
Harrisburg, PA 17120
P: (717) 783-8322
F: (717) 782-2961

**Bizzarro, Ryan A. (D, 3)**
G01 Irvis Office Building
P.O. Box 202003
Harrisburg, PA 17120
P: (717) 772-2297
F: (717) 780-4767

**Bloom, Stephen (R, 199)**
B8 Main Capitol Building
P.O. Box 202199
Harrisburg, PA 17120
P: (717) 772-2280
F: (717) 705-2012

**Boback, Karen (R, 117)**
314C Main Capitol
P.O. Box 202117
Harrisburg, PA 17120
P: (717) 787-1117
F: (717) 705-1889
E: kboback@pahousegop.com

**Boyle, Kevin J. (D, 172)**
226 Irvis Office Building
P.O. Box 202172
Harrisburg, PA 17120
P: (717) 783-4944

**Bradford, Matthew (D, 70)**
323 Main Capitol Building
P.O. Box 202070
Harrisburg, PA 17120
P: (717) 772-2572
F: (717) 772-2360

**Briggs, Tim (D, 149)**
527E Main Capitol Building
P.O. Box 202149
Harrisburg, PA 17120
P: (717) 705-7011
F: (717) 772-9860

**Brown, Rosemary M. (R, 189)**
164A East Wing
P.O. Box 202189
Harrisburg, PA 17120
P: (717) 260-6171

**Brown, Vanessa Lowery (D, 190)**
325 Irvis Office Building
P.O. Box 202190
Harrisburg, PA 17120
P: (717) 783-3822
F: (717) 772-2384

**Bullock, Donna (D, 195)**
105A East Wing
P.O. Box 202195
Harrisburg, PA 17120
P: (717) 787-3480
F: (717) 772-9853

**Burns, Frank (D, 72)**
324 Main Capitol Building
P.O. Box 202072
Harrisburg, PA 17120
P: (717) 772-8056
F: (717) 772-9965

**Caltagirone, Thomas R. (D, 127)**
106 Irvis Office Building
P.O. Box 202127
Harrisburg, PA 17120
P: (717) 787-3525
F: (717) 772-5401
E: tcaltagi@pahouse.net

**Carroll, Mike (D, 118)**
300 Main Capitol Building
P.O. Box 202118
Harrisburg, PA 17120
P: (717) 787-3589
F: (717) 780-4763
E: mcarroll@pahouse.net

**Causer, Martin T. (R, 67)**
41B East Wing
P.O. Box 202067
Harrisburg, PA 17120
P: (717) 787-5075
F: (717) 705-7021
E: mcauser@pahousegop.com

**Cephas, Morgan (D, 192)***
103A East Wing
P.O. Box 200192
Harrisburg, PA 17120
P: (717) 783-2192
F: (717) 787-2960

**Charlton, Alexander (R, 165)***
53A East Wing
P.O. Box 202165
Harrisburg, PA 17120
P: (717) 787-1248
F: (717) 782-2956

# Pennsylvania

**Christiana, Jim (R, 15)**
107 Ryan Office Building
P.O. Box 202015
Harrisburg, PA 17120
P: (717) 260-6144
F: (717) 782-2919
E: jchristi@pahousegop.com

**Comitta, Carolyn T.
(D, 156)***
25A East Wing
P.O. Box 202156
Harrisburg, PA 17120
P: (717) 705-2075

**Conklin, H. Scott (D, 77)**
314 Irvis Office Building
P.O. Box 202077
Harrisburg, PA 17120
P: (717) 787-9473
F: (717) 780-4764
E: sconklin@pahouse.net

**Cook, Bud (R, 49)***
B15 Main Capitol Building
P.O. Box 202049
Harrisburg, PA 17120
P: (717) 783-8655

**Corbin, Becky (R, 155)**
52A East Wing
P.O. Box 202155
Harrisburg, PA 17120
P: (717) 783-2520
F: (717) 782-2927

**Corr, Michael N. (R, 150)***
153A East Wing
P.O. Box 202150
Harrisburg, PA 17120
P: (717) 705-7164
F: (717) 705-7164

**Costa, Dom (D, 21)**
217 Irvis Office Building
P.O. Box 202021
Harrisburg, PA 17120
P: (717) 783-9114
F: (717) 780-4761

**Costa, Paul (D, 34)**
33 Main Capitol Building
P.O. Box 202034
Harrisburg, PA 17120
P: (717) 783-1914
F: (717) 705-2564
E: pcosta@pahouse.net

**Cox, Jim (R, 129)**
209 Ryan Office Building
P.O. Box 202129
Harrisburg, PA 17120
P: (717) 772-2435
F: (717) 705-1849
E: jcox@pahousegop.com

**Cruz, Angel (D, 180)**
528E Main Capitol Building
P.O. Box 202180
Harrisburg, PA 17120
P: (717) 787-1407
F: (717) 780-4769
E: acruz@pahouse.net

**Cutler, Bryan (R, 100)**
121 Main Capitol Building
P.O. Box 202100
Harrisburg, PA 17120
P: (717) 783-6424
F: (717) 772-9859

**Daley, Mary Jo (D, 148)**
115A East Wing
P.O. Box 202148
Harrisburg, PA 17120
P: (717) 787-9475
F: (717) 787-0861

**Davidson, Margo L. (D, 164)**
38A East Wing
P.O. Box 202164
Harrisburg, PA 17120
P: (717) 783-4907
F: (717) 780-4750

**Davis, Tina M. (D, 141)**
G14 Irvis Office Building
P.O. Box 202141
Harrisburg, PA 17120
P: (717) 783-4903

**Dawkins, Jason (D, 179)**
26A East Wing
P.O. Box 202179
Harrisburg, PA 17120
P: (717) 797-1354

**Day, Gary (R, 187)**
163B East Wing
P.O. Box 202187
Harrisburg, PA 17120
P: (717) 787-3017
F: (717) 705-1951

**Dean, Madeleine (D, 153)**
32 East Wing
P.O. Box 202153
Harrisburg, PA 17120
P: (717) 783-7619
F: (717) 780-4754

**Deasy, Daniel J. (D, 27)**
323 Irvis Office Building
P.O. Box 202027
Harrisburg, PA 17120
P: (717) 772-8187

**DeLissio, Pamela A.
(D, 194)**
109B East Wing
P.O. Box 202194
Harrisburg, PA 17120
P: (717) 783-4945

**Delozier, Sheryl M. (R, 88)**
141A East Wing
P.O. Box 202088
Harrisburg, PA 17120
P: (717) 783-5282
F: (717) 772-9994
E: sdelozie@pahousegop.com

**DeLuca, Anthony M. (D, 32)**
115 Irvis Office Building
P.O. Box 202032
Harrisburg, PA 17120
P: (717) 783-1011
F: (717) 772-9937
E: tdeluca@pahouse.net

**Dermody, Frank (D, 33)**
423 Main Capitol Building
P.O. Box 202033
Harrisburg, PA 17120
P: (717) 787-3566
F: (717) 787-8060
E: fdermody@pahouse.net

**Diamond, Russ (R, 102)**
145B East Wing
P.O. Box 202102
Harrisburg, PA 17120
P: (717) 787-2686

**DiGirolamo, Gene (R, 18)**
49 East Wing
P.O. Box 202018
Harrisburg, PA 17120
P: (717) 783-7319
F: (717) 772-2414
E: gdigirol@pahousegop.com

**Donatucci, Maria P.
(D, 185)**
101 Irvis Office Building
P.O. Box 202185
Harrisburg, PA 17120
P: (717) 783-8634
F: (717) 772-9888

**Dowling, Matthew D.
(R, 51)***
53B East Wing
P.O. Box 202051
Harrisburg, PA 17120
P: (717) 783-5173
F: (717) 782-2963

**Driscoll, Mike (D, 173)**
27A East Wing
P.O. Box 202173
Harrisburg, PA 17120
P: (717) 787-4331
F: (717) 772-9962

**Dunbar, George (R, 56)**
147A East Wing
P.O. Box 202056
Harrisburg, PA 17120
P: (717) 260-6132
F: (717) 782-2880

**Dush, Cris (R, 66)**
161A East Wing
P.O. Box 202066
Harrisburg, PA 17120
P: (717) 787-3845
F: (717) 782-2946

**Ellis, Brian (R, 11)**
110 Ryan Office Building
P.O. Box 202011
Harrisburg, PA 17120
P: (717) 787-7686
F: (717) 782-2907
E: bellis@pahousegop.com

**Emrick, Joe (R, 137)**
160B East Wing
P.O. Box 202137
Harrisburg, PA 17120
P: (717) 260-6159

**English, Harold A. (R, 30)**
406 Irvis Office Building
P.O. Box 202030
Harrisburg, PA 17120
P: (717) 260-6407
F: (717) 783-5740

**Evankovich, Eli (R, 54)**
3 East Wing
P.O. Box 202054
Harrisburg, PA 17120
P: (717) 260-6129

**Everett, Garth D. (R, 84)**
400 Irvis Office Building
P.O. Box 202084
Harrisburg, PA 17120
P: (717) 787-5270
F: (717) 772-9958

**Fabrizio, Florindo J.
(D, 2)**
200 Irvis Office Building
P.O. Box 202002
Harrisburg, PA 17120
P: (717) 787-4358
F: (717) 780-4774
E: ffabrizi@pahouse.net

**Farry, Frank (R, 142)**
52B East Wing
P.O. Box 202142
Harrisburg, PA 17120
P: (717) 260-6140
F: (717) 782-2916
E: Ffarry@pahousegop.com

**Fee, Mindy (R, 37)**
164B East Wing
P.O. Box 202037
Harrisburg, PA 17120
P: (717) 772-5290
F: (717) 783-1904

**Fitzgerald, Isabella
(D, 203)***
25B East Wing
P.O. Box 202203
Harrisburg, PA 17120
P: (717) 783-4111
F: (717) 780-4753

**Flynn, Marty (D, 113)**
G05 Irvis Office Building
P.O. Box 202113
Harrisburg, PA 17120
P: (717) 787-8981
F: (717) 705-1958

**Frankel, Dan B. (D, 23)**
417 Main Capitol Building
P.O. Box 202023
Harrisburg, PA 17120
P: (717) 705-1875
F: (717) 705-2034
E: dfrankel@pahouse.net

**Freeman, Robert L. (D, 136)**
207 Irvis Office Building
P.O. Box 202136
Harrisburg, PA 17120
P: (717) 783-3815
F: (717) 783-2152
E: rfreeman@pahouse.net

**Fritz, Jonathan (R, 111)***
414 Irvis Office Building
P.O. Box 202111
Harrisburg, PA 17120
P: (717) 783-2910
F: (717) 782-2957

**Gabler, Matt (R, 75)**
210 Ryan Office Building
P.O. Box 202075
Harrisburg, PA 17120
P: (717) 260-6142

**Gainey, Ed (D, 24)**
116B East Wing
P.O. Box 202024
Harrisburg, PA 17120
P: (717) 783-1017

**Galloway, John T. (D, 140)**
301 Irvis Office Building
P.O. Box 202140
Harrisburg, PA 17120
P: (717) 787-1292
F: (717) 780-4780

**Gergely, Marc J. (D, 35)**
325 Main Capitol Building
P.O. Box 202035
Harrisburg, PA 17120
P: (717) 783-1018
F: (717) 780-4779
E: mgergely@pahouse.net

**Gillen, Mark M. (R, 128)**
408 Irvis Office Building
P.O. Box 202128
Harrisburg, PA 17120
P: (717) 787-8550

**Gillespie, Keith J. (R, 47)**
45 East Wing
P.O. Box 202047
Harrisburg, PA 17120
P: (717) 705-7167
F: (717) 782-2914
E: kgillesp@pahousegop.com

**Godshall, Robert W. (R, 53)**
150 Main Capitol Building
P.O. Box 202053
Harrisburg, PA 17120
P: (717) 783-6428
F: (717) 787-7424
E: rgodshal@pahousegop.com

**Goodman, Neal P. (D, 123)**
512-E Main Capitol Building
P.O. Box 202123
Harrisburg, PA 17120
P: (717) 787-2798
F: (717) 772-9948
E: ngoodman@pahouse.net

**Greiner, Keith J. (R, 43)**
54B East Wing
P.O. Box 202043
Harrisburg, PA 17120
P: (717) 783-6422
F: (717) 782-2926

**Grove, Seth (R, 196)**
7 East Wing
P.O. Box 202196
Harrisburg, PA 17120
P: (717) 783-2655
F: (717) 260-6482

**Haggerty, Kevin (D, 112)**
103B East Wing
P.O. Box 202112
Harrisburg, PA 17120
P: (717) 783-5043
F: (717) 787-1231

**Hahn, Marcia M. (R, 138)**
402 A Irvis Office Building
P.O. Box 202138
Harrisburg, PA 17120
P: (717) 783-8573
F: (717) 783-3899

**Hanna, Michael K. (D, 76)**
428 Main Capitol Building
P.O. Box 202076
Harrisburg, PA 17120
P: (717) 772-2283
F: (717) 787-4137
E: mhanna@pahouse.net

**Harkins, Patrick J. (D, 1)**
202 Irvis Office Building
P.O. Box 202001
Harrisburg, PA 17120
P: (717) 787-7406
F: (717) 780-4775
E: pharkins@pahouse.net

**Harper, Kate (R, 61)**
216 Ryan Office Building
P.O. Box 202061
Harrisburg, PA 17120
P: (717) 787-2801
F: (717) 787-2022
E: kharper@pahousegop.com

**Harris, C. Adam (R, 82)**
115 Ryan Office Building
P.O. Box 202082
Harrisburg, PA 17120
P: (717) 783-7830
F: (717) 782-9869
E: aharris@pahousegop.com

**Harris, Jordan A. (D, 186)**
328 Irvis Office Building
P.O. Box 202186
Harrisburg, PA 17120
P: (717) 783-1792
F: (717) 787-7172

**Heffley, Doyle (R, 122)**
403 Irvis Office Building
P.O. Box 202122
Harrisburg, PA 17120
P: (717) 260-6139
F: (717) 772-8418

**Helm, Susan C. (R, 104)**
420 Irvis Office Building
P.O. Box 202104
Harrisburg, PA 17120
P: (717) 787-1230
F: (717) 787-7375
E: shelm@pahousegop.com

**Hennessey, Tim (R, 26)**
313 Main Capitol Building
P.O. Box 202026
Harrisburg, PA 17120
P: (717) 787-3431
F: (717) 787-9864
E: thenness@pahousegop.com

**Hickernell, David S.
(R, 98)**
43A East Wing
P.O. Box 202098
Harrisburg, PA 17120
P: (717) 783-2076
F: (717) 787-9175
E: dhickern@pahousegop.com

**Hill, Kristin (R, 93)**
123B East Wing
P.O. Box 202093
Harrisburg, PA 17120
P: (717) 783-8389

**Hill-Evans, Carol (D, 95)***
28A East Wing
P.O. Box 202095
Harrisburg, PA 17120
P: (717) 787-7514
F: (717) 780-4765

**Irvin, Rich (R, 81)**
5 East Wing
P.O. Box 202081
Harrisburg, PA 17120
P: (717) 787-3335
F: (717) 782-2884

**James, R. Lee (R, 64)**
145A East Wing
P.O. Box 202064
Harrisburg, PA 17120
P: (717) 783-8188

**Jozwiak, Barry (R, 5)**
155B East Wing
P.O. Box 202005
Harrisburg, PA 17120
P: (787) 772-9940
F: (787) 782-2925

**Kampf, Warren (R, 157)**
153B East Wing
P.O. Box 202157
Harrisburg, PA 17120
P: (717) 260-6166
F: (717) 782-2888

**Kaufer, Aaron (R, 120)**
B16 Main Capitol Building
P.O. Box 202120
Harrisburg, PA 17120
P: (717) 787-3798
F: (717) 782-2950

**Kauffman, Rob W. (R, 89)**
312 Main Capitol Building
P.O. Box 202089
Harrisburg, PA 17120
P: (717) 705-2004
F: (717) 787-9840
E: rkauffma@pahousegop.com

**Kavulich, Sid Michaels
(D, 114)**
103 Irvis Office Building
P.O. Box 202114
Harrisburg, PA 17120
P: (717) 783-4874

**Keefer, Dawn W. (R, 92)***
423 Irvis Office Building
P.O. Box 202092
Harrisburg, PA 17120
P: (717) 783-8783
F: (717) 782-2920

**Keller, Fred (R, 85)**
428 Irvis Office Building
P.O. Box 202085
Harrisburg, PA 17120
P: (717) 787-3443
F: (717) 782-2887

# Pennsylvania

**Keller, Mark K. (R, 86)**
108 Ryan Office Building
P.O. Box 202086
Harrisburg, PA 17120
P: (717) 783-1593
F: (717) 782-2894
E: mkeller@pahousegop.com

**Keller, William F. (D, 184)**
326 Main Capitol Building
P.O. Box 202184
Harrisburg, PA 17120
P: (717) 787-5774
F: (717) 705-2088
E: wkeller@pahouse.net

**Kim, Patty (D, 103)**
G01 Irvis Office Building
P.O. Box 202103
Harrisburg, PA 17120
P: (717) 783-9342
F: (717) 787-8957

**Kinsey, Stephen (D, 201)**
317 Irvis Office Building
P.O. Box 202201
Harrisburg, PA 17120
P: (717) 787-3181
F: (717) 772-4038

**Kirkland, Brian (D, 159)***
101B East Wing
P.O. Box 202159
Harrisburg, PA 17120
P: (717) 787-5881
F: (717) 780-4762

**Klunk, Kate (R, 169)**
123A East Wing
P.O. Box 202169
Harrisburg, PA 17120
P: (717) 787-4790

**Knowles, Jerry (R, 124)**
155A East Wing
P.O. Box 202124
Harrisburg, PA 17120
P: (717) 787-9029
F: (717) 782-2908

**Kortz, William C. (D, 38)**
114 Irvis Office Building
P.O. Box 202038
Harrisburg, PA 17120
P: (717) 787-8175
F: (717) 780-4783

**Krueger-Braneky, Leanne (D, 161)**
115B East Wing
P.O. Box 202161
Harrisburg, PA 17120
P: (717) 705-2567
F: (717) 705-7000

**Kulik, Anita Astorino (D, 45)***
106B East Wing
P.O. Box 202045
Harrisburg, PA 17120
P: (717) 783-3780
F: (717) 780-4773

**Lawrence, John A. (R, 13)**
211 Ryan Office Building
P.O. Box 202013
Harrisburg, PA 17120
P: (717) 260-6117

**Lewis, Harry (R, 74)**
159A East Wing
P.O. Box 202074
Harrisburg, PA 17120
P: (717) 787-1806
F: (717) 782-2947

**Longietti, Mark (D, 7)**
127 Irvis Office Building
P.O. Box 202007
Harrisburg, PA 17120
P: (717) 772-4035
F: (717) 780-4785

**Mackenzie, Ryan E. (R, 134)**
160A East Wing
P.O. Box 202134
Harrisburg, PA 17120
P: (717) 787-1000
F: (717) 782-2893

**Madden, Maureen (D, 115)***
28B East Wing
P.O. Box 202115
Harrisburg, PA 17120
P: (717) 787-5811
F: (717) 705-1920

**Maher, John A. (R, 40)**
113 Ryan Office Building
P.O. Box 202040
Harrisburg, PA 17120
P: (717) 783-1522
F: (717) 783-8332
E: jmaher@pahousegop.com

**Mako, Zachary (R, 183)***
402 Irvis Office Building
P.O. Box 202183
Harrisburg, PA 17120
P: (717) 772-5398
F: (717) 783-7667

**Maloney Sr., David M. (R, 130)**
6B East Wing
P.O. Box 202130
Harrisburg, PA 17120
P: (717) 260-6161
F: (717) 782-2883

**Markosek, Joseph F. (D, 25)**
512E Main Capitol Building
P.O. Box 202025
Harrisburg, PA 17120
P: (717) 783-1540
F: (717) 787-2334
E: jmarkose@pahouse.net

**Marshall, Jim (R, 14)**
106 Ryan Office Building
P.O. Box 202014
Harrisburg, PA 17120
P: (717) 260-6432
F: (717) 782-2918
E: jmarshal@pahousegop.com

**Marsico, Ron S. (R, 105)**
315J Main Capitol Building
P.O. Box 202105
Harrisburg, PA 17120
P: (717) 783-2014
F: (717) 705-2010
E: rmarsico@pahousegop.com

**Masser, Kurt A. (R, 107)**
128 Main Capitol Building
P.O. Box 202107
Harrisburg, PA 17120
P: (717) 260-6134
F: (717) 787-9463

**Matzie, Robert (D, 16)**
121 Irvis Office Building
P.O. Box 202016
Harrisburg, PA 17120
P: (717) 787-4444
F: (717) 780-4772

**McCarter, Stephen (D, 154)**
26B East Wing
P.O. Box 202154
Harrisburg, PA 17120
P: (717) 783-1079
F: (717) 787-2713

**McClinton, Joanna E. (D, 191)**
105B East Wing
P.O. Box 202191
Harrisburg, PA 17120
P: (717) 772-9850
F: (717) 783-1516

**McGinnis, John D. (R, 79)**
429 Irvis Office Building
P.O. Box 202079
Harrisburg, PA 17120
P: (717) 787-6419
F: (717) 782-2923

**McNeill, Daniel (D, 133)**
101A East Wing
P.O. Box 202133
Harrisburg, PA 17120
P: (717) 772-9902

**Mehaffie, Thomas (R, 106)***
159B East Wing
P.O. Box 202106
Harrisburg, PA 17120
P: (717) 787-2684
F: (717) 787-7557

**Mentzer, Steven C. (R, 97)**
51A East Wing
P.O. Box 202097
Harrisburg, PA 17120
P: (717) 787-1776
F: (717) 705-2031

**Metcalfe, Daryl (R, 12)**
144 Main Capitol Building
P.O. Box 202012
Harrisburg, PA 17120
P: (717) 783-1707
F: (717) 787-4771
E: dmetcalf@pahousegop.com

**Metzgar, Carl (R, 69)**
111 Ryan Office Building
P.O. Box 202069
Harrisburg, PA 17120
P: (717) 783-8756
F: (717) 782-2911

**Miccarelli, Nick (R, 162)**
432 Irvis Office Building
P.O. Box 202162
Harrisburg, PA 17120
P: (717) 787-3472
F: (717) 787-8215
E: NickMicc@pahousegop.com

**Millard, David (R, 109)**
316 Main Capitol Building
P.O. Box 202109
Harrisburg, PA 17120
P: (717) 783-1102
F: (717) 772-0094
E: dmillard@pahousegop.com

**Miller, Brett (R, 41)**
54A East Wing
P.O. Box 202041
Harrisburg, PA 17120
P: (717) 705-7161

**Miller, Daniel L. (D, 42)**
116A East Wing
P.O. Box 202042
Harrisburg, PA 17120
P: (717) 783-1850
F: (717) 780-4756

**Milne, Duane (R, 167)**
150A East Wing
P.O. Box 202167
Harrisburg, PA 17120
P: (717) 787-8579
F: (717) 787-1295
E: dmilne@pahousegop.com

**Moul, Dan (R, 91)**
G32 Irvis Office Building
P.O. Box 202091
Harrisburg, PA 17120
P: (717) 783-5217
F: (717) 772-5499
E: dmoul@pahousegop.com

**Mullery, Gerald J. (D, 119)**
120 Irvis Office Building
P.O. Box 202119
Harrisburg, PA 17120
P: (717) 783-4893
F: (717) 780-4782

**Murt, Thomas P. (R, 152)**
410 Irvis Office Building
P.O. Box 202152
Harrisburg, PA 17120
P: (717) 787-6886
F: (717) 782-2886
E: tmurt@pahousegop.com

**Mustio, T. Mark (R, 44)**
416 Irvis Office Building
P.O. Box 202044
Harrisburg, PA 17120
P: (717) 787-6651
F: (717) 782-2889
E: mmustio@pahousegop.com

**Neilson, Ed (D, 174)**
107 East Wing
P.O. Box 202174
Harrisburg, PA 17120
P: (717) 772-4032
F: (717) 783-1579

**Nelson, Eric (R, 57)**
117B East Wing
P.O. Box 202057
Harrisburg, PA 17120
P: (717) 260-6146

**Nesbit, Tedd (R, 8)**
121A East Wing
P.O. Box 202008
Harrisburg, PA 17120
P: (717) 783-6438
F: (717) 782-2943

**Neuman, Brandon P. (D, 48)**
225 Irvis Office Building
P.O. Box 202048
Harrisburg, PA 17120
P: (717) 783-4834
F: (717) 705-1887

**Oberlander, Donna (R, 63)**
152 Main Capitol Building
P.O. Box 202063
Harrisburg, PA 17120
P: (717) 772-9908
F: (717) 782-2912
E: Doberlan@pahousegop.com

**O'Brien, Michael H. (D, 175)**
302 Main Capitol Building
P.O. Box 202175
Harrisburg, PA 17120
P: (717) 783-8098
F: (717) 780-4787
E: mobrien@pahouse.net

**O'Neill, Bernie T. (R, 29)**
47 East Wing
P.O. Box 202029
Harrisburg, PA 17120
P: (717) 705-7170
F: (717) 783-3278
E: boneill@pahousegop.com

**Ortitay, Jason (R, 46)**
125B East Wing
P.O. Box 202046
Harrisburg, PA 17120
P: (717) 787-1281

**Pashinski, Eddie Day (D, 121)**
203 Irvis Office Building
P.O. Box 202121
Harrisburg, PA 17120
P: (717) 783-0686
F: (717) 772-2284

**Peifer, Michael (R, 139)**
157 East Wing
P.O. Box 202139
Harrisburg, PA 17120
P: (717) 783-2037
F: (717) 782-2910
E: mpeifer@pahousegop.com

**Petrarca, Joseph A. (D, 55)**
220 Irvis Office Building
P.O. Box 202055
Harrisburg, PA 17120
P: (717) 787-5142
F: (717) 705-2014
E: jpetrarc@pahouse.net

**Petri, Scott A. (R, 178)**
105 Ryan Office Building
P.O. Box 202178
Harrisburg, PA 17120
P: (717) 787-9033
F: (717) 705-1802
E: spetri@pahousegop.com

**Pickett, Tina (R, 110)**
315-A Main Capitol Building
P.O. Box 202110
Harrisburg, PA 17120
P: (717) 783-8238
F: (717) 782-2881
E: tpickett@pahousegop.com

**Pyle, Jeffrey P. (R, 60)**
218 Ryan Office Building
P.O. Box 202060
Harrisburg, PA 17120
P: (717) 783-5327
F: (717) 782-2904
E: jpyle@pahousegop.com

**Quigley, Thomas (R, 146)**
125A East Wing
P.O. Box 202146
Harrisburg, PA 17120
P: (717) 772-9963
F: (717) 782-2951
E: tquigley@pahousegop.com

**Quinn, Christopher B. (R, 168)**
405 Irvis Office Building
P.O. Box 202168
Harrisburg, PA 17120
P: (717) 772-0855

**Quinn, Marguerite (R, 143)**
141B East Wing
P.O. Box 202143
Harrisburg, PA 17120
P: (717) 772-1413
F: (717) 783-3793
E: mquinn@pahousegop.com

**Rabb, Christopher M. (D, 200)***
106A East Wing
P.O. Box 202200
Harrisburg, PA 17120
P: (717) 783-2178
F: (717) 783-9755

**Rader Jr., Jack (R, 176)**
423 Irvis Office Building
P.O. Box 202176
Harrisburg, PA 17120
P: (717) 787-7732

**Rapp, Kathy L. (R, 65)**
143 East Wing
P.O. Box 202065
Harrisburg, PA 17120
P: (717) 787-1367
F: (717) 787-5854
E: klrapp@pahousegop.com

**Ravenstahl, Adam (D, 20)**
322 Irvis Office Building
P.O. Box 202020
Harrisburg, PA 17120
P: (717) 787-5470
F: (717) 783-0407

**Readshaw, Harry A. (D, 36)**
221 Irvis Office Building
P.O. Box 202036
Harrisburg, PA 17120
P: (717) 783-0411
F: (717) 705-2007
E: hreadsha@pahouse.net

**Reed, Dave (R, 62)**
110 Main Capitol Building
P.O. Box 202062
Harrisburg, PA 17120
P: (717) 705-7173
F: (717) 705-1947
E: dreed@pahousegop.com

**Reese, Mike (R, 59)**
147B East Wing
P.O. Box 202059
Harrisburg, PA 17120
P: (717) 783-9311
F: (717) 782-2900
E: Mreese@pahousegop.com

**Roae, Brad (R, 6)**
162B East Wing
P.O. Box 202006
Harrisburg, PA 17120
P: (717) 787-2353
F: (717) 260-6505
E: broae@pahousegop.com

**Roe, Eric (R, 158)***
117A East Wing
P.O. Box 202158
Harrisburg, PA 17120
P: (717) 783-1574
F: (717) 782-2970

**Roebuck, Jim (D, 188)**
208 Irvis Office Building
P.O. Box 202188
Harrisburg, PA 17120
P: (717) 783-1000
F: (717) 783-1665
E: jroebuck@pahouse.net

**Rothman, Greg (R, 87)**
163A East Wing
P.O. Box 202087
Harrisburg, PA 17120
P: (717) 783-2063
F: (717) 782-2897

**Rozzi, Mark (D, 126)**
111 Irvis Office Building
P.O. Box 202126
Harrisburg, PA 17120
P: (717) 783-3290
F: (717) 787-7517

**Ryan, Francis X. (R, 101)***
149A East Wing
P.O. Box 202101
Harrisburg, PA 17120
P: (717) 783-1815
F: (717) 782-2937

**Saccone, Rick (R, 39)**
430 Irvis Office Building
P.O. Box 202039
Harrisburg, PA 17120
P: (717) 260-6122

# Pennsylvania

**Sainato, Chris (D, 9)**
30 East Wing
P.O. Box 202009
Harrisburg, PA 17120
P: (717) 772-2436
F: (717) 783-8536
E: csainato@pahouse.net

**Samuelson, Steve (D, 135)**
34 East Wing
P.O. Box 202135
Harrisburg, PA 17120
P: (717) 705-1881
F: (717) 772-2469
E: ssamuels@pahouse.net

**Sankey, Tommy (R, 73)**
149B East Wing
P.O. Box 202073
Harrisburg, PA 17120
P: (717) 787-7099
F: (717) 782-2922

**Santora, James (R, 163)**
432 Irvis Office Building
P.O. Box 202163
Harrisburg, PA 17120
P: (717) 783-8808
F: (717) 782-2955

**Saylor, Stan (R, 94)**
245 Main Capitol Building
P.O. Box 202094
Harrisburg, PA 17120
P: (717) 783-6426
F: (717) 783-7655
E: ssaylor@pahousegop.com

**Schemel, Paul (R, 90)**
121B East Wing
P.O. Box 202090
Harrisburg, PA 17120
P: (717) 783-5218
F: (717) 782-2903

**Schlegel Culver, Lynda (R, 108)**
402 Irvis Office Building
P.O. Box 202108
Harrisburg, PA 17120
P: (717) 787-3485
F: (717) 782-2892

**Schlossberg, Michael H. (D, 132)**
331 Irvis Office Building
P.O. Box 202132
Harrisburg, PA 17120
P: (717) 705-1869

**Schweyer, Peter (D, 22)**
104 Irvis Office Building
P.O. Box 202022
Harrisburg, PA 17120
P: (717) 787-2909
F: (717) 787-2176

**Simmons, Justin J. (R, 131)**
5 East Wing
P.O. Box 202131
Harrisburg, PA 17120
P: (717) 783-1673
F: (717) 705-7012

**Sims, Brian (D, 182)**
104B East Wing
P.O. Box 202182
Harrisburg, PA 17120
P: (717) 783-4072
F: (717) 787-5066

**Snyder, Pam (D, 50)**
112 Irvis Office Building
P.O. Box 202050
Harrisburg, PA 17120
P: (717) 783-3797
F: (717) 772-3605

**Solomon, Jared G. (D, 202)***
104A East Wing
P.O. Box 202202
Harrisburg, PA 17120
P: (717) 787-4117

**Sonney, Curtis G. (R, 4)**
161B East Wing
P.O. Box 202004
Harrisburg, PA 17120
P: (717) 783-9087
F: (717) 787-2005
E: csonney@pahousegop.com

**Staats, Craig (R, 145)**
412 Irvis Office Building
P.O. Box 202145
Harrisburg, PA 17120
P: (717) 783-3154
F: (717) 260-6521

**Stephens, Todd (R, 151)**
4A East Wing
P.O. Box 202151
Harrisburg, PA 17120
P: (717) 260-6163

**Sturla, P. Michael (D, 96)**
414 Main Capitol Building
P.O. Box 202096
Harrisburg, PA 17120
P: (717) 787-3555
F: (717) 705-1923
E: msturla@pahouse.net

**Tallman, Will (R, 193)**
427 Irvis Office Building
P.O. Box 202193
Harrisburg, PA 17120
P: (717) 783-8875
F: (717) 787-7588
E: Wtallman@pahousegop.com

**Taylor, John J. (R, 177)**
214 Ryan Office Building
P.O. Box 202177
Harrisburg, PA 17120
P: (717) 787-3179
F: (717) 260-6519
E: jtaylor@pahousegop.com

**Thomas, W. Curtis (D, 181)**
214 Irvis Office Building
P.O. Box 202181
Harrisburg, PA 17120
P: (717) 787-9471
F: (717) 787-7297
E: cthomas@pahouse.net

**Tobash, Mike (R, 125)**
4B East Wing
P.O. Box 202125
Harrisburg, PA 17120
P: (717) 260-6148

**Toepel, Marcy (R, 147)**
116 Main Capitol Building
P.O. Box 202147
Harrisburg, PA 17120
P: (717) 787-9501
F: (717) 787-8215

**Toohil, Tarah (R, 116)**
B14 Main Capitol Building
P.O. Box 202116
Harrisburg, PA 17120
P: (717) 260-6136
F: (717) 782-2921

**Topper, Jesse (R, 78)**
409 Irvis Office Building
P.O. Box 202078
Harrisburg, PA 17120
P: (717) 787-7076
F: (717) 782-2933

**Turzai, Mike (R, 28)**
139 Main Capitol
P.O. Box 202028
Harrisburg, PA 17120
P: (717) 772-9943
F: (717) 772-2470
E: mturzai@pahousegop.com

**Vitali, Greg (D, 166)**
38B East Wing
P.O. Box 202166
Harrisburg, PA 17120
P: (717) 787-7647
F: (717) 705-2089
E: gvitali@pahouse.net

**Walsh, Justin M. (R, 58)***
B12 Main Capitol Building
P.O. Box 202058
Harrisburg, PA 17120
P: (717) 783-3825

**Ward, Judy (R, 80)**
413 Irvis Office Building
P.O. Box 202080
Harrisburg, PA 17120
P: (717) 787-9020
F: (717) 260-6521

**Warner, Ryan (R, 52)**
B12 Main Capitol Building
P.O. Box 202052
Harrisburg, PA 17120
P: (717) 787-1540
F: (717) 782-2882

**Warren, Perry S. (D, 31)***
27B East Wing
P.O. Box 202031
Harrisburg, PA 17120
P: (717) 787-5475

**Watson, Katharine M. (R, 144)**
41A East Wing
P.O. Box 202144
Harrisburg, PA 17120
P: (717) 787-5452
F: (717) 783-8934
E: kwatson@pahousegop.com

**Wentling, Parke (R, 17)**
162A East Wing
P.O. Box 202017
Harrisburg, PA 17120
P: (717) 783-5008
F: (717) 705-1948

**Wheatley, Jake (D, 19)**
36 East Wing
P.O. Box 202019
Harrisburg, PA 17120
P: (717) 783-3783
F: (717) 780-4753
E: jwheatley@pahouse.net

**Wheeland, Jeff (R, 83)**
415 Irvis Office Building
P.O. Box 202083
Harrisburg, PA 17120
P: (717) 787-2885
F: (717) 782-2948

**White, Martina (R, 170)**
B13 Main Capitol Building
P.O. Box 202170
Harrisburg, PA 17120
P: (717) 787-6740
F: (717) 782-2929

**Youngblood, Rosita C. (D, 198)**
331 Main Capitol Building
P.O. Box 202198
Harrisburg, PA 17120
P: (717) 787-7727
F: (717) 772-1313
E: ryoungbl@pahouse.net

**Zimmerman, David (R, 99)**
51B East Wing
P.O. Box 202099
Harrisburg, PA 17120
P: (717) 787-3531
F: (717) 705-1986

# Puerto Rico

## Executive

### Governor

**The Honorable Ricky Rosello (NPP)**
Governor
La Fortaleza
P.O. Box 9020082
San Juan, PR 00902
P: (787) 721-7000
F: (787) 721-5072

### Lieutenant Governor

*Puerto Rico does not have the office of the lieutenant governor. The secretary of state is appointed by the governor and is next in line of succession to the governorship.*

### Attorney General

**The Honorable Cesar R. Miranda-Rodriguez**
Attorney General
G.P.O. Box 902192
San Juan, PR 00902
P: (787) 721-2900

### Auditor

**Ms. Yesmin Valdivieso-Galib** (appointed)
Comptroller
P.O. Box 366069
San Juan, PR 00963
P: (787) 250-3300
F: (787) 751-6768
E: ocpr@ocpr.gov.pr

### Treasurer

**The Honorable Raul Maldonado**
Secretary of Treasury
P.O. Box 9024140
San Juan, PR 00902
P: (787) 721-2020
F: (787) 721-6213

## Judiciary

### Supreme Court (GA)

**Ms. Patricia Oton Oliveri**
Secretary of Supreme Court
P.O. Box 9022392
San Juan, PR 00902
P: (787) 723-6033
F: (787) 723-9199

**The Honorable Maite Oronoz Rodriguez**
Chief Justice
**The Honorable Roberto Cintron Feliberti**
**The Honorable Angel Colon-Perez**
**The Honorable Luis Estrella Martinez**
**The Honorable Erick V. Kolthoff Caraballo**
**The Honorable Rafael L. Martinez Torres**
**The Honorable Mildred G. Pabon Charneco**
**The Honorable Edgardo Rivera Garcia**
**The Honorable Anabelle Rodriguez**

## Legislative

## Senate

### Senate President

**Senator Thomas Rivera Schatz (NPP)**
Senate President
The Capitol
P.O. Box 9023431
San Juan, PR 00902
P: (787) 724-2030 Ext. 3008
E: trivera@senado.pr.gov

### President Pro Tempore of the Senate

**Senator Lawrence Seilhamer Rodriguez (NPP)**
Senate Vice President
The Capitol
P.O. Box 9023431
San Juan, PR 00902
P: (787) 724-2030 Ext. 1623
E: lseilhamer@senado.pr.gov

### Senate Majority Leader

**Senator Carmelo J. Rios (NPP)**
Senate Majority Leader
The Capitol
P.O. Box 9023431
San Juan, PR 00902
P: (787) 724-2030 Ext. 2668
E: crios@senado.pr.gov

### Senate Minority Leader

**Senator Eduardo Bhatia (PDP)**
Senate Minority Leader
The Capitol
P.O. Box 9023431
San Juan, PR 00902
P: (787) 724-2030 Ext. 3031
E: ebhatia@senado.pr.gov

### Secretary of the Senate

**Ms. Tania Barbarossa**
Secretary of the Senate
The Capitol
P.O. Box 9023431
San Juan, PR 00902
P: (787) 724-2030 ext. 2266

### Members of the Senate

**Berdiel Rivera, Luis (NPP, 5)**
The Capitol
P.O. Box 9023431
San Juan, PR 00902
P: (787) 724-2030
E: lberdiel@senadopr.us

**Bhatia, Eduardo (PDP, At-Large)**
The Capitol
P.O. Box 9023431
San Juan, PR 00902
P: (787) 724-2030 Ext. 3031
E: ebhatia@senado.pr.gov

**Correa Rivera, Eric (NPP, 8)**
The Capitol
P.O. Box 9023431
San Juan, PR 00902
P: (787) 724-2030
E: ecorrea@senado.pr.gov

**Cruz, Nelson (NPP, 5)***
The Capitol
P.O. Box 9023431
San Juan, PR 00902
P: (787) 724-2030
E: ncruz@senado.pr.gov

**Dalmau Ramírez, Juan (PIP, At-Large)***
The Capitol
P.O. Box 9023431
San Juan, PR 00902
P: (787) 724-2030
E: jdalmau@senado.pr.gov

**Dalmau Santiago, Jose L. (PDP, 7)**
The Capitol
P.O. Box 9023431
San Juan, PR 00902
P: (787) 724-2030 Ext. 2357
E: jldalmau@senado.pr.gov

**Laboy, Zoé (NPP, At-Large)***
The Capitol
P.O. Box 9023431
San Juan, PR 00902
P: (787) 724-2030
E: zlaboy@senado.pr.gov

**Laureano, Miguel (NPP, 7)***
The Capitol
P.O. Box 9023431
San Juan, PR 00902
P: (787) 724-2030
E: milaureano@senado.pr.gov

**Lopez Leon, Rossana (PDP, At-Large)**
The Capitol
P.O. Box 9023431
San Juan, PR 00902
P: (787) 724-2030 Ext. 1020
E: rolopez@senado.pr.gov

**Martinez Santiago, Angel (NPP, 3)**
The Capitol
P.O. Box 9023431
San Juan, PR 00902
P: (787) 724-2030 Ext. 2762
E: anmartinez@senado.pr.gov

**Muñiz Cortes, Luis Daniel (NPP, 4)**
The Capitol
P.O. Box 9023431
San Juan, PR 00902
P: (787) 724-2030

**Nadal Power, Jose R. (PDP, At-Large)**
The Capitol
P.O. Box 9023431
San Juan, PR 00902
P: (787) 724-2030 Ext. 2000
E: jnadal@senado.pr.gov

**Nazario Quinones, Abel (NPP, At-Large)***
The Capitol
P.O. Box 9023431
San Juan, PR 00902
P: (787) 724-2030
E: abnazario@senado.pr.gov

**Neumann, Henry (NPP, 1)***
The Capitol
P.O. Box 9023431
San Juan, PR 00902
P: (787) 724-2030
E: hneumann@senado.pr.gov

**Nolasco Santiago, Margarita (NPP, At-Large)**
The Capitol
P.O. Box 9023431
San Juan, PR 00902
P: (787) 724-2030 Ext. 2909
E: mnolasco@senado.pr.gov

**Padilla Alvelo, Migdalia (NPP, 2)**
The Capitol
P.O. Box 9023431
San Juan, PR 00902
P: (787) 724-2030 Ext. 2221
E: mpadilla@senado.pr.gov

**Peña Ramirez, Itzamar (NPP, At-Large)**
The Capitol
P.O. Box 9023431
San Juan, PR 00902
P: (787) 723-2030 Ext. 2383
E: ipena@senado.pr.gov

**Pereira Castillo, Miguel A. (PDP, At-Large)**
The Capitol
P.O. Box 9023431
San Juan, PR 00902
P: (787) 724-2030 Ext. 2504
E: mpereira@senado.pr.gov

**Perez Rosa, Jose O. (NPP, 3)**
The Capitol
P.O. Box 9023431
San Juan, PR 00902
P: (787) 724-2030 Ext. 2337
E: josperez@senado.pr.gov

**Rios, Carmelo J. (NPP, 2)**
The Capitol
P.O. Box 9023431
San Juan, PR 00902
P: (787) 724-2030 Ext. 2668
E: crios@senado.pr.gov

**Rivera Schatz, Thomas (NPP, At-Large)**
The Capitol
P.O. Box 9023431
San Juan, PR 00902
P: (787) 724-2030 Ext. 3008
E: trivera@senado.pr.gov

**Rodríguez Mateo, Carlos (NPP, 6)\***
The Capitol
P.O. Box 9023431
San Juan, PR 00902
P: (787) 724-2030
E: cjrodriguez
@senado.pr.gov

**Romero, Miguel (NPP, 1)\***
The Capitol
P.O. Box 9023431
San Juan, PR 00902
P: (787) 724-2030
E: maromero@senado.pr.gov

**Roque, Axel (NPP, 6)\***
The Capitol
P.O. Box 9023431
San Juan, PR 00902
P: (787) 724-2030
E: airoque@senado.pr.gov

**Seilhamer Rodriguez, Lawrence (NPP, 5)**
The Capitol
P.O. Box 9023431
San Juan, PR 00902
P: (787) 724-2030 Ext. 1623
E: lseilhamer@senado.pr.gov

**Tirado Rivera Jr., Cirilo (PDP, At-Large)**
The Capitol
P.O. Box 9023431
San Juan, PR 00902
P: (787) 724-2030 Ext. 2226
E: ctirado@senado.pr.gov

**Torres Torres, Anibal J. (PDP, At-Large)**
The Capitol
P.O. Box 9023431
San Juan, PR 00902
P: (787) 724-2030 Ext. 2100
E: ajtorres@senado.pr.gov

**Vargas Vidot, José Antonio (I, At-Large)\***
The Capitol
P.O. Box 9023431
San Juan, PR 00902
P: (787) 724-2030
E: jvargas@senado.pr.gov

**Vazquez Nieves, Evelyn (NPP, 4)**
The Capitol
P.O. Box 9023431
San Juan, PR 00902
P: (787) 724-2030

**Venegas Brown, Nayda (NPP, 8)\***
The Capitol
P.O. Box 9023431
San Juan, PR 00902
P: (787) 724-2030
E: nvenegas@senado.pr.gov

# House
## Speaker of the House
**Representative Carlos Mendez Nuñez (NPP)**
Speaker of the House
The Capitol
P.O. Box 9022228
San Juan, PR 00902
P: (787) 722-3539
F: (787) 721-3644
E: cmendez
@camaraderepresentantes.org

## Speaker Pro Tempore of the House
**Representative Jose Torres Zamora (NPP)**
House Speaker Pro Tempore
The Capitol
P.O. Box 902228
San Juan, PR 00902

## House Majority Leader
**Representative Gabriel Rodríguez Aguiló (NPP)**
House Majority Leader
The Capitol
P.O. Box 9022228
San Juan, PR 00902
P: (787) 723-0109
F: (787) 622-4387
E: gfrodriguez
@camaraderepresentantes.org

## House Minority Leader
**Representative Urayoan Hernandez Alvarado (NPP)**
House Minority Leader
The Capitol
P.O. Box 9022228
San Juan, PR 00902
P: (787) 725-4431
F: (787) 723-2746
E: uhernandez
@camaraderepresentantes.org

## Clerk of the House
**Ms. Brunilda Ortiz-Rodriguez**
Clerk of the House
P.O. Box 9022228
San Juan, PR 00902
P: (787) 722-0830
F: (787) 723-4342

# Members of the House
**Alonso, Nestor (NPP, At-Large)\***
The Capitol
P.O. Box 9022228
San Juan, PR 00902

**Aponte, Javier (PDP, 38)**
The Capitol
P.O. Box 9022228
San Juan, PR 00902
P: (787) 722-7780
F: (787) 622-4963
E: apontedalmau
@camaraderepresentantes.org

**Aponte Hernández, José F. (NPP, At-Large)**
The Capitol
P.O. Box 9022228
San Juan, PR 00902
P: (787) 723-1090
F: (787) 722-5106
E: japonte
@camaraderepresentantes.org

**Banchs Alemán, José A. (NPP, 24)\***
The Capitol
P.O. Box 9022228
San Juan, PR 00902

**Bianchi Anglero, Carlos (PDP, 20)**
The Capitol
P.O. Box 9022228
San Juan, PR 00902
P: (787) 977-2456
F: (787) 721-3644
E: cbianchi
@camaraderepresentantes.org

**Bulerín Ramos, Angel L. (NPP, 37)**
The Capitol
P.O. Box 9022228
San Juan, PR 00902
P: (787) 722-2508
F: (787) 721-6608
E: abulerin
@camaraderepresentantes.org

**Charbonier, Eddie (NPP, 1)\***
The Capitol
P.O. Box 9022228
San Juan, PR 00902

**Charbonier Laureano, Maria M. (NPP, At-Large)**
The Capitol
P.O. Box 9022228
San Juan, PR 00902
P: (787) 721-1190
F: (787) 723-2139
E: mcharbonier
@camaraderepresentantes.org

# Puerto Rico

**Cruz Burgos, Ramon Luis (PDP, 34)**
The Capitol
P.O. Box 9022228
San Juan, PR 00902
P: (787) 622-3802
F: (787) 725-0437
E: rcruz
@camaraderepresentantes.org

**Del Valle Colón, Nelson E. (NPP, 9)**
The Capitol
P.O. Box 9022228
San Juan, PR 00902

**Diaz Collazo, Jose Anibal (PDP, 29)**
The Capitol
P.O. Box 9022228
San Juan, PR 00902
P: (787) 622-4885

**Franqui Atiles, Joel (NPP, 15)***
The Capitol
P.O. Box 902228
San Juan, PR 00902

**Hernandez Alvarado, Urayoan (NPP, 26)**
The Capitol
P.O. Box 9022228
San Juan, PR 00902
P: (787) 725-4431
F: (787) 723-2746
E: uhernandez
@camaraderepresentantes.org

**Hernández Montañez, Rafael (PDP, 11)**
The Capitol
P.O. Box 9022228
San Juan, PR 00902
P: (787) 622-4997
F: (787) 723-1732
E: rahernandez
@camaraderepresentantes.org

**Lassalle, Felix (NPP, 16)***
The Capitol
P.O. Box 9022228
San Juan, PR 00902

**Lebrón Rodríguez, Yashira (NPP, 8)**
The Capitol
P.O. Box 9022228
San Juan, PR 00902
P: (787) 721-6040
F: (787) 622-4710

**López De Arrarás, Brenda (PDP, At-Large)**
The Capitol
P.O. Box 9022228
San Juan, PR 00902
P: (787) 725-2771
F: (787) 622-4970
E: blopez
@camaraderepresentantes.org

**Márquez Lebrón, Denis (PIP, At-Large)***
The Capitol
P.O. Box 9022228
San Juan, PR 00902

**Mas Rodríguez, Maricarmen (NPP, 19)***
The Capitol
P.O. Box 9022228
San Juan, PR 00902

**Matos Garcia, Angel (PDP, 40)**
The Capitol
P.O. Box 9022228
San Juan, PR 00902
P: (787) 721-4039
F: (787) 722-5483
E: amatos
@camaraderepresentantes.org

**Melendez Ortiz, Jose E. (NPP, At-Large)**
The Capitol
P.O. Box 9022228
San Juan, PR 00902
P: (787) 725-9189
F: (787) 721-6062
E: jem
@camaraderepresentantes.org

**Mendez Nuñez, Carlos (NPP, 36)**
The Capitol
P.O. Box 9022228
San Juan, PR 00902
P: (787) 722-3539
F: (787) 721-3644
E: cmendez
@camaraderepresentantes.org

**Méndez Silva, Lydia (PDP, 21)**
The Capitol
P.O. Box 9022228
San Juan, PR 00902
P: (787) 722-0801
F: (787) 721-0483
E: lmendez
@camaraderepresentantes.org

**Miranda Rivera, Guillermo (NPP, 12)***
The Capitol
P.O. Box 9022228
San Juan, PR 00902

**Morales, Juan Oscar (NPP, 3)***
The Capitol
P.O. Box 9022228
San Juan, PR 00902

**Natal Albelo, Manuel (PDP, At-Large)**
The Capitol
P.O. Box 9022228
San Juan, PR 00902
P: (787) 721-8011
F: (787) 977-2496
E: mnatal
@camaraderepresentantes.org

**Navarro Suárez, Jorge (NPP, 5)**
The Capitol
P.O. Box 9022228
San Juan, PR 00902
P: (787) 724-4465
F: (787) 723-4711
E: jnavarro
@camaraderepresentantes.org

**Ortiz, Jesús Manuel (PDP, At-Large)***
The Capitol
P.O. Box 9022228
San Juan, PR 00902

**Ortiz Lugo, Luis R. (PDP, 30)**
The Capitol
P.O. Box 9022228
San Juan, PR 00902
P: (787) 721-5545
F: (787) 725-6669
E: lortiz
@camaraderepresentantes.org

**Pagán Cuadrado, Samuel (NPP, 34)***
The Capitol
P.O. Box 9022228
San Juan, PR 00902

**Parés, Victor (NPP, 4)***
The Capitol
P.O. Box 9022228
San Juan, PR 00902

**Peña Ramírez, Angel (NPP, 33)**
The Capitol
P.O. Box 9022228
San Juan, PR 00902
P: (787) 622-4961
F: (787) 622-4995
E: anpena
@camaraderepresentantes.org

**Pérez Cordero, José (NPP, 18)***
The Capitol
P.O. Box 9022228
San Juan, PR 00902

**Pérez Ortiz, Luis (NPP, 7)**
The Capitol
P.O. Box 9022228
San Juan, PR 00902
P: (787) 724-6262
F: (787) 723-9551
E: lperez
@camaraderepresentantes.org

**Quinones, Michael A. (NPP, 22)***
The Capitol
P.O. Box 9022228
San Juan, PR 00902
P: (787) 721-6040

**Ramos, María (NPP, At-Large)**
The Capitol
P.O. Box 9022228
San Juan, PR 00902
P: (787) 721-6040
F: (787) 622-4882
E: lramos
@camaraderepresentantes.org

**Rivera Guerra, José L. (NPP, 17)**
The Capitol
P.O. Box 9022228
San Juan, PR 00902

**Rivera Ortega, Rafael (NPP, 28)**
The Capitol
P.O. Box 9022228
San Juan, PR 00902
P: (787) 977-2417
F: (787) 725-4290
E: rarivera
@camaraderepresentantes.org

**Rodriguez, Ramón Luis (NPP, 27)***
The Capitol
P.O. Box 9022228
San Juan, PR 00902

**Rodriguez, Jacqueline (NPP, 25)***
The Capitol
P.O. Box 9022228
San Juan, PR 00902

**Rodríguez Aguiló, Gabriel (NPP, 13)**
The Capitol
P.O. Box 9022228
San Juan, PR 00902
P: (787) 723-0109
F: (787) 622-4387
E: gfrodriguez
@camaraderepresentantes.org

**Santa Rodriguez, Jesus**
**(PDP, 31)**
The Capitol
P.O. Box 9022228
San Juan, PR 00902
P: (787) 725-5595
F: (787) 725-3411
E: jsanta
@camaraderepresentantes.org

**Santiago Guzman, Pedro J.**
**(NPP, 10)**
The Capitol
P.O. Box 9022228
San Juan, PR 00902
P: (787) 725-3350
F: (787) 721-6608
E: psantiago
@camaraderepresentantes.org

**Soto Torres, Antonio L.**
**(NPP, 6)**
The Capitol
P.O. Box 9022228
San Juan, PR 00902
P: (787) 725-2698
F: (787) 977-2477
E: ansoto
@camaraderepresentantes.org

**Torres, Victor (NPP, 23)\***
The Capitol
P.O. Box 9022228
San Juan, PR 00902

**Torres Cruz, Luis R.**
**(PDP, 2)**
The Capitol
P.O. Box 9022228
San Juan, PR 00902
P: (787) 723-1816
F: (787) 722-3573
E: ltorres
@camaraderepresentantes.org

**Torres Zamora, Jose**
**(NPP, At-Large)**
The Capitol
P.O. Box 902228
San Juan, PR 00902

**Varela Fernández, José M.**
**(PDP, 32)**
The Capitol
P.O. Box 9022228
San Juan, PR 00902
P: (787) 725-3928
F: (787) 723-4711
E: jvarela
@camaraderepresentantes.org

**Vega Ramos, Luis R.**
**(PDP, At-Large)**
The Capitol
P.O. Box 9022228
San Juan, PR 00902
P: (787) 725-3898
F: (787) 622-4875
E: lvega
@camaraderepresentantes.org

# Rhode Island

## Executive

### Governor

**The Honorable Gina M. Raimondo (D)**
Governor
State House
Providence, RI 02903
P: (401) 222-2080
F: (401) 222-8096
E: governor@governor.ri.gov

### Lieutenant Governor

**The Honorable Daniel McKee (D)**
Lieutenant Governor
116 State House
Providence, RI 02903
P: (401) 222-2371
F: (401) 222-2012

### Attorney General

**The Honorable Peter F. Kilmartin (D)**
Attorney General
150 South Main Street
Providence, RI 02903
P: (401) 274-4400

### Auditor

**Mr. Dennis E. Hoyle**
(appointed by the Legislature)
Auditor General
86 Weybosset Street
Providence, RI 02903
P: (401) 222-2435 Ext. 3038
F: (401) 222-2111
E: ag@oag.ri.gov

### Secretary of State

**The Honorable Nellie Gorbea**
Secretary of State
82 Smith Street, Room 217
Providence, RI 02903
P: (401) 222-2357
F: (401) 222-1356
E: nmgorbea@sos.ri.gov

### Treasurer

**The Honorable Seth Magaziner (D)**
General Treasurer
102 State House
Providence, RI 02903
P: (401) 222-2397
F: (401) 222-6140
E: generaltreasurer
@treasury.ri.gov

## Judiciary

### Supreme Court (LA)

**Ms. Debra A. Saunders**
Supreme Court Clerk
Frank Licht Judicial Complex
250 Benefit Street
Providence, RI 02903
P: (401) 222-3272
E: dsaunders@courts.ri.gov

**The Honorable Paul A. Suttell**
Chief Justice
**The Honorable Francis X. Flaherty**
**The Honorable Maureen M. Goldberg**
**The Honorable Gilbert V. Indeglia**
**The Honorable William P. Robinson III**

## Legislative

## Senate

### Senate President

**Senator M. Teresa Paiva-Weed (D)**
Senate President
82 Smith Street
Providence, RI 02903
P: (401) 276-2555
E: sen-paivaweed
@rilegislature.gov

### Senate Majority Leader

**Senator Dominick J. Ruggerio (D)**
Senate Majority Leader
82 Smith Street
Providence, RI 02903
P: (401) 276-2555
E: sen-ruggerio
@rilegislature.gov

### Senate Minority Leader

**Senator Dennis L. Algiere (R)**
Senate Minority Leader
82 Smith Street
Westerly, RI 02891
P: (401) 222-2708
E: sen-algiere
@rilegislature.gov

## Secretary of the Senate

**Mr. Joseph Brady**
Secretary of the Senate
82 Smith Street
Providence, RI 02903
P: (401) 276-5558
E: jbrady@rilin.state.ri.us

## Members of the Senate

**Algiere, Dennis L. (R, 38)**
82 Smith Street
Westerly, RI 02891
P: (401) 222-2708
E: sen-algiere
@rilegislature.gov

**Archambault, Stephen R. (D, 22)**
82 Smith Street
Smithfield, RI 02917
P: (401) 276-5589
E: sen-archambault
@rilegislature.gov

**Calkin, Jeanine (D, 30)***
82 Smith Street
Providence, RI 02903

**Ciccone III, Frank A. (D, 7)**
82 Smith Street
Providence, RI 02909
P: (401) 275-0949
E: sen-ciccone
@rilegislature.gov

**Conley Jr., William J. (D, 18)**
82 Smith Street
Providence, RI 02903
P: (401) 276-2555
E: sen-conley
@rilegislature.gov

**Cote, Marc A. (D, 24)**
82 Smith Street
Providence, RI 02903
P: (401) 276-2555
E: sen-cote
@rilegislature.gov

**Coyne, Cynthia (D, 32)**
82 Smith Street
Providence, RI 02903
P: (401) 276-2555
E: sen-coyne
@rilegislature.gov

**Crowley, Elizabeth A. (D, 16)**
82 Smith Street
Providence, RI 02903
P: (401) 276-2555
E: sen-crowley
@rilegislature.gov

**DaPonte, Daniel (D, 14)**
82 Smith Street
Providence, RI 02903
P: (401) 276-2555
E: sen-daponte
@rilegislature.gov

**DiPalma, Louis P. (D, 12)**
82 Smith Street
Providence, RI 02903
P: (401) 276-2555
E: sen-dipalma
@rilegislature.gov

**Doyle II, James E. (D, 8)**
82 Smith Street
Providence, RI 02903
P: (401) 276-2555
E: sen-doyle
@rilegislature.gov

**Felag Jr., Walter S. (D, 10)**
82 Smith Street
Providence, RI 02903
P: (401) 276-2555
E: sen-felag
@rilegislature.gov

**Fogarty, Paul W. (D, 23)**
82 Smith Street
Providence, RI 02903
P: (401) 276-2555
E: sen-fogarty
@rilegislature.gov

**Gallo, Hanna M. (D, 27)**
82 Smith Street
Providence, RI 02903
P: (401) 276-2555
E: sen-gallo
@rilegislature.gov

**Gee, Mark (R, 35)**
82 Smith Street
Providence, RI 02903
P: (401) 276-2555
E: sen-gee
@rilegislature.gov

**Goldin, Gayle L. (D, 3)**
82 Smith Street
Providence, RI 02903
P: (401) 276-2555
E: sen-goldin
@rilegislature.gov

**Goodwin, Maryellen (D, 1)**
82 Smith Street
Providence, RI 02903
P: (401) 276-2555
E: sen-goodwin
@rilegislature.gov

**Jabour, Paul V. (D, 5)**
82 Smith Street
Providence, RI 02903
P: (401) 276-2555
E: sen-jabour
@rilegislature.gov

**Kettle, Nicholas D. (R, 21)**
82 Smith Street
Providence, RI 02903
P: (401) 276-2555
E: sen-kettle
@rilegislature.gov

**Lombardi, Frank S. (D, 26)**
82 Smith Street
Providence, RI 02903
P: (401) 276-2555
E: sen-lombardi
@rilegislature.gov

**Lombardo III, Frank (D, 25)**
82 Smith Street
Providence, RI 02903
P: (401) 276-2555
E: sen-lombardo
@rilegislature.gov

**Lynch Prata, Erin (D, 31)**
82 Smith Street
Providence, RI 02903
P: (401) 276-2555
E: sen-lynch
@rilegislature.gov

**McCaffrey, Michael J. (D, 29)**
82 Smith Street
Providence, RI 02903
P: (401) 276-2555
E: sen-mccaffrey
@rilegislature.gov

**Metts, Harold M. (D, 6)**
82 Smith Street
Providence, RI 02903
P: (401) 276-2555
E: sen-metts
@rilegislature.gov

**Miller, Joshua B. (D, 28)**
82 Smith Street
Providence, RI 02903
P: (401) 276-2555
E: sen-miller
@rilegislature.gov

**Morgan, Elaine (R, 34)**
82 Smith Street
Providence, RI 02903
P: (401) 276-2555
E: sen-morgan
@rilegislature.gov

**Nesselbush, Donna (D, 15)**
82 Smith Street
Providence, RI 02903
P: (401) 276-2555
E: sen-nesselbush
@rilegislature.gov

**Paiva-Weed, M. Teresa (D, 13)**
82 Smith Street
Providence, RI 02903
P: (401) 276-2555
E: sen-paivaweed
@rilegislature.gov

**Paolino, Thomas (R, 17)\***
82 Smith Street
Providence, RI 02903
P: (401) 276-2555

**Pearson, Ryan (D, 19)**
82 Smith Street
Providence, RI 02903
P: (401) 276-2555
E: sen-pearson
@rilegislature.gov

**Picard, Roger A. (D, 20)**
82 Smith Street
Providence, RI 02903
P: (401) 276-2555
E: sen-picard
@rilegislature.gov

**Quezada, Ana B. (D, 2)\***
82 Smith Street
Providence, RI 02903
P: (401) 276-2555
E: sen-quezada
@rilegislature.gov

**Raptakis, Leonidas P. (D, 33)**
82 Smith Street
Providence, RI 02903
P: (401) 276-2555
E: sen-raptakis
@rilegislature.gov

**Ruggerio, Dominick J. (D, 4)**
82 Smith Street
Providence, RI 02903
P: (401) 276-2555
E: sen-ruggerio
@rilegislature.gov

**Satchell, Adam J. (D, 9)**
82 Smith Street
Providence, RI 02903
P: (401) 276-2555
E: sen-satchell
@rilegislature.gov

**Seveney, James A. (D, 11)\***
82 Smith Street
Providence, RI 02903
P: (401) 276-2555

**Sheehan, James C. (D, 36)**
82 Smith Street
Providence, RI 02903
P: (401) 276-2555
E: sen-sheehan
@rilegislature.gov

**Sosnowski, V. Susan (D, 37)**
82 Smith Street
Providence, RI 02903
P: (401) 276-2555
E: sen-sosnowski
@rilegislature.gov

# House

## Speaker of the House

**Representative Nicholas A. Mattiello (D)**
House Speaker
82 Smith Street
Providence, RI 02903
P: (401) 222-1478
E: rep-mattiello
@rilegislature.gov

## House Majority Leader

**Representative K. Joseph Shekarchi (D)**
House Majority Leader
82 Smith Street
Providence, RI 02903
P: (401) 222-1478
E: rep-shekarchi
@rilegislature.gov

## House Minority Leader

**Representative Patricia L. Morgan (R)**
House Minority Leader
82 Smith Street
Providence, RI 02903
P: (401) 222-1478
E: rep-morgan
@rilegislature.gov

## Clerk of the House

**Mr. Frank McCabe**
Clerk of the House
82 Smith Street
Providence, RI 02903
P: (401) 222-3580

## Members of the House

**Abney, Marvin L. (D, 73)**
82 Smith Street
Providence, RI 02903
P: (401) 222-1478
E: rep-abney
@rilegislature.gov

**Ackerman, Mia A. (D, 45)**
82 Smith Street
Providence, RI 02903
P: (401) 222-1478
E: rep-ackerman
@rilegislature.gov

**Ajello, Edith H. (D, 1)**
82 Smith Street
Providence, RI 02903
P: (401) 222-1478
E: rep-ajello
@rilegislature.gov

**Almeida, Joseph S. (D, 12)**
82 Smith Street
Providence, RI 02903
P: (401) 222-1478
E: rep-almeida
@rilegislature.gov

**Amore, Gregg (D, 65)**
82 Smith Street
Providence, RI 02903
P: (401) 222-1478
E: rep-amore
@rilegislature.gov

**Azzinaro, Samuel A. (D, 37)**
82 Smith Street
Providence, RI 02903
P: (401) 222-1478
E: rep-azzinaro
@rilegislature.gov

**Barros, Jean (D, 59)**
82 Smith Street
Providence, RI 02903
P: (401) 222-1478
E: rep-barros
@rilegislature.gov

**Bennett, David A. (D, 20)**
82 Smith Street
Providence, RI 02903
P: (401) 222-1478
E: rep-bennett
@rilegislature.gov

**Blazejewski, Christopher R. (D, 2)**
82 Smith Street
Providence, RI 02903
P: (401) 222-1478
E: rep-blazejewski
@rilegislature.gov

**Canario, Dennis M. (D, 71)**
82 Smith Street
Providence, RI 02903
P: (401) 222-1478
E: rep-canario
@rilegislature.gov

# Rhode Island

**Carson, Lauren (D, 75)**
82 Smith Street
Providence, RI 02903
P: (401) 222-1478
E: rep-carson
   @rilegislature.gov

**Casey, Stephen (D, 50)**
82 Smith Street
Providence, RI 02903
P: (401) 222-1478
E: rep-casey
   @rilegislature.gov

**Casimiro, Julie (D, 31)***
82 Smith Street
Providence, RI 02903
P: (401) 222-1478
E: rep-casimiro
   @rilegislature.gov

**Chippendale, Michael W.
   (R, 40)**
82 Smith Street
Providence, RI 02903
P: (401) 222-1478
E: rep-chippendale
   @rilegislature.gov

**Corvese, Arthur J. (D, 55)**
82 Smith Street
Providence, RI 02903
P: (401) 222-1478
E: rep-corvese
   @rilegislature.gov

**Costantino, Gregory J.
   (D, 44)**
82 Smith Street
Providence, RI 02903
P: (401) 222-1478
E: rep-costantino
   @rilegislature.gov

**Coughlin, David (D, 60)**
82 Smith Street
Providence, RI 02903
P: (401) 222-1478
E: rep-coughlin
   @rilegislature.gov

**Craven Sr., Robert E.
   (D, 32)**
82 Smith Street
Providence, RI 02903
P: (401) 222-1478
E: rep-craven
   @rilegislature.gov

**Cunha, Helder (D, 64)***
82 Smith Street
Providence, RI 02903
P: (401) 222-1478
E: rep-cunha
   @rilegislature.gov

**Diaz, Grace (D, 11)**
82 Smith Street
Providence, RI 02903
P: (401) 222-1478
E: rep-diaz
   @rilegislature.gov

**Donovan, Susan (D, 69)***
82 Smith Street
Providence, RI 02903
P: (401) 222-1478
E: rep-donovan
   @rilegislature.gov

**Edwards, John G. (D, 70)**
82 Smith Street
Providence, RI 02903
P: (401) 222-1478
E: rep-edwards
   @rilegislature.gov

**Fellela, Deborah A. (D, 43)**
82 Smith Street
Providence, RI 02903
P: (401) 222-1478
E: rep-fellela
   @rilegislature.gov

**Filippi, Blake A. (I, 36)**
82 Smith Street
Providence, RI 02903
P: (401) 222-1478
E: rep-filippi
   @rilegislature.gov

**Fogarty, Kathleen (D, 35)**
82 Smith Street
Providence, RI 02903
P: (401) 222-1478
E: rep-fogarty
   @rilegislature.gov

**Giarrusso, Antonio (R, 30)**
82 Smith Street
Providence, RI 02903
P: (401) 222-1478
E: rep-giarrusso
   @rilegislature.gov

**Hagan McEntee, Carol
   (D, 33)**
82 Smith Street
Providence, RI 02903
P: (401) 222-1478
E: rep-mcentee
   @rilegislature.gov

**Handy, Arthur (D, 18)**
82 Smith Street
Providence, RI 02903
P: (401) 222-1478
E: rep-handy
   @rilegislature.gov

**Hearn, Joy (D, 66)**
82 Smith Street
Providence, RI 02903
P: (401) 222-1478
E: rep-hearn
   @rilegislature.gov

**Hull, Raymond (D, 6)**
82 Smith Street
Providence, RI 02903
P: (401) 222-1478
E: rep-hull
   @rilegislature.gov

**Jacquard, Robert B. (D, 17)**
82 Smith Street
Providence, RI 02903
P: (401) 222-1478
E: rep-jacquard
   @rilegislature.gov

**Johnston Jr., Raymond H.
   (D, 61)**
82 Smith Street
Providence, RI 02903
P: (401) 222-1478
E: rep-johnston
   @rilegislature.gov

**Kazarian, Katherine S.
   (D, 63)**
82 Smith Street
Providence, RI 02903
P: (401) 222-1478
E: rep-kazarian
   @rilegislature.gov

**Keable, Cale (D, 47)**
82 Smith Street
Providence, RI 02903
P: (401) 222-1478
E: rep-keable
   @rilegislature.gov

**Kennedy, Brian Patrick
   (D, 38)**
82 Smith Street
Providence, RI 02903
P: (401) 222-1478
E: rep-kennedy
   @rilegislature.gov

**Knight, Jason (D, 67)***
82 Smith Street
Providence, RI 02903
P: (401) 222-1478
E: rep-knight
   @rilegislature.gov

**Lancia, Robert (R, 16)**
82 Smith Street
Providence, RI 02903
P: (401) 222-1478
E: rep-lancia
   @rilegislature.gov

**Lima, Charlene M. (D, 14)**
82 Smith Street
Providence, RI 02903
P: (401) 222-1478
E: rep-lima
   @rilegislature.gov

**Lombardi, John J. (D, 8)**
82 Smith Street
Providence, RI 02903
P: (401) 222-1478
E: rep-lombardi
   @rilegislature.gov

**Maldonado, Shelby (D, 56)**
82 Smith Street
Providence, RI 02903
P: (401) 222-1478
E: rep-maldonado
   @rilegislature.gov

**Marshall, Kenneth A.
   (D, 68)**
82 Smith Street
Providence, RI 02903
P: (401) 222-1478
E: rep-marshall
   @rilegislature.gov

**Marszalkowski, Alex**
82 Smith Street
Providence, RI 02903
P: (401) 222-1478
E: rep-marszalkowski
   @rilegislature.gov

**Mattiello, Nicholas A.
   (D, 15)**
82 Smith Street
Providence, RI 02903
P: (401) 222-1478
E: rep-mattiello
   @rilegislature.gov

**McKiernan, Daniel (D, 7)**
82 Smith Street
Providence, RI 02903
P: (401) 222-1478
E: rep-mckiernan
   @rilegislature.gov

**McLaughlin, James N.
   (D, 57)**
82 Smith Street
Providence, RI 02903
P: (401) 222-1478
E: rep-mclaughlin
   @rilegislature.gov

**McNamara, Joseph M. (D, 19)**
82 Smith Street
Providence, RI 02903
P: (401) 222-1478
E: rep-mcnamara
   @rilegislature.gov

**Mendonca, Kenneth (R, 72)***
82 Smith Street
Providence, RI 02903
P: (401) 222-1478
E: rep-mendonca
@rilegislature.gov

**Messier, Mary Duffy (D, 62)**
82 Smith Street
Providence, RI 02903
P: (401) 222-1478
E: rep-messier
@rilegislature.gov

**Morgan, Patricia L. (R, 26)**
82 Smith Street
Providence, RI 02903
P: (401) 222-1478
E: rep-morgan
@rilegislature.gov

**Morin, Michael A. (D, 49)**
82 Smith Street
Providence, RI 02903
P: (401) 222-1478
E: rep-morin
@rilegislature.gov

**Nardolillo, Robert (R, 28)**
82 Smith Street
Providence, RI 02903
P: (401) 222-1478
E: rep-nardolillo
@rilegislature.gov

**Newberry, Brian C. (R, 48)**
82 Smith Street
Providence, RI 02903
P: (401) 222-1478
E: rep-newberry
@rilegislature.gov

**Nunes, Jared R. (D, 25)**
82 Smith Street
Providence, RI 02903
P: (401) 222-1478
E: rep-nunes
@rilegislature.gov

**O'Brien, William W. (D, 54)**
82 Smith Street
Providence, RI 02903
P: (401) 222-1478
E: rep-obrien
@rilegislature.gov

**O'Grady, Jeremiah T.
(D, 46)**
82 Smith Street
Providence, RI 02903
P: (401) 222-1478
E: rep-ogrady
@rilegislature.gov

**Perez, Ramon (D, 13)***
82 Smith Street
Providence, RI 02903
P: (401) 222-1478
E: rep-perez
@rilegislature.gov

**Phillips, Robert (D, 51)**
82 Smith Street
Providence, RI 02903
P: (401) 222-1478
E: rep-phillips
@rilegislature.gov

**Price, Justin (R, 39)**
82 Smith Street
Providence, RI 02903
P: (401) 222-1478
E: rep-Price
@rilegislature.gov

**Quattrocchi, Robert
(R, 41)***
82 Smith Street
Providence, RI 02903
P: (401) 222-1478
E: rep-quattrocchi
@rilegislature.gov

**Ranglin-Vassell, Marcia**
82 Smith Street
Providence, RI 02903
P: (401) 222-1478
E: rep-ranglin-vassell
@rilegislature.gov

**Regunberg, J. Aaron (D, 4)**
82 Smith Street
Providence, RI 02903
P: (401) 222-1478
E: rep-regunberg
@rilegislature.gov

**Roberts, Sherry (R, 29)**
82 Smith Street
Providence, RI 02903
P: (401) 222-1478
E: rep-roberts
@rilegislature.gov

**Ruggiero, Deborah L.
(D, 74)**
82 Smith Street
Providence, RI 02903
P: (401) 222-1478
E: rep-ruggiero
@rilegislature.gov

**Serpa, Patricia A. (D, 27)**
82 Smith Street
Providence, RI 02903
P: (401) 222-1478
E: rep-serpa
@rilegislature.gov

**Shanley, Evan P. (D, 24)***
82 Smith Street
Providence, RI 02903
P: (401) 222-1478
E: rep-shanley
@rilegislature.gov

**Shekarchi, K. Joseph
(D, 23)**
82 Smith Street
Providence, RI 02903
P: (401) 222-1478
E: rep-shekarchi
@rilegislature.gov

**Slater, Scott (D, 10)**
82 Smith Street
Providence, RI 02903
P: (401) 222-1478
E: rep-slater
@rilegislature.gov

**Solomon, Joseph (D, 22)**
82 Smith Street
Providence, RI 02903
P: (401) 222-1478
E: rep-solomon
@rilegislature.gov

**Tanzi, Teresa Ann (D, 34)**
82 Smith Street
Providence, RI 02903
P: (401) 222-1478
E: rep-tanzi
@rilegislature.gov

**Tobon, Carlos (D, 58)**
82 Smith Street
Providence, RI 02903
P: (401) 222-1478
E: rep-tobon
@rilegislature.gov

**Ucci, Stephen R. (D, 42)**
82 Smith Street
Providence, RI 02903
P: (401) 222-1478
E: rep-ucci
@rilegislature.gov

**Vella-Wilkinson, Camille
(D, 21)***
82 Smith Street
Providence, RI 02903
P: (401) 222-1478
E: rep-vella-wilkinson
@rilegislature.gov

**Walsh, Moira (D, 3)***
82 Smith Street
Providence, RI 02903
P: (401) 222-1478
E: rep-walsh
@rilegislature.gov

**Williams, Anastasia P.
(D, 9)**
82 Smith Street
Providence, RI 02903
P: (401) 222-1478
E: rep-williams
@rilegislature.gov

**Winfield, Thomas (D, 53)**
82 Smith Street
Providence, RI 02903
P: (401) 222-1478
E: rep-winfield
@rilegislature.gov

# South Carolina

## Executive

### Governor

The Honorable Henry D. McMaster (R)
Governor
1205 Pendleton Street
Columbia, SC 29201
P: (803) 734-2100
F: (803) 734-5167

### Lieutenant Governor

The Honorable Kevin L. Bryant (R)
Lieutenant Governor
P.O. Box 142
Columbia, SC 29202
P: (803) 734-2080
F: (803) 734-2082
E: KevinBryant@scsenate.gov

### Adjutant General

Major General Robert E. Livingston Jr.
Adjutant General
1 National Guard Road
Columbia, SC 29201
P: (803) 299-2500
F: (803) 806-4468
E: bob.livingston
@us.army.mil

### Commissioner of Agriculture

Mr. Hugh E. Weathers (R)
Commissioner
Wade Hampton Office Building
P.O. Box 11280
Columbia, SC 29211
P: (803) 734-2179
F: (803) 734-2192

### Attorney General

The Honorable Alan Wilson (R)
Attorney General
Rembert C. Dennis Office Building
P.O. Box 11549
Columbia, SC 29211
P: (803) 734-3970

### Auditor

Mr. George L. Kennedy III
(appointed)
State Auditor
1401 Main Street, Suite 1200
Columbia, SC 29201
P: (803) 253-4160 Ext. 203
F: (803) 343-0723
E: gkennedy@osa.sc.gov

### Comptroller

The Honorable Richard Eckstrom (R)
Comptroller General
305 Wade Hampton Office Building
1200 Senate Street
Columbia, SC 29201
P: (803) 734-2588
F: (803) 734-1765
E: reckstrom@cg.sc.gov

### Secretary of State

The Honorable Mark Hammond (R)
Secretary of State
1205 Pendleton Street, Suite 525
Columbia, SC 29201
P: (803) 734-2170
F: (803) 734-1661
E: rdaggerhart@sos.sc.gov

### Superintendent of Education

The Honorable Molly M. Spearman (R)
Superintendent of Education
1429 Senate Street
Columbia, SC 29201
P: (803) 734-8500
F: (803) 734-3389
E: SCSuptEd@ed.sc.gov

### Treasurer

The Honorable Curtis Loftis (R)
State Treasurer
P.O. Box 11778
Columbia, SC 29211
P: (803) 734-2101
F: (803) 734-2690
E: treasurer@sto.sc.gov

## Judiciary

### Supreme Court (LA)

Mr. Daniel E. Shearouse
Clerk of Court
1231 Gervais Street
P.O. Box 11330
Columbia, SC 29211
P: (803) 734-1080
F: (803) 734-1499

The Honorable Donald W. Beatty
Chief Justice
The Honorable John Cannon Few
The Honorable Kaye G. Hearn
The Honorable George C. Jones Jr.
The Honorable John W. Kittredge

## Legislative Senate

### Senate President

The Honorable Kevin L. Bryant (R)
Lieutenant Governor
P.O. Box 142
Columbia, SC 29202
P: (803) 734-2080
F: (803) 734-2082
E: KevinBryant@scsenate.gov

### President Pro Tempore of the Senate

Senator Hugh K. Leatherman Sr. (R)
Senate President Pro Tempore
111 Gressette Building
P.O. Box 142
Columbia, SC 29202
P: (803) 212-6640

### Senate Majority Leader

Senator A. Shane Massey (R)
Senate Majority Leader
311 Gressette Building
P.O. Box 142
Columbia, SC 29202
P: (803) 212-6024
E: ShaneMassey@scsenate.gov

### Senate Minority Leader

Senator Nikki G. Setzler (D)
Senate Minority Leader
510 Gressette Building
P.O. Box 142
Columbia, SC 29202
P: (803) 212-6140
E: NikkiSetzler
@scsenate.gov

### Secretary of the Senate

Mr. Jeffrey S. Gossett
Clerk of the Senate
P.O. Box 142
Columbia, SC 29202
P: (803) 212-6200
E: JeffreyGossett
@scsenate.gov

### Members of the Senate

Alexander, Thomas C. (R, 1)
313 Gressette Building
P.O. Box 142
Columbia, SC 29202
P: (803) 212-6220
E: ThomasAlexander
@scsenate.gov

Allen, Karl B. (D, 7)
610 Gressette Building
P.O. Box 142
Columbia, SC 29202
P: (803) 212-6040
E: KarlAllen@scsenate.gov

Bennett, Sean (R, 38)
601 Gressette Building
P.O. Box 142
Columbia, SC 29202
P: (803) 212-6116
E: SeanBennett@scsenate.gov

Bryant, Kevin L. (R, 3)
P.O. Box 142
Columbia, SC 29202
P: (803) 734-2080
F: (803) 734-2082
E: KevinBryant@scsenate.gov

Campbell Jr., Paul G. (R, 44)
205 Gressette Building
P.O. Box 142
Columbia, SC 29202
P: (803) 212-6016
E: PaulCampbell
@scsenate.gov

Campsen III, George E. (R, 43)
305 Gressette Building
P.O. Box 142
Columbia, SC 29202
P: (803) 212-6340
E: GeorgeCampsen
@scsenate.gov

Climer, Wes (R, 15)*
604 Gressette Building
P.O. Box 142
Columbia, SC 29202
P: (803) 212-6016
E: wesclimer@scsenate.gov

**Corbin, Thomas D. (R, 5)**
501 Gressette Building
P.O. Box 142
Columbia, SC 29202
P: (803) 212-6100
E: TomCorbin@scsenate.gov

**Courson, John E. (R, 20)**
412 Gressette Building
P.O. Box 142
Columbia, SC 29202
P: (803) 212-6250
E: JohnCourson@scsenate.gov

**Cromer, Ronnie W. (R, 18)**
410 Gressette Building
P.O. Box 142
Columbia, SC 29202
P: (803) 212-6330
E: RonnieCromer
    @scsenate.gov

**Davis, Tom (R, 46)**
404 Gressette Building
P.O. Box 142
Columbia, SC 29202
P: (803) 212-6008
E: TomDavis@scsenate.gov

**Fanning, Mike (D, 17)***
606 Gressette Building
P.O. Box 142
Columbia, SC 29202
P: (803) 212-6024
E: mikefanning@schouse.gov

**Gambrell, Michael W. (R, 4)**
610 Gressette Building
P.O. Box 142
Columbia, SC 29202
P: (803) 212-6040
E: MikeGambrell
    @scsenate.gov

**Goldfinch Jr., Stephen
(R, 34)**
P.O. Box 142
Columbia, SC 29202
P: (803) 212-6927
E: StephenGoldfinch
    @scsenate.gov

**Gregory, Chauncey K.
(R, 16)**
512 Gressette Building
P.O. Box 142
Columbia, SC 29202
P: (803) 212-6024
E: ChaunceyGregory
    @scsenate.gov

**Grooms, Lawrence K. (R, 37)**
203 Gressette Building
P.O. Box 142
Columbia, SC 29202
P: (803) 212-6400
E: LawrenceGrooms
    @scsenate.gov

**Hembree, Greg (R, 28)**
604 Gressette Building
P.O. Box 142
Columbia, SC 29202
P: (803) 212-6016
E: GregHembree@scsenate.gov

**Hutto, C. Bradley (D, 40)**
510 Gressette Building
P.O. Box 142
Columbia, SC 29202
P: (803) 212-6140
E: BradHutto@scsenate.gov

**Jackson, Darrell (D, 21)**
612 Gressette Building
P.O. Box 142
Columbia, SC 29202
P: (803) 212-6048
E: DarrellJackson
    @scsenate.gov

**Johnson, Kevin L. (D, 36)**
606 Gressette Building
P.O. Box 142
Columbia, SC 29202
P: (803) 212-6048
E: KevinJohnson
    @scsenate.gov

**Kimpson, Marlon E. (D, 42)**
508 Gressette Building
P.O. Box 142
Columbia, SC 29201
P: (803) 212-6056
E: MarlonKimpson
    @scsenate.gov

**Leatherman Sr., Hugh K.
(R, 31)**
111 Gressette Building
P.O. Box 142
Columbia, SC 29202
P: (803) 212-6640

**Malloy, Gerald (D, 29)**
513 Gressette Building
P.O. Box 142
Columbia, SC 29202
P: (803) 212-6172
E: GeraldMalloy
    @scsenate.gov

**Martin, Shane R. (R, 13)**
211 Gressette Building
P.O. Box 142
Columbia, SC 29202
P: (803) 212-6100
E: ShaneMartin@scsenate.gov

**Massey, A. Shane (R, 25)**
311 Gressette Building
P.O. Box 142
Columbia, SC 29202
P: (803) 212-6024
E: ShaneMassey@scsenate.gov

**Matthews Jr., John W.
(D, 39)**
613 Gressette Building
P.O. Box 142
Columbia, SC 29202
P: (803) 212-6056
E: JohnMatthews
    @scsenate.gov

**Matthews, Margie Bright
(D, 45)**
502 Gressette Building
P.O. Box 142
Columbia, SC 29202
P: (803) 212-6056
E: MargieMatthews
    @scsenate.gov

**McElveen III, J. Thomas
(D, 35)**
508 Gressette Building
P.O. Box 142
Columbia, SC 29556
P: (803) 212-6132
E: ThomasMcElveen
    @scsenate.gov

**McLeod, Mia (D, 22)**
506 Gressette Building
P.O. Box 142
Columbia, SC 29202
P: (803) 212-6124
E: MiaMcLeod@scsenate.gov

**Nicholson, Floyd (D, 10)**
610 Gressette Building
P.O. Box 142
Columbia, SC 29202
P: (803) 212-6000
E: FloydNicholson
    @scsenate.gov

**Peeler Jr., Harvey S.
(R, 14)**
213 Gressette Building
P.O. Box 142
Columbia, SC 29202
P: (803) 212-6430
E: HarveyPeeler
    @scsenate.gov

**Rankin Sr., Luke A. (R, 33)**
101 Gressette Building
P.O. Box 142
Columbia, SC 29202
P: (803) 212-6410
E: LukeRankin@scsenate.gov

**Reese, Glenn G. (D, 11)**
502 Gressette Building
P.O. Box 142
Columbia, SC 29202
P: (803) 212-6108
E: GlennReese@scsenate.gov

**Rice, Rex F. (R, 2)**
501 Gressette Building
P.O. Box 142
Columbia, SC 29202
P: (803) 212-6100
E: rexrice@scsenate.gov

**Sabb, Ronnie A. (D, 32)**
504 Gressette Building
P.O. Box 142
Columbia, SC 29202
P: (803) 212-6032
E: RonnieSabb@scsenate.gov

**Scott Jr., John L. (D, 19)**
506 Gressette Building
P.O. Box 142
Columbia, SC 29202
P: (803) 212-6124
E: JohnScott@scsenate.gov

**Senn, Sandy (R, 41)***
513 Gressette Building
P.O. Box 142
Columbia, SC 29202
P: (803) 212-6172
E: sandysenn@scsenate.gov

**Setzler, Nikki G. (D, 26)**
510 Gressette Building
P.O. Box 142
Columbia, SC 29202
P: (803) 212-6140
E: NikkiSetzler
    @scsenate.gov

**Shealy, Katrina Frye
(R, 23)**
303 Gressette Building
P.O. Box 142
Columbia, SC 29202
P: (803) 212-6108
E: KatrinaShealy
    @scsenate.gov

**Sheheen, Vincent A. (D, 27)**
504 Gressette Building
P.O. Box 142
Columbia, SC 29202
P: (803) 212-6032
E: VincentSheheen
    @scsenate.gov

**Talley, Scott F. (R, 12)**
612 Gressette Buidling
P.O. Box 142
Columbia, SC 29202
P: (803) 212-6048
E: scotttalley@scsenate.gov

**Timmons, William (R, 6)***
602 Gressette Building
P.O. Box 142
Columbia, SC 29202
P: (803) 212-6008
E: williamtimmons
    @scsenate.gov

# South Carolina

**Turner, Ross (R, 8)**
512 Gressette Building
P.O. Box 142
Columbia, SC 29202
P: (803) 212-6148
E: RossTurner@scsenate.gov

**Verdin III, Daniel B.
(R, 9)**
402 Gressette Building
P.O. Box 142
Columbia, SC 29202
P: (803) 212-6230
E: DanielVerdin
@scsenate.gov

**Williams, Kent M. (D, 30)**
608 Gressette Building
P.O. Box 142
Columbia, SC 29202
P: (803) 212-6000
E: KentWilliams
@scsenate.gov

**Young Jr., Thomas R.
(R, 24)**
608 Gressette Building
P.O. Box 142
Columbia, SC 29202
P: (803) 212-6124
E: TomYoung@schouse.gov

# House

## Speaker of the House

**Representative James H.
Lucas (R)**
Speaker of the House
506 Blatt Building
P.O. Box 11867
Columbia, SC 29211
P: (803) 734-3125
E: JayLucas@schouse.gov

## Speaker Pro Tempore of the House

**Representative Thomas E.
Pope (R)**
House Speaker Pro Tempore
505 Blatt Building
P.O. Box 11867
Columbia, SC 29211
P: (803) 734-2701
E: TommyPope@schouse.gov

## House Majority Leader

**Representative Bruce W.
Bannister (R)**
House Majority Leader
312B Blatt Building
P.O. Box 11867
Columbia, SC 29211
P: (803) 734-3138
E: BruceBannister
@schouse.gov

## House Minority Leader

**Representative J. Todd
Rutherford (D)**
House Minority Leader
335B Blatt Building
P.O. Box 11867
Columbia, SC 29211
P: (803) 734-9441
E: ToddRutherford
@schouse.gov

## Clerk of the House

**Mr. Charles F. Reid**
Clerk
P.O. Box 11867
Columbia, SC 29211
P: (803) 734-2403
F: (803) 734-0201

## Members of the House

**Alexander, Terry (D, 59)**
314C Blatt Building
P.O. Box 11867
Columbia, SC 29211
P: (803) 734-3004
E: TerryAlexander
@schouse.gov

**Allison, Rita (R, 36)**
429 Blatt Building
P.O. Box 11867
Columbia, SC 29211
P: (803) 734-3053
E: RitaAllison@schouse.gov

**Anderson, Carl L. (D, 103)**
304C Blatt Building
P.O. Box 11867
Columbia, SC 29211
P: (803) 734-2933
E: CarlAnderson@schouse.gov

**Anthony, Michael A. (D, 42)**
432C Blatt Building
P.O. Box 11867
Columbia, SC 29211
P: (803) 734-3060
E: MichaelAnthony
@schouse.gov

**Arrington, Katherine E.
(R, 94)\***
308A Blatt Building
P.O. Box 11867
Columbia, SC 27211
P: (803) 212-6871
E: KatieArrington
@schouse.gov

**Atkinson, Frank (D, 57)\***
333D Blatt Building
P.O. Box 11867
Columbia, SC 29211
P: (803) 212-6936
E: LucasAtkinson
@schouse.gov

**Atwater, Todd K. (R, 87)**
320D Blatt Building
P.O. Box 11867
Columbia, SC 29211
P: (803) 212-6924
E: ToddAtwater@schouse.gov

**Bales, Jimmy C. (D, 80)**
503A Blatt Building
P.O. Box 11867
Columbia, SC 29211
P: (803) 734-3107
E: JimmyBales@schouse.gov

**Ballentine, Nathan (R, 71)**
320B Blatt Building
P.O. Box 11867
Columbia, SC 29211
P: (803) 734-2969
E: NathanBallentine
@schouse.gov

**Bamberg, Justin (D, 90)**
335D Blatt Building
P.O. Box 11867
Columbia, SC 29211
P: (803) 212-6907
E: JustinBamberg
@schouse.gov

**Bannister, Bruce W. (R, 24)**
312B Blatt Building
P.O. Box 11867
Columbia, SC 29211
P: (803) 734-3138
E: BruceBannister
@schouse.gov

**Bedingfield, Eric M.
(R, 28)**
202 Blatt Building
P.O. Box 11867
Columbia, SC 29211
P: (803) 734-2962
E: EricBedingfield
@schouse.gov

**Bennett, Linda (R, 114)\***
414D Blatt Building
P.O. Box 11867
Columbia, SC 29211
P: (803) 212-6948
E: LinBennett@schouse.gov

**Bernstein, Beth E. (D, 78)**
532C Blatt Building
P.O. Box 11867
Columbia, SC 29211
P: (803) 212-6940
E: BethBernstein
@schouse.gov

**Blackwell, Bart T. (R, 81)\***
416D Blatt Building
P.O. Box 11867
Columbia, SC 29211
P: (803) 212-6884
E: bartblackwell
@schouse.gov

**Bowers, William K. (D, 122)**
310C Blatt Building
P.O. Box 11867
Columbia, SC 29211
P: (803) 734-2959
E: BillBowers@schouse.gov

**Bradley, Jeff (R, 123)**
320A Blatt Building
P.O. Box 11867
Columbia, SC 29211
P: (803) 212-6928
E: JeffBradley@schouse.gov

**Brown, Robert L. (D, 116)**
330D Blatt Building
P.O. Box 11867
Columbia, SC 29211
P: (803) 734-3170
E: RobertBrown@schouse.gov

**Burns, James (R, 17)**
326B Blatt Building
P.O. Box 11867
Columbia, SC 29211
P: (803) 212-6891

**Caskey IV, Micajah P.
(R, 89)\***
323D Blatt Building
P.O. Box 11867
Columbia, SC 29211
P: (803) 212-6959
E: micahcaskey@schouse.gov

**Chumley, William M. (R, 35)**
326A Blatt Building
P.O. Box 11867
Columbia, SC 29211
P: (803) 212-6894
E: BillChumley@schouse.gov

**Clary, Gary (R, 3)**
402D Blatt Building
P.O. Box 11867
Columbia, SC 29211
P: (803) 212-6908
E: GaryClary@schouse.gov

**Clemmons, Alan D. (R, 107)**
519C Blatt Building
P.O. Box 11867
Columbia, SC 29211
P: (803) 734-3113
E: AlanClemmons@schouse.gov

**Clyburn, William (D, 82)**
416C Blatt Building
P.O. Box 11867
Columbia, SC 29211
P: (803) 734-3033
E: BillClyburn@schouse.gov

**Cobb-Hunter, Gilda (D, 66)**
309C Blatt Building
P.O. Box 11867
Columbia, SC 29211
P: (803) 734-2809
E: GildaCobbHunter
@schouse.gov

**Cogswell Jr., William Scott (R, 110)***
530A Blatt Building
P.O. Box 11867
Columbia, SC 29211
P: (803) 212-6950
E: williamcogswell
@schouse.gov

**Cole Jr., J. Derham (R, 32)**
402B Blatt Building
P.O. Box 11867
Columbia, SC 29211
P: (803) 212-6790
E: DerhamCole@schouse.gov

**Collins, Neal (R, 5)**
418C Blatt Building
P.O. Box 11867
Columbia, SC 29211
P: (803) 212-6913
E: NealCollins@schouse.gov

**Crawford, Heather Ammons (R, 68)**
522A Blatt Building
P.O. Box 11867
Columbia, SC 29211
P: (803) 212-6933
E: HeatherCrawford
@schouse.gov

**Crosby, William E. (R, 117)**
310D Blatt Building
P.O. Box 11867
Columbia, SC 29211
P: (803) 212-6879
E: BillCrosby@schouse.gov

**Daning, Joseph S. (R, 92)**
310B Blatt Building
P.O. Box 11867
Columbia, SC 29211
P: (803) 734-2951
E: JoeDaning@schouse.gov

**Davis, Sylleste (R, 100)**
414A Blatt Building
P.O. Box 11867
Columbia, SC 29211
P: (803) 212-6930
E: SyllesteDavis
@schouse.gov

**Delleney Jr., F. Gregory (R, 43)**
512 Blatt Building
P.O. Box 11867
Columbia, SC 29211
P: (803) 734-3120
E: GregDelleney@schouse.gov

**Dillard, Chandra (D, 23)**
414B Blatt Building
P.O. Box 11867
Columbia, SC 29211
P: (803) 212-6791
E: ChandraDillard
@schouse.gov

**Douglas, MaryGail (D, 41)**
314B Blatt Building
P.O. Box 11867
Columbia, SC 29211
P: (803) 212-6789
E: MaryGailDouglas
@schouse.gov

**Duckworth, Greg (R, 104)**
434C Blatt Building
P.O. Box 11867
Columbia, SC 29211
P: (803) 212-6918
E: GregDuckworth
@schouse.gov

**Elliott, Jason (R, 22)***
312D Blatt Building
P.O Box 11867
Columbia, SC 29211
P: (803) 212-6877
E: jasonelliott@schouse.gov

**Erickson, Shannon S. (R, 124)**
320C Blatt Building
P.O. Box 11867
Columbia, SC 29211
P: (803) 734-3261
E: shannonerickson
@schouse.gov

**Felder, Raye (R, 26)**
402A Blatt Building
P.O. Box 11867
Columbia, SC 29211
P: (803) 212-6892
E: RayeFelder@schouse.gov

**Finlay III, Kirkman (R, 75)**
532A Blatt Building
P.O. Box 11867
Columbia, SC 29211
P: (803) 212-6943
E: KirkmanFinlay
@schouse.gov

**Forrest, Cally R. (R, 39)***
323A Blatt Building
P.O Box 11867
Columbia, SC 29211
P: (803) 212-6938
E: CalForrest@schouse.gov

**Forrester, P. Michael (R, 34)**
402C Blatt Building
P.O. Box 11867
Columbia, SC 29211
P: (803) 212-6792
E: MikeForrester
@schouse.gov

**Fry, Russell W. (R, 106)**
522D Blatt Building
P.O. Box 11867
Columbia, SC 29211
P: (803) 212-6781

**Funderburk, Laurie Slade (D, 52)**
422C Blatt Building
P.O. Box 11867
Columbia, SC 29211
P: (803) 734-3044
E: LaurieFunderburk
@schouse.gov

**Gagnon, Craig A. (R, 11)**
436A Blatt Building
P.O. Box 11867
Columbia, SC 29211
P: (803) 212-6934
E: CraigGagnon@schouse.gov

**Govan Jr., Jerry N. (D, 95)**
530B Blatt Building
P.O. Box 11867
Columbia, SC 29211
P: (803) 734-3012
E: JerryGovan@schouse.gov

**Hamilton, Dan (R, 20)**
312C Blatt Building
P.O. Box 11867
Columbia, SC 29211
P: (803) 212-6795
E: DanHamilton@schouse.gov

**Hardee, Kevin (R, 105)**
306C Blatt Building
P.O. Box 11867
Columbia, SC 29211
P: (803) 212-6796
E: KevinHardee@schouse.gov

**Hart, Christopher R. (D, 73)**
432B Blatt Building
P.O. Box 11867
Columbia, SC 29211
P: (803) 734-3061
E: ChristopherHart
@schouse.gov

**Hayes, Jackie E. (D, 55)**
333C Blatt Building
P.O. Box 11867
Columbia, SC 29211
P: (803) 734-3099
E: JackieHayes@schouse.gov

**Henderson, Phyllis (R, 21)**
522B Blatt Building
P.O. Box 11867
Columbia, SC 29211
P: (803) 212-6883
E: PhyllisHenderson
@schouse.gov

**Henegan, Pat (D, 54)**
333B Blatt Building
P.O. Box 11867
Columbia, SC 29211
P: (803) 212-6896
E: PatHenegan@schouse.gov

**Herbkersman, William G. (R, 118)**
308B Blatt Building
P.O. Box 11867
Columbia, SC 29211
P: (803) 734-3063
E: BillHerbkersman
@schouse.gov

**Hewitt, Lee (R, 108)***
327D Blatt Building
P.O. Box 11867
Columbia, SC 29211
P: (803) 212-6927
E: lee.hewitt@schouse.gov

**Hill, Jonathan (R, 8)**
434A Blatt Building
P.O. Box 11867
Columbia, SC 29211
P: (803) 212-6919
E: JonathanHill@schouse.gov

**Hiott, David R. (R, 4)**
411 Blatt Building
P.O. Box 11867
Columbia, SC 29211
P: (803) 734-3022
E: DavidHiott@schouse.gov

# South Carolina

**Hixon, William M. (R, 83)**
416A Blatt Building
P.O. Box 11867
Columbia, SC 29211
P: (803) 212-6898
E: BillHixon@schouse.gov

**Hosey, Lonnie (D, 91)**
404B Blatt Building
P.O. Box 11867
Columbia, SC 29211
P: (803) 734-2829
E: LonnieHosey@schouse.gov

**Howard, Leon (D, 76)**
425 Blatt Building
P.O. Box 11867
Columbia, SC 29211
P: (803) 734-3046
E: LeonHoward@schouse.gov

**Huggins, Chip (R, 85)**
323B Blatt Building
P.O. Box 11867
Columbia, SC 29211
P: (803) 734-2971
E: ChipHuggins@schouse.gov

**Jefferson Jr., Joseph H. (D, 102)**
304B Blatt Building
P.O. Box 11867
Columbia, SC 29211
P: (803) 734-2936
E: JosephJefferson
@schouse.gov

**Johnson, Jeff (R, 58)**
434B Blatt Building
P.O. Box 11867
Columbia, SC 29211
P: (803) 212-6946
E: Jeff.Johnson@schouse.gov

**Jordan Jr., Wallace H. (R, 63)**
327A Blatt Building
P.O. Box 11867
Columbia, SC 29211
P: (803) 212-6785
E: JayJordan@schouse.gov

**King, John Richard C. (D, 49)**
309D Blatt Building
P.O. Box 11867
Columbia, SC 29211
P: (803) 212-6873
E: JohnKing@schouse.gov

**Kirby, Roger (D, 61)**
314D Blatt Building
P.O. Box 11867
Columbia, SC 29211
P: (803) 212-6947
E: RogerKirby@schouse.gov

**Knight, Patsy G. (D, 97)**
306B Blatt Building
P.O. Box 11867
Columbia, SC 29211
P: (803) 734-2960
E: PatsyKnight@schouse.gov

**Loftis, Dwight A. (R, 19)**
522C Blatt Building
P.O. Box 11867
Columbia, SC 29211
P: (803) 734-3101
E: DwightLoftis@schouse.gov

**Long, Steven Wayne (R, 37)***
304A Blatt Building
P.O. Box 11867
Columbia, SC 29211
P: (803) 212-6878
E: stevenlong@schouse.gov

**Lowe, Phillip D. (R, 60)**
327B Blatt Building
P.O. Box 11867
Columbia, SC 29211
P: (803) 734-2975
E: PhillipLowe@schouse.gov

**Lucas, James H. (R, 65)**
506 Blatt Building
P.O. Box 11867
Columbia, SC 29211
P: (803) 734-3125
E: JayLucas@schouse.gov

**Mack III, David J. (D, 109)**
328D Blatt Building
P.O. Box 11867
Columbia, SC 29211
P: (803) 734-3192
E: DavidMack@schouse.gov

**Magnuson, Josiah (R, 38)***
304D Blatt Building
P.O. Box 11867
Columbia, SC 29211
P: (803) 212-6876
E: josiahmagnuson
@schouse.gov

**Martin, Richard (R, 40)***
418D Blatt Building
P.O. Box 11867
Columbia, SC 29211
P: (803) 212-6951
E: RickMartin@schouse.gov

**McCoy Jr., Peter M. (R, 115)**
420D Blatt Building
P.O. Box 11867
Columbia, SC 29211
P: (803) 212-6872
E: PeterMcCoy@schouse.gov

**McCravy III, John R. (R, 13)***
420A Blatt Building
P.O. Box 11867
Columbia, SC 29211
P: (803) 212-6939
E: johnmccravy@schouse.gov

**McEachern, Joseph A. (D, 77)**
330B Blatt Building
P.O. Box 11867
Columbia, SC 29211
P: (803) 212-6875
E: JoeMcEachern@schouse.gov

**McKnight, Cezar (D, 101)**
314A Blatt Building
P.O. Box 11867
Columbia, SC 29211
P: (803) 212-6926
E: CezarMcKnight
@schouse.gov

**Merrill, James H. (R, 99)**
308C Blatt Building
P.O. Box 11867
Columbia, SC 29211
P: (803) 734-3072
E: JamesMerrill@schouse.gov

**Mitchell Jr., Harold (D, 31)**
414C Blatt Building
P.O. Box 11867
Columbia, SC 29211
P: (803) 734-6638
E: HaroldMitchell
@schouse.gov

**Moss, Dennis C. (R, 29)**
503B Blatt Building
P.O. Box 11867
Columbia, SC 29211
P: (803) 734-3073
E: DennisMoss@schouse.gov

**Moss, V. Stephen (R, 30)**
418B Blatt Building
P.O. Box 11867
Columbia, SC 29211
P: (803) 212-6885
E: StephenMoss@schouse.gov

**Murphy, Christopher J. (R, 98)**
308D Blatt Building
P.O. Box 11867
Columbia, SC 29211
P: (803) 212-6925
E: ChrisMurphy@schouse.gov

**Newton, Brandon Michael (R, 45)***
404D Blatt Building
P.O. Box 11867
Columbia, SC 29211
P: (803) 212-6874
E: brandon.newton
@schouse.gov

**Newton, Weston J. (R, 120)**
228 Blatt Building
P.O. Box 11867
Columbia, SC 29211
P: (803) 212-6810
E: WestonNewton@schouse.gov

**Norrell, Mandy Powers (D, 44)**
422B Blatt Building
P.O. Box 11867
Columbia, SC 29211
P: (803) 212-6937
E: MandyNorrell@schouse.gov

**Ott, Russell L. (D, 93)**
306D Blatt Building
P.O. Box 11867
Columbia, SC 29211
P: (803) 212-6945
E: RussellOtt@schouse.gov

**Parks, J. Anne (D, 12)**
434D Blatt Building
P.O. Box 11867
Columbia, SC 29211
P: (803) 734-3069
E: AnneParks@schouse.gov

**Pitts, Michael A. (R, 14)**
519B Blatt Building
P.O. Box 11867
Columbia, SC 29211
P: (803) 734-2830
E: MichaelPitts@schouse.gov

**Pope, Thomas E. (R, 47)**
505 Blatt Building
P.O. Box 11867
Columbia, SC 29211
P: (803) 734-2701
E: TommyPope@schouse.gov

**Putnam, Joshua A. (R, 10)**
436D Blatt Office Building
P.O. Box 11867
Columbia, SC 29211
P: (803) 212-6931
E: JoshuaPutnam@schouse.gov

**Quinn, Rick (R, 69)**
532D Blatt Building
P.O. Box 11867
Columbia, SC 29211
P: (803) 212-6897
E: RickQuinn@schouse.gov

**Ridgeway III, Robert L.
(D, 64)**
422A Blatt Building
P.O. Box 11867
Columbia, SC 29211
P: (803) 212-6929
E: RobertRidgeway
@schouse.gov

**Rivers Sr., Michael F.
(D, 121)***
432D Blatt Building
P.O. Box 11867
Columbia, SC 29211
P: (803) 212-6952
E: michaelrivers
@schouse.gov

**Rivers Jr., Samuel (R, 15)**
530C Blatt Building
P.O. Box 11867
Columbia, SC 29211
P: (803) 212-6890
E: SamuelRivers@schouse.gov

**Robinson-Simpson, Leola C.
(D, 25)**
330A Blatt Building
P.O. Box 11867
Columbia, SC 29211
P: (803) 212-6941
E: LeolaRobinson-Simpson
@schouse.gov

**Rutherford, J. Todd (D, 74)**
335B Blatt Building
P.O. Box 11867
Columbia, SC 29211
P: (803) 734-9441
E: ToddRutherford
@schouse.gov

**Ryhal, Mike (R, 56)**
404A Blatt Building
P.O. Box 11867
Columbia, SC 29211
P: (803) 212-6935
E: MikeRyhal@schouse.gov

**Sandifer III, William E.
(R, 2)**
407 Blatt Building
P.O. Box 11867
Columbia, SC 29211
P: (803) 734-3015
E: BillSandifer@schouse.gov

**Simrill, J. Gary (R, 46)**
518C Blatt Building
P.O. Box 11867
Columbia, SC 29211
P: (803) 734-3040
E: GarySimrill@schouse.gov

**Smith Jr., G. Murrell
(R, 67)**
420B Blatt Building
P.O. Box 11867
Columbia, SC 29211
P: (803) 734-3042
E: MurrellSmith@schouse.gov

**Smith, Garry R. (R, 27)**
534 Blatt Building
P.O. Box 11867
Columbia, SC 29211
P: (803) 734-3141
E: GarrySmith@schouse.gov

**Smith Jr., James E. (D, 72)**
335C Blatt Building
P.O. Box 11867
Columbia, SC 29211
P: (803) 734-2997
E: JamesSmith@schouse.gov

**Sottile, F. Michael
(R, 112)**
310A Blatt Building
P.O. Box 11867
Columbia, SC 29211
P: (803) 212-6880
E: MikeSottile@schouse.gov

**Spires, L. Kit (R, 96)**
326D Blatt Building
P.O. Box 11867
Columbia, SC 29211
P: (803) 734-3010
E: KitSpires@schouse.gov

**Stavrinakis, Leonidas E.
(D, 119)**
420C Blatt Building
P.O. Box 11867
Columbia, SC 29211
P: (803) 734-3039
E: LeonStavrinakis
@schouse.gov

**Stringer, Tommy (R, 18)**
312A Blatt Building
P.O. Box 11867
Columbia, SC 29211
P: (803) 212-6881
E: TommyStringer
@schouse.gov

**Tallon Sr., Edward R.
(R, 33)**
518B Blatt Building
P.O. Box 11867
Columbia, SC 29211
P: (803) 212-6893
E: EddieTallon@schouse.gov

**Taylor, Bill (R, 86)**
416B Blatt Building
P.O. Box 11867
Columbia, SC 29211
P: (803) 212-6923
E: BillTaylor@schouse.gov

**Thayer, Anne J. (R, 9)**
436B Blatt Building
P.O. Box 11867
Columbia, SC 29211
P: (803) 212-6889
E: AnneThayer@schouse.gov

**Thigpen, Ivory Torrey
(D, 79)***
333A Blatt Building
P.O. Box 11867
Columbia, SC 29211
P: (803) 212-6794
E: IvoryThigpen@schouse.gov

**Toole, McLain R. (R, 88)**
323C Blatt Building
P.O. Box 11867
Columbia, SC 29211
P: (803) 734-2973
E: MacToole@schouse.gov

**Weeks, J. David (D, 51)**
330C Blatt Building
P.O. Box 11867
Columbia, SC 29211
P: (803) 734-3102
E: DavidWeeks@schouse.gov

**West IV, John Taliaferro
(R, 7)***
432A Blatt Building
P.O. Box 11867
Columbia, SC 29211
P: (803) 212-6954
E: JayWest@schouse.gov

**Wheeler III, William W.
(D, 50)***
422D Blatt Building
P.O. Box 11867
Columbia, SC 29211
P: (803) 212-6958
E: WIllWheeler@schouse.gov

**Whipper, J. Seth (D, 113)**
328C Blatt Building
P.O. Box 11867
Columbia, SC 29211
P: (803) 734-3191
E: SethWhipper@schouse.gov

**White, W. Brian (R, 6)**
525 Blatt Building
P.O. Box 11867
Columbia, SC 29211
P: (803) 734-3144
E: BrianWhite@schouse.gov

**Whitmire, William R. (R, 1)**
436C Blatt Building
P.O. Box 11867
Columbia, SC 29211
P: (803) 734-3068
E: BillWhitmire@schouse.gov

**Williams, Robert Q. (D, 62)**
328B Blatt Building
P.O. Box 11867
Columbia, SC 29211
P: (803) 734-3142
E: RobertWilliams
@schouse.gov

**Willis, Mark N. (R, 16)**
326C Blatt Building
P.O. Box 11867
Columbia, SC 29211
P: (803) 212-6882
E: MarkWillis@schouse.gov

**Yow, Richie (R, 53)**
327C Blatt Building
P.O. Box 11867
Columbia, SC 29211
P: (803) 212-6949

# South Dakota

## Executive

### Governor
**The Honorable Dennis Daugaard (R)**
Governor
500 East Capitol Avenue
Pierre, SD 57501
P: (605) 773-3212
F: (605) 773-4711

### Lieutenant Governor
**The Honorable Matthew Michels (R)**
Lieutenant Governor
500 East Capitol Street
Pierre, SD 57501
P: (605) 773-3661
F: (605) 773-4711

### Attorney General
**The Honorable Marty J. Jackley (R)**
Attorney General
1302 East Highway 14, Suite 1
Pierre, SD 57501
P: (605) 773-3215
F: (605) 773-4106
E: atghelp@state.sd.us

### Auditor
**Mr. Martin Guindon**
Auditor General
500 East Capitol Avenue
Pierre, SD 57501
P: (605) 773-3595
F: (605) 773-6454
E: marty.guindon
@state.sd.us

### Commissioner of School & Public Lands
**The Honorable Ryan Brunner (R)**
Commissioner
500 East Capitol Avenue
Pierre, SD 57501
P: (605) 773-3303
F: (605) 773-5520
E: ryan.brunner@state.sd.us

## Public Utilities Commission
**The Honorable Kristie Fiegen (R)**
Commissioner
State Capitol
500 East Capitol Avenue
Pierre, SD 57501
P: (605) 773-3201
F: (866) 757-6031
E: kristie.fiegen
@state.sd.us

**The Honorable Gary W. Hanson (R)**
Commissioner
State Capitol, 500 East Capitol Avenue
Pierre, SD 57501
P: (605) 773-3201
F: (866) 757-6031
E: gary.hanson@state.sd.us

**Mr. Chris Nelson (R)**
Chairman
State Capitol
500 East Capitol Avenue
Pierre, SD 57501
P: (605) 773-3201
F: (866) 757-6031
E: Chris.Nelson@state.sd.us

## Secretary of State
**The Honorable Shantel Krebs (R)**
Secretary of State
500 E Capitol Ave Ste 204
Pierre, SD 57501
P: (605) 773-3537
F: (605) 773-6580
E: shantel.krebs
@state.sd.us

## Treasurer
**The Honorable Rich L. Sattgast (R)**
State Treasurer
500 East Capitol Avenue
Pierre, SD 57501
P: (605) 773-3378
F: (605) 773-3115
E: rich.sattgast
@state.sd.us

## Judiciary
### Supreme Court (MR)
**Ms. Shirley A. Jameson-Fergel**
Clerk
500 East Capitol Avenue
Pierre, SD 57501
P: (605) 773-3511
F: (605) 773-6128

**The Honorable David Gilbertson**
Chief Justice
**The Honorable Janine M. Kern**
**The Honorable Glen Severson**
**The Honorable Lori S. Wilbur**
**The Honorable Steven L. Zinter**

## Legislative
## Senate
### Senate President
**The Honorable Matthew Michels (R)**
Lieutenant Governor
500 East Capitol Street
Pierre, SD 57501
P: (605) 773-3661
F: (605) 773-4711

### President Pro Tempore of the Senate
**Senator Brock L. Greenfield (R)**
Senate President Pro Tempore
State Capitol
500 East Capitol Avenue
Pierre, SD 57501
E: brock.greenfield
@sdlegislature.gov

### Senate Majority Leader
**Senator R. Blake Curd (R)**
Senate Majority Leader
State Capitol
500 East Capitol Avenue
Pierre, SD 57501
P: (605) 773-3821
F: (605) 731-2225
E: blake.curd
@sdlegislature.gov

### Senate Minority Leader
**Senator Billie H. Sutton (D)**
Senate Minority Leader
State Capitol
500 East Capitol Avenue
Pierre, SD 57501
E: billie.sutton
@sdlegislature.gov

## Secretary of the Senate
**Ms. Kay Johnson**
Secretary of the Senate
State Capitol, Room 330
500 East Capitol Avenue
Pierre, SD 57501
P: (605) 773-3825
F: (605) 773-6806
E: kay.johnson
@sdlegislature.gov

## Members of the Senate
**Bolin, Jim (R, 16)**
State Capitol
500 East Capitol Avenue
Pierre, SD 57501
E: jim.bolin
@sdlegislature.gov

**Cammack, Gary L. (R, 29)**
State Capitol
500 East Capitol Avenue
Pierre, SD 57501
E: gary.cammack
@sdlegislature.gov

**Cronin, Justin R. (R, 23)**
State Capitol
500 East Capitol Avenue
Pierre, SD 57501
E: justin.cronin
@sdlegislature.gov

**Curd, R. Blake (R, 12)**
State Capitol
500 East Capitol Avenue
Pierre, SD 57501
P: (605) 773-3821
F: (605) 731-2225
E: blake.curd
@sdlegislature.gov

**Ewing, Bob (R, 31)**
State Capitol
500 East Capitol Avenue
Pierre, SD 57501
E: bob.ewing
@sdlegislature.gov

**Frerichs, Jason (D, 1)**
State Capitol
500 East Capitol Avenue
Pierre, SD 57501
E: jason.frerichs
@sdlegislature.gov

**Greenfield, Brock L. (R, 2)**
State Capitol
500 East Capitol Avenue
Pierre, SD 57501
E: brock.greenfield
@sdlegislature.gov

**Haverly, Terri (R, 35)**
State Capitol
500 East Capitol Avenue
Pierre, SD 57501
E: terri.haverly
@sdlegislature.gov

**Heinert, Troy (D, 26)**
State Capitol
500 East Capitol Avenue
Pierre, SD 57501
E: troy.heinert
@sdlegislature.gov

**Jensen, Phil (R, 33)**
State Capitol
500 East Capitol Avenue
Pierre, SD 57501
E: phil.jensen
@sdlegislature.gov

**Kennedy, Craig (D, 18)***
State Capitol
500 East Capitol Avenue
Pierre, SD 57501
E: craig.kennedy
@sdlegislature.gov

**Killer, Kevin (D, 27)**
State Capitol
500 East Capitol Avenue
Pierre, SD 57501
E: kevin.killer
@sdlegislature.gov

**Klumb, Joshua (R, 20)**
State Capitol
500 East Capitol Avenue
Pierre, SD 57501
E: joshua.klumb
@sdlegislature.gov

**Kolbeck, Jack (R, 13)***
State Capitol
500 East Capitol Avenue
Pierre, SD 57501
E: jack.kolbeck
@sdlegislature.gov

**Langer, Kris (R, 25)**
State Capitol
500 East Capitol Avenue
Pierre, SD 57501
E: kris.langer
@sdlegislature.gov

**Monroe, Jeff (R, 24)**
State Capitol
500 East Capitol Avenue
Pierre, SD 57501
E: jeff.monroe
@sdlegislature.gov

**Nelson, Stace (R, 19)**
State Capitol
500 East Capitol Avenue
Pierre, SD 57501
E: stace.nelson
@sdlegislature.gov

**Nesiba, Reynold (D, 15)***
State Capitol
500 East Capitol Avenue
Pierre, SD 57501
E: reynold.nesiba
@sdlegislature.gov

**Netherton, Jenna (R, 10)**
State Capitol
500 East Capitol Avenue
Pierre, SD 57501
E: jenna.haggar
@sdlegislature.gov

**Novstrup, Al (R, 3)**
State Capitol
500 East Capitol Avenue
Pierre, SD 57501
E: al.novstrup
@sdlegislature.gov

**Otten, Ernie (R, 6)**
State Capitol
500 East Capitol Avenue
Pierre, SD 57501
E: ernie.otten
@sdlegislature.gov

**Partridge, Jeff (R, 34)**
State Capitol
500 East Capitol Avenue
Pierre, SD 57501
E: jeffrey.partridge
@sdlegislature.gov

**Peters, Deb (R, 9)**
State Capitol
500 East Capitol Avenue
Pierre, SD 57501
E: deb.peters
@sdlegislature.gov

**Rusch, Arthur (R, 17)**
State Capitol
500 East Capitol Avenue
Pierre, SD 57501
E: arthur.rusch
@sdlegislature.gov

**Russell, Lance S. (R, 30)**
State Capitol
500 East Capitol Avenue
Pierre, SD 57501
E: lance.russell
@sdlegislature.gov

**Soholt, Deb (R, 14)**
State Capitol
500 East Capitol Avenue
Pierre, SD 57501
E: deb.soholt
@sdlegislature.gov

**Solano, Alan D. (R, 32)**
State Capitol
500 East Capitol Avenue
Pierre, SD 57501
E: alan.solano
@sdlegislature.gov

**Stalzer, Jim (R, 11)**
State Capitol
500 East Capitol Avenue
Pierre, SD 57501
E: jim.stalzer
@sdlegislature.gov

**Sutton, Billie H. (D, 21)**
State Capitol
500 East Capitol Avenue
Pierre, SD 57501
E: billie.sutton
@sdlegislature.gov

**Tapio, Neal (R, 5)***
State Capitol
500 East Capitol Avenue
Pierre, SD 57501
E: neal.tapio
@sdlegislature.gov

**Tidemann, Larry (R, 7)**
State Capitol
500 East Capitol Avenue
Pierre, SD 57501
E: larry.tidemann
@sdlegislature.gov

**White, Jim (R, 22)**
State Capitol
500 East Capitol Avenue
Pierre, SD 57501
E: jim.white
@sdlegislature.gov

**Wiik, John (R, 4)**
State Capitol
500 East Capitol Avenue
Pierre, SD 57501
E: john.wiik
@sdlegislature.gov

**Youngberg, Jordan (R, 8)***
State Capitol
500 East Capitol Avenue
Pierre, SD 57501
E: jordan.youngberg
@sdlegislature.gov

# House

## Speaker of the House

**Speaker G. Mark Mickelson (R)**
Speaker of the House
State Capitol
500 East Capitol Avenue
Pierre, SD 57501
E: mark.mickelson
@sdlegislature.gov

## Speaker Pro Tempore of the House

**Representative Don Haggar (R)**
House Speaker Pro Tempore
State Capitol
500 East Capitol Avenue
Pierre, SD 57501
E: don.haggar
@sdlegislature.gov

**Speaker G. Mark Mickelson (R)**
Speaker of the House
State Capitol
500 East Capitol Avenue
Pierre, SD 57501
E: mark.mickelson
@sdlegislature.gov

## House Majority Leader

**Representative Lee Qualm (R)**
House Majority Leader
State Capitol
500 East Capitol Avenue
Pierre, SD 57501
E: lee.qualm
@sdlegislature.gov

## House Minority Leader

**Representative Spencer Hawley (D)**
House Minority Leader
State Capitol
500 East Capitol Avenue
Pierre, SD 57501
P: 605-773-3851
E: spencer.hawley
@sdlegislature.gov

# South Dakota

## Clerk of the House

**Ms. Arlene Kvislen**
Chief Clerk of the House
State Capitol, Room 362
500 East Capitol Avenue
Pierre, SD 57501
P: (605) 773-3842
F: (605) 773-6806

## Members of the House

**Ahlers, Dan (D, 25)**
State Capitol
500 East Capitol Avenue
Pierre, SD 57501
E: dan.ahlers
    @sdlegislature.gov

**Anderson, David (R, 16)**
State Capitol
500 East Capitol Avenue
Pierre, SD 57501
P: (605) 764-5781
E: david.anderson
    @sdlegislature.gov

**Bartels, Hugh (R, 5)\***
State Capitol
500 East Capitol Avenue
Pierre, SD 57501
E: hugh.bartels
    @sdlegislature.gov

**Bartling, Julie (D, 21)**
State Capitol
500 East Capitol Avenue
Pierre, SD 57501
E: julie.bartling
    @sdlegislature.gov

**Beal, Arch (R, 12)**
State Capitol
500 East Capitol Avenue
Pierre, SD 57501
E: arch.beal
    @sdlegislature.gov

**Bordeaux, Shawn (D, 26A)**
State Capitol
500 East Capitol Avenue
Pierre, SD 57501
E: shawn.bordeaux
    @sdlegislature.gov

**Brunner, Thomas J. (R, 29)**
State Capitol
500 East Capitol Avenue
Pierre, SD 57501
P: (605) 257-2336
F: (605) 257-2336
E: thomas.brunner
    @sdlegislature.gov

**Campbell, Blaine (R, 35)**
State Capitol
500 East Capitol Avenue
Pierre, SD 57501
E: blaine.campbell
    @sdlegislature.gov

**Carson, Lance (R, 20)**
State Capitol
500 East Capitol Avenue
Pierre, SD 57501
E: Lance.Carson
    @sdlegislature.gov

**Chase, Roger (R, 22)\***
State Capitol
500 East Capitol Avenue
Pierre, SD 57501
E: roger.chase
    @sdlegislature.gov

**Clark, Michael (R, 9)\***
State Capitol
500 East Capitol Avenue
Pierre, SD 57501
E: michael.clark
    @sdlegislature.gov

**Conzet, Kristin A. (R, 32)**
State Capitol
500 East Capitol Avenue
Pierre, SD 57501
E: kristin.conzet
    @sdlegislature.gov

**Dennert, Drew (R, 3)\***
State Capitol
500 East Capitol Avenue
Pierre, SD 57501
E: drew.dennert
    @sdlegislature.gov

**DiSanto, Lynne (R, 35)**
State Capitol
500 East Capitol Avenue
Pierre, SD 57501
E: lynne.disanto
    @sdlegislature.gov

**Duvall, Mary (R, 24)**
State Capitol
500 East Capitol Avenue
Pierre, SD 57501
E: mary.duvall
    @sdlegislature.gov

**Frye-Mueller, Julie (R, 30)\***
State Capitol
500 East Capitol Avenue
Pierre, SD 57501
E: julie.fryemueller
    @sdlegislature.gov

**Glanzer, Bob (R, 22)\***
State Capitol
500 East Capitol Avenue
Pierre, SD 57501
E: bob.glanzer
    @sdlegislature.gov

**Goodwin, Tim (R, 30)\***
State Capitol
500 East Capitol Avenue
Pierre, SD 57501
E: tim.goodwin
    @sdlegislature.gov

**Gosch, Spencer (R, 23)\***
State Capitol
500 East Capitol Avenue
Pierre, SD 57501
E: spencer.gosch
    @sdlegislature.gov

**Greenfield, Lana (R, 2)**
State Capitol
500 East Capitol Avenue
Pierre, SD 57501
E: lana.greenfield
    @sdlegislature.gov

**Haggar, Don (R, 10)**
State Capitol
500 East Capitol Avenue
Pierre, SD 57501
E: don.haggar
    @sdlegislature.gov

**Haugaard, Steven (R, 10)**
State Capitol
500 East Capitol Avenue
Pierre, SD 57501
E: steven.haugaard
    @sdlegislature.gov

**Hawley, Spencer (D, 7)**
State Capitol
500 East Capitol Avenue
Pierre, SD 57501
P: 605-773-3851
E: spencer.hawley
    @sdlegislature.gov

**Heinemann, Leslie J. (R, 8)**
State Capitol
500 East Capitol Avenue
Pierre, SD 57501
E: leslie.heinemann
    @sdlegislature.gov

**Holmes, Tom (R, 14)**
State Capitol
500 East Capitol Avenue
Pierre, SD 57501
E: Thomas.Holmes
    @sdlegislature.gov

**Howard, Taffy (R, 33)\***
State Capitol
500 East Capitol Avenue
Pierre, SD 57501
E: taffy.howard
    @sdlegislature.gov

**Hunhoff, Jean M. (R, 18)**
State Capitol
500 East Capitol Avenue
Pierre, SD 57501
E: jean.hunhoff
    @sdlegislature.gov

**Jamison, Greg (R, 12)\***
State Capitol
500 East Capitol Avenue
Pierre, SD 57501
E: greg.jamison
    @sdlegislature.gov

**Jensen, Kevin (D, 9)\***
State Capitol
500 East Capitol Avenue
Pierre, SD 57501
E: kevin.jensen
    @sdlegislature.gov

**Johns, Timothy R. (R, 31)**
State Capitol
500 East Capitol Avenue
Pierre, SD 57501
E: timothy.johns
    @sdlegislature.gov

**Johnson, David (R, 33)\***
State Capitol
500 East Capitol Avenue
Pierre, SD 57501
E: david.johnson
    @sdlegislature.gov

**Kaiser, Dan (R, 3)**
State Capitol
500 East Capitol Avenue
Pierre, SD 57501
P: (605) 228-4988
E: dan.kaiser
    @sdlegislature.gov

**Karr, Chris (R, 11)\***
State Capitol
500 East Capitol Avenue
Pierre, SD 57501
E: chris.karr
    @sdlegislature.gov

**Kettwig, Jason W. (R, 4)\***
State Capitol
500 East Capitol Avenue
Pierre, SD 57501
E: jason.kettwig
    @sdlegislature.gov

**Lake, John (R, 23)***
State Capitol
500 East Capitol Avenue
Pierre, SD 57501
E: john.lake
  @sdlegislature.gov

**Latterell, Isaac (R, 6)**
State Capitol
500 East Capitol Avenue
Pierre, SD 57501
E: isaac.latterell
  @sdlegislature.gov

**Lesmeister, Oren (D, 28A)***
State Capitol
500 East Capitol Avenue
Pierre, SD 57501
E: oren.lesmeister
  @sdlegislature.gov

**Livermont, Steve (R, 27)***
State Capitol
500 East Capitol Avenue
Pierre, SD 57501
E: steve.livermont
  @sdlegislature.gov

**Lust, David (R, 34)**
State Capitol
500 East Capitol Avenue
Pierre, SD 57501
E: david.lust
  @sdlegislature.gov

**Marty, J. Sam (R, 28B)**
State Capitol
500 East Capitol Avenue
Pierre, SD 57501
E: sam.marty
  @sdlegislature.gov

**May, Elizabeth (R, 27)**
State Capitol
500 East Capitol Avenue
Pierre, SD 57501
E: elizabeth.may
  @sdlegislature.gov

**McCleerey, Steven (D, 1)**
State Capitol
500 East Capitol Avenue
Pierre, SD 57501
E: steven.mccleerey
  @sdlegislature.gov

**McPherson, Sean (R, 32)***
State Capitol
500 East Capitol Avenue
Pierre, SD 57501
E: sean.mcpherson
  @sdlegislature.gov

**Mickelson, G. Mark (R, 13)**
State Capitol
500 East Capitol Avenue
Pierre, SD 57501
E: mark.mickelson
  @sdlegislature.gov

**Mills, John (R, 4)***
State Capitol
500 East Capitol Avenue
Pierre, SD 57501
E: john.mills
  @sdlegislature.gov

**Otten, Herman (R, 6)**
State Capitol
500 East Capitol Avenue
Pierre, SD 57501
E: herman.otten
  @sdlegislature.gov

**Peterson, Kent (R, 19)**
State Capitol
500 East Capitol Avenue
Pierre, SD 57501
E: kent.peterson
  @sdlegislature.gov

**Peterson, Sue (R, 13)***
State Capitol
500 East Capitol Avenue
Pierre, SD 57501
P: (605) 773-3851
E: sue.peterson
  @sdlegislature.gov

**Pischke, Tom (R, 25)***
State Capitol
500 East Capitol Avenue
Pierre, SD 57501
E: tom.pischke
  @sdlegislature.gov

**Qualm, Lee (R, 21)**
State Capitol
500 East Capitol Avenue
Pierre, SD 57501
E: lee.qualm
  @sdlegislature.gov

**Rasmussen, Nancy (R, 17)**
State Capitol
500 East Capitol Avenue
Pierre, SD 57501
E: nancy.rasmussen
  @sdlegislature.gov

**Reed, Tim (R, 7)***
State Capitol
500 East Capitol Avenue
Pierre, SD 57501
E: tim.reed
  @sdlegislature.gov

**Rhoden, Larry (R, 29)***
State Capitol
500 East Capitol Avenue
Pierre, SD 57501
E: larry.rhoden
  @sdlegislature.gov

**Ring, Ray (D, 17)**
State Capitol
500 East Capitol Avenue
Pierre, SD 57501
E: ray.ring
  @sdlegislature.gov

**Rounds, Tim (R, 24)**
State Capitol
500 East Capitol Avenue
Pierre, SD 57501
E: tim.rounds
  @sdlegislature.gov

**Rozum, Tona (R, 20)**
State Capitol
500 East Capitol Avenue
Pierre, SD 57501
E: tona.rozum
  @sdlegislature.gov

**Schaefer, James G. (R, 26B)**
State Capitol
500 East Capitol Avenue
Pierre, SD 57501
E: james.schaefer
  @sdlegislature.gov

**Schoenfish, Kyle (R, 19)**
State Capitol
500 East Capitol Avenue
Pierre, SD 57501
E: kyle.schoenfish
  @sdlegislature.gov

**Smith, Jamie (D, 15)***
State Capitol
500 East Capitol Avenue
Pierre, SD 57501
E: jamie.smith
  @sdlegislature.gov

**Soli, Karen L. (D, 15)**
State Capitol
500 East Capitol Avenue
Pierre, SD 57501
E: karen.soli
  @sdlegislature.gov

**Steinhauer, Wayne H. (R, 9)**
State Capitol
500 East Capitol Avenue
Pierre, SD 57501
P: (605) 773-3851
E: wayne.steinhauer
  @sdlegislature.gov

**Stevens, Mike (R, 18)**
State Capitol
500 East Capitol Avenue
Pierre, SD 57501
E: mike.stevens
  @sdlegislature.gov

**Tieszen, Craig (R, 34)**
State Capitol
500 East Capitol Avenue
Pierre, SD 57501
E: craig.tieszen
  @sdlegislature.gov

**Tulson, Burt E. (R, 2)**
State Capitol
500 East Capitol Avenue
Pierre, SD 57501
E: burt.tulson
  @sdlegislature.gov

**Turbiville, Charles M.
  (R, 31)**
State Capitol
500 East Capitol Avenue
Pierre, SD 57501
E: charles.turbiville
  @sdlegislature.gov

**Wiese, Marli (R, 8)***
State Capitol
500 E Capitol Ave
Pierre, SD 57501
P: (605) 773-3851
E: marli.wiese
  @sdlegislature.gov

**Willadsen, Mark K. (R, 11)**
State Capitol
500 East Capitol Avenue
Pierre, SD 57501
P: (605) 773-3851
E: mark.willadsen
  @sdlegislature.gov

**Wismer, Susan (D, 1)**
State Capitol
500 East Capitol Avenue
Pierre, SD 57501
E: susan.wismer
  @sdlegislature.gov

**York, Nancy (R, 5)***
State Capitol
500 East Capitol Avenue
Pierre, SD 57501
E: nancy.york
  @sdlegislature.gov

**Zikmund, Larry (R, 14)**
State Capitol
500 East Capitol Avenue
Pierre, SD 57501
E: larry.zikmund
  @sdlegislature.gov

# Tennessee

## Executive

### Governor

**The Honorable Bill Haslam (R)**
Governor
State Capitol
Nashville, TN 37243
P: (615) 741-2001
F: (615) 532-9711
E: bill.haslam@tn.gov

### Lieutenant Governor

**The Honorable Randy McNally**
(elected by the Senate)
Lieutenant Governor/Speaker of the Senate
Suite 13, Legislative Plaza
301 6th Avenue North
Nashville, TN 37243
P: (615) 741-6806
F: (615) 253-0285
E: lt.gov.randy.mcnally
@capitol.tn.gov

### Attorney General

**The Honorable Herbert Slatery III**
(appointed)
Attorney General
425 5th Avenue North
Nashville, TN 37243
P: (615) 741-3491
F: (615) 741-2009

### Auditor

**Mr. Justin P. Wilson**
Comptroller of the Treasury
505 Deaderick Street, Suite 1500
Nashville, TN 37243
P: (615) 741-2501
F: (615) 741-7328
E: justin.wilson@tn.gov

### Secretary of State

**The Honorable Tre Hargett**
(elected by the Legislature)
Secretary of State
First Floor, State Capitol
Nashville, TN 37243
P: (615) 741-2819
F: (615) 741-5962
E: tre.hargett@tn.gov

## Treasurer

**The Honorable David H. Lillard Jr.**
(elected by the Legislature)
State Treasurer
State Capitol, First Floor
600 Charlotte Avenue
Nashville, TN 37243
P: (615) 741-2956
F: (615) 253-1591
E: david.lillard@tn.gov

## Judiciary

### Supreme Court (PE)

**Mr. James Hivner**
Appellate Court Clerk
Supreme Court Building
401 7th Avenue, North
Nashville, TN 37219
P: (615) 741-2681
F: (615) 532-8757

**The Honorable Jeffrey Bivins**
Chief Justice
**The Honorable Cornelia Clark**
**The Honorable Holly Kirby**
**The Honorable Sharon G. Lee**
**The Honorable Roger A. Page**

## Legislative

## Senate

### Speaker of the Senate

**The Honorable Randy McNally (R)**
Lieutenant Governor/Speaker of the Senate
Suite 13, Legislative Plaza
301 6th Avenue North
Nashville, TN 37243
P: (615) 741-6806
F: (615) 253-0285
E: lt.gov.randy.mcnally
@capitol.tn.gov

### Speaker Pro Tempore of the Senate

**Senator Jim Tracy (R)**
Senate Speaker Pro Tempore
Suite 2, Legislative Plaza
301 6th Avenue North
Nashville, TN 37243
P: (615) 741-1066
F: (615) 741-2255
E: sen.jim.tracy
@capitol.tn.gov

### Senate Majority Leader

**Senator Mark Norris (R)**
Senate Majority Leader
Suite 9A, Legislative Plaza
301 6th Avenue North
Nashville, TN 37243
P: (615) 741-1967
F: (615) 253-0194
E: sen.mark.norris
@capitol.tn.gov

### Senate Minority Leader

**Senator Lee Harris (D)**
Senate Minority Leader
Suite 318, War Memorial Building
301 6th Avenue North
Nashville, TN 37243
P: (615) 741-1767
F: (615) 253-0357
E: sen.lee.harris
@capitol.tn.gov

### Secretary of the Senate

**Mr. Russell Humphrey**
Chief Clerk of the Senate
State Capitol, 2nd Floor
Nashville, TN 37243
P: (615) 741-2730
E: russell.humphrey
@capitol.tn.gov

### Members of the Senate

**Bailey, Paul (R, 15)**
Suite 2, Legislative Plaza
301 6th Avenue North
Nashville, TN 37243
P: (615) 741-3978
F: (615) 253-0381
E: sen.paul.bailey
@capitol.tn.gov

**Beavers, Mae (R, 17)**
Suite 6, Legislative Plaza
301 6th Avenue North
Nashville, TN 37243
P: (615) 741-2421
F: (615) 253-0205
E: sen.mae.beavers
@capitol.tn.gov

**Bell, Mike (R, 9)**
Suite 309, War Memorial Building
301 6th Avenue North
Nashville, TN 37243
P: (615) 741-1946
F: (615) 253-0374
E: sen.mike.bell
@capitol.tn.gov

**Bowling, Janice (R, 16)**
Suite 310A, War Memorial Building
301 6th Avenue North
Nashville, TN 37243
P: (615) 741-6694
F: (615) 253-0260
E: sen.janice.bowling
@capitol.tn.gov

**Briggs, Richard (R, 7)**
Suite 317, War Memorial Building
301 6th Avenue North
Nashville, TN 37243
P: (615) 741-1766
F: (615) 253-0199
E: sen.richard.briggs
@capitol.tn.gov

**Crowe, Rusty (R, 3)**
Suite 8, Legislative Plaza
301 6th Avenue North
Nashville, TN 37243
P: (615) 741-2468
F: (615) 253-0359
E: sen.rusty.crowe
@capitol.tn.gov

**Dickerson, Steven (R, 20)**
Suite 310, War Memorial Building
301 6th Avenue North
Nashville, TN 37243
P: (615) 741-6679
F: (615) 253-0275
E: sen.steven.dickerson
@capitol.tn.gov

**Gardenhire, Todd (R, 10)**
Suite 11A, Legislative Plaza
301 6th Avenue North
Nashville, TN 37243
P: (615) 741-6682
F: (615) 253-0209
E: sen.todd.gardenhire
@capitol.tn.gov

**Green, Mark (R, 22)**
Suite 4, Legislative Plaza
301 6th Avenue North
Nashville, TN 37243
P: (615) 741-2374
F: (615) 253-0193
E: sen.mark.green
@capitol.tn.gov

**Gresham, Dolores (R, 26)**
Suite 308, War Memorial Building
301 6th Avenue North
Nashville, TN 37243
P: (615) 741-2368
F: (615) 253-0204
E: sen.dolores.gresham
@capitol.tn.gov

**Haile, Ferrell (R, 18)**
Suite 10A, Legislative Plaza
301 6th Avenue North
Nashville, TN 37243
P: (615) 741-1999
F: (615) 253-0207
E: sen.ferrell.haile
@capitol.tn.gov

**Harper, Thelma (D, 19)**
Suite 303, War Memorial
Building
301 6th Avenue North
Nashville, TN 37243
P: (615) 741-2453
F: (615) 253-0268
E: sen.thelma.harper
@capitol.tn.gov

**Harris, Lee (D, 29)**
Suite 318, War Memorial
Building
301 6th Avenue North
Nashville, TN 37243
P: (615) 741-1767
F: (615) 253-0357
E: sen.lee.harris
@capitol.tn.gov

**Hensley, Joey (R, 28)**
Suite 309, War Memorial
Building
301 6th Avenue North
Nashville, TN 37243
P: (615) 741-3100
F: (615) 253-0231
E: sen.joey.hensley
@capitol.tn.gov

**Jackson, Ed (R, 27)**
Suite 3, Legislative Plaza
301 6th Avenue North
Nashville, TN 37243
P: (615) 741-1810
F: (615) 253-0179
E: sen.ed.jackson
@capitol.tn.gov

**Johnson, Jack (R, 23)**
Suite 11, Legislative Plaza
301 6th Avenue North
Nashville, TN 37243
P: (615) 741-2495
F: (615) 253-0321
E: sen.jack.johnson
@capitol.tn.gov

**Kelsey, Brian K. (R, 31)**
Suite 7, Legislative Plaza
301 6th Avenue North
Nashville, TN 37243
P: (615) 741-3036
F: (615) 253-0266
E: sen.brian.kelsey
@capitol.tn.gov

**Ketron, Bill (R, 13)**
Suite 5, Legislative Plaza
301 6th Avenue North
Nashville, TN 37243
P: (615) 253-0282
F: (615) 741-7200
E: sen.bill.ketron
@capitol.tn.gov

**Kyle, Sara (D, 30)**
Suite 305, War Memorial
Building
301 6th Avenue North
Nashville, TN 37243
P: (615) 741-4167
F: (615) 253-0221
E: sen.sara.kyle
@capitol.tn.gov

**Lundberg, Jon (R, 4)**
304 War Memorial Building
301 6th Avenue North
Nashville, TN 37243
P: (615) 741-5761
E: sen.jon.lundberg
@capitol.tn.gov

**Massey, Becky Duncan (R, 6)**
Suite 6A, Legislative Plaza
301 6th Avenue North
Nashville, TN 37243
P: (615) 741-1648
F: (615) 253-0270
E: sen.becky.massey
@capitol.tn.gov

**McNally, Randy (R, 5)**
Suite 13, Legislative Plaza
301 6th Avenue North
Nashville, TN 37243
P: (615) 741-6806
F: (615) 253-0285
E: lt.gov.randy.mcnally
@capitol.tn.gov

**Niceley, Frank S. (R, 8)**
Suite 9, Legislative Plaza
301 6th Avenue North
Nashville, TN 37243
P: (615) 741-2061
F: (615) 253-0255
E: sen.frank.niceley
@capitol.tn.gov

**Norris, Mark (R, 32)**
Suite 9A, Legislative Plaza
301 6th Avenue North
Nashville, TN 37243
P: (615) 741-1967
F: (615) 253-0194
E: sen.mark.norris
@capitol.tn.gov

**Overbey, Doug (R, 2)**
Suite 306, War Memorial
Building
301 6th Avenue North
Nashville, TN 37243
P: (615) 741-0981
F: (615) 253-0224
E: sen.doug.overbey
@capitol.tn.gov

**Roberts, Kerry (R, 25)**
Suite 321, War Memorial
Building
301 6th Avenue North
Nashville, TN 37243
P: (615) 741-4499
F: (615) 253-0302
E: sen.kerry.roberts
@capitol.tn.gov

**Southerland, Steve (R, 1)**
Suite 10, Legislative Plaza
301 6th Avenue North
Nashville, TN 37243
P: (615) 741-3851
F: (615) 253-0330
E: sen.steve.southerland
@capitol.tn.gov

**Stevens, John (R, 24)**
Suite 302, War Memorial
Building
301 6th Avenue North
Nashville, TN 37243
P: (615) 741-4576
F: (615) 253-0161
E: sen.john.stevens
@capitol.tn.gov

**Tate, Reginald (D, 33)**
Suite 320, War Memorial
Building
301 6th Avenue North
Nashville, TN 37243
P: (615) 741-2509
F: (615) 253-0167
E: sen.reginald.tate
@capitol.tn.gov

**Tracy, Jim (R, 14)**
Suite 2, Legislative Plaza
301 6th Avenue North
Nashville, TN 37243
P: (615) 741-1066
F: (615) 741-2255
E: sen.jim.tracy
@capitol.tn.gov

**Watson, Bo (R, 11)**
Suite 307, War Memorial
Building
301 6th Avenue North
Nashville, TN 37243
P: (615) 741-3227
F: (615) 253-0280
E: sen.bo.watson
@capitol.tn.gov

**Yager, Ken (R, 12)**
Suite G-19, War Memorial
Building
301 6th Avenue North
Nashville, TN 37243
P: (615) 741-1449
F: (615) 253-0237
E: sen.ken.yager
@capitol.tn.gov

**Yarbro, Jeff (D, 21)**
Suite 312, War Memorial
Building
301 6th Avenue North
Nashville, TN 37243
P: (615) 741-3291
F: (615) 253-0198
E: sen.jeff.yarbro
@capitol.tn.gov

# House

## Speaker of the House

**Representative Beth Harwell (R)**
House Speaker
Suite 19, Legislative Plaza
301 6th Avenue North
Nashville, TN 37243
P: (615) 741-0709
F: (615) 741-4917
E: speaker.beth.harwell
@capitol.tn.gov

## Speaker Pro Tempore of the House

**Representative Curtis G. Johnson (R)**
House Speaker Pro Tempore
Suite 15, Legislative Plaza
301 6th Avenue North
Nashville, TN 37243
P: (615) 741-4341
F: (615) 253-0269
E: rep.curtis.johnson
@capitol.tn.gov

## House Majority Leader

**Representative Glen Casada (R)**
House Republican Leader
Suite 25, Legislative Plaza
301 6th Avenue North
Nashville, TN 37243
P: (615) 741-4389
F: (615) 253-0229
E: rep.glen.casada
@capitol.tn.gov

# Tennessee

## House Minority Leader

**Representative Craig Fitzhugh (D)**
House Democratic Leader
Suite 33, Legislative Plaza
301 6th Avenue North
Nashville, TN 37243
P: (615) 741-2134
F: (615) 741-1446
E: rep.craig.fitzhugh
@capitol.tn.gov

## Clerk of the House

**Mr. Joe McCord**
Chief Clerk of the House
State Capitol, 2nd Floor
Nashville, TN 37243
P: (615) 741-2901
E: joe.mccord
@capitol.tn.gov

## Members of the House

**Akbari, Raumesh (D, 91)**
Suite 35, Legislative Plaza
301 6th Avenue North
Nashville, TN 37243
P: (615) 741-3830
F: (615) 253-0335
E: rep.raumesh.akbari
@capitol.tn.gov

**Alexander, David (R, 39)**
Suite 107, War Memorial
Building
301 6th Avenue North
Nashville, TN 37243
P: (615) 741-8695
F: (615) 253-0314
E: rep.david.alexander
@capitol.tn.gov

**Beck, Bill (D, 51)**
Suite 24, Legislative Plaza
301 6th Avenue North
Nashville, TN 37243
P: (615) 741-3229
F: (615) 253-0233
E: rep.bill.beck
@capitol.tn.gov

**Brooks, Harry (R, 19)**
Suite 117, War Memorial
Building
301 6th Avenue North
Nashville, TN 37243
P: (615) 741-6879
F: (615) 253-0212
E: rep.harry.brooks
@capitol.tn.gov

**Brooks, Kevin (R, 24)**
Suite 103, War Memorial
Building
301 6th Avenue North
Nashville, TN 37243
P: (615) 741-1350
F: (615) 253-0346
E: rep.kevin.brooks
@capitol.tn.gov

**Butt, Sheila (R, 64)**
Suite 106, War Memorial
Building
301 6th Avenue North
Nashville, TN 37243
P: (615) 741-3005
F: (615) 253-0365
E: rep.sheila.butt
@capitol.tn.gov

**Byrd, David (R, 71)**
Suite 110, War Memorial
Building
301 6th Avenue North
Nashville, TN 37243
P: (615) 741-2190
F: (615) 253-0377
E: rep.david.byrd
@capitol.tn.gov

**Calfee, Kent (R, 32)**
Suite 219, War Memorial
Building
301 6th Avenue North
Nashville, TN 37243
P: (615) 741-7658
F: (615) 253-0163
E: rep.kent.calfee
@capitol.tn.gov

**Camper, Karen D. (D, 87)**
Suite 32, Legislative Plaza
301 6th Avenue North
Nashville, TN 37243
P: (615) 741-1898
F: (615) 253-0211
E: rep.karen.camper
@capitol.tn.gov

**Carr, Dale (R, 12)**
Suite 214, War Memorial
Building
301 6th Avenue North
Nashville, TN 37243
P: (615) 741-5981
F: (615) 253-0303
E: rep.dale.carr
@capitol.tn.gov

**Carter, Mike (R, 29)**
Suite G-3, War Memorial
Building
301 6th Avenue North
Nashville, TN 37243
P: (615) 741-3025
F: (615) 253-0241
E: rep.mike.carter
@capitol.tn.gov

**Casada, Glen (R, 63)**
Suite 25, Legislative Plaza
301 6th Avenue North
Nashville, TN 37243
P: (615) 741-4389
F: (615) 253-0229
E: rep.glen.casada
@capitol.tn.gov

**Clemmons, John (D, 55)**
Suite 38, Legislative Plaza
301 6th Avenue North
Nashville, TN 37243
P: (615) 741-4410
F: (615) 253-0202
E: rep.john.ray.clemmons
@capitol.tn.gov

**Coley, Jim (R, 97)**
Suite 207, War Memorial
Building
301 6th Avenue North
Nashville, TN 37243
P: (651) 741-8201
F: (615) 253-0267
E: rep.jim.coley
@capitol.tn.gov

**Cooper, Barbara Ward (D, 86)**
Suite 38, Legislative Plaza
301 6th Avenue North
Nashville, TN 37243
P: (615) 741-4295
F: (615) 253-0327
E: rep.barbara.cooper
@capitol.tn.gov

**Crawford, John (R, 1)***
20 Legislative Plaza
301 6th Avenue North
Nashville, TN 37243
P: (615) 741-7623
F: (615) 253-0272
E: rep.john.crawford
@capitol.tn.gov

**Curcio, Michael (R, 69)***
301 6th AVenue North
Nasvhille, TN 37243
P: (615) 741-3513
F: (615) 253-0244
E: rep.michael.curcio
@capitol.tn.gov

**Daniel, Martin (R, 18)**
Suite 109, War Memorial
Building
301 6th Avenue North
Nashville, TN 37243
P: (615) 741-2287
F: (615) 253-0348
E: rep.martin.daniel
@capitol.tn.gov

**DeBerry Jr., John J. (D, 90)**
Suite 26, Legislative Plaza
301 6th Avenue North
Nashville, TN 37243
P: (615) 741-2239
F: (615) 253-0292
E: rep.john.deberry
@capitol.tn.gov

**Doss, Barry (R, 70)**
Suite 106, War Memorial
Building
301 6th Avenue North
Nashville, TN 37243
P: (615) 741-7476
F: (615) 253-0258
E: rep.barry.doss
@capitol.tn.gov

**Dunn, Bill (R, 16)**
Suite 115, War Memorial
Building
301 6th Avenue North
Nashville, TN 37243
P: (615) 741-1721
F: (615) 253-0276
E: rep.bill.dunn
@capitol.tn.gov

**Eldridge, Jimmy A. (R, 73)**
Suite 208, War Memorial
Building
301 6th Avenue North
Nashville, TN 37243
P: (615) 741-7475
F: (615) 253-0373
E: rep.jimmy.eldridge
@capitol.tn.gov

**Faison, Jeremy (R, 11)**
Suite 202, War Memorial
Building
301 6th Avenue North
Nashville, TN 37243
P: (615) 741-6871
F: (615) 253-0225
E: rep.jeremy.faison
@capitol.tn.gov

**Farmer, Andrew (R, 17)**
Suite 109, War Memorial
Building
301 6th Avenue North
Nashville, TN 37243
P: (615) 741-4419
F: (615) 253-0203
E: rep.andrew.farmer
@capitol.tn.gov

**Favors, JoAnne (D, 28)**
Suite 35, Legislative Plaza
301 6th Avenue North
Nashville, TN 37243
P: (615) 741-2702
F: (615) 253-0351
E: rep.joanne.favors
@capitol.tn.gov

**Fitzhugh, Craig (D, 82)**
Suite 33, Legislative Plaza
301 6th Avenue North
Nashville, TN 37243
P: (615) 741-2134
F: (615) 741-1446
E: rep.craig.fitzhugh
@capitol.tn.gov

**Forgety, John (R, 23)**
Suite 109, War Memorial
Building
301 6th Avenue North
Nashville, TN 37243
P: (615) 741-1725
F: (615) 253-0309
E: rep.john.forgety
@capitol.tn.gov

**Gant, Ron (R, 94)\***
Suite 18A, Legislative Plaza
301 6th Avenue North
Nashville, TN 37243
P: (615) 741-6890
F: (615) 253-0380
E: rep.ron.gant
@capitol.tn.gov

**Gilmore, Brenda (D, 54)**
Suite 26, Legislative Plaza
301 6th Avenue North
Nashville, TN 37243
P: (615) 741-1997
F: (615) 253-0361
E: rep.brenda.gilmore
@capitol.tn.gov

**Goins, Tilman (R, 10)**
Suite 207, War Memorial
Building
301 6th Avenue North
Nashville, TN 37243
P: (615) 741-6877
F: (615) 253-0182
E: rep.tilman.goins
@capitol.tn.gov

**Gravitt, Marc (R, 30)**
Suite 107, War Memorial
Building
301 6th Avenue North
Nashville, TN 37243
P: (615) 741-1934
F: (615) 253-0271
E: rep.marc.gravitt
@capitol.tn.gov

**Halford, Curtis (R, 79)**
Suite 108, War Memorial
Building
301 6th Avenue North
Nashville, TN 37243
P: (615) 741-7478
F: (615) 253-0218
E: rep.curtis.halford
@capitol.tn.gov

**Hardaway, G. A. (D, 93)**
Suite 37, Legislative Plaza
301 6th Avenue North
Nashville, TN 37243
P: (615) 741-5625
F: (615) 253-0185
E: rep.ga.hardaway
@capitol.tn.gov

**Harwell, Beth (R, 56)**
Suite 19, Legislative Plaza
301 6th Avenue North
Nashville, TN 37243
P: (615) 741-0709
F: (615) 741-4917
E: speaker.beth.harwell
@capitol.tn.gov

**Hawk, David (R, 5)**
Suite 201, War Memorial
Building
301 6th Avenue North
Nashville, TN 37243
P: (615) 741-7482
F: (615) 253-0210
E: rep.david.hawk
@capitol.tn.gov

**Hazlewood, Patsy (R, 27)**
Suite 20, Legislative Plaza
301 6th Avenue North
Nashville, TN 37243
P: (615) 741-2746
F: (615) 253-0304
E: rep.patsy.hazlewood
@capitol.tn.gov

**Hicks, Gary (R, 9)**
Suite 205, War Memorial
Building
301 6th Avenue North
Nashville, TN 37243
P: (615) 741-7480
F: (615) 253-0307
E: rep.gary.hicks
@capitol.tn.gov

**Hill, Matthew (R, 7)**
Suite 23, Legislative Plaza
301 6th Avenue North
Nashville, TN 37243
P: (615) 741-2251
F: (615) 253-0299
E: rep.matthew.hill
@capitol.tn.gov

**Hill, Timothy (R, 3)**
Suite 23, Legislative Plaza
301 6th Avenue North
Nashville, TN 37243
P: (615) 741-2050
F: (615) 253-0298
E: rep.timothy.hill
@capitol.tn.gov

**Holsclaw Jr., John (R, 4)**
Suite G-24, War Memorial
Building
301 6th Avenue North
Nashville, TN 37243
P: (615) 741-7450
F: (615) 253-0310
E: rep.john.holsclaw
@capitol.tn.gov

**Holt, Andy (R, 76)**
Suite 205, War Memorial
Building
301 6th Avenue North
Nashville, TN 37243
P: (615) 741-7847
F: (615) 253-0293
E: rep.andy.holt
@capitol.tn.gov

**Howell, Dan (R, 22)**
Suite 110, War Memorial
Building
301 6th Avenue North
Nashville, TN 37243
P: (615) 741-7799
F: (615) 253-0252
E: rep.dan.howell
@capitol.tn.gov

**Hulsey, Bud (R, 2)**
Suite 204, War Memorial
Building
301 6th Avenue North
Nashville, TN 37243
P: (615) 741-2886
F: (615) 253-0247
E: rep.bud.hulsey
@capitol.tn.gov

**Jernigan, Darren (D, 60)**
Suite 24, Legislative Plaza
301 6th Avenue North
Nashville, TN 37243
P: (615) 741-6959
F: (615) 253-0331
E: rep.darren.jernigan
@capitol.tn.gov

**Johnson, Curtis G. (R, 68)**
Suite 15, Legislative Plaza
301 6th Avenue North
Nashville, TN 37243
P: (615) 741-4341
F: (615) 253-0269
E: rep.curtis.johnson
@capitol.tn.gov

**Jones, Sherry (D, 59)**
Suite 26, Legislative Plaza
301 6th Avenue North
Nashville, TN 37243
P: (615) 741-2035
F: (615) 253-0290
E: rep.sherry.jones
@capitol.tn.gov

**Kane, Roger (R, 89)**
Suite 202A, War Memorial
Building
301 6th Avenue North
Nashville, TN 37243
P: (615) 741-4110
F: (615) 253-0195
E: rep.roger.kane
@capitol.tn.gov

**Keisling, Kelly (R, 38)**
Suite 108, War Memorial
Building
301 6th Avenue North
Nashville, TN 37243
P: (615) 741-6852
F: (615) 253-0234
E: rep.kelly.keisling
@capitol.tn.gov

**Kumar, Sabi (R, 66)**
Suite G-28, War Memorial
Building
301 6th Avenue North
Nashville, TN 37243
P: (615) 741-2860
F: (615) 253-0283
E: rep.sabi.kumar
@capitol.tn.gov

**Lamberth, William (R, 44)**
Suite 22, Legislative Plaza
301 6th Avenue North
Nashville, TN 37243
P: (615) 741-1980
F: (615) 253-0336
E: rep.william.lamberth
@capitol.tn.gov

**Littleton, Mary (R, 78)**
Suite 212, War Memorial
Building
301 6th Avenue North
Nashville, TN 37243
P: (615) 741-7477
F: (615) 253-0279
E: rep.mary.littleton
@capitol.tn.gov

# Tennessee

**Lollar, Ron (R, 99)**
Suite 214, War Memorial
Building
301 6th Avenue North
Nashville, TN 37243
P: (615) 741-7084
F: (615) 253-0294
E: rep.ron.lollar
　@capitol.tn.gov

**Love Jr., Harold M. (D, 58)**
Suite 35, Legislative Plaza
301 6th Avenue North
Nashville, TN 37243
P: (615) 741-3831
F: (615) 253-0323
E: rep.harold.love
　@capitol.tn.gov

**Lynn, Susan M. (R, 57)**
Suite 102, War Memorial
Building
301 6th Avenue North
Nashville, TN 37243
P: (615) 741-7462
F: (615) 253-0353
E: rep.susan.lynn
　@capitol.tn.gov

**Marsh, Pat (R, 62)**
Suite G19-A, War Memorial
Building
301 6th Avenue North
Nashville, TN 37243
P: (615) 741-6824
F: (615) 253-0344
E: rep.pat.marsh
　@capitol.tn.gov

**Matheny, Judd (R, 47)**
Suite 215, War Memorial
Building
301 6th Avenue North
Nashville, TN 37243
P: (615) 741-7448
F: (615) 253-0226
E: rep.judd.matheny
　@capitol.tn.gov

**Matlock, Jimmy (R, 21)**
Suite 219, War Memorial
Building
301 6th Avenue North
Nashville, TN 37243
P: (615) 741-3736
F: (615) 253-0312
E: rep.jimmy.matlock
　@capitol.tn.gov

**McCormick, Gerald (R, 26)**
Suite 206A, War Memorial
Building
301 6th Avenue North
Nashville, TN 37243
P: (615) 741-2548
F: (615) 253-0305
E: rep.gerald.mccormick
　@capitol.tn.gov

**McDaniel, Steve (R, 72)**
Suite 18, Legislative Plaza
301 6th Avenue North
Nashville, TN 37243
P: (615) 741-0750
F: (615) 253-0213
E: rep.steve.mcdaniel
　@capitol.tn.gov

**Miller, Larry J. (D, 88)**
Suite 36, Legislative Plaza
301 6th Avenue North
Nashville, TN 37243
P: (615) 741-4453
F: (615) 253-0329
E: rep.larry.miller
　@capitol.tn.gov

**Mitchell, Bo (D, 50)**
Suite 37, Legislative Plaza
301 6th Avenue North
Nashville, TN 37243
P: (615) 741-4317
F: (615) 741-0360
E: rep.bo.mitchell
　@capitol.tn.gov

**Moody, Debra (R, 81)**
Suite 205, War Memorial
Building
301 6th Avenue North
Nashville, TN 37243
P: (615) 741-3774
F: (615) 253-0263
E: rep.debra.moody
　@capitol.tn.gov

**Parkinson, Antonio (D, 98)**
Suite 36B, Legislative Plaza
301 6th Avenue North
Nashville, TN 37243
P: (615) 741-4575
F: (615) 253-0347
E: rep.antonio.parkinson
　@capitol.tn.gov

**Pitts, Joe (D, 67)**
Suite 32, Legislative Plaza
301 6th Avenue North
Nashville, TN 37243
P: (615) 741-2043
F: (615) 253-0200
E: rep.joe.pitts
　@capitol.tn.gov

**Pody, Mark (R, 46)**
Suite 203, War Memorial
Building
301 6th Avenue North
Nashville, TN 37243
P: (615) 741-7086
F: (615) 253-0206
E: rep.mark.pody
　@capitol.tn.gov

**Powell, Jason (D, 53)**
Suite 34, Legislative Plaza
301 6th Avenue North
Nashville, TN 37243
P: (615) 741-6861
F: (615) 741-0325
E: rep.jason.powell
　@capitol.tn.gov

**Powers, Dennis (R, 36)**
Suite G-27, War Memorial
Building
301 6th Avenue North
Nashville, TN 37243
P: (615) 741-3335
F: (615) 253-0296
E: rep.dennis.powers
　@capitol.tn.gov

**Ragan, John (R, 33)**
Suite G-24, War Memorial
Building
301 6th Avenue North
Nashville, TN 37243
P: (615) 741-4400
F: (615) 253-0297
E: rep.john.ragan
　@capitol.tn.gov

**Ramsey, Bob (R, 20)**
Suite 212, War Memorial
Building
301 6th Avenue North
Nashville, TN 37243
P: (615) 741-3560
F: (615) 253-0376
E: rep.bob.ramsey
　@capitol.tn.gov

**Reedy, Jay (R, 74)**
Suite 22, Legislative Plaza
301 6th Avenue North
Nashville, TN 37243
P: (615) 741-7098
F: (615) 253-0315
E: rep.jay.reedy
　@capitol.tn.gov

**Rogers, Courtney (R, 45)**
Suite 110A, War Memorial
Building
301 6th Avenue North
Nashville, TN 37243
P: (615) 741-3893
F: (615) 253-0350
E: rep.courtney.rogers
　@capitol.tn.gov

**Rudd, Tim (R, 34)***
Suite 107, War Memorial
Building
301 6th Avenue North
Nashville, TN 37243
P: (615) 741-2804
F: (615) 253-0322
E: rep.tim.rudd
　@capitol.tn.gov

**Sanderson, Bill (R, 77)**
Suite 204, War Memorial
Building
301 6th Avenue North
Nashville, TN 37243
P: (615) 741-0718
F: (615) 253-0214
E: rep.bill.sanderson
　@capitol.tn.gov

**Sargent, Charles Michael
(R, 61)**
Suite 206, War Memorial
Building
301 6th Avenue North
Nashville, TN 37243
P: (615) 741-6808
F: (615) 253-0217
E: rep.charles.sargent
　@capitol.tn.gov

**Sexton, Cameron (R, 25)**
Suite 114, War Memorial
Building
301 6th Avenue North
Nashville, TN 37243
P: (615) 741-2343
F: (615) 253-0230
E: rep.cameron.sexton
　@capitol.tn.gov

**Sexton, Jerry (R, 35)**
Suite 113, War Memorial
Building
301 6th Avenue North
Nashville, TN 37243
P: (615) 741-2534
F: (615) 253-0273
E: rep.jerry.sexton
　@capitol.tn.gov

**Shaw, Johnny (D, 80)**
Suite 36C, Legislative Plaza
301 6th Avenue North
Nashville, TN 37243
P: (615) 741-4538
F: (615) 253-0356
E: rep.johnny.shaw
　@capitol.tn.gov

**Sherrell, Paul (R, 43)***
301 6th Avenue North
Nashville, TN 37243
P: (615) 741-1963
F: (615) 253-0207
E: rep.paul.sherrell
　@capitol.tn.gov

**Smith, Eddie (R, 13)**
Suite 207, War Memorial
Building
301 6th Avenue North
Nashville, TN 37243
P: (615) 741-2031
F: (615) 253-0192
E: rep.eddie.smith
   @capitol.tn.gov

**Sparks, Mike (R, 49)**
Suite 113, War Memorial
Building
301 6th Avenue North
Nashville, TN 37243
P: (615) 741-6829
F: (615) 253-0332
E: rep.mike.sparks
   @capitol.tn.gov

**Staples, Rick (D, 15)***
Suite 34, Legislative Plaza
301 6th Avenue North
Nashville, TN 37243
P: (615) 741-0768
F: (615) 253-0316
E: rep.rick.staples
   @capitol.tn.gov

**Stewart, Mike (D, 52)**
Suite 33, Legislative Plaza
301 6th Avenue North
Nashville, TN 37243
P: (615) 741-2184
F: (615) 253-0181
E: rep.mike.stewart
   @capitol.tn.gov

**Swann, Art (R, 8)**
Suite G-19A, War Memorial
Building
301 6th Avenue North
Nashville, TN 37243
P: (615) 741-5481
F: (615) 253-0220
E: rep.art.swann
   @capitol.tn.gov

**Terry, Bryan (R, 48)**
Suite 114, War Memorial
Building
301 6th Avenue North
Nashville, TN 37243
P: (615) 741-2180
F: (615) 253-0372
E: rep.bryan.terry
   @capitol.tn.gov

**Thompson, Dwayne (D, 96)***
Suite 32, Legislative Plaza
301 6th Avenue North
Nashville, TN 37243
P: (615) 741-1920
F: (615) 253-0232
E: rep.dwayne.thompson
   @capitol.tn.gov

**Tillis, Thomas R. (R, 92)***
Suite 209, War Memorial
Building
301 6th Avenue North
Nashville, TN 37243
P: (615) 741-4170
F: (615) 253-0274
E: rep.rick.tillis
   @capitol.tn.gov

**Towns Jr., Joe (D, 84)**
Suite 37, Legislative Plaza
301 6th Avenue North
Nashville, TN 37243
P: (615) 741-2189
F: (615) 253-0201
E: rep.joe.towns
   @capitol.tn.gov

**Travis, Ron (R, 31)**
Suite G-3, War Memorial
Building
301 6th Avenue North
Nashville, TN 37243
P: (615) 741-1450
F: (615) 253-0262
E: rep.ron.travis
   @capitol.tn.gov

**Turner, Johnnie (D, 85)**
Suite 38, Legislative Plaza
301 6th Avenue North
Nashville, TN 37243
P: (615) 741-6954
F: (615) 253-0339
E: rep.johnnie.turner
   @capitol.tn.gov

**Van Huss, James Micah
   (R, 6)**
Suite 23, Legislative Plaza
301 6th Avenue North
Nashville, TN 37243
P: (615) 741-1717
F: (615) 253-0301
E: rep.micah.vanhuss
   @capitol.tn.gov

**Weaver, Terri Lynn (R, 40)**
Suite 105, War Memorial
301 6th Avenue North
Nashville, TN 37243
P: (615) 741-2192
F: (615) 253-0378
E: rep.terri.lynn.weaver
   @capitol.tn.gov

**White, Dawn (R, 37)**
Suite 209A, War Memorial
Building
301 6th Avenue North
Nashville, TN 37243
P: (615) 741-6849
F: (615) 253-0264
E: rep.dawn.white
   @capitol.tn.gov

**White, Mark (R, 83)**
Suite 217, War Memorial
Building
301 6th Avenue North
Nashville, TN 37243
P: (615) 741-4415
F: (615) 253-0349
E: mark.white
   @capitol.tn.gov

**Whitson, Sam (R, 65)***
Suite 209, War Memorial
Building
301 6th Avenue North
Nashville, TN 37243
P: (615) 741-1864
F: (615) 253-0228
E: rep.sam.whitson
   @capitol.tn.gov

**Williams, Ryan (R, 42)**
Suite 17, Legislative Plaza
301 6th Avenue North
Nashville, TN 37243
P: (615) 741-1875
F: (615) 253-0160
E: rep.ryan.williams
   @capitol.tn.gov

**Windle, John Mark (D, 41)**
Suite 24, Legislative Plaza
301 6th Avenue North
Nashville, TN 37243
P: (615) 741-1260
F: (615) 253-0328
E: rep.john.windle
   @capitol.tn.gov

**Wirgau, Tim (R, 75)**
Suite G-2, War Memorial
Building
301 6th Avenue North
Nashville, TN 37243
P: (615) 741-6804
F: (615) 253-0239
E: rep.tim.wirgau
   @capitol.tn.gov

**Zachary, Jason (R, 14)**
Suite 104, War Memorial
Building
301 6th Avenue North
Nashville, TN 37243
P: (615) 741-2264
F: (615) 253-0317
E: Rep.Jason.Zachary
   @capitol.tn.gov

# Texas

## Executive

### Governor
The Honorable Greg
  Abbott (R)
Governor
P.O. Box 12428
Austin, TX 78711
P: (512) 463-2000
F: (512) 463-5571

### Lieutenant Governor
The Honorable Dan
  Patrick (R)
Lieutenant Governor
Capitol Station
P.O. Box 12068
Austin, TX 78711
P: (512) 463-0001
F: (512) 463-0677

### Commissioner of Agriculture
The Honorable Sid
  Miller (R)
Commissioner
P.O. Box 12847
Capitol Station
Austin, TX 78711
P: (512) 463-7567
F: (512) 463-1104

### Attorney General
The Honorable Ken
  Paxton (R)
Attorney General
Capitol Station
P.O. Box 12548
Austin, TX 78711
P: (512) 463-2100
F: (512) 475-2994
E: ken.paxton
  @texasattorneygeneral.gov

### Auditor
Ms. Lisa Collier
  (appointed by the Legislature)
First Assistant State Auditor
1501 North Congress, 4th Floor
P.O. Box 12067
Austin, TX 78701
P: (512) 936-9500
F: (512) 936-9400

## Commissioner of the General Land Office
The Honorable George P.
  Bush (R)
Commissioner
1700 North Congress Avenue,
Suite 935
Austin, TX 78701
P: (512) 463-5001

## Railroad Commission
The Honorable Christi
  Craddick
Chair
P.O. Box 12967
Austin, TX 78711
P: (512) 463-7140
F: (512) 463-7161
E: christi.craddick
  @rrc.state.tx.us

The Honorable Ryan
  Sitton (R)
Commissioner
1701 North Congress Avenue
P.O. Box 12967
Austin, TX 78711
P: (512) 463-7144
F: (512) 462-7161
E: ryan.sitton
  @rrc.state.tx.us

## Secretary of State
The Honorable Rolando
  Pablos (R)
  (appointed)
Secretary of State
1100 Congress Avenue
Austin, TX 78701
P: (512) 463-5770

## Treasurer
The Honorable Glenn
  Hegar (R)
Comptroller of Public Accounts
LBJ State Office Building, 1st
Floor
111 East 17th Street
Austin, TX 78774
P: (512) 463-4444
F: (512) 463-4902
E: glenn.hegar
  @cpa.state.tx.us

## Judiciary
### Supreme Court (PE)
Mr. Blake A. Hawthorne
Clerk of the Court
201 West 14th Street, Room 104
P.O. Box 12248
Austin, TX 78711
P: (512) 463-1312
F: (512) 463-1365

The Honorable Nathan L.
  Hecht
Chief Justice
The Honorable Jeffrey S.
  Boyd
The Honorable Jeff Brown
The Honorable Phillip
  Devine
The Honorable Paul Green
The Honorable Eva Guzman
The Honorable Phil Johnson
The Honorable Debra
  Lehrmann
The Honorable Don R.
  Willett

## Legislative
### Senate
#### Senate President
The Honorable Dan
  Patrick (R)
Lieutenant Governor
Capitol Station
P.O. Box 12068
Austin, TX 78711
P: (512) 463-0001
F: (512) 463-0677

#### President Pro Tempore of the Senate
Senator Kel Seliger (R)
President Pro Tempore
Capitol Office Room 1E.12
P.O. Box 12068
Austin, TX 78711
P: (512) 463-0131
F: (512) 475-3733
E: Kel.Seliger
  @senate.state.tx.us

## Secretary of the Senate
Ms. Patsy Spaw
Secretary of the Senate
P.O. Box 12068
Austin, TX 78711
P: (512) 463-0100
F: (512) 463-6034
E: patsy.spaw
  @senate.state.tx.us

## Members of the Senate
Bettencourt, Paul (R, 7)
Capitol Office Room 3E.16
P.O. Box 12068
Austin, TX 78711
P: (512) 463-0107
E: Paul.Bettencourt
  @senate.state.tx.us

Birdwell, Brian (R, 22)
Capitol Office Room E1.706
P.O. Box 12068
Austin, TX 78711
P: (512) 463-0122
F: (512) 475-3729
E: Brian.Birdwell
  @senate.state.tx.us

Buckingham, Dawn (R, 24)*
Capitol Office Room GE.5
P.O. Box 12068
Austin, TX 78711
P: (512) 463-0124
E: Dawn.Buckingham
  @senate.state.tx.us

Burton, Konni (R, 10)
Capitol Office Room 3E.2
P.O. Box 12068
Austin, TX 78711
P: (512) 463-0110
E: Konni.Burton
  @senate.state.tx.us

Campbell, Donna (R, 25)
Capitol Office Room 3E.8
P.O. Box 12068
Austin, TX 78711
P: (512) 463-0125
F: (512) 463-7794
E: Donna.Campbell
  @senate.state.tx.us

Creighton, Brandon (R, 4)
Capitol Office Room E1.606
P.O. Box 12068
Austin, TX 78711
P: (512) 463-0104
F: (512) 463-6373
E: Brandon.Creighton
  @senate.state.tx.us

**Estes, Craig (R, 30)**
Capitol Office Room 3E.18
P.O. Box 12068
Austin, TX 78711
P: (512) 463-0130
F: (512) 463-8874
E: Craig.Estes
@senate.state.tx.us

**Garcia, Sylvia (D, 6)**
Capitol Office Room 3E.12
P.O. Box 12068
Austin, TX 78711
P: (512) 463-0106
E: Sylvia.Garcia
@senate.state.tx.us

**Hall, Bob (R, 2)**
Capitol Office Room E1.808
P.O. Box 12068
Austin, TX 78711
P: (512) 463-0102
F: (512) 463-7202
E: Bob.Hall
@senate.state.tx.us

**Hancock, Kelly (R, 9)**
Capitol Office Room 1E.9
P.O. Box 12068
Austin, TX 78711
P: (512) 463-0109
E: Kelly.Hancock
@senate.state.tx.us

**Hinojosa, Juan (D, 20)**
Capitol Office Room 3E.16
P.O. Box 12068
Austin, TX 78711
P: (512) 463-0120
F: (512) 463-0229
E: Juan.Hinojosa
@senate.state.tx.us

**Huffines, Don (R, 16)**
Capitol Office Room E1.608
P.O. Box 12068
Austin, TX 78711
P: (512) 463-0116
E: Don.Huffines
@senate.state.tx.us

**Huffman, Joan (R, 17)**
Capitol Office Room 1E.15
P.O. Box 12068
Austin, TX 78711
P: (512) 463-0117
E: Joan.Huffman
@senate.state.tx.us

**Hughes, Bryan (R, 1)**
Capitol Office Room GE.7
P.O. Box 12068
Austin, TX 78971
P: (512) 463-0101
E: Bryan.Hughes
@senate.state.tx.us

**Kolkhorst, Lois W. (R, 18)**
Capitol Office Room GE.4
P.O. Box 12068
Austin, TX 78711
P: (512) 463-0118
E: Lois.Kolkhorst
@senate.state.tx.us

**Lucio Jr., Eddie (D, 27)**
Capitol Office Room 3S.5
P.O. Box 12068
Austin, TX 78711
P: (512) 463-0127
F: (512) 463-0061
E: Eddie.Lucio
@senate.state.tx.us

**Menendez, Jose (D, 26)**
Capitol Office Room E1.712
P.O. Box 12068
Austin, TX 78711
P: (512) 463-0126
E: Jose.Menendez
@senate.state.tx.us

**Miles, Borris L. (D, 13)**
Capitol Office Room 3S.3
P.O. Box 2910
Austin, TX 78768
P: (512) 463-0518
F: (512) 463-0941
E: Borris.Miles
@senate.state.tx.us

**Nelson, Jane (R, 12)**
Capitol Office Room 1E.5
P.O. Box 12068
Austin, TX 78711
P: (512) 463-0112
F: (512) 463-0923
E: Jane.Nelson
@senate.state.tx.us

**Nichols, Robert (R, 3)**
Capitol Office Room E1.704
P.O. Box 12068
Austin, TX 78711
P: (512) 463-0103
E: Robert.Nichols
@senate.state.tx.us

**Perry, Charles Lee (R, 28)**
Capitol Office Room E1.810
P.O. Box 12068
Austin, TX 78711
P: (512) 463-0128
F: (512) 463-2424
E: Charles.Perry
@senate.state.tx.us

**Rodriguez, Jose (D, 29)**
Capitol Office Room E1.610
P.O. Box 12068
Austin, TX 78711
P: (512) 463-0129
E: Jose.Rodriguez
@senate.state.tx.us

**Schwertner, Charles (R, 5)**
Capitol Office Room E1.806
P.O. Box 12068
Austin, TX 78711
P: (512) 463-0105
F: (512) 463-5713

**Seliger, Kel (R, 31)**
Capitol Office Room 1E.12
P.O. Box 12068
Austin, TX 78711
P: (512) 463-0131
F: (512) 475-3733
E: Kel.Seliger
@senate.state.tx.us

**Taylor, Larry (R, 11)**
Capitol Office Room 3E.10
P.O. Box 12068
Austin, TX 78711
P: (512) 463-0111
E: Larry.Taylor
@senate.state.tx.us

**Taylor, Van (R, 8)**
Capitol Office, Room E1.708
P.O. Box 12068
Austin, TX 78711
P: (512) 463-0108
F: (512) 463-1021
E: Van.Taylor
@house.state.tx.us

**Uresti, Carlos (D, 19)**
Capitol Office Room 4E.2
P.O. Box 12068
Austin, TX 78711
P: (512) 463-0119
F: (512) 463-1017
E: Carlos.Uresti
@senate.state.tx.us

**Watson, Kirk (D, 14)**
Capitol Office Room E1.804
P.O. Box 12068
Austin, TX 78711
P: (512) 463-0114
F: (512) 463-5949
E: Kirk.Watson
@senate.state.tx.us

**West, Royce (D, 23)**
Capitol Office Room 1E.3
P.O. Box 12068
Austin, TX 78711
P: (512) 463-0123
F: (512) 463-0299
E: Royce.West
@senate.state.tx.us

**Whitmire, John (D, 15)**
Capitol Office Room 1E.13
P.O. Box 12068
Austin, TX 78711
P: (512) 463-0115
E: John.Whitmire
@senate.state.tx.us

**Zaffirini, Judith (D, 21)**
Capitol Office Room 1E.14
P.O. Box 12068
Austin, TX 78711
P: (512) 463-0121
E: Judith.Zaffirini
@senate.state.tx.us

# House

## Speaker of the House

**Representative Joe Straus (R)**
House Speaker
Capitol Office Room 2W.13
P.O. Box 2910
Austin, TX 78768
P: (512) 463-1000
F: (512) 463-0675
E: Joe.Straus
@house.state.tx.us

## Speaker Pro Tempore of the House

**Representative Dennis Bonnen (R)**
House Speaker Pro Tempore
Capitol Office Room 1W.6
P.O. Box 2910
Austin, TX 78768
P: (512) 463-0564
F: (512) 463-8414
E: Dennis.Bonnen
@house.state.tx.us

## Clerk of the House

**Mr. Robert Haney**
Chief Clerk of the House
Capitol Room 2W.29
P.O. Box 2910
Austin, TX 78768
P: (512) 463-0845
F: (512) 463-5896
E: robert.haney
@house.state.tx.us

## Members of the House

**Allen, Alma A. (D, 131)**
Capitol Office Room GW.5
P.O. Box 2910
Austin, TX 78768
P: (512) 463-0744
F: (512) 463-0761
E: Alma.Allen
@house.state.tx.us

# Texas

**Alonzo, Roberto R. (D, 104)**
Capitol Office Room 1N.12
P.O. Box 2910
Austin, TX 78768
P: (512) 463-0408
F: (512) 463-1817
E: Roberto.Alonzo
@house.state.tx.us

**Alvarado, Carol (D, 145)**
Capitol Office Room GW.6
P.O. Box 2910
Austin, TX 78768
P: (512) 463-0732
F: (512) 463-4781
E: Carol.Alvarado
@house.state.tx.us

**Anchia, Rafael (D, 103)**
Capitol Office Room 1N.9
P.O. Box 2910
Austin, TX 78768
P: (512) 463-0746
F: (512) 463-0044
E: Rafael.Anchia
@house.state.tx.us

**Anderson, Charles (R, 56)**
Capitol Office Room GW.8
P.O. Box 2910
Austin, TX 78768
P: (512) 463-0135
F: (512) 463-0642
E: Charles.Anderson
@house.state.tx.us

**Anderson, Rodney (R, 105)**
Capitol Office Room E1.414
P.O. Box 2910
Austin, TX 78768
P: (512) 463-0641
F: (512) 463-0044
E: Rodney.Anderson
@house.state.tx.us

**Arevalo, Diana (D, 116)\***
Capitol Office Room E2.304
P.O. Box 2910
Austin, TX 78768
P: (512) 463-0616
E: diana.arevalo
@house.state.tx.us

**Ashby, Trent (R, 57)**
Capitol Office Room E2.414
P.O. Box 2910
Austin, TX 78768
P: (512) 463-0508
F: (512) 463-5896
E: Trent.Ashby
@house.state.tx.us

**Bailes, Ernest (R, 18)\***
Capitol Office Room E1.316
P.O. Box 2190
Austin, TX 78768
P: (512) 463-0570
F: (512) 463-0315
E: ernest.bailes
@house.state.tx.us

**Bell, Cecil (R, 3)**
Capitol Office Room E2.708
P.O. Box 2910
Austin, TX 78768
P: (512) 463-0650
F: (512) 463-0575
E: Cecil.Bell
@house.state.tx.us

**Bernal, Diego (D, 123)**
Capitol Office Room E1.220
P.O. Box 2910
Austin, TX 78768
P: (512) 463-0532
E: Diego.Bernal
@house.state.tx.us

**Biedermann, Kyle (R, 73)\***
Capitol Office Room E1.412
P.O. Box 2910
Austin, TX 78768
P: (512) 463-0325
E: kyle.biedermann
@house.state.tx.us

**Blanco, Cesar (D, 76)**
Capitol Office Room E1.218
P.O. Box 2910
Austin, TX 78768
P: (512) 463-0622
F: (512) 463-0931
E: Cesar.Blanco
@house.state.tx.us

**Bohac, Dwayne (R, 138)**
Capitol Office Room GS.6
P.O. Box 2910
Austin, TX 78768
P: (512) 463-0727
F: (512) 463-0681
E: Dwayne.Bohac
@house.state.tx.us

**Bonnen, Dennis (R, 25)**
Capitol Office Room 1W.6
P.O. Box 2910
Austin, TX 78768
P: (512) 463-0564
F: (512) 463-8414
E: Dennis.Bonnen
@house.state.tx.us

**Bonnen, Greg (R, 24)**
Capitol Office Room E2.504
P.O. Box 2910
Austin, TX 78768
P: (512) 463-0729
E: Greg.Bonnen
@house.state.tx.us

**Burkett, Cindy (R, 113)**
Capitol Office Room GN.10
P.O. Box 2910
Austin, TX 78768
P: (512) 463-0464
F: (512) 463-9295
E: Cindy.Burkett
@house.state.tx.us

**Burns, DeWayne (R, 58)**
Capitol Office Room E1.322
P.O. Box 2910
Austin, TX 78768
P: (512) 463-0538
F: (512) 463-0897
E: DeWayne.Burns
@house.state.tx.us

**Burrows, Dustin (R, 83)**
Capitol Office Room E2.710
P.O. Box 2910
Austin, TX 78768
P: (512) 463-0542
F: (512) 463-0671
E: Dustin.Burrows
@house.state.tx.us

**Button, Angie Chen (R, 112)**
Capitol Office Room 4N.5
P.O. Box 2910
Austin, TX 78768
P: (512) 463-0486
E: AngieChen.Button
@house.state.tx.us

**Cain, Briscoe (R, 128)\***
Capitol Office Room E1.418
P.O. Box 2910
Austin, TX 78768
P: (512) 463-0733
F: (512) 463-1323
E: briscoe.cain
@house.state.tx.us

**Canales, Terry (D, 40)**
Capitol Office Room E2.910
P.O. Box 2910
Austin, TX 78768
P: (512) 463-0426
F: (512) 463-0043
E: Terry.Canales
@house.state.tx.us

**Capriglione, Giovanni
(R, 98)**
Capitol Office Room E2.610
P.O. Box 2910
Austin, TX 78768
P: (512) 463-0690
F: (512) 463-1004
E: Giovanni.Capriglione
@house.state.tx.us

**Clardy, Travis (R, 11)**
Capitol Office Room E2.908
P.O. Box 2910
Austin, TX 78768
P: (512) 463-0592
F: (512) 463-8792
E: Travis.Clardy
@house.state.tx.us

**Coleman, Garnet F. (D, 147)**
Capitol Office Room 4N.10
P.O. Box 2910
Austin, TX 78768
P: (512) 463-0524
F: (512) 463-1260
E: Garnet.Coleman
@house.state.tx.us

**Collier, Nicole (D, 95)**
Capitol Office Room E2.318
P.O. Box 2910
Austin, TX 78768
P: (512) 463-0716
F: (512) 463-1516
E: Nicole.Collier
@house.state.tx.us

**Cook, Byron (R, 8)**
Capitol Office Room GW.7
P.O. Box 2910
Austin, TX 78768
P: (512) 463-0730
F: (512) 463-2506
E: Byron.Cook
@house.state.tx.us

**Cortez, Philip (D, 117)**
Capitol Office Building E2.714
P.O. Box 2910
Austin, TX 78768
P: (512) 463-0269
F: (512) 463-1096
E: Philip.Cortez
@house.state.tx.us

**Cosper, Scott (R, 54)\***
Capitol Office Building E2.816
P.O. Box 2910
Austin, TX 78768
P: (512) 463-0684
F: (512) 436-8987
E: scott.cosper
@house.state.tx.us

**Craddick, Tom R. (R, 82)**
Capitol Office Room 1W.09
P.O. Box 2910
Austin, TX 78768
P: (512) 463-0500
F: (512) 463-7722
E: Tom.Craddick
@house.state.tx.us

**Cyrier, John (R, 17)**
Capitol Office Room E2.314
P.O. Box 2910
Austin, TX 78768
P: (512) 463-0682
F: (512) 463-9955
E: John.Cyrier
    @house.state.tx.us

**Dale, Tony (R, 136)**
Capitol Office Room E2.602
P.O. Box 2910
Austin, TX 78768
P: (512) 463-0696
F: (512) 463-9333
E: Tony.Dale
    @house.state.tx.us

**Darby, Drew (R, 72)**
Capitol Office Room E1.308
P.O. Box 2910
Austin, TX 78768
P: (512) 463-0331
F: (512) 463-0517
E: Drew.Darby
    @house.state.tx.us

**Davis, Sarah (R, 134)**
Capitol Office Room GW.4
P.O. Box 2910
Austin, TX 78768
P: (512) 463-0389
F: (512) 463-1374
E: Sarah.Davis
    @house.state.tx.us

**Davis, Yvonne (D, 111)**
Capitol Office Room 4N.9
P.O. Box 2910
Austin, TX 78768
P: (512) 463-0598
F: (512) 463-2297
E: Yvonne.Davis
    @house.state.tx.us

**Dean, Jay (R, 7)***
Capitol Office Room E2.716
P.O. Box 2190
Austin, TX 78768
P: (512) 463-0750
F: (512) 463-9085
E: jay.dean
    @house.state.tx.us

**Deshotel, Joe D. (D, 22)**
Capitol Office Room GW.12
P.O. Box 2910
Austin, TX 78768
P: (512) 463-0662
F: (512) 463-8381
E: Joe.Deshotel
    @house.state.tx.us

**Dukes, Dawnna (D, 46)**
Capitol Office Room E2.302
P.O. Box 2910
Austin, TX 78768
P: (512) 463-0506
F: (512) 463-7864
E: Dawnna.Dukes
    @house.state.tx.us

**Dutton Jr., Harold V.
    (D, 142)**
Capitol Office Room 3N.5
P.O. Box 2910
Austin, TX 78768
P: (512) 463-0510
F: (512) 463-8333
E: Harold.Dutton
    @house.state.tx.us

**Elkins, Gary (R, 135)**
Capitol Office Room 4N.03
P.O. Box 2910
Austin, TX 78768
P: (512) 463-0722
F: (512) 463-2331
E: Gary.Elkins
    @house.state.tx.us

**Faircloth, Wayne (R, 23)**
Capitol Office Room E2.812
P.O. Box 2910
Austin, TX 78768
P: (512) 463-0502
F: (512) 936-4260
E: Wayne.Faircloth
    @house.state.tx.us

**Fallon, Pat (R, 106)**
Capitol Office Room E2.722
P.O. Box 2910
Austin, TX 78768
P: (512) 463-0694
F: (512) 463-1130
E: Pat.Fallon
    @house.state.tx.us

**Farrar, Jessica C. (D, 148)**
Capitol Office Room 1N.8
P.O. Box 2910
Austin, TX 78768
P: (512) 463-0620
F: (512) 463-0894
E: Jessica.Farrar
    @house.state.tx.us

**Flynn, Dan (R, 2)**
Capitol Office Room 1N.10
P.O. Box 2910
Austin, TX 78768
P: (512) 463-0880
F: (512) 463-2188
E: Dan.Flynn
    @house.state.tx.us

**Frank, James (R, 69)**
Capitol Office Room E2.604
P.O. Box 2910
Austin, TX 78768
P: (512) 463-0534
F: (512) 463-8161
E: James.Frank
    @house.state.tx.us

**Frullo, John (R, 84)**
Capitol Office Room 4N.6
P.O. Box 2910
Austin, TX 78768
P: (512) 463-0676
F: (512) 463-0072
E: John.Frullo
    @house.state.tx.us

**Geren, Charlie (R, 99)**
Capitol Office Room GW.15
P.O. Box 2910
Austin, TX 78768
P: (512) 463-0610
F: (512) 463-8310
E: Charlie.Geren
    @house.state.tx.us

**Gervin-Hawkins, Barbara
    (D, 120)***
Capitol Office Room E1.208
P.O. Box 2910
Austin, TX 78768
P: (512) 463-0708
F: (512) 463-7071

**Giddings, Helen (D, 109)**
Capitol Office Room GW.11
P.O. Box 2910
Austin, TX 78768
P: (512) 463-0953
F: (512) 463-5887
E: Helen.Giddings
    @house.state.tx.us

**Goldman, Craig (R, 97)**
Capitol Office Room E2.606
P.O. Box 2910
Austin, TX 78768
P: (512) 463-0608
F: (512) 463-8342
E: Craig.Goldman
    @house.state.tx.us

**Gonzales, Larry (R, 52)**
Capitol Office Room E2.418
P.O. Box 2910
Austin, TX 78768
P: (512) 463-0670
F: (512) 463-1469
E: Larry.Gonzales
    @house.state.tx.us

**Gonzalez, Mary (D, 75)**
Capitol Office Room E2.204
P.O. Box 2910
Austin, TX 78768
P: (512) 463-0613
F: (512) 463-1237
E: Mary.Gonzalez
    @house.state.tx.us

**Gooden, Lance (R, 4)**
Capitol Office Room E1.204
P.O. Box 2910
Austin, TX 78768
P: (512) 463-2040
E: Lance.Gooden
    @house.state.tx.us

**Guerra, Robert (D, 41)**
Capitol Office Room E2.818
P.O. Box 2910
Austin, TX 78768
P: (512) 463-0578
F: (512) 463-1482
E: Bobby.Guerra
    @house.state.tx.us

**Guillen, Ryan (D, 31)**
Capitol Office Room 1W.3
P.O. Box 2910
Austin, TX 78768
P: (512) 463-0416
F: (512) 463-1012
E: Ryan.Guillen
    @house.state.tx.us

**Gutierrez, Roland (D, 119)**
Capitol Office Room GN.7
P.O. Box 2910
Austin, TX 78768
P: (512) 463-0452
F: (512) 463-1447
E: Roland.Gutierrez
    @house.state.tx.us

**Hefner, Cole (R, 5)***
Capitol Office Room E1.416
P.O. Box 2190
Austin, TX 78768
P: (512) 463-0271
F: (512) 463-1515
E: cole.hefner
    @house.state.tx.us

**Hernandez, Ana E. (D, 143)**
Capitol Office Room 4S.3
P.O. Box 2910
Austin, TX 78768
P: (512) 463-0614
F: (512) 463-0612
E: Ana.Hernandez
    @house.state.tx.us

# Texas

**Herrero, Abel (D, 34)**
Capitol Office Room 4S.6
P.O. Box 2910
Austin, TX 78768
P: (512) 463-0462
F: (512) 463-1705
E: Abel.Herrero
    @house.state.tx.us

**Hinojosa, Gina (D, 48)***
Capitol Office Room E2.316
P.O. Box 2910
Austin, TX 78768
P: (512) 463-0668
F: (512) 463-0957
E: gina.hinojosa
    @house.state.tx.us

**Holland, Justin (R, 33)***
Capitol Office Room E2.804
P.O. Box 2910
Austin, TX 78768
P: (512) 463-0484
F: (512) 463-7834
E: justin.holland
    @house.state.tx.us

**Howard, Donna (D, 48)**
Capitol Office Room E1.504
P.O. Box 2910
Austin, TX 78768
P: (512) 463-0631
F: (512) 463-0901
E: Donna.Howard
    @house.state.tx.us

**Huberty, Daniel G. (R, 127)**
Capitol Office Room E2.408
P.O. Box 2910
Austin, TX 78768
P: (512) 463-0520
F: (512) 463-1606
E: Daniel.Huberty
    @house.state.tx.us

**Hunter, Todd A. (R, 32)**
Capitol Office Room 1W.11
P.O. Box 2910
Austin, TX 78768
P: (512) 463-0672
E: Todd.Hunter
    @house.state.tx.us

**Isaac, Jason (R, 45)**
Capitol Office Room E1.320
P.O. Box 2910
Austin, TX 78768
P: (512) 463-0647
F: (512) 463-3573
E: Jason.Isaac
    @house.state.tx.us

**Israel, Celia (D, 50)**
Capitol Office Room E2.212
P.O. Box 2910
Austin, TX 78768
P: (512) 463-0821
E: Celia.Israel
    @house.state.tx.us

**Johnson, Eric (D, 100)**
Capitol Office Room 1N.7
P.O. Box 2910
Austin, TX 78768
P: (512) 463-0586
F: (512) 463-8147
E: Eric.Johnson
    @house.state.tx.us

**Johnson, Jarvis (D, 139)**
Capitol Office Room E1.424
P.O. Box 2910
Austin, TX 78768
P: (512) 463-0554
F: (512) 463-8380
E: jarvis.johnson
    @house.state.tx.us

**Kacal, Kyle (R, 12)**
Capitol Office Room E2.412
P.O. Box 2910
Austin, TX 78768
P: (512) 463-0412
F: (512) 463-9059
E: Kyle.Kacal
    @house.state.tx.us

**Keough, Mark (R, 15)**
Capitol Office Room E2.402
P.O. Box 2910
Austin, TX 78768
P: (512) 463-0797
F: (512) 463-0898
E: Mark.Keough
    @house.state.tx.us

**King, Ken (R, 88)**
Capitol Office Room E2.410
P.O. Box 2910
Austin, TX 78768
P: (512) 463-0736
F: (512) 463-0211
E: Ken.King
    @house.state.tx.us

**King, Phil (R, 61)**
Capitol Office Room 1N.5
P.O. Box 2910
Austin, TX 78768
P: (512) 463-0738
F: (512) 463-1957
E: Phil.King
    @house.state.tx.us

**King, Tracy O. (D, 80)**
Capitol Office Room GW.16
P.O. Box 2910
Austin, TX 78768
P: (512) 463-0194
F: (512) 463-1220
E: Tracy.King
    @house.state.tx.us

**Klick, Stephanie (R, 91)**
Capitol Office Room E2.904
P.O. Box 2910
Austin, TX 78768
P: (512) 463-0599
F: (512) 463-0751
E: Stephanie.Klick
    @house.state.tx.us

**Koop, Linda (R, 102)**
Capitol Office Room E1.406
P.O. Box 2910
Austin, TX 78768
P: (512) 463-0454
F: (512) 463-1121
E: Linda.Koop
    @house.state.tx.us

**Krause, Matt (R, 93)**
Capitol Office Room E2.214
P.O. Box 2910
Austin, TX 78768
P: (512) 463-0562
F: (512) 463-2053
E: Matt.Krause
    @house.state.tx.us

**Kuempel, John (R, 44)**
Capitol Office Room E2.422
P.O. Box 2910
Austin, TX 78768
P: (512) 463-0602
F: (512) 480-0391
E: John.Kuempel
    @house.state.tx.us

**Lambert, Stan (R, 71)***
Capitol Office Room E2.820
P.O. Box 2910
Austin, TX 78768
P: (512) 463-0718
F: (512) 463-0994
E: stan.lambert
    @house.state.tx.us

**Landgraf, Brooks (R, 81)**
Capitol Office Room E1.312
P.O. Box 2910
Austin, TX 78768
P: (512) 463-0546
F: (512) 463-8067
E: Brooks.Landgraf
    @house.state.tx.us

**Lang, Mike (R, 60)***
Capitol Office Room E1.410
P.O. Box 2910
Austin, TX 78768
P: (512) 463-0656
E: mike.lang
    @house.state.tx.us

**Larson, Lyle T. (R, 122)**
Capitol Office Room E2.406
P.O. Box 2910
Austin, TX 78768
P: (512) 463-0646
F: (512) 463-0893
E: Lyle.Larson
    @house.state.tx.us

**Laubenberg, Jodie (R, 89)**
Capitol Office Room 1W.4
P.O. Box 2910
Austin, TX 78768
P: (512) 463-0186
F: (512) 463-5896
E: Jodie.Laubenberg
    @house.state.tx.us

**Leach, Jeff (R, 67)**
Capitol Office Room GN.9
P.O. Box 2910
Austin, TX 78768
P: (512) 463-0544
F: (512) 463-9974
E: Jeff.Leach
    @house.state.tx.us

**Longoria, Oscar (D, 35)**
Capitol Office Room E1.510
P.O. Box 2910
Austin, TX 78768
P: (512) 463-0645
F: (512) 463-0559
E: Oscar.Longoria
    @house.state.tx.us

**Lozano, Jose Manuel (R, 43)**
Capitol Office Room GN.11
P.O. Box 2910
Austin, TX 78768
P: (512) 463-0463
F: (512) 463-1765
E: JoseManuel.Lozano
    @house.state.tx.us

**Lucio III, Eddie (D, 38)**
Capitol Office Room GN.8
P.O. Box 2910
Austin, TX 78768
P: (512) 463-0606
F: (512) 463-0660
E: Eddie.Lucio
    @house.state.tx.us

**Martinez, Armando (D, 39)**
Capitol Office Room 4N.4
P.O. Box 2910
Austin, TX 78768
P: (512) 463-0530
F: (512) 463-0849
E: mando.martinez
@house.texas.gov

**Metcalf, Will (R, 16)**
Capitol Office Room E1.314
P.O. Box 2910
Austin, TX 78768
P: (512) 463-0726
F: (512) 463-8428
E: Will.Metcalf
@house.state.tx.us

**Meyer, Morgan (R, 108)**
Capitol Office Room E1.318
P.O. Box 2910
Austin, TX 78768
P: (512) 463-0367
F: (512) 463-0078
E: Morgan.Meyer
@house.state.tx.us

**Miller, Rick (R, 26)**
Capitol Office Room E2.822
P.O. Box 2910
Austin, TX 78768
P: (512) 463-0710
F: (512) 463-0711
E: Rick.Miller
@house.state.tx.us

**Minjarez, Ina (D, 124)**
Capitol Office Room E2.312
P.O. Box 2910
Austin, TX 78768
P: (512) 463-0634
F: (512) 463-7668
E: Ina.Minjarez
@house.state.tx.us

**Moody, Joseph (D, 78)**
Capitol Office Room E1.420
P.O. Box 2910
Austin, TX 78768
P: (512) 463-0728
F: (512) 463-0397
E: Joseph.Moody
@house.state.tx.us

**Morrison, Geanie (R, 30)**
Capitol Office Room 3S.2
P.O. Box 2910
Austin, TX 78768
P: (512) 463-0456
F: (512) 463-0158
E: Geanie.Morrison
@house.state.tx.us

**Munoz Jr., Sergio (D, 36)**
Capitol Office Room 4S.4
P.O. Box 2910
Austin, TX 78768
P: (512) 463-0704
F: (512) 463-5364
E: Sergio.Munoz
@house.state.tx.us

**Murphy, Jim (R, 133)**
Capitol Office Room E1.506
P.O. Box 2910
Austin, TX 78768
P: (512) 463-0514
F: (512) 463-8715
E: Jim.Murphy
@house.state.tx.us

**Murr, Andrew S. (R, 53)**
Capitol Office Room E1.306
P.O. Box 2910
Austin, TX 78768
P: (512) 463-0536
F: (512) 463-1449
E: Andrew.Murr
@house.state.tx.us

**Neave, Victoria (D, 107)***
Capitol Office Room E1.216
P.O. Box 2910
Austin, TX 78768
P: (512) 463-0244
F: (512) 463-9967
E: victoria.neave
@house.state.tx.us

**Nevarez, Poncho (D, 74)**
Capitol Office Room E1.508
P.O. Box 2910
Austin, TX 78768
P: (512) 463-0566
F: (512) 463-0220
E: Poncho.Nevarez
@house.state.tx.us

**Oliveira, Rene O. (D, 37)**
Capitol Office Room 3N.06
P.O. Box 2910
Austin, TX 78768
P: (512) 463-0640
F: (512) 463-8186
E: Rene.Oliveira
@house.state.tx.us

**Oliverson, Tom (R, 130)***
Capitol Office Room E2.720
P.O. Box 2910
Austin, TX 78768
P: (512) 463-0661
F: (512) 463-4130
E: tom.oliverson
@house.state.tx.us

**Ortega, Evelina (D, 77)***
Capitol Office Room E2.704
P.O. Box 2910
Austin, TX 78768
P: (512) 463-0638
F: (512) 463-8908
E: evelina.ortega
@house.state.tx.us

**Paddie, Chris (R, 9)**
Capitol Office Room E2.502
P.O. Box 2910
Austin, TX 78768
P: (512) 463-0556
F: (512) 463-5896
E: Chris.Paddie
@house.state.tx.us

**Parker, Tan (R, 63)**
Capitol Office Room 4S.2
P.O. Box 2910
Austin, TX 78768
P: (512) 463-0688
F: (512) 480-0694
E: Tan.Parker
@house.state.tx.us

**Paul, Dennis (R, 129)**
Capitol Office Room E2.814
P.O. Box 2910
Austin, TX 78768
P: (512) 463-0734
F: (512) 479-6955
E: Dennis.Paul
@house.state.tx.us

**Perez, Mary Ann (D, 144)**
Capitol Office Room E1.212
P.O. Box 2910
Austin, TX 78768
P: (512) 463-0460
F: (512) 463-0763
E: MaryAnn.Perez
@house.state.tx.us

**Phelan, Dade (R, 21)**
Capitol Office Room E1.324
P.O. Box 2910
Austin, TX 78768
P: (512) 463-0706
F: (512) 463-1861
E: Dade.Phelan
@house.state.tx.us

**Phillips, Larry (R, 62)**
Capitol Office Room 4N.7
P.O. Box 2910
Austin, TX 78768
P: (512) 463-0297
F: (512) 463-1561
E: Larry.Phillips
@house.state.tx.us

**Pickett, Joe C. (D, 79)**
Capitol Office Room 1W.05
P.O. Box 2910
Austin, TX 78768
P: (512) 463-0596
F: (512) 463-6504
E: Joe.Pickett
@house.state.tx.us

**Price, Walter (R, 87)**
Capitol Office Room E2.902
P.O. Box 2910
Austin, TX 78768
P: (512) 463-0470
E: Walter.Price
@house.state.tx.us

**Raney, John (R, 14)**
Capitol Office Room E2.808
P.O. Box 2910
Austin, TX 78768
P: (512) 463-0698
F: (512) 463-5109
E: John.Raney
@house.state.tx.us

**Raymond, Richard Pena (D, 42)**
Capitol Office Room 1W.2
P.O. Box 2910
Austin, TX 78768
P: (512) 463-0558
F: (512) 463-6296
E: Richard.Raymond
@house.state.tx.us

**Reynolds, Ron (D, 27)**
Capitol Office Room E2.308
P.O. Box 2910
Austin, TX 78768
P: (512) 463-0494
F: (512) 463-1403
E: Ron.Reynolds
@house.state.tx.us

**Rinaldi, Matt (R, 115)**
Capitol Office Room E2.508
P.O. Box 2910
Austin, TX 78768
P: (512) 463-0468
F: (512) 463-1044
E: Matt.Rinaldi
@house.state.tx.us

**Roberts, Kevin (R, 126)***
P.O. Box 2910
Austin, TX 78768
E: kevin.roberts
@house.state.tx.us

# Texas

**Rodriguez, Eddie (D, 51)**
Capitol Office Room 4S.5
P.O. Box 2910
Austin, TX 78768
P: (512) 463-0674
F: (512) 463-0314
E: Eddie.Rodriguez
@house.state.tx.us

**Rodriguez, Justin (D, 125)**
Capitol Office Room E2.306
P.O. Box 2910
Austin, TX 78768
P: (512) 463-0669
F: (512) 463-5074
E: Justin.Rodriguez
@house.state.tx.us

**Romero Jr., Ramon (D, 90)**
Capitol Office Room E2.210
P.O. Box 2910
Austin, TX 78768
P: (512) 463-0740
F: (512) 463-1075
E: Ramon.Romero
@house.state.tx.us

**Rose, Toni (D, 110)**
Capitol Office Room E2.310
P.O. Box 2910
Austin, TX 78768
P: (512) 463-0664
F: (512) 463-0476
E: Toni.Rose
@house.state.tx.us

**Sanford, Scott (R, 70)**
Capitol Office Room E2.322
P.O. Box 2910
Austin, TX 78768
P: (512) 463-0356
F: (512) 463-0701
E: Scott.Sanford
@house.state.tx.us

**Schaefer, Matt (R, 6)**
Capitol Office Room E2.510
P.O. Box 2910
Austin, TX 78768
P: (512) 463-0584
E: Matt.Schaefer
@house.state.tx.us

**Schofield, Mike (R, 132)**
Capitol Office Room E1.402
P.O. Box 2910
Austin, TX 78768
P: (512) 463-0528
F: (512) 463-7820
E: Mike.Schofield
@house.state.tx.us

**Schubert, Leighton (R, 13)**
Captiol Office Room E1.512
P.O. Box 2910
Austin, TX 78768
P: (512) 463-0600
F: (512) 463-5240
E: Leighton.Schubert
@house.state.tx.us

**Shaheen, Matt (R, 66)**
Capitol Office Room E2.208
P.O. Box 2910
Austin, TX 78768
P: (512) 463-0594
F: (512) 463-1021
E: Matt.Shaheen
@house.state.tx.us

**Sheffield, J.D. (R, 59)**
Capitol Office Room E2.810
P.O. Box 2910
Austin, TX 78768
P: (512) 463-0628
F: (512) 463-3644
E: JD.Sheffield
@house.state.tx.us

**Shine, Hugh (R, 55)***
Capitol Office Room E2.806
P.O. Box 2910
Austin, TX 78768
P: (512) 463-0630
F: (512) 463-0937
E: hugh.shine
@house.state.tx.us

**Simmons, Ron (R, 65)**
Capitol Office Room E2.608
P.O. Box 2910
Austin, TX 78768
P: (512) 463-0478
F: (512) 463-2089
E: Ron.Simmons
@house.state.tx.us

**Smithee, John T. (R, 86)**
Capitol Office Room 1W.10
P.O. Box 2910
Austin, TX 78768
P: (512) 463-0702
F: (512) 476-7016
E: John.Smithee
@house.state.tx.us

**Springer, Drew (R, 68)**
Capitol Office Room E2.706
P.O. Box 2910
Austin, TX 78768
P: (512) 463-0526
F: (512) 463-1011
E: Drew.Springer
@house.state.tx.us

**Stephenson, Phil (R, 85)**
Capitol Office Room E2.906
P.O. Box 2910
Austin, TX 78768
P: (512) 463-0604
F: (512) 463-5244
E: Phil.Stephenson
@house.state.tx.us

**Stickland, Jonathan (R, 92)**
Capitol Office Room E1.404
P.O. Box 2910
Austin, TX 78768
P: (512) 463-0522
F: (512) 463-9529
E: Jonathan.Stickland
@house.state.tx.us

**Straus, Joe (R, 121)**
Capitol Office Room 2W.13
P.O. Box 2910
Austin, TX 78768
P: (512) 463-1000
F: (512) 463-0675
E: Joe.Straus
@house.state.tx.us

**Stucky, Lynn (R, 64)***
Capitol Office Room E2.420
P.O. Box 2910
Austin, TX 78768
P: (512) 463-0582
F: (512) 463-0471
E: lynn.stucky
@house.state.tx.us

**Swanson, Valoree (R, 150)***
Capitol Office Room E2.802
P.O. Box 2910
Austin, TX 78768
P: (512) 463-0518
F: (512) 463-0941
E: valoree.swanson
@house.state.tx.us

**Thierry, Shawn (D, 146)***
P.O. Box 2910
Austin, TX 78768
E: shawn.thierry
@house.state.tx.us

**Thompson, Ed (R, 29)**
Capitol Office Room E2.506
P.O. Box 2910
Austin, TX 78768
P: (512) 463-0707
F: (512) 463-8717
E: Ed.Thompson
@house.state.tx.us

**Thompson, Senfronia (D, 141)**
Capitol Office Room 3S.6
P.O. Box 2910
Austin, TX 78768
P: (512) 463-0720
F: (512) 463-6306
E: Senfronia.Thompson
@house.state.tx.us

**Tinderholt, Tony (R, 94)**
Capitol Office Room E1.422
P.O. Box 2910
Austin, TX 78768
P: (512) 463-0624
F: (512) 463-8386
E: Tony.Tinderholt
@house.state.tx.us

**Turner, Chris (D, 101)**
Capitol Office Room E1.408
P.O. Box 2910
Austin, TX 78768
P: (512) 463-0574
F: (512) 463-1481
E: Chris.Turner
@house.state.tx.us

**Uresti, Tomas (D, 118)***
Capitol Office Room E2.712
P.O. Box 2910
Austin, TX 78768
P: (512) 463-0714
F: (512) 463-1458
E: tomas.uresti
@house.state.tx.us

**VanDeaver, Gary (R, 1)**
Capitol Office Room E1.310
P.O. Box 2910
Austin, TX 78768
P: (512) 463-0692
F: (512) 463-0902
E: Gary.VanDeaver
@house.state.tx.us

**Villalba, Jason (R, 114)**
Capitol Office Room E2.404
P.O. Box 2910
Austin, TX 78768
P: (512) 463-0576
F: (512) 463-7827
E: Jason.Villalba
@house.state.tx.us

**Vo, Hubert (D, 149)**
Capitol Office Room 4N.8
P.O. Box 2910
Austin, TX 78768
P: (512) 463-0568
F: (512) 463-0548
E: Hubert.Vo
@house.state.tx.us

**Walle, Armando Lucio (D, 140)**
Capitol Office Room GW.18
P.O. Box 2910
Austin, TX 78768
P: (512) 463-0924
F: (512) 463-1510
E: ArmandoLucio.Walle
@house.state.tx.us

**White, James E. (R, 19)**
Capitol Office Room GN.12
P.O. Box 2910
Austin, TX 78768
P: (512) 463-0490
F: (512) 463-9059
E: James.White
@house.state.tx.us

**Wilson, Terry (R, 20)\***
Capitol Office Room E2.702
P.O. Box 2910
Austin, TX 78768
P: (512) 463-0309
F: (512) 463-0049
E: terry.wilson
@house.state.tx.us

**Workman, Paul Daniel (R, 47)**
Capitol Office Room E1.304
P.O. Box 2910
Austin, TX 78768
P: (512) 463-0652
F: (512) 463-0565
E: PaulDaniel.Workman
@house.state.tx.us

**Wray, John (R, 10)**
Capitol Office Room E1.302
P.O. Box 2910
Austin, TX 78768
P: (512) 463-0516
F: (512) 463-1051
E: John.Wray
@house.state.tx.us

**Wu, Gene (D, 137)**
Capitol Office Room E2.718
P.O. Box 2910
Austin, TX 78768
P: (512) 463-0492
F: (512) 463-1182
E: Gene.Wu
@house.state.tx.us

**Zedler, Bill (R, 96)**
Capitol Office Room GS.2
P.O. Box 2910
Austin, TX 78768
P: (512) 463-0374
F: (512) 463-0364
E: Bill.Zedler
@house.state.tx.us

**Zerwas, John (R, 28)**
Capitol Office Room GW.17
P.O. Box 2910
Austin, TX 78768
P: (512) 463-0657
F: (512) 236-0713
E: John.Zerwas
@house.state.tx.us

# U.S. Virgin Islands

## Executive

### Governor
**The Honorable Kenneth Mapp (I)**
Governor
Government House
21-22 Kongens Gade
St. Thomas, VI 00802
P: (340) 774-0001
F: (340) 693-4374

### Lieutenant Governor
**The Honorable Osbert Potter (I)**
Lieutenant Governor
1331 Kings Street, Suite 101
St. Croix, VI 00802
P: (340) 773-6449
F: (340) 773-0330

### Secretary of State
*The U.S. Virgin Islands do not have the office of secretary of state. Some of the duties of the secretary of state are performed by the office of lieutenant governor.*

### Attorney General
**The Honorable Claude E. Walker**
(appointed)
Attorney General
34-38 Kronprinsdens Gade
GERS Building, 2nd Floor
St. Thomas, VI 00802
P: (340) 774-5666

### Auditor
**Mr. Steven G. Van Beverhoudt**
Inspector General
2315 Kronprindsens Gade #75
Charlotte Amalie
St. Thomas, VI 00802
P: (340) 774-3388
F: (340) 774-6431
E: svanbeverhoudt@viig.org

### Treasurer
**Mr. Valdamier Collens**
(appointed)
Treasury Division
2314 Kronprindsens Gade
St. Thomas, VI 00802
P: (340) 774-4750
F: (340) 776-4028

## Judiciary

### Supreme Court (GA)
**Ms. Veronica J. Handy**
Clerk of the Court
P.O. Box 590
St. Thomas, VI 00804
P: (340) 774-2237
F: (340) 774-2258

**The Honorable Rhys S. Hodge**
Chief Justice
**The Honorable Maria M. Cabret**
**The Honorable Ive Arlington Swan**

## Legislative

## Senate

### Senate President
**Senator Myron D. Jackson (D)**
Senate President
Capitol Building, Charlotte Amalie
P.O. Box 1690
St. Thomas, VI 00804
P: (340) 774-0880
F: (340) 693-3634
E: mjackson@legvi.org

### Vice President of the Senate
**Senator Janette Millin Young (D)**
Senate Vice President
Capitol Building, Charlotte Amalie
P.O. Box 1690
St. Thomas, VI 00804
P: (340) 774-0880
F: (340) 693-3634
E: jmyoung@legvi.org

### Secretary of the Senate
**Senator Janette Millin Young (D)**
Senate Vice President
Capitol Building, Charlotte Amalie
P.O. Box 1690
St. Thomas, VI 00804
P: (340) 774-0880
F: (340) 693-3634
E: jmyoung@legvi.org

## Members of the Senate

**Blyden, Marvin A. (D, STTHOMAS)**
Capitol Building, Charlotte Amalie
P.O. Box 1690
St. Thomas, VI 00804
P: (340) 774-0880
F: (340) 693-3639
E: mblyden@legvi.org

**DeGraff, Dwayne (I, STTHOMAS)\***
P.O. Box 1690
St. Thomas, VI 00804
P: (340) 774-0880
F: (340) 693-3634

**Forde, Jean (D, STTHOMAS)**
Capitol Building, Charlotte Amalie
P.O. Box 1690
St. Thomas, VI 00804
P: (340) 774-0880
F: (340) 693-3642
E: jforde@legvi.org

**Francis Jr., Novelle E. (D, STCROIX)**
#1 Lagoon Street Complex
Frederiksted
St. Croix, VI 00840
P: (340) 773-2424
F: (340) 712-2372
E: nfrancis@legvi.org

**Hansen, Alicia Chucky (I, STCROIX)\***
Legislature of the Virgin Islands
#1 Lagoon Street Complex,
Frederiksted
St. Croix, VI 00804
P: (340) 712-2269
F: (340) 712-2376
E: ahansen@legvi.org

**Jackson, Myron D. (D, STTHOMAS)**
Capitol Building, Charlotte Amalie
P.O. Box 1690
St. Thomas, VI 00804
P: (340) 774-0880
F: (340) 693-3634
E: mjackson@legvi.org

**James, Neville A. (D, STCROIX)**
#1 Lagoon Street Complex
Frederiksted
St. Croix, VI 00804
P: (340) 773-2424
F: (340) 712-2242
E: njames@legvi.org

**Nelson, Terrence "Positive" (ICM, STCROIX)**
#1 Lagoon Street Complex
Frederiksted
St. Croix, VI 00850
P: (340) 773-2424
F: (340) 712-2374
E: positivetimez@gmail.com

**Rivera-O'Reilly, Nellie (I, STCROIX)**
#1 Lagoon Street Complex
Frederiksted
St. Croix, VI 00840
P: (340) 773-2424
F: (340) 712-2378
E: teamnellie@gmail.com

**Roach, Tregenza (I, STTHOMAS)**
Capitol Building, Charlotte Amalie
P.O. Box 1690
St. Thomas, VI 00804
P: (340) 774-0880
F: (340) 693-3660
E: troach@legvi.org

**Sanes, Sammuel (D, STCROIX)**
#1 Lagoon Street Complex
Frederiksted
St. Croix, VI 00840
P: (340) 773-2424
F: (340) 712-2380
E: sammuelsanes@yahoo.com

**Smith, Brian A. (D, At-Large)**
P.O. Box 1690
St. Thomas, VI 00804
P: (340) 774-0880
F: (340) 693-3634

**Vialet, Kurt (D, STCROIX)**
#1 Lagoon Street Complex
Frederiksted
St. Croix, VI 00840
P: (340) 773-2424
F: (340) 712-2376
E: kvialet@legvi.org

**Young, Janette Millin**
  **(D, STTHOMAS)**
Capitol Building, Charlotte
Amalie
P.O. Box 1690
St. Thomas, VI 00804
P: (340) 774-0880
F: (340) 693-3634
E: jmyoung@legvi.org

# Utah

## Executive

### Governor

**The Honorable Gary R. Herbert (R)**
Governor
State Capitol, Suite 200
Salt Lake City, UT 84114
P: (801) 538-1000
F: (801) 538-1557

### Lieutenant Governor

**The Honorable Spencer J. Cox (R)**
Lieutenant Governor
P.O. Box 142325
Salt Lake City, UT 84114
P: (801) 538-1041
F: (801) 538-1133

### Secretary of State

*Utah does not have the office of secretary of state. Some of the duties of the secretary of state are performed by the office of the lieutenant governor.*

### Attorney General

**The Honorable Sean D. Reyes (R)**
Attorney General
State Capitol, Room 236
Salt Lake City, UT 84114
P: (801) 538-9600
F: (801) 538-1121
E: uag@utah.gov

### Treasurer

**The Honorable David Damschen (R)**
350 North State Street, Suite 180
P.O. Box 142315
Salt Lake City, UT 84114
P: (801) 538-1042
F: (801) 538-1042
E: sto@utah.gov

## Judiciary

### Supreme Court (MR)

**Vacant**
450 South State Street, 5th Floor
P.O. Box 140210
Salt Lake City, UT 84114
P: (801) 238-7974
F: (801) 578-3999

**The Honorable Matthew B. Durrant**
Chief Justice
**The Honorable Christine M. Durham**
**The Honorable Constandinos Himonas**
**The Honorable Thomas R. Lee**
**The Honorable John A. Pearce**

## Legislative Senate

### Senate President

**Senator Wayne Niederhauser (R)**
Senate President
320 State Capitol
P.O. Box 145115
Salt Lake City, UT 84114
P: (801) 538-1035
F: (801) 326-1475
E: wniederhauser @le.utah.gov

### Senate Majority Leader

**Senator Ralph Okerlund (R)**
Majority Leader
320 State Capitol
P.O. Box 145115
Salt Lake City, UT 84114
P: (801) 538-1035
F: (801) 326-1475
E: rokerlund@le.utah.gov

### Senate Minority Leader

**Senator Gene Davis (D)**
Minority Leader
320 State Capitol
P.O. Box 145115
Salt Lake City, UT 84114
P: (801) 538-1035
F: (801) 326-1475
E: gdavis@le.utah.gov

## Secretary of the Senate

**Ms. Leslie D. McLean**
Secretary of the Senate
320 State Capitol
P.O. Box 145115
Salt Lake City, UT 84114
P: (801) 538-1458
F: (801) 326-1475
E: lmclean@utahsenate.org

## Members of the Senate

**Adams, Stuart (R, 22)**
320 State Capitol
P.O. Box 145115
Salt Lake City, UT 84114
P: (801) 538-1035
F: (801) 326-1475
E: jsadams@le.utah.gov

**Anderegg, Jacob L. (R, 13)**
320 State Capitol
Po Box 145115
Salt Lake City, UT 84114
P: (801) 538-1035
F: (801) 326-1544
E: janderegg@le.utah.gov

**Bramble, Curtis S. (R, 16)**
320 State Capitol
P.O. Box 145115
Salt Lake City, UT 84114
P: (801) 538-1035
F: (801) 326-1475
E: curt@cbramble.com

**Buxton, D. Gregg (R, 20)**
320 State Capitol
PO Box 145115
Salt Lake City, UT 84114
P: (801) 538-1035
F: (801) 326-1475
E: gbuxton@le.utah.gov

**Christensen, Allen M. (R, 19)**
320 State Capitol
P.O. Box 145115
Salt Lake City, UT 84114
P: (801) 538-1035
F: (801) 326-1475
E: achristensen@le.utah.gov

**Dabakis, Jim (D, 2)**
320 State Capitol
P.O. Box 145115
Salt Lake City, UT 84114
P: (801) 538-1035
F: (801) 326-1475
E: jdabakis@le.utah.gov

**Davis, Gene (D, 3)**
320 State Capitol
P.O. Box 145115
Salt Lake City, UT 84114
P: (801) 538-1035
F: (801) 326-1475
E: gdavis@le.utah.gov

**Dayton, Margaret (R, 15)**
320 State Capitol
P.O. Box 145115
Salt Lake City, UT 84114
P: (801) 538-1035
F: (801) 326-1475
E: mdayton@le.utah.gov

**Escamilla, Luz (D, 1)**
320 State Capitol
P.O. Box 145115
Salt Lake City, UT 84114
P: (801) 538-1035
F: (801) 326-1475
E: lescamilla@le.utah.gov

**Fillmore, Lincoln (R, 10)**
320 State Capitol
P.O. Box 145115
Salt Lake City, UT 84114
P: (801) 538-1035
F: (801) 326-1475
E: lfillmore@le.utah.gov

**Harper, Wayne A. (R, 6)**
320 State Capitol
P.O. Box 145115
Salt Lake City, UT 84114
P: (801) 538-1035
F: (801) 326-1475
E: wharper@le.utah.gov

**Hemmert, Daniel (R, 14)\***
320 State Capitol
PO Box 145115
Salt Lake City, UT 84114
P: (801) 538-1035
F: (801) 326-1475
E: dhemmert@le.utah.gov

**Henderson, Deidre M. (R, 7)**
320 State Capitol
P.O. Box 145115
Salt Lake City, UT 84114
P: (801) 538-1035
F: (801) 326-1475
E: dhenderson@le.utah.gov

**Hillyard, Lyle W. (R, 25)**
320 State Capitol
P.O. Box 145115
Salt Lake City, UT 84114
P: (801) 538-1035
F: (801) 326-1475
E: lhillyard@le.utah.gov

**Hinkins, David P. (R, 27)**
320 State Capitol
P.O. Box 145115
Salt Lake City, UT 84114
P: (801) 538-1035
F: (801) 326-1475
E: dhinkins@le.utah.gov

**Ipson, Don L. (R, 29)**
320 State Capitol
Po Box 145115
Salt Lake City, UT 84114
P: (801) 538-1035
F: (801) 326-1475
E: dipson@le.utah.gov

**Iwamoto, Jani (D, 4)**
320 State Capitol
P.O. Box 145115
Salt Lake City, UT 84114
P: (801) 538-1035
F: (801) 326-1475
E: jiwamoto@le.utah.gov

**Knudson, Peter C. (R, 17)**
320 State Capitol
P.O. Box 145115
Salt Lake City, UT 84114
P: (801) 538-1035
F: (801) 326-1475
E: pknudson@le.utah.gov

**Mayne, Karen (D, 5)**
320 State Capitol
P.O. Box 145115
Salt Lake City, UT 84114
P: (801) 538-1035
F: (801) 326-1475
E: kmayne@le.utah.gov

**Millner, Ann (R, 18)**
320 State Capitol
P.O. Box 145115
Salt Lake City, UT 84114
P: (801) 538-1035
F: (801) 326-1475
E: amillner@le.utah.gov

**Niederhauser, Wayne (R, 9)**
320 State Capitol
P.O. Box 145115
Salt Lake City, UT 84114
P: (801) 538-1035
F: (801) 326-1475
E: wniederhauser
  @le.utah.gov

**Okerlund, Ralph (R, 24)**
320 State Capitol
P.O. Box 145115
Salt Lake City, UT 84114
P: (801) 538-1035
F: (801) 326-1475
E: rokerlund@le.utah.gov

**Shiozawa, Brian E. (R, 8)**
320 State Capitol
P.O. Box 145115
Salt Lake City, UT 84114
P: (801) 538-1035
F: (801) 326-1475
E: bshiozawa@le.utah.gov

**Stephenson, Howard A. (R, 11)**
320 State Capitol
P.O. Box 145115
Salt Lake City, UT 84114
P: (801) 538-1035
F: (801) 326-1475
E: hstephenson@le.utah.gov

**Stevenson, Jerry W. (R, 21)**
320 State Capitol
P.O. Box 145115
Salt Lake City, UT 84114
P: (801) 538-1035
F: (801) 326-1475
E: jwstevenson@le.utah.gov

**Thatcher, Daniel W. (R, 12)**
320 State Capitol
P.O. Box 145115
Salt Lake City, UT 84114
P: (801) 538-1035
F: (801) 326-1475
E: dthatcher@le.utah.gov

**Van Tassell, Kevin (R, 26)**
320 State Capitol
P.O. Box 145115
Salt Lake City, UT 84114
P: (801) 538-1035
F: (801) 326-1475
E: kvantassell@le.utah.gov

**Vickers, Evan J. (R, 28)**
320 State Capitol
P.O. Box 145115
Salt Lake City, UT 84114
P: (801) 538-1035
F: (801) 326-1475
E: evickers@le.utah.gov

**Weiler, Todd (R, 23)**
320 State Capitol
P.O. Box 145115
Salt Lake City, UT 84114
P: (801) 538-1035
F: (801) 326-1475
E: tweiler@le.utah.gov

# House
## Speaker of the House
**Representative Gregory H. Hughes (R)**
Speaker of the House
350 North State, Suite 350
P.O. Box 145030
Salt Lake City, UT 84114
P: (801) 538-1029
F: (801) 326-1544
E: greghughes@le.utah.gov

## House Majority Leader
**Representative Brad R. Wilson (R)**
Majority Leader
350 North State, Suite 350
P.O. Box 145030
Salt Lake City, UT 84114
P: (801) 538-1029
F: (801) 326-1544
E: bradwilson@le.utah.gov

## House Minority Leader
**Representative Brian S. King (D)**
Minority Leader
350 North State, Suite 350
P.O. Box 145030
Salt Lake City, UT 84114
P: (801) 538-1029
F: (801) 326-1544
E: briansking@le.utah.gov

## Clerk of the House
**Ms. Sandy D. Tenney**
Chief Clerk of the House
350 North State, Suite 350
P.O. Box 145030
Salt Lake City, UT 84114
P: (801) 538-1029
F: (801) 326-1544
E: stenney@le.utah.gov

## Members of the House
**Albrecht, Carl (R, 70)\***
350 North State, Suite 350
Po Box 145030
Salt Lake City, UT 84114
P: (801) 538-1029
F: (801) 326-1544
E: carlalbrecht@le.utah.gov

**Arent, Patrice (D, 36)**
350 North State, Suite 350
P.O. Box 145030
Salt Lake City, UT 84114
P: (801) 538-1029
F: (801) 326-1544
E: parent@le.utah.gov

**Barlow, Stewart (R, 17)**
350 North State, Suite 350
P.O. Box 145030
Salt Lake City, UT 84114
P: (801) 538-1029
F: (801) 326-1544
E: sbarlow@le.utah.gov

**Briscoe, Joel K. (D, 25)**
350 North State, Suite 350
P.O. Box 145030
Salt Lake City, UT 84114
P: (801) 538-1029
F: (801) 326-1544
E: jbriscoe@le.utah.gov

**Brooks, Walt (R, 75)\***
350 North State, Suite 350
Po Box 145030
Salt Lake City, UT 84114
P: (801) 538-1029
F: (801) 326-1544
E: wbrooks@le.utah.gov

**Chavez-Houck, Rebecca (D, 24)**
350 North State, Suite 350
P.O. Box 145030
Salt Lake City, UT 84114
P: (801) 538-1029
F: (801) 326-1544
E: rchouck@le.utah.gov

**Chew, Scott H. (R, 55)**
350 North State, Suite 350
P.O. Box 145030
Salt Lake City, UT 84114
P: (801) 538-1029
F: (801) 326-1544
E: scottchew@le.utah.gov

**Christensen, LaVar (R, 32)**
350 North State, Suite 350
P.O. Box 145030
Salt Lake City, UT 84114
P: (801) 538-1029
F: (801) 326-1544
E: lavarchristensen
  @le.utah.gov

**Christofferson, Kay J. (R, 56)**
350 North State, Suite 350
P.O. Box 145030
Salt Lake City, UT 84114
P: (801) 538-1029
F: (801) 326-1544
E: kchristofferson
  @le.utah.gov

**Coleman, Kim (R, 42)**
350 North State, Suite 350
P.O. Box 145030
Salt Lake City, UT 84114
P: (801) 538-1029
F: (801) 326-1544
E: kimcoleman@le.utah.gov

**Cutler, Bruce R. (R, 44)**
350 North State, Suite 350
P.O. Box 145030
Salt Lake City, UT 84114
P: (801) 538-1029
F: (801) 326-1544
E: brucecutler@le.utah.gov

# Utah

**Daw, Brad M. (R, 60)**
350 North State, Suite 350
P.O. Box 145030
Salt Lake City, UT 84114
P: (801) 538-1029
F: (801) 326-1544
E: bdaw@le.utah.gov

**Duckworth, Susan (D, 22)**
350 North State, Suite 350
P.O. Box 145030
Salt Lake City, UT 84114
P: (801) 538-1029
F: (801) 326-1544
E: sduckworth@le.utah.gov

**Dunnigan, James A. (R, 39)**
350 North State, Suite 350
P.O. Box 145030
Salt Lake City, UT 84114
P: (801) 538-1029
F: (801) 326-1544
E: jdunnigan@le.utah.gov

**Edwards, Rebecca (R, 20)**
350 North State, Suite 350
P.O. Box 145030
Salt Lake City, UT 84114
P: (801) 538-1029
F: (801) 326-1544
E: beckyedwards@le.utah.gov

**Eliason, Steve (R, 45)**
350 North State, Suite 350
P.O. Box 145030
Salt Lake City, UT 84114
P: (801) 538-1029
F: (801) 326-1544
E: seliason@le.utah.gov

**Fawson, Justin L. (R, 7)**
350 North State, Suite 350
P.O. Box 145030
Salt Lake City, UT 84114
P: (801) 538-1029
F: (801) 326-1544
E: justinfawson@le.utah.gov

**Froerer, Gage (R, 8)**
350 North State, Suite 350
P.O. Box 145030
Salt Lake City, UT 84114
P: (801) 538-1029
F: (801) 326-1544
E: gfroerer@le.utah.gov

**Gardiner, Adam (R, 43)\***
350 North State, Suite 350
Po Box 145030
Salt Lake City, UT 84114
P: (801) 537-1029
F: (801) 326-1544
E: adamgardiner@le.utah.gov

**Gibson, Francis D. (R, 65)**
350 North State, Suite 350
P.O. Box 145030
Salt Lake City, UT 84114
P: (801) 538-1029
F: (801) 326-1544
E: fgibson@le.utah.gov

**Greene, Brian M. (R, 57)**
350 North State, Suite 350
P.O. Box 145030
Salt Lake City, UT 84114
P: (801) 538-1029
F: (801) 326-1544
E: bgreene@le.utah.gov

**Grover, Keith (R, 61)**
350 North State, Suite 350
P.O. Box 145030
Salt Lake City, UT 84114
P: (801) 538-1029
F: (801) 326-1544
E: keithgrover@le.utah.gov

**Hall, Craig (R, 33)**
350 North State, Suite 350
P.O. Box 145030
Salt Lake City, UT 84114
P: (801) 538-1029
F: (801) 326-1544
E: chall@le.utah.gov

**Handy, Stephen G. (R, 16)**
350 North State, Suite 350
P.O. Box 145030
Salt Lake City, UT 84114
P: (801) 538-1029
F: (801) 326-1544
E: stevehandy@le.utah.gov

**Hawkes, Timothy D. (R, 18)**
350 North State, Suite 350
P.O. Box 145030
Salt Lake City, UT 84114
P: (801) 538-1029
F: (801) 326-1544
E: thawkes@le.utah.gov

**Hemingway, Lynn N. (D, 40)**
350 North State, Suite 350
P.O. Box 145030
Salt Lake City, UT 84114
P: (801) 538-1029
F: (801) 326-1544
E: lhemingway@le.utah.gov

**Hollins, Sandra (D, 23)**
350 North State, Suite 350
P.O. Box 145030
Salt Lake City, UT 84114
P: (801) 538-1029
F: (801) 326-1544
E: shollins@le.utah.gov

**Hughes, Gregory H. (R, 51)**
350 North State, Suite 350
P.O. Box 145030
Salt Lake City, UT 84114
P: (801) 538-1029
F: (801) 326-1544
E: greghughes@le.utah.gov

**Hutchings, Eric K. (R, 38)**
350 North State, Suite 350
P.O. Box 145030
Salt Lake City, UT 84114
P: (801) 538-1029
F: (801) 326-1544
E: ehutchings@le.utah.gov

**Ivory, Ken (R, 47)**
350 North State, Suite 350
P.O. Box 145030
Salt Lake City, UT 84114
P: (801) 538-1029
F: (801) 326-1544
E: kivory@le.utah.gov

**Kennedy, Michael S. (R, 27)**
350 North State, Suite 350
P.O. Box 145030
Salt Lake City, UT 84114
P: (801) 538-1029
F: (801) 326-1544
E: mikekennedy@le.utah.gov

**King, Brian S. (D, 28)**
350 North State, Suite 350
P.O. Box 145030
Salt Lake City, UT 84114
P: (801) 538-1029
F: (801) 326-1544
E: briansking@le.utah.gov

**Knotwell, John (R, 52)**
350 North State, Suite 350
P.O. Box 145030
Salt Lake City, UT 84114
P: (801) 538-1029
F: (801) 326-1544
E: jknotwell@le.utah.gov

**Kwan, Karen (D, 34)\***
350 North State, Suite 350
Po Box 145030
Salt Lake City, UT 84114
P: (801) 538-1029
F: (801) 326-1544
E: kkwan@le.utah.gov

**Last, Bradley G. (R, 71)**
350 North State, Suite 350
P.O. Box 145030
Salt Lake City, UT 84114
P: (801) 538-1029
F: (801) 326-1544
E: blast@le.utah.gov

**Lisonbee, Karianne (R, 14)\***
350 North State, Suite 350
Po Box 145030
Salt Lake City, UT 84114
P: (801) 538-1029
F: (801) 326-1544
E: karilisonbee@le.utah.gov

**Maloy, A. Cory (R, 6)\***
350 North State, Suite 350
Po Box 145030
Salt Lake City, UT 84114
P: (801) 538-1029
F: (801) 326-1544
E: corymaloy@le.utah.gov

**McCay, Daniel (R, 41)**
350 North State, Suite 350
P.O. Box 145030
Salt Lake City, UT 84114
P: (801) 538-1029
F: (801) 326-1544
E: dmccay@le.utah.gov

**McKell, Mike K. (R, 66)**
350 North State, Suite 350
P.O. Box 145030
Salt Lake City, UT 84114
P: (801) 538-1029
F: (801) 326-1544
E: mmckell@le.utah.gov

**Miles, Kelly B. (R, 11)\***
350 North State, Suite 350
Po Box 145030
Salt Lake City, UT 84114
P: (801) 538-1029
F: (801) 326-1544
E: kmiles@le.utah.gov

**Moss, Jefferson (R, 2)\***
350 North State, Suite 350
PO Box 145030
Salt Lake City, UT 84114
P: (801) 538-1029
F: (801) 326-1544
E: jeffersonmoss
@le.utah.gov

**Nelson, Merrill F. (R, 68)**
350 North State, Suite 350
P.O. Box 145030
Salt Lake City, UT 84114
P: (801) 538-1029
F: (801) 326-1544
E: mnelson@le.utah.gov

**Noel, Michael E. (R, 73)**
350 North State, Suite 350
P.O. Box 145030
Salt Lake City, UT 84114
P: (801) 538-1029
F: (801) 326-1544
E: mnoel@kanab.net

**Owens, Derrin (R, 58)**
350 North State, Suite 350
P.O. Box 145030
Salt Lake City, UT 84114
P: (801) 538-1029
F: (801) 326-1544
E: derrinowens@le.utah.gov

**Perry, Lee B. (R, 29)**
350 North State, Suite 350
P.O. Box 145030
Salt Lake City, UT 84114
P: (801) 538-1029
F: (801) 326-1544
E: leeperry@le.utah.gov

**Peterson, Jeremy A. (R, 9)**
350 North State, Suite 350
P.O. Box 145030
Salt Lake City, UT 84114
P: (801) 538-1029
F: (801) 326-1544
E: jeremyapeterson
   @le.utah.gov

**Peterson, Val (R, 59)**
350 North State, Suite 350
P.O. Box 145030
Salt Lake City, UT 84114
P: (801) 538-1029
F: (801) 326-1544
E: vpeterson@le.utah.gov

**Pitcher, Dixon M. (R, 10)**
350 North State, Suite 350
P.O. Box 145030
Salt Lake City, UT 84114
P: (801) 538-1029
F: (801) 326-1475
E: dpitcher@le.utah.gov

**Potter, Val (R, 3)***
350 North State, Suite 350
PO Box 145030
Salt Lake City, UT 84114
P: (801) 538-1029
F: (801) 326-1544
E: valpotter@le.utah.gov

**Poulson, Marie H. (D, 46)**
350 North State, Suite 350
P.O. Box 145030
Salt Lake City, UT 84114
P: (801) 538-1029
F: (801) 326-1544
E: mariepoulson@le.utah.gov

**Pulsipher, Susan (R, 50)***
350 North State, Suite 350
Po Box 145030
Salt Lake City, UT 84114
P: (801) 538-1029
F: (801) 326-1544
E: susanpulsipher
   @le.utah.gov

**Quinn, Tim (R, 54)***
350 North State, Suite 350
Po Box 145030
Salt Lake City, UT 84114
P: (801) 538-1029
F: (801) 326-1544
E: tquinn@le.utah.gov

**Ray, Paul (R, 13)**
350 North State, Suite 350
P.O. Box 145030
Salt Lake City, UT 84114
P: (801) 538-1029
F: (801) 326-1544
E: pray@le.utah.gov

**Redd, Edward H. (R, 4)**
350 North State, Suite 350
P.O. Box 145030
Salt Lake City, UT 84114
P: (801) 538-1029
F: (801) 326-1544
E: eredd@le.utah.gov

**Roberts, Marc K. (R, 67)**
350 North State, Suite 350
P.O. Box 145030
Salt Lake City, UT 84114
P: (801) 538-1029
F: (801) 326-1544
E: mroberts@le.utah.gov

**Romero, Angela (D, 26)**
350 North State, Suite 350
P.O. Box 145030
Salt Lake City, UT 84114
P: (801) 538-1029
F: (801) 326-1544
E: angelaromero@le.utah.gov

**Sagers, Douglas (R, 21)**
350 North State, Suite 350
P.O. Box 145030
Salt Lake City, UT 84114
P: (801) 538-1029
F: (801) 326-1544
E: dougsagers@le.utah.gov

**Sandall, Scott (R, 1)**
350 North State, Suite 350
P.O. Box 145030
Salt Lake City, UT 84114
P: (801) 538-1029
F: (801) 326-1544
E: ssandall@le.utah.gov

**Sanpei, Dean (R, 63)**
350 North State, Suite 350
P.O. Box 145030
Salt Lake City, UT 84114
P: (801) 538-1029
F: (801) 326-1544
E: dsanpei@le.utah.gov

**Schultz, Mike (R, 12)**
350 North State, Suite 350
P.O. Box 145030
Salt Lake City, UT 84114
P: (801) 538-1029
F: (801) 326-1544
E: mikeschultz@le.utah.gov

**Snow, V.Lowry (R, 74)**
350 North State, Suite 350
P.O. Box 145030
Salt Lake City, UT 84114
P: (801) 538-1029
F: (801) 326-1544
E: vlsnow@le.utah.gov

**Spackman Moss, Carol
(D, 37)**
350 North State, Suite 350
P.O. Box 145030
Salt Lake City, UT 84114
P: (801) 538-1029
F: (801) 326-1544
E: csmoss@le.utah.gov

**Spendlove, Robert (R, 49)**
350 North State, Suite 350
P.O. Box 145030
Salt Lake City, UT 84114
P: (801) 538-1029
F: (801) 326-1544
E: rspendlove@le.utah.gov

**Stanard, Jon E. (R, 62)**
350 North State, Suite 350
P.O. Box 145030
Salt Lake City, UT 84114
P: (801) 538-1029
F: (801) 326-1544
E: jstanard@le.utah.gov

**Stratton, Keven J. (R, 48)**
350 North State, Suite 350
P.O. Box 145030
Salt Lake City, UT 84114
P: (801) 538-1029
F: (801) 326-1544
E: kstratton@le.utah.gov

**Thurston, Norman (R, 64)**
350 North State, Suite 350
P.O. Box 145030
Salt Lake City, UT 84114
P: (801) 538-1029
F: (801) 326-1544
E: normthurston@le.utah.gov

**Ward, Raymond (R, 19)**
350 North State, Suite 350
P.O. Box 145030
Salt Lake City, UT 84114
P: (801) 538-1029
F: (801) 326-1544
E: rayward@le.utah.gov

**Watkins, Christine F.
(D, 69)**
350 North State, Suite 350
P.O. Box 145030
Salt Lake City, UT 84114
P: (801) 538-1029
F: (801) 326-1544
E: christinewatkins
   @le.utah.gov

**Webb, R.Curt (R, 5)**
350 North State, Suite 350
P.O. Box 145030
Salt Lake City, UT 84114
P: (801) 538-1029
F: (801) 326-1544
E: curtwebb@le.utah.gov

**Weight, Elizabeth (D, 31)***
350 North State, Suite 350
P.O. Box 145030
Salt Lake City, UT 84114
P: (801) 538-1029
F: (801) 326-1544
E: elizabethweight
   @le.utah.gov

**Westwood, John R. (R, 72)**
350 North State, Suite 350
P.O. Box 145030
Salt Lake City, UT 84114
P: (801) 538-1029
F: (801) 326-1544
E: jwestwood@le.utah.gov

**Wheatley, Mark A. (D, 35)**
350 North State, Suite 350
P.O. Box 145030
Salt Lake City, UT 84114
P: (801) 538-1029
F: (801) 326-1544
E: markwheatley@le.utah.gov

**Wilde, Logan (R, 53)***
350 North State, Suite 350
Po Box 145030
Salt Lake City, UT 84114
P: (801) 538-1029
F: (801) 326-1544
E: loganwilde@le.utah.gov

**Wilson, Brad R. (R, 15)**
350 North State, Suite 350
P.O. Box 145030
Salt Lake City, UT 84114
P: (801) 538-1029
F: (801) 326-1544
E: bradwilson@le.utah.gov

**Winder, Mike (R, 30)***
350 North State, Suite 350
Po Box 145030
Salt Lake City, UT 84114
P: (801) 538-1029
F: (801) 326-1544
E: mikewinder@le.utah.gov

# Vermont

## Executive

### Governor

**The Honorable Phil Scott (R)**
Governor
109 State Street
Montpelier, VT 05609
P: (802) 828-3333
F: (802) 828-3339

### Lieutenant Governor

**The Honorable David Zuckerman (D)**
Lieutenant Governor
115 State Street
Monpelier, VT 05633
P: (802) 828-2226
F: (802) 828-3198
E: dzuckerman
@leg.state.vt.us

### Attorney General

**The Honorable TJ Donovan (D)**
Attorney General
109 State Street
Montpelier, VT 05609
P: (802) 828-3171
F: (802) 828-3187

### Auditor

**The Honorable Douglas R. Hoffer (D)**
State Auditor
132 State Street
Montpelier, VT 05633
P: (802) 828-2281
F: (802) 828-2198
E: doug.hoffer@state.vt.us

### Secretary of State

**The Honorable Jim Condos (D)**
Secretary of State
128 State Street
Montpelier, VT 05633
P: (802) 828-2148
F: (802) 828-2496
E: jim.condos
@sec.state.vt.us

### Treasurer

**The Honorable Elizabeth Pearce**
State Treasurer
109 State Street
Montpelier, VT 05609
P: (802) 828-3322
F: (802) 828-2772
E: Beth.Pearce@state.vt.us

## Judiciary

### Supreme Court (MC)

**Ms. Patricia Gabel**
Court Administrator & Clerk
109 State Street
Montpelier, VT 05609
P: (802) 828-3278
F: (802) 828-4750

**The Honorable Paul L. Reiber**
Chief Justice
**The Honorable John A. Dooley III**
**The Honorable Harold Eaton**
**The Honorable Beth Robinson**
**The Honorable Marilyn S. Skoglund**

## Legislative

## Senate

### Senate President

**The Honorable David Zuckerman (D)**
Lieutenant Governor
115 State Street
Monpelier, VT 05633
P: (802) 828-2226
F: (802) 828-3198
E: dzuckerman
@leg.state.vt.us

### President Pro Tempore of the Senate

**Senator Tim Ashe (D)**
President Pro Tempore
115 State Street
Montpelier, VT 05633
P: (802) 828-2228
E: tashe@leg.state.vt.us

### Senate Majority Leader

**Senator Becca Balint (D)**
Senate Majority Leader
115 State Street
Montpelier, VT 05633
P: (802) 828-2228
E: bbalint@leg.state.vt.us

### Senate Minority Leader

**Senator Dustin Allard Degree (R)**
Senate Minority Leader
115 State Street
Montpelier, VT 05633
P: (802) 828-2228
E: ddegree@leg.state.vt.us

### Secretary of the Senate

**Mr. John H. Bloomer Jr.**
Secretary of the Senate
115 State Street
Montpelier, VT 05633
P: (802) 828-2241
F: (802) 828-1272
E: jbloomer@leg.state.vt.us

### Members of the Senate

**Ashe, Tim (D, SP4)**
115 State Street
Montpelier, VT 05633
P: (802) 828-2228
E: tashe@leg.state.vt.us

**Ayer, Claire D. (D, SP1)**
115 State Street
Montpelier, VT 05633
P: (802) 828-2228
E: cayer@leg.state.vt.us

**Balint, Becca (D, SP12)**
115 State Street
Montpelier, VT 05633
P: (802) 828-2228
E: bbalint@leg.state.vt.us

**Baruth, Philip (D, SP4)**
115 State Street
Montpelier, VT 05633
P: (802) 828-2228
E: pbaruth@leg.state.vt.us

**Benning, Joe (R, SP3)**
115 State Street
Montpelier, VT 05633
P: (802) 828-2228
E: jbenning@leg.state.vt.us

**Branagan, Carolyn Whitney (R, SP6)**
115 State Street
Montpelier, VT 05633
P: (802) 828-2228
E: cbranagan
@leg.state.vt.us

**Bray, Christopher A. (D, SP1)**
115 State Street
Montpelier, VT 05633
P: (802) 828-2228
F: (802) 329-2256
E: cbray@leg.state.vt.us

**Brooks, Francis K. (D, SP11)**
115 State Street
Montpelier, VT 05633
P: (802) 828-2228
E: fbrooks@leg.state.vt.us

**Campion, Brian (D, SP2)**
115 State Street
Montpelier, VT 05633
P: (802) 828-2228
E: bcampion@leg.state.vt.us

**Clarkson, Alison H. (D, SP13)**
115 State Street
Montpelier, VT 05633
P: (802) 828-2228
E: aclarkson
@leg.state.vt.us

**Collamore, Brian P. (R, SP10)**
115 State Street
Montpelier, VT 05633
P: (802) 828-2228
E: bcollamore
@leg.state.vt.us

**Cummings, Ann E. (D, SP11)**
115 State Street
Montpelier, VT 05633
P: (802) 828-2228
E: acummings
@leg.state.vt.us

**Degree, Dustin Allard (R, SP6)**
115 State Street
Montpelier, VT 05633
P: (802) 828-2228
E: ddegree@leg.state.vt.us

**Flory, Peg (R, SP10)**
115 State Street
Montpelier, VT 05633
P: (802) 828-2228
E: pflory@leg.state.vt.us

**Ingram, Debbie (D, SP4)***
115 State Street
Montpelier, VT 05633
P: (802) 828-2228
E: dingram@leg.state.vt.us

**Kitchel, M. Jane (D, SP3)**
115 State Street
P.O. Box 82
Montpelier, VT 05633
P: (802) 828-2228
E: jkitchel@leg.state.vt.us

**Lyons, Virginia (D, SP4)**
115 State Street
Montpelier, VT 05633
P: (802) 828-2228
E: vlyons@leg.state.vt.us

**MacDonald, Mark A. (D, SP9)**
115 State Street
Montpelier, VT 05633
P: (802) 828-2228
F: (802) 433-1035
E: mmacdonald
@leg.state.vt.us

**Mazza, Richard T. (D, SP7)**
115 State Street
Montpelier, VT 05633
P: (802) 828-2228
F: (802) 859-9215

**McCormack, Richard J.
(D, SP13)**
115 State Street
Montpelier, VT 05633
P: (802) 828-2228
E: rmccormack
@leg.state.vt.us

**Mullin, Kevin J. (R, SP10)**
115 State Street
Montpelier, VT 05633
P: (802) 828-2228
E: kjmbjm@aol.com

**Nitka, Alice W. (D, SP13)**
115 State Street
Montpelier, VT 05633
P: (802) 828-2228
E: anitka@leg.state.vt.us

**Pearson, Christopher A.
(P, SP4)**
115 State Street
Monpelier, VT 05633
P: (802) 828-2228
E: cpearson@leg.state.vt.us

**Pollina, Anthony (P, SP11)**
115 State Street
Montpelier, VT 05633
P: (802) 828-2228
E: apollina@leg.state.vt.us

**Rodgers, John S. (D, SP5)**
115 State Street
Montpelier, VT 05633
P: (802) 828-2228
E: jrodgers@leg.state.vt.us

**Sears Jr., Richard W.
(D, SP2)**
115 State Street
Montpelier, VT 05633
P: (802) 828-2228
E: rsears@leg.state.vt.us

**Sirotkin, Michael (D, SP4)**
115 State Street
Montpelier, VT 05633
P: (802) 828-2228
E: msirotkin
@leg.state.vt.us

**Starr Jr., Robert A.
(D, SP5)**
115 State Street
Montpelier, VT 05633
P: (802) 828-2228
E: rstarr@leg.state.vt.us

**Westman, Richard A.
(R, SP8)**
115 State Street
Montpelier, VT 05633
P: (802) 828-2228
F: (802) 644-2297
E: rawestman@gmail.com

**White, Jeanette K.
(D, SP12)**
115 State Street
Montpelier, VT 05633
P: (802) 828-2228
E: jwhite@leg.state.vt.us

# House

## Speaker of the House

**Representative Mitzi
Johnson (D)**
Speaker of the House
115 State Street
Montpelier, VT 05633
P: (802) 828-2228
E: mjohnson@leg.state.vt.us

## House Majority Leader

**Representative Sarah
Copeland-Hanzas (D)**
House Majority Leader
115 State Street
Montpelier, VT 05633
P: (802) 828-2228
E: scopelandhanzas
@leg.state.vt.us

## House Minority Leader

**Representative Donald H.
Turner (R)**
House Minority Leader
115 State Street
Montpelier, VT 05633
P: (802) 828-2228
F: (802) 893-3467
E: dturner@leg.state.vt.us

## Clerk of the House

**Mr. William Monroe Magill**
Clerk of the House
115 State Street
Monpelier, VT 05633
P: (802) 828-2247
F: (802) 828-0724

## Members of the House

**Ainsworth, David M.
(R, SP115)**
115 State Street
Montpelier, VT 05633
P: (802) 828-2228
E: dainsworth
@leg.state.vt.us

**Ancel, Janet (D, SP95)**
115 State Street
Montpelier, VT 05633
P: (802) 828-2228
E: janetancel@earthlink.net

**Bancroft, Robert L.
(R, SP51)**
115 State Street
Montpelier, VT 05633
P: (802) 828-2228
E: rbancroft
@leg.state.vt.us

**Bartholomew, John
(D, SP108)**
115 State Street
Montpelier, VT 05633
P: (802) 828-2228
E: jbartholomew
@leg.state.vt.us

**Baser, Fred K. (R, SP17)**
115 State Street
Montpelier, VT 05633
P: (802) 828-2228
E: fbaser@leg.state.vt.us

**Batchelor, Lynn (R, SP74)**
115 State Street
Montpelier, VT 05633
P: (802) 828-2228
E: lbatchelor
@leg.state.vt.us

**Beck, Scott (R, SP28)**
115 State Street
Montpelier, VT 05633
P: (802) 828-2228
E: sbeck@leg.state.vt.us

**Belaski, Paul (D, SP106)***
115 State Street
Montpelier, VT 05633
P: (802) 828-2228
E: pbelaski@leg.state.vt.us

**Beyor, Steve (R, SP62)**
115 State Street
Montpelier, VT 05633
P: (802) 828-2228
E: sbeyor@leg.state.vt.us

**Bissonnette, Clem (D, SP44)**
115 State Street
Montpelier, VT 05633
P: (802) 828-2228
E: cbissonnette
@leg.state.vt.us

**Bock, Thomas (D, SP110)***
115 State Street
Montpelier, VT 05633
P: (802) 828-2228
E: tbock@leg.state.vt.us

**Botzow, Bill (D, SP20)**
115 State Street
Montpelier, VT 05633
P: (802) 828-2228
E: bbotzow@leg.state.vt.us

**Brennan, Patrick M.
(R, SP53)**
115 State Street
Montpelier, VT 05633
P: (802) 828-2228
E: pbrennan@leg.state.vt.us

**Briglin, Tim (D, SP116)**
115 State Street
Montpelier, VT 05633
P: (802) 828-2228
E: tbriglin@leg.state.vt.us

**Browning, Cynthia (D, SP24)**
115 State Street
Montpelier, VT 05633
P: (802) 828-2228
E: cbrowning
@leg.state.vt.us

**Brumsted, Jessica (D, 37)***
115 State Street
Montpelier, VT 05633
P: (802) 828-2228
E: jbrumsted
@leg.state.vt.us

**Buckholz, Susan (D, SP112)***
115 State Street
Montpelier, VT 05633
P: (802) 828-2228
E: sbuckholz
@leg.state.vt.us

**Burditt, Tom (R, SP79)**
115 State Street
Montpelier, VT 05633
P: (802) 828-2228
E: tburditt@leg.state.vt.us

**Burke, Mollie S. (P, SP100)**
115 State Street
Montpelier, VT 05633
P: (802) 828-2228
E: mburke@leg.state.vt.us

# Vermont

**Canfield, William (R, SP80)**
115 State Street
Montpelier, VT 05633
P: (802) 828-2228
E: wcanfield
@leg.state.vt.us

**Carr, Steve (D, SP86)**
115 State Street
Montpelier, VT 05633
P: (802) 828-2228
E: scarr@leg.state.vt.us

**Chesnut-Tangerman, Robin (D, SP87)**
115 State Street
Montpelier, VT 05633
P: (802) 828-2228
E: rchesnut-tangerman
@leg.state.vt.us

**Christensen, Annmarie (D, SP109)\***
115 State Street
Montpelier, VT 05633
P: (802) 828-2228
E: achristensen
@leg.state.vt.us

**Christie, Kevin (D, SP113)**
115 State Street
Montpelier, VT 05633
P: (802) 828-2228
E: kchristie
@leg.state.vt.us

**Cina, Brian (P, SP41)\***
115 State Street
Montpelier, VT 05633
P: (802) 828-2228
E: bcina@leg.state.vt.us

**Colburn, Selene (P, SP41)\***
115 State Street
Montpelier, VT 05633
P: (802) 828-2228
E: scolburn@leg.state.vt.us

**Condon, Jim (D, SP52)**
115 State Street
Montpelier, VT 05633
P: (802) 828-2228
E: jimcondon@lycos.com

**Conlon, Peter (D, SP15)\***
115 State Street
Montpelier, VT 05633
P: (802) 828-2228
E: pconlon@leg.state.vt.us

**Connor, Dan (D, SP63)**
115 State Street
Montpelier, VT 05633
P: (802) 828-2228
E: dconnor@leg.state.vt.us

**Conquest, Chip (D, SP73)**
115 State Street
Montpelier, VT 05633
P: (802) 828-2228
E: cconquest
@leg.state.vt.us

**Copeland-Hanzas, Sarah (D, SP71)**
115 State Street
Montpelier, VT 05633
P: (802) 828-2228
E: scopelandhanzas
@leg.state.vt.us

**Corcoran, Timothy R. (D, SP21)**
115 State Street
Montpelier, VT 05633
P: (802) 828-2228
E: tcorcoran
@leg.state.vt.us

**Cupoli, Larry (R, SP83)**
115 State Street
Montpelier, VT 05633
P: (802) 828-2228
F: (802) 775-3179
E: lcupoli@leg.state.vt.us

**Dakin, Maureen P. (D, SP53)**
115 State Street
Montpelier, VT 05633
P: (802) 828-2228
E: mdakin@leg.state.vt.us

**Deen, David L. (D, SP103)**
115 State Street
Montpelier, VT 05633
P: (802) 828-2228
F: (802) 869-1103
E: ddeen@leg.state.vt.us

**Devereux, Dennis J. (R, SP89)**
115 State Street
Route 155
Montpelier, VT 05633
P: (802) 828-2228
E: ddevereux
@leg.state.vt.us

**Dickinson, Eileen (R, SP60)**
115 State Street
Montpelier, VT 05633
P: (802) 828-2228
F: (802) 527-3767
E: edickinson
@leg.state.vt.us

**Donahue, Anne B. (R, SP90)**
115 State Street
Montpelier, VT 05633
P: (802) 828-2228
E: adonahue@leg.state.vt.us

**Donovan, Johannah Leddy (D, SP42)**
115 State Street
Montpelier, VT 05633
P: (802) 828-2228
E: jdonovan@leg.state.vt.us

**Dunn, Betsy (D, SP49)\***
115 State Street
Montpelier, VT 05633
P: (802) 828-2228
E: bdunn@leg.state.vt.us

**Emmons, Alice M. (D, SP111)**
115 State Street
Montpelier, VT 05633
P: (802) 828-2228
E: aemmons@leg.state.vt.us

**Fagan, Peter J. (R, SP82)**
115 State Street
Montpelier, VT 05633
P: (802) 828-2228
E: pfagan@leg.state.vt.us

**Feltus, Marty (R, SP29)**
115 State Street
Montpelier, VT 05633
P: (802) 828-2228
E: martyfeltus@gmail.com

**Fields, Rachael (D, SP21)**
115 State Street
Montpelier, VT 05633
P: (802) 828-2228
E: rfields@leg.state.vt.us

**Forguites, Robert (D, SP111)**
115 State Street
Montpelier, VT 05633
P: (802) 828-2228
E: rforguites
@leg.state.vt.us

**Frenier, Robert (R, SP70)\***
115 State Street
Montpelier, VT 05633
P: (802) 828-2228
E: rfrenier@leg.state.vt.us

**Gage, Doug (R, SP85)**
115 State Street
Montpelier, VT 05633
P: (802) 828-2228
E: dgage@leg.state.vt.us

**Gamache, Marianna (R, SP61)**
115 State Street
Montpelier, VT 05633
P: (802) 828-2228
E: mgamache@leg.state.vt.us

**Gardner, Marica (D, SP31)\***
115 State Street
Montpelier, VT 05633
P: (802) 828-2228
E: mgardner@leg.state.vt.us

**Giambatista, Dylan (D, SP50)\***
115 State Street
Montpelier, VT 05633
P: (802) 828-2228
E: dgiambatista
@leg.state.vt.us

**Gonzalez, Diana (P, SP44)**
115 State Street
Montpelier, VT 05633
P: (802) 828-2228
E: dgonzalez
@leg.state.vt.us

**Grad, Maxine Jo (D, SP96)**
115 State Street
Montpelier, VT 05633
P: (802) 828-2228
F: (802) 496-6104
E: mgrad@leg.state.vt.us

**Graham, Rodney (R, SP70)**
115 State Street
Montpelier, VT 05633
P: (802) 828-2228
E: rgraham@leg.state.vt.us

**Greshin, Adam (I, SP96)**
115 State Street
Montpelier, VT 05633
P: (802) 828-2228
E: agreshin@leg.state.vt.us

**Haas, Sandy (P, SP117)**
115 State Street
Montpelier, VT 05633
P: (802) 828-2228
E: shaas@leg.state.vt.us

**Head, Helen (D, SP47)**
115 State Street
Montpelier, VT 05633
P: (802) 828-2228
E: helen@helenhead.com

**Hebert, Michael (R, SP98)**
115 State Street
Montpelier, VT 05633
P: (802) 828-2228
F: (802) 254-3660
E: mhebert@leg.state.vt.us

**Helm, Robert (R, SP80)**
115 State Street
Montpelier, VT 05633
P: (802) 828-2228
E: rhelm@leg.state.vt.us

**Higley, Mark A. (R, SP77)**
115 State Street
Montpelier, VT 05633
P: (802) 828-2228
E: mhigley@leg.state.vt.us

**Hill, Matthew (D, SP67)***
115 State Street
Montpelier, VT 05633
P: (802) 828-2228
E: mhill@leg.state.vt.us

**Hooper, Jay (D, SP72)***
115 State Street
Montpelier, VT 05633
P: (802) 828-2228
E: jhooper@leg.state.vt.us

**Hooper, Mary (D, SP93)**
115 State Street
Montpelier, VT 05633
P: (802) 828-2228
E: mhooper@leg.state.vt.us

**Houghton, Lori (D, SP50)***
115 State Street
Montpelier, VT 05633
P: (802) 828-2228
E: lhoughton
    @leg.state.vt.us

**Howard, Mary (D, SP84)***
115 State Street
Montpelier, VT 05633
P: (802) 828-2228
E: mhoward@leg.state.vt.us

**Hubert, Ronald E. (R, SP54)**
115 State Street
Montpelier, VT 05633
P: (802) 828-2228
F: (802) 893-3814
E: rhubert@leg.state.vt.us

**Jessup, Kimberly (D, SP94)***
115 State Street
Montpelier, VT 05633
P: (802) 828-2228
E: kjessup@leg.state.vt.us

**Jickling, Ben (I, SP72)***
115 State Street
Montpelier, VT 05633
P: (802) 828-2228
E: bjickling
    @leg.state.vt.us

**Johnson, Mitzi (D, SP65)**
115 State Street
Montpelier, VT 05633
P: (802) 828-2228
E: mjohnson@leg.state.vt.us

**Joseph, Ben W. (D, SP65)***
115 State Street
Montpelier, VT 05633
P: (802) 828-2228
E: bjoseph@leg.state.vt.us

**Juskiewicz, Bernie
    (R, SP68)**
115 State Street
Montpelier, VT 05633
P: (802) 828-2228
E: bjuskiewicz
    @leg.state.vt.us

**Keefe, Brian (R, SP24)***
115 State Street
Montpelier, VT 05633
P: (802) 828-2228
E: bkeefe@leg.state.vt.us

**Keenan, Kathleen C.
    (D, SP59)**
115 State Street
Montpelier, VT 05633
P: (802) 828-2228
E: kkeenan@leg.state.vt.us

**Kimbell, Charlie
    (D, SP114)***
115 State Street
Montpelier, VT 05633
P: (802) 828-2228
E: ckimbell@leg.state.vt.us

**Kitzmiller, Warren F.
    (D, SP93)**
115 State Street
Montpelier, VT 05633
P: (802) 828-2228
E: wkitzmiller
    @leg.state.vt.us

**Krowinski, Jill (D, SP40)**
115 State Street
Montpelier, VT 05633
P: (802) 828-2228
E: jkrowinskiz
    @leg.state.vt.us

**LaClair, Rob (R, SP91)**
115 State Street
Montpelier, VT 05633
P: (802) 828-2228
E: rlaclair@leg.state.vt.us

**LaLonde, Martin (D, SP45)**
115 State Street
Montpelier, VT 05633
P: (802) 828-2228
E: mlalonde@leg.state.vt.us

**Lanpher, Diane (D, SP16)**
115 State Street
Montpelier, VT 05633
P: (802) 828-2228
E: dlanpher@leg.state.vt.us

**Lawrence, Richard (R, SP29)**
115 State Street
Montpelier, VT 05633
P: (802) 828-2228
F: (802) 626-8081
E: rlawrence
    @leg.state.vt.us

**Lefebvre, Paul D. (R, SP56)**
115 State Street
Montpelier, VT 05633
P: (802) 828-2228
E: plefebvre
    @leg.state.vt.us

**Lewis, Patti J. (R, SP90)**
115 State Street
Montpelier, VT 05633
P: (802) 828-2228
E: plewis@leg.state.vt.us

**Lippert Jr., William J.
    (D, SP35)**
115 State Street
Montpelier, VT 05633
P: (802) 828-2228
F: (802) 482-3528
E: wlippert@leg.state.vt.us

**Long, Emily (D, SP104)**
115 State Street
Montpelier, VT 05633
P: (802) 828-2228
E: elong@leg.state.vt.us

**Lucke, Gabrielle (D, SP113)**
115 State Street
Montpelier, VT 05633
P: (802) 828-2228
E: glucke@leg.state.vt.us

**Macaig, Terence (D, SP32)**
115 State Street
Montpelier, VT 05633
P: (802) 828-2228
E: tmacaig@leg.state.vt.us

**Marcotte, Michael J.
    (R, SP75)**
115 State Street
Montpelier, VT 05633
P: (802) 828-2228
E: mmarcotte
    @leg.state.vt.us

**Martel, Marcia Robinson
    (R, SP26)**
115 State Street
Montpelier, VT 05633
P: (802) 828-2228
E: mmartel@leg.state.vt.us

**Masland, Jim (D, SP116)**
115 State Street
Monpelier, VT 05633
P: (802) 828-2228
E: jmasland@leg.state.vt.us

**McCormack, Curt (D, SP40)**
115 State Street
Montpelier, VT 05633
P: (802) 828-2228
E: cmccormack
    @leg.state.vt.us

**McCoy, Patricia A.
    (R, SP78)**
115 State Street
Montpelier, VT 05633
P: (802) 828-2228
E: pmccoy@leg.state.vt.us

**McCullough, Jim (D, SP32)**
115 State Street
Montpelier, VT 05633
P: (802) 828-2228
E: jim_mccullough
    @myfairpoint.net

**McFaun, Francis (R, SP91)**
115 State Street
Montpelier, VT 05633
P: (802) 828-2228
E: fmcfaun@leg.state.vt.us

**Miller, Alice (D, SP23)**
115 State Street
Montpelier, VT 05633
P: (802) 828-2228
F: (802) 442-9825
E: amiller@leg.state.vt.us

**Morris, Kiah (D, SP22)**
115 State Street
Montpelier, VT 05633
P: (802) 828-2228
E: kmorris@leg.state.vt.us

**Morrissey, Mary A.
    (R, SP22)**
115 State Street
Montpelier, VT 05633
P: (802) 828-2228
E: mmorrissey
    @leg.state.vt.us

**Mrowicki, Mike (D, SP103)**
115 State Street
Montpelier, VT 05633
P: (802) 828-2228
E: mmrowicki
    @leg.state.vt.us

**Murphy, Barbara S.
    (I, SP58)**
115 State Street
Montpelier, VT 05633
P: (802) 828-2228
E: bmurphy@leg.state.vt.us

**Myers, Linda K. (R, SP49)**
115 State Street
Montpelier, VT 05633
P: (802) 828-2228
E: lmyers@leg.state.vt.us

**Nolan, Gary (R, SP69)***
115 State Street
Montpelier, VT 05633
P: (802) 828-2228
E: gnolan@leg.state.vt.us

# Vermont

**Norris, Terry (I, SP19)***
115 State Street
Montpelier, VT 05633
P: (802) 828-2228
E: tnorris@leg.state.vt.us

**Noyes, Daniel (D, SP67)***
115 State Street
Montpelier, VT 05633
P: (802) 828-2228
E: dnoyes@leg.state.vt.us

**Ode, Carol (D, SP38)***
115 State Street
Montpelier, VT 05633
P: (802) 828-2228
E: code@leg.state.vt.us

**Olsen, Oliver K. (I, SP107)**
115 State Street
Montpelier, VT 05633
P: (802) 828-2228
E: oliver@oliverolsen.com

**O'Sullivan, Jean (D, SP39)**
115 State Street
Montpelier, VT 05633
P: (802) 828-2228
F: (802) 658-0492
E: josullivan
   @leg.state.vt.us

**Parent, Corey (R, SP59)**
115 State Street
Montpelier, VT 05633
P: (802) 828-2228
E: cparent@leg.state.vt.us

**Partridge, Carolyn W.
   (D, SP102)**
115 State Street
Montpelier, VT 05633
P: (802) 828-2228
F: (802) 874-4182
E: cpartridge
   @leg.state.vt.us

**Pearce, Albert (R, SP62)**
115 State Street
Montpelier, VT 05633
P: (802) 828-2228
E: apearce@leg.state.vt.us

**Poirier, Paul N. (I, SP92)**
115 State Street
Montpelier, VT 05633
P: (802) 828-2228
E: ppoirier@leg.state.vt.us

**Potter, Dave (D, SP79)**
115 State Street
Montpelier, VT 05633
P: (802) 828-2228
E: dpotter@leg.state.vt.us

**Pugh, Ann D. (D, SP46)**
115 State Street
Montpelier, VT 05633
P: (802) 828-2228
E: apugh@leg.state.vt.us

**Quimby, Connie (R, SP55)**
115 State Street
Montpelier, VT 05633
P: (802) 828-2228
E: cquimby@leg.state.vt.us

**Rachelson, Barbara
   (D, SP43)**
115 State Street
Montpelier, VT 05633
P: (802) 828-2228
E: brachelson
   @leg.state.vt.us

**Rosenquist, Carl J.
   (R, SP57)**
115 State Street
Montpelier, VT 05633
P: (802) 828-2228
E: crosenquist
   @leg.state.vt.us

**Savage, Brian K. (R, SP61)**
115 State Street
Montpelier, VT 05633
P: (802) 828-2228
E: bsavage@leg.state.vt.us

**Scheu, Robin (D, SP14)***
115 State Street
Montpelier, VT 05633
P: (802) 828-2228
E: rscheu@leg.state.vt.us

**Scheuermann, Heidi E.
   (R, SP66)**
115 State Street
Montpelier, VT 05633
P: (802) 828-2228
F: (802) 253-2275
E: hscheuermann
   @leg.state.vt.us

**Sharpe, David (D, SP17)**
115 State Street
Montpelier, VT 05633
P: (802) 828-2228
E: dsharpe@leg.state.vt.us

**Shaw, Butch (R, SP86)**
115 State Street
Montpelier, VT 05633
P: (802) 828-2228
E: bshaw@leg.state.vt.us

**Sheldon, Amy (D, SP14)**
115 State Street
Montpelier, VT 05633
P: (802) 828-2228
E: asheldon@leg.state.vt.us

**Sibilia, Laura (I, SP106)**
115 State Street
Montpelier, VT 05633
P: (802) 828-2228
E: lsibilia@leg.state.vt.us

**Smith, Brian (R, SP74)***
115 State Street
Montpelier, VT 05633
P: (802) 828-2228
E: bsmith@leg.state.vt.us

**Smith, Harvey T. (R, SP18)**
115 State Street
Montpelier, VT 05633
P: (802) 828-2228
E: hsmith@leg.state.vt.us

**Squirrell, Trevor
   (D, SP33)***
115 State Street
Montpelier, VT 05633
P: (802) 828-2228
E: tsquirrell
   @leg.state.vt.us

**Stevens, Tom (D, SP97)**
115 State Street
Montpelier, VT 05633
P: (802) 828-2228
E: tstevens@leg.state.vt.us

**Strong, Vicki (R, SP73)**
115 State Street
Montpelier, VT 05633
P: (802) 828-2228
E: vstrong@leg.state.vt.us

**Stuart, Valerie A.
   (D, SP99)**
115 State Street
Montpelier, VT 05633
P: (802) 828-2228
E: vstuart@leg.state.vt.us

**Sullivan, Linda (D, SP25)***
115 State Street
Montpelier, VT 05633
P: (802) 828-2228
E: lsullivan
   @leg.state.vt.us

**Sullivan, Mary M. (D, SP42)**
115 State Street
Montpelier, VT 05633
P: (802) 828-2228
E: msullivan
   @leg.state.vt.us

**Tate, Job (R, SP88)**
115 State Street
Montpelier, VT 05633
P: (802) 828-2228
E: jtate@leg.state.vt.us

**Taylor, Curt (D, SP52)***
115 State Street
Montpelier, VT 05633
P: (802) 828-2228
E: ctaylor@leg.state.vt.us

**Terenzini, Thomas (R, SP81)**
115 State Street
Montpelier, VT 05633
P: (802) 828-2228
E: tterenzini
   @leg.state.vt.us

**Till, George (D, SP33)**
115 State Street
Montpelier, VT 05633
P: (802) 828-2228
F: (802) 878-6131
E: gtill@leg.state.vt.us

**Toleno, Tristan (D, SP101)**
115 State Street
Montpelier, VT 05633
P: (802) 828-2228
E: ttoleno@leg.state.vt.us

**Toll, Kitty (D, SP30)**
115 State Street
Montpelier, VT 05633
P: (802) 828-2228
E: ktoll@leg.state.vt.us

**Townsend, Maida (D, SP48)**
115 State Street
Montpelier, VT 05633
P: (802) 828-2228
E: mtownsend
   @leg.state.vt.us

**Trieber, Matthew (D, SP102)**
115 State Street
Montpelier, VT 05633
P: (802) 828-2228
E: matrieber@gmail.com

**Troiano, Chip (D, SP27)**
115 State Street
Montpelier, VT 05633
P: (802) 828-2228
E: ctroiano@leg.state.vt.us

**Turner, Donald H. (R, SP54)**
115 State Street
Montpelier, VT 05633
P: (802) 828-2228
F: (802) 893-3467
E: dturner@leg.state.vt.us

**Van Wyck, Warren (R, SP16)**
115 State Street
Montpelier, VT 05633
P: (802) 828-2228
E: wvanwyck@leg.state.vt.us

**Viens, Gary (R, SP75)**
115 State Street
Montpelier, VT 05633
P: (802) 828-2228
E: gviens@leg.state.vt.us

**Walz, Tommy (D, SP92)**
115 State Street
Montpelier, VT 05633
P: (802) 828-2228
E: twalz@leg.state.vt.us

**Webb, Kate (D, SP36)**
115 State Street
Montpelier, VT 05633
P: (802) 828-2228
E: kwebb@leg.state.vt.us

**Weed, Cindy (P, SP64)**
115 State Street
Montpelier, VT 05633
P: (802) 828-2228
E: cweed@leg.state.vt.us

**Willhoit, Janssen (R, SP28)**
115 State Street
Montpelier, VT 05633
P: (802) 828-2228
E: jwillhoit
    @leg.state.vt.us

**Wood, Theresa (D, SP97)**
115 State Street
Montpelier, VT 05633
P: (802) 828-2228
E: twood@leg.state.vt.us

**Wright, Kurt (R, SP38)**
115 State Street
Montpelier, VT 05633
P: (802) 828-2228
E: kwright@leg.state.vt.us

**Yacovone, David (D, SP69)***
115 State Street
Montpelier, VT 05633
P: (802) 828-2228
E: dyacovone
    @leg.state.vt.us

**Yantachka, Mike (D, SP34)**
115 State Street
Montpelier, VT 05633
P: (802) 828-2228
E: myantachka
    @leg.state.vt.us

**Young, Sam (D, SP76)**
115 State Street
Montpelier, VT 05633
P: (802) 828-2228
E: syoung@leg.state.vt.us

# Virginia

## Executive

### Governor
**The Honorable Terry McAuliffe (D)**
Governor
State Capitol, Third Floor
Richmond, VA 23219
P: (804) 786-2211
F: (804) 371-6351

### Lieutenant Governor
**The Honorable Ralph S. Northam (D)**
Lieutenant Governor
102 Governor Street
Richmond, VA 23219
P: (804) 786-2078
F: (804) 786-7514
E: ltgov@ltgov.virginia.gov

### Attorney General
**The Honorable Mark R. Herring (D)**
Attorney General
900 East Main Street
Richmond, VA 23219
P: (804) 786-2071

### Auditor
**Ms. Martha Mavredes**
(appointed by the Legislature)
Auditor of Public Accounts
P.O. Box 1295
Richmond, VA 23218
P: (804) 225-3350
F: (804) 225-3357
E: martha.mavredes
@apa.virginia.gov

### Secretary of the Commonwealth
**The Honorable Kelly Thomasson**
(appointed)
Secretary of the Commonwealth
P.O. Box 2454
Address 2
Richmond, VA 23218
P: (804) 786-2441
F: (804) 371-0017
E: socmail
@governor.virginia.gov

## Treasurer
**The Honorable Manju Ganeriwala**
(appointed)
State Treasurer
P.O. Box 1879
Richmond, VA 23219
P: (804) 225-3131
F: (804) 786-0833
E: Manju.Ganeriwala
@trs.virginia.gov

## Judiciary

### Supreme Court (LA)
**Ms. Patricia L. Harrington**
Clerk
100 North 9th Street, 5th Floor
P.O. Box 1315
Richmond, VA 23219
P: (804) 786-2251

**The Honorable Donald W. Lemons**
Chief Justice
**The Honorable S. Bernard Goodwyn**
**The Honorable D. Arthur Kelsey**
**The Honorable Elizabeth A. McClanahan**
**The Honorable Stephen R. McCullough**
**The Honorable William C. Mims (R)**
**The Honorable Cleo E. Powell**

## Legislative
## Senate

### Senate President
**The Honorable Ralph S. Northam (D)**
Lieutenant Governor
102 Governor Street
Richmond, VA 23219
P: (804) 786-2078
F: (804) 786-7514
E: ltgov@ltgov.virginia.gov

## President Pro Tempore of the Senate
**Senator Stephen D. Newman (R)**
President Pro Tempore
General Assembly Building,
Room 621
P.O. Box 396
Richmond, VA 23218
P: (804) 698-7523
F: (804) 698-7651
E: district23
@senate.virginia.gov

## Senate Majority Leader
**Senator Thomas K. Norment Jr. (R)**
Senate Majority Leader
General Assembly Building,
Room 626
P.O. Box 396
Richmond, VA 23218
P: (804) 698-7503
F: (804) 698-7651
E: district03
@senate.virginia.gov

## Senate Minority Leader
**Senator Richard L. Saslaw (D)**
Senate Minority Leader
General Assembly Building,
Room 613
P.O. Box 396
Richmond, VA 23218
P: (804) 698-7535
F: (804) 698-7651
E: district35
@senate.virginia.gov

## Secretary of the Senate
**Ms. Susan Clarke Schaar**
Clerk of the Senate
P.O. Box 396
Richmond, VA 23218
P: (804) 698-7400
F: (804) 698-7670
E: sschaar
@senate.virginia.gov

## Members of the Senate
**Barker, George L. (D, 39)**
General Assembly Building,
Room 315
P.O. Box 396
Richmond, VA 23218
P: (804) 698-7539
F: (804) 698-7651
E: district39
@senate.virginia.gov

**Black, Richard H. (R, 13)**
General Assembly Building,
Room 311
P.O. Box 396
Richmond, VA 23218
P: (804) 698-7513
F: (804) 698-7651
E: district13
@senate.virginia.gov

**Carrico Sr., Charles W. (R, 40)**
General Assembly Building,
Room 330
P.O. Box 396
Richmond, VA 23218
P: (804) 698-7540
F: (804) 698-7651
E: district40
@senate.virginia.gov

**Chafin Jr., A. Benton (R, 38)**
General Assembly Building,
Room 428
P.O. Box 396
Richmond, VA 23218
P: (804) 698-7538
F: (804) 698-7651
E: district38
@senate.virginia.gov

**Chase, Amanda F. (R, 11)**
General Assembly Building,
Room 319
P.O. Box 396
Richmond, VA 23218
P: (804) 698-7511
F: (804) 698-7651
E: district11
@senate.virginia.gov

**Cosgrove Jr., John A. (R, 14)**
General Assembly Building,
Room 323
P.O. Box 396
Richmond, VA 23218
P: (804) 698-7514
F: (804) 698-7651
E: district14
@senate.virginia.gov

# Virginia

**Dance, Rosalyn R. (D, 16)**
General Assembly Building,
Room 320
P.O. Box 396
Richmond, VA 23218
P: (804) 698-7516
F: (804) 698-7651
E: district16
@senate.virginia.gov

**Deeds, R. Creigh (D, 25)**
General Assembly Building,
Room 432
P.O. Box 396
Richmond, VA 23218
P: (804) 698-7525
F: (804) 698-7651
E: district25
@senate.virginia.gov

**DeSteph Jr., William R.
(R, 8)**
General Assembly Building,
Room 306
P.O. Box 396
Richmond, VA 23218
P: (804) 698-7508
F: (804) 698-7651
E: district08
@senate.virginia.gov

**Dunnavant, Siobhan S.
(R, 12)**
General Assembly Building,
Room 307
P.O. Box 396
Richmond, VA 23218
P: (804) 698-7512
F: (804) 698-7651
E: district12
@senate.virginia.gov

**Ebbin, Adam P. (D, 30)**
General Assembly Building,
Room 328
P.O. Box 396
Richmond, VA 23218
P: (804) 698-7530
F: (804) 698-7651
E: district30
@senate.virginia.gov

**Edwards, John S. (D, 21)**
General Assembly Building,
Room 301
P.O. Box 396
Richmond, VA 23218
P: (804) 698-7521
F: (804) 698-7651
E: district21
@senate.virginia.gov

**Favola, Barbara A. (D, 31)**
General Assembly Building,
Room 316
P.O. Box 396
Richmond, VA 23218
P: (804) 698-7531
F: (804) 698-7651
E: district31
@senate.virginia.gov

**Hanger Jr., Emmett W.
(R, 24)**
General Assembly Building,
Room 326
P.O. Box 396
Richmond, VA 23218
P: (804) 698-7524
F: (804) 698-7651
E: district24
@senate.virginia.gov

**Howell, Janet D. (D, 32)**
General Assembly Building,
Room 321
P.O. Box 396
Richmond, VA 23218
P: (804) 698-7532
F: (804) 698-7651
E: district32
@senate.virginia.gov

**Lewis Jr., Lynwood W.
(D, 6)**
General Assembly Building,
Room 430
P.O. Box 406
Richmond, VA 23218
P: (804) 698-7506
F: (804) 698-7651
E: district06
@senate.virginia.gov

**Locke, Mamie E. (D, 2)**
General Assembly Building,
Room 427
P.O. Box 396
Richmond, VA 23218
P: (804) 698-7502
F: (804) 698-7651
E: district02
@senate.virginia.gov

**Lucas, L. Louise (D, 18)**
General Assembly Building,
Room 426
P.O. Box 396
Richmond, VA 23218
P: (804) 698-7518
F: (804) 698-7651
E: district18
@senate.virginia.gov

**Marsden, David W. (D, 37)**
General Assembly Building,
Room 429
P.O. Box 396
Richmond, VA 23218
P: (804) 698-7537
F: (804) 698-7651
E: district37
@senate.virginia.gov

**Mason, T. Montgomery (D, 1)**
General Assembly Building
P.O. Box 396
Richmond, VA 23218
P: (804) 698-7501
E: district01
@senate.virginia.gov

**McClellan, Jennifer L.
(D, 9)**
General Assembly Building,
Room 310
P.O. Box 396
Richmond, VA 23218
P: (804) 698-7509
F: (804) 698-7961
E: district09
@senate.virginia.gov

**McDougle, Ryan T. (R, 4)**
General Assembly Building,
Room 314
P.O. Box 396
Richmond, VA 23218
P: (804) 698-7504
F: (804) 698-7943
E: district04
@senate.virginia.gov

**McPike, Jeremy S. (D, 29)**
General Assembly Building,
Room 317
P.O. Box 396
Richmond, VA 23218
P: (804) 698-7529
F: (804) 698-7651
E: district29
@senate.virginia.gov

**Newman, Stephen D. (R, 23)**
General Assembly Building,
Room 621
P.O. Box 396
Richmond, VA 23218
P: (804) 698-7523
F: (804) 698-7651
E: district23
@senate.virginia.gov

**Norment Jr., Thomas K.
(R, 3)**
General Assembly Building,
Room 626
P.O. Box 396
Richmond, VA 23218
P: (804) 698-7503
F: (804) 698-7651
E: district03
@senate.virginia.gov

**Obenshain, Mark D. (R, 26)**
General Assembly Building,
Room 331
P.O. Box 396
Richmond, VA 23218
P: (804) 698-7526
F: (804) 698-7651
E: district26
@senate.virginia.gov

**Peake, Mark J. (R, 22)***
General Assembly Building,
Room 322
P.O. Box 396
Richmond, VA 23218
P: (804) 698-7522
F: (804) 698-7651
E: district22
@senate.virginia.gov

**Petersen, Chapman (D, 34)**
General Assembly Building,
Room 329
P.O. Box 396
Richmond, VA 23218
P: (804) 698-7534
F: (804) 698-7651
E: district34
@senate.virginia.gov

**Reeves, Bryce (R, 17)**
General Assembly Building,
Room 312
P.O. Box 396
Richmond, VA 23218
P: (804) 698-7517
F: (804) 698-7651
E: district17
@senate.virginia.gov

**Ruff Jr., Frank M. (R, 15)**
General Assembly Building,
Room 431
P.O. Box 396
Richmond, VA 23218
P: (804) 698-7515
F: (804) 698-7651
E: district15
@senate.virginia.gov

# Virginia

**Saslaw, Richard L. (D, 35)**
General Assembly Building, Room 613
P.O. Box 396
Richmond, VA 23218
P: (804) 698-7535
F: (804) 698-7651
E: district35
@senate.virginia.gov

**Spruill Sr., Lionell (D, 5)**
General Assembly Building
P.O. Box 396
Richmond, VA 23218
P: (804) 698-7505
E: district05
@senate.virginia.gov

**Stanley Jr., William M. (R, 20)**
General Assembly Building, Room 313
P.O. Box 396
Richmond, VA 23218
P: (804) 698-7520
F: (804) 698-7651
E: district20
@senate.virginia.gov

**Stuart, Richard H. (R, 28)**
General Assembly Building, Room 302
P.O. Box 396
Richmond, VA 23218
P: (804) 698-7528
F: (804) 698-7651
E: district28
@senate.virginia.gov

**Sturtevant Jr., Glen H. (R, 10)**
General Assembly Building, Room 318
P.O. Box 396
Richmond, VA 23218
P: (804) 698-7510
F: (804) 698-7651
E: district10
@senate.virginia.gov

**Suetterlein, David R. (R, 19)**
General Assembly Building, Room 322
P.O. Box 396
Richmond, VA 23218
P: (804) 698-7519
F: (804) 698-7651
E: district19
@senate.virginia.gov

**Surovell, Scott A. (D, 36)**
General Assembly Building, Room 308
P.O. Box 396
Richmond, VA 23218
P: (804) 698-7536
F: (804) 698-7651
E: district36
@senate.virginia.gov

**Vogel, Jill Holtzman (R, 27)**
General Assembly Building, Room 309
P.O. Box 396
Richmond, VA 23218
P: (804) 698-7527
F: (804) 698-7651
E: district27
@senate.virginia.gov

**Wagner, Frank W. (R, 7)**
General Assembly Building, Room 304
P.O. Box 396
Richmond, VA 23218
P: (804) 698-7507
F: (804) 698-7651
E: district07
@senate.virginia.gov

**Wexton, Jennifer T. (D, 33)**
General Assembly Building, Room 327
P.O. Box 396
Richmond, VA 23218
P: (804) 698-7533
F: (804) 698-7651
E: district33
@senate.virginia.gov

# House

## Speaker of the House

**Delegate William J. Howell (R)**
House Speaker
General Assembly Building, Room 635
P.O. Box 406
Richmond, VA 23218
P: (804) 698-1028
F: (804) 698-6728
E: DelWHowell
@house.virginia.gov

## House Majority Leader

**Delegate M. Kirkland Cox (R)**
House Majority Leader
General Assembly Building, Room 607
P.O. Box 406
Richmond, VA 23218
P: (804) 698-1066
F: (804) 698-6766
E: DelKCox
@house.virginia.gov

## House Minority Leader

**Delegate David J. Toscano (D)**
House Minority Leader
General Assembly Building, Room 614
P.O. Box 406
Richmond, VA 23218
P: (804) 698-1057
F: (804) 698-6757
E: DelDToscano
@house.virginia.gov

## Clerk of the House

**Mr. G. Paul Nardo**
Clerk of the House
General Assembly Building, Third Floor
P.O. Box 406
Richmond, VA 23218
P: (804) 698-1619
F: (804) 698-1800
E: GPNardo
@house.virginia.gov

## Members of the House

**Adams, Leslie R. (R, 16)**
General Assembly Building, Room 719
P.O. Box 406
Richmond, VA 23218
P: (804) 698-1016
F: (804) 698-6716
E: DelLAdams
@house.virginia.gov

**Aird, Lashrecse D. (D, 63)**
General Assembly Building, Room 817
P.O. Box 406
Richmond, VA 23218
P: (804) 698-1063
F: (804) 698-6763
E: DelLAird
@house.virginia.gov

**Albo, David B. (R, 42)**
General Assembly Building, Room 529
P.O. Box 406
Richmond, VA 23218
P: (804) 698-1042
F: (804) 698-6742
E: DelDAlbo
@house.virginia.gov

**Anderson, Richard L. (R, 51)**
General Assembly Building, Room 406
P.O. Box 406
Richmond, VA 23218
P: (804) 698-1051
F: (804) 698-6751
E: DelRAnderson
@house.virginia.gov

**Austin, Terry L. (R, 19)**
General Assembly Building, Room 412
P.O. Box 406
Richmond, VA 23218
P: (804) 698-1019
F: (804) 698-6719
E: DelTAustin
@house.virginia.gov

**Bagby, Lamont (D, 74)**
General Assembly Building, Room 513
P.O. Box 406
Richmond, VA 23218
P: (804) 698-1074
F: (804) 698-6774
E: DelLBagby
@house.virginia.gov

**Bell, John J. (D, 87)**
General Assembly Building, Room 423
P.O. Box 406
Richmond, VA 23218
P: (804) 698-1087
F: (804) 698-6787
E: DelJBell
@house.virginia.gov

**Bell, Richard P. (R, 20)**
General Assembly Building, Room 517
P.O. Box 406
Richmond, VA 23218
P: (804) 698-1020
F: (804) 698-6720
E: DelDBell
@house.virginia.gov

**Bell, Robert B. (R, 58)**
General Assembly Building,
Room 801
P.O. Box 406
Richmond, VA 23218
P: (804) 698-1058
F: (804) 698-6758
E: DelRBell
 @house.virginia.gov

**Bloxom Jr., Robert S.
 (R, 100)**
General Assembly Building,
Room 405
P.O. Box 406
Richmond, VA 23218
P: (804) 698-1000
E: DelRBloxom
 @house.virginia.gov

**Bourne, Jeffrey M. (D, 71)***
General Assembly Building,
Room 715
P.O. Box 406
Richmond, VA 23218
P: (804) 698-1071
E: DelJBourne
 @house.virginia.gov

**Boysko, Jennifer B. (D, 89)**
General Assembly Building,
Room 816
P.O. Box 406
Richmond, VA 23218
P: (804) 698-1086
F: (804) 698-6786
E: DelJBoysko
 @house.virginia.gov

**Bulova, David L. (D, 37)**
General Assembly Building,
Room 402
P.O. Box 406
Richmond, VA 23218
P: (804) 698-1037
F: (804) 698-6737
E: DelDBulova
 @house.virginia.gov

**Byron, Kathy J. (R, 22)**
General Assembly Building,
Room 411
P.O. Box 406
Richmond, VA 23218
P: (804) 698-1022
F: (804) 698-6722
E: DelKByron
 @house.virginia.gov

**Campbell, Jeffrey L. (R, 6)**
General Assembly Building,
Room 708
P.O. Box 406
Richmond, VA 23218
P: (804) 698-1006
F: (804) 698-6706
E: DelJCampbell
 @house.virginia.gov

**Carr, Betsy B. (D, 69)**
General Assembly Building,
Room 527
P.O. Box 406
Richmond, VA 23218
P: (804) 698-1069
F: (804) 698-6769
E: DelBCarr
 @house.virginia.gov

**Cline, Benjamin L. (R, 24)**
General Assembly Building,
Room 722
P.O. Box 406
Richmond, VA 23218
P: (804) 698-1024
F: (804) 698-6724
E: DelBCline
 @house.virginia.gov

**Cole, Mark L. (R, 88)**
General Assembly Building,
Room 822
P.O. Box 406
Richmond, VA 23218
P: (804) 698-1088
F: (804) 698-6788
E: DelMCole
 @house.virginia.gov

**Collins, Christopher E.
 (R, 29)**
General Assembly Building,
Room 509
P.O. Box 406
Richmond, VA 23218
P: (804) 698-1029
F: (804) 698-6729
E: DelCCollins
 @house.virginia.gov

**Cox, M. Kirkland (R, 66)**
General Assembly Building,
Room 607
P.O. Box 406
Richmond, VA 23218
P: (804) 698-1066
F: (804) 698-6766
E: DelKCox
 @house.virginia.gov

**Davis Jr., Glenn R. (R, 84)**
General Assembly Building,
Room 416
P.O. Box 406
Richmond, VA 23218
P: (804) 698-1084
E: DelGDavis
 @house.virginia.gov

**Dudenhefer, L. Mark (R, 2)**
General Assembly Building,
Room 407
P.O. Box 406
Richmond, VA 23218
P: (804) 698-1002
F: (804) 698-6702
E: DelMDudenhefer
 @house.virginia.gov

**Edmunds II, James E.
 (R, 60)**
General Assembly Building,
Room 805
P.O. Box 406
Richmond, VA 23218
P: (804) 698-1060
F: (804) 698-6760
E: DelJEdmunds
 @house.virginia.gov

**Fariss, C. Matthew (R, 59)**
General Assembly Building,
Room 808
P.O. Box 406
Richmond, VA 23218
P: (804) 698-1059
F: (804) 698-6759
E: DelMFariss
 @house.virginia.gov

**Farrell, Peter F. (R, 56)**
General Assembly Building,
Room 528
P.O. Box 406
Richmond, VA 23218
P: (804) 698-1056
F: (804) 698-6756
E: DelPFarrell
 @house.virginia.gov

**Filler-Corn, Eileen (D, 41)**
General Assembly Building,
Room 414
P.O. Box 406
Richmond, VA 23218
P: (804) 698-1041
F: (804) 698-6741
E: DelEFiller-Corn
 @house.virginia.gov

**Fowler Jr., Hyland F.
 (R, 55)**
General Assembly Building,
Room 810
P.O. Box 406
Richmond, VA 23218
P: (804) 698-1055
F: (804) 698-6755
E: DelBFowler
 @house.virginia.gov

**Freitas, Nicholas J.
 (R, 30)**
General Assembly Building,
Room 718
P.O. Box 406
Richmond, VA 23218
P: (804) 698-1030
F: (804) 698-6730
E: DelNFreitas
 @house.virginia.gov

**Garrett, T. Scott (R, 23)**
General Assembly Building,
Room 524
P.O. Box 406
Richmond, VA 23218
P: (804) 698-1023
F: (804) 698-6723
E: DelSGarrett
 @house.virginia.gov

**Gilbert, C. Todd (R, 15)**
General Assembly Building,
Room 511
P.O. Box 406
Richmond, VA 23218
P: (804) 698-1015
F: (804) 698-6715
E: DelTGilbert
 @house.virginia.gov

**Greason, Thomas A. (R, 32)**
General Assembly Building,
Room 703
P.O. Box 406
Richmond, VA 23218
P: (804) 698-1032
F: (804) 698-6732
E: DelTGreason
 @house.virginia.gov

**Habeeb, Gregory D. (R, 8)**
General Assembly Building,
Room 713
P.O. Box 406
Richmond, VA 23218
P: (804) 698-1008
F: (804) 698-6708
E: DelGHabeeb
 @house.virginia.gov

# Virginia

**Hayes Jr., C.E. (D, 77)\***
General Assembly Building,
Room 418
P.O. Box 406
Richmond, VA 23218
P: (804) 698-1077
E: DelCHayes
   @house.virginia.gov

**Head, Chris T. (R, 17)**
General Assembly Building,
Room 408
P.O. Box 406
Richmond, VA 23218
P: (804) 698-1017
F: (804) 698-6717
E: DelCHead
   @house.virginia.gov

**Helsel, Gordon C. (R, 91)**
General Assembly Building,
Room 812
P.O. Box 406
Richmond, VA 23218
P: (804) 698-1091
E: DelGHelsel
   @house.virginia.gov

**Heretick, Stephen E.
(D, 79)**
General Assembly Building,
Room 809
P.O. Box 406
Richmond, VA 23218
P: (804) 698-1079
F: (804) 698-6779
E: DelSHeretick
   @house.virginia.gov

**Herring, Charniele L.
(D, 46)**
General Assembly Building,
Room 504
P.O. Box 406
Richmond, VA 23218
P: (804) 698-1046
F: (804) 698-6746
E: DelCHerring
   @house.virginia.gov

**Hester, Daun Sessoms
(D, 89)**
General Assembly Building,
Room 813
P.O. Box 406
Richmond, VA 23218
P: (804) 698-1089
F: (804) 698-6789
E: DelDHester
   @house.virginia.gov

**Hodges, M. Keith (R, 98)**
General Assembly Building,
Room 821
P.O. Box 406
Richmond, VA 23218
P: (804) 698-1098
F: (804) 698-6798
E: DelKHodges
   @house.virginia.gov

**Holcomb III, Rocky (R, 85)\***
General Assembly Building,
Room 515
P.O. Box 406
Richmond, VA 23218
P: (804) 698-1085
F: (804) 698-6776
E: DelRHolcomb
   @house.virginia.gov

**Hope, Patrick A. (D, 47)**
General Assembly Building,
Room 712
P.O. Box 406
Richmond, VA 23218
P: (804) 698-1047
F: (804) 698-6747
E: DelPHope
   @house.virginia.gov

**Howell, William J. (R, 28)**
General Assembly Building,
Room 635
P.O. Box 406
Richmond, VA 23218
P: (804) 698-1028
F: (804) 698-6728
E: DelWHowell
   @house.virginia.gov

**Hugo, Timothy D. (R, 40)**
General Assembly Building,
Room 523
P.O. Box 406
Richmond, VA 23218
P: (804) 698-1040
F: (804) 698-6740
E: DelTHugo
   @house.virginia.gov

**Ingram, Riley E. (R, 62)**
General Assembly Building,
Room 404
P.O. Box 406
Richmond, VA 23218
P: (804) 698-1062
F: (804) 698-6762
E: DelRIngram
   @house.virginia.gov

**James, Matthew (D, 80)**
General Assembly Building,
Room 803
P.O. Box 406
Richmond, VA 23218
P: (804) 698-1080
F: (804) 698-6780
E: DelMJames
   @house.virginia.gov

**Jones, S. Chris (R, 76)**
General Assembly Building,
Room 948
P.O. Box 406
Richmond, VA 23218
P: (804) 698-1076
F: (804) 698-6776
E: DelCJones
   @house.virginia.gov

**Keam, Mark L. (D, 35)**
General Assembly Building,
Room 507
P.O. Box 406
Richmond, VA 23218
P: (804) 698-1035
F: (804) 698-6735
E: DelMKeam
   @house.virginia.gov

**Kilgore, Terry G. (R, 1)**
General Assembly Building,
Room 704
P.O. Box 406
Richmond, VA 23218
P: (804) 698-1001
F: (804) 698-6701
E: DelTKilgore
   @house.virginia.gov

**Knight, Barry D. (R, 81)**
General Assembly Building,
Room 415
P.O. Box 406
Richmond, VA 23218
P: (804) 698-1081
F: (804) 698-6781
E: DelBKnight
   @house.virginia.gov

**Kory, Kaye (D, 38)**
General Assembly Building,
Room 707
P.O. Box 406
Richmond, VA 23218
P: (804) 698-1038
F: (804) 698-6738
E: DelKKory
   @house.virginia.gov

**Krizek, Paul E. (D, 44)**
General Assembly Building,
Room 422
P.O. Box 406
Richmond, VA 23218
P: (804) 698-1044
F: (804) 698-6744
E: DelPKrizek
   @house.virginia.gov

**Landes, R. Steven (R, 25)**
General Assembly Building,
Room 947
P.O. Box 406
Richmond, VA 23218
P: (804) 698-1025
F: (804) 698-6725
E: DelSLandes
   @house.virginia.gov

**LaRock, David A. (R, 33)**
General Assembly Building,
Room 721
P.O. Box 406
Richmond, VA 23218
P: (804) 698-1033
F: (804) 698-6733
E: DelDLaRock
   @house.virginia.gov

**Leftwich Jr., James A.
(R, 78)**
General Assembly Building,
Room 417
P.O. Box 406
Richmond, VA 23218
P: (804) 698-1078
F: (804) 698-6778
E: DelJLeftwich
   @house.virginia.gov

**LeMunyon, James M. (R, 67)**
General Assembly Building,
Room 419
P.O. Box 406
Richmond, VA 23218
P: (804) 698-1067
F: (804) 698-6767
E: DelJLeMunyon
   @house.virginia.gov

**Levine, Mark (D, 45)**
General Assembly Building,
Room 709
P.O. Box 406
Richmond, VA 23218
P: (804) 698-1045
F: (804) 698-6745
E: DelMLevine
   @house.virginia.gov

**Lindsey, Joseph C. (D, 90)**
General Assembly Building,
Room 505
P.O. Box 406
Richmond, VA 23218
P: (804) 698-1090
F: (804) 698-6790
E: DelJLindsey
@house.virginia.gov

**Lingamfelter, L. Scott
(R, 31)**
General Assembly Building,
Room 804
P.O. Box 406
Richmond, VA 23218
P: (804) 698-1031
F: (804) 698-6731
E: DelSLingamfelter
@house.virginia.gov

**Lopez, Alfonso (D, 49)**
General Assembly Building,
Room 716
P.O. Box 406
Richmond, VA 23218
P: (804) 698-1049
F: (804) 698-6749
E: DelALopez
@House.virginia.gov

**Loupassi, G. Manuel (R, 68)**
General Assembly Building,
Room 520
P.O. Box 406
Richmond, VA 23218
P: (804) 698-1068
F: (804) 698-6768
E: DelMLoupassi
@house.virginia.gov

**Marshall III, Daniel W.
(R, 14)**
General Assembly Building,
Room 702
P.O. Box 406
Richmond, VA 23218
P: (804) 698-1014
F: (804) 698-6714
E: DelDMarshall
@house.virginia.gov

**Marshall, Robert G. (R, 13)**
General Assembly Building,
Room 501
P.O. Box 406
Richmond, VA 23218
P: (804) 698-1013
F: (804) 698-6713
E: DelBMarshall
@house.virginia.gov

**Massie III, James P.
(R, 72)**
General Assembly Building,
Room 516
P.O. Box 406
Richmond, VA 23218
P: (804) 698-1072
F: (804) 698-6772
E: DelJMassie
@house.virginia.gov

**McQuinn, Delores L. (D, 70)**
General Assembly Building,
Room 522
P.O. Box 406
Richmond, VA 23218
P: (804) 698-1070
F: (804) 698-6770
E: DelDMcQuinn
@house.virginia.gov

**Miller, Jackson H. (R, 50)**
General Assembly Building,
Room 720
P.O. Box 406
Richmond, VA 23218
P: (804) 698-1050
F: (804) 698-6750
E: DelJMiller
@house.virginia.gov

**Minchew, J. Randy (R, 10)**
General Assembly Building,
Room 525
P.O. Box 406
Richmond, VA 23218
P: (804) 698-1010
F: (804) 698-6710
E: DelRMinchew
@house.virginia.gov

**Miyares, Jason S. (R, 82)**
General Assembly Building,
Room 410
P.O. Box 406
Richmond, VA 23218
P: (804) 698-1082
F: (804) 698-6782
E: DelJMiyares
@house.virginia.gov

**Morefield, James W. (R, 3)**
General Assembly Building,
Room 714
P.O. Box 406
Richmond, VA 23218
P: (804) 698-1003
F: (804) 698-6703
E: DelJMorefield
@house.virginia.gov

**Morris, Richard L. (R, 64)**
General Assembly Building,
Room 807
P.O. Box 406
Richmond, VA 23218
P: (804) 698-1064
F: (804) 698-6764
E: DelRMorris
@house.virginia.gov

**Mullin, Michael P. (D, 93)\***
General Assembly Building
P.O. Box 406
Richmond, VA 23218
P: (804) 698-1093
E: DelMMullin
@house.virginia.gov

**Murphy, Kathleen J. (D, 34)**
General Assembly Building,
Room 413
P.O. Box 406
Richmond, VA 23218
P: (804) 698-1034
F: (804) 698-6734
E: DelKMurphy
@house.virginia.gov

**O'Bannon III, John M.
(R, 73)**
General Assembly Building,
Room 521
P.O. Box 406
Richmond, VA 23218
P: (804) 698-1073
F: (804) 698-6773
E: DelJOBannon
@house.virginia.gov

**O'Quinn, Israel D. (R, 5)**
General Assembly Building,
Room 705
P.O. Box 406
Richmond, VA 23218
P: (804) 698-1005
F: (804) 698-6705
E: DelIOQuinn
@house.virginia.gov

**Orrock Sr., Robert D.
(R, 54)**
General Assembly Building,
Room 701
P.O. Box 406
Richmond, VA 23218
P: (804) 698-1054
F: (804) 698-6754
E: DelBOrrock
@house.virginia.gov

**Peace, Christopher Kilian
(R, 97)**
General Assembly Building,
Room 820
P.O. Box 406
Richmond, VA 23218
P: (804) 698-1097
F: (804) 698-6797
E: DelCPeace
@house.virginia.gov

**Pillion, Todd E. (R, 4)**
General Assembly Building,
Room 706
P.O. Box 406
Richmond, VA 23218
P: (804) 698-1004
F: (804) 698-6704
E: DelTPillion
@house.virginia.gov

**Plum, Kenneth R. (D, 36)**
General Assembly Building,
Room 401
P.O. Box 406
Richmond, VA 23218
P: (804) 698-1036
F: (804) 698-6736
E: DelKPlum
@house.virginia.gov

**Pogge, Brenda L. (R, 96)**
General Assembly Building,
Room 403
P.O. Box 406
Richmond, VA 23218
P: (804) 698-1096
F: (804) 698-1196
E: DelBPogge
@house.virginia.gov

**Poindexter, Charles D.
(R, 9)**
General Assembly Building,
Room 802
P.O. Box 406
Richmond, VA 23218
P: (804) 698-1009
F: (804) 698-6709
E: DelCPoindexter
@house.virginia.gov

**Price, Marcia S. (D, 95)**
General Assembly Building,
Room 818
P.O. Box 406
Richmond, VA 23218
P: (804) 698-1095
F: (804) 698-6795
E: DelMPrice
@house.virginia.gov

# Virginia

**Ransone, Margaret Bevans (R, 99)**
General Assembly Building,
Room 512
P.O. Box 406
Richmond, VA 23218
P: (804) 698-1099
F: (804) 786-6310
E: DelMRansone
@house.virginia.gov

**Rasoul, Sam (D, 11)**
General Assembly Building,
Room 814
P.O. Box 406
Richmond, VA 23218
P: (804) 698-1011
F: (804) 698-6711
E: DelSRasoul
@house.virginia.gov

**Robinson, Roxann L. (R, 27)**
General Assembly Building,
Room 409
P.O. Box 406
Richmond, VA 23218
P: (804) 698-1027
F: (804) 698-6727
E: DelRRobinson
@house.virginia.gov

**Rush, L. Nick (R, 7)**
General Assembly Building,
Room 519
P.O. Box 406
Richmond, VA 23218
P: (804) 698-1007
F: (804) 698-6707
E: DelNRush
@house.virginia.gov

**Sickles, Mark D. (D, 43)**
General Assembly Building,
Room 711
P.O. Box 406
Richmond, VA 23218
P: (804) 698-1043
F: (804) 698-6743
E: DelMSickles
@house.virginia.gov

**Simon, Marcus B. (D, 53)**
General Assembly Building,
Room 710
P.O. Box 406
Richmond, VA 23218
P: (804) 698-1053
F: (804) 698-6753
E: DelMSimon
@house.virginia.gov

**Stolle, Christopher P. (R, 83)**
General Assembly Building,
Room 420
P.O. Box 406
Richmond, VA 23218
P: (804) 698-1083
F: (804) 698-6783
E: DelCStolle
@house.virginia.gov

**Sullivan Jr., Richard C. (D, 48)**
General Assembly Building,
Room 819
P.O. Box 406
Richmond, VA 23218
P: (804) 698-1048
F: (804) 698-6748
E: DelRSullivan
@house.virginia.gov

**Torian, Luke E. (D, 52)**
General Assembly Building,
Room 508
P.O. Box 406
Richmond, VA 23218
P: (804) 698-1052
F: (804) 698-6752
E: DelLTorian
@house.virginia.gov

**Toscano, David J. (D, 57)**
General Assembly Building,
Room 614
P.O. Box 406
Richmond, VA 23218
P: (804) 698-1057
F: (804) 698-6757
E: DelDToscano
@house.virginia.gov

**Tyler, Roslyn C. (D, 75)**
General Assembly Building,
Room 506
P.O. Box 406
Richmond, VA 23218
P: (804) 698-1075
F: (804) 698-6775
E: DelRTyler
@house.virginia.gov

**Villanueva, Ronald A. (R, 21)**
General Assembly Building,
Room 503
P.O. Box 406
Richmond, VA 23218
P: (804) 698-1021
F: (804) 698-6721
E: DelRVillanueva
@house.virginia.gov

**Ward, Jeion A. (D, 92)**
General Assembly Building,
Room 502
P.O. Box 406
Richmond, VA 23218
P: (804) 698-1092
F: (804) 698-6792
E: DelJWard
@house.virginia.gov

**Ware Jr., R. Lee (R, 65)**
General Assembly Building,
Room 421
P.O. Box 406
Richmond, VA 23218
P: (804) 698-1065
F: (804) 698-6765
E: DelLWare
@house.virginia.gov

**Watts, Vivian E. (D, 39)**
General Assembly Building,
Room 514
P.O. Box 406
Richmond, VA 23218
P: (804) 698-1039
F: (804) 698-6739
E: DelVWatts
@house.virginia.gov

**Webert, Michael J. (R, 18)**
General Assembly Building,
Room 510
P.O. Box 406
Richmond, VA 23218
P: (804) 698-1018
F: (804) 698-6718
E: DelMWebert
@house.virginia.gov

**Wilt, Tony O. (R, 26)**
General Assembly Building,
Room 526
P.O. Box 406
Richmond, VA 23218
P: (804) 698-1026
F: (804) 698-6726
E: DelTWilt
@house.virginia.gov

**Wright Jr., Thomas C. (R, 61)**
General Assembly Building,
Room 811
P.O. Box 406
Richmond, VA 23218
P: (804) 698-1061
F: (804) 698-6761
E: DelTWright
@house.virginia.gov

**Yancey, David E. (R, 94)**
General Assembly Building,
Room 717
P.O. Box 406
Richmond, VA 23218
P: (804) 698-1094
F: (804) 698-6794
E: DelDYancey
@house.virginia.gov

**Yost, Joseph R. (R, 12)**
General Assembly Building,
Room 518
P.O. Box 406
Richmond, VA 23218
P: (804) 698-1012
F: (804) 698-6712
E: DelJYost
@House.virginia.gov

# Washington

## Executive

### Governor
**The Honorable Jay Inslee (D)**
Governor
P.O. Box 40002
Olympia, WA 98504
P: (360) 902-4111
F: (360) 753-4110

### Lieutenant Governor
**The Honorable Cyrus Habib (D)**
Lieutenant Governor
416 14th Avenue Southwest
P.O. Box 40448
Olympia, WA 98504
P: (360) 786-7694
F: (360) 786-7749

### Attorney General
**The Honorable Bob Ferguson (D)**
Attorney General
1125 Washington Street, Southeast
P.O. Box 40100
Olympia, WA 98504
P: (360) 753-6200
F: (360) 664-0228
E: bob.ferguson@atg.wa.gov

### Auditor
**The Honorable Pat McCarthy (D)**
State Auditor
P.O. Box 40021
Olympia, WA 98504
P: (360) 902-0370
F: (360) 753-0646
E: auditor@sao.wa.gov

### Commissioner of Insurance
**The Honorable Mike Kreidler (D)**
Commissioner
P.O. Box 40256
Olympia, WA 98504
P: (360) 725-7000
F: (360) 586-3535
E: askMike@oic.wa.gov

### Commissioner of Public Lands
**The Honorable Hilary Franz (D)**
Commissioner of Public Lands
111 Washington Street, Southeast
P.O. Box 47000
Olympia, WA 98504
P: (360) 902-1000
F: (360) 902-1775
E: cpl@dnr.wa.gov

### Secretary of State
**Ms. Kim Wyman (R)**
Secretary of State
P.O. Box 40220
Olympia, WA 98504
P: (360) 902-4151
F: (360) 586-5629
E: kim.wyman@sos.wa.gov

### Superintendent of Public Instruction
**The Honorable Chris Reykdal**
Superintendent of Public Instruction
Old Capitol Building
Olympia, WA 98504
P: (360) 725-6115
F: (360) 753-6712

### Treasurer
**The Honorable Duane Davidson (R)**
State Treasurer
P.O. Box 40200
Olympia, WA 98504
P: (360) 902-9001
F: (360) 902-9037

## Judiciary

### Supreme Court (NE)
**Ms. Susan Carlson**
Clerk
415 12th Avenue, Southwest
P.O. Box 40929
Olympia, WA 98504
P: (360) 357-2077

**The Honorable Mary E. Fairhurst**
Chief Justice
**The Honorable Steven C. Gonzalez**
**The Honorable Charles W. Johnson**
**The Honorable Barbara A. Madsen**
**The Honorable Sheryl Gordon McCloud**
**The Honorable Susan J. Owens**

**The Honorable Debra L. Stephens**
**The Honorable Charlie Wiggins**
**The Honorable Mary Yu**

## Legislative Senate

### Senate President
**The Honorable Cyrus Habib (D)**
Lieutenant Governor
416 14th Avenue Southwest
P.O. Box 40448
Olympia, WA 98504
P: (360) 786-7694
F: (360) 786-7749

### President Pro Tempore of the Senate
**Senator Tim Sheldon (D)**
President Pro Tempore
312 Legislative Building
P.O. Box 40435
Olympia, WA 98504
P: (360) 786-7668
F: (360) 786-1999
E: timothy.sheldon @leg.wa.gov

### Senate Majority Leader
**Senator Mark Schoesler (R)**
Senate Majority Leader
307 Legislative Building
P.O. Box 40409
Olympia, WA 98504
P: (360) 786-7620
F: (360) 786-1999
E: mark.schoesler @leg.wa.gov

### Senate Minority Leader
**Senator Sharon Nelson (D)**
Senate Democratic Leader
316 Legislative Building
P.O. Box 40434
Olympia, WA 98504
P: (360) 786-7667
E: sharon.nelson@leg.wa.gov

### Secretary of the Senate
**Mr. Hunter G. Goodman**
Secretary of the Senate
418 Legislative Building
P.O. Box 40482
Olympia, WA 98504
P: (360) 786-7550
E: hunter.goodman @leg.wa.gov

### Members of the Senate
**Angel, Jan (R, 26)**
203A Irv Newhouse Building
P.O. Box 40426
Olympia, WA 98504
P: (360) 786-7650
E: jan.angel@leg.wa.gov

**Bailey, Barbara (R, 10)**
407 Legislative Building
P.O. Box 40410
Olympia, WA 98504
P: (360) 786-7618
E: barbara.bailey @leg.wa.gov

**Baumgartner, Michael (R, 6)**
404 Legislative Building
P.O. Box 40406
Olympia, WA 98504
P: (360) 786-7610
E: michael.baumgartner @leg.wa.gov

**Becker, Randi (R, 2)**
305 Legislative Building
P.O. Box 40402
Olympia, WA 98502
P: (360) 786-7602
E: randi.becker@leg.wa.gov

**Billig, Andy (D, 3)**
412 Legislative Building
P.O. Box 40403
Olympia, WA 98504
P: (360) 786-7604
E: andy.billig@leg.wa.gov

**Braun, John (R, 20)**
303 John A. Cherberg Building
P.O. Box 40420
Olympia, WA 98504
P: (360) 786-7638
E: john.braun@leg.wa.gov

**Brown, Sharon (R, 8)**
202 Irv Newhouse Building
P.O. Box 40408
Olympia, WA 98504
P: (360) 786-7614
E: sharon.brown@leg.wa.gov

# Washington

**Carlyle, Reuven (D, 36)**
213 John A. Cherberg Building
P.O. Box 40436
Olympia, WA 98504
P: (360) 786-7670
E: reuven.carlyle
    @leg.wa.gov

**Chase, Maralyn (D, 32)**
224 John A. Cherberg Building
P.O. Box 40432
Olympia, WA 98504
P: (360) 786-7662
E: maralyn.chase@leg.wa.gov

**Cleveland, Annette (D, 49)**
220 John A. Cherberg Building
P.O. Box 40449
Olympia, WA 98504
P: (360) 786-7696
E: Annette.Cleveland
    @leg.wa.gov

**Conway, Steve (D, 29)**
241 John A. Cherberg Building
P.O. Box 40429
Olympia, WA 98504
P: (360) 786-7656
E: steve.conway@leg.wa.gov

**Darneille, Jeannie (D, 27)**
237 John A. Cherberg Building
P.O. Box 40427
Olympia, WA 98504
P: (360) 786-7652
E: jeannie.darneille
    @leg.wa.gov

**Ericksen, Doug (R, 42)**
414 Legislative Building
P.O. Box 40442
Olympia, WA 98504
P: (360) 786-7682
E: doug.ericksen@leg.wa.gov

**Fain, Joe (R, 47)**
309 Legislative Building
P.O. Box 40447
Olympia, WA 98504
P: (360) 786-7692
E: joe.fain@leg.wa.gov

**Fortunato, Phil (R, 31)\***
201 Irv Newhouse Building
P.O. Box 40431
Olympia, WA 98504
P: (360) 786-7660
E: Phil.Fortunato
    @leg.wa.gov

**Frockt, David (D, 46)**
227 John A. Cherberg Building
P.O. Box 40446
Olympia, WA 98504
P: (360) 786-7690
E: david.frockt@leg.wa.gov

**Hasegawa, Bob (D, 11)**
223 John A. Cherberg Building
P.O. Box 40411
Olympia, WA 98504
P: (360) 786-7616
E: bob.hasegawa@leg.wa.gov

**Hawkins, Brad (R, 12)**
107 Irv Newhouse Building
P.O. Box 40412
Olympia, WA 98504
P: (360) 786-7832
E: brad.hawkins@leg.wa.gov

**Hobbs, Steve (D, 44)**
239 John A. Cherberg Building
P.O. Box 40444
Olympia, WA 98504
P: (360) 786-7686
E: steve.hobbs@leg.wa.gov

**Honeyford, Jim (R, 15)**
112 Irv Newhouse Building
P.O. Box 40415
Olympia, WA 98504
P: (360) 786-7684
F: (360) 786-1999
E: jim.honeyford@leg.wa.gov

**Hunt, Sam (D, 22)**
405 Legislative Building
P.O. Box 40622
Olympia, WA 98504
P: (360) 786-7992
E: sam.hunt@leg.wa.gov

**Keiser, Karen (D, 33)**
219 John A. Cherberg Building
P.O. Box 40433
Olympia, WA 98504
P: (360) 786-7664
F: (360) 786-1999
E: karen.keiser@leg.wa.gov

**King, Curtis (R, 14)**
305 John A. Cherberg Building
P.O. Box 40414
Olympia, WA 98504
P: (360) 786-7626
F: (360) 786-1999
E: curtis.king@leg.wa.gov

**Kuderer, Patty (D, 48)**
411 Legislative Building
P.O. Box 40448
Olympia, WA 98504
P: (360) 786-7694
E: patricia.kuderer
    @leg.wa.gov

**Liias, Marko (D, 21)**
416 Legislative Building
P.O. Box 40421
Olympia, WA 98504
P: (360) 786-7640
E: marko.liias@leg.wa.gov

**McCoy, John (D, 38)**
314 Legislative Building
P.O. Box 40438
Olympia, WA 98504
P: (360) 786-7674
E: john.mccoy@leg.wa.gov

**Miloscia, Mark (R, 30)**
105 Irv Newhouse Building
P.O. Box 40430
Olympia, WA 98504
P: (360) 786-7658
E: mark.miloscia@leg.wa.gov

**Mullet, Mark (D, 5)**
415 Legislative Building
P.O. Box 40405
Olympia, WA 98504
P: (360) 786-7608
E: mark.mullet@leg.wa.gov

**Nelson, Sharon (D, 34)**
316 Legislative Building
P.O. Box 40434
Olympia, WA 98504
P: (360) 786-7667
E: sharon.nelson@leg.wa.gov

**O'Ban, Steve (R, 28)**
102 Irv Newhouse Building
P.O. Box 40428
Olympia, WA 98504
P: (360) 786-7654
E: steve.oban@leg.wa.gov

**Padden, Mike (R, 4)**
106 Irv Newhouse Building
P.O. Box 40404
Olympia, WA 98504
P: (360) 786-7606
E: mike.padden@leg.wa.gov

**Palumbo, Guy (D, 1)\***
402 Legislative Building
P.O. Box 40401
Olympia, WA 98504
P: (360) 786-7600
E: Guy.Palumbo@leg.wa.gov

**Pearson, Kirk (R, 39)**
115D Irv Newhouse Building
P.O. Box 40439
Olympia, WA 98504
P: (360) 786-7676
E: kirk.pearson@leg.wa.gov

**Pedersen, Jamie (D, 43)**
235 John A. Cherberg Building
P.O. Box 40443
Olympia, WA 98504
P: (360) 786-7628
E: jamie.pedersen
    @leg.wa.gov

**Ranker, Kevin (D, 40)**
215 John A. Cherberg Building
P.O. Box 40440
Olympia, WA 98504
P: (360) 786-7678
E: kevin.ranker@leg.wa.gov

**Rivers, Ann (R, 18)**
204 Irv Newhouse Building
P.O. Box 40418
Olympia, WA 98504
P: (360) 786-7634
E: ann.rivers@leg.wa.gov

**Rolfes, Christine (D, 23)**
233 John A. Cherberg Building
P.O. Box 40423
Olympia, WA 98504
P: (360) 786-7644
E: christine.rolfes
    @leg.wa.gov

**Schoesler, Mark (R, 9)**
307 Legislative Building
P.O. Box 40409
Olympia, WA 98504
P: (360) 786-7620
F: (360) 786-1999
E: mark.schoesler
    @leg.wa.gov

**Sheldon, Tim (D, 35)**
312 Legislative Building
P.O. Box 40435
Olympia, WA 98504
P: (360) 786-7668
F: (360) 786-1999
E: timothy.sheldon
    @leg.wa.gov

**Short, Shelly (R, 7)**
409  Legislative Building
P.O. Box 40407
Olympia, WA 98504
P: (340) 786-7612
E: shelly.short@leg.wa.gov

**Takko, Dean (D, 19)**
226 John A. Cherberg Building
P.O. Box 40419
Olympia, WA 98504
P: (360) 786-7636
E: dean.takko@leg.wa.gov

**Van De Wege, Kevin (D, 24)**
212 John A. Cherberg Building
P.O. Box 40624
Olympia, WA 98504
P: (360) 786-7916
E: kevin.vandewege
    @leg.wa.gov

**Walsh, Maureen (R, 16)**
205 Irv Newhouse Building
P.O. Box 40416
Olympia, WA 98504
P: (360) 786-7836
E: maureen.walsh@leg.wa.gov

**Warnick, Judy (R, 13)**
103 Irv Newhouse Building
P.O. Box 40413
Olympia, WA 98504
P: (360) 786-7624
E: judy.warnick@leg.wa.gov

**Wellman, Lisa (D, 41)***
218 John A. Cherberg Building
P.O. Box 40401
Olympia, WA 98504
P: (360) 786-7641
E: Lisa.Wellman@leg.wa.gov

**Wilson, Lynda (R, 17)**
110 Irv Newhouse Building
P.O. Box 40617
Olympia, WA 98504
P: (360) 786-7994
E: lynda.wilson@leg.wa.gov

**Zeiger, Hans (R, 25)**
109 Irv Newhouse Building
P.O. Box 40625
Olympia, WA 98504
P: (360) 786-7968
E: hans.zeiger@leg.wa.gov

# House

## Speaker of the House

**Representative Frank Chopp (D)**
House Speaker
339C Legislative Building
P.O. Box 40600
Olympia, WA 98504
P: (360) 786-7920
E: frank.chopp@leg.wa.gov

## Speaker Pro Tempore of the House

**Representative Tina L. Orwall (D)**
Speaker Pro Tempore
326 John L. O'Brien Building
P.O. Box 40600
Olympia, WA 98504
P: (360) 786-7834
E: tina.orwall@leg.wa.gov

## House Majority Leader

**Representative Pat Sullivan (D)**
House Majority Leader
339A Legislative Building
P.O. Box 40600
Olympia, WA 98504
P: (360) 786-7858
E: pat.sullivan@leg.wa.gov

## House Minority Leader

**Representative Dan Kristiansen (R)**
House Minority Leader
335C Legislative Building
P.O. Box 40600
Olympia, WA 98504
P: (360) 786-7967
E: dan.kristiansen@leg.wa.gov

## Clerk of the House

**Mr. Bernard Dean**
Chief Clerk
P.O. Box 40600
Olympia, WA 98504
P: (360) 786-7750
E: bernard.dean@leg.wa.gov

## Members of the House

**Appleton, Sherry (D, 23)**
132F Legislative Building
P.O. Box 40600
Olympia, WA 98504
P: (360) 786-7934
E: sherry.appleton@leg.wa.gov

**Barkis, Andrew (R, 2)**
122D Legislative Building
P.O. Box 40600
Olympia, WA 98504
P: (360) 786-7824
E: andrew.barkis@leg.wa.gov

**Bergquist, Steve (D, 11)**
322 John L. O'Brien Building
P.O. Box 40600
Olympia, WA 98504
P: (360) 786-7862
E: steve.bergquist@leg.wa.gov

**Blake, Brian (D, 19)**
437A Legislative Building
P.O. Box 40600
Olympia, WA 98504
P: (360) 786-7870
E: brian.blake@leg.wa.gov

**Buys, Vincent (R, 42)**
465 John L. O'Brien Building
P.O. Box 40600
Olympia, WA 98504
P: (360) 786-7854
E: vincent.buys@leg.wa.gov

**Caldier, Michelle (R, 26)**
409 John L. O'Brien Building
P.O. Box 40600
Olympia, WA 98504
P: (360) 786-7802
E: michelle.caldier@leg.wa.gov

**Chandler, Bruce (R, 15)**
427B Legislative Building
P.O. Box 40600
Olympia, WA 98504
P: (360) 786-7960
E: bruce.chandler@leg.wa.gov

**Chapman, Mike (D, 24)***
132B Legislative Building
P.O. Box 40600
Olympia, WA 98504
P: (360) 786-7916
E: Mike.Chapman@leg.wa.gov

**Chopp, Frank (D, 43)**
339C Legislative Building
P.O. Box 40600
Olympia, WA 98504
P: (360) 786-7920
E: frank.chopp@leg.wa.gov

**Clibborn, Judy (D, 41)**
415 John L. O'Brien Building
P.O. Box 40600
Olympia, WA 98504
P: (360) 786-7926
E: judy.clibborn@leg.wa.gov

**Cody, Eileen (D, 34)**
303 John L. O'Brien Building
P.O. Box 40600
Olympia, WA 98504
P: (360) 786-7978
E: eileen.cody@leg.wa.gov

**Condotta, Cary (R, 12)**
425B Legislative Building
P.O. Box 40600
Olympia, WA 98504
P: (360) 786-7954
E: cary.condotta@leg.wa.gov

**DeBolt, Richard (R, 20)**
425A Legislative Building
P.O. Box 40600
Olympia, WA 98504
P: (360) 786-7896
E: richard.debolt@leg.wa.gov

**Dent, Tom (R, 13)**
437 John L. O'Brien Building
P.O. Box 40600
Olympia, WA 98504
P: (360) 786-7932
E: tom.dent@leg.wa.gov

**Doglio, Beth (D, 22)***
317 John L. O'Brien Building
P.O. Box 40600
Olympia, WA 98504
P: (360) 786-7992
E: Beth.Doglio@leg.wa.gov

**Dolan, Laurie (D, 22)***
318 John L. O'Brien Building
P.O. Box 40600
Olympia, WA 98504
P: (360) 786-7940
E: Laurie.Dolan@leg.wa.gov

**Dye, Mary (R, 9)**
432 John L. O'Brien Building
P.O. Box 40600
Olympia, WA 98504
P: (360) 786-7942
E: Mary.Dye@leg.wa.gov

**Farrell, Jessyn (D, 46)**
370 John L. O'Brien Building
P.O. Box 40600
Olympia, WA 98504
P: (360) 786-7818
E: jessyn.farrell@leg.wa.gov

**Fey, Jake (D, 27)**
414 John L. O'Brien Building
P.O. Box 40600
Olympia, WA 98504
P: (360) 786-7974
E: jake.fey@leg.wa.gov

**Fitzgibbon, Joe (D, 34)**
305 John L. O'Brien Building
P.O. Box 40600
Olympia, WA 98504
P: (360) 786-7952
E: joe.fitzgibbon@leg.wa.gov

**Frame, Noel (D, 36)**
319 John L. O'Brien Building
P.O. Box 40600
Olympia, WA 98504
P: (360) 786-7814
E: noel.frame@leg.wa.gov

**Goodman, Roger (D, 45)**
436B Legislative Building
P.O. Box 40600
Olympia, WA 98504
P: (360) 786-7878
E: roger.goodman@leg.wa.gov

**Graves, Paul (R, 5)***
469 John L. O'Brien Building
P.O. Box 40600
Olympia, WA 98504
P: (360) 786-7876
E: Paul.Graves@leg.wa.gov

# Washington

**Gregerson, Mia (D, 33)**
328 John L. O'Brien Building
P.O. Box 40600
Olympia, WA 98504
P: (360) 786-7868
E: mia.gregerson@leg.wa.gov

**Griffey, Daniel (R, 35)**
410 John L. O'Brien Building
P.O. Box 40600
Olympia, WA 98504
P: (360) 786-7966
E: dan.griffey@leg.wa.gov

**Haler, Larry (R, 8)**
122H Legislative Building
P.O. Box 40600
Olympia, WA 98504
P: (360) 786-7986
E: larry.haler@leg.wa.gov

**Hansen, Drew (D, 23)**
369 John L. O'Brien Building
P.O. Box 40600
Olympia, WA 98504
P: (360) 786-7842
E: drew.hansen@leg.wa.gov

**Hargrove, Mark (R, 47)**
436 John L. O'Brien Building
P.O. Box 40600
Olympia, WA 98504
P: (360) 786-7918
E: mark.hargrove@leg.wa.gov

**Harmsworth, Mark (R, 44)**
466 John L. O'Brien Building
P.O. Box 40600
Olympia, WA 98504
P: (360) 786-7892
E: mark.harmsworth
   @leg.wa.gov

**Harris, Paul (R, 17)**
403 John L. O'Brien Building
P.O. Box 40600
Olympia, WA 98504
P: (360) 786-7976
E: paul.harris@leg.wa.gov

**Hayes, Dave (R, 10)**
467 John L. O'Brien Building
P.O. Box 40600
Olympia, WA 98504
P: (360) 786-7914
E: dave.hayes@leg.wa.gov

**Holy, Jeff (R, 6)**
405 John L. O'Brien Building
P.O. Box 40600
Olympia, WA 98504
P: (360) 786-7962
E: jeff.holy@leg.wa.gov

**Hudgins, Zack (D, 11)**
438A Legislative Building
P.O. Box 40600
Olympia, WA 98504
P: (360) 786-7956
E: zack.hudgins@leg.wa.gov

**Irwin, Morgan (R, 31)\***
430 John L. O'Brien Building
PO Box 40600
Olympia, WA 98504
P: (360) 786-7866
E: morgan.irwin@leg.wa.gov

**Jenkin, William (R, 16)\***
417 John L. O'Brien Building
P.O. Box 40600
Olympia, WA 98504
P: (360) 786-7836
E: Bill.Jenkin@leg.wa.gov

**Jinkins, Laurie A. (D, 27)**
308 John L. O'Brien Building
P.O. Box 40600
Olympia, WA 98504
P: (360) 786-7930
E: laurie.jinkins
   @leg.wa.gov

**Johnson, Norm (R, 14)**
122C Legislative Building
P.O. Box 40600
Olympia, WA 98504
P: (360) 786-7810
E: norm.johnson@leg.wa.gov

**Kagi, Ruth (D, 32)**
320 John L. O'Brien Building
P.O. Box 40600
Olympia, WA 98504
P: (360) 786-7910
E: ruth.kagi@leg.wa.gov

**Kilduff, Christine (D, 28)**
334 John L. O'Brien Building
P.O. Box 40600
Olympia, WA 98504
P: (360) 786-7958
E: christine.kilduff
   @leg.wa.gov

**Kirby, Steve (D, 29)**
437B Legislative Building
P.O. Box 40600
Olympia, WA 98504
P: (360) 786-7996
E: steve.kirby@leg.wa.gov

**Klippert, Brad (R, 8)**
122A Legislative Building
P.O. Box 40600
Olympia, WA 98504
P: (360) 786-7882
E: brad.klippert@leg.wa.gov

**Kloba, Shelley (D, 1)\***
132A Legislative Building
P.O. Box 40600
Olympia, WA 98504
P: (360) 786-7900
E: Shelley.Kloba@leg.wa.gov

**Koster, John (R, 39)**
122G Legislative Building
P.O. Box 40600
Olympia, WA 98504
P: (360) 786-7994
E: Josh.Koster@leg.wa.gov

**Kraft, Vicki (R, 17)\***
418 John L. O'Brien Building
P.O. Box 40600
Olympia, WA 98504
P: (360) 786-7994
E: Vicki.Kraft@leg.wa.gov

**Kretz, Joel (R, 7)**
335A Legislative Building
P.O. Box 40600
Olympia, WA 98504
P: (360) 786-7988
E: joel.kretz@leg.wa.gov

**Kristiansen, Dan (R, 39)**
335C Legislative Building
P.O. Box 40600
Olympia, WA 98504
P: (360) 786-7967
E: dan.kristiansen
   @leg.wa.gov

**Lovick, John (D, 44)**
429B Legislative Building
P.O. Box 40600
Olympia, WA 98504
P: (360) 786-7804
E: john.lovick@leg.wa.gov

**Lytton, Kristine (D, 40)**
368 John L. O'Brien Building
P.O. Box 40600
Olympia, WA 98504
P: (360) 786-7800
E: kristine.lytton
   @leg.wa.gov

**MacEwen, Drew (R, 35)**
434 John L. O'Brien Building
P.O. Box 40600
Olympia, WA 98504
P: (360) 786-7902
E: drew.macewen@leg.wa.gov

**Macri, Nicole (D, 43)\***
311 John L. O'Brien Building
P.O. Box 40600
Olympia, WA 98504
P: (360) 786-7826
E: Nicole.Macri@leg.wa.gov

**Manweller, Matt (R, 13)**
470 John L. O'Brien Building
P.O. Box 40600
Olympia, WA 98504
P: (360) 786-7808
E: matt.manweller
   @leg.wa.gov

**Maycumber, Jacquelin
   (R, 7)\***
411 John L. O'Brien Building
P.O. Box 40600
Olympia, WA 98504
P: (360) 786-7908
E: jacquelin.maycumber
   @leg.wa.gov

**McBride, Joan (D, 48)**
335 John L. O'Brien Building
P.O. Box 40600
Olympia, WA 98504
P: (360) 786-7848
E: joan.mcbride@leg.wa.gov

**McCabe, Gina (R, 14)**
431 John L. O'Brien Building
P.O. Box 40600
Olympia, WA 98504
P: (360) 786-7856
E: gina.mccabe@leg.wa.gov

**McCaslin Jr., Bob (R, 4)**
425 John L O'Brien Building
PO Box 40600
Olympia, WA 98504
P: (360) 786-7946
E: bob.mccaslin@leg.wa.gov

**McDonald, Joyce (R, 25)**
406 John L. O'Brien Building
P.O. Box 40600
Olympia, WA 98504
P: (360) 786-7968
E: Joyce.McDonald
   @leg.wa.gov

**Morris, Jeff (D, 40)**
436A Legislative Building
P.O. Box 40600
Olympia, WA 98504
P: (360) 786-7970
E: jeff.morris@leg.wa.gov

**Muri, Dick (R, 28)**
424 John L. O'Brien Building
P.O. Box 40600
Olympia, WA 98504
P: (360) 786-7890
E: dick.muri@leg.wa.gov

**Nealey, Terry (R, 16)**
404 John L. O'Brien Building
P.O. Box 40600
Olympia, WA 98504
P: (360) 786-7828
E: terry.nealey@leg.wa.gov

**Orcutt, Ed (R, 20)**
408 John L. O'Brien Building
P.O. Box 40600
Olympia, WA 98504
P: (360) 786-7990
E: ed.orcutt@leg.wa.gov

**Ormsby, Timm (D, 3)**
315 John L. O'Brien Building
P.O. Box 40600
Olympia, WA 98504
P: (360) 786-7946
E: timm.ormsby@leg.wa.gov

**Ortiz-Self, Lillian (D, 21)**
330 John L. O'Brien Buidling
P.O. Box 40600
Olympia, WA 98504
P: (360) 786-7972
E: lillian.ortiz-self
   @leg.wa.gov

**Orwall, Tina L. (D, 33)**
326 John L. O'Brien Building
P.O. Box 40600
Olympia, WA 98504
P: (360) 786-7834
E: tina.orwall@leg.wa.gov

**Pellicciotti, Mike (R, 30)\***
304 John L. O'Brien Building
P.O. Box 40600
Olympia, WA 98504
P: (360) 786-7898
E: Mike.Pellicciotti
   @leg.wa.gov

**Peterson, Strom (D, 21)**
324 John L. O'Brien Building
P.O. Box 40600
Olympia, WA 98504
P: (360) 786-7950
E: strom.peterson
   @leg.wa.gov

**Pettigrew, Eric (D, 37)**
434B Legislative Building
P.O. Box 40600
Olympia, WA 98504
P: (360) 786-7838
E: eric.pettigrew
   @leg.wa.gov

**Pike, Liz (R, 18)**
122B Legislative Building
P.O. Box 40600
Olympia, WA 98504
P: (360) 786-7812
E: liz.pike@leg.wa.gov

**Pollet, Gerry (D, 46)**
132C Legislative Building
P.O. Box 40600
Olympia, WA 98504
P: (360) 786-7886
E: gerry.pollet@leg.wa.gov

**Reeves, Kristine (D, 30)\***
132D Legislative Building
P.O. Box 40600
Olympia, WA 98504
P: (360) 786-7830
E: Kristine.Reeves
   @leg.wa.gov

**Riccelli, Marcus (D, 3)**
434A Legislative Building
P.O. Box 40600
Olympia, WA 98504
P: (360) 786-7888
E: marcus.riccelli
   @leg.wa.gov

**Robinson, June (D, 38)**
332 John L. O'Brien Building
P.O. Box 40600
Olympia, WA 98504
P: (360) 786-7864
E: june.robinson@leg.wa.gov

**Rodne, Jay (R, 5)**
420 John L. O'Brien Building
P.O. Box 40600
Olympia, WA 98504
P: (360) 786-7852
E: jay.rodne@leg.wa.gov

**Ryu, Cindy (D, 32)**
325 John L. O'Brien Building
P.O. Box 40600
Olympia, WA 98504
P: (360) 786-7880
E: cindy.ryu@leg.wa.gov

**Santos, Sharon Tomiko
   (D, 37)**
321 John L. O'Brien Building
P.O. Box 40600
Olympia, WA 98504
P: (360) 786-7944
E: sharontomiko.santos
   @leg.wa.gov

**Sawyer, David (D, 29)**
306 John L. O'Brien Building
P.O. Box 40600
Olympia, WA 98504
P: (360) 786-7906
E: david.sawyer@leg.wa.gov

**Schmick, Joe (R, 9)**
426B Legislative Building
P.O. Box 40600
Olympia, WA 98504
P: (360) 786-7844
E: joe.schmick@leg.wa.gov

**Sells, Mike (D, 38)**
438B Legislative Building
P.O. Box 40600
Olympia, WA 98504
P: (360) 786-7840
E: mike.sells@leg.wa.gov

**Senn, Tana (D, 41)**
309 John L. O'Brien Building
P.O. Box 40600
Olympia, WA 98504
P: (360) 786-7894
E: tana.senn@leg.wa.gov

**Shea, Matthew (R, 4)**
427A Legislative Building
P.O. Box 40600
Olympia, WA 98504
P: (340) 786-7984
E: matt.shea@leg.wa.gov

**Slatter, Vandana (D, 48)\***
336 John L. O'Brien Building
P.O. Box 40600
Olympia, WA 98504
P: (360) 786-7936
E: vandana.slatter
   @leg.wa.gov

**Smith, Norma (R, 10)**
435 John L. O'Brien Building
P.O. Box 40600
Olympia, WA 98504
P: (360) 786-7884
E: norma.smith@leg.wa.gov

**Springer, Larry (D, 45)**
132E Legislative Building
P.O. Box 40600
Olympia, WA 98504
P: (360) 786-7822
E: larry.springer
   @leg.wa.gov

**Stambaugh, Melanie (R, 25)**
122E Legislative Building
P.O. Box 40600
Olympia, WA 98504
P: (360) 786-7948
E: melanie.stambaugh
   @leg.wa.gov

**Stanford, Derek (D, 1)**
327 John L. O'Brien Building
P.O. Box 40600
Olympia, WA 98504
P: (360) 786-7928
E: derek.stanford
   @leg.wa.gov

**Steele, Mike (R, 12)\***
122F Legislative Building
P.O. Box 40600
Olympia, WA 98504
P: (360) 786-7832
E: Mike.Steele@leg.wa.gov

**Stokesbary, Drew (R, 31)**
426 John L. O'Brien Building
P.O. Box 40600
Olympia, WA 98504
P: (360) 786-7846
E: drew.stokesbary
   @leg.wa.gov

**Stonier, Monica Jurado
   (D, 49)**
331 John L. O'Brien Building
P.O. Box 40600
Olympia, WA 98504
P: (360) 786-7872
E: monica.stonier
   @leg.wa.gov

**Sullivan, Pat (D, 47)**
339A Legislative Building
P.O. Box 40600
Olympia, WA 98504
P: (360) 786-7858
E: pat.sullivan@leg.wa.gov

**Tarleton, Gael (D, 36)**
429A Legislative Building
P.O. Box 40600
Olympia, WA 98504
P: (360) 786-7860
E: gael.tarleton@leg.wa.gov

**Taylor, David (R, 15)**
421 John L. O'Brien Building
P.O. Box 40600
Olympia, WA 98504
P: (360) 786-7874
E: david.taylor@leg.wa.gov

**Tharinger, Steve (D, 24)**
314 John L. O'Brien Building
P.O. Box 40600
Olympia, WA 98504
P: (360) 786-7904
E: steve.tharinger
   @leg.wa.gov

**Van Werven, Luanne (R, 42)**
419 John L. O'Brien Building
PO Box 40600
Olympia, WA 98504
P: 360-786-7980
E: luanne.vanwerven
   @leg.wa.gov

**Vick, Brandon (R, 18)**
468 John L. O'Brien Building
P.O. Box 40600
Olympia, WA 98504
P: (360) 786-7850
E: Brandon.Vick@leg.wa.gov

**Volz, Mike (R, 6)\***
427 John L. O'Brien Building
P.O. Box 40600
Olympia, WA 98504
P: (360) 786-7922
E: Mike.Volz@leg.wa.gov

**Walsh, Jim (R, 19)\***
428 John L. O'Brien Building
P.O. Box 40600
Olympia, WA 98504
P: (360) 786-7806
E: Jim.Walsh@leg.wa.gov

# Washington

**Wilcox, J.T. (R, 2)**
426A Legislative Building
P.O. Box 40600
Olympia, WA 98504
P: (360) 786-7912
E: jt.wilcox@leg.wa.gov

**Wylie, Sharon (D, 49)**
310 John L. O'Brien Building
P.O. Box 40600
Olympia, WA 98504
P: (360) 786-7924
E: sharon.wylie@leg.wa.gov

**Young, Jesse (R, 26)**
422 John L. O'Brien Building
P.O. Box 40600
Olympia, WA 98504
P: (360) 786-7964
E: jesse.young@leg.wa.gov

# West Virginia

## Executive

### Governor
**The Honorable Jim Justice (D)**
Governor
State Capitol Complex
1900 Kanawha Boulevard East
Charleston, WV 25305
P: (304) 558-2000

### Lieutenant Governor
**Senator Mitch Carmichael (R)**
(elected by the Legislature)
Senate President/Lieutenant Governor
Room 227M, Building 1
1900 Kanawha Boulevard, East
Charleston, WV 25305
P: (304) 357-7855
E: mitch.carmichael
    @wvsenate.gov

### Commissioner of Agriculture
**The Honorable Kent Leonhardt (R)**
Commissioner
1900 Kanawha Boulevard, East
State Capitol, Room E-28
Charleston, WV 25305
P: (304) 558-3550
F: (304) 558-2203

### Attorney General
**The Honorable Patrick Morrisey (R)**
Attorney General
State Capitol
1900 Kanawha Boulevard, East
Charleston, WV 25305
P: (304) 558-2021
F: (304) 558-0140

### Auditor
**The Honorable John McCuskey (R)**
State Auditor
Building 1, Room W-100
State Capitol Complex
Charleston, WV 25305
P: (304) 558-2251 Ext. 116
F: (304) 558-5200

### Secretary of State
**The Honorable Mac Warner (R)**
Secretary of State
Building 1, Suite 157K
1900 Kanawha Boulevard
Charleston, WV 25305
P: (304) 558-6000
F: (304) 558-0900
E: wvsos@wvsos.com

### Treasurer
**The Honorable John D. Perdue (D)**
State Treasurer
State Capitol Complex
Building 1, Room E-145
Charleston, WV 25305
P: (304) 558-5000
F: (304) 558-4097

## Judiciary

### Supreme Court of Appeals (PE)
**Mr. Rory L. Perry II**
Clerk of Court
State Capitol, Room E-317
1900 Kanawha Boulevard, East
Charleston, WV 25305
P: (304) 558-2601
F: (304) 558-3815

**The Honorable Allen H. Loughry II**
Chief Justice
**The Honorable Robin Jean Davis**
**The Honorable Menis Ketchum II (D)**
**The Honorable Elizabeth Walker**
**The Honorable Margaret L. Workman (D)**

## Legislative

## Senate

### Senate President
**Senator Mitch Carmichael (R)**
Senate President/Lieutenant Governor
Room 227M, Building 1
1900 Kanawha Boulevard, East
Charleston, WV 25305
P: (304) 357-7855
E: mitch.carmichael
    @wvsenate.gov

### President Pro Tempore of the Senate
**Senator Donna J. Boley (R)**
Senate President Pro Tempore
Room 206W, Building 1
1900 Kanawha Boulevard, East
Charleston, WV 25305
P: (304) 357-7905
E: donnaboley
    @suddenlink.net

### Senate Majority Leader
**Senator Ryan Ferns (R)**
Majority Leader
Room 223M, Building 1
1900 Kanawha Boulevard, East
Charleston, WV 25305
P: (304) 357-7918
E: ryan.ferns@wvsenate.gov

### Senate Minority Leader
**Senator Roman Prezioso (D)**
Minority Leader
Room 245M, Building 1
1900 Kanawha Boulevard, East
Charleston, WV 25305
P: (304) 357-7961
E: roman.prezioso
    @wvsenate.gov

### Clerk of the Senate
**Mr. Clark S. Barnes**
Clerk of the Senate
Room 211M, Building 1
State Capitol Complex
Charleston, WV 25305
P: (304) 357-7800
E: senate.clerk
    @wvsenate.gov

### Members of the Senate
**Azinger, Mike (R, 3)**
Room 223W, Building 1
1900 Kanawha Boulevard, East
Charleston, WV 25305
P: (304) 357-7970
E: mike.azinger
    @wvsenate.gov

**Beach, Robert D. (D, 13)**
Room 204W, Building 1
1900 Kanawha Boulevard, East
Charleston, WV 25305
P: (304) 357-7919
E: bob.beach@wvsenate.gov

**Blair, Craig (R, 15)**
Room 217W, Building 1
1900 Kanawha Boulevard, East
Charleston, WV 25305
P: (304) 357-7867
E: craig@craigblair.com

**Boley, Donna J. (R, 3)**
Room 206W, Building 1
1900 Kanawha Boulevard, East
Charleston, WV 25305
P: (304) 357-7905
E: donnaboley
    @suddenlink.net

**Boso, Greg (R, 11)**
Room 441M, Building 1
1900 Kanawha Boulevard, East
Charleston, WV 25305
P: (304) 357-7973
E: greg.boso@wvsenate.gov

**Carmichael, Mitch (R, 4)**
Room 227M, Building 1
1900 Kanawha Boulevard, East
Charleston, WV 25305
P: (304) 357-7855
E: mitch.carmichael
    @wvsenate.gov

**Clements, Charles (R, 2)***
Room 218W, Building 1
1900 Kanawha Boulevard, East
Charleston, WV 25305
P: (304) 357-7827
E: charles.clements
    @wvsenate.gov

**Cline, Sue (R, 9)**
Room 216W, Building 1
1900 Kanawha Boulevard, East
Charleston, WV 25305
P: (304) 357-7807
E: sue.cline@wvsenate.gov

**Facemire, Douglas E. (D, 12)**
Room 213W, Building 1
1900 Kanawha Boulevard, East
Charleston, WV 25305
P: (304) 357-7845
E: douglas.facemire
    @wvsenate.gov

**Ferns, Ryan (R, 1)**
Room 223M, Building 1
1900 Kanawha Boulevard, East
Charleston, WV 25305
P: (304) 357-7918
E: ryan.ferns@wvsenate.gov

**Gaunch, Ed (R, 8)**
Room 441M, Building 1
1900 Kanawha Boulevard, East
Charleston, WV 25305
P: (304) 357-7841
E: ed.gaunch@wvsenate.gov

# West Virginia

**Hall, Mike (R, 4)**
Room 451M, Building 1
1900 Kanawha Boulevard, East
Charleston, WV 25305
P: (304) 357-7901
E: mike.hall@wvsenate.gov

**Jeffries, Glenn (D, 8)***
Room 203W, Building 1
1900 Kanawha Boulevard, East
Charleston, WV 25168
P: (304) 357-7866
E: Glenn.Jeffries
    @wvsenate.gov

**Karnes, Robert L. (R, 11)**
Room 417M, Building 1
1900 Kanawha Boulevard, East
Charleston, WV 25305
P: (304) 357-7906
E: robert.karnes
    @wvsenate.gov

**Mann, Kenny W. (R, 10)***
Room 417M, Building 1
1900 Kanawha Boulevard, East
Charleston, WV 25305
P: (304) 357-7849
E: kenny.mann@wvsenate.gov

**Maroney, Mike (R, 2)***
Room 218W, Building 1
1900 Kanawha Boulevard, East
Charleston, WV 25305
P: (304) 357-7902
E: mike.maroney
    @wvsenate.gov

**Maynard, Mark R. (R, 6)**
Room 206W, Building 1
1900 Kanawha Boulevard, East
Charleston, WV 25305
P: (304) 357-7808
E: Mark.Maynard
    @wvsenate.gov

**Miller, Ronald F. (D, 10)**
Room 229W, Building 1
1900 Kanawha Boulevard, East
Charleston, WV 25305
P: (304) 357-7959
E: ronald.miller
    @wvsenate.gov

**Mullins, Jeff (R, 9)**
Room 217W, Building 1
1900 Kanawha Boulevard, East
Charleston, WV 25305
P: (304) 357-7831
E: jeff.mullins
    @wvsenate.gov

**Ojeda II, Richard N.
    (D, 7)***
Room 213W, Building 1
1900 Kanawha Boulevard, East
Charleston, WV 25305
P: (304) 357-7857
E: richard.ojeda
    @wvsenate.gov

**Palumbo, Corey L. (D, 17)**
Room 209W, Building 1
1900 Kanawha Boulevard, East
Charleston, WV 25305
P: (304) 357-7854
E: corey.palumbo
    @wvsenate.gov

**Plymale, Robert H. (D, 5)**
Room 204W, Building 1
1900 Kanawha Boulevard, East
Charleston, WV 25305
P: (304) 357-7937
E: robert.plymale
    @wvsenate.gov

**Prezioso, Roman (D, 13)**
Room 245M, Building 1
1900 Kanawha Boulevard, East
Charleston, WV 25305
P: (304) 357-7961
E: roman.prezioso
    @wvsenate.gov

**Romano, Mike (D, 12)**
Room 200W, Building 1
1900 Kanawha Boulevard, East
Charleston, WV 25305
P: (304) 357-7904
E: mike.romano@wvsenate.gov

**Rucker, Patricia (R, 16)***
Room 223W, Building 1
1900 Kanawha Boulevard, East
Charleston, WV 25305
P: (304) 357-7957
E: Patricia.Rucker
    @wvsenate.gov

**Smith, Randy (R, 14)**
Room 214W, Building 1
1900 Kanawha Boulevard, East
Charleston, WV 25305
P: (304) 340-3396
E: randy.smith@wvsenate.gov

**Stollings, Ron (D, 7)**
Room 209W, Building 1
1900 Kanawha Boulevard, East
Charleston, WV 25305
P: (304) 357-7939
E: ron.stollings
    @frontier.com

**Swope, Chandler (R, 6)***
Room 229W, Building 1
1900 Kanawha Boulevard, East
Charleston, WV 25305
P: (304) 357-7843
E: chandler.swope
    @wvsenate.gov

**Sypolt, Dave (R, 14)**
Room 214W, Building 1
1900 Kanawha Boulevard, East
Charleston, WV 25305
P: (304) 357-7914
E: dave.sypolt@wvsenate.gov

**Takubo, Tom (R, 17)**
Room 439M, Building 1
1900 Kanawha Boulevard, East
Charleston, WV 25305
P: (304) 357-7990
E: drtomtakubo@gmail.com

**Trump IV, Charles S.
    (R, 15)**
Room 210W, Building 1
1900 Kanawha Boulevard, East
Charleston, WV 25305
P: (304) 357-7880
F: (304) 340-3315
E: charles.trump
    @wvsenate.gov

**Unger II, John (D, 16)**
Room 200W, Building 1
1900 Kanawha Boulevard, East
Charleston, WV 25305
P: (304) 357-7933
E: john.unger@wvsenate.gov

**Weld, Ryan W. (R, 1)**
Room 216W, Building 1
1900 Kanawha Boulevard, East
Charleston, WV 25305
P: (304) 340-3367
E: ryan.weld@wvsenate.gov

**Woelfel, Mike (D, 5)**
Room 203W, Building 1
1900 Kanawha Boulevard, East
Charleston, WV 25305
P: (304) 357-7956
E: mike.woelfel
    @wvsenate.gov

# House

## Speaker of the House

**Delegate Tim Armstead (R)**
Speaker of the House
Room 228M, Building 1
1900 Kanawha Boulevard, East
Charleston, WV 25305
P: (304) 340-3210
E: armstead@wvhouse.gov

## Speaker Pro Tempore of the House

**Delegate John
    Overington (R)**
Speaker Pro Tempore
Room 242M, Building 1
1900 Kanawha Boulevard, East
Charleston, WV 25305
P: (304) 340-3148
E: john@overington.com

## House Majority Leader

**Delegate Daryl E.
    Cowles (R)**
House Majority Leader
Room 228M, Building 1
1900 Kanawha Boulevard, East
Charleston, WV 25305
P: (304) 340-3220
E: daryl.cowles@wvhouse.gov

## House Minority Leader

**Delegate Tim Miley (D)**
House Minority Leader
Room 264M, Building 1
1900 Kanawha Boulevard, East
Charleston, WV 25305
P: (304) 340-3240
E: tim.miley@wvhouse.gov

## Clerk of the House

**Mr. Steve Harrison**
Clerk of the House
Room 212M, Building 1
1900 Kanawha Boulevard, East
Charleston, WV 25305
P: (304) 340-3200
E: house.clerk@wvhouse.gov

## Members of the House

**Ambler, George (R, 42)**
Room 203E, Building 1
1900 Kanawha Boulevard, East
Charleston, WV 25305
P: (304) 340-3129
E: george.ambler
    @wvhouse.gov

**Anderson, Bill (R, 8)**
Room 200E-C, Building 1
1900 Kanawha Boulevard, East
Charleston, WV 25305
P: (304) 340-3168
E: bill.anderson
    @wvhouse.gov

**Armstead, Tim (R, 40)**
Room 228M, Building 1
1900 Kanawha Boulevard, East
Charleston, WV 25305
P: (304) 340-3210
E: armstead@wvhouse.gov

**Arvon, Lynne (R, 31)**
Room 211E, Building 1
1900 Kanawha Boulevard, East
Charleston, WV 25305
P: (304) 340-3384
E: karen.arvon@wvhouse.gov

**Atkinson III, Martin
(R, 11)**
Room 208E, Building 1
1900 Kanawha Boulevard, East
Charleston, WV 25305
P: (304) 340-3185
E: martin.atkinson
@wvhouse.gov

**Baldwin Jr., Stephen
(D, 42)***
Room 150R, Building 1
1900 Kanawha Boulevard East
Charleston, WV 25305
P: (304) 340-3131
E: Duane.Borchers
@wvhouse.gov

**Barrett, Jason (D, 61)**
Room 4R, Building 1
1900 Kanawha Boulevard, East
Charleston, WV 25305
P: (304) 340-3188
E: jason.barrett
@wvhouse.gov

**Bates, Mick (D, 30)**
Room 150R, Building 1
1900 Kanawha Boulevard, East
Charleston, WV 25305
P: (304) 340-3180
E: mick.bates@wvhouse.gov

**Blair, Saira (R, 59)**
Room 221E, Building 1
1900 Kanawha Boulevard, East
Charleston, WV 25305
P: (304) 340-3122
E: saira.blair@wvhouse.gov

**Boggs, Brent (D, 34)**
Room 258M, Building 1
1900 Kanawha Boulevard, East
Charleston, WV 25305
P: (304) 340-3142
E: brent.boggs@wvhouse.gov

**Brewer, Scott (D, 13)***
Room 231E, Building 1
1900 Kanawha Boulevard, East
Charleston, WV 25305
P: (304) 340-3146
E: Scott.Brewer@wvhouse.gov

**Butler, Jim (R, 14)**
Room 222E, Building 1
1900 Kanawha Boulevard, East
Charleston, WV 25305
P: (304) 340-3199
E: jim.butler@wvhouse.gov

**Byrd, Andrew D. (D, 35)**
Room 151R, Building 1
1900 Kanawha Boulevard, East
Charleston, WV 25305
P: (304) 340-3362
E: andrew.byrd@wvhouse.gov

**Canestraro, Joe (D, 4)***
Room 151R, Building 1
1900 Kanawha Boulevard, East
Charleston, WV 25305
P: (304) 340-3151
E: Joe.Canestraro
@wvhouse.gov

**Capito, Moore (R, 35)***
Room 220E, Building 1
1900 Kanawha Boulevard, East
Charleston, WV 25305
P: (304) 340-3340
E: Moore.Capito@wvhouse.gov

**Caputo, Mike (D, 50)**
Room 258M, Building 1
1900 Kanawha Boulevard, East
Charleston, WV 25305
P: (304) 340-3249
E: mike.caputo@wvhouse.gov

**Cooper, Roy G. (R, 28)**
Room 203E, Building 1
1900 Kanawha Boulevard, East
Charleston, WV 25305
P: (304) 340-3119
E: roy.cooper@wvhouse.gov

**Cowles, Daryl E. (R, 58)**
Room 228M, Building 1
1900 Kanawha Boulevard, East
Charleston, WV 25305
P: (304) 340-3220
E: daryl.cowles@wvhouse.gov

**Criss, Vernon (R, 10)***
Room 224E, Building 1
1900 Kanawha Boulevard, East
Charleston, WV 25305
P: (304) 340-3202
E: Vernon.Criss@wvhouse.gov

**Dean, Mark (R, 21)***
Room 218E, Building 1
1900 Kanawha Boulevard, East
Charleston, WV 25305
P: (304) 340-3304
E: Mark.Dean@wvhouse.gov

**Deem, Frank (R, 10)**
Room 276M, Building 1
1900 Kanawha Boulevard, East
Charleston, WV 25305
P: (304) 340-3137
F: (304) 357-7829
E: frank.deem@wvhouse.gov

**Diserio, Phil (D, 2)**
Room 230E, Building 1
1900 Kanawha Boulevard, East
Charleston, WV 25305
P: (304) 340-3367
E: phillip.diserio
@wvhouse.gov

**Eldridge, Jeff (D, 22)**
Room 230E, Building 1
1900 Kanawha Boulevard, East
Charleston, WV 25305
P: (304) 340-3113
E: jeff.eldridge
@wvhouse.gov

**Ellington, Joe (R, 27)**
Room 215E-A, Building 1
1900 Kanawha Boulevard, East
Charleston, WV 25305
P: (304) 340-3269
E: joe.ellington
@wvhouse.gov

**Espinosa, Paul (R, 66)**
Room 434M, Building 1
1900 Kanawha Boulevard, East
Charleston, WV 25305
P: (304) 340-3130
E: paul.espinosa
@wvhouse.gov

**Evans, Allen V. (R, 54)**
Room 216E, Building 1
1900 Kanawha Boulevard, East
Charleston, WV 25305
P: (304) 340-3399
E: allen.evans@wvhouse.gov

**Evans, Ed (D, 26)***
Room 150R, Building 1
1900 Kanawha Boulevard, East
Charleston, WV 25305
P: (304) 340-3165
E: Ed.Evans@wvhouse.gov

**Fast, Tom (R, 32)**
Room 220E, Building 1
1900 Kanawha Boulevard, East
Charleston, WV 25305
P: (304) 340-3170
E: tom.fast@wvhouse.gov

**Ferro, Michael T. (D, 4)**
Room 230E, Building 1
1900 Kanawha Boulevard, East
Charleston, WV 25305
P: (304) 340-3111
E: mike.ferro@wvhouse.gov

**Fleischauer,
Barbara Evans (D, 51)**
Room 151R, Building 1
1900 Kanawha Boulevard, East
Charleston, WV 25305
P: (304) 340-3127
E: barbaraf@wvhouse.gov

**Fluharty, Shawn (D, 3)**
Room 4R, Building 1
1900 Kanawha Boulevard, East
Charleston, WV 25305
P: (304) 340-3270
E: shawn.fluharty
@wvhouse.gov

**Folk, Michael (R, 63)**
Room 229E, Building 1
1900 Kanawha Boulevard, East
Charleston, WV 25305
P: (304) 340-3350
E: michael.folk@wvhouse.gov

**Foster, Geoff (R, 15)**
Room 223E, Building 1
1900 Kanawha Boulevard, East
Charleston, WV 25305
P: (304) 340-3121
E: geoff.foster@wvhouse.gov

**Foster, Nancy Reagan
(R, 38)***
Room 221E, Building 1
1900 Kanawha Boulevard, East
Charleston, WV 25305
P: (304) 340-3392
E: Nancy.Foster@wvhouse.gov

**Frich, Cindy (R, 51)**
Room 205E, Building 1
1900 Kanawha Boulevard, East
Charleston, WV 25305
P: (304) 340-3125
E: cindy.frich@wvhouse.gov

**Gearheart, Marty (R, 27)**
Room 200E-A, Building 1
1900 Kanawha Boulevard, East
Charleston, WV 25305
P: (304) 340-3179
E: marty.gearheart
@wvhouse.gov

**Hamilton, Bill (R, 45)**
Room 216E, Building 1
1900 Kanawha Boulevard, East
Charleston, WV 25305
P: (304) 340-3167
E: bill.hamilton
@wvhouse.gov

**Hamrick, Danny (R, 48)**
Room 206E, Building 1
1900 Kanawha Boulevard, East
Charleston, WV 25305
P: (304) 340-3141
E: danny.hamrick
@wvhouse.gov

# West Virginia

**Hanshaw, Roger (R, 33)**
Room 408M, Building 1
1900 Kanawha Boulevard, East
Charleston, WV 25305
P: (304) 340-3135
E: roger.hanshaw
@wvhouse.gov

**Harshbarger, Jason S.
(R, 7)***
Room 225E, Building 1
1900 Kanawha Boulevard, East
Charleston, WV 25305
P: (304) 340-3195
E: Jason.Harshbarger
@wvhouse.gov

**Hartman, William G. (D, 43)**
Room 231E, Building 1
1900 Kanawha Boulevard, East
Charleston, WV 25305
P: (304) 340-3178
E: billhartman
@suddenlink.net

**Hicks, Ken (D, 19)**
Room 150R, Building 1
1900 Kanawha Boulevard, East
Charleston, WV 25305
P: (304) 340-3155
E: ken.hicks@wvhouse.gov

**Higginbotham, Joshua Kurt
(R, 13)***
Room 223E, Building 1
1900 Kanawha Boulevard, East
Charleston, WV 25305
P: (304) 340-3118
E: Joshua.Higginbotham
@wvhouse.gov

**Hill, Jordan (R, 41)**
Room 228E, Building 1
1900 Kanawha Boulevard, East
Charleston, WV 25305
P: (304) 340-3352
E: jordan.hill@wvhouse.gov

**Hollen, Ray (R, 9)***
Room 224E, Building 1
1900 Kanawha Boulevard, East
Charleston, WV 25305
P: (304) 340-3136
E: Ray.Hollen@wvhouse.gov

**Hornbuckle, Sean (D, 16)**
Room 150R, Building 1
1900 Kanawha Boulevard, East
Charleston, WV 25305
P: (304) 340-3395
E: sean.hornbuckle
@wvhouse.gov

**Householder, Eric L.
(R, 64)**
Room 472M, Building 1
1900 Kanawha Boulevard, East
Charleston, WV 25305
P: (304) 340-3274
E: eric.householder
@wvhouse.gov

**Howell, Gary G. (R, 56)**
Room 213E, Building 1
1900 Kanawha Boulevard, East
Charleston, WV 25305
P: (304) 340-3192
E: gary.howell@wvhouse.gov

**Iaquinta, Richard J.
(D, 48)**
Room 231E, Building 1
1900 Kanawha Boulevard, East
Charleston, WV 25305
P: (304) 340-3161
E: richard.iaquinta
@wvhouse.gov

**Isner, Phil (D, 43)***
Room 151R, Building 1
1900 Kanawha Boulevard, East
Charleston, WV 25305
P: (304) 340-3145
E: Phil.Isner@wvhouse.gov

**Kelly, John R. (R, 10)**
Room 201E, Building 1
1900 Kanawha Boulevard, East
Charleston, WV 25305
P: (304) 340-3394
E: john.kelly@wvhouse.gov

**Kessinger, Kayla (R, 32)**
Room 227E, Building 1
1900 Kanawha Boulevard, East
Charleston, WV 25305
P: (304) 340-3197
E: kayla.kessinger
@wvhouse.gov

**Lane, Charlotte R. (R, 35)***
Room 227E, Building 1
1900 Kanawha Boulevard, East
Charleston, WV 25305
P: (304) 340-3183
E: Charlotte.Lane
@wvhouse.gov

**Lewis, Tony J. (R, 52)***
Room 209E, Building 1
1900 Kanawha Boulevard, East
Charleston, WV 25305
P: (304) 340-3396
E: Tony.Lewis@wvhouse.gov

**Longstreth, Linda (D, 50)**
Room 6U-A, Building 1
1900 Kanawha Boulevard, East
Charleston, WV 25305
P: (304) 340-3124
E: linda.longstreth
@wvhouse.gov

**Love, Shirley D. (D, 32)**
Room 223E, Building 1
1900 Kanawha Boulevard, East
Charleston, WV 25305
P: (304) 340-3337
E: shirley.love@wvhouse.gov

**Lovejoy, Chad (D, 17)***
Room 151R, Building 1
1900 Kanawha Boulevard, East
Charleston, WV 25305
P: (304) 340-3280
E: Chad.Lovejoy@wvhouse.gov

**Lynch, Dana (D, 44)**
Room 6R, Building 1
1900 Kanawha Boulevard, East
Charleston, WV 25305
P: (304) 340-3916
E: dana.lynch@wvhouse.gov

**Marcum, Justin (D, 20)**
Room 150R, Building 1
1900 Kanawha Boulevard, East
Charleston, WV 25305
P: (304) 340-3126
E: justin.marcum
@wvhouse.gov

**Martin, Patrick S. (R, 46)***
Room 228E, Building 1
1900 Kanawha Boulevard, East
Charleston, WV 25305
P: (304) 340-3123
E: Patrick.Martin
@wvhouse.gov

**Maynard, Zack (R, 22)***
Room 204E, Building 1
1900 Kanawha Boulevard, East
Charleston, WV 25305
P: (304) 340-3152
E: Zack.Maynard@wvhouse.gov

**McGeehan, Pat (R, 1)**
Room 226E, Building 1
1900 Kanawha Boulevard, East
Charleston, WV 25305
P: (304) 340-3397
F: (304) 340-3315
E: pat.mcgeehan@wvhouse.gov

**Miley, Tim (D, 48)**
Room 264M, Building 1
1900 Kanawha Boulevard, East
Charleston, WV 25305
P: (304) 340-3240
E: tim.miley@wvhouse.gov

**Miller, Carol (R, 16)**
Room 246M, Building 1
1900 Kanawha Boulevard, East
Charleston, WV 25305
P: (304) 340-3176
E: carol.miller@wvhouse.gov

**Miller, Rodney A. (D, 23)***
Room 150R, Building 1
1900 Kanawha Boulevard, East
Charleston, WV 25305
P: (304) 340-3184
E: Rodney.Maynard
@wvhouse.gov

**Moore, Riley (R, 67)***
Room 225E, Building 1
1900 Kanawha Boulevard, East
Charleston, WV 25305
P: (304) 340-3248
E: Riley.Moore@wvhouse.gov

**Moye, Ricky (D, 29)**
Room 2R, Building 1
1900 Kanawha Boulevard, East
Charleston, WV 25305
P: (304) 340-3162
E: rmoyewvhouse@yahoo.com

**Nelson, Eric (R, 35)**
Room 462M, Building 1
1900 Kanawha Boulevard, East
Charleston, WV 25305
P: (304) 340-3230
E: nelson@wvhouse.gov

**O'Neal IV, John D. (R, 28)**
Room 214E, Building 1
1900 Kanawha Boulevard, East
Charleston, WV 25305
P: (304) 340-3164
E: john.oneal@wvhouse.gov

**Overington, John (R, 62)**
Room 242M, Building 1
1900 Kanawha Boulevard, East
Charleston, WV 25305
P: (304) 340-3148
E: john@overington.com

**Paynter, Tony (R, 25)***
Room 222E, Building 1
1900 Kanawha Boulevard, East
Charleston, WV 25305
P: (304) 340-3163
E: Tony.Paynter@wvhouse.gov

**Pethtel, Dave (D, 5)**
Room 230E, Building 1
1900 Kanawha Boulevard, East
Charleston, WV 25305
P: (304) 340-3158
E: dave.pethtel@wvhouse.gov

**Phillips Jr., Rupert (D, 24)**
Room 476M, Building 1
1900 Kanawha Boulevard, East
Charleston, WV 25305
P: (304) 340-3174
E: rupert.phillips
@wvhouse.gov

**Pushkin, Mike (D, 37)**
Room 6U-B, Building 1
1900 Kanawha Boulevard, East
Charleston, WV 25305
P: (304) 340-3106
E: mike.pushkin@wvhouse.gov

**Pyles, Rodney (D, 51)\***
Room 231E, Building 1
1900 Kanawha Boulevard, East
Charleston, WV 25305
P: (304) 340-3153
E: Rodney.Pyles@wvhouse.gov

**Queen, Ben (R, 48)\***
Room 206E, Building 1
1900 Kanawha Boulevard, East
Charleston, WV 25305
P: (304) 340-3171
E: Ben.Queen@wvhouse.gov

**Robinson, Andrew (D, 36)\***
Room 151R, Building 1
1900 Kanawha Boulevard, East
Charleston, WV 25305
P: (304) 340-3156
E: Andrew.Robinson
@wvhouse.gov

**Rodighiero, Ralph (D, 24)**
Room 2R, Building 1
1900 Kanawha Boulevard, East
Charleston, WV 25305
P: (304) 340-3297
F: (304) 340-3315
E: ralph.rodighiero
@wvhouse.gov

**Rohrbach, Matthew (R, 17)**
Room 209E, Building 1
1900 Kanawha Boulevard, East
Charleston, WV 25305
P: (304) 340-3221
E: matthew.rohrbach
@wvhouse.gov

**Romine, C.E. (R, 16)\***
Room 207E, Building 1
1900 Kanawha Boulevard, East
Charleston, WV 25305
P: (304) 340-3277
E: Chuck.Romine@wvhouse.gov

**Romine, William R. (R, 6)**
Room 210E, Building 1
1900 Kanawha Boulevard, East
Charleston, WV 25305
P: (304) 340-3226
E: roger.romine@wvhouse.gov

**Rowan, Ruth (R, 57)**
Room 210E, Building 1
1900 Kanawha Boulevard, East
Charleston, WV 25305
P: (304) 340-3157
E: ruth.rowan@wvhouse.gov

**Rowe, Larry L. (D, 36)**
Room 6R-A, Building 1
1900 Kanawha Boulevard, East
Charleston, WV 25305
P: (304) 340-3287
F: (304) 357-7829
E: larry.rowe@wvhouse.gov

**Shott, John (R, 27)**
Room 418M, Building 1
1900 Kanawha Boulevard, East
Charleston, WV 25305
P: (304) 340-3252
E: john.shott@wvhouse.gov

**Sobonya, Kelli (R, 18)**
Room 207E, Building 1
1900 Kanawha Boulevard, East
Charleston, WV 25305
P: (304) 340-3175
E: kelli.sobonya
@wvhouse.gov

**Sponaugle, Isaac (D, 55)**
Room 258M, Building 1
1900 Kanawha Boulevard, East
Charleston, WV 25305
P: (304) 340-3154
E: isaac.sponaugle
@wvhouse.gov

**Statler, Joe (R, 51)**
Room 442M, Building 1
1900 Kanawha Boulevard, East
Charleston, WV 25305
P: (304) 340-3900
E: joe.statler@wvhouse.gov

**Storch, Erikka (R, 3)**
Room 202E, Building 1
1900 Kanawha Boulevard, East
Charleston, WV 25305
P: (304) 340-3378
E: erikka.storch
@wvhouse.gov

**Summers, Amy (R, 49)**
Room 215E-A, Building 1
1900 Kanawha Boulevard, East
Charleston, WV 25305
P: (304) 340-3139
E: amy.summers@wvhouse.gov

**Sypolt, Terry Funk (R, 52)\***
Room 219E, Building 1
1900 Kanawha Boulevard, East
Charleston, WV 25305
P: (304) 340-3160
E: Terry.Sypolt@wvhouse.gov

**Thompson, Robert (D, 19)\***
Room 150R, Building 1
1900 Kanawha Boulevard, East
Charleston, WV 25305
P: (304) 340-3355
E: Robert.Thompson
@wvhouse.gov

**Upson, Jill (R, 65)**
Room 219E, Building 1
1900 Kanawha Boulevard, East
Charleston, WV 25305
P: (304) 340-3366
E: jill.upson@wvhouse.gov

**Wagner, Danny (R, 47)**
Room 226E, Building 1
1900 Kanawha Boulevard, East
Charleston, WV 25305
P: (304) 340-3398
E: danny.wagner@wvhouse.gov

**Walters, Ron (R, 39)**
Room 212E, Building 1
1900 Kanawha Boulevard, East
Charleston, WV 25305
P: (304) 340-3194
E: ron.walters@wvhouse.gov

**Ward, Guy (R, 50)\***
Room 208E, Building 1
1900 Kanawha Boulevard, East
Charleston, WV 25305
P: (304) 340-3331
E: Guy.Ward@wvhouse.gov

**Westfall, Steve (R, 12)**
Room 204E, Building 1
1900 Kanawha Boulevard, East
Charleston, WV 25305
P: (304) 340-3140
E: steve.westfall
@wvhouse.gov

**White, Brad (R, 36)**
Room 218E, Building 1
1900 Kanawha Boulevard, East
Charleston, WV 25305
P: (304) 340-3138
E: brad.white@wvhouse.gov

**Williams, John (D, 51)\***
Room 6R-A, Building 1
1900 Kanawha Boulevard, East
Charleston, WV 25305
P: (304) 340-3173
E: John.Williams
@wvhouse.gov

**Wilson, S. Marshall (R, 60)\***
Room 229E, Building 1
1900 Kanawha Boulevard, East
Charleston, WV 25305
P: (304) 340-3147
E: Marshall.Wilson
@wvhouse.gov

**Zatezalo, Mark (R, 1)**
Room 201E, Building 1
1900 Kanawha Boulevard, East
Charleston, WV 25305
P: (304) 340-3120
E: mark.zatezalo
@wvhouse.gov

# Wisconsin

## Executive

### Governor
The Honorable Scott K. Walker (R)
Governor
115 East State Capitol
Madison, WI 53707
P: (608) 266-1212
F: (608) 267-8983

### Lieutenant Governor
The Honorable Rebecca Kleefisch (R)
Lieutenant Governor
Room 19, East State Capitol
P.O. Box 2043
Madison, WI 53702
P: (608) 266-3516
F: (608) 267-3571

### Attorney General
The Honorable Brad Schimel (R)
Attorney General
State Capitol, Suite 114 East
P.O. Box 7857
Madison, WI 53707
P: (608) 266-1221

### Auditor
Mr. Joe Chrisman
  (appointed by the Legislature)
State Auditor
22 East Mifflin Street, Suite 500
Madison, WI 53703
P: (608) 266-2818
F: (608) 267-0410
E: joe.chrisman
  @legis.wisconsin.gov

### Secretary of State
The Honorable Douglas J. La Follette (D)
Secretary of State
P.O. Box 7848
Madison, WI 53707
P: (608) 266-8888
F: (608) 266-3159
E: doug.lafollette
  @sos.state.wi.us

## Superintendent of Public Instruction
The Honorable Anthony Evers
Superintendent of Public Instruction
125 South Webster Street
Madison, WI 53707
P: (608) 266-3390
E: anthony.evers@dpi.wi.gov

## Treasurer
The Honorable Matt Adamczyk (R)
State Treasurer
P.O. Box 8982
Madison, WI 53708
P: (608) 266-3714
F: (608) 266-2647
E: Matt.Adamczyk
  @wisconsin.gov

## Judiciary

### Supreme Court (NE)
Ms. Diane M. Fremgen
Clerk of the Supreme Court
100 East Main Street, Suite 215
P.O. Box 1688
Madison, WI 53701
P: (608) 261-4300
F: (608) 267-0640
E: Diane.Fremgen
  @courts.state.wi.us

The Honorable Patience D. Roggensack
Chief Justice
The Honorable Shirley S. Abrahamson
The Honorable Ann Walsh Bradley
The Honorable Rebecca G. Bradley
The Honorable Michael J. Gableman
The Honorable Daniel Kelly
The Honorable Annette K. Ziegler

## Legislative Senate

### Senate President
Senator Roger J. Roth Jr. (R)
Senate President
220-S, State Capitol
P.O. Box 7882
Madison, WI 53707
P: (608) 266-0718
E: sen.Roth@legis.wi.gov

## President Pro Tempore of the Senate
Senator Howard Marklein (R)
Senate President Pro Tempore
8-S, State Capitol
P.O. Box 7882
Madison, WI 53707
P: (608) 266-0703
E: sen.Marklein
  @legis.wi.gov

## Senate Majority Leader
Senator Scott L. Fitzgerald (R)
Senate Majority Leader
211-S, State Capitol
P.O. Box 7882
Madison, WI 53707
P: (608) 266-5660
F: (608) 267-6795
E: Sen.Fitzgerald
  @legis.wi.gov

## Senate Minority Leader
Senator Jennifer Shilling (D)
Senate Minority Leader
206-S, State Capitol
P.O. Box 7882
Madison, WI 53707
P: (608) 266-5490
F: (608) 282-3572
E: Sen.Shilling
  @legis.wisconsin.gov

## Chief Clerk of the Senate
Mr. Jeffery Renk
Senate Chief Clerk & Director of Operations
Room B205 South, State Capitol
P.O. Box 7882
Madison, WI 53707
P: (608) 266-2517
F: (608) 266-0643
E: jeff.renk
  @legis.wisconsin.gov

## Members of the Senate
Bewley, Janet (D, 25)
126-S, State Capitol
P.O. Box 7882
Madison, WI 53707
P: (608) 266-3510
E: sen.Bewley@legis.wi.gov

Carpenter, Tim (D, 3)
109-S, State Capitol
P.O. Box 7882
Madison, WI 53707
P: (608) 266-8535
F: (608) 282-3543
E: Sen.Carpenter
  @legis.wi.gov

Cowles, Robert L. (R, 2)
118-S, State Capitol
P.O. Box 7882
Madison, WI 53707
P: (608) 266-0484
F: (608) 267-0304
E: Sen.Cowles@legis.wi.gov

Craig, David (R, 28)
104-S, State Capitol
P.O. Box 7882
Madison, WI 53707
P: (608) 266-5400
E: Sen.Craig
  @legis.wisconsin.gov

Darling, Alberta (R, 8)
317-E, State Capitol
P.O. Box 7882
Madison, WI 53707
P: (608) 266-5830
F: (608) 267-0588
E: Sen.Darling
  @legis.wisconsin.gov

Erpenbach, Jon B. (D, 27)
7-S, State Capitol
P.O. Box 7882
Madison, WI 53707
P: (608) 266-6670
F: (608) 266-2508
E: Sen.Erpenbach
  @legis.wi.gov

Feyen, Dan (R, 18)*
Room 306 South, State Capitol
P.O. Box 7882
Madison, WI 53707
P: (608) 266-5300
E: sen.feyen@legis.wi.gov

Fitzgerald, Scott L. (R, 13)
211-S, State Capitol
P.O. Box 7882
Madison, WI 53707
P: (608) 266-5660
F: (608) 267-6795
E: Sen.Fitzgerald
  @legis.wi.gov

Hansen, Dave (D, 30)
106-S, State Capitol
P.O. Box 7882
Madison, WI 53707
P: (608) 266-5670
F: (608) 267-6791
E: Sen.Hansen
  @legis.wisconsin.gov

**Harsdorf, Sheila (R, 10)**
122-S, State Capitol
P.O. Box 7882
Madison, WI 53707
P: (608) 266-7745
F: (608) 267-0369
E: Sen.Harsdorf
@legis.wisconsin.gov

**Johnson, LaTonya (D, 6)**
22-S, State Capitol
P.O. Box 7882
Madison, WI 53707
P: (608) 266-5580
F: (608) 282-3617
E: Sen.Johnson
@legis.wisconsin.gov

**Kapenga, Chris (R, 33)**
15 S, State Capitol
P.O. Box 7882
Madison, WI 53707
P: (608) 266-9174
E: Sen.Kapenga@legis.wi.gov

**Larson, Chris (D, 7)**
20-S, State Capitol
P.O. Box 7882
Madison, WI 53707
P: (608) 266-7505
F: (608) 282-3547
E: Sen.Larson@legis.wi.gov

**Lasee, Frank G. (R, 1)**
316-S, State Capitol
P.O. Box 7882
Madison, WI 53707
P: (608) 266-3512
F: (608) 267-6792
E: Sen.Lasee@legis.wi.gov

**LeMahieu, Devin (R, 9)**
Room 323 South, State Capitol
P.O. Box 7882
Madison, WI 53707
P: (608) 266-2056
E: sen.lemahieu
@legis.wi.gov

**Marklein, Howard (R, 17)**
8-S, State Capitol
P.O. Box 7882
Madison, WI 53707
P: (608) 266-0703
E: sen.Marklein
@legis.wi.gov

**Miller, Mark (D, 16)**
19-S, State Capitol
P.O. Box 7882
Madison, WI 53707
P: (608) 266-9170
F: (608) 282-3556
E: Sen.Miller
@legis.wisconsin.gov

**Moulton, Terry A. (R, 23)**
310-S, State Capitol
P.O. Box 7882
Madison, WI 53707
P: (608) 266-7511
F: (608) 282-3563
E: Sen.Moulton@legis.wi.gov

**Nass, Stephen L. (R, 11)**
10-S, State Capitol
P.O. Box 7882
Madison, WI 53707
P: (608) 266-2635
F: (608) 282-3631
E: sen.Nass@legis.wi.gov

**Olsen, Luther S. (R, 14)**
313-S, State Capitol
P.O. Box 7882
Madison, WI 53707
P: (608) 266-0751
F: (608) 267-4350
E: Sen.Olsen
@legis.wisconsin.gov

**Petrowski, Jerry (R, 29)**
123-S, State Capitol
P.O. Box 7882
Madison, WI 53707
P: (608) 266-2502
E: Sen.Petrowski
@legis.wi.gov

**Ringhand, Janis (D, 15)**
3-S, State Capitol
P.O. Box 8952
Madison, WI 53707
P: (608) 266-2253
E: sen.Ringhand
@legis.wi.gov

**Risser, Fred A. (D, 26)**
130-S, State Capitol
P.O. Box 7882
Madison, WI 53707
P: (608) 266-1627
F: (608) 266-1629
E: Sen.Risser
@legis.wisconsin.gov

**Roth Jr., Roger J. (R, 19)**
220-S, State Capitol
P.O. Box 7882
Madison, WI 53707
P: (608) 266-0718
E: sen.Roth@legis.wi.gov

**Shilling, Jennifer (D, 32)**
206-S, State Capitol
P.O. Box 7882
Madison, WI 53707
P: (608) 266-5490
F: (608) 282-3572
E: Sen.Shilling
@legis.wisconsin.gov

**Stroebel, Duey (R, 20)**
18-S, State Capitol
P.O. Box 7882
Madison, WI 53707
P: (608) 266-7513
E: sen.stroebel
@legis.wisconsin.gov

**Taylor, Lena C. (D, 4)**
5-S, State Capitol
P.O. Box 7882
Madison, WI 53707
P: (608) 266-5810
F: (608) 282-3544
E: Sen.Taylor
@legis.wisconsin.gov

**Testin, Patrick (R, 24)\***
Room 131 South, State Capitol
P.O. Box 7882
Madison, WI 53707
P: (608) 266-3123
E: sen.testin@legis.wi.gov

**Tiffany, Thomas (R, 12)**
409-S, State Capitol
P.O. Box 7882
Madison, WI 53707
P: (608) 266-2509
E: Sen.Tiffany@legis.wi.gov

**Vinehout, Kathleen (D, 31)**
108-S, State Capitol
P.O. Box 7882
Madison, WI 53707
P: (608) 266-8546
F: (608) 267-2871
E: Sen.Vinehout
@legis.wi.gov

**Vukmir, Leah (R, 5)**
415-S, State Capitol
P.O. Box 7882
Madison, WI 53707
P: (608) 266-2512
F: (608) 267-0367
E: Sen.Vukmir@legis.wi.gov

**Wanggaard, Van (R, 21)**
319-S, State Capitol
P.O. Box 7882
Madison, WI 53707
P: (608) 266-1832
F: (608) 282-3561
E: Sen.Wanggaard
@legis.wi.gov

**Wirch, Robert W. (D, 22)**
127-S, State Capitol
P.O. Box 7882
Madison, WI 53707
P: (608) 267-8979
F: (608) 267-0984
E: Sen.Wirch
@legis.wisconsin.gov

## Assembly

### Speaker of the Assembly

**Speaker Robin J. Vos (R)**
Speaker of the Assembly
211-W, State Capitol
P.O. Box 8953
Madison, WI 53708
P: (608) 266-9171
F: (608) 282-3663
E: Rep.Vos@legis.wi.gov

### Speaker Pro Tempore of the Assembly

**Representative Tyler August (R)**
Speaker Pro Tempore
119-W, State Capitol
P.O. Box 8952
Madison, WI 53708
P: (608) 266-1190
F: (608) 282-3632
E: Rep.August
@legis.wisconsin.gov

### Assembly Majority Leader

**Representative Jim Steineke (R)**
Assembly Majority Leader
115-W, State Capitol
P.O. Box 8953
Madison, WI 53708
P: (608) 266-2418
F: (608) 282-3605
E: Rep.Steineke
@legis.wisconsin.gov

### Assembly Minority Leader

**Representative Peter W. Barca (D)**
Assembly Minority Leader
201-W, State Capitol
P.O. Box 8952
Madison, WI 53708
P: (608) 266-5504
F: (608) 282-3664
E: Rep.Barca@legis.wi.gov

# Wisconsin

## Clerk of the Assembly

**Mr. Patrick Fuller**
Chief Clerk of the Assembly
17 West Main Street, Room 401
P.O. Box 8952
Madison, WI 53708
P: (608) 266-1501
F: (608) 266-5617
E: patrick.fuller
@legis.wisconsin.gov

## Members of the Assembly

**Allen, Scott (R, 97)**
8-W, State Capitol
P.O. Box 8952
Madison, WI 53708
P: (608) 266-8580
E: rep.allen@legis.wi.gov

**Anderson, Jimmy (D, 47)***
Room 9 North, State Capitol
P.O. Box 8952
Madison, WI 53708
P: (608) 266-8570
E: rep.anderson
@legis.wi.gov

**August, Tyler (R, 32)**
119-W, State Capitol
P.O. Box 8952
Madison, WI 53708
P: (608) 266-1190
F: (608) 282-3632
E: Rep.August
@legis.wisconsin.gov

**Ballweg, Joan A. (R, 41)**
210-N State Capitol
PO Box 8952
Madison, WI 53708
P: (608) 266-8077
F: (608) 282-3641
E: Rep.Ballweg
@legis.wisconsin.gov

**Barca, Peter W. (D, 64)**
201-W, State Capitol
P.O. Box 8952
Madison, WI 53708
P: (608) 266-5504
F: (608) 282-3664
E: Rep.Barca@legis.wi.gov

**Berceau, Terese (D, 77)**
104-N, State Capitol
P.O. Box 8952
Madison, WI 53708
P: (608) 266-3784
F: (608) 282-3676
E: Rep.Berceau@legis.wi.gov

**Bernier, Kathleen (R, 68)**
314-N, State Capitol
P.O. Box 8952
Madison, WI 53708
P: (608) 266-9172
F: (608) 282-3668
E: Rep.Bernier@legis.wi.gov

**Billings, Jill (D, 95)**
307-W, State Capitol
P.O. Box 8952
Madison, WI 53708
P: (608) 266-5780
E: Rep.Billings
@legis.wi.gov

**Born, Mark (R, 39)**
320-E, State Capitol
P.O. Box 8952
Madison, WI 53708
P: (608) 266-2540
F: (608) 282-3639
E: Rep.Born
@legis.wisconsin.gov

**Bowen, David (D, 10)**
3-N, State Capitol
P.O. Box 8952
Madison, WI 53708
P: (608) 266-7671
E: rep.bowen
@legis.wisconsin.gov

**Brandtjen, Janel (R, 22)**
221-N, State Capitol
P.O. Box 8952
Madison, WI 53708
P: (608) 266-2367
E: rep.brandtjen
@legis.wisconsin.gov

**Brooks, Edward (R, 50)**
20-N, State Capitol
P.O. Box 8952
Madison, WI 53708
P: (608) 266-8531
F: (608) 282-3650
E: Rep.Brooks@legis.wi.gov

**Brooks, Robert (R, 60)**
309-N, State Capitol
P.O. Box 8953
Madison, WI 53708
P: (608) 267-2369
E: rep.brooks@legis.wi.gov

**Brostoff, Jonathan (D, 19)**
420-N, State Capitol
P.O. Box 8952
Madison, WI 53708
P: (608) 266-0650
E: jbrostoff
@legis.wisconsin.gov

**Considine, Dave (D, 81)**
303-W, State Capitol
P.O. Box 8952
Madison, WI 53708
P: (608) 266-7746
E: rep.considine
@legis.wi.gov

**Crowley, David (D, 17)***
Room 5 North, State Capitol
P.O. Box 8952
Madison, WI 53708
P: (608) 266-5580
E: rep.crowley@legis.wi.gov

**Czaja, Mary (R, 35)**
321-E, State Capitol
P.O. Box 8953
Madison, WI 53708
P: (608) 266-7694
F: (608) 282-3635
E: Rep.Czaja
@legis.wisconsin.gov

**Doyle, Steve (D, 94)**
124-N, State Capitol
P.O. Box 8952
Madison, WI 53708
P: (608) 266-0631
F: (608) 282-3694
E: Rep.Doyle@legis.wi.gov

**Duchow, Cindi (R, 99)**
304-N, State Capitol
P.O. Box 8952
Madison, WI 53708
P: (608) 266-3007
E: rep.duchow@legis.wi.gov

**Edming, James W. (R, 87)**
109-W, State Capitol
P.O. Box 8952
Madison, WI 53708
P: (608) 266-7506
E: rep.edming@legis.wi.gov

**Fields, Jason (D, 11)**
412-N, State Capitol
P.O. Box 7882
Madison, WI 53708
P: (608) 266-3756
E: rep.fields@legis.wi.gov

**Gannon, Bob (R, 58)**
12-W, State Capitol
P.O. Box 8952
Madison, WI 53708
P: (608) 264-8486
E: rep.gannon@legis.wi.gov

**Genrich, Eric (D, 90)**
320-W, State Capitol
P.O. Box 8952
Madison, WI 53708
P: (608) 266-0616
F: (608) 282-3690
E: Rep.Genrich@legis.wi.gov

**Goyke, Evan (D, 18)**
322-W, State Capitol
P.O. Box 8952
Madison, WI 53708
P: (608) 266-0645
F: (608) 282-3618
E: Rep.Goyke
@legis.wisconsin.gov

**Hebl, Gary A. (D, 46)**
120-N, State Capitol
P.O. Box 8952
Madison, WI 53708
P: (608) 266-7678
F: (608) 282-3646
E: Rep.Hebl@legis.wi.gov

**Hesselbein, Dianne (D, 79)**
119-N, State Capitol
P.O. Box 8952
Madison, WI 53708
P: (608) 266-5340
F: (608) 282-3679
E: Rep.Hesselbein
@legis.wi.gov

**Hintz, Gordon (D, 54)**
109-N, State Capitol
P.O. Box 8952
Madison, WI 53708
P: (608) 266-2254
E: Rep.Hintz@legis.wi.gov

**Horlacher, Cody (R, 33)**
214-N, State Capitol
P.O. Box 8952
Madison, WI 53708
P: (608) 266-5715
E: rep.horlacher
@legis.wisconsin.gov

**Hutton, Rob (R, 13)**
220-N, State Capitol
P.O. Box 8952
Madison, WI 53708
P: (608) 267-9836
F: (608) 282-3613
E: Rep.Hutton
@legis.wisconsin.gov

**Jacque, Andre (R, 2)**
212-N, State Capitol
P.O. Box 8953
Madison, WI 53708
P: (608) 266-9870
F: (608) 282-3602
E: Rep.Jacque@legis.wi.gov

**Jagler, John (R, 37)**
316-N, State Capitol
P.O. Box 8952
Madison, WI 53708
P: (608) 266-9650
F: (608) 282-3637
E: Rep.Jagler
@legis.wisconsin.gov

**Jarchow, Adam (R, 28)**
19-N, State Capitol
P.O. Box 8952
Madison, WI 53708
P: (608) 267-2365
E: rep.jarchow
  @legis.wisconsin.gov

**Katsma, Terry (R, 26)**
Room 208 North, State Capitol
PO Box 8952
Madison, WI 53708
P: (608) 266-0656
E: rep.katsma
  @legis.wisconsin.gov

**Kerkman, Samantha (R, 61)**
315-N, State Capitol
P.O. Box 8952
Madison, WI 53708
P: (608) 266-2530
F: (608) 282-3666
E: Rep.Kerkman@legis.wi.gov

**Kessler, Frederick P.
  (D, 12)**
111-N, State Capitol
P.O. Box 8952
Madison, WI 53708
P: (608) 266-5813
F: (608) 282-3612
E: Rep.Kessler
  @legis.wisconsin.gov

**Kitchens, Joel C. (R, 1)**
10-W, State Capitol
P.O. Box 8952
Madison, WI 53708
P: (608) 266-5350
E: rep.kitchens
  @legis.wisconsin.gov

**Kleefisch, Joel M. (R, 38)**
216-N, State Capitol
P.O. Box 8952
Madison, WI 53708
P: (608) 266-8551
F: (608) 282-3638
E: Rep.Kleefisch
  @legis.wisconsin.gov

**Knodl, Dan (R, 24)**
218-N, State Capitol
P.O. Box 8952
Madison, WI 53708
P: (608) 266-3796
F: (608) 282-3624
E: Rep.Knodl
  @legis.wisconsin.gov

**Kolste, Debra (D, 44)**
8-N, State Capitol
P.O. Box 8952
Madison, WI 53708
P: (608) 266-7503
F: (608) 282-3644
E: Rep.Kolste@legis.wi.gov

**Kooyenga, Dale (R, 14)**
324-E, State Capitol
P.O. Box 8952
Madison, WI 53708
P: (608) 266-9180
F: (608) 282-3614
E: Rep.Kooyenga
  @legis.wisconsin.gov

**Kremer, Jesse (R, 59)**
17-W, State Capitol
P.O. Box 8952
Madison, WI 53708
P: (608) 266-9175
E: rep.kremer@legis.wi.gov

**Krug, Scott (R, 72)**
207-N, State Capitol
P.O. Box 8952
Madison, WI 53708
P: (608) 266-0215
F: (608) 282-3672
E: Rep.Krug@legis.wi.gov

**Kuglitsch, Mike (R, 84)**
129-W, State Capitol
P.O. Box 8952
Madison, WI 53708
P: (608) 267-5158
F: (608) 282-3684
E: Rep.Kuglitsch
  @legis.wi.gov

**Kulp, Bob (R, 69)**
15-W, State Capitol
P.O. Box 8952
Madison, WI 53708
P: (608) 267-0280
F: (608) 282-3669
E: Rep.Kulp@legis.wi.gov

**Loudenbeck, Amy (R, 31)**
304-E, State Capitol
P.O. Box 8952
Madison, WI 53708
P: (608) 266-9967
F: (608) 282-3645
E: Rep.Loudenbeck
  @legis.wisconsin.gov

**Macco, John (R, 88)**
308-N, State Capitol
P.O. Box 8952
Madison, WI 53708
P: (608) 266-0485
E: rep.macco
  @legis.wisconsin.gov

**Mason, Cory (D, 66)**
6-N, State Capitol
P.O. Box 8953
Madison, WI 53708
P: (608) 266-0634
F: (608) 282-3662
E: Rep.Mason@legis.wi.gov

**Meyers, Beth (D, 74)**
409-N, State Capitol
P.O. Box 8953
Madison, WI 53708
P: (608) 266-7690
E: rep.meyers@legis.wi.gov

**Milroy, Nick (D, 73)**
126-N, State Capitol
P.O. Box 8953
Madison, WI 53708
P: (608) 266-0640
F: (608) 282-3673
E: Rep.Milroy@legis.wi.gov

**Murphy, David (R, 56)**
318-N, State Capitol
P.O. Box 8953
Madison, WI 53708
P: (608) 266-7500
F: (608) 282-3656
E: Rep.Murphy@legis.wi.gov

**Mursau, Jeffrey L. (R, 36)**
113-W, State Capitol
P.O. Box 8953
Madison, WI 53708
P: (608) 266-3780
F: (608) 282-3636
E: Rep.Mursau
  @legis.wisconsin.gov

**Nerison, Lee (R, 96)**
310-N, State Capitol
P.O. Box 8953
Madison, WI 53708
P: (608) 266-3534
F: (608) 282-3696
E: Rep.Nerison@legis.wi.gov

**Neylon, Adam (R, 98)**
125-W, State Capitol
P.O. Box 8953
Madison, WI 53708
P: (608) 266-5120
E: Rep.Neylon@legis.wi.gov

**Novak, Todd (R, 51)**
312-N, State Capitol
P.O. Box 8953
Madison, WI 53708
P: (608) 266-7502
E: rep.novak@legis.wi.gov

**Nygren, John (R, 89)**
309-E, State Capitol
P.O. Box 8953
Madison, WI 53708
P: (608) 266-2343
E: Rep.Nygren@legis.wi.gov

**Ohnstad, Tod (D, 65)**
128-N, State Capitol
P.O. Box 8953
Madison, WI 53708
P: (608) 266-0455
F: (608) 282-3665
E: Rep.Ohnstad@legis.wi.gov

**Ott, Jim (R, 23)**
317-N, State Capitol
P.O. Box 8953
Madison, WI 53708
P: (608) 266-0486
E: Rep.OttJ
  @legis.wisconsin.gov

**Petersen, Kevin David
  (R, 40)**
105-W, State Capitol
P.O. Box 8953
Madison, WI 53708
P: (608) 266-3794
E: Rep.Petersen
  @legis.wisconsin.gov

**Petryk, Warren (R, 93)**
103-N, State Capitol
P.O. Box 8953
Madison, WI 53708
P: (608) 266-0660
F: (608) 282-3693
E: Rep.Petryk@legis.wi.gov

**Pope, Sondy (D, 80)**
118-N, State Capitol
P.O. Box 8953
Madison, WI 53708
P: (608) 266-3520
F: (608) 282-3679
E: Rep.Pope@legis.wi.gov

**Pronschinske, Treig
  (R, 92)\***
Room 18 West, State Capitol
P.O. Box 8953
Madison, WI 53708
P: (608) 266-7015
E: rep.pronschinske
  @legis.wi.gov

**Quinn, Romaine Robert
  (R, 75)**
323-N, State Capitol
P.O. Box 8953
Madison, WI 53708
P: (608) 266-2519
E: rep.quinn@legis.wi.gov

**Riemer, Daniel (D, 7)**
122-N, State Capitol
P.O. Box 8953
Madison, WI 53708
P: (608) 266-1733
F: (608) 282-3607
E: Rep.Riemer
  @legis.wisconsin.gov

**Ripp, Keith (R, 42)**
223-N, State Capitol
P.O. Box 8953
Madison, WI 53708
P: (608) 266-3404
F: (608) 282-3647
E: Rep.Ripp@legis.wi.gov

# Wisconsin

**Rodriguez, Jessie (R, 21)**
204-N, State Capitol
P.O. Box 8953
Madison, WI 53708
P: (608) 266-0610
F: (608) 282-3621
E: Rep.Rodriguez
@legis.wisconsin.gov

**Rohrkaste, Mike (R, 55)**
321-E, State Capitol
P.O. Box 8953
Madison, WI 53708
P: (608) 266-5719
E: rep.rohrkaste
@legis.wi.gov

**Sanfelippo, Joe (R, 15)**
306-N, State Capitol
P.O. Box 8953
Madison, WI 53708
P: (608) 266-0620
F: (608) 282-3615
E: Rep.Sanfelippo
@legis.wisconsin.gov

**Sargent, Melissa (D, 48)**
321-W, State Capitol
P.O. Box 8953
Madison, WI 53708
P: (608) 266-0960
F: (608) 282-3648
E: Rep.Sargent@legis.wi.gov

**Schraa, Michael (R, 53)**
107-W, State Capitol
P.O. Box 8953
Madison, WI 53708
P: (608) 267-7990
F: (608) 282-3653
E: Rep.Schraa@legis.wi.gov

**Shankland, Katrina (D, 71)**
304-W, State Capitol
P.O. Box 8953
Madison, WI 53708
P: (608) 267-9649
F: (608) 282-3671
E: Rep.Shankland
@legis.wi.gov

**Sinicki, Christine (D, 20)**
114-N, State Capitol
P.O. Box 8953
Madison, WI 53708
P: (608) 266-8588
F: (608) 282-3620
E: Rep.Sinicki
@legis.wisconsin.gov

**Skowronski, Ken (R, 82)**
209-N, State Capitol
P.O. Box 8953
Madison, WI 53708
P: (608) 266-8590
F: (608) 282-3682
E: Rep.Skowronski
@legis.wi.gov

**Snyder, Patrick (R, 85)\***
Room 9 West, State Capitol
P.O. Box 8953
Madison, WI 53708
P: (608) 266-0654
E: rep.snyder@legis.wi.gov

**Spiros, John (R, 86)**
15-N, State Capitol
P.O. Box 8953
Madison, WI 53708
P: (608) 266-1182
F: (608) 282-3686
E: Rep.Spiros@legis.wi.gov

**Spreitzer, Mark (D, 45)**
113-N, State Capitol
P.O. Box 8953
Madison, WI 53708
P: (608) 266-1192
E: rep.spreitzer
@legis.wi.gov

**Stafsholt, Rob (R, 29)\***
Room 17 North, State Capitol
P.O. Box 8953
Madison, WI 53708
P: (608) 266-7683
E: rep.stafsholt
@legis.wi.gov

**Steffen, David (R, 4)**
21-N, State Capitol
P.O. Box 8953
Madison, WI 53708
P: (608) 266-5840
E: rep.steffen
@legis.wisconsin.gov

**Steineke, Jim (R, 5)**
115-W, State Capitol
P.O. Box 8953
Madison, WI 53708
P: (608) 266-2418
F: (608) 282-3605
E: Rep.Steineke
@legis.wisconsin.gov

**Stuck, Amanda (D, 57)**
4-W, State Capitol
P.O. Box 8953
Madison, WI 53708
P: (608) 266-3070
E: rep.stuck@legis.wi.gov

**Subeck, Lisa (D, 78)**
418-N, State Capitol
P.O. Box 8953
Madison, WI 53708
P: (608) 266-7521
E: Rep.subeck@legis.wi.gov

**Summerfield, Rob (R, 67)\***
Room 7 West, State Capitol
P.O. Box 8953
Madison, WI 53708
P: (608) 266-1194
E: rep.summerfield
@legis.wi.gov

**Swearingen, Rob (R, 34)**
123-W, State Capitol
P.O. Box 8953
Madison, WI 53708
P: (608) 266-7141
F: (608) 282-3634
E: Rep.Swearingen
@legis.wisconsin.gov

**Tauchen, Gary (R, 6)**
13-W, State Capitol
P.O. Box 8953
Madison, WI 53708
P: (608) 266-3097
E: Rep.Tauchen
@legis.wisconsin.gov

**Taylor, Chris (D, 76)**
306-W, State Capitol
P.O. Box 8953
Madison, WI 53708
P: (608) 266-5342
F: (608) 282-3648
E: Rep.Taylor@legis.wi.gov

**Thiesfeldt, Jeremy (R, 52)**
16-W, State Capitol
P.O. Box 8953
Madison, WI 53708
P: (608) 266-3156
F: (608) 282-3652
E: Rep.Thiesfeldt
@legis.wi.gov

**Tittl, Paul (R, 25)**
219-N, State Capitol
P.O. Box 8953
Madison, WI 53708
P: (608) 266-0315
F: (608) 282-3625
E: Rep.Tittl
@legis.wisconsin.gov

**Tranel, Travis (R, 49)**
302-N, State Capitol
P.O. Box 8952
Madison, WI 53708
P: (608) 266-1170
E: Rep.Tranel@legis.wi.gov

**Tusler, Ron (R, 3)\***
Room 22 West, State Capitol
P.O. Box 8953
Madison, WI 53708
P: (608) 266-5831
E: rep.tusler@legis.wi.gov

**VanderMeer, Nancy Lynn
(R, 70)**
11-W, State Capitol
P.O. Box 8953
Madison, WI 53708
P: (608) 266-8366
E: rep.vandermeer
@legis.wi.gov

**Vorpagel, Tyler (R, 27)**
127-W, State Capitol
P.O. Box 8953
Madison, WI 53708
P: (608) 266-8530
E: rep.vorpagel
@legis.wisconsin.gov

**Vos, Robin J. (R, 63)**
211-W, State Capitol
P.O. Box 8953
Madison, WI 53708
P: (608) 266-9171
F: (608) 282-3663
E: Rep.Vos@legis.wi.gov

**Vruwink, Don (D, 43)\***
Room 5 North, State Capitol
P.O. Box 8953
Madison, WI 53708
P: (608) 266-3790
E: rep.vruwink
@legis.wisconsin.gov

**Wachs, Dana (D, 91)**
107-N, State Capitol
P.O. Box 8953
Madison, WI 53708
P: (608) 266-7461
F: (608) 282-3691
E: Rep.Wachs@legis.wi.gov

**Weatherston, Thomas (R, 62)**
307-N, State Capitol
P.O. Box 8953
Madison, WI 53708
P: (608) 266-0731
F: (608) 282-3691
E: Rep.Weatherson
@legis.wi.gov

**Wichgers, Chuck (R, 83)\***
Room 121 West, State Capitol
P.O. Box 8953
Madison, WI 53708
P: (608) 266-3363
E: rep.wichgers
@legis.wi.gov

**Young, Leon D. (D, 16)**
11-N, State Capitol
P.O. Box 8953
Madison, WI 53708
P: (608) 266-3786
F: (608) 282-3616
E: Rep.Young
@legis.wisconsin.gov

**Zamarripa, JoCasta (D, 8)**
112-N, State Capitol
P.O. Box 8953
Madison, WI 53708
P: (608) 267-7669
F: (608) 282-3608
E: Rep.Zamarripa
   @legis.wi.gov

**Zepnick, Josh (D, 9)**
7-N, State Capitol
P.O. Box 8953
Madison, WI 53708
P: (608) 266-1707
F: (608) 282-3609
E: Rep.Zepnick
   @legis.wisconsin.gov

**Zimmerman, Shannon (R, 30)***
Room 18 North, State Capitol
P.O. Box 8953
Madison, WI 53708
P: (608) 266-1526
E: rep.zimmerman
   @legis.wi.gov

# Wyoming

## Executive

### Governor
**The Honorable Matthew Mead (R)**
Governor
State Capitol Building, Room 124
Cheyenne, WY 82002
P: (307) 777-7434
F: (307) 632-3909

### Lieutenant Governor
*This state does not have the office of lieutenant governor. The secretary of state is next in line of succession to the governorship.*

### Attorney General
**The Honorable Peter K. Michael**
(appointed)
Attorney General
State Capitol Building
Cheyenne, WY 82002
P: (307) 777-7841
F: (307) 777-6869

### Auditor
**The Honorable Cynthia I. Cloud (R)**
State Auditor
State Capitol, Suite 114
200 West 24th Street
Cheyenne, WY 82002
P: (307) 777-7831
F: (307) 777-6983
E: SAOAdmin@wyo.gov

### Secretary of State
**The Honorable Ed Murray (R)**
Secretary of State
2020 Carey Avenue, Suite 600 & 700
Cheyenne, WY 82002
P: (307) 777-7378
F: (307) 777-6217
E: secofstate@wyo.gov

## Superintendent of Public Instruction
**The Honorable Jillian Balow (R)**
Superintendent of Public Instruction
2300 Capitol Avenue
Cheyenne, WY 82002
P: (307) 777-7675
F: (307) 777-6234
E: superintendent@wyo.gov

### Treasurer
**The Honorable Mark Gordon**
State Treasurer
200 West 24th Street
Cheyenne, WY 82002
P: (307) 777-7408
F: (307) 777-3731
E: treasurer@wyo.gov

## Judiciary

### Supreme Court (MR)
**Ms. Carol Thompson**
Clerk of Court
2301 Capitol Avenue
Cheyenne, WY 82002
P: (307) 777-7316
F: (307) 777-6129
E: cthompson @courts.state.wy.us

**The Honorable E. James Burke**
Chief Justice
**The Honorable Michael K. Davis**
**The Honorable Kate Fox**
**The Honorable William U. Hill**
**The Honorable Keith G. Kautz**

## Legislative

## Senate

### Senate President
**Senator Eli D. Bebout (R)**
President of the Senate
213 State Capitol Building
Cheyenne, WY 82002
P: (307) 777-7881
F: (307) 777-5466
E: Eli.Bebout@wyoleg.gov

## Vice President of the Senate
**Senator Michael Von Flatern (R)**
Senate Vice President
213 State Capitol Building
Cheyenne, WY 82002
P: (307) 777-7881
F: (307) 777-5466
E: Michael.VonFlatern @wyoleg.gov

## Senate Majority Leader
**Senator Drew A. Perkins (R)**
Senate Majority Floor Leader
213 State Capitol Building
Cheyenne, WY 82002
P: (307) 777-7881
F: (307) 777-5466
E: Drew.Perkins@wyoleg.gov

## Senate Minority Leader
**Senator Chris Rothfuss (D)**
Senate Minority Floor Leader
213 State Capitol Building
Cheyenne, WY 82002
P: (307) 777-7881
F: (307) 777-5466
E: Chris.Rothfuss @wyoleg.gov

## Secretary of the Senate
**Ms. Ellen Thompson**
Chief Clerk of the Senate
213 State Capitol Building
Cheyenne, WY 82002

## Members of the Senate
**Agar, Wyatt (R, 20)***
213 State Capitol Building
Cheyenne, WY 82002
P: (307) 777-7881
F: (307) 777-5466
E: Wyatt.Agar@wyoleg.gov

**Anderson, James Lee (R, 28)**
213 State Capitol Building
Cheyenne, WY 82002
P: (307) 777-7881
F: (307) 777-5466
E: Jameslee.Anderson @wyoleg.gov

**Anselmi-Dalton, Liisa (D, 12)***
213 State Capitol Building
Cheyenne, WY 82002
P: (307) 777-7881
F: (307) 777-5466
E: Liisa.Anselmi-Dalton @wyoleg.gov

**Baldwin, Fred A. (R, 14)**
213 State Capitol Building
Cheyenne, WY 82002
P: (307) 777-7881
F: (307) 777-5466
E: Fred.Baldwin@wyoleg.gov

**Barnard, Paul (R, 15)**
213 State Capitol Building
Cheyenne, WY 82002
P: (307) 777-7881
F: (307) 777-5466
E: Paul.Barnard@wyoleg.gov

**Bebout, Eli D. (R, 26)**
213 State Capitol Building
Cheyenne, WY 82002
P: (307) 777-7881
F: (307) 777-5466
E: Eli.Bebout@wyoleg.gov

**Boner, Brian (R, 2)**
213 State Capitol Building
Cheyenne, WY 82002
P: (307) 777-7881
F: (307) 777-5466
E: brian.boner@wyoleg.gov

**Bouchard, Anthony (R, 6)***
213 State Capitol Building
Cheyenne, WY 82002
P: (307) 777-7881
F: (307) 777-5466
E: Anthony.Bouchard @wyoleg.gov

**Burns, Bruce (R, 21)**
213 State Capitol Building
Cheyenne, WY 82002
P: (307) 777-7881
F: (307) 777-5466
E: Bruce.Burns@wyoleg.gov

**Case, Cale (R, 25)**
213 State Capitol Building
Cheyenne, WY 82002
P: (307) 777-7881
F: (307) 777-5466
E: Cale.Case@wyoleg.gov

**Christensen, Leland G. (R, 17)**
213 State Capitol Building
Cheyenne, WY 82002
P: (307) 777-7881
F: (307) 777-5466
E: Leland.Christensen @wyoleg.gov

**Coe, Henry H.R. (R, 18)**
213 State Capitol Building
Cheyenne, WY 82002
P: (307) 777-7881
F: (307) 777-5466
E: Hank.Coe@wyoleg.gov

**Dockstader, Dan (R, 16)**
213 State Capitol Building
Cheyenne, WY 82002
P: (307) 777-7881
F: (307) 777-5466
E: Dan.Dockstader
@wyoleg.gov

**Driskill, Ogden (R, 1)**
213 State Capitol Building
Cheyenne, WY 82002
P: (307) 777-7881
F: (307) 777-5466
E: Ogden.Driskill
@wyoleg.gov

**Ellis, Affie (R, 8)***
213 State Capitol Building
Cheyenne, WY 82002
P: (307) 777-7881
F: (307) 777-5466
E: Affie.Ellis@wyoleg.gov

**Emerich, Fred (R, 5)**
213 State Capitol Building
Cheyenne, WY 82002
P: (307) 777-7881
F: (307) 777-5466
E: Fred.Emerich@wyoleg.gov

**Hastert, John M. (D, 13)**
213 State Capitol Building
Cheyenne, WY 82002
P: (307) 777-7881
F: (307) 777-5466
E: John.Hastert@wyoleg.gov

**Hicks, Larry (R, 11)**
213 State Capitol Building
Cheyenne, WY 82002
P: (307) 777-7881
F: (307) 777-5466
E: Larry.Hicks@wyoleg.gov

**Kinskey, Dave (R, 22)**
213 State Capitol Building
Cheyenne, WY 82002
P: (307) 777-7881
F: (307) 777-5466
E: Dave.Kinskey@wyoleg.gov

**Landen, Bill (R, 27)**
213 State Capitol Building
Cheyenne, WY 82002
P: (307) 777-7881
F: (307) 777-5466
E: Bill.Landen@wyoleg.gov

**Meier, Curt (R, 3)**
213 State Capitol Building
Cheyenne, WY 82002
P: (307) 777-7881
F: (307) 777-5466
E: Curt.Meier@wyoleg.gov

**Moniz, Glenn (R, 10)**
213 State Capitol Building
Cheyenne, WY 82002
P: (307) 777-7881
F: (307) 777-5466
E: glenn.moniz@wyoleg.gov

**Nethercott, Tara (R, 4)***
213 State Capitol Building
Cheyenne, WY 82002
P: (307) 777-7881
F: (307) 777-5466
E: Tara.Nethercott
@wyoleg.gov

**Pappas, Stephan (R, 7)**
213 State Capitol Building
Cheyenne, WY 82002
P: (307) 777-7881
F: (307) 777-5466
E: Stephan.Pappas
@wyoleg.gov

**Perkins, Drew A. (R, 29)**
213 State Capitol Building
Cheyenne, WY 82002
P: (307) 777-7881
F: (307) 777-5466
E: Drew.Perkins@wyoleg.gov

**Peterson, R. Ray (R, 19)**
213 State Capitol Building
Cheyenne, WY 82002
P: (307) 777-7881
F: (307) 777-5466
E: Ray.Peterson@wyoleg.gov

**Rothfuss, Chris (D, 9)**
213 State Capitol Building
Cheyenne, WY 82002
P: (307) 777-7881
F: (307) 777-5466
E: Chris.Rothfuss
@wyoleg.gov

**Scott, Charles K. (R, 30)**
213 State Capitol Building
Cheyenne, WY 82002
P: (307) 777-7881
F: (307) 777-5466
E: Charles.Scott@wyoleg.gov

**Von Flatern, Michael
(R, 24)**
213 State Capitol Building
Cheyenne, WY 82002
P: (307) 777-7881
F: (307) 777-5466
E: Michael.VonFlatern
@wyoleg.gov

**Wasserburger, Jeff (R, 23)**
213 State Capitol Building
Cheyenne, WY 82002
P: (307) 777-7881
F: (307) 777-5466
E: Jeff.Wasserburger
@wyoleg.gov

# House

## Speaker of the House

**Representative Steve
Harshman (R)**
Speaker of the House
213 State Capitol Building
Cheyenne, WY 82002
P: (307) 777-7881
F: (307) 777-5466
E: Steve.Harshman
@wyoleg.gov

## Speaker Pro Tempore of the House

**Representative Donald E.
Burkhart Jr. (R)**
Speaker Pro Tempore
213 State Capitol Building
Cheyenne, WY 82002
P: (307) 777-7881
F: (307) 777-5466
E: Donald.Burkhart
@wyoleg.gov

## House Majority Leader

**Representative David R.
Miller (R)**
Majority Floor Leader
213 State Capitol Building
Cheyenne, WY 82002
P: (307) 777-7881
F: (307) 777-5466
E: David.Miller@wyoleg.gov

## House Minority Leader

**Representative Cathy
Connolly (D)**
Minority Floor Leader
213 State Capitol Building
Cheyenne, WY 82002
P: (307) 777-7881
F: (307) 777-5466
E: Cathy.Connolly
@wyoleg.gov

# Clerk of the House

**Ms. Wendy Harding**
Chief Clerk of the House
P.O. Box 2831
Cheyenne, WY 82003
P: (307) 777-7852

# Members of the House

**Allen, Jim (R, 33)**
213 State Capitol Building
Cheyenne, WY 82002
P: (307) 777-7881
F: (307) 777-5466
E: Jim.Allen@wyoleg.gov

**Baker, Mark (R, 48)**
213 State Capitol Building
Cheyenne, WY 82002
P: (307) 777-7881
F: (307) 777-5466
E: Mark.Baker@wyoleg.gov

**Barlow, Eric (R, 3)**
213 State Capitol Building
Cheyenne, WY 82002
P: (307) 777-7881
F: (307) 777-5466
E: Eric.Barlow@wyoleg.gov

**Biteman, Bo (R, 51)***
213 State Capitol Building
Cheyenne, WY 82002
P: (307) 777-7881
F: (307) 777-5466
E: bo.biteman@wyoleg.gov

**Blackburn, Jim (R, 42)**
213 State Capitol Building
Cheyenne, WY 82002
P: (307) 777-7881
F: (307) 777-5466
E: Jim.Blackburn@wyoleg.gov

**Blake, Stan (D, 39)**
213 State Capitol Building
Cheyenne, WY 82002
P: (307) 777-7881
F: (307) 777-5466
E: Stan.Blake@wyoleg.gov

**Bovee, Debbie (D, 36)***
213 State Capitol Building
Cheyenne, WY 82002
P: (307) 777-7881
F: (307) 777-5466
E: debbie.bovee@wypleg.gov

**Brown, Landon (R, 9)***
213 State Capitol Building
Cheyenne, WY 82002
P: 301-777-7881
F: (307) 777-5466
E: landon.brown@wyleg.gov

# Wyoming

**Burkhart Jr., Donald E. (R, 15)**
213 State Capitol Building
Cheyenne, WY 82002
P: (307) 777-7881
F: (307) 777-5466
E: Donald.Burkhart
@wyoleg.gov

**Byrd, James W. (D, 44)**
213 State Capitol Building
Cheyenne, WY 82002
P: (307) 777-7881
F: (307) 777-5466
E: James.Byrd@wyoleg.gov

**Clausen, Aaron (R, 6)***
213 State Capitol Building
Cheyenne, WY 82002
P: 301-777-7881
F: (307) 777-5466
E: aaron.clausen@wyloeg.gov

**Clem, Scott (R, 31)**
213 State Capitol Building
Cheyenne, WY 82002
P: (307) 777-7881
F: (307) 777-5466
E: Scott.Clem@wyoleg.gov

**Connolly, Cathy (D, 13)**
213 State Capitol Building
Cheyenne, WY 82002
P: (307) 777-7881
F: (307) 777-5466
E: Cathy.Connolly
@wyoleg.gov

**Court, Scott B. (R, 24)***
213 State Capitol Building
Cheyenne, WY 82002
P: (307) 777-7881
F: (307) 777-5466
E: scott.court@wyoleg.gov

**Crank, Thomas (R, 18)***
213 State Capitol Building
Cheyenne, WY 82002
P: (307) 777-7881
F: (307) 777-5466
E: thomas.crank@wyoleg.gov

**Dayton, JoAnn (D, 17)**
213 State Capitol Building
Cheyenne, WY 82002
P: (307) 777-7881
F: (307) 777-5466
E: JoAnn.Dayton@wyoleg.gov

**Edwards, Roy (R, 53)**
213 State Capitol Building
Cheyenne, WY 82002
P: (307) 777-7881
F: (307) 777-5466
E: Roy.Edwards@wyoleg.gov

**Eklund, John (R, 10)**
213 State Capitol Building
Cheyenne, WY 82002
P: (307) 777-7881
F: (307) 777-5466
E: John.Eklund@wyoleg.gov

**Erye, Daniel (R, 19)***
213 State Capitol Building
Cheyenne, WY 82002
P: (307) 777-7881
F: (307) 777-5466
E: danny.eyre@wyoleg.gov

**Flitner, Jamie (R, 26)***
213 State Capitol Building
Cheyenne, WY 82002
P: (307) 777-7881
F: (307) 777-5466
E: jamie.flitner@wyoleg.gov

**Freeman, John (D, 60)**
213 State Capitol Building
Cheyenne, WY 82002
P: (307) 777-7881
F: (307) 777-5466
E: John.Freeman@wyoleg.gov

**Furphy, Dan (R, 14)***
213 State Capitol Building
Cheyenne, WY 82002
P: 307-777-7881
F: (307) 777-5466
E: dan.furphy@wyoleg.gov

**Gierau, Mike (D, 16)***
213 State Capitol Building
Cheyenne, WY 82002
P: (307) 777-7881
F: (307) 777-5466
E: mike.gierau@wyoleg.gov

**Gray, Chuck (R, 57)***
213 State Capitol Building
Cheyenne, WY 82002
P: (307) 777-7881
F: (307) 777-5466
E: chuck.gray@wyoleg.gov

**Greear, Mike (R, 27)**
213 State Capitol Building
Cheyenne, WY 82002
P: (307) 777-7881
F: (307) 777-5466
E: Mike.Greear@wyoleg.gov

**Haley, Bill (R, 46)***
213 State Capitol Building
Cheyenne, WY 82002
P: (307) 777-7881
F: (307) 777-5466
E: bill.haley@wyoleg.gov

**Hallinan, Timothy (R, 32)**
213 State Capitol Building
Cheyenne, WY 82002
P: (307) 777-7881
F: (307) 777-5466
E: tim.hallinan@wyoleg.gov

**Halverson, Marti (R, 22)**
213 State Capitol Building
Cheyenne, WY 82002
P: (307) 777-7881
F: (307) 777-5466
E: Marti.Halverson
@wyoleg.gov

**Harshman, Steve (R, 37)**
213 State Capitol Building
Cheyenne, WY 82002
P: (307) 777-7881
F: (307) 777-5466
E: Steve.Harshman
@wyoleg.gov

**Henderson, Bill (R, 41)***
213 State Capitol Building
Cheyenne, WY 82002
P: (307) 777-7881
F: (307) 777-5466
E: bill.henderson
@wyoleg.gov

**Hunt, Hans (R, 2)**
213 State Capitol Building
Cheyenne, WY 82002
P: (307) 777-7881
F: (307) 777-5466
E: Hans.Hunt@wyoleg.gov

**Jennings, Mark (R, 30)**
213 State Capitol Building
Cheyenne, WY 82002
P: (307) 777-7881
F: (307) 777-5466
E: Mark.Jennings@wyoleg.gov

**Kinner, Mark S. (R, 29)**
213 State Capitol Building
Cheyenne, WY 82002
P: (307) 777-7881
F: (307) 777-5466
E: Mark.Kinner@wyoleg.gov

**Kirkbride, Dan R. (R, 4)**
213 State Capitol Building
Cheyenne, WY 82002
P: (307) 777-7881
F: (307) 777-5466
E: Dan.Kirkbride@wyoleg.gov

**Larsen, Lloyd Charles (R, 54)**
213 State Capitol Building
Cheyenne, WY 82002
P: (307) 777-7881
F: (307) 777-5466
E: Lloyd.Larsen@wyoleg.gov

**Laursen, Dan (R, 25)**
213 State Capitol Building
Cheyenne, WY 82002
P: (307) 777-7881
F: (307) 777-5466
E: Dan.Laursen@wyoleg.gov

**Lindholm, Tyler (R, 1)**
213 State Capitol Building
Cheyenne, WY 82002
P: (307) 777-7881
F: (307) 777-5466
E: Tyler.Lindholm
@wyoleg.gov

**Lone, Lars (R, 12)***
213 State Capitol Building
Cheyenne, WY 82002
P: 307-777-7881
F: (307) 777-5466
E: laes.lone@wyoleg.gov

**Loucks, Bunky (R, 59)**
213 State Capitol Building
Cheyenne, WY 82002
P: (307) 777-7881
F: (307) 777-5466
E: Bunky.Loucks@wyoleg.gov

**MacGuire, Joe (R, 35)***
213 State Capitol Building
Cheyenne, WY 82002
P: (307) 777-7881
F: (307) 777-5466
E: Joe.MacGuire@wyoleg.gov

**Madden, Michael K. (R, 40)**
213 State Capitol Building
Cheyenne, WY 82002
P: (307) 777-7881
F: (307) 777-5466
E: Mike.Madden@wyoleg.gov

**McKim, Robert M. (R, 21)**
213 State Capitol Building
Cheyenne, WY 82002
P: (307) 777-7881
F: (307) 777-5466
E: Robert.McKim@wyoleg.gov

**Miller, David R. (R, 55)**
213 State Capitol Building
Cheyenne, WY 82002
P: (307) 777-7881
F: (307) 777-5466
E: David.Miller@wyoleg.gov

**Nicholas, Bob (R, 8)**
213 State Capitol Building
Cheyenne, WY 82002
P: (307) 777-7881
F: (307) 777-5466
E: Bob.Nicholas@wyoleg.gov

**Northrup, David (R, 50)**
213 State Capitol Building
Cheyenne, WY 82002
P: (307) 777-7881
F: (307) 777-5466
E: David.Northrup
@wyoleg.gov

**Obermueller, Jerry (R, 56)***
213 State Capitol Building
Cheyenne, WY 82002
P: (307) 777-7881
F: (307) 777-5466
E: jerry.obermueller
  @wyoleg.gov

**Olsen, Jared (R, 11)***
213 State Capitol Building
Cheyenne, WY 82002
P: (307) 777-7881
F: (307) 777-5466
E: jared.olsen@wyoleg.gov

**Paxton, Jerry D. (R, 47)**
213 State Capitol Building
Cheyenne, WY 82002
P: (307) 777-7881
F: (307) 777-5466
E: Jerry.Paxton@wyoleg.gov

**Pelkey, Charles F. (D, 45)**
213 State Capitol Building
Cheyenne, WY 82002
P: (307) 777-7881
F: (307) 777-5466
E: Charles.Pelkey
  @wyoleg.gov

**Piiparinen, Garry C.
  (R, 49)**
213 State Capitol Building
Cheyenne, WY 82002
P: (307) 777-7881
F: (307) 777-5466
E: Garry.Piiparinen
  @wyoleg.gov

**Pownall, William (R, 52)**
213 State Capitol Building
Cheyenne, WY 82002
P: (307) 777-7881
F: (307) 777-5466
E: Bill.Pownall@wyoleg.gov

**Salazar, Tim (R, 34)***
213 State Capitol Building
Cheyenne, WY 82002
P: (307) 777-7881
F: (307) 777-5466
E: tim.salazar@wyoleg.gov

**Schwartz, Andy (D, 23)**
213 State Capitol Building
Cheyenne, WY 82002
P: (307) 777-7881
F: (307) 777-5466
E: Andy.Schwartz@wyoleg.gov

**Sommers, Albert (R, 20)**
213 State Capitol Building
Cheyenne, WY 82002
P: (307) 777-7881
F: (307) 777-5466
E: Albert.Sommers
  @wyoleg.gov

**Steinmetz, Cheri (R, 5)**
213 State Capitol Building
Cheyenne, WY 82002
P: (307) 777-7881
F: (307) 777-5466
E: Cheri.Steinmetz
  @wyoleg.gov

**Sweeney, Pat (R, 58)***
213 State Capitol Building
Cheyenne, WY 82002
P: (307) 777-7881
F: (307) 777-5466
E: patrick.sweeney
  @wyoleg.gov

**Walters, Tom (R, 38)**
213 State Capitol Building
Cheyenne, WY 82002
P: (307) 777-7881
F: (307) 777-5466
E: Tom.Walters@wyoleg.gov

**Wilson, Sue (R, 7)**
213 State Capitol Building
Cheyenne, WY 82002
P: (307) 777-7881
F: (307) 777-5466
E: Sue.Wilson@wyoleg.gov

**Winters, Nathan (R, 28)**
213 State Capitol Building
Cheyenne, WY 82002
P: (307) 777-7881
F: (307) 777-5466
E: Nathan.Winters
  @wyoleg.gov

**Zwonitzer, Dan (R, 43)**
213 State Capitol Building
Cheyenne, WY 82002
P: (307) 777-7881
F: (307) 777-5466
E: Dan.Zwonitzer@wyoleg.gov

# Massachusetts District Table

*This table lists the full name of the district. To find the legislator's district name, please refer to the "SP" code in parenthesis next to each name.*

| Code | District Name | Code | District Name | Code | District Name |
|------|---------------|------|---------------|------|---------------|
| SP1 | = First Barnstable | SP65 | = Sixth Middlesex | SP129 | = Sixth Suffolk |
| SP2 | = Second Barnstable | SP66 | = Seventh Middlesex | SP130 | = Seventh Suffolk |
| SP3 | = Third Barnstable | SP67 | = Eighth Middlesex | SP131 | = Eighth Suffolk |
| SP4 | = Fourth Barnstable | SP68 | = Ninth Middlesex | SP132 | = Ninth Suffolk |
| SP5 | = Fifth Barnstable | SP69 | = Tenth Middlesex | SP133 | = Tenth Suffolk |
| SP6 | = Barnstable, Dukes, Nantucket | SP70 | = Eleventh Middlesex | SP134 | = Eleventh Suffolk |
| SP7 | = First Berkshire | SP71 | = Twelfth Middlesex | SP135 | = Twelfth Suffolk |
| SP8 | = Second Berkshire | SP72 | = Thirteenth Middlesex | SP136 | = Thirteenth Suffolk |
| SP9 | = Third Berkshire | SP73 | = Fourteenth Middlesex | SP137 | = Fourteenth Suffolk |
| SP10 | = Fourth Berkshire | SP74 | = Fifteenth Middlesex | SP138 | = Fifteenth Suffolk |
| SP11 | = First Bristol | SP75 | = Sixteenth Middlesex | SP139 | = Sixteenth Suffolk |
| SP12 | = Second Bristol | SP76 | = Seventeenth Middlesex | SP140 | = Seventeenth Suffolk |
| SP13 | = Third Bristol | SP77 | = Eighteenth Middlesex | SP141 | = Eighteenth Suffolk |
| SP14 | = Fourth Bristol | SP78 | = Nineteenth Middlesex | SP142 | = Nineteenth Suffolk |
| SP15 | = Fifth Bristol | SP79 | = Twentieth Middlesex | SP143 | = First Worcester |
| SP16 | = Sixth Bristol | SP80 | = Twenty-first Middlesex | SP144 | = Second Worcester |
| SP17 | = Seventh Bristol | SP81 | = Twenty-second Middlesex | SP145 | = Third Worcester |
| SP18 | = Eighth Bristol | SP82 | = Twenty-third Middlesex | SP146 | = Fourth Worcester |
| SP19 | = Ninth Bristol | SP83 | = Twenty-fourth Middlesex | SP147 | = Fifth Worcester |
| SP20 | = Tenth Bristol | SP84 | = Twenty-fifth Middlesex | SP148 | = Sixth Worcester |
| SP21 | = Eleventh Bristol | SP85 | = Twenty-sixth Middlesex | SP149 | = Seventh Worcester |
| SP22 | = Twelfth Bristol | SP86 | = Twenty-seventh Middlesex | SP150 | = Eighth Worcester |
| SP23 | = Thirteenth Bristol | SP87 | = Twenty-eighth Middlesex | SP151 | = Ninth Worcester |
| SP24 | = Fourteenth Bristol | SP88 | = Twenty-ninth Middlesex | SP152 | = Tenth Worcester |
| SP25 | = First Essex | SP89 | = Thirtieth Middlesex | SP153 | = Eleventh Worcester |
| SP26 | = Second Essex | SP90 | = Thirty-first Middlesex | SP154 | = Twelfth Worcester |
| SP27 | = Third Essex | SP91 | = Thirty-second Middlesex | SP155 | = Thirteenth Worcester |
| SP28 | = Fourth Essex | SP92 | = Thirty-third Middlesex | SP156 | = Fourteenth Worcester |
| SP29 | = Fifth Essex | SP93 | = Thirty-fourth Middlesex | SP157 | = Fifteenth Worcester |
| SP30 | = Sixth Essex | SP94 | = Thirty-fifth Middlesex | SP158 | = Sixteenth Worcester |
| SP31 | = Seventh Essex | SP95 | = Thirty-sixth Middlesex | SP159 | = Seventeenth Worcester |
| SP32 | = Eighth Essex | SP96 | = Thirty-seventh Middlesex | SP160 | = Eighteenth Worcester |
| SP33 | = Ninth Essex | SP97 | = First Norfolk | SP161 | = Berkshire, Hampshire, Franklin, Hampden |
| SP34 | = Tenth Essex | SP98 | = Second Norfolk | SP162 | = Bristol, Norfolk |
| SP35 | = Eleventh Essex | SP99 | = Third Norfolk | SP163 | = First Bristol, Plymouth |
| SP36 | = Twelfth Essex | SP100 | = Fourth Norfolk | SP164 | = Second Bristol, Plymouth |
| SP37 | = Thirteenth Essex | SP101 | = Fifth Norfolk | SP165 | = Cape, Islands |
| SP38 | = Fourteenth Essex | SP102 | = Sixth Norfolk | SP166 | = First Essex, Middlesex |
| SP39 | = Fifteenth Essex | SP103 | = Seventh Norfolk | SP167 | = Second Essex, Middlesex |
| SP40 | = Sixteenth Essex | SP104 | = Eighth Norfolk | SP168 | = Third Essex, Middlesex |
| SP41 | = Seventeenth Essex | SP105 | = Ninth Norfolk | SP169 | = Hampden |
| SP42 | = Eighteenth Essex | SP106 | = Tenth Norfolk | SP170 | = First Hampden, Hampshire |
| SP43 | = First Franklin | SP107 | = Eleventh Norfolk | SP171 | = Second Hampden, Hampshire |
| SP44 | = Second Franklin | SP108 | = Twelfth Norfolk | SP172 | = Hampshire, Franklin, Worcester |
| SP45 | = First Hampden | SP109 | = Thirteenth Norfolk | SP173 | = Middlesex, Essex |
| SP46 | = Second Hampden | SP110 | = Fourteenth Norfolk | SP174 | = First Middlesex, Norfolk |
| SP47 | = Third Hampden | SP111 | = Fifteenth Norfolk | SP175 | = Second Middlesex, Norfolk |
| SP48 | = Fourth Hampden | SP112 | = First Plymouth | SP176 | = Middlesex, Suffolk |
| SP49 | = Fifth Hampden | SP113 | = Second Plymouth | SP177 | = Middlesex, Worcester |
| SP50 | = Sixth Hampden | SP114 | = Third Plymouth | SP178 | = Norfolk, Bristol, Plymouth |
| SP51 | = Seventh Hampden | SP115 | = Fourth Plymouth | SP179 | = Norfolk, Bristol, Middlesex |
| SP52 | = Eighth Hampden | SP116 | = Fifth Plymouth | SP180 | = Norfolk, Plymouth |
| SP53 | = Ninth Hampden | SP117 | = Sixth Plymouth | SP181 | = Plymouth, Barnstable |
| SP54 | = Tenth Hampden | SP118 | = Seventh Plymouth | SP182 | = First Plymouth, Bristol |
| SP55 | = Eleventh Hampden | SP119 | = Eighth Plymouth | SP183 | = Second Plymouth, Bristol |
| SP56 | = Twelfth Hampden | SP120 | = Ninth Plymouth | SP184 | = Plymouth, Norfolk |
| SP57 | = First Hampshire | SP121 | = Tenth Plymouth | SP185 | = First Suffolk, Middlesex |
| SP58 | = Second Hampshire | SP122 | = Eleventh Plymouth | SP186 | = Second Suffolk, Middlesex |
| SP59 | = Third Hampshire | SP123 | = Twelfth Plymouth | SP187 | = Suffolk, Norfolk |
| SP60 | = First Middlesex | SP124 | = First Suffolk | SP188 | = Worcester, Hampden, Hampshire, Middlesex |
| SP61 | = Second Middlesex | SP125 | = Second Suffolk | | |
| SP62 | = Third Middlesex | SP126 | = Third Suffolk | SP189 | = Worcester, Middlesex |
| SP63 | = Fourth Middlesex | SP127 | = Fourth Suffolk | SP190 | = Worcester, Norfolk |
| SP64 | = Fifth Middlesex | SP128 | = Fifth Suffolk | | |

# New Hampshire District Table

*This table lists the full name of the district. To find the legislator's district name, please refer to the "SP" code in parenthesis next to each name.*

| Code | District Name | Code | District Name | Code | District Name | Code | District Name |
|---|---|---|---|---|---|---|---|
| SP1 = | Belknap 1 | SP52 = | Grafton 12 | SP103 = | Merrimack 1 | SP154 = | Rockingham 23 |
| SP2 = | Belknap 2 | SP53 = | Grafton 13 | SP104 = | Merrimack 2 | SP155 = | Rockingham 24 |
| SP3 = | Belknap 3 | SP54 = | Grafton 14 | SP105 = | Merrimack 3 | SP156 = | Rockingham 25 |
| SP4 = | Belknap 4 | SP55 = | Grafton 15 | SP106 = | Merrimack 4 | SP157 = | Rockingham 26 |
| SP5 = | Belknap 5 | SP56 = | Grafton 16 | SP107 = | Merrimack 5 | SP158 = | Rockingham 27 |
| SP6 = | Belknap 6 | SP57 = | Grafton 17 | SP108 = | Merrimack 6 | SP159 = | Rockingham 28 |
| SP7 = | Belknap 7 | SP58 = | Hillsborough 1 | SP109 = | Merrimack 7 | SP160 = | Rockingham 29 |
| SP8 = | Belknap 8 | SP59 = | Hillsborough 2 | SP110 = | Merrimack 8 | SP161 = | Rockingham 30 |
| SP9 = | Belknap 9 | SP60 = | Hillsborough 3 | SP111 = | Merrimack 9 | SP162 = | Rockingham 31 |
| SP10 = | Carroll 1 | SP61 = | Hillsborough 4 | SP112 = | Merrimack 10 | SP163 = | Rockingham 32 |
| SP11 = | Carroll 2 | SP62 = | Hillsborough 5 | SP113 = | Merrimack 11 | SP164 = | Rockingham 33 |
| SP12 = | Carroll 3 | SP63 = | Hillsborough 6 | SP114 = | Merrimack 12 | SP165 = | Rockingham 34 |
| SP13 = | Carroll 4 | SP64 = | Hillsborough 7 | SP115 = | Merrimack 13 | SP166 = | Rockingham 35 |
| SP14 = | Carroll 5 | SP65 = | Hillsborough 8 | SP116 = | Merrimack 14 | SP167 = | Rockingham 36 |
| SP15 = | Carroll 6 | SP66 = | Hillsborough 9 | SP117 = | Merrimack 15 | SP168 = | Rockingham 37 |
| SP16 = | Carroll 7 | SP67 = | Hillsborough 10 | SP118 = | Merrimack 16 | SP169 = | Strafford 1 |
| SP17 = | Carroll 8 | SP68 = | Hillsborough 11 | SP119 = | Merrimack 17 | SP170 = | Strafford 2 |
| SP18 = | Cheshire 1 | SP69 = | Hillsborough 12 | SP120 = | Merrimack 18 | SP171 = | Strafford 3 |
| SP19 = | Cheshire 2 | SP70 = | Hillsborough 13 | SP121 = | Merrimack 19 | SP172 = | Strafford 4 |
| SP20 = | Cheshire 3 | SP71 = | Hillsborough 14 | SP122 = | Merrimack 20 | SP173 = | Strafford 5 |
| SP21 = | Cheshire 4 | SP72 = | Hillsborough 15 | SP123 = | Merrimack 21 | SP174 = | Strafford 6 |
| SP22 = | Cheshire 5 | SP73 = | Hillsborough 16 | SP124 = | Merrimack 22 | SP175 = | Strafford 7 |
| SP23 = | Cheshire 6 | SP74 = | Hillsborough 17 | SP125 = | Merrimack 23 | SP176 = | Strafford 8 |
| SP24 = | Cheshire 7 | SP75 = | Hillsborough 18 | SP126 = | Merrimack 24 | SP177 = | Strafford 9 |
| SP25 = | Cheshire 8 | SP76 = | Hillsborough 19 | SP127 = | Merrimack 25 | SP178 = | Strafford 10 |
| SP26 = | Cheshire 9 | SP77 = | Hillsborough 20 | SP128 = | Merrimack 26 | SP179 = | Strafford 11 |
| SP27 = | Cheshire 10 | SP78 = | Hillsborough 21 | SP129 = | Merrimack 27 | SP180 = | Strafford 12 |
| SP28 = | Cheshire 11 | SP79 = | Hillsborough 22 | SP130 = | Merrimack 28 | SP181 = | Strafford 13 |
| SP29 = | Cheshire 12 | SP80 = | Hillsborough 23 | SP131 = | Merrimack 29 | SP182 = | Strafford 14 |
| SP30 = | Cheshire 13 | SP81 = | Hillsborough 24 | SP132 = | Rockingham 1 | SP183 = | Strafford 15 |
| SP31 = | Cheshire 14 | SP82 = | Hillsborough 25 | SP133 = | Rockingham 2 | SP184 = | Strafford 16 |
| SP32 = | Cheshire 15 | SP83 = | Hillsborough 26 | SP134 = | Rockingham 3 | SP185 = | Strafford 17 |
| SP33 = | Cheshire 16 | SP84 = | Hillsborough 27 | SP135 = | Rockingham 4 | SP186 = | Strafford 18 |
| SP34 = | Coos 1 | SP85 = | Hillsborough 28 | SP136 = | Rockingham 5 | SP187 = | Strafford 19 |
| SP35 = | Coos 2 | SP86 = | Hillsborough 29 | SP137 = | Rockingham 6 | SP188 = | Strafford 20 |
| SP36 = | Coos 3 | SP87 = | Hillsborough 30 | SP138 = | Rockingham 7 | SP189 = | Strafford 21 |
| SP37 = | Coos 4 | SP88 = | Hillsborough 31 | SP139 = | Rockingham 8 | SP190 = | Strafford 22 |
| SP38 = | Coos 5 | SP89 = | Hillsborough 32 | SP140 = | Rockingham 9 | SP191 = | Strafford 23 |
| SP39 = | Coos 6 | SP90 = | Hillsborough 33 | SP141 = | Rockingham 10 | SP192 = | Strafford 24 |
| SP40 = | Coos 7 | SP91 = | Hillsborough 34 | SP142 = | Rockingham 11 | SP193 = | Strafford 25 |
| SP41 = | Grafton 1 | SP92 = | Hillsborough 35 | SP143 = | Rockingham 12 | SP194 = | Sullivan 1 |
| SP42 = | Grafton 2 | SP93 = | Hillsborough 36 | SP144 = | Rockingham 13 | SP195 = | Sullivan 2 |
| SP43 = | Grafton 3 | SP94 = | Hillsborough 37 | SP145 = | Rockingham 14 | SP196 = | Sullivan 3 |
| SP44 = | Grafton 4 | SP95 = | Hillsborough 38 | SP146 = | Rockingham 15 | SP197 = | Sullivan 4 |
| SP45 = | Grafton 5 | SP96 = | Hillsborough 39 | SP147 = | Rockingham 16 | SP198 = | Sullivan 5 |
| SP46 = | Grafton 6 | SP97 = | Hillsborough 40 | SP148 = | Rockingham 17 | SP199 = | Sullivan 6 |
| SP47 = | Grafton 7 | SP98 = | Hillsborough 41 | SP149 = | Rockingham 18 | SP200 = | Sullivan 7 |
| SP48 = | Grafton 8 | SP99 = | Hillsborough 42 | SP150 = | Rockingham 19 | SP201 = | Sullivan 8 |
| SP49 = | Grafton 9 | SP100 = | Hillsborough 43 | SP151 = | Rockingham 20 | SP202 = | Sullivan 9 |
| SP50 = | Grafton 10 | SP101 = | Hillsborough 44 | SP152 = | Rockingham 21 | SP203 = | Sullivan 10 |
| SP51 = | Grafton 11 | SP102 = | Hillsborough 45 | SP153 = | Rockingham 22 | SP204 = | Sullivan 11 |

# Vermont District Table

This table lists the full name of the district. To find the legislator's district name, please refer to the "SP" code in parenthesis next to each name.

| Code | District Name | Code | District Name | Code | District Name |
|------|---------------|------|---------------|------|---------------|
| SP1 = | Addison | SP41 = | Chittenden-6-4 | SP81 = | Rutland-4 |
| SP2 = | Bennington | SP42 = | Chittenden-6-5 | SP82 = | Rutland-5-1 |
| SP3 = | Caledonia | SP43 = | Chittenden-6-6 | SP83 = | Rutland-5-2 |
| SP4 = | Chittenden | SP44 = | Chittenden-6-7 | SP84 = | Rutland-5-3 |
| SP5 = | Essex, Orleans | SP45 = | Chittenden-7-1 | SP85 = | Rutland-5-4 |
| SP6 = | Franklin | SP46 = | Chittenden-7-2 | SP86 = | Rutland-6 |
| SP7 = | Grand Isle | SP47 = | Chittenden-7-3 | SP87 = | Rutland, Bennington |
| SP8 = | Lamoille | SP48 = | Chittenden-7-4 | SP88 = | Rutland, Windsor-1 |
| SP9 = | Orange | SP49 = | Chittenden-8-1 | SP89 = | Rutland, Windsor-2 |
| SP10 = | Rutland | SP50 = | Chittenden-8-2 | SP90 = | Washington-1 |
| SP11 = | Washington | SP51 = | Chittenden-8-3 | SP91 = | Washington-2 |
| SP12 = | Windham | SP52 = | Chittenden-9-1 | SP92 = | Washington-3 |
| SP13 = | Windsor | SP53 = | Chittenden-9-2 | SP93 = | Washington-4 |
| SP14 = | Addison-1 | SP54 = | Chittenden-10 | SP94 = | Washington-5 |
| SP15 = | Addison-2 | SP55 = | Essex, Caledonia | SP95 = | Washington-6 |
| SP16 = | Addison-3 | SP56 = | Essex, Caledonia, Orleans | SP96 = | Washington-7 |
| SP17 = | Addison-4 | SP57 = | Franklin-1 | SP97 = | Washington, Chittenden |
| SP18 = | Addison-5 | SP58 = | Franklin-2 | SP98 = | Windham-1 |
| SP19 = | Addison, Rutland | SP59 = | Franklin-3-1 | SP99 = | Windham-2-1 |
| SP20 = | Bennington-1 | SP60 = | Franklin-3-2 | SP100 = | Windham-2-2 |
| SP21 = | Bennington-2-1 | SP61 = | Franklin-4 | SP101 = | Windham-2-3 |
| SP22 = | Bennington-2-2 | SP62 = | Franklin-5 | SP102 = | Windham-3 |
| SP23 = | Bennington-3 | SP63 = | Franklin-6 | SP103 = | Windham-4 |
| SP24 = | Bennington-4 | SP64 = | Franklin-7 | SP104 = | Windham-5 |
| SP25 = | Bennington, Rutland | SP65 = | Grand Isle, Chittenden | SP105 = | Windham-6 |
| SP26 = | Caledonia-1 | SP66 = | Lamoille-1 | SP106 = | Windham, Bennington |
| SP27 = | Caledonia-2 | SP67 = | Lamoille-2 | SP107 = | Windham, Bennington, |
| SP28 = | Caledonia-3 | SP68 = | Lamoille-3 | | Windsor |
| SP29 = | Caledonia-4 | SP69 = | Lamoille, Washington | SP108 = | Windsor-1 |
| SP30 = | Caledonia, Washington | SP70 = | Orange-1 | SP109 = | Windsor-2 |
| SP31 = | Chittenden-1 | SP71 = | Orange-2 | SP110 = | Windsor-3-1 |
| SP32 = | Chittenden-2 | SP72 = | Orange, Washington, Addison | SP111 = | Windsor-3-2 |
| SP33 = | Chittenden-3 | SP73 = | Orange, Caledonia | SP112 = | Windsor-4-1 |
| SP34 = | Chittenden-4-1 | SP74 = | Orleans-1 | SP113 = | Windsor-4-2 |
| SP35 = | Chittenden 4-2 | SP75 = | Orleans-2 | SP114 = | Windsor-5 |
| SP36 = | Chittenden-5-1 | SP76 = | Orleans, Caledonia | SP115 = | Windsor, Orange-1 |
| SP37 = | Chittenden-5-2 | SP77 = | Orleans, Lamoille | SP116 = | Windsor, Orange-2 |
| SP38 = | Chittenden-6-1 | SP78 = | Rutland-1 | SP117 = | Windsor, Rutland |
| SP39 = | Chittenden-6-2 | SP79 = | Rutland-2 | | |
| SP40 = | Chittenden-6-3 | SP80 = | Rutland-3 | | |